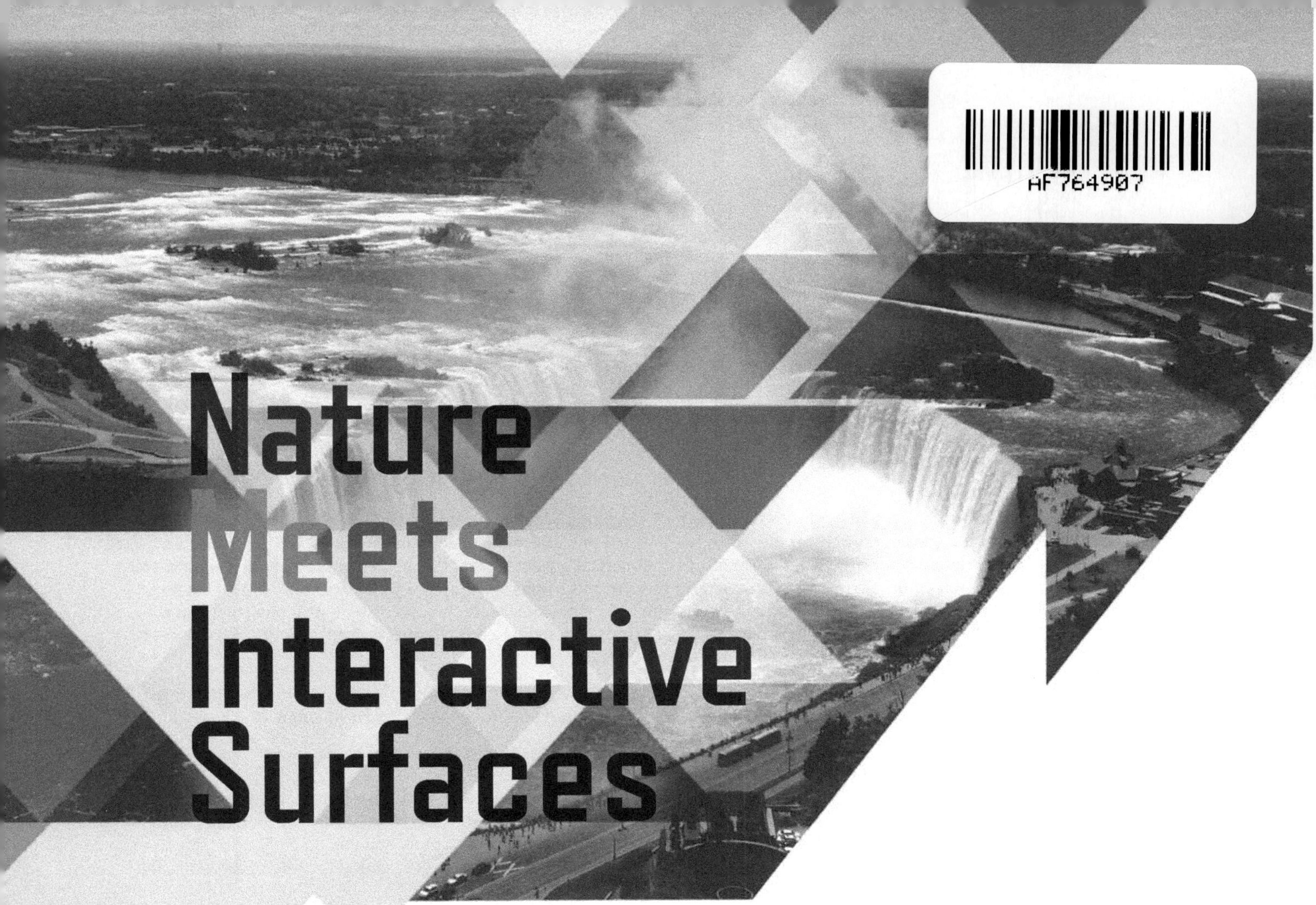

Nature Meets Interactive Surfaces

Proceedings of the 2016 ACM International Conference on

INTERACTIVE SURFACES AND SPACES

ISS 2016

November 6-9 2016 | Niagara Falls, Canada

iss2016.acm.org

SIGCHI

Association for Computing Machinery

Association for
Computing Machinery

Advancing Computing as a Science & Profession

The Association for Computing Machinery
2 Penn Plaza, Suite 701
New York, New York 10121-0701

ISBN: 978-1-4503-4248-3 (Digital)

ISBN: 978-1-4503-4712-9 (Print)

Additional copies may be ordered prepaid from:

ACM Order Department
PO Box 30777
New York, NY 10087-0777, USA

Phone: 1-800-342-6626 (USA and Canada)
+1-212-626-0500 (Global)
Fax: +1-212-944-1318
E-mail: acmhelp@acm.org
Hours of Operation: 8:30 am – 4:30 pm ET

Printed in the USA

Welcome to ISS 2016

It is our pleasure to welcome you to the 2016 ACM International Conference on Interactive Surfaces and Spaces (ISS 2016). ISS is the premier venue for research addressing the design, development and use of new and emerging digital surfaces and multi-surface technologies. Located right at the border between Canada and the US, the scenic view of the magnificent Niagara Falls and its vibrant city life will be the ideal host for this 11th annual event in the conference series, and the first year with our new conference name. Over the years ISS has been a venue for research and applications of interactive surfaces as well as spaces, which has been acknowledged by the incorporation of 'Spaces' into our conference name for this year. Interactive Surfaces *and* Spaces increasingly pervade our everyday life, appearing in various sizes, shapes, and application contexts, offering a rich variety of ways to interact. Our conference is the venue to discuss all those innovations in many different areas including design, software, hardware, understanding of use, and applications or deployments of interactive surfaces and spaces.

Sponsored by ACM SIGCHI and generously supported by Microsoft, ISS brings together researchers and practitioners from a variety of backgrounds and interest areas. Thanks to all authors submitting novel and innovative research, and the hard work of our program committee, we again have an engaging and high quality conference program. As in previous years, we kept the single track conference structure, split over four days. We had 119 submissions for the main paper track and selected 33 of them. In addition, the program covered a doctoral colloquium, workshops, tutorials, studios and posters and demos.

To recognize influential research published at our previous conferences we award the *10-Year Impact Award* at ISS for the second time. This year the award goes to Meredith Ringel Morris, AJ Bernheim Brush, and Brian R. Meyers for their submission “Reading revisited: Evaluating the usability of digital display surfaces for active reading tasks". Their contribution to TABLETOP'07 10 years ago addressed the much considered, but still contested, challenge of understanding the differences between reading and annotating text on paper, and reading and annotating text within digital media. The paper revisited the issue from the perspective of workplace tasks, and through a range of qualitative and quantitative studies considered a number of configurations of single and dual displays in horizontal and vertical configurations. Inevitably the conclusions were nuanced, including a set of considerations for the suitability of different set-ups for annotation, navigation, spatial management, composition, and ergonomic comfort. Ten years on and the impact of the paper is clearly seen in the many citations made to the paper by other researchers. These have come in waves of secondary studies as new reading technologies have emerged; and with the emergence of e-readers as commercial products and an increase in research on multi-device document reading and annotation, the work has genuinely stood the test of time, with citation rates actually increasing in recent years.

For the opening and closing keynotes this year we invited two excellent speakers. The conference opening keynote will be by Ali Mazalek, Canada Research Chair in Digital Media and Innovation and Associate Professor in the RTA School of Media at Ryerson University. In her talk, she will provide some perspectives on the role of physical movements and materials in the way we engage with and construct knowledge in the world, highlighting research from the Synaesthetic Media Lab that supports creativity, discovery and learning across the physical and digital worlds. Camille Utterback, an internationally acclaimed artist and pioneer in the field of digital and interactive art and Assistant Professor in the Art and Art History Department at Stanford University, will then close the conference on the last day with her keynote on the aesthetic and experiential possibilities of linking computational systems to human movement and physicality in visually layered ways. This will include her work ranging from interactive gallery installations, to intimate reactive sculptures, to architectural scale site-specific works.

To make this conference happen, we would like to thank a large number of volunteers that have contributed so much of their efforts to the organization of the conference, reviewing, venue arrangement, web presence, and publicity for ISS 2016.

Mark Hancock

Nicolai Marquardt

Johannes Schöning

Melanie Tory

Table of Contents

Session 3: Infoviz

Session Chair: Rina Rene *(University of Waterloo)*

Session 4: Cross Devices

Session Chair: Steven Houben *(UCL)*

Session 5: Interactions

Session Chair: Sheelagh Carpendale *(University of Calgary)*

Session 6: Large Displays

Session Chair: Edward Tse *(SMART Technologies)*

Session 7: Applications

Session Chair: Jo Vermeulen *(University of Calgary)*

Posters

Demos

Workshops & Tutorials

ISS 2016 Conference Organization

General Chairs: Mark Hancock *(University of Waterloo, Canada)*
Nicolai Marquardt *(University College London, UK)*

Program Chairs: Johannes Schöning *(Hasselt University, Belgium)*
Melanie Tory (*Tableau Research, USA)*

Local Arrangements Chairs: James Wallace (*University of Waterloo, Canada)*
Rina R. Wehbe (*University of Waterloo, Canada)*

Panels Chairs: Daniel Vogel (*University of Waterloo, Canada)*
Fabrice Matulic (*University of Waterloo, Canada)*

Proceedings Chair: Simon Voelker *(RWTH Aachen University , Germany)*

Posters Chairs: Miriam Sturdee *(Lancaster University, UK)*
Jo Vermeulen *(University of Calgary, Canada)*

Demos Chairs: Pedro Campos *(University of Madeira, Portugal)*
Florian Echtler *(Bauhaus-Universität Weimar, Germany)*

Web Chair: Victor Cheung *(University of Waterloo, Canada)*

Graphics Chair: Mojgan Ghare *(University of Waterloo, Canada)*

Tutorials, Workshops and Studios Chairs: Edward Tse *(SMART Technologies, Canada)*
Shah Rukh Humayoun *(University of Kaiserslautern, Germany)*

Doctoral Symposium Chairs: Stacey Scott *(University of Waterloo, Canada)*
Bongshin Lee *(Microsoft Research, USA)*

Student Volunteers Chairs: Steve Funke *(Chemnitz University of Technology, Germany)*
Diane Watson *(Waterloo University, Canada)*

Publicity Chairs: Craig Anslow *(Middlesex University, UK)*
Jun Kato *(National Institute of Advanced Industrial Science and Technology, Japan)*

Sponsorship & Industry Chairs: Carl Gutwin *(University of Saskatchewan, Canada)*
Harald Reiterer *(University of Konstanz, Germany)*

Madness Chair: Teddy Seyed (*University of Calgary, Canada)*

Mobile Chair: Fateme Rajabiyazdi (*University of Calgary, Canada)*

Program Committee: Craig Anslow (Middlesex University, London, UK)
Mirijam Augstein (FH Hagenberg, Austria)
Jason Alexander (Lancaster University, UK)
Tom Bartindale (University of Newcastle, UK)
Hrvoje Benko (Microsoft, USA)
Andrea Bellucci (University Carlos III of Madrid, Spain)
Pedro Campos (M-ITI, Portugal)
Paloma Diaz (University Madrid, Spain)
Augusto Esteves (Edinburgh Napier, UK)
Morten Fjeld (Chalmers University of Technology, Sweden)
Carl Gutwin (University of Saskatchewan, Canada)
Uta Hinrichs (St. Andrews, UK)
Jonathan Hook (University of York, UK)
Christian Holz (Microsoft, USA)
Steven Houben (UCL, UK)
Daisuke Iwai (University of Osaka, Japan)
Judy Kay (University of Sydney, Australia)
Ahmed Kharuffa (Reflective Thinking, UK)
Hideki Koike (Tokyo Institute of Technology, Japan)
Bongshin Lee (Microsoft, USA)
Andres Lucero (Syddansk Universitet, Denmark)
Rainer Malaka (University of Bremen, Germany)
Roberto Martinez-Maldonado (Univ. of Technology Sydney, Australia)
Alexandra Mendes (Teesside University, UK)
Jeff Nichols (Google, USA)
Clemens Nylandsted Klokmose (Aarhus University, Denmark)
Narges Mahyar (Univ. of British Columbia, Canada)
Harald Reiterer (University of Konstanz, Germany)
Anne Rodaut (University of Bristol, UK)
Yvonne Rogers (UCL, UK)
Stacey D. Scott (University of Waterloo, Canada))
Edward Tse (SMART, Canada)
Simon Voelker (RWTH Aachen, Germany)
Charles Perin (University of Calgary, Canada)
Giulio Jacucci (University of Helsinki, Finland)
Marc Herrlich (University of Bremen, Germany)
Dimitar Valkov (University of Münster, Germany)
Jo Vermeulen (University of Calgary, Canada)

Additional reviewers:

David Ahlström
Ali Alavi
Dzmitry Aliakseyeu
Ragaad AlTarawneh
Christopher Andrews
Thi Anh Ngoc Nguyen
Michelle Annett
Lisa P Anthony
Caroline Appert
Ahmed Arif
Ignacio Martin Avellino
Sriram Karthik Badam
Saskia Bakker
Olivier Bau
Michel Beaudouin-Lafon
Steve Benford
Ben Bengler
Peter D Bennett
Sourav Bhattacharya
Nadia Bianchi-Berthouze
Andrea Bianchi
Jacob T Biehl
Jon Bird
Rachel Blagojevic
Florian Block
David Bonnet
Sebastian Boring
Cati Boulanger
LouAnne E. Boyd
Michael Boyle
Luca Brayda
Constantin Brosda
Gerd Bruder
Frederik Brudy
Erin Buehler
Simon Butscher
Diogo Cabral
Jorge C. S. Cardoso
Lucila Carvalho
Géry Casiez
Alejandro Catala
Amira Chalbi
Tsung-Hsiang Chang
Olivier Chapuis
Fred Charles
Christian Cherek
Victor Cheung
Pei-Yu (Peggy) Chi
"Ming Ki" Chong
Christopher Clarke
Loraine E Clarke
Christopher Clarke
Andrew Clayphan
Andy Cockburn
Stéphane Conversy
Christian Corsten
Florian Daiber
Andreea Danielescu
Elisabeth Davenport
Nigel Davies
Alexander De Luca
Luigi De Russis
Rob Diaz-Marino
Paul Dietz
Andreas Dippon
Tao Dong
Carlos Duarte
Rachel Eardley
Vanessa Echeverría
Michael D Ekstrand
Niklas Elmqvist
Alex Endert
Jackson F Feijó Filho
Joao F. Ferreira
Bruce Ferwerda
Joel Fischer
Angus Forbes
Erik Jon Karl Forsström
Sebastian Franken
Christopher Frauenberger
Dustin E.R. Freeman
Joep Frens
Thomas Friedrichs
Bernd Froehlich
Kentaro Fukuchi
Steve Funke
Ana Cristina Garcia
Juan Camilo Garcia
Sven Gehring
Hans Gellersen
Audrey Girouard
Antonio Gomes

Additional reviewers (continued):

Nicholas Graham
Celeste Groenewald
Jens Grubert
Anselm Grundhöfer
Gabriele Guidi
Jonna R Häkkilä
Michael Haller
Nur Al-huda Hamdan
Peter Hamilton
Tracy A Hammond
Chris Harrison
Shoichi Hasegawa Hasegawa
Florian Heller
Javier Hernandez Rivera
Thomas Herrmann
Phil Heslop
Keita Higuchi
Otmar Hilliges
Ken Hinckley
Uta Hinrichs
Jussi Holopainen
Kasper Hornbæk
Eva Hornecker
Juan Pablo Hourcade
Shah Rukh Humayoun
Ke Huo
Stephane Huot
Alexandra Ion
Pourang Irani
Petra Isenberg
Tobias Isenberg
Mikkel R. Jakobsen
Ghita Jalal
Satnam Jaswal
Sampath Jayarathna
Mads Møller Jensen
Heejin Jeong
Hans-Christian Jetter
Tero Jokela
Hyunggu Jung
Shingo Kagami
Ulrike Kister
Aniket Kittur
Jesper Kjeldskov
Jarrod Knibbe
Takafumi Koike
Henrik Korsgaard
Thomas Kubitza
Alexander D. Kulik
Andreas M. W. Kunz
Daniel Kurz
Benjamin Lafreniere
Christian Lander
Gierad Laput
Shaimaa Lazem
Khanh-Duy Le
Eric Lecolinet
David Ledo
Sang-won Leigh
Daniel Leithinger
Yang Li
Q. Vera Liao
Tomas Lindén
David Lindlbauer
Stephen Colin Lindsay
Lars Lischke
Cindy Hsin Liu Kao
Can Liu
Can Liu Liu
Markus Löchtefeld
Zhihan Lu
Paul Boguslaw Lubos
Karon E MacLean
Scott Mail
Horia Alexandru Maior
Regan L Mandryk
Nicolai Marquardt
Mark T. Marshall
Diego Martinez Plasencia
Fabio Marton
Nolwenn Maudet
Laura Maye
Sven Mayer
Sinziana Mazilu
Dan McReynolds
Hongying Meng
Sarah Mennicken
Emma M Mercier
Yajie Miao
Toni Georg Michel
Klaus Miesenberger
Chulhong Min

Additional reviewers (continued):

Mohammed Mohanna
Kyle Montague
Simone Mora
Meredith Morris
Gerald Morrison
Stefanie Mueller
Jörg Müller
Maximilian Müller
Miguel Nacenta
Mathieu Nancel
Timothy Neate
Michael Nebeling
Keith Nesbitt
Thomas Nescher
James Nicholson
Christian Nitschke
Alexander Nolte
Mohamed Noordeen
Chris L North
Diana Nowacka
Marianna Obrist
Dietmar Offenhuber
Hyunjoo Oh
Leif Oppermann
Francisco Raul Ortega
João Gilberto Orvalho
Pablo Paredes
Alison Park-Douglas
Prajwal Paudyal
Simon T Perrault
Anthony Perritano
Ulrike Pfeil
Ken Pfeuffer Pfeuffer
Katrin Plaumann
Beryl Plimmer
Henning Pohl
Aura Pon
Martin Porcheron
Wendy A Powell
Manoj Prasad
Bonnie L Presser
Luis P. Prieto
Parinya Punpongsanon
Filipe Quintal
Roman Rädle
Roope Raisamo
Aarne Ranta
Umar Rashid
Sebastian Felix Rauh
Janet Read
Stephan R Richter
Markus Rittenbruch
Katja Rogers
Joan Roo
Chris Rooney
Gustavo Rovelo Ruiz
Jeffrey Rzeszotarski
Ramik Sadana
Alan Said
Daisuke Sakamoto
Amir Esmaeil Sarabadani Tafreshi
Ali Sarvghad
Yann SAVOYE
Florian Schaub
Aaron Scherzinger
Simone Schnall
Bertrand Schneider
Guy Schofield
Johannes Schöning
Sue Ann Seah
Ted Selker
Marcos Serrano
Teddy Seyed
Ehud Sharlin
Timothy Shaw
Buntarou Shizuki
Anton Sigitov
Beat Signer
Itiro Siio
Adalberto L Simeone
Mike Sinclair
Maurício Sousa
Marcus Specht
Viraj Srivastava
Oliver Staadt
Sophie Stellmach
Wolfgang Stuerzlinger
Maki Sugimoto
Aurélien Tabard
Kazuki Takashima
Masahiro Takatsuka
John C. Tang

Additional reviewers (continued):

Anthony Tang
Aneesh P Tarun
Robyn Taylor
Kate Thompson
Gustavo Fortes Tondello
Melanie K Tory
Giovanni Maria Troiano
Edward Tse
Umair ul Hassan
Nina Valkanova
Dimitar Valkov
Jean Vanderdonckt
Christina Vasiliou
Eduardo Velloso
Jo Vermeulen
Frederic D Vernier
Roel Vertegaal
Akos Vetek
Andrea Vianello
Simon Voelker
Daniel Vogel
Elena Volodina
Romain Vuillemot
Chat Wacharamanotham
Julie Wagner
Jagoda Walny
Robert Walter
Yi Wang
Daniel Wessolek
Mark Edmond Whiting
Alexander Wiethoff
Gerard Wilkinson
Andrew D Wilson
Raphael Wimmer
Gavin Wood
Jonathan Woodruff
Paweł W Woźniak
Peta Wyeth
Robert Xiao
Xiao Xiao
Anbang Xu
Xing-Dong Yang
Asim Evren Yantaç
YoungSeok Yoon
Sang Ho Yoon
Shunsuke Yoshimoto
Nicola Yuill
Beste Filiz Yuksel
Cheng Zhang
Zhong Zhou
Kening Zhu

ISS 2016 Sponsors & Supporters

ISS 2016 gratefully acknowledges our sponsoring SIG and the support of the following organizations:

Sponsor: SIGCHI · acm Association for Computing Machinery

Bronze Sponsors: Microsoft

Academic Sponsor: University of Waterloo

Movement, Material, Mind: Tangible and Embodied Interactions for Discovery and Learning

Ali Mazalek
RTA School of Media
Ryerson University, Canada
mazalek@ryerson.ca

ABSTRACT
We are increasingly tethered to pixelated boxes of varying shapes and sizes. These devices are ever present in our lives, transporting us daily into vast information and computational realms. And while our interactions with digital devices are arguably becoming more fluid and "natural", they still make only limited use of our motor system and largely isolate us from our immediate physical surroundings. Yet a gradual shift in the cognitive sciences toward embodied paradigms of human cognition can inspire us to think about why and how computational media should engage our bodies and minds together. What is the role of physical movements and materials in the way we engage with and construct knowledge in the world? This talk will provide some perspectives on this question, highlighting research from the Synaesthetic Media Lab [1] that supports creativity, discovery and learning across the physical and digital worlds.

ACM Classification Keywords
H.5.2. User Interfaces

BIOGRAPHY

Dr. Ali Mazalek has spent nearly 20 years trying to get digital technologies to fit better into her physical world and life, rather than letting them drag her into the pixelated depths of her computer screens. At the same time, she has a deep interest in how computational media can support and enhance creative practices and processes, supporting new forms of expression and new ways of thinking and learning. She is a Canada Research Chair in Digital Media and Innovation and Associate Professor in the RTA School of Media at Ryerson University. Her Synaesthetic Media Lab [1] is a playground where physical materials, analog sensors, and digital media happily co-exist and come together in novel ways to support creativity and expression across both science and art disciplines. Mazalek received M.S. and Ph.D. degrees from the MIT Media Lab and a Hon. B.Sc. in computer science and mathematics from the University of Toronto. She is a member of the inaugural cohort of the Royal Society of Canada's College of New Scholars, Artists and Scientists.

REFERENCE
1. Synaesthetic Media Lab http://synlab.ca/

ISS 2016, November 6–9, 2016, Niagara Falls, ON, Canada.
ACM ISBN 978-1-4503-4530-9/16/11.
http://dx.doi.org/10.1145/2992154.3003474

An Artist's Perspective on Interactive Surfaces and Spaces

Camille Utterback
Art & Art History Department
Stanford University, CA, USA
camille@camilleutterback.com

ABSTRACT

In her talk, Utterback will use examples of her own ground-breaking computer vision based artwork along with other art historical and contemporary examples to explore interaction design from a creative and sometimes radical perspective. While we often think our current technological innovations are completely new, a deeper look to the past provides intriguing visions, alternate possibilities, and provocations for the present. For example, many artists in the 1960's created projections onto multiple layers of glass or other transparent surfaces, including moving and sculptural surfaces. A closer look at these works reveals new possibilities for current work, which may also now be more feasible due to technological progress. Along with introducing inspiring examples from the past, Utterback will outline her current research into transparent, shaped and moving surfaces for interactive projections. Her current projects include multi-sided interactive installations using sets of scrims, fabric, LCD and OLED surfaces, and projections into custom formed glass – both multi-layered glass surfaces, and hand blown or cast glass. At Stanford, Utterback recently taught two quarters of a course titled "Sculptural Screens" and will also share some of her students' innovative projects. An important element of Utterback's artistic research is questioning how technology can be designed to either ignore or enhance our embodied selves. She will highlight this aspect of her work along with lessons she has learned in her near 20 years working as a professional artist at the intersection of art and technology.

ACM Classification Keywords

H.5.2. User Interfaces

BIOGRAPHY

Camille Utterback is an internationally acclaimed artist and pioneer in the field of digital and interactive art. Her work ranges from gallery installations, to intimate reactive sculptures, to architectural scale site-specific works.

Utterback's work explores theaesthetic and experiential possibilities of linking computational systems to human movement and physicality in visually layered ways. Utterback's extensive exhibit history includes more than fifty shows on four continents. In addition to a MacArthur "Genius" Fellowship (2009), other honors include a Creative Work Fund Media Arts Grant (2015), IBM Innovation Merit Award (2007), Transmediale International Media Art Festival Award (2005), Rockefeller Foundation New Media Fellowship (2002), and MIT's Technology Review's TR100 - the top 100 innovators of the year under 35 (2002). Public commissions include works for the Santa Cruz Museum of Art and History (2016), Liberty Mutual Group (2013), FOR-SITE Foundation (2012), the City of Sacramento, California (2011), the City of San Jose, California (2010), the City of St. Louis Park, Minnesota (2009), and the Whitney Museum's ArtPort website (2002). Camille's Text Rain installation, created with Romy Achituv in 1999, was recently acquired by the Smithsonian American Art Museum. Utterback holds a BA in Art from Williams College, and a Masters degree from the Interactive Telecommunications Program at NYU's Tisch School of the Arts. She is an Assistant Professor at Stanford University in the Department of Art and Art History, and by courtesy in the department of Computer Science. She is also Academic Director of the Stanford Graduate Design Program.

REFERENCE

1. Camille Utterback, http://camilleutterback.com

ISS 2016, November 6–9, 2016, Niagara Falls, ON, Canada.
ACM ISBN 978-1-4503-4530-9/16/11.
http://dx.doi.org/10.1145/2992154.3003475

Less Is More: Efficient Back-of-Device Tap Input Detection Using Built-in Smartphone Sensors

Emilio Granell
PRHLT, Universitat Politècnica de València
egranell@dsic.upv.es

Luis A. Leiva
Sciling
name@sciling.com

ABSTRACT

Back-of-device (BoD) interaction using current smartphone sensors (e.g. accelerometer, microphone, or gyroscope) has recently emerged as a promising novel input modality. Researchers have used a different number of features derived from these commodity sensors, however it is unclear what sensors and which features would allow for practical use, since not all sensor measurements have an equal value for detecting BoD interactions reliably and efficiently.

In this paper, we primarily focus on constructing and selecting a subset of features that is a good predictor of BoD tap-based input while ensuring low energy consumption. As a result, we build several classifiers for a variety of use cases (e.g. single or double taps with the dominant or non-dominant hand). We show that a subset of just 5 features provides high discrimination power and results in high recognition accuracy. We also make our software publicly available, so that others can build upon our work.

Author Keywords

BoD interaction; Tap-based input; Sensors; Machine learning; Feature selection

ACM Classification Keywords

H.5.2 User Interfaces: Input devices and strategies; Interaction styles; I.5.4 Pattern Recognition: Applications

INTRODUCTION

Current smartphones have enough capabilities to serve for many tasks. Increases in mobile performance, along with their high availability and range, are expanding further their capabilities and uses. One prominent use case is back-of-device (BoD) interaction, which enables eyes-free indirect input. BoD interaction can address severe occlusion problems on small touchscreens [1], has shown to be useful in increasing privacy by preventing shoulder-surfing attacks [3, 13], and can be used to control screen sharing apps such as multi-player games [2] or even to predict users' intention by the way they hold the device [15].

ISS '16, November 06–09, 2016, Niagara Falls, ON, Canada

ISBN 978-1-4503-4248-3/16/11... $15.00

http://dx.doi.org/10.1145/2992154.2992166

BoD interactions are largely dependent on sensors. Recently, it has been shown that this input modality can be accomplished on today's mobile devices with their built-in hardware like accelerometers, microphones, or gyroscopes [21, 24]. For this, many different features derived from sensor readings have been proposed, like sound volume, device motion, or frequency analysis. However, it is unclear which features would allow for practical use, since not all sensor measurements have an equal value for detecting BoD interactions reliably and efficiently. And while modern smartphones are incorporating low-power coprocessors for managing the built-in sensors, energy consumption is still a matter of great concern [20, 22, 24]. Our technique is the first to address this concern for BoD tap-based input detection, by analyzing which sensor features are most appropriate and removing thus unnecessary computations that could drain battery life after extended periods of use. Further, our technique is segmentation-free and provides high accuracy, which allows for practical, real-world use cases such as gaming or casual applications; see some examples below.

Today, one-handed input is widely recognized as a desirable property for mobile interaction [6, 9, 13], as the other hand is often occupied with a primary or secondary task [10]. For this reason, we mainly focus on detecting BoD taps with one hand. Some common scenarios of BoD tap-based interaction on smartphones include e.g. scroll a web page, take a picture, stop/resume a video, mute an incoming call, or play one-button games like Badland or FlappyBird. In sum, BoD taps enable an alternative set of interactions to augment (rather than replace) touchscreen input.

This paper presents a detection technique grounded on machine learning principles that enables highly accurate and practical BoD tap-based interaction using current hardware and sensors, without the need to instrument the mobile device. Concretely, this paper offers the following contributions:

- **Feature engineering.** We construct and select a subset of features that is a good predictor of BoD tap-based input, showing that a small subset thereof provides high discrimination power and results in high recognition accuracy.

- **BoD tap modeling.** We build several classifiers for a variety of real-world use cases; e.g. single or double taps with the dominant or non-dominant hand.

- **Release of the software.** We believe that making our software publicly available will be useful for others to enable efficient BoD interaction on current smartphones.

RELATED RESEARCH

Overall, sensing the mobile device with additional hardware has been very popular for enabling BoD interactions. For example, using a touchpad [1] or touch-sensitive surface [11], a stethoscope [14], tactile landmarks [2], or an external accelerometer attached to the device [12]. However, today's smartphones already include sophisticated built-in sensors, such as gyroscope, accelerometer, or gravity sensors. Therefore, in the remainder of this section we discuss previous works that focus on BoD interaction using current hardware and sensors.

ForceTap [8], JerkTilts [16], and TimeTilt [19] investigated motion as input using built-in accelerometers. However, these techniques seem unsuitable for continuous input. TapBack [18] relies on the sound created when tapping on the case of the phone, although recognition rates were found to be insufficient for practical use. BackPat [21] added frequency analysis and was primarily focused on finger differentiation, concluding that users preferred interacting with the index finger. Finally, BackTap [25] used sound volume and device motion for classifying BoD taps on a tablet's corners. This work was extended in BeyondTouch [24] to support more interactions, achieving encouraging results.

Altogether, previous works have relied on an unknown or a relatively arbitrary choice of sensors and features. For example, TimeTilt [19] looks at jerk movements over the Z axis (6 features), BackPat [21] uses an unknown number of features derived from gyroscope and sound frequency analysis, and BeyondTouch [24] uses 241 features sampled at 100 Hz. It is thus unclear how many features and what sensors would actually perform better for detecting BoD taps reliably. Our work is the first systematic examination in this regard.

On the other hand, researchers have been mainly concerned with accurate BoD tap event *segmentation*, and have approached this problem either from manual or ad-hoc perspectives. For example, relying on the user long-tapping on the screen for activation [21], waiting for a stable frame of 300 ms in the acceleration variation [19], or examing all available sensors and looking for a predefined threshold [22, 24]. In contrast, our technique is segmentation-free, based on solid machine learning procedures, so no previous knowledge is required to detect BoD tap-based input. Further, previous works were tested on a single smartphone, which calls into question how they would work across devices; as the position of sensors and thus the sensing values can differ from one device to another. In this regard, we have analyzed 9 different smartphones (Table 4), contributing thus with new knowledge on the feasibility and applicability of BoD tap input detection.

METHOD

Taking into account the sensors already included in most of today's smartphones, and considering the previous work on BoD interactions as well, we analyzed the accelerometer, gyroscope, gravity, and microphone. Altogether, these sensors measure, respectively: device acceleration, device angular speed, influence of the gravity acceleration, and environmental loudness.

Sensor Signals

We considered different signals derived from the sensors mentioned above. First, we computed the triaxial values and magnitude from accelerometer, gyroscope, and gravity sensors. Second, we measured environmental loudness with and without a "no tap" reference, in order to consider the influence of background noise while interacting. As in previous works [24, 25] the sound signal was treated in a decibel scale, by computing the logarithmic ratio between the measured value P and a reference value P_{ref}. Concretely, P_{ref} was set to 1 for the signal without "no tap" reference, whereas for the signal with "no tap" reference P_{ref} was set to the mean value of the first second previous to the tap acquisition. Finally, we computed the fraction of the acceleration attributed to the user's force, by subtracting the gravity acceleration to the measured device acceleration. This signal thus accounts for the actual force applied by the user while tapping. In sum, we eventually considered 18 different sensor signals for analysis, as listed in Table 1.

No.	Signal sources
4	Device acceleration (triaxial + magnitude)
4	Device angular velocity (triaxial + magnitude)
4	Gravity acceleration (triaxial + magnitude)
2	Environmental loudness (with and without "no tap" reference)
4	User acceleration (triaxial + magnitude)

Table 1: We analyzed 18 different signals derived from the smartphone sensors.

Sampling and Labeling

We conducted a preliminary experiment with 4 users to gain insights about the data we would collect afterward. Users were simply told to tap on the back of the device with their index finger within 1 second, followed by 3 seconds to rest. This was repeated up to 10 times. The Experimental Evaluation section provides more details of the procedure.

First of all, we should decide an appropriate sampling rate that would aim for lowering both computational cost and energy consumption. Based on the preliminary experiment, we observed that a BoD tap usually occurs in a time span of around 200 ms of duration (M=198, SD=11). Therefore, we measured the power consumption [26] of acquiring the sensor signals (Table 1) with the usual sampling rate of 100 Hz and by using the minimum rate that satisfies the Nyquist frequency, which in this case is a sampling rate of 10 Hz. Table 2 shows the results.

Sampling Rate (Hz)	Power Consumption (mW/s)
10	29.3 ± 6.6
100	126.3 ± 14.7

Table 2: Power consumption in the signal acquisition using different sample rates.

Together with the observed pattern of BoD taps (see an example in Figure 1), we conclude that a sampling rate of 10 Hz is enough to detect a BoD tap while ensuring minimum power consumption. Notice that this sampling rate is one order of magnitude lower than in previous works; e.g. [21, 24]. Eventually, the obtained signals were sampled using a fixed-width sliding window of 300 ms with 50% of overlapping context.

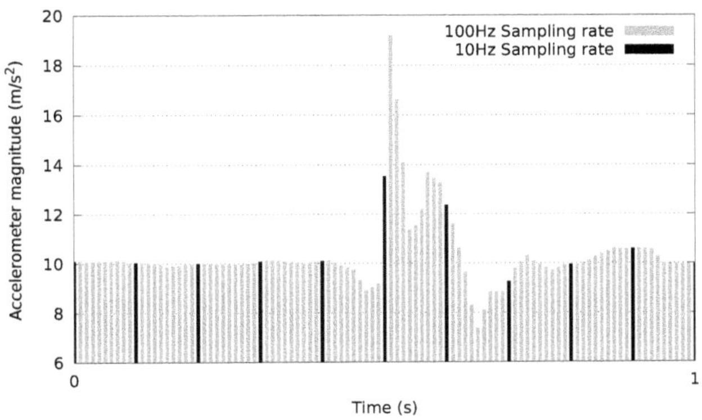

Figure 1: Sampling the accelerometer magnitude signal at 100 and 10 Hz for 1 second. When a BoD tap occurs, the detection pattern is equivalent in both cases.

Initially, during data acquisition, all samples were automatically labeled, at the frame level. That is, the samples included in the 1-second window were automatically labeled as tap frames, and the samples included in the 3-second window were automatically labeled as no-tap frames. Nonetheless, these labels were not accurate enough as not all frames in the 1-second window are actual tap frames. Thus, in order to provide a solid ground truth (i.e., the gold standard), all tap frames were ultimately supervised and manually annotated (10 814 out of 32 130 frames in total).

Feature Computation

Finally, a set of 24 functions was applied to each windowed sample. Eight of them were in the temporal domain, according to the research literature: root mean squared (RMS) and its derivative (RMS'), mean, median (Mdn), variance (σ^2), maximum (Max) and minimum (Min) values, and the Max/Min ratio. The other 16 functions were in the frequency domain, based on a Discrete Fourier Transform (DFT) [17] of 9 bins with a bandwidth of 0.625 Hz in the 0–5 Hz frequency range.[1] Table 3 depicts the functions used to parameterize each signal (both in time and frequency domains) listed in Table 1. In sum, we are considering an overall set of 18 sensors $\times$ 24 functions = 432 features for analysis.

Feature	Description
RMS	Root mean squared value
RMS'	Derivative of the RMS
Mean	Mean value
Mdn	Median value
σ^2	Variance
Max	Largest value
Min	Smallest value
Max/Min	Ratio between largest and smallest values
DFT	Discrete Fourier Transform (16 functions)

Table 3: Functions used as features of each signal sample.

[1]Regarding our frame size, the DFT input was padded with zeros.

Feature Selection

The purpose of feature selection is three-fold [5]: improving the prediction performance of the features, providing faster and more cost-effective features, and providing a better understanding of the underlying process that generated the data. In general, feature selection methods are used to identify and remove unneeded, irrelevant and redundant attributes from data that do not contribute to the accuracy of a predictive model or may in fact decrease it because of overfitting.

Step-wise, recursive strategies seem to be particularly computationally advantageous for feature selection. They come primarily in two flavors: forward selection and backward elimination. In forward selection, features are progressively incorporated into larger and larger subsets, whereas in backward elimination one starts with the set of all features and progressively eliminates the least promising ones. Both methods yield nested subsets of features, although backward elimination is usually preferred because in forward selection a feature added early may become redundant afterward. Therefore, in order to select the best subset of features for BoD tap-based input, we used backward feature elimination.

Recursive Backward Feature Elimination Algorithm

Formally, the algorithm for backward feature elimination is described as follows. Let $S = \{S_1, \ldots, S_n\}$ be a sequence of candidates for the number of features to retain ($S_1 > S_2, \ldots$). First, the algorithm fits a chosen model to *all* features (S_1) and each feature is ranked according to its importance to the model, using a normalized score that accounts for prediction errors and correlations between features. Then, at each iteration, the top S_i ranked features are retained, the model is refit, and performance is assessed. At the end of the algorithm, a consensus ranking is used to determine the best features to retain.

EXPERIMENTAL EVALUATION

To begin, we acquired sensor data from different users, who tested different conditions of BoD tap-based input on different smartphones. Then, several algorithms for feature selection were tested; among which we chose random forests, an ensemble learning method for classification that is well suited to non-linear modeling and has been proved robust against noise and overfitting [7]. Finally, we compared different classifiers for the most promising feature subset found.

Participants

We recruited 9 participants aged 25–35 (*M*=28, *SD*=2.3) using our University's mailing lists. We intentionally wanted users with rather broad backgrounds and so we recruited participants from e.g. Mechanical Engineering, Computer Science, or Physics. There was no economic compensation for the participants, who just provided us with raw sensor data.

Apparatus

Each participant tested two devices: their own smartphone and another participant's smartphone. This way, we can cover a range of usage scenarios. First, by using each participant's own smartphone, we ensure that the user is familiar with the device itself. Second, by using other participant's smartphone, we can gather insights about first-time usage of a BoD-capable device. Table 4 describes the smartphones used in our experiments. No smartphone was equipped with a protection case. We developed for Android, since it currently dominates the smartphone market.

Manufacturer	Device model	Size (mm)	Weight (g)	Android ver.
Samsung	Galaxy Note 3	151 x 79 x 8	168	4.4.4
	Galaxy S3 mini	122 x 63 x 10	112	5.0.2
	Galaxy S6 edge+	154 x 76 x 7	153	5.1.1
Google/LG	Nexus 4	134 x 69 x 9	139	5.1.1
	Nexus 5	138 x 69 x 9	130	6.0.0
Sony	Xperia Z	139 x 71 x 8	146	4.4.4
OnePlus	One	153 x 76 x 9	162	5.1.1
BQ	Aquaris M5	69 x 143 x 8	144	5.0.2
Motorola	Moto G2	141 x 71 x 11	149	5.0.2

Table 4: Smartphones used in our experiments. The 'Size' column denotes height x width x thickness.

Design

We acquired sensor readings for one-handed BoD tap input with the index finger, considering 2 factors: *Tap* (2 levels: single, double) and *Hand* (2 levels: dominant, non-dominant). This choice of factors and levels is motivated by previous works which suggested that users generally prefer tapping with the index finger and using one hand; c.f. Introduction section.

Both classification accuracy and the kappa statistic were considered the main outcome for analysis. The kappa statistic [23] gives a strong indicator of how a classifier performed across all instances, as compared to merely using accuracy for comparison. Further, the kappa statistic for one model is directly comparable to the kappa statistic for any other model used for the same classification task; akin the effect sizes used in statistical testing.

Procedure

We conducted the study in an open office environment; i.e., there were no fixed partitions or private rooms. Participants were seated during the whole study in the center of the office, surrounded by 15 employees. This way, we could strive for a balance between a carefully controlled setting and a real-world setting, where environmental noise and distractions may happen. In fact, different types of distractions actually happened, as reported by the participants. For instance, some participants found distracting the environmental noise coming from computer fans and people talking or laughing. One participant pointed out that the occasional movement of office chairs prevented him from being fully concentrated in the acquisition study. Finally, another participant mentioned that the mobile phone fell off his hands once. All these eventual distractions therefore reduced cognitive performance, which mimic a range of typical everyday scenarios. In sum, we acquired both positive (taps) and negative samples (ambient data) reflecting everyday smartphone usage.

We used a repeated measures within-subjects design, i.e., all participants tested all combinations (4 conditions in total). We ensured we would collect the same amount of data for each user: each participant had to perform 10 BoD taps with their index finger (both hands) on 2 smartphones, resulting in 40 session logs per participant and smartphone, 720 logs in total, 32 130 annotated frames overall (with tap or no-tap labels). As mentioned in the previous section, all tap-labeled data (10 814 frames) were manually supervised.

We used Latin squares to counterbalance the order of the conditions and mitigate learning effects between trials. This procedure reduces learning effects as well as asymmetrical skill transfer across conditions. We also used Latin squares to decide which device would be used by each user (both their own phone and another participant's phone).

Participants were able to practice and get accustomed to each condition before actually testing it. We developed an Android application that requested participants to enter a BoD tap within 1 second, followed by 3 seconds to prepare for the next BoD tap acquisition. We used a Wizard of Oz procedure, which informed participants only that they advanced to the next BoD tap acquisition.

Data Preprocessing and Analysis

We normalize the feature values (zero mean and unit variance) so that values that fall in greater numeric ranges do not dominate those in smaller numeric ranges. We consider user-independent tests, aiming at producing a subset of features that is a good predictor of BoD tap-based input for general use. We use 80% of the data for training (feature selection) and the remaining 20% for testing different classifiers. We balance the training data of positive (tap) and negative (no-tap) samples to avoid negatively skewing the classifiers.

To get performance estimates that incorporate the variation attributed to feature selection, we use the Area Under the ROC Curve (AUC) as the measure to optimize. The Receiver Operating Characteristic (ROC) curve is a plot of the true positive rate (TPR, also called specificity or recall) against the false positive rate (FPR, also called sensivity or fallout) of a classifier. In Section 4.6 we conduct a follow-up analysis in this regard.

By optimizing for the AUC (with regularization) we prevent overfitting and also exclude noisy features that do not contribute to the accurate discrimination of our classes (tap/no-tap). Next, we perform a 10-fold cross-validation using stratified sampling, to create balanced splits of the data that preserve the overall class distributions. We then choose the most promising feature subset and evaluate its performance against several classifiers on the testing partition.

Results

We report the results of detecting either single or double BoD taps. Actually, a double tap is detected when two consecutive taps are separated by a short amount of time; concretely, less than 300 ms according to our observations (M=287.52, SD=94.10). We first split the results by hand (dominant and no-dominant) and then analyze the different classifiers over the full testing partition (considering the data from both hands).

All experiments were performed in a user-independent setting, since user-independent tests allow us to generalize the results to potentially any user. In contrast, user-dependent tests are harder to deploy for real-world use, since each user would require a dedicated model, with a dedicated number of training and testing samples.

As observed in Figure 2, a small number of features is able to achieve competitive results. For example, using 5–10 features it is possible to achieve 98% of accuracy, which is an excellent result for real-world use. Furthermore, the Kappa statistics for subsets of 5 features and above suggest a high practical importance of the results.

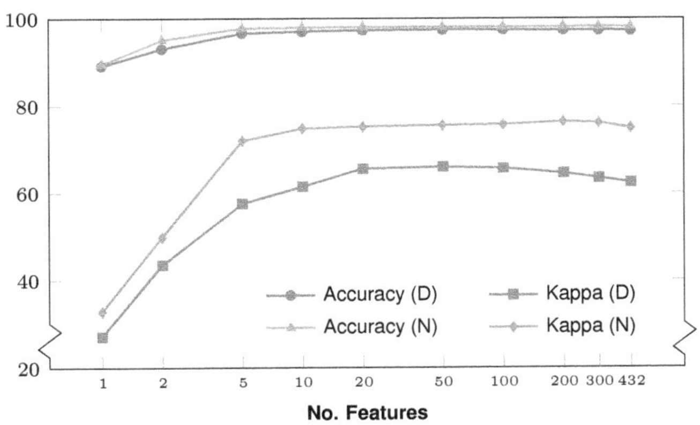

Figure 2: Results of BoD tap input detection, either single or double taps with the dominant (D) and non-dominant (N) hand.

Interestingly, slightly better results were observed for the BoD taps performed with the non-dominant hand. This is explained by the fact that users proceed a bit more carefully in comparison to their dominant hand, a well-known observation that has been reported in the research literature [4].

Surprisingly, we observed that the top-5 features were the same in all experiments; see Table 5. This is an interesting result, since a single general model can be implemented to detect BoD taps with either hand. More interestingly, the top-10 features are all related to the Fourier transform, which proves advantageous since they are really fast to compute. Also interestingly, we can conclude that the values of the higher frequency bins of the DFT from user acceleration are the features with most discriminative power overall.

In light of these observations, we decided to use the top-5 feature subset and build several classifiers. The choice of these classifiers was informed by previous works and their popularity in machine learning experiments. Concretely, we tested Partial Least Squares (PLS), Linear Discriminant Analysis (LDA), Generalized Linear Models (GLM), Generalized Boosted Models (GBM), and Support Vector Machines (SVM). We processed the data for both the dominant and non-dominant hand, aiming for general-purpose classifiers. Table 6 shows the classification results.

By way of baseline, in these experiments we include a PLS classifier that takes into account all the 432 features (PLS0). We also include SVMb, which is the same classifier with the same feature set used in BeyondTouch [24], by way of comparison with the most recent approach to detecting BoD taps.

Rank	Feature	Signal	Importance
1	$\Re(\text{DFT}_{4.375})$	| User acc. |	14.95
2	$\Re(\text{DFT}_{5})$	| User acc. |	13.82
3	$\Re(\text{DFT}_{3.75})$	| User acc. |	12.56
4	$\Im(\text{DFT}_{3.125})$	| User acc. |	12.09
5	$\Im(\text{DFT}_{2.5})$	| User acc. |	9.95
6	$\Im(\text{DFT}_{2.5})$	User acc. Z axis	9.75
7	$\Im(\text{DFT}_{3.75})$	| User acc. |	9.48
8	$\Im(\text{DFT}_{2.5})$	| Acc. |	8.15
9	$\Im(\text{DFT}_{4.375})$	| User acc. |	8.12
10	$\Im(\text{DFT}_{3.125})$	Gyro X axis	7.85

Table 5: Rank of the top-10 most discriminative features. $\Re(\text{DFT}_i)$ and $\Im(\text{DFT}_i)$ represent the real and imaginary parts of the bin centered in the ith frequency (in Hz), $|\cdot|$ denotes the magnitude of the triaxial signals, and "acc." stands for "acceleration."

Classifier	Accuracy (%)	95% Conf. Interval
PLS0	95.12	[93.87, 96.19]
PLS	96.75	[95.69, 97.61]
GLM	97.10	[96.09, 97.91]
LDA	97.10	[96.09, 97.91]
SVM	97.53	[96.58, 98.27]
SVMb	97.10	[96.09, 97.91]
GBM	97.46	[96.50, 98.21]

Table 6: Classification accuracy for BoD tap input with either hand, using the set of top-5 features. PLS0 indicates a PLS classifier trained with all the 432 features. SVMb denotes the BeyondTouch classifier.

As can be observed, using all features proves disadvantageous in many senses. Not only recognition accuracy is significantly degraded, but also a classifier that uses all features will result in less discriminative power (Table 7) and will require more computational resources than e.g. a GLM that uses just the top-5 discriminative features. This is an important result because selecting the right features can mean a difference between low performance with long computation times and high performance with short computation times.

Also an interesting result is the fact that BeyondTouch could perform a bit better if our set of discriminant features were used. More important, we should note that BeyondTouch uses 241 features sampled at 100 Hz and the equivalent SVM we tested uses 5 features sampled at 10 Hz.

ROC Analysis

One of the harder parts of implementing BoD taps is not about detecting the tap itself, but rather about not raising false positives. These false positives could happen when the user is doing any other activity with the mobile device that may shake it. For this reason, we decided to conduct an additional study on this matter.

The ROC curve (true positive rate *vs.* false positive rate) has many interesting properties:

1. It shows the tradeoff between sensitivity and specificity: any increase in sensitivity will be accompanied by a decrease in specificity.
2. The area under the curve is a measure of classification accuracy.
3. The closer the curve follows the left-hand border and then the top border of the ROC space, the more accurate the classifier.
4. The closer the curve comes to the 45-degree diagonal of the ROC space, the less accurate the classifier.

Classifier	PLS0	PLS	GLM	LDA	SVM	SVMb	GBM
AUC	0.500	0.704	0.782	0.831	0.805	0.768	0.833

Table 7: Testing the discriminative power of different classifiers with the Area Under the ROC Curve (AUC). PLS0 indicates a PLS classifier trained with all the 432 features. SVMb denotes the BeyondTouch classifier.

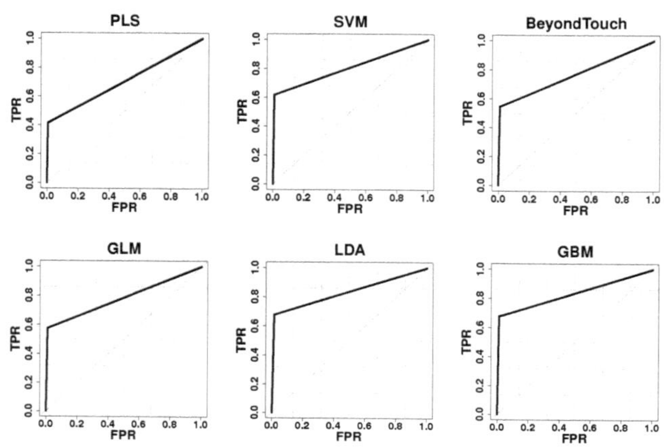

Figure 3: ROC curves of the different classifiers. The PLS0 curve is the 45-degree diagonal, so it is omitted.

A perfect ROC curve will be shaped with a sharp bend. As observed in Figure 3, the performance achieved by most of the tested classifiers is near perfect separation, with GBM and LDA achieving the best results. PLS0 achieved the worst results (its ROC curve is the 45-degree diagonal line). We should mention that the angle-shape elbow appears in logistic regression, i.e., when both the ground truth output and the prediction are binary (tap, no-tap).

Taken together, our results suggest that GLM, LDA, SVM, and GBM are the most competitive classifiers overall, given their accuracy (Table 6) and discriminative power (Table 7 and Figure 3). We hope this evaluation, together with the rest of the paper, will inform researchers and developers interested in incorporating robust BoD tap-based interactions to their prototypes or applications.

SOFTWARE IMPLEMENTATION

We have developed a background service that abstracts the logic for BoD tap input detection. The service implements a GLM-based classifier and does not provide a user interface, this way developers simply have to instantiate the service in their own apps. Moreover, the service runs in a single background thread. This allows it to detect BoD tap input without affecting the user interface's responsiveness.

In order to avoid interfering with unintended motion data, the service does not read the device sensors unless some application requests using the service. This also helps to reduce energy consumption to a great extent, since BoD tap detection is performed only when an app explicitly requires it.

Our implementation provides single and double BoD taps detection off-the-shelf. Therefore, the service can be used to handle basic interactions such as controlling a music player or selecting text onscreen. The service can also be used to complement traditional interactions such as muting an incoming call or playing one-button games. At the moment, the software is available for the Android operating system and can be downloaded from https://kant3.prhlt.upv.es/btap/.

LIMITATIONS

Apart from the "usual suspects" in lab-based studies (number of participants, age, etc.), we should mention a number of limitations worth discussing about this work. We believe that understanding these will be useful to researchers and developers interested in detecting BoD tap-based interactions reliably.

Firstly, we decided that our technique should detect only two location-unaware BoD taps (namely, single and double BoD taps anywhere on the smartphone's case). This decision was informed by previous works; see Related Research section. Eventually, considering more tap locations (1) requires the user positioning his hand more precisely [15] and, most important, (2) decreases accuracy to a great extent [24]. We believe that this would deter real-world use, however it is an interesting research avenue to consider in future work; see next section.

Secondly, we have not tested the use of protection cases, which are relatively common among smartphone users. It is expected that different case materials and thicknesses would have an impact on recognition accuracy. However, this is essentially the subject of a different paper.

Lastly, we should mention that the frequency range we considered was aimed at minimizing energy consumption (see Table 2) and thus it precludes the use of more advanced BoD interactions. For example, any tap can be decomposed into much shorter events (e.g., onset of contact, application of force, release of contact) that unfortunately are hard to detect within a sampling rate of 10 Hz.

FUTURE WORK

At present, we plan to explore how our BoD taps detection technique could be applied in other interaction domains. Namely, *off-screen* interactions such as patting with the thumb on the side of the device [21] and *around-device* interactions such as detecting slide gestures on a nearby surface [24].

On the other hand, we only considered sound frequencies in the subaudible range of 0–5 Hz, therefore the microphone sensor seems irrelevant in our experiments, discriminative wise. Nevertheless, richer interactions can be considered if we incorporate features derived from this sensor. For example, the above-mentioned around-device sliding gestures for scroll, zoom, etc. Although it is important to notice that the microphone, despite being an excellent sensor to detect BoD taps alone, is very sensible to ambient noise and thus it often raises many false positives. Therefore, it must be intelligently combined with other features to ensure a practical use.

CONCLUSION

We have proposed an efficient and reliable technique for detecting BoD tap-based input on current smartphones using commodity sensors. The value of our technique lies in the fact that we use low-cost yet highly discriminative features. We have made our software public so that others can build upon our work. The software can be easily incorporated into production-ready applications, as developers simply have to instantiate a background activity that abstracts the logic for BoD tap input detection.

Device manufacturers can benefit from this work by selecting an appropriate BoD tap detection feature subset that is performance-friendly and relatively easy to implement. Overall, BoD interaction can be used either as a means of direct input or as a complementary input aid. Ultimately, our work provides designers, researchers, and practitioners with new understanding on robust and efficient BoD tap input detection.

ACKNOWLEDGMENTS

Work partially supported by SmartWays (MINECO, RTC-2014-1466-4) and CoMUN-HaT (MINECO/FEDER, TIN2015-70924-C2-1-R).

REFERENCES

1. Baudisch, P., and Chu, G. Back-of-device interaction allows creating very small touch devices. In *Proc. CHI* (2009).
2. Corsten, C., Cherek, C., Karrer, T., and Borchers, J. HaptiCase: Back-of-device tactile landmarks for eyes-free absolute indirect touch. In *Proc. CHI* (2015).
3. De Luca, A., von Zezschwitz, E., Nguyen, N. D. H., Maurer, M.-E., Rubegni, E., Scipioni, M. P., and Langheinrich, M. Back-of-device authentication on smartphones. In *Proc. CHI* (2013).
4. Gignac, G. E., and Vernon, P. A. Reaction time and the dominant and non-dominant hands: An extension of Hick's law. *Personality and Individual Differences 36*, 3 (2004).
5. Guyon, I., and Elisseeff, A. An introduction to variable and feature selection. *J. Mach. Learn. Res. 3* (2003).
6. Hassan, N., Rahman, M., Irani, P., and Graham, P. Chucking: A one-handed document sharing technique. In *Proc. INTERACT*, vol. 5727 of *LNCS*. 2009.
7. Hastie, T., Tibshirani, R., and Friedman, J. *The Elements of Statistical Learning*, 2nd ed. Springer-Verlag, 2009.
8. Heo, S., and Lee, G. ForceTap: extending the input vocabulary of mobile touch screens by adding tap gestures. In *Proc. MobileHCI* (2011).
9. Hinckley, K., and Song, H. Sensor synesthesia: touch in motion, and motion in touch. In *Proc. CHI* (2011).
10. Hirotaka, N. Reassessing current cell phone designs: using thumb input effectively. In *Proc. CHI EA* (2003).
11. Holman, D., Hollatz, A., Banerjee, A., and Vertegaal, R. Unifone: Designing for auxiliary finger input in one-handed mobile interactions. In *Proc. TEI* (2013).
12. Hudson, S. E., Harrison, C., Harrison, B. L., and LaMarca, A. Whack gestures: inexact and inattentive interaction with mobile devices. In *Proc. TEI* (2010).
13. Leiva, L. A., and Catalá, A. BoD Taps: An improved back-of-device authentication technique on smartphones. In *Proc. MobileHCI* (2014).
14. Lopes, P., Jota, R., and Jorge, J. A. Augmenting touch interaction through acoustic sensing. In *Proc. ITS* (2011).
15. Mohd Noor, M. F. Exploring back-of-device interaction. In *Adj. Proc. UIST* (2013).
16. Oakley, I., and Park, J. A motion-based marking menu system. In *Proc. CHI EA* (2007).
17. Proakis, J. G., and Manolakis, D. K. *Digital Signal Processing*, 4th ed. Prentice Hall, 2006.
18. Robinson, S., Rajput, N., Jones, M., Jain, A., Sahay, S., and Nanavati, A. TapBack: Towards richer mobile interfaces in impoverished contexts. In *Proc. CHI* (2011).
19. Roudaut, A., Baglioni, M., and Lecolinet, E. Timetilt: using sensor-based gestures to travel through multiple applications on a mobile device. In *Proc. INTERACT*, vol. 5726 of *LNCS*. 2009.
20. Saeedi, R., Schimert, B., and Ghasemzadeh, H. Cost-sensitive feature selection for on-body sensor localization. In *Adj. Proc. UbiComp* (2014).
21. Seipp, K., and Devlin, K. BackPat: One-handed off-screen patting gestures. In *Proc. MobileHCI* (2014).
22. Serrano, M., Lecolinet, E., and Guiard, Y. Bezel-Tap gestures: Quick activation of commands from sleep mode on tablets. In *Proc. CHI* (2013).
23. Siegel, S., and Castellan, N. J. *Nonparametric Statistics for the Behavioural Sciences*, 2nd ed. McGraw-Hill, 1988.
24. Zhang, C., Guo, A., Zhang, D., Southern, C., Arriaga, R., and Abowd, G. BeyondTouch: Extending the input language with built-in sensors on commodity smartphones. In *Proc. IUI* (2015).
25. Zhang, C., Parnami, A., Southern, C., Thomaz, E., Reyes, G., Arriaga, R., and Abowd, G. D. BackTap: Robust four-point tapping on the back of an off-the-shelf smartphone. In *Adj. Proc. UIST* (2013).
26. Zhang, L., Tiwana, B., Qian, Z., Wang, Z., Dick, R. P., Mao, Z. M., and Yang, L. Accurate online power estimation and automatic battery behavior based power model generation for smartphones. In *Proc. CODES+ISSS* (2010).

TapSkin: Recognizing On-Skin Input for Smartwatches

Cheng Zhang, Abdelkareem Bedri, Gabriel Reyes, Bailey Bercik
Omer T. Inan, Thad E. Starner, Gregory D. Abowd
chengzhang, akareem.bedri, greyes, baileybercik, thad, abowd@gatech.edu; omer.inan@ece.gatech.edu
Georgia Institute of Technology

ABSTRACT
The touchscreen has been the dominant input surface for smartphones and smartwatches. However, its small size compared to a phone limits the richness of the input gestures that can be supported. We present TapSkin, an interaction technique that recognizes up to 11 distinct tap gestures on the skin around the watch using only the inertial sensors and microphone on a commodity smartwatch. An evaluation with 12 participants shows our system can provide classification accuracies from 90.69% to 97.32% in three gesture families – number pad, d-pad, and corner taps. We discuss the opportunities and remaining challenges for widespread use of this technique to increase input richness on a smartwatch without requiring further on-body instrumentation.

Author Keywords
Smartwatch interaction; acoustic sensing; inertial sensing; machine learning; input technology

ACM Classification Keywords
H.5.m. Information Interfaces and Presentation (e.g. HCI): Miscellaneous

INTRODUCTION
Most wearable devices such as the smartwatch, by necessity, are relatively small compared to traditional computing devices (e.g., laptop, smartphone). Input technologies for traditional computing devices cannot be easily replicated on wearable devices because of its size and form factor disparity. For instance, wearing an additional keyboard, even an optimized one [17], is inconvenient for most users and may limit the functionality of the hand. Therefore, providing an input technique for wearable devices that is both lightweight and always available is of much interest to the HCI community.

As a modern representative of wearable devices, the smartwatch uses a built-in capacitive multitouch screen as the surface for both input and output. Unfortunately, the relatively small size of the screen limits the richness of interactions. Many successful interactions on smartphones cannot be reproduced on smartwatches, such as multitouch gestures. Furthermore, these interaction issues, such as a large finger occluding parts of the screen, may seem insignificant on a smartphone, but are exaggerated on a smartwatch.

ISS'16, November 06-09, 2016, Niagara Falls, ON, Canada
 ISBN 978-1-4503-4248-3/16/11...$15.00
DOI: http://dx.doi.org/10.1145/2992154.2992187

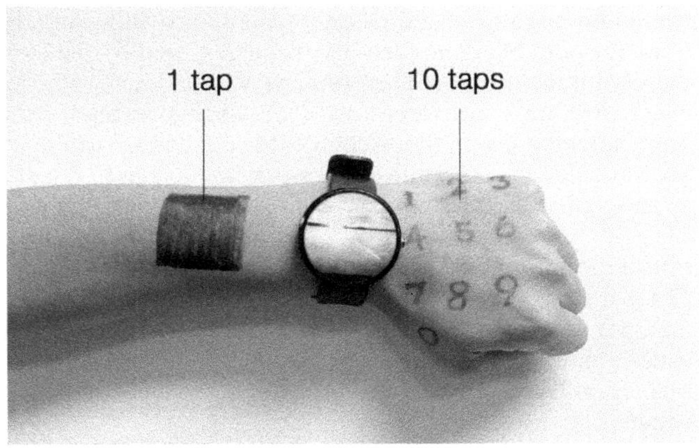

Figure 1. The TapSkin interaction technique. Drawings on the skin are only for clarity to indicate where input events can be performed.

These issues motivate us to look at the area surrounding the smartwatch, specifically the skin on the back of the hand, as a potential input surface. By extending the input outward to the skin, the user can view the screen while interacting, similar to the indirect interaction provided by a trackpad on a laptop. Although approaching the skin as the input surface has been previously explored [12, 29], those approaches have exploited additional instrumentation of the body to achieve the interaction. We demonstrate providing a rich set of tapping gestures that work with the current sensing capabilities of a smartwatch, specifically its microphone and inertial sensors.

We present TapSkin, a novel interaction technique that provides a family of tap gestures (up to 11 tap locations) on the skin around the wrist area without additional instrumentation, by only using the inertial measurement unit (IMU) and the microphone on a commodity smartwatch. Our approach offers a more practical solution for detecting on-skin tap gestures for a wrist-mounted device.

We provide the following contributions in this paper:

- The design and implementation of a family of tap gestures on the skin around the wrist area with the IMU and microphone on a smartwatch.

- An evaluation of the tapping gestures with 12 participants in a lab-based environment.
- User-dependent, independent, and user adaptive models are built to evaluate the challenges of personalizing on-skin gesture models for different participants.
- An extensive discussion of the challenges for the future practical deployment of this technique.

RELATED WORK

Though smartwatch and wearable devices have only started becoming popular in the past few years, providing interactions for portable computers has been explored by the community for many years. Therefore, we will first review the relevant work on smartphones and then discuss research about novel interactions on the wearable devices and smartphones. We conclude by examining past work that has used the skin as an input surface.

Interaction for smart phones

Compared with the traditional computers (e.g., desktops or laptops), the smartphone has a relatively small screen and is usually in the possession of its owner. Therefore, they share many similar interaction design challenges with the smartwatch.

Starting in the early 2000's, researchers have explored extending interactions on smartphones [13]. Some of the research focused on extending the input experience on the touchscreen by designing new gestures [26], improving the touch input accuracy [4], and detecting touch pressure [9]. Other researchers extended the interactions beyond the touchscreen, by providing novel motion gestures [27], or recognizing gestures on the back or the side of the case [2, 19, ?].

Interaction for wearable devices

Early explorations of input for wearable computing used an additional wearable device with physical buttons to provide text input (e.g., Twiddler [18]). These methods were able to provide reliable and fast input with training. More recent work has explored instrumenting different parts of the body, such as the fingers [5, 21, 34] or the arm [6, 12, 28] to provide a more limited input vocabulary, typically a small set of discrete gestures. However, all these works require the user to wear an additional device on the body, which is inconvenient and impractical for always-on devices such as smartwatches.

Interaction for smartwatches

As wrist-mounted devices (e.g., health activity monitors and smartwatches) dominate the wearable device market, more interest has been raised on improving the interactions with them, especially the input on the smartwatch. The approaches used have varied from increasing the size of the touchscreen by adding additional screens around the wrist [16], to using an active stylus which allows finer manipulation than the fingers [31], or designing specific finger/hand gestures [3, 33, 30, 23].

Different parts of the watch have also been appropriated for interaction to provide a richer input vocabulary. Perrault [24] and Funk [8] turned the watch band into an input surface for gestures and text input. Nenya [1] used a magnetic ring to provide gestures for the smartwatch by detecting a changing magnetic field. Xiao [32] showed the feasibility of using the screen as a joystick to provide more input events. WatchOut [36] extends the interaction to the case and band of the watch with only IMU sensors.

The input space for a smartwatch can also be extended by considering the larger area around the watch. Kim *et al.*[14] demonstrated a gesture watch using an array of IR proximity sensors to detect intuitive and gross hand gestures above the watch face.

Approaching the skin as the input surface

Though not demonstrated in the context of wrist-worn device interaction, Harrison *et al.*'s demonstration of OmniTouch [11] showed how depth sensing can be used to enhance interaction around the hand and wrist, and specifically using the skin as the interaction surface. Indeed, a person's skin is a good alternative input surface for wearable devices[29], because of its proximity to the smartwatch.

Obviously, defining the skin as the input surface has great potential in the space of gesture design. To recognize gestures on the skin, a variety of sensing modalities have been explored, including capacitance [25], vision [11], muscle activation via electromyography [28], infrared proximity sensors [15], motion/inertial and force [6], electricity[37] as well as sound [7, 12, 20, 22].

These solutions all require the user to wear additional device to accommodate the input technique, which is not ideal. Our solution, TapSkin, will demonstrate the feasibility of using a combination of sensors already in a smartwatch and a smartphone to detect a family of on-skin gestures, providing a more practical solution.

DESIGN AND IMPLEMENTATION OF TAPSKIN

TapSkin is demonstrated on commodity smarwatches (Sony SmartWatch3, Moto 360) using available sensor data from the gyroscope, accelerometer, and microphone. A Google Nexus 6 phone is used to running the recognition algorithm. We first explain the intuition behind moving from skin taps to recognized gestures in TapSkin. Then, we discuss the design of our TapSkin gesture sets. Lastly, we present details of the gesture recognition implementation we used for our validation experiments.

Theory of Operation

When touching the skin around the wrist, sound propagates from the point of contact towards the microphone in the smartwatch. We observed that the sounds of tapping on different locations of the hand are distinguishable from each other. As Figure 2 shows, tapping on the number 3 (depicted as N3 on the top right of Figure 2 and shown in Figure 1) would have more energy at higher frequencies compared with the tapping event on the number 1 (depicted as N1 on the top left of Figure 2 and shown in Figure 1). This is because the thickness of the tissue, the ratio of fat, and the structure of the bone underneath are all different at different locations along the back of the hand and along the top of the forearm. For instance, the position of number 3 is closer to the knuckle, which has more bone underneath. Therefore, the sound of a tap at that position has more energy at lower frequencies.

In addition, the act of tapping will induce a movement of the arm that the smartwatch is mounted on. As Figure 3 shows, tapping on different locations on the back of the hand, would introduce different kinds of movement. For instance, tapping on the number 7 and 9 (graphs N7 and N9 in Figure 3) would first have a positive peak on the x-axis of the gyroscope and then a negative peak, while tapping on the number 1 and 3 (graphs N1 and N3 in Figure 3) would first generate the negative peak along the y-axis and then a positive peak.

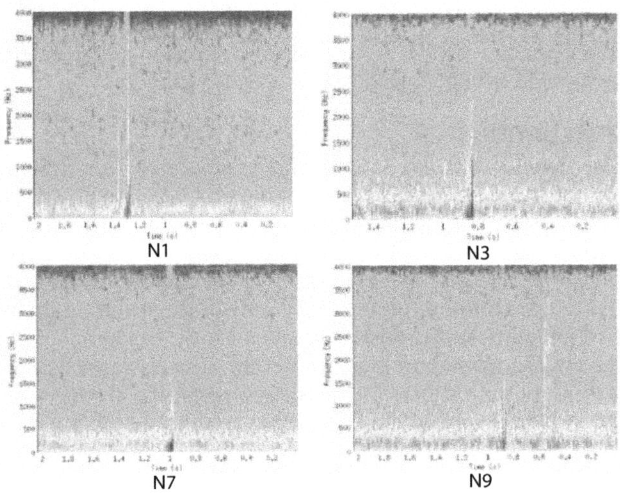

Figure 2. Comparing the acoustic response of taps at different location around the smartwatch.

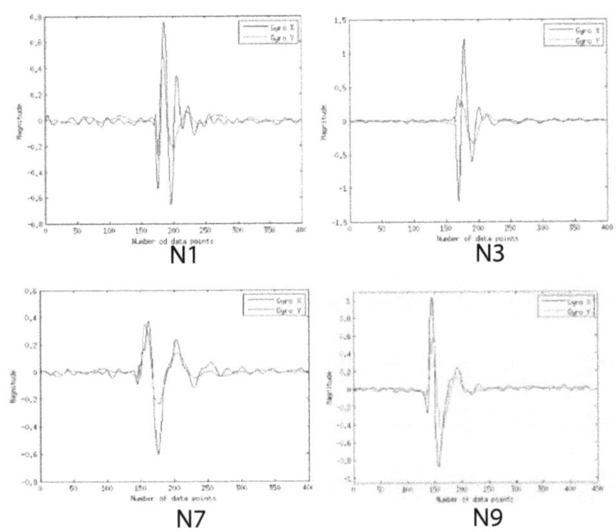

Figure 3. Comparing gyroscope sensor response of taps at different locations around the smartwatch.

These visually apparent differences across the various sensing modalities strongly suggest that with appropriate data acquisition and analysis, we should be able to distinguish different locations of a tap on the skin around the smartwatch. Therefore, we choose to use the gyroscope and accelerometer to characterize arm displacement and the microphone to record the acoustic response of the tap.

Gesture Design and Applications

With this intuitive and theoretical motivation, we first consider three sets of tapping gestures that can map into useful input: the NumPad, the DPad, and the CornerPad. Figure 4 depicts these three gesture sets. For each set, there is also a single tap on the top of the forearm beyond the smartwatch (depicted as a gray rectangular patch).

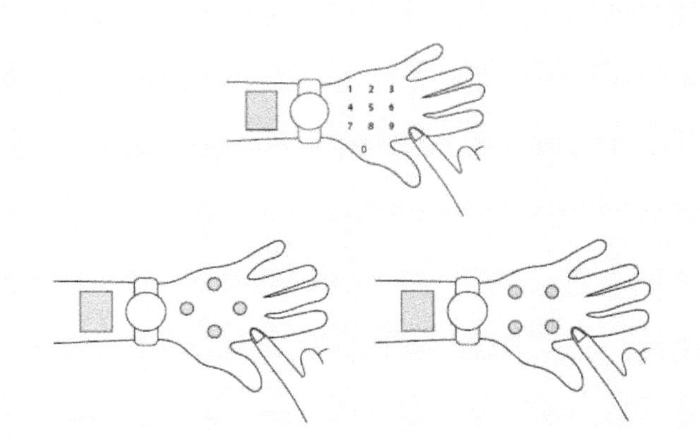

Figure 4. The TapSkin gesture sets: NumPad (top), DPad (bottom left), and CornerPad (bottom right).

NumPad

The NumPad gesture family simulates the layout of a number pad, which provides 10 distinct tap locations on the back of the hand and one tap location to the left side of the watch (as seen in Figure 4). It can potentially be used for entering numbers or even text (through multi-tap or T9), which is currently difficult on a small touch screen. The tap gesture on the left of the watch (TapLeft) is designed for two purposes: one is to serve as the activation gesture, informing our recognizer when it should pay attention for skin gesture input. The other is to undo the last gesture, such that the user can revise their input.

DPad

As Figure 4 shows, DPad contains the TapLeft gesture as well as four tap gestures located at the top, bottom, left, and right parts of the back of the hand. It can be used for directional controls or scrolling through a list of items on the smartwatch. For instance, the most common operation on a smartwatch touchscreen is to scroll down the menu vertically and horizontally. This operation can be naturally mapped to the four tap gestures using DPad. The TapLeft gesture is used for activation as well as for confirming the selection of a menu item or application.

This main advantage of the TapSkin DPad will be seen with applications that display a lot of information. DPad will reduce occlusion while still providing an intuitive means of interaction.

CornerPad

The CornerPad includes the four corners on the back of the hand. The two gestures on the left are close to the wrist joint, and the other two gestures on the right are close to the knuckles at the base of two fingers. These four distinct tap gestures can be used as shortcuts to certain applications on a smartwatch. The TapLeft gesture again serves as the activation gesture into CornerPad.

Gesture Recognition

We apply a traditional machine learning pipeline to recognize the gestures, which consists of two steps: gesture event detection and gesture classification. To identify events, we first apply a sliding window of 1.2 seconds with 75% overlap on the synchronized data streams of the gyroscope, accelerometer, and the microphone. Within each window, we detect whether there is a gesture event. If a gesture is detected, we pass the event window for feature extraction, which is then passed to a Support Vector Machine (SVM) to classify the gesture events. We use the sequential minimal optimization (SMO) of SVM provided by Weka for building our training models and for real-time classification in our prototype system [10].

Event Detection

To detect whether there is a gesture event in each 1.2 second sliding window, we inspect the window to determine if either the gyroscope or accelerometry data passes an empirically-determined threshold value based on the maximum energy in the window. If one of the thresholds is satisfied, we continue to the next step in the pipeline to define an *event window*.

Within the original sliding window used for event detection, we locate the position of the maximum absolute value of each sensor signal. Note that the max points may be at different times for each sensor. We then define an event window of data values for each sensor stream balanced around that maximum point. The size of event window is 0.5 seconds both IMU data (accelerometer and gyroscope) and acoustic data. If the maximum point is too close to the edge of the original sliding window, we advance into the previous or next sliding window. We now assume there is a gesture within that event window, so the raw data is passed along for feature selection.

Feature extraction

For each event window, we calculate a vector with 286 features.

For each axis of the linear acceleration and the gyroscope data, we first derived virtual sensors by taking the derivative of each axis. Then for each axis of the raw sensor and virtual sensors, we extracted a set of statistical features including the maximum, minimum, mean, median, standard deviation, root-mean-square(RMS), variance, zero-crossing rate, and the values of peaks and their differences. To capture the relationship between the different axes of each IMU sensor, we also calculate the ratio and differences of the energy, first and second absolute peak values of each two axes on each sensor. We also perform a Fast Fourier Transform (FFT) on the gyroscope data (50 points), which results in 24 features (abandoned the first bin) for each axis. Since the frequency of our gesture is under 6kHz, we only add the values of first three bins of the FFT results and the entropy across the values of different bins into a feature vector.

For the acoustic data, we extracted features in the frequency domain. We divided the window into 30ms frames with 50% overlap. We first extract 26 Mel-frequency cepstral coefficients (MFCC) features, based on the observation that the sounds generated by these on-skin gestures are mostly under 4kHz, which is similar to the range of the human voice. For each frame of data, we also calculate the FFT and average the results across different frames. We only keep the first 30 values of the FFT results, which represent the magnitude of frequencies between 0Hz to 500Hz, which we determined empirically as the most informative frequency band for the sound of our gestures. The center of mass across the frequencies is also added to the feature vector.

The feature vector is used to train a support vector machine to recognize which gesture has been performed.

EVALUATION

We conducted a user study to understand how our technique would work across different people and how we could build optimal machine learning models for each gesture set. We collect gesture examples first and apply offline analysis to build our models. We evaluate the system offline instead of using a real-time prototype. By collecting gesture examples first and performing an offline analysis, we can better explore the classification problem. At present, there is a practical limitation for running the data processing pipeline in real-time on the watch, so we offload that computational task to a paired smartphone. Therefore, the sensor data needs to be transmitted from the watch to the phone. However, continuously transmitting acoustic data via Bluetooth in real-time is limited by the bandwidth between the mobile phone and smartwatch. The data transmission would introduce a non-negligible latency while the system is running the real-time. This is the current limitation of the system implementation. However, as the processing power of the smartwatches are expected to increase over time, we would expect the whole system to run exclusively on the watch in the near future.

Apparatus

We evaluated our technology on a Sony SmartWatch 3 (Android Wear) for data collection and a Nexus 6 (Android 5.1) for running our machine learning algorithm. We specify the highest sampling rate available for the gyroscope (200Hz) and the linear acceleration (250Hz), but we intentionally lower the sampling rate for the microphone to 8kHz, as the sound generated by the tap event on the skin is mostly under 4kHz, and the lower sampling rate reduces power consumption. The lower sampling rate also minimizes the data transmission time between the watch and the phone, reducing the latency for eventual real-time classification results.

Study Design

To evaluate TapSkin, we recruited 12 participants (6 male) from our university campus with an average age of 26 years.

The study was conducted in an open space at a university building, where the sound from the air conditioner as well

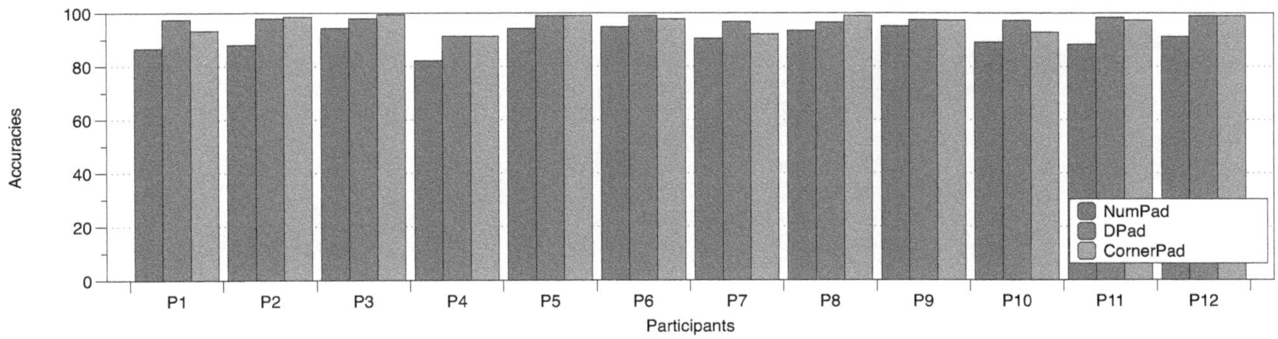

Figure 5. The classification accuracy for each participant

as people's talking and movement can be heard. Each participant was asked to complete surveys before and after the study gauging their experience. At the beginning of the study, we asked the participants to wear the watch on the left wrist and use the right hand to perform the gesture. We advised them to wear the watch closer to the hand and adjust the band tightly but comfortably on the wrist. For consistency and helping participants remember the locations of each tap gesture, a number pad as seen in figure 1 was drawn on the back of each participant's hand.

A researcher then demonstrated the entire gesture set and asked the participant to practice. The formal study consisted of 8 sessions. During each session, the participant performed all the gestures while sitting in front of a table, where they could rest their elbow during the study. The participants were asked to take breaks for a few minutes between sessions to reduce fatigue. During these breaks, they could walk around or take the watch off if desired. The whole study lasted approximately 45 minutes on average.

During each session, they were asked to follow the stimuli displayed on the screen of the watch to perform the NumPad gestures. DPad and CornerPad are a subset of the NumPad gesture family. The sequence of the stimuli was randomized. Five instances of each gesture were collected per session, and 11*5 = 55 total gesture events were collected per session. Each gesture event was saved into 2-second raw data files for further analysis. In total, we collected 5*11*8 = 440 gesture instances from each of the 12 participants. We recorded video of the sessions for later analysis.

Results

We first removed instances where the researcher observed the participant tapping at the wrong position or missing the event. Only the remaining gesture instances were used for the offline analysis. As a result, we collected 5264 gesture instances from 12 users in total.

During the study, each participant provided gesture instances through 8 separate sessions. To understand how the system works when the training data came from different sessions, we applied a "leave-one-session-out" method to evaluate the system. For each participant, we iteratively used the instances from one session as the testing data, while using the instances from the rest seven sessions as the training data to build the model.This step was repeated eight times for each participant and we reported the overall results.

Gesture Event Detection Results

In our data processing pipeline, the first step is to detect the gesture event. If we failed to detect any gesture event in any sliding window in the offline files representing a gesture instance, we counted this instance as a false-negative error. If we detected more than one gesture event representing a gesture instance in the files' sliding windows, we counted these instances as false-positive errors. We did not run these instances with errors through gesture classification. As a result, 9 false-positive errors and 162 false-negative errors were detected out of 5264 gesture instances (NumPad). The false positive rate are 0.17%, 0.17%, 0.21%, and the false negative rate are 3.08%, 2.68%, 2.84% respectively for NumPad, DPad and CornerPad.

NumPad Classification Results

The average accuracy across 12 users for NumPad in the leave-one-session-out evaluation is 90.69%. The accuracy for each participant is shown in Figure 5. Participant 9 (P9) provided the gesture instances with the highest accuracy (95.14%) and P4 provided the instances resulting in the lowest accuracy at 82.09%. We reviewed the video from P4's data collection session and found that the way the participant performed the tap gesture was apparently lighter than others. We further examined the data and discovered that the microphone barely captured the sound of some gesture events, resulting in the lower reported accuracy. We present the confusion matrix of NumPad in Figure 6.

The lowest precision of 85.62% was provided by N8. Most of the confusion exists between adjacent tap locations. For instance, 3.05% and 7.19% of the instances of N8 were misclassified as N7 and N9. The N0 and LeftTap are the most accurate gestures at 97.15% and 96.55%, respectively. We believe this is due to the fact that the position of these two gestures are distinct from others on the back of the hand. The closer the two tap locations are, the more similar displacement patterns are during the tap captured on the wrist.

DPad Classification Results

The DPad gesture family is a subset of NumPad gestures. The four tap gesture is mapped to the N2, N4, N6, and N8 in the NumPad gesture set. The layout of the these four tap locations

	N0	N1	N2	N3	N4	N5	N6	N7	N8	N9	TapLeft
N0	97.15%	0.22%	0.44%	0.44%	0.00%	0.00%	0.00%	0.66%	0.88%	0.22%	0.00%
N1	0.22%	85.81%	6.88%	1.29%	2.80%	0.43%	0.22%	1.08%	0.00%	0.43%	0.86%
N2	0.00%	4.70%	86.75%	5.56%	0.43%	1.71%	0.85%	0.00%	0.00%	0.00%	0.00%
N3	0.43%	0.22%	3.70%	93.26%	0.00%	0.87%	1.30%	0.00%	0.22%	0.00%	0.00%
N4	0.22%	0.43%	0.43%	0.00%	90.91%	5.19%	0.43%	0.87%	0.00%	0.65%	0.87%
N5	0.00%	0.44%	1.54%	0.44%	3.96%	89.43%	2.86%	0.44%	0.88%	0.00%	0.00%
N6	0.00%	0.21%	0.21%	1.27%	0.21%	3.82%	93.84%	0.00%	0.21%	0.21%	0.00%
N7	1.08%	0.87%	0.43%	0.43%	1.52%	0.22%	0.00%	89.59%	3.69%	1.74%	0.43%
N8	1.74%	0.00%	0.00%	0.22%	0.65%	1.31%	0.22%	3.05%	85.62%	7.19%	0.00%
N9	0.85%	0.21%	0.00%	0.21%	0.63%	0.42%	1.27%	0.21%	7.40%	88.79%	0.00%
TapLeft	0.00%	0.43%	0.43%	0.22%	0.86%	0.22%	0.00%	0.86%	0.22%	0.22%	96.55%

Figure 6. Confusion Matrix for NumPad

is similar to a control pad, which can be used to navigate in the up, down, left and right directions.

The average accuracy for DPad across 12 participants is 97.33%. P4 and P5 provided the gestures with the lowest accuracy (91.28%) and highest accuracy(98.99%), respectively. As the confusion matrix in Figure 7 shows, TapLeft has the highest accuracy 97.84% and N4 offered the lowest at 96.75%.

	N2	N4	N6	N8	TapLeft
N2	97.22%	0.64%	1.71%	0.43%	0.00%
N4	0.65%	96.75%	1.30%	0.43%	0.87%
N6	0.64%	1.27%	97.66%	0.42%	0.00%
N8	0.65%	1.09%	0.65%	97.17%	0.44%
TapLeft	0.43%	1.51%	0.22%	0.00%	97.84%

Figure 7. Confusion Matrix for DPad

CornerPad Classification Results

The layout of the CornerPad gestures is mapped to the four corners on the back of the hand. By locations, they are mapped to the N1, N3, N7, and N9 gesture of the NumPad set. The average accuracy across 12 participants is 96.64%. The gesture instances from P3 achieved the highest accuracy of 99.48%. P4 offered the gesture instances with the lowest accuracies of 91.32% in the cross evaluation.

The confusion matrix of the CornerPad is shown in Figure 8. The most accurate gesture is N9 with an accuracy of 98.52% and the least accurate gesture is N7 with an accuracy of 94.36%. Interestingly, we noticed the TapLeft gesture was mostly confused with N1 and N7, which are the closest tap locations to TapLeft in the CornerPad.

	N1	N3	N7	N9	TapLeft
N1	94.41%	2.15%	1.51%	0.65%	1.29%
N3	0.87%	98.04%	0.43%	0.65%	0.00%
N7	1.08%	0.65%	94.36%	3.25%	0.65%
N9	0.42%	0.63%	0.42%	98.52%	0.00%
TapLeft	0.65%	0.43%	1.08%	0.00%	97.84%

Figure 8. Confusion Matrix for CornerPad

DISCUSSION

Evaluation with more practical models

The results of leave-one-session-out validation provide a good estimate of how well the classifier performs on recognizing different gestures across different sessions. However,

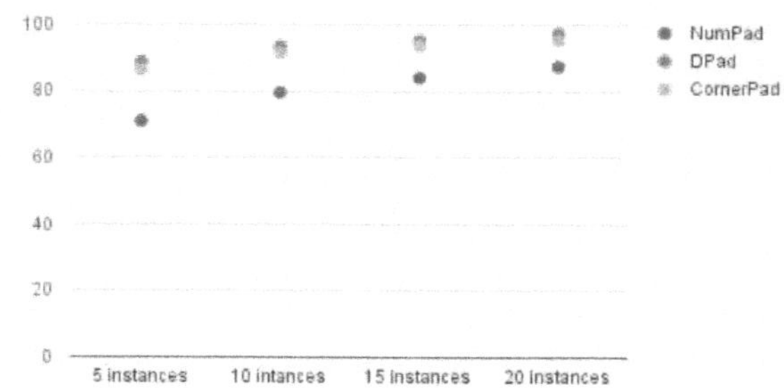

Figure 9. Accuracy of different number of training instances for user-dependent models

in practice, building a real-time gesture recognition model would face more challenges, such as how many training instances are needed to build a model for a person, whether the model can be built for user-independent operation, and how many calibration instances would be necessary to improve the classification accuracy. To answer these questions, we conducted another set of experiments by building user-dependent, user-independent(leave-one-participant-out), and user-adaptive models. Similarly, we simulate the real-time classification pipeline by applying a sliding window of 1.2 seconds with 75% overlap for all the files we collected in all the models we built in this section.

User-Dependent Models

User-dependent models only use the data from the same participant to train a model which will be then used for classifying his/her own gestures. Usually, a model trained with more training instances provide higher recognition accuracies, but also require longer time to collect the data from the participant, which can be annoying. Therefore, to investigate how many instances are needed to train a user-dependent model, we built user-dependent models for each participant by using the first 5, 10, 15, and 20 collected instances per gesture from that same participant to train an SVM model. We used the remaining instances of that participant to test the model. Evaluating TapSkin with user-dependent models across the data collected in different sessions would be similar to how the system would work in practice. A user provides the data in the first few sessions, which will be used to build models evaluated in the later sessions. The results are shown in Figure 9. When only using 5 instances to build a model, the overall accuracy for NumPad, DPad and CornerPad across 12 participants were 70.97%, 88.69% and 86.3%. The highest accuracies were 87.33%, 97.09%, and 95.23% respectively for NumPad, DPad and CornerPad, when we trained the user-dependent models with 20 instances per gesture for each participant.

User-Independent and User-Adaptive Models

Compared with user-dependent models, user-independent models(Leave-one-user-out) do not require the user to provide any training data before using the technique. It would improve the user experience by reducing the workload on the side of the user, but it places a higher standard for the reliability of the gesture models.

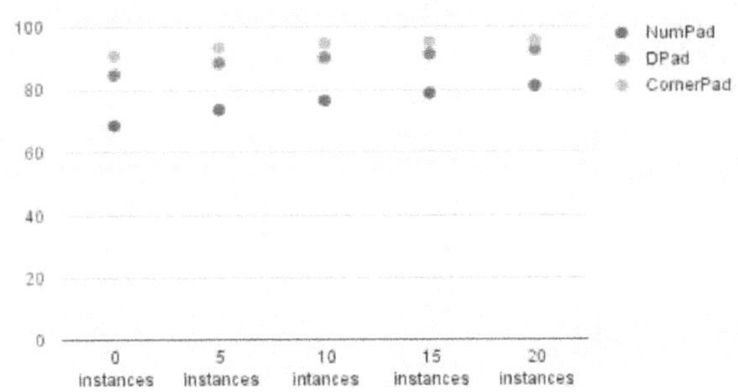

Figure 10. Accuracies of User-independent and user-adaptive Models. Along the x-axis, a value of 0 instances is the same as a user-independent model.

We used the data of 11 participants from the total 12 participants to train a support vector machine, which is then tested with data from the remaining participant. The average accuracy across 12 participants for the NumPad, DPad and CornerPad are 68.65%, 84.78% and 90.35% as shown in Figure 10.

The user-adaptive model falls in between the user-independent and user-dependent models, considering the amount of effort required for each user to provide training instances. It strengthens the user-independent models by adding a few number of instances per gesture from an individual user as demonstrated by [35]. We evaluated our technique on user-adaptive models by incrementally adding 5, 10, 15, and 20 instances per gesture from each participant to the user-independent training set. As Figure 10 shows, the more personalization data is added to the models, the higher the average accuracies are. The highest accuracies are reached when 20 instances are added to the models, which are 81.13%, 92.64%, and 95.66% for NumPad, DPad and CornerPad.

We notice that the accuracies of user-adaptive models with 20 instances per gesture are lower than the accuracies of user-dependent models built with similar number of training instances. We believe this is due to tap locations being different from person to person based on different hand sizes. For example, tapping at the same location of the hand (e.g., knuckle) can generate a different sound from person to person. Therefore, adding more training data from others may not necessarily help improve the recognition accuracy.

However, the user-independent model may work for a smaller set of gestures. CornerPad achieved 90.35% accuracy with user-independent models. With 5 and 10 instances added, the accuracy further increased to 93.32% and 94.72%. We believe it is because the distances between the tapping locations in CornerPad are longest, which potentially provides more distinguishable characteristics in different gestures. A practical approach is to ask the user to test each gesture before using it and only provide a few calibration gestures for those gestures that may be misclassified.

Addressing the false-positive and negative errors

One important practical challenge for this gesture recognition technique for wearable devices is how it works when being deployed in a real device which is worn by the user all day long. In real scenarios, this may trigger false-positive (FP) and false-negative (FN) errors, which is critical to the perceived user experience.

Therefore, we conducted a more detailed analysis into these errors. In the above experiment, our system triggered 9 (0.17%) FP and 162 (3.08%) FN errors out of 5264 gesture instances. We first looked into the 162 FN errors. We found only 13 of the FN errors were caused by not passing the predefined thresholds.The rest 149 FN errors were introduced by not being able to capture the whole 0.5 feature extraction window after the peak localization. After reviewing the video and the sensor data, we found three reasons.

The first one is that if the participant (E.g. P4) made weak taps, the peak localization may not capture the peak as expected. The second reason is that the participant performed the gestures either too early or too late, such that only part of the gesture fell into the 2-second window which were saved into sensor files. The third reason is that the audio data was not synchronized with IMU data while saving to files, which introduces a misalignment on the time-stamp. As a result, one of the sensor (mostly the audio) files failed to capture the whole gesture. This happens more when the watch is over heated after performing the heavy computing workload for a certain period of time. As the watches become more powerful in the future, it is reasonable to expect that the last two kinds of FN errors can be reduced by running the whole system online exclusively on the watch.

Although our system only triggered 9 FP errors, avoiding the FP errors is still quite a challenging task. On one hand, the results caused by FP errors can be very frustrating to a user. For instance, if TapSkin is used to control the dial pad, FP errors may result in unwanted phone calls when the user even does not notice it at all. On the other hand, all the gesture instances were captured in a daily office area in a static posture(sitting), where only gentle noise (e.g. talking, walking, air conditioning) existed compared with outdoor noise. To address this FP issue in real scenarios, one way is to apply more advanced signal processing technique (e.g. band-pass filter) and build another classifier in the gesture event detection step with carefully collected noise data. The other method is to use an activation gesture for TapSkin. Only when an activation gesture is detected, the system begins recognizing the whole gesture set. The activation gesture should be both intuitive to perform, has less confusion with other gestures, and providing low FN and FP error rates. We observed that the tap on the left side of the watch satisfies these criterion by providing the highest classification accuracy and relatively low FN and FP error rates. Therefore, we chose this gesture as the activation gesture for all TapSkin gesture families. In practice, in order to further reduce the false-positive errors, a double tap instead of a single tap on the left of the watch can be used as the activation gesture.

Improving the Sensing Unit

TapSkin uses both inertial sensing (gyroscope, accelerometer) and acoustic sensing (microphone) to detect the tap events on the skin. To understand which sensing unit is more informative in recognizing the on-skin tap gestures, we conducted an additional experiment by using only the data from IMU or the microphone in a traditional 10-fold-cross-validation for the NumPad gesture set on each participant. The overall results across 12 participants are presented in Table 1. The table shows that the IMU data provides more discriminative power than the acoustic data, but together still provide significantly better classification results.

Table 1. Accuracies with different sensor combinations

	IMU	Acoustic	Both
Accuracy	88.82	65.72	92.96

We are currently using the built-in microphone on a smartwatch to capture the on-skin sound, which is not designed to capture with the body transmit ed sound. Potentially, the quality of the acoustic information can be improved by using a more sensitive sensor (e.g. contact mic) that can be better coupled to the body rather than the air.

Improving the Gesture Design

The current gesture design is based on the layout of a number pad (NumPad), a control pad (DPad) and the corners of a square shape (CornerPad). To help the experimental participants learn the tap locations, we drew the layout on the skin, a solution that may not be desirable in practice. One challenge is to design a gesture set that is both memorable as well as machine recognizable.

One way to enhance recognition is to provide a small set of tap gestures, which are located at greater distances between each other (e.g., DPad, CornerPad). Therefore, the user can easily memorize the location of each tap gesture. A drawing layout may not be needed in such a case. Since there is a larger space between the two tap locations, variance between different taps for the same gesture can be tolerated by the system and used for recognition.

Another method to prevent drawing icons on the skin is to utilize the natural layout of the hand and map gestures to different parts of the body. For instance, each hand consists of 4 knuckles. If we map each of them with a tap gesture, a user can easily repeat the tap even without any marker on the skin.

However, painting on the hand may not always be unacceptable for some users, if the drawn picture is well designed. For instance, many people have already a tattoo on their skin. Therefore, we can redesign the whole drawn layout of TapSkin which makes it more like a tattoo, such that people will not feel uncomfortable with a 'Tattoo" style layout on their skin.

System Limitations and Future Work

There are several important limitations of our results and system to consider before applying TapSkin to real applications.

First, in our validation experiment, gesture instances were collected while the participants were holding their arms in a static position. In practical scenarios, the users may use TapSkin while they are in motion (e.g., while walking). Tapping on the skin in motion would influence the inertial signals, as well as potentially the accuracy of the tapping locations. Our current technique may exhibit higher classification errors and more false-positive errors. However, we can build separate models for when the user is in motion (or different states of motion, such as stationary, walking or running). To classify a gesture, we need to first classify the user's motion state (using something like Google's Activity Recognition service) and choose the appropriate classifier for that motion state. To reduce the potential false-positive errors while the user is in motion, a high-pass filter can be applied to the IMU data to remove the low-frequency motion(such as walking). And a separate binary classifier for noise detection can be built for event detection too. We plan to further explore this issue in the future.

Second, all the processing work is not processed solely on the watch but using an external phone. The data transmission between the watch and the phone introduces a high latency, which influence the perceived user experience. We plan to further improve the user experience by optimizing the processing pipeline to reduce the delay.

Another limitation of the work is that the sound generated by the tapping event may change in different situations. For instance, if the hands sweat or are otherwise moistened, the wet skin will change the acoustic signature of the tap, providing an unknown influence on the system's performance. We also have not considered the effect of clothing covering the arm or gloves on either the tapping or receiving hand. This introduces an even more complicated recognition problem beyond determining the motion state of the user. We note that these issues also cause problems with the normal touchscreen interaction, suggesting a more general problem for future research on wearable interaction techniques.

Figure 5 shows variance on the classification accuracies across different participants. After reviewing the video, we found that certain participants made weak taps on the back of their hand, tending to result in a higher amount of false-negative errors. The overall classification accuracies were also influenced by the strength of the tap being too light. This can be one potential limitation of TapSkin.

Somewhat related to this last point, we intentionally instructed our participants to wear the smartwatch near the wrist in a tightly fit fashion. This is helpful for collecting useful IMU data, but may cause a problem for those who dislike a tight-fitting wrist-mounted device. We are aware that some users like wearing the watch loosely, where the watch may slide along the arm. Such a movement may cause both motion and acoustic noise, which introduces more false-positive and classification errors. This is another limitation of our technique.

Furthermore, the current gesture family only contains tap gestures. However, we have received encouraging results by applying the similar technology on detecting slide gestures on the back skin of the hand. We would expect in the future to be able to expand the gesture set to include more elaborate sliding sequences, ultimately allowing a user to do a Grafiti-style text input language.

CONCLUSION

In order to increase the richness of input to a smartwatch without introducing any further on-body instrumentation, we introduced TapSkin, which uses the on-board sensing of the smartwatch to classify a variety of tapping gestures. Our results for classifying tap events are good enough for everyday use in a variety of application scenarios. We can identify up to 11 on-skin tap gestures (Number Pad with an activation patch) around the wrist area with an accuracy of 90.69% in a leave-one-session-out validation with 12 participants. These results increase to 97.33% and 96.64% for reduced tap locations of a DPad and CornerPad, each with 4 tap locations and an activation patch. While there are still some limitations to our approach for practical deployment, we provided an extensive discussion to address those issues for the practical deployment.

ACKNOWLEDGMENTS

We would like to thank Ning Xu for the help on the video and visual graphs, all the reviewers for their detailed feedback and the participants in the user study. This work is supported by Georgia Tech Wearable Computing Center Engagement Grant and the Intel Science and Technology Center for Pervasive Computing (ISTC-PC).

REFERENCES

1. Ashbrook, D., Baudisch, P., and White, S. Nenya: Subtle and eyes-free mobile input with a magnetically-tracked finger ring. In *Proceedings of the SIGCHI Conference on Human Factors in Computing Systems*, CHI '11, ACM (New York, NY, USA, 2011), 2043–2046.
2. Baudisch, P., and Chu, G. Back-of-device interaction allows creating very small touch devices. In *Proceedings of the 27th international conference on Human factors in computing systems - CHI 09*, Association for Computing Machinery (ACM) (2009).
3. Bernaerts, Y., Druwé, M., Steensels, S., Vermeulen, J., and Schöning, J. The office smartwatch: development and design of a smartwatch app to digitally augment interactions in an office environment. In *Proceedings of the 2014 companion publication on Designing interactive systems*, ACM (2014), 41–44.
4. Bi, X., Li, Y., and Zhai, S. FFitts law. In *Proceedings of the SIGCHI Conference on Human Factors in Computing Systems - CHI 13*, Association for Computing Machinery (ACM) (2013).
5. Chen, K.-Y., Lyons, K., White, S., and Patel, S. utrack. In *Proceedings of the 26th annual ACM symposium on User interface software and technology - UIST 13*, Association for Computing Machinery (ACM) (2013).
6. Dementyev, A., and Paradiso, J. A. Wristflex. In *Proceedings of the 27th annual ACM symposium on User interface software and technology - UIST 14*, Association for Computing Machinery (ACM) (2014).
7. Deyle, T., Palinko, S., Poole, E. S., and Starner, T. Hambone: A bio-acoustic gesture interface. In *2007 11th IEEE International Symposium on Wearable Computers*, Institute of Electrical & Electronics Engineers (IEEE) (oct 2007).
8. Funk, M., Sahami, A., Henze, N., and Schmidt, A. Using a touch-sensitive wristband for text entry on smart watches. In *Proceedings of the extended abstracts of the 32nd annual ACM conference on Human factors in computing systems - CHI EA 14*, Association for Computing Machinery (ACM) (2014).
9. Goel, M., Wobbrock, J., and Patel, S. Gripsense. In *Proceedings of the 25th annual ACM symposium on User interface software and technology - UIST 12*, Association for Computing Machinery (ACM) (2012).
10. Hall, M., Frank, E., Holmes, G., Pfahringer, B., Reutemann, P., and Witten, I. H. The weka data mining software: an update. *ACM SIGKDD explorations newsletter 11*, 1 (2009), 10–18.
11. Harrison, C., Benko, H., and Wilson, A. D. Omnitouch: wearable multitouch interaction everywhere. In *Proceedings of the 24th annual ACM symposium on User interface software and technology*, ACM (2011), 441–450.
12. Harrison, C., Tan, D., and Morris, D. Skinput: appropriating the body as an input surface. In *Proceedings of the SIGCHI Conference on Human Factors in Computing Systems*, ACM (2010), 453–462.
13. Hinckley, K., and Horvitz, E. Toward more sensitive mobile phones. In *Proceedings of the 14th annual ACM symposium on User interface software and technology*, ACM (2001), 191–192.
14. Kim, J., He, J., Lyons, K., and Starner, T. The gesture watch: A wireless contact-free gesture based wrist interface. In *2007 11th IEEE International Symposium on Wearable Computers*, Institute of Electrical & Electronics Engineers (IEEE) (oct 2007).

15. Laput, G., Xiao, R., Chen, X. ., Hudson, S. E., and Harrison, C. Skin buttons. In *Proceedings of the 27th annual ACM symposium on User interface software and technology - UIST 14*, Association for Computing Machinery (ACM) (2014).

16. Lyons, K., Nguyen, D., Ashbrook, D., and White, S. Facet. In *Proceedings of the 25th annual ACM symposium on User interface software and technology - UIST 12*, Association for Computing Machinery (ACM) (2012).

17. Lyons, K., Starner, T., Plaisted, D., Fusia, J., Lyons, A., Drew, A., and Looney, E. Twiddler typing: one-handed chording text entry for mobile phones. In *Proceedings of the SIGCHI conference on Human factors in computing systems*, ACM (2004), 671–678.

18. Lyons, K., Starner, T., Plaisted, D., Fusia, J., Lyons, A., Drew, A., and Looney, E. W. Twiddler typing. In *Proceedings of the 2004 conference on Human factors in computing systems - CHI 04*, Association for Computing Machinery (ACM) (2004).

19. McGrath, W., and Li, Y. Detecting tapping motion on the side of mobile devices by probabilistically combining hand postures. In *Proceedings of the 27th annual ACM symposium on User interface software and technology*, ACM (2014), 215–219.

20. Merrill, D., and Raffle, H. The sound of touch. In *CHI'07 Extended Abstracts on Human Factors in Computing Systems*, ACM (2007), 2807–2812.

21. Nanayakkara, S., Shilkrot, R., Yeo, K. P., and Maes, P. Eyering: a finger-worn input device for seamless interactions with our surroundings. In *Proceedings of the 4th Augmented Human International Conference*, ACM (2013), 13–20.

22. Nandakumar, R., Iyer, V., Tan, D., and Gollakota, S. Fingerio: Using active sonar for fine-grained finger tracking. In *Proceedings of the 2016 CHI Conference on Human Factors in Computing Systems*, ACM (2016), 1515–1525.

23. Oakley, I., Lee, D., Islam, M. R., and Esteves, A. Beats. In *Proceedings of the 33rd Annual ACM Conference on Human Factors in Computing Systems - CHI 15*, Association for Computing Machinery (ACM) (2015).

24. Perrault, S. T., Lecolinet, E., Eagan, J., and Guiard, Y. Watchit. In *Proceedings of the SIGCHI Conference on Human Factors in Computing Systems - CHI 13*, Association for Computing Machinery (ACM) (2013).

25. Rekimoto, J. GestureWrist and GesturePad: unobtrusive wearable interaction devices. In *Proceedings Fifth International Symposium on Wearable Computers*,

26. Roudaut, A., Huot, S., and Lecolinet, E. TapTap and MagStick. In *Proceedings of the working conference on Advanced visual interfaces - AVI 08*, Association for Computing Machinery (ACM) (2008).

27. Ruiz, J., Li, Y., and Lank, E. User-defined motion gestures for mobile interaction. In *Proceedings of the SIGCHI Conference on Human Factors in Computing Systems*, ACM (2011), 197–206.

28. Saponas, T. S., Tan, D. S., Morris, D., Balakrishnan, R., Turner, J., and Landay, J. A. Enabling always-available input with muscle-computer interfaces. In *Proceedings of the 22nd annual ACM symposium on User interface software and technology*, ACM (2009), 167–176.

29. Weigel, M., Mehta, V., and Steimle, J. More than touch: Understanding how people use skin as an input surface for mobile computing. In *Proceedings of the SIGCHI Conference on Human Factors in Computing Systems*, CHI '14, ACM (New York, NY, USA, 2014), 179–188.

30. Wen, H., Ramos Rojas, J., and Dey, A. K. Serendipity: Finger gesture recognition using an off-the-shelf smartwatch. In *Proceedings of the 2016 CHI Conference on Human Factors in Computing Systems*, ACM (2016), 3847–3851.

31. Xia, H., Grossman, T., and Fitzmaurice, G. Nanostylus. In *Proceedings of the 28th Annual ACM Symposium on User Interface Software & Technology - UIST 15*, Association for Computing Machinery (ACM) (2015).

32. Xiao, R., Laput, G., and Harrison, C. Expanding the input expressivity of smartwatches with mechanical pan, twist, tilt and click. In *Proceedings of the 32nd annual ACM conference on Human factors in computing systems - CHI 14*, Association for Computing Machinery (ACM) (2014).

33. Xu, C., Pathak, P. H., and Mohapatra, P. Finger-writing with smartwatch: A case for finger and hand gesture recognition using smartwatch. In *Proceedings of the 16th International Workshop on Mobile Computing Systems and Applications*, ACM (2015), 9–14.

34. Yang, X.-D., Grossman, T., Wigdor, D., and Fitzmaurice, G. Magic finger: always-available input through finger instrumentation. In *Proceedings of the 25th annual ACM symposium on User interface software and technology*, ACM (2012), 147–156.

35. Zhang, C., Guo, A., Zhang, D., Southern, C., Arriaga, R., and Abowd, G. Beyondtouch: Extending the input language with built-in sensors on commodity smartphones. In *Proceedings of the 20th International Conference on Intelligent User Interfaces*, IUI '15, ACM (New York, NY, USA, 2015), 67–77.

36. Zhang, C., Yang, J., Southern, C., Starner, T., and Abowd, G. D. Watchout: Extending interactions on a smartwatch with inertial sensing. In *2016 20th IEEE International Symposium on Wearable Computers* (2016).

37. Zhang, Y., Zhou, J., Laput, G., and Harrison, C. Skintrack: Using the body as an electrical waveguide for continuous finger tracking on the skin. In *Proceedings of the 2016 CHI Conference on Human Factors in Computing Systems*, ACM (2016), 1491–1503.

RootCap: Touch Detection on Multi-electrodes using Single-line Connected Capacitive Sensing

Masaya Tsuruta, Shuta Nakamae, and Buntarou Shizuki
University of Tsukuba
Tennodai 1-1-1, Tsukuba, Ibaraki 305-8573, Japan
{tsuruta,nakamae,shizuki}@iplab.cs.tsukuba.ac.jp

ABSTRACT
In designing interactive products, it is important for designers to test the product's usability by manufacturing its shape and interface iteratively through rapid prototyping. The goal of our research is to provide the designers with an additional touch sensing method for rapid prototyping interactive products with flat, curved, or flexible surface. In this paper, we present RootCap, a capacitive touch sensing method that can detect a touch on a multi-electrode input surface while maintaining the characteristics of a single-line connection. The key concept behind realizing this goal is the imposition of unique capacitance on each electrode (including the capacitor connected to the touch electrode) branching from the single-line connection. Moreover, we developed a technique for creating a capacitor by printing silver nanoparticle ink on both sides of a sheet of paper, supporting designers in the creation of a multi-electrode input surface, on which each electrode has a unique capacitance.

Author Keywords
Touch Surface; Capacitive Sensors; Rapid Prototyping; Paper Prototyping; Digital Fabrication; Conductive Ink; Paper Circuit; Double-Sided Circuit; Flexible Sensor; Gesture Detection.

ACM Classification Keywords
H.5.2. Information interfaces and presentation: User Interfaces - Input Devices and Strategies.

INTRODUCTION
In designing interactive products, it is important for designers to test the product's usability by manufacturing its shape and interface iteratively through rapid prototyping. To this end, manufacturing methods such as stereolithography [10] and fused deposition modeling (FDM) were developed and used, allowing designers to manufacture a small-scale prototypes quickly without using a mold or lathe. In interface manufacturing, many devices—including traditional mechanical devices (e.g., buttons, switches, and sliders) as well as recent touch sensing tools, such as integrated circuits (ICs)—are available. Ready-made multi-electrode touch sensor ICs suite rapid prototyping; they allow designers to place many touchable "buttons" on the surface of their prototypes (even on curved or flexible one), while facilitating the mounting process compared to solder-connected mechanical buttons. Moreover, it also allows the designers to design such buttons in free-form (e.g., circular, star-shaped, and heart-shaped ones).

ISS 2016, November 6–9, 2016, Niagara Falls, ON, Canada.

http://dx.doi.org/10.1145/2992154.2992180

The goal of our research is to provide the designers with an additional touch sensing method for rapid prototyping interactive products with flat, curved, or flexible surface. Generally, a capacitive touch sensor consists of a touch electrode, a sensing circuit, and a wire that connects the touch electrode and the sensing circuit. As a result, if the designers wish to use N touch electrodes, N sensing circuits and N wires are also necessary. While reducing the number of sensing circuit is made possible by using a multiplexer, this implementation still involves significant complicated wiring and its structures and logic are difficult to implement.

Thus far, myriad touch sensing methods have been developed that may be applied to prototypes with flexible shapes, such as in [9, 14, 4, 15, 16, 8, 7]. Based on this previous work, our focus herein is on:

- Decreasing the number of connections between the sensing circuit and touch sensing electrodes while increasing the number of available touch sensing electrode, and
- Expanding the degree of freedom for the shape and layout of touch sensing electrodes.

In this paper, we present RootCap, a capacitive touch sensing method that can detect a touch on a multi-electrode input surface while maintaining the characteristics of a single-line connection, as illustrated in Figure 1. The key concept behind realizing this goal is the imposition of unique capacitance on each electrode (including the capacitor connected to the touch electrode) branching from the single-line connection. As the result, when the user touches a touch electrode, a different capacitance is observed via the single-line connection according to which electrode is touched.

The contributions of this paper are as follows:

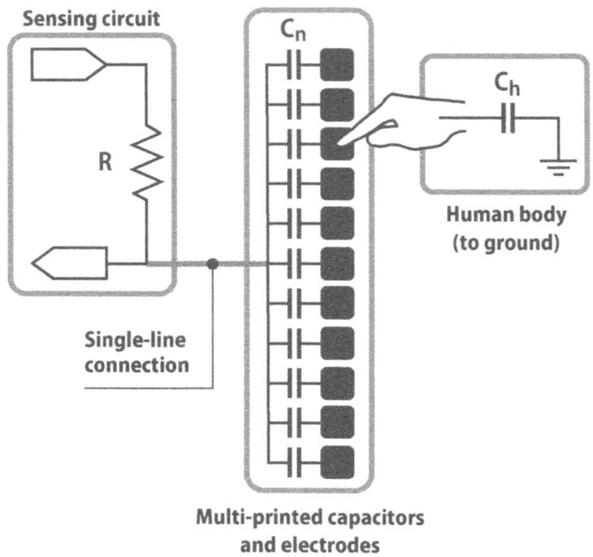

Figure 1. RootCap Concept.

1. We developed a touch sensing method that can detect touch to an electrode on a multi-electrode input surface with a single-line connection.
2. We developed a technique for creating a capacitor by printing silver nanoparticle ink on both sides of a sheet of paper, supporting designers in the creation of a multi-electrode input surface, on which each electrode has a unique capacitance.
3. We obtained high detection accuracy of touched electrodes and gestures on a multi-electrode input surface. Thus, we demonstrate the feasibility of this method for use in rapid prototyping.

RELATED WORK

Input Methods for Rapid Prototyping

Since it is important for designers to test usability of interactive products through rapid prototyping, many input methods for rapid prototyping have been researched; specifically, there has been intensive research on touch sensing methods. Touché [20] is a technology that adds touch sensitivity to electrically conductive objects. It observes impedance by attaching a conducting wire to the target object and imposing an electrical current; it detects how the object is touched by using machine learning, since the impedance changes depending on the way in which the object is touched. Touch & Activate [17] and Acoustruments [11] are methods that sense touch through sound. While their concept for touch detection are similar to that of Touché, it can add touch-sensitivity to objects without electrical conductivity, using sound instead. In contrast to these approaches, our method can even detect gestures by using multiple touch electrodes while our method uses dedicated touch electrodes.

Instant Inkjet Circuits [9] utilize home-use ink-jet printer to print circuits with silver nanoparticle ink on paper such as wires, resisters, and free-form electrodes. Karataş et al. [7] used this method to create multi-key controllers by printing a resister and switches. This printed circuit works as a voltage divider; when the user shorts any printed switch by touching it, the sensing circuit connected to the voltage divider can detect which printed switch was touched by observing the divided voltage. In contrast to this method, which requires a two-line connection between the voltage divider and the sensing circuit, our method uses a single-line connection.

Of the touch sensing method, a capacitive touch sensing [19, 2, 24, 5, 6] is well-studied. One merit of the capacitive sensing method is that it requires only a single-line connection between the sensing circuit and a touch electrode when the system has a single electrode.

There have been some studies based on the capacitive sensing method in which touch sensors were built using silver nanoparticle ink or print boards as touch-sensitive electrodes [9, 14, 4, 15, 16, 8]. For example, Instant Inkjet Circuits [9] printed a comb-like capacitor with silver nanoparticle ink to serve as a two-line connected touch sensor. Olberding et al. [14, 16, 15] attempted to use surfaces printed with silver nanoparticle or luminous ink in prototyping objects with touch sensitivity. Extension Sticker [8] extended touch sensitivity out of the capacitive touch screen by adding stripes printed with silver nanoparticle ink. By contrast, we focus on detecting touch to an electrode on a multi-electrode input surface using a single-line connection.

Touch Detection by a Single-line Connected Electrode

Detecting a touch and/or touch gestures using a single-line connection has also previously been explored by many researchers. Wimmer et al. [23] detected a touched point on a single conductive wire, by observing the reflection of the Time Domain Reflectometry (TDR) pulse caused by touch. Kawahara et al. [9] showed that silver nanoparticle ink can be used to print the Hilbert pattern in [23], which was then used as a touch electrode. While they used a complicated sensing process requiring a reflectometer or network analyzer, our method uses a simple sensing circuit and can detect a touched electrode by imposing unique capacitance on each one. Manabe et al. [12, 13] proposed a method to detect the number of fingers used to swipe, and their direction using two electrodes; they used a single-line connection for their capacitive sensing method. While our method also uses a single-line connection, it can detect a touched electrode among multi-electrodes, which can be used to detect touch gestures such as swipes. Takada et al. [22] extended Manabe's method [12, 13] and devised a pattern of electrodes, that can detect five touch gestures: a tap and swipes in four directions. The pattern was connected with a single-line connection to a sensing circuit. In contrast, our method can detect one touched electrode among multi-electrodes.

Conductive Ink Capacitors

The idea of using conductive ink, including silver nanoparticle ink, to form a capacitor is not new. There was a comb-like capacitor that was formed by printing silver nanoparticle ink on one side of a paper [9]. In contrast to the comb-like capacitor, whose shape and layout are limited, our method gives designers a greater degree of freedom in shape design.

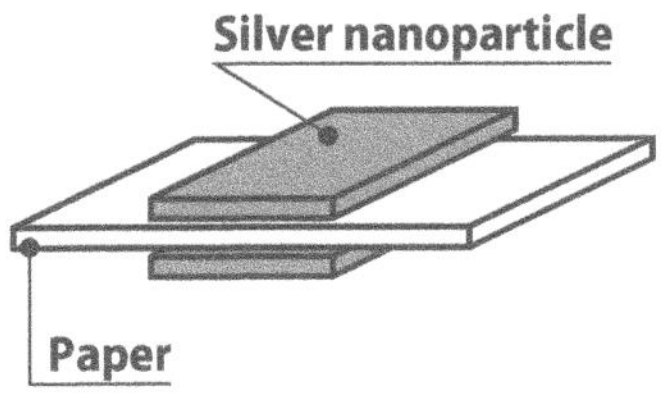

Figure 2. Structure of the double-printed capacitor.

Ta et al. [21] printed silver nanoparticle ink on both sides of a sheet of paper to form a multilayered circuit; Olberding et al. [16] printed conductive ink in multiple layers to form a capacitive touch sensor using screen-printing. We simply print silver nanoparticle ink on both sides of a sheet of paper to form a capacitor.

ROOTCAP

RootCap is a capacitive touch sensing method that can detect a touch on a multi-electrode input surface while maintaining the characteristics of a single-line connection as illustrated in Figure 1. This is realized by imposing unique capacitance on each electrode (including the capacitor connected to the touch electrode) branched from the single-line connection. As a result, when the user touches an electrode, a specific capacitance is observed via the single-line connection in accordance with the electrode that was touched. Therefore, by observing the capacitance of the single-line connection using a sensing circuit (the left side of Figure 1), the touched electrode can be detected. Moreover, supporting designers in the creation of a multi-electrode input surface, each of electrode has unique capacitance, is an important issue. To this end, we present a technique for creating a capacitor by printing silver nanoparticle ink on both sides of a sheet of paper, as illustrated in Figure 2. We call this capacitor a *double-printed capacitor*. Note that designers can also easily print a touch electrode with silver nanoparticle ink, including the wire that connects it with a double-printed capacitor.

In this section, we describe the double-printed capacitor, a touch sensing circuit that measures capacitance, and an example application using RootCap.

The Double-Printed Capacitor

A double-printed capacitor is structured as shown in Figure 2. The sheet of paper serves as a dielectric; the silver nanoparticle ink printed on both sides of the paper serves as a conductor. Conductors can be printed with silver nanoparticle ink as filled-in shapes at the same position on both sides of the paper. Thus, their capacitance can be designed by changing the area of each shapes.

In contrast to the comb-like capacitor [9], our method gives designers a greater degree of freedom in designing capacitor shape, such as the ones shown in Figure 3. Moreover, printing technology using silver nanoparticle ink is now being used in rapid prototyping of circuits on paper, including components such as wires, registers, free-form electrodes, and even touch sensors [9, 7, 14, 4, 15, 16, 8]. Therefore, our double-printed capacitors can be used in combination with such technologies, supporting designers in rapidly prototyping more complex circuits.

Figure 3. Free-form double-printed capacitors.

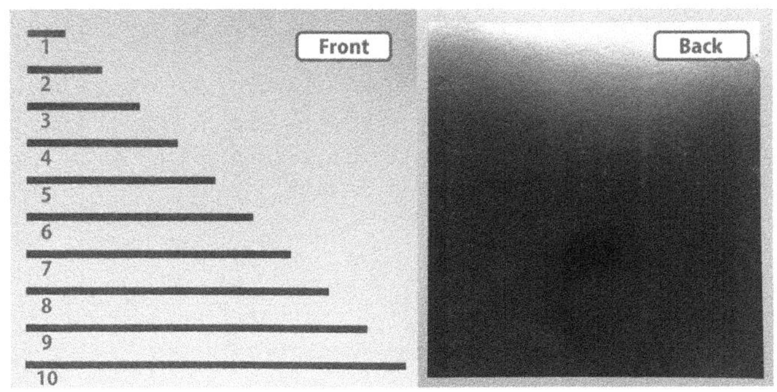

Figure 4. Tested double-printed capacitors.

Apparatus and Materials

In this implementation, we used a Brother DCP-J525N printer, Mitsubishi Paper Mills Limited NBSIJ-MU01 silver nanoparticle ink, and KOKUYO KJ-G23A4-30 paper.

Measuring Capacitance

We tested the relationship between the printed area of a double-printed capacitor and its capacitance. We created capacitors of 10 different sizes (labeled with IDs 1–10 from top to bottom), as shown in Figure 4, whose areas were $100\ \text{mm}^2$, $200\ \text{mm}^2, \cdots, 1000\ \text{mm}^2$. We measured each capacitance by using an LCR meter (DER EE LCR METER DE-5000). Figure 5 shows the result. The horizontal axis represents each capacitor's ID; the vertical axis represents capacitance. This result shows that area and capacitance have a linear relationship, which is consistent with the theory that the capacitance of a parallel plate capacitor is proportional to the plate's area.

Design Guideline

Since our method detects a touched electrode by observing the capacitance of the single-line connection, and capacitance is measured as a function of the capacitor's charging time (i.e., the time required for the capacitor to become charged),

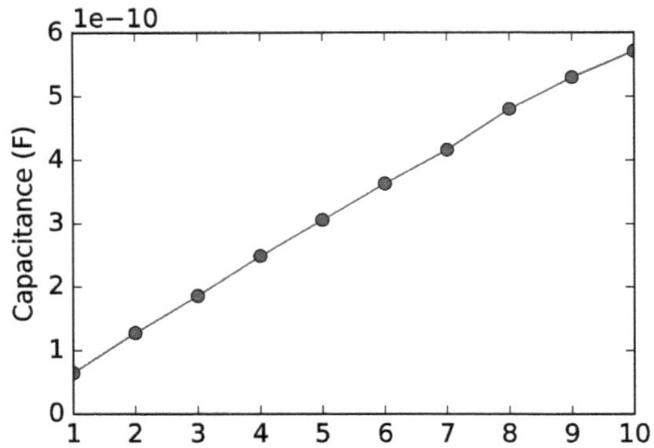

Figure 5. Capacitance of each strip.

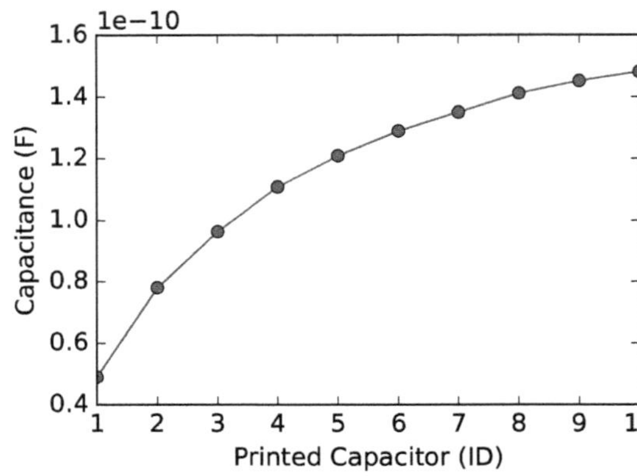

Figure 7. Combined capacitance of C_n and C_h

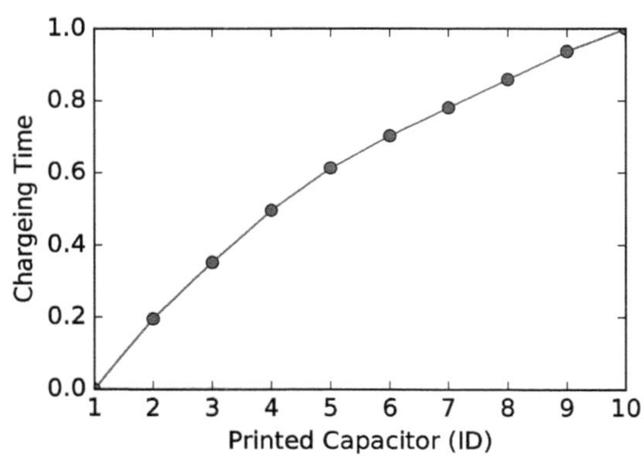

Figure 6. Charging time for each capacitor measured by our circuit.

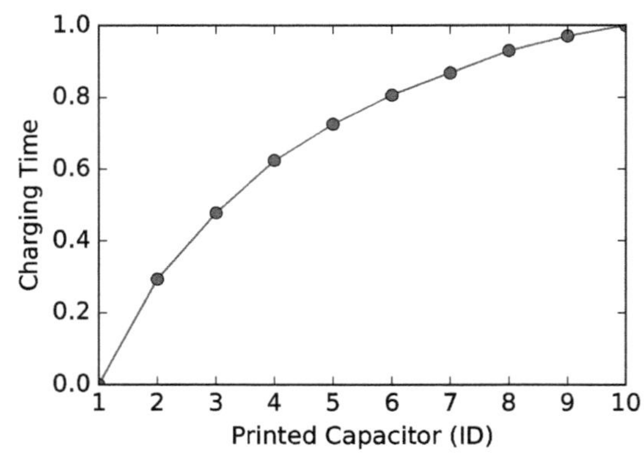

Figure 8. Theoretical charging time.

the difference in charging times should be large enough between the touch electrodes to avoid noise, which affects the design of touch electrodes.

First, we observed charging time, using a sensing circuit shown in Figure 1, when touching the double-printed capacitors one-by-one. The result is shown in Figure 6. The horizontal axis represents each capacitor's ID; the vertical axis represents measured charging time, which is normalized for later comparison.

On the other hand, the theoretical charging time t of a capacitor with the capacitance C is

$$t = -RCln(1 - \frac{V_t}{V_0}). \tag{1}$$

In this equation, R is the resistance in Figure 1; V_t is a threshold voltage; V_0 is the voltage applied to the capacitor. Since the logarithm term is constant, Equation 1 can be simplified by defining $A = ln(1 - Vt/V0)$ as

$$t = -ARC. \tag{2}$$

By transforming Equation 2, the observed capacitance can be represented as

$$C = -\frac{t}{AR}. \tag{3}$$

Note that the observed capacitance is the combined capacitance of C_n (the capacitance of the double-printed capacitor) and C_h (the users body capacitance). Because C_n and C_h are connected serially as illustrated in Figure 1, C is

$$C = \frac{C_n C_h}{C_h + C_n}. \tag{4}$$

To understand the relationship between C_n of a touch electrode and the observed capacitance (the charging time) in the single-line connection (the center panel in Figure 1) in conjunction with C_h, we first measured C_h with our touch-sensing circuit (the left side of Figure 1). When one of the authors touched the single-line connection having inserting neither any electrodes nor a capacitor, t was $3\,\mu$s. Using Equation 1, C_h was calculated as 221 pF with $R = 10\,\mathrm{k}\Omega$, $V_t = 2.5\,\mathrm{V}$, and $V_0 = 3.3\,\mathrm{V}$ (we defined $R = 10\,\mathrm{k}\Omega$ and $V_t = 2.5\,\mathrm{V}$ empirically). This result matches [3] and [18], which measured human body capacitance. From this result, we calculated the combined capacitance C of each C_n (measured with an LCR meter) and C_h (i.e., 221 pF) using Equation 4 and plotted the result in Figure 7. The horizontal axis represents each capacitor's ID; the vertical axis represents the combined capacitance. We also calculated the theoretical charging time using Equation 2 with $R = 10\,\mathrm{k}\Omega$ and the calculated combined capacitance in Figure 7, and plotted the result in Figure 8. The horizontal axis represents each capacitor's ID; the vertical axis represents theoretical charging time, which is normalized for comparison with Figure 6. When comparing Figure 8 with Figure 6, we observe that the theo-

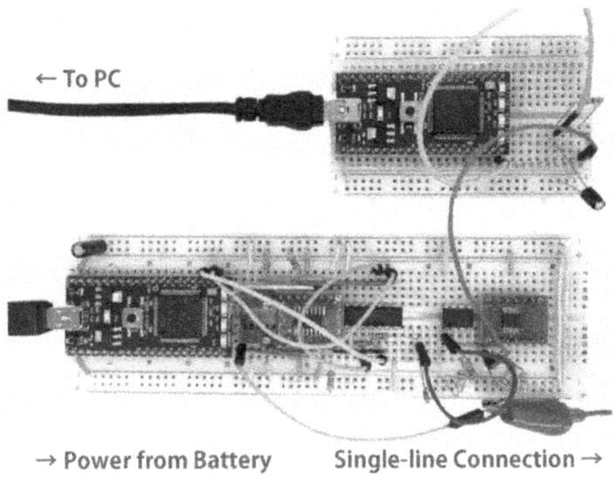

Figure 9. Touch sensing circuit (prototype).

retical and measured charging times match well. Therefore, Equation 1 can be used as a model to estimate capacitance from the charging time measured with the sensing circuit in Figure 1.

For further analysis, we then formulate $C_n = aS$ where a is a constant that depends on the paper and ink; S is the area of a double-printed capacitor. Inserting this into Equation 1 yields

$$t = -AR\frac{aSC_h}{C_h + aS}. \quad (5)$$

Equation 5 shows that as the area of a double-printed capacitor grows, the growth in charging time gradually slows down. This observation also appears in Figures 6 and 8, in which the growth rate of the charging time converges around double-printed capacitor 10, whose area was $1000\,\mathrm{mm}^2$. Therefore, in this implementation, with $R = 10\,\mathrm{k}\Omega$, we recommend that the printed capacitor's area should not exceed $1000\,\mathrm{mm}^2$, and that the gap between capacitor of this area and others should be as large as possible. Additionally, the upper limit of the area is also affected by R. Therefore, if designers want to create a larger printed capacitor, they should use smaller R, and vice versa. Besides, there is no limitations when designing touch electrodes, because there is no limitations in the area of the touch electrode connected to the printed capacitor part.

Touch Sensing Circuit

We implemented a touch sensing circuit (Figure 9) based on a capacitive sensing method described in [12]. Its simplified circuit diagram is depicted in Figure 10. Figure 9 contains two sets of the circuit depicted in Figure 10 (excluding a wire for touch electrodes and one for sensor output) for noise reduction. Among some approaches to measure capacitance or to detect the alteration of capacitance, such as measuring the charging time or observing the resonant frequency, we adopted a simple approach which measures the charging time. While most of the following logic can be implemented by programming a microcomputer, we implemented it via hardware, which enabled rapid capacitance measurement.

To measure the charging time, we need two rectangular pulse signals: one for charging the touch electrode (Pulse A), which is deformed when the electrode is touched, and the other for measuring the charging time (Pulse B). We also measure the

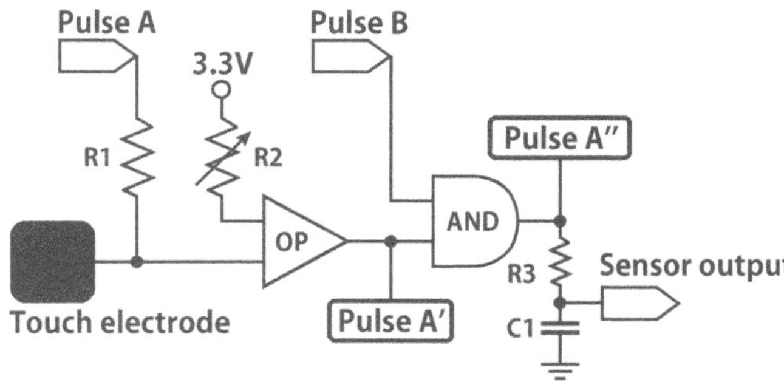

Figure 10. Touch sensing circuit.

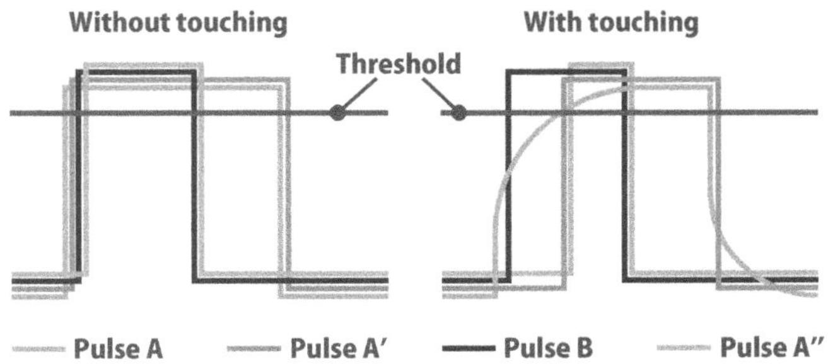

Figure 11. Pulses for sensing.

discharging time for noise reduction, which can be measured with the same mechanism for charging. Therefore, we use four pulse signals as shown in Figure 11 for sensing. Below are the methods by which these components allow us to acquire the charging time. To charge the touch electrode, we use Pulse A, a pulse with a duty cycle 1/2. We arrange Pulse B so that its rising edge matches that of Pulse A and its falling edge does not exceed that of Pulse A. We also determine a threshold voltage (R2). When Pulse A passes R2, we determine the time as the finish time of charging. When the touch electrode is touched, Pulse A rises slowly (the right in Figure 11) because the human body is also charged. Thus, it takes more time for Pulse A to reach R2 when touched, compared to when not touched. Therefore, comparing the voltage of Pulse A and R2 with a comparator (OP in Figure 10) generates a signal (Pulse A') which is HI while Pulse A is passing R2. Since the falling edge of Pulse A leans to the right when touched, passing Pulse A and Pulse B to an AND gate (AND in Figure 10) generates Pulse A which becomes wide when not touched and narrow when touched. A low-pass filter (R3 and C1 in Figure 10) converts the duration of Pulse A to its moving average (i.e., the longer the duration is, the higher the voltage is, and vice versa). Thus, by using an ADC, we can obtain the charging time as a discrete one dimensional value.

We used the pseudo-differential measurement [1] also used in [12] to decrease noises such as the one from a commercial power supply. Generally, this method decrease noise by summing the noisy signal (i.e., the signal for measuring the charging time in our case) and a signal with the reverse-phased noise. For the reverse-phased noise, we used the signal for measuring discharge time, which is acquired by the same mechanism as charging time. Figure 9 contains two

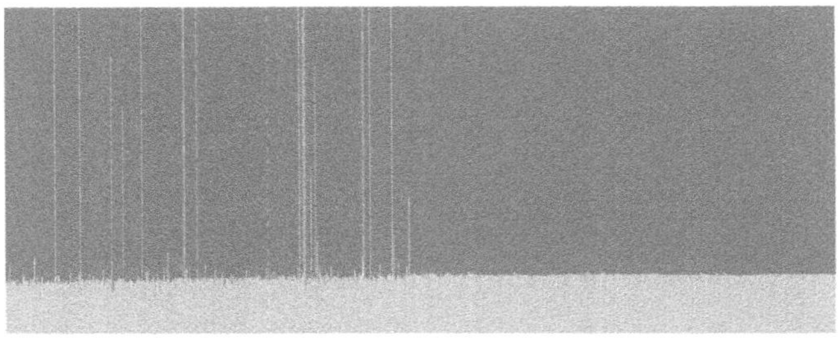

Figure 12. Figure 12. Effect of low-pass filters by both hardware and software; horizontal axis: time; vertical axis: sensor value where length of blue represents charging time. Half left: sensor value with low-pass filters. Half right: sensor value without low-pass filters.

sets of the circuit in Figure 10 (excluding a touch electrode and sensor output)—one each for acquiring charging and discharge times—to implement the pseudo-differential.

In addition, we added some contrivances to measure the charging time stably. First, we enabled it to adjust the sensitivity of the capacitance sensor value by allowing the threshold to vary (R2 in Figure 10), which determines the charging completion time of pulse A. For example, to obtain a large difference of charging time when the difference of charging time is so small between touch electrodes causing detection errors, the threshold for charging should be adjusted larger and the one for discharging should be adjusted smaller. Next, we added low-pass filters by both hardware and software to decrease the noise that could not be absorbed by pseudo-differential measurement. The half left of Figure 12 shows the measured charging time without this noise reduction; the half right shows one with this noise reduction. Third, we omitted a voltage follower placed near the electrode, which was used in [12]. This omission was due to large voltage drop, which was an adverse effect for observing detailed capacitance variations. Instead, we attached ferrite clamps to the single-line connection and power line to decrease the noise. Moreover, this circuit can be driven by a commercial power supply or bus power from a PC, but when a clear signal is required, a battery should be used.

Example Application

To evaluate the detection accuracy of multiple electrodes on a single-line connection, we developed an evaluation application: a numeric keypad. The keypad is composed of touch electrodes connected with 10 double-printed capacitors (Figure 13), a touch-sensing circuit (Figure 9), and PC software for detection (Figure 14).

Printed Numeric Keypad

The numeric keypad we developed (Figure 13) consists of two parts: the capacitor (top) and the touch electrode (bottom).

The capacitor is formed by printing silver nanoparticles onto both sides of a sheet of paper. The front surface is arranged from 10 differently sized parts, each of which is U-shaped in order to increase the printed area. A single rectangle that covers the entire surface of the capacitor component is printed on the back surface of the paper; this forms 10 double-printed

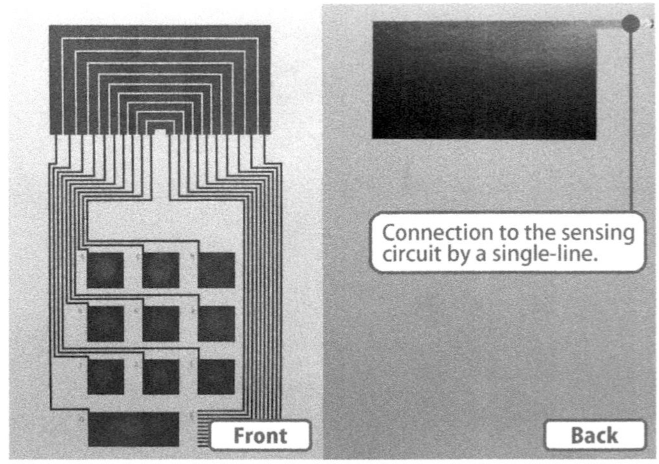

Figure 13. Numeric keypad.

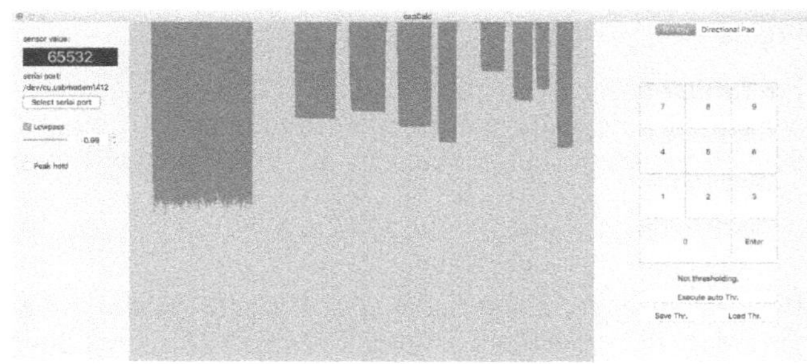

Figure 14. PC software for detection.

capacitors with the 10 areas on the front surface. A single-line connection is connected from the back surface to the sensing circuit.

The touch electrode part has electrodes connected to the double-printed capacitors, each of which serves as a numeric key. In addition to the 10 numeric keys, we designed the enter key as a stripe pattern; when the user touches the enter key, all of the double-printed capacitors are touched at once, resulting in the largest capacitance observed on the single-line connection. This design shows a possibility where the designers can increase touch electrodes while reducing the number of double-printed capacitors.

PC software for detection

We implemented PC-based software (Figure 14) that detects the numeric key touched and shows the result.

The software has three display areas. The area on the left displays the sensor value, and provides a GUI for choosing the serial port and controlling the software low-pass filter. The center area plots the sensor values. The horizontal axis represents time; the vertical axis represents the sensor value. The plot colored green represents sensor value. The smaller the sensor value, the larger the capacitance when touched. The area on the right displays the virtual keys.

The software uses the sensor values, which are sent to the PC via USB from the touch-sensing circuit, to detect the numeric key (i.e., the touched electrode) with a threshold-based ap-

Touched \ Detected	none	Enter	9	8	7	6	5	4	3	2	1	0
none	1											
Enter		0.96										0.04
9	0.08		0.92									
8			0.04	0.96								
7					1							
6						1						
5							1					
4							0.04	0.96				
3									1			
2										1		
1											0.88	0.13
0												1

Figure 15. Multi-electrode numeric keypad detection accuracy.

proach. Therefore, the software requires an initial calibration: the user touches each electrode in order before using the numeric keypad. The software automatically binds the touched electrode to the corresponding virtual key using this sensor value. The calibration is completed when the user touches all of the electrodes. After the calibration, when the user touches an electrode, the software highlights the bound virtual key on the display.

EVALUATION

Because touch gestures can be categorized into discrete and continuous ones, we conducted two experiments. The first one is for evaluating the detection accuracy of touches with multiple-electrodes, as an example of a discrete gesture. The second one is for evaluating the detection accuracy of vertical and horizontal swipes as an example of a continuous gesture.

Multi-electrode Detection

We carried out an experiment to evaluate the detection accuracy of touch electrodes connected by a single-line connection. In this evaluation, we used the touch electrode shown in Figure 13. This is a numeric keypad with 11 keys, which are numbers from 0 to 9 and Enter. Enter has the largest capacitance, 0 has the second largest, and 9 has the smallest. Each of the participants (8 persons whose ages ranged from 21 to 24) touched each electrode in order before using the numeric key for calibration. Next, the participants touched the electrodes in order to evaluate the systems accuracy. Each key was touched 3 times by a participant; all keys were touched 264 times by the 8 participants. We recorded the keys touched and whether the software responded to the correct key to evaluate detection accuracy.

The result of this experiment is shown in Figure 15 as a confusion matrix. The vertical axis represents the key which the participant actually touched; the horizontal axis represents the key which the software detected. The average detection accuracy was 97.2%. The accuracy in detecting the key corresponding to the number 1 was the lowest. Key 1 is third-largest in capacitance size, at 530 pF. In referring to the design guideline, we know that it is difficult to observe capacitance size near the capacitor. From Equation 4, the combined capacitance when touching Key 1 is 156 pF which is

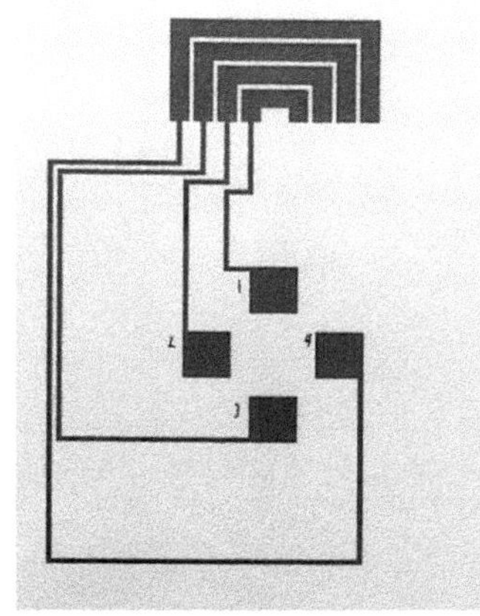

Figure 16. Gesture pad.

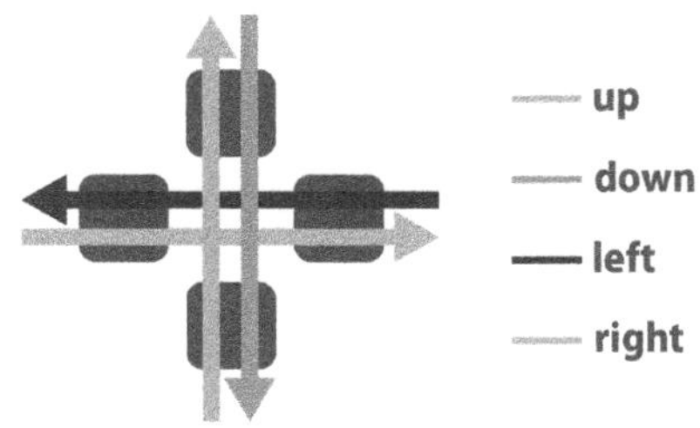

Figure 17. Detection of 4 touch gestures: up, down, left, right swipes.

calculated by substituting $C_n = 530\,\text{pF}$ and $C_h = 222\,\text{pF}$ to Equation 4. On the other hand, from Figure 7 which shows the combined capacitance, we can observe that the growth rate of the combined capacitance converges stronger at around 140 pF, making it difficult to observe the change in the combined capacitance around Key 1, thus decreasing detection accuracy.

Gesture Detection

We conducted an experiment to detect 4 touch gestures: up, down, left, right swipes. The design of the electrode is shown in Figure 16, and has 4 types of printed capacitor with electrodes connected to each one. The participants touched the electrode shown in (Figure 17), and can input 4 distinct swipe gestures. In each swipe gesture, two electrodes are touched. As the result, the sensor values for each gesture appear in Figure 18. In this signal, gestures can be detected from the difference in the two continuing signals that are emitted from a single gesture. The software for this experiment shows the detected gesture. The participant in this part of the experiment was 24 years old. The participant performed 4 gestures in a random order 10 times for a single trial. Ten trials were carried out in total, thus each gesture was input 100 times.

The result of this experiment is shown in Figure 19 as a confusion matrix. The vertical axis represents the gesture that the participant actually performed; the horizontal axis represents the gesture that the software detected. Average accuracy of detection was 96.8%. From the result, we observed that the up and left gestures tended to be confused with each other. This would occur because the sensor values of the up and left

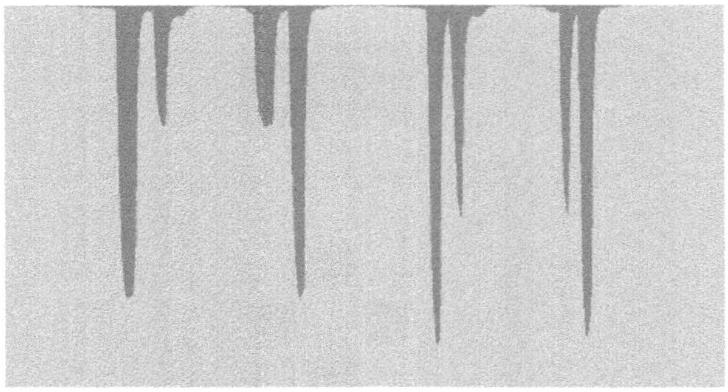

Figure 18. Sensor values for 4 gestures. From from left to right, the gesture directions are up, down, left, and right.

Gestured \ Detected	up	down	left	right
up	0.89	0.01	0.09	0.01
down		1		
left	0.02		0.98	
right				1

Figure 19. Accuracy of gesture detection.

gestures tended to be similar and because it was harder to slide the finger upwards, which made the sensor values unstable.

EXAMPLES OF PROTOTYPING

Ergonomic Keypad

By using the numeric keypad which we used for evaluation, the designers can design a keypad with flat, curved, or flexible surface. We show the example of ergonomic keypad on Figure 20. As this figure, designers can hide printed capacitors inside of the prototype and only single-line wire to the sensing circuit should be connected. This allows designers to raise the degree of freedom for the shape and layout of touch electrodes and whole shape of the prototype.

Slider

A slider can be implemented by lining up stripes (i.e., electrodes) with different capacitance. When sliding the finger over the stripes, the finger rides on several stripes. This results in continuous bumpy waves in sensor values, which denote the direction and length of the slide. We can also recognize where the finger stopped.

Interactive Christmas Ornament

We can use our method to create simple controllers made of paper with only a single-line connection, which we can use as decorations. By touching the star of the ornament shown in Figure 21, the user can control the light. For example, by touching the top edge of the star, all the lights are turned on. The two edges on the bottom are controllers that switch between white and red lights.

Control Panel Prototype of Car or Consumer Electronics

When developing a UI for consumer electronics and large touch panels for cars, it is necessary to iterate the design many times. Additionally, panels with free curved surfaces have begun to be marketed, and it is likely that such surfaces will become more prevalent at technology improves. Rapid prototyping of touch interfaces on such operation panels with our method, which can create flexible shaped touch surfaces any where with a single-line, will contribute to design efficiency.

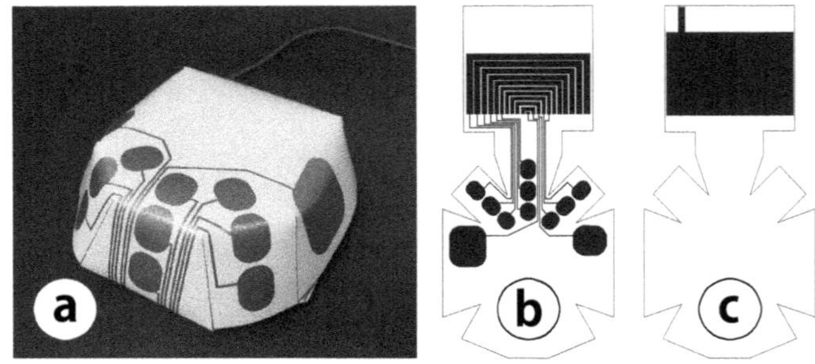

Figure 20. Ergonomic keypad. a) Overview of the ergonomic keypad with a single-line connection. b) Front side. c) Bottom side.

Figure 21. Interactive Christmas ornament.

Touch Interactive Architecture Prototype

Our method could also be used in the field of architecture. For example, when creating complex architecture models from styrene or paper board, the designers can assemble and implement touch-operating panels for multiple illuminations with our method. Such models could reduce the cost of wiring, connecting and, and designing operating panels.

DISCUSSION AND FUTURE WORK

In this paper, we discussed a limit the resolution of detection. Thereby, we presented a design guideline for the maximum limit of the area of a double-printed capacitor. Therefore, our immediate future work is to explore further design guidelines to help the designers determine the number and areas of double-printed capacitors.

There are also possibilities on reducing the implementation area in gesture detection, because only requires 3 types of capacitors in minimum to detect 6 directions gestures as shown in Figure 22. By extending our method, it may also be feasible to solve the electrode margin restrictions shown in [22].

Furthermore, in a pilot study, our method could detect gestures such as hover, double taps, and triple taps with each electrode. Since the design of our sensing circuit is simple, we are planning to miniaturize and package this. We also can imagine other applications. For example, our method makes it possible to implement a touch panel with high-speed responses by decreasing the number of connections and multiplexer processes. As another future work, we are planning to devise the system for simultaneous multi-touch.

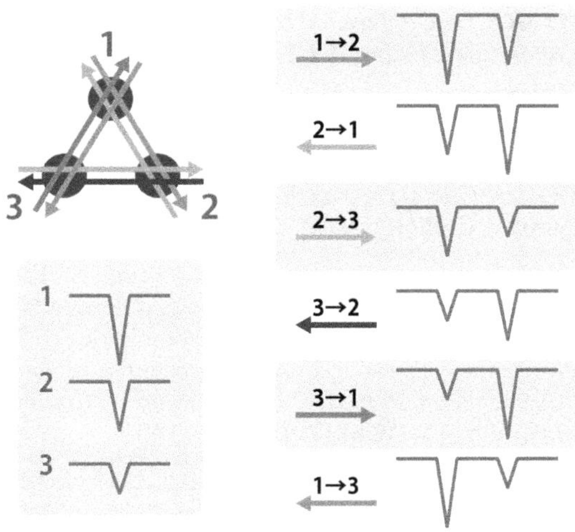

Figure 22. Six touch gestures with 3 types of capacitors.

CONCLUSIONS

In this paper, we present RootCap, a capacitive touch sensing method that can detect a touch on a multi-electrode input surface while maintaining the characteristics of a single-line connection, as illustrated in Figure 1. From the preliminary research, we were able to derive the relational expression of capacitance, area of printed capacitor, and the charging time when touched by human. For a single-line connection, we set a design guideline limiting the largest area to $1000\,\mathrm{mm}^2$, knowing that 10 stages were the most useful number of electrodes. In addition, we did an experiment to determine whether we could detect 11 stages of keys correctly with only a single-line connection. As a result, the total detection accuracy for our numeric keypad was 97.2% We also did an experiment to understand if we could detect 4 gestures by using a 4 staged single-line connection. We also carried out an experiment to confirm whether we could detect 4 gestures using a 4-stage single-line connection. As a result, the total detection accuracy of gestures was 96.8%. Therefore, we were able to reduce connections in order to rapidly create touch sensors, and were also able to reduce the implementation area of touch sensors which could detect multiple types of input. Moreover, we show a technique call for creating a capacitor, which we call a double-printed capacitor, by printing silver nanoparticle ink on both sides of a sheet of paper. This technique supports designers in the creation of a multi-electrode input surface, on which each electrode has a unique capacitance with a greater degree of freedom in shape design. RootCap meets the requirements of touch input methods for rapid prototyping: the number of connections between the sensing circuit and touch electrodes is decreased while the number of available touch electrode is increased, and raising the degree of freedom for the shape and layout of touch electrodes. As a result, we were able to demonstrate the feasibility of our method for use in rapid prototyping.

REFERENCES

1. Chan, V., and Underwood, S. MSP430 capacitive single-touch sensor design guide. `http://www.ti.com/lit/an/slaa379/slaa379.pdf`.
2. Dietz, P., and Leigh, D. DiamondTouch: A multi-user touch technology. In *Proceedings of the 14th Annual ACM Symposium on User Interface Software and Technology*, UIST '01, ACM (2001), 219–226.
3. Fujiwara, O., and Ikawa, T. Numerical calculation of human-body capacitance by surface charge method. *The IEICE Transactions on Communications 84*, 10 (2001), 1841–1847. (in Japanese).
4. Gong, N.-W., Steimle, J., Olberding, S., Hodges, S., Gillian, N. E., Kawahara, Y., and Paradiso, J. A. PrintSense: A versatile sensing technique to support multimodal flexible surface interaction. In *Proceedings of the SIGCHI Conference on Human Factors in Computing Systems*, CHI '14, ACM (2014), 1407–1410.
5. Grosse-Puppendahl, T., Berghoefer, Y., Braun, A., Wimmer, R., and Kuijper, A. OpenCapSense: A rapid prototyping toolkit for pervasive interaction using capacitive sensing. In *2013 IEEE International Conference on Pervasive Computing and Communications (PerCom)* (2013), 152–159.
6. Grosse-Puppendahl, T., Herber, S., Wimmer, R., Englert, F., Beck, S., von Wilmsdorff, J., Wichert, R., and Kuijper, A. Capacitive near-field communication for ubiquitous interaction and perception. In *Proceedings of the 2014 ACM International Joint Conference on Pervasive and Ubiquitous Computing*, UbiComp '14, ACM (2014), 231–242.
7. Karataş, Ç., and Gruteser, M. Printing multi-key touch interfaces. In *Proceedings of the 2015 ACM International Joint Conference on Pervasive and Ubiquitous Computing*, UbiComp '15, ACM (2015), 169–179.
8. Kato, K., and Miyashita, H. Extensionsticker: A proposal for a striped pattern sticker to extend touch interfaces and its assessment. In *Proceedings of the 33rd Annual ACM Conference on Human Factors in Computing Systems*, CHI '15, ACM (2015), 1851–1854.
9. Kawahara, Y., Hodges, S., Cook, B. S., Zhang, C., and Abowd, G. D. Instant Inkjet Circuits: Lab-based inkjet printing to support rapid prototyping of ubicomp devices. In *Proceedings of the 2013 ACM International Joint Conference on Pervasive and Ubiquitous Computing*, UbiComp '13, ACM (2013), 363–372.
10. Kodama, H. Automatic method for fabricating a threedimensional plastic model with photohardening polymer. *Review of Scientific Instruments 52*, 11 (1981).
11. Laput, G., Brockmeyer, E., Hudson, S. E., and Harrison, C. Acoustruments: Passive, acoustically-driven, interactive controls for handheld devices. In *Proceedings of the 33rd Annual ACM Conference on Human Factors in Computing Systems*, CHI '15, ACM (2015), 2161–2170.
12. Manabe, H., and Inamura, H. Multi-touch gesture recognition by single touch sensor. *IPSJ Journal 56*, 4 (2014), 1193–1202. (in Japanese).

13. Manabe, H., and Inamura, H. Single capacitive touch sensor that detects multi-touch gestures. In *Proceedings of the 2014 ACM International Symposium on Wearable Computers*, ISWC '14, ACM (2014), 137–138.

14. Olberding, S., Gong, N.-W., Tiab, J., Paradiso, J. A., and Steimle, J. A cuttable multi-touch sensor. In *Proceedings of the 26th Annual ACM Symposium on User Interface Software and Technology*, UIST '13, ACM (2013), 245–254.

15. Olberding, S., Soto Ortega, S., Hildebrandt, K., and Steimle, J. Foldio: Digital fabrication of interactive and shape-changing objects with foldable printed electronics. In *Proceedings of the 28th Annual ACM Symposium on User Interface Software and Technology*, UIST '15, ACM (2015), 223–232.

16. Olberding, S., Wessely, M., and Steimle, J. PrintScreen: Fabricating highly customizable thin-film touch-displays. In *Proceedings of the 27th Annual ACM Symposium on User Interface Software and Technology*, UIST '14, ACM (2014), 281–290.

17. Ono, M., Shizuki, B., and Tanaka, J. Touch & Activate: Adding interactivity to existing objects using active acoustic sensing. In *Proceedings of the 26th Annual ACM Symposium on User Interface Software and Technology*, UIST '13, ACM (2013), 31–40.

18. Ott, H. W. *Electromagnetic Compatibility Engineering*. Wiley, 2009.

19. Rekimoto, J. SmartSkin: An infrastructure for freehand manipulation on interactive surfaces. In *Proceedings of the SIGCHI Conference on Human Factors in Computing Systems*, CHI '02, ACM (2002), 113–120.

20. Sato, M., Poupyrev, I., and Harrison, C. Touché: Enhancing touch interaction on humans, screens, liquids, and everyday objects. In *Proceedings of the SIGCHI Conference on Human Factors in Computing Systems*, CHI '12, ACM (2012), 483–492.

21. Ta, T., Fukumoto, M., Narumi, K., Shino, S., Kawahara, Y., and Asami, T. Interconnection and double layer for flexible electronic circuit with instant inkjet circuits. In *Proceedings of the 2015 ACM International Joint Conference on Pervasive and Ubiquitous Computing*, UbiComp '15, ACM (2015), 181–190.

22. Takada, R., Shizuki, B., and Tanaka, J. MonoTouch: Single capacitive touch sensor that differentiates touch gestures. In *Proceedings of the 2016 CHI Conference Extended Abstracts on Human Factors in Computing Systems*, CHI EA '16, ACM (2016), 2736–2743.

23. Wimmer, R., and Baudisch, P. Modular and deformable touch-sensitive surfaces based on time domain reflectometry. In *Proceedings of the 24th Annual ACM Symposium on User Interface Software and Technology*, UIST '11, ACM (2011), 517–526.

24. Zimmerman, T. G., Smith, J. R., Paradiso, J. A., Allport, D., and Gershenfeld, N. Applying electric field sensing to human-computer interfaces. In *Proceedings of the SIGCHI Conference on Human Factors in Computing Systems*, CHI '95, ACM Press/Addison-Wesley Publishing Co. (1995), 280–287.

Ballumiere: Real-Time Tracking and Spherical Projection for High-Speed Moving Balls

Shio Miyafuji, Masato Sugasaki, Hideki Koike
Tokyo Institute of Technology
2-12-1, Ookayama, Meguro-ku, Tokyo 152-8550, JAPAN
{miyafuji.s.aa, sugasaki.m.ab}@m.titech.ac.jp, koike@cs.titech.ac.jp

Figure 1. Projections on balls thrown in the air and bouncing on a floor

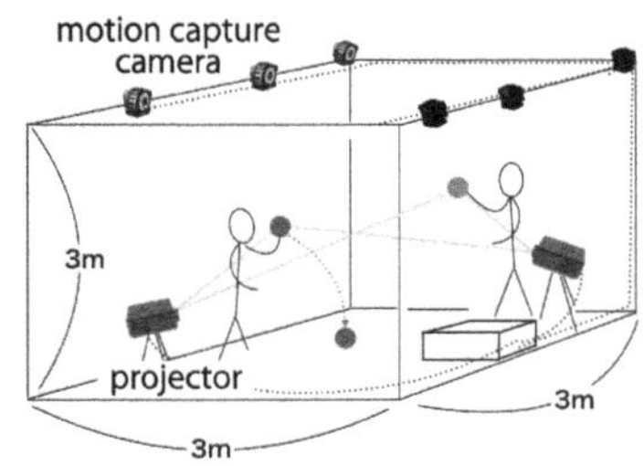

Figure 2. System overview

ABSTRACT
Projections on moving objects have a problem in that the projection may slip because of the delay between tracking and projection. Here, we propose a new prediction method combining a Kalman filter and a three-frame feedback model that switches between these models according to the ball's state of motion. We developed a real-time tracking and projection system named "Ballumiere", which uses motion-capture cameras for tracking and multiple projectors for spherical projection. We conducted a comparative experiment with an existing prediction model and showed that our method minimizes slipping and increases the accuracy of the projection.

Author Keywords
Spherical display; Dynamic projection; Projection mapping; Touch sensitive device

ACM Classification Keywords
I.4.8 Computing Methodologies: Scene Analysis; H.5.1 Information Systems: Multimedia Information Systems

INTRODUCTION
Projection mappings are popular events at entertainment and commercial showcases, and large-scale projection mappings have been done on historical buildings throughout the world.

ISS 2016, November 6–9, 2016, Niagara Falls, ON, Canada.

http://dx.doi.org/10.1145/2992154.2992181

However, almost all of the projection mapping techniques only allow projections on static objects or targets that move slowly. To offer a high-quality experience, a technology for projecting onto moving objects is required. Some researchers have tackled the problem of projecting images onto moving balls [4, 5, 8]. However, they have a problem in that the projection accuracy deteriorates when the movement direction of the ball changes. To address this issue, we propose a new method combining a Kalman filter and a three-frame prediction model wherein these prediction models are switched according to the motion of the balls. In experiments, we succeeded in minimizing slipping of the projection (Figure 1).

RELATED WORK

Projection Mapping
Shader Lamps [9] enables computer graphics to be rendered on real objects in three-dimensional space by using projectors. This research is the cornerstone of projection mapping. However, up till now, almost all the projection mapping techniques can only project on static objects and objects that move slowly. The conventional projection mapping is unsatisfactory for tracking and projecting onto moving objects because of the delay between tracking and projection. IllumiRoom [2] and RoomAlive [1] transform a room into displays for games with multi-surface projection including on the walls and floor. These developments enable various new physical interactions with the room itself. However, they render a 3D projection image only on plane surfaces. ViBall [3] uses projectors placed outside of a ball to display spherical images on the ball. This approach to spherical mapping is almost the same as ours. However, in that system, the ball cannot be lifted or moved freely, and spherical images cannot be projected on moving balls.

Dynamic Projection Mapping

Lincoln et al. [6] and Zheng et al. [10] map images onto a real moving object with low latency through an optical see-through head mounted display, but not in terms of projection mapping. Several studies have attempted to project images onto moving objects. Lumipen [8] tracks and projects on a small object in real time by using a high-speed vision sensor and a projector combination using a high-speed optical gaze controller. Although the system can project images on a high-speed moving object, only one object is allowed to be a projection target because the optical axes of the vision sensor and the projector must be the same. LumoSpheres [5] and Knibbe et al. [4] perform real-time tracking and projection onto flying balls. LumoSpheres [5] uses motion capture cameras, and Knibbe et al. [4] uses Kinect to track balls in the air. These studies both overcome the delay issue by using a prediction method incorporating a Kalman filter. Knibbe et al. [4] also uses a memory lookup model at catching points where the projections tend to overshoot. As they indicate in their study, a Kalman filter is useful when balls are thrown in the air. However, their work still has the problem of low projection accuracy when the speed of the ball changes rapidly. To address this issue, we propose a new method combining a Kalman filter and a three-frame prediction model, wherein we switch these prediction models according to the ball's motion and thereby succeed in minimizing the projection slipping (Figure1).

TECHNOLOGY

Figure 2 is an overview of our real-time tracking and projection system, named "Ballumiere". The system consists of six motion tracking cameras (OptiTrack S250e, 120fps), two (or more) projectors (BenQ TH681), and a PC for making the prediction calculation of the balls' coordinates and for rendering images. To capture the ball's position with mocap cameras, the balls are wrapped with retroreflective sheets. This does not influence the quality of the displayed images. The three-dimensional position of the ball is immediately obtained by the motion tracking system and is sent to the PC for rendering that takes into account the viewing angle from each projector.

Real Time Spherical Projection

We developed a real-time 360-degree projection on flying balls. Figure 3 illustrates how this system renders images for multiple projectors. The positional relationships between the ball and the projectors are calculated by transforming the projector positions in the real world to the camera coordinate system. By combining three-dimensional ball positions from the motion tracking system, the system generates projection images corresponding to each projector's position.

Figure 4 shows an example of sphere mapping. Different images are projected using multiple projectors from different directions to cover almost the whole surface of the ball while at the same time accounting for the ball's position and orientation. To assure real-time projection, the system overlays images precisely at the same position from each projector without considering the overlapping part. Moreover, the system can change projection images corresponding to the positions

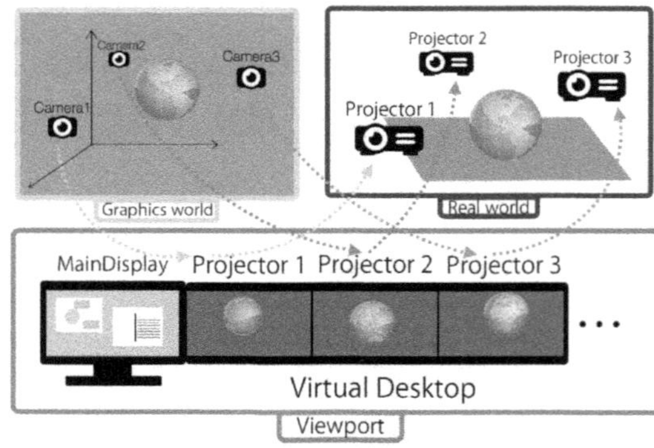

Figure 3. Spherical projection mapping with multiple projectors

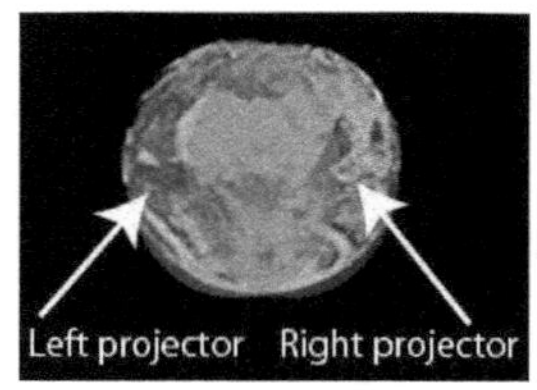

Figure 4. Spherical projection mapping

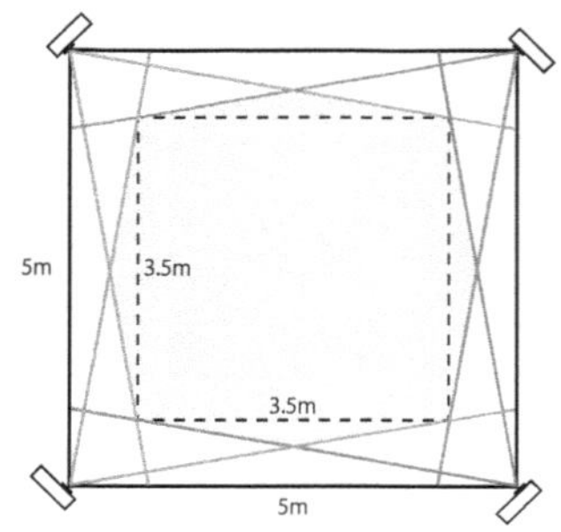

Figure 5. Projection area example

and movements of the balls, which enables users to interact with the balls. The field of view of the projectors is about 70 degrees. Figure 5 represents the projection area of our system. As the figure shows, we can perform an entire circumferential mapping in a 3.5 m x 3.5 m volume a 5 m x 5 m room.

Prediction

Since there is latency in the cameras, PCs, and projectors, the position of the ball captured by the cameras will be different from the position where the image is projected. Some of the previous studies overcame this issue by using a Kalman filter with a parabolic motion model [4, 5]. They, however, still faced the problem of the projection slipping when the ball's speed changed suddenly, for example when the ball was caught by the user. To address this problem, we used two prediction models, a Kalman filter and the three-frame feedback prediction model (Figure 6) and switched between these two models according to the ball's motion.

Three-Frame Feedback Model

We designed the three-frame feedback model to overcome the projection slipping problem affecting the previous research. It is similar to the FIR filter known in the field of control engineering. Exp.1 shows the predicted position of a ball in a projector space P_n at frame n.

$$P_n = p_n + Q_n R_n \tag{1}$$

$$Q_n = \alpha_1 d_n + \alpha_2 (d_n - d_{n-1}) \tag{2}$$

$$R_n = \begin{cases} |d_n| & (|d_n| < 0.001) \\ 1 & (|d_n| >= 0.001) \end{cases} \tag{3}$$

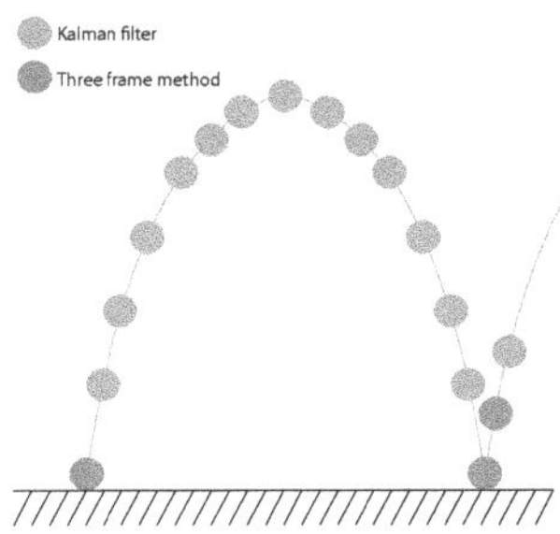

Figure 6. Adaptive model switching: switching between Kalman filter and three-frame feedback model according to the motion of a ball

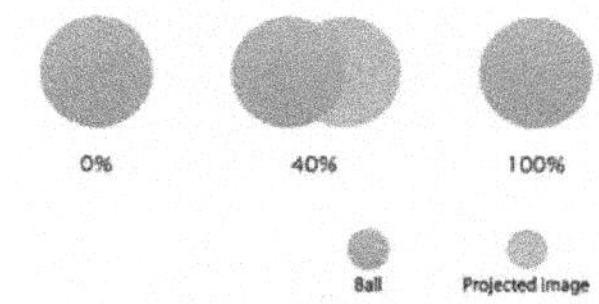

Figure 7. Projection accuracy example

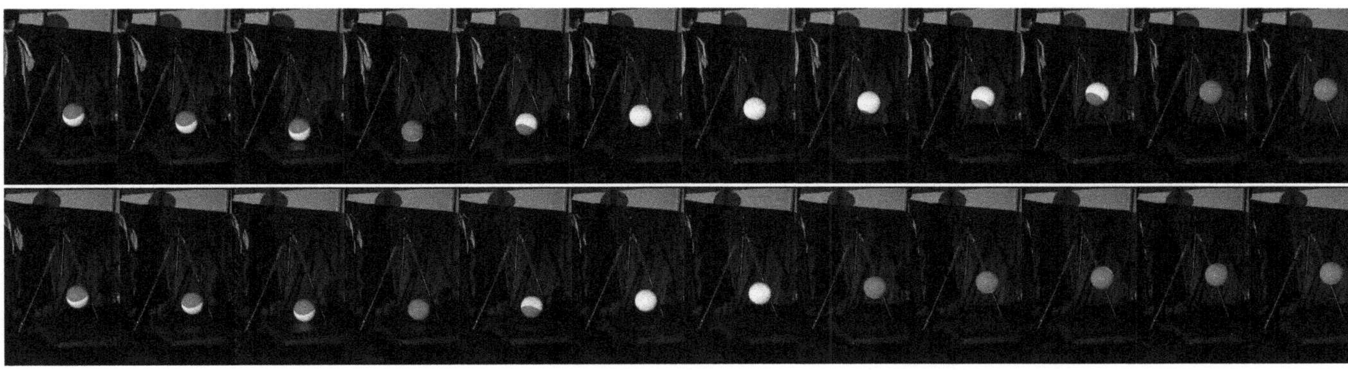

Figure 8. Comparison of Kalman filter prediction model (top) and our new prediction model (bottom)

Where p_n is the current position of the ball captured by the cameras, α is a correction coefficient for the delay at the cameras, projectors, and program (Exp.2). d_n is the distance between the positions at the present and one frame before. The values of α and the threshold value for d_n (i.e. 0.001) are determined empirically because they depend on the frame rate of the camera. There is an error component for the acceleration because this system calculates acceleration by using data from motion capture cameras. The weighting terms of the equation with α work to minimize the effect of errors. P_n, the predicted position, is corrected using Q_n, a function of d_n as a velocity correction, using $d_n - d_{n-1}$ as an acceleration correction, and using R_n, a function for weighting by distance. Weighting using R_n(Exp.3) reduces the projection slipping caused by the error of tracking.

Adaptive Model Switching

To improve prediction accuracy, we switch prediction models when state of the ball's motion changes. We estimate the ball motion from the y-axis acceleration, which is calculated from data of a ball tracked with motion capture cameras. Our prediction system uses a Kalman filter under the influence of gravity and switches the method to the three frame feedback model under other conditions.

Evaluation

We conducted the following comparative experiment. A ball was dropped from 135 cm high with zero initial velocity along the y-axis (i.e. the vertical direction), and it bounced off the floor. Video was captured with a high-speed camera (120 fps) beside the projector that projected an image onto the ball. The accuracy of the projection was calculated with Exp.4 for each frame.

$$\text{Accuracy}[\%] = \frac{\text{image projected area[pixel]}}{\text{projection target area[pixel]}} \times 100 \quad (4)$$

Figure 7 illustrates how the projection accuracy was calculated. The projection accuracy of the left ball on which nothing was projected was 0%. That of the middle ball whose projection slipped by its radius was 40%, and that of the right ball on which the same-size image was perfectly projected was 100%.

We compared our method with a no prediction model and a Kalman filter with a kinetic model. Figure 9, Figure 10, Figure 11, and Figure 12 show the projection accuracies of the no prediction model, that of the Kalman filter with the kinetic model, that of the three-frame feedback model only, and that of our method (i.e. the combination of a Kalman filter and three-frame feedback model), respectively. The averages projection accuracies of no prediction, Kalman filter and kinetic model, three-frame feedback model, and the proposed method were 51.89[%], 70.26[%], 86.08[%], and 89.79[%], respectively. Figure 9 shows that accuracy of the projection gets worse when the ball is falling. This is because the speed of the ball gets faster while it is falling. The other evaluation results are more accurate than the no prediction model in the same situation. Comparing Figure 10 and Figure 12, we found that our new model is more accurate than the others especially around the starting point and just after the bounce point as indicated with red circles. The projection went back to the correct position 12 frames faster in our method than in the Kalman filter model (Figure 8).

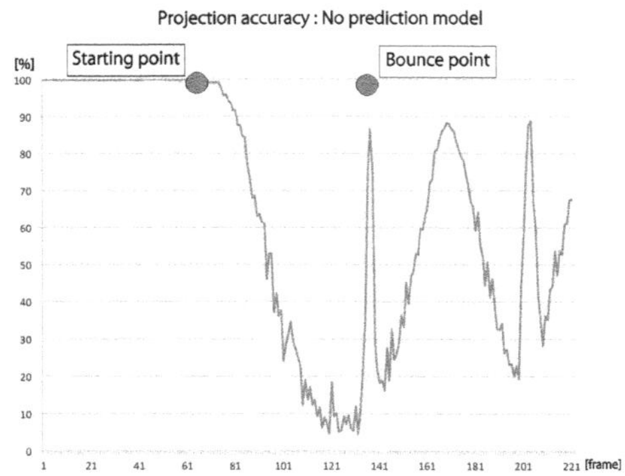

Figure 9. No prediction model

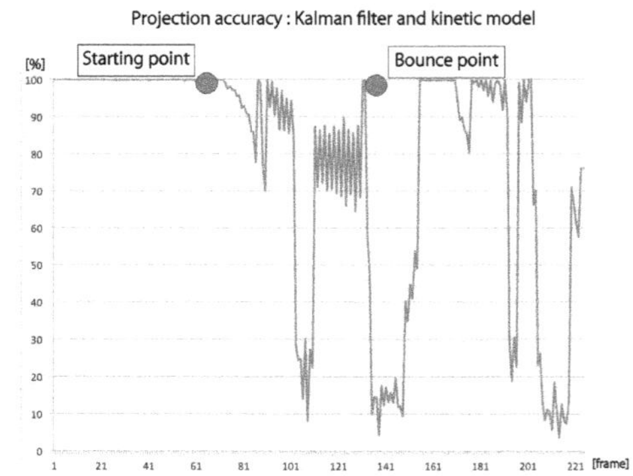

Figure 10. Kalman filter and kinetic model

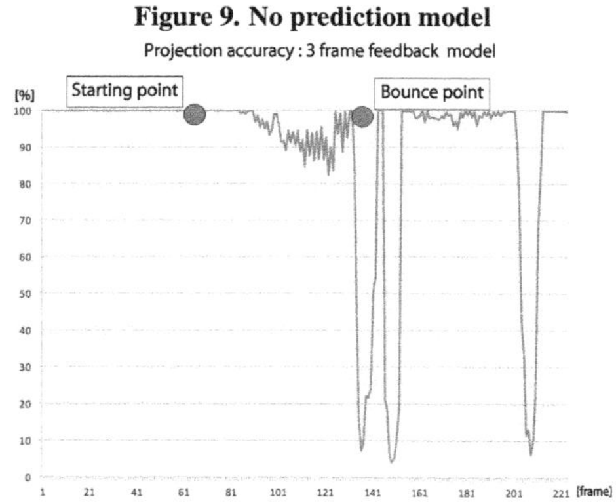

Figure 11. Three-frame feedback model

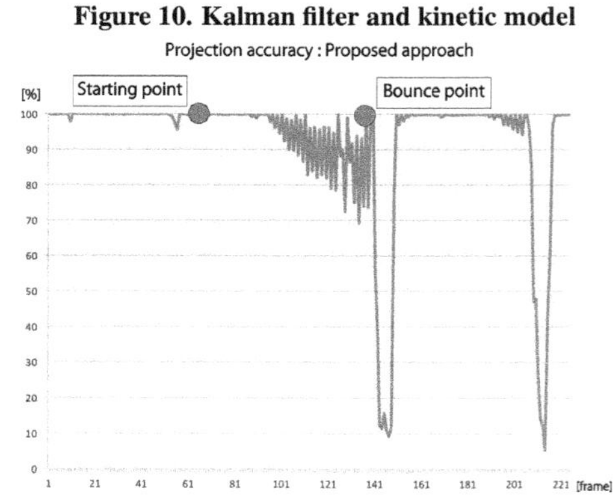

Figure 12. Proposed approach

DISCUSSION

As is mentioned in LumoSpheres [5], the frame rate of projectors is 60 fps and that of video cameras used in the evaluation experiments are 120 fps, which causes frame skips upon projection. This means that when a system predicts images for two frames, while the projectors can only project one frame. Therefore, even if this system predicts the ball's position correctly at 120 fps, projectors project that image every two frames. This frame skip causes a small vibration in the graph, which can be seen in Figure 9, 10, 11, and 12.

Although we succeeded in improving projection accuracy, there are still frames where projection slipping occurs when the acceleration changes. It will be possible to decrease the number of projection slips at bounce points if the locations of the floor and objects in collision with the ball are provided.

Currently, our prediction switching is conducted outside the Kalman filter; we will see if it is feasible to include the three-frame feedback model in the Kalman filter.

This system would be useful in sports and entertainment, for example, projection mapping on basket balls, soccer balls in freestyle, juggling balls, and so on. We believe that our system can perform projection mapping onto various moving objects such as vehicles. Moreover, by detecting bouncing and other states of a ball's motion and taking these actions as inputs by users, this system enables users to interact with balls.

Spherical projection from multiple projectors makes an overlapping part that might be unnaturally bright. We may be able to overcome this problem by rendering the image while calculating the intensity of every pixel.

Although we have not yet conducted formal user studies, we demonstrated the system at SIGGRAPH ASIA 2015 [7] and at Laval Virtual 2016, where over 100 people experienced the system. In the demonstration, slipping of the projection was hardly visible and the concept of the projection mapping onto moving balls was well received. Once anything changed in our system from the position where it was, the projection became blurred. Automatic calibration may overcome this problem.

CONCLUSION

We described a system for real-time tracking and real-time spherical projection onto flying balls, where a spherical image is projected on the balls by using multiple projectors. We proposed a combination of a Kalman filter and a three-frame feedback model as a new prediction model for the ball's position. The results of comparative experiments show that our approach is better than the existing Kalman filter model. Our results obtained 89.79%, a high projection accuracy, on a moving and bouncing ball; this is an increase of 19.35% over that of the Kalman-only model. We believe this system is compelling for a variety of projection mapping purposes, including sports and entertainment.

REFERENCES

1. Jones, B., Sodhi, R., Murdock, M., Mehra, R., Benko, H., Wilson, A., Ofek, E., MacIntyre, B., Raghuvanshi,

N., and Shapira, L. RoomAlive: Magical experiences enabled by scalable, adaptive projector-camera units. In *Proceedings of the 27th Annual ACM Symposium on User Interface Software and Technology*, UIST '14, ACM (New York, NY, USA, 2014), 637–644.

2. Jones, B. R., Benko, H., Ofek, E., and Wilson, A. D. IllumiRoom: Peripheral projected illusions for interactive experiences. In *ACM SIGGRAPH 2013 Emerging Technologies*, SIGGRAPH '13, ACM (New York, NY, USA, 2013), 7:1–7:1.

3. Kettner, S., Madden, C., and Ziegler, R. Direct rotational interaction with a spherical projection. *Creativity & Cognition Symposium on Interaction: Systems, Plactice and Theory.* (2004).

4. Knibbe, J., Benko, H., and Wilson, A. D. Juggling the effects of latency: Software approaches to minimizing latency in dynamic projector-camera systems. In *Adjunct Proceedings of the 28th Annual ACM Symposium on User Interface Software & Technology*, UIST '15 Adjunct, ACM (New York, NY, USA, 2015), 93–94.

5. Koike, H., and Yamaguchi, H. Lumospheres: Real-time tracking of flying objects and image projection for a volumetric display. In *Proceedings of the 6th Augmented Human International Conference*, AH '15, ACM (New York, NY, USA, 2015), 93–96.

6. Lincoln, P., Blate, A., Singh, M., Whitted, T., State, A., Lastra, A., and Fuchs, H. From motion to photons in 80 microseconds: Towards minimal latency for virtual and augmented reality. *IEEE Trans Vis Comput Graph 22*, 4 (Apr 2016), 1367–1376.

7. Miyafuji, S., and Koike, H. Ballumiere: Real-time tracking and projection system for high-speed flying balls. In *SIGGRAPH Asia 2015 Emerging Technologies*, SA '15, ACM (New York, NY, USA, 2015), 2:1–2:1.

8. Okumura, K., Oku, H., and Ishikawa, M. Lumipen: Projection-based mixed reality for dynamic objects. In *Proceedings of the 2012 IEEE International Conference on Multimedia and Expo*, ICME '12, IEEE Computer Society (Washington, DC, USA, 2012), 699–704.

9. Raskar, R., Welch, G., Low, K.-L., and Bandyopadhyay, D. Shader Lamps: Animating real objects with image-based illumination. In *Proceedings of the 12th Eurographics Workshop on Rendering Techniques*, Springer-Verlag (London, UK, UK, 2001), 89–102.

10. Zheng, F., Whitted, T., Lastra, A., Lincoln, P., State, A., Maimone, A., and Fuchs, H. Minimizing latency for augmented reality displays: Frames considered harmful. In *Mixed and Augmented Reality (ISMAR), 2014 IEEE International Symposium on* (Sept 2014), 195–200.

AnyLight: Programmable Ambient Illumination via Computational Light Fields

Yuichiro Takeuchi
yutak@acm.org

Shunichi Suwa
Shunichi.Suwa@jp.sony.com

Kunihiko Nagamine
Kunihiko.Nagamine@jp.sony.com

Sony Computer Science Laboratories Inc.
3-14-13 Higashigotanda
Shinagawa-ku, Tokyo 141-0022 Japan

ABSTRACT
In this paper we describe AnyLight, a lighting device that uses computational light fields to offer highly programmable illumination for architectural environments. Relying on *integral imaging*—a technique commonly used to realize stereoscopic 3D displays—AnyLight can mimic the illumination effects of various light sources, both real and imagined. A combination of high-output, narrow-beam LED backlight and custom, 3D printed optics give the device the capacity to shoot out strong, targeted light rays from its surface in arbitrary directions. The paper will provide extensive discussions covering the device's technical details, usage scenarios, and possibilities for future extensions; quantitative and qualitative results from our initial evaluation sessions will be reported as well.

Author Keywords
Integral illumination; integral imaging; computational light field; light field display; robotic/responsive architecture; programmable lighting.

ACM Classification Keywords
H.5.m. Information Interfaces and Presentation (e.g. HCI): Miscellaneous

INTRODUCTION
Integral imaging, a technique originally invented more than a century ago, has found popular use as a relatively simple way to implement stereoscopic 3D displays in the past several decades. Potential uses of the technique are by no means limited to stereoscopic displays, however—and ongoing advances in lighting technology (e.g., LEDs) and the recent introduction of 3D printable optics have now put us in a position where we can easily (and also *cheaply*) explore alternative applications of the technique.

In this paper, we explore one of such alternative uses of integral imaging, namely its potential to realize a highly programmable lighting (*integral illumination*) system for architectural environments. We have developed a prototype system, called AnyLight, which aims to mimic the lighting effects of a wide range of both real and imaginary light sources, e.g., spotlight, chandelier, sunlight, etc. While our prototype is still small in scale, room-sized implementations are theoretically possible by tiling multiple devices in a 2D grid layout. In a room fully furnished with an array of AnyLights, occupants will be able to freely control its lighting, and thereby also its ambience, to a degree unachievable using existing lighting technologies—with as much effort as switching wallpaper images on PCs or mobile devices.

Figure 1. AnyLight: an integral illumination device.

Hardware-wise, AnyLight employs a design similar to that of a conventional, integral imaging-based 3D display, involving a combination of a spatially modulated light source (we use a standard LCD with a custom-designed backlight in our prototype) and lenticular optics. However, the difference in objective between a display and a programmable lighting system—in particular the fact that we cannot determine a fixed *viewing area* for AnyLight—creates distinct technical challenges that we counter through several measures, e.g., a "hybrid" optical design where transparent and opaque elements coexist within a single lenticular sheet. Software-wise, we have developed a simple desktop controller application designed to allow users to intuitively harness the power of AnyLight without needing to understand low-level optical phenomena.

The paper will explain the technical principles underlying the design of AnyLight and illustrate the details of our prototype implementation, highlighting the major technical hurdles and our strategies to overcome them. We will describe several potential usage scenarios of the device within architectural environments, and discuss how the hardware may be optimized to suit different use cases and installment locations. We will also report results obtained from our initial evaluation sessions, including quantitative measurements of hardware performance and informal feedback gathered through a user study.

ISS 2016, November 06–09, 2016, Niagara Falls, ON, Canada
 ISBN 978-1-4503-4248-3/16/11...$15.00
DOI: http://dx.doi.org/10.1145/2992154.2992188

The paper's main contributions can be summarized as below:

- Introduces the concept and design of AnyLight, a programmable lighting system for architectural environments based on the principle of integral illumination
- Identifies the key technical challenges the aforementioned concept entails, and delineates strategies to solve them
- Explores the design space of AnyLight, illustrating through examples how the system may be optimized or extended to suit different applications and use cases
- Presents evaluation results that verify the soundness of the AnyLight concept, which should assist future efforts to design similar or derivative systems

RELATED WORK

Stereoscopic Displays

Integral imaging, first described by Lippmann [17] in 1908, is a technique to record and reproduce 4D plenoptic light fields using a planar array of tiny convex lenses. In the final decades of the 20th century, the technique had been revived to realize stereoscopic/multiscopic 3D displays, and a range of new developments has been spurred [37] as a result. Notable examples include the use of slanted 1D lenticulars to increase perceived spatial resolution [4], achieving actual high resolution using a projector array instead of an LCD [18], expanding the viewing angle using an extra, passive optical screen [8], and realizing variable-focus integral imaging using liquid lenses [29]. Recently, 3D printable optics [36] has begun to be used for integral imaging as well [27]. Active development is also taking place regarding the development of light field cameras (i.e., the use of integral imaging to capture 3D content), where lenticular sheets are placed on top of photosensors instead of displays [19, 35].

Besides integral imaging, a number of other techniques to implement stereoscopic displays exist, for example parallax barriers [20], holography [23], polarized glasses [12], volumetric displays [11], and time-multiplexed LCD stacks [32] (a comprehensive overview of existing 3D display technologies can be found in [16]).

Programmable Lighting

The notion of realizing "programmable" lighting using digital technology is an old one—a recurring idea (that has routinely been featured in concept images/videos meant to demonstrate the potential of Ubiquitous Computing) is to use projectors as reconfigurable illumination appliances [15, 21, 30]. However, limitations such as the fixed (and often narrow) projection angle, low spatial resolution, etc. makes their use as ambient illumination devices still rather impractical. On the other hand, simpler, more economic programmable lighting devices such as color-changing LED bulbs [1, 24] have been gaining popularity as part of a *smart home* [7] setup. Smart lighting is also finding usages other than illumination per se, for example visible light communication [13].

We do not claim that AnyLight is the world's first system that appropriates integral imaging for programmable illumination; a number of precedents do exist in this area [5, 14, 38]. However, instead of targeting architectural or ambient illumination as we do with AnyLight, in prior efforts only relatively small objects positioned inside a limited, predefined area are illuminated. This is an important distinction; whereas in prior work on integral illumination, only light rays that hit the target objects (more precisely, only light rays that enter the predefined area containing the target objects) need to be controlled, AnyLight needs to have command over *all* rays that emanate from its surface. This presents a unique challenge to the hardware design; we will revisit this fact later in the paper when we discuss the issue of "ghosting" and our tactics to counter it.

Robotic/Responsive Architecture

Within the spatial design professions (e.g., architecture, stage design, interior design, installation art, etc.) lighting has long been considered a key factor that influences the quality of architectural space, and one can find numerous instances where innovative lighting has been used to create distinct spatial experiences [2]. Such regard for the power of lighting is corroborated by environmental psychology literature [3]; lighting is known to have wide-ranging, and often subconscious, effects on our behaviors, thoughts, emotions, etc.

In light of such facts, a building furnished with architectural-scale programmable lighting may well be viewed as a type of *robotic, or responsive architecture* [22]—a class of architectural structures and environments that dynamically alter their shapes and/or appearances using sensors, displays, kinetic actuators, etc. In our previous work [26], we positioned robotic/responsive architecture as one of the key technical approaches that may lead to a world built of *habitable bits*, where the built environment itself becomes infused with the "distinctive plasticity and interactivity of digital bits"—the classic, Weiserian [31] vision of *overlaying* myriad computers on top of the environment is replaced by an inseparable integration of digital technology and the physical environment.

Though we expect AnyLight to be a versatile technology that can provide benefit in a wide range of applications, costs will likely be prohibitive at first for individual, domestic uses, and initially the most practical application domain for the technology may be *media facades* [10, 33]—large-scale LED/LCD displays installed as part of building exteriors, found in commercial city centers all over the world such as Times Square in New York. AnyLight may be used to build more expressive successors to such displays.

HARDWARE

Figure 2 shows the basic hardware configuration of AnyLight. As can be seen, the overall architecture is roughly identical to that of a conventional integral imaging 3D display, employing a combination of an LED backlight, an LCD panel and a lenticular sheet, assembled linearly. Again, as with conventional integral imaging setups, the backlight and the LCD panel can be swapped with other forms of spatially modulated lighting, such as a projector, LED/OLED display, etc. LCD panels are notoriously inefficient (a typical color LCD can only transmit less than 10% of incoming light), and thus our use of an LCD may seem to be a questionable choice, especially considering

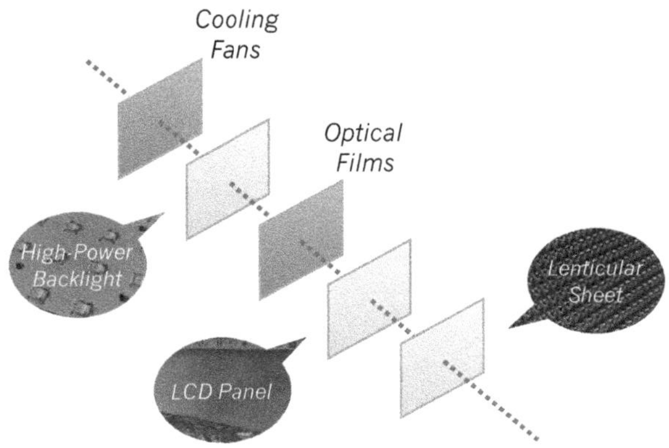

Figure 2. AnyLight hardware configuration.

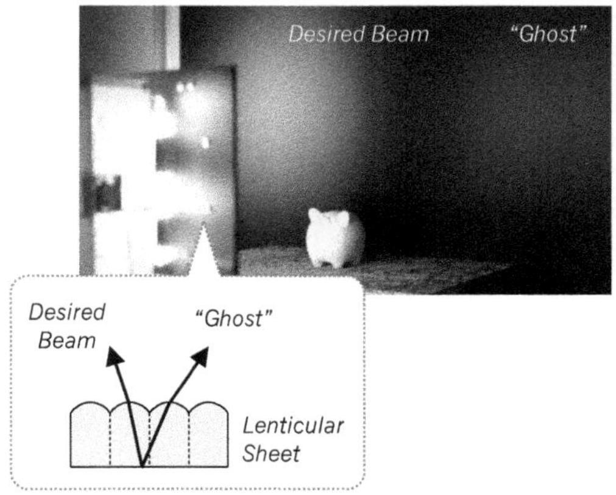

Figure 3. Cross-talk between lenslets, and the resulting ghost.

the decreasing costs of LED matrix displays. However, if we set aside the issue of energy use, no other technology can currently offer the combination of high pixel density, high brightness, low cost, and compact form factor. As we are still in the early prototyping stage, we deemed energy usage to not be as important as the quality of user experience; LCDs are the best option we have now to simulate what LED/OLED-based implementations may be able to provide in the near- to mid-term future, assuming continuous technical advances.

Although the general architecture is similar, several important differences set AnyLight apart from existing integral imaging displays. For example, the power output of the LED backlight is much higher (with an upper limit of 271,200 lumens in our brightest setup), and the printed lenticular sheet sports a custom design that mixes clear and opaque elements. In order to manage the considerable heat generated by the LEDs, we rely on both passive and active cooling technologies, including a set of two powerful fans (24V/2.3A) installed on the back of the device. When assembled, the entire setup measures 43.4 × 16.5 × 26.8cm. (We built several versions of the prototype, each with a slightly different form factor; the above measurements were taken from our main setup, which we used in all of our evaluations.)

An idealized, "true" integral imaging display can simulate the presence of any 3D object/environment positioned beneath its surface. Similarly, AnyLight can simulate any light source(s) positioned beneath the LCD panel, albeit within practical limitations regarding physical size, power output, spatial/angular resolutions, field of view, etc.

Busting "Ghosts"

Bluntly speaking, it is not a mistake to describe the AnyLight hardware as merely an integral imaging display with a significantly more powerful backlight. However, naively increasing the power output of an integral imaging display produces unwelcome optical effects, which we refer to as *ghosts*.

Ghosts are a result of *cross-talk* between neighboring lenslets on a lenticular sheet. Figure 3 illustrates how such cross-talks arise; here, the right-side LCD pixels underneath each lenslet are illuminated, which should result in a narrow beam of light emanating leftward from each lenslet. However, as light from the illuminated LCD pixels can also travel rightward into the neighboring lenslet, another, somewhat weaker beam of light emanates from each lenslet as well—thereby creating a *ghost*. The top photo in Figure 3 shows AnyLight shooting out a leftward, circular spotlight (realized by only turning on the rightmost pixels beneath lenslets located in the central area of the AnyLight LCD), with a ghost clearly visible to the right. Note that even with the same hardware configuration, whether and how strongly ghosts appear will differ based on the illumination effect produced by AnyLight, which in turn is decided by the 2D pixel pattern shown on the underlying LCD. As a general rule, ghosts are weakest (usually nonexistent) when only pixels under the central region of each lenslet are illuminated (so light is emitted roughly perpendicular to the LCD screen) and become strongest when pixels near the perimeter of each lenslet are illuminated. Another fact worth mentioning is that ghost rays always emanate outside the lenslet's angle of view.

This phenomenon of ghosting is not unique to AnyLight, but is shared among integral imaging systems in general—the *repeating* of content on lenticular postcards (often sold as souvenirs at tourist destinations) is caused by the same cross-talk, for example. Nevertheless, the issue is of much higher importance for AnyLight, than it is for other systems. As illustrated in Figure 4, stereoscopic displays have predefined *viewing areas* from which viewers see the display, and conventional integral illumination systems have predefined *projection areas* in which objects to be illuminated are placed. Light that does

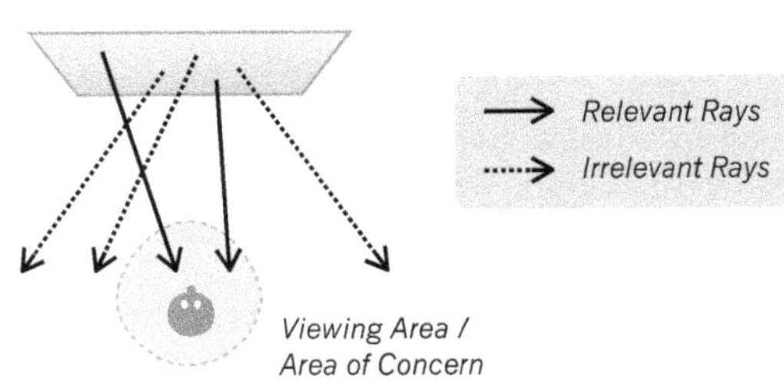

Figure 4. In conventional integral imaging setups, only rays that enter "areas of concerns" need to be controlled.

Figure 5. Hybrid lenticular design with clear and opaque elements.

Figure 6. Optimization software and resulting lenticular designs.

not enter these *areas of concerns* is considered irrelevant and thus does not need to be controlled (note that "ghost" rays always fall into this category, as areas of concerns are naturally designed to exist within the lenslets' angle of view). Ambient illumination systems like AnyLight do not have this luxury as we cannot define any specific areas of concern, and hence *all* rays coming out of the device are relevant; they either need to be controlled, or in cases where that is not possible they need to be at least suppressed.

In order to reduce ghosting as much as possible, in our implementations we employ the following two techniques:

Hybrid Lenticulars

There are several variations to lenticular sheets used for integral imaging; a 1D array of narrow, cylindrical lenses may be used where content only needs to change along a single axis, or a 2D array of circular lenses (e.g., fly-eye lens) can be used if it needs to change along both the x and y axes. In any case, the lenticular sheets are wholly made out of transparent, optical grade glass or plastic. However, as we have seen in Figure 3, within lenticular sheets entirely made out of clear materials there is no mechanism to curb the cross-talk between lenslets, and consequently the creation of ghosts.

For AnyLight, we take advantage of 3D printing to design and fabricate custom lenticulars with opaque "walls" built around each lenslet, in effect optically isolating the lenslets from each other (Figure 5). The sheets are printed using a Stratasys Connex 3D printer, with clear parts made of VeroClear (refractive index $= 1.47$) and opaque parts made of VeroBlackPlus. The opaque, black walls absorb incoming light, and hence prevent inter-lenslet transmission of light rays. (3D printed lenticulars with similar designs have been described in [28], although not for illumination purposes).

The LCD panel in our prototype was sourced by taking apart an Asus MB168+ 15-inch external display, with a screen resolution of 1920 $\times$ 1080px and a pixel pitch of 0.179mm. We designed each lenslet to have a diameter exactly 20 times the pixel pitch (3.58mm), and made variations of the sheets with two different wall thicknesses (0.179mm and 0.358mm). We also tested using a grayscale LCD (Totoku MS25i2) in one of our alternative implementations; in this case the system loses the ability to adjust the color of light rays, but the light output will be significantly higher due to the lack of color filters. (In a typical color LCD, the color filters alone shut out two thirds of the incoming light).

In designing lenslets we followed an approach similar to that described in [27], and wrote a custom numerical optimization program that employs a Monte Carlo method to minimize focusing errors among rays passing through different points on the lens surface. The program supports designs of both spherical and aspherical lenses, and we have made a series of custom lenticulars, as shown in Figure 6. We will report the comparative performances of these lenses later in the paper.

Narrow-Beam Backlight

Unfortunately, even if the opaque walls succeed in absorbing 100% (i.e., no reflection) of inter-lenslet rays we will still see some level of ghosting, as light rays can traverse freely within the thin, clear layer of glass protecting the LCD panel (Figure 7). Taking off this glass layer, or embedding walls inside this layer may perhaps be possible but is impractical and thus we rely on a different approach, that is to modify the backlight to limit the angle with which light rays are emitted.

Figure 8 shows our backlight. We use a total of 240 Lumiled LUXEON M high power LEDs, which can be switched on/off in batches of 8 to enable local dimming (which contributes to more efficient energy use, and also higher contrast). Covering the LEDs are several layers of optical sheets—diffuser, prism sheets (one each for x and y directions), and 3M DBEF (Dual Brightness Enhancement Film), respectively—a routine configuration found in many off-the-shelf LCDs. We handpicked the sheets from a group of alternatives to find the combination that produces the narrowest beam possible; however in reality we found little variance in performance among the options (it appears that products on the market are already optimized for LCDs, and are manufactured to similar specifications). Thus we were unable to limit beam angles to our desired levels with optical sheets alone (we will report performance details later in the evaluations section).

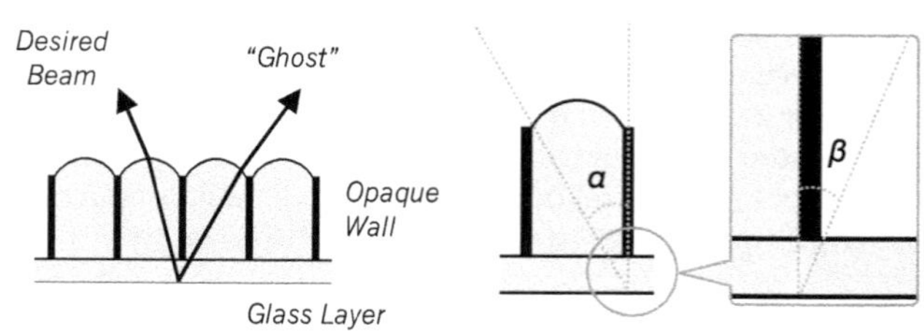

Figure 7. Cross-talk arising from glass protection layer.

Figure 8. LED backlight.

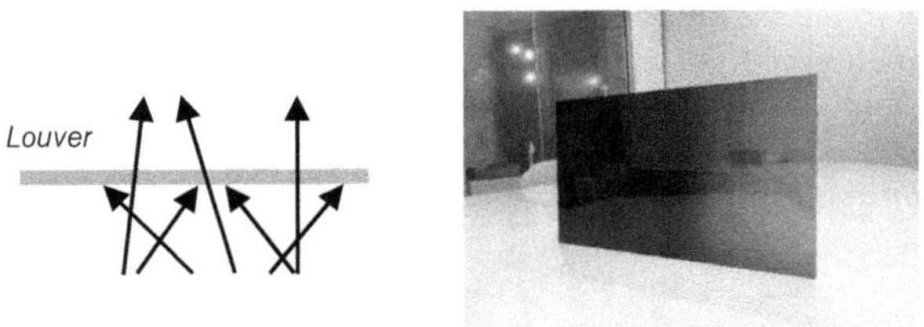

Figure 9. Limiting beam angle with louver film.

A number of optical arrangements exist that can further limit the beam angle. However, to maintain the compact form factor and the low cost of the prototype, we chose to simply add an extra sheet of *louver film* in front of the DBEF sheet. Commonly marketed as privacy filters for PC/smartphone screens, louver films absorb all light entering at angles greater than its *cutoff* value (Figure 9). Although this approach has the virtue of easy installation, owing to its reliance on absorption louver films are inevitably less energy efficient than refraction-based or reflection-based optical arrangements (e.g., using collimators). Exactly how much we should limit the beam angle is a design decision that depends multiple factors, but the louver's cutoff angle should be somewhere between α and β in Figure 7; choosing a value close to β will produce less ghosting but reduce overall light output, whereas a value close to α has the opposite effect. Any value outside this range will either lead to a needless increase in ghosting ($> \alpha$), or a similarly needless reduction of light output ($< \beta$). For our implementations, we used a 3M louver film with a cutoff of ± 30 degrees.

Our current implementation relies on an LCD, but as we mentioned earlier we expect them to be eventually replaced by superior technologies, e.g., LED matrix displays. Many of such technologies will negate the need of a backlight, but the issue of ghosting and requirement for limiting beam angles will still persist; thus experimental results obtained through our prototype will still be relevant to such future designs.

SOFTWARE

Figure 10 illustrates the relation between on/off states of LCD pixels and the emitted light ray. Here, the vector (x, y, z) can be computed using the following equations, in which n_{air} and n_{lens} denote the respective refractive indices of air (1.00029) and the lens material (1.47). The color of the light will mirror

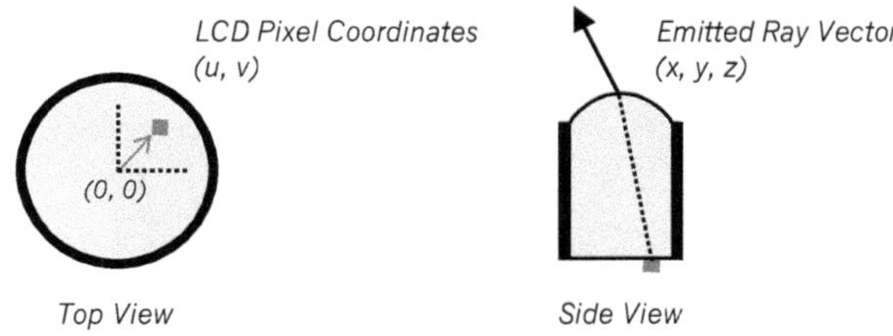

Figure 10. Relation between LCD pixel position and emitted light ray.

that of the LCD pixel. Computing the inverse, i.e., determining which pixel needs to be lit up to produce the desired light rays, is equally straightforward as well.

$$x = \frac{-u}{\sqrt{u^2 + v^2}} \cdot w \tag{1}$$

$$y = \frac{-v}{\sqrt{u^2 + v^2}} \cdot w \tag{2}$$

$$z = \sqrt{1 - w^2} \tag{3}$$

Where:

$$w = \frac{\sqrt{u^2 + v^2}}{\sqrt{h^2 + u^2 + v^2}} \cdot \frac{n_{lens}}{n_{air}} \tag{4}$$

The AnyLight software continuously modulates the LCD pixels to obtain the desired light output, while shutting down the backlight locally for any region in which all pixels are black, i.e., $(R, G, B) = (0, 0, 0)$. (The hardware is capable of more sophisticated backlight dimming, but we currently use binary on/off for simplicity's sake.) Cooling fans are not controlled by the software—instead they are kept running whenever the system's main power is turned on.

User Interface

As we have just seen, running AnyLight is simply a matter of dynamically modulating LCD pixels, and writing the driving software can hence be a quite straightforward process. However, to make the system usable we will also need an easy-to-use user interface. Directly manipulating pixel values to control light rays is an incredibly complex task, difficult even for those with deep knowledge of lenticular optics and the intricate details of our prototype hardware. We need an interface that provides a proper level of abstraction, while retaining the system's distinctive high degree of freedom.

Figure 11 shows our user interface application. States of each LCD pixel are completely hidden from users, and instead they choose a light source from several alternatives (e.g., spotlight, spherical light) and adjust parameters such as position, number, orientation, color, etc. by clicking and dragging on a 3D rendering view showing models of light sources, emitted rays, and the device's surface panel. The application automatically modulates LCD pixels to simulate the virtual light sources on the screen as accurately as possible. One drawback of this interface is that, due to its reliance on real-world metaphors, the

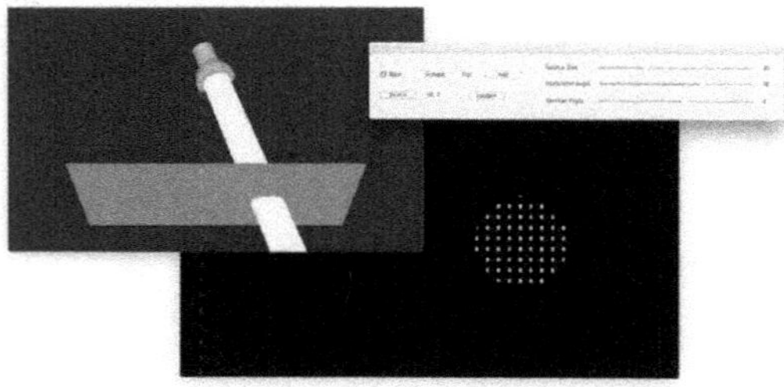

Figure 11. User interface application.

application is unable to produce purely imaginary lighting effects that cannot be synthesized using a combination of actual light sources. Although the application only supports manual controls at this stage, we are also interested in fully automatic lighting adjustment, e.g., making a spotlight continually track a person or an object.

APPLICATIONS

We expect AnyLight to have potential uses in a wide range of settings, some of which are listed below.

Home/Office Lighting The device may act as a more versatile lighting system for living/working environments, possibly assisting with relaxation, concentration, etc.

Media Facades The device may serve as a more interactive and dynamic alternative to existing media facades in urban centers, providing both commercial and aesthetic values

Stage Lighting The device may be used as a dynamically reconfigurable stage lighting, giving scenic designers higher degrees of artistic freedom

Photography The device could possibly serve as a substitute for existing lighting equipment in photography studios

Therapy The device may potentially be used in light therapy [6], for treating Seasonable Affective Disorders (SADs)

Not all of the above applications will become practical simultaneously. For example, commercial uses like media facades should become viable sooner than individual ones, and some applications will naturally be more demanding than others in terms of technical specifications (e.g., stage lighting will need higher power output compared to normal ambient lighting).

Theoretically, an integral illumination device can simulate the presence of arbitrary objects, including but not limited to light sources, situated within a virtual 3D space underneath the device's surface. Though there needs to be a series of improvements regarding spatial/angular resolutions, light output, etc., allowing ourselves to be a bit speculative, we can envision a future room with a large AnyLight device covering the entire ceiling—which can quickly switch from showing a simulated twilight sunbeam that can actually be blinding, to rendering a virtual Bohemian chandelier that actually looks breathtaking (perhaps a partial realization of Sutherland's *ultimate display* concept [25]). Note that since integral illumination is a variant of integral imaging, AnyLight can function as a display as well; users can look up to the ceiling and see realistically visualized light sources, not just their resulting effects. (Again, however, this is contingent on future technical advances—our current prototype's low spatial resolution makes for a terribly crude display at the moment).

The difference between integral illumination and the existing *projectors-as-illumination* ideas [30] may warrant a brief discussion. Roughly speaking, integral illumination can produce effects akin to a 2D grid of projectors, albeit with higher spatial resolution, lower angular resolution, and much lower cost of implementation. Light rays emitted from a single projector all originate from essentially the same point in space; consequently its capacity to produce variable directional lighting is severely limited. This is easy to understand if we consider its use in photography sessions; a task as simple as switching the direction of light cast onto the subject cannot be fulfilled with a single projector-based lighting.

Application-Specific Lenticular Design

An ideal integral illumination device would be universal—the same optical design would provide equally good performance in all situations and scenarios. However, real-world design of such devices involves a number of performance tradeoffs, and a universal optical design may well be one that only achieves mediocre performance for all situations.

By making use of the freedom of design offered by 3D printed lenses, we can customize the lenticular optics of AnyLight to provide better performances for specific uses, situations, and installment locations. Below we provide several examples to demonstrate this potential, along with photographs of custom lenticulars that we have actually fabricated (Figure 12). (Note that the experimental lens designs described here have not yet been tested, and we make no guarantee that they will perform as planned in practice.)

Wider/Narrower Angle of View

When considering indoor uses, an ideal lenslet for AnyLight will have an angle of view just wide enough to cover the entire area that needs to be illuminated; anything wider will amount to a waste of angular resolution (unless we are pursuing some artistic indirect lighting effects). For example, installing AnyLight overhead in a large room with a low ceiling would benefit from a wider angle of view, whereas one installed in a tiny room with a high ceiling would call for a narrower angle. For spherical lenslets, the general rule is that a large curvature radius widens the angle of view, while a smaller radius narrows it down—which will also make the lens taller, if optimized to minimize focus errors.

Directional Lenticulars

Not all installations of AnyLight call for light to be spread out equally in a radially symmetrical manner, 360 degrees around the device. For example, a ceiling light installed near a corner of a room may only need to emit light in the direction opposite to the walls, and an AnyLight media facade might not need to shoot out light upwards into the sky. In such situations, more efficient use of spatial resolution may be achieved by adding directionality to the lenslets—i.e., modifying their designs so that light from LCD pixels will only be refracted in directions that are necessary under the context of installation. We have

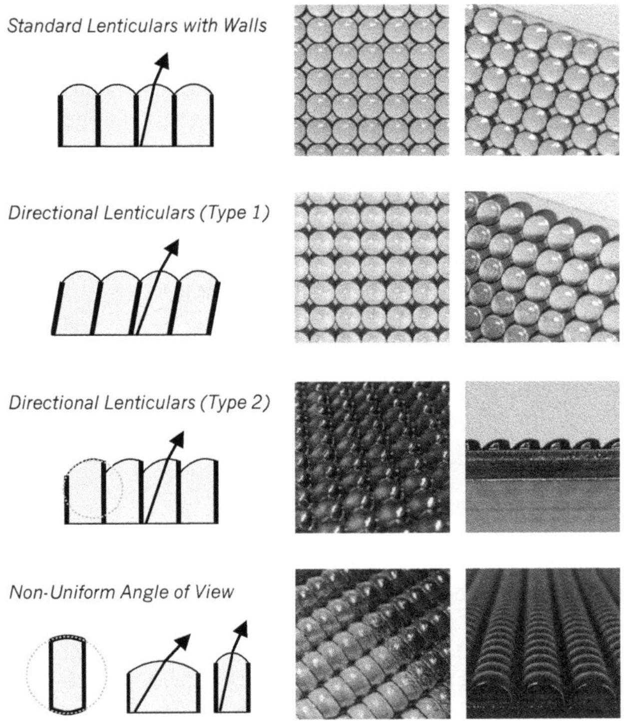

Figure 12. Application-specific lenticular sheets.

designed two alternative lenticulars that may fulfill this function: one where the cylindrical base of each lenslet is slanted diagonally, and another where each lenslet is actually a non-concentric cutout from a larger lenslet shape.

Non-Uniform Angles of View

We have already discussed how the angle of view of the lenslets may be adjusted to accommodate for differences in room geometries, but problems arise for rooms with with vastly different dimensions along the x and y axes—for example a long hallway. In such cases, it might make sense to design lenslets with different angles of view for each direction. We designed one lenticular sheet that may provide this function; the rectangular lenslet shape was derived by carving out a sliver from a larger, radially symmetrical lenslet.

Combining Different Lenslets

Lenslets laid out on a single lenticular sheet do not necessarily need to be uniform in design, and we can mix different lenslets to realize unique illumination effects, compensate for the weakness of each design, etc. For example, by using a combination of lenslets whose angles of view are slanted outward in different directions, we can give AnyLight a wider angular coverage than is possible with uniform lenslets.

EVALUATIONS

To test the validity of the AnyLight concept and our prototype design, we have performed the following two evaluations: 1) quantitative performance measurement of our prototype hardware, with a particular focus on assessing the effectiveness of our *anti-ghosting* measures, and 2) an informal, unstructured user study to gather qualitative feedback on the user interface and overall thoughts regarding the AnyLight concept.

Figure 13. Measuring luminance values.

Hardware Performance Measurement

Using a setup as pictured in Figure 13, we measured the luminance values of light emitted from our AnyLight prototype at varying angles (-80° to 80°, at 5° intervals), under the 13 conditions outlined below.

1–5: Prototype simulates front-facing spotlight, using lenticular sheets ABCDE, respectively

6–9: Prototype simulates side-facing spotlight, using lenticular sheets ABCD, respectively

10, 11: Backlight only (no lenticular sheet), with and without louver film

12–14: Prototype simulates side-facing spotlight, with louver film, using lenticular sheets ABC, respectively

Here, lenticular sheets A through C all share the same spherical lenslet design, with a curvature radius of 1.933mm and a 64.17° angle of view. Lens A is wholly transparent (no walls), whereas Lens B and C contain opaque walls with thicknesses of 0.179mm and 0.358mm, respectively (i.e., 1× or 2× of the LCD's pixel pitch).

Sheet D has a slightly different, but still spherical lenslet design, taller than sheets A through C (6.153mm, as opposed to 4.859mm for ABC) and with a curvature radius of 2.227mm, 49.17° angle of view, and and walls of 0.179mm thickness.

Sheet E is our only sheet with aspherical lenslets, which theoretically should result in significantly lower focusing errors. The lenslets have a 64.18° angle of view and 0.179mm walls.

All lenslets have a diameter of 3.58mm, and are arranged in a rectilinear manner on the lenticular sheets. Distances between lenslets are identical for all sheets with no walls or 0.179mm walls (i.e., sheets ABDE), while sheet C has a wider gap between lenslets to make room for the thicker walls.

Figure 14 shows the performance measurement results.

The top five graphs show the results for conditions **1** through **5**. A clear, strong peak can be observed for all five conditions, demonstrating how our prototype can direct light in small angles, as per our design intentions. In the graph for condition **1** we can see two small peaks at wider angles (around ±50°), presumably caused by ghosting. These peaks are diminished in conditions **2** to **5**, which demonstrate how the opaque walls

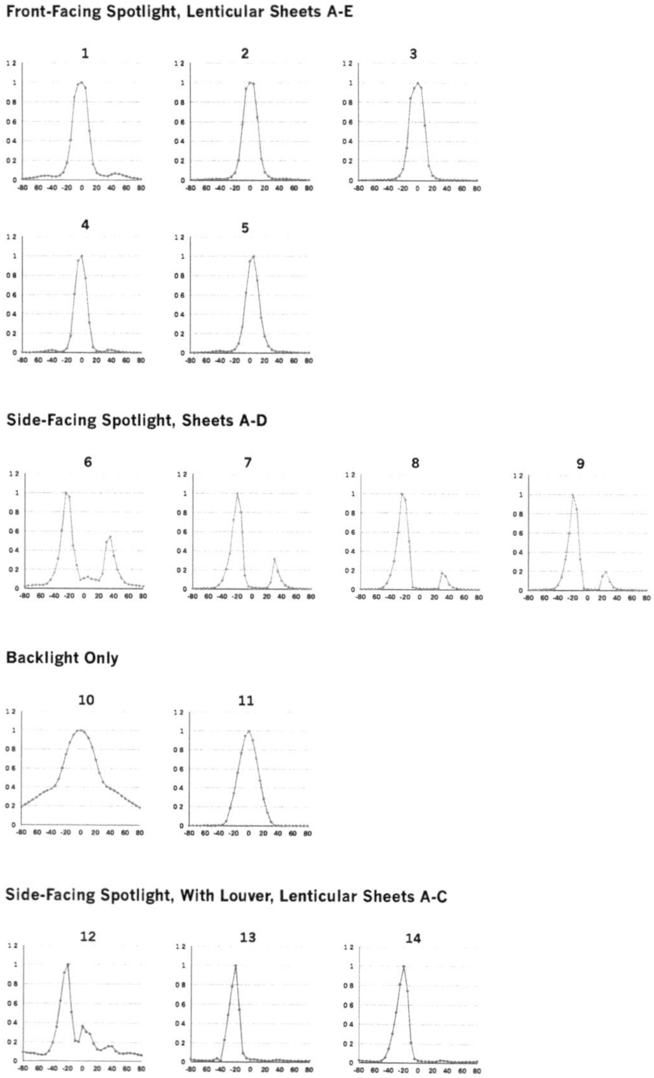

Figure 14. Performance measurement results. Horizontal axis denotes angle (in degrees), vertical axis denotes luminance value (standardized).

successfully suppress ghosting by cutting down on cross-talk between lenslets. Results for condition **5** (sheet E, aspherical lenslets) do not show any clear advantages over the other conditions; theoretically the low focusing errors of the aspherical design would lead to a narrower, clearer peak, but perhaps the limited accuracy of our 3D printer (30 microns) had hindered the lens from fulfilling its intended performance.

The next batch of four graphs shows the results for conditions **6** to **9**. With spotlights cast in a side-facing manner, these are the conditions most susceptible to the formation of ghosts. As expected, we can see significant *ghost peaks* in addition to the main peaks created by simulated spotlights. Comparing conditions **6**, **7**, and **8**, we can readily see how effective the walls are in suppresssing ghosts—unsurprisingly, thicker walls and wider gaps between lenslets yield even better suppression performance. Comparing the results for conditions **7** and **9**, we can see how taller lenslets lead to weaker ghosts, which again is in line with our understanding of how ghosts are formed.

The graph for condition **10** shows measurements taken using the backlight only; as can be seen, the backlight emits a moderately diffuse light in all directions. Comparing this with the graph for condition **11**, we can see how a simple addition of a louver film can give a strong directionality to the light. (Note that luminance values in the graphs are standardized; in absolute values, using the louver film has led to an approximately 30% drop in luminance at the 0° direction.)

The final batch of graphs shows the results for conditions **12** to **14**. We can see how ghosts can be all but eliminated using both a walled lenticular design and a louver film, although the sizable drop in luminance from the louver film holds true here as well.

Informal User Study

To collect some initial feedback about our user interface software and general reception towards the AnyLight concept, we gathered 8 subjects (6 male and 2 female, ages 20–30, median age 26) to conduct an informal user study. In terms of technical proficiency the subjects were sort of a mixed bag, including engineering students and self-proclaimed "luddites". The study did not have a clear structure; subjects were invited into a room one at a time (one or more of the authors stayed in the same room for the duration of each study), received a brief introduction to AnyLight, and were asked to freely interact with the prototype through our user interface application. Subjects were instructed to provide feedback anytime during the study through speech (we took notes of all conversations), and also immediately after the study through a written report. The duration of the study was 20 to 30 minutes per subject. We will discuss some of our findings below.

On the User Interface

Overall, reactions to our interface were mixed. While none of the subjects gave truly negative feedback toward our software per se, many explicitly questioned our decision to use a desktop app as a controller; three of the subjects suggested the use of levers, joysticks or other physical interfaces, one suggested a large touchscreen, and two others suggested an augmented reality interface and mid-air gesture control, respectively. The strong preference for *Natural User Interfaces (NUIs)* [34] and the spontaneous ways in which it was raised by subjects came as a surprise to us—it appeared to us that the subjects saw the desktop app as an awkward filter preventing them from more directly engaging with the immediate, physical functionality offered by AnyLight. However, it must be noted that subjects were wildly diverse with regards to the exact type of *natural* interface they think would be suited for AnyLight, suggesting the need for several iterations of trial and error before we can settle on a single design approach.

If we set aside the skepticism regarding our choice of a desktop application platform, subjects were overall positive about the ease of use of the software itself, though we received several complaints regarding the perceived lack of freedom with which lighting effects can be designed. (Our application does not allow users to design freeform light sources from scratch;

they can only pick a source type from a predefined list of options and then adjust its parameters).

On the Overall Concept
Subjects' responses toward the overall concept were positive, with numerous suggestions about its potential uses in theater, theme parks, nightclubs / concert halls, high-end retail stores, etc. Interestingly, only one of the subjects spontaneously gave home/offices as a suitable setting for the device, and generally subjects seemed to view AnyLight as a device to create *spectacle*, rather than something that can subtly enhance everyday life as per our original intent.

While we doubtlessly take these results seriously, there is one factor that we believe, in hindsight, may have influenced subjects' views on this topic. During the test, when subjects were first presented with the user interface app, the default screen always showed a single spotlight emitting a brightly-colored beam; subjects were first instructed to try to move around and change parameters of this spotlight, before switching to other types of light sources. This first encounter may have colored subjects' opinions, and perhaps we would have received different responses had we begun with a different light source as the starting point.

DISCUSSION
Evaluation results show that our prototype generally works as well as we had expected. However, the prototype is too small to qualify as an architectural illumination device, and thus we have yet to gain good insights regarding the true user experience of AnyLight. To make the most out of AnyLight's ability to freely control not only the color/intensity but also the directions of light rays, the device needs to be fairly large relative to the illuminated objects. Thus our prototype can render various eye-catching effects when illuminating reasonably small objects, but when used as a ceiling light in a real architectural environment its expressive power becomes reduced to such a degree that the effects are no more striking compared to what can be done using a common LCD/DLP projector.

We will need to create a larger prototype—preferably around 2m $\times$ 2m large—before we can conduct more detailed studies and make accurate assessments of AnyLight's potential as an ambient illumination device.

Figure 15 shows some examples of lighting effects produced by AnyLight, and also several of the different hardware setups we have implemented so far.

CONCLUSION AND FUTURE WORK
In this paper we have introduced AnyLight, a novel illumination device that uses the principle of integral imaging to offer highly programmable ambient illumination in varied environmental settings. We described the overall design of the system and our current LCD-based implementation, proposed several measures to tackle the issue of "ghosting", and illustrated potential use cases for the system and how the technology may be extended to suit different scenarios and objectives. Evaluation results demonstrate that our prototype works as intended, and also verifies the effectiveness of our anti-ghost tactics. In

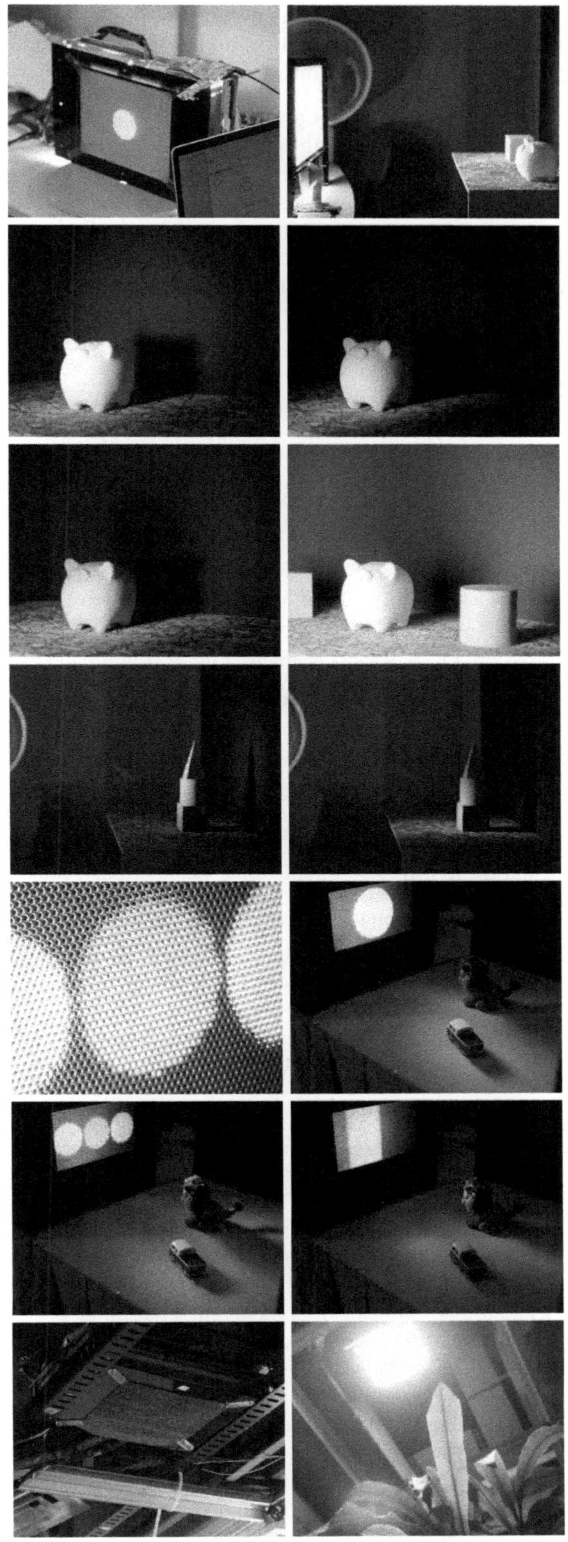

Figure 15. Photographs of AnyLight prototypes and lighting effects.

the user study, subjects were generally supportive of the overall concept of AnyLight, and offered helpful feedback regarding the design of the user interface.

One serious flaw with our current, LCD-based prototype is its energy inefficiency; solving this issue is critical if we wish to bring this technology to the market. We are currently working on a specialized backlight design that would allow it to focus light rays into a narrow beam without the use of a louver, and also discussing with manufacturers of LED displays to investigate the possibility of abandoning LCDs altogether.

REFERENCES

1. Philips Hue (http://www2.meethue.com). Retrieved on Sep. 9, 2016.
2. The Weather Project (http://olafureliasson.net/archive/artwork/WEK101003/the-weather-project). Retrieved on Sep. 9, 2016.
3. Bell, P.A., Greene, T.C., Fisher, J.D., Baum, A. Environmental Psychology (Fifth Edition). Lawrence Erlbaum Associates. 2001.
4. Berkel, C.V. Image preparation for 3D-LCD. Proc. SPIE Stereoscopic Displays and Virtual Reality Systems 3639, pp.84-91. 1999.
5. Cossairt, O., Nayar, S., Ramamoorthi, R. Light Field Transfer: Global Illumination Between Real and Synthetic Objects. ACM Trans. Graph. (Proc. SIGGRAPH) 27(3). 57:1-57:6. 2008.
6. Glickman, G., Byrne, B., Pineda, C., Hauck, W.W., Brainard, G.C. Light therapy for seasonal affective disorder with blue narrow-band light-emitting diodes (LEDs). Biological Psychiatry 59(6). pp.502-507. 2006.
7. Han, D.M., Lim, J.H. Smart Home Energy Management System Using IEEE 802.15.4 and Zigbee. IEEE Trans. on Consumer Electronics 56(3). pp.1403-1410. 2010.
8. Hirsch, M., Wetzstein, G., Raskar, R. A Compressive Light Field Projection System. ACM Trans. Graph. (Proc. SIGGRAPH) 33(4). Article 58. 2014.
9. Jacobs, A., Mather, J., Winlow, R., Montgomery, D., Jones, G., Willis, M., Tillin, M., Hill, L., Khazova, M., Stevenson, H., Bourhill, G. 2D/3D Switchable Displays. Sharp Technical Journal 4. pp.15-18. 2003.
10. Khoo, C.K., Salim, F.D. Lumina: A Soft Kinetic Material for Morphing Architectural Skins and Organic User Interfaces. Proc. UbiComp 2013. pp.53-62.
11. Kimura, H., Uchiyama, T., Yoshikawa, H. Laser Produced 3D Display in the Air. SIGGRAPH 2006 Emerging Technologies. pp.20. 2006.
12. Kitamura, Y., Konishi, T., Yamamoto, S., Kishino, F. Interactive Stereoscopic Display for Three or More Users. Proc. SIGGRAPH 2001. pp.231-240.
13. Komine, T., Nakagawa, M. Fundamental Analysis for Visible-Light Communication System Using LED Lights. IEEE Trans. on Consumer Electronics 50(1). pp.100-107. 2004.
14. Levoy, M., Ng, R., Adams, A., Footer, M., Horowitz, M. Light Field Microscopy. ACM Trans. Graph. (Proc. SIGGRAPH) 25(3). pp.924-934. 2006.
15. Linder, N., Maes, P. LuminAR: Portable Augmented Reality Interface Design and Prototype. In Adjunct Proc. of UIST 2010. pp.395-396.
16. Lueder, E. 3D Displays. Wiley. 2012.
17. Lippmann, G.M. La Photographie Integrale. Comptes-Rendus 146. pp.446-451. 1908.
18. Matusik, W., Pfister, H. A Scalable System for Real-Time Acquisition, Transmission, and Autostereoscopic Display of Dynamic Scenes. ACM Trans. Graph. (Proc. SIGGRAPH) 23(3). pp.814-824. 2004.
19. Ng, R., Levoy, M., Bredif, M., Duval, G., Horowitz, M., Hanrahan, P. Light Field Photography with a Hand-Held Plenoptic Camera. Computer Science Technical Report CSTR, Jan 2005.
20. Perlin, K., Paxia, S., Kollin, J.S. An Autostereoscopic Display. Proc. SIGGRAPH 2000. pp.319-326.
21. Raskar, R., von Baar, J., Beardsley, P., Willwacher, T., Rao, S., Forlines, C. iLamps: Geometrically Aware and Self-Configuring Projectors. Proc. SIGGRAPH 2006. pp.809-818.
22. Negroponte, N. Soft Architecture Machines. MIT Press. 1975.
23. St. Hillaire, P., Lucente, M., Sutter, J., Pappu, R., Sparrell, C.J., Benton, S. Scaling Up the MIT Holographic Video System. Proc. Fifth International Symposium on Display Holography. SPIE. pp.374-480. 1995.
24. Schubert, E.F., Kim, J.K. Solid-State Light Sources Getting Smart. Science 308 (5726). pp.1274-1278. 2005.
25. Sutherland, I. The Ultimate Display. In Proc. of IFIP Congress 1965. pp.506-508.
26. Takeuchi, Y. Towards Habitable Bits: Digitizing the Built Environment. Proc. ITS 2014. pp.209-218.
27. Tompkin, J., Heinzle, S., Kautz, J., Matusik, W. Content-Adaptive Lenticular Prints. ACM Trans. Graph. (Proc. SIGGRAPH) 32(4). 133:1-133:10. 2013.
28. Tompkin, J., Muff, S., McCann, J., Pfister, H., Kautz, J., Alexa, M., Matusik, W. Joint 5D Pen Input for Light Field Displays. Proc. UIST 2015. pp.637-647.
29. Ueda, K., Koike, T., Takahashi, K., Naemura, T. Adaptive integral photography imaging with variable-focus lens array. Proc. SPIE 6803. 2008.
30. Underkoffler, J., Ullmer, B., Ishii, H. Emancipated Pixels: Real-World Graphics in the Luminous Room. Proc. SIGGRAPH 1999. pp.385-392.
31. Weiser, M. The Computer for the 21st Century. Scientific American, 264 (3). pp.94-104. 1991.
32. Wetzstein, G., Lanman, D., Hirsch, M., Raskar, R. Tensor Displays: Compressive Light Field Synthesis Using Multilayer Displays with Directional Backlighting. Proc. SIGGRAPH 2012. pp.1-11.
33. Wiethoff, A., Gehring, S. Designing Interaction with Media Facades: A Case Study. Proc. DIS 2012. pp.308-317.
34. Wigdor, D., Wixon, D. Brave NUI World. Morgan Kauffman. 2011.
35. Wilburn, B., Smulski, M., Lee, K.H., Horowitz, M. The Light Field Video Camera. Proc. SPIE Conference on Media Processors 4674. pp.29-36. 2002.
36. Willis, K., Brockmeyer, E., Hudson, S., Poupyrev, I. Printed Optics: 3D Printing of Embedded Optical Elements for Interactive Devices. Proc. UIST 2012. pp.589-598.
37. Xiao, X., Javidi, B., Martinez-Corral, M., Stern, A. Advances in Three-Dimensional Integral Imaging: Sensing, Display, and Applications. Applied Optics 52(4). pp.546-560. 2013.
38. Zhou, Z., Yu, T., Qiu, X., Yang, R., Zhao, Q. Light field projection for lighting reproduction. Proc. IEEE VR 2015. pp.135-142.

Ketsuro-Graffiti: an Interactive Display with Water Condensation

Yuki Tsujimoto **Yuichi Itoh** **Takao Onoye**
Graduate School of Information Science and Technology, Osaka University
1-5 Yamadaoka, Suita, Osaka, Japan
{tsujimoto.yuki, itoh, onoye}@ist.osaka-u.ac.jp

ABSTRACT
In this paper, we propose a novel interactive display, *Ketsuro-Graffiti*, that provides information with water condensation. Recently, a lot of substantial displays have been proposed that utilize various types of physical material. These displays enable users to touch each pixel freely. Water condensation exists ubiquitously in daily life, and drawing on it is familiar. Therefore, a display with water condensation achieves an intuitive and familiar interaction between users and information. We propose a method to control generation and evaporation of water condensation and implement two prototypes of Ketsuro-Graffiti using peltier devices. One prototype uses an open loop control system and the other uses a PID closed loop control system with thermistors. Our evaluation of system performance indicates that both prototypes can control generation, evaporation, and thickness of water condensation.

Author Keywords
Substantial Display; Water Condensation; Peltier Device; Thermistor

ACM Classification Keywords
H.5.2. Information Interfaces and Presentation: User Interfaces

INTRODUCTION
Water condensation (called "Ketsuro" in Japanese) exists ubiquitously in daily life. For example, it appears on window surfaces in the winter and on glasses holding a cold drink. People often enjoy writing or drawing pictures on water condensation, and it can be regarded as one of the most familiar everyday canvasses. In addition, artists such as Haacke and Kneffel have produced works related to water condensation [1, 5]. It is considered that water condensation is something fascinating that compels us to touch it. We think these features are very good affordance to develop an interactive display.

On the other hand, many researchers have proposed substantial displays that provide information using various types of physical materials. These displays have the following features: users can directly touch physically represented pixels, information can be provided in a familiar and not disturbing way, and we can utilize features unique to the physical material. However, there are few substantial displays utilizing water condensation. Parkes proposed Dewy, which shows a pattern of water condensation by heating wet felt [11]. In this system, however, water condensation is generated at an area users cannot touch and the system is not interactive.

In this paper, we propose a novel interactive display, *Ketsuro-Graffiti,* which shows images with water condensation and allows users to interact with them intuitively and freely. Users can write or apply graffiti with their fingers on a pattern of water condensation as shown in Figure 1. Our contributions in this paper are as follows:

- implement a mechanism to control generation, evaporation, and thickness of water condensation on a mirror-type surface.

- detect a user's touch on the surface by using a part of the mechanism for generating water condensation.

- evaluate the performance of the system and propose some applications.

Figure 1. Ketsuro-Graffiti shows images with a pattern of water condensation and enables users to interact with water condensation freely

ISS '16, November 06-09, 2016, Niagara Falls, ON, Canada
© 2016 ACM. ISBN 978-1-4503-4248-3/16/11...$15.00
DOI: http://dx.doi.org/10.1145/2992154.2992159

RELATED WORK

We first describe substantial displays that utilize various types of physical material. We then summarize displays that use temperature changes to provide tactile experiences or to produce visual changes of a certain object.

Substantial displays

Shaboned Display [2] is one substantial display that uses soap bubbles in a matrix form as both pixels of a display and input tools. This display allows users to interact with soap bubbles freely and can be applied as an ambient display. MOSS-xels [4] is one that utilizes blocks of moss in a matrix form as pixels. The display can create various patterns by controlling the timing of water provided and can be applied as an ambient display that can blend into the natural environment. Offenhuber presents contextual strategies for staging ambient interfaces in public space, and one of which is "Embracing unstable Display Media" [10]. He argues the display composed of ephemeral materials represent information blended with environmental influences and this approach might contribute an additional dimension to the display. We can say that these systems described above also use the same strategy.

Some systems utilize features of water to display something. FogScreen [14] is a display that adopts fog as a screen, and it tackles the limitation of projection screens in that users cannot see or touch behind them. MisTable [9] is a tabletop system that combines personal screens using fog with a horizontal interactive surface. Since a fog screen is see-through and reach-through, a user can interact with a tabletop surface behind the fog screen. LiquiTouch [16] uses water for tactile feedback on touchscreens. The system can provide various stimuli such as pressure, temperature or viscosity with water.

We described various types of substantial displays. Though these displays utilize features of physical materials (e.g. soap bubbles, moss, water), these materials are not usually used for expression. As described in the last chapter, we often enjoy drawing pictures on water condensation, and it can be considered to be a familiar canvas. Therefore, an interactive display using water condensation enables users to interact with information in a familiar way, e.g. deleting information by swiping and reproducing information by breathing on the surface.

Temperature-based displays

In our proposed system, we control water condensation by controlling the temperature of the display surface.

Thermoesthesia [8] is an interactive surface that allows users to feel the temperature of the visually displayed objects. Thermo-Pict neo [6] is a display that combines a thermal sense display and a thermograph sheet. This system can visualize the temperature of the surface without a projector. Thermo-Paradox [7] is a thermal sense display that can create thermal tactile physiological illusions by patterns of warm and cool temperatures. These systems utilize temperature changes to produce thermal tactile sensation in addition to visual information, thereby exploring the potential of temperature-based displays. Though, in most of these systems, the temperature is controlled by peltier devices in a matrix form, the temperature of the surface is not fed back to the control system. Thus, since the temperature is controlled in an open loop control system, the resolution of the temperature is not high and can be affected by environmental conditions.

Mosaic Textile [19] is a wearable substantial display using temperature changes to control the color of textile modules. The system utilizes conductive yarns to heat and visually change textile coated by liquid crystal ink. Ambikraf [13] is also a color-changing fabric display that utilizes peltier devices to control the temperature of thermochromic ink fabric. These systems explore the potential of color-changing fabric displays, which can be adapted to the environment and applied as ambient displays.

Dewy [11] is a display that utilizes condensation as information. The system employs peltier devices in a 3x5 matrix to heat wet felt and generate water vapor. Water vapor attaches to a sheet of clear acrylic and shows visual images. Though Dewy utilizes water condensation as pixels, water condensation is generated inside a casing including a sheet of acrylic and a steel surface. Therefore, users are unable to touch and interact with the water condensation. This means that the system does not fully utilize the features of water condensation. Our proposed system utilizes the affordance of touching, that is, the system generates water condensation on the display surface and affords touch interaction. This affordance achieves applications such as digital signage, which users feel like touching, and a picture-drawing device useful for entertainment.

KETSURO-GRAFFITI

In Ketsuro-Graffiti, we propose a mechanism to control generation, evaporation, and thickness of water condensation on a mirror-type surface. We first describe the material of the display surface and the mechanism of water condensation generation. We next describe the implementation of the two prototypes and a touch-sensing system.

Material of display

The important characteristics of the display surface are high visibility and time responsiveness. We conducted a preliminary experiment to choose material for the surface. In consideration of visibility, we evaluated six types of mirror-type materials as follows: polyvinyl chloride (PVC) mirror (0.5 and 1.7 mm thick), glass mirror (1 mm thick), stainless steel plate (0.5 mm thick), aluminum plate (0.5 mm thick), and copper plate (0.5 mm thick). We put each material on a peltier device and cooled the surface. After the size of water condensation became the same as the size of a peltier device, we stopped the cooling. The size of a peltier device is 8.3 x 8.3 mm. We measured the generation

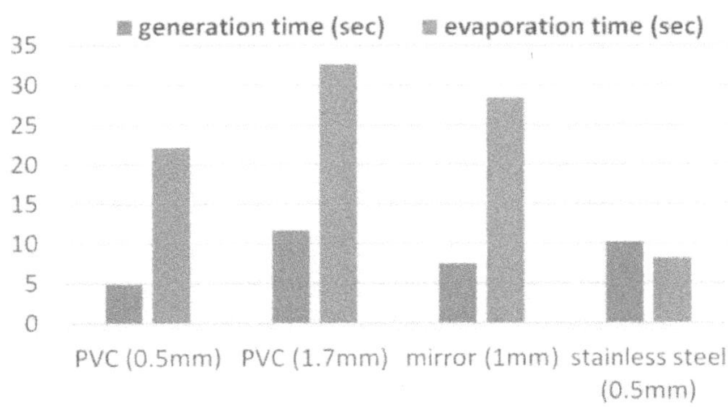

Figure 2. Results of preliminary experiment showing time required for generation and evaporation of water condensation

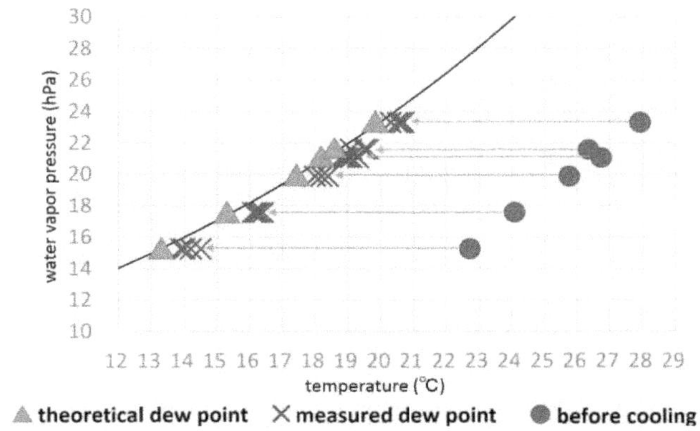

Figure 3. Results of preliminary experiment showing measured dew points and theoretical dew points

time (from the start of cooling to the start of generation) and the evaporation time (from the end of cooling to complete evaporation) of water condensation. We defined the start of generation as when the condensation on the area of a peltier device began to appear visually. Similarly, we defined the completion of evaporation as when the condensation completely disappeared from the area of peltier device. In this measurement, the temperature of the room was 20.8°C and the humidity was 57%. We conducted the measurement five times for each material and calculated the average.

Figure 2 shows the results. Since aluminum and copper have excellent thermal conductivities and the coldness is conducted to the outside of the area touched by the peltier device, water condensation was not generated on the aluminum plate and the copper plate. From the results, water condensation was generated most quickly on the PVC mirror (0.5 mm thick) and evaporated most quickly on stainless steel. Though both generation time and evaporation time are preferred to be short, we think it is possible to shorten the evaporation time by reversing the current flow for a peltier device or blowing hot air on the surface for heating. Therefore, we chose the PVC mirror as a display surface.

Generation of water condensation

We propose a mechanism to freely control generation and evaporation of water condensation. Water condensation is the change of water from gas phase into liquid phase. Water vapor changes to liquid water when its temperature falls below the dew point. A dew point is generally associated with the relationship between temperature and water vapor pressure. This relationship is formulated as Tetens' formula [18]:

$$p(T) = 6.1078 \times 10^{\frac{7.5T}{T+237.3}} \tag{1}$$

where T is temperature in °C and $p(T)$ is saturated water vapor pressure in hectopascals. A dew point is calculated as follows:

$$T_{dew} = \left(237.3 \log_{10} \frac{6.1078}{p(T_{room}) \cdot Rh/100}\right) \div \left(\log_{10} \frac{p(T_{room}) \cdot Rh/100}{6.1078} - 7.5\right) \tag{2}$$

where T_{dew} is the dew point in °C, T_{room} is the temperature of the room in °C, and Rh is the relative humidity of the room in percentages. It is considered that we can control generation or evaporation of water condensation by controlling the temperature of the surface below or above the dew point. Moreover, it is considered that we can control the thickness of water condensation by controlling the difference in temperature between the surface and the dew point.

We use peltier devices to control the temperature of the display surface. A peltier device is a thermoelectric element generally used for CPU coolers or mini refrigerators. It can both heat and cool depending on the direction of the current flow. Its ability to rapidly control temperature across a wide range is suited for our proposed system.

We conducted another preliminary experiment to examine whether the dew points accord with the saturated water vapor pressure curve and to confirm that we can control generation and evaporation of water condensation using peltier devices. We put a PVC mirror (0.5 mm thick) on a peltier device (75 x 75 mm) and supplied power to it. We measured the temperature when water condensation was generated in six environments where the temperature and humidity of the room were different. We conducted measurement five times in each of the six environments. In this experiment, the temperature of the display was measured with a radiation thermometer (DT8580, SainSonic) and the temperature and humidity of the room were measured with a digital thermometer and a hygrometer (AD-5682, A&D Co., Ltd.).

From the results shown in Figure 3, it is suggested that the measured dew points accord with the saturated water vapor pressure curve. The gaps between the theoretical values and measured values are approximately 0.3 – 0.5°C, which are

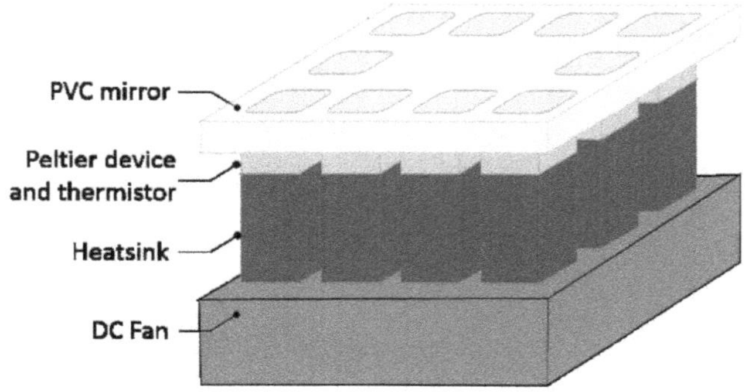

Figure 4. System overview of Ketsuro-Graffiti

within the error margin of the radiation thermometer, ±2°C. Therefore, we can apply the saturated water vapor pressure curve to estimate the conditions under which water condensation is generated, and it is suggested that we can control the generation and evaporation of water condensation using theoretical dew points. We conducted an additional experiment and confirmed that the temperature of the PVC mirror falls below about -15°C, which is the dew point when the water vapor pressure is 8.72 hPa (e.g., 5°C, 20%). Therefore, we can cool the display below the dew point and control the generation of water condensation in a general indoor environment.

System Configuration

Figure 4 shows the system overview of Ketsuro-Graffiti. We implemented two prototypes using peltier devices in a matrix form. One prototype controls matrix-placed peltier devices with open loop control. This prototype is easy to implement and control. In the other prototype, each peltier device is equipped with a thermistor and controlled with a PID (proportional–integral–derivative) closed loop process. This prototype is able to accurately control the temperature of the surface.

Prototype using open loop control system

Figure 5 shows the implementation of the prototype using open loop control. A matrix is comprised of 100 peltier devices (TEFC1-03112, Nippon Tecmo). The size of each peltier device is 8.3 x 8.3 x 2.4 mm, about the same size as a fingertip of an adult person. Peltier devices are placed on heatsinks with heat-dissipating silicone grease and DC fans release heat from the heatsinks. We use two Arduino Megas to drive the peltier devices with 100 power metal–oxide–semiconductor field-effect transistors (MOSFET) (2SK4017, Toshiba).

With this prototype, we control the generation of water condensation by manually manipulating the pulse width modulation (PWM) duty cycle. For example, when water condensation is generated with a 30% duty cycle, we can make it thicker with a 60% duty cycle and evaporate with a 0% duty cycle. Figure 6 shows the changes in thickness by manipulating the duty cycle. Each percentage represents the PWM duty cycle. Since this prototype does not need to measure the environmental condition and the temperature of the surface, we can easily implement and control the system. However, it is difficult to accurately control the temperature of the surface, and this means we have to attempt several conditions of the duty cycle to control the density of the water condensation. In addition, even if the condition of the duty cycle is the same, the thickness of the water condensation might depend on the environmental conditions, including the temperature and humidity of the room.

Figure 5. Implementation of open loop control system

(a) 33% (b) 66% (c) 100%

Figure 6. Example changes in thickness with open loop control system. Each percentage represents the PWM duty cycle.

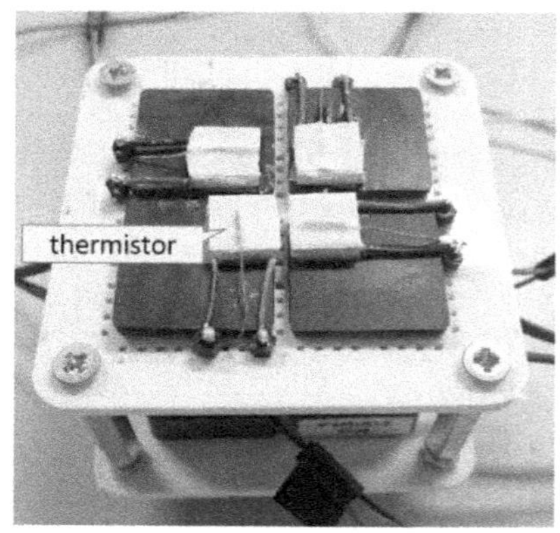

Figure 7. Implementation of PID closed loop system

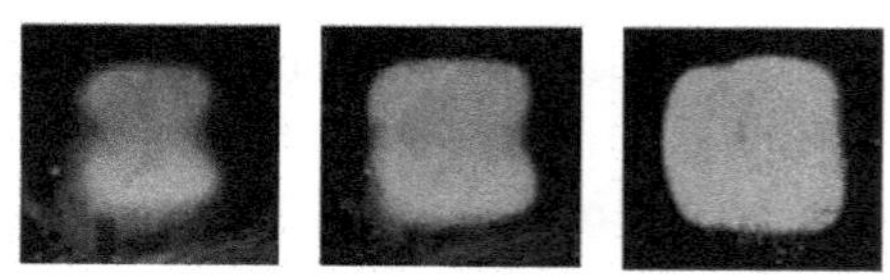

(a) – 1°C (b) – 2°C (c) – 3°C

Figure 8. Example changes in thickness with PID closed loop system. Each temperature represents difference between temperature of surface and dew point

Prototype using PID closed loop control system

Figure 7 shows the implementation of the prototype using PID closed loop control. A matrix is comprised of four peltier devices (TEFC1-03112, Nippon Tecmo). Peltier devices are placed on heatsinks with heat-dissipating silicone grease and DC fans release heat from the heatsinks. A thermistor (56A1002-C3, Alpha Technics) is placed on each peltier device with heat-conductive double-sided tape. We use an Arduino UNO to drive the peltier devices with four power MOSFETs (2SK4017, Toshiba) and to measure the temperature with thermistors. We use an RC circuit to eliminate noise on each thermistor.

In this prototype, we adopt a PID closed loop control system in order to accurately control the temperature on the surface and the generation of water condensation. A PID closed loop control system is commonly used in industrial control systems and is able to accurately control temperature by using feedback from temperature sensors. With this control system, we can maintain an arbitrary surface temperature. By controlling the difference in temperature between the display and the theoretical dew point, we can control the thickness of water condensation. For example, when water condensation is generated by setting the temperature of the surface to be 1°C lower than the dew point, it would become thicker when the temperature is 5°C lower than the dew point and evaporate when the temperature is 1°C higher than the dew point. Figure 8 shows an example of changes in thickness by controlling the temperature. Each temperature represents the difference between the temperature of the surface and the dew point: (a) 1°C lower than the dew point, (b) 2°C lower than the dew point, (c) 3°C lower than the dew point. Since the PID closed loop system accurately controls the temperature, it is considered that it can control the thickness independently of the environmental conditions and more accurately than the open loop control system shown in Figure 6.

Touch Sensing

A PID closed loop control system is able to accurately maintain an arbitrary surface temperature. This means that the system can detect a user's touch interaction through the sudden rise in temperature. This touch-sensing principle does not require any additional hardware such as a camera. Peiris et al. also propose a touch-sensing system using a temperature sensor [12].

Figure 9 shows an example of the changes in temperature when a user touches the surface. It is revealed that the temperature and the differential value of it suddenly rise when the surface is touched, and the system can detect a user's touch interaction by observing whether the differential value exceeds a threshold. In this case, we can set 1.0 °C/s as the threshold.

EVALUATION

We conducted a technical experiment to evaluate the performance of the thickness control of the water

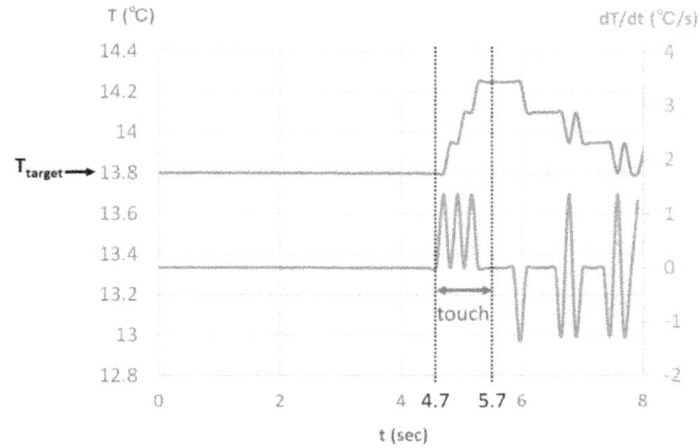

Figure 9. Changes in temperature caused by a user's touch

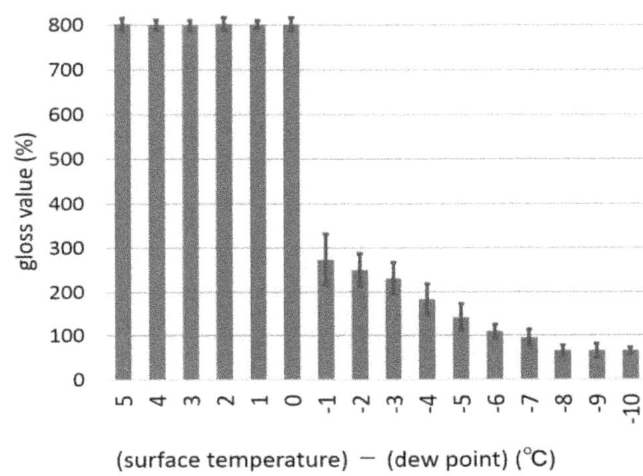

Figure 10. Surface temperature vs. gloss value

condensation. When water condensation is generated on the surface, it causes a diffuse reflection and the specular reflectivity is reduced. It is considered that the thicker the water condensation is, the lower the specular reflectivity becomes. Therefore, we can evaluate the thickness control by measuring the specular gloss of the display. ISO 2813 [3] defines the gloss value as "ratio multiplied by 100 of the luminous flux reflected from a specimen to that reflected by a glass surface with a refractive index of 1,567 at a wavelength of 587.6 nm in specular direction for a specified reflection angle and specified aperture angles of light source and receptor". It also defines a method for gloss measurement. We conducted an experiment based on this measurement method.

With the prototype using a PID closed loop control system, we kept the temperature of the display at 16 target temperatures and measured the gloss values. The target temperatures are from 5°C higher than the dew point to 10°C lower than the dew point with decrements of 1°C. We measured 10 times for each target temperature and calculated the average. The experiment was carried out in a

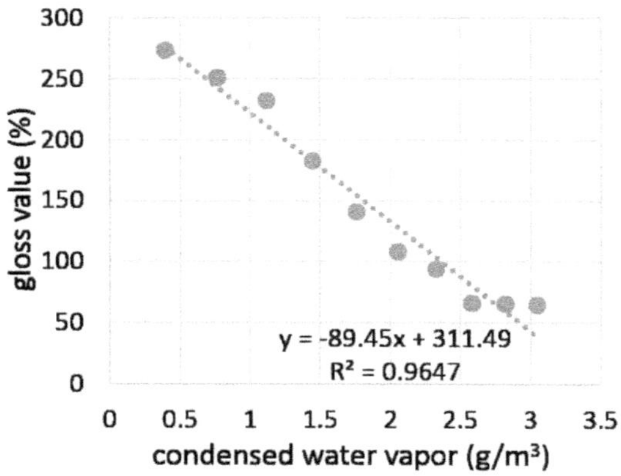

Figure 11. Condensed water vapor vs. gloss value

laboratory room (temperature: 19.3°C, humidity: 34.4%). The gloss value was measured with a gloss checker (IG-410, Horiba, Ltd.), whose measurement range is 0-1,000, and the room temperature and humidity were measured with a digital humidity sensor (HTU21D, SparkFun). The dew point of the room was 3.22°C, calculated with equation 2.

Figure 10 shows the results of average gloss values. The gloss value sharply declines when the temperature falls below the dew point and water condensation is generated. Under the conditions where the temperatures are lower than the dew point, the gloss values range from 273.5% to 65.0%.

Figure 11 shows the relationships between the amount of condensed water vapor (the horizontal axis) and the gloss value (the vertical axis). The amount of condensed water vapor indicates the thickness of water condensation and can be calculated by applying the temperature of the surface, the room's temperature, and the room's humidity to equation 2. The graph suggests that the relationships between the amount of condensed water vapor and the gloss value can be expressed by a linear regression equation. The coefficient of determination is 0.9647. Under the conditions where the differences between the temperature of the surface and the theoretical dew point are from -1°C to -8°C, the gloss values are sufficiently identified. Under the conditions where the differences are greater than -8°C, there seems not to be much of a significant difference. There seem to be two reasons as follows. One is that the display was cooled for a long time and eventually frozen. The other is that the amount of condensed water vapor per unit area was saturated.

On the other hand, Serikawa and Shimomura argue that glossiness defined in some measurement methods does not correspond with psychological glossiness perceived by the human eye, and it is necessary to measure psychological glossiness [17]. Therefore, it is not clear whether users can identify the difference in the thickness of water condensation even if we accurately control the thickness. It remains as future work for us to conduct a subject experiment to determine how much difference between each thickness users can distinguish.

APPLICATION

Ketsuro-Graffiti has certain features: users can directly touch the information represented with water condensation, information can be provided with some objects existing in the living space (e.g. mirrors and windows), and users feel like touching the display. There are some attractive applications utilizing these features.

If a mirror with our proposed display is installed in an entrance or a washstand, it can provide such modest information as weather forecasts, daily schedules or weight changes with a pattern of water condensation. Since most people wash their face as soon as they get up in the morning, the mirror would enable them to never forget to obtain such information.

On the other hand, it is considered that many people are familiar with writing or drawing pictures on water condensation since childhood, and water condensation has some attractiveness that makes people touch it. A promising application utilizing this attractiveness is digital signage that users feel like approaching and touching. This application is considered to be useful for mirrors in various stores and restaurants. Such displays can provide sales information and recommended menu items.

Another application is a picture-drawing device useful for entertainment. A drawing function can be implemented by generating water condensation where users touch. Supporting various interactions (e.g. swiping and breathing on the surface) can make for a more attractive drawing device. Moreover, the system can extend the interaction with water condensation. Though we are usually unable to undo or redo pictures on water condensation existing on surfaces in the environment, our proposed system achieves these features. Additionally, some features that are supported by general drawing software can be achieved by our proposed system (e.g. saving, reproduction and deletion).

As described above, the specular reflectivity changes according to the thickness of water condensation. This feature enables to develop a programmable mirror that can control the specular reflectivity of its partial square areas independently. The area with high specular reflectivity can be used as a mirror and the area with low specular reflectivity can be used as a screen. By using these properly, a programmable mirror can be applied for a virtual try-on system by being combined with a projector and a camera. It is considered that this system can provide more real experience than existing systems with a display and a camera. Another application is real-world pixelization on a mirror. Rekimoto proposes a programmable window system, Squama [15], which can control transparency of a window in a modular way and can be used to satisfy the openness and privacy needs. A programmable mirror also satisfies privacy needs in public space, e.g., toilet and public bath, by using mirror area and non-mirror area properly according to movement of users.

CONCLUSION

We proposed a novel interactive display called Ketsuro-Graffiti that provides information with a pattern of water condensation and can be applied as digital signage, ambient displays, and drawing installations. We investigated the system to control generation, evaporation, and thickness of water condensation and implemented two prototypes using peltier devices. We conducted a technical evaluation and it suggested the proposed system can control the thickness of water condensation. Future work is to implement a high-resolution display, evaluate the psychological glossiness, and achieve various types of interaction.

REFERENCES

1. Haacke, H. Condensation Cube. *Leonardo*, 36.4 (2003), 265-265.
2. Hirayama, S. and Kakehi, Y. Shaboned display: an interactive substantial display using soap bubbles. In *ACM SIGGRAPH 2010 Emerging Technologies*, ACM (2010), 21:1-21:1.
3. ISO 2813 (2014) Paints and varnishes-determination of gloss value at 20 degrees, 60 degrees and 85 degrees.
4. Kimura, T. and Kakehi, Y. MOSS-xels: slow changing pixels using the shape of racomitrium canescens. In *ACM SIGGRAPH 2014 Posters*, ACM (2014), 20:1-20:1.
5. Kneffel, K. Untitled. (2011), http://www.gagosian.com/exhibitions/karin-kneffel--september-12-2012 (accessed 2016-06-29).
6. Kushiyama, K., Baba, T., Doi, K., and Sasada, S. Temperature design display device to use peltier elements and liquid crystal thermograph sheet: "Thermo-Pict neo". In *ACM SIGGRAPH 2010 Posters*, ACM (2010), 42:1-42:1.
7. Kushiyama, K., Baba, T., Doi, K., and Sasada, S. Thermal design display device to use the thermal tactile illusions: "Thermo-Paradox". In *ACM SIGGRAPH 2010 Posters*, ACM (2010), 99:1-99:1.
8. Kushiyama, K., Inose, M., Yokomatsu, R., Fujita, K., Kitazawa, T., Tamura, M., and Sasada, S. Thermoesthesia: about collaboration of an artist and a scientist. In *ACM SIGGRAPH 2006 Educators program*, ACM (2006), 23:1-23:2.
9. Martinez P.D., Joyce, E., and Subramanian, S. MisTable: reach-through personal screens for tabletops. In *Proc. CHI '2014*, ACM (2014), 3493-3502.
10. Offenhuber, D. The invisible display-design strategies for ambient media in the urban context. In Proc. *International Workshop on Ambient Information Systems, Colocated with Ubicomp 2008.*
11. Parkes, A. and Offenhuber, D. Dewy: a condensation display. In *ACM SIGGRAPH 2007 posters*, ACM (2007), 44:1-44:1.
12. Peiris, R.L. and Nakatsu, R. TempTouch: a novel touch sensor using temperature controllers for surface based textile displays. In *Proc. ITS '13*, ACM (2013), 105-114.
13. Peiris, R.L., Tharakan, M.J., Cheok, A.D., and Newton, O.N. AmbiKraf: a ubiquitous non-emissive color changing fabric display. In *Proc. MindTrek '11*, ACM (2011), 320-322.
14. Rakkolainen, I., DiVerdi, S., Olwal, A., Candussi, N., Hüllerer, T., Laitinen, M., Piirto, M., and Palovuori, K. The interactive FogScreen. In *ACM SIGGRAPH 2005 Emerging technologies*, ACM (2005), 8:1-8:1.
15. Rekimoto, J. Squama: modular visibility control of walls and windows for programmable physical architectures. In Proc. *AVI '12*, ACM (2012), 168-171.
16. Richter, H., Manke, F. and Seror, M. LiquiTouch: liquid as a medium for versatile tactile feedback on touch surfaces. In *Proc. TEI '13*, ACM (2013), 315-318.
17. Serikawa, S. and Shimomura, T. Method for measuring glossiness of plane surfaces based on psychological sensory scale. *IEICE transactions on Fundamentals of Electronics, Communications and Computer Sciences*, IEICE (1993), 439-446.
18. Tetens, O. Über einige meteorologiche Begriffe. *Z. Geophys.*, 6, (1930), 297-309.
19. Wakita, A. and Shibutani, M. Mosaic textile: wearable ambient display with non-emissive color-changing modules. In *Proc. ACE '06*, ACM (2006), 48:1-48:7.

EV-Pen: Leveraging Electrovibration Haptic Feedback in Pen Interaction

Qinglong Wang [1,3], Xiangshi Ren[1,2], Sayan Sarcar[2], Xiaoying Sun[3]
wesleypk.cn@gmail.com, {ren.xiangshi, sayan.sarcar}@kochi-tech.ac.jp, sunxy@jlu.edu.cn
[1]Center for Human-Engaged Computing, Kochi University of Technology, Kochi, Japan
[2]School of Information, Kochi University of Technology, Kochi, Japan
[3]College of Communication Engineering, Jilin University, Changchun, China

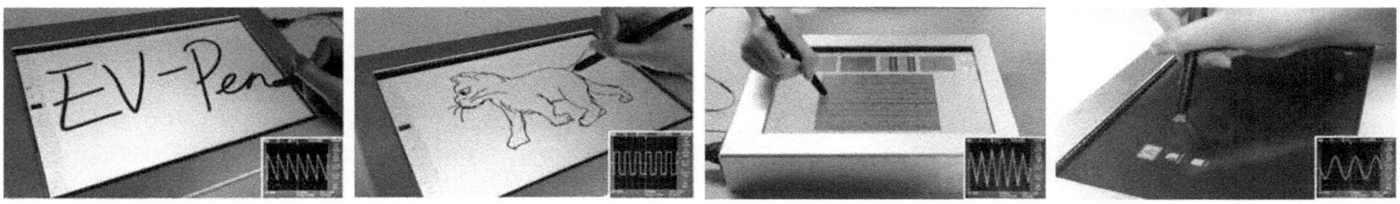

(a) Handwriting (b) Drawing (c) Texture Simulations (d) GUI Elements with Haptic Feedback

Figure 1. Demo applications with electrovibration haptic feedback created for our EV-Pen.

ABSTRACT
This paper presents an Electrovibration Pen (EV-Pen) which incorporates electrovibration technology into pen interactions. The EV-Pen has two unique characteristics: precise interaction and pen-on-paper feeling. We conducted four experiments for evaluating the EV-Pen. Experiment 1 was to determine preliminary characteristics of the EV-Pen. Experiments 2 and 3 were to evaluate precise interaction task performance through a steering task and a tracing task. We compared user performance between the EV-Pen, a mechanical-vibration pen, a normal pen without feedback and electrovibration-based finger interaction. Experimental results indicated that the EV-Pen outperformed the other devices in precise task interactions. Experiment 4 tested pen-on-paper feeling in drawing and handwriting tasks, and it was observed that the EV-Pen significantly enhances user experience. Based on the experimental results, we discuss implications and potential benefits for the design of the EV-Pen.

Author Keywords
pen; electrovibration; haptic feedback; steering task; tracing task; drawing; handwriting

ACM Classification Keywords
H.5.2 [Information Interfaces and Presentation]: User Interfaces; Haptic I/O, Input devices and strategies

INTRODUCTION
Recently, pen-based devices are widely used in computer graphics systems by designers, artists and architects [11, 13]. Pen-based interaction has also become a de-facto standard input method for large screen smartphones and tablet computers. Some pen-based products have been launched, such as the Apple Pencil, the Microsoft Surface Pen, and the Samsung S-Pen. These have shown real potential but there is room for significant improvement.

For example, currently available products do not consider feedback and material properties that could simulate a real pen-on-paper experience. To overcome this issue, pen devices with haptic feedback based on mechanical technology were developed [2,6,7,12,14,15,20]. However, in such pens, traditional vibrotactile feedback, which is generated by mechanical motors [5], may shake the whole pen and the hand, thus making it difficult to perform precise operations.

For performing precise operations and implementing real pen-on-paper feeling, we developed the EV-Pen by leveraging *electrovibration* technology [16] in pen interaction (Figure 1). It controls electrostatic friction [4] between the pen-tip and the touch surface to produce multisensory feedback. The EV-Pen has two unique characteristics: 1) precise interaction enhances human performance (e.g., menu navigation, tracing) because unlike conventional vibrotactile feedback pen, the EV-Pen has no mechanical actuator to disturb movement of the pen-tip; 2) pen-on-paper feeling enhances user satisfaction (e.g., drawing, handwriting) because it allows users to perceive different textures.

In this paper, we first review the related work and describe the implementation of the EV-Pen. We then present an experiment to determine preliminary characteristics of the EV-Pen (Experiment 1), and evaluate two unique characteristics (precise interaction in Experiments 2 and 3, and pen-on-paper feeling in Experiment 4). Concretely, *Experiment 1* was to determine the basic characteristics of the EV-Pen, which also provided the basic parameter values for Experiment 2, 3 and 4. *Experiment 2* was a fundamental study to look *theoretically* at whether the steering law holds well with our EV-Pen,

ISS '16, November 06-09, 2016, Niagara Falls, ON, Canada
© 2016 ACM. ISBN 978-1-4503-4248-3/16/11...$15.00
DOI: http://dx.doi.org/10.1145/2992154.2992161

i.e., whether the EV-Pen can perform basic HCI tasks. *Experiment 3* was an empirical study which *quantitatively* investigated the performance of the EV-Pen through the tracing task. *Experiment 4* was performed to *qualitatively* understand the user experience when interacting with the EV-Pen in practice through drawing and handwriting.

The experiment results confirmed that the EV-Pen has two unique characteristics: precise interaction which enhances human performance (e.g., menu navigation, tracing); pen-on-paper feeling which enhances user satisfaction (e.g., drawing, handwriting).

RELATED WORK

Our work focuses on leveraging electrovibration haptic feedback for pen interaction. This section summarizes previous studies related to haptic perception for pen and electrovibration for finger interaction.

Haptic Perception for Pen

Pen devices with haptic perception features have been explored in many studies. The works can be classified into three subcategories based on the technology used. (1) *Haptic feedback through vibration actuator*: these pen devices provided vibrotactile haptic feedback to users by augmenting different kinds of vibration actuators such as linear resonant actuators, piezo-ceramic actuators [6], vibration motors [2, 12], TouchEngine actuators [20], solenoid actuators [14, 15] and Maxon motors [7]. (2) *Haptic feedback through retractable machinery*: to provide a greater degree of freedom in pen motion apart from the feedback, researchers adopted retractable technology. By using different kinds of motors, these pen devices can be changed in length [18, 28] and shape [10] while interacting on screens. (3) *Haptic feedback through electromagnetic technology*: Wintergerst et al. [27] designed a reflective haptic pen operated through changing friction between the steel ball and a screen by the electromagnetic coil.

First, undesirable forces, vibration and noise are unavoidably produced in motors because of bearings, sliding contacts, imbalance, geared power transmissions and friction force [5]. So, when motors or some other mechanical actuators are used to provide haptic feedback, the feedback may shake the whole pen and the hand, making it difficult to perform precise operations with the pen. Furthermore, the noise produced by mechanical actuators can be annoying, causing distraction which leads to a non-immersive experience.

Second, previous works focused on haptic texture rendering and modelling [17, 22] to re-create paper-like textures with haptic pen using actuators, but they have focused less on discussing a natural pen-on-paper feeling to improve the performance of pen interaction in HCI (e.g., steering, tracing).

We have developed the EV-Pen which provides haptic feedback *without* mechanical actuator. Thus, our EV-Pen feedback is silent and does not cause disturbance because no physical motion ever happens inside the pen. Also, as the feedback of the EV-Pen is generated by controlling friction between pen-tip and touch surface, this passive (frictional) nature supports precise interactions. However, haptic feedback using a mechanical actuator is active (i.e. making energy).

Electrovibration for Finger

The effect of "electrovibration" was discovered by Mallinckrodt et al. [16] while a finger was touched on a surface with a high-voltage (110 V) AC conductor coated with a thin layer of insulation. Applications based on the electrovibration effect on a touchscreen have been developed by some researchers [3, 4, 26], such as TeslaTouch and REVEL which allowed users to feel different textures and friction between objects.

However, extreme temperatures and humidity can interfere with the sensation of electrovibration on the human body [9] when the human skin becomes moist. Furthermore, users felt numb and uncomfortable after extended use with voltages (more than 250V, 6-8 minutes). This fact was revealed through our pilot studies.

Moreover, due to *"fat finger"* problems [23], it is difficult to perform accurate movement tasks, such as drawing and gesturing [25]. For handwriting and drawing tasks, studies [21, 25] have shown that users prefer a pen over a finger.

Our EV-Pen augments electrovibration technology into the pen device, where sensation is barely influenced by extreme environments and human body. By contrast, numbness was not experienced during experiments with our EV-Pen. Participants found EV-Pen haptic feedback to be comfortable. At the same time, the EV-Pen inherits all the advantages of pen interactions, particularly in supporting precise interaction (e.g., drawing and handwriting).

In summary, no previous study has focused on electrovibration for pen interaction. Also, little study has explored possible application scenarios for effective haptic pen interaction including analyzing the task performance quality and satisfaction of the users. Thus, we leverage electrovibration into pen interactions to enhance user experience and performance.

THE IMPLEMENTATION OF EV-PEN

Our prototype of the EV-Pen provides haptic feedback which is based on the primary principle of electrovibration without using any form of mechanical actuator. The system structure of the EV-Pen is shown in Figure 2a.

Prototype Design

To create the EV-Pen, we modified a capacitive pen which was originally designed for capacitive-based touch surfaces. The pen is about 100mm long and 7 mm wide. The pen-tip diameter is 5 mm. We connected the tail of the pen to a signal generator. Then, the pen was covered with insulation tape.

To activate the principle of electrovibration, a 3M Microtouch panel was used (model number: $SCT3250EX$). It is composed of an ITO transparent electrode sheet applied to a glass

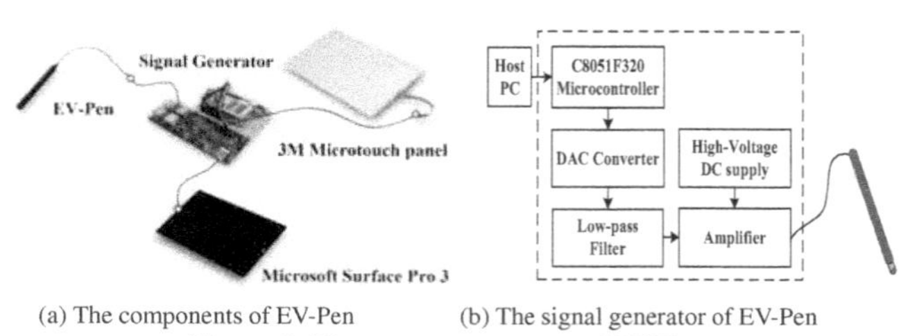

(a) The components of EV-Pen (b) The signal generator of EV-Pen

Figure 2. The system structure of EV-Pen.

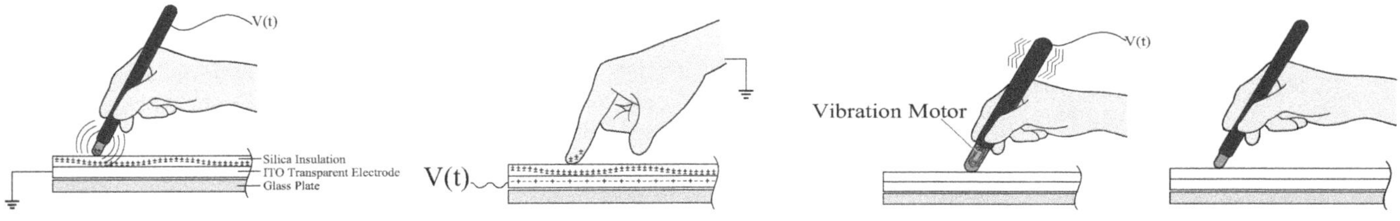

(a) EV-Pen (b) EV-Finger (c) V-Pen (d) N-Pen

Figure 3. Four different input devices tested in experiment.

plate coated with a layer of silica insulation. The thickness of the silica insulation layer is one micron. The thickness of the ITO transparent electrode layer is 40 nanometers. The signal generator and the transparent electrode sheet of the 3M Microtouch were electrically coupled to a common ground to create a return ground path for the signal.

The signal generator provided the drive signal for the EV-Pen (Figure 2b). A Silicon $C8051F320$ microcontroller generated a low-amplitude signal using an 8 bit digital-to-analog converter ($DAC0832$). Various signal shapes were stored in the microcontroller's flash memory and their frequencies and amplitudes were controlled by the host computer. The signal was smoothed using a low-pass filter and amplified using a transistor amplifier with high-voltage DC supply. The low pass filter cutoff frequency was 3 KHz, which would scarcely distort the low-frequency wave. We tested the waveform on an oscilloscope. Finally, the signal was injected to the EV-Pen. The drive signal frequency range was 10 Hz to 1000 Hz, and the amplitude range was 0 V to 400 V. The current was limited to 0.5mA, which was considered safe.

Theory of Operation

When the EV-Pen (Figure 3a) slides over the 3M Microtouch panel, the signal generator creates various signals V(t) of sufficient amplitude to affect the pen. An electrostatic force of attraction develops between the sliding EV-Pen and the underlying electrode. The attractive force increases the dynamic friction between the EV-Pen and the 3M Microtouch surface. This friction can be controlled by modulating the waveform, amplitude and frequency of the drive signal. Thus, users can feel haptic feedback during pen motion and no feedback while the pen is stationary according to the principle of electrovibration technology.

By contrast with TeslaTouch [4], we reversed the electrovibration path: the signal was injected to the EV-Pen and the surface was grounded, which enhances haptic feedback and supports multi-point feedback.

EXPERIMENT 1: PRELIMINARY CHARACTERIZATION

Designing effective haptic interfaces based on the EV-Pen requires an understanding of the basic factors and usability characteristics of electrovibration for a pen. What are the lowest signal levels that users can feel? What about the subjective feelings of users toward our EV-Pen? To answer these questions, we conducted detection threshold pilot studies and subjective evaluation studies.

Detection Threshold Pilot Study

To judge the perception-based characteristics of the EV-Pen, it is essential to measure the absolute detection threshold. This psychological measure fixes the baseline of human sensitivity. In the case of the EV-Pen, we calculated the minimum voltage amplitude that creates a just noticeable difference at a typical frequency. We were obviously unable to consider the voltages below the detection threshold, as those are not effective in creating haptic sensations.

We estimated the detection and discrimination thresholds for seven frequencies: 50, 100, 150, 200, 250, 300 and 350 Hz. We randomized the order of frequencies to minimize the order effect. A widely used one-up/two-down adaptive staircase procedure [4] was implemented. We then estimated absolute detection thresholds by using a two-alternative forced-choice paradigm. The touchscreen canvas was split into two areas; one had haptic feedback, while the other had none. In each trial, we randomly assigned stimulus to one of the two areas and participants determined which area had haptic sensation.

Six participants (3 males, 3 females, aged from 21 to 27 years old, mean age 23.8 years old, all right handed) took part in the pilot study. They conducted between 50 and 100 trials for each of the 7 reference frequencies. Total experiment time was around 45 minutes.

Results and Discussion

The detection threshold results are shown in Figure 4. We found: (1) frequency influences the detection threshold of a sine waveform, (2) frequency barely influences the detection threshold of a square waveform, (3) the detection threshold of a square waveform is lower than that of a sine waveform, (4) the detection threshold of sine waveform for the EV-Pen is lower than that of TeslaTouch [4].

The experiment provides important guidelines for designing the EV-Pen interfaces. For example, the results inform the designer that at each frequency the applied voltage must be above the corresponding detection threshold level in order to provide a haptic sensation that a user can perceive. Also, results show that the EV-Pen is operable in low power mode, so it can be applied in mobile devices.

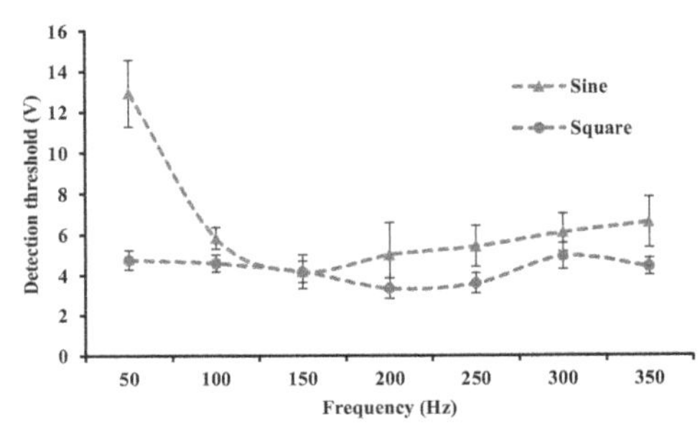

Figure 4. Mean detection threshold with standard error bars.

Parameters	Values	
Waveform	Sine	Square
Frequency	Low:50Hz	High:200Hz
Amplitude	Low:100V	High:250V

Table 1. The different parameters tested in experiment

Subjective Evaluation Study

We conducted subjective evaluation to better understand how users feel the haptic feedback produced by the EV-Pen.

Participants

Twelve volunteers (6 males, 6 females, aged from 21 to 35 years old, average age 27.6 years, all right handed) participated in the experiment. None had prior exposure to this technology and none had worked with a stylus.

Task and Procedure

Participants felt eight kinds of haptic feedback from the EV-Pen produced by six amplitude & frequency & waveform combinations (Table 1). We chose two frequencies that are within the sensitivity range of human perception, and a low amplitude that is strong enough to be perceived, whereas the high amplitude is not so strong as to make the users uncomfortable. These were determined through pilot studies.

Participants were asked to draw the gestures for as long as they wished with each feedback type of the EV-Pen. The feedback types were presented to the user randomly. After each feedback experience, participants filled out a two-session questionnaire. In the first session, participants were asked to describe each feedback type in their own words as comprehensively as possible (e.g., the feeling is like using paper). In the second session, participants used a set of 7-point Likert scales to record their evaluations of the following characteristics: hardness (1 = softness to 7 = hardness), roughness (1 = roughness to 7 = smooth), friction (1 = sticky to 7 = slippery), pleasant (1 = unpleasant to 7 = pleasant) [4, 19]. The sessions took about 35 minutes.

Results and Discussion

First session results are as follows (Table 2). For the sine waveform with low frequency and low amplitude (50Hz, 100V), five participants described the feeling as various kinds of pen (e.g., pen, water oil pen, fountain pen) and two participants described it as various kinds of paper (e.g., paper, cardboard paper). However, for the sine waveform with high frequency and high amplitude (200Hz, 250V), five participants described it as various kinds of paper (e.g., paper, rough paper, plastic paper, sand paper). For the square waveform with low frequency and low amplitude (50Hz, 100V), three participants described the feeling as various kinds of paper or pen (e.g., paper, paper box, ballpen). However, for the square waveform with high frequency and low amplitude (200Hz, 100V), five participants described it as various kinds of paper or pen (e.g., paper, toilet paper, sand paper, pencil). Other participants described it as rubber, stone, sand and skin.

Voltage \ Participant		1	2	3	4	5	6	7	8	9	10	11	12
Sine	50Hz 100V	smooth cloth	marker pen	glass	paper	fountain pen	silk	carton paper	water oil pen	pen	crayon	glass	silk
Sine	50Hz 250V	rubber	rubber	sand	high electricity	rubber	stone	electricity on metal	touching cat	brush	glass	sand	jeans
Sine	200Hz 100V	hard rough wood	fountain pen	frosted glass	wall	smooth glass	dull polish	glass not clean	marker pen	rubber string	silk	glass	fur
Sine	200Hz 250V	rubber	water pen on rough paper	thin sand paper	sand	paper	sand paper	plastic paper	clean glass	water	sand	ballpen	plastic
Square	50Hz 100V	paper	ballpen	silk	baby skin	plastic	paper box	silk	leather	glass	stone	skin	skin
Square	50Hz 250V	like gauze	gauze	rubber	rock	jeans	rough wood	insect movement	sand	water string	motor	stone	sand
Square	200Hz 100V	smooth plastic	pencil	leather	toilet paper	frosted glass	rubber	leather or plastic	marker pen	paper	gauze	skin	sand paper
Square	200Hz 250V	hard leather	thick comb	rough plastic	old man hand	sand paper	glass	silk	like using drill	rubber	cut wood	stone	stone

Table 2. Participants' subjective feelings of the EV-Pen.

Second session results are presented in Figure 5. Indeed, amplitude had a significant effect on perception of hardness ($\chi^2(2) = 5.33$, $p < 0.05$): low amplitudes were associated with sensations of softness, while high amplitudes felt like hardness. Amplitude had a significant effect on perception of roughness ($\chi^2(2) = 12.00$, $p < 0.01$): low amplitudes were associated with roughness sensations, while high amplitudes felt smooth. Amplitude had a significant effect on perception of friction ($\chi^2(2) = 8.33$, $p < 0.01$): low amplitudes were associated with slippery sensations, while high amplitudes felt sticky. Waveform also had a significant effect on perception of friction ($\chi^2(2) = 5.33$, $p < 0.05$): sine waveforms were associated with slippery sensations, while square waveforms felt sticky. Haptic feedback with high amplitudes were rated less pleasant than lower amplitude, with a mean rating of 4.5 versus 3.3 ($\chi^2(2) = 5.33$, $p < 0.05$).

The results of subjective evaluation studies provide important guidelines for designing the EV-Pen interfaces. For example, the square wave with high amplitude produces unpleasant feedback which may act as "*error feedback*". However, the sine waveform with low amplitude means pleasant feedback which may act as "*affirmative feedback*". Participants also expressed their feeling as real *pen-on-paper*. These kinds of natural feelings are helpful when handwriting and drawing.

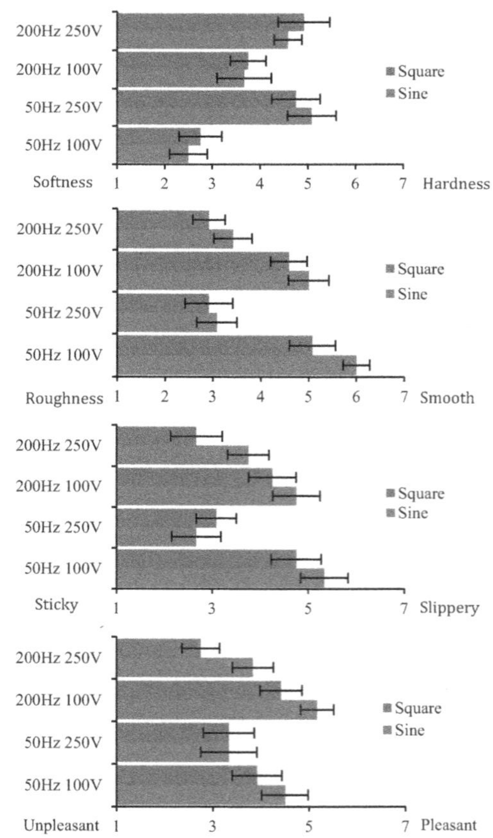

Figure 5. Ratings of hardness, roughness, friction and pleasure.

EXPERIMENT 2: STEERING TASK

To examine the effectiveness of the EV-Pen, we conducted a steering task experiment. The choice of a steering task for our experiment was based on careful consideration. Steering tasks can be used in many daily tasks like navigation in hierarchical menus and other trajectory-based manipulations. Our EV-Pen is a new device so we modeled it on the steering law which has been widely used as a theoretical framework for computer input device evaluation [1,20].

We compared the EV-Pen with two conventional haptic input modes (Table 3): mechanical-vibration pen input (V-Pen) and electrovibration-based finger input (EV-Finger). For comparison with a V-Pen, we chose a typical type of general vibration actuated V-Pen. EV-Finger and the EV-Pen are based on the same principle.

For the steering task, while the pen or finger was moving along the circular steering tunnel, haptic feedback was presented to the participants on the boundaries and outside the tunnel, i.e., we built a "*haptic tunnel wall*" to indicate that participants were inside the tunnel. Haptic feedback indicated "*error feedback*" [24] for participants.

Apparatus

The experiment was conducted on a Microsoft Surface Pro 3 tablet PC running Windows 8.1 pro. The screen size was 12-inches with a resolution of 2160 × 1440 pixels. The experimental software was developed in C++.

For the EV-Pen, the stimulating signal was a square wave with an amplitude of 300V, and a frequency of 120Hz. We chose these parameters based on Experiment 1 because the square wave with high amplitude provided more unpleasant feelings to users. This frequency of 120 Hz was easily detected, according to our experiment of device characteristics. This combination was therefore suitable for "error feedback". We tested the parameters through pilot studies with four participants. The feedback was easily perceived and the device was steady and comfortable to use.

For the V-Pen (Figure 3c), a vibration motor (2.0 V to 3.0 V, $LA4-503AC2$) was mounted in the capacitive pen body. The body of the same type of capacitive pen was used for the EV-Pen. The size of the motor was 4.3 × 10.7 mm. We used adhesive tape to mount the motor inside the pen, 15 mm from the pen-tip. The electrical signal was controlled by a Silicon $C8051F320$ microcontroller. For fair device comparison, the stimuli intensity with V-Pen was set as close as possible to the EV-Pen. We conducted pilot studies with four participants to determine suitable feedback parameters. As a result, the motor was supplied with 2.0 Vdc/55 mA.

Devices	EV-Pen	V-Pen	EV-Finger
Implement	Pen	Pen	Finger
Mechanism	Electrovibration	Vibration	Electrovibration
Feature	No motor inside the pen	Motor inside the pen	Visual occlusion by finger-tip
	Precise interaction	Imprecise interaction	Affected by humidity etc.

Table 3. Three input devices tested in Experiment 2.

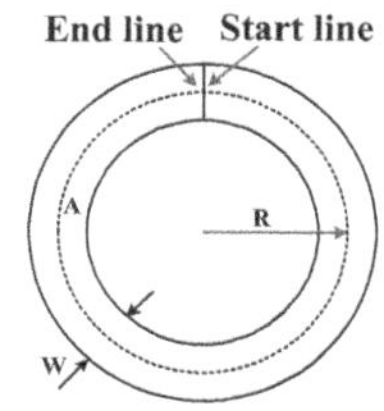

Figure 6. The steering task.

For EV-Finger (Figure 3b), it was similar to TeslaTouch [4]. The drive signal was the same as the one used in the EV-Pen.

Participants

Twelve volunteers (7 males, 5 females, aged from 22 to 37 years old, average age 31.6 years, all right handed) participated in the experiment. Only one had worked with a stylus.

Task and Procedure

We chose a non-liner steering task because the circular steering task is more complex than a straight line steering task. For a circular tunnel, the movement distance A was equal to the circle's circumference, i.e., $2\pi R$, where R is the radius. The tunnel width was W. According to the steering law, the *index of difficulty* for steering through a circular tunnel was $ID = A/W$. The movement time T could then be expressed in the formula: $T = a + bID$, where a and b are empirically determined constants.

All participants conducted the experiment in sitting postures. Participants were asked to move along a circular tunnel from the start line to the end line as accurately and as fast as possible in a clockwise direction using a pen or finger (Figure 6).

We measured the movement time T (time taken to move from the start line to the end line). To measure the accuracy of the trajectory produced, we calculated its lateral standard deviation SD (standard deviation of the distances between trajectory points and the center of the circular tunnel) and out of path movement OPM (percentage of trajectory points outside the tunnel boundaries). For both SD and OPM, higher values indicate lower accuracy.

After finishing the trials, the participants were asked to fill in a questionnaire to evaluate their subjective performances on 7-point Likert scales with ratings from 1 (worst) to 7 (best).

Design

The experiment employed a within-subject factorial design. The independent variables were: tunnel width W (30, 40, and 50 pixels), tunnel distance A (1000, 1500 and 1800 pixels), and three devices (EV-Pen, V-Pen, EV-Finger). Participants were exposed to three devices, whose order of appearance was balanced using a Latin square. For each device, participants were asked to perform the task in all combinations of tunnel widths and tunnel distances 3 times in random order.

The experiment consisted of: 12 participants × 3 tunnel widths × 3 tunnel distances × 3 devices × 3 repetitious = 972 trials.

The temperature in the lab was 25.0°C – 27.5°C with a relative humidity of 62.3% – 77.0% during experiments.

Results

Movement Time (T)

A repeated-measures ANOVA (analysis of variance) showed that there was no significant effect for devices on T. The overall means of T were 2.57s for the EV-Pen, 2.25s for the V-Pen and 2.23s for the EV-Finger.

The regression analysis on T and ID indicated that all three devices proved to fit the steering law with correlations greater than 0.90. The linear regression between the steering time (in s) and steering ID produced the following equations for each of the three input devices:

EV-Pen: $T = 0.0436ID + 0.9422\ (R^2 = 0.9322)$

V-Pen: $T = 0.0357ID + 0.9133\ (R^2 = 0.9176)$

EV-Finger: $T = 0.0301ID + 1.0957\ (R^2 = 0.9057)$

Our results showed that the steering law holds well with our EV-Pen $(R^2 = 0.93)$.

Out of Path Movement (OPM)

A repeated-measures ANOVA showed that there was a statistically significant effect for devices on OPM $(F_{2,22} = 22.35, p < 0.001)$. The overall means of OPM were 8.76% for the EV-Pen, 11.84% for the V-Pen and 21.80% for the EV-Finger (Figure 7a).

Pair-wise comparison tests showed that the participants produced significantly lower OPM $(p < 0.05)$ with the EV-Pen compared to other devices.

Standard Deviation (SD)

A repeated-measures analysis showed that there was a statistically significant effect for devices on SD $(F_{2,22} = 16.25, p < 0.001)$. The overall means of SD were 15.63 for the EV-Pen, 19.06 for the V-Pen and 24.26 for the EV-Finger (Figure 7b).

Pair-wise comparison tests showed that the participants produced significantly lower SD $(p < 0.05)$ with the EV-Pen compared to other devices.

Subjective Evaluation

According to the results of the questionnaire, half of the participants (6/12) preferred the EV-Pen over other devices to negotiate the tunnel. The participants also commented that the haptic feedback of the EV-Pen was more comfortable than with the V-Pen. The majority of participants (9/12) reported that it was difficult to complete the tasks with EV-Finger.

A repeated-measures analysis showed that there was a statistically significant effect for devices on *satisfaction* $(F_{2,22} = 7.90, p < 0.05)$. The overall means of *satisfaction* were 5.75 for the EV-Pen, 5.41 for the V-Pen and 4.08 for the EV-Finger. *Satisfaction* was the highest with the EV-Pen.

Discussion

The results showed that the OPM and the SD with the EV-Pen were the lowest. This indicates that participants performed the task most accurately with the EV-Pen. This is because the haptic feedback of the V-Pen comes from the body of the pen. As a result, the smooth movement of the pen is disturbed by the vibrating motor which is mounted inside the pen. By

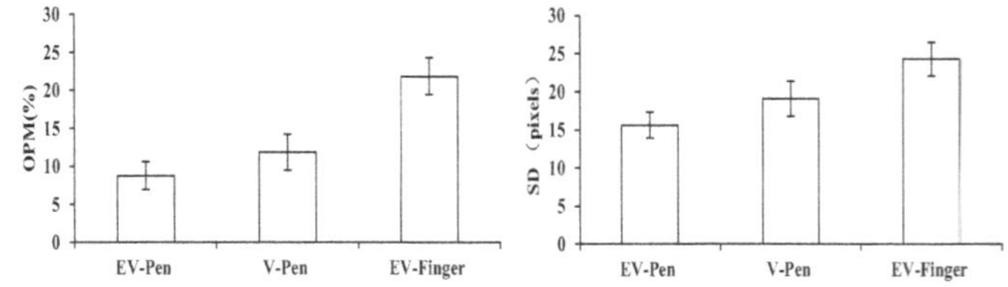

(a) Mean OPM with standard error bars. (b) Mean SD with standard error bars.

Figure 7. The results of steering task with three different input devices.

contrast, the EV-Pen produces haptic feedback from the pen-tip when the pen-tip touches the screen surface and this allows users to perform more precise interactions.

The experiment showed that T with the EV-Pen was slightly longer than with the others. This is caused mainly by friction between the pen and the touch surface due to the electrovibration. When participants moved outside the tunnel erroneously, the friction between the EV-Pen and touch surface increased to provide haptic feedback to indicate such errors. In other words, the EV-Pen acts as a "*brake*" and "*caution*". By contrast, the V-Pen acts only as a "*caution*".

Half of the participants preferred the EV-Pen. They stated that the EV-Pen was comfortable and easy to use. Besides, the majority of participants (9/12) reported that it was difficult to complete the tasks with the EV-Finger. Indeed, it is difficult to perform the task when the tunnel is narrow because of visual occlusion caused by the thickness of the finger-tip.

EV-Finger interaction is affected by the users skin properties (electric impedance), temperature and humidity [3, 9]. The temperature and humidity in our experiment constituted mild weather (temperature was 25.0°C – 27.5°C and humidity was 62.3% – 77.0%). We could predict that if temperature and humidity became very high, the EV-Finger would not work very well. By contrast, weather conditions and human body barely affect the haptic feedback of our EV-Pen.

EXPERIMENT 3: TRACING TASK

Experiment 1 confirmed that our EV-Pen could provide haptic feedback just like pen-on-paper feeling. Experiment 2 confirmed that our EV-Pen outperformed the other input modes in precise navigation interactions. Therefore, Experiment 3 was aimed to quantitatively investigate the performance of the EV-Pen in a tracing task because tracing is also a fundamental skill for people to learn writing or drawing.

As a pen is the main device for tracing tasks, we compared our EV-Pen with two conventional pen modes: mechanical-vibration pen (V-Pen) and normal pen (N-Pen, i.e. pen without haptic feedback). By contrast with the steering task experiment, haptic feedback was presented to the participants in the tunnels to guide tracing while the pen was moving along the tracing tunnel, so the participants could feel haptic feedback most of the time. In this task, haptic feedback indicated "affirmative feedback" to the participants.

Apparatus

The apparatus for this experiment was similar to that used in Experiment 2.

Figure 8. Three different shapes tested in Experiment 3.

For the EV-Pen, the stimulating signal was a sine wave with an amplitude of 200 V, and a frequency of 120 Hz. We chose these parameters based on the results of Experiment 1 because sine waves with lower amplitudes could provide more pleasant sensations to users. This frequency of 120 Hz was easily detected according to our experiment of device characteristics. This combination was suitable for navigating the tunnel. We tested the parameters through pilot studies with four participants. The feedback was easily perceived and the device was steady and comfortable to use.

For the V-Pen (Figure 3c), the device was the same as that used in Experiment 2. For fair device comparison, the stimuli intensity with V-Pen was set as close as possible to the EV-Pen. We conducted pilot studies with four participants to determine suitable feedback parameters. As a result, the motor was supplied with 1.5 Vdc/30 mA.

For the N-Pen (Figure 3d), the same type of capacitive pen was used, but without feedback.

Participants

Twelve volunteers (6 males, 6 females, aged from 21 to 35 years old, average age 26.83 years, all right handed) participated in the experiment. None had worked with a stylus.

Task and Procedure

All participants conducted the experiment in sitting postures. Participants were instructed to trace over the shape in one stroke, beginning at the start line to the end line in a clockwise direction (Figure 8). They traced over the shape once for each pen, the EV-Pen, the V-Pen and the N-Pen. The participants were asked to move as accurately and as quickly as possible.

For a trial, we collected the following metrics: *Tracing time* (time taken to completely trace a shape) and *Error rate* (percentage of trajectory points outside the tunnel). We also saved a screenshot of each completed trial. After finishing the trials, participants were asked to fill in a questionnaire to evaluate their subjective performances on 7-point Likert scales with ratings from 1 (worst) to 7 (best).

Design

The experiment employed a within-subject factorial design. The independent variables were: shapes (circle, star and puzzle), tunnel width (30 and 60 pixels), and three devices (EV-Pen, V-Pen and N-Pen). The shape size was 1200 pixels. Participants were exposed to all three devices, whose order of appearance was balanced using a Latin square. For each device, participants were asked to perform the task in all combinations of shapes and tunnel widths 3 times in random order.

The experiment consisted of: 12 participants $\times$ 3 shapes $\times$ 2 tunnel widths $\times$ 3 devices $\times$ 3 repetitious = 648 trials.

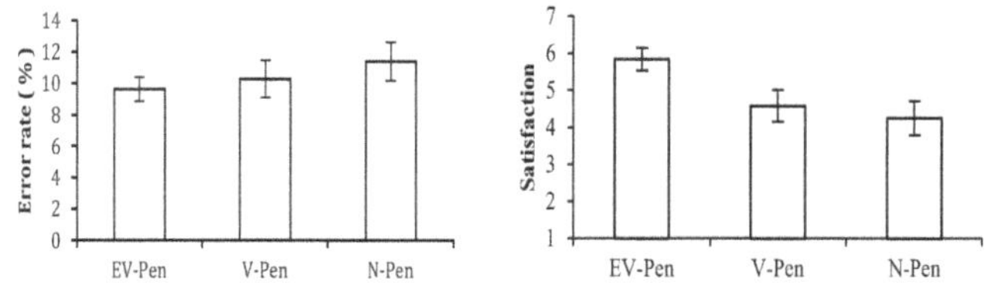

(a) Mean error rate with standard error bars. (b) Mean satisfaction with standard error bars.

Figure 9. The results of tracing task with three different input devices.

Results

Tracing Time (T)

A repeated-measures ANOVA showed no significant effect for devices on T. The overall means of T were 13.96s for the EV-Pen, 14.04s for the V-Pen and 13.68s for the N-Pen.

Error rate

A repeated-measures ANOVA showed that there was a statistically significant effect for devices on *error rate* ($F_{2,22} = 3.669, p < 0.05$). The overall means of *error rate* were 9.64% for the EV-Pen, 10.29% for the V-Pen and 11.41% for the N-Pen (Figure 9a).

Pair-wise comparison tests showed that the participants produced a significantly lower *error rate* ($p < 0.05$) with the EV-Pen compared to N-Pen.

Subjective Evaluation

According to the questionnaire results, nine participants (9/12) preferred the EV-Pen to other devices to negotiate the tunnel. They also commented that the haptic feedback of the EV-Pen was more comfortable than the V-Pen.

The overall means of *satisfaction* were 5.83 for the EV-Pen, 4.58 for the V-Pen and 4.25 for the N-Pen (Figure 9b). A repeated-measures analysis showed that there a was statistically significant effect on *satisfaction* ($F_{2,22} = 4.25, p < 0.05$). *Satisfaction* with the EV-Pen was the highest.

Discussion

The experimental results showed that the *error rate* with the EV-Pen was the lowest. This indicates that participants performed the task most accurately with the EV-Pen. Furthermore, nine participants (9/12) preferred the EV-Pen over the other input devices. The feedback provided by the EV-Pen was the most pleasant of all input devices. Participants stated that the movement of the EV-Pen was easy to control and it was easy to complete the task with the EV-Pen. This is mainly because our EV-Pen produces haptic feedback from the pen-tip rather than from the pens body and this allows users to perform more precise interactions.

By contrast, the participants stated that feedback provided by the V-Pen was a little shaky. When they used it for a long time it felt unnatural and uncomfortable. This is because haptic feedback from the V-Pen comes from the body of the pen resulting in disturbed movement which requires more effort to control and to maintain accuracy tracing.

The participants stated that N-Pen was too smooth for writing on the touchscreen. They could not control it very well because there was no haptic feedback.

EXPERIMENT 4: DRAWING AND HANDWRITING

There are many touchscreen applications where the EV-Pen can be implemented to perform specific tasks. However, our EV-Pen uniquely supports applications where precise and controlled pen movements are required. Moreover, the superior waveform, frequency & amplitude range and unique characteristics of the EV-Pen yield more accurate haptic representations and allow for richer user experiences.

Therefore, to understand user experience with the EV-Pen, we chose drawing and handwriting applications to imitate real world experiences because they are common for user tasks. Also, these applications are suited to continuous feedback which can improve the quality of the artwork and user experience.

Participants

Six participants (3 males, 3 females, aged from 19 to 35 years old, average age 25 years, all right handed) took part in the drawing and handwriting applications. All of them had moderate to good sketching and illustration skills. Three of them had drawing experience on computers.

Task and Procedure

We designed drawing and handwriting applications aligned with our previous experiments. Six different kinds of haptic feedback of the EV-Pen were presented to users and users freely chose the one that best suited them. The thickness of the line could be changed, meanwhile different intensities of haptic feedback were provided.

Participants performed the experiment in the sitting posture. After training, they were asked to (1) freely experiment with the EV-Pen to create artworks of their own, and then (2) write five phrases ("Good afternoon", "Hello", "Happy Birthday", "Handwriting" and "Drawing") in the most natural way. We conducted an open-ended interview with a subjective questionnaire during the experiment. On an average, participants took 45 minutes to complete the whole experiment.

Results

Overall, participants responded positively regarding the effectiveness of our EV-Pen. All participants appreciated the unique haptic feedback of our EV-Pen.

P3: "I think it is interesting. It is difficult to tell the feeling, but I like it. The feedback made me think that I was drawing. I prefer to use it always. "

P5: "The haptic feedback is very important for drawing and handwriting because you can express the feeling from it."

P6: "The haptic experience of writing or drawing with pen now can be transferable from real pen-on-paper to the computer environment."

Drawing

Some artworks created by participants are shown in Figure 10. Participants expressed that the EV-Pen provided haptic feedback just like using a real pen to draw on real paper.

P3: "The feeling is like pencil drawing on paper. If I change the line thickness, the feedback is changed to other pencil."

(a) (b)

Figure 10. Artworks created by participants using the EV-Pen.

They also stated that the feeling was good and it helped to improve the quality of their computer-based drawing.

P6: "It can provide the feeling of texture. The feeling is like drawing on real paper. It is better than my previous drawing experience on computers."

Handwriting

Similar to drawing, participants were satisfied with the haptic feedback as they could relate to real pen-on-paper writing.

P1: " The feeling of the friction with the pen is like a pencil sliding on real paper. This feeling is amazing."

Participants also believed that the continuous haptic feeling enriched their experience and enhanced their writing ability.

P4: " This haptic feedback makes me immersed in writing on touchscreens."

Potential Applications

Participants pointed out their desire to use our EV-Pen in a variety of applications. Also, they provided some good ideas for future enhancements.

P3: "If a professional drawing software application can provide haptic feedback like this, that will be perfect."

P4: "This can be used to teach children about sketching and writing in computers."

P6: "If different pen pressures can change the thickness of the line and the haptic feedback of the pen, that will be helpful."

Discussion

The overall experience of participants revealed their appreciation for the unique capabilities of our EV-Pen. They felt that our EV-Pen kept them engaged while drawing and handwriting. Also, participants agreed that they drew and wrote more correctly with haptic feedback. Whether the character shapes were curly, straight, mixed etc., it was easy for participants to control their pen movements on the touchscreen (just as with real pen and paper). They enjoyed the tasks and were satisfied with their experiences during the experiment. The feedback was natural and harmonious, so they were able to draw complex sketches and shaped letters easily with the system. The results showed that our EV-Pen can enhance user experience, efficiency and accuracy when drawing and handwriting.

GENERAL DISCUSSION

We designed the EV-Pen that leverages electrovibration haptic feedback in pen interaction by controlling electrostatic friction between the pen and the touch surface. Therefore, the EV-Pen can produce multisensory feedback. In other words, the electrostatic friction is controlled by the voltage, which is further parameterized by changing the waveform, amplitude and frequency. Thus, this potentially offers three channels of haptic information. Moreover, the haptic feedback can be dynamically changed according to the circumstances while the pen is moving on the surface.

Implications and Opportunities

The four experiments showed that our EV-Pen can enhance user performance and experience for precise tasks with real pen-on-paper feeling. More than that, a set of new haptic interactions can be implemented. We have implemented "*Texture Simulations*" and "*GUI Elements with Haptic Feedback*" (described below). We have further explored some interaction opportunities of the EV-Pen (shown below).

Texture Simulations (Figure 1c)

Apart from augmenting the pen device with electrovibration, we also characterized the feedback strengths which were responsible for distinct feelings. We offered three dynamic haptic feedback channels of information depending on amplitude, frequency and waveform. The results showed that our EV-Pen can simulate different kinds of haptic interaction, such as simulating friction between objects, feeling different textural patterns, implementing different feedback modes and intensities for different commands on touchscreens.

GUI Elements with Haptic Feedback (Figure 1d)

There are many interesting ways through which we can augment haptic feedback of the GUI elements for EV-Pen interaction. For example, users can feel different kinds of haptic feedback when they drag different files (e.g., doc, pdf, jpg) on touchscreens. These functions will help improve user satisfaction and experience in EV-Pen interactions.

Haptic Information Layers

In our experiments, we have tested the characterization and user feeling for some typical combinations of waveform, frequency and amplitude. The results support additional feedback channels which open up the possibility of perceiving non-visual information layers. For example, users can choose and draw on different layers with different types of haptic feedback from the EV-Pen when they work with Photoshop.

Pen Simulations

Most of the participants commented that interaction with the EV-Pen is more helpful, satisfactory, more engaging and it enhances their ability to draw or write well. This is because the feeling when drawing and writing is very similar to the physical and intimate interaction with a pen on real paper. We can further extend the user experience by simulating haptic feedback modes for different kinds of pen (e.g., pencil, ballpen, crayon, brush) on different kinds of paper.

Multi-point Haptic Feedback (Figure 11a)

More than one EV-Pen can be utilized to interact simultaneously on a multi-point touchscreen by being injected with different drive signals. For example, two EV-Pens can be injected with different drive signals providing two kinds of feedback (e.g., one for drawing and the other for handwriting), which is useful for collaborative work.

(a) Multi-point Haptic Feedback (b) Pen-Finger Simultaneous Operation

Figure 11. Interaction opportunities of the EV-Pen.

Pen-Finger Simultaneous Operation (Figure 11b)

Based on the capacity to perform multi-point haptic feedback using electrovibration, we can combine electrovibration in pen and finger technology for simultaneous operation. The EV-Pen and fingers could employ two handed operations on a single touchscreen. For example, the non-dominant hand could perform a gross manipulation with fingers, such as zoom in/out and rotating, while the dominant hand simultaneously performs a fine-grained interaction with the EV-Pen, such as gesturing, writing and drawing [8]. Both the EV-Pen and fingers can feel respective haptic feedback at the same time. This could be an interesting area for future exploration.

Limitations and Future work

Our prototype EV-Pen is wired with external hardware. To make it commercial and convenient to use, we can miniaturize the signal generator and put it inside the pen. The user's body can act as a common ground; when one hand holds the metal body of the mobile device (connected to the ground of the touch panel) and the other holds the EV-Pen (connected to the ground of the EV-Pen), the user can feel the haptic feedback. Current flow will be limited for safety.

In addition, we plan to put pressure, accelerometer and orientation sensors into the EV-Pen. Thus, haptic feedback will be controlled by pressure, tilt, rolling and azimuth of the pen [29]. Also we can dynamically change the waveform, frequency and amplitude by considering the pen location, velocity and direction, which can help simulate textures more precisely. This work will increase the interaction bandwidth and give sufficient choices to users who access the EV-Pen.

This paper focuses on pen interaction rather than presenting an entirely perceptual study. Thus, we only determined the basic detection threshold and a subjective evaluation study. Future work may include human perception (e.g., proximal stimuli, magnitude estimation) to enhance the efficiency of the EV-Pen. To make the "pen-on-paper" feeling and other textures even more realistic, we will explore more complex combinations of waveform & frequency & amplitude.

CONCLUSION

We presented the EV-Pen for touchscreens providing variable intensity electrovibration feedback without any mechanical actuator. We demonstrated the effectiveness of the EV-Pen through four experiments. The results confirmed that employing the EV-Pen enhances the user experience to perform precise tasks with real pen-on-paper feeling. We are still at an early stage in exploring electrovibration for pen interactions. We believe that this work will open up a wide range of possibilities for both electrovibration and pen interactions.

ACKNOWLEDGMENTS
We thank all members of the Center for Human-Engaged Computing at Kochi University of Technology for their support. This study has been partially supported by the "User Interface Design for the Ageing Population" project of JST's FY2014 Strategic International Collaborative Research Program (SICORP) in Japan and National Key Research and Development Program of China (No. 2016YFB1001300).

REFERENCES
1. Accot, J., and Zhai, S. Performance evaluation of input devices in trajectory-based tasks: an application of the steering law. In *Proc. CHI '99*, 466–472.
2. Arasan, A., Basdogan, C., and Sezgin, T. M. Haptic stylus with inertial and vibro-tactile feedback. In *Proc. WHC '13*, 425–430.
3. Bau, O., and Poupyrev, I. Revel: tactile feedback technology for augmented reality. *ACM Trans. on Graphics, 31*, 4 (2012), 89.
4. Bau, O., Poupyrev, I., Israr, A., and Harrison, C. Teslatouch: electrovibration for touch surfaces. In *Proc. UIST '10*, 283–292.
5. Bertolini, T., and Fuchs, T. *Vibrations and Noises in Small Electric Motors: Measurement, Analysis, Interpretation, Optimization*. Süddeutscher Verlag onpact, 2011.
6. Chen, D., Song, A., and Tian, L. A novel miniature multi-mode haptic pen for image interaction on mobile terminal. In *Proc. HAVE '15*, 1–6.
7. DiFilippo, D., and Pai, D. K. The ahi: An audio and haptic interface for contact interactions. In *Proc. UIST '00*, 149–158.
8. Hinckley, K., Yatani, K., Pahud, M., Coddington, N., Rodenhouse, J., Wilson, A., Benko, H., and Buxton, B. Pen+ touch= new tools. In *Proc. UIST '10*, 27–36.
9. Kaczmarek, K. A., Nammi, K., Agarwal, A. K., Tyler, M. E., Haase, S. J., and Beebe, D. J. Polarity effect in electrovibration for tactile display. *IEEE Trans. on Biomedical Engineering, 53*, 10 (2006), 2047–2054.
10. Kamuro, S., Minamizawa, K., Kawakami, N., and Tachi, S. Ungrounded kinesthetic pen for haptic interaction with virtual environments. In *Proc. RO-MAN '09*, 436–441.
11. Ko, C.-H. The evaluation of pen gestures in a digital painting environment. In *Ubiquitous Computing Application and Wireless Sensor*. Springer, 2015, 385–391.
12. Kyung, K.-U., and Park, J.-S. Ubi-pen: Development of a compact tactile display module and its application to a haptic stylus. In *Proc. World Haptics '07*, 109–114.
13. Lee, D., Son, K., Lee, J. H., and Bae, S.-H. Phantompen: virtualization of pen head for digital drawing free from pen occlusion & visual parallax. In *Proc. UIST '12*, 331–340.
14. Lee, J. C., Dietz, P. H., Leigh, D., Yerazunis, W. S., and Hudson, S. E. Haptic pen: a tactile feedback stylus for touch screens. In *Proc. UIST '04*, 291–294.
15. Liao, C., Guimbretière, F., and Loeckenhoff, C. E. Pen-top feedback for paper-based interfaces. In *Proc. UIST '06*, 201–210.
16. Mallinckrodt, E., Hughes, A., and Sleator Jr, W. Perception by the skin of electrically induced vibrations. *Science* (1953).
17. McMahan, W., and Kuchenbecker, K. J. Dynamic modeling and control of voice-coil actuators for high-fidelity display of haptic vibrations. In *Proc. HAPTICS '14*, 115–122.
18. Nagasaka, S., Uranishi, Y., Yoshimoto, S., Imura, M., and Oshiro, O. Haptylus: haptic stylus for interaction with virtual objects behind a touch screen. In *Proc. SIGGRAPH Asia '14*, 9.
19. Okamoto, S., Nagano, H., and Yamada, Y. Psychophysical dimensions of tactile perception of textures. *IEEE Trans. on Haptics, 6*, 1 (2013), 81–93.
20. Poupyrev, I., Okabe, M., and Maruyama, S. Haptic feedback for pen computing: directions and strategies. In *Proc. CHI'04*, 1309–1312.
21. Prattichizzo, D., Meli, L., and Malvezzi, M. Digital handwriting with a finger or a stylus: A biomechanical comparison. *IEEE Trans. on Haptics, 8*, 4 (2015), 356–370.
22. Romano, J. M., and Kuchenbecker, K. J. Creating realistic virtual textures from contact acceleration data. *IEEE Trans. on Haptics, 5*, 2 (2012), 109–119.
23. Siek, K. A., Rogers, Y., and Connelly, K. H. Fat finger worries: how older and younger users physically interact with pdas. In *Proc. INTERACT '05*. Springer, 267–280.
24. Sun, M., Ren, X., and Cao, X. Effects of multimodal error feedback on human performance in steering tasks. *Journal of Information Processing 18* (2010), 284–292.
25. Tu, H., Ren, X., and Zhai, S. Differences and similarities between finger and pen stroke gestures on stationary and mobile devices. *ACM Trans. on Computer-Human Interaction, 22*, 5 (2015), 22.
26. Wijekoon, D., Cecchinato, M. E., Hoggan, E., and Linjama, J. Electrostatic modulated friction as tactile feedback: intensity perception. In *Proc. EuroHaptics '12*, 613–624.
27. Wintergerst, G., Jagodzinski, R., Hemmert, F., Müller, A., and Joost, G. Reflective haptics: enhancing stylus-based interactions on touch screens. In *Proc. EuroHaptics '10*, 360–366.
28. Withana, A., Kondo, M., Makino, Y., Kakehi, G., Sugimoto, M., and Inami, M. Impact: Immersive haptic stylus to enable direct touch and manipulation for surface computing. *Computers in Entertainment, 8*, 2 (2010), 9.
29. Xin, Y., Bi, X., and Ren, X. Acquiring and pointing: an empirical study of pen-tilt-based interaction. In *Proc. CHI '11*, 849–858.

In-Place-Ink: Toward More Direct Handwriting Interfaces

Jiseong Gu
HCI Lab., School of Computing, KAIST
Daejeon, Republic of Korea
jiseong.gu@kaist.ac.kr

Geehyuk Lee
HCI Lab., School of Computing, KAIST
Daejeon, Republic of Korea
geehyuk@gmail.com

ABSTRACT

An indirect handwriting interface using a separate window is a de facto standard interface in most of major pen computing systems. In this paper, we study the potential of the other less explored handwriting interfaces, which we call In-Place-Ink (IPI) interfaces, where a user writes directly on a target text input area. We first conducted a preliminary experiment to determine the optimal input area dimensions for direct handwriting input, and based on the results designed two IPI interfaces: a discrete IPI (DIPI) interface and a continuous IPI (CIPI) interface. We then conducted a main experiment using form-filling tasks to evaluate their efficiencies and collect user feedback about them in comparison with a conventional indirect writing (IW) interface. The experiment results showed that CIPI required significantly lower completion time for a form-filling task than other interfaces, and was comparable to the IW interface in terms of user preference. We hope our report of designing and evaluating the two IPI interfaces may stimulate future research efforts toward more direct handwriting interfaces.

Author Keywords

In-Place-Ink; direct writing interfaces; indirect writing interfaces; pen computers

ACM Classification Keywords

H.5.2 User Interfaces: Input devices and strategies (e.g., mouse, touchscreen)

INTRODUCTION

Text entry on pen computers usually requires a series of steps as shown in Figure 1a. First, the user places a text cursor in the text control, and then the system shows a pop-up window for pen input. A user then writes on the pop-up window, and then the system converts the ink into typed text. A user may then perform gestures or use buttons on the pop-up window to correct entered text, if needed, and press a button to accept and insert the entered text into the text control. Such a pen text entry interface may be called an Indirect Writing (IW) interface because writing is not performed directly to the text control, but is performed indirectly via a separate pop-up window. IW is now a de facto standard for pen text entry, being used in most of major pen computing systems.

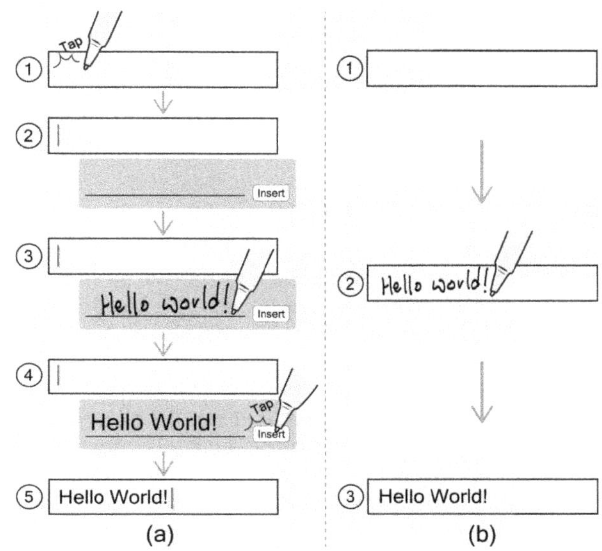

Figure 1. (a) Indirect Writing (IW) vs. (b) In-Place-Ink (IPI)

It seems that IW has become popular for the following two reasons. First, its large pop-up window allows the user to write more easily in large letters. Writing in large letters may require less physical and mental loads, and higher resolution ink inputs through a large pop-up window may benefit the handwriting recognizer. Second, IW is compatible with the traditional GUI where text entry is done via a text cursor. The pop-up window of IW plays the role of a keyboard by sending a recognized ink input to the GUI system as a keyboard does. In other words, IW does not require a major change to the traditional text-cursor-based GUI. On the other hand, IW also has drawbacks. First, it requires an additional step of placing a text cursor in a target area before starting to write in the pop-up window. This additional step would not be necessary if the user could write in the target area directly. Second, it may require frequent visual focus shifts between the pop-up window and the target area because the user writes on the pop-up window whereas the result is inserted into the target area. Third, the pop-up window may occupy or occlude a substantial part of the screen area.

The most distinguishing feature of a pen-based GUI compared to the traditional GUI is its directness; a pen interacts

ISS'16, November 06-09, 2016, Niagara Falls, ON, Canada.

DOI: http://dx.doi.org/10.1145/2992154.2992184

with target objects directly whereas a mouse interacts with target objects indirectly through a cursor. It is interesting that text entry only is done in an indirect way whereas other operations are done in a direct way in a pen-based GUI. Would it be a bad idea to allow the user to write directly into a text input area? Figure 1b illustrates this alternative. As a pen input is performed where it is needed, no separate text cursor or no separate pop-up window for pen input is needed. We call this alternative way of pen text entry as In-Place-Ink (IPI) in this paper. The defining property of IPI is its *directness*; it enables writing directly in the area where a text input should be inserted. IPI is not in fact a new concept, but is found in the early history of pen computing [19, 6, 15]. IPI, However, disappeared at some point, and IW became the main interface. We conducted a literature survey about handwriting text entry interface[6, 14, 19, 5, 10, 15, 18, 21, 1, 13, 4], but, we could not find any empirical study to point out a critical problem with IPI and explain its discontinuation. As pen interface technologies improved significantly since the early days of pen computing, and the shape and role of computers has changed dramatically in recent years, we think that we may give another chance to IPI.

In this study we examined the advantages and problems of IPI in comparison with IW by designing and implementing working IPI interface examples, a discrete IPI (DIPI) interface and a continuous IPI (CIPI) interface, and evaluating them in the context of form-filling tasks. The DIPI interface supports character-wise text entry while the CIPI interface supports word-wise text entry. The In-Place-Ink Interfaces section describes them in detail. We selected form-filling tasks because they require the user to switch between text entry and GUI manipulation frequently, and will benefit most from the directness of IPI. In addition, form filling tasks are not uncommon; many computer tasks are performed via a form, such as an online order form for buyer and order information and a test application form for examinee and test option information.

The remainder of the paper is organized as follows. In Related Work section, we summarize a brief review of previous studies related to the current study. In IPI section, we define IPI and summarize its advantages and disadvantages. In DIPI and CIPI sections, respectively, we define DIPI and CIPI, and explain their design details of their prototypes. In the next three sections, we explain the design and result of two experiments. The goal of the first experiment was to determine the best input box size for a DIPI interface. In the second experiment, we compared the DIPI and CIPI interfaces with an IW interface counterpart in terms of a few performance metrics including task completion time. In Discussion section we provide further interpretations of the experimental results and comments on the limitations of the current study. In the Conclusion section, we summarize the main results, the contributions of the current study, and immediate future work.

RELATED WORK

Most of handwriting interface studies have been focused on improving handwriting recognition. This may be because the accuracy of handwriting recognition is most important for user satisfaction [2, 3]. LaLomia showed by an experiment using a Wizard of Oz method that handwriting recognition was acceptable when the character-by-character accuracy was over 97%[10]. Recent years have seen significant advances in handwriting recognition technologies, and state-of-the-art products these days show an error rate of around 1% after sufficient training [9], and handwriting recognition technologies now seem to have achieved the user satisfaction goal. Nevertheless, a handwriting interface is not yet preferred to a keyboard despite the recent wide adoption of pen computers [8]. This may suggest that the interaction aspect of a handwriting interface now deserves a due research focus. In this section, we review past studies related to the IPI interfaces, past studies on the diverse design parameters of handwriting user interfaces, and past studies on user interface designs to support error correction.

In-Place-Ink interfaces in the past

Studies related to the IPI concept are found in the early literature of pen computing. Windows for Pen Computing [19] was a Windows 3.1x add-on package for tablet computers. It supported three different ways of text entry: typing with a software keyboard, handwriting in a pop-up windows (IW interface), and handwriting in a target text input area (IPI interface). Until 1994, examples of an IPI interface were not rare [6, 15], but nearly disappeared afterward and IW interfaces became the main stream. Recently, IPI-like interfaces are seen in some of note-taking applications. In addition, a tablet computer maker introduced an add-on package to support an IPI interface[1]. The revival of IPI interfaces in the market may mean that the verdict on the future of the IPI interfaces is yet to be reached. We need empirical data to help designers and developers make informed decision about the future of handwriting interfaces.

Exploring parameters for handwriting interface

There have been many studies on the various design parameters of handwriting interfaces, including input symbol sets[21, 5, 18], the size of input boxes [13], the quality of handwriting recognition [10], the design of an input window (letter-wise / line-wise / free form) [14, 4], and the position, time, and duration of the visual feedback of a recognition result [14, 1, 6]. Among various possible input symbol sets, unistroke symbol sets were popular because they have less ambiguity than the roman alphabet. Unistroke symbols sets showed an improved recognition rate and text entry speed, but demanded users the overhead of learning a new set of symbols [21, 5, 18]. In an experiment to find an optimal box size for letter-wise handwriting input, Ren et al. showed that a box size of 12 x 14 mm was the best considering input performance and user preference [13].

In a study on handwriting input window design, Santos et al. [14] reported that a letter-wise input showed a better handwriting recognition, and a continuous input allowed users feel less constrained. In a more recent study by Gao et al. [4], however, a continuous input exhibited the best accuracy in alphanumeric handwriting recognition. We also explore the

[1]Lenovo WRITEit, http://www.lenovo.com/us/en/apps/writeit/

two cases of a discrete input and a continuous input in the current research, and expect that the latter will be a more practical option based on these previous studies. Regarding the visual feedback of a recognition result, Santos et al. [14] conducted an experiment and reported that visual feedback in close proximity was helpful for novice users, but makes no different for expert users. Bouteruche et al. [1] reported that visual feedback away from the locus of writing with some amount of time delay is not helpful.

Whereas there have been many studies on the various design parameters of handwriting interfaces, there have been few studies on the directness of handwriting interfaces. The current study will be the first empirical study on the effect of the directness of handwriting interfaces in the modern tablet computer context.

Interface design for error correction

Although handwriting recognition technologies are advancing, handwriting recognition is intrinsically error-prone due to the diversity and irregularity of human handwriting skill, and therefore a usable handwriting interface should provide functions for error recovery. Schomaker [15] introduced as a cheap trick to recover from an incorrect handwriting recognition a method that allows a user to choose one of the other alternative recognition results. Goodisman [6] and Mankoff et al. [12] proposed a marking-gesture-based interface to recover from an incorrect recognition result. Goodisman [6] also proposed an interface where a user can replace the current recognition result with the second-best recognition result by tapping in the box before handwriting recognition is completed. Hurst et al. [7] proposed a method to distinguish pen strokes for repairing errors and pen strokes for text entry. Shilman et al. [16] proposed a way to impose a constraint on handwriting recognition using a gesture. This method allows a user to correct a recognition result without re-writing.

These prior work suggests that any usable handwriting interface should provide an interface for correcting errors. Therefore, we implemented editing functions in the handwriting interfaces that we implemented for our user studies. We expect that these editing functions will be more effective in IPI interfaces because text entry and editing occur in the same space in IPI interfaces.

IN-PLACE-INK INTERFACES

With an IPI interface, the user can write on a target text input area with a pen directly as we write on the paper with a pen in a real physical world. Figure 1 compares IPI and IW interfaces. The most distinguishing feature of IPI is that it does not need a text cursor because the action of writing itself specifies the text entry point in IPI. Selecting, inserting, and deleting text are done without a text cursor. No text cursor means no need to place a text cursor in a target area first before text entry, which is usually the first step of text entry in IW interfaces. The next distinguishing feature is the absence of a separate pop-up window, which means no need to switch the visual focus between the pop-up window and a text input area and no occlusion problem by the pop-up window.

In addition to these advantages, IPI also has problems to solve before it can be a practical handwriting interface. First, IPI may require a text input control larger than that of the traditional GUI because the text input control of IPI is for handwriting while the text input control of the traditional GUI is for typed text. Indeed, blank cells for handwriting input in a paper-based form is large compared with typed letters. The large text input controls of IPI may consume more screen space and may not go well with other GUI components such as buttons and list boxes. For the design of a practical IPI interface, we may need to answer first what would be the minimal size of the text input controls that would not affect handwriting efficiency too much. The goal of the first experiment of the current research was to answer this question.

Second, a mismatch between handwriting and typed text in their sizes and styles may introduce discontinuities in text entry, e.g., a periodic rearrangement of entered text. This is not a problem in IW interfaces because handwriting in this case occurs in a separate space (a pop-up window) and a target text control needs to handle typed text only. This is an inherent problem of IPI interfaces because handwriting and typed text share the same space. A novel design to enable a smooth transition from handwriting to typed text is necessary for IPI to be a practical interface option. In the current research, we considered DIPI first which is free from this mismatch problem because it is a letter-wise interface. After studying more basic questions about IPI interfaces using DIPI, we continued with CIPI, which is a word-wise interface.

In the following subsections we describe the two IPI interface designs: DIPI and CIPI interfaces. A DIPI interface supports character-wise text entry while a CIPI interface supports word-wise text entry. Both were implemented in C# language using the Microsoft Ink library (default recognizer for English). We used Microsoft Surface Pro 3 running Windows 8.1 with .Net Framework 4.5.1 throughout the user experiments. The two IPI interfaces are not meant to be anything optimal or representative. There were numerous design options that we had to decide on at our discretion. A systematic study on the design options will be certainly required once the concept of IPI turns out to be optimistic.

The DIPI Interface

Figure 2 illustrates the DIPI interface. It uses a series of boxes for letter-wise writing, and therefore is called "discrete" IPI. As a series of boxes defines the positions of input letters, we can avoid the problem of mismatch between handwriting and typed text. A guideline for census form design[17] suggested that the optimal aspect ratio of an input box for digits and upper-case letter is 5(width) : 6(height). In our case, we needed to consider lower-case letters, too, some of which need space for descenders, and therefore determined the aspect ratio of the input box to be 9:5. In order to indicate the area for descenders clearly, we added a baseline in the boxes as shown in Figure 2. The optimal size of the input boxes will depend on many factors such as a pen technology and a usage environment. Based on the results of Experiment 1, we determine it to be 8 mm (width) by 14.4 mm (height).

Figure 2 explains the text entry process of the DIPI interface using the example of entering the text. Each input box can be in one of the following three states: Ink-only state, Overlapping state, and Text-only state. Figure 2 shows input boxes in different states. Initially, an input box is in the Text-only state. An input box switches to the Ink-only state when the user starts to write in it. In the Ink-only state, an input box contains input strokes only and does not start handwriting recognition. An input box switches to the Overlapping state when the user starts to write in one of the other boxes or when 1 second passes after the user finishes writing. In the Overlapping state, an input box shows input strokes and a recognition result together. If the user adds a stroke to an input box during the Overlapping state, the recognition result disappears and the new stroke is added to the existing strokes. An input box makes transition to the Text-only state when no input box receives an input for 5 seconds or when an editing operation, which is described next, is started. In the Text-only state, an input box contains a recognition result only. If the user writes in an input box in the Text-only state, the input box deletes the recognition result and makes transition to the Ink-only state.

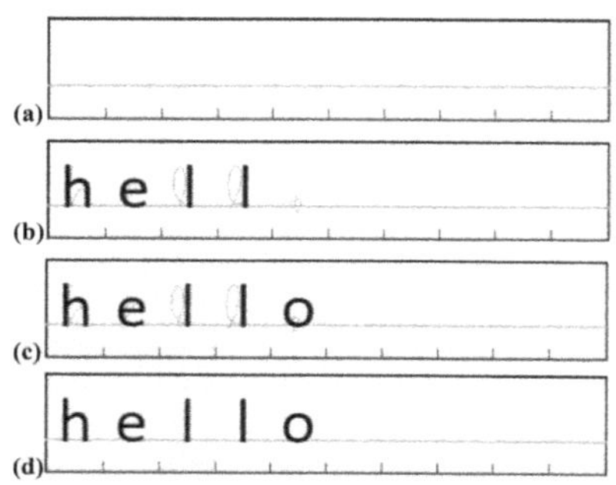

Figure 2. The DIPI interface (a) when it is empty (All boxes are in the Text-only state.), (b) when digital ink is being written (The first four boxes are in the Overlapping state and the fifth box is in the Ink-only state.), (c) when the ink is completely recognized after a second (The first five boxes are in the Overlapping state.), and (d) when the ink disappears after additional four seconds (All boxes are back in the Text-only state.).

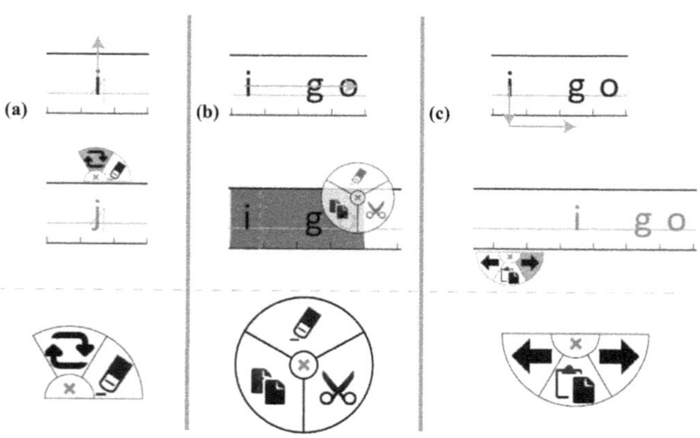

Figure 3. Text manipulation using exit strokes in the DIPI interface: (a) an Up-stroke from a box to correct or delete letter, (b) a Left/Right-stroke from a box to select text, and (c) a Down-stroke from a box to move text or paste copied text. Blue arrows show pen traces to invoke each operation.

The DIPI interface also provides functions for editing entered text, and the user can invoke these functions using "exit strokes". An exit stroke is a pen stroke that starts inside an input box and continue beyond the boundary of the input box by some margin. In the DIPI interface, strokes for text entry do not leave the input box, and therefore exit strokes are distinguished from strokes for text entry. An exit stroke can be upward, downward, leftward, or rightward, and is called Up-stroke, Down-stroke, Left-stroke, or Right-stroke, respectively.

Figure 3 explains the use of the four exit strokes. Figure 3a shows how to use an Up-stroke to correct a recognition result. An Up-stroke invokes a pie menu. The upper icon in the menu is for overwriting the current recognition result with the second best recognition result. The right icon in the menu is for deleting ink and the recognition result in the current box. Figure 3b shows how to use a Left-stroke or a Right-stroke to select a range of text from the current box to the box at the end point of the stroke. On the completion of the text selection, a pie menu with the following four icons appears: Copy, Cut, Delete, and Replace. The first three functions are self-explanatory. The Replace function is for replacing the current selection with the text in the clipboard. Figure 3c shows how to move a range of text using a Down-stroke. A Down-stroke invokes a pie menu. Continuing the stroke to the left or right moves the text in the current box and the subsequent boxes to the left or right. This operation can be used to create a space or remove a space between words. The lower icon in the menu is for inserting text in the clipboard at the current point.

The CIPI Interface

Figure 4 illustrates the CIPI interface. It allows the user to write in the box continuously, and therefore it is called "continuous" IPI. After the user write in the box, handwritten letters should be converted into typed letters. In the CIPI interface, this conversion is done in two steps. When the user pauses for a second while writing, the interface performs handwriting recognition on the inputted digital ink. The recognition result is shown in typed letters overlapped on the digital ink as shown in Figure 4c; the CIPI interface uses fonts in various sizes to maximize overlaps between the inputted digital ink and the recognition result in typed letters. As the user continues to write and pause, recognition of a new digital ink and presentation of the results in overlapping typed letters repeat. When the user finish writing the whole line and pushes on "Done" button at the end of the input box, the CIPI interface irons out irregularities in the typed letters, i.e., it converts the typed letters in various font sizes into typed letters in a uniform, predefined font size as shown in Figure 4d.

The CIPI interface provides editing functions which are similar to that of the DIPI interface but are word-wise rather than letter-wise. As shown in Figure 4c, the CIPI interface presents a recognition result word-wise, i.e., every word is shown in a grey rectangle. A user can use an exit stroke to invoke an editing function on the current word by starting an exit stroke from the inside of the gray rectangle.

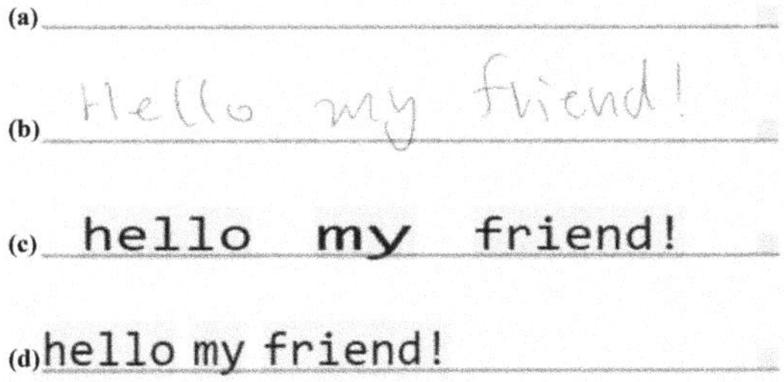

Figure 4. The CIPI interface (a) when it is empty, (b) when digital ink is written, (c) when the ink is recognized, and (d) when "Done" button is pushed.

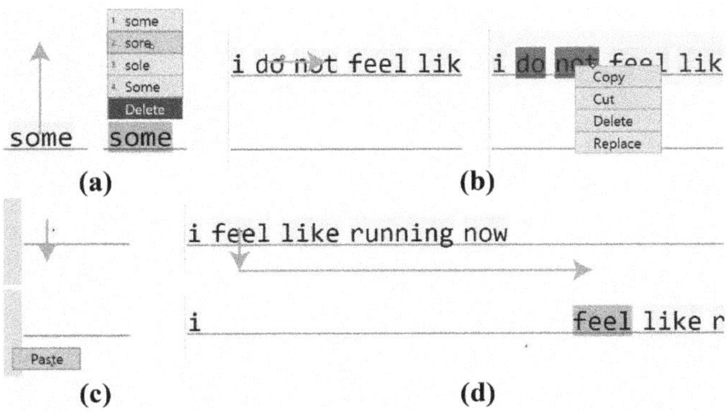

Figure 5. Text manipulation using exit strokes in the CIPI interface: (a) a up-stroke from a word to invoke an edit menu, (b) an right-stroke from a word to select text, (c) a down-stroke from an empty space to paste copied text, and (d) a down-stroke from a word to move text. Blue arrows show pen movements.

Figure 5 explains the use of the four exit strokes. Figure 5a shows how to use a up-stroke to correct a recognition result. A up-stroke invokes a menu with the next four recognition candidates, and the user can select one of them to substitute for the current recognition result. The menu also contains a delete icon for deleting the current word. Figure 5b shows how to use a left- or right-stroke to select a series of words. On the completion of the selection, a pie menu with Copy, Cut, Delete, and Replace commands appears. These can be used similarly as in the case of the DIPI interface. Figure 5c shows how to paste copied text. Figure 5d shows how to move the current word using a down-stroke. As in the case of the DIPI interface, a down-stroke followed by a left or right movement moves the current and subsequent words to the left or right. This operation can be used to create a space or remove a space between words.

PRELIMINARY EXPERIMENT

The goal of the preliminary experiment was to determine the optimal dimensions of an input box for the DIPI interface. A smaller input box will allow a better utilization of the screen space, but will render handwriting difficult. In particular, it might be difficult to write a letter neatly confined in a small box. The optimal choice will be a trade-off between efficient space utilization and easy handwriting. In addition, we expected that the two opposing factors would also affect the text entry speed of the DIPI interface. Therefore, our hypotheses in this experiment were as follows.

H1 The handwriting speed will change as the input box size increases. (a) Handwriting speed will increase until a certain input box size. (b) Handwriting speed will decrease after the certain input box size.

H2 Writing characters in a given input box will be easier as the input box size increases. (a) User will correct an input less frequently as the box size increases. (b) Unintended exit-strokes will occur less frequently as the box size increases. (c) User will perceive less burden as the box size increases.

H3 Handwriting recognition will be more accurate as the input box size increases.

Apparatus

Figure 6 shows the task application used in the experiment. The application was run on Microsoft Surface Pro 3. A sentence to write was presented, and participants wrote the sentence in the provided input cells. No handwriting recognition was active during the experiment in order not to interrupt a natural writing skill. All ink inputs were saved and were batch-processed later using a handwriting recognition engine to compare recognition rates in different conditions. The sentences used in the experiment were randomly selected from MacKenzie Phrase Set [11], and participants were instructed to write in lower-case letters.

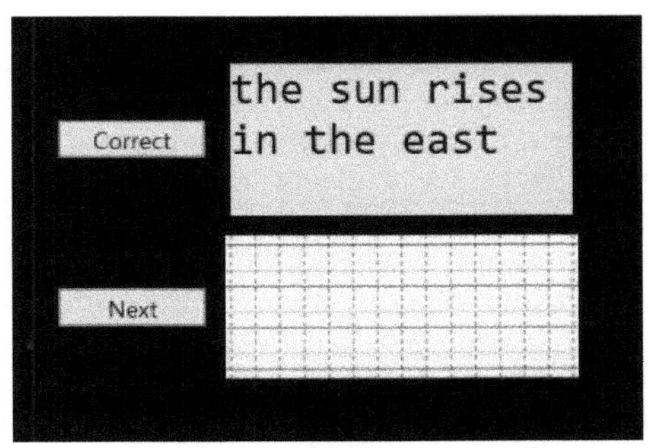

Figure 6. A snapshot of the task application used in the preliminary experiment.

Line changes during handwriting may have a negative effect on the writing performance and experience. Therefore, the number of rows and the number of cells in a row were kept constant irrespective of the cell size: 3 rows and 14 cells in a row. If a mistake is found, one could remove all strokes in a cell by tapping on the cell during a correction mode which is activated by pressing the Correct button. The Correct button was located on the left side of presented text to prevent an accidental touch by the hand (All participants were right-handed.). In a pilot experiment, we observed that the handwritten letters were not aligned well, suggesting a need for a base line, and therefore we added a line across the input cells at the 1/4 level as shown in Figure 6.

Participants

Twelve participants (6 female, average age = 21.75 (SD = 2.89)) were recruited from our university. One of them was a graduate student, and others were undergraduate students. All of them have engineering background, and four of them had a prior experience with handwriting text entry. None of the participants were native English speakers, but their official language in class was English. They were more familiar with separate-letter writing than joined-up (cursive) writing.

Design

The experiment was a within-subject design; the independent variable was *CellSize* (input cell size). There were six input cell sizes, and they were counterbalanced using a Latin Square.

We measured the following metrics in each trial.

- *CompletionTime* is the difference between the time when the first stylus-down event occurred and the time when Next button was clicked.
- *CorrectionFrequency* is the total number of taps on non-empty cells during the correction mode.
- *ProtrusionRate* is the number of strokes crossing the boundary of an originating cell by the total number of strokes.
- *RecognitionAccuracy* is the number of correctly recognized characters divided by the total number of input characters. We excluded empty spaces in this calculation.

Procedure

First, participants were given a brief introduction to the goal and procedure of the experiment. Next, they were allowed three minutes to find a comfortable posture for handwriting while writing sentences in a grid with a cell size of 6 mm x 10.8 mm. Next, the pen system was calibrated for individual participants. Next, six blocks of trials for six different input cell sizes were repeated. The six cell sizes were 2 mm x 3.6 mm, 4 mm x 7.2 mm, 6 mm x 10.8 mm, 8 mm x 14.4 mm, 10 mm x 18 mm, and 12 mm x 21.6 mm (the aspect ratios in all cases = 5:9). In each block, participants transcribed 25 sentences and then were given 5 minutes to answer a NASA TLX questionnaire. Each block lasted from 10 to 15 minutes. After finishing all blocks, participants were asked to rank their preferences over the six cell sizes (*PreferenceRank*).

Results

Figure 7 shows changes in the four objective metrics as the cell size increases. *CellSize* had a significant effect on *CompletionTime* ($F_{5,55}$ = 10.050, $p < 0.001$), on *CorrectionFrequency* ($F_{5,55}$ = 4.169, $p < 0.005$), on *ProtrusionRate* ($F_{1.695,18.641}$ = 39.881, $p < 0.001$), and on *RecognitionAccuracy* ($F_{2.239,24.630}$ = 8.496, $p < 0.005$). Post-hoc comparisons with Bonferroni adjustment between all *CellSize* pairs were done, and their results are shown on the graphs.

- *CompletionTime* decreases as *CellSize* increases. There is no significant decrease after *CellSize* reaches 4 mm. H1a is supported, but H1b is not supported.
- *CorrectionFrequency* decreases as *CellSize* increases. There is no significant decrease after *CellSize* reaches 4 mm. H2a is supported.
- *ProtrusionRate* decreases as *CellSize* increases. There is no significant decrease after *CellSize* reaches 8 mm. H2b is supported.
- *RecognitionAccuracy* increases as *CellSize* increases. There is no significant increase after *CellSize* reaches 6 mm. H3 is supported.

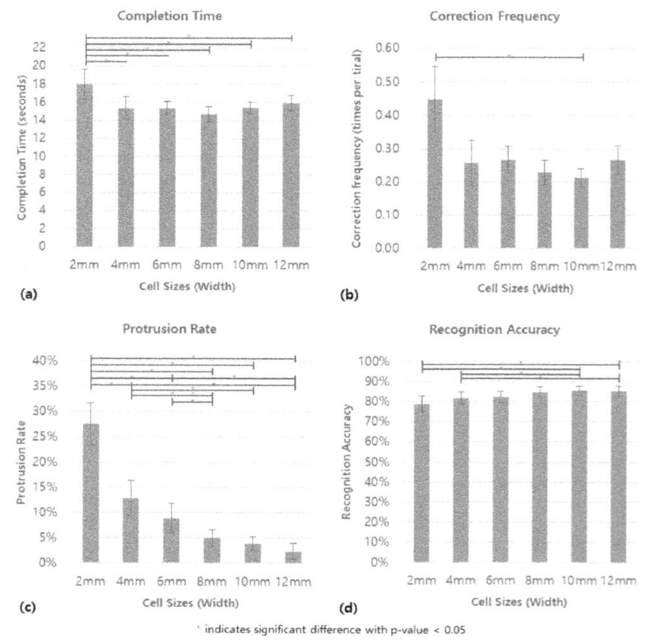

Figure 7. The four objective metrics in the preliminary experiment: (a) *CompletionTime*, (b) *CorrectionFrequency*, (c) *ProtrusionRate*, and (d) *RecognitionAccuracy*.

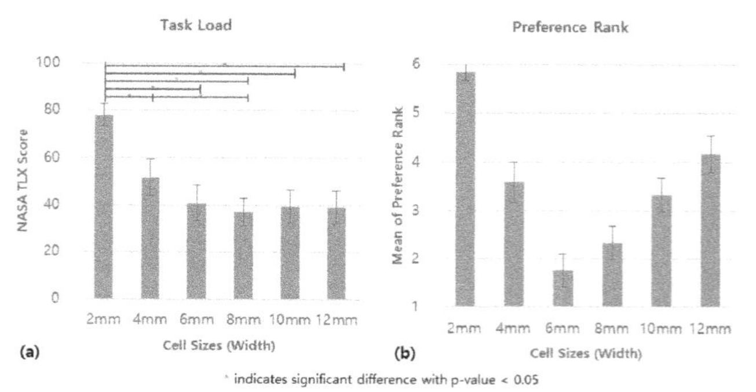

Figure 8. The two subjective metrics in the preliminary experiment.

Figure 8 shows changes in *TaskLoad* and *PreferenceRank* as the cell size changes. ANOVA after Aligned Rank Transform (ART) [20] showed that *CellSize* has a significant effect on *TaskLoad* ($F_{2.131,23.440}$ = 9.611, $p < 0.005$) and on *PreferenceRank* ($F_{2.353,25.888}$ = 16.723, $p < 0.001$). Post-hoc comparisons between all *CellSize* pairs were done and their results are shown on the graphs.

- *TaskLoad* decreases as *CellSize* increases, but its change is not statistically significant after *CellSize* reaches 6 mm. H2c is supported.

- There are significant differences between all pairs except between 6 mm and 8 mm ($p = 1.000$ for both); both 6 mm and 8 mm are most preferred.

In almost all aspects, 2 mm *CellSize* was significantly worse than others. The main conclusion was that no significant performance improvement was seen after 8 mm *CellSize*.

Discussion

All hypotheses were supported except H1b. H1b was not supported possibly because the maximum box size was not large enough to enable us to observe a negative effect of a large size on writing speed.

Ren et al. [13] suggested 12 mm x 14 mm as an optimal input box size for alphanumeric handwriting, which is different from our result. There may be many reasons for this difference. First, their writing environment was different. Their participants wrote on a PDA held in the hand, whereas our participants wrote on a large tablet resting the hand on it. Second, we fixed the aspect ratio of an input box at 5:9 in the early stage of the design, and this ratio was not considered in Ren et al.. Third, their participants wrote in two input boxes alternatingly, whereas our participants wrote in a series of input boxes, from left to right. In short, it is difficult to compare our conclusion with theirs.

The recognition accuracy results were in fact unexpectedly low. Using a per-letter analysis of recognition accuracy, we found that a significant portion of the errors were due to 'i' and 'j': the recognition accuracies for the two letters were both around 50%. This was because many participants tends to write the two letters in a non-standard stroke order. We could observe an accuracy improvement by about 5% in each size condition when we excluded 'i' and 'j' from the accuracy analysis.

MAIN EXPERIMENT

The goal of the experiment was comparing our DIPI and CIPI interfaces with an IW interface counterpart using form-filling tasks. We measured a few performance metrics including task completion time, and identified problems to be addressed in the future from observation and participant feedback.

Our hypotheses were as follows.

H1 Users will complete the form-filling tasks faster with the IPI interfaces than with the IW interface.

H2 Users will perceive less burden using the IPI interfaces.

H3 Users will prefer the IPI interfaces for the form-filling tasks.

Apparatus

We used Surface Pro 3 running Microsoft Windows 8.1. We blocked touch inputs in the input boxes of the IPI interfaces to prevent unintentional handwriting or command input by the hand. Touch inputs outside the input boxes were unaffected, and therefore one could use drag gestures to scroll the view.

We designed two forms, Form 1 and 2, in this experiment. Figure 9 and 11 show snapshots of the three different versions of Form 1 and 2 for the three interfaces. We chose the input cell size of DIPI at 8 mm x 14.4 mm based on the results of the preliminary experiment. The height of an input line in CIPI was set to be the same as that of the DIPI cell. We used the default handwriting IME for English in Windows 8.1 as an IW interface counterpart.

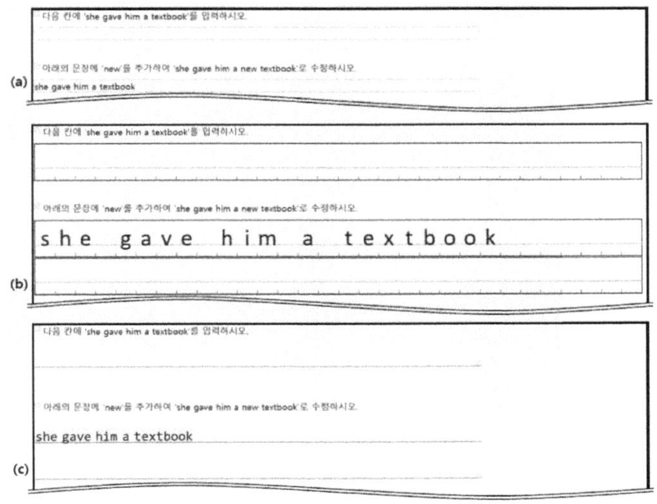

Figure 9. The snapshots of Form 1 (a) in the IW interface, (b) in the DIPI interface, and (c) in the CIPI interface.

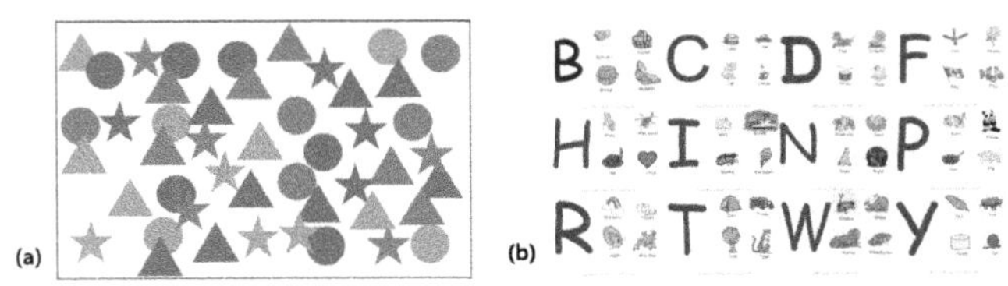

Figure 10. Example images (a) for the *CountObject* **task and (b) for the** *TranscribeWords* **task.**

Form 1 consists of four sections. The first section consists of a *EditText* task, which in turn consists of transcription, insertion, deletion, and modification subtasks around a short sentence. Figure 9 shows a *EditText* task. The second section consists of three *CountObject* tasks around a picture as shown in Figure 10a. A *CountObject* task is to count objects in a certain shape or in a certain color in a picture. The third section consists of three *EditText* tasks. The fourth section consists of three *TranscribeWords* tasks around a word table as shown in Figure 10b. A word table consists of 3 x 4 cells, and each cell contains a letter and four words (with pictures) starting with the letter. A *TranscribeWords* task is to write down three randomly chosen words from a specified card.

In a practice session, Form 1a was used. Form 1a is similar to Form 1, but was designed to provide more chances to practice text manipulation functions. The main difference of Form 1a is that the *EditText* task has copy-and-paste subtasks between transcription and insertion. A copy-and-paste subtask is to copy words in a given text and paste them to a target text box in a given order. For example, one has to copy and paste words from 'him she gave textbook a' to target box to make a sentence 'she gave him a textbook'. Another difference of Form 1a is that the third section has two *EditText* tasks instead of three.

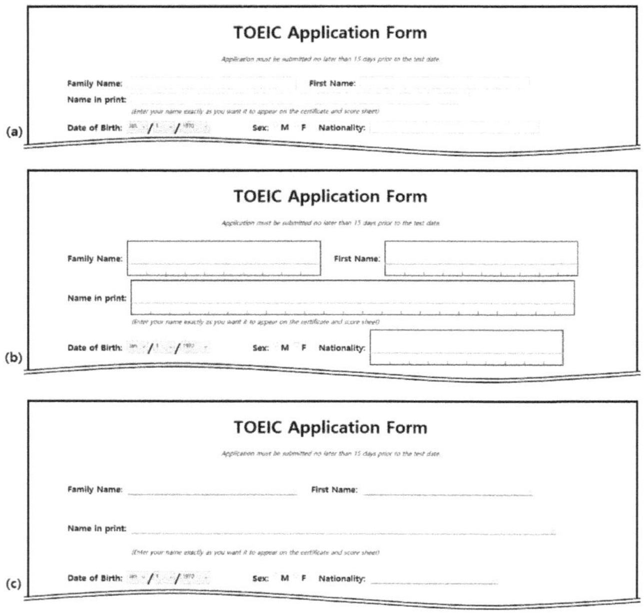

Figure 11. The snapshots of Form 2 (a) in the IW interface, (b) in the DIPI interface, and (c) in the CIPI interface.

Form 2 was designed after a TOEIC application form of a university (paper form). We replaced some of the fields in the form, such as date of birth, sex, and payment method, with non-text-box GUI components such as radio buttons and drop-down menus.

In both cases of Form 1 and 2, undo and redo buttons were always available at the top of the screen so that participants might easily recover from an error such as unintentional exit strokes.

Participants

Twelve participants (3 female, average age = 20.58 (SD = 2.07)) were recruited from our university. One of them was a graduate student and others were undergraduate students. All of them have engineering background and eight of them had a prior experience with handwriting text entry. None of them took part in Experiment 1. None of the participants were native English speakers, but their official language in class was English. They were more familiar with separate-letter writing than with joined-up (cursive) writing.

Design

The independent variable was *Technique* (IW, DIPI, and CIPI), and the experiment was a within-subject design. The order of the interface techniques was fully counter-balanced across participants using a Latin Square.

The dependent variables were *CompletionTime*1, *CompletionTime*2, *TextEntrySpeed*, *TaskLoad*, and *PreferenceRank*. *CompletionTime* 1 and 2 were the task completion times of Form 1 and 2, respectively. *TextEntrySpeed* was estimated using the completion time of the transcription subtask of the *EditText* task in Form 1. *TaskLoad* was measured using the NASA TLX test, and *PreferenceRank* was based on questionnaire answers.

Procedure

First, participants were given a brief introduction to the goal and procedure of the experiment. Next, they were allowed three minutes to find a comfortable posture. Next, the pen system was calibrated for individual participants. Finally, three experimental sessions for the three interfaces were repeated with 5 minute break between sessions.

Each session consisted of a practice block and a main block. In the practice block, participants were given an introduction to the interface and an instruction on how to finish each task in Form 1a, and then completed Form 1a. In the main block, they completed Form 1. The two blocks lasted approximately 25 and 20 minutes, respectively, and there was a 3 minutes break between the two blocks. After each session, participants answered a NASA TLX questionnaire.

After the three sessions, participants were answered a short questionnaire. The questionnaire consisted of 7-point Likert-scale questions about preferences for interfaces, a perceived recognition accuracy (*PerceivedAccuracy*), the convenience of text manipulation (*EditConvenience*), and ease of use (*EaseOfUse*) of each interface technique.

Result

Figure 12 shows *TextEntrySpeed*, *CompletionTime*1, and *CompletionTime*2 for each (*Technique*). Repeated measures ANOVA tests showed that *Technique* had no significant effect on *TextEntrySpeed* ($F_{1.282,14.106} = 2.611$, $p = 0.123$) or on *CompletionTime2* ($F_{2,22} = 3.081$, $p = 0.066$). On the other hand, *Technique* had a significant effect on *CompletionTime*1 ($F_{2,22} = 25.529$, $p < 0.001$). Post-hoc pairwise comparisons with Bonferroni correction indicated that (IW, CIPI) and (DIPI, CIPI) pairs in *CompletionTime*1 were significantly different ($p < 0.001$ for both).

Figure 13 shows the NASA TLX results for each *Techniques*. Repeated measures ANOVA tests after ART showed that *Technique* had no significant effect on the total score ($F_{2,22} = 3.152$, $p = 0.063$), but had a significant effect on *MentalDemand* ($F_{2,22} = 5.473$, $p < 0.05$) and on *PhysicalDemand* ($F_{2,22} = 5.672$, $p < 0.05$). Post-hoc pairwise comparisons with Bonferroni correction indicated that the (IW, DIPI) and (DIPI, CIPI) pairs were significantly different in *MentalDemand*. However, there was no significant difference in *PhysicalDemand* between any pairs.

Figure 14 shows the results of usability questions and mean preference ranks for each *Techniques*. Repeated measures ANOVA tests after ART showed that *Technique* had a significant effect on *PerceivedAccuracy* ($F_{2,22} = 9.689$, $p < 0.005$), on *EaseOfUse*($F_{2,22} = 7.646$, $p < 0.005$), and on

$PreferenceRank$ ($F_{2,22} = 8.084$, $p < 0.005$), but had no significant effect on $EditConvenience$ ($F_{1.378,15.161} = 3.003$, $p = 0.094$). Post-hoc pairwise comparison with Bonferroni correction indicated that the (IW, DIPI) pair was significantly different in $PerceivedAccuracy$, and the (IW, DIPI) and (DIPI, CIPI) pairs were significantly different in $PreferenceRank$. However, there was no significant difference in $EaseOfUse$ between any pairs.

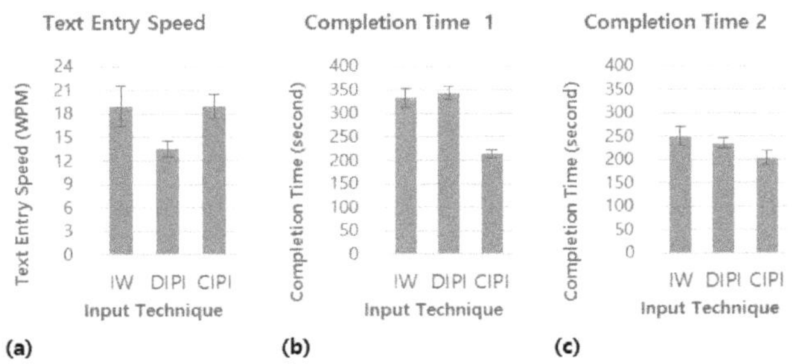

Figure 12. The objective metrics of the main experiment: (a) $TextEntrySpeed$**, (b)** $CompletionTime1$**, and (c)** $CompletionTime2$**, for each** $Technique$**.**

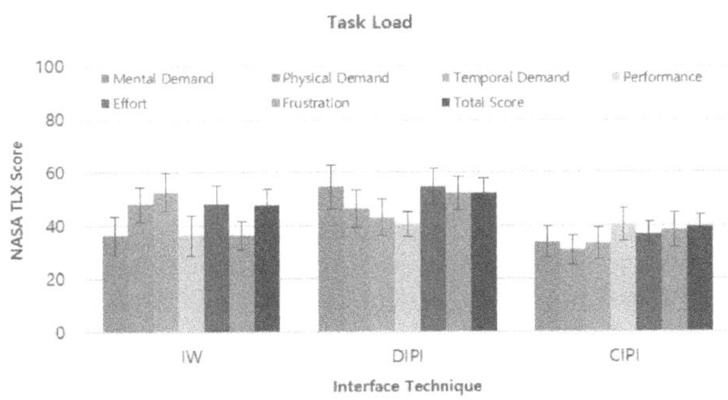

Figure 13. The NASA TLX results of the main experiment.

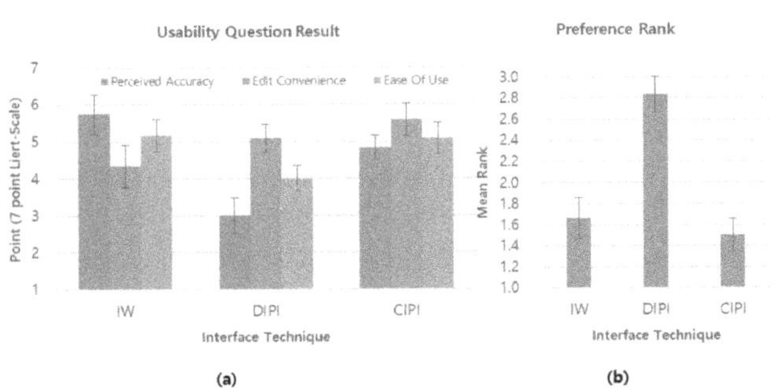

Figure 14. The questionnaire results of the main experiment: (a) usability questions and (b) $PreferenceRank$

All participants commented that the DIPI interface had the lowest recognition accuracy, and eight of them commented that the boxed style of DIPI was annoying. Five participants commented that text manipulation was more convenient while using the IPI interfaces. Five participants commented that correcting recognition errors was much more convenient while using the IW interface. Three participants commented that the indirectness of IW was cumbersome. Two participants commented that the IW interface occluded too much portion of the display, but one of them also commented that the IW interface was better for writing text because it allows writing in larger letters.

Discussion

The CIPI interface was significantly faster than the IW interface in terms of $CompletionTime1$, but the difference in $TextEntrySpeed$ between the two interfaces was not significant. This may mean that the CIPI interface was faster than the IW interface mainly due to its directness, which could support more efficient text manipulation and better integration of writing and GUI operations.

The DIPI interface was worst in terms of almost all performance metrics. The main reason may be that DIPI is based on letter-wise writing and recognition, whereas CIPI and IW are based on line-wise writing and recognition. In fact, the majority of the participants commented that the boxed styles of the DIPI interface was annoying. It seems that letter-wise writing interface should be avoided whenever possible. The main trend of pen computing is also in favor of line-wise interfaces. Letter-wise interfaces were the main stream until a decade ago, but have been replaced by line-wise interfaces with the advances in the handwriting recognition technology.

The perceive recognition accuracy of the DIPI interface was significantly lower than that of other interfaces. This result may sound counter-intuitive because the input boxes of DIPI may encourage participants to write more clearly in separate letters. This result may be due to the way the DIPI interface recognize inputs and present recognition results. The DIPI interface tries to recognize strokes in a box as soon as a stroke is entered in the next box. It uses a word-level recognizer, but tries to recognize incomplete words, and may present wrong recognition results until a complete word is entered. The intermediate wrong recognition feedback must have given a negative impression to participants even though the actual recognition accuracy might not be different from that of the CIPI interface.

GENERAL DISCUSSION

One of the main goals of the current study was to show the directness benefit of the IPI interfaces in comparison with the IW interface, but the IW interface that we used in the main experiment was not only different in directness but also in many other aspects from the IPI interfaces. For instance, the IW interface, as a mature commercial product, supports rich markup style gestures for text manipulation, whereas the CIPI interface does not provide such letter-level editing functions. This difference was actually mentioned often in the experiment by the participants, and one of the main reasons for preferring the IW interface was in fact this difference. For a more controlled study, we had to design and implement our own IW interface that is as similar as possible to the IPI interfaces except for the directness aspect of the interface. It is desired to include both our own IW interface and an external IW implementation in a future comparison study for more controlled experiment and also for external validity.

We could learn many insights for the future directions of the IPI interfaces from the experiment results and user observations in the experiment. One of the clear lessons was the superiority of the CIPI interface over the DIPI interface, and therefore the CIPI interface will be with our future. The CIPI interface as it is has very limited functionalities because it was developed for a very early exploration. We will add more functionalities to the CIPI interface to make it a usable interface. For example, the CIPI interface will have functions for editing recognition results letter-wise as the IW interface that we used in the main experiment does. For another example, the CIPI interface will have functions for manipulating white-spaces between words; the current CIPI design does not have functions for adding a new line character or multiple consecutive spaces between words.

CONCLUSION

In order to explore the potential of the IPI interfaces, we designed two example designs, the DIPI and CIPI interfaces, and evaluated them in comparison with an IW interface in a series of user experiments. Some of the main results of the experiments follow. 1) CIPI showed a significantly lower completion time for the Form 1 task than others. 2) DIPI required significantly higher mental demand. 3) DIPI were least preferred and IW and CIPI were comparable. The experience of designing the two IPI interfaces and evaluating them with participants enabled us to have a better insight into the future directions of the IPI interfaces. Immediate future work is to improve the CIPI interface based on what we learned from the current study, and evaluate it with a more ecologically valid tasks.

ACKNOWLEDGEMENTS

This work was supported by Hancom Inc. Its intellectual property rights reserved by KAIST and Hancom.

REFERENCES

1. Bouteruche, F., Deconde, G., Anquetil, E., and Jamet, E. Design and evaluation of handwriting input interfaces for small-size mobile devices In *Proc. of the Workshop on Improving and Assessing Pen-Based Input Techniques* (2005), 49-56.
2. Chang, L., and MacKenzie, I. S. A comparison of two handwriting recognizers for pen-based computers. In *Proc. of CASCR'94*, IBM Press (1994), 9.
3. Frankish, C., Hull, R., and Morgan, P. Recognition accuracy and user acceptance of pen interfaces. In *Proc. CHI'95*, ACM Press. (1995), 503–510.
4. Gao, Q., Zhu, B., Rau, P.-L. P., Vyas, S., Chen, C., and Li, H. User experience with chinese handwriting input on touch-screen mobile phones. In *Cross-Cultural Design. Methods, Practice, and Case Studies*. Springer. (2013), 384–392.
5. Goldberg, D., and Richardson, C. Touch-typing with a stylus. In *Proc. INTERACT'93 and CHI'93*, ACM (1993), 80–87.
6. Goodisman, A. *A Stylus-Based User Interface for Text: Entry and Editing*. PhD thesis, MIT, Dept. of Electrical Engineering and Computer Science, 1991.
7. Huerst, W., Yang, J., and Waibel, A. Interactive error repair for an online handwriting interface. In *Proc. CHI'98*, ACM (1998), 353–354.
8. Kim, J., and Sin, B.-K. Online handwriting recognition. In *Handbook of Document Image Processing and Recognition*. Springer, 2014, 887–915.
9. Kristensson, P. O., and Denby, L. C. Text entry performance of state of the art unconstrained handwriting recognition: a longitudinal user study. In *Proc. CHI'09*, ACM (2009), 567–570.
10. LaLomia, M. User acceptance of handwritten recognition accuracy. In *Proc. CHI'94*, ACM (1994), 107–108.
11. MacKenzie, I. S., and Soukoreff, R. W. Phrase sets for evaluating text entry techniques. In *Proc. the CHIEA'03* , ACM (2003), 754–755.
12. Mankoff, J., Hudson, S. E., and Abowd, G. D. Interaction techniques for ambiguity resolution in recognition-based interfaces. In *Proc. UIST'00*, ACM (2000), 11–20.
13. Ren, X., and Zhou, X. The optimal size of handwriting character input boxes on pdas. *Intl. Journal of Human–Computer Interaction 25*, 8 (2009), 762–784.
14. Santos, P. J., Baltzer, A. J., Badre, A. N., Henneman, R. L., and Miller, M. S. On handwriting recognition system performance: Some experimental results. In *Proceedings of the Human Factors and Ergonomics Society Annual Meeting*, vol. 36, SAGE Publications (1992), 283–287.
15. Schomaker, L. From handwriting analysis to pen-computer applications. *Electronics & Communication Engineering Journal 10*, 3 (1998), 93–102.
16. Shilman, M., Tan, D. S., and Simard, P. Cuetip: a mixed-initiative interface for correcting handwriting errors. In *Proc. UIST'06*, ACM (2006), 323–332.
17. Top Image Systems. Guidelines for census form design, 2008. [Online; accessed 22-September-2015].
18. Wikipedia. Graffiti (palm os) (2015) [Online; accessed 22-September-2015].
19. Wikipedia. Windows for pen computing (2015) [Online; accessed 22-September-2015].
20. Wobbrock, J. O., Findlater, L., Gergle, D., and Higgins, J. J. The aligned rank transform for nonparametric factorial analyses using only anova procedures. In *Proc. CHI'11*, ACM (2011), 143–146.
21. Wobbrock, J. O., Myers, B. A., and Kembel, J. A. Edgewrite: a stylus-based text entry method designed for high accuracy and stability of motion. In *Proc. UIST'03*, ACM (2003), 61–70.

ShadowHands: High-Fidelity Remote Hand Gesture Visualization using a Hand Tracker

Erroll Wood[1,2] **Jonathan Taylor**[1] **John Fogarty**[1] **Andrew Fitzgibbon**[1] **Jamie Shotton**[1]

[1]Microsoft [2]University of Cambridge

ABSTRACT

This paper presents *ShadowHands* – a novel technique for visualizing a remote user's hand gestures using a single depth sensor and hand tracking system. Previous work has shown that making distributed users better aware of each other's gestures facilitates remote collaboration. These systems presented virtual embodiments as a stream of raw 2D or 3D data – this data is noisy, and requires high bandwidth and favorable camera positions. Instead, our work uses a hand tracker to capture gestures which we visualize with a high-fidelity hand model. Our system is practical, requiring only a single depth sensor placed below the screen, and can be used without per-user calibration. As we use a 3D model rather than raw data, we can augment the hand's appearance to improve saliency and aesthetics. We alpha-blend this visualization over a shared workspace, so the local user perceives the remote user's hand as if they were separated by a transparent display. We conducted an experiment to compare traditional hand embodiments with our new technique, showing a quantitative improvement in selection accuracy and qualitative improvements in feelings of mutual understanding and engagement.

Author Keywords

Remote Collaboration; Hand Gestures; Hand Tracking

ACM Classification Keywords

H.5.3 Group and Organization Interfaces: Computer-supported cooperative work

INTRODUCTION

During remote collaboration, the remote user is often portrayed with a virtual embodiment. Popular systems, e.g. Skype, generally display only a video of the collaborator's face, either adjacent to or super-imposed onto the shared workspace. Improving upon this has been a research goal for some time, and previous work has shown that more advanced embodiments such as "phantom" hand visualizations [9] or whole-body 3D representations [23] can improve cooperation. These allow the communication of important visual cues including hand gestures, eye gaze, and facial expressions. As a result, collaborators are able to understand each other better, and make their actions and intentions clear.

ISS 2016, November 6–9, 2016, Niagara Falls, ON, Canada.

ACM ISBN 978-1-4503-4248-3/16/11 ...$15.00.
http://dx.doi.org/10.1145/2992154.2992169

Figure 1: A remote user guiding a collaborator through an inking task using ShadowHands (white 3d hand model), visualized on top of a shared workspace.

In this work we present *ShadowHands* – a novel technique for visualizing remote hand gestures. Using a hand tracking system, we capture the gestures of a remote user, and render them onto a shared digital workspace. The virtual hand is presented as if the distributed users are separated by a transparent display (Figure 1). Embodiments in previous work used *image-based* techniques – portraying gestures through streams of 2D images or 3D depth data. Despite careful segmentation and post-processing, this data is noisy and requires high bandwidth to transmit. Instead, our approach is *model-based* – we use a state-of-the-art system to track hands in real-time, and reconstruct them by cleanly rendering a posed 3D hand model. These gestures can then be efficiently encoded in a handful of pose parameters, rather than a dense image representation. Furthermore, while previous systems require complex hardware setups including multiple favorably positioned sensors, our approach requires only a single commodity depth camera placed below the screen.

Comparing the effects of different embodiments is an under-researched problem [4]. We conducted an experiment to compare ShadowHands to two alternative embodiments: a point cloud of RGB-D data [23, 6] and a simple lazer pointer. Participants cooperated to complete three tasks: a pointing task, a maze solving task, and a house sketching task. Results showed that our ShadowHands visualization led to fewer selection errors than the point cloud, and was considered easier to use and less distracting. In summary, the contributions of this work are threefold: i) a novel 3D visualization technique that tracks and portrays hand gestures with high-fidelity: they are noise-free, aesthetically pleasing, and visually salient. ii) a simple and flexible hardware setup that uses a single depth camera, and can work with both small and large displays. iii) a study that compared ShadowHands with previous visualization techniques, demonstrating both the quantitative and qualitative benefits of our approach.

RELATED WORK

Facilitating better awareness between distributed users has been a challenge in computer supported cooperative work (CSCW) research for some time. Gestures enhance communication in two main ways: they are either *expressive* – aiding speech production and interpretation, or *deictic* – referring to objects or a task at hand [18]. So if we don't allow users to produce or observe guestures, collaboration may suffer.

Virtual hand embodiments

Early CSCW research identified the importance of being able to see the remote user. VideoDraw [19] and Clearboard [8] presented remote collaborators as if they were on the other side of a shared interactive surface. These systems streamed videos of a remote user's hands, face, and body under a local workspace, allowing users to collaborate in drawing tasks. However, bulky and impractical hardware setups were required to capture and transmit video, and it was found that simply overlaying digital ink over a user's video feed was distracting [8]. Following work addressed these issues, using modern equipment and computer vision to relax hardware requirements and display improved visualizations.

VideoArms [18], DigiTable [2], and T3 [21] used webcams and simple computer vision techniques to transmit videos of a user's arms as they interacted in video conferencing scenarios. These 2D image-based systems segmented arm images from the background in a video, allowing them to be selectively composited onto a shared digital workspace. For DigiTable this involved a geometric and photometric analysis of the display-facing video feed, segementing out hand pixels that could not be mapped onto the displayed image. C-Slate [9, 1] proposed an alternative low-cost solution that used polarization filters for segmenting the hands for a *phantom presence* visualization. The hand-to-screen distance was also used to modulate the visualization's transparency and bluriness, mitigating occlusion issues and providing an additional channel for communication.

The introduction of commoditity RGB-D sensors [22] and body tracking [16] has allowed researchers to extend these 2D image-based embodiments to 3D, representing a remote user with a stream of 3D point cloud data. 3D-Board [23] is a wall-sized system that presents a 3D image-based embodiment of a whole user, conveying their eye gaze, facial expresssions, and hand gestures. The remote user is rendered locally by fusing together multiple RGB-D streams from two Kinects mounted above the screen. Immserseboard [6] explored novel visualization styles for the whole body, rendering the remote user as if they were writing side-by-side with the local user, or on a shared mirror. Both these systems reported limitations in terms of the 3D image quality. To improve upon this, Zillner et al. [23] proposed improved noise filtering techniques, and

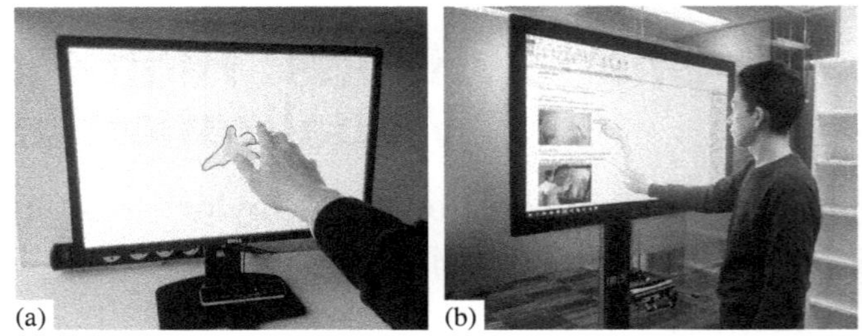

Figure 2: ShadowHands can be deployed on screens both small, 24-inch (a); and large, 55-inch (b).

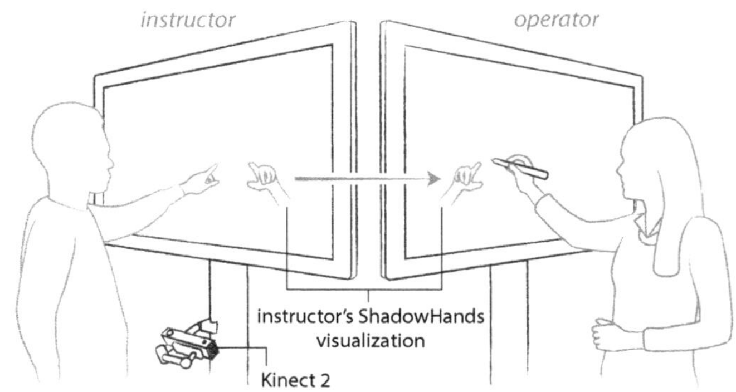

Figure 3: A remote *instructor* performs hand gestures which are tracked using our system and a Kinect V2. The ShadowHands visualization is then blended onto the *operator*'s workspace, who conducts a task using their interactive display.

Higuchi et al. [6] proposed using better quality sensors. Another solution is to cleanly render 3D body models instead of noisy depth data – we examine this approach in our work.

Comparing different embodiments

Though virtual arm embodiments are a common feature of remote collaboration systems in research, there has been little work on directly comparing different types of visualization. [14, 4]. Doucette et al. [4] compared several different hand embodiments: a thin line, 2D shadows, and stretched 2D arm photos. Interestingly, they found that increasing the "level of realism" of the hand embodiment had no effect, though increasing the embodiment's thickness made people better aware of their partner. This suggests that visual prominence is an important factor for collaboration, while realism may not be. However, this study was limited in that it only examined 2D embodiments – it is unclear if these results generalize to the 3D visualizations that are common nowadays.

THE SHADOWHANDS SYSTEM

ShadowHands is a new visualization technique for hand gestures that addresses the limitations of previous work, while relaxing the hardware requirements. We provide a noise-free, visually salient, and aesthetically pleasing hand embodiment, requiring only a single depth camera placed below a screen. To create the impression of looking through a transparent display, we first capture the hand movements of one user using a hand tracker, render these using a 3D model, and finally alpha-blend

Figure 4: The ShadowHands visualization process: Data from the depth sensor (a) is processed by our hand tracker, producing a coarse 3D hand model (b). We then smooth the model using subdivision, shade it with image-based lighting (c), and add black outlines (d). Additionally, our hand pose information allows us to provide alternate stylized visualizations (e).

the rendered image onto both users' screens. In this section we describe the the core components of the ShadowHands system, and the hardware that drives them.

Apparatus

Our hardware setup is practical, requiring only a single depth camera placed below the screen. As can be seen in Figure 2, ShadowHands can be used with both small and large displays. We used an Intel RealSense [7] for close-range desktop operation, or a Kinect V2 [12] for longer-range digital whiteboard use. This paper focusses on the large display scenario: two distributed users collaborating using digital whiteboards.

Figure 3 shows the large screen ShadowHands setup. We use two 55-inch displays: 1) a passive display for a remote instuctor, and 2) an interactive display for a local operator. During our studies, both large displays were situated next to each other, back-to-back. This separated the users so they could not see each other, though they could still hear each other. For convenience, both displays were driven by a single PC which performed both the hand tracking and rendering (3.5GHz CPU, 8 GB memory, K2000 GPU).

Hand tracking

We use a state-of-the-art hand tracker to recover the pose of a user's hand from depth data. It uses machine learning for initialization and recovery; and iterative model-fitting optimization for precise pose and shape alignment. For each input depth frame, the tracker: 1) pre-processes the data to locate the hand, 2) generates a set of initial pose hypotheses, 3) optimizes a smooth fitting energy for each hypothesis, and 4) returns the hand pose that fit best. It can track hands up to several meters away, and is robust against sensor noise. It runs in real time on the CPU only, freeing up the GPU for rendering ShadowHands visualizations in high detail. For more details on the hand tracker, please see previous work [20, 10, 15].

Rendering ShadowHands

We implemented a number of graphics techniques to provide a high-fidelity visualization that was both aesthetically pleasing and visually salient. The output of our hand tracker is a posed mesh of 520 vertices in camera-space (Figure 4b). To create the illusion of viewing the other user's hand in front of them, we first use the camera's intrinsic and extrinsic calibration to re-project this hand mesh as if it were seen from a fixed point 50cm from the centre of the screen.

If visualized directly, this low-resolution mesh would appear unnaturally sharp and blocky, so we instead render a smoothed subdivided mesh (Figure 4c) that better represents the smooth surface of skin. This smoothed mesh is derived by applying two steps of Loop subdivision [11] to the tracked hand mesh. We quickly discovered that users had strong opinions about the appearance of their virtual hands. We therefore experimented with a number of different rendering techniques, including realistic high-resolution skin textures and artistic sketch-style effects. We settled on a clean "toon-style" rendering that users found aesthetically pleasing (Figure 4d), using image-based lighting [3] to illuminate the model. We wanted different hand gestures to be easily identifiable against different workspace backgrounds, so we added black strokes to the outlines of the hand and fingers (Figure 4d). These strokes were added with a post-process: we detected outlines (or edges) as image-space discontinuities in surface normals and depth by filtering with a Laplacian kernel ∇^2 [5].

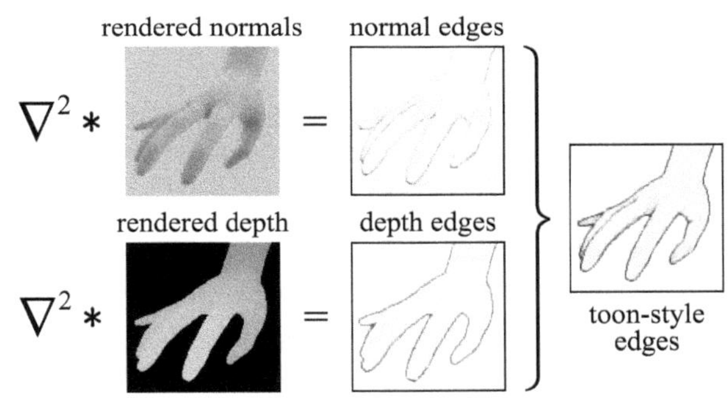

Figure 5 show the improved visual saliency of ShadowHands compared to rendering processed RGB-D sensor data, as done by previous work [23, 6]. This is especially apparent for poses where the sensor cannot see parts of the hand (Figure 5b), or when the RGB sensor is over or under-exposed in difficult lighting conditions (Figure 5c). See the experiment section for details of our sensor data visualizaiton.

Additionally, as our tracker outputs hand pose information in the form of finger-joint angles, we can easily re-pose alternative models to target a user's gestures. This allows for playful communication with non-traditional embodiments e.g. a skeleton hand (Figure 4e) – something that would not be possible without the hand pose data from the hand tracker. All graphics effects were implemented with DirectX.

Blending onto a workspace

The ShadowHands visualization is displayed in a transparent window that appears on top of all other desktop windows.

In this way, it can be used with any other software. While previous work displayed virtual embodiments with a fixed opacity [23], we instead provide a depth-cue by varying the opacity of different parts of the hand model based on their tracked depth. This is done by applying depth-based per-pixel alpha blending in a pixel shader.

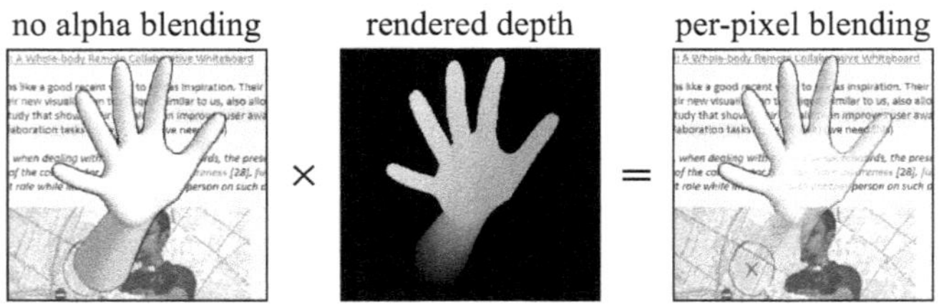

We initially render all our 3D geometry with 100% opacity, and then scale the alpha channel for each pixel based on distance to the screen. So a pixel for a finger touching the screen (0cm away) would appear fully opaque ($\alpha = 1.0$), while a forearm pixel 50cm away or more would appear fully transparent ($\alpha = 0.0$). This allows users to control how visible their gestures are: they can draw attention to themselves by gesturing close to the screen; or remove themselves from a discussion by withdrawing away from the screen. Additionally, this prevents the hand visualization from fully obscuring what's underneath it – this can be inconvenient if the remote user is trying to read their screen under the visualization. These transparent window effects were implemented with WINAPI [13].

EXPERIMENT

We conducted an experiment with three tasks to compare our ShadowHands visualization with techniques used in previous work. We focussed on large interactive screen collaboration scenarios, like those between two meeting rooms in two different places. For each experiment we used the same apparatus and compared the same set of virtual hand embodiments.

Participants 14 volunteers (6 male, 8 female) from a universtiy and research lab participated in the experiment, with average age 29.2 ± 4.07[1]. The participants performed all tasks in pairs, with one participant (the remote *instructor*) giving guidance to the other (the local *operator*). The instructors used hand gestures and their voice to give commands, and the operators interpreted these and acted accordingly. 86% of participants reported that they often used video conferencing software for remote collaboration as part of their work. 21% were familiar with large interactive touch screens, and 36% were familiar with hand tracking systems.

Embodiments We compared the effects of using three different virtual hand embodiments:

1. *ShadowHands*: Our high-fidelity tracked hand model.
2. *Point cloud*: This technique was chosen as a comparison to previous work [23, 6]. Similarly to 3D-Board [23], we project the camera's depth image into world space using its intrinsic and extrinsic parameters. Each 3D point is then expanded into a hexagon using a geometry shader, colored using the camera's color image, and rendered from the same virtual camera as ShadowHands. Using tracking information, we only display data from the segmented hand region to reduce background clutter. Furthermore, we median filter the raw RGB-D data to reduce noise.
3. *Laser pointer*: A small red dot in the style of a laser pointer, similar to that used for gesturing in presentation software. This dot was made to follow the user's index finger using the hand tracker.

[1]Results are reported as MEAN ± STD.DEV.

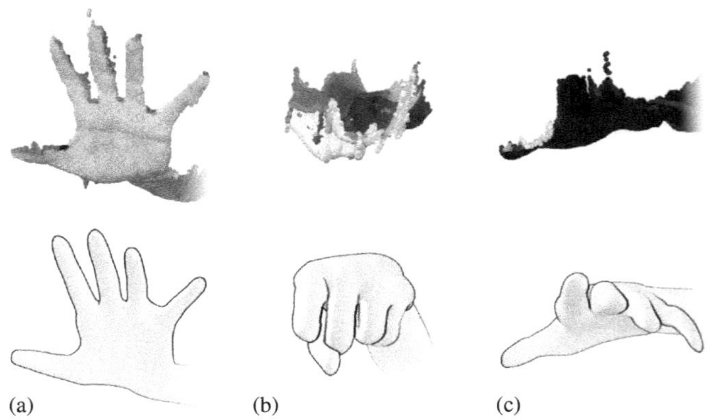

Figure 5: A comparison between rendering RGB-D sensor data (top row), and ShadowHands (bottom row). RGB-D data can be ambiguous for certain hand poses (b) or difficult underexposed lighting conditions (c).

Procedure At the beginning of the session, both participants filled out a pre-study questionnaire on their prior experience with remote collaboration, and the hardware and software used in the experiment. They then performed three tasks: 1) a pointing task, 2) a maze solving task, and 3) a house sketching task. The instructor and operator experienced asymmetric views of each task, so the solution or goal was always visible to the instructor, who had to communicate this to the operator. Before each task, the participants were given as much time as they desired to practice each embodiment as both instructor and operator. The order of embodiments was counterbalanced to reduce learning effects. For the first two tasks, half the participants were operator first, and half the participants were instructor first. After these three tasks were completed, the participants filled out a post-study questionnaire which measured their attitudes towards each different embodiment. The experiment took about an hour to complete in total.

Task 1: Target selection

In the first part of the experiment we investigated the performance characteristics of different embodiments when guiding a user through an abstracted pointing task (Figure 6). This task was chosen to see if ShadowHands provided any improvements for task selection over previous embodiments.

Task design

This task involved the instructor guiding the operator to select circular targets in an 8×8 grid. Before each trail, all targets started off unselected. On beginning the trail, a randomized set of targets in a line chain were highlighted for the instructor

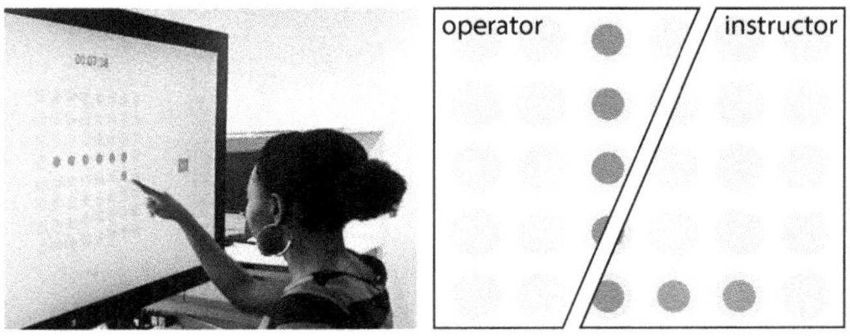

Figure 6: Pointing task: this task involved the operator selecting targets from a grid. The instructor was presented with the candidates for selection, and had to communicate these to the operator using hand gestures only.

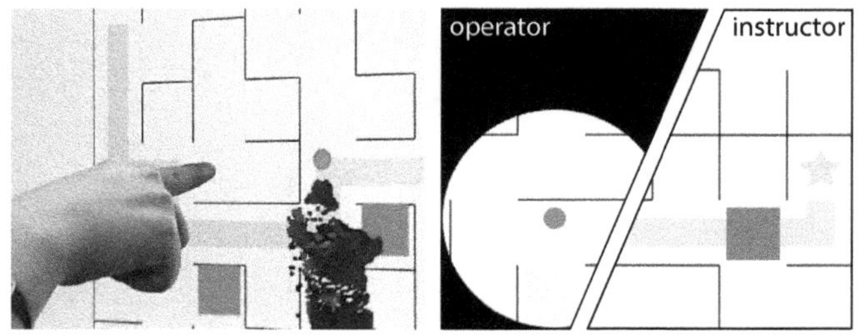

Figure 7: Maze task: the instructor sees the whole maze and must guide the operator through it using guestures and voice. The operator only sees a small region of the maze.

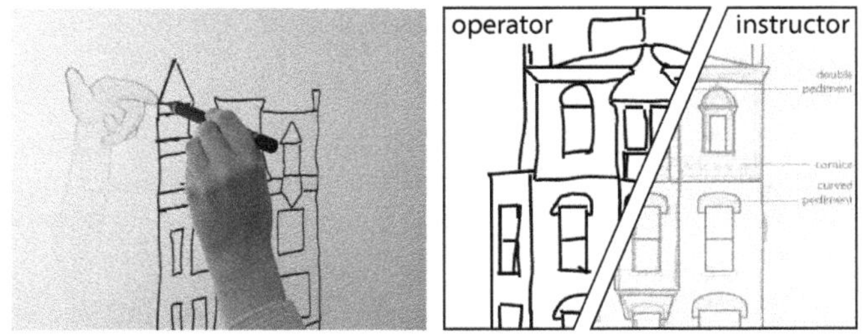

Figure 8: Drawing task: the instructor was presented with a target house design, and the operator was given a plain canvas and a sketching interface. The instructor's goal was to guide the operator so they replicated the target design.

only, marking them as candidates for selection. The instructor then pointed these targets out to the operator, who selected them by touching them. The correct and incorrect selections were visible to the instructor. The participants were told to complete each trial as quickly as possible and were not allowed to talk during this experiment. We measured completion time and selection errors over ten trials for each different embodiment. Once the first operator had completed ten selection trials for each embodiment, the two participants swapped roles and the second operator completed another full set of trials – ten for each embodiment.

Results

Average completion times were 7.05s $\pm$ 1.91s for ShadowHands, 7.31s $\pm$ 2.09s for point cloud, and 7.23s $\pm$ 2.76s for laser pointer. Wilcoxon signed-rank tests showed no significant differences between times for ShadowHands and point cloud ($Z=4247.5, p=0.15$), ShadowHands and laser pointer ($Z=4485.0, p=0.35$), and point cloud and laser pointer ($Z=4138.0, p=0.10$). On average there were 7.10 ± 1.61 targets per trial. Total selection errors were measured as false positives + false negatives. Average errors per trial were 0.41 ± 1.09 for ShadowHands, 0.77 ± 0.12 for point cloud, and 0.21 ± 0.56 for laser pointer. A two-way ANOVA was conducted on the influence of independent variables (embodiment, role) on the number of errors made. The main effect for embodiment type yielded $F(2,414)=7.26, p<0.001$, showing significant effect. The main effect for participant role yielded $F(1,414)=2.18, p=0.14$, indicating that it was not significant whether participants were operator or instructor first. Wilcoxon signed-ranks tests showed that the point cloud resulted in more errors than ShadowHands ($Z=463.0, p<0.05$) and the laser pointer ($Z=328.0, p<0.001$). No significant difference in error rate was found between ShadowHands and the laser pointer ($Z=435.0, p=0.15$).

Task 2: Maze solving

In the second part of the experiment we examined how hand embodiments were used during a maze solving game (Figure 7). This task was chosen to see if ShadowHands helped instructors communicate spatial and temporal guidance.

Task design

In this task the instructor guided the operator through a randomly generated maze with moving hazard objects. The goal of the operator was to move a blue dot through the maze to touch a gold star, without hitting any red hazards on the way. If the operator collided with a hazard, they were moved backwards in the maze. The instructor and operator experienced asymmetric views: the instructor could see the entire maze while the operator could only see a small region around the blue dot. The participants completed three mazes for each different embodiment. As in the previous task, once the first operator completed three mazes for each embodiment, the participants swapped roles and the second operator completed a further three mazes for each embodiment. We measured maze completion time and hazard collision rate.

Results

Average maze completion times were: 29.9s $\pm$ 15.4s for ShadowHands, 31.7s $\pm$ 12.0s for the point cloud, and 28.7 $\pm$ 16.3s for the laser pointer. Wilcoxon signed-rank tests showned no significant differences between times for ShadowHands and laser pointer ($Z=335.0, p=0.15$), ShadowHands and point cloud ($Z=391.0, p=0.45$), and point cloud and laser pointer ($Z=287.0, p=0.05$). Hazard collision rate per trial was measured as the number of collisions / number of hazards. Average collision rates were 0.54 ± 0.56 for ShadowHands, 0.37 ± 0.43 for the point cloud, and 0.53 ± 0.47 for the laser pointer. Wilcoxon signed-rank tests showned no significant differences between collision rates for ShadowHands and laser pointer ($Z=32.5, p=0.18$), ShadowHands and point cloud ($Z=28.0, p=0.17$), and point cloud and laser pointer ($Z=25.0, p=0.78$).

Figure 9: Three sketches of the same house design done by different participants. Note that some participants ran out of time before they could finish a sketch (middle sketch).

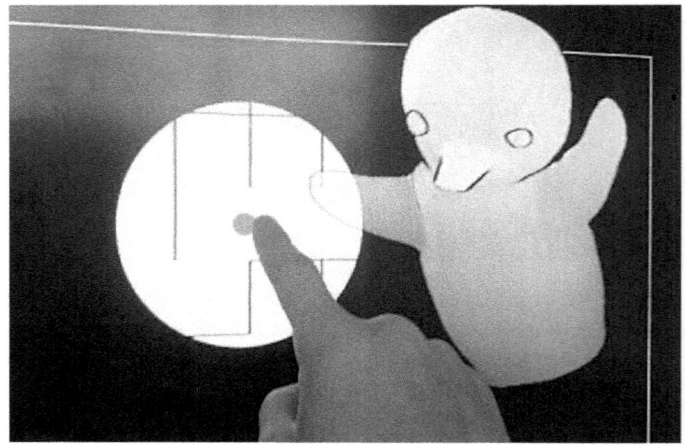

Figure 11: An example of emergent behaviour: some participants role-played using hand puppet visualizations.

Task 3: Sketching a house design

The final task was a collaborative sketching exercise. This task was chosen as we wanted to see how hand embodiments might be used in a more complex and realistic remote collaboration scenario.

Task design

As shown in Figure 8, this task involved sketching a house design. The participants role played as an architect (the operator) being guided through a house design process by a client (the instructor). The instructor was shown an annotated target house design that they communicated to the operator using voice and gestures, while the operator was shown a blank canvas, and was asked to sketch a house design as guided by the instructor. The goal was for the operator's sketch to end up as close as possible to the target design. Four different house designs of the same style [17] were chosen – one to practice on and one for each different embodiment. The participants completed one design per embodiment, and were given a 5 minute time limit for each design. Given the time required, and to prevent fatigue, the participants did not swap roles.

Results

All participants took the maximum time available for each trail. Some examples of the resulting house design sketches can be seen in Figure 9.

Qualitative feedback

Following these tasks, the participants filled out a post-study questionnaire. This included 5-point Likert scale questions to gauge their attitudes towards the different embodiments, and free-form text fields where they could elaborate on what they liked or disliked. The responses to the Likert scale questions can be seen in Figure 10. Significance was measured using the Mann-Whitney U-test.

ShadowHands received positive feedback concerning its appearance – participants found it *"visually appealing"* and appreciated that it *"blended well with the background"*. They reported ShadowHands was *"clear and easy to follow"*, and found it less distracting than the Point Cloud ($U = 158.5, p < 0.005$). The biggest issue with ShadowHands was hand tracking failure – *"when it works, it's super, but I feel like half the time that did not happen"*. 43% of participants reported some level of issue with tracking, ranging from minor glitches (*"sometimes switches from showing only the index finger to two fingers"*) to serious frequent tracking failure (*"hand gesture often wrong"*). Despite this, most participants still found it easy to make themselves understood.

Using the point cloud, participants found it harder to make themselves understood compared to ShadowHands ($U = 44.5, p < 0.005$) or the laser pointer ($U = 39.0, p < 0.005$). As instructors, they found themselves awkwardly positioning their hands *"to get into a shape that would be easily understood by the operator"*, for example, positioning their hand *"away from [their] finger for it to be seen"*. Operators reported that it was *"often hard to see where the hand actually is pointing"*, and were confused by the unnatural hand gestures – *"it was hard to tell which was the thumb and/or index finger"*. Furthermore, they complained that the point cloud visualization was distracting – *"I did not like that it was so pixelated and easily dissolved"*. They therefore found it harder to understand point cloud gestures compared to ShadowHands ($U = 28.5, p < 0.001$) or the laser pointer ($U = 30.0, p < 0.001$). Some participants appreciated that the point cloud was *"predictable"* and did not exhibit tracking glitches like ShadowHands.

The laser pointer was a popular technique, with most participants finding it easy to use and understand – *"it was very easy to follow"*. However, some participants felt they missed out on more complex signals – *"there was no way to signal other intentions than an exact point"*. While they liked that the pointer was precise, some participants found it was easy to obscure (*"I kept obscuring the pointer with my finger"*) or lose track of (*"it was hard to locate"*). The biggest complaint was that the laser pointer felt *"impersonal"*, with fewer participants feeling a sense of engagement compared to ShadowHands ($U = 46.0, p < 0.01$).

Emergent behaviour

We were interested in discovering if ShadowHands afforded any communication techniques that we did not expect. The maze and sketching tasks were therefore designed to be fun

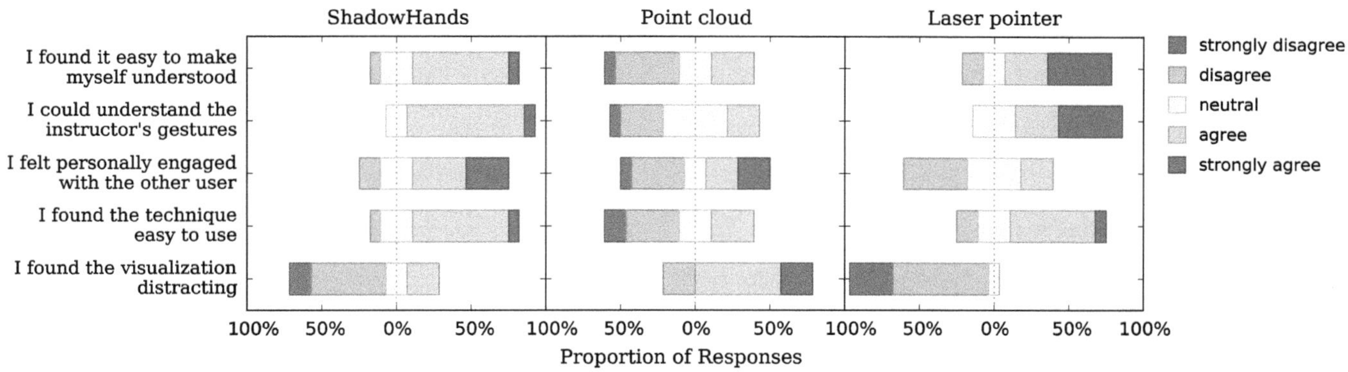

Figure 10: Stacked diverging bar charts of our Likert Scale responses (bars show the number of participants deviating from neutral response). ShadowHands was more popular than Point Cloud in terms of understanding, ease of use, and distraction. Attitudes towards ShadowHands and Laser Pointer were similar, except for feelings of personal engagement.

and complex, to encourage participants to use hand gestures beyond simply pointing at the screen.

We found that ShadowHands were used in several ways beyond pointing. During the maze task, we observed participants holding their palm up to the screen in a "stop" gesture to prevent the operator colliding with nearby hazards. We also observed the ShadowHands being used as a measurement tool during the drawing task: one participant used the width of their fingers to express the width of different architectural features – something tricky to do with only a pointer.

We also observed playful behaviour. During the maze task, a participant accidentally enabled an alternative ShadowHands visualization: a hand-puppet. They then proceeded to role-play as the puppet, gesturing with the puppets arms and head to guide the operator out of the maze[2]. While it is unlikely this provided any measurable benefit to task performance, the participants enjoyed being able to experience the game in this different way.

DISCUSSION

We now summaraize our key findings from the study. In our pointing task we discovered that ShadowHands led to higher accuracy than the point cloud. This was supported by qualitative feedback, with more participants finding ShadowHands easy to use and understand than the point cloud. Current commodity sensors cannot provide good enough RBG-D data for clearly representing hand gestures in our usage scenario. Participants were therefore confused by the ambiguity of the point cloud, preferring the clean ShadowHands visualizations. This finding corroborates previous work suggesting the importance of visual prominence for remote embodiments [4].

As might be expected, the participants felt more personally engaged when using ShadowHands or the point cloud compared to the laser pointer. However, no difference in personal engagement could be found between the point cloud and the laser pointer. This suggests that realism might not be as important for awareness between remote users as previously thought. If we can render stylised model-based embodiments that faithfully represent a user's gestures, we might improve gesture clarity without affecting awareness.

Though users did not feel personally engaged when they used the laser pointer, this did not lead to any empirical differences in task performance compared to ShadowHands. Furthermore, participant attitutudes towards ShadowHands and the laser pointer were similar, apart from feelings of engagement. This suggests that simple visualization techniques like a pointer are sufficient for many tasks, and future work should include it as a baseline when comparing new visualization techniques.

CONCLUSION

We introduced ShadowHands– a novel technique for visualizing hand gestures to assist remote collaboration. Rather than streaming 2D or 3D data, ShadowHands uses a hand tracker to capture a user's hand gestures, and presents them to a their collaborator. We ensure this visualization is aesthetically pleasing and visually prominent through toon-style shading and per-pixel alpha blending. We ran an experiment to compare ShadowHands to previous visualization techniques. Participants were quantitatively better at selecting targets with ShadowHands (compared with a point cloud), and this translated qualitatively into improved attitudes towards mutual understanding, ease of use, and distraction.

The primary complaint with ShadowHands was that it was unpredictable – some users experienced glitches in hand tracking that they found frustrating. As hand tracking techniques continue to improve, we hope this issue can be resolved in the future. We also discovered that participants enjoyed using playful non-hand visualizations, and would like to investigate these interactions more formally in future work.

ACKNOWLEDGEMENTS

We would like to thank Jeff Han for suggesting we explore this idea. We would also like to thank the reviewers for their detailed and helpful feedback.

[2]Data from these trials were not recorded for the experiment.

REFERENCES

1. Agarwal, A., Izadi, S., Chandraker, M., and Blake, A. High precision multi-touch sensing on surfaces using overhead cameras. In *Workshop on Horizontal Interactive Human-Computer Systems, TABLETOP'07*, IEEE (2007).
2. Coldefy, F., and Louis-dit Picard, S. Digitable: an interactive multiuser table for collocated and remote collaboration enabling remote gesture visualization. In *IEEE CVPR'07*, IEEE (2007).
3. Debevec, P. Image-based lighting. *IEEE Computer Graphics and Applications* (2002).
4. Doucette, A., Gutwin, C., Mandryk, R. L., Nacenta, M., and Sharma, S. Sometimes when we touch: how arm embodiments change reaching and collaboration on digital tables. In *Proc. CSCW'13*, ACM (2013).
5. Gonzalez, R. C., and Woods, R. E. Digital image processing. *Nueva Jersey* (2008).
6. Higuchi, K., Chen, Y., Chou, P. A., Zhang, Z., and Liu, Z. Immerseboard: Immersive telepresence experience using a digital whiteboard. In *Proc. ACM CHI'15* (2015).
7. Intel. Intel realsense camera f200. http://www.intel.com/content/www/us/en/architecture-and-technology/realsense-shortrange.html, 2016. Accessed: 2016-07-07.
8. Ishii, H., and Kobayashi, M. Clearboard: a seamless medium for shared drawing and conversation with eye contact. In *Proc. ACM CHI'92*, ACM (1992).
9. Izadi, S., Agarwal, A., Criminisi, A., Winn, J., Blake, A., and Fitzgibbon, A. C-slate: a multi-touch and object recognition system for remote collaboration using horizontal surfaces. In *Workshop on Horizontal Interactive Human-Computer Systems, TABLETOP'07*, IEEE (2007).
10. Joseph Tan, D., Cashman, T., Taylor, J., Fitzgibbon, A., Tarlow, D., Khamis, S., Izadi, S., and Shotton, J. Fits like a glove: Rapid and reliable hand shape personalization. In *Proc. CVPR'16* (2016).
11. Loop, C. Smooth subdivision surfaces based on triangles.
12. Microsoft. Kinect for windows. https://developer.microsoft.com/en-us/windows/kinect/, 2016. Accessed: 2016-07-07.
13. Microsoft. Windows api index. https://msdn.microsoft.com/en-gb/library/windows/desktop/ff818516(v=vs.85).aspx, 2016. Accessed: 2016-07-07.
14. Pinelle, D., Nacenta, M., Gutwin, C., and Stach, T. The effects of co-present embodiments on awareness and collaboration in tabletop groupware. In *Proceedings of graphics interface 2008*, Canadian Information Processing Society (2008).
15. Sharp, T., Keskin, C., Robertson, D., Taylor, J., Shotton, J., Kim, D., Rhemann, C., Leichter, I., Vinnikov, A., Wei, Y., et al. Accurate, robust, and flexible real-time hand tracking. In *Proc. CHI'15*, ACM (2015).
16. Shotton, J., Sharp, T., Kipman, A., Fitzgibbon, A., Finocchio, M., Blake, A., Cook, M., and Moore, R. Real-time human pose recognition in parts from single depth images. *Communications of the ACM* (2013).
17. Survey, H. A. B. Chapline street row historic district, 2301 to 2319 chapline street. In *Library of Congress* (1933).
18. Tang, A., Neustaedter, C., and Greenberg, S. Videoarms: embodiments for mixed presence groupware. In *People and Computers XX-Engage*. Springer, 2007.
19. Tang, J. C., and Minneman, S. L. Videodraw: a video interface for collaborative drawing. *ACM Transactions on Information Systems (TOIS)* (1991).
20. Taylor, J., Bordeaux, L., Cashman, T., Corish, B., Keskin, C., Soto, E., Sweeney, D., Valentin, J., Luff, B., Topalian, A., Wood, E., Khamis, S., Kohli, P., Sharp, T., Izadi, S., Banks, R., Fitzgibbon, A., and Shotton, J. Efficient and precise interactive hand tracking through joint, continuous optimization of pose and correspondences. In *ACM SIGGRAPH* (2016).
21. Tuddenham, P., and Robinson, P. T3: Rapid prototyping of high-resolution and mixed-presence tabletop applications. In *Workshop on Horizontal Interactive Human-Computer Systems, TABLETOP'07*, IEEE (2007).
22. Zhang, Z. Microsoft kinect sensor and its effect. *IEEE multimedia* (2012).
23. Zillner, J., Rhemann, C., Izadi, S., and Haller, M. 3d-board: a whole-body remote collaborative whiteboard. In *Proc. UIST'14*, ACM (2014).

DIRECT: Making Touch Tracking on Ordinary Surfaces Practical with Hybrid Depth-Infrared Sensing

Robert Xiao **Scott Hudson** **Chris Harrison**
Carnegie Mellon University, Human-Computer Interaction Institute
5000 Forbes Avenue, Pittsburgh, PA 15213
{brx, scott.hudson, chris.harrison}@cs.cmu.edu

ABSTRACT

Several generations of inexpensive depth cameras have opened the possibility for new kinds of interaction on everyday surfaces. A number of research systems have demonstrated that depth cameras, combined with projectors for output, can turn nearly any reasonably flat surface into a touch-sensitive display. However, even with the latest generation of depth cameras, it has been difficult to obtain sufficient sensing fidelity across a table-sized surface to get much beyond a proof-of-concept demonstration. In this paper we present DIRECT, a novel touch-tracking algorithm that merges depth and infrared imagery captured by a commodity sensor. This yields significantly better touch tracking than from depth data alone, as well as any prior system. Further extending prior work, DIRECT supports arbitrary user orientation and requires no prior calibration or background capture. We describe the implementation of our system and quantify its accuracy through a comparison study of previously published, depth-based touch-tracking algorithms. Results show that our technique boosts touch detection accuracy by 15% and reduces positional error by 55% compared to the next best-performing technique.

Author Keywords

Touch tracking; depth sensing; sensor fusion.

ACM Classification Keywords

H.5.2. Information interfaces and presentation (e.g. HCI): User interfaces: Input devices and strategies.

INTRODUCTION

Touch interfaces have become ubiquitous for small screens due to the popularity of touchscreen-based smartphones and tablets. However, for much larger displays, touchscreens remain expensive and can be intrusive to install in some environments. On the other hand, walls, tables, and other relatively flat surfaces are already present in many spaces.

ISS '16, November 06-09, 2016, Niagara Falls, ON, Canada
© 2016 ACM. ISBN 978-1-4503-4248-3/16/11···$15.00
DOI: http://dx.doi.org/10.1145/2992154.2992173

The introduction of digital projectors and low-cost depth camera technologies raises the possibility of transforming these everyday surfaces into large, touch-sensitive computing experiences.

While free-space hand and finger tracking research spans several decades of research, starting with seminal work by Krueger in the Video Place System [10], comparatively little research has examined finger and touch tracking on ordinary, unmodified surfaces. This can be attributed to the difficult challenge of first segmenting a finger from the background to extract its spatial position and then undertaking the even more challenging task of sensing when a finger has physically contacted a surface (vs. merely hovering close to it).

The advent of inexpensive depth cameras offered a promising potential solution for addressing this challenge. Early work by Wilson et al. [24] demonstrated the potential of this approach for detecting touches on arbitrary surfaces.

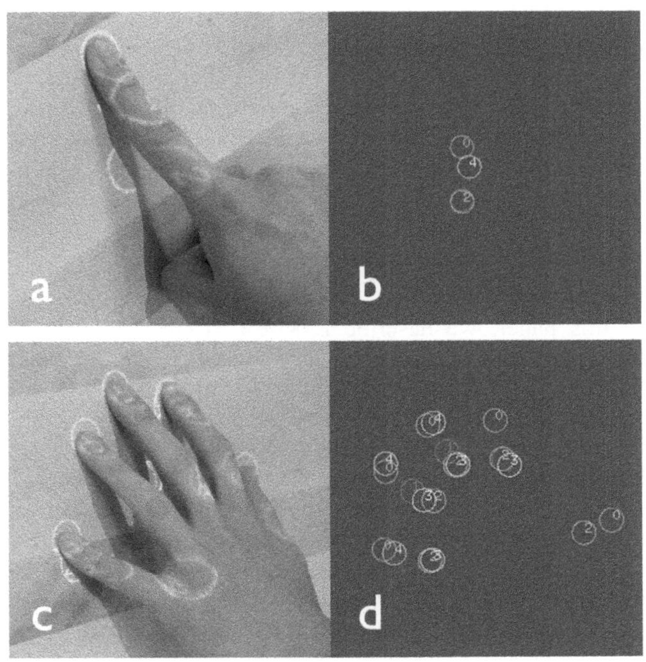

Figure 1. Comparison of depth-camera-based touch tracking methods. Our method (DIRECT) is shown in green and labeled 0. Comparison methods are single-frame model (1/red), maximum distance model [24] (2/orange), statistical model [7, 25] (3/yellow) and slice finding [6] (4/cyan).

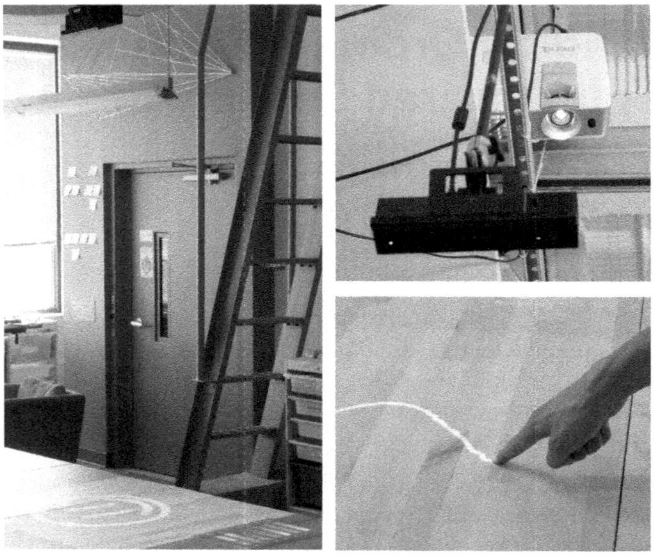

Figure 2. The system setup. Left: the Kinect depth camera is mounted 1.6 m from the table surface. Top right: the projector and Kinect are rigidly mounted and calibrated to each other (but not the surface). Bottom right: The table surface functions as a touchscreen.

While prior approaches have demonstrated that depth-based touch tracking should be viable, full exploration of the design space requires input sensing, which exhibits high stability and positional accuracy, as well as reliable touch segmentation/detection with both low false positives and low false negatives.

Unfortunately, attaining this very high accuracy strains the capabilities of even the latest generation of depth cameras. The depth resolution and noise characteristics of current generation sensors means that fingertips simply merge into the surface at distances needed to cover reasonably sized work surfaces (Figure 3a), making precise touch tracking extremely difficult. This has made it challenging to move beyond the first proof-of-concept research systems to practical use in real deployments.

CONTRIBUTIONS

In this paper, we describe DIRECT (Depth and IR Enhanced Contact Tracking), a new touch-tracking approach that merges depth and infrared image data (from a single sensor) to provide significantly enhanced finger tracking (Figures 1 and 2). Infrared imagery provides precise finger boundaries, while depth imagery provides precise contact detection. Additionally, the use of infrared data allows the system to more robustly reject tracking errors arising from noisy depth data. This approach allows DIRECT to provide touch tracking precision to within a single pixel in the depth image, and overall, finger tracking accuracy approaching that of conventional touch-screens. Additionally, our approach makes no assumptions about user position or orientation (in contrast to all prior systems, which require *a priori* knowledge of finger orientation to correct for undetected fingertips), nor does it require prior calibration or background capture.

We describe in detail the technical implementation of DIRECT and discuss its capabilities and unique characteristics relative to other touch tracking approaches. We further contribute a multi-technique comparison study – the first evaluation of its type – where we compare four previously published methods against one another, as well as against DIRECT. As we will show, DIRECT readily outperforms these prior techniques with respect to viable distance, touch precision, touch stability, multi-finger segmentation, and touch detection false positives and false negatives.

Additionally, to encourage research in this domain, as well as facilitate replication and comparative studies, we have made implementations of DIRECT and our four comparative methods available for download and review at https://github.com/nneonneo/direct-handtracking.

RELATED WORK

There are many different approaches for touch tracking on large surfaces. The simplest approach is to create a special purpose surface, using *e.g.* cameras [5, 13] or capacitive sensors [11]. Alternatively, existing surfaces can be retrofitted with sensors, such as acoustic sensors to detect the sound of a tap [16], or infrared emitters and receivers to detect occlusion from a finger. There are also methods that can operate on ad hoc, uninstrumented surfaces. These systems most often use optical sensors (*e.g.*, cameras [9] or LIDAR [15]).

Detecting whether a finger has contacted a surface is challenging with conventional RGB or infrared cameras, which has inspired several approaches. PlayAnywhere [22] demonstrated a touch tracking approach based on analyzing the shadows cast by a finger near the surface. Sugita et al. [19] detect touches by tracking the visual change in the fingernail when it is pressed against a surface. TouchLight [23] uses a stereo pair of cameras, detecting touches when the finger images pass beyond a virtual plane. Many other systems use finger dwell time or an external sensor (accelerometer [8], microphone, or acoustic sensor [16, 26]) to detect touch events.

Most related to our present technique are depth camera-based touch-tracking systems. Depth cameras sense the physical distance from the sensor to each point in the field of view, making it possible (in concept) to innately sense whether a finger has contacted a surface or not. Broadly, these systems can be placed into two categories:

Background modeling approaches compute and store a model or snapshot of the depth background. Touches are detected where the live depth data differs from the background depth map in specific ways. Wilson [24] uses a background snapshot computed from the maximum depth point observed at each pixel over a small window of time. KinectFusion [7] uses a background model developed by analyzing the 3D structure of the scene from multiple angles (SLAM), effectively producing a statistically derived background map. WorldKit [25] also uses a statistical approach, computing the mean and standard deviation for

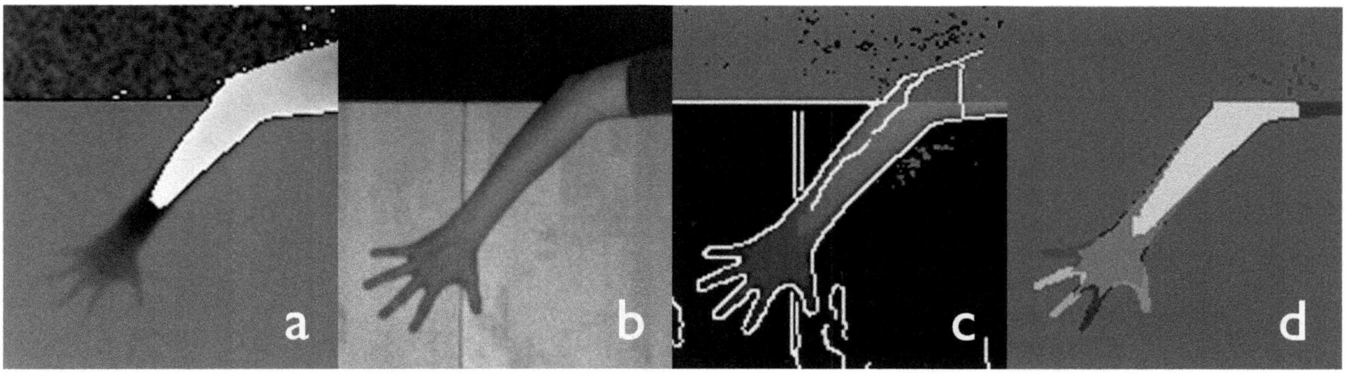

Figure 3. Close-up of touch tracking process for five fingers laid flat on the table. (a) depth image, (b) infrared image, (c) infrared edges overlaid on z-score map, (d) segmentation result. In (d), *arm* pixels are cyan, *hand* pixels are blue-green, and *finger* pixels are combined with *fingertip* pixels and shown in various shades of green.

each pixel, modeling both the background and noise. Finally, MirageTable [1] captures a background mesh and renders foreground hands as particles.

Finger modeling approaches attempt to segment fingers based on their physical characteristics, and generally do not require background data. OmniTouch [6] used a template-finding approach to label finger-like cylindrical slices within depth images. The slices are then merged into fingers, and finally touch contacts. FlexPad [18] detected and removed hands by analyzing the subsurface scattering of the Kinect's structured infrared light pattern, allowing the background to be uniquely segmented.

Surprisingly few systems attempt to fuse depth sensing with other sensing modalities for touch tracking. Of the existing literature on sensor fusion depth-sensing systems, only the Dante Vision project [17] uses a multisensory approach for touch tracking, combining depth sensing with thermal imaging infrared camera. This is used to improve touch contact detection accuracy (a thermal imprint is left on the surface upon physical touch), though at the expense of continuous tracking and high contact latency (~200 ms).

IMPLEMENTATION

We implemented our touch tracking algorithm and comparison techniques in C++ on a 2.66 GHz 3-core Windows PC, with a Kinect for Windows 2 providing the depth and infrared imagery. The Kinect 2 is a time-of-flight depth camera, which uses active infrared illumination to determine the distances to objects in the scene. It provides 512x424 pixel depth and infrared images at 30 frames per second. A BenQ W1070 projector with a resolution of 1920x1080 is also mounted above our test surface (a wooden table) to provide visual feedback.

The Kinect 2 is mounted 1.60 meters above a large table surface, and the projector is 2.35 meters above the surface (Figure 2). At the horizontal edges of the Kinect's field of view, the table surface is 2.0 meters from the Kinect. Both the projector and Kinect are securely mounted to the ceiling, and were calibrated to each other using multiple views of a planar calibration target.

The present configuration allows the projector to project a 1.0×2.0 meter image onto the table surface, with the Kinect capable of sensing objects across the entire projected area. At this distance, each projected pixel is 1.0 mm square, and each Kinect depth pixel is 4.4 mm square at the table surface. Thus, even with this second generation sensor, a typical fingertip resting on the table is less than 3 depth image pixels wide, underscoring the sensing challenge.

Our approach combines background modeling and anthropometric modeling approaches. More specifically, DIRECT models both the background *and* the user's arms, hands, and fingers using separate processes. Our processing pipeline is carefully optimized so that it runs at camera frame rate (30 FPS) using a single core of the PC.

The touch-tracking pipeline is illustrated in Figures 3 and 4. Figure 3 shows a hand laid flat on the table, which is challenging for depth-based touch tracking approaches because the fingertips generally fuse with the background due to sensor imprecision and noise (Figure 3a). In Figure 3d, we show that DIRECT can still segment the fingers (labeled in different colors) right down to the fingertip. Figure 4 shows another challenging case - a single extended finger raised 60°. This is problematic because there are very few depth pixels available for the fingertip itself. As before, DIRECT is able to segment the crucial fingertip.

Background Modeling

Our system uses a statistical model of the background, inspired in part by the implementation in WorldKit [25]. At every pixel, we maintain a rolling window of five seconds of depth data and compute the mean and standard deviation. This model allows us to establish both a highly accurate mean depth background, as well as a noise profile at every pixel in the scene.

With these rolling windows, we support *dynamic* updating of the background model. If the standard deviation exceeds a certain depth-dependent threshold (accounting for higher average noise further from the sensor), the pixel is temporarily "stunned" and its background model mean and standard deviation will be held constant until the moving average

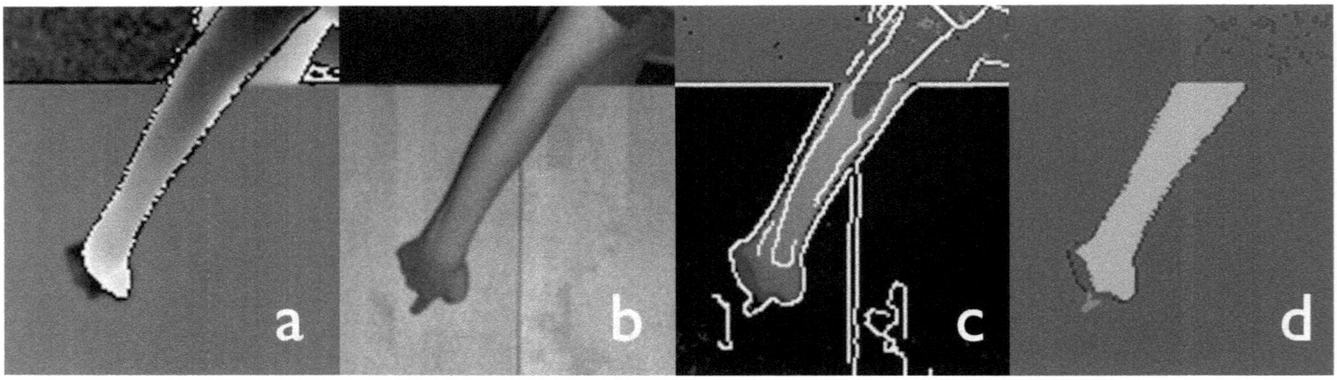

Figure 4. Close-up of touch tracking process for a finger angled at 60° vertically. (a) depth, (b) infrared, (c) edges and depth map z-scores, and (d) filled blobs. Refer to Figure 3 for a full color key.

drops below the threshold. This approach accurately tracks long-term changes in the environment (*e.g.*, objects moved around), while ignoring short-term changes (*e.g.*, actively-interacting hands and fingers). In our present implementation, the background is updated in a separate thread, running at 15 fps to avoid excessively frequent updates. This type of dynamic background updating is crucial for long-running systems to deal with shifts in the environment (*e.g.*, movement of objects residing on the surface), yet most existing systems (*e.g.*, [24, 25]) use only a single static background model captured during initial setup. We note that highly stationary hands and fingers could be "integrated into the background" with this approach, though we observed that, in practice, users rarely stay stationary for several seconds over top of active touch interfaces.

Infrared Edge Detection

We use the infrared image primarily to detect the boundary between the fingertip and the surrounding surface. As such, our first step is to detect edges in the infrared image. The Kinect 2's infrared image comes from the same sensor as the depth data, and thus it is precisely registered to the depth image. We use a Canny edge filter [2] to locate candidate edge pixels in the image (7x7 Sobel filter, with hysteresis thresholds of 4000 and 8000), with results shown in Figure 5. Note the parameters are not specific to the operating depth or objects in the scene.

After running the Canny edge filter, some edges may have gaps. These can occur due to *e.g.,* multiple edges meeting. A common gap-filling technique, image dilation followed by erosion, is inappropriate for our case due to the small size of the fingertip. Instead, we employ an *edge-linking* [12] algorithm across the edge map, which walks along Canny edge boundaries and bridges one-pixel breaks between neighboring edges. After applying this algorithm, fingertips and hands are usually fully enclosed (Figures 3c and 4c, pale yellow lines).

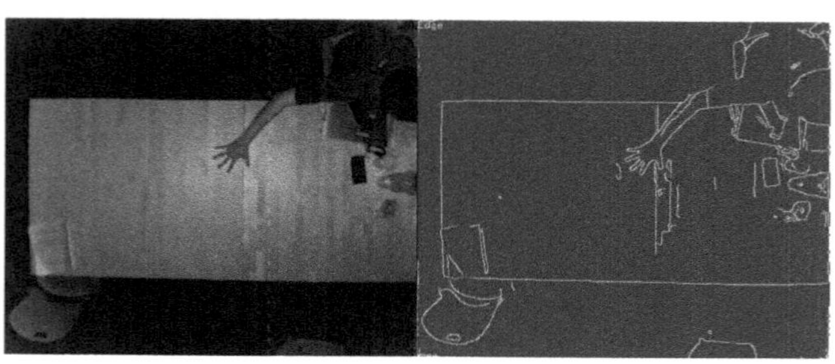

Figure 5. Canny edge detection.
Left: Kinect IR image. Right: Edge map.

Surfaces with a very similar infrared albedo to skin could cause issues for edge finding. However, anecdotally, we have found that the shadows cast by the arm and hand (illuminated by the active IR emitter found in many depth cameras), even near the fingertip, helps to increase contrast (as seen in Figures 3b and 4b).

Iterative Flood-Fill Segmentation

Our touch tracking pipeline consists of a sequence of iterative flood fills, each responsible for a different pixel type: arm filling, hand filling, finger filling, and fingertip filling. When each flood fill completes, it triggers the next fill in the sequence, starting from pixels on its boundary. Critically, each flooded area is *linked* to the parent area from which it was seeded (*e.g.* the finger fill starts from the hand that it is attached to), forming a hierarchy of filled objects that match their respective anthropometric requirements derived from [3, 4, 14, 21]. For a finger to be successfully segmented (and passed as input to an interface), a complete hierarchy must exist – a process that robustly rejects finger-like objects that are not connected to hands, arms and so on (*e.g.*, a whiteboard marker laying on a tabletop).

Arm Stage

The first stage is labeling arm pixels, and merging them into connected *arm blobs* (Figures 3d and 4d, light blue). Arm pixels are defined as pixels that are at least 5 cm closer to the sensor than the background mean, *i.e.* pixels that are at least 5 cm above the surface. This high threshold is chosen both to unambiguously distinguish human activity from background noise (standard deviations at the edge of the depth map can reach ~1.5 cm, so 5 cm is more than 3 standard deviations away), and to detect human forearms even when laid *totally* flat on the table (6.3 cm is the 2.5^{th} percentile diameter of a human forearm).

Hand Stage

Then, for all arm blobs, our algorithm flood fills downwards towards the hand pixels, defined as pixels that are at least 12 mm from the surface. This threshold was chosen to segment individual fingers apart from the hand (12 mm is the 2.5^{th} percentile thickness of a human finger, allowing us to detect even small fingers laying flat on a table). During this step, the fill is constrained to avoid pixels with high depth variance in their local neighborhood. This constraint ensures that this flood fill does not simply fill into noisy pixels surrounding the arm. The result is a *hand blob* attached to the parent arm blob (Figure 3d and 4d, dark blue blob). If multiple hand blobs are found, only the largest is taken (to avoid noise-induced "phantom hands").

Finger Stage

In the third stage, the algorithm fills from the hand blob into finger pixels, which are defined as pixels that are at least one standard deviation above from the surface mean. These pixels are above noise, but are otherwise very close to the surface. Because of this, we constrain the fill to stay within the boundaries derived from the infrared edge map. In the event of a hole in the edge map, the fill will stop at below-noise pixels and thus will not fill too far. This process produces a number of *finger blobs* attached to the hand blob, and the point at which the finger attaches to the hand is called the *finger base*.

Fingertip Stage

Finally, for each finger blob, the algorithm fills further into the below-noise pixels (fingertip pixels). At this point, the depth map is not used (as fingers generally merge with noise), and only the infrared edge constrains the fill. A vast majority of frames fill successfully, however occasionally, a gap in the edge map will cause the flood to escape outside the finger. To mitigate this, our flood fill stops and flags an *overfill error* if the fill extends more than 15 cm from the finger base. This value allows for both the longest human fingers (mean length 8.6 cm, SD 0.5) and is 2 standard deviations above the mean palm center to fingertip length (mean 12.9 cm, SD 0.8), which is the worst-case scenario if the hand fill stage was only partially successful in flooding into the hand. Additionally, this permits the use of grasped pens, markers or styluses used as pointing devices, while still rejecting out-of-control flood fills that spill out onto the background.

If an overfill condition is detected, DIRECT deletes the flooded fingertip pixels and returns a failure indication. This allows the system to gracefully fall back to depth-only touch tracking in the event that the IR image is unusable for any reason (*e.g.* because there are holes in the edge image). Crucially, this enables the algorithm to work in cluttered or complex environments when the edge image may be damaged or unusable, albeit with reduced performance. Otherwise, if no overfill occurs, the fingertip pixels are added to the parent finger blob. The resulting finger blobs are seen in Figure 3d and 4d (varying shades of green).

Touch Point Extraction

During both the finger fill and tip fill, we record the distance of each finger pixel to the finger base. For each detected finger, we simply place the fingertip at the pixel with the highest such distance. We found that this pixel correlates extremely well with the fingertip's actual location, and furthermore that this point is stable enough that touch position smoothing is unnecessary.

If the tip filling failed due to an over-fill, the fingertip's position can be estimated using forward projection, by using the arm and hand positions to determine the orientation of the finger. However, the resulting estimate will be substantially noisier, a fact which can be conveyed to a higher-level filtering or smoothing algorithm.

Touch Contact Detection

To detect if the fingertip is in contact with the surface behind it (*i.e.* to distinguish *hover* from *contact*), we examine the 5x5 neighborhood around the tip pixel. If any pixel is more than 1 cm from the background, we mark the finger as hovering, otherwise the finger is marked as touching the surface. We then apply hysteresis to avoid rapid changes in touch state. Although this touch detection approach is simplistic, it is surprisingly robust; we attribute this to the high precision of our fingertip tracking.

Touch Tracking Properties

The DIRECT approach merges aspects of optical tracking, background modeling and anthropometric finger modeling approaches, and therefore exhibits some unique properties relative to other methods. Compared to depth-only methods, the touch points detected by DIRECT are more stable, as the infrared estimation provides pixel-accurate detection of the fingertip. Consequently, DIRECT requires no temporal touch smoothing to work well, allowing it to have very low latency (15 ms average latency from input depth data to output touch point) without sacrificing accuracy.

While DIRECT uses ideas from finger modeling, it does not directly model the shape of fingers, nor does it make assumptions about the shape of the touch contact area. Therefore, DIRECT is capable of tracking touches when the fingers assume unusual configurations, such as holding all fingers together, performing gestural touches, or holding objects such as pens and styli.

Lastly, DIRECT provides some additional information about the hand and fingers beyond just the touch point. Specifically, it also provides the orientation of the finger (the vector from the finger base to fingertip), the pose of the hand, and the arm associated with each touch. This metadata could be used to implement interaction techniques beyond simple multitouch, *e.g.* using the finger angles for rotational input [20], or to manipulate 3D objects [27], and using the arm data to enable bimanual interactions.

COMPARATIVE TECHNIQUES

To compare the performance of our technique, we implemented four representative depth-camera-based touch tracking methods from the literature (see also Related Work). An example frame of tracking output from these implementations can be seen in Figure 1 (see also Video Figure).

Of note, many of our comparison techniques were originally developed using the predecessor of the Kinect 2 we use (the "Kinect for Windows", henceforth called Kinect 1 for simplicity). The Kinect 1 sensor uses structured light, which projects an infrared speckle pattern, as opposed to the time-of-flight method used in the Kinect 2. The speckle pattern renders the infrared image virtually unusable for tracking, precluding DIRECT-style sensing. The Kinect 1 features both lower depth image pixel resolution and lower depth resolution (~4 mm per depth unit at a distance of 2 meters) than the Kinect 2. We have thus adjusted and tuned the comparison techniques to work with the Kinect 2 sensor as best possible.

We also did not use any calibration with these techniques. Touch tracking systems often employ a calibration stage where a user touches several points to establish a mapping between the sensor and known physical points. However, if the user calibrates without significantly changing their orientation, this calibration can mask certain orientation-dependent biases (as we show in our results) and make the system dependent on the user and finger orientation. Hence, in our study, we apply only a global calibration between the depth camera and the projector, and do not calibrate using detected finger positions.

All of our comparison techniques have a certain number of "magic numbers" that must be tuned for correct operation of the system. Furthermore, precise adjustments of these numbers can be used to trade off between *e.g.* touch accuracy and false touch detection. For the study, we tuned these numbers to keep false positives acceptably low, as these are especially damaging to the user experience. Specifically, we aimed to reduce false positives to less than one false-positive per five seconds within our target area (2 m^2) when no fingers are present. Although this is still a high rate of false positives, we found that attempting to further reduce this rate led to unacceptable insensitivity in two of our comparison techniques. We tuned each comparison technique independently, communicating with the system's authors when necessary to best reproduce the technique.

Tests on all techniques were done without smoothing of the touch data. Smoothing could be applied to the output of any of these approaches and might increase accuracy. However, this would come at the cost of increased latency and would tend to hide the merits of the technique itself.

Single-Frame Background Model

Our first comparison technique is a common, naïve technique often used for simple touch tracking. It uses a background model consisting of a single captured depth frame. Candidate touch pixels are simply those that lie between a minimum and maximum distance threshold from the background (in our implementation, between 7 and 15 mm from the surface).

For all background model implementations, we apply a low-pass boxcar filter followed by thresholding. A connected-components pass then extracts touch blobs, following the implementation in [24]. Although most naïve implementations do not perform this filtering, we found it necessary to avoid excessive noise in the contact tracking.

Maximum Distance Background Model

The second comparison technique models the background using the *maximum* depth value seen over a window of time. This effectively implements a conservative noise model of the background. Like the single-frame approach, the captured depth is then processed through a low-pass filter and thresholded, followed by a connected-components pass to segment finger touches.

Wilson [24] implements a variation on this technique (pers. comm.), using a histogram to choose *e.g.*, the 90th percentile depth value at each pixel to eliminate outliers in the original Kinect data. With the Kinect 2, we did not observe such outliers, and so our maximum distance model is effectively the same as the histogram method. Wilson tested their system using a Kinect at a maximum distance of 1.5 metres from a table. At that distance, Wilson reported anecdotally that the positional tracking error was about 1.5 cm.

Statistical Background Model

The final background modeling method uses a statistical approach. This implementation uses the same mean and standard deviation calculation as the DIRECT method. New depth frames are converted into Z-scores based on their differences from the background (specifically, the value of each pixel, minus the mean, divided by the standard deviation), and the Z-scores are then filtered, thresholded and connected as in the other methods.

This method closely resembles the background differencing approach used in WorldKit [25]. It also aims to capture the essence of the KinectFusion SLAM touch tracking approach [7], in that it integrates the background profile gradually over time, building a statistical model of the environment that is much more accurate than any single frame. However, our replicated approach lacks the spatial averaging of KinectFusion.

Slice Finding and Merging

For our final comparison technique, we chose to implement the slice-finding approach used in OmniTouch [6]. This approach locates cylindrical slices in the depth image using an elastic template, and then links together adjacent slices to form fingers. Of note, unlike the other approaches, OmniTouch requires that the fingers be clearly separated in the depth image. Furthermore, as it does not use a background model, it may detect erroneous touches on the surface due to objects already in the scene; therefore, for the study, we cleared the table surface of all objects.

The original OmniTouch implementation only supported fingers oriented horizontally. We therefore extended OmniTouch by implementing biaxial template matching – locating candidate finger slices in both the X- and Y-axes –

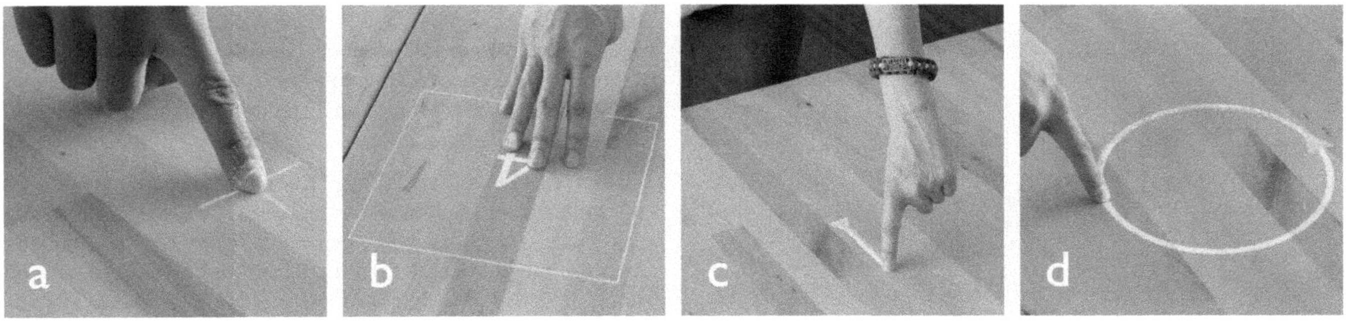

Figure 6. Tasks performed by users in our study. (a) crosshair task, (b) multitouch box task, (c) line shape tracing task, (d) circle shape tracing task.

and then merging the centroids of these slices into fingers. Our approach demonstrably locates fingers oriented in any direction. To best replicate OmniTouch's true performance, we also implemented the system's finger forward-projection method. As noted previously, because the fingers fuse with the depth background upon touch, it is difficult to estimate the true tip position. In response, OmniTouch uses the detected finger's orientation to extend the estimated touch position 15 mm towards the un-sensed tip [pers. comm.]. This improvement is not directly applicable to the previously discussed background-subtraction methods, as they do not model the finger orientation or shape. Of note, the original OmniTouch system was designed to operate at a distance of just 40 cm.

EVALUATION

To assess the accuracy of DIRECT, we ran an evaluation with 12 participants (3 female; average age 25). All users were familiar with touch interfaces. Each study session lasted for roughly 30 minutes, and participants were compensated $10 USD for their time.

Participants were simply told that the table surface was a touchscreen from the outset, and to touch the surface as they would any ordinary touchscreen. Users were permitted to use either hand (including interchangeably) and to use any finger pose they found comfortable. Users were not required to remove jewelry or roll up sleeves – several users conducted the study while wearing long sleeved shirts, bracelets, watches and rings. Our experiment system ran all five touch-tracking methods (DIRECT plus the four comparison techniques) simultaneously at a consistent 30 fps (the frame rate of the depth sensor). Please also refer to the Video Figure.

Tasks

Participants completed a series of small tasks, organized into three categories. Task order was randomized per participant to mitigate order effects. For each task, users were instructed to stand along one of the two long edges of our test table (thus changing the orientation of their touches).

Crosshair: Participants placed their fingertip on a projected crosshair (Figure 6a), after which the experimenter manually advanced the trial and the touches detected by each tracker were recorded. This task measured the positional accuracy of each finger tracking method and touch segmentation accuracy. Crosshairs were arranged in a 4x8 grid spanning the table surface, but were shown one at a time and in random order. This task was performed twice for each edge of the table.

Multitouch Segmentation: Participants were instructed to place a specific number of fingers within a projected 20 cm square on the table (Figure 6b). The experimenter manually advanced the trial and the number of touches reported within the box for each tracker was recorded. This task was intended to measure the multitouch contact reporting accuracy of each technique (*i.e.*, false positive and false negative touches). Six boxes were specified across the length of the table, and the number of fingers varied from 1-5 for a total of 30 trials, randomly ordered. This task was also performed twice for each edge of the table.

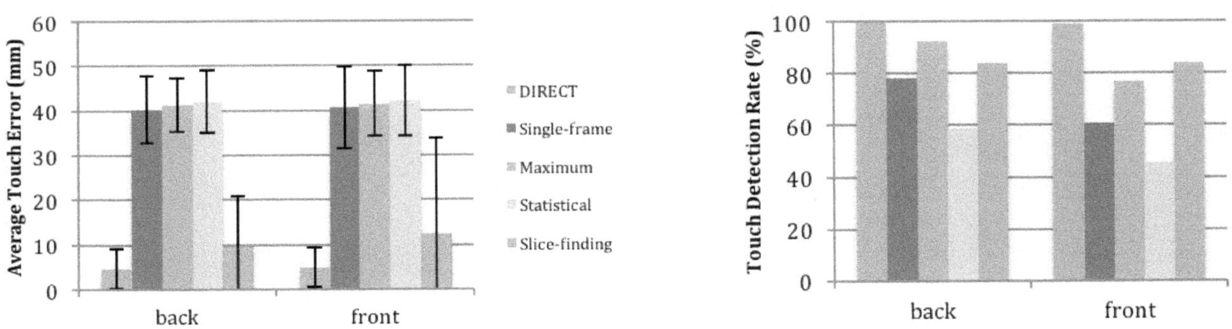

Figure 7. Average touch positional error (left) and touch detection rate (right) for each of the five touch tracking methods. Error bars are standard error.

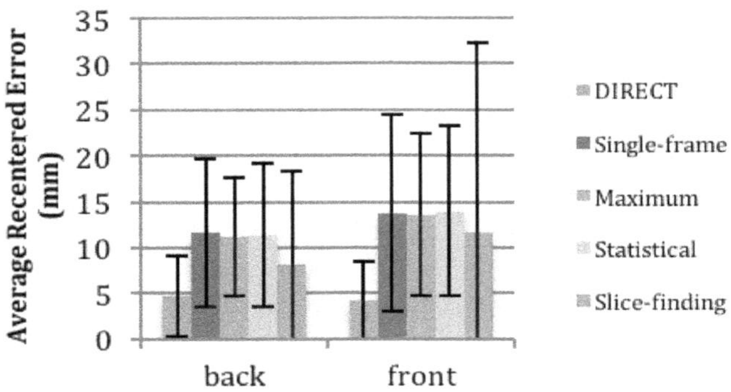

Figure 8. Average positional error after removing the average offset vector and assuming *a priori* knowledge of the user's orientation. Error bars are Standard Error.

Shape Tracing: Participants were instructed to trace a particular projected shape, beginning at the start position indicated with a green triangle (Figures 6c, 6d), and tracing to the end of the path. For each frame between the start and end of the trial, we recorded the touch coordinates for each method. This task was intended to replicate the tracing task used in OmniTouch [6]. There were three instances of this task per table edge, one for each shape: horizontal line, vertical line, and circle.

RESULTS AND DISCUSSION

In our results, we denote the two edges of the table as "back" and "front". The top of the Kinect's image corresponded to the front edge of the table.

Crosshair

The crosshair task allowed us to test both touch positional accuracy and touch detection rate. Due to potential spuriously-detected touches, we measured accuracy as the mean distance from the finger to the *nearest* detected touch point for each tracker. Touches further than 200 mm from the finger were not counted, since those touches would clearly be erroneous. If no touches were detected in range for a particular tracker, the tracker was considered to have failed to detect the touch.

In total, we collected 768 trials for each side of the table. The touch positional accuracy results are summarized in Figure 7. The accuracy results show a slight but consistent increase in accuracy across all trackers when users stood at the front edge of the table.

DIRECT achieved an average Euclidean-distance positional error of 4.8 mm across all trials, with a 99.3% touch detection rate. The next best technique, slice finding, had an average positional error of 11.1 mm and a touch detection rate of 83.9%. The background modeling methods all performed poorly, with average positional errors of over 40 mm and touch detection rates ranging from 52.1% to 84.8%. Put simply, these methods do not have the necessary sophistication to segment small finger contacts at the noise level present when sensing at 1.6 meters.

During development, we noticed that the slice finding method without forward projection performed very poorly (~20 mm average error), so it was clear that finger forward projection was crucial to obtain good accuracy. This is because these methods cannot accurately locate the fingertip in the noise, and so they instead locate a point somewhere along the finger.

Therefore, we also analyzed the accuracy of the four competing approaches by applying a mean offset vector (*i.e.*, a post hoc global offset). This vector depends on knowing the precise finger orientation, and thus the offset correction corresponds to a "calibrating" of the touch algorithm from a *fixed* user position and assuming the finger is extended perpendicular to the table. Consequently, we computed offsets separately for the front and back user positions. Because the prior systems recognize neither the user position nor finger orientation, this result is purely *hypothetical*, but serves as a useful benchmark.

The resulting average *offset-corrected* errors (Figure 8) were 4.46 mm for DIRECT (a negligible 0.3 mm improvement), 9.9 mm for the slice finding method (a modest 1.2 mm improvement), and 12.3-12.7 mm for the back-

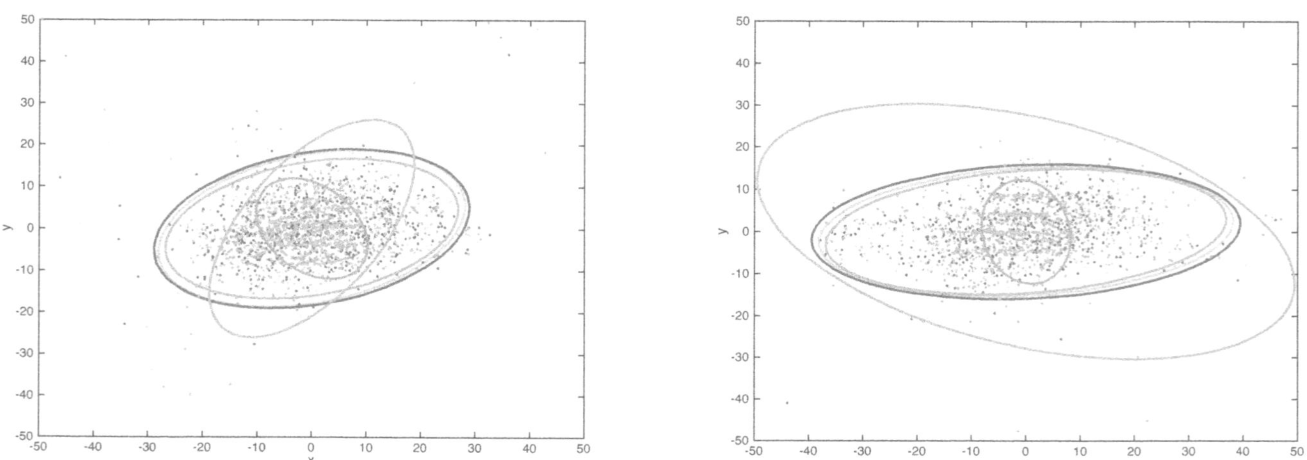

Figure 9. 95% confidence ellipses for crosshair task from the back of the table (left) and front of the table (right). X and Y units are in millimetres; colours are as in Figure 8.

ground modeling approaches (a significant 20-30 mm improvement). To visualize these errors, we also computed the 95% confidence ellipsoids (Figure 9) for each tracker (note that the offset correction corresponds to recentering the ellipsoids). These errors are consistent with prior results from Wilson [24] and OmniTouch [6], suggesting that our offset-corrected comparison implementations are reasonably close to the original implementations.

Multitouch Segmentation

With the multitouch segmentation task, we aimed to measure the false positive and false negative rates for touch detection with multiple fingers present in a small region. Under these conditions, touch trackers might merge adjacent fingers or detect spurious touches between fingers. The differences between the back and front sides were not significant in this task, so the results have been combined. In total, 1440 trials were collected.

Detecting a single extended finger is the easiest task. In single finger trials, DIRECT detected the correct number 95.8% of the time. Single-frame background, maximum frame background and statistical model background achieved 52.8%, 66.3% and 35.1% respectively. Slice-finding was 75.0% accurate.

Detecting several fingers in close proximity is much more challenging when sensing at 1.6 meters. With all trials combined, DIRECT detected the correct number of fingers in 75.5% of trials, more fingers than were present in 2.4% of trials and fewer fingers than were present in 22.1% of trials. The three background modeling approaches – single-frame, maximum frame and statistical model – detected the correct number of fingers 22.2%, 29.2% and 17.3% of the time. Very few trials reported more fingers than were present: 9, 7 and 4 trials respectively (<0.1% of all trials). Instead, these methods tended to miss fingers (77.1%, 70.2%, and 82.4% of trials respectively). Finally, the slice-finding approach detected more fingers in just 9 trials (<0.1% of trials), fewer fingers in 75.4% of trials, and the true number of fingers in 24.0% of trials.

We tuned the comparison technique implementations to minimize spurious touches while nothing was touching the table. However, our multitouch segmentation results suggest that optimizing for this criterion could have rejected too many legitimate touches, reducing touch detection rates. On the other hand, increasing touch sensitivity significantly increases noise and errant touches. For example, decreasing the "low boundary" depth threshold in the maximum-distance background model tracker by a single millimeter results in hundreds of errant touches detected on the surface every second, which is clearly not acceptable.

Shape Tracing

Tracking moving fingers is extra challenging as the exposure time of the depth camera produces motion blur across the moving parts of the frame, reducing accuracy. Further, as already mentioned above, our comparative methods are prone to missing fingers. In the case of finger movement, this will manifest as loss of finger tracking for several frames. During this period, spurious input would often cause the traced path to zigzag. For this reason, it was simply not possible to complete a realistic and useful analysis with our study data.

However, we can use results reported in OmniTouch [6] as one point of comparison. Specifically, OmniTouch reports a mean error of 6.3 mm (SD=3.9 mm) at a sensing distance of 40 cm on a flat notepad. For comparison, DIRECT achieves a mean error of 2.9 mm (mean SD=2.7 mm) at a sensing distance of 160 cm (on a flat table).

CONCLUSION

We have presented DIRECT, a touch tracking system which strategically merges depth and infrared data from an off-the-shelf infrared depth camera to enable highly accurate touch tracking, even at significant distances from the sensor. Overall, DIRECT demonstrates greatly improved touch tracking accuracy (mean error of 4.9 mm) and detection rate (>99%) – roughly twice as good as the next best method in the literature, and nearly ten times better than classic approaches.

There are also immediate ways to further improve our system. For example, in our present implementation, DIRECT outputs integer coordinates on the depth map, which quantizes the X/Y position to 4.4 mm (mean error due to quantization: 3.1 mm). Averaging pixels at the tip could provide a sub-pixel estimate, further boosting accuracy. Additionally, we could apply temporal smoothing to improve touch position stability at the expense of latency.

To conclude, we hope that DIRECT's significantly improved finger tracking accuracy can open new opportunities in ad hoc touch interfaces and better allow this emerging computing modality to be explored. We also believe this advance can help move depth-driven systems from proof-of-concept to more practical and widespread use.

ACKNOWLEDGMENTS

This research was generously supported by the David and Lucile Packard Foundation, Qualcomm, and a Google Faculty Research Award.

REFERENCES

1. Benko, H., Jota, R. and Wilson, A. Miragetable: freehand interaction on a projected augmented reality tabletop. In *Proc. CHI '12*. 199–208.
2. Canny, J. A Computational Approach To Edge Detection. *IEEE Trans. Pattern Analysis and Machine Intelligence*, 8(6), 1986, 679-698.
3. Eastman Kodak Company. Kodak's Ergonomic Design for People at Work, 2nd Edition. 2003, pp. 48-49.
4. Haley, J. Anthropometry and mass distribution for human analogues. Volume 1, 1988. Aerosp. Med. Res. Lab Wright-Patterson, Ohio.

5. Han, J. Y. Low-cost multi-touch sensing through frustrated total internal reflection. In *Proc. UIST '05*. 115-118.
6. Harrison, C., Benko, H. and Wilson, A.D. OmniTouch: wearable multitouch interaction everywhere. In *Proc. UIST '11*. 441-450.
7. Izadi, S., Kim, D., Hilliges, O., Molyneaux, D., Newcombe, R., Kohli, P., Shotton, J., Hodges, S., Freeman, D., Davison, A. and Fitzgibbon, A. KinectFusion: Real-time 3D Reconstruction and Interaction Using a Moving Depth Camera. In *Proc. UIST '11*. 559-568.
8. Kane, S., Avrahami, D., Wobbrock, J., Harrison, B., Rea, A., Philipose, M. and LaMarca, A. Bonfire: a nomadic system for hybrid laptop-tabletop interaction. In *Proc. UIST '09*. 129-138.
9. Koike, H., Sato, Y. and Kobayashi, Y. Integrating paper and digital information on EnhancedDesk: a method for realtime finger tracking on an augmented desk system. *ACM Trans. on Computer-Human Inter.*, 8(4), 307-322.
10. Krueger, M. W., Gionfriddo, T. and Hinrichsen, K. VIDEOPLACE — an artificial reality. In *Proc. CHI '85*. 35-40.
11. Lee, S. K., Buxton, W. and Smith, K. C. A multi-touch three dimensional touch-sensitive tablet. In *Proc. CHI '85*. 21-25.
12. Maeda, J., Iizawa, T., Ishizaka, T., Ishikawa, C. and Suzuki, Y. Segmentation of Natural Images Using Anisotropic Diffusion and Linking of Boundary Edges. Pattern Recognition, 31(12), 1998.
13. Matsushita, N. and Rekimoto, J. HoloWall: designing a finger, hand, body, and object sensitive wall. In *Proc. UIST '97*. 209-210.
14. NASA. Anthropometry and Biomechanics. NASA-STD-3000: Man-Systems Integration Standards, Volume 1, Section 3. Revision B, July 1995.
15. Paradiso, J., Hsiao, K., Strickon, J., Lifton, J. and Adler, A. Sensor Systems for Interactive Surfaces. IBM Systems Journal, Volume 39, Nos. 3 & 4, October 2000, pp. 892-914.
16. Paradiso, J., Leo, C., Checka, N. and Hsiao, K. Passive acoustic sensing for tracking knocks atop large interactive displays. In *Proc. IEEE Sensors '02*. 521-527.
17. Saba, E.N., Larson, E.C. and Patel, S.N. Dante vision: In-air and touch gesture sensing for natural surface interaction with combined depth and thermal cameras. In *Proc. IEEE ESPA '12*. 167-170.
18. Steimle, J., Jordt, A. and Maes, P. Flexpad: highly flexible bending interactions for projected handheld displays. In *Proc. CHI '13*. 237-246.
19. Sugita, N., Iwai, D. and Sato K. Touch Sensing by Image Analysis of Fingernail. In *Proc. SICE Annual Conference '08*. 1520-1525.
20. Wang, F. and Ren, X. Empirical evaluation for finger input properties in multi-touch interaction. In *Proc. CHI '09*. 1063-1072.
21. White, R. M. *Comparative anthropometry of the hand*. No. NATICK/CEMEL-229. Army Natrick Research and Development Labs, MA. Clothing Equipment and Materials Engineering Lab, 1980.
22. Wilson, A. PlayAnywhere: A Compact Interactive Tabletop Projection-Vision System. In *Proc. UIST '05*. 83-92.
23. Wilson, A. TouchLight: An Imaging Touch Screen and Display for Gesture-Based Interaction. In *Proc. ICMI '04*. 69-76.
24. Wilson, A. Using a depth camera as a touch sensor. In *Proc. ITS '10*. 69-72.
25. Xiao, R., Harrison, C. and Hudson, S. E. WorldKit: Rapid and Easy Creation of Ad-hoc Interactive Applications on Everyday Surfaces. In *Proc. CHI '13*. 879-888.
26. Xiao, R., Lew, G., Marsanico, J., Hariharan, D., Hudson, S.E. and Harrison, C. Toffee: enabling ad hoc, around-device interaction with acoustic time-of-arrival correlation. In *Proc. MobileHCI '14*. 67-76.
27. Xiao, R., Schwarz, J. and Harrison, C. Estimating 3D Finger Angle on Commodity Touchscreens. In *Proc. ITS '15*. 47-50.

Are Kindergarten Children Ready for Indirect Drag Interactions?

Vicente Nacher[1], Alfredo Ferreira[2], Javier Jaen[1], Fernando Garcia-Sanjuan[1]
[1]ISSI Group, Dpto. Sistemas Informáticos y Computación, Universitat Politècnica de València.
[2]Instituto Superior Técnico, INESC-ID/IST/Technical University of Lisbon, Lisbon, Portugal.
vnacher@dsic.upv.es; alfredo.ferreira@ist.utl.pt; {fjaen, fegarcia}@dsic.upv.es

ABSTRACT
Several studies have shown the suitability of the direct manipulation style and the multi-touch technology for kindergarteners and, as a result, direct dragging has been established as the standard way of interaction when supporting drag manipulations for them. However, there are scenarios in which direct dragging is not appropriate. For example, when the object to be dragged has to move at a fixed speed or performing an animation independent of the actual direct movement speed or trajectory of the user's hand. However, nobody has yet explored the suitability of indirect dragging interaction mechanisms that allow designers to effectively implement these scenarios. This paper evaluates different mechanisms of indirect dragging manipulations (Tap-based, Accelerometer-based and Buttons-based) in order to identify those that could be used by kindergarteners in scenarios where the direct dragging is not suitable. The results show that even though kindergarten children are able to effectively use different types of indirect dragging techniques, some considerations in terms of completion time and precision must be taken into account.

Author Keywords
Multi-touch interaction; usability evaluation; kindergarten; guidelines

ACM Classification Keywords
H.5.2. [Information interfaces and presentation]: User Interfaces - Evaluation/methodology, Interaction Styles.

INTRODUCTION
Children's use of interactive surfaces in distinct form-factors has become common in the last few years [5]. Ranging from smartphones to interactive tables and walls, these devices rely on touchscreens and are classified as natural user interfaces (NUI), often being labeled as "natural" to use. However, this might not be the case [3,9]. While children appear to "naturally" interact with touch-screen devices, a great deal of attention has been given to validate this assertion. Previous studies on the usage of touchscreen devices by children have provided insightful information on this topic and point out the suitability of using the direct manipulation style concept defined by Shneiderman and Plaisant [11]. Though, none has focused on the appropriateness and effectiveness of direct and indirect techniques for the dragging operation by under six-year-olds. This evaluation is relevant because, although direct dragging has been established as the de facto standard, there are scenarios in which direct dragging is not appropriate. For example, when the object to be dragged has to move at a fixed speed or performing a predefined animation (jumping or flying or affected by gravity) independently of the actual direct movement speed or trajectory of the user's hand.

In this context, we aimed to understand which approaches to the dragging operation are best suited for (pre)kindergarten children. We conducted a series of tests on a tablet-sized handheld device, involving children aged from 2 to 6 years. One direct and three indirect dragging alternatives were compared. The widely used direct drag manipulation was compared against tap-based drag, accelerometer-based drag, and button-based drag.

The results of this study show the direct dragging approach as the most effective, efficient and precise technique for all (pre-)kindergarten age groups. In a context in which direct dragging cannot be applied, the most appropriate technique depends on several factors such as the effectivity, efficiency or precision required. We believe these results will help developers of touch-based interfaces for children to choose the most suitable technique for each context.

RELATED WORK
Children's interactions with touch screen devices have recently received a great deal of attention and several studies have assessed the use of touch interaction by (pre)kindergarten children. Nacher et al. [4] evaluated a basic set of multi-touch gestures with pre-kindergarten children (2 to 3 years old) and their results showed that they are able to perform basic gestures such as tap, drag, scale up, scale down and one finger rotation, even when requiring accuracy in the termination phase for some of these gestures [6]. Moreover, more complex gestures such as double tap and long press can also be achieved when some assistive techniques are used [8]. Vatavu et al [12] also evaluat-

ISS '16, November 06-09, 2016, Niagara Falls, ON, Canada

DOI: http://dx.doi.org/10.1145/2992154.2992186

ed touch gestures such as tap, double tap, drag & drop and multiple drag & drop with children aged between 3 and 6 years old on tablets and smartphones. They concluded that, although performance increases significantly with age, all the children had high success rates when performing these gestures on both devices.

Other previous studies [1][2] chose four applications and evaluated the interaction needed to play with them. Gestures such as tap, drag, rotation, drag and drop, pinch, spread and flick were tested with children aged from 2 to 4. The authors concluded that children aged 4 were able to perform all the evaluated gestures and those aged 3 only had problems with the spread task. Finally, 2-year-olds were less effective with the more complex gestures such as drag and drop and pinch but were able to perform the tap and drag gestures properly and quickly learnt to perform the flick gesture.

These previous works reveal that direct manipulations are feasible interaction mechanisms for (pre)kindergarten children but, as pointed out in the previous section, these may not always be appropriate manipulations in some specific scenarios. To our knowledge, indirect interaction mechanisms have not yet been evaluated for these very young children. Therefore, in this paper we start addressing this issue by evaluating alternative indirect manipulations for the direct drag operation. The selection of this specific type of gesture is motivated by the requirement of some applications in which digital elements have to be moved across the surface in an indirect way.

EXPERIMENTAL STUDY

The overall goal of our experimental study is to evaluate the suitability of different drag operations on a hand-held device and assess possible differences between them in terms of success, completion time and precision. More specifically, the research questions of the study are formulated as follows:

RQ1: Is the degree of success independent of the drag interaction style?

RQ2: Is the degree of success independent of the age group?

RQ3: Is the completion time independent of the drag interaction style?

RQ4: Is the completion time independent of the age group?

RQ5: Is the number of collisions independent of the drag interaction style?

RQ6: Is the number of collisions independent of the age group?

Drag operations overview

The drag operations that will be evaluated in this study involve the standard direct drag operation and three indirect alternatives:

-Direct drag: Using the direct manipulation style, this natural interaction mechanism allows users to move the target element by dragging it with one finger.

-Tap-based drag: In this case, the users have to deal with a mediated interaction by tapping on the destination point to which they want to move the target, which moves in a straight line from its location to the tapped point in an animated way. While the target is moving, the point tapped is marked with a cross in order to make it visible. If the moving target collides with an obstacle or a screen border it stops.

-Accelerometer-based drag: The accelerometer is a natural interaction which allows users to move the target by tilting the device in the desired direction. As a result, the target "slides" or moves in the direction specified.

-Button-based drag: In this case four arrow-shaped buttons are used to move the target object in the four basic directions (i.e. up, down, left and right). These buttons were placed at the bottom-center of the screen (see Figure 1-Bottom). This mediated interaction mechanism allows users to move the target by tapping and holding one finger on the button that symbolizes the desired direction.

Participants

Forty-nine children (20 girls and 29 boys) from two different kindergarten schools and aged between 2 and 6 years old took part in the experiment (Mean (M) = 3.82, Standard Deviation (SD) = 0.94). The children do not use touch devices in the school as a learning tool but had occasional prior experience with them in the home environment. The children were split up into three balanced age groups, i.e. they were grouped by age, with each age group a comprising the ages in $[a - 0.5, a + 0.5[$. The distribution of the age groups is shown in Table 1.

Age group	#Participants
3	17
4	16
5	16

Table 1. Number of participants by age group

APPARATUS

The interaction framework for the experiment was implemented in Java using the LibGDX framework. The devices used for the experiment were a Samsung Galaxy Note 10.1 and a BQ Edison 3 tablet with Android 3.2 and Android 4.4 respectively. Both tablets equipped with capacitive multi-touch screens.

Task

A static image of an animal appears in a position on the screen and the same (reference) image appears in a white profile in another position. In order to force the children to perform drag operations which are not just simple straight lines but instead force them to change the dragging direction, either one, two or three obstacles (three difficulty levels) are placed between the two images (examples with two obstacles are shown in Figure 1). The subjects are requested to move the target to the reference image with a specific interaction mechanism (direct, tap, accelerometer or button-based). The task is marked as successful when the target image reaches the location of the reference image with a precision of less than 30 pixels on both the X and Y axes.

Procedure

The experiment was carried out on four consecutive days. Each day, the children performed twelve repetitions (4 by difficulty level) for a given task using one of the interaction mechanisms described above. The order in which the difficulty levels were presented and the order in which the interaction mechanisms were evaluated each day were randomized per subject to avoid learning effects.

For each task, the children participated in a 2-minute learning session with an instructor. Then, the experimental platform asked them to perform the task with no external adult intervention. When the gesture was successfully completed, the platform gave a positive audiovisual feedback. If the instructor observed that the participant did not carry out the task in a given time, it was marked as undone and the child went on to the next one.

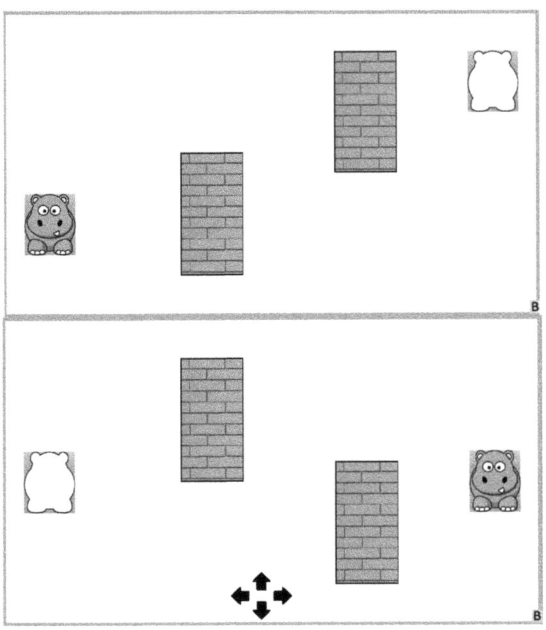

Figure 1. Example of a task with two obstacles for the drag, accelerometer, tap (top) and buttons (bottom) interaction.

Design

Three dependent variables were defined; *success rate*, *completion time* and *collisions*. A mixed design was made and as all the participants experimented the four interaction mechanisms, a repeated measures ANOVA (with an $\alpha = 0.05$) was carried out with the within-subject factor *Interaction mechanism* with four levels (Direct vs. Tap vs. Accelerometer vs. Buttons) and the between-subject factor *age group* (3 years vs. 4 years vs. 5 years). A Mauchly's Test of Sphericity was carried out in order to determine whether the data met the sphericity assumptions. The tasks that did not comply with these assumptions were applied a Greenhouse-Geisser correction and were reported in the results section with F-values with fractional degrees of freedom.

RESULTS

Success

In order to aggregate the success variable over the twelve repetitions, the variable was expressed as a percentage according to the number of repetitions performed successfully. The success rate of each interaction mechanism is shown in Figure 2 for each group.

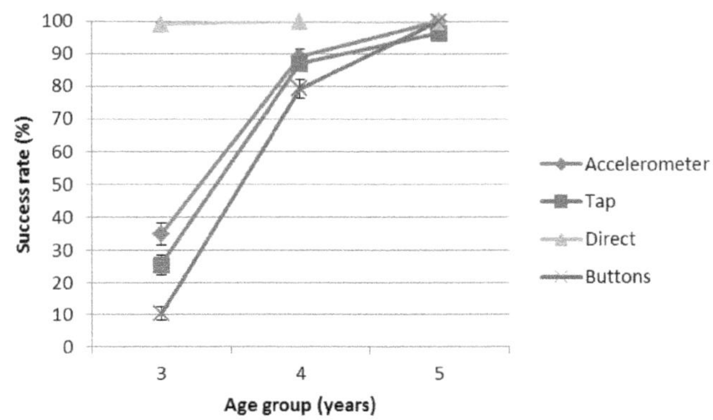

Figure 2. Success rate by interaction mechanism and age group.

The repeated measures ANOVA revealed significant differences in the success rate in the within-subject factor *Interaction Mechanism* [$F(2.555,117.508) = 34.926$, $p < .001$] and the between-subject factor *Age group* [$F(2,46) = 56.267$, $p < .001$]. The post-hoc tests revealed significant differences between all the interaction mechanisms. The interaction mechanisms can be sorted by decreasing success rate as follows: *Direct*, *Accelerometer*, *Tap* and *Buttons*.

Moreover, the analysis of the *Interaction Mechanism*Age group* interaction revealed significant main effects [$F(5.109, 19.466) = 56.267$, $p < .001$]. As can be observed in Figure 2 these differences arise because there is a trend for children to be more successful with age in the *Accelerometer*, *Tap* and *Buttons* interactions. However, in the case of the *Direct* interaction there is no evolution in the success rates, since even the youngest group had a success rate close to 100 per cent.

Completion time

The average of each subject's successful tasks is used to obtain the completion time aggregated by users. The unsuccessful tests were excluded in the completion time analysis.

The completion time is shown in Figure 3 by interaction mechanism and age group.

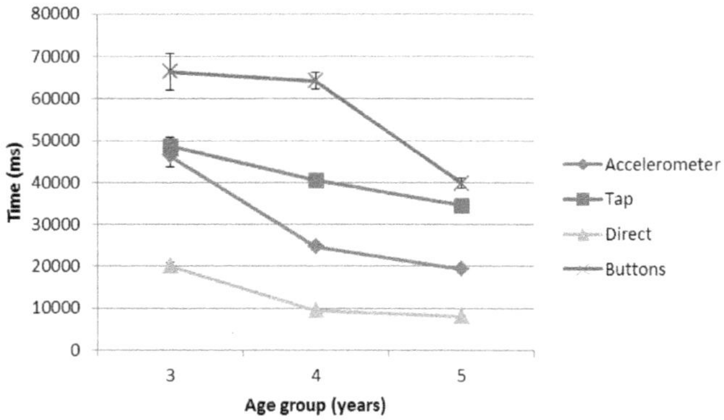

Figure 3. Completion time by interaction mechanism and age group.

Evaluating the completion time of the task, the analysis revealed significant differences in the within-subject factor *Interaction Mechanism* [F(3,93) = 166.809, p < .001] and the between-subject factor *Age group* [F(2,31) = 25.674, p < .001]. The conducted post-hoc tests revealed that there are differences between all the interaction mechanisms in terms of completion time.

The analysis of the *Interaction Mechanism**Age group* interaction also revealed significant main effects [F(6,93) = 11.964, p < .001]. As can be seen in Figure 3, the evolution of time with age is not the same for all the interactions. In the case of the *Buttons* interaction there are no differences between children in the 3 and 4 year-old groups, but those in the 5 year-old group needed significantly less time to achieve the task. On the other hand, in the *Tap* and *Accelerometer* interaction there are significant differences between all age groups. Finally, in the *Direct* interaction children aged 4 and 5 needed less time than those aged 3 when achieving the task, but no differences were found between the two former groups.

Precision

In order to evaluate the precision when moving an object on the screen, we analyzed the number of collisions that this object had with the placed obstacles or the edge of the screen. According to this, the number of collisions by interaction mechanism and age group is shown in Figure 4.

Evaluating the number of collisions when performing the task, the analysis revealed significant differences in the within-subject factor *Interaction Mechanism* [F(3,99) = 49.594, p < .001] and the between-subject factor *Age group* [F(2,31) = 25.674, p < .001]. The post-hoc tests revealed that with the *Direct* interaction users had a significantly lower number of collisions and with the *Accelerometer* interaction users had a significantly higher number of collisions. Finally, no significant differences were found between the *Tap* and *Buttons* interactions in terms of collisions.

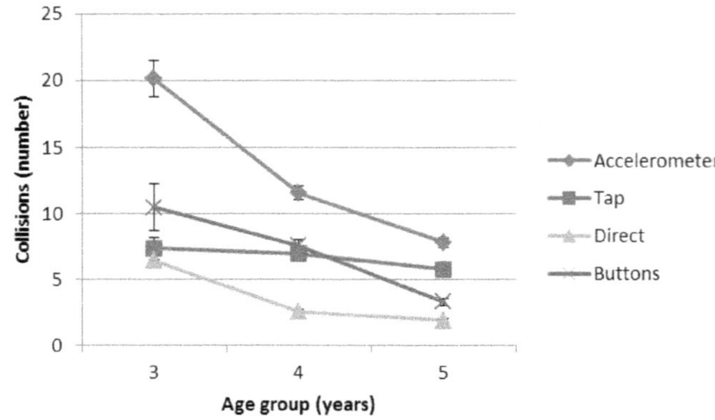

Figure 4. Collisions by interaction mechanism and age group.

The analysis of the *Interaction Mechanism**Age group* interaction also revealed significant main effects [F(6,99) = 11.295, p < .001]. Analyzing the differences in the evolution of the collisions by age group we can see that in the *Tap* interaction the number of collisions remains nearly constant for all age groups. However, in the *Accelerometer* and the *Buttons* interaction there is a significant continuous improvement of the children's precision with age. Finally, in the *Direct* interaction children aged 4 and 5 were more precise than those aged 3 because the former made a significantly lower number of collisions. No differences were found between children aged 4 and 5 for the number of collisions in this interaction mechanism.

DISCUSSION

In response to RQ1, the results show that the interaction mechanism used affects the success rate. As expected *Direct* interaction is the most effective with a 99.66% of the second most effective (73.81%) followed by the *Tap* (68.71%) interaction. Finally, the *Buttons* (62.07%) interaction is the worst in terms of success. As can be seen, the two natural interaction mechanisms evaluated *(Direct & Accelerometer)* overcome the two mediated interactions (*Tap & Buttons)*. The cognitive effort required to map mediated interactions to actual object movements have an impact at these early ages as will be discussed later.

The RQ2, on whether the degree of success is independent of the age group, is answered negatively. This is an expected result given that children are continuously developing their motor and cognitive skills. However, the degree of improvement is also affected by the nature of the interaction mechanism. This is confirmed by the results obtained related to the *Interaction Mechanism**Age group* statistical interaction. On the one hand, the *Direct* style is the less demanding and, hence, the most effective. Even the youngest children evaluated (those in the 3 years-old group) are able to perform it with success rates close to 100%. Hence, there is no evolution with age, since all the children achieved the task with success rates near 100%. On the other hand, the three indirect approaches (*Accelerometer, Tap* and *Buttons*) follow a similar evolution, with the success rate increasing with age. Our results show that the three techniques are unsuitable for children aged 3 and younger. Nevertheless, these techniques have success rates higher than 80% with children in the 4 year-old group and success rates close to 100% in the 5 years-old age group. Hence, even though these techniques are not suitable for the youngest children, they can be effectively used when the application is designed for children aged 4 or older. Finally, as can be seen in Figure 2, no differences in terms of success are found between the four interaction mechanisms evaluated with children in the 5 years-old group. At this age, children are able to achieve the task with success rates higher that 95% in all the interaction mechanisms. Therefore, our results confirm that children at this age have developed the required motor and cognitive skills to succeed when performing the evaluated indirect dragging manipulations.

RQ3 is negatively answered since the completion time is dependent on the interaction mechanism. The order from more to less effective in terms of completion time is the same as the one pointed out for the success rate. The *Direct* interaction is, as expected, the fastest one, since it allows children to move the target with the velocity they choose by moving their finger at the desired speed. Button-based dragging is the worst in terms of completion time because children need to perform repeated vertical and horizontal drag operations when a diagonal trajectory has to be followed and this is time consuming. This is not the case with the accelerometer and tap based operations, in which diagonal movements are directly supported by the interaction style. Finally, if we take a closer look at these two interactions we observe that using an accelerometer is better than using tap interactions in terms of completion time because the change of direction is easily achieved by simply tilting the tablet in the right direction (see Figure 5). In order to achieve the same effect with the tap operation, children need to move their hand across the surface to reach the desired tap point, which is less effective than tilting.

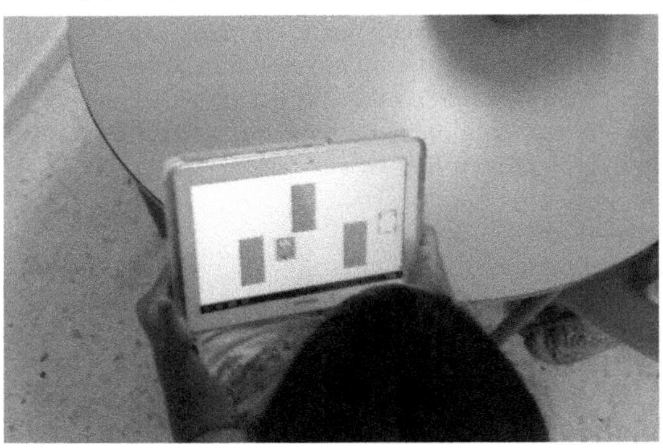

Figure 5. Kindergarten child performing the accelerometer task.

Answering RQ4, on whether age has an impact on the completion time, our results show that the required time to complete the task always decreases with age for all the evaluated interaction styles (see Figure 3). Again, as with success rates, this is consistent with the existing literature on motor and cognitive development in young children [10].

Although the efficiency of all interaction mechanisms increases with age, even the most skilled children (those in the 5 year-old age group) spend a significant amount of time completing the tasks with the *Buttons* and *Tap* interaction styles, respectively. Therefore, designers of applications for kindergarteners requiring very fast indirect drag operations should implement accelerometer-based interactions instead of tap or button-based ones. In fact, the *Accelerometer* interaction has a significantly lower completion time with children aged 4 ($M_{4\text{-years}}$= 24.71s) and children aged 5 ($M_{5\text{-years}}$= 19.34s). Of course, if direct interaction is suitable for the application being designed, it would be the best style, because of its excellent results in terms of efficiency and completion time ($M_{3\text{-years}}$= 20.08s, $M_{4\text{-years}}$= 9.43s, $M_{5\text{-years}}$= 8.18s).

Regarding the children's precision when performing the tasks, the number of collisions is dependent on the interaction mechanism and therefore the response to RQ5 is negative. The *Accelerometer* interaction is the most challenging for children in terms of precision. This occurs because kindergarten children have still not fully developed their fine and gross motor skills and, hence, they are not able to hold the device upright without tilting it. Most of the times, they tilt the device downwards and the target object collides with the bottom edge of the screen repeatedly. No differences are found in terms of collisions between the two mediated interactions (*Tap* & *Buttons*). However, an interesting unexpected issue arose with the *Tap* interaction. We observed during the experiments that children do not have enough cognitive development to estimate in advance the path that the target object is going to follow as a result of a tap operation when obstacles are in their way and so they are not able to prevent the collisions. In the *Buttons* interaction, we also observed an interesting behavior. Kindergarten children very often held a given button until the object to be moved collided with an obstacle or the edge of the screen and then they lifted their finger and tapped another button.

Finally, regarding the effect of the age group on the precision of children (RQ6), once more the superior fine motor skills of the older age groups allows them to be more accurate when performing the task, resulting in a lower number of collisions (see Figure 4).

In addition, evaluating the *Interaction Mechanism*Age group* interaction, the analysis shows that in the *Accelerometer* interaction the number of collisions is reduced significantly with age. However, despite the reduction in the number of collisions, the most skilled children (those in the 5 years-old group) still had a considerable number of collisions (M= 7.81). Hence, designers should take into account that maybe this interaction mechanism is not suitable for children aged 2 to 6 in scenarios in which precision is a mandatory requirement.

Regarding the *Buttons* interaction, no significant differences are found between children aged 3 and 4. However, children aged 5 are significantly more accurate than the youngest groups, with a mean of 3.32 collisions per task. Therefore, when precision is a mandatory requirement the *Buttons* interaction is more appropriate for children aged 5 or older.

On the other hand, no significant improvement in terms of accuracy is observed in the *Tap* interaction. Hence, the cognitive skills required to overcome the intellectual demand to foresee the path that the object will follow and then tap the correct location to avoid collisions is not fully developed in children younger than 6 years old. Thus, this interaction mechanism should be avoided by designers when developing applications targeted at kindergarten children in scenarios requiring high levels of precision.

Finally, in the *Direct* drag manipulation, children in the 3 years-old group are significantly less accurate than those in the 4 and 5 years-old group. In addition, no differences are found between the two older age groups, since these children have a low number of collisions ($M_{4\text{-years}}$= 2.58 & $M_{5\text{-years}}$= 1.93). Therefore, the *Direct* drag interaction mechanism could be used when the scenario requires accuracy in the manipulation with children aged from 4 onwards and there are no restrictions on the use of direct techniques.

In summary, in terms of design recommendations, there are several considerations to be taken into account by developers of applications for these children. First, the three indirect techniques are unsuitable for children aged 3 and younger. These children would need specific assistance strategies if any of the indirect techniques would be applied in this age range. Second, for those applications that need fast indirect dragging manipulations the recommended interaction style would be accelerometer-based followed by tap-based in case the devices to be used do not support the former interaction style. Finally, if precision is a requirement the recommended indirect dragging technique is the button-based one because, as it was discussed above, children have cognitive difficulties to estimate future trajectories of objects when using the tap-based approach.

There are some threats in terms of the generalization of the findings of this study to other contexts and environments and several precautions must be taken. The fact that children had only two minutes of training and they may have previous experiences with the direct drag technique could have influenced the results favoring it in the comparison with the other techniques. Hence, further research should be carried out in order to obtain a more comprehensive comparison between the direct-dragging and the indirect techniques.

CONCLUSIONS AND FUTURE WORK

In this paper we evaluated several indirect alternative dragging mechanisms (accelerometer, tap and buttons based) with kindergarten children as potential candidate interaction styles when direct dragging operations are not suitable. These indirect mechanisms may be mandatory when implementing games or educational tablet applications for kindergarteners, in which the interactive elements to be moved across the surface have to exhibit specific behaviors which are independent of the actual direct movement speed or trajectory of the user's hand.

The results of this study show that the direct dragging approach is the most effective, efficient and precise technique for all pre-kindergarten age groups. In a context in which direct dragging cannot be applied, the most appropriate technique depends on several factors. The three indirect approaches are similarly effective, but unsuitable for three-year-olds or younger children. Indeed, while the success rate with direct dragging is close to one-hundred percent for all age groups, task completion with indirect techniques increases greatly with age. From an efficiency perspective, children under three perform faster with tap and accelerometer techniques than when using buttons, but the evolution with age is not the same for all. At age five, children are more efficient with the accelerometer than using tap or buttons. Regarding precision, while the accelerometer-based dragging proved worse than other techniques for all age groups, the number of collisions decreases with age for all the alternatives. We believe these results will help developers of touch-based interfaces for children to choose the most suitable technique for each context.

Our future work will evaluate the implementation of assistive techniques to overcome some of the problems related to precision that were identified in our experiments. In addition, we also plan to evaluate the ability of kindergarteners to use these indirect dragging mechanisms to move interactive characters in open 2D spaces. The design of visual semiotics [7] to indicate to kindergarteners the direction to follow in open 2D spaces would pave the way for the implementation of educational adventure experiences in which kindergarten children could freely explore the available 2D space. In our opinion these types of games have not yet been fully exploited for this very young age range.

ACKNOWLEDGMENTS

Work supported by the Spanish MECD (FPU14/00136), the GVA (ACIF/2014/214), and by Spanish MINECO and funded by EDRF-FEDER with Project SUPEREMOS TIN2014-60077-R.

REFERENCES

1. Abdul Aziz, N.A., Batmaz, F., Stone, R., and Paul, C. Selection of touch gestures for children's applications. *Proceedings of the Science and Information Conference*, (2013), 721–726.
2. Abdul Aziz, N.A., Mat, N.S., Batmaz, F., Stone, R., and

Paul, C. Selection of Touch Gestures for Children's Applications: Repeated Experiment to Increase Reliability. *International Journal of Advanced Computer Science and Applications 5*, 4 (2014), 97–102.
3. Malizia, A. and Bellucci, A. The artificiality of natural user interfaces. *Communications of the ACM 55*, 3 (2012), 36.
4. Nacher, V., Jaen, J., Navarro, E., Catala, A., González, P. Multi-touch gestures for pre-kindergarten children. *International Journal of Human-Computer Studies 73*, (2015), 37–51.
5. Nacher, V., Garcia-Sanjuan, F., Jaen, J. Interactive Technologies for Preschool Game-Based Instruction: Experiences and Future Challenges. *Entertainment Computing 17, (2016): 19–29.* http://doi.org/10.1016/j.entcom.2016.07.001
6. Nacher, V. and Jaen, J. Evaluating the Accuracy of Pre-kindergarten Children Multi-touch Interaction. In *IFIP TC.13 International Conference on Human-Computer Interaction - INTERACT*. Bamberg, 2015, 549–556.
7. Nacher, V., Jaen, J., and Catala, A. Evaluating Multitouch Semiotics to Empower Prekindergarten Instruction with Interactive Surfaces. *Interacting with Computers*, (2016).
8. Nacher, V., Jaen, J., Catala, A., Navarro, E., and Gonzalez, P. Improving Pre-Kindergarten Touch Performance. *Proceedings of the 9th ACM International Conference on Interactive Tabletops and Surfaces*, ACM (2014), 163–166.
9. Norman, D.A. The way I see it: Natural user interfaces are not natural. *interactions 17*, 3 (2010), 6–10.
10. Piaget, J. *The Child and Reality.* Grossman, New York, 1973.
11. Shneiderman, B. and Plaisant, C. *Designing the User Interface: Strategies for Effective Human-Computer Interaction.* Addison-Wesley, Boston, 2004.
12. Vatavu, R., Cramariuc, G., and Schipor, D.M. Touch interaction for children aged 3 to 6 years : Experimental findings and relationship to motor skills. *International Journal of Human-Computer Studies 74*, (2015), 54–76.

Effect of Touch Latency on Elementary vs. Bimanual Composite Tasks

Elie Cattan
University of Grenoble
LIG, UJF
Grenoble, France
elie.cattan@imag.fr

Amélie Rochet-Capellan
University of Grenoble
Gipsa-lab, CNRS
Grenoble, France
amelie.rochet-capellan@gipsa-lab.grenoble-inp.fr

François Bérard
University of Grenoble
LIG, Grenoble-INP
Grenoble, France
francois.berard@imag.fr

ABSTRACT

Touch latency has been shown to reduce users' performances but most studies focus on one-handed elementary tasks such as pointing or tracking a single object. The everyday use of touch devices is made, however, of more complex "composite" tasks combining several objects with potential bimanual interaction. Such a composite task may increase users' cognitive load which makes latency less perceivable [2]. We thus expected that the impact of latency on users' performances should be smaller in composite tasks than in elementary tasks.

We tested this hypothesis by comparing the degradation effect of latency on users' performances in an elementary vs. a composite task. The elementary task consisted in positioning a single object. The composite task involved sorting and positioning objects with a two-handed interaction, inducing more complex planning and motor strategies that could be seen as an additional cognitive load. Contrary to expectations, the degradation effect was comparable in the two tasks. This study indicates that the substantial hindrance of latency, demonstrated on elementary tasks, also exists in more complex tasks that better represent the every day use of touch devices. This strengthens the motivation to question the interaction between the task properties and latency effect and to adapt commercial devices and applications accordingly.

Author Keywords

latency; direct-touch; dragging task; composite task; bimanual interaction; target acquisition; user performances

ACM Classification Keywords

H.5.2 User Interfaces: Input devices and strategies (e.g., mouse, touchscreen)

INTRODUCTION

Touch latency, the delay between a user's action on a touchscreen and the corresponding feedback, has been proved to deteriorate users' performances, even at levels as low as 25ms [5, 10]. These results were obtained with target acquisition tasks, following the Fitts' law paradigm [6]. Target acquisition, as well as the tracking and steering studied in the mouse-latency literature, are elementary tasks: they involve the independent repetition of a single gesture. Elementary tasks are implicitly considered to be the building block of everyday interaction. However, out of the lab, interactions happen in complex contexts with multiple items and targets. When available, users also perform bimanual interactions, which supports some degree of parallelism and improves performance [11]. Everyday interactions can thus be seen as "composite tasks" in which the elementary tasks studied in the literature are interleaved with other higher level cognitive tasks, such as dealing with distractors [3], planning the order of execution of the subtasks, or allocating the dominant and non-dominant hand to the subtasks. All could be seen as an increase of cognitive load.

Recent studies have shown that, as the cognitive load of a task increases, participants' ability to perceive latency decreases [2]. In addition, if the non-dominant hand is engaged in accurate gestures, its motions are slower than those of the dominant hand [12], which also makes latency less perceivable. When less perceivable, the effect of latency on users' performances is expected to be milder. The main motivation of this work is to study how the strong negative effect of touch-latency, measured on simple laboratory tasks, applies to a more complex task that is similar to the tasks performed in everyday use. In particular, a weaker effect of latency on composite tasks could account for the widespread use of touch devices despite having high levels of latency, i.e. significantly higher than the latencies tested in the lab studies.

We studied the difference of the effect of touch-latency on users' performances between an elementary dragging task and a composite sorting task. The composite task is made of several dragging actions, similar to those of the elementary task, but performed with the two hands. We considered that it increases the cognitive load, compared with the elementary task, as it requires sorting decisions and planification in relation with the coordination of the two hands. We expected latency to have a smaller effect in the composite task than in the elementary task, but the results did not reveal any significant difference. We discuss the results in relation to possible

ISS 2016, November 6–9, 2016, Niagara Falls, ON, Canada.

ACM ISBN 978-1-4503-4248-3/16/11 ...$15.00.
http://dx.doi.org/10.1145/2992154.2992160

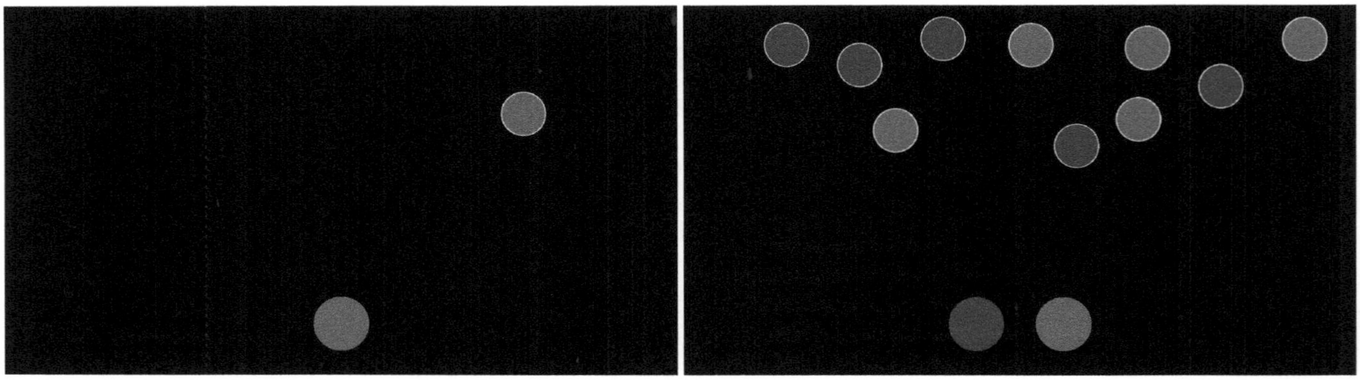

Figure 1. Display at the beginning of an elementary task (left) and at the beginning of a composite task (right). Users have to drag the disc objects located in the top half of the display within the targets located in the bottom side. The composite task is executed with the two index fingers and requires matching the color of objects and targets.

explanations and consider the general implication for touch interaction.

RELATED WORK

The effect of latency on users' performances in *mouse* interaction was studied using various elementary tasks such as pointing [7, 13], 2d tracking [17], 3d aiming [9] or steering [7]. All these studies reveal a clear negative impact of latency on users' performances. In the case of *touch* interaction, the effect of latency on users' performances was only investigated using Fitts' target acquisition tasks [6]. The degradation is demonstrated even at latency levels smaller than 25ms [5, 10]. The effect of latency on users' performances was always considered on elementary tasks, i.e. the repetition of a task requiring a single gesture, but not studied for more demanding tasks. In particular, the effect of latency was not studied in the case of two-handed multi-touch interaction on composite tasks.

System latency was also considered in more complex situations, but to evaluate users' ability to *perceive* latency rather than to measure the effect of latency on users' performances. Meehan et al. studied the effect of latency on the feeling of immersion in stressful virtual environments; they found that immersion was better at 50ms of latency than at 90ms [14]. Anderson et al. asked users to rate the usability of various desktop applications at different levels of latency [1]. Usability was rated low at high levels of latency, but with a clear effect only over 280ms, a latency higher than those of current commercial devices. Annett et al. used drawing and writing tasks to show that the ability to perceive system latency decreases with an increase of task complexity [2]. The perception threshold jumps from 6ms for dragging a square with a pen [15] to 61ms when drawing a star [2]. These studies indicate that, when performing a task with a high cognitive cost, the threshold of *latency perception* is higher than when performing a simple task. As latency becomes less perceivable, we expect users' performances to be less affected.

In our *composite* experimental task, one way to increase participant's cognitive load is the requirement for bimanual interaction. Kabbash et al. demonstrated that the use of two hands could improve performances for direct manipulation tasks [11]. However, the addition of a second hand does not simply double users' performances. Two-handed interaction engages a complex behavior where the partition of the work performed by the dominant and non-dominant hand is not symmetric [8, 12]. In a bimanual sorting task, attention, decision making and fine motor control has to be phased with the coordination of the two hands. Together with the slower motion of the non-dominant hand, this should increase the threshold of latency perception.

USER STUDY

The main objective of this experiment is to examine if and how the strong negative effect of latency on users' performances, previously measured on elementary tasks, applies to more demanding composite tasks. An "in the wild" study would provide a faithful depiction of everyday use. However, "in the wild" studies are not well suited for an accurate measurement of users' performances variations, which is best performed with repeated measurement of a controlled task. We thus designed a laboratory study, which included an elementary task and a composite task. Our rational was that the composite task, even if not an actual everyday use of the system, is more similar to everyday use than the elementary task.

For the elementary task, we use the dragging of an object to a target. For comparison purposes, we chose the composite task to be very similar to the elementary task in term of movements trajectory and indices of difficulty. However, in the composite task users are presented with *a set* of objects instead of a single object, and they must drag each object in a bimanual interaction to one of two targets depending on their color. Examples of the graphical display in the elementary and composite tasks are shown in Figure 1.

Compared to the elementary task, the composite task adds a simple sorting subtask (objects go to targets of matching color), a planning subtask (participants optimize the sequence of drags of the objects), the planning of hand allocation to objects and the motor coordination of the two hands in a two-handed interaction. The composite task is designed explicitly to impose more cognitive load on the subjects. It is an "orthogonal assemblage" [11] where each hand executes independent subtasks which could "impose a considerable cognitive load on subjects" [11]. Parallelizing actions also adds a lot of visual diversion: users visual focus constantly switches between the two hands, which can also affect the cognitive load [11] and reduce the attentional ressources available to perceive latency.

As a first step, we test both tasks in a low vs high latency design. We selected two latency levels: 25ms is the lowest achievable latency of our system, and 100ms is a relatively high level where a clear effect of latency should appear, at least on the elementary task [5, 10]. By choosing two values that are clearly apart (a 300% increase from low to high latency), we expect to enhance the difference between the tasks and make a potential effect clearly visible. We test both the elementary and composite tasks at 25ms and 100ms, and we assess users' performances degradation in both cases.

Apparatus

Current commercial touch devices exhibit latency in the order of 80ms or more. Custom made low-latency devices are thus used to experiment with low levels of latency [2, 5, 16]. Following Cattan et al. [5], we use optical tracking to reproduce a system with 25ms of baseline latency. A 24 inches screen is set horizontally on the desk and touch is simulated with optical tracking. Five cameras track the position of markers taped on participants' index fingers. We use custom developed C++ software for rendering. In addition to the 25ms baseline latency of the system, idle time is used in the event queue to simulate a 100ms latency system. Latency levels are regularly controlled using a predictive method [4].

Design

The main factor of the experiment is TASK_TYPE, which has two conditions: *elementary* and *composite*. In both conditions participants have to drag disc *objects* (radius 1.78cm) into disc *targets* (radius 2.20cm) of the same color. Each time an object is released, i.e. participant lift their finger from the surface, a feedback is given: the color of the target flashes for 0.1s to green (resp. red) if the drag succeeds (resp. fails). A drag is successful if the object is released when entirely within the target's boundary. Participants are asked to execute the tasks "as fast as possible while attempting to avoid failures". Pauses are offered regularly to avoid fatigue effects. During pauses, a turtle or a rabbit is displayed to announce whether the next block will be with low or high latency. This warning reduces the surprise effect of a change of latency and avoid outliers at the beginning of a block. Participants choose when to end the pause by touching a button in the elementary task, or two buttons in the composite task. The buttons are displayed at the targets' locations to ensure that the participants' fingers are at the same position at the beginning of each trial.

In the elementary condition a blue target is displayed at a fixed position at the bottom center of the screen. Blue disc objects appear sequentially at pseudo-random locations in the upper half of the screen. A *trial* consists of dragging the object on top of the target with the index of the dominant hand and lifting the finger from the display. As soon as the object is released and the feedback provided, a new disc appear for the next trial. Trials are grouped by *blocks* of 40, each trial having a unique initial position of the object (Fitts' indexes of difficulty range from 5.08 to 6.19). Blocks of 40 trials are presented first with low latency, then with high latency. This sequence is repeated five times for a total of 400 dragging actions: [40 (drags) x 2 (latencies)] x 5 (repetitions). Hence, latency conditions were interleaved, always starting with the smallest latency as it allows training with the task in "natural condition". Interleaving blocks is then a way to control for order effect as in this design, low latency occurs 5 times before and 4 times after the high latency and conversely. The initial positions of the objects are also randomized within each block to avoid sequence learning. A pause is offered between each block.

For the composite condition, two targets, one purple, one blue, are displayed 7cm apart in the bottom half of the screen. At the beginning of each trial, 10 disc objects, 5 purple and 5 blue, appear simultaneously in the upper half of the screen. A trial consists of dragging the 10 objects to the appropriate target. The index fingers of the two hands are used. A trial ends when the 10 objects have been moved and released. There are 4 different starting sets of 10 objects, which, grouped together, include the 40 object-to-target relative positions used in the elementary task. The four sets are presented first with low latency, then with high latency. This sequence is repeated five times for a total of 400 dragging actions: [10 (drags) x 4 (sets) x 2 (latencies)] x 5 (repetitions). Hence, latency conditions were interleaved as in the elementary condition. A pause is provided between each trial to ensure that participants' hands go back to the initial position before the next trial.

In a within subject design, 12 participants (3 females) executed both conditions of TASK_TYPE in *two parts* of the experiment. They were all right handed with an average age of 28.3 years old (range [24..38]). In the first part, half of the participants started with the elementary task and the other half with the composite task.

Measurements

Our goal is to assess the *impact of latency* depending on TASK_TYPE. This requires a delicate choice of the measured variable as different tasks inherently yield different durations: if the same duration increase, expressed in seconds, is observed for a long vs. a short task, then it denotes a latency impact that is actually stronger for the short task than for the long task. In order to compare the latency impact across tasks of various durations, we have to measure the *relative* increase of *dragging time*, in percentage, from the low to the high levels of latency.

For the *error*, measuring the increase of failed targets as an absolute value or as a percentage of the total number of target is similar since the number of targets to acquire in each "latency x task type" condition is the same (200 targets). Hence, we measure the impact of latency on *error* as an absolute difference between the two latency conditions that we can compare across TASK_TYPEs.

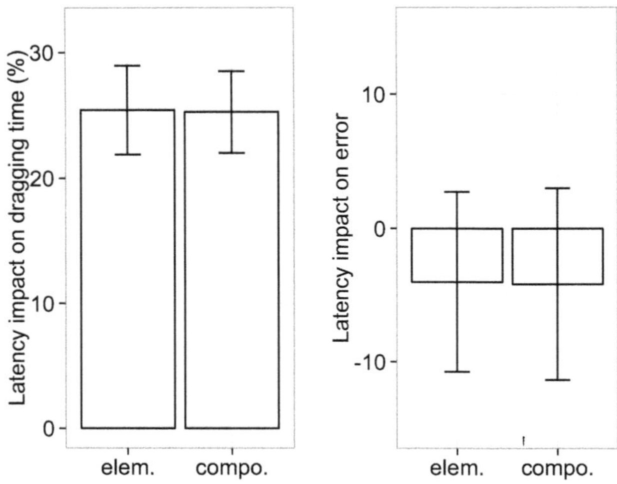

Figure 2. Effect of the task type (elementary vs. composite) on the latency impact on dragging time (left) and errors (right).

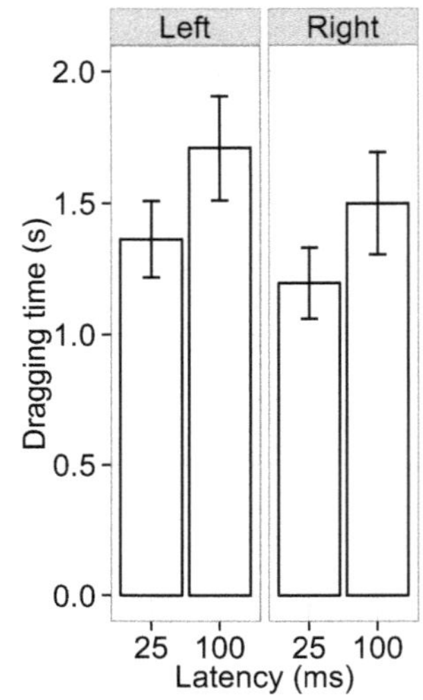

Figure 3. Effect of HAND and LATENCY on the dragging time during the composite task.

	time_impact (%)		*error_impact*	
	elem.	compo.	elem.	compo.
average	25.4	25.3	-4.0	-4.2
min	21.1	16.0	-21	-25
max	40.8	34.9	13	13
stddev	5.54	5.11	10.6	11.3

Table 1. Values measured on the dependent variables depending on the task type (elementary vs. composite).

We thus record two dependent variables:

- the latency *time_impact* on dragging time: the *relative* increase of the average *dragging time* when latency increases from 25ms to 100ms, measured as a percentage.
- the latency *error_impact*: the increase of the number of failed targets when latency increases from 25ms to 100ms.

The expected effects of TASK_TYPE and LATENCY on *dragging time* and *error* were verified with a repeated measure ANOVA. The effect of TASK_TYPE on the two dependent variables was then tested with paired sample t-tests.

Results

As expected, the average dragging time (for a unique dragging action) was higher in the composite condition than in the elementary condition (1.44s. vs 0.94s, $F_{1,11} = 169, p < 1e-07$). This would indicate a greater cognitive demand of the composite condition. There is also a clear effect of LATENCY on the *dragging time* ($F_{1,11} = 255, p < 1e-08$). In the elementary condition, the average *time_impact* across participants was 25.4%. This is consistent with results from the literature [5, 10]. The time_impact in the composite condition was very similar at 25.3%. The difference was not found significant with a paired sample t-test ($t(11) = 0.097, p = .92$).

The number of errors was significantly higher in the composite condition than in the elementary condition (25.6 errors vs 20.9 erros, $F_{1,11} = 5.4, p = .04$), but there was no significant effect of LATENCY ($F_{1,11} = 2.0, p > .18$). In the elementary condition, the average number of failed targets per participant decreased by 4 from 22.9 to 18.9 with the latency increase. In the composite condition, the decrease was 4.2 from 27.7 to 23.5. Less errors at higher levels of latency may be explained by participants being more cautious when they feel that the system does not respond as they expect. The difference between the elementary and the composite task was not found significant with a paired sample t-test ($t(11) = 0.07, p = .95$).

In summary, TASK_TYPE was found to have an effect neither on *time_impact* nor on *error_impact*. An absence of effect can not be statistically proved, but a significant effect with more participants or longer sessions seems unlikely with p-values above 0.9. In any cases, these results indicate that even if a significant difference of the impact of latency could be observed, the impact would still be very similar accross TASK_TYPE.

The results of the influence of TASK_TYPE on the dependent variables is reported in Table 1 and illustrated on Figure 2.

DISCUSSION

Latency has been shown to significantly reduce users' performances, but only in the case of elementary tasks and single-handed interaction. In addition, recent research efforts have demonstrated that users are less capable of perceiving latency as the cognitive demand of the task increases [2]. In this study, we worked on the assumption that when users' perception of latency is reduced, then their performances should be less affected. We attempted to observe such a reduction of latency's influence, but the results don't support this assumption. The higher average dragging time in the composite condition is a sign of a higher cognitive demand compared to the elementary condition. However, latency has a very similar influence in both conditions: a 25.4% vs 25.3% increase of dragging times when going from 25ms to 100ms.

We investigated how the non-dominant hand could have influenced the results. Focusing on the composite task, we performed a repeated measure ANOVA to study how the factors HAND and LATENCY influenced the object dragging time. As all our participants are right-handed, we use the levels *left* and *right* for the non-dominant and dominant hands, respectively. The main effect of HAND supports what is expected: as our dragging task requires a good amount of precision, the dragging time is significantly higher for the left hand (1.54s.) than for the right hand (1.35s.) ($F_{1,11} = 10, p = .009$). More interestingly, latency clearly makes both hands' dragging time increase ($F_{1,11} = 142, p < 1e-06$) but there is no evidence of an interaction between HAND and LATENCY ($F_{1,11} = 1.3, p > 0.25$): the effect of latency on performances appears to be as strong on the left hand as on the right hand. Focusing back to our main result, the introduction of the non-dominant hand cannot explain the stronger than expected influence of latency in the composite task.

We also interviewed participants at the end of the experiment to get their subjective impression. We asked them to rate four sentences on a Likert scale from 1 (strongly disagree) to 5 (strongly agree). Participants "clearly noticed the difference between the two delay conditions" in both tasks, but they better perceived latency in the elementary task ($M = 4.83, SD = 0.39$) compared to the composite task ($M = 4.5, SD = 0.52$), $t(11) = 2.35, p = .039$. This is consistent with the results from Annett et al. on latency perception [2]: with a greater cognitive load, latency is less perceived. Participants felt that "the delay strongly impacted their performances" on the elementary task ($M = 4.5, SD = 0.80$) and on the composite task ($M = 4, SD = 1.0$), but the difference is not significant ($t(11) = 1.11, p = 0.29$). The subjective questionnaire is consistent with the quantitative results: even if latency is less perceivable in the composite task than in the elementary task, there is no clear agreement on a weaker effect on performance in the composite task.

This study, revealing the unexpected strong effect of latency on demanding tasks, opens the way to further fundamental research that should question the detrimental mechanisms of latency. In particular, we need to understand how latency can keep the same influence on users' performances when its perception by users is reduced. This will require further investigations, such as a fine analysis of finger trajectories with feedback (delayed or not) and no feedback at all.

In term of touch system design, our experiment emphasizes the crucial importance of low latency even in an every day use context. It reveals that the negative influence of latency on users' performances, previously exposed on elementary tasks, might generalize to a broader range of tasks, in particular tasks that resemble the every day use of touch surfaces. Hence, efforts to improve touch detection in hardware [16] or software [5] should be pursued, as any improvement should have immediate benefits for the users. More user studies are also required to understand the interaction between the latency of the system and the properties of the task. This could open new alternative for task-specific design.

CONCLUSION

In this paper, we compared the effect of a touch-system's latency on an elementary dragging task and a bimanual composite task more similar to the everyday use of touch devices. We expected that the more demanding composite task would reduce participants' ability to perceive latency and thus limit latency's influence on participants' performances. We observed, however, that the latency's negative influence on performance, shown in many previous studies, was similar in the more demanding composite task. Regarding the everyday use of touch surfaces, we contemplated the idea that a smaller effect of latency on composite tasks could account for the success of touch devices despite their high levels of latency. Rather, our study indicates that the reason of the success may lie elsewhere. This study opens the way to further reasearch questionning the detrimental mechanisms of latency and its interaction with task properties. In addition, it reinforces the expectation of a clearly noticeable benefit of latency reduction in commercial touch devices.

ACKNOWLEDGMENTS

This work has been partially supported by the LabEx PERSYVAL-Lab (ANR-11-LABX-0025-01).

REFERENCES

1. Anderson, G., Doherty, R., and Ganapathy, S. User perception of touch screen latency. In *International Conference of Design, User Experience, and Usability*, Springer (2011), 195–202.

2. Annett, M., Ng, A., Dietz, P., Bischof, W. F., and Gupta, A. How low should we go?: Understanding the perception of latency while inking. In *Proceedings of Graphics Interface (GI)* (2014).

3. Blanch, R., and Ortega, M. Benchmarking pointing techniques with distractors: adding a density factor to fitts' pointing paradigm. In *Proceedings of the SIGCHI Conference on Human Factors in Computing Systems*, ACM (2011), 1629–1638.

4. Cattan, E., Rochet-Capellan, A., and Bérard, F. A predictive approach for an end-to-end touch-latency measurement. In *Proceedings of the 2015 International Conference on Interactive Tabletops & Surfaces*, ACM (2015), 215–218.

5. Cattan, E., Rochet-Capellan, A., Perrier, P., and Bérard, F. Reducing latency with a continuous prediction: Effects on users' performance in direct-touch target acquisitions. In *Proceedings of the 2015 International Conference on Interactive Tabletops & Surfaces*, ACM (2015), 205–214.

6. Fitts, P. M. The information capacity of the human motor system in controlling the amplitude of movement. *Journal of Experimental Psychology 47*, 6 (1954), 381–391.

7. Friston, S., Karlstrom, P., and Steed, A. The effects of low latency on pointing and steering tasks.

8. Guiard, Y. Asymmetric division of labor in human skilled bimanual action: The kinematic chain as a model. *Journal of motor behavior 19*, 4 (1987), 486–517.
9. Ivkovic, Z., Stavness, I., Gutwin, C., and Sutcliffe, S. Quantifying and mitigating the negative effects of local latencies on aiming in 3d shooter games. In *Proceedings of ACM CHI* (2015).
10. Jota, R., Ng, A. N., Dietz, P., and Wigdor, D. How fast is fast enough? a study of the effects of latency in direct-touch pointing tasks. In *ACM CHI*, ACM (2013).
11. Kabbash, P., Buxton, W., and Sellen, A. Two-handed input in a compound task. In *Proceedings of the SIGCHI Conference on Human Factors in Computing Systems*, ACM (1994), 417–423.
12. Kabbash, P., MacKenzie, I. S., and Buxton, W. Human performance using computer input devices in the preferred and non-preferred hands. In *Proceedings of the INTERACT'93 and CHI'93 Conference on Human Factors in Computing Systems*, ACM (1993), 474–481.
13. MacKenzie, I. S., and Ware, C. Lag as a determinant of human performance in interactive systems. In *Proceedings of ACM CHI* (1993), 488–493.
14. Meehan, M., Razzaque, S., Whitton, M. C., and Brooks Jr, F. P. Effect of latency on presence in stressful virtual environments. In *Virtual Reality, 2003. Proceedings. IEEE*, IEEE (2003), 141–148.
15. Ng, A., Annett, M., Dietz, P., Gupta, A., and Bischof, W. F. In the blink of an eye: Investigating latency perception during stylus interaction. In *ACM CHI*, ACM (2014), 1103–1112.
16. Ng, A., Lepinski, J., Wigdor, D., Sanders, S., and Dietz, P. Designing for low-latency direct-touch input. In *Proceedings of ACM UIST*, ACM (2012), 453–464.
17. Pavlovych, A., and Gutwin, C. Assessing target acquisition and tracking performance for complex moving targets in the presence of latency and jitter. In *Proceedings of the 2012 Graphics Interace Conference*, Canadian Information Processing Society (2012), 109–116.

UD Co-Spaces: A Table-Centred Multi-Display Environment for Public Engagement in Urban Design Charrettes

Narges Mahyar, Kelly J. Burke, Jialiang (Ernest) Xiang, Siyi (Cathy) Meng, Kellogg S. Booth, Cynthia L. Girling, and Ronald W. Kellett
The University of British Columbia, Vancouver, BC V6T 1Z4, CANADA
{nmayhar, jlxiang, mengxixi, ksbooth}@cs.ubc.ca,
kelly.burke@ubc.ca, and {cgirling, rkellett}@sala.ubc.ca

ABSTRACT
UD Co-Spaces (Urban Design Collaborative Spaces) is an integrated, tabletop-centered multi-display environment for engaging the public in the complex process of collaborative urban design. We describe the iterative user-centered process that we followed over six years through a close interdisciplinary collaboration involving experts in urban design and neighbourhood planning. Versions of UD Co-Spaces were deployed in five real-world charrettes (planning workshops) with 83 participants, a heuristic evaluation with three domain experts, and a qualitative laboratory study with 37 participants. We reflect on our design decisions and how multi-display environments can engage a broad range of stakeholders in decision making and foster collaboration and co-creation within urban design. We examine the parallel use of different displays, each with tailored interactive visualizations, and whether this affects what people can learn about the consequences of their choices for sustainable neighborhoods. We assess UD Co-Spaces using seven principles for collaborative urban design tools that we identified based on literature in urban design, CSCW, and public engagement.

Author Keywords
Charrette, collaboration, interaction design, interdisciplinary design, public engagement, sustainability, urban design, user-centered design, visualization

ACM Classification Keywords
H.5.2-3. Information Interfaces and Presentation: User Interfaces, Group and Organization Interfaces

INTRODUCTION
This application paper describes UD Co-Spaces (Urban Design Collaborative Spaces), an interactive multi-display collaborative environment to support complex urban design exercises. Urban design is the process of designing neighbourhoods and larger urban areas. It typically focuses on the relationships of buildings, streets and public spaces to make urban areas functional, livable and sustainable.

ISS '16, November 06-09, 2016, Niagara Falls, ON, Canada

DOI: http://dx.doi.org/10.1145/2992154.2992163

UD Co-Spaces is centered on a multi-user tabletop display that enables stakeholders to collaboratively design the future of a neighbourhood through direct multi-touch manipulation of planning options, interactively explore design alternatives, and cross-check with sustainability indicators in real time during a session. It includes auxiliary wall displays and hand-held individual displays that extend the functionality of the tabletop to better support Arnstein's notion of *engagement* for users [2]. The interdisciplinary project is a long-term collaboration involving a team of human-computer interaction (HCI), computer-supported cooperative work (CSCW), urban design, and public engagement researchers.

Definitions and terms. Our target application is urban design charrettes (or simply *charrettes*), one common method for engaging the public in complex planning for urban design. Charrettes are intensive multi-day processes during which a team of professionals and a diverse set of community stakeholders create a holistic development plan through a series of iterative feedback loops [7, 9, 15]. Charrettes often utilise direct manipulation of physical representations of urban design precedents or *cases*, such as buildings, streets, or parks. A case has information such as its footprint (for a building and its associated surroundings), height, volume, energy usage, and other attributes. A *pattern* is a spatial layout of cases that constitutes a possible urban design. Increasingly, urban design considers sustainability and uses *indicators* such as building occupancy levels, commercial and residential capacities, density, dwelling types, energy usage, land use, jobs, transportation utilisation, walkability indices for neighborhoods, and other measures related to sustainability that help estimate the environmental and social consequences of a proposed urban design pattern. Indicators are calculated based on the spatial layout and attributes of an urban design pattern, often using heuristics derived from urban design models.

In this paper, the term "design" is overloaded. It could mean designing urban environments or it could mean designing environments to support urban design. We try to make clear which is meant each time we use the term, but usually we mean designing urban environments.

Real-world application: the urban design charrette. Charrettes have been characterised as "an impossible problem in an absurdly short time" where the constraints are an essential characteristic of the process [7]. Charrette participants include facilitators, design professionals (architects, urban designers), experts (planners, engineers, scientists), and public stakeholders who have a vested interest in the project. These are our users. In this process, participants explore multiple variables and possible solutions. Charrettes still rely heavily on "hand" drawings completed by design professionals. They often lack rigorous evaluation, particularly in real time. Where digital tools such as GIS mapping have been introduced, they remain expert driven so that non-expert participants remain passive consumers of information [5, 7, 15]. A bottleneck in the adoption of these tools is that software developers are too far removed from the planning environment [17], so they lack important contextual knowledge concerning the diverse interests that steer the interactions of growing numbers of stakeholders. We spent considerable time learning about existing charrette processes and workflows, and the shortcomings of current practice. Our research examines how surface interaction techniques on multiple interconnected displays can better support user engagement in complex processes of urban design during charrettes.

Value hypothesis: surfaces promote engagement. Stakeholders with different knowledge, expertise, and objectives participate in public consultation phases of urban design. Our main goals are: (a) engaging different groups of stakeholders to actively interact with design options, (b) fostering collaboration and co-creation of urban design through the use of touch-based interaction and surface technology, and (c) enabling stakeholders to understand consequences of their choices using simple visual encodings that connect sustainability indicators to urban form.

Design process and principles: domain and user centered. System design choices for UD Co-Spaces were informed by various literature in CSCW, planning support systems, and public engagement. We followed an iterative user-centered process to identify appropriate surface-based interaction tools that promote common ground among stakeholders with various backgrounds and objectives. We examined how different display form factors might increase engagement with both the process and the group. Through our observations of the system in use, we considered which collaboration and visualization technologies enable stakeholders to interactively design solutions and better understand the consequences of their designs. Three major system iterations each added a new display type to UD Co-Spaces to support collaboration and visualization activities identified in formative evaluations.

One challenge we faced was lack of design guidelines for charrettes that address engagement, collaboration, and other domain-specific requirements. Although our system design choices were informed by collocated collaborative visualization guidelines on tabletops [12, 20], we also reviewed literature in urban design and public engagement and adopted principles from Arnstein [2], and Snyder [22] to the narrower challenge of building engaging Collaborative Planning Support Systems (CPSS) for the urban design charrette process.

Based on these principles and our own observations of UD Co-Spaces in use, we synthesised a set of seven principles for

Figure 1. The third iteration of UD Co-Spaces, a multi-display collaborative environment where multiple users can simultaneously interact with 2D maps on a tabletop, with 3D views on the wall, and with two applications on hand-held iPads.

urban design charrettes: (1) ***engagement***, (2) ***collaboration***, (3) ***interactive visualization***, (4) ***accessibility***, (5) ***iteration***, (6) ***understanding consequences***, and (7) ***transparency***. In our discussion we describe the principles and explain how the features in UD Co-Spaces work together to address them.

Next best alternative: traditional planning systems. Collaborative and visualization technology can play an important role in increasing public engagement in urban design, but few systems support the complexity and interactivity required for a truly collaborative decision-making process. Many current tools use powerful GIS-based visualizations, however, they are expert-intensive, non-collaborative, and rarely provide real-time feedback because they require significant effort to produce visual encodings of indicators.

Contributions and overview of the paper. We describe UD Co-Spaces (Fig. 1) and the iterative user-centered design process we followed over six years in close collaboration with experts in urban design and neighbourhood planning. We reflect on system design decisions and how multi-display environments can engage a broad range of stakeholders in decision making and foster collaboration and co-creation for urban design. We examine the parallel use of different displays, each with tailored interactive visualizations, and whether this affects what people learn about the consequences of their choices for sustainable neighborhoods. Finally, we assess UD Co-Spaces using the seven design principles that we identified for collaborative urban design tools that target charrette-style processes.

After summarizing prior research on the charrette process in urban design, planning support system software, interactive visualization and collaboration tools, multi-display environments, and guidelines for assessing urban design tools and processes, we describe the iterative development of UD Co-Spaces and its deployment and evaluation through three prototypes. We conclude with a discussion of lessons learned and suggestions for future work to support the charrette process using the framework adapted from the literature.

RELATED WORK

There is a rich body of research in CSCW and tabletop applications for collocated collaboration, visual analytics, and decision making. We focus only on urban design tabletop applications and charrette-style processes where the goals are to provide tools that help users understand the consequences of design choices and promote a sense of empowerment that encourages broad-based public engagement.

Planning support systems. There are many digital Planning Support Systems (PSS) under development that are used to engage the public with long-range decision-making around climate change [6,8]. Built primarily upon GIS and decision-support tools, PSS are digital systems that integrate spatial and non-spatial analysis with simulation and visualization capacity specifically tailored to the needs and processes of planning-analysis, prediction and prescription [14]. Our goal is to address the challenge of public engagement identified by researchers [11] by providing comparative data about spatial scenarios that is accessible and understandable by the general public.

Interactive visualization. Computers can provide visualization methods to increase understanding, actively engage with lay people, and expand the reach of public engagement processes. The Planning and Urban Design Standards [3] define visualization in this context as "the process of taking abstract ideas or data and translating them into easily understood or interpreted images to enhance planning, urban design and decision-making processes." Visualization tools can display urban forms in two and three dimensions with associated data: computerised versions of traditional maps, perspective drawings, and data plots [1].

Most similar to our work are PSS tools that link and visualize complex information so non-professional stakeholders can better engage and understand long-range consequences of decisions.[1] These PSS support 3D scenario development linked to preset planning parameters, source data customised to location and application, integration of spatial and non-spatial data, trial and error scenario testing, and plan revision. However, many of these tools are suited only to a narrow range of scale (spatial extent) and do not adjust well to other scales. For example, MetroQuest is well suited to study policy questions at the city or metropolitan scale, whereas CommunityViz is better suited to urban form scenarios at only the district scale [8]. The level of expertise needed to use each system varies widely. Some are relatively user friendly, whereas others require significant expertise [8]. For planners to engage and use PSS in their day-to-day work, the systems must be more flexible and adaptable to different circumstances, easier to learn, and better at providing interfaces for the public [14].

Tabletop systems. There has been previous work on collaborative tabletop systems for urban planning [4,10,13,17,23]. Perhaps best known is URP, from the MIT Media Lab [23]. It is a workbench environment with a tangible user interface that allows urban planners to study how architectural structures will affect light, wind, and other factors that have an impact on urban design. The same group developed Luminous Table [13] to address limitations in URP. Luminous Table is an augmented or mixed reality system that blends digital tabletop objects with physical objects integrating 2D drawings, 3D models, and computational simulations. Physical models of buildings can be placed on the table and they will be recognised by the system and then simulations calculate shadows and wind flows that can be rendered on the table. A 2D drawing can be provided as a background image for the study area.

Multi-display environments. Some research has utilised multiple displays used in conjunction with collaborative tabletops. For example, Wagner et al. [25] developed a mixed-reality system for urban planning using both tabletop and wall displays with physical objects on the table. The objects are only used as tokens instead of being actual scale models of buildings as in Luminous Table [13]. However, the application is more a presentation tool for previously developed urban designs, with little support for interactive design. ETH's ValueLab [10] is a collaborative environment that brings together large interactive displays and visualizations to facilitate public participation in the planning of megacities (what ETH researchers refer to as "Future Cities"). GIS data and visualization software is used to simulate design choices. ColorTable [17] is an interactive round table designed to facilitate communication between diverse stakeholders. It utilises a tangible user interface and tokens placed on the table to represent design elements, such as buildings or streets. It uses a physical map augmented with 2D images and 3D objects to lend the design area more realism. A perspective view of the design is provided by a projected image on a wall display.

Tangible vs. digital. Our goal is different from other systems. We target urban design activities and explicitly focus on user engagement, collaboration, and awareness of design consequences. The collaborative and interactive environments of ColorTable and Value Lab are the most similar to UD Co-Spaces in terms of their goals, which are focused on collaboration and public participation. However, the system architecture of each is quite different from that of UD Co-Spaces: Value Lab relies on GIS data and 3D animations for its visualization needs, while ColorTable's tangible user interface relies on physical tokens to represent design features. Evaluation of the ColorTable revealed "that participants had troubles following long workflows, organizing the number of objects, and interpreting which physical object is linked to which digital counterpart in the case of large differences in size" [17].

The obvious advantages of tangibility are, in our opinion, outweighed by the overhead of providing physical artifacts appropriate to a range of urban settings. Our research provides a totally digital solution, with the possibility of supporting tangible objects in the future. UD Co-Spaces uses external systems as components to provide flexibility and extensibility of geographic areas and building types for planning exercises. Neither Value Lab nor ColorTable incorporates hand-held devices; UD Co-Spaces is unique in this respect.

[1]Examples of commercial tools include: Community Viz (placeways.com/communityviz), INDEX (www.crit.com/sparc), MetroQuest (metroquest.com), and UrbanSim (www.urbansim.org)

Principles for engagement in collaborative urban design. Planning support tools have a diverse range of objectives that have their own guidelines. Design charrettes are a specific type of collaboration with unique characteristics such as limited time, multivariate data, multiple users with different levels of expertise, etc. These characteristics pose new challenges for designing support tools for this domain space.

While guidelines from collaborative visualization [12,20] address the use of collaborative technology and design of visualizations for multiple users, CPSS requires additional guidelines specific to the domain and to the challenge of engaging various stakeholders in the design process. Engaging stakeholders with different backgrounds, expertise, and expectations is a prominent challenge for design charrettes. Arnstein's widely adopted **Ladder of Public Engagement** [2] proposes an eight-level hierarchy of *manipulation, therapy, informing, consultation, placation, partnership, delegated power*, and *citizen control* to assess the degree of engagement in general settings.

In the context of urban planning, Snyder [22] proposes a 13-point "wish list" for urban design tools including *interactive and usable at multiple levels of expertise, accessible and affordable, adaptable and maintainable, having an open architecture, utilising high quality data, operating at local and regional scale, providing comprehensive coverage and integration of issues, supporting impact analysis including short-, medium- and long-term effects, engaging citizens and supporting face-to-face interactions, visual imagery, values, causes, and effects, promoting identification of design options*, and *regular monitoring and reporting*. However, there are no specific guidelines in urban design that target all of the requirements for CPSS specific to design charrettes. Based on these principles, and our own observations of UD Co-Spaces in use, we synthesised a set of principles for urban design charrettes that we describe in the Discussion.

ITERATIVE DEVELOPMENT OF UD Co-Spaces

There were three major iterations of UD Co-Spaces, each adding a new display type to support collaboration and visualization activities identified in formative evaluations. For each iteration we discuss key lessons learned during field deployments that affect the final system, including challenges and design rationale.

Iteration 1: A multi-user, multi-touch tabletop. A proof-of-concept prototype on a SMART Technology Digital Vision Touch (DViT) tabletop (91.5cm x 74cm top surface, 65.4cm height, 57.2cm x 42.9cm screen with 1024x768 pixels) ran custom software developed entirely in C# using SMART's Table SDK. The code base had 15 classes, 135 methods, and 4795 lines of code.

Cases and patterns. The tabletop's horizontal form factor provides a natural collaborative platform where individuals can explore options in parallel by dragging cases from a *side bar* (Fig. 2A) along the edge of the display to locations on a 2D map at the center of the display. The side bar has a full set of cases that are colour-coded according to building type and usage. Cases can be moved and rotated at any time. Tapping

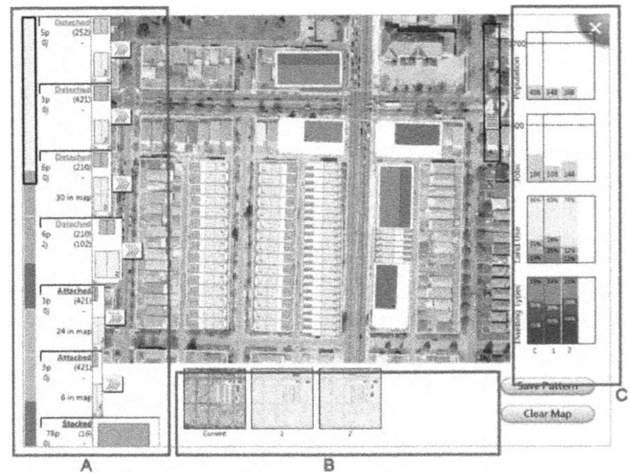

Figure 2. The first iteration of UD Co-Spaces, where the center of the tabletop is a map view of the *current pattern*, with (A) a *side bar* displaying a list of available cases that can be dragged onto the map, (B) a *bottom bar* showing a list of saved patterns, and (C) a comparison of the current and saved patterns based on a fixed set of indicators.

on a case opens a pop-up window with detailed information (floor area, number of bedrooms, alternate views, etc.). The shared map in the center of the tabletop is the only place to create urban design solutions. This was done to encourage collaborative co-creation of urban designs.

Understanding design consequences. Four summary charts provide quantitative visuals for key sustainability indicators in a reserved display area (Fig. 2C). These show target values (thresholds) so users can track how close they are to reaching their goals. Charts update automatically any time cases are added or removed. Users cannot interact with charts directly, they only make changes and then see how the charts respond. Previous patterns can be recalled from the *bottom bar* (Fig. 2B) that serves as a primitive history mechanism.

Challenges and lessons learned. The biggest problem with the initial prototype was limited screen real estate. Display size was not enough for robust design exercises. A lot of space was occupied by visualizations showing sustainability indicators that were considered too sophisticated for novice users. There was no 3D view in this version. The software was specific to a particular tabletop manufacturer. The background map had to be provided as an image file. The need to manually prepare maps put constraints on how much they could be scaled and thus limited the areas for which urban design could be explored using the prototype.

Iteration 2: Adding a wall display. We added an auxiliary wall display with a 3D aerial view and a custom-designed indicator dashboard (Fig. 3). Based on advice from domain experts, a simpler visual encoding using bar and donut charts (with simple infographics in the middle) to help users better understand the indicators was developed [24]. The natural up-down orientation of the 3D view and indicators was more appropriate for a vertical display. This freed up valuable real estate on the horizontal tabletop display, so it could be devoted to the 2D map and case bar for interaction (Fig. 4). 3D viewing parameters such as viewing angle, zoom level, and

Figure 3. The auxiliary wall display in the second iteration of UD Co-Spaces, with a 3D view (top) and new visual encodings for sustainability indicators (bottom).

Figure 4. The touch-table interface in the second iteration of UD Co-Spaces, with a map of the study area in the center and a case bar along each edge of the display to allow individual exploration of options.

elevation were dynamically controlled using a custom widget on the tabletop.

Revised architecture with federated services. UD Co-Spaces integrates three independent applications: a 2D map server to replace manually loaded map images, live access to a database where cases can be obtained, and a third-party renderer to display urban design patterns in 3D with cases at their correct locations. Dashboards were implemented so they update their views when callbacks notify them that the pattern on the tabletop has changed. To provide compatibility with future technology, the software uses a layered approach that introduces abstractions for the 2D and 3D displays and for the case database. *RabbitMQ* provides a bulletin-board-style messaging layer in which requests are broadcast and listeners associated with each federated component provide asynchronous responses. The federated architecture proved fortuitous when personal displays were added in the third iteration.

Device and service abstractions. Bindings were written to support SMART Technologies, Microsoft Surface, and PQ Labs multi-touch surfaces for the 2D tabletop (each device has about four times the area of the initial prototype), *Google Earth* for 3D rendering, *Google Map* and Microsoft *Bing* for 2D map content, and *elementsDB*, a database of cases developed previously by the researchers. Trimble's *Sketchup* was used to convert *elementsDB* case geometry into 2D images for the tabletop and 3D models that *Google Earth*'s API "inserts" at the appropriate locations and orientations for rendering by an *Apache* web server and display in a full-screen browser window on the wall.

Indicators. A new custom-designed dashboard provides visual encodings of key indicators that can have target values specified for "are we there yet?" interaction. These indicators can be used to determine near-optimal designs for a particular urban area.

Deployment. The second iteration was tested in a series of 26 workshop sessions with 44 citizens and planners in the British Columbia city of Revelstoke and 18 professionals in Vancouver. Sessions were video taped and data gathered through questionnaires and focus groups, yielding insights about the system design, collaborative interaction, engagement, and the value of immediate live feedback during the urban design process. We received positive responses from stakeholders that UD Co-Spaces was *fun*, *easy to understand and interact with*, *encouraging*, and *instructive* about the consequences of decisions: participants' feedback indicated that the system helped them see the impact of their designs, understand city planning and its complexity, and learn from each other. Those in the Revelstoke workshop remarked that the "tools were helpful in understanding some impacts of choices," "I learned a lot from [a developer] and [a planner] about how developers and planners think," it was "interesting to see everyone's views," "there are a lot of details to consider when doing urban planning!" and the process helped "understand city planning and its ramifications."

Features that both professionals and the public liked were *fast and early feedback*, *number and variety of alternatives*, and *visualization linked to the indicators*. The system was well received by professional planners, even though we had thought it would be mainly of interest only to non-experts. The Vancouver field trials involved six city planners and 12 other municipal staff in half-day design workshops. In follow-up interviews, they reported that seeing 2D and 3D concurrently with "live" indicators, enabled them to effectively engage with non-planner colleagues to generate and evaluate numerous alternatives. All of them reported that it raised their confidence about proposed solutions and they subsequently requested to use the tool set for additional work sessions.

Challenges and lessons learned. Analysis of videos, questionnaires and focus groups indicated some important limitations: lack of personal work spaces on the displays, difficulty interacting in parallel with the 3D view on the wall display, and low user engagement with sustainability indicators now that they were shown on the wall rather than at the center of attention on the tabletop. Adding indicators at the bottom of the wall display also created a display real estate problem: indicators took space on the wall that was supposed to be used for 3D. The set of indicators and target values were statically chosen; there was no opportunity to customise them for individual use. Some participants commented that the tabletop was so engaging that they did not pay much attention to the indicators on the wall. We addressed these issues in the third iteration of the system by adding personal hand-held devices to control the 3D view and for viewing indicators, thus free-

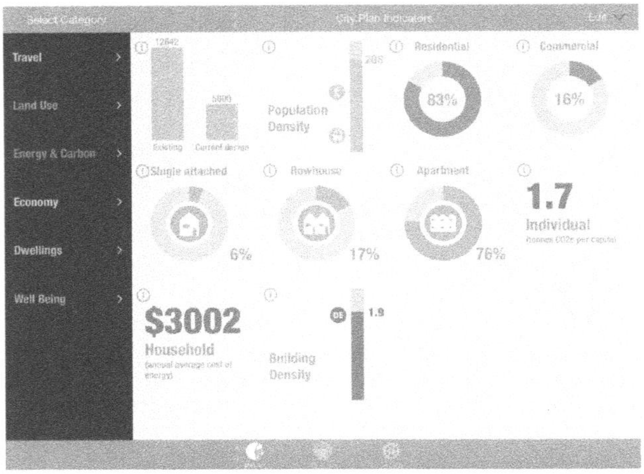

Figure 5. A dashboard on the iPad shows visual feedback about sustainability indicators for the current design. The left side is a toolbox of colour-coded indicator categories, the right side is a canvas showing the selected indicators. Users drag indicators from the toolbar to the canvas and can select target thresholds for each indicator.

ing up the wall display for 3D while also encouraging more interaction with the sustainability indicators.

Iteration 3: Adding personal hand-held displays. Our current version of UD Co-Spaces is an integrated multi-display environment (Fig. 1) whose activities are anchored in a multi-touch tabletop workspace augmented with both large-screen wall displays for shared viewing and smaller hand-held displays for individual access and customization. The federated use of services abstracted into layers and the message paradigm to support asynchronous communication continues. We improved interaction with the 3D wall display and added new functionality for interacting with indicators by introducing Apple iPad tablets that remotely manipulate the 3D view and configure and display personal indicator dashboards for parallel investigation of sustainability indicators. iPad applications use WiFi to communicate with the server that manages the tabletop and 3D display through agents resident on the server that respond to task-specific RabbitMQ messages.

iPad 3D view control. As in the second iteration, a direct manipulation multi-touch view controller on the tabletop initially sets the location of a virtual camera and its direction of view and elevation relative to a "look-at" point in the urban design. A new custom remote control iPad app then allows pan and scroll of the look-at point by one-finger movement, camera distance and orientation by two-finger pinch-expand and twist gestures, and camera elevation by two-finger virtual sliding. Our assumption that ubiquitous experience with personal computers, hand-held smart phones, and tablets has created a level of sophistication in the general public that implies that gestures such as zoom and pinch will be familiar to many people was definitely borne out in our testing.

iPad sustainability indicators. Dashboard indicators give visual feedback about sustainability indicators for the current design. Indicators can be grouped to display related information. A *dashboard* is a collection of indicators. Dashboards can be displayed on the tabletop or on the wall or on the iPads. On iPads, indicators can be dragged from a toolbox (Fig. 5) to build custom dashboards that display the indicators that matter most to users. We added a fixed bar on the top of the iPad using one-fifth of the display space to show default indicators that were most relevant to the design task. This was done for the lay people who were not necessarily familiar enough with the context of urban design to select the relevant indicators. The bar can be hidden if users need more space.

As in the second iteration, indicators are updated automatically whenever a change takes place on the tabletop, so they always show current data to everyone. Indicators are drawn from computational models in the *elementsDB* urban design database. To encourage more interactivity and transparency about how indicators are set, users can select target thresholds for indicators using the iPad. This also allows facilitators to interactively guide sessions if they want to explore a variety of scenarios with different thresholds.

Challenges and lessons learned. After deploying the third iteration we conducted formal and informal evaluations that we describe in the next section.

EVALUATION

UD Co-Spaces is intended to serve a large range of stakeholders. A primary concern is usability of UD Co-Spaces for different groups of stakeholders and to observe and analyze its effects on collaboration and engagement. All of our system design decisions and development processes were based on close collaboration with both academic and professional domain experts: urban planners in both Revelstoke and Vancouver, who used UD Co-Spaces in actual planning charrettes in the two cities, which served as field trials for our system.

An example of a low-level system design decision is when users control the 3D viewer from the tabletop. They need to hold a finger down on the table for 4 seconds to activate the 3D viewer camera controller. When using an iPad to control the 3D, they got confused about where the 3D camera is looking. We added an "eye" icon displayed at the center of the 2D tabletop to indicate that the camera for the 3D viewer is always looking at that point no matter how the viewing parameters change. When users let go of their fingers, the eye icon disappears automatically.

We also took the opportunity during a demo of our system to 28 high school students (two groups each of 14 girls) to test whether multiple users could smoothly use the iPads to control the 3D view. Each demo took 45 minutes. During the demos we provided 10 minutes of introduction, then we observed the students working freely with five iPads to control the 3D view on the wall display. Most of the students quickly learned how to perform rudimentary actions, confirming that (at least for younger stakeholders) almost-ubiquitous exposure to personal surface interaction can be assumed. In addition to this and many other informal evaluations that are part of normal iterative system design, we conducted two formal evaluations.

Heuristic Evaluation. A heuristic evaluation for both of the iPad applications was conducted with three experts in urban design and public engagement. We had one task for each application (3D viewer and indicator dashboard), and gave each expert 20 minutes to try each feature. After each task, an expert provided verbal comments about each application and provided us with suggestions to improve them. Each expert was tested separately for about 60 minutes. All three experts said hand-held devices were valuable. After comparing 3D navigation on the tabletop to navigation using iPad, Expert 1 stated that "iPad is easier to use for posture, it gives you better opportunity to find the 3D view, and it is more comfortable because of the posture (standing up and looking at the wall display on the wall)." Expert 2 said "controlling 3D is more intuitive on the iPad than controlling the 3D from the table" but that while he was comfortable with both "as facilitator [I] would be more comfortable on the table where everyone can see the interactions, but iPad is easier to get into than the table itself." Expert 1 said "gestures feel better on the iPad than the table, it takes some getting used to navigate on the table while looking up at the wall." Expert 3 made similar comments.

All three experts were also positive about how easy the indicators were to navigate and operate. Expert 1 mentioned "being able to modify the key/value pairs in the design task ... to react to people's interest is very important, being able to customise indicators for each group based on what they care [about] most is important." Similarly, Expert 2 liked "the ability to modify the indicators in accordance with the priorities of a group or a workshop." Expert 3 said "the combination of numbers and visuals [and] infographics is great" to visually encode indicators.

Formal user study. To evaluate the effect of UD Co-Spaces on engagement and collaboration, we conducted a user study comparing our current tool to the traditional paper map-based approach still widely in use. We recruited eight groups of 4-5 participants, most of whom were students at our university. Each group had a mix of people from different backgrounds. In each group there was at least one person who was familiar with urban design. Due to space limitations, we focus on results related to the use of UD Co-Spaces. Our qualitative results suggest that UD Co-Spaces promotes engagement, fosters collaboration, and helps users better learn about the consequences of their design choices compared to a traditional paper-based approach.

In general, UD Co-Spaces provided a highly collaborative environment for participants. Participants often worked in parallel, breaking off into smaller groups of 2-3 to discuss design issues and options. While the paper condition had a lower learning threshold, overall the interaction style of UD Co-Spaces was not a deterrent; participants quickly learned how to manipulate the table and the iPads. Our observations of many interactions with the wall display in UD Co-Spaces suggest that the 3D view is integral for engagement with the design process because it allows participants to see an approximate visualization of the neighbourhood as they design. We believe that UD Co-Spaces allowed participants to better understand how cases impacted the design by linking the information attached to each case to visual encodings of key sustainability indicators. Feedback from participants has corroborated the positive value of adding individual displays to engage people and allowing them to explore and customise data based on personal needs.

DISCUSSION

We adapted Arnstein's ladder and Snyder's principles to the narrower challenge of designing a CPSS targeted to the charrette process. Based on these principles, urban design experts' feedback, and our own observations of UD Co-Spaces in use, we synthesised a set of seven principles for urban design charrettes. We examine how UD Co-Spaces supports these principles using comments obtained from informants in our user studies.

1. Engagement. Based on our observations, we believe support systems for charrettes need to engage users on an individual and a group level in order to capitalize on the diversity of stakeholders. Engagement primarily refers to users engaging with one another, but it can also refer to how users engage with the system as well. Therefore, the system should act as a common space that engages participants with each other while also engaging individuals in the design task through features that are innovative and easy to use and learn. Our study results show that using diverse displays, including the tabletop, the 3D wall display, and the hand-held devices, contributed to a highly engaging environment. Users interacted with various displays, which in turn resulted in increased interaction among the group members. As one participant stated, "The visual aspect of it is really engaging. You become kind of engrossed in it. I thought it worked really well in terms of getting people engaged in the actual process" (Revelstoke workshop). The collaborative tabletop was a space where multiple users could interact with the system simultaneously, allowing users to work individually or in groups, supporting engagement at both of these levels. Additionally, the 2D and 3D visualizations with familiar, easy-to-use interaction techniques made the system relatively easy to learn in a short amount of time, which makes engaging with the system more likely.

2. Collaboration. A main goal of design charrettes and our system is to foster collaboration through co-creation of designs [7,9]. In order to achieve this goal we deployed a multi-display, multi-user system that has a single solution space. Evaluation of previous iterations of our system indicated that the size of the design space mattered, and that limited space hampered collaboration by making the information difficult to access and manage. Subsequent iterations of the system included a large wall-display and hand-held devices in order to mitigate the issue of limited real estate. Indicators were moved from the wall display to the hand-held devices to save space, which had the added benefit of allowing individuals to customise indicators in which they were most interested.

Tabletop. In line with previous research, we chose a tabletop to provide a collaborative platform to encourage collaboration [16,20]. There are other collaborative PSS tools that achieve collaboration through the use of tabletops [10,13,17]. While we provided access to cases (building types) on each edge of the table to enable individual exploration, we deliberately provided only one shared space for the final solution in the middle of the table to encourage collaboration and co-creation of design.

Wall Display. Due to the spatial nature of urban forms, extra display space is needed to show the 3D view of a neighbourhood. Our studies, as well as other relevant studies, suggest that augmenting the tabletop collaborative platform with a vertical 3D view is beneficial. Therefore, we chose to display a 3D rendering of the design on the wall because the vertical nature of urban form suggests that wall displays would be more appropriate [10, 17]. Our observations suggest that the 3D view plays an important role in the design process.

Personal Displays. In the first iteration, indicators were shown on the table. Feedback indicated that the real estate on the tabletop was needed for interaction with the design. In the second iteration we moved the indicators to the bottom of the wall display to free up valuable real-estate on the tabletop. While professionals actively referenced the real time feedback of indicators, we observed that lay people did not interact much with the indicators. Indicators were far from reach, took up valuable space on the wall, and the choice of indicators was determined by the system. Therefore, we provided personal space through the addition of hand-held devices in the third iteration of UD Co-Spaces. This enabled individual exploration and customization of the indicators dashboard (indicators can still be displayed on the wall or the tabletop if desired). We received positive feedback about adding personal devices to improve interactions both with the wall and with the indicators. One participant said "I definitely really liked how everything was synced, specially with regards to the projection and the iPad and the table itself. Being able to rotate it so we could get a better view, and just being able to see everything unfold in real time" (Revelstoke workshop), which supports our decision to add hand-held devices to our system.

3. Interactive visualizations. The use of interactive visualizations in our system provided a number of benefits for participants, who represented diverse stakeholders in the design process. In line with previous research [1], our findings indicate that the interactive visualizations we provided helped foster participant engagement in the design process. Additionally, participants better understood the design process because they could visually see how their design decisions impacted sustainability issues through the use of indicators that changed in real-time as they explored designs iteratively. According to Salter and Campbell [19], "most true group interactions with the technology have been limited and remain somewhat reactive, rather than fully interactive." Despite our visualizations being little more than a dashboard, with limited interactivity, user study participant stated that "each interaction, including touch, move cases, [and then] drag, drop, and manipulate them will make a big difference" and he added that "the different representations including map, 3D, indicators, and back and forth between those adds a richness to participants' understanding." We observed a lot more attention being paid to the indicators in the third iteration.

There were at least 1-2 people in each group who interacted throughout the session with the indicators and communicated to the rest of the group how indicators were changing as cases were added or deleted from the design space. In each group, there were significant interactions with the wall display, with the 3D view providing important contextual information that helped participants make decisions about their designs. As one participant stated, "I think I like [the] combination of all of them together because I could see all the information on one wall, I could see the 3D view on one, I could manipulate the view on the table, and I could see all the changes on the tablet. So for me it was the combination" (Revelstoke workshop).

4. Accessibility. In order to encourage participation of stakeholders with different backgrounds, expertise, and often different expectations, special attention is needed to make the system accessible and usable for different groups of users [9, 22]. Specifically, the system should be easy to learn and use, with effective and efficient work-spaces. It should provide numerous types of information including 2D maps, 3D views, examples of cases, and data visualizations, as well as numeric data to reach people with different learning styles.

To address users' needs, we observed charrette participants and their various concerns and objectives. A simple categorization of users in this context divides them into professionals and the public (or lay people). For professional planners, the ability to create and compare a diverse range of alternatives against indicators of performance is important. For public stakeholders the main considerations are increasing the level of engagement, understanding the process, social learning, collaboration, and trust. Therefore, we used familiar visualization and interaction techniques and put a lot of effort into making access equitable by providing for individual exploration and input. We iteratively improved visualization and selected data representations for each display based on our evaluations. Our results suggest UD Co-Spaces might have a leveling effect on power and control. Based on observations during the formal user study, we noticed that the case bar allowed participants better access to and understanding of the information attached to each case, which impacted overall design choices made collaboratively. In addition, participants seemed more democratic in what they contributed to the design, whereas in the paper condition we noticed more "gatekeeper" roles emerge where one participant acted as a dominant voice, to the point of removing cases without any discussion or debate.

One participant in the user study said "We all subconsciously took on different roles in the project based on the areas that we felt more comfortable with ... [that] will definitely help in a real setting ... towards collaboration, ... we also learn from one another by being able to engage in real time with each other, with the knowledge that we brought to the table, and with the data that we were using" (Participant P13). Another said "Having this tabletop put every stakeholder involved so they can make changes themselves, see those changes right away, [which] promotes collaboration" (P15).

5. Iteration. It is well-known that iteration in design is a valuable exercise that can contribute to a better final design due to exploring many different alternatives [18, 27]. While using traditional paper-based methods limits the chances that participants in a public workshop will explore lots of alternatives, digital tools provide opportunities to create and evaluate alternatives much faster. UD Co-Spaces supports multiple urban design iterations by providing fast and early feedback through 3D views and sustainability indicators. As one planning student noted, "Having the tabletop in terms of its usability and our ability to go back and revise and edit ... was superior to paper in that format. Instead going back and then erasing and then redrawing it out again, especially if you need to actually draw it out instead of arranging it by paper blocks. Definitely being able to edit on the fly and change on the fly helped a lot" (P13). This was apparent even in relatively short user study sessions. "We learned everything we needed to know from the software within the time period, but ... a longer workshop ... given different targets ... would just give more opportunity for more iterations of designs" (P11).

6. Understanding Consequences. One high-level goal of design charrettes is helping stakeholders understand and assess the consequences of their designs and therefore make more informed decisions. However, in conventional approaches this is a long and time-consuming process. Usually planners need to invite participants back for a second workshop session after the analysis and visualizations are ready when they all discuss the consequences and possible changes necessary.

UD Co-Spaces from the very first iteration included a visualization of indicators, although many users did not really understand the visualizations. In the second iteration we paid special attention to make them more accessible by different groups of users. Based on domain experts' input, we used only donut charts with simple infographics in the middle and, when information was more appropriate for bar charts, we marked the target value on the bar as well as the current value to help see how close an urban design is to achieving its target value. These dashboards were added and tested during the deployments. While professionals really appreciated the new dashboards, lay people again did not use them much. The reason was different this time: one participant reported "the tabletop was so engaging that I did not look up to check the [indicators]" and another said "I looked up only to check the 3D but I did not really pay attention to the [indicators]" (Revelstoke workshop).

In the third iteration we enabled users to customise and get information about the indicators on iPads, which helped users improve their urban designs and understand the consequences of the designs. Multiple features were considered helpful in understanding consequences. "Having [indicators] and having that in real time definitely helped me understand ... the role that each decision was having both [in] terms of density [and] in terms of the lifestyle that was being lead to just through the indirect stats that we were getting. ... I definitely feel like that radically altered how we approached the project" and "the sync between all the devices [meant we were] able to make one change and then almost immediately see the impact that that change had both visually and statistically from the data ... the immediate interplay between the two" (P13). Similarly, each device brought a different understanding. "The iPad ... added an additional information source that gave me more context. [H]aving those different [indicators] that I could look at was really helpful to see, okay, what is the larger impact ... it was almost like stepping out and saying, okay, what did we actually do and what is the impact?" (P35).

7. Transparency. In order to engage the public in urban design, gaining trust is absolutely necessary [21]. "People are suspicious of 'blackbox' computer-generated answers. Models and assumptions should be as transparent as possible" [22]. UD Co-Spaces makes the process much more transparent by enabling users to customise indicators, set targets, and directly interact with them. We believe that this transparency creates better opportunity for understanding the indicators and trusting the outcome at the end.

"[Indicators] provide an orientation of what you're trying to accomplish and making a connection to that. But, not to limit it just to those [indicators] is another consideration because you don't want to go too far in one direction where you're only considering active transit and commercial space because then you lose out on all the other [indicators]" (P36).

There were also misgivings. "I think [the indicators are] a bunch of data that isn't necessarily useful to the public if it's not translated ... the indicators seemed very arbitrary" (P25). This suggests that true transparency may require much deeper explanation of how indicators are calculated and what they mean. One expert who saw value in our design pointed out the possible irony that municipal planning departments might not welcome our system: "one caveat about all of this is that cities are reluctant to use this tool, because it is very open."

CONCLUSION AND FUTURE WORK

We designed, developed, and iteratively improved UD Co-Spaces to engage the public in participatory urban design. Evaluations showed that it strongly impacted engagement by providing a collaborative platform where multiple users could interact with 2D, 3D, and indicator visualizations in real time. We assessed UD Co-Spaces using seven design principles for supporting design charrettes that offer guidance for developers of future systems. We suggest three areas for research.

Street view, overlays, and more. UD Co-Spaces currently lacks a street-view on the wall display, information overlay layers on the tabletop, detailed information about existing buildings in the planning area, and rich interactive control over indicators by facilitators.

More sophisticated interactive visualization. Visualizations in UD Co-Spaces are still very basic and need improvement. Cases could give previews of indicator changes using feed-forward techniques such as "scented widgets" [26].

History. UD Co-Spaces logs key iPad and tabletop events. A rudimentary *history browser* on the iPad can be used during or after a session to review the options that were explored. The log includes time of day, the tabletop group associated with an event (if multiple tabletops are in use), an optional event name, an extensible set of tags, and a snapshot of the design pattern at the time of the event. There are many questions still to explore, such as how to coordinate views when loading a pattern from the history to the table, how to interactively compare indicators across patterns, and how to best support browsing in the history. Our proof-of-concept history browser uses visual coding to identify events. We have not yet evaluated the coding. We suspect different history mechanisms are needed for facilitators and the public because they have different mental models of urban design.

ACKNOWLEDGMENTS

Funding from GRAND, NSERC, SSHRC, and research infrastructure from CFI, CIRS and ICICS supported the research. The UBC BREB gave ethics approval. We thank the planners in Revelstoke and Vancouver, all of the participants in the user study and the field trials, and our colleagues Jon Salter, Maged Senbel, Melanie Tory, and Mike vander Laan for their valuable feedback.

REFERENCES

1. Al-Kodmany, K. Visualization tools and methods in community planning : From freehand sketches to virtual reality. *J. Planning Literature 17*, 2 (2002), 189–211.
2. Arnstein, S. R. A ladder of citizen participation. *J. American Institute of Planners 35*, 4 (1969), 216–224.
3. Association, A. P. *Planning and urban design standards*. John Wiley & Sons, 2006.
4. Ben-Joseph, E., Ishii, H., Underkoffler, J., Piper, B., and Yeung, L. Urban simulation and the luminous planning table bridging the gap between the digital and the tangible. *J. Planning Education & Research 21*, 2 (2001), 196–203.
5. Bond, S., and Thompson-Fawcett, M. Public participation and new urbanism: A conflicting agenda? *Planning Theory & Practice 8*, 3 (2007), 449–472.
6. Brail, R. K. *Planning support systems for cities and regions*. Lincoln Institute of Land Policy, Cambridge, MA, 2008.
7. Condon, P. *Design charrettes for sustainable communities*. Island Press, Washington, DC, 2007.
8. Condon, P. M., Cavens, D., and Miller, N. *Urban planning tools for climate change mitigation*. Lincoln Institute of Land Policy, Cambridge, MA, 2009.
9. Girling, C., Kellett, R., and Johnstone, S. Informing design charrettes: Tools for participation in neighbourhood-scale planning. *The Integrated Assessment Journal 6*, 4 (2006), 109–130.
10. Halatsch, J., Kunze, A., and Schmitt, G. Value lab: A collaborative environment for the planning of future cities. In *Proc. 27th eCAADe* (Brussels, 2009), 507–514.
11. Harris, B., and Batty, M. Locational models, geographic information and planning support systems. In *Planning support systems: integrating geographic information systems, models, & visualization tools*, R. K. Brail and R. E. Klosterman, Eds. ESRI, Redlands, CA, 2001.
12. Isenberg, P. *Collaborative information visualization in co-located environments*. PhD thesis, U. Calgary, 2009.
13. Ishii, H., Underkoffler, J., Chak, D., Piper, B., Ben-Joseph, E., Yeung, L., and Kanji, Z. Augmented Urban Planning Workbench: Overlaying Drawings, Physical Models and Digital Simulation. In *Proc. Inter. Symp. Mixed & Augmented Reality*, IEEE Computer Society (Los Alamitos, CA, 2002), 203–211.
14. Klosterman, R. E. Planning support systems: A new perspective on computer-aided planning. *J. Planning Education & Research 17*, 1 (1997), 45–54.
15. Lennertz, B. The charrette as an agent for change. *New Urbanism: Comprehensive report & best practices guide* (2003), 12–28.
16. Mahyar, N., Sarvghad, A., Tory, M., and Weeres, T. Observations of record-keeping in co-located collaborative analysis. In *46th Hawaii Int'l. Conf. on System Sciences*, IEEE (2013), 460–469.
17. Maquil, V. Towards understanding the design space of tangible user interfaces for collaborative urban planning. *Interacting with Computers* (2015), 1–20.
18. Milburn, L.-A. S., and Brown, R. D. The relationship between research and design in landscape architecture. *Landscape & Urban Planning 64*, 1-2 (2003), 47–66.
19. Salter, J. D., Campbell, C., Journeay, M., and Sheppard, S. R. The digital workshop: Exploring the use of interactive and immersive visualisation tools in participatory planning. *J. environmental management 90*, 6 (2009), 2090–2101.
20. Scott, S., Grant, K., and Mandryk, R. System guidelines for co-located, collaborative work on a tabletop display. *ECSCW 2003*, 5 (2003), 159–178.
21. Shipley, R., and Utz, S. Making it count: A review of the value and techniques for public consultation. *J. Planning Literature 27*, 1 (2012), 22–42.
22. Snyder, K. Tools for community design and decision making. In *Planning Support Systems in Practice*, S. Geertman and J. Stillwell, Eds. Springer, NY, 2003, 99–120.
23. Underkoffler, J., and Ishii, H. URP: A luminous-tangible workbench for urban planning and design. In *Proc. SIGCHI '99*, ACM (NY, 1999), 386–393.
24. van der Laan, M., Kellet, R., Girling, C., Senbel, M., and Su, T. A collaborative multi-touch, multi-display, urban futures tool. In *Proc. Symp. Simulation for Architecture & Urban Design*, Society for Computer Simulation Int'l. (San Diego, CA, 2013), 1–4.
25. Wagner, I., Basile, M., Ehrenstrasser, L., Maquil, V., Terrin, J.-J., and Wagner, M. Supporting the formation of communities of practice: Urban planning in the MR-Tent. *Sprouts: Working Papers on Information Systems 9* (2009), 1–11.
26. Willett, W., Heer, J., and Agrawala, M. Scented widgets: Improving navigation cues with embedded visualizations. *IEEE Trans. on Visualization & Computer Graphics 13*, 6 (2007), 1129–1136.
27. Zeisel, J. *Inquiry by design*. W. W. Norton, NY, 2006.

Towards Road Traffic Management with Forecasting on Wall Displays

Arnaud Prouzeau **Anastasia Bezerianos** **Olivier Chapuis**
LRI, Univ Paris-Sud, CNRS, Inria, Université Paris-Saclay
F-91405 Orsay, France

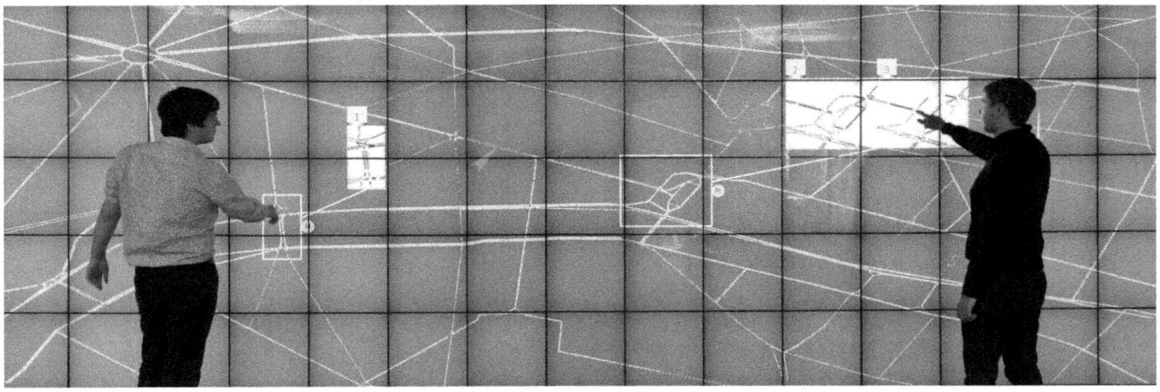

Figure 1. Visualization of traffic in a city with two "DragMagics" (white rectangles) showing one (left) and two (right) simulations associated with different possible interventions on the traffic. The simulation visualizations use difference color maps to highlight differences with the real traffic.

ABSTRACT
Road traffic control centers are of vital importance to modern cities. Interviews with controllers in two such centers identified the need to incorporate the visualization of results from predictive traffic models with real traffic, to help operators choose among different interventions on the network. We explore this idea in a prototype that runs on a wall display, and supports direct touch and input from workstations and mobile devices. Apart from basic functionality to manage the current traffic such as changing traffic light duration or speed limits, the prototype incorporates traffic simulations for forecasting results of possible actions, highlighting their differences to current traffic. Based on needs identified in our interviews, we offer two techniques that visually combine simulated and real situations, taking advantage of the large display space: multiple independent views and DragMagic, a variation of magic lenses. A preliminary laboratory experiment suggests that both techniques are viable design options, even for monitoring several simulations and areas of interest, contrary to expectations from previous work. However DragMagics are easier to master. An informal feedback session with our experts showed promising early feedback.

Author Keywords
Traffic monitoring; wall display; road traffic model; traffic forecast; DragMag; magic lens

ISS 2016, November 6–9, 2016, Niagara Falls, ON, Canada.

http://dx.doi.org/10.1145/2992154.2992158

ACM Classification Keywords
H.5.2 Information interfaces and presentation (e.g., HCI): User Interfaces – Graphical user interfaces.

INTRODUCTION
Traffic congestion in major cities and highways is a growing problem in most countries. Perturbations such as accidents and breakdowns, or exceptional events such as demonstrations, can overload a road network that may already be operating at its limit, e.g. during rush hour. To prevent and to react efficiently to incidents and perturbations, road traffic in cities and highways is monitored in dedicated control centers.

Even for experienced operators, it is often challenging to evaluate the impact of an intervention on the network. While they are equipped with predefined traffic plans (sets of compatible interventions on a sector or area), it is still sometimes unclear which plan will work best for the current state of the network, in particular during exceptional events. This is where simulation models of road-traffic can help operators better understand and chose among possible intervention alternatives.

Road-traffic is a complex system with multiple agents (cars) that can behave in a non-deterministic manner. Researchers approximate road-traffic using methods from physics [16] or statistics and machine learning [43]. Their simulations can perform short-term traffic forecasting, identify problematic sectors with high-risk of traffic-congestion, and test new concepts to improve road-traffic such as dynamic adjustment of speed limits. Nevertheless, there is little work that looks at incorporating these results visually in traffic control centers.

Following interviews and observations of road-traffic control centers, we extracted user needs and designed a prototype system for road-traffic monitoring that runs on a touch enabled ultra high-resolution wall display[1]. Taking advantage of their high resolution and large real-estate, our prototype extends the visualizations currently used in road-traffic control centers, to allow operators to concurrently explore and visualize results from multiple simulations testing alternative interventions on the network, both in a local and global scale.

We propose two techniques for viewing multiple simulations in combination with real traffic: (i) *multiple views* [21, 41, 45] to show the global state of the network; and (ii) *DragMagic*, a combination of DragMags [46] and magic lenses [8], to visualize localized sectors (Figure 1). We adapt and combine these techniques to visualize and compare several forecast visualizations using wall displays in control centers.

To better understand the performance of these techniques in our context, we compared them in a lab experiment. Participants performed well in comparison tasks of up to 6 different simulations, contrary to previous findings [30] that predicted decreased performance with the increase of comparisons. Our results also suggest that DragMagic is easier to master and may be beneficial when the number of simulations to compare is high, but that both techniques are viable alternatives. Early feedback on our prototype from experts also indicates a preference for DragMagic.

Our *contributions* are: (i) The user-centered design motivating a wall display prototype, building on interviews and observations of expert users, and the needs derived from them. (ii) Combining interaction and visualization techniques to present *multiple* simulated and real situations in the context of traffic management, something not seen in previous work. (iii) The first controlled study to evaluate these visualization techniques using an adapted situation-awareness task.

BACKGROUND

We discuss wall displays and Multi-Display Environments (MDE) for control rooms, and road traffic visualization.

Wall Displays & MDE for Control Rooms

Control rooms are used to monitor complex systems like telescopes [28], power plants [26] or transportation networks [39]. They are usually equipped with a large display showing an overview of the situation and general information for all operators, and with individual workstations where operators act on the system (Figure 2).

Designers of such systems have recognized early on the importance of human factors and interaction in their work, and in particular the benefit of visualization walls and other shared displays. For instance, Smith et al. [38] study the control room of the London subway and highlight that a shared visualization can improve group awareness and communication in the team. And later, Starke et al. [39] studied how operators gathered and integrated information across displays in a simulated "object in the road" scenario.

Shared displays in control rooms are often treated as large monitors, and interaction is done using mice and keyboards. More recent work has focused on direct interaction with tabletops in crisis management [32, 13]. Others have combined tabletops and tangible tools in power plant control centers [26], and tabletops and paper in air-traffic control [17]. Finally, recent work combined tabletops with shared vertical screens present in most control centers. For example, Bader et al. [5] combine a digital table map, a vertical screen with additional information, and a tablet to overlay personal information on the map. And Chokshi et al. [11] use tabletops to perform actions collaboratively on a central wall display.

In the above work, operators interact with the wall display indirectly, through mice/keyboards or tabletops. In few approaches, such as ours, interaction takes place directly on the wall displays. For example, in a scenario of police officers monitoring cars on a wall display, Ion et al. [19] use DragMags to focus on an area, with cut-offs of interesting items outside it connected with a folded strip. Our approach differs from previous work in control rooms. Beyond *directly* interacting with the wall display [19], we further propose using the wall display as a *central interactive* surface where operators can *solve problems*, not just monitor situations.

Irrespective of interaction platform, this previous work often relies on general purpose interaction and visualization techniques related to focusing and monitoring one or more areas of interest, such as space folding [14], magic lenses [8], DragMags [46] and multi-focus techniques [22, 25]. This is due to the need in such contexts to monitor several specific areas in detail, while still having an overview of the situation. For example Ion et al. [19] use DragMags with attached cut-offs; Schwarz et al. [37] use local semantic magnification with a Manhattan lens or a deported view on the wall, and multiple space-folds to visualize multiple areas with context-sensitive information at higher resolution [9, 37].

Our work poses visualization challenges that go beyond those seen in previous work, as it not only needs to allow operators to monitor multiple areas of interest simultaneously, but it also combines real data with *simulation and forecasting* visualizations. Thus the progress and results of one or even more simulations need to be viewed and understood concurrently with the actual road traffic data on multiple areas of interest.

Road Traffic Visualization

Trajectory visualization [2] focuses often on vessel traffic, marine [23, 34, 36] and air [18, 35], and on an a-posteriori analysis of movement patterns over long time periods, using sophisticated interaction and visualization mechanisms such as aggregating paths, brushing and linking views, advanced statistics on selections, etc.

Similarly, most work on *road traffic* focuses on a-posteriori analysis and visualization of traffic patterns. For example, Andrienko et al. [1] extract and visualize meaningful places within movement data, and cluster spatio-temporal events or trajectories. Tominski et al. [40] visualize trajectories at different points in time, by stacking them on the 3rd dimension.

For real time traffic data visualizations, Wang et al. [44] visualize macro-traffic data recorded by transportation cells, using a combination of aggregated trajectories and of individ-

[1] an earlier version of the prototype alone has been presented in French as a Work in Progress (poster presentation) [31].

Figure 2. PC Lutèce and PC Berlier traffic control centers in Paris.

ual views for each cell showing vehicle animations. Nevertheless, the majority of modern traffic control centers, and studies conducted around them (see previous section), visualize real traffic data by coloring road segments based on traffic density or average vehicle speed, similarly to tools like Google Maps, Bing Maps, etc. As we saw, this visualization is often coupled with techniques that aid monitoring of different locations on wall displays, most notably variations of Magic lenses [8] and DragMags [30, 46].

We also use visualization lenses, but for a different purpose. As our goal is to augment real time traffic with results of simulations, lenses are used to provide side-by-side comparisons between the current situation and simulations in an area of interest. As an alternative to lenses, we also provide multiple juxtaposed views of the entire network [21, 41, 45], with real or simulated data. Another approach taken by Andrienko et al. [3] superimposed on a map the simulated results of road traffic bands in a time cube. Nevertheless, they focused on the simulation visualization and did not combine this visualization with real-time traffic. More recently, they presented a complete framework [4] to analyze road traffic, and model how additional cars will influence the network. To compare the impact of different possible interventions, they visualize results using difference maps, time cubes and statistics. Our work is orthogonal, as we focus on the user-centered design of a system to be incorporated in the shared wall of a control center, using visualizations to monitor multiple simulations and points of interest at a given time.

OBSERVATIONS AND INTERVIEWS

To understand the tasks, tools and needs of traffic operators, we visited two control centers: PC Lutèce that handles traffic for the city of Paris (Figure 2 left), and PC Berlier (Figure 2 right) that monitors the Périphérique, a motorway surrounding Paris. We observed two operators in PC Lutèce and interviewed one in depth (1h) as well as an operations engineer (1h); and we observed another two operators in PC Berlier and interviewed one (1/2h) and the operator supervisor (1h).

General Observations. Both control centers are furnished with a large shared visualization wall showing the monitored network, surrounded by smaller screens with live camera feeds from the streets in PC Lutèce, and from the Périphérique and its tunnels in PC Berlier. Road segments are colored depending on traffic congestion from green (no congestion), to yellow, orange, and red (high congestion). Gray is used to indicate segments with faulty loop detectors. Arrows are used to highlight areas in which an intervention was done, either by the system (green arrow) or by an operator (yellow arrow if the system agrees with the intervention and red if it disagrees). Individual operator workstations are located in front of the wall, also displaying the network visualization (see Figure 2), alerts and other statistical information.

Due to the small scale and resolution of their monitors (w.r.t. the scale of the monitored network), operators tend to focus on localized areas of the network in their workstations, using mouse and keyboard to navigate. While they look at their individual workstations more, they all use the wall as an awareness monitor to acquire the "big picture" of the network state.

PC Lutèce. An automated system (SURF3) manages the traffic lights for approximately 1500 Parisian intersections, with more than 800.000 cars and 2.5 million pedestrian movements daily. It includes a library of "Traffic Light Plans" (a collection of consistent traffic light durations), and automatically choses the most appropriate plan, depending on the current traffic situation, the day of the week and the time of day. Under normal conditions (outside special events) the priority is public transport and pedestrian flow.

Operators can switch plans for specific sectors, or change traffic light duration of individual intersections for specific events or when incidents occur. Our interviewees explained that operators have a lot of experience in handling incidents in the city and can very accurately predict the impact of their actions and interventions in a local scale, such as a crossroad. Nevertheless, they explained it is difficult to access the impact of actions at a more global scale, e.g., it is often unclear how a change in a crossroad will impact other connected crossroads in the *local sector* or even the *entire network*.

PC Berlier. The center manages the traffic flow in the Périphérique motorway (IPER-REPER system), that hosts daily approximately 1.2 million car movements of commuters between Paris and its suburbs (60% of traffic in the region, 2002). Operators have to constantly monitor traffic in the motorway and its tunnels in order to spot incidents and congestions. To optimize traffic flow, they can activate/deactivate lanes and reroute drivers using variable message signs, in particular since they face almost daily maintenance of lanes that requires reflow of traffic. To ensure safety in tunnels, operators can trigger and follow emergency plans, including evacuation, activation of smoke control systems, or closing tunnels in coordination with firefighter forces on the ground.

Our interviewees explained that a rerouting plan is in place for closing off sections of the motorway or tunnels. But they are hard pressed to apply it as it is difficult to assess the impact of such a drastic measure in each traffic situation. They described an incident with a tunnel flooded in both directions for 11 hours, where they considered applying this plan but could not risk it without a clear picture of potential *global* effects on the rest of the network.

The operator supervisor organizes shifts, oversees the good operation of the center and is involved in training new operators. She added that face the challenge of boredom: monitoring traffic feeds and messages from the public to detect incidents early is monotonous and operator attention can wander, and she felt that occasional task switching, such as forecast planning, could increase operator interest and focus.

Other Control Centers. Road-traffic control centers around the world use different technologies and methods. In Paris, the traffic light control cycle is controlled by timing plans, while dynamic modification of the green light duration is not allowed. Other centers, like in London (SCOOT system[2]) allow such modifications. Interestingly, some centers started using predictive modeling to assess the impact of incidents and to help decision-making, such as in the Piemont Control Center in Italy (PTV Optima[3] software). However, to our knowledge no control center combines forecasting and real-time traffic visualizations.

Motivation and User Needs. Our interviews and knowledge of existing centers suggest that: (i) It would be beneficial to incorporate *visualization of predictive models* with real-time monitoring tools, as the impact of actions is often hard to predict. (ii) Operators should be provided with likely outcomes of their interventions both *globally* on the entire network, and *locally* on specific sectors or intersections. (iii) Forecast visualizations increase the amount of information to be displayed, but are needed *periodically*, not on a constant basis. Given the advances in wall displays, i.e., their interactive support and their ability to display a large amount of information, wall displays can be a good platform for the next generation of road traffic systems, going beyond awareness monitors to also incorporate forecast analysis and visualization when needed.

Current control center setups also suffer from divided attention issues [37], with operators monitoring live camera feeds, the entire network on the visualization wall, and interacting through their individual workstations. If we consider additionaly visually displaying the results of predictive models, the already challenging task of monitoring real-time traffic can become increasingly difficult. As such, for our prototype we decided to show the visualization of the prediction models on the main visualization, and test the limits of how many such prediction models users can comfortably monitor.

PROTOTYPE

In order to explore solutions for integrating the results of forecasting models to real-time traffic monitoring, we implemented a set of visualizations and interaction techniques within a functional prototype. The prototype is developed using Java and the ZVTM Cluster library [29] that allows it to run simultaneously on desktops and on a wall driven by a computer cluster. Several desktop computers can share the view seen on the wall, but at different scales, as is currently done in control centers. On desktops, operators interact with mice and keyboard and their actions are mirrored on the wall.

On the wall we support two types of inputs: direct touch, and indirect touch using mobiles and tablets via the Smarties toolkit [10]. This dual input enables implicit zooming and context switching through movement [6, 7], leverages the benefits of wall displays in high information density tasks [24], and provides new opportunities for collaborative data analysis [20]. Such interaction requires physical navigation

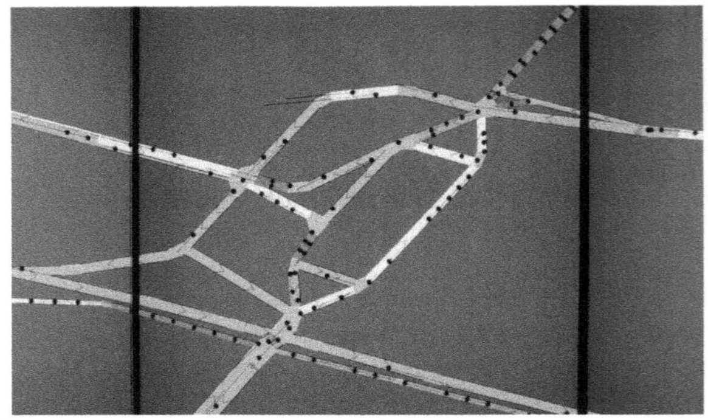

Figure 3. View of "Place de la Concorde" in Paris on our prototype.

[6], that could fatigue operators working long hours. We instead envision they'll be used occasionally: operators generally sit in front of their workstation, but when they address critical incidents or conduct planning sessions, they get up and interact with the wall. Focusing on a single shared screen could better support group work and awareness [15], and reduce the visual attention switch that occurs in MDE [33].

Traffic data and modeling

In our prototype, we represent each road network as a directed graph, with roads as links and intersections as nodes. The topography of existing road networks is extracted from OpenStreetMap data, or can be generated artificially (randomly) given a number of intersections and a desired road density.

Our system can process and display real-time streaming traffic-density data (e.g. data from the SURF3 system). To predict the evolution of current traffic, or of possible operator interventions, our prototype also models traffic. Roads are assigned speed limits, and intersection traffic-lights are assigned a duration. The duration of multiple lights (e.g. on a single road) can be synchronized as a group.

The current forecasting model is an extension of the Nagel and Schreckenberg one [27] developed by Chrobrok et al. [12]. It is based on cellular automata, and can model road networks with several lanes. At each intersection cars have a predefined probability of taking one of the available roads; this probability is calculated using real data, or the network topology favoring multi-lane roads.

A given state of the network can be cloned and used to run a forecasting model (accelerated) to (i) see a likely outcome of the current traffic, or (ii) see and compare the impact of possible interventions that adjust different parameters of the network (e.g. speed limit, lane closing, traffic light duration).

Our model is only a simplification of real road traffic, and more complex models have been developed in the field of traffic prediction using real-time data (e.g [4]). Nevertheless, our goal is not to develop a more accurate model, but rather to focus on the design of interaction and visualization techniques that can combine real time data and data from (multiple) forecasting simulations. Thus the traffic model is a plug-in in our prototype, so as to be able to incorporate and test different models in the future.

[2] http://www.scoot-utc.com/ [3] http://vision-traffic.ptvgroup.com

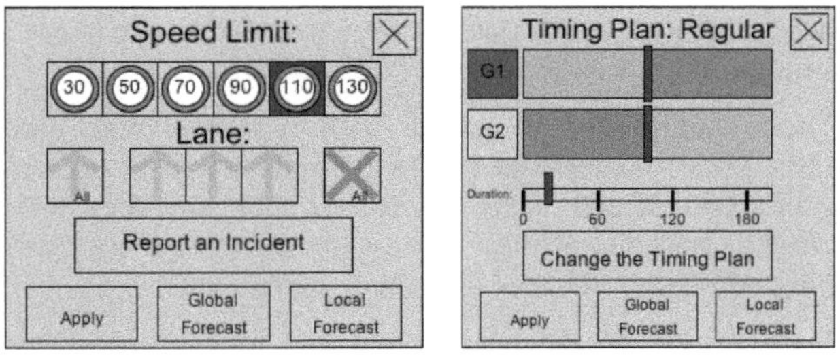

Figure 4. Context aware tool-palettes for modifying road (left) and intersection settings (right).

Real Traffic, Visualization & Interaction

To visualize real-time data, we follow the conventions used in traffic control that operators are familiar with. Traffic density is represented by a progressive color scale: green (fluid), yellow, orange and red (saturated). Depending on data availability, individual cars can also be displayed as circles with a line representing their direction and speed vector (Figure 3).

Operators can invoke context-aware tool palettes (left click for mouse, long tap for touch) to manage roads or intersections. For a road they can alter the speed limit, open or close individual (or all) lanes, and report accidents (Figure 4-left). For an intersection, they can act on light duration: change the proportion of red/green light time, change the cycle duration, or change the current timing plan with another (Figure 4-right). These changes can either be applied immediately to the traffic, or clone the traffic and create a forecast visualization (discussed next).

Operator interventions on real traffic are reported on the map with arrows. By selecting an intervention arrow they can undo the action, or "lock" it so that it cannot be undone, suppressing the marker.

Forecasts, Visualization & Interaction

We are interested in combining real traffic visualization, with likely *forecasts* of the potential future of this traffic, or of the impact of an intervention (e.g., closing a lane or changing light duration), calculated by traffic models. When operators invoke the tool palette to intervene on real traffic, instead of applying their changes, they can choose to instead start a forecast simulation. This clones the state of the real traffic and models the possible outcome of applying the changes, or the predicted outcome of the current situation sped-up.

Operators can intervene further on a forecast visualization, by changing road or intersection settings in the same way they do in the real-time visualization. They can choose to apply their changes to this particular forecast visualization, to the real traffic, or even clone the forecast simulation and apply the changes to the clone. Thus, they can generate multiple branching alternative simulations if desired.

As operators often want to compare the result of forecasts to the baseline traffic to see if there is an improvement, we use difference maps (as Lampe et al. [23]): colors do not indicate an absolute measure (e.g. density), but rather a positive or negative distance from a baseline situation (real traffic). The selection of an appropriate color map is important to highlight differences [42]. We use a diverging color scheme, adapted

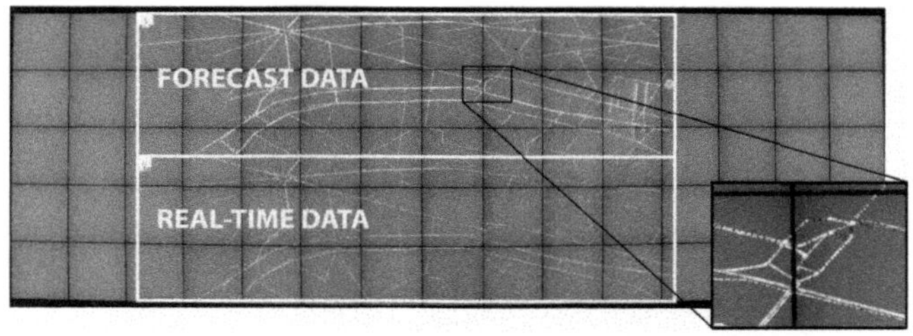

Figure 5. Global visualization of real traffic (bottom) and forecast (top) using MultiViews. A difference color map is used in forecast (cutout).

to be clearly visible on a wall (Figure 5 top & Figure 6 DragMagic views). Three blue hues indicate improvement, three brown deterioration, and white color indicates a similar traffic density. These 7 colors represent all the possible amplitudes of the difference between real traffic and forecasts.

Based on our interviews, operators need to see two types of forecast results: *Global*, that show the forecast for the entire network; or *Local*, that are focused on a few neighboring roads and intersections, that we call an "area of interest".

Global (MultiViews). When operators are interested in forecast visualizations focusing on global outcomes, they can create a new view of the entire network for each simulation, following the idea of small multiples [21]. One view always represents the real time traffic, while the others are forecasts calculated by the predictive model (Figure 5).

Apart from using the tool palette, operators can also create new global forecast visualizations by tracing a vertical line inside a simulation to "split" its view, and create a perfect clone of it. Simulations are laid out on the wall using a grid optimization algorithm.

On the top left corner, global forecast visualizations have a unique identification number based on the order in which they were spawned, and a legend explaining the color range used in the view. They also have a button for invoking a tool palette, through which operators can change simulation settings, such as setting the prediction time frame with a slider from 0 to 30 minutes (a time duration considered to provide reliable results for our forecasting algorithm).

Local (DragMagic). When operators want to focus on particular areas of interest, they can invoke a variation of magic lenses [8, 25] that displays the forecast only for that area. This local view is placed at an offset position to avoid obscuring the real traffic at this area. A DragMagic can also be created by tracing a corner shaped gesture to define the area to be cloned in the DragMagic. As with a DragMag [46], the forecast visualization can be dragged, and is linked visually to the area of interest that is itself highlighted. Several forecast visualizations of different intervention simulations, focusing on the same area of interest, can be displayed side-by-side to show the possible outcomes (Figure 6).

Similarly to the global forecast visualization, DragMagics have a number identifying the simulation they are displaying, and a button to invoke the settings palette (Figure 6). This can be useful if operators want to monitor the results of a single simulation on more than one area of interest. It can be used

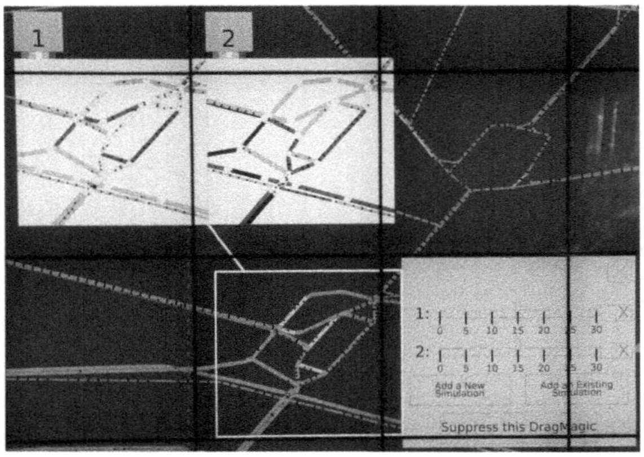

Figure 6. A DragMagic with two forecast visualizations (top left) linked to its area of focus (inside white rectangle), and its menu open (right).

for example to aid operators visualize the impact of an action on critical areas not directly linked to the location of the action, that may be far away. Such areas include vital pathways for access to hospitals, sensitive locations such as long tunnels, or central traffic hubs.

MULTIPLE VIEWS VS. DRAGMAGIC

An important and novel functionality of our prototype is the visualization of forecasts in combination with real traffic, using *MultiViews* to provide a global view of the models' prediction for the entire network, and *DragMagic* to visualize locally the predictions for specific areas.

MultiViews are well adapted for situations where operators need to see the impact for the entire network, as they show global forecasts. When they are interested in a single small area of the network, *DragMagic*s are better for showing local effects. However, the situation is more complex when operators need to consider several areas of interest (critical areas) on the network. Due to the higher number and sparsity of areas of interest, this task is neither clearly local nor global, and thus it is unclear which technique fares best. *DragMagic* likely works well for few areas of interest, but as their number increases they approximate the entire network, and as such *MultiViews* may be better. Moreover, it is unclear how hard it is to follow multiple simulations running at the same time in order to decide between alternatives, using either technique. We thus designed an experiment to compare viewers' performance using *DragMagic* and *MultiViews* for this intermediate case, varying the number of simulations and areas of interest.

Our factors are: two techniques TECH, *DragMagic* and *MultiViews*; number of simulations #SIMU, with 3 values $\{2,4,6\}$ (to simplify, we consider real-time traffic as a simulation); and number of areas of interest #AOI, with 3 values $\{3,5,7\}$.

In a trial, we showed participants several traffic simulations, where one ("simulation 0") is considered the reality and is coded with the classic red to green color coding. The rest use difference maps with simulation 0 (see Prototype). In *MultiViews*, on each simulation the areas of interest are highlighted using white rectangles. In *DragMagic* only simulation 0 is shown fully, and a DragMagic per area of interest is used to display the remaining simulations. For consistency, in the experiment all areas of interest contained exactly two roads, and simulations were updated every 10 seconds.

The layout of *MultiViews* was such that simulations had the same size, and were as big as possible while fitting on the wall. *DragMagic*s were positioned such that they were as close as possible of their area of interest, while not overlapping with other areas of interest or *DragMagic*.

In each trial, participants were asked four questions, separated by intervals of about 30 sec. Two questions were on the present state of the areas of interest, and two on their past history (inspired by tests accessing situation awareness that alternate and repeat questions on present and past, as in [19]):

Q_{pres} "At the present moment, which simulation is the best for the areas of interest?". Asked 1st and 3rd.

Q_{hist} "From the beginning of this trial, which simulation was the best for the areas of interest?". Asked 2nd and 4th.

When it was time for a question, an alarm rung, the simulations paused, and the question was displayed at the top of the wall. Participants gave their answer (the simulation number) using a smartphone. They were instructed to be as fast as possible while minimizing errors. We explicitly told participants not to perform a detailed comparison, but to give us their overall impression, especially for Q_{pres} where a detailed comparison is tedious but possible. Trials lasted 2 minutes plus the time taken by participants to answer the questions.

Our first working hypothesis is that:

H1 *DragMagic* will perform better than *MultiViews*, as viewers have to monitor a smaller area.

Following Plumlee and Ware [30] that link performance with the number of visual comparisons in a task, it is reasonable to hypothesize that increasing the number of simulations #SIMU and areas of interest #AOI will decrease performance overall. However, our experiment was not designed to evaluate the effects of #SIMU and #AOI, but rather to evaluate a possible interaction of TECH with #SIMU and #AOI. According to Plumlee and Ware [30] distance between comparisons can also deteriorate performance:

H2 *DragMagic* will perform better with a larger number of simulations #SIMU as the distance of the areas being compared is reduced; while *MultiViews* will perform better with more areas of interest #AOI, as its global view will be a good approximation of all the #AOI's.

Experimental Design

Participants. Sixteen volunteers took part in the experiment (8 female, 8 male), aged 23 to 32, with normal or corrected-to-normal vision. As participants needed to tell the difference between several shades of the same color, they took the Ishihara Color Blindness test before the experiment to ensure they did not suffer from color-blindness. As our experiment is perceptual in nature (tracking of color changes over time) with no domain knowledge requirements, we believe that designing with experts and experimenting initially with non-experts is valid for measuring perceptual situation awareness (similarly to previous work, e.g., [19]).

Effect for *Time*	n,d	$F_{n,d}$	p	
TECHORDER	1,14	2.48	0.137	
TECH	1,14	5.28	0.038	⋆
#SIMU	2,28	31.8	<0.001	⋆
#AOI	2,28	3.77	0.036	⋆
TECHORDER×TECH	1,14	6.44	0.024	⋆
TECHORDER×#SIMU	2,28	4.20	0.025	⋆
TECHORDER×#AOI	2,28	0.56	0.565	
TECH×#SIMU	2,28	2.61	0.091	·
TECH×#AOI	2,28	0.44	0.650	
#SIMU×#AOI	4,56	5.38	<0.001	⋆

(a)

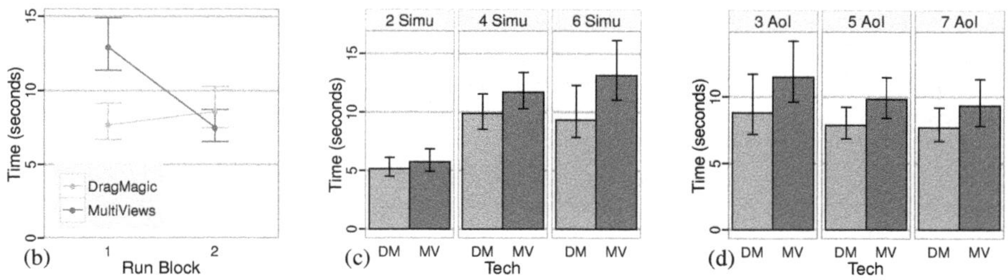

Figure 7. ***Time*** **to answer for question Q_{pres}: (a) Results of the degree 2 ANOVA in the mixed model TECHORDER × TECH × #SIMU × #AOI ×** ***Rand*****(PARTICIPANT) (there is no significant interaction of degree > 2, all p's > 0.4); statistically significant results (p < .05) are starred, whereas a dot marks statistical trends (p < .1). (b) Time by TECH depending on whether a technique was run in the 1st block or in the 2nd one. (c) Time for each TECH by #SIMU. (d) Time for each TECH by #AOI. In (c) and (d), DM stands for** ***DragMagic*** **and MV for** ***MultiViews*****.**

Apparatus. We used an interactive wall (5.9m × 1.96m wide, with a resolution of 14 400 × 4800 pixels), made of 75 LCD displays (21.6 inches, 3mm bezels each), seen in Figure 1. The wall was driven by a rendering cluster of 10 computers. The experimental software, built on our prototype, ran on a master machine connected to the cluster through 1Gbit Ethernet. Participants answered questions using a smartphone.

Procedure and Design. The experiment is a [2×3×3] within-participants design with factors TECH (*MultiViews* and *DragMagic*), #SIMU (2, 4 and 6) and #AOI (3, 5 and 7). We blocked by TECH and the order was counter-balanced between participants: half started with *DragMagic* and half with *MultiViews*. For each TECH, a first trial was used to explain the task, questions and the visualization (e.g., color code, areas of interest, simulation). Then participants conducted 3 training trials before proceeding to the 9 (=3×3) measured trials. For these 9 trials, the #SIMU increased gradually (first 2, then 4 and 6). And for each simulation number condition, the #AOI also increases gradually (3, then 5 and 7). We started with the a-priori easier tasks to try to reduce learning effects.

The network used are the main roads in Paris city center. Using our prototype we built 13 sets of simulations (4 for the training and 9 for the measured trials), by generating a large number of 2 min simulations and selecting ones with a similar number of color changes (about 1000 per simulation). Real traffic (sim 0) was also generated this way for consistency. To ensure a fair comparison across techniques, we took the original simulation sets, and built another 13 ones by changing the simulations order. TECH presentation order was counter-balanced consistently with the sets.

Sessions lasted 1 hour, and at the end participants completed a questionnaire on strategy, workload (customized NASA TLX questionnaire) and preference.

Measures. We recorded the time to answer the questions *Time*, and participants' answers. Time is important in a control room context, as operators need to evaluate situations and act quickly. In our experiment, slower answer times can indicate that in some conditions assessing a situation is harder and requires more reflection. When two or more simulations are displayed, a given imperfect answer could be better than another, as simulations have an order when it comes to improvement over the real situation. Thus, we define *NError* as: $(R - 1)/(\#Simu - 1)$ where R is the rank of the simulation when ordered from best to worst. Using #SIMU ensures we normalize the error per number of simulations. We also report on absolute number of errors per condition (*Err*).

Results

We first look at the results for Q_{pres}, the results for Q_{hist} are similar and discussed next. We noticed that the presentation order of TECH has an impact on the results, thus we report on the between-subject factor TECHORDER. Error bars in our images represent 95% CI computed with all the data points using BCa bootstrapping. For post-hoc tests we use paired t-test with Holm correction.

Time

Figure 7-a shows the detailed ANOVA for *Time*. TECH has a significant effect on *Time* (*DragMagic* being faster), but we also have a significant TECH × TECHORDER interaction. A post-hoc test shows that *DragMagic* is significantly faster than *MultiViews* (p = 0.007, a speed-up of 33%) for participants starting with *MultiViews*, but not for participants starting with *DragMagic* (p = 0.753, almost the same mean *Time*). See Figure 7-b. Thus, *H1* is only satisfied when participants are mastering the techniques and task.

Note that the *Time* for *DragMagic* for both TECHORDERs, and for *MultiViews* when seen second are very similar, and all three significantly faster than *MultiViews* when seen first (p's < 0.009). We see a positive learning transfer from *DragMagic* to *MultiViews*, while the time for *DragMagic* is similar irrespective of order indicating it is easier to master.

There is a significant effect of #SIMU and #AOI on *Time*, with significant interactions TECHORDER × #SIMU and #SIMU × #AOI, but no significant interaction with TECH (next paragraph). Post-hoc tests show that participants were overall faster with 2 simulations than with 4 and 6 (p's < 0.001, no significant difference between 4 and 6 simulations, p = 0.648; see Figure 7-c). When starting with *MultiViews* this difference between 2 simulations and 4 or 6 simulations are bigger than when starting with *DragMagic* (the TECHORDER × #SIMU interaction). Surprisingly, when it comes to #AOI, participants were overall significantly slower with 3 AoIs than with 7 AoIs (p = 0.025; no other significant difference between the AoIs; see Figure 7-d). This difference is mainly caused by the case of 6 simulations (the #SIMU × #AOI interaction) and suggests that participants were able to use the time in between questions to select and focus on a few promising simulations, reducing the number of comparisons at answer time.

The TECH × #SIMU interaction is not significant ($p = 0.091$). However, the difference between the better performance of *DragMagic* over *MultiViews* grows with #SIMU and becomes significant with 6 simulations: $5.1s$ vs. $5.7s$ for 2 simulations ($p = 0.466$), $9.9s$ vs. $11.7s$ for 4 ($p = 0.146$), and $9.3s$ vs. $13.1s$ for 6 simulations ($p = 0.038$). Thus, the first part of *H2* is partially confirmed. Results do not confirm the second part of *H2*, as there is no effect of #AOI on TECH.

Normilized Errors

Regarding normalized errors, the only significant result is an effect of #SIMU ($F_{2,28} = 7.48$, $p = 0.002$). Participants made significantly more errors with 4 simulations (on average 0.13) than with 2 simulations (on average 0.06, $p = 0.02$. And trend for more errors with 4 simulations than with 6 simulations (average of 0.08, $p = 0.065$). We note that statistical trends with absolute number of errors are similar, with the additional difference between 2 and 6 simulations ($p < .001$). Mean absolute error was 0.06, 0.27, 0.20 for 2,4, and 6 simulations respectively.

An important remark is that *DragMagic* and *MultiViews* exhibit very similar average normalized error, overall (0.087 vs. 0.086), and also depending on whether they are seen first or second (0.106 vs. 0.097 for block one and 0.068 vs. 0.076 for block two). The same holds for absolute error (0.18 vs. 0.185). Thus, the above results on *Time* cannot be attributed to a speed-accuracy trade-off.

The Q_{hist} Question vs. the Q_{pres} Question

Result trends for Q_{hist} are very similar to Q_{pres}, we thus omit a detailed presentation of the results. For instance, we have a significant TECHORDER × TECH interaction ($F_{1,14} = 5.43$, $p = 0.035$), *DragMagic* is significantly faster than *MultiViews* for the participants starting with *MultiViews* ($p = 0.002$, a 26% speed-up), but not for the participants starting with *DragMagic*. Moreover, the *Time* for *DragMagic* for both TECHORDER and *MultiViews* for the participants starting with *DragMagic* are very close. Average errors are almost the same for the 4 conditions considered above.

Participants were overall significantly faster with Q_{pres} than with Q_{hist} ($p < 0.001$, $6.5s$ vs. $9.2s$), and made significantly less errors ($p < 0.001$, 0.09 vs. 0.25). This is a reasonable result as Q_{hist} is more complex since it relies more heavily on memory.

Subjective Results

Eleven out of sixteen participants preferred to use *DragMagic* over *MultiViews*, a slight – non significant – preference for *DragMagic* ($\chi^2_{1,16} = 2.25$, $p = 0.134$). Seven out of the eight participants that started with *MultiViews* preferred *DragMagic* ($\chi^2_{1,8} = 4.5$, $p = 0.034$), while from the participants that started with *DragMagic*, four indicate a preference for *DragMagic* and four for *MultiViews*. Thus, TECH preference matches closely the results on time.

Regarding subjective mental workload, a TECHORDER × TECH interaction is again present. Participants starting with *MultiViews* reported a significantly higher mental workload for *MultiViews* than for *DragMagic* ($p = 0.008$, 4.8 vs. 3.9 on a 1–7 scale). While for participants starting with *DragMagic* reported mental workload was similar between *MultiViews* (4.2) and *DragMagic* (4.1).

When reporting strategies, 10 participants explicitly mentioned they always chose 2-3 promising simulations to focus on, even when more simulations were running.

Summary and Discussion

Participants starting with *MultiViews* were slower with this technique (without making less errors): participants starting with *DragMagic* were 33% faster with both *DragMagic* and with *MultiViews*, when compared to participants that started with *MultiViews*. The speed of *DragMagic* was fairly consistent across ordering conditions. The subjective results (preference and mental workload) show a similar trend. Even if there is a learning effect on *MultiViews*, there is no such effect on *DragMagic*, which suggests that participants mastered the use of *DragMagic* faster than *MultiViews*. Moreover, using *DragMagic* has a positive learning impact on *MultiViews*.

DragMagic exhibits slightly better performance than *MultiViews* as the number of simulations increases, indicating that, as expected, reducing the distance between the simulations to be compared can be beneficial. Nevertheless, we did not measure any difference between *MultiViews* and *DragMagic* when the number of areas of interest increased.

Contrary to the model of Plumlee and Ware [30], we do not have a clear growing relation between *Time* and the number of comparisons needed to perform the task, in particular when it comes to the increase of areas of interests and number of simulations. This can be explained by the temporal nature of our task. Based on their comments, participants continuously compared simulations in the time between questions, not just at question time, and were thus able to identify and ignore ahead of time non-promising simulations, providing answers more quickly. Thus, the Plumlee and Ware model does not extend to tasks that have a temporal continuity.

When considering the traffic control context, our results indicate that both techniques can be effective for comparison of simulation results of possible interventions, without a strong performance difference once users become familiar with them. We feel this shows both designs as viable alternatives in terms of performance, and thus designers can choose based on other criteria, like space requirements, positioning of operators in the control room, areas to be monitored, etc.

Our study is perceptual in nature, thus we felt 16 non-expert participants were appropriate. Nevertheless, a larger number of participants could have provided more power to our results. Moreover, our study did not evaluate the interactive aspect of creating, managing and rearranging the *DragMagic* or the *MultiViews*. Finally, to ensure a realistic experiment duration, we fixed the time interval and changes between questions, but verifying that our results hold under varying intervals would strengthen our findings. These remain future work.

EARLY FEEDBACK FROM EXPERTS

A user feedback session was conducted with three of our original users, using a combination of a desktop demo and a video of the prototype used on the wall.

Our interviewees found the idea of interleaving the results of real time traffic data and model predictions very useful. However, all explained that these visualizations would not be used constantly, rather occasionally in situations when the results of possible actions are hard to predict. Operators mentioned they would most likely interact with them from their workstations. Nevertheless, the operations manager explained that the setup of the walk-up and use wall (away from their workstation) could benefit operators in two ways: first by helping them focus on the task at hand without distractions such as camera feeds, etc. And second it could shift their attention away from the monotonous monitoring tasks, and thus alleviating boredom and improving overall performance.

All interviewees seemed to be more interested in the DragMagic visualization for comparing real and forecast data, as they give operators the information they need in the areas of interest "and also the state of the traffic around it".

Two operators thought separately of another use for our system not envisioned before. They felt our techniques can help them diagnose and predict problematic situations by comparing "benchmark" traffic data (past data recorded under normal conditions) with current traffic. As one explained, the system could suggest to operators to open the comparative visualizations when a big enough difference is detected. The visualizations could then provide context and help operators determine if the unusual behavior is a potential unreported incident that requires further investigation, or if the traffic situation is deteriorating and requires intervention.

They also highlighted the need to incorporate some additional functionality, such as the ability to update messages on electronic signs around the city and motorway for the public, and to integrate multiple global traffic light timing plans used currently in the city that we did not have access to initially.

One operator and the operations engineer are currently involved in the development of new systems that may include predictive models (without visualization). Both explained that our setup could also be very useful to their colleagues that work on improving traffic modeling for control centers. Their algorithms require careful tuning and they often need to run multiple small variations of them, that are hard to visualize concurrently on desktop screens.

CONCLUSION

We propose using interactive wall displays in road-traffic control centers for interacting with real-time and simulated traffic data. After visiting two such centers, we designed a prototype that allows to monitor and act on the traffic (or on simulations) and, more importantly, to compare real traffic and several forecast simulations. To this end we use two visualization techniques: MultiViews and DragMagic, that we compared in a lab experiment in terms of situation awareness.

The results show that DragMagic is easier to master, but that both techniques are reasonable design options for control centers, even for several simulations and areas of interest. It seems that the speed of monitoring tasks, that are temporal in nature, is not drastically affected by the number of comparisons in multiple views (predicted by the Plumlee and Ware model [30]). Viewers can identify and ignore non-promising forecasts, reducing the number of effective comparisons. Revising such models is interesting future work.

Expert users provided encouraging feedback and suggestions after seeing the prototype, appreciating in particular the use of DragMagic to follow forecast simulations while keeping the context of real traffic. They also found the prototype useful to compare real and past data to help identify possible problematic situations.

We next plan to study collaboration in control centers, in particular the use of several DragMagics, and cases where some operators interact with the wall and others with their workstation, a functionality we already support.

ACKNOWLEDGMENT

We thank P. Goatin, L. Charansonney and N. Acherar for their availability. We also thank C. Appert, E. Pietriga, O. Gladin and the members of the ILDA team. This research was partially supported by EquipEx Digiscope (ANR-10-EQPX-26-01).

REFERENCES

1. Andrienko G., Andrienko N., Hurter C., Rinzivillo S. & Wrobel S. From movement tracks through events to places: Extracting and characterizing significant places from mobility data. *VAST '11*, IEEE (2011), 161–170.
2. Andrienko N. & Andrienko G. Visual analytics of movement: An overview of methods, tools and procedures. *Info. Vis. 12*, 1 (2013), 3–24.
3. Andrienko N., Andrienko G. & Rinzivillo S. Exploiting spatial abstraction in predictive analytics of vehicle traffic. *ISPRS Int. J. Geo-Inf. 4*, 2 (2015), 591–606.
4. Andrienko N., Andrienko G. & Rinzivillo S. Leveraging spatial abstraction in traffic analysis and forecasting with visual analytics. *Info. Sys. 57* (2016), 172–194.
5. Bader T., Meissner A. & Tscherney R. Digital map table with fovea-tablett®: Smart furniture for emergency operation centers. *ISCRAM '08*, ISCRAM (2008), 2033–2034.
6. Ball R., North C. & Bowman D. A. Move to improve: promoting physical navigation to increase user performance with large displays. *CHI '07*, ACM (2007), 191–200.
7. Bezerianos A. & Isenberg P. Perception of visual variables on tiled wall-sized displays for information visualization applications. *IEEE TVCG 18*, 12 (2012), 2516–2525.
8. Bier E. A., Stone M. C., Pier K., Buxton W. & DeRose T. D. Toolglass and magic lenses: The see-through interface. *SIGGRAPH '93*, ACM (1993), 73–80.
9. Butscher S., Hornbæk K. & Reiterer H. Spacefold and physiclenses: Simultaneous multifocus navigation on touch surfaces. *AVI '14*, ACM (2014), 209–216.
10. Chapuis O., Bezerianos A. & Frantzeskakis S. Smarties: An input system for wall display development. *CHI '14*, ACM (2014), 2763–2772.
11. Chokshi A., Seyed T., Marinho Rodrigues F. & Maurer F. ePlan multi-surface: A multi-surface environment for

emergency response planning exercises. *ITS '14*, ACM (2014), 219–228.

12. Chrobok R., Hafstein S. F. & Pottmeier A. Olsim: A new generation of traffic information systems. *Forschung und wissenschaftliches Rechnen, GWDG-Berichte Nr. 63* (2004), 11–25.
13. Doeweling S., Tahiri T., Sowinski P., Schmidt B. & Khalilbeigi M. Support for collaborative situation analysis and planning in crisis management teams using interactive tabletops. *ITS '13*, ACM (2013), 273–282.
14. Elmqvist N., Henry N., Riche Y. & Fekete J.-D. Melange: Space folding for multi-focus interaction. *CHI '08*, ACM (2008), 1333–1342.
15. Gutwin C. & Greenberg S. A descriptive framework of workspace awareness for real-time groupware. *JCSCW 11*, 3 (2002), 411–446.
16. Helbing D. Traffic and related self-driven many-particle systems. *Rev. Mod. Phys. 73*, 4 (2001), 1067–1141.
17. Hurter C., Lesbordes R., Letondal C., Vinot J.-L. & Conversy S. Strip'TIC: Exploring augmented paper strips for air traffic controllers. *AVI '12*, ACM (2012), 225–232.
18. Hurter C., Tissoires B. & Conversy S. Fromdady: Spreading aircraft trajectories across views to support iterative queries. *IEEE TVCG 15*, 6 (2009), 1017–1024.
19. Ion A., Chang Y.-L. B., Haller M., Hancock M. & Scott S. D. Canyon: Providing location awareness of multiple moving objects in a detail view on large displays. *CHI '13*, ACM (2013), 3149–3158.
20. Jakobsen M. R. & Hornbæk K. Up close and personal: Collaborative work on a high-resolution multitouch wall display. *ACM ToCHI 21*, 2 (2014), 11:1–11:34.
21. Javed W. & Elmqvist N. Exploring the design space of composite visualization. *PacificVis '12*, IEEE (2012), 1–8.
22. Javed W., Ghani S. & Elmqvist N. Polyzoom: Multiscale and multifocus exploration in 2D visual spaces. *CHI '12*, ACM (2012), 287–296.
23. Lampe O. D., Kehrer J. & Hauser H. Visual analysis of multivariate movement data using interactive difference views. *VMV '10*, EG (2010), 315–322.
24. Liu C., Chapuis O., Beaudouin-Lafon M., Lecolinet E. & Mackay W. Effects of display size and navigation type on a classification task. *CHI '14*, ACM (2014), 4147–4156.
25. Lobo M.-J., Pietriga E. & Appert C. An evaluation of interactive map comparison techniques. *CHI '15*, ACM (2015), 3573–3582.
26. Müller J., Schwarz T., Butscher S. & Reiterer H. Back to tangibility: A post-wimp perspective on control room design. *AVI '14*, ACM (2014), 57–64.
27. Nagel K. & Schreckenberg M. A cellular automaton model for freeway traffic. *J. Phys. I 2*, 12 (1992), 2221–2229.
28. Pietriga E., et al. Interaction design challenges and solutions for ALMA operations monitoring and control. In *SPIE 8451, Software and Cyberinfrastructure for Astronomy II*, SPIE (2012), 10:1–10:16.
29. Pietriga E., Huot S., Nancel M. & Primet R. Rapid development of user interfaces on cluster-driven wall displays with jBricks. *EICS '11*, ACM (2011), 185–190.
30. Plumlee M. D. & Ware C. Zooming versus multiple window interfaces: Cognitive costs of visual comparisons. *ACM ToCHI 13*, 2 (2006), 179–209.
31. Prouzeau A., Bezerianos A. & Chapuis O. Surveillance du trafic routier avec un mur d'écrans. *IHM TeC '15*, ACM (2015), 6 pages.
32. Qin Y., Liu J., Wu C. & Shi Y. uEmergency: A collaborative system for emergency management on very large tabletop. *ITS '12*, ACM (2012), 399–402.
33. Rashid U., Nacenta M. A. & Quigley A. Factors influencing visual attention switch in multi-display user interfaces: A survey. *PerDis '12*, ACM (2012), 1:1–1:6.
34. Riveiro M. Evaluation of normal model visualization for anomaly detection in maritime traffic. *ACM TIIS 4*, 1 (2014), 5:1–5:24.
35. Scheepens R., Hurter C., van de Wetering H. & van Wijk J. Visualization, selection, and analysis of traffic flows. *IEEE TVCG 22*, 1 (2016), 379–388.
36. Scheepens R., Willems N., van de Wetering H., Andrienko G., Andrienko N. & van Wijk J. J. Composite density maps for multivariate trajectories. *IEEE TVCG 17*, 12 (2011), 2518–2527.
37. Schwarz T., Butscher S., Mueller J. & Reiterer H. Content-aware navigation for large displays in context of traffic control rooms. *AVI '12*, ACM (2012), 249–252.
38. Smith P., Blandford A. & Back J. Questioning, exploring, narrating and playing in the control room to maintain system safety. *Cognition, Technology & Work 11*, 4 (2009), 279–291.
39. Starke S., Cooke N., Howes A., Morar N. & Baber C. Visual sampling in a road traffic management control room task. In *International Conference on Ergonomics & Human Factors*, Taylor & Francis (2015), 503–511.
40. Tominski C., Schumann H., Andrienko G. & Andrienko N. Stacking-based visualization of trajectory attribute data. *IEEE TVCG 18*, 12 (2012), 2565–2574.
41. Tufte E. R. *The Visual Display of Quantitative Information*. Graphics Press, Cheshire, CT, USA, 1986.
42. Verma V. & Pang A. Comparative flow visualization. *IEEE TVCG 10*, 6 (2004), 609–624.
43. Vlahogianni E. I., Golias J. C. & Karlaftis M. G. Short-term traffic forecasting: Overview of objectives and methods. *Transport reviews 24*, 5 (2004), 533–557.
44. Wang Z., Ye T., Lu M., Yuan X., Qu H., Yuan J. & Wu Q. Visual exploration of sparse traffic trajectory data. *IEEE TVCG 20*, 12 (2014), 1813–1822.
45. Wang Baldonado M. Q., Woodruff A. & Kuchinsky A. Guidelines for using multiple views in information visualization. *AVI '00*, ACM (2000), 110–119.
46. Ware C. & Lewis M. The dragmag image magnifier. *CHI '95*, ACM (1995), 407–408.

Active Pathways: Using Active Tangibles and Interactive Tabletops for Collaborative Modeling in Systems Biology

Meghna Mehta[1], Ahmed Sabbir Arif[2], Apurva Gupta[1], Sean DeLong[2], Roozbeh Manshaei[2], Graceline Williams[1], Manasvi Lalwani[1], Sanjay Chandrasekharan[3], Ali Mazalek[1,2]

Synaesthetic Media Laboratory
Georgia Institute of Technology, Atlanta, GA, USA[1]
Ryerson University, Toronto, ON, Canada[2]

Homi Bhabha Centre for Science Education[3]
Tata Institute of Fundamental Research
Mumbai, India

meghna80791@gmail.com, asarif@ryerson.ca, apurva.gupta@gatech.edu, sean.delong@ryerson.ca, roozbeh.manshaei@ryerson.ca, racelwill17@gmail.com, manasvi.lalwani@gatech.edu, sanjayen@gmail.com, mazalek@gatech.edu

ABSTRACT

We present *Active Pathways*, an active tangible and tabletop system that aims to support collaborative discovery and learning in biochemical modeling. Our work extends ideas from embodied cognition that suggest that interactive systems that support model building by coupling actions made with the motor system to the dynamic properties of external and internal models can enhance the potential for insight and discoveries. We describe the motivation for our work and the design and development of our system. We also present the results of a user study with pairs of novice modelers, which suggest that our system is not only easy to use and learn but also successful at facilitating an understanding of complex systems and supporting collaboration.

Author Keywords

Tangibles; tabletop; computational science; systems biology; modeling; collaboration.

ACM Classification Keywords

H.5.2 Information Interfaces and Presentation (*e.g.*, HCI): User Interfaces—Input devices and strategies, interaction styles, user-centered design; I.6.7 Simulation and Modeling: Simulation Support Systems—Environments.

INTRODUCTION

Since age old times we have incessantly tried to unveil the inner workings of nature. With the development of computational techniques, we have slowly moved from just offloading basic computations to exploring new avenues of discovery using computers. The complexity of these computational problems demands the use of complex tools, which are used by novice students and researchers as well as experts. Yet these tools often fail to balance the complexity required to support discovery and the simplicity required to enable learning. Furthermore, few of them provide support for collaboration among students and researchers from various backgrounds. The problem thus, is not merely how to facilitate computation, but how to utilize these tools to enhance our abilities to discover and learn collaboratively.

We propose to harness knowledge from the cognitive sciences to solve the above problem. Theories in embodied cognition underline the importance the physical world and the body play in our cognitive processes [20, 21, 32]. In particular, the common coding theoretical framework can be used to understand this phenomenon [9]. This framework posits that our imagination and perception of movements are linked with our actions (motor system). Building upon this theory, researchers have shown that the act of building computational models, particularly models with dynamic visualizations, can support conceptual understanding and lead to new discoveries [8, 9]. The theory argues that movement acts as a common language between our small-scale internal models (that we form to understand the world) and external models. Hence, manipulating a physical model can help evolve our mental models, leading to comprehension and discovery. One of the most prominent examples of an external model that led to a breakthrough discovery is the DNA model. Watson and Crick created this 3D physical model to help "fit" the experimental data, which helped them solve the mystery of DNA. In parallel, a growing body of research in the field of Tangible and Embodied Interaction (TEI) tries to bridge the gap between the physical and the digital worlds [37, 40] and goes hand in hand with theories of embodied cognition. We believe that bringing together knowledge from embodied cognition with TEI research and design can help us develop tools for supporting learning and discovery in areas of computational scientific practice.

In this paper, we present *Active Pathways*, a tangible system that facilitates collaborative discovery and learning in the modeling of biochemical processes by novice researchers and students. It brings together computational modeling, embodied cognition, and TEI to enable novice students and expert researchers to build and manipulate external models

ISS '16, November 06-09, 2016, Niagara Falls, ON, Canada
© 2016 ACM. ISBN 978-1-4503-4248-3/16/11...$15.00
DOI: http://dx.doi.org/10.1145/2992154.2992176

that lend spatial and dynamic properties to abstract scientific problems.

In the following section, we discuss related work. Next, we discuss the cognitive foundations of our work, as well as our overarching research question and design goals. We then describe the design and implementation of the proposed *Active Pathways* system and present results of a user study conducted with novice modelers. We then conclude with a discussion of future work.

RELATED WORK

Researchers have investigated how learning abilities can be enhanced through haptic channels. For instance, Brooks et al. [6] developed Project GROPE to display 6-D force fields of interacting protein molecules augmented with haptic interaction. Their work revealed that the combination of visual and haptic displays improves users' perception and understanding of the force fields. Similarly, Chan and Black [7] conducted a user study to understand how students use cognitive processing to understand structure, purposes, and functional relations among system entities. They taught Newtonian mechanics to a group of students using different methods, including sound, touch, and visuals. Results of the study showed that using haptic channels enhanced students' learning capabilities. None of these projects, however, focus on collaboration or model construction.

There have been several attempts to provide users with flexible Graphical User Interface (GUI) based tools for the visualization of biological pathways. For example, a Web-based system called VisANT [16] provides a framework for visualizing and analyzing different types of networks of biological interactions and associations. Another system called Cytoscape [31] supports the visualization and integration of molecular interaction networks and biological pathways. Neither system allows model construction, but manipulation of the data through using various filters. They also do not facilitate learning or collaborative exploration.

Many projects have also focused on tangible interfaces to support scientific practices. Mackay et al. [19], for example, developed augmented laboratory notebooks, termed *a*-books, for linking paper, physical artifacts such as lab specimens, and online data. While both novices and experts can benefit from a-books, it does not allow complex model construction. It also does not support collaboration directly, but allows users to share notes with each other. In a different project, Schkolne et al. [29] used a number of tangible input devices along with a stereoscopic display for DNA molecule design. The system, however, is designed for experts, and therefore does not facilitate learning. It is also unclear if the system enables collaboration among the users or allows model construction. Augmented Chemistry [13, 14] is an augmented reality based tool that employs tangibles to help teach organic chemistry. It combines the strengths of graphical and tangible user interfaces to provide an involved learning experience to students by helping them construct and visualize molecules in 3D. However, the system does not support a collaborative environment.

Many researchers have designed scientific support systems based on interactive tabletops. For example, the eLabBench [35] is a digital tabletop-based laboratory bench that supports molecular biologists in both capturing experimental work and working with standard tools such as spreadsheets using a combination of stylus, mouse and keyboard, and tangibles. This system supports learning and collaboration among the users, but does not support modeling. It does, however, allow users to apply various statistical tests on a dataset. Other examples include the G-nome Surfer [30], a multi-touch tabletop system for collaborative exploration of genomic databases; SynFlo [39], a tangible tabletop for introducing synthetic biology concepts to non-experts, and Eugenie [15], a tangible tabletop interface for helping synthetic biologists to explore of large datasets through the construction of complex queries. A more recent tabletop and active tangible-based system called Sparse Tangibles [1] supports cross-platform collaborative gene network exploration using a Web interface. It enables query construction and filtering the data both on- and off-the-table using the active tangibles. None of these techniques provide the support for model construction.

Technique	Interaction Modalities	Learning	Collaboration	Modeling
Project GROPE [6]	Visual and haptic displays	Yes	Unclear	No
Direct-manipulation animations [7]	Interactive animations with auditory, visual, haptic feedback	Yes	No	No
VisANT [16]	Conventional desktop interactions on a Web browser	No	No	Partially
Cytoscape [31]	Conventional desktop interactions	No	No	Partially
Augmented Chemistry [13, 14]	Desktop and tangible interactions, and augmented reality	Yes	No	Yes
a-book [19]	Augmented notebooks as active tangibles and stylus	Yes	Partially	No
Immersive interface for DNA [29]	Various tangible 3D input devices	No	Unclear	Unclear
eLabBench [35]	Stylus, mouse/keyboard, tangibles, and physical buttons	Yes	Yes	Partially
The G-nome Surfer [30]	Multi-touch tabletop	Yes	Yes	No
Systems Dynamics [27]	Tabletop and tangibles, and external display	Unclear	Yes	Unclear
SynFlo [39]	Tabletop and active tangibles	Yes	Unclear	No
Eugenie [15]	Tabletop and active tangibles	Yes	Yes	No
Sparse Tangibles [1]	Tabletop and active tangibles	Yes	Yes	No
Kinesthetic Pathways [38]	Tabletop and active tangibles	Yes	Yes	No
Active Pathways	Tabletop and active tangibles	Yes	Yes	Yes

Table 1. An overview of the most relevant data visualization and manipulation projects.

Systems Dynamics [27] is a tangible-tabletop system for studying complex feedback systems in fields such as business and social sciences. It allows users to change various parameters of computer models to simulate the outcome. However, it is unclear how the system can aid the process of learning.

Arias et al. [1] developed a research platform that explores a socio-technical environment to bring together people from different backgrounds to frame and solve complex problems. They employ tabletop computing and tangibles to combine action and reflection spaces, and to create "boundary objects" that help people communicate and build a common ground. The research, spanning over two decades, explains how such an environment can support design, creativity and learning. While their explorations are more geared towards open ended problems where human opinions are the parameters, we employ these methods in mathematical "what-if" situations.

Kinesthetic Pathways [38] is a tangible tabletop system for visualizing biochemical reaction networks. It was developed as a result of a two-year ethnographic study conducted in two systems biology research labs. The studied labs build Ordinary Differential Equation (ODE) models that represent how the concentrations of different metabolites change over time for a particular pathway. Without any visualization tools specific to their practice, they have to work with bare chemical and ODE equations. Most of them resort to drawing sketches on paper to augment their mental model of the pathway. Kinesthetic Pathways provided a tabletop visualization of a built-in chemical network to facilitate exploration of parameters to fit model data using a limited set of passive tangibles (*e.g.*, [22]). It did not support model construction.

Figure 1. Users collaboratively building a biochemical pathway model using the *Active Pathways* system.

MOTIVATION

Motivated by the idea that building computational models can support conceptual understanding as discussed above [8, 9], our research aims to extend the tabletop visualization work of Kinesthetic Pathways in order to support collaborative model construction for graduate students and novice researchers [38]. The ethnographic research conducted in systems biology labs outlined the practices and problems of novice graduate students from various backgrounds, including engineering, mathematics, and biology, as they build biochemical pathways to understand different natural phenomena [38]. Often these students also take modeling courses, many of which have adopted problem-based learning approaches that are grounded in real research problems. This type of classroom setting provides an interesting context for our research as students not only try to gain new knowledge, but also try to apply it to solve real problems. Additionally, these classes bring together students from varying backgrounds with differing levels of biomedical engineering or modeling expertise to work on complex scientific problems.

For modeling, the students receive experimental data, often in tables or spreadsheets, which can be used to develop the pathway and validate the model. The modeling phase is divided into three main phases, namely *building*, *fitting* and *perturbation*. These models usually deal with metabolic processes and are often sketched on paper as a network, *i.e.*, nodes connected by arrows, where the nodes represent molecules and the arrows represent the reactions between them. Ordinary Differential Equations (ODEs) are derived from the pathway to describe the change of concentration of metabolites over time and coded in a numerical computation language such as MATLAB. The parameters (*i.e.*, kinetic order and rate constant) are then iteratively estimated and simulations are run to check the "fit" of the model with the experimental data [9, 38].

It is evident from the description above that the elements of the modeling process are scattered across different representations, *i.e.*, numerical, graphical, computational, etc., and it is up to the student to bring all of these together and create a coherent mental model. Moreover, with students of varying backgrounds coming together to solve these problems, there is a need for a platform to share and gain knowledge. Our research operates within this problem domain, and seeks to apply TEI approaches to facilitate collaboration, learning, and discovery in systems biology by novice students and researchers. The following questions encompass our broad research goals.

- *What functionality is required for supporting collaborative modeling of biochemical pathway in terms of model construction, data fitting/testing, validation, and collaborative tasks?*
- *What combinations of control and representation effectively capture and support the modeling process and allow researchers to work together in building, navigating, and testing the model?*
- *Can the designed system facilitate peer-level collaboration in and understanding of the modeling task for novice researchers from different backgrounds?*

DESIGN OBJECTIVES

Transforming abstract data into physical form is challenging. In an investigation, Shaer et al. [30] listed several challenges of computational scientific practices and pointed towards possible TEI interventions with respect to understanding complex problems, visualizing biological data, enabling large collaboration, and supporting diverse audiences. During the design process, we looked into each of these in greater detail, in an attempt to introduce new interaction techniques that employ active tokens and interactive tabletops in a robust system for building and simulating biochemical models and fitting them to experimental datasets.

Similar to the existing Eugenie [15] and SyFlo [39] systems, we employ active tangibles in combination with an interactive tabletop, however we focus more on the building, as well as the visualization and exploration of dynamic models to support conceptual understanding. To achieve this, we extended the Kinesthetic Pathways project to provide a complete system for both model construction and fitting tasks that is based on the use of multiple active tangibles, programmable physical objects with integrated display, sensing, or actuation technologies, that can be used both off and on an interactive tabletop display surface. Kinesthetic Pathways focused on visualizing a dynamic system on an interactive tabletop with manipulation of parameters using passive tangible controls. In contrast, our aim was to provide users with a comprehensive system that would let users build, edit, manipulate, and simulate their model, as well as test its performance against imported real-world experimental results. The use of active tangibles is central to this goal, as they can serve not only as controls for manipulating visualized data, but can also physically become components of the dynamic system that have changing properties over time, such as molecules and reactions.

Our research team is interdisciplinary, and includes six human-computer interaction researchers, two biomedical engineers, and one cognitive scientist. The human-computer interaction researchers worked closely with the biomedical engineers, who provided domain expertise in systems biology in order to inform the design of the system's features and functionality. The cognitive scientist provided theoretical and empirical knowledge in embodied cognition to inform the design of tangible interactions and visualizations that could facilitate model construction and the development of shared conceptual models by novice and expert users. To fully utilize the interdisciplinary nature of our research team, we adopted an iterative design process where all design decisions were evaluated and analyzed by the team members, and interactions were redesigned until every member found them satisfactory. This process was particularly beneficial, as the experienced biomedical engineers on our team are can also be identified as potential users of the system. Primarily, we attempted to achieve the following goals while designing and testing/pre-evaluating the system.

- *Easy to learn and use:* As our system targets both novice and experienced biologists, and collaboration among them, our primary goal was to make input and interactions with the system intuitive and easy to learn.
- *Facilitates understanding of complex systems:* Through an external model that resonates with the complex analogical problem, we attempted to support the development of a mental model and a way to explore the problem space [23]. We also tried to strengthen the understanding of relationships among the different components by enabling users to see the effect on the system of changing any of its parts.
- *Facilitates discovery and problem solving:* Attempts were also made to assist the process of discovery by exploiting the connection between mental and physical models through tangible interactions. While changing the external model helps novices discover new states, visualizations help shape their imagination and nudge their internal models into new states [9]. This also supports problem solving by allowing users to gauge the accuracy of the solution and a gradual evolution of their internal models.
- *Facilitates collaboration:* With multiple tangibles as inputs and a tabletop system that can accommodate several people, we attempted to create a common space for users to work together. With the shared external model that can be perceived by several people at once, we potentially enable the creation of shared mental models that can help users work together in real time and reach a consensus.
- *The learning and discovery process is enjoyable:* Enjoyment is created not only through involvement of different senses (visual, touch), but also through satisfaction gained from a better understanding of the task at hand.

ACTIVE PATHWAYS

We designed and developed *Active Pathways*, an active tangible and tabletop application for collaborative modeling of biochemical reaction networks. The system seeks to help novice students and researchers in the processes of discovery and learning through building external models. It also explores the use of active tangibles as a means to provide flexible physical attributes to digital data.

Tangible Interactions

The interaction flow is defined around the two major tasks involved in modeling biochemical pathways. First, building the model, and second, fitting the model to experimental data by adjusting parameters. Multiple active tangibles, *i.e.*, Sifteo Cubes [33], are used both on and off the tabletop for both model construction and fitting tasks. Unlike tangible widgets [28], the cubes contain a hierarchy of menu options. We categorize the menu into two initial high-level options: "Model" for creating and editing components and "Data" for uploading experimental data, each having multiple options to choose from, illustrated in Figure 2 (a). Grouping the building and fitting functions creates an agile environment wherein users can quickly build, modify, and test their pathways iteratively without having to switch context. One can switch between the options inside each of these categories by tilting the cube. A selection is made by a single tap on the cube's screen. Shaking the cube takes one back to the parent category. A good analogy to understand the navigation is a tree structure. For the purpose of this prototype we use three Sifteo cubes. Among these, two can be used to build and fit, while one is reserved to play and stop the simulation.

The "Model" Category

This includes the options to create and modify molecules, enzymes, and reactions. Each of these components is a menu in itself and holds an array of related actions that can be performed on the respective components.

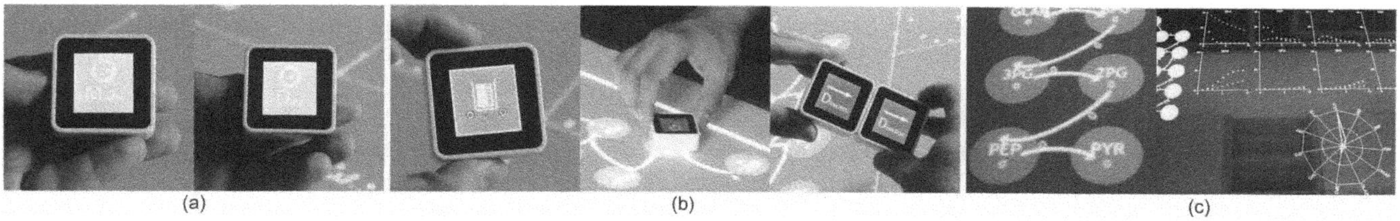

Figure 2. (a) The top-level menus on the active tangibles. (b) Model creation with active tangibles. Here, the user first selects the "Concentration" option from the menu on the tangible, places it on a molecule on the table, and then uses it like a dial to adjust the concentration parameter. S/he can also create a reaction by touching two molecules together and tilting to set the direction. (c) Data visualization in *Active Pathways*. The directional graph visualization represents the pathway, while the radial chart and scatterplot visualizations are for comparing model and experimental data.

For example, consider that two users, Sara and Rahul, want to create the pathway GLC→G6P with enzyme Hexokinase acting on it. Towards that, Sara takes a cube, navigates to the desired molecule (GLC), places the cube on the table, and then taps. This creates the molecule GLC on the table that is now "bound" to that cube, *i.e.*, 'GLC' can now be controlled using that cube. She moves the cube to place the molecule at a desired position on the interactive table. She sets the initial concentration of the molecule by navigating and selecting "Concentration" and then rotating the cube like a VCR dial, *i.e.*, clockwise to increase and anti-clockwise to reduce, till it reflects the value she wants. See Figure 2 (b).

Rahul follows a similar process to create G6P. He then "unbinds" the cube from the molecule by shaking it so that he can create the Hexokinase enzyme. He later realizes that he forgot to initialize the concentration of G6P, so he puts the cube back on the molecule G6P and taps on "Molecule". This enables him to make the necessary changes. Sara and Rahul now bring together the two cubes bound to the molecules to create a reaction between them. See Figure 2 (b). The direction is set by the action of "pouring" the cube bound to the reactant (GLC) onto the one bound to the product (G6P). The rate constant of the reaction is set by binding a cube to it and then rotating the cube. Since the Hexokinase enzymes acts on the GLC→G6P reaction, the enzyme is connected to the reaction by touching a cube bound to the enzyme with a cube bound to the reaction.

A scatter plot can be viewed for each molecule by tapping on the option "Graph" inside the molecule category. Once the pathway is set up, Sara and Rahul can run the simulation by hitting play and see how their model fits the experimental data in real time. The process can be repeated until a good fit is obtained.

The "Data" Category

We users with the ability to input the experimental data using a .CSV or .XLS file via a Web form. Once the file is uploaded, a Data cube can be used to transfer data points from the file onto the model on the table. Users can choose the files associated with the model and go inside the menu to look for the Root Mean Square (RMS) error related to each of them.

Visualizations

The visualizations of our system were inspired by the design and evaluation of Kinesthetic Pathways [38]. While different modelers have different ways of representing pathways, we borrow the directional graph, which is evidently a common representation used by most [38]. This depicts molecules and enzymes as nodes with reactions as arrows connecting them, illustrated in Figure 2 (a). We use fill color to differentiate between molecules and enzymes. We incorporate animations like "breathing" of molecules to make the pathway feel more organic. The name and concentration of the molecule are placed within the circle, whereas the rate constants are situated above a reaction arrow.

Keeping in mind the importance of graphs to validate the accuracy of the results, we use scatter plots and radial charts as graphical aids to realize a fit, illustrated in Figure 2 (c). It has also been shown that different people like to organize the same pathway in different ways to suit their mental models. With the aim of providing a comprehensive representation and the flexibility of arranging their own models, we provide the freedom to move around the different components on the interactive table.

Hardware Implementation

Active Pathways is a tangible tabletop system built around three main components: Sifteo Cubes as active tangibles, a Diffused Surface Illumination (DSI) interactive table, and the CCV and ReacTIVision computer vision framework. Figure 3 illustrates the setup.

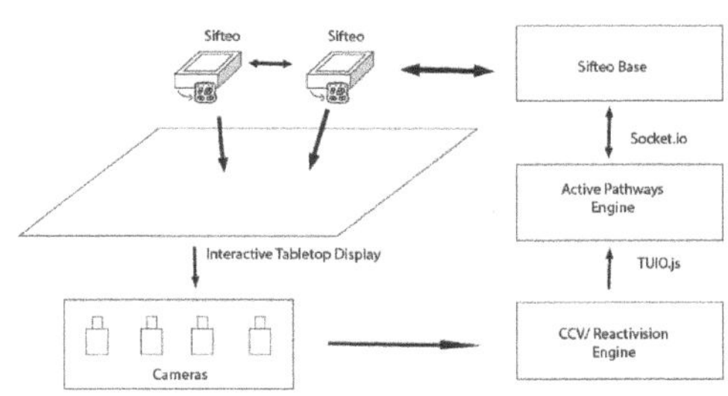

Figure 3. The *Active Pathways* system setup.

We selected Sifteo Cubes to prototype the active tangibles in our system, as each cube has a small Liquid-Crystal Display (LCD) and built-in sensors that detect shake, touch, tilt, and adjacency with other cubes. They communicate wirelessly with a base that is connected to a computer via USB. They can thus communicate bi-directionally with the computer in the interactive table and can be easily programmed to listen to and create events that are communicated via WebSockets.

In our system, ReacTIVision fiducial markers [17] are affixed to the base of the cubes, allowing them to be manipulated both on and off the tabletop. The size of the Sifteo Cubes also factored into our decision to use them in our system: they are small enough to not take up significant screen real-estate and occlude visualizations on the table, but big enough to be held comfortably in hand.

We use a DSI table constructed with four PS3 Eye Cameras viewing the four quadrants of the table from underneath. The PS3 Eye Camera is a webcam that can record an image of 640×480 at 60 Hz or 320×240 at 120 Hz. We use a short-throw projector to rear-project an image on the table's 43.3×30.9-inch active surface. The pictures from different cameras are stitched together by the Community Core Vision (CCV) engine [25] to form a single image. It tracks both the position and orientation of the small ReacTIVision fiducial markers attached to the cubes as they are moved around the tabletop.

Software Implementation

Active Pathways is built on top of Web technologies, *i.e.*, Node.js [24], JavaScript, and HTML 5, for easy portability to other potential platforms, such as tablets and smartphones. For tabletop interactions, we use the CCV computer vision engine, which recognizes the ReacTIVision fiducial markers and touch events on the DSI table. CCV communicates the events occurring on the table using the TUIO protocol. We use the TUIO.js JavaScript library [36] to detect touch and tangible interactions on a Web browser. We use the Sifteo SDK to communicate with the Sifteo Cubes and Socket.IO [34] as the pipeline between the table and the Sifteos. As users interact with the cubes, events are created that are broadcast via Socket.IO. We use the D3.js JavaScript library [4] to create and manage our visualizations and animations. Formation of ODEs is an integral part of modeling and these are created behind the scenes as the model is built. We use the Numeric.js JavaScript library [26] to solve these equations as the simulation is run while performing fitting tasks.

A USER STUDY

We conducted an empirical study to gauge the usability and usefulness of *Active Pathways* for collaborative modeling and fitting tasks.

Apparatus

The user studies were conducted in a lab on a Windows 7 machine. The interactive table was 124×90×94 centimeters in dimension, with an active surface of 110×78.5 centimeters resolution of 1280×800 pixels. The application does not have any touch capabilities hence the touch sensitivity was turned off to ensure proper behavior. The indoor lights were turned off while using the DSI table for proper detection of the fiducial markers. All sessions were video-recorded with due permissions from the participants for the purpose of analysis.

Participants

Since almost all existing work on supporting systems biology modeling on an interactive tabletop has focused on expert users while our system is targeted primarily at novice researchers, we recruited novice modelers for our study. Fourteen paid participants from the university community participated in the study. Twelve of them were from the age group 18-24 and the remaining two were from 25-39. Ten of them were male and four of them were female. They all had prior experience with modeling through coursework, *i.e.*, about four months on average, but had never used an interactive table before. Since we aim to support collaborative modeling, the study was conducted in pairs. Each participant was given a $10.00 Starbucks gift card for participating in the study.

Procedure

The user study started with a semi-structured interview to understand the background of the participants and their familiarity with modeling practices. Since this is a novel approach towards modeling and not many people are familiar with a tabletop system, the interview was followed by a brief demo of the functionalities of the system. Participants were then given some time to get familiar with the system, at the end of which they were asked to fill in a perceived usefulness and ease of use questionnaire, *i.e.*, pre-task questionnaire. It used a 7-point Likert scale and was based on a combination of the System Usability Scale (SUS) [5], the Technology Acceptance Model (TAM) [10], and our own questions regarding specific features of the system. Participants were instructed to rate the evaluated system in comparison with the system they use most frequently for modeling tasks.

We then gave them a small modeling task, in which they were asked to first build the Glycolysis pathways and then to perform a fitting task based on the experimental data already fed into the system. Glycolysis is the metabolic pathway that converts glucose into pyruvate. This particular pathway is commonly used to teach the process of modeling to novices. Although, in practice experimental data is obtained through research, we used synthetic data for simplicity. We manually selected initial concentration values for each molecule, *i.e.*, higher values for reactant and lower values for products, and rate constants for each reaction. The simulation then produced the value for each molecule per unit of time for a total of 10 units.

Participants were given 20 minutes to complete the task. This was decided in consultation with several expert modelers, who responded that it would take them less than 20 minutes to complete the presented task with conventional tools. Upon completion of the task, they were asked to revisit the usefulness and ease of use questions, *i.e.*, post-task questionnaire. We ended each session with a short subjective debrief interview to gather additional feedback.

RESULTS

We converted user response on seven-point Likert scales to three-point scales using linear transformation to calculate ratios (%). All ratings below four were mapped to one, all fours to twos, and all ratings above four were mapped to three. We also converted some responses to binomial data. That is, everything above four was rated as "accept" and below four as "reject" or vice versa, depending on the phrasing of the question. Ratings of four were disregarded. Such a mapping is common practice in statistics [11].

Popular Modeling Tools

Results revealed that most participants use MATLAB for data visualization and modeling tasks. The remaining use various tools, including SolidWorks, AutoCAD, Microsoft Excel, and Simulink. See Figure 4. Interestingly, about 57% participants responded that they often use paper or whiteboard along with these tools. In regard to usability of the tools, half of them responded that they often find these difficult to use, especially when working with large datasets. It is also takes extra time to discover and learn a previously unknown feature due to the systems' unintuitive user interface. Therefore, most participants (80%) felt that more user friendly and responsive systems can improve their modeling performance. Regarding collaboration, most participants (80%) responded that they often collaborate with their peers.

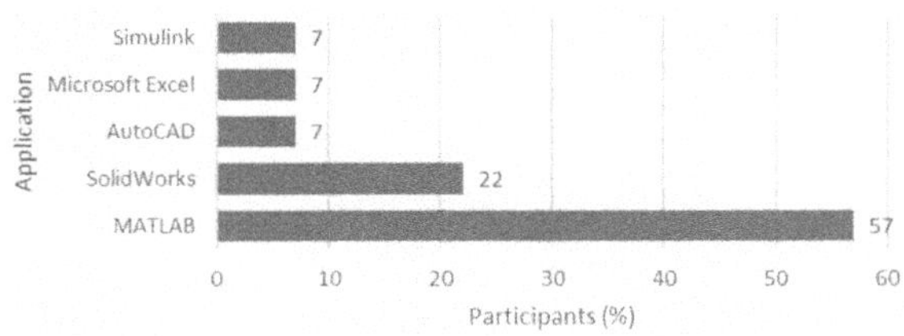

Figure 4. The most used data visualization and modeling tools.

Usability

When asked about the perceived learnability and ease of use of the system in the pre-task questionnaire, most participants (93%) responded that they think that the system will be easy to learn and use. Their responses did not deviate much after using the system. In the post-task questionnaire, most participants responded that the system either met or exceeded their expectations, both in terms of learnability (80%) and ease of use (71%). The remaining 20% and 29% participants found the system more difficult to learn and use, respectively, than they initially expected. See Figure 5.

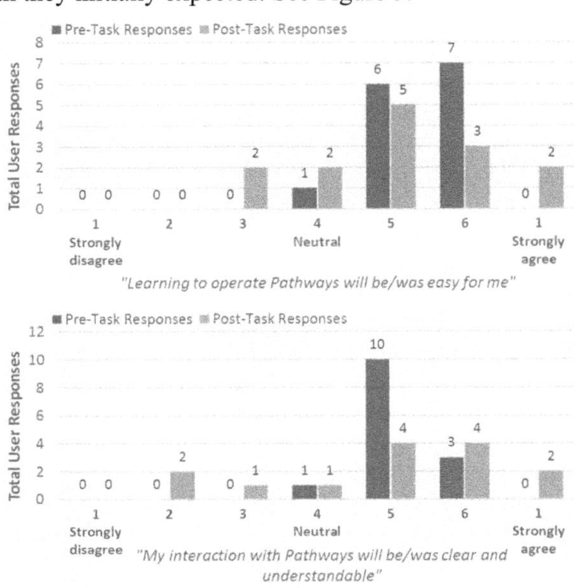

Figure 5. User responses regarding learnability and ease of use, respectively.

Functionality

In the pre-task questionnaire, most participants (about 90%) responded that they found the various functions are well integrated in the system and data visualization on the tabletop is beneficial. Similar to usability, their responses regarding functionality did not deviate much after using the system. In the post-task questionnaire, most participants responded that the system either met or exceeded their expectations in terms of various function integrations (57%) and data visualization (71%). Nevertheless, about 43% and 29% participants did not find the functions as well integrated and the visualizations as useful, respectively, as they initially expected. See Figure 6.

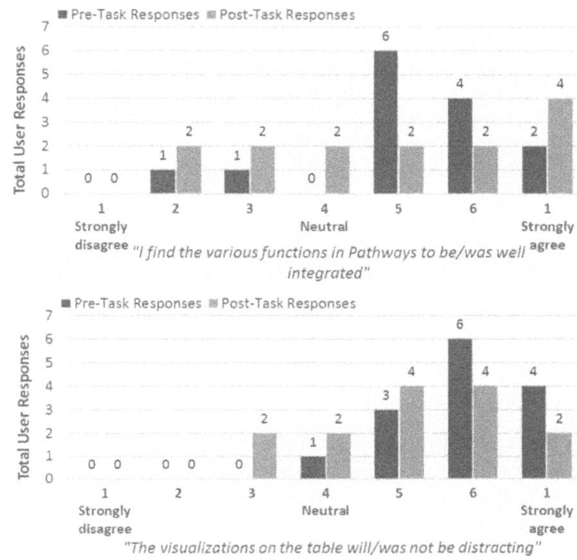

Figure 6. User responses regarding function integration and data visualization, respectively.

Usefulness

In the pre-task questionnaire, all participants (100%) felt that the system will make them better understand the model, the molecules, the reactions, and the relationships between them. They all believed that this will make fitting process easier, as a result make them more confident performing fitting tasks (93%) and enhance their effectiveness on the job (71%). Likewise, in the post-task questionnaire, 86% responded that the system either met or exceeded their expectations in terms of its effectiveness on their performance. However, the remaining 14% were not as convinced. See Figure 7.

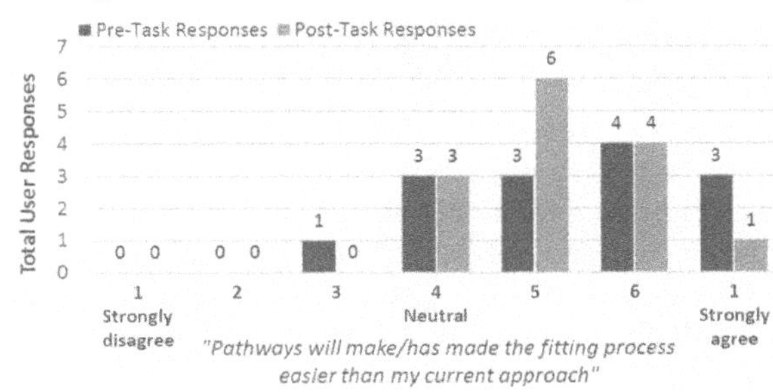

Figure 7. User responses regarding the easiness of the fitting process.

Collaboration

The complete session lasted for about one hour, including demonstration, interviews, questionnaires, and breaks. Each modeling session lasted for about 20 minutes (on average 19 minutes, SD = 3.6). Four out of seven groups (57%) were able to complete the model and run at least one simulation, while the remaining three groups (43%) failed to complete the task. This is not surprising, considering that we recruited novice modelers to perform a task that is usually performed by experts. In the pre-task questionnaire, most participants (80%) replied that the system will most probably make collaboration easier. Their responses did not deviate much after using the system. In the post-task questionnaire, about 80% of them stuck with their initial responses, when the remaining 21% found it less collaboration-friendly then they anticipated. See Figure 8.

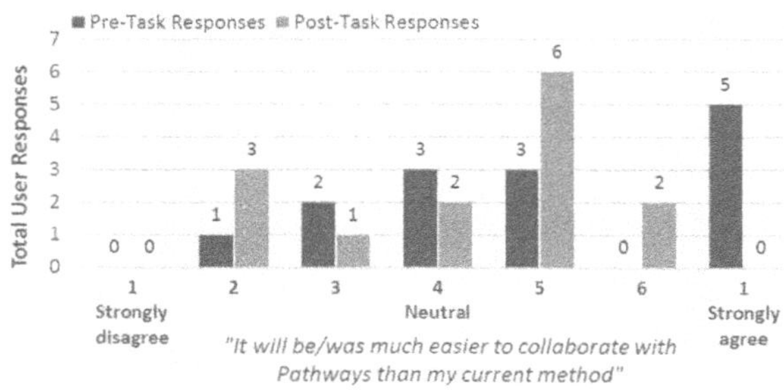

Figure 8. User responses regarding collaboration.

To better understand how well the examined system supports collaboration, we studied the video recordings of the sessions to observe if participants worked exclusively or collaboratively, and if both participants were handling the active tangibles and performing actions or if only one participant was actively performing tasks when the other was either providing directions or passively watching. We then classified the groups based on Shaer et al.'s [30] classification of roles taken by pairs of users working together on a task: Independent, Driver-Passenger, Driver-Navigator, and Turn-Taker.

Based on our observations, all of our groups can be classified as Turn-Takers. That is, both participants in all groups were equally involved in the task, actively participated, and accepted suggestions from their partner. Even in cases where one participant was more knowledgeable, the other was still actively involved with the system, making suggestions and trying actions to move through the tasks. In all groups, each participant assumed ownership of one tangible throughout the duration of the experiment.

User Experience

In the pre-task questionnaire, most participants (over 90%) responded that they will enjoy using the system and can see themselves using it for modeling tasks in the future. However, after using the system about 36% did not find the system as enjoyable as they initially expected. About 21% also changed their minds about using it in the future. See Figure 8.

DISCUSSION

Active Pathways aims to help students and researchers in the processes of systems biology learning and discovery by building external models using active tangible and tabletop interaction. The results of the study provide an opportunity to revisit our design goals.

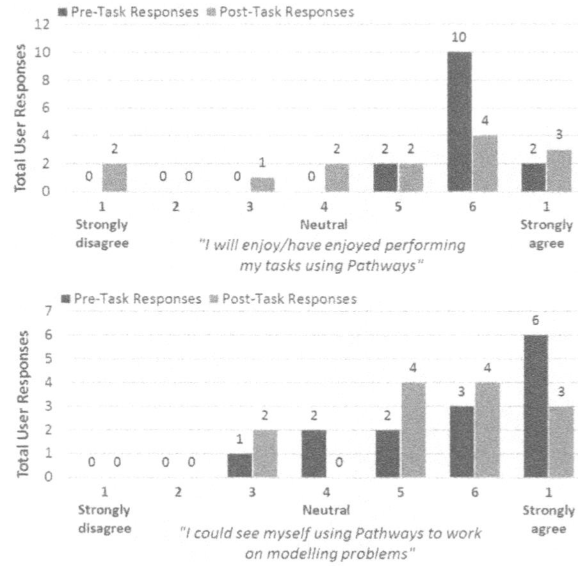

Figure 9. User responses regarding whether the system was enjoyable (above) and whether they see themselves using it in the future (below).

Several participants mentioned that seeing and feeling the model helped their understanding. One group liked how binding makes it feel like one is holding the molecule and another mentioned how physically putting things together helped them "see" better, which is hard to do in MATLAB. Moreover, they found the approach better than paper, as one can easily modify the pathway.

Roughly half the groups were able to complete the task and we received mixed feedback with respect to how well the system supports problem solving. This appears to be due to a combination of reasons. First, as all our participants were new to modeling tasks, it is not surprising that they would require more time for the tasks than expert modelers. Instead, the fact that about the half the groups (57.14%) were able to compete the tasks without having any prior knowledge of the system or the tasks assigned to them highlights the system's usability and how both experts and novices can be productive with it. Second, the accuracy of detection and the limited interactions using active tangibles affected participants' experiences with the system. Since the tabletop interactions in the system currently are entirely based on the positioning and movement of active tangibles on the tabletop (*i.e.*, no support for multi-touch), their detection needs to be accurate and smooth. It can get frustrating for a user if a molecule is constructed at an unexpected position. In the post-study interviews, some also complained about the absence of real-time feedback on parameter changes. There were also some disagreements among the participants regarding how many active tangibles are required to perform the tasks. Some complained that there were not enough active tangibles for the given tasks, while some suggested that not many tangibles are required. A male participant, 25-39 years, commented, "*...everything can be accomplished with one cube (active tangible)*". Nevertheless, we aim to improve these limitations in future revisions.

From the perspective of collaboration, it is evident from the study that in all the groups both participants worked together not just while planning the next steps but also while performing the tasks. Relevantly, a female participant, 18-24 years, commented, "*(the) tasks were easily divisible between partners.*" We speculate that having multiple tangibles to hold, as opposed to simply a large shared display, encouraged joint action and turn-taking, hence increasing focus on the task, opening up a space for discussion, and fostering collaboration among participants. However, we acknowledge the fact that all our participants took courses together may have contributed to this behavior, thus further investigation is necessary to fully understand collaboration behaviors with the system.

While most participants agreed that working on the system would be enjoyable, post task some of them felt it was not as enjoyable as they had initially expected. As active tangibles were a novel form of interaction to all users, several of them did not feel comfortable with the interactions based around the tangibles alone (*i.e.*, without multi-touch), or would have liked more active tangibles. This feedback can be easily incorporated into future iterations of the system. It is worth noting that the system needs to strike the right balance between using tangibles as a novel interaction to most users [18], and providing interactions that they are familiar and comfortable with. For example, swiping the screen to scroll through the options has become so ingrained in us that it was hard for some of our participants to get accustomed to tilting a cube to change the menu. Future design iterations could employ new kinds of active tangibles that address some of these issues.

Lastly, our goal of facilitating discovery is difficult to assess at this stage of the research. Boden [1] describes how individuals generate knowledge that is either new to them as individuals ("P-Creative"), or new to humanity as a whole ("H-Creative"). Assessing how well the system facilitates discovery will require deploying the system in actual learning or research settings to evaluate its impact on individual and/or broader creativity.

The foundation for our work lies in the ideas advanced by embodied cognition, which suggest that interactive systems that couple actions made with the motor system to the movement properties of internal models can enhance the potential for insight and discoveries. While much TEI research focuses on improving ease-of-use and collaboration in a given task, there remain unexplored avenues when it comes to understanding how we can design scientific support systems that can better leverage the connection between our motor, perceptual and cognitive processes. We hope *Active Pathways* can help further the research in this direction and possibly be extended to computational modeling in areas beyond systems biology.

CONCLUSION

Based on ideas from embodied cognition, we designed and developed *Active Pathways*: an active tangible and tabletop system that aims to support collaborative discovery and learning in biochemical modeling. We evaluated the system in a user study with pairs of novice modelers. Results of the study suggest that the system is easy to use and learn and can facilitate an understanding of complex systems and collaboration.

FUTURE WORK

Our future plans include refining the tangible and tabletop interactions based on the feedback collected in the study, including more tangibles and exploring the combination of tangibles and multi-touch on the tabletop. Additionally, we are beginning to explore additional tangible devices to better support the fitting task by providing simultaneous control over multiple parameters. Ultimately, we aim to incorporate additional features to provide a more comprehensive tool to support modeling practices in the systems biology classroom or research lab. On the empirical side, we plan to deploy the system in an undergraduate modeling class to understand how it may aid novice modelers in the process of collaborative learning and discovery of complex systems.

ACKNOWLEDGMENTS

This work has been supported by NSF grant IIS-1320350, NSERC, Canada Research Chairs program, Canada Foundation for Innovation (CFI), and the Ontario Ministry of Research and Innovation (MRI).

REFERENCES

1. Arias, E. G., Eden, H., and Fischer, G. *The envisionment and discovery collaboratory (EDC*. Morgan & Claypool Publishers, Williston, VT, 2015.
2. Arif, A. S., Manshaei, R., DeLong, S., East, B., Kyan, M., and Mazalek, A. Sparse Tangibles: Collaborative exploration of gene networks using active tangibles and interactive tabletops. *TEI '16*, ACM (2016), 287-295.
3. Boden, M. A. *The creative mind: Myths and mechanisms*. Psychology Press, New York, NY, 2004.
4. Bostock, M., Ogievetsky, V., and Heer, J. D^3 data-driven documents. *IEEE Transactions on Visualization and Computer Graphics 17*, 12 (2011), 2301-2309.
5. Brooke, J. SUS-A quick and dirty usability scale. *Usability Evaluation* in Industry *189*, 194 (1996), 4-7.
6. Brooks, Jr., F. P., Ouh-Young, M., Batter, J. J., and Kilpatrick, P. J. Project GROPE - Haptic displays for scientific visualization. *SIGGRAPH '90*, ACM (1990), 177-185.
7. Chan, M. S. and Black, J. B. Direct-manipulation animation: Incorporating the haptic channel in the learning process to support middle school students in science learning and mental model acquisition. *ICLS '06*, International Society of the Learning Sciences (2006), 64-70.

8. Chandrasekharan, S. and Nersessian, N. J. Building cognition: The construction of computational representations for scientific discovery. *Cognitive Science 39*, 8 (2015), 1727-1763.
9. Chandrasekharan, S. Building to discover: A common coding model. *Cognitive Science 33*, 6 (2009), 1059-1086.
10. Davis, F. D. Perceived usefulness, perceived ease of use, and user acceptance of information technology. *MIS Quarterly 13*, 3 (1989), 319-340.
11. Dawes, J. G. Do data characteristics change according to the number of scale points used? An experiment using 5 point, 7 point and 10 point scales. *International Journal of Market Research 51*, 1 (2008).
12. Do-Lenh, S., Kaplan, F., Sharma, A., and Dillenbourg, P. Multi-finger interactions with papers on augmented tabletops. *TEI '09*, ACM (2009), 267-274.
13. Fjeld, M., Fredriksson, J., Ejdestig, M., Duca, F., Bötschi, K., Voegtli, B., and Juchli, P. Tangible user interface for chemistry education: Comparative evaluation and re-design. *CHI '07*, ACM (2007), 805-808.
14. Fjeld, M., Hobi, D., Winterthaler, L., Voegtli, B., and Juchli, P. Teaching electronegativity and dipole moment in a TUI. *ICALT '04*, IEEE (2004), 792-794.
15. Grote, C., Segreto, E., Okerlund, J., Kincaid, R., and Shaer, O. 2015. Eugenie: Multi-touch and tangible interaction for bio-design. *TEI '15*, ACM (2015), 217-224.
16. Hu, Z., Mellor, J., Wu, J., Yamada, T., Holloway, D., and DeLisi, C. VisANT: Data-integrating visual framework for biological networks and modules. *Nucleic Acids Research 33*, 2 (2005), W352-W357.
17. Kaltenbrunner, M. and Bencina, R. reacTIVision: A computer-vision framework for table-based tangible interaction. *TEI '07*, ACM (2007), 69-74.
18. Lucchi, A, Jermann, P., Zufferey, G., and Dillenbourg, P. An empirical evaluation of touch and tangible interfaces for tabletop displays. *TEI '10*, ACM (2010), 177-184.
19. Mackay, W. E., Pothier, G., Letondal, C., Bøegh, K., and Sørensen, H. E. The missing link: Augmenting biology laboratory notebooks. *UIST '02*, ACM (2002), 41-50.
20. Markova, M. S., Wilson, S., and Stumpf, S. Tangible user interfaces for learning. *Int. J. Technol. Enhanc. Learn. 4*, 3/4 (2012), 139-155.
21. Marshall, P. Do tangible interfaces enhance learning? *TEI '07*, ACM (2007), 163-170.
22. Nagel, T., Heidmann, F., Condotta, M., and Duval, E. Venice unfolding: A tangible user interface for exploring faceted data in a geographical context. *NordiCHI '10*, ACM (2010), 743-746.
23. Nersessian, N. J. and Chandrasekharan, S. Hybrid analogies in conceptual innovation in science. *Cognitive Systems Research 10*, 3 (2009), 178-188.
24. Node.js. https://nodejs.org/en
25. NUI Group. http://ccv.nuigroup.com
26. Numeric JavaScript. http://www.numericjs.com
27. Patten, J., Ishii, H., Hines, J., and Pangaro, G. Sensetable: A wireless object tracking platform for tangible user interfaces. *CHI '01*, ACM (2001), 253-260.
28. Rangoni, Y., Maquil, V., Tobias, E., and Ras, E. Implementing widgets using Sifteo cubes for visual modelling on tangible user interfaces. *EICS '14*, ACM (2014), 205-210.
29. Schkolne, S., Ishii, H., and Schroder, P. Immersive design of DNA molecules with a tangible interface. *VIS '04*, IEEE (2004), 227-234.
30. Shaer, O., Strait, M., Valdes, C., Wang, H., Feng, T., Lintz, M., Ferreirae, M., Grote, C., Tempel, K., and Liu, S. The design, development, and deployment of a tabletop interface for collaborative exploration of genomic data. *International Journal of Human-Computer Studies 70*, 10 (2012), 746-764.
31. Shannon, P., Markiel, A., Ozier, O., Baliga, N. S., Wang, J. T., Ramage, D., Amin, N., Schwikowski, B., and Ideker, T. Cytoscape: A software environment for integrated models of biomolecular interaction networks. *Genome Research 13*, 11 (2003), 2498-2504.
32. Shapiro, L. *The Routledge handbook of embodied cognition*. Routledge, Abingdon, UK, 2014.
33. Sifteo. https://youtu.be/fEqq8JykQoQ
34. Socket.IO. http://socket.io
35. Tabard, A., Ramos, J. D. H., and Bardram, J. The eLabBench in the wild: Supporting exploration in a molecular biology lab. *CHI '12*, ACM (2012), 3051-3060.
36. TUIO.JS. http://protium-labs.co/Tuio.js
37. Ullmer, B. and Ishii, H. Emerging frameworks for tangible user interfaces. *IBM Systems Journal 39*, 3.4 (2000), 915-931.
38. Wu, A., Yim, J., Caspary, E., Mazalek, A., Chandrasekharan, S., and Nersessian, N. J. Kinesthetic Pathways: A tabletop visualization to support discovery in systems biology. *C&C '11*, ACM (2011), 21-30.
39. Xu, W., Chang, K., Francisco, N., Valdes, C., Kincaid, R., and Shaer, O. From wet lab bench to tangible virtual experiment: SynFlo. *TEI '13*, ACM (2013), 399-400.
40. Zuckerman, O., Arida, S., and Resnick, M. Extending tangible interfaces for education: Digital Montessori-inspired manipulatives. *CHI '05*, ACM (2005), 859-868.

MultiLens: Fluent Interaction with Multi-Functional Multi-Touch Lenses for Information Visualization

Ulrike Kister, Patrick Reipschläger, Raimund Dachselt
Interactive Media Lab Dresden
Technische Universität Dresden, Germany
{firstname}.{lastname}@tu-dresden.de

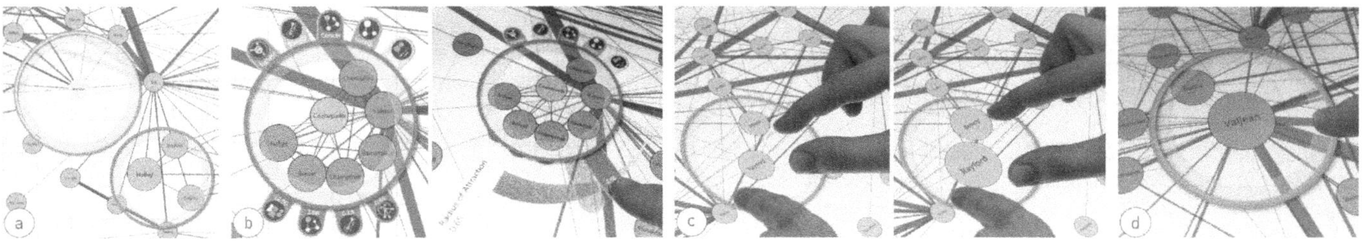

Figure 1. a) single and multi-function lenses; b) radial menu and slider for parameter adjustment; c) continuous gestures; and d) combination of lenses.

ABSTRACT
Interactive lenses have proven to be useful for many visualization applications where exploratory analysis is a primary task. Up to now, interaction with lenses is mostly limited to single-user, single-function lenses operated by mouse, keyboard and traditional parameter menus. To overcome these limitations, we propose *MultiLens*, touch-enabled magic lenses for fluently manipulating functions, parameters, and combinations of lenses on interactive surfaces. We contribute a novel multi-touch menu technique for magic lenses using a widget-based approach with a *drag-snap slider* for relative parameter adjustment. We also propose a *continuous gesture set* for rapidly changing lenses and their primary parameters in one seamless phrase. In addition, by supporting the combination of various lens functions, we create a generic multi-purpose lens tool. We illustrate our approach by investigating and implementing the concepts for the field of graph exploration. The prototype was evaluated in a user study with 22 participants comparing it to traditional parameter menus operated with both mouse and touch.

Author Keywords
Multi-touch interaction; information visualization; magic lenses; focus+context; graph exploration; graph lenses.

ACM Classification Keywords
H.5.2. Information Interfaces and Presentation (e.g. HCI): User Interfaces

ISS'16, November 06 - 09, 2016, Niagara Falls, ON, Canada.

ACM 978-1-4503-4248-3/16/11...$15.00
DOI: http://dx.doi.org/10.1145/2992154.2992168

INTRODUCTION
Magic lenses [5] are established focus and context tools that have been applied to very diverse application domains. An important area where lenses are used is information visualization, where they can support exploration and understanding of very diverse information spaces and data types such as temporal or geo-spatial data. Magic lenses in visualization are defined as interactive tools temporarily altering a selected part of the data's representation [39]. The function of the lens can be an enlargement or distortion of content, like the most commonly used magnification lens, or other effects, e.g., to highlight or sample parts of the data. For this work, we use graph exploration as an exemplary visualization task as it is important in both research and practice: Graphs represent social networks for understanding social patterns, publication networks, or semantic ontologies. In biology, graphs visualizing metabolic pathways can improve comprehension of chemical processes in a cell. Examination and analysis of these networks can be valuable to very different users and domains. Lenses can help analyze these networks by highlighting relations, neighborhood, or patterns.

Many lens solutions have been proposed for data exploration, such as the RouteLens [1], the labeling lens [4], fisheye views for graphs [33], or the Bring Neighbors Lens [38]. However, many of them are limited to mouse-based positioning and global menus or dialog boxes for adjusting parameters. This decouples lens interaction from actual data exploration and creates discontinuities within the workflow. We expect large interactive surfaces to play a dominant role in both professional and private contexts. As soon as they are widely available, they can also be used for interactive exploration of information visualizations. Large interactive surfaces further lend themselves to collaborative data analysis supporting work of multiple people. With the advent of Natural User Interface techniques, novel ways of interacting with lenses have been proposed, among them multi-touch as a predominant input modality. However, the full potential of touch-enabled magic lenses has not yet been unleashed, especially in the field of information visualization. So far, research has mostly focused on simply repositioning and resizing a lens [6, 20, 34]. However, this does not sufficiently utilize the power of interactive lenses. For their effective and efficient use for the exploration of visualizations, the lens function and its parameters have to be adjusted and manipulated as well. In this paper, we propose *MultiLens*, multi-purpose, multi-touch lenses that allow the application of different functions within the same lens. By synthesizing a collection of our own interaction concepts and existing principles, we contribute a functional multi-purpose magic lens system. We present multiple concepts for adjusting the lens function and its parameters and provide tools for their fluent adjustment using alternative manipulation techniques (see Figure 1). We contribute a widget-based approach with a *radial touch menu* for in-place interaction at the lens border that includes a novel *drag-snap slider* technique for efficient and fast manipulation of lens function parameters. We also propose a set of *continuous gestures* for both lens function activation and immediate adjustment of parameters in a seamless phrase. Additionally, our design allows the interactive combination of multiple lenses with different functions into one composite lens. While our general principles are applicable to other contexts, we implemented and evaluated our concepts for the specific context of graph exploration.

In the following sections, we will first provide an overview of related work focusing on magic lenses, their interaction and specific lenses for graphs. We will furthermore discuss our design of *MultiLens*, presenting both interaction techniques individually and then describe the combination of lenses. Finally, we report on a comparative study in which we evaluated our radial touch lens manipulation concept in contrast to global adjustment approaches with both mouse and touch.

RELATED WORK

There has been a variety of research on different aspects of magic lenses. While we focus on interaction, this paper is rooted in several of these earlier approaches. In the following, we will present related work in the context of magic lenses, their interaction and combination, as well as previous work in our example application context of graph exploration.

Magic Lenses and Defining the Lens' Selection

Magic lenses [5] are user interface tools of arbitrary shape, defining a focus region in which the representation of contained objects is altered, leaving the surrounding visualization as the context. As we cannot address all research on magic lenses, we refer to the survey by Tominski et al. [39] which presents a summary of data and tasks addressed by magic lenses in the context of visualization. It describes the three most important aspects of the lens: the *selection*, the *lens function*, and the *join* with the base visualization. Focus of most research on lenses are novel lens functions for specific use cases. Magnification is one obvious lens function in use, but reconfiguring, encoding, and filtering tasks can also be accomplished using lenses [39]. Contrary to the focus on developing new lens functions, in this work we advance the interaction concepts for magic lenses. Instead of the visualization side, we focus on the often disregarded interaction side within information visualization applications [25].

The *selection*, i.e., the region of interest, is mostly defined by the position of the lens. For mouse interaction, an improvement on this aspect has been discussed by Appert et al. [2] who address target selection by taking the mouse cursor's input velocity into account. Similarly, Alvina et al. [1] improve interactions for the *lens' selection* by using the metadata about routes on maps to counteract overshooting when moving the lens along a path. Next to position size, shape, and orientation also influence the *lens' selection* [39]. The labeling lens by Bertini et al. [4] improves exploration by automatically adjusting its size according to data density. Pindat et al.'s JellyLens [28] takes this further by dynamically adapting the shape of the lens to the content below.
When lenses are adjusted using the mouse, interaction is limited to subsequent changes of one parameter at a time, sometimes even on separate global widgets. Instead, multi-touch interaction allows for fast and convenient direct manipulation of elements.

Initially, lenses were used to improve touch or pen target aquisition using magnification. Ramos et al. [29] apply stylus triggered lenses for small target selection and conceptionally propose the adjustment of the zoom by direction-dependent crossing of the lens border. FingerGlass [20] presents fluent creation and re-positioning of lenses using touch for enhanced target selection which is made possible through bimanual interactions. However, position and size were the only lens parameters adjusted. Similarly, Schmidt et al. [35] present a PushLens for graph exploration where only creation and re-positioning is possible. The lens-like telescope views of Khan et al. [21] include a fisheye magnification that can be moved and allows GUI-based adjustment of a zoom factor. Furthermore, Bortolaso et al. [6] apply magnification lenses to maps on interactive tabletops and a touch-enabled magnification lens for scatterplots has been introduced by Sadana and Stasko [31]. The PhysicLenses of Butscher et al. [7] further advance the use of lenses by applying multiple lenses to the same map data and discussing comparison possibilities. Smarties [11] uses magnification lenses for map data presented on a large display. These lenses' size and magnification factor can be remotely controlled by pinching on a mobile device.

All these examples apply multi-touch interaction to magic lenses for their specific use case and use repositioning and resizing to manipulate the *selection*. However, while the *lens' selection* is an important initial parameter that defines the data in focus, adjusting the lens function and its parameters is a second important aspect to make the lens effective to support the task and goals of the user. In previous work, parametrization was rarely used if at all, with the exception of a zoom factor. There are no solutions that accomodate flexible lens function parametrization and lenses with multiple functions. In this paper, we therefore primarily address the adjustment of the lens function and its parameters beside just basic repositioning.

Combination of Lens Functions

Existing lenses from related work often present one single lens function at a time. Yet, the combination of functions can improve efficiency [37] and create new lens functions [38]. The technical aspects of defining lenses to be able to compose them has previously been discussed by Fox [14]. Thiede et al. [37] focus on lenses as operators and base the possible combination on the Data State Reference Model. We use this as a foundation to create an interactive combination of lenses. For tangible interaction, combination of layered filters for image data has been presented in both embodied lenses [22] and TangibleRings [12]. However, these transparencies and rings are inflexible in size and cannot be easily parametrized.

Graph Interaction and Lenses for Graph Exploration

We selected graph exploration as our use case because it is a common task in information visualization which can be useful in a multitude of application cases, such as biology, social analysis, and database exploration. For graph exploration, Schmidt et al. [35] present a set of novel touch techniques for edge and connectivity exploration by plucking, pinning, strumming, and bundling edges, and Riche et al. [30] further discuss multi-touch gestures for control of edge bundling. To improve visibility in graph exploration, specific node magnification lenses have been developed as early as 1992 [32]. Carpendale et al. [9, 10] apply various parameters to magnification lenses, including different shapes, several fisheye functions and drop-offs for the effect. Tominski et al. [38] present a Bring Neighbors Lens that pulls in adjacent nodes of the ones in the *selection* for more information on the connectivity.

Multiple lenses have also been presented to counteract edge congestion, which is one major problem when exploring graphs. Wong et al. [41] propose an Edge Lens that uses distortion around a central point to push away all edges in proximity. The PushLens [35] takes this further by distorting edges around a circular lens area. The LocalEdge Lens [38] deals with local clutter by distinguishing relevant from irrelevant edges. Edges connected to nodes in the *selection* remain unchanged while all other edges crossing the lens are visually removed. Hurter et al. [19] apply different degrees of edge bundling and unbundling to edges in the *lens' selection*. Altogether there are other graph lenses for specific types of node-link diagrams and graph data [39], we only presented a selection of lens functions. While most of the lenses address graph exploration, few works like the EditLens [17] use them for manipulation.

Other than mouse and touch interaction, novel spatial interaction modalities were applied to lenses for the specific case of graph exploration. Spindler et al. [36] present semantic zooming on graph nodes through spatial movement of Tangible Views. Another approach was presented in BodyLenses [24] where the user's body is used to reposition and resize lenses on a display wall to explore a graph.

MAGIC TOUCH LENSES

As described in the previous section, lens manipulation in the past was mostly limited to positioning and resizing of lenses using mouse (e.g., [1, 38]) or very basic movement of touch-enabled lenses (e.g., [6, 31, 35]). We believe that magic lenses as tools need to be able to be configured according to the users' needs to support them as best as possible in their current task and therefore need to support dynamically adjusting individual function parameters. We propose a touch interaction concept for magic lenses, called *MultiLens*, including manipulation and adjustment of the lens function, specifically focusing on fluent and seamless interaction. For that, we deliberately develop lenses as individual tools without global menus to keep the user's focus primarily on the selected data in a local context. This also supports the use on tabletops and wall-sized displays where global menus are not appropriate. In additional, multi-user scenarios are possible as lenses are created and manipulated independently of each other. Additionally, we designed the lens to resemble a ring to allow touch-through interaction to elements below the lens. This creates the significant advantage that elements within the region of interest can be further examined or manipulated.

As we address the combination of lenses, we distinguish the terms function and lens in this paper: A *lens* is the actual tool that can be manipulated. The *function* describes the effect or type of the lens, e.g., magnification or filtering. Each lens can have one or multiple functions with different parameters to consider. As it is the most commonly used form, our proposed lenses are of circular shape. The border is the visual representation of the lens and allows manipulation. As the border itself is rather thin to reduce occlusion of data, we widen the touchable area around it with a semi-transparent area. The color of the lens border encodes its current function. As multiple functions can be active in one lens, the border can consist of multiple colored rings (see Figure 1d).

Lens Functions and Parametrization

We use a set of graph-related lens functions as examples to illustrate our design. Our interaction concepts could also be applied to other data types and visualization techniques. However, this would require a different set of lens functions, e.g., ColorLens [13] for image data. Our set consists of the functions *Fisheye*, *Bring Neighbors*, *K-Neighborhood* and *Local Edge*. They were chosen for their diverse properties, addressing rendering, layout, or filtering of graph elements. Most research on lenses presented in prior work focus on the function itself, seldom offering the ability to dynamically change certain aspects of the function [39]. We analyzed these functions and identified a number of parameters that influence their effect. In the following, we describe our exemplary lens functions and their respective parameters.

The *Fisheye* function [10, 32] magnifies the content of the lens with continuous distortion toward the border. The power of the distortion can be altered by the repulsion parameter and the zoom level parameter changes the magnification. For the *Bring Neighbors* function [38], adjacent nodes are pulled in toward the lens. While the original concept only affected direct neighbors of the nodes in focus, we expanded it with a parameter controlling the degree of neighborhood at which nodes are affected. We call this the *K-Neighborhood* function. Nodes are arranged in concentric circles around a cen-

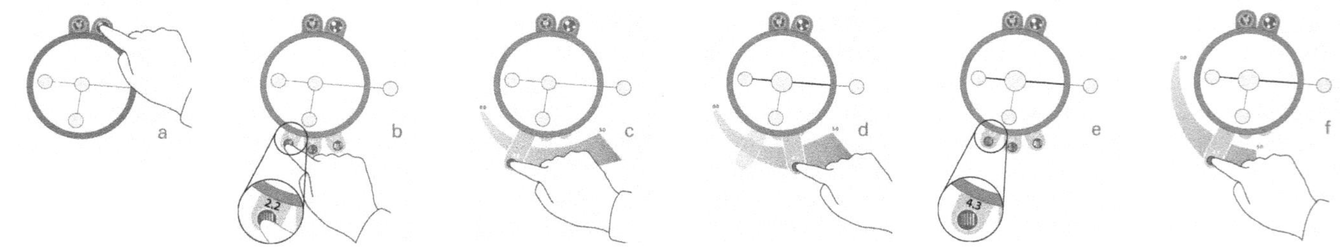

Figure 2. While the upper menu allows selection of desired lens functions (a), the lower handles allow parameter adjustments. The handle is *dragged* out (b-c) to adjust the value(c-d). On handle release, the handle *snaps* back to its original position (e). When pulled out again the position of the slider is automatically adjusted to the new value (f) again allowing relative manipulation.

ter node according to their degree (similar to Bring & Go by Moscovich et al. [27]), with an adjustable radius for the circles. The last parameter is the intensity with which the affected nodes are pulled towards the center node. The *Local Edge* function [38] declutters the view by removing crossing edges that are not connected to the selected nodes. We added a parameter which controls the transparency of the affected edges. Another parameter enables omitting all edges below a certain weight, with the transparency being only applied to the remaining edges.

Basic Manipulations of the Lens

We designed interactions for creating lenses as well as manipulating their position and size. Creation can be accomplished by holding five fingers in close proximity onto the interactive surface, similar to Smarties [11]. This gesture was chosen as the fingers form a circle which resembles the lens. The fingers provide a diameter as an initial lens size value. As the border embodies the lens as a whole, dragging on the lens border is used for translation of the lens, and scaling can be done using the well-known pinch gesture on the lens border. Furthermore, lenses can be removed by scaling them down to a certain minimal threshold which will create a fade-out effect and removes the lens if it is not resized or touched again.

Manipulation of Lens Functions and their Parameters

After being created, the generic lens has no active function yet. In this section, we present the *MultiLens* concepts to adjust a lens by selecting its function and by modifying function-dependent parameters. We first introduce a menu-based approach and then a gesture-only interaction technique.

Radial Touch Menu. To support novices or the infrequent use of *MultiLens*, we make the functionality explicit by using graphical widgets around the lens border, similar to GeoLens [40]. While GeoLens uses a fixed timescale around a circular element, we present a flexible tool for parameter adjustment. A radial context menu along the border of the lens exposes all possible functions and parameters to the user, enabling in-place interaction close to the data. Visibility of this menu can be toggled with a tap on the border. To support differentiation of lens functions and parameters, we separated the radial menu in two major groups. The handles at the top toggle the different lens functions, e.g., Fisheye or Local Edge, and are activated by a tap. Multiple active functions are supported, with the parameter handles for each function placed at the bottom of the lens. Parameter handles are only visible when the respective function is activated. Each function has a unique color, which is used consistently for the lens border and all corresponding handles. For manipulating parameters, we propose two different interaction styles, one with sequential actions and the other with a seamless interaction phrase.

Discrete Tapping. Generally, a *discrete tap* on a parameter menu handle extends the handle and a slider appears around the lens. Simultaneously, other handles are miniaturized to make room (Figure 2c). Movement of the handle along the slider adjusts the parameter of the function. Parameters are either continuous with free handle movement or discrete where the handle snaps to defined steps. Another tap on the handle hides the slider again. We ensure that every parameter handle is always located at the same position on the lens border, using the user's spatial memory to facilitate fast navigation.

Drag-Snap Technique. In our experience, function parameters are often not set to specific values but instead relative to the current value, e.g., bigger or smaller. For more efficient and fluent interaction, we propose a novel continuous technique for relative parameter adjustment on sliders called *drag-snap technique* as an alternative to discrete tapping. Parameter handles can be pulled out and smoothly dragged along the border of the lens to change a value in one continuous movement (Figure 2b-d). As soon as the finger is lifted, the handle snaps back to its original position on the lens border, selecting the chosen value. The slider automatically disappears while the selected value is still visible in the handle (Figure 2e). On dragging out the same handle again, the slider will have automatically adjusted its position (Figure 2f, cf. 2c). Therefore, relative adjustment is again possible. To summarize, if the user wants to change a parameter, she has to drag the handle outwards, move it to adjust the value, and release the touch.

In allowing both discrete, sequential tapping as well as smooth, continuous movement, we support inexperienced users as well as the transition to more fluent interaction for advanced users within the same widget-based approach. Additionally, all parameter handles are positioned at the bottom of the lens to allow observation of the current change to the visualization in the center of the lens while rotating the handle along the slider.

Continuous Gestures. To complement manipulating parameters using widgets, we propose a set of multi-touch gestures for the efficient and fast interaction with lenses. Together with the radial touch menu, *MultiLens* offers a joint interaction concept with different approaches to cater for different usage styles. Both allow triggering different functions within a single lens (see the accompanying video demonstrating the techniques). As tools are often immediately configured to suit the individual needs of a user, we developed continuous gestures allowing for a fluent transition from first activating the lens function to subsequently adjusting its primary parameter without lifting the finger. We thereby support an unbroken kinesthetic tension as previously discussed by Buxton [8] and recently presented by Gupta and McGuffin [18] for improved command selection and argument manipulation in radial menus.
To distinguish lens gestures from interaction with the underlying visualization, the user touches the lens' border with the non-dominant hand to set the frame of reference [3] for the interaction of the dominant hand. Besides decoupling gestures affecting the visualization from gestures affecting the lens, this also avoids complex gestures and provides easily remembered shortcuts for expert users. We present the following iconic gestures for the selected example lenses.

The *Fisheye* function is triggered using a pinch gesture (Figure 3a), which also allows seamlessly changing the degree of magnification. We employ this gesture as the resulting magnification is quite similar to zooming which is predominantly done using pinch-to-zoom gestures. For the classic *Bring Neighbors* function, affecting only direct neighbors, we deliberately designed the gesture mimicking the physical action: The user has to place her fingers onto the surface in form of a grabbing gesture, moving four or five fingers towards the lens center (Figure 3b). This also immediately manipulates the attraction radius. The *K-Neighborhood* function is triggered using a spiral drawing gesture (Figure 3c) which is similar to the concentric rings formed by the lens. Outward or inward spiral movement controls the degree of neighborhood, and the distance to the lens' center changes the radius of the circles. This gesture has also been examined in CycloZoom+ [26] where it was used for zooming purposes. Finally, triggering the *Local Edge* function is performed with a drag gesture resulting in a straight line from within the lens area towards the border of the lens, symbolizing dragging an edge away from the lens area (Figure 3d). Transparency of the edges is directly controlled by the distance of the touch to the lens' center.

To summarize, the proposed gestures provide a seamless transition from activation to adjustment of the lens function, seamlessly phrasing together individual interaction steps [8].

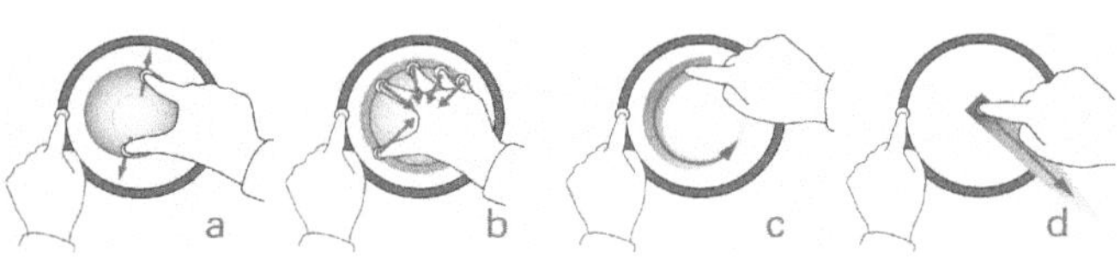

Figure 3. A recognized gesture switches the lens function while the continuation of the gesture allows for adjustment of a primary parameter.

Figure 4. When lenses of about the same size overlap, they can be combined to form one lens. Here both Fisheye (blue) and Local Edge (pink) function are active.

Experts can trigger functions efficiently and fluently adjust the main parameters within their workflow. Similar to Frisch et al. [16], with *MultiLens* we advocate the creation of interaction techniques for both novices and experts, emphasizing the need for effective multi-touch techniques for fluent use. To support all users, a switch between gesture and menu-based interaction is possible at any time without explicit mode switches.

Combination of Lenses

Similar to the presented parameter adjustment of lenses, *MultiLens* supports alternative ways of combining multiple lens functions. Moving two lenses on top of each other applies their individual lens functions onto the shared selection. This is a very clear interaction for novice users. If both lenses are similar in size (below a certain threshold) and would cover the same area, a colored ring inside the lens indicates that the lenses may be combined. Releasing the touch when feedback is visible confirms the combination. The feedback vanishes when the lens is held for a second, keeping the lenses from snapping together. Lenses of different size can be moved on top of each other without automatic combination. A combination of *Fisheye* and *Local Edge* function can be seen in Figure 4. This combination presents a new tool in itself that supports focusing on central nodes. It can be moved as one lens. Separation of lenses can be accomplished by holding a finger on the border of the lens. This will split the lens border into individually colored segments representing the currently active functions which can then be dragged out from the lens to be removed.

While this interaction for combining lenses requires two lenses already in place, simply adding a function to an existing lens can also be useful. Therefore, we distinguish two modes when using the expert gestures: replace or add. These modes are differentiated by the number of fingers placed on the lens border with the non-dominant hand, again setting the frame of reference for the interaction. We use two fingers to activate the alternative action, similar to [15]. Performing the gesture with two fingers on the lens border will add the new function to the lens instead of replacing the existing one(s).

EVALUATION: COMPARISON STUDY

We conducted a user study to assess our *MultiLens* concept aiming at gaining insights for further iterations as well as evaluating its usability and suitability for practical use. Since the flexible radial menu including the *drag-snap slider technique* is a central aspect of our approach, we investigated its comprehensibility and efficiency. In this work, we focus on the basic approach suitable for all users and leave the study of the advanced gestures for experts for future work. We decided to compare the radial menu concept to state-of-the-art implementations of magic lenses. Since there are no comparable solutions on large displays, we use a single-user single-display setup. Most state-of-the-art lens implementations use mouse interaction and global menus or dialogs for the parameter adjustments [39]. Therefore, we use a traditional side menu for comparison. However, to distinguish between changes resulting from the interaction modality, we decided to evaluate both touch and mouse interaction for the traditional menu. This results in three conditions: mouse + traditional menu (M+TM), touch + traditional menu (T+TM), and our own approach touch + radial menu (T+RM).

We hypothesized that the radial touch menu (T+RM) as part of our *MultiLens* is more efficient in terms of required time per action than the current state-of-the-art menu versions (both M+TM and T+TM) because of shorter distances between lens and menu. Furthermore, we believed that users will prefer the directness of the novel *MultiLens* implementation over the state-of-the-art as interaction is less decoupled from the focus (i.e., the selected data).

Participants. We recruited 22 unpaid participants (all right handed, 5 female) to take part in this comparative evaluation study. The participants were students of the math, computer science, and engineering departments of our university. Their age ranged from 21 to 36 ($M = 24.7, SD = 3.3$). All but two reported daily use of mobile touch-enabled devices, of which eight had occasional to frequent use of larger touch-surfaces (interactive white-boards or wall-sized displays) and eight had never worked with touch on devices larger than tablets. 13 had no or very little experience with graphs, while nine stated they work with graphs occasionally, e.g., for UML diagrams or research projects. Magic lenses were completely unknown or never used by 14, three had little experience and only five had worked with magic lenses occasionally up to frequently for research or student projects.

Apparatus. We implemented our *MultiLens* concept in a C#/WPF application for graph exploration (extended from our conference demo [23]). We also created a state-of-the-art implementation where lenses can be dragged and selected on their border. To manipulate their function and parameter, we also designed a side menu with WPF menu elements for use with either touch or mouse interaction. The touch conditions (both T+TM and T+RM) ran on a 27" Perceptive Pixel[1] display with a resolution of 2560x1440 which was slightly tilted for comfort. For M+TM, we used a standard vertical PC display setup with the same resolution and size to represent a state-of-the-art setup for comparison (see Figure 5). Both displays were connected to the same PC.

Methodology and Procedure. The time used for the experiment per participant was approx. 50 min. Prior to data collection, participants completed a questionnaire on their demographic details and experience. All participants were introduced to the effect of each lens function that was used in the study by being presented with images on paper. Afterwards, they were instructed to make themselves comfortable in front of either the PC display (for mouse condition) or the Perceptive Pixel display (for touch conditions). The experiment was a within-subject design and the order of conditions was counterbalanced for 21 participants. An additional 22nd participant was recruited to replace an outlier (see observations below).

[1]http://www.perceptivepixel.com

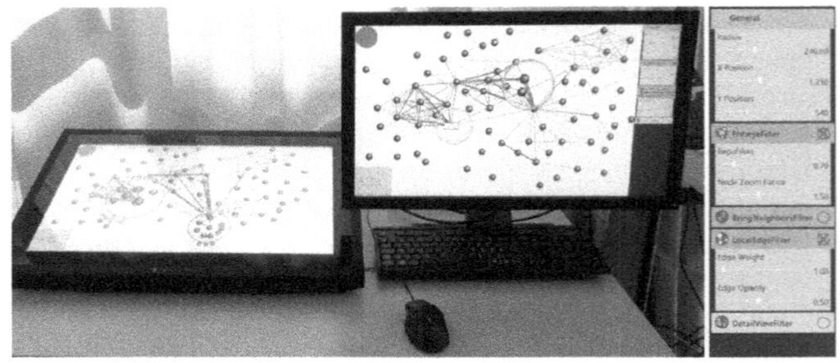

Figure 5. The study was conducted using a slightly tilted display for both touch conditions and a vertical PC display for the mouse condition. The traditional menu (right) was used both with mouse and touch for comparison with our radial touch menu.

For each condition the participant started with a training phase where a researcher explained the basic functionality of each menu, starting with the basic repositioning of the lens to individual lens function parameter adjustments. The participants were given time to make themselves familiar with the interactions until they felt comfortable using the condition ($M = 3.1\ min$). They could then trigger the beginning of the experiment. In each task, participants were presented with the task description and they had time to carefully read the instructions before pressing the start button and moving to the graph. We created three social graphs with random names as the study's data sets. To balance complexity, the number of elements (77 nodes, 254 edges) and node degrees were the same. Using a force-directed layout, each graph was arranged differently. They were counterbalanced so that each graph was used equally often among conditions.

We designed the experiment to include two groups of tasks: six *process tasks (A)* and three *exploration tasks (B)*. In the first group (A), for each task participants were given a list of specific instructions stating up to four individual manipulation steps. Examples include (1) "Trigger lens function Local Edge", (2) "Set function parameter Edge Opacity to 0.2", etc. We designed the process tasks to conform with normal lens exploration processes. Hence, the tasks often started or ended with a move of the lens onto a specific, highlighted node. For *process tasks*, we measured task completion times and logged times of individual interaction steps. *Exploration tasks* (B) were less specific in which interaction steps to take. They included questions such as "Find and select the vegetarian among the friends of Frida" or "Select all neighbors of Lorenzo". We designed each graph for these tasks to include the same problems (e.g., edge clutter, so that the node in question had unconnected edges running through and using the *Local Edge* function was necessary). We also logged completion times for these tasks, but their exploratory char-

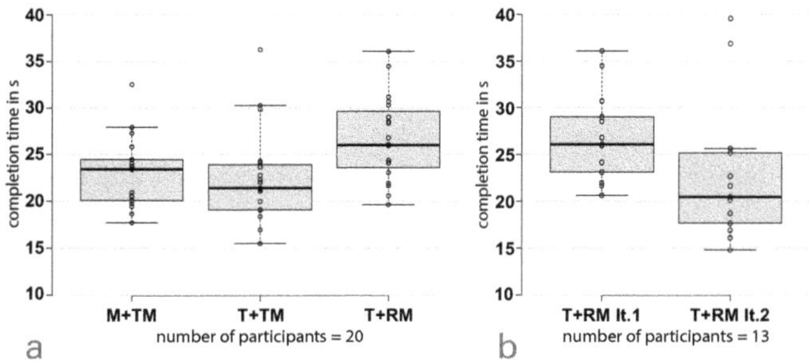

Figure 6. Box plots using quartiles with Tukey whiskers (created with http://boxplot.tyerslab.com). a) T+RM is significantly, albeit in regard to absolute time only slightly slower than M+TM and T+TM. However, b) the second iteration of T+RM is significantly faster than the first one.

acter makes it difficult to tell how much of the time was affected by the menu technique. These tasks primarily served for observing the exploration process. Furthermore, we video recorded the interactions of each user for later analysis and took notes of our observations during the task completion.

After every condition, the participants filled out a separate questionnaire of NASA TLX questions with a 7-point scale to evaluate the physical and mental demand and stated the perceived ease while manipulating the lens. After completing all three conditions, the users were asked to complete a final comparing questionnaire, checking which of the conditions was perceived as most and least helpful, fastest, most comfortable in use, and applicable in everyday work.

Observations and Results

The analysis of the completion times for the process tasks showed outliers for two participants who we also noticed had problems reading the descriptions or partially disregarded the instructions. We removed those two participants for all conditions. As a Shapiro-Wilk test indicated that the assumption of normal distribution was violated, we used Friedman's ANOVA showing a significant difference between T+RM and the other conditions ($\chi^2(2) = 17.1, p \leq .001$). There was no significant difference between M+TM and T+TM. Even though we hypothesized a better performance, T+RM ($M = 26.59\ s$) was slightly slower than M+TM ($M = 22.95\ s$) and T+TM ($M = 22.45\ s$) (see Figure 6a). We hypothesize that a potential reason for this result was the novelty of the menu and the little experience most participants had with larger displays and magic lenses. Therefore, we asked 13 of the participants to perform an additional repetition of the six process tasks using T+RM to evaluate potential learning effects. We statistically analyzed the difference between their first and their second iteration with T+RM (normally distributed, ANOVA with Bonferroni correction). These participants were significantly faster ($F_{1,12} = 13.39, p \leq .05$) in the second run ($M = 22,79\ s$), with an average of 15.2% increase in speed (see Figure 6b). This shows that experience is an essential factor in this scenario. While with further training all conditions will likely improve, the interaction principles of traditional menus are well-estabilshed, so that the strong improvements with the novel condition suggest that the differences between conditions might even disappear.

The evaluation of the NASA TLX questionnaires found no significant differences (ANOVA) between the conditions regarding mental or physical demand, effort, or frustration. While no assertion can be made, we see no evidence for a difference in perceived demand between techniques. In the final questionnaire, the participants were asked to compare the three conditions. 62% of participants selected T+RM as the condition they felt supported them best. Comfort of use was also considered best with T+RM by 57% of participants. When asked to guess the fastest of the conditions, 43% of the participants selected T+TM, 33% T+RM and only 24% checked M+TM. Although we tried to hide which of the conditions were our own design, we cannot rule out a possible bias due to the novelty effect which might have influenced the participant's selection.

Beside the questionnaire, we used the video data and our own observations during both the *process* but also especially the *exploration tasks* to further assess the participant's interactions, concentrating on our T+RM technique to gain insight on how participants worked with the lenses. One aspect of T+RM, which we frequently observed, was that participants had problems identifying parameters based on their icons. They needed to expand the handle to be able to read the label, often resulting in trying out several handles before discovering the right one. This may have been partially responsible for the slower task completion times.

Participants were offered free choice between using tap or drag-snap for manipulating parameters. We observed that of the 22 participants, 14 mainly used the *drag-snap technique*, only three used *discrete tapping* primarily and five participants frequently switched techniques. We noticed that using tap often coincided with situations where participants were unsure on how to proceed or which parameter to select. This assumption is further supported by the questionnaires, where the three users of *discrete tapping* belonged to the group which had little to no experience with large touch displays, graphs, and magic lenses. In all three conditions, some tasks required using two lenses while other tasks provided two lenses that could be used freely. We noticed that when given the choice, 16 of 22 participants used only a single lens, combining various lens functions instead of assigning a unique function to each lens.

DISCUSSION

In this work, we focused on a multi-purpose lens design which is capable of unifying multiple functions in one lens tool. Even though *MultiLens* was slower in our study, time differences in terms of overall time were generally small, and our evaluation shows that more experience and training results in improved efficiency. Furthermore, contrary to traditional menus, *MultiLens* is applicable to large displays and multi-user scenarios because of its support for in-place manipulation and local adjustment of the tool. With all interaction taking place directly around the explored data, minimizing the distraction resulting from gaze switches, the user can better immerse herself in her current task.

Our study uncovered a flaw in our design as our participants had to expand handles of individual function parameters to reveal their labels when the handle icon itself was not sufficient. This needs to be addressed in a future iteration and is especially important for domain novices, which are still in the learning process and therefore unsure about individual parameters. With the increased use of multi-touch for more complex functionality and without the help of tooltips, there is a hightened need for a diverse set of well-designed icons. This results in a challenge for HCI designers to improve the distinguishability of parameters, making them easily recognizable even for novice users. Short textual labels can complement the icons and improve recognition.

Furthermore, our study indicated that users prefer to extend the functionality of a single lens instead of using multiple independent lenses. This observation strengthens our approach of supporting flexible combination of multiple lens functions into a single tool. Nonetheless, it raises the question to further research if single adjustable tools with rich, complex functions are to be preferred to multiple single purpose tools. However, one limitation of the radial menu is that the space for menu handles is dependent on the size of the lens, which limits the possible number of lens functions and parameters. This needs to be investigated further.

An important contribution of our work is the flexible parametrization and combination of lens functions. Related work on touch-enabled lenses [6, 11, 20, 31] focused mostly on magnification, only sometimes allowing the adjustment of a zoom factor. Their interaction principles were relatively limited and did not support flexible lens functions nor their parametrization. However, we believe lenses can be a rich tool applicable to many use cases with diverse lens functions. Their combination further encourages this toolbox-like character. Nevertheless, to support these functionalities additional interaction concepts are necessary. We hence took existing related work and extended it by applying lenses to a more advanced use case that goes beyond simple magnification of content. As a result, our approach supports both the combination of lenses as well as the individual parametrization of lens functions. Our interaction concepts are strongly integrated into the overall approach of the lens, allowing manipulation in-place, and – as we observed in the study – were found pleasant to use.

In our prototype, we used *MultiLens* for graph exploration. Nevertheless, our interaction design principles are also applicable to other visualizations, e.g., examination of medical images by applying additional image filters. We think that professional tasks like these will soon be accomplished using natural user interfaces on mobile devices and large interactive surfaces. However, appropriate gestures for these other domains need to be designed. An advantage of our system are the diverse, redundant interaction possibilities that can be used to trigger functionality. Participants in our study switched between techniques (discrete tapping, continuous drag-snap) depending on context, confidence, and experience. In joining these menu and slider techniques with our continuous gestures, we designed a flexible system, offering easy adjustment of functions and parameters while supporting personally preferred interaction styles. We think that providing tools with both smooth widget-based and gestural interaction capabilities yields improved interaction and has potential for efficiently supporting the work of a larger range of users. These principles can be generalized and extended to other designs where tool creation and parameter adjustments are in focus. Especially for information visualization, interactive surfaces can improve interaction by providing tools that allow casual exploration and direct feel of the data while also providing precise input capabilities for efficiency. By fluently combining and adjusting lens functions using multi-touch, we advocate a novel way of more direct interaction with information visualizations.

CONCLUSION

We contributed *MultiLens*, novel multi-touch-enabled visualization lenses that provide multiple lens functions within one generic lens tool. As previous work focused on single-function lenses, we apply existing principles and improve on the interaction with lenses considering a) basic interactions, b) activation of different functions, c) the adjustment of function-dependent parameters, and d) the combination of lens functions. In a comparative evaluation, we found slower task completion compared to traditional menus with mouse and touch. However, further training resulted in significant performance improvements. In contrast to traditional approaches, our lenses support seamless in-place manipulations and adjustments which contribute to the user's flow of interaction. We proposed multiple ways of function and parameter adjustments presenting both a widget-based approach using a novel *drag-snap technique* and a set of *continuous gestures*. Both enable fluent interaction in uninterrupted phrases. Furthermore, the combination of lenses yields entirely new lens functions. With this, we contributed another step in using the potential of interactive surfaces for information visualization by presenting a flexible tool with different interaction alternatives.

For future work, we plan to apply our *MultiLens* concept to other visualization domains and their lens functions. This would offer the possibility for in-depth evaluation of our extended approach together with domain experts. Additionally, even though *MultiLens* already supports basic multi-user scenarios, we want to further investigate their special requirements and the necessary additions to our concepts.

ACKNOWLEDGMENTS

The authors would like to thank Mathias Frisch and the students Martin Zenker, Elisabeth Wienß, and Sara Groß for their involvement in this project. This project was in part funded by the DFG (DA 1319/3-1) and the Excellence Initiative of the German Federal and State Governments (Institutional Strategy, measure "support the best").

REFERENCES

1. Alvina, J., Appert, C., Chapuis, O., and Pietriga, E. Routelens: Easy route following for map applications. In *Proc.*, AVI '14, ACM (2014), 125–128.

2. Appert, C., Chapuis, O., and Pietriga, E. High-precision magnification lenses. In *Proc.*, CHI '10, ACM (2010), 273–282.

3. Balakrishnan, R., and Hinckley, K. The role of kinesthetic reference frames in two-handed input performance. In *Proc.*, UIST '99, ACM (1999), 171–178.
4. Bertini, E., Rigamonti, M., and Lalanne, D. Extended excentric labeling. In *Proc.*, EuroVis'09, The Eurographs Association (2009), 927–934.
5. Bier, E. A., Stone, M. C., Pier, K., Buxton, W., and DeRose, T. D. Toolglass and magic lenses: The see-through interface. In *Proc.*, SIGGRAPH'93, ACM (1993), 73–80.
6. Bortolaso, C., Oskamp, M., Phillips, G., Gutwin, C., and Graham, T. N. The effect of view techniques on collaboration and awareness in tabletop map-based tasks. In *Proc.*, ITS '14, ACM (2014), 79–88.
7. Butscher, S., Hornbæk, K., and Reiterer, H. Spacefold and physiclenses: Simultaneous multifocus navigation on touch surfaces. In *Proc.*, AVI '14, ACM (2014), 209–216.
8. Buxton, W. A. S. Human-computer interaction. Morgan Kaufmann Publishers Inc., San Francisco, CA, USA, 1995, ch. Chunking and Phrasing and the Design of Human-computer Dialogues, 494–499.
9. Carpendale, M. S. T., and Montagnese, C. A framework for unifying presentation space. In *Proc.*, UIST '01, ACM (2001), 61–70.
10. Carpendale, S., Ligh, J., and Pattison, E. Achieving higher magnification in context. In *Proc.*, UIST '04, ACM (2004), 71–80.
11. Chapuis, O., Bezerianos, A., and Frantzeskakis, S. Smarties: An input system for wall display development. In *Proc.*, CHI '14, ACM (New York, NY, USA, 2014), 2763–2772.
12. Ebert, A., Weber, C., Cernea, D., and Petsch, S. Tangiblerings: Nestable circular tangibles. In *Ext. Abstracts CHI*, CHI EA '13, ACM (2013), 1617–1622.
13. Elmqvist, N., Dragicevic, P., and Fekete, J.-D. Color lens: Adaptive color scale optimization for visual exploration. *IEEE Trans. Vis. Comput. Graphics 17*, 6 (June 2011), 795–807.
14. Fox, D. Composing magic lenses. In *Proc.*, CHI '98, ACM (1998), 519–525.
15. Frisch, M., Heydekorn, J., and Dachselt, R. Diagram editing on interactive displays using multi-touch and pen gestures. In *Proc.*, Diagrams '10, Springer (Aug. 2010), 182–196.
16. Frisch, M., Langner, R., and Dachselt, R. Neat: a set of flexible tools and gestures for layout tasks on interactive displays. In *Proc.*, ITS '11, ACM (2011), 1–10.
17. Gladisch, S., Schumann, H., Ernst, M., Füllen, G., and Tominski, C. Semi-automatic editing of graphs with customized layouts. *Computer Graphics Forum 33*, 3 (June 2014), 381–390.
18. Gupta, S., and McGuffin, M. J. Multitouch radial menu integrating command selection and control of arguments with up to 4 degrees of freedom. In *Proc.*, AVI '16, ACM (2016), 256–263.
19. Hurter, C., Telea, A., and Ersoy, O. Moleview: An attribute and structure-based semantic lens for large element-based plots. *IEEE Trans. Vis. Comput. Graphics 17*, 12 (2011), 2600–2609.
20. Käser, D. P., Agrawala, M., and Pauly, M. Fingerglass: efficient multiscale interaction on multitouch screens. In *Proc.*, CHI '11, ACM (2011), 1601–1610.
21. Khan, A., Fitzmaurice, G., Almeida, D., Burtnyk, N., and Kurtenbach, G. A remote control interface for large displays. In *Proc.*, UIST '04, ACM (2004), 127–136.
22. Kim, K., and Elmqvist, N. Embodied lenses for collaborative visual queries on tabletop displays. *Information Visualization 11*, 4 (Oct. 2012), 319–338.
23. Kister, U., Reipschläger, P., and Dachselt, R. Multi-touch manipulation of magic lenses for information visualization. In *Proc.*, ITS '14, ACM (2014), 431–434.
24. Kister, U., Reipschläger, P., Matulic, F., and Dachselt, R. Bodylenses: Embodied magic lenses and personal territories for wall displays. In *Proc.*, ITS '15, ACM (2015), 117–126.
25. Lee, B., Isenberg, P., Riche, N. H., and Carpendale, S. Beyond mouse and keyboard: Expanding design considerations for information visualization interactions. *IEEE Trans. Vis. Comput. Graphics 18*, 12 (2012), 2689–2698.
26. Malacria, S., Lecolinet, E., and Guiard, Y. Clutch-free panning and integrated pan-zoom control on touch-sensitive surfaces: the cyclostar approach. In *Proc.*, CHI '10, ACM (2010), 2615–2624.
27. Moscovich, T., Chevalier, F., Henry, N., Pietriga, E., and Fekete, J.-D. Topology-aware navigation in large networks. In *Proc.*, CHI '09, ACM (2009), 2319–2328.
28. Pindat, C., Pietriga, E., Chapuis, O., and Puech, C. Jellylens: content-aware adaptive lenses. In *Proc.*, UIST '12, ACM (2012), 261–270.
29. Ramos, G., Cockburn, A., Balakrishnan, R., and Beaudouin-Lafon, M. Pointing lenses: Facilitating stylus input through visual-and motor-space magnification. In *Proc.*, CHI '07, ACM (2007), 757–766.
30. Riche, N. H., Dwyer, T., Lee, B., and Carpendale, S. Exploring the design space of interactive link curvature in network diagrams. In *Proc.*, AVI '12, ACM (2012), 506–513.
31. Sadana, R., and Stasko, J. Designing and implementing an interactive scatterplot visualization for a tablet computer. In *Proc.*, AVI '14, ACM (2014), 265–272.

32. Sarkar, M., and Brown, M. H. Graphical fisheye views of graphs. In *Proc.*, CHI '92, ACM (1992), 83–91.

33. Sarkar, M., and Brown, M. H. Graphical fisheye views. *Commun. ACM 37*, 12 (Dec. 1994), 73–83.

34. Schmidt, D., Chong, M. K., and Gellersen, H. Idlenses: Dynamic personal areas on shared surfaces. In *Proc.*, ITS '10, ACM (2010), 131–134.

35. Schmidt, S., Nacenta, M. A., Dachselt, R., and Carpendale, S. A set of multi-touch graph interaction techniques. In *Proc.*, ITS '10, ACM (2010), 113–116.

36. Spindler, M., Tominski, C., Schumann, H., and Dachselt, R. Tangible views for information visualization. In *Proc.*, ITS '10, ACM (2010), 157–166.

37. Thiede, C., Fuchs, G., and Schumann, H. Smart lenses. In *Smart Graphics*, vol. 5166 of *SG '08*. Springer-Verlag, 2008, 178–189.

38. Tominski, C., Abello, J., van Ham, F., and Schumann, H. Fisheye tree views and lenses for graph visualization. In *Proc.*, IV '06, IEEE Computer Society (2006), 17–24.

39. Tominski, C., Gladisch, S., Kister, U., Dachselt, R., and Schumann, H. Interactive lenses for visualization: An extended survey. *Computer Graphics Forum* (2016).

40. von Zadow, U., Daiber, F., and Schöning, J. GeoLens: Multi-User interaction with rich geographic information. *Workshop DEXIS* (2012), 16–19.

41. Wong, N., Carpendale, S., and Greenberg, S. Edgelens: an interactive method for managing edge congestion in graphs. In *Proc.*, InfoVis'03, IEEE Computer Society (2003), 51–58.

Expanding Selection for Information Visualization Systems on Tablet Devices

Ramik Sadana
Georgia Institute of Technology
ramik@gatech.edu

John Stasko
Georgia Institute of Technology
stasko@cc.gatech.edu

ABSTRACT
Selection is a fundamental operation in interactive visualization applications. Although techniques such as clicking and lassoing items of interest are sufficient for basic selections, a more sophisticated interaction mechanism is required for expressing complex queries to modify or generalize existing selections. The ability to perform these advanced selections is critical for effective analysis within visualization systems. On touch-based devices such as tablets, however, expressing advanced selections is difficult due to the absence of a cursor and modifier keys. In this work, we address this limitation by presenting new interaction techniques that leverage a person's non-dominant hand. We use these techniques for advanced selection operations such as expanding, modifying, and replicating existing selections. Further, we introduce a method for performing generalized selection on tablet devices that provides a fluid mechanism to control the attributes and parameters of selection.

Author Keywords
Information visualization, selection, multi-touch, tablets

ACM Classification Keywords
H.5.m. Info Interfaces and Presentation (e.g. HCI): Misc.

INTRODUCTION
Selection is a fundamental operation in interactive visualization applications [36]. It can be used for finding details about an item or as an initial step for subsequent operations such as filtering, brushing, and deletion. While basic techniques for selection such as clicking/tapping and lassoing are robust and employed across domains, performing an advanced selection (e.g., adding to an existing selection) often requires expressing more complex and nuanced queries. This complexity is a direct consequence of the modes associated with the selection operation, including add-to-selection, remove-from-selection, intersect-with-selection, replace-selection, and toggle-selection [32].

In commercial operating systems, modifier keys (Cmd, Ctrl and Shift) are used to augment the basic selection by enabling two additional modes — add-to-selection and remove-from-selection. For example, a control click on a file icon in MS Windows adds that file to the existing selection set. Graphics applications such as Photoshop extend support for all five modes, with each using an explicit button for activation. Advanced selection behavior is also evident within desktop visualization systems. Applications such as Tableau and Spotfire support three selection modes – replace, add, and remove.

While advanced selection behavior is common across desktop-based visualization systems, the same is not true for visualization applications on touch devices. In fact, currently there are inconsistencies in the way basic selection itself is supported in applications. For example, Kinetica [26] supports a limited form of selection, employing it only for grouping tasks. Vizable [2] supports selection for details-on-demand on linecharts, but does not provide selection on barcharts. Sadana and Stasko employ selection more extensively in their system [27], using it for brushing, filtering, and details-on-demand. However, their system only supports the basic (replace) selection mode.

Since advanced selection is important for visualization applications, there is a clear need to explore and understand it in more detail. However, several challenges must be addressed to bring advanced selection to visualizations on touch-devices. First, it is not immediately clear which modes should be supported. Further, identifying touch gestures to use for these operations is also challenging. The predominant trend in touch-based visualization systems has been to adopt a standard vocabulary of gestures, i.e., a combination of tap, pan, pinch, and rotate [4, 26, 27]. Since these interactions are typically already employed for other critical operations, identifying alternate interactions becomes even more difficult.

In this design-focused research, we introduce a new approach for providing powerful selection capabilities in touch-based visualization systems. First, by leveraging a person's non-dominant hand, we extend the standard vocabulary of gestures available within these systems. Next, we use the new interactions to support advanced selection operations such as expanding, modifying, and duplicating existing selections. Finally, we present a novel interaction technique to perform a special type of advanced selection — generalized selection.

BACKGROUND

Advanced Selection on Multitouch Devices
On touch-devices with finger-based input, a person typically selects items by tapping on the intended targets or by lassoing around them. Usually, this is less precise than on desk-

ISS'16, November 06 - 09, 2016, Niagara Falls, ON, Canada

ACM 978-1-4503-4248-3/16/11$15.00
DOI: http://dx.doi.org/10.1145/2992154.2992157

top computers because of people's inaccuracy in touching the screen with their finger(s) [19] and the occlusion that results from it [24]. These issues of imprecision have been well documented in the past, and researchers have presented several techniques to mitigate them. Previous work includes *take-off* [24] that placed the cursor at a fixed offset from the touch location, and *zoom-pointing* [5] and *sliding-widgets* [22] that both enhanced the touch areas to allow precise selection of the target.

Enhanced selection techniques have also been proposed for improving selection of an item from a dense cluster of items, a task that is central to visualizations. In LinearDragger [3], users begin by initiating a drag gesture at the position of the target object. This reveals a zoomed-in view of the area, with the object nearest to touch location selected. As the user drags the finger away, the system sequentially scrubs through all the neighboring objects. Lifting the finger commits the selection.

The other way of countering imprecision is by modifying erroneous selections. Several advanced selection techniques for modifying selections on touch-screens have been proposed. For example, Wu et al. [35] described a Pile-n-Browse gesture for selecting objects by scooping them between both hands. Wilson et al. [33] presented an approach to select multiple objects by placing multiple fingers on them. We considered these techniques for our work, but due to their focus on large surfaces and the use of bimanual interactions, their applicability to tablet-based visualizations is limited.

Benko et al. [6] highlighted the value in making selection simple, since the ability to directly touch an object to select it is a very appealing aspect of touch screens. This was further confirmed by the guessability study conducted by Wobbrock et al. [34] where participants preferred the use of tap and lasso gestures for both single and group selection tasks. However, so far the adoption of advanced selection on tablet devices has been limited. In the space of commercial applications for tablets, only those in the graphics domain, such as Photoshop and Paper, provide support for advanced selection modes such as add-to-selection and remove-from-selection.

Advanced Selection in Information Visualization

Selection is a cornerstone of interaction within visualization systems [32, 36]. The key role of selection is in assigning *reference*: indicating data item(s) of interest that can subsequently be operated upon. If there are multiple coordinated views, selected items can also be highlighted and brushed across views [10]. Alternatively, selecting an item can reveal specific details about the item in a details-on-demand view.

Advanced selection is also critical to visualizations and advanced operations are common across desktop visualization systems, such as Tableau and Spotfire. Typically, these systems extend the behavior that the operating system provides and support modes such as add-to-selection and remove-from-selection. These modes are often operated with modifier keys (Ctrl, Alt, Shift) or mode-switches. However, as ubiquitous as these selections are on desktop visualization systems, they are noticeably absent across touch-based visualization systems such as Kinetica [26], Vizable [2], and TouchWave [4].

North et al. [23] earlier explored selection operations on large touchscreen displays. Through a user study, they compared the use of one and two-handed postures for group selection tasks within a glyph-based visualization technique. More recently, Willett et al. [31] gathered user-elicited gestures for selection in interactive graphics on large vertical displays. Their results indicated a preference for one-finger and one-handed interactions over two-handed interactions. However, the tasks they employed were referential in nature ('Select all the peaks' or 'Select three lowest data points'), and differed from the advanced selection operations that are the focus of our work, such as modify or duplicate selection.

ADVANCED SELECTION FOR TABLET VISUALIZATIONS

In this work, we focus on tablets: portable, handheld devices with a touchscreen display ranging from 7 to 13-inches. Several research and commercial data visualization applications have been developed for such devices recently [2, 4, 26, 27]. Our goal was to design support for advanced selection operations within these applications. Our design process involved two main steps. First, we identified the selection modes that are applicable to tablet-based visualization systems. Second, we identified appropriate touch interactions for enabling and operating these modes.

Modes for Advanced Selection

Because selection modes are not mutually exclusive and a combination of a few modes can be sufficiently powerful and expressive [32], not all modes need to necessarily be supported in a system. Identifying relevant selection modes is crucial, however. One option is to replicate the functionality provided within comparable systems on desktops, such as Tableau and Spotfire. This would help address the typical use case for advanced selection in visualizations, wherein users want to perform a selection task, but are unable to express the query using the standard selection operations. However, on touch-devices, another unique set of use-cases also emerge as a consequence of the input being (imprecise) finger-based instead of cursor-based. Below, we describe these diverse use-cases for advanced selection on touch-based tablets. For each case, we identify the selection mode(s) that best represents the use-case.

View-driven Selections

V1. Compound filter - A filter query may be expressed over multiple attributes (e.g., for movies: 1998 < Year < 2008 AND Genre = Comedy OR Drama). This filter operation can be executed by clicking on or lassoing around data items in the view that match the filter criteria, and activating "keep only" or "exclude" options. However, advanced selection techniques are needed here since target items may be placed at distant locations, on different axes, or in entirely different views. Relevant selection modes: *add-to-selection* and *intersect-with-selection.*

V2. Brushing & Linking - Selecting items in one view to track them in a different view is a key operation in visualization applications. Often this operation is one of creating a selection window and subsequently modifying it to observe the effect in other views. Modifications that are useful are resizing (or adding and removing items), translation, and duplication of selection windows. Relevant selection modes: *add-to-selection*, *remove-from-selection*, and *duplicate-selection*.

Challenges of Touch Input

T1. Imprecision of touch - Touch input is inherently imprecise as the finger is many times larger than a target pixel on the display [19]. This imprecision affects selections made with drag or lasso operations, such as range selections made by dragging a finger on an axis [27]. Imprecision causes the fingers to overshoot or undershoot the intended boundaries of selection. Thus, the user may want to resize the selection window. Relevant selection modes: *add-to-selection* and *remove-from-selection*.

T2. Occlusion by hand - The hand manipulating the display often covers the majority of the visualization. This issue is particularly notable on multi-view configurations where selections are dependent on observing data items across views (or brushing). Thus, frequent hand lift-offs are required, which subsequently imply features for readjusting the selection window. Relevant selection modes: *add-to-selection* and *remove-from-selection*.

The above use cases highlight the need for four selection modes—add-to-selection, remove-from-selection, duplicate-selection, and intersect-with-selection. In the following section, we design interaction techniques to operate these modes.

Interaction Techniques for Advanced Selection

The advanced selection interactions typically consist of the user enabling a mode and then performing a selection, or performing a selection first and then picking a mode. In both implementations, communicating the mode to the system is required. On touchscreens, this can be done in a number of ways. The three main approaches are *multitouch menus*, *touch overloading*, and *quasimodes*.

Multitouch Menus

As the number of gestures employed in a system increases, the cognitive overhead of remembering the gestures also increases. Using menus can help reduce this overhead by encouraging recognition over recall. A common example on touch-devices are the marking menus. These menus can be activated with a gesture and typically appear around the touch point. The options in the menu can be accessed either by tapping, using a stroke [21], or through a chorded action of the fingers [20].

The use of menus for advanced selection is common in desktop applications such as Photoshop and Sketch. Similar behaviors can easily be replicated in tablets – a menu can either be persistent or can appear automatically once selection is made. However, the drawback of the first approach is that persistent menus take up valuable space on the screen. The second case, on-demand marking-menus, may occlude sections of the view that contain information needed to select a mode. Further, introducing marking-menus within a system that does not already use them has the potential to impose unneeded complexity. If the behavior is unique, the discoverability of the menu, at least initially, is low. Conversely, once users gain experience with the menu, they are likely to expect menus for other operations as well.

Touch Overloading

A second approach involves *touch overloading*: differentiating between touch events, based on their properties, to enable distinct actions. Commonly used properties include location on the screen, input type (finger vs. stylus), duration, and direction of movement. More recently, other properties have also been shown to be effective for differentiating touches, such as velocity, shear [14], and pressure [17].

Any of these properties can be adapted to create interactions for advanced selection operations. For example, tapping the screen with pressure could activate the add-to-selection mode. However, the disadvantage of touch overloading is similar to that of marking-menus. Novel interactions that are considerably different from ones already used in the system require significant effort from the user to learn and remember. Further, since the touch properties themselves do not have any direct relationship with advanced selection (akin to, say, pressure and thickness), the learning effort is further amplified.

Quasimodes

Modes are states that a system enters wherein all user actions pertain to a specific category of tasks. While the use of modes is common in desktop computers, they are also popular on mobile devices. A common example is lists—tap and drag gestures in a list map to selection and scrolling, but by enabling the edit mode, the same gestures map to operations such as removing and reordering of items.

Modes can operate in one of two manners—*persistent* and *transient*. Persistent modes, also known as "latching" modes [13], stay in effect until cancelled or changed. For instance, the edit list operation is an example of a latching mode. Research has revealed that these modes tend to lead to more errors [28] since users often forget their state and struggle to identify how to cancel the mode if they realize they have made an error.

Transient modes, or "quasimodes" [25], stay in effect only as long as the user maintains the action required to activate the mode. These modes provide an easy and reliable way to return to the default application state and have been shown to significantly reduce mode errors compared to persistent modes [28]. On desktops, most examples of quasimodes make use of modifier keys, such as Shift, Command, Ctrl, and Alt. A similar idea can be adopted for tablets, but a replacement for those modifier keys must be found.

ADVANCED SELECTION INTERACTION DESIGN

Based upon the considerations discussed above, we used quasimodes to provide advanced selection on tablets. In the absence of keyboards with shift and control keys, a different modifier was needed to trigger the mode. To address this need, we leveraged the use of a person's non-dominant hand. The complementary roles of dominant and non-dominant hands have been studied extensively [12]. In HCI research, two-handed interactions have been employed for drawing and selection tasks, and for techniques such as ToolGlasses [7].

Most of these applications, though, assume stable configurations of use, where both hands are free to provide input to the system. On tablet devices, however, the non-dominant hand is often restricted to holding the tablet. As a result, the range of movement available to the non-dominant hand is severely constrained. Based on the way the tablet is held, people can only perform basic tap, hold, and drag gestures at the edges of the screen using either the thumb or the fingers.

Wagner et al. [29] initially explored this idea for handheld tablet devices. By observing how people typically held tablets, they introduced three categories of bimanual interactions — *bimanual taps*, *bimanual chords*, and *bimanual gestures*. Each of these assigned specific operations to the non-dominant hand, e.g., in the case of chords and gestures, finger(s) manipulated specific widgets on the screen, such as menus and lists. While these interactions are certainly more complex than we require, the bimanual tap configuration is more relevant for our use. The authors employ these gestures, which consist of tapping or holding on the edge of the screen, for actions such as activating a marking menu or displaying the *keypad* mode on the soft keyboard.

We build on these results, but simplify the interaction to match the role of a modifier. Modifiers only act as precursors to the primary action. Thus, we only require a single bit of information—whether the modifier was performed or not. Since a basic hold gesture provides this information, we employ it as a modifier.

The Clutch Modifier Technique

We define *Clutch*[1] as the action of the non-dominant hand performing a hold (or long-press) gesture on the screen. We utilize this Clutch action as a modifier in the system. The behavior of our implementation differs from modifiers on desktops. There, a modifier typically does not align to a unique category of tasks. For example, the tasks performed with a Shift key cannot be classified together into a single category. We employ Clutch to introduce interactions that all map to the same category of tasks—advanced selection.

To introduce Clutch on tablets, we had to define the locations on the screen where the action would be permissible. This choice of locations depends on the way people hold tablets. Wagner et al. [29] conducted an initial study to observe people's grips when holding a tablet and found five configurations: ThumbBottom, ThumbCorner, ThumbSide, FingersTop, and FingersSide. In their observation of 8 participants, they identified FingersSide as the most preferred option.

While their results are applicable to our work, they are notably different from our informal observations of people using tablets under both regular and controlled conditions today. The predominant posture we observe is a combination of ThumbSide and ThumbCorner. These observations are also consistent with the patterns that are found in the results from a Google Image Search for terms *tablet*, *grip*, *ipad*, and *holding*. The difference in observations can partly be explained by the significant drop in the weight of tablets since the original study was conducted in 2012. For instance, the weight of an Apple iPad, the dominant tablet in the market, has declined by over 30% since 2012. The weight of a device has a strong bearing on how people hold it, as acknowledged by the authors of the original study.

Ultimately, our design choice was to relax the location requirement and support Clutch on all four edges of the screen. We provide a 100 pixels wide zone that runs along the edges. Since Clutch is a single discrete action, the effort required to operate it is small. Enabling it on all edges further reduces this effort. Moreover, it better supports the division of labor model since Clutch is not restricted to any single hand. Depending on where the primary action needs to be performed, either hand can be used to activate Clutch. When a Clutch is detected, a bright blue halo image appears beneath the clutching finger to provide visual feedback to the user.

To demonstrate the utility of Clutch gestures for advanced selection, we add them to a system providing multi-coordinated visualizations on tablets [27]. The system supports several methods for selecting glyphs in charts such as scatterplots and bar graphs. Individual glyphs can be selected by tapping on them, while multiple glyphs can be selected by lassoing around them. Swiping on the axes selects glyphs between a range of values. Finally, via brushing, glyphs selected in one chart are also highlighted in the other chart.

Mapping Clutch to Selection Modes

Using Clutch as a modifier, we are able to augment and reuse all the primary gestures, such as tap, drag, and pinch. In mapping these modified gestures to advanced selection tasks, we sought a correspondence between the roles of the original gesture A and the modified gesture Clutch + A. We achieved this in the following manner: gestures that create a new selection in the original state do the same in the modified state, but with a different selection mode enabled. Similarly, gestures that modify an existing selection in the original state modify a copy of the selection in the new state. Enabling the Clutch behavior that is consistent with the behavior of modifiers on desktops should help promote learnability of the gestures. In the following section, we describe the role of each modified gesture in detail. The accompanying video illustrates the dynamics of each operation as well.

Clutch + Tap

The Clutch + tap gesture is performed by activating Clutch and tapping with a finger anywhere on the screen (Figure 1). This gesture augments the standard tap behavior that selects the glyph placed beneath the finger. Whereas the non-clutched tap deselects previously selected glyphs, Clutch + tap simply adds the new glyph to the existing selection. If the tapped glyph is already selected, Clutch + tap deselects the glyph and removes it from existing selection.

Clutch + Drag

Similar to Clutch + tap, Clutch + drag is performed by activating a Clutch and dragging a finger on the screen. We use

[1] We use the term "Clutch" much like a car clutch, different from that as used in a thread of existing touch interaction research [9].

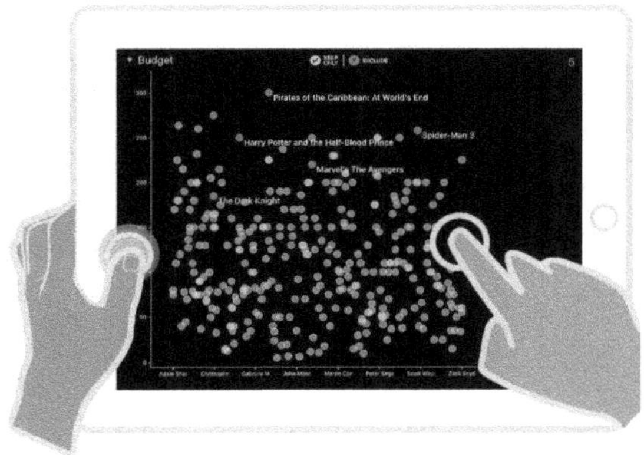

Figure 1: Clutch + tap gesture to select multiple glyphs.

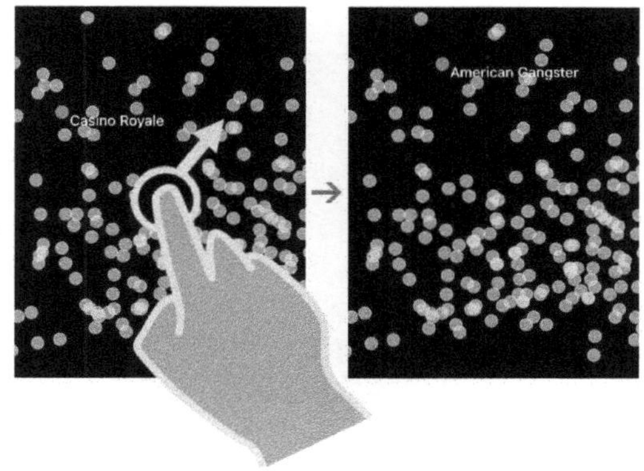

Figure 2: When a single glyph is selected, Clutch + drag translates the selection to a neighboring glyph that is located in the direction of the drag.

this gesture to enable different selection modes depending on the type of selection currently active in the system.

1. Single glyph selected – A single glyph is selected by either tapping on it or lassoing around it. Since identifying a glyph in a dense region is fairly imprecise [19], we use Clutch + drag gesture to assist in selecting a target glyph.

The technique works in the following manner. When a Clutch + drag is initiated with one glyph selected, the system projects the drag movement further in that direction to identify the glyph placed closest to the selected glyph. Once identified, the system holds for the user to move the finger by the same amount as the distance between the two glyphs. For target glyphs placed further away, we use a control-display gain to expand the magnitude of movement. When the movement exceeds the distance between the glyphs, the selection snaps to the other glyph, deselecting the original glyph (Figure 2). This also reveals a label depicting the primary key of the selected glyph for additional feedback. The overall effect of the operation resembles that of using a trackpad where finger's movement maps to the movement of a cursor. Similar to BubbleCursor [11], the selection is snapped to a glyph at all times, i.e. there is no transitional state in the middle when no glyph is selected.

Our design is also similar to the LinearDragger technique for selecting an item from a dense cluster of items [3], with three key differences. First, the user does not need to place their finger near the dense area of points and can perform the action from a distance. Second, instead of mapping the selection to one-dimensional movement, we use both dimensions of the movement to allow more precise access to the neighboring glyphs. Finally, we provide details for each glyph, helping users differentiate them from one another.

2. Multiple glyphs selected – Dragging on the view draws a lasso path and selects all points that lie within the path. Using a Clutch augments this behavior by enabling the add-to-selection mode. Thus, new glyphs are selected without deselecting previously selected glyphs. This is similar to Clutch + tap. However, Clutch + lasso does not support remove-from-selection. If the lasso region contains glyphs that are already selected, their selection state is *not* toggled.

3. Rectangular selection – If a view contains an active selection rectangle on any axis, the Clutch + drag gesture responds based on the position where the drag is initiated.

A. Clutch + drag on the axis: Clutch + drag in this case creates a new rectangular selection without dismissing existing selections (Figure 3). However, the selection mode employed depends on whether the existing selections and the new selection are on the same axis or on different axes. In case of the former, the add-to-selection mode is activated and all glyphs that lie within any of the selection rectangles are selected. For the latter, we considered both union and intersection as potential options. We debated providing both as a toggle option, but ultimately concluded that the need for union of selections on independent axes was fairly small. Thus, we solely use an intersection operation on selections belonging to different axes. We use color variation to differentiate the selected region from the unselected region (Figure 3).

B. Clutch + drag inside selection: Dragging inside a selection without Clutch moves the selection along the axis. Dragging with Clutch results in a similar effect, but instead of moving the original rectangle, it moves a copy of the selection, by activating the duplicate-selection mode (Figure 4). The glyphs that lie within either of the rectangles are selected, i.e. we use union of the rectangles for selection.

Clutch + Pinch

The Clutch + pinch gesture is performed by activating a Clutch and executing a two-finger pinch gesture on the view. We utilize this gesture for modifying existing selections by increasing and decreasing the size of the selection area.

1. Clutch + pinch for multiple selected glyphs – If the view contains multiple selected glyphs, the Clutch + pinch gesture can be used for scaling the size of this selection (Figure 5). When the gesture is initiated, the system creates a convex hull that encloses all the selected glyphs. The pinch gesture then controls the size of the hull. We utilize a flexible aspect ratio pinch on the region, i.e. the horizontal and vertical scaling of the hull individually depend on the movement of the fingers in the x and y direction respectively.

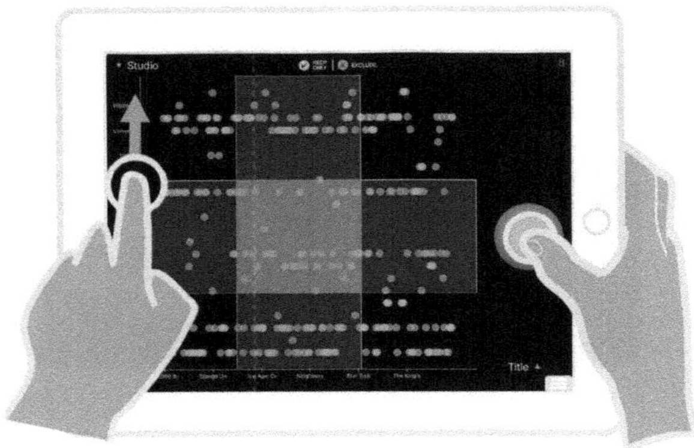

Figure 3: Clutch + drag on the axis creates a new rectangular selection that intersects with existing selections. Notice the color difference in selected and non-selected portions. Here, the right hand is performing the Clutch action.

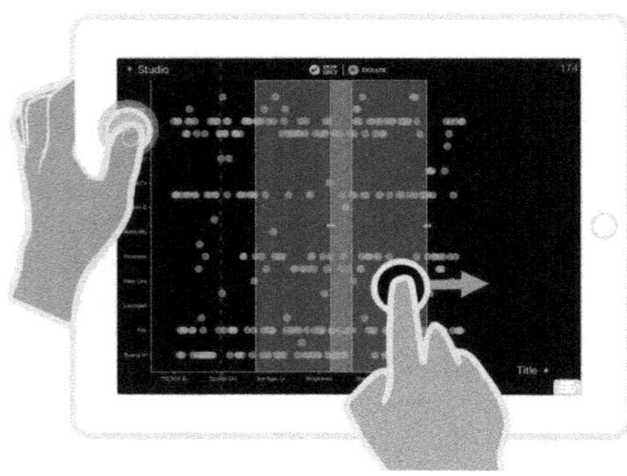

Figure 4: Clutch + drag inside a rectangular selection creates a duplicate.

2. *Clutch + pinch for selection rectangles* – For rectangular selections, the movement of each finger in the pinch gesture is mapped to the ends of the active rectangle. As the fingers move, the size of the active rectangle changes accordingly.

Clutch + Drag + Pinch

The Clutch + drag + pinch gesture is a special configuration of the Clutch + drag gesture, where the user begins by dragging a finger and, without lifting that finger, performs a pinch gesture using another finger. We currently utilize this gesture to further augment the Clutch + drag operation on single glyph selections. There, we utilized the gesture to scrub through the neighboring glyphs. In configurations when the glyphs are located in a densely packed region, executing the pinch-out gesture reveals a lens at that location with the region zoomed in (Figure 6). The user can now lift her second finger and continue dragging with the first finger. This cycles through the glyphs in the scaled up view in the lens. If the target glyph is situated outside the region in the lens, the lens appropriately shifts to the new location. Once the task is complete, the user can close the lens by either pinching-in or lifting all the fingers.

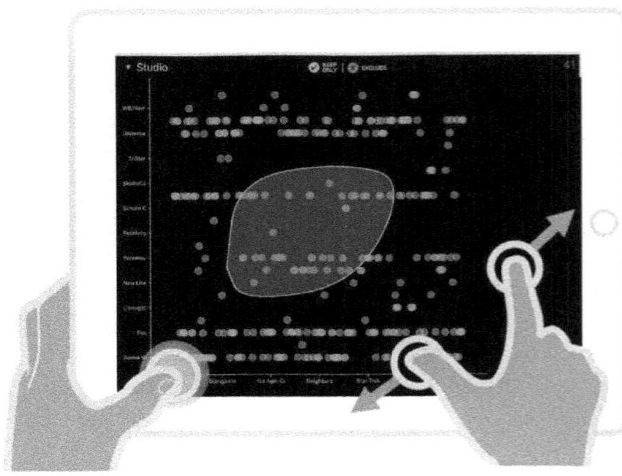

Figure 5: Clutch + pinch for multiple glyphs grows or shrinks the selection area.

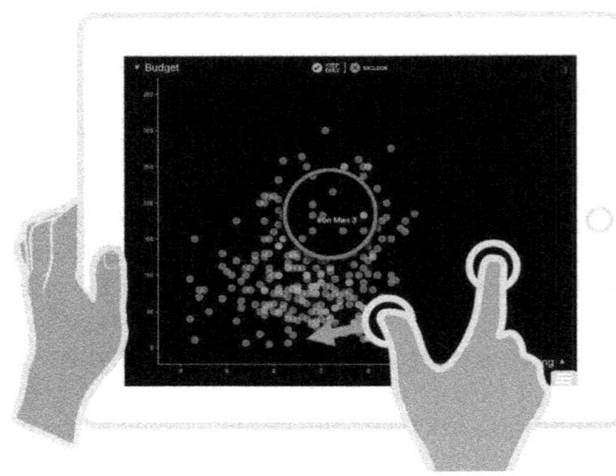

Figure 6: Clutch + drag + pinch for single selections reveals a lens with zoomed in region.

Low-Tension Clutch

The Clutch-modified gestures presented above can be described as *phrases*. Buxton [8] defines phrases as chunks of subtasks "glued together" into a routine that can be performed in a single continuous action. The physical tension that "chunks" or ties together the actions of a phrase is called phrase tension [18]. For the above gestures, the Clutch action behaves as the phrase tension.

Hinckley et al. [18] define three categories of phrase tension—full-, half-, and low-tension. These differ based on the duration for which the user keeps the physical tension active. In the current implementation of the Clutch-modified gestures, keeping the Clutch active for the entire duration is unnecessary since the Clutch info is only utilized at the start of the gestures. We thus configured the Clutch as a low-tension modifier—for all Clutch-modified gestures, users can lift the Clutch immediately after they begin the gesture with their primary hand (as demonstrated in Figure 6).

A low-tension Clutch helps in reducing discomfort that may occur in manipulating the screen with both hands simultaneously, while also supporting the tablet with one hand. It also further differentiates the behavior of the Clutch modifier from a desktop modifier. On desktops, when selecting text using Shift and arrow keys, the user cannot release the Shift key until the selection is complete, even though the arrow key is continuously pressed.

GENERALIZED SELECTION INTERACTION DESIGN

Conceptual Foundation

Selections can broadly be classified into two categories: view-driven and data-centric. View-driven selections are the "standard" selections where targets are identified based on the visual properties of the glyphs, such as position or size. Conversely, in data-centric selections, targets are identified based on a value or range of values of an attribute in the data. For example, data items with a specific value for a categorical attribute can be selected by mapping the attribute to a visual property such as color or shape, and using the legend.

Generalized selection is an advanced selection operation that combines these view-driven and data-centric selections. Here, the user identifies a target using a visual property, e.g. position or color, and subsequently intends to select other items that are similar to this item based on certain attributes of the data. For example, in a scatterplot of movies with *rating* and *profit* on x and y-axis, the user highlights the movie that is furthest towards the top right and wants to view other movies by the same director. This selection differs from the data-centric selection since the user may not be interested in knowing who the director is, but is only interested in the ratings and profit of the other movies made by him/her.

Heer et al. [16] described generalized selection as a "select objects like this" query, and presented a method to perform it in scatterplots on desktops. In their system, users invoke a context menu on a selected glyph and pick an attribute from a list. This selects all other glyphs in the view with the same value for the attribute as the originally selected glyph. If the attribute contains hierarchical information, selection can be cycled through different levels of the hierarchy by repeatedly clicking on the originally selected glyph. For example, if the attribute is a date, repeated clicks expand the selection to include items from the same day, same week, same month, and then the same year.

Generalizing a selection in the absence of a specialized method is fairly cumbersome, however. For instance, to perform the selection in the above example without a context menu, one needs the following steps: identify the director of the movie, switch the axis attribute to directors, lasso-select all movies by the specific director, and finally switch back to the original axis attributes to view the spread of the selected movies. An alternate method would be to add a second view, such as a barchart with directors on the x-axis, and use brushing between the views. Selecting the movie in the scatterplot would highlight the bar representing the director in the barchart. Subsequently, selecting this bar would select all connected movies in the scatterplot.

All these alternatives involve multiple steps, each of which alters users' context by changing the views. Since such context switches are undesirable, we created a specialized method to perform generalized selection in a tablet visualization system.

We designed a novel interaction technique that provides fluid access to attributes of data. Our implementation expands the operations originally presented in [16] by applying it to additional attribute types and adding methods for users to control the parameters of the selection.

Selection Variations — The outcome of generalizing a selection varies based on the size of the existing selection and the attribute used for generalizing it.

1. Single object selections: For a single selected glyph, outcome varies with the type of attribute as follows:
   (a) Categorical: For categorical attributes, the selection expands to include all data items that have the same value for the attribute as the selected glyph. (e.g., genre = 'Action')
   (b) Hierarchy: For attributes with hierarchical properties, selection expands to include the data items that match the value of the selected glyph at the lowest level of the hierarchy. For example, for the date attribute, we begin by matching the exact date of the data items (i.e., date = '07/13/2016').
   (c) Quantitative: For quantitative attributes, the selection expands include to data items that fall within a neighborhood around the value of the selected glyph. (e.g., profit $\in$ [90, 110]).
2. Multiple object selections: Generalizing selections for multiple selected glyphs behaves similar to the single selected glyph, but expands the matching criteria to include values of the attribute from all the selected glyphs. For categorical attributes and hierarchical attributes, the union of all the values is used for selection, while for quantitative values, a range going from the minimum and maximum value of the attribute is used.

Interaction Design

The key component for the generalized selection operation is a list of attributes from which the user picks one. The necessity of displaying this list differentiates the operation from the other advanced selection operations we presented earlier.

Our interaction design consists of a widget that appears in the periphery of the selected data glyph(s). The widget is hidden by default, and can be introduced on demand. To circumvent the need for a persistent UI element to initialize the operation, we utilize a unique gesture — a *two-finger tap*. If one or more glyphs are selected, performing a two-finger tap gesture anywhere on the view presents the widget.

The widget consists of a single label that, initially, gives a description of the operation (Figure 7a). In the background, the widget contains a vertically scrollable list of options that remain hidden from the user. The widget operates in a manner emulating trackpad input with the entire screen behaving as a touchpad. The user can place her finger anywhere on the screen and drag vertically up or down to scroll through the options (Figure 7b). As an option becomes visible, the glyphs in the chart update to reflect the selection that is generalized with respect to the attribute the option represents.

To enable users to explore all available options, the widget maintains two separate selections. The primary selection maps to the originally selected glyphs and remains static throughout the operation. The secondary selection represents glyphs selected through generalization, and updates each time the user scrolls to a different option. By separating the selections, the user is able to explore the options over multiple drag gestures and finger lifts, and is not required to complete the entire selection in a single continuous stroke. To commit a selection, the user can tap outside the list. This merges the secondary selection into the primary selection. Alternatively, to cancel the operation and return to the original state, the user can either scroll the list to the top or perform a two-finger tap gesture to dismiss the widget.

The second step in generalizing a selection is controlling the parameters of the chosen attribute. As we discussed earlier, the parameters are dependent on the type of the attribute. Our design displays the options for modifying the parameters in a separate control that appears below the original widget (Figure 7c). This additional control only appears when the user halts on a particular option for more than 500 ms (i.e., scrolls to an option and lifts her finger).

For attributes with hierarchical properties, the secondary control presents the level of hierarchy being used for expanding the selection. Initially, this is the lowest level for that attribute (e.g. date). The other levels appear as columns of a horizontally scrollable list view contained within the control (Figure 7c). Users can switch to any other level by swiping left or right. Similar to vertical swiping in the attribute list, this horizontal swiping can be performed anywhere on the view.

Finally, for quantitative attributes, the secondary control contains a slider widget that depicts the range of values used for generalizing the selection (Figure 7d). When the initial selection is a single glyph, we use a 10 percent threshold around the value of the attribute. For multiple glyphs, the range extends from the minimum to the maximum value of the attribute for the selected glyphs. The slider widget extends from the minimum to the maximum across the entire dataset, with the selected range highlighted using handles. Since manipulating the small handles directly is difficult, their position can be controlled with a two-finger pinch operation (Figure 7d). The gesture can be performed anywhere on the screen. Dragging a finger causes the corresponding handle to move by an equivalent amount. Finally, we also embellish the widget with the distribution of the values for the attribute using the scented-widgets technique [30].

DISCUSSION

The Clutch technique we introduce in this paper extends the selection capabilities and features of touch-based visualization systems. However, the technique can also be applied to operations other than selection. In this section, we discuss a few extensions of the technique and reflect on the drawbacks and limitations of the current design.

Potential Extensions

We envision the Clutch gestures being applied for other operations such as layout-modification. For instance, in a system

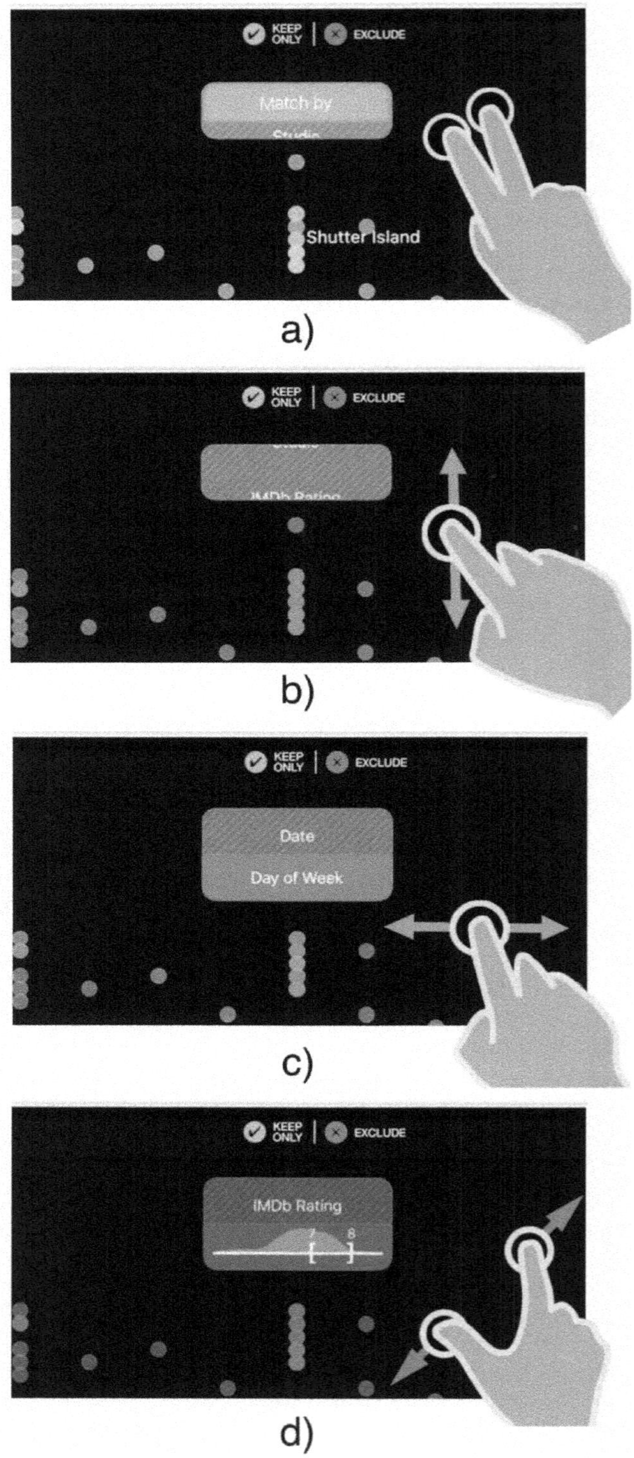

Figure 7: Generalized selection. a) User taps on the screen with two fingers to activate the generalized selection menu. b) To scroll through the list of attributes, user drags a finger vertically. c) For hierarchical attributes, user drags horizontally to access other levels of hierarchy. d) For quantitative attributes, the scented widget displays the selected and overall range of selection. Using a two finger pinch, user can modify the extents of the selection.

with multiple stacked views (e.g., [27]), Clutch + drag could be used for reordering or removing views from the screen. Clutch + pinch could be used for ad hoc scaling of certain views, in case the user wants more space for precise actions, or if views contain only a few glyphs. Finally, one could utilize Clutch + tap or double-tap to disconnect a view from other views. This would permit localized filtering of data for situations when users wish to compare views filtered differently. Alternatively, Clutch + tap also could be used for bookmarking the state of a view that users can revert to later.

While the Clutch gesture has applicability to a broad set of operations, the Clutch action itself is only one of many possible modifier techniques. With a modifier, one ultimately wants to supply a single unit of information to the system before performing a gesture. A non-preferred hand modifier has the benefit that it conforms with the division of labor model—the role of the non-dominant hand is that of framing the detailed action that the dominant hand performs. It also prevents the need for the preferred hand to perform a complex gesture. However, other properties of touch can be leveraged that permit the modifier to also be supplied by the preferred hand without adding difficulty. One potential option is to use pressure. Recently, 3D Touch [1] was introduced on Apple iPhones that adds pressure sensitivity to the screen. A modifier on this screen could be force-pressing the screen once before performing the gesture normally. Alternatively, a touch could be treated as a modifier if it is performed using the knuckle or nail of the finger [15]. In fact, many touch overloading techniques we presented earlier are suitable for use as modifier actions.

Drawbacks and Limitations

Although the Clutch modifier technique holds promise for touch-based visualization systems, it exhibits a number of potential limitations as well. First, the Clutch action is potentially disruptive and likely requires users to switch their grip. This can be particularly cumbersome if the user is mobile rather than stationary. Another limitation is the ergonomics of performing Clutch. It may be difficult to maintain the Clutch action for a continuous period of time. Although the low-tension mode we discussed earlier addresses this limitation to an extent, repeated Clutch actions over a short time period can still strain the hands and affect performance over time.

Perhaps the biggest limitation of the technique is discoverability and affordance. Discoverability is an issue both for the Clutch action itself and the mapping to the advanced selection operations. Since the Clutch action is not self revealing, users are less likely to discover or "guess" it on their own without guidance. Providing an affordance for the action is, thus, critical, although it is difficult to ascertain what the affordance should be. Further, if users discover the clutch action on their own, they still need some guidance for mapping the action to the advanced selection operations. The activation region of the Clutch action overlaps with the location of a few other operations, such as drag on axes and swipe-in from edges. This likely increases the probability of accidental Clutch activations. Nonetheless we believe that self-revelation affordances need to be integrated with the Clutch technique in the future.

Finally, user studies of the Clutch techniques compared to other approaches such as marking menus or alternative touch gestures are clearly needed to better understand each's strengths and weaknesses. The design-oriented research in this article has focused on introducing the idea of using Clutch gestures for advanced selections operations. Earlier, we presented the reasons that make us believe that the quasi-mode approach can succeed, but only user testing and actual trial usage will discover how people perceive and react to the different methods.

CONCLUSION

In this paper, we explore novel interactions for performing advanced selections on tablet-based visualization systems. We present the *Clutch* modifier technique and employ it for advanced selection tasks. The benefit of this approach is that it extends the vocabulary by augmenting existing gestures in place of introducing new and complex interactions. We also describe the design of interactions to provide generalized selection, and we extend the technique to include operations for parameterized control of the selections.

Much further work remains. For example, the generalized selection technique can be extended beyond selections made within charts, and into other components, such as the cells, rows or columns of the data table, or the filter badges that represent the active "keep only' or "exclude" filters. Opportunities also exist for providing compound generalized selections, such as generalization on multiple attributes (e.g., select all movies by same director OR same genre AND same release year). Similarly, the interaction techniques we introduce could be used for providing different types of operations, such as layout-modifications.

The potential to extend the interactions and feature-space of touch-based visualization tools is immense. The use of a Clutch operation augments everyday gestures that are familiar to people, and thus extends a command set (e.g., advanced selection) while helping to keep the interactions approachable and accessible. We hope that such design contributions can help spur further advances in touch-based visualizations, with the aim of achieving parity with desktops in the efficiency of data analysis.

ACKNOWLEDGEMENTS

This work was supported by a Google Faculty Research Award and by the National Science Foundation via award IIS-1320537.

REFERENCES

1. 3d Touch - iOS - Apple Developer. https://apple.com/ios/3d-touch/.
2. Vizable by Tableau. https://vizable.tableau.com/.
3. Au, O. K.-C., Su, X., and Lau, R. W. LinearDragger: A Linear Selector for One-finger Target Acquisition. In *Proc. of ACM CHI '14* (2014), 2607–2616.
4. Baur, D., Lee, B., and Carpendale, S. TouchWave: Kinetic Multi-touch Manipulation for Hierarchical Stacked Graphs. In *Proc. of ITS '12* (2012), 255–264.

5. Bederson, B. B., and Hollan, J. D. Pad++: A Zoomable Graphical Interface System. In *ACM CHI Conference Companion* (1995), 23–24.

6. Benko, H., Wilson, A. D., and Baudisch, P. Precise Selection Techniques for Multi-touch Screens. In *Proc. of ACM CHI '06* (2006), 1263–1272.

7. Bier, E. A., Stone, M. C., Pier, K., Buxton, W., and DeRose, T. D. Toolglass and Magic Lenses: The See-through Interface. In *Proc. of ACM SIGGRAPH '93* (1993), 73–80.

8. Buxton, W. A. S. Chunking and phrasing and the design of human-computer dialogues. In *Human-computer Interaction*, R. M. Baecker, J. Grudin, W. A. S. Buxton, and S. Greenberg, Eds. Morgan Kaufmann Publishers Inc., San Francisco, CA, USA, 1995, 494–499.

9. Casiez, G., Vogel, D., Pan, Q., and Chaillou, C. Rubberedge: Reducing Clutching by Combining Position and Rate Control with Elastic Feedback. In *Proc. of ACM UIST '07* (2007), 129–138.

10. Chen, H. Compound brushing [dynamic data visualization]. In *Information Visualization, 2003. INFOVIS 2003. IEEE Symposium on*, IEEE (2003), 181–188.

11. Grossman, T., and Balakrishnan, R. The Bubble Cursor: Enhancing Target Acquisition by Dynamic Resizing of the Cursor's Activation Area. In *Proc. of ACM CHI '05* (2005), 281–290.

12. Guiard, Y. Asymmetric division of labor in human skilled bimanual action. *Journal of Motor Behavior 19*, 4 (1987), 486–517.

13. Hackett, M., and Cox, P. T. Touchscreen Interfaces for Visual Languages. Tech. Rep. CS-2011-05, Dalhousie University, July 2011.

14. Harrison, C., and Hudson, S. Using Shear As a Supplemental Two-dimensional Input Channel for Rich Touchscreen Interaction. In *Proc. of ACM CHI '12* (2012), 3149–3152.

15. Harrison, C., Schwarz, J., and Hudson, S. E. TapSense: Enhancing Finger Interaction on Touch Surfaces. In *Proc. of ACM UIST '11* (2011), 627–636.

16. Heer, J., Agrawala, M., and Willett, W. Generalized Selection via Interactive Query Relaxation. In *Proc. of ACM CHI '08* (2008), 959–968.

17. Heo, S., and Lee, G. Force Gestures: Augmenting Touch Screen Gestures with Normal and Tangential Forces. In *Proc. of ACM UIST '11* (2011), 621–626.

18. Hinckley, K., Baudisch, P., Ramos, G., and Guimbretiere, F. Design and Analysis of Delimiters for Selection-action Pen Gesture Phrases in Scriboli. In *Proc. of ACM CHI '05* (2005), 451–460.

19. Holz, C., and Baudisch, P. Understanding Touch. In *Proc. of ACM CHI '11* (2011), 2501–2510.

20. Lepinski, G. J., Grossman, T., and Fitzmaurice, G. The Design and Evaluation of Multitouch Marking Menus. In *Proc. of ACM CHI '10* (2010), 2233–2242.

21. Luo, Y., and Vogel, D. Pin-and-Cross: A Unimanual Multitouch Technique Combining Static Touches with Crossing Selection. In *Proc. of ACM UIST '15* (2015), 323–332.

22. Moscovich, T. Contact Area Interaction with Sliding Widgets. In *Proc. of ACM UIST '09* (2009), 13–22.

23. North, C., Dwyer, T., Lee, B., Fisher, D., Isenberg, P., Robertson, G., and Inkpen, K. Understanding multi-touch manipulation for surface computing. In *Proc. of INTERACT '09*, Springer-Verlag (2009), 236–249.

24. Potter, R. L., Weldon, L. J., and Shneiderman, B. Improving the Accuracy of Touch Screens: An Experimental Evaluation of Three Strategies. In *Proc. of ACM CHI '88* (1988), 27–32. 00328.

25. Raskin, J. *The Humane Interface: New Directions for Designing Interactive Systems*. ACM Press/Addison-Wesley Publishing Co., 2000.

26. Rzeszotarski, J. M., and Kittur, A. Kinetica: Naturalistic Multi-touch Data Visualization. In *Proc. of ACM CHI '14* (2014), 897–906.

27. Sadana, R., and Stasko, J. Designing Multiple Coordinated Visualizations for Tablets. In *Computer Graphics Forum*, vol. 35 (2016), 261–270.

28. Sellen, A. J., Kurtenbach, G. P., and Buxton, W. A. S. The Prevention of Mode Errors Through Sensory Feedback. *Hum.-Comput. Interact. 7*, 2 (June 1992), 141–164.

29. Wagner, J., Huot, S., and Mackay, W. BiTouch and BiPad: Designing Bimanual Interaction for Hand-held Tablets. In *Proc. of ACM CHI '12* (2012), 2317–2326.

30. Willett, W., Heer, J., and Agrawala, M. Scented Widgets: Improving Navigation Cues with Embedded Visualizations. *IEEE TVCG 13*, 6 (Nov. 2007), 1129–1136.

31. Willett, W., Lan, Q., and Isenberg, P. Eliciting Multi-touch Selection Gestures for Interactive Data Graphics. In *EuroVis Short-Paper Proceedings* (2014).

32. Wills, G. J. Selection: 524,288 ways to say "this is interesting". In *Proc. of IEEE InfoVis '96* (1996), 54–60.

33. Wilson, A. D., Izadi, S., Hilliges, O., Garcia-Mendoza, A., and Kirk, D. Bringing Physics to the Surface. In *Proc. of UIST '08*, UIST '08 (2008), 67–76.

34. Wobbrock, J. O., Morris, M. R., and Wilson, A. D. User-defined Gestures for Surface Computing. In *Proc of ACM SIGCHI '09* (2009), 1083–1092.

35. Wu, M., Shen, C., Ryall, K., Forlines, C., and Balakrishnan, R. Gesture registration, relaxation, and reuse for multi-point direct-touch surfaces. In *Proc. of IEEE TABLETOP '06* (2006), 185–192.

36. Yi, J. S., Kang, Y., and Stasko, J. Toward a Deeper Understanding of the Role of Interaction in Information Visualization. *IEEE TVCG 13*, 6 (Nov. 2007), 1224–1231.

CurationSpace: Cross-Device Content Curation Using Instrumental Interaction

Frederik Brudy, Steven Houben, Nicolai Marquardt, Yvonne Rogers
University College London, UCL Interaction Centre and ICRI Cities, Gower Street, London, UK
f.brudy@cs.ucl.ac.uk, {s.houben, n.marquardt, y.rogers}@ucl.ac.uk

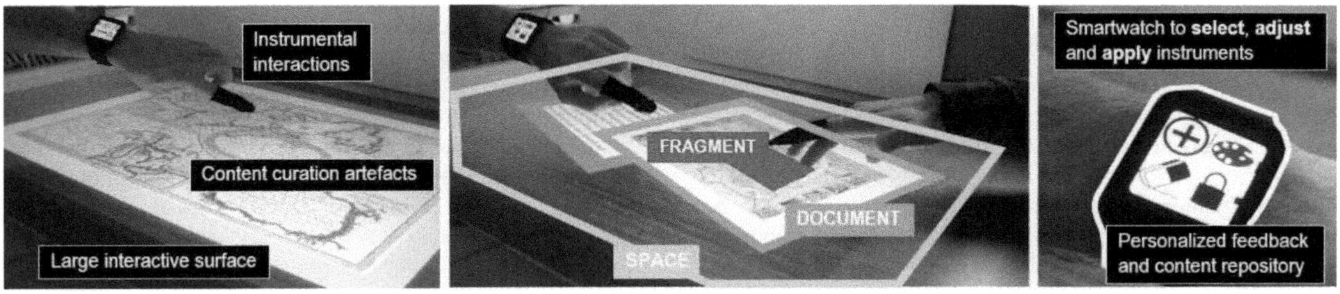

Figure 1. ***CurationSpace*** **provides a shared collaboration space for content curation based on instrumental interactions.**

ABSTRACT
For digital content curation of historical artefacts, curators collaboratively collect, analyze and edit documents, images, and other digital resources in order to display and share new representations of that information to an audience. Despite their increasing reliance on digital documents and tools, current technologies provide little support for these specific collaborative content curation activities. We introduce *CurationSpace* – a novel cross-device system – to provide more expressive tools for curating and composing digital historical artefacts. Based on the concept of Instrumental Interaction, *CurationSpace* allows users to interact with digital curation artefacts on shared interactive surfaces using personal smartwatches as selectors for *instruments* or *modifiers* (applied to either the whole curation space, individual documents, or fragments). We introduce a range of novel interaction techniques that allow individuals or groups of curators to more easily create, navigate and share resources during content curation. We report insights from our user study about people's use of instruments and modifiers for curation activities.

Author Keywords
Instrumental Interaction; Cross-Device Collaboration; Curation Work; Content Curation; Smartwatch Interaction

ACM Classification Keywords
H.5.m. Information interfaces and presentation (e.g., HCI): Miscellaneous.

ISS '16, November 06 - 09, 2016, Niagara Falls, ON, Canada

ACM 978-1-4503-4248-3/16/11…$15.00
DOI: http://dx.doi.org/10.1145/2992154.2992175

INTRODUCTION
There are many different curation practices, extending beyond the more traditional interpretation of a professional museum curator. One of these practices is *content curation*, which can be defined as the process of *collecting, analyzing, displaying* and *sharing* information in order to derive new insights and knowledge and present these findings to a broader audience [33]. Curating content often requires *specialized knowledge* and *collaborative artefact discovery*. One example of such content curation is that of historical documents, often done by (non-professional) historic societies or charities who collaboratively create curated data sets, formulate conclusions, and create new representations. Over the years, technology has resulted in a growing amount of information, allowing for new ways of conducting curation processes. Moreover, it enables groups to work collaboratively, using the various resources, bringing together people with expertise from different backgrounds [40]. The focus of our research is on curation work for ad hoc collocated resource collation. Specifically, we explore how content curation tasks, such as collecting, organizing, reviewing, displaying and sharing digital content (e.g. images, maps or notes), can be supported effectively through using multiple tools and devices at hand for group work.

Curating digital content in a group setting, however, using *multiple* digital devices can be challenging because it requires a large amount of configuration work [16] when setting up devices and sharing resources. Furthermore, even though people use computationally powerful and interconnected devices, most of these devices are not designed to support in situ collaborative work [34]. Which devices might be put to good use in order to support ad hoc curation work? Large displays can be used for shared curation work in combination with other hand held technologies. These offer a high resolution interaction space and allow for collaboration and exploration of large datasets [2]. However, several problems arise from using large and public displays for content curation, such as the positioning of control instruments on large screens [1, 39], territoriality [37], or privacy when working with private data [8]. The use of personal devices with large displays offers ways of overcoming these while also providing new methods for controlling and interacting with content. In particular, using a worn device with a tabletop allows users to personalize systems with their own content. Compared with using phones for personalized input with a larger interactive surface (e.g., [35]), the use of a smartwatch does not require to be held, leaving users' hands free for interactions.

CurationSpace was designed as a personalized sharing system that leverages the functionality of (i) an individual user's *smartwatch* for *instrumental interactions* [4] and (ii) a shared interaction space (e.g., a large, touch-enabled tabletop or wall display). It was motivated by how we interact with tools in the real world, in which there exists a many-to-many relation between tools (like pens, scissors, markers) and objects of interest (paper, plastic, fabric).

The smartwatch is used to identify its user, to store and share personal information, provide the user with customized views or interfaces, while also allowing protection of private and sensitive information which a user does not want to share publicly. It is a *mediator* between the user and the interaction space that supports collaborative working with a focus on content curation. The shared public space is a multi-touch surface that multiple users can interact with.

The contribution of this paper is a new instrumental interaction approach for collocated curation work that (i) separates space, domain object and individual fragments as interaction entities, and (ii) uses a smartwatch to augment human touch with configurable tools that act upon these entities.

INSTRUMENTAL INTERACTION FOR SMARTWATCHES

The vision behind ubiquitous computing and cross-device interactions is to allow users to seamlessly interact with digital information where and when needed. As Bødker [7] argues, users do not interact with technology but rather "*through the interface*". Computer devices, systems, and applications are mediating tools or instruments that allow users to act upon information using systems from their environment.

The notion of Instrumental Interaction was originally proposed by Beaudouin-Lafon [4] as a POST-WIMP interaction model in which there is a strong conceptual separation between the information, data or other domain objects, and the *instruments* or *tools* that are used to act upon those domain objects. Instruments are a combination of hardware and software components that mediate the interaction between the human and the domain objects that are of interest to the user. The user interacts with instruments that translate its actions to the underlying data and provide feedback to the user. This instrumental interaction model is inspired from the observation that "*our interaction with the physical world is governed by our use of tools.*" [4]. Instrumental interaction is based on three design principles [5]: (i) reification, the process of objectifying instruments and interactions, (ii) polymorphism, the property that allows for a single instrument to be applied to any domain object, and (iii) reuse, the process of leveraging previous defined objects for future use.

This Instrumental Interaction model was extended by Klokmose et al. [22] into a Ubiquitous Instrumental Interaction model, in which instruments were made much more explicit in the form of reusable interchangeable artefacts that could be used on different types of domain models across different types of surfaces. Instruments can migrate from one device to another, from one data structure to another. Although instruments can break on certain types of domain objects, they should provide an operational consistency across domain objects and interactive surfaces. Klokmose et al. [22] did not differentiate between types of devices, but rather see instruments as hardware-independent digital constructs that themselves should be easy to manipulate by other instruments.

In this paper, we differentiate between types of devices, and more specifically their role towards supporting instruments. By wearing a watch, we can automatically identify users through their touch input and gestures, which can help auto-select instruments, and more generally *augment the human touch capabilities*. Rather than using physical instruments, the watch can be leveraged to contextually reshape the instruments executed by our hands, as well as our human touch. The watch can in this way be used to configure and execute the instruments that are applied to a range of different document types available in *CurationSpace.*

RELATED WORK

Wrist-based Interactions and Smartwatches

Previous research has shown that the wrist is a good place to position a device that needs to be accessed quickly or frequently [3]. DeskJockey [44] offloaded interface elements by projecting them onto its surroundings. Similarly, Mayer et al. [26] introduced user interface beaming, leveraging a smartwatch to interact with smart objects in the environment. Duet [10] extended the input space on a phone with a smartwatch, e.g. the smartwatch acts as a tool palette when editing input on the phone, and Expressy combined a wrist-worn IMU to expand the expressiveness of touch interactions [41]. In *CurationSpace* the smartwatch acts as tool selector, augmenting the user's touch, and can therefore be seen as an extension of the shared surface screen. It declutters the shared surface from menu items while, similar to Local Tools [6], allowing for quick access to the commonly used instruments.

Although researchers have explored using a smartwatch as a public display [28], a smartwatch is a personal, body-worn device, which is predominantly owned and operated by a single person. Reading personal notifications is the second most common usage of a smartwatch (after reading the time), and denotes overall the longest interaction time with a smartwatch [29]. Leveraging the one-user-per-device property, *CurationSpace* allows users to personalize input and bring private content to a shared surface. GestureWrist [31] introduced hand and arm posture recognition on the wrist, Gesture Watch [20] detected gestures above and around a smartwatch, and Haptic Wristwatch [27] allowed users to perform gestures, such as covering the watch-face, or interact with the bevel of a wristwatch.

Sensemaking on Large Surfaces and Across Devices

Previous research has explored how a single user can work with large collections of digital data, for example, on large screens [2], tabletops [12] or using multiple devices [13]. While public displays offer a high resolution interaction space for collaboration [1], it was pointed out that territoriality [37] and privacy [8] have to be considered. Augmented Surfaces [32] introduced hybrid and collaborative digital/physical interaction space and UbiTable [38] explored the design space of tabletops when used in a kiosk-style walk-up-and-use scenario. Similarly, *CurationSpace* was developed for sharing and exploring digital content on a large interactive surface in walk-up-and-use collaborations.

Using a phone as an input device for large displays has been explored, e.g. in Touch & Interact [14] a phone could be used to interact with a display similar to a stylus on a PDA. Schmidt et al. built on this input vocabulary [36] and detected a phone's touch on a tabletop to, for example, allow data transfer or tool selection and extension of the input and output space [35].

Cross-device Interactions

Using mobile devices for cross-device sensemaking has been used for example by United Slates [9] and Conductor [13]. In more recent years researches have focused more and more on cross-device interaction with body worn devices, such as SleeD [43], Duet [10] and WatchConnect [17]. Schmidt et al. [35] explored the design space of mobile+surface interactions. A taxonomy for surface gestures, together with a user-defined gesture set was presented [42]. More recently, Webstrates [21] provides an environment for collaborative, real-time sharing and editing.

No prior work has explored how smartwatches can be used in conjunction with a shared space for collaborative content curation. *CurationSpace* introduces a collaborative document presentation system that allows users to modify its content through a number of instruments that can be selected, adjusted, and applied using a personal smartwatch. Leveraging the fact that smartwatches are body-worn and personal devices, *CurationSpace* allows users to bring personal content into a shared space, customizing their input using instruments selected on the watch. Further, the watch can provide personal feedback through its easily visible display, not occupying any space of the shared area. *CurationSpace* allows for touch input on the smartwatch as well as gesture input using the smartwatch's internal sensors.

SCENARIO DESCRIPTION

Our content creation scenario describes the process of groups **collecting**, **analyzing**, **displaying** and **sharing** information – for example historic documents – in order to present it to audiences in new ways [33]:

Lisa is interested in the history of the street on which she lives. She joined a volunteer-driven historic society that preserves the history of her street, through collecting, analyzing, and reworking various sources of historic material, including maps, photographs, and locals' memories. Lisa is working together with John on a report about the history of the local hospital. They split up their work to research different facets online, in local archives, libraries. In order to collaboratively organize and analyze their information, they meet in a library using the CurationSpace system.

Lisa and John connect their smartwatches to the system. John shows Lisa a chapter of the report he has been working on. Lisa edits the text and images of the section using various instruments. Lisa also extends her collection of photos of historic maps with the ones that John has found. They review and finish the editing on one of the chapters of their building report. After two hours of exploring and sharing, they have created a new visual history of the hospital, loaded their work onto their watches so that they can continue their work at a later stage and vacate CurationSpace.

Throughout this paper, we refer back to the key curation activities from this scenario.

CURATIONSPACE

The design of *CurationSpace* is inspired by the observations of how people collaborate and interact with *physical documents* during a group session [23]. First, people often organize the table into distinct *spaces* that serve several purposes (e.g. often the middle of the table is used to share or present content to each other, while the edges closer to the users are used to store personal notes or documents [37]). Second, to discuss and reflect on content, people often place documents (reports or collages that are composed of smaller fragments, such as images, photos, texts, maps or other relevant resources) onto the table, which also facilitates sharing of documents or fragments with others. Third, users utilize tools (e.g. pens, markers, tape, pencils, scissors) to modify, annotate and create content while interacting with the *documents* or *fragments*. Importantly, tools can be applied to different types of documents, e.g., a pen can be used to write new text, to annotate a map, or to sketch a new figure.

Inspired by Beaudouin-Lafon's ideas on Instrumental Interaction [4] and Kay's vision of dynamic media [18], *CurationSpace*'s design provides a new document presentation and interaction model that follows this clear separation between (i) the cross-device interaction *space* that is being used as part of the curation work, (ii) the *documents* that are shared in the space, (iii) the individual *fragments* that make up each document, and (iv) the *instruments* that people are using to modify and create content during the curation process (Figure 1 middle). We extend established interaction techniques [6, 10, 17, 36] to explore a system implementation of this vision for supporting content curation tasks on a shared surface, using personal devices. *CurationSpace* uses smartwatches as instrument selection devices that enable people to reconfigure their hands into different tools needed to perform curation work. Based on the principles of Instrumental Interaction [5], *CurationSpace* is built around three main principles:

1. **Dynamic resources** – To allow for reification [5], information is structured within three levels of abstractions: documents, fragments and spaces. These atomic units of interaction are exchangeable, combinable and controllable to create high level information structures.
2. **Tool multiplicity** – A basic set of tools are provided that can be applied to any resource. Tools or instruments can be applied to a variety of dynamic media, allowing for polymorphism across objects types and reuse of the same tool across a suite of information resources [5].
3. **Personal and shared objects** – Tools and objects can be personal or shared with other people. Both the hierarchical resource structure as well as the tool multiplicity are constrained by user roles and access models.

CurationSpace components

CurationSpace consists of two components: a smartwatch application and a touch-enabled large interactive surface. The smartwatch allows users to select instruments ("interaction instruments" in Instrumental Interaction [4]), which they can apply to documents on shared spaces to change their properties. Each instrument acts on a multitude of different documents and fragments, but to the user it only appears as a single instrument (e.g. "colorize", "delete", or "create"). On the surface side (Figure 1 left and middle), *CurationSpace* consists of three nested modules. These represent the domain objects of instrumental interaction. At the broadest level, there is an *interaction space* which is shared among all users and spans one or multiple interactive surfaces. Using *instruments*, a user creates or interacts with *documents*. Each document is owned by a user; however, they can share access to a document. Each document in return can contain one or multiple *fragments*, e.g. text, images, or a canvas.

The smartwatch (Figure 1 right) acts as a *mediator* between the user, the interaction space and the objects within, by providing a variety of instruments. Since every smartwatch is owned and worn by one individual person, they can be used to personalize the input, provide access to personal data, and allow for personal feedback. Using a smartwatch as an instrument selector reduces the need for cumbersome menu selection on the shared surface, allows for hands-free interaction and does not occupy space on shared surface.

General interaction with CurationSpace

CurationSpace starts with an empty interaction space. A user interacts with the space by applying instruments. For example, touching the interaction space will automatically use the *create instrument* to produce an empty rectangular shaped document. Documents can be resized and repositioned. Each document is either private or public, defining who can interact with it and blocking access to unauthorized users. Authenticated users (the *owner*) can manipulate their own documents using multi-touch gestures on the surface, which are defined by the selected instrument on the smartwatch. A private document can be made public (shared) by the authenticated user using the *share instrument*, allowing everyone to interact with it. One or multiple fragments can be added to each document. Fragments contain either text, images, or a canvas and can also be manipulated using instruments. When interacting with their own document, the user's smartwatch lights up in a matching color to indicate the connection. The watch also shows the currently selected instrument.

Instrument selection may occur automatically, based on the current context, or manually through explicit user selection. The user interacts with the shared space using the selected instrument. An instrument can be deselected either implicitly by selecting a new instrument, or explicitly by tilting the smartwatch. The functionality of some instruments is contextual, based on the type of domain object with which the user is interacting. This contextual difference lies in the nature of instrumental interaction and the system has to mediate [22]. This mediation is integrated into our system's underlying architecture: domain objects "understand" how to react to the application of instruments (through an event model) and therefore mediate the instruments' effect on them. The connection with the shared space can be broken by covering the smartwatch. This results in all documents being removed from the space and offloaded to the smartwatch.

Technical implementation of CurationSpace

CurationSpace is implemented on a modified Microsoft Surface 1.0 SP1 tabletop running Windows 7. The system runs a distributed message and content server based on SignalR that connects the watches (and potentially other devices) to the surface application. We used a Sony SWR50 SmartWatch 3, running Android Wear, connected to an Android smartphone via Bluetooth connection. The phone acts as a proxy between the smartwatch and the tabletop, allowing for a network connection between tabletop and smartwatch. The smartwatch transmits sensor data, instruments, and content selection to the tabletop, and receives system status updates.

A touch on the surface is considered *authenticated*, when it can be associated with a particular user. In our setup, a user wears a glove with fiducial markers attached to the finger (similar to [25]). Since each smartwatch belongs to an individual person, it can provide the fiducial marker IDs of its user to the system, therefore identifying the user to the system. It also acts as a private content repository, allowing a user to bring in their own data. The smartwatch has touch input, and its integrated IMU can be used for gesture recognition (e.g. the user disconnects from the system by covering the light sensor of the watch; or performs a tilt gesture to deselect the selected instrument). Further, it extends the shared surface to provide personalized, private feedback. Available instruments are shown in a grid-layout (Figure 1, right) and content in a scrollable list (Fig. 3, top) on the watch's screen.

CurationSpace represents the core ideas of Instrumental Interaction in its underlying distributed system architecture, in which instruments are *object events* that can be triggered on domain objects. It is not the instrument that defines its effect, but the domain object that reacts to the event of instrument-application. Introducing new instruments means simply introducing a new object event, implementing the receiver on the domain objects and its reaction to the event. If no event listener is implemented, the domain object will simply ignore the application of that instrument. Instrument mediation and instruments' many-to-many relation with objects is therefore integrated into our system's architecture: domain objects "understand" how to react to the application of instruments (object events) and therefore mediate how to react to an instrument's application. Furthermore, when no tool is selected, some domain objects trigger automatic tool selection upon a user's touch, e.g., when no tool is selected and the user touches the interaction space, the "create" instrument will be automatically selected.

CurationSpace instruments

Instruments customize users' touch input, which extends it beyond the normal binary touch. As laid out in the instrumental interaction model [4], the conceptual separation between domain objects (documents in *CurationSpace*) and instruments frees instruments to be reusable artefacts which can be applied on different domain models. While one instrument's usage is consistent across domain objects, the underlying interpretation on the data depends on the domain object. Differing from the work by Klokmose et al. [22], *CurationSpace does* employ device boundaries, differentiating between each user's smartwatch and the shared spaces. We argue that using the watch as an explicit instrument selector allows the differentiation between an individual's instrument and work, and thus allows group collaboration on a shared interaction space. Each user's smartwatch serves as an instrument selector and a personal identifier, receives personal system feedback, and provides a personal content repository. Using and adapting these instruments allows users to contextually re-configure and augment touch input.

Our set of instruments is informed by the key curation tasks of our user scenario. Depending on the current system state the instrument is being applied to, these affect and alter the domain objects in different ways.

- **Create instrument:** Allows users to create documents and fragments. The watch acts as an identifier and holds users' personal data to be shared with the space. This instrument is the default instrument when interacting with the space itself while no other instrument is selected.
- **Manipulate instrument:** Selecting an object or fragment allows the user to change its position, rotation, size, and to crop it using multi-finger gestures. The smartwatch acts as an identifier and tool selector for further operations. This instrument is the default instrument when interacting with a document or fragment while no instrument is selected.
- **Color instrument:** Using the smartwatch a user can select a color on their smartwatch. The color instrument can be applied to different domain object, e.g. it can be used to draw on a canvas, highlight parts of an image or color text.
- **Increase / decrease instrument:** These instruments allow the user to zoom in on a picture, increase the font size of a text, or show a document in full screen mode or vice versa.
- **Erase instrument:** The erase instrument acts as an eraser on a canvas, can be used to delete text through selection, remove images by touching them inside a document, or eradicate an entire document from the space.
- **Copy instrument:** This instrument allows the user to duplicate a document or image fragment, or to copy and paste text through selection.
- **Share instrument:** Created documents are owned by one user. Sharing a document allows other users to manipulate the documents.

These instruments should be seen as an example list of tools demonstrating the concepts of using Instrumental Interaction for content curation tasks, rather than an exhaustive set.

INTERACTION TECHNIQUES FOR CURATION TASKS

In the following we illustrate how these atomic instruments support collaborative content curation, by using the smartwatch for instrument selection, feedback display, and personal content repository. We illustrate the nuances of these techniques with our scenario application.

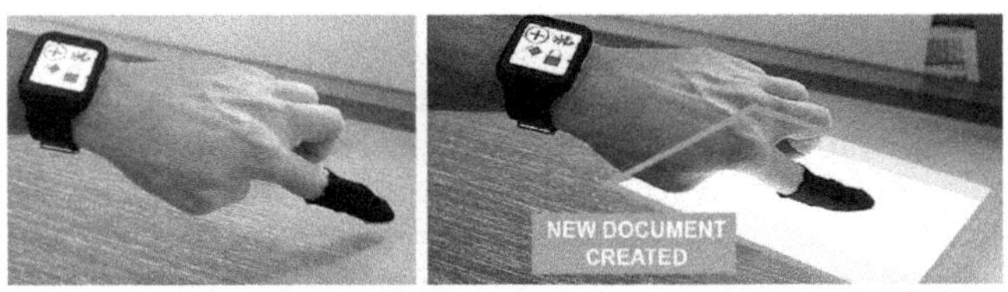

Figure 2. Using the implicitly selected *create instrument* (left) a user creates a new document on the interaction space (right). A green marker shows the authenticated interaction (middle).

Creating documents and adding content into fragments

Creating new documents for arranging curation content is one of the key content curation tasks. We designed instrumental interaction smartwatch techniques to facilitate the ad hoc creation of documents and adding content directly in context: *John wants to share photos of historic maps he has found in the archives. To start, he touches an empty area on the interaction space. After a 1.5 second dwelling time (to prevent accidental document-creation) a new document is created (Figure 2). The system selects this function automatically because on the empty interaction space no other instrument than the create instrument has an effect. After creating a new document, John wants to add pictures. He explicitly selects the create instrument on his watch, which then presents him with thumbnails of the content he can share from the watch (Figure 3 small inlay top). He can cycle through the text and images through touch gestures, and select the desired image of the map, adding it as a new image fragment to the document. The content is added the document he last activated through interacting (touch or move) with it.*

Figure 3 shows a screenshot of interaction space containing five documents, of which two are docked to the side. Two documents are owned by John (green border), two by Lisa (purple border), and one has been shared publicly, allowing everyone to access it (white border). *CurationSpace* supports different document types. Currently implemented are text (Figure 3, middle right), images (Figure 3, middle left), and canvas (Figure 3, bottom right). Documents' borders are marked in their owner's color (here: green and purple; white borders indicate public access), and can be docked to the size to declutter the interaction space (Figure 3, bottom).

Figure 3. The smartwatch acts as a personal content repository (inlay top), allowing users to share their personal data.

Manipulate and organize documents and fragments

When sorting through documents, people employ the space around them [2]. Using the document system, *CurationSpace* allows users to spatially arrange their content. The manipulate instrument is the default instrument when interacting with documents while no other instrument is selected, and can be used to position, resize, and rotate documents. For better overview, documents can be docked to the sides of the display, shrinking them to small preview icons (Figure 3), or enlarged to take up the whole screen. This allows for a large number of documents to be used, while not cluttering the interaction space. The *increase / decrease instrument* can also be used to resize documents by touching their borders and to zoom in on images or increase text font size (Figure 4).

Figure 4. Using the *increase* instrument.

Since Lisa sits opposite John, he uses the manipulate instrument to spatially organize documents on the surface, by moving them around, rotating them using simple gestures, or to resize them. The manipulate instrument can be used on whole documents, as well as image and canvas fragments. John looks through the photos. Using the manipulate instrument, he can crop, resize, and rotate the image fragments. John shows Lisa the text he has been working on. He increases the font size, for easier reading.

Share access to a document with other users

Finding and sharing artefacts (digital and physical) with collaborators is one of the key curation activities, allowing more insight to be gained [33, 40]. However, not all content should be editable by everyone as people care about their personal data and boundaries [8, 37]. In *CurationSpace* documents are therefore owned by an individual person and cannot be manipulated by others unless explicitly shared. Using the share instrument, the ownership of multiple documents can be changed through the touch of an authenticated finger.

Lisa wants to erase a paragraph of text in a document. She selects the erase instrument on her watch and attempts to erase the text. However, John has not granted her access to the document so she can view it, but not edit it. In order to share the document, John selects the share instrument on his watch, and applies it to the document with an authenticated touch. This transfers the ownership of the document to the public, making it editable by anyone. Lisa can apply the same instrument to the public document, transferring ownership to her.

Edit content, documents, and fragments

As part of the curation activities, documents are also analyzed and reworked into new representations. Text needs to be deleted, important area marked on a map, or essential paragraphs in a text highlighted. In *CurationSpace* various editing instruments (e.g. color instrument to draw, highlight or change text color, see Figure 5) are available for these tasks. Using instruments, a user can rapidly multitask between different objects. For example, John can highlight sections of text as well as visually mark sections on a map.

Figure 5. Using the color instrument, the user can set the paint of his drawings or change the color of text.

John has a draft chapter about the hospital at home, on which he wants to work further with Lisa, while also marking key spots on a map. He uses the create instrument to add a text fragment to a document. He then uses the color instrument to change the color of text when highlighting it and to draw on the map. Together Lisa and John mark places on the map with their occurrence in the text in the same color.

Erase to delete content, fragments, and documents

The erase instrument works on fragments or their contents, but also on whole documents. Once selected, a user can for example erase drawings on a canvas (Figure 6 top) or selected text, remove images, or delete entire documents (Figure 6 bottom). This helps to keep the curation space clean by quickly erasing unneeded content.

One of the photos is irrelevant for the current chapter. Lisa selects the erase instrument and applies it to the image. In fact, she can delete any fragment or entire objects by touching their borders. Applying the erase instrument to the inside of a fragment allows her to remove part of the content, for example to erase parts of a drawing on a canvas or an image, or to delete parts of a text by selecting it.

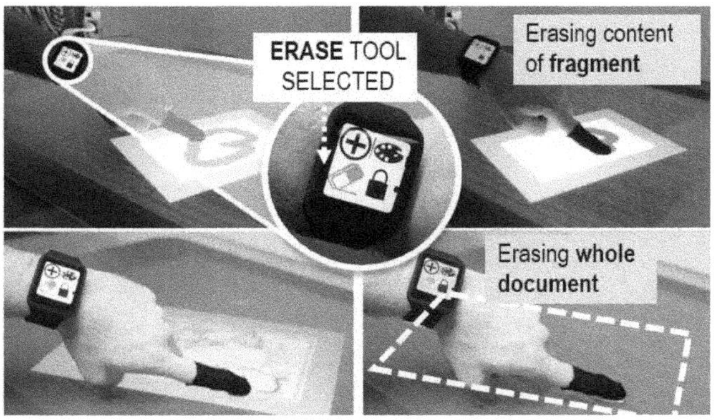

Figure 6. The *erase instrument* can be used to erase drawings on a canvas or image (top) and to erase documents (bottom).

The watch as a clipboard and document repository

Non-public documents are marked in their owner's color. When disconnecting from *CurationSpace* by covering the watch with the entire hand, all documents are saved on the owner's smartwatch, removing all private documents from the shared space. To clear up space, documents can be docked as icons to the sides of the interaction space using the manipulate instrument (Figure 3) or the decrease instrument.

Lisa wants to continue working on a text at home, and gives John a copy of the text. She uses the copy instrument to duplicate the document, and transfers ownership of one of them to John using the share instrument. When disconnecting, the documents are offloaded to their smartwatches. At a later time, instead of creating new documents, they load previously used documents from their watch: when using the create instrument, previously created documents are available.

USER EVALUATION

To evaluate people's interaction with the instruments in *CurationSpace*, we conducted a scenario-based user study. The goal was to learn from participants' appropriation of *CurationSpace* for curation tasks and gather user feedback about the understanding of its basic concepts and techniques.

Procedure

We recruited 8 participants (4 female; 27-35 years old, mean 30) from different backgrounds (historian, librarian, financial consultant, civil servant, researcher). Participants rated themselves as average to experienced computer users (median=3.5; iqr=1 on 5-point Likert scale) and to be experienced using multiple devices (average number of owned devices=4.12; stdev=0.6 including smartphones, smartwatches, tablets, e-reader, laptop and desktop PCs). Participants were introduced to the task, signed a consent form and answered a pre-questionnaire. We then asked them to complete a scenario using *CurationSpace*. Each smartwatch was preloaded with photos, text, and maps. Participants were asked to complete both individual and collaborative tasks; a researcher acted as their collaborator. They were guided through their tasks and asked to think aloud. After completion, a semi-structured interview and post-study questionnaire followed.

Participants enacted the following scenario: they are meeting with a collaborator to work on a report about architecture and landscapes in London. The report should eventually consist of images and text about the topic. Prior to the meeting they created a pre-selection of images and text and preloaded them to their smartwatch. They were asked to add content (images, drawings, text) to the shared space; explore images, maps and text; create new sketches; highlight sections of images or text; delete parts of drawings, text or entire documents; group and arrange content; and share it with their collaborator. These tasks required users to go through the content on the watch, add them to the interaction space and use various instruments (color, erase, increase, decrease, create). The aim was to explore the core tasks of curation supported in *CurationSpace* (collecting, analyzing, editing, sharing).

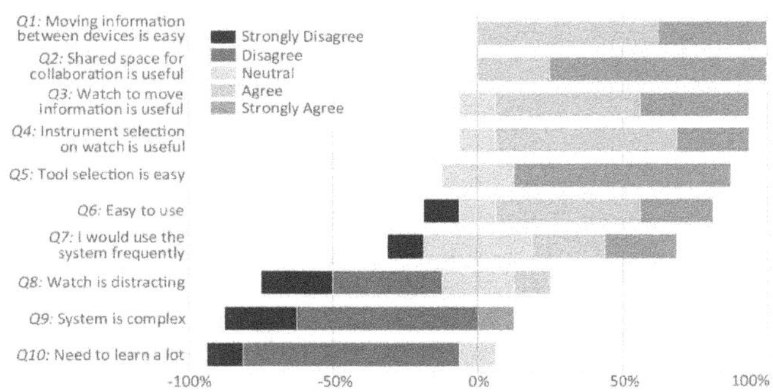

Figure 7. Results of the 5-point-Likert-scale of all 8 participants to the post-study questionnaire about CurationSpace.

Results

User Feedback: Figure 7 shows an overview of participants' answers from the post-study questionnaire. Participants found the system easy to use (Q6. Md=4; iqr=1.5 on 5-point Likert scale). Although one participant found that the watch distracted him from his main task, most participants found the watch useful (Q8. Md=2; iqr=1.75) and it was generally seen as a useful companion for tool selection (Q4. Md=4; iqr=0.75). Participants found it useful to share personal data from the smartwatch to the shared space (Q3. Md=4; iqr=1) and all participants agreed that moving information between watch and shared space was easy (Q1. Md=4; iqr=0).

Understanding of instruments: The scenario was set up in a way that participants' learned the system on-the-fly. They explored the functionality of the smartwatch and its interaction with the shared surface through the task and did not have a high learning barrier (Q10. Md=2; iqr=0). Users understood that instruments were atomic tools that could be applied to the space, a document or the content of a document. For example, P7 used the increase/decrease instruments to change picture and document sizes. Later, she wanted to replace an image with a different one and decided to try the erase instrument because she thought it could be applied in a similar way as learned before with the other instruments.

Order of applying instruments: *CurationSpace* follows the principles of reification, polymorphism and reuse [5], in that an instrument can be applied to different objects of interest. Users expected instruments to work similar to existing tools in GUI (such as Microsoft Word), where the order of application is different: object selection first, tool selection after, whereas in *CurationSpace* it is the other way around. Although all users understood how instruments worked after experiencing one instrument across multiple domain objects, initially different expectation about their mode of operation sometimes led to confusion. P3 summarized his understanding of how tools work: *"the tools seem to work forward, rather than on previous selections. Rather than selecting something and then selecting the tool, I have to select a tool and then apply it to something. Which is counterintuitive to what I am used to in a desktop PC.*" He continued: "*this system differs very much from my current working style. For example, I see that [the erase tool] works like a regular eraser with a pencil drawing, but I feel like I need to unlearn a lot of things [in order to use it]."* On the contrary, P4 argued: *"once you know which way it works it's easy. [Pick up an] instrument and go"* and P8 notes: *"It's different from how I use [tools] on a computer, but similar to a pencil. So I guess it's just a mind-set."* P6 suggested a new *transparent-instrument*, which could reverse the order of operation: First he selects an object using this instrument and then applies, say, the color instrument afterwards.

Awareness and conflicts: The smartwatch provides personalized feedback to the user, showing which tool was currently selected. When moving their attention away from the watch to collaborate on the shared space, we observed situations where users forgot which tool was selected. For example, after deleting some text, a participant sat back to proofread the result. She then wanted to rotate the document to share it with her collaborator. Since the erase-instrument was still selected, the entire document disappeared: "*I expected it to confirm first. But it's handy, you just have to know that it's gone once you apply it*" - P7. As a solution P2 said "*I'm a forgetful person. So I imagine if you have done a lot of work together and then erase a little bit and forget to switch it off, I might accidentally erase something. [...] A small pictogram of the selected instrument on the shared screen or confirmation if you are about to delete something would be good*". P3 suggested a timeout to automatically deselect a tool after an amount of time not using it.

Use in real world practices: Overall, most participants could imagine themselves using *CurationSpace* in their curation workflows (Q7. Md=3.5; iqr=1.75): "*it is much easier to share information between multiple people rather than watching it behind your screen*" (P2). P7 adds that she "*can be selective and only share what [her] colleague needs, who in return can then select [what] he wants to have on his watch and not bombarding him with all the documents*". P5 reported that she does not see any application of the system in her current work: "*I do everything electronically and send it and talk about it via email*". P3 suggested "*if [the shared space] were in a different format, say a large whiteboard, where it was more a presentation format, rather than an intimate format, then I'd see much more of an application for this*". P3's mentioned that he does not see any advantage of using *CurationSpace* in his work: "*I print everything and it's a lot easier to do all of these things with paper*". P7's perspective differs: "*we have all the documents online and it's not like we print anything anymore. I was working with a colleague earlier, and we had to squeeze in font of one computer, but couldn't work together at the same time*".

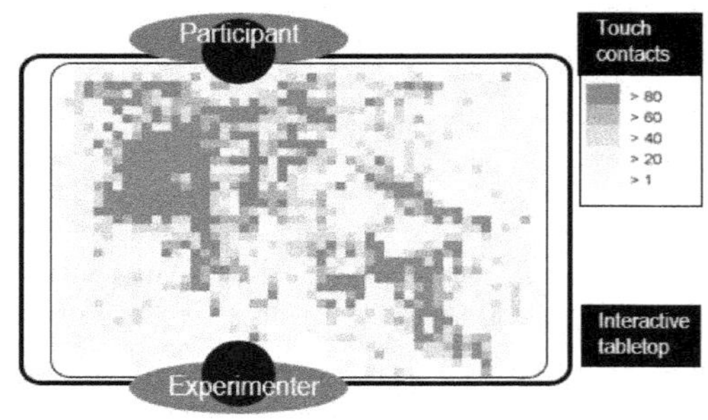

Figure 8: Heatmap of participants' touch patterns on the shared space, showing the main interaction zones.

Usage of space: Participants appreciated a shared space for group work (Q2. Md=5; iqr=0.75). The instruments of *CurationSpace* did not hinder the interaction with the tabletop, as the observed usage pattern reflect similar observations in prior work [37], where group, personal and storage territories exists. Figure 8 shows the usage patterns across the shared surface of *CurationSpace* (except P3, as this data file was corrupted) . Participants were seated to the top left, their collaborator was seated across from them (bottom left). Participants usually started their interaction in the space in front of them and then shared documents by moving them to free space on their collaborator's side (bottom right).

Privacy: Most participants saw the benefits for co-located group work and using a personal device for selecting shareable data. "*There is an element of privacy when selecting documents from a smartwatch. If you are using it in a really collaborative setting I am happy for everyone to see everything. But with different stakeholders or sensitive data, then it is much better to use it on a personal device*" (P1). P2 compared it using the smartwatch to opening images from a folder: "*It depends a bit on what information you are sharing with who. If it's a good friend, I wouldn't mind that they see pictures I didn't want them to see. If it's my boss, I would not* *want them to see everything. [CurationSpace] is much better in only showing what I want to show.*" And P1 added "*I have most of the information already located on a cloud based service [which is connected to my] smartwatch. So I wouldn't need to bring a USB stick or anything else.*"

Suggestions for tools: Participants suggested further instruments: P8 wanted to rearrange 12 different documents on the shared space and felt it was cumbersome to do so with the manipulate instrument because it meant rotating, moving and resizing every single one. She suggested to add predefined sizes, positions, rotations and orientations within the manipulate instrument that could be applied with a single touch to any document. P2 suggested a share instrument to "*save everything on the table itself, but also you could select if you want to save it only on your watch or on the other's watch*". This could also be extended to save the entire state of the system, allowing users to resume a curation session later.

DISCUSSION AND CONCLUSIONS

CurationSpace was designed to provide a new document presentation system that applies the concepts of Instrumental Interaction [4] and dynamic media [18] to content curation of historical documents on interactive surface. A distinguishing feature from other cross-device systems is a clear separation between the interaction space, the high level documents of interest, the atomic fragments that make up the documents, and the instruments that are used to modify or create content. The interaction techniques and document model presented provide an example of how smartwatches can be utilized to augment human touch with a vocabulary of interactive instruments that allow for menu-less content curation resembling interactions with physical documents.

Hardware limitations: To authenticate a user on the tabletop display, our system uses fiducial marker attached to the fingertips of a glove (similar to TouchID [25]). However, with the advent of novel touch sensing technologies, in the future screens will be able to identify a finger through internal sensors, e.g. as proposed in DiamondTouch [11], with IMU sensors such as in SwipeID [19], through fingerprint sensors in a touch screen [15], or use top-mounted tracking systems (e.g. GroupTogether [24] or HuddleLamp [30]) combined with gesture recognition on the smartwatch.

Use of smartwatches for instrumental interaction: Although previous systems have proposed related interaction techniques to allow for cross-device information management, privacy applications, and personalized content, these are mostly based on smartphones interacting with the table. Compared to watches, smartphones are harder to manipulate, take up space on the table, and are not particularly suitable for many of the instruments introduced in *CurationSpace.* Furthermore, the ability for users to pass around or share tablets and phones as (semi) shared devices creates operational inconsistencies connected to identifying the user, or maintaining the user's personal information repository. In contrast, smartwatches are rarely passed around and thus are a much more suitable personal "passport" of the user.

Through the user study we found that *CurationSpace* in its current form is easy to use and participants found it well suited for collaborative tasks. The tasks in the user study followed our initially introduced scenario. We found the main curation tasks were effectively supported; participants were able to review, edit and share documents with their collaborator. Although the order of applying instruments to domain objects follows the interaction mode with physical tools (pick up first, then use) rather than GUIs (selection first, then pick tool), this model was understood by participants but needed learning. In particular, with sensitive content or in more formal social settings, participants saw benefits of a private, body-worn content repository. Although the smartwatch application showed the currently selected instrument at any time, some participants, while discussing their curations works, forgot which tool was selected. This should be considered in any future work, for example, the system could either provide mediation (e.g. timeout or confirmation with the erase instrument) or a more prominent status feedback, in particular with critical instruments. The user study lasted approximately one hour and throughout this this time we saw how participants got accustomed in sharing and editing documents. However, real world curation activities usually last longer and might span across multiple sessions different days.

Generalizability: The concepts, document model, and watch-centric instrumental interactions can be applied to other domains, applications, and user groups beyond content curation. *CurationSpace* introduces users to a reconfigurable shared and instrumented configuration space [16] that allows users to modify any content that can be modeled, visualized, and shared in the `<space, document, fragment, instrument>` structure. Furthermore, the intrinsic separation between instruments and documents allows for great flexibility to extend the system with many new instruments, or even customized combinations of instruments.

We are currently expanding *CurationSpace*'s concepts to further curation tasks, including expanding the document model to the physical space, allowing users to use both physical and digital documents. By creating consistency between how people interact with digital and physical documents, the aim is to provide users with a uniform interaction model across digital devices and physical tools for curation work.

ACKNOWLEDGMENTS

We thank the anonymous reviewers for their helpful feedback and all of our study participants for their time and valuable insights. This work has been supported by Microsoft Research through its PhD Scholarship Programme.

REFERENCES

1. Andrews, C. et al. 2011. Information visualization on large, high-resolution displays: Issues, challenges, and opportunities. *Information Visualization.* 10, 4.
2. Andrews, C. et al. 2010. Space to think: large high-resolution displays for sensemaking. *Proc. of CHI '10.*

3. Ashbrook, D.L. et al. 2008. Quickdraw: the impact of mobility and on-body placement on device access time. *Proc. of CHI '08*. ACM.
4. Beaudouin-Lafon, M. 2000. Instrumental interaction: an interaction model for designing post-WIMP user interfaces. *Proc. of CHI '00*. ACM.
5. Beaudouin-Lafon, M. and Mackay, W.E. 2000. Reification, Polymorphism and Reuse: Three Principles for Designing Visual Interfaces. *Proc. of AVI '00*. ACM.
6. Bederson, B.B. et al. 1996. Local Tools: An Alternative to Tool Palettes. *Proc. of UIST '96*. ACM.
7. Bødker, S. 1990. *Through the Interface - a Human Activity Approach to User Interface Design*. CRC Press.
8. Brudy, F. et al. 2014. Is Anyone Looking? Mitigating Shoulder Surfing on Public Displays through Awareness and Protection. *Proc. of PerDis '14*. ACM.
9. Chen, N. et al. 2012. Designing a multi-slate reading environment to support active reading activities. *ACM Transactions on Computer-Human Interaction*. 19, 3.
10. Chen, X. et al. 2014. Duet: exploring joint interactions on a smart phone and a smart watch. *Proc. of CHI '14*.
11. Dietz, P. and Leigh, D. 2001. DiamondTouch: a multi-user touch technology. *Proc. of UIST '01*. ACM.
12. Everitt, K. et al. 2006. MultiSpace: Enabling electronic document micro-mobility in table-centric, multi-device environments. *Proc. of TABLETOP '06*. IEEE.
13. Hamilton, P. and Wigdor, D.J. 2014. Conductor: enabling and understanding cross-device interaction. *Proc. of CHI '14*. ACM.
14. Hardy, Robert 2008. Touch & Interact: Touch-based Interaction of Mobile Phones with Displays. *Proc. of MobileHCI '08*. ACM.
15. Holz, C. and Baudisch, P. 2013. Fiberio: a touchscreen that senses fingerprints. *Proc. of UIST '13*. ACM.
16. Houben, S. et al. 2014. ActivitySpace: Managing Device Ecologies in an Activity-Centric Configuration Space. *Proc. of ITS '14*. ACM.
17. Houben, S. and Marquardt, N. 2015. WatchConnect: A Toolkit for Prototyping Smartwatch-Centric Cross-Device Applications. *Proc. of CHI '15*. ACM.
18. Kay, A. and Goldberg, A. 1977. Personal dynamic media. *Computer*. 10, 3, 31–41.
19. Kharrufa, A. et al. 2015. Using IMUs to Identify Supervisors on Touch Devices. *Human-Computer Interaction – INTERACT 2015*. J. Abascal et al., eds. Springer International Publishing. 565–583.
20. Kim, J. et al. 2007. The gesture watch: A wireless contact-free gesture based wrist interface. *Proc. ISWC '07*.
21. Klokmose, C.N. et al. 2015. Webstrates: Shareable Dynamic Media. *Proc. of UIST '15*. ACM.
22. Klokmose, C.N. and Beaudouin-Lafon, M. 2009. VIGO: instrumental interaction in multi-surface environments. *Proc. of CHI '09*. ACM.
23. Kruger, R. et al. 2003. How People Use Orientation on Tables: Comprehension, Coordination and Communication. *Proc. of GROUP '03*. ACM.
24. Marquardt, N. et al. 2012. Cross-device interaction via micro-mobility and f-formations. *Proc. of UIST '12*.
25. Marquardt, N. et al. 2011. Designing user-, hand-, and handpart-aware tabletop interactions with the TouchID toolkit. *Proc. of ITS '11*. ACM.
26. Mayer, S. and Soros, G. 2014. User Interface Beaming - Seamless Interaction with Smart Things Using Personal Wearable Computers. *Proc. of BSN '14*. IEEE.
27. Pasquero, J. et al. 2011. A haptic wristwatch for eyes-free interactions. *Proc. of CHI '11*. ACM.
28. Pearson, J. et al. 2015. It's About Time: Smartwatches as Public Displays. *Proc. of CHI '15*. ACM.
29. Pizza, S. et al. 2016. Smartwatch in vivo. *Proc. of CHI '16*. ACM.
30. Rädle, R. et al. 2014. HuddleLamp: Spatially-Aware Mobile Displays for Ad-hoc Around-the-Table Collaboration. *Proc. of ITS '14*. ACM.
31. Rekimoto, J. 2001. Gesturewrist and gesturepad: Unobtrusive wearable interaction devices. *Proc. of ISWC '01*.
32. Rekimoto, J. and Saitoh, M. 1999. Augmented surfaces: a spatially continuous work space for hybrid computing environments. *Proc. of CHI '99*. ACM.
33. Rotman, D. et al. 2012. Supporting content curation communities: The case of the Encyclopedia of Life. *Journal of the American Society for Information Science and Technology*. 63, 6, 1092–1107.
34. Santosa, S. and Wigdor, D. 2013. A field study of multi-device workflows in distributed workspaces. *Proc. of UbiComp '13*. ACM.
35. Schmidt, D. et al. 2012. A cross-device interaction style for mobiles and surfaces. *Proc. of DIS '12*. ACM.
36. Schmidt, D. et al. 2010. PhoneTouch: a technique for direct phone interaction on surfaces. *Proc. of UIST '10*.
37. Scott, S.D. et al. 2004. Territoriality in collaborative tabletop workspaces. *Proc. of CSCW '04*. ACM.
38. Shen, C. et al. 2003. UbiTable: Impromptu face-to-face collaboration on horizontal interactive surfaces. *Proc. of UbiComp '03*. Springer.
39. Shen, H. et al. 2006. Informing the design of direct-touch tabletops. *Computer Graphics and Applications, IEEE*. 26, 5, 36–46.
40. Streitz, N.A. et al. 1999. i-LAND: an interactive landscape for creativity and innovation. *Proc. of CHI '99*.
41. Wilkinson, G. et al. 2016. Expressy: Using a Wrist-worn Inertial Measurement Unit to Add Expressiveness to Touch-based Interactions. *Proc. of CHI '16*. ACM.
42. Wobbrock, J.O. et al. 2009. User-defined gestures for surface computing. *Proc. of CHI '09*. ACM.
43. von Zadow, U. et al. 2014. SleeD: Using a Sleeve Display to Interact with Touch-sensitive Display Walls. *Proc. of ITS '14*. ACM.
44. Ziola, R. et al. 2007. DeskJockey: exploiting passive surfaces to display peripheral information. *Proc. of INTERACT '07*. Springer.

CapCam: Enabling Quick, Ad-Hoc, Position-Tracked Interactions Between Devices

Robert Xiao **Scott Hudson** **Chris Harrison**
Carnegie Mellon University, Human-Computer Interaction Institute
5000 Forbes Avenue, Pittsburgh, PA 15213
{brx, scott.hudson, chris.harrison}@cs.cmu.edu

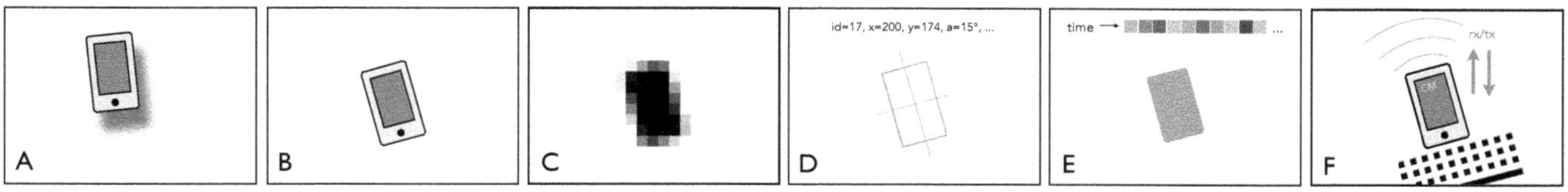

Figure 1. A: CapCam is used to pair two devices, a "cap" device (background is a large touchscreen display) and a "cam" device (here, a smartphone). B: The phone is pressed to the display. C: The phone body creates a characteristic signal on the touchscreen's capacitive sensor. D: CapCam extracts the shape, position and orientation of the phone from this capacitive image. E: CapCam encodes pairing data (e.g., IP, port and password) as a flashing color pattern, rendered beneath the phone body. F: The phone's rear camera captures the pattern, and uses it to establish a conventional two-way wireless link (e.g., WiFi). With both devices paired and communicating, interactive applications can be launched, such as this virtual keyboard.

ABSTRACT
We present CapCam, a novel technique that enables smartphones (and similar devices) to establish quick, ad-hoc connections with a host touchscreen device, simply by pressing a device to the screen's surface. Pairing data, used to bootstrap a conventional wireless connection, is transmitted optically to the phone's rear camera. This approach utilizes the near-ubiquitous rear camera on smart devices, making it applicable to a wide range of devices, both new and old. CapCam also tracks phones' physical positions on the host capacitive touchscreen without any instrumentation, enabling a wide range of targeted interactions. We quantify the communication performance of our pairing approach and demonstrate data transmission rates up to four times faster than prior camera-based techniques. To demonstrate the unique capability and utility of our system, we built a series of example applications, highlighting different interaction techniques CapCam enables.

Author Keywords
Large displays; ad-hoc connections; capacitive sensing; device pairing; cross-device interaction.

ACM Classification Keywords
H.5.2. Information interfaces and presentation (e.g., HCI): User interfaces: Input devices and strategies.

ISS '16, November 06-09, 2016, Niagara Falls, ON, Canada
© 2016 ACM. ISBN 978-1-4503-4248-3/16/11···$15.00
DOI: http://dx.doi.org/10.1145/2992154.2992182

INTRODUCTION
Large touchscreen displays, such as public kiosks, digital whiteboards and interactive tabletops have become increasingly popular as prices have fallen. Similarly, mobile devices, such as smartphones and tablets, have achieved ubiquity. While such devices are reasonably smart on their own, cross-device interactions hold much promise for making interactive experiences even more powerful [14].

However, interacting *across* devices is rarely straightforward. Although many mobile devices support e.g., Bluetooth pairing, such pairing options are generally time-consuming and cumbersome (i.e., on the order of 5 seconds, see Table 1). Often, users must confirm or manually enter connection parameters (e.g., device, network identifier) and security parameters (e.g., PIN) [27]. Short-range NFC, an emerging technology, aims to mitigate many of these issues. However, it requires specific hardware on both devices, and more importantly, only indicates device presence, not position (unless receivers are tiled into an matrix [35] or combined with another method, like optical fiducial tags [1]). Thus, it only allows for coarse device-to-device pairing, precluding metadata such as spatial position and rotation of devices, as well as rich multi-device experiences. Moreover, NFC is not commonly available on larger devices, such as laptops, tablets, and interactive surfaces – the class of surfaces we chiefly target.

CAPCAM
In this work, we describe *CapCam*, a new technique that provides rapid, ad-hoc connections between two devices. CapCam pairs a "cap" device with a capacitive touchscreen to a "cam" device with a camera sensor (Figure 1A). For example, typical smartphones and tablets can be paired with each other, and these devices can be paired to even larger touchscreens, such as smart whiteboards and

Method	Pair Time	Notes
Bluetooth	4.8 sec (SD 2.5)	Starting from Bluetooth config screen of smartphone with device already in discoverable mode. Mean of: Hyundai Elantra (2012), Samsung HM3500 Headset, Plantronics BackBeat 903 headset, Beats Studio Wireless headset.
Wifi WPS	5.1 sec (SD 1.3)	Starting in WiFi settings of smartphone, from moment of WPS button press. Mean of: LinkSys E3200 router, MyQ Garage door opener, Technicolor 582n router, D-Link N300 router.
NFC	1.3 sec (SD 0.3)	With item to send or NFC application already open, from time to tap devices together to time of visible response ("beam" prompt, notification, etc.). Mean of: Nexus 7, LG NFC Tag, WhizTag, Sony Xperia Z, Samsung Galaxy Nexus.
FlashLight [12]	2.64 sec (Tx only)	Pairing data transmission time alone, calculated from the paper. 100 ms camera synchronization time, plus 84-bit payload at 33 bits/sec (the highest throughput achievable without significant error). Data rate assumes error correction is not needed.
BlueTable [37]	3 sec (Tx only)	Pairing data transmission time alone, calculated using the statistics quoted in the paper. This system transmits 8-bit pairing codes at 2.67 bits/sec.
CapCam	1.21 sec (SD 0.1)	With app open, from time to tap Cam device to time of visible Cap device response (including network connection overhead). 84-bit message + 42 additional ECC bits. Time measured using worst-performing device (Microsoft Surface). **0.83** seconds to transmit the 126-bit pairing packet alone (for comparison with FlashLight and BlueTable). See also Video Figure.

Table 1. Informal comparison of different pairing methods.

touchscreen monitors. CapCam uses the cap device's touchscreen to detect and track the cam device (Figure 1, C and D), and renders color-modulated pairing data that is captured by the cam device's rear camera (Figure 1E).

This pairing data contains configuration information necessary to establish a bidirectional link (e.g., IP address, port and password). In this way, CapCam provides a unidirectional communication mechanism from the touchscreen to the camera, which is then used to bootstrap a full bidirectional, high-speed link (Figure 1F). Because CapCam also provides precise, continuous spatial tracking, we can enable rich synergistic applications utilizing both (or many) devices at once.

Overall, we believe CapCam exhibits six desirable properties – it enables *zero-configuration* pairing via automatically transmitted pairing codes; it is *rapid*, capable of establishing links in roughly one second; *anonymous*, in that it requires no identifying information to be exchanged; pairing is explicitly initiated by users through a *purposeful* pressing of a device to a host screen; it enables *targeted* interactions on said screen via position tracking; and, it allows for *multiple devices* to be paired and used on the same cap device simultaneously.

Although many prior systems have independently addressed pairing or spatial interaction, few have *combined* these into a single system. CapCam provides both pairing and spatial interaction as phases of a single interactive transaction, enabling rapid, ad hoc interactions, e.g,. walking up to a public display and initiating rich, spatial interactions nearly instantaneously.

In addition to describing our CapCam implementation, we also offer several applications and interactions enabled by our technique. We further contribute an evaluation of the technical aspects of our approach, including pairing latency, pairing code bandwidth and bit error rate across three exemplary devices.

RELATED WORK

CapCam intersects with several distinct areas of the literature, which we now review.

Device Pairing Interactions

Interaction techniques for establishing an ad hoc connection between devices in a convenient but secure fashion have been proposed in a large number of research systems. Chong et al. provide a survey of systems in [9] and review relevant usability factors in [8]. Systems differ in terms of the actions users must undertake to establish an association between devices: using e.g., pre-shared codes [20], simple placement of a phone in view of a camera on a specially augmented surface [37], gestures performed by the user with a mobile device [15, 25], or synchronous motion, vibration or other input on two devices [6, 13, 14, 15, 24, 28], among others.

Pairing Techniques using Optical Communication

A number of systems have explored optical transmission methods for device pairing [21, 26, 30, 31, 37]. Several use color encoding, e.g., [22] which uses hue differentials for coding; [38], which exploits the rolling-shutter effect to present imperceptible visual tags; and [12, 34], which use color transitions for coding. However, only one prior system, FlashLight [12] has demonstrated optical transmission of data between a display (a diffuse illumination touch table) and a coupled phone.

Augmenting Interactions Using Spatial Tracking

A phone or other device with knowledge of its spatial location can be used as an auxiliary input and/or display device to augment interaction on a larger device (see e.g., [17, 19, 23, 36]). For example, it could be used as a magic lens [2], providing physical detail+context [29], or as a *peephole* display [39] in a larger context. Other systems use specially-designed tangible widgets which can be tracked and identified by a capacitive touchscreen, e.g., TUIC [40] and CapStones and ZebraWidgets [7]. The phone's camera can also be used to infer the phone's position relative to a remote display, to enable various interactions [3, 4].

One exemplary system is PhoneTouch [32, 33], which lets users tap a phone onto a display surface and perform targeted interactions. This is achieved by merging two disparate events: an impact registered by the phone's accelerometer and the appearance of a new blob on an FTIR display.

This requires devices to be pre-paired and have synchronized clocks. Similarly, the Thaw system [18] uses a hue encoding technique to encode x-y positions on a display, which can be interpreted by the camera of a pre-paired phone. As previously mentioned, NFC pairs one device to another, without fine grain targeting. In response, Touch & Select [35] uses a special grid of NFC tags operating behind the display to provide rough position tracking of a phone while using NFC. Finally, Echtler et al. [10] use a camera-driven interactive table to recognize devices based on the shadows they cast, and combine this with Bluetooth signal strength to establish a connection, thus requiring no modification to e.g., smartphones.

Closely Related Systems

A few systems deserve special mention for their proximity to the present work. BlueTable [37] tracks phones on a surface using an overhead camera, and pairs with them via infrared flashes from the IrDA transceiver. BlueTable was able to transfer data at 2.67 bits per second using binary encoding. FlashLight [12] is a system that transmits pairing data from a diffuse illumination touch table to a phone resting on it; a basic color transition scheme is used to transmit approximately one bit per frame to the phone's camera, achieving a transmission rate of 33 bits per second.

In contrast to these systems, CapCam is the first to use commodity, off-the-shelf capacitive touchscreens, meaning our technique is *immediately portable* to most touchscreen devices today (as opposed to optical touch tables used in e.g., [10, 37]). Additionally, CapCam offers significantly higher data transmission rates – up to 150 bits per second – allowing for almost instant pairing. Table 1 offers findings from an informal comparison of commercial systems, BlueTable and FlashLight. Beyond offering competitive pairing ease and speed, CapCam also significantly extends prior work with respect to our exploration of the interactions enabled; please also see our Video Figure.

IMPLEMENTATION

The cap device in CapCam can be any capacitive touchscreen device, ranging from large public kiosks to small mobile phones. To demonstrate this range, we used several different off-the-shelf, consumer devices for development and testing. Importantly, these devices represent a wide range of sizes and pixel densities.

Smartphone – We used a stock Nexus 5 running Android 5.0.1, which features a 5" diagonal screen with a resolution of 1080x1920 pixels (445 pixels per inch) running at 60 fps, and a touchscreen update rate of 120 Hz.

Laptop – Laptops increasingly feature touchscreens, and so we chose a laptop as our second display platform. In order to directly compare transmission performance with FlashLight [12], we use a MacBook Pro. Because this particular computer lacks a touchscreen, we only evaluated data transmission rates with this device. The MacBook has a 15" screen with a resolution of 2880x1800 pixels (220 PPI) running at 60 fps.

Figure 2. A hand and smartphone resting on our Microsoft Surface display. The capacitive image is seen above (offset vertically for illustrative purposes).

Large Interactive Surface – As a demonstration of large CapCam-enabled interactions, we use a 55" Microsoft Surface touchscreen display, with a resolution of 1920x1080 pixels (40 PPI) at 60 Hz. The touchscreen has an update rate of 120 Hz.

Cam Device

As an example cam device, we used an unmodified Nexus 5 smartphone running Android 5.0.1. Android 5 provides low-level control over many parameters of the phone's camera, enabling specialized imaging applications like ours. Specifically, it allows full-manual control over shutter speed, exposure, focus and color compensation. Although few devices currently support this full-control API, the underlying features are present on nearly all image sensors at a low level (readily available to system integrators and hardware manufacturers).

Despite our control over the camera's focus parameters, the images are nonetheless blurred because the camera cannot focus at such short distances. We use the camera in manual-control video mode, which provides 640x480 resolution images at 30 FPS.

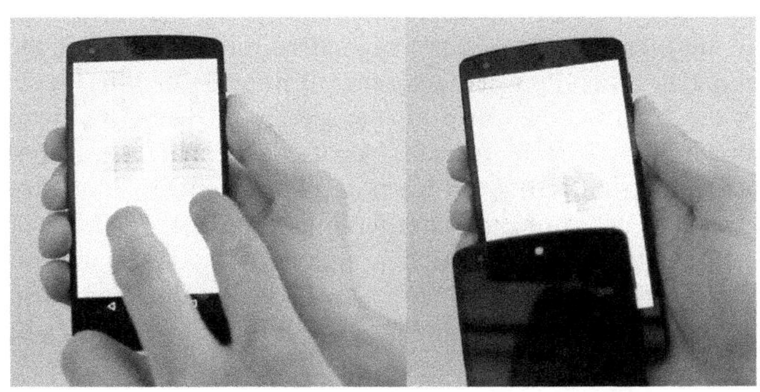

Figure 3. Capacitive images from our Nexus 5 smartphone showing the signal obtained from finger touches (left) and a phone contact (right). The camera ring of the contacting phone is visible at right. For illustrative purposes, the signal is offset vertically to avoid occlusion.

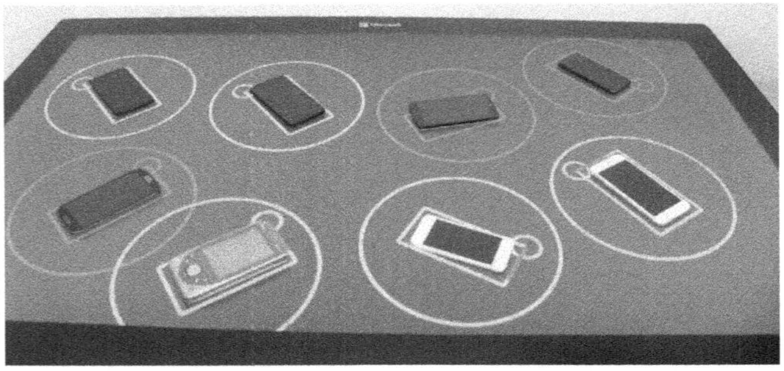

Figure 4. Multiple devices (of many models) simultaneously tracked on the Microsoft screen by our algorithm. Rectangles display the recognized phone's shape, orientation and position. A red line denotes a device's x-axis; the upper-left corner is marked with a hollow circle.

Capacitive Image Processing and Tracking

Capacitive touchscreens function by sensing changes in the electric field near the surface of the display. Typically, the field is sensed at points on a regularly-spaced electrode grid, resulting in a low-resolution "capacitive image". The touch controller processes this image internally to extract touch data (most typically, the X/Y position of touch contacts), which is then passed up to the operating system.

Most touch controllers, however, offer a "debug" interface that enables the complete capacitive image to be retrieved. On the Nexus 5 smartphone, we modified the Linux kernel to provide access to the Synaptics S3350 touch controller's capacitive image (a capability previously exploited in e.g., CapAuth [11] and BodyPrint [16]). On the Microsoft Surface display, we developed a user-space USB driver for OS X integrated into the cap application, which retrieves the image over the USB connection. We use the raw capacitive image (Figures 2 and 3) produced by the touchscreen controller to implement our own tracking algorithms, which we designed for finding phones and touches simultaneously (Figure 4 and Video Figure).

On our large interactive display, we find phones by tracking the rectangular capacitive imprint (Figure 2, right). When a phone is placed on the surface, the phone creates a characteristic electric field disturbance under the entire area of the phone. Although the capacitive measurement of the phone is generally lower than that of fingers, the noise level of the Microsoft Surface display precludes using a simple threshold approach. Instead, we use a connected components algorithm to detect blobs in the image. The blob size is used to determine whether the blob represents a phone or a finger touch. A natural consequence of this simple approach is that large touch contacts, such as palms, may also be recognized as "phones". However, since non-camera device contacts will not pair with the screen, they can be rejected quickly.

For phones, we then fit a rectangle to the contact blob to extract the approximate bounding box of the phone (Figure 4). To obtain the phone's angle, the algorithm selects the orientation angle that minimizes the bounding box size. After the phone establishes a connection with the display, it can optionally transmit its physical dimensions to the display to enable more precise tracking.

On the Nexus 5 smartphone, the touchscreen controller's built-in auto-calibration feature, which integrates large, weak capacitive blobs into the background profile over time, precluded us from similarly tracking the body of the other phone. Consequently, we track other phones (*i.e.*, cam devices) by identifying and tracking the metallic ring that often surrounds camera modules (seen in Figure 3, right). We use a connected-components algorithm (flood fill algorithm) to locate the ring, and distinguish it from fingers by comparing the maximum signal value against a threshold – the capacitive measurement of the ring is significantly lower than any finger.

Of note, the lower resolution of our Surface's touchscreen prevents us from reliably segmenting the camera module from the rest of the phone's blob. Instead, we treat any contact point inside the phone's area as a potential camera. In order to accurately discern the camera's position, we vary the pairing data (e.g., using different passcodes) rendered beneath the phone by position (e.g., quadrants) – the unique pairing data that eventually connects thus reveals the camera location. As camera modules are almost always located at the top of devices, we can further infer the orientation of devices (Figure 4, top left corner denoted with a circle).

Transmitting the Pairing Data

We encode pairing data as visible light beneath the device. Pairing data is encoded into sequential frames, where each frame consists of a color. Thus, the pairing data appears visually as a series of flashing solid colors on the display (see Video Figure). To match the frame rate of the camera, the frames are transmitted at 30 Hz (thus, when displayed at 60 Hz we simply repeat each color frame twice).

Each packet of pairing data begins with a three-frame header, consisting of one frame each of solid green, red and blue (Figure 5). This sequence is highly unlikely to occur in the wild or at random, especially at precisely 30 Hz, and so it neatly delineates packets. Furthermore, as we describe later, this known and "pure-color" header data is used to automatically color calibrate the camera to the particular display for improved payload decoding.

Figure 5. A sample packet as encoded by the display. The packet starts with a three-frame green-red-blue header, followed by 21 color frames containing 6 bits each (using 4 color levels per channel). The raw transmitted bits are noted below each frame.

Figure 6. Two consecutive camera frames captured by our Nexus 5, showing our GRB packet header (Figure 5). Image rows are captured sequentially in time due to the rolling shutter. Left: the green header frame, followed by the start of the red frame. Right: the next frame shows the end of the red frame and the start of the blue frame. White dots represent the sampling points used to extract the packet.

Following the header, the pairing data is encoded into the RGB color values of each frame (Figure 5), depending on the number of color levels configured. For example, if we use 4 color levels per channel (e.g., color channel values of 0, 85, 170, and 255), then each color channel encodes 2 bits of data (00, 01, 10 and 11 respectively). Since we can independently manipulate R, G and B output on the display, each frame encodes 6 bits. Using this scheme, a 162-bit message can be transmitted in one second (30 frames total, three header frames plus 27 data frames). Increasing the number of levels per channel provides higher theoretical throughput, but also raises the error rate. Consequently, the number of levels should be chosen to optimize the error-corrected bit rate (Figure 9).

Modern operating systems perform sophisticated color correction to match display characteristics with human perception. These color corrections include gamma corrections, chromatic shifts, white-point adjustments, and gross brightness/contrast control. Although these are useful for presenting accurate colors to humans, they cause unpredictable changes in the displayed color data across monitors. We therefore bypass these color correction algorithms by specifying that our color data is pre-corrected to the sRGB color space, thus allowing us to display "raw" RGB values.

As LCD displays vary in emission spectra and brightness, there will still be a color mismatch between the display and the camera. We use our GRB packet header (Figures 5 and

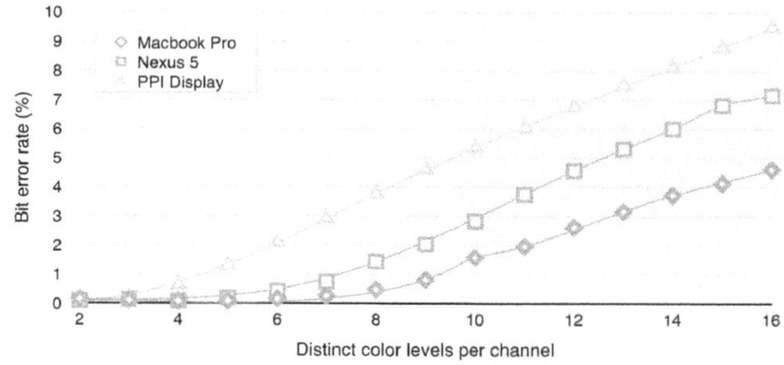

Figure 7. Raw bit error rate (% of bits flipped) as a function of color level density.

6) to calibrate the camera, computing a color-calibration matrix that reduces the observed cross-talk between different channels and normalizes the sensitivity of the camera's response to each channel. After this correction, there is still some residual noise, for example, some LCD displays exhibit slow switching times, resulting in intermediate color values being received by the camera. Because of this, some level of error correction is required to accurately transmit packets. Furthermore, these effects may reduce the number of usable color levels per channel.

Capturing the Connection String with the Camera

Our example displays all have a refresh rate of 60 Hz, accurate to within fractions of a Hz. Due to the rolling shutter on the phone's camera (true for most cameras used in smartphones), the camera frame will usually contain part of one display frame, the vertical blanking interval, and part of the next display frame (Figure 6). The point in the image at which the blanking interval appears will move as the camera moves in and out of sync with the display. If the break moves across the image too quickly, the captured frames will skip or lag with respect to the display, invalidating the received data.

Thus, we configure the phone's shutter speed so that it captures frames as close to 30 Hz as possible, by setting the sensor frame duration as close to 33.3 ms as the hardware will allow. On the Nexus 5, we can do so to within 0.3 Hz (33.1 ms), so that the blanking interval moves at most 1/3 of the camera frame per second. This is sufficiently stable for our use. We used the same camera settings for all smartphones and cap devices.

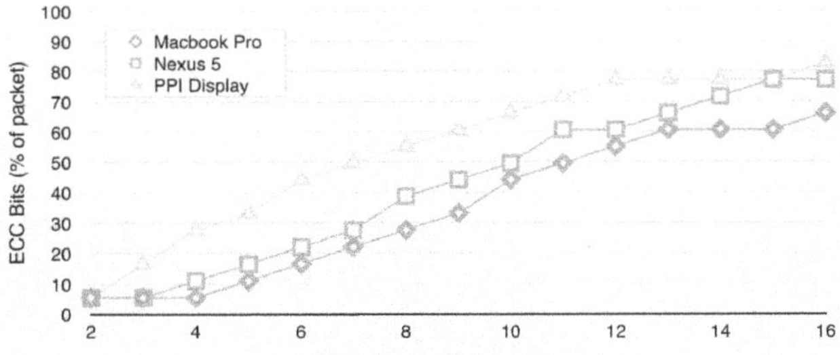

Figure 8. Percentage of 126-bit packet needed for error correction to attain a packet loss rate of 1%, as a function of color level density.

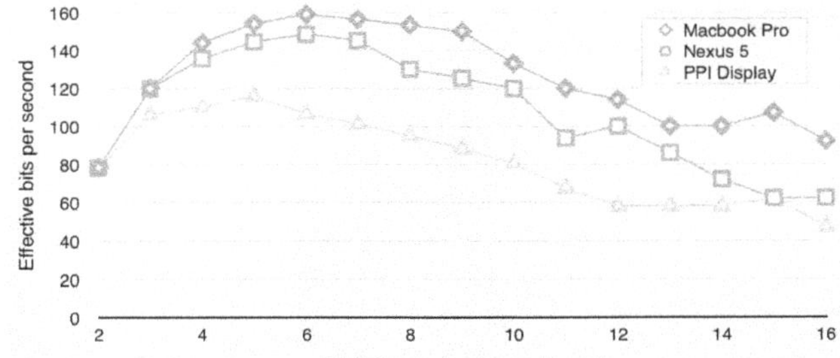

Figure 9. Effective payload data transmission rate as a function of color level density, after applying the error correction necessary for a target packet loss rate of 1%.

Figure 10. Keyboard example. The screen provides a large on-screen keyboard for paired phones, easing text input.

On the cam device, we select eight sample points across the height of the camera frame (Figure 6, white dots). At each sample point, we attempt to decode the observed color sequence as a packet. Because we synchronize closely to the display's frame rate, there will be at least one sample point that is not affected by the rolling shutter break for the duration of the transmission, allowing that sample point to receive the message and decode it successfully.

Connection Creation

Once the cam device receives and decodes the pairing data packet, it initiates a connection to the display. In our proof-of-concept implementation, the connection is made over WiFi, though any wireless protocol could be used (e.g., cellular). The pairing data contains all data necessary to establish this connection. For example, it could contain a Bluetooth hardware address and PIN, a WiFi ad-hoc BSSID and WPA2 key, or an IP address and port if the devices are on a shared network (e.g., cellular network or WiFi access point). The pairing data packet also contains a one-time use passcode (i.e., nonce), which further identifies the cam device to the cap device.

Error Correction

Due to inherent noise and non-uniformity in the camera hardware, color space differences, and LCD imperfections, some level of error correction is needed to ensure reliable data transmission. In our implementation, we employ a BCH error-correcting code [5] appended to each transmitted packet. The precise code configuration used can be optimized based on the capabilities of the screen; for our implementation, we used a 42-bit code appended to an 84-bit message, capable of correcting any 6 erroneous bits within a 126-bit packet. These parameters were chosen to give a 99% packet transmission rate on the Microsoft Surface device (which exhibited the most challenging transmission characteristics, as seen in Figure 7).

Connection Tear Down

When the cam device is removed from the display, the cap device immediately detects the loss of capacitive tracking and can optionally terminate the connection if no further interaction is desired. This facilitates rapid and effortless creation and destruction of ephemeral pairings between the devices. Moreover, this serves to require physical proximity for pairings to exist, which is not possible with a purely wireless solution. Alternatively, applications can choose to retain the pairing after the phone leaves the display, using CapCam as a general-purpose device pairing solution.

Privacy

Although CapCam was not designed for security-sensitive applications, it does exhibit several properties that make it reasonably robust against simple attacks (e.g., compared to that of entering a PIN into an ATM).

A co-located attacker with line of sight could conceivably intercept the data sent from the display to the phone. This line of sight is significantly hindered by the fact we render our visible light handshake under the device, thus requiring a camera to be at an oblique angle relative to the display and with a large depth of field. We could further obfuscate data transmission with false patterns presented around the camera module.

Even if the attacker is successful in visually intercepting the connection data, they would only gain access to the host display (not the client) and then, only for an extremely short period of time. Only one connection is permitted per port/passcode. Thus, the attacker would have to decode the CapCam packet before the phone; when the true client phone does attempt to connect (perhaps a few tens of milliseconds later), the server can terminate both connections on grounds of suspicious activity.

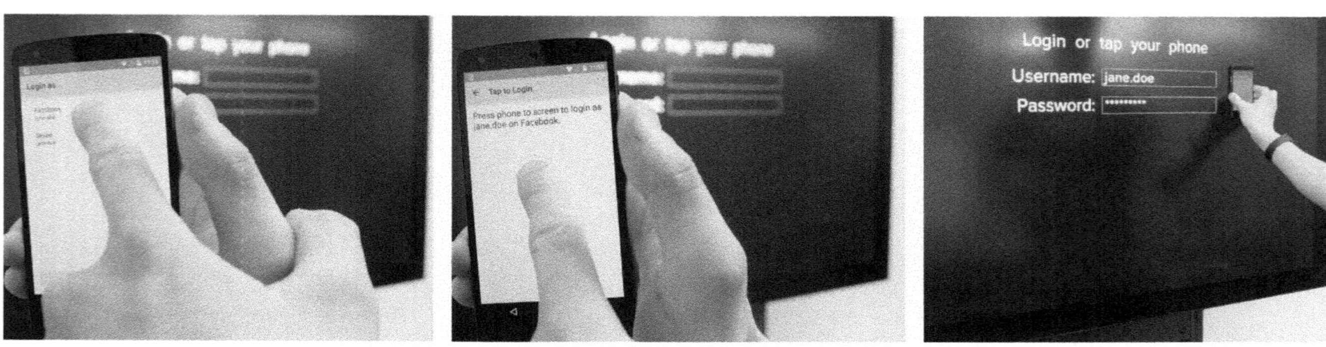

Figure 11. Authentication demo. Instead of entering a password on a highly-visible on-screen keyboard, users select an account (left) on their phone. The credentials are automatically sent after pressing the phone to the screen (right).

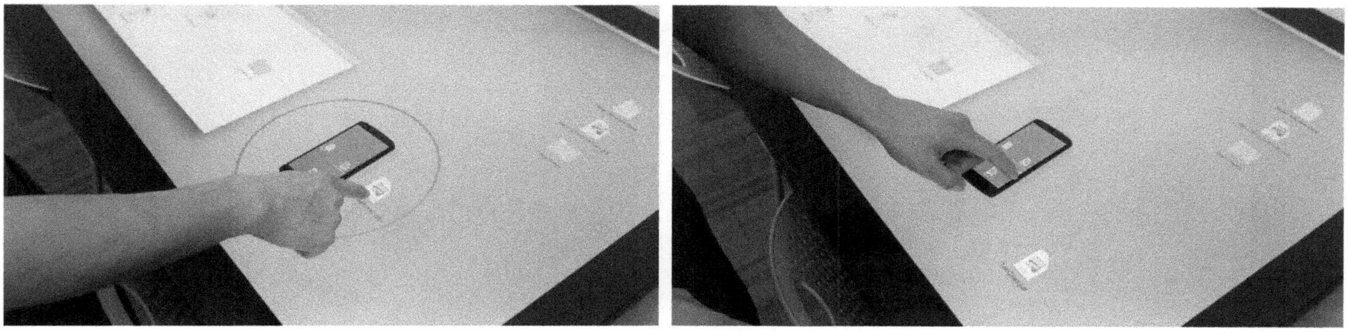

Figure 12. Data transfer between a phone and a desktop. Left: desktop files can be dropped onto the phone. Right: dragging files to the bezel of the phone drops them on the desktop.

In general, after successfully establishing a two-way wireless connection between legitimate devices, the host/client can negotiate an encrypted channel using e.g., Transport Layer Security (TLS) to thwart passive listening attacks.

EVALUATION

We conducted an evaluation to determine the transmission characteristics of CapCam: the bit error rate, packet drop rate, and effective transmission rates over a range of different transmission encodings and devices. Our evaluation was performed on our three test devices: a Nexus 5 smartphone, a MacBook Pro laptop, and a Microsoft Surface 55" multitouch display. A Nexus 5 smartphone was used in all three cases to receive the data.

Each of the host displays was configured to repeatedly flash a random data packet encoded with a random number of color levels (from 2-16 levels per channel) and a random packet length (from 10-20 display frames per packet), with no error correction applied. In each case, the packet was preceded and followed by the standard G,R,B header. After the display flashes the packet, the phone sends back the received packet (or reports a failure if the packet was not detected) and the result is compared against the original sent packet to determine the bit error rate.

RESULTS AND PERFORMANCE

Each display device was tested over a period of eight hours, during which the smartphone was placed on the cap device and configured to continually receive pairing data. In total, 113,957 packets were sent (over 32,000 per device); 64 packets were lost, for a packet loss rate of less than 0.06%. In total, 5,106,848 bits of information were transmitted.

For each device and number of color levels, we computed the total raw bit error rate, shown in Figure 7. The error rate increases as the number of color levels increases, due to the decreasing separation between adjacent color levels. We then calculated the minimum amount of error correction needed to ensure that 99% of packets are corrected (a packet loss rate of 1%) for each encoding level; the error correction levels are shown in Figure 8 for a packet size of 126 bits. In all cases, a BCH error correction scheme was used.

Finally, based on the resulting effective payload sizes, we computed the net throughput of the system, shown in Figure 9. The results show that there is a consistent "peak" of throughput around 4-6 color levels, past which the increased raw throughput is outweighed by the increase in error rate.

As our implementation is designed for a power-of-two number of color levels (for simplicity), we chose 8 color levels for the MacBook and 4 color levels for the Nexus 5 and Microsoft Surface implementations, for bit rates of 150, 135 and 110 bits per second, respectively. These rates are sufficient to send a full setup packet (32-bit IP address, 16-bit port, 32-bit passcode) in under one second on all devices. For higher-security applications, 1.5 seconds would allow for a 128-bit key to be transmitted.

Overall, our encoding scheme, coupled with our greater control over the camera's shutter timing and color correction, allows us to achieve speeds much higher than the color transition approach shown in e.g., [12,34].

Figure 13. Business card exchange. After a meeting, electronic business cards are exchanged. Simply pressing one phone's camera to the other's screen initiates CapCam pairing and downloads the requested card.

Figure 14. Image gallery example. Users simply press their phone to a desired image to download it.

EXAMPLE APPLICATIONS AND INTERACTIONS

To illustrate the potential of CapCam, we built seven example applications demonstrating different use cases. Please also see our Video Figure, which underscores the speed and robustness of our approach – *all* demos shown are functional and real-time.

Facilitating Input

We built a simple application that allows the user to enter text on their phone using a larger, on-screen keyboard (Figure 10). The user places their phone on a cap device (oriented like a table), causing a position-tracked keyboard to appear below the phone. Multiple devices can be paired to the same cap device, each given their own keyboard, which transmits keystrokes only to its respective device.

We also built a demo in which the phone transmits data to the host cap device. With public kiosks, users often have to enter their authentication credentials on a large touchscreen, where they can be easily observed. In this example, users can press their phone to the display to automatically transmit their credentials rapidly and securely (Figure 11).

File & Information Transfer

Data transfer between a phone and a computer is often challenging. In our desktop demo application, users simply press their phone to the display to enable bidirectional drag-and-drop file transfer. Dragging files off the phone causes them to be copied to the desktop (Figure 12, right), and vice-versa (Figure 12, left). The cap device tracks the

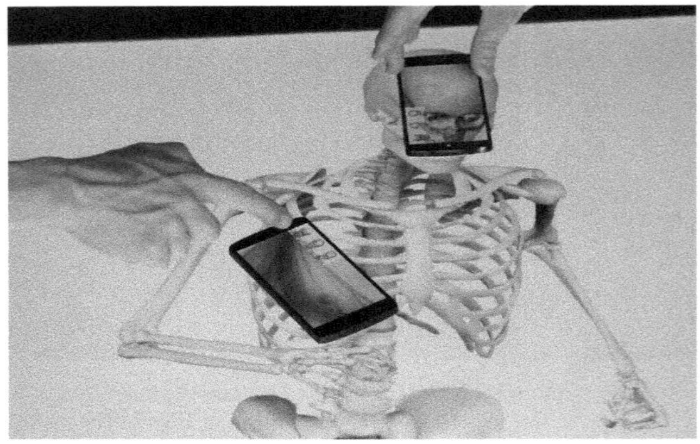

Figure 15. Context+Focus demo. The phones display high-resolution imagery that corresponds to the devices' position on screen. Users can also switch anatomical layers and change zoom levels.

location of the phone, allowing its physical location to serve as a drop target. Additionally, we stream file icons and relative radial position to render a live preview of the drop location.

Alternately, users can select files to download by pressing the phone directly onto documents. In our gallery demo, users can download a high-res image simply by placing their phone camera to it (Figure 14). CapCam transmits a URL for the desired content to the phone, which then downloads and displays the image. We note in this example that, from the user's perspective, the act of pairing the devices has disappeared into the main interaction itself.

The cap device need not always be a large display. We created a phone-to-phone business card demo, where two users can exchange business cards by pressing their phones together (Figure 13). CapCam transmits an appropriate pairing code (e.g., Bluetooth device ID and PIN) and automatically downloads the selected card file.

Phone as Accessory

The phone can also be used as an accessory for larger displays. As an example, we created a context+focus demo where the phone (445 ppi) is used as a focus display for the larger, low-resolution (~40 ppi) cap device (Figure 15). The phone's position and orientation is precisely tracked and transmitted from the cap device to the phone, allowing a seamless overlay of shared content.

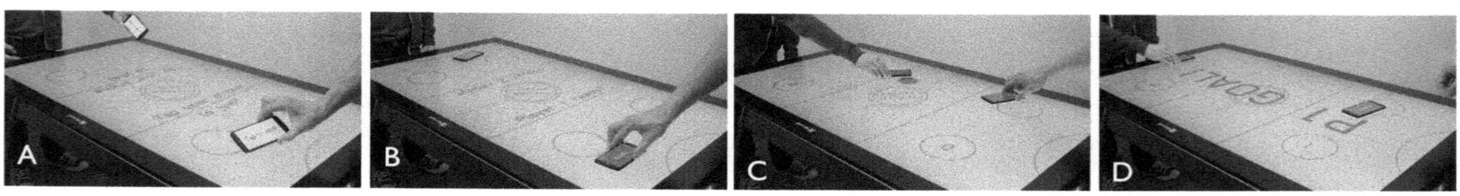

Figure 16. CapCam air hockey. (A) Players are invited to join the game. (B) When players press their phones to the table, CapCam rapidly and anonymously pairs the phones to the display. When two phones are paired, the game begins. (C) Players use their physical phones to deflect the virtual puck. CapCam tracks the phones and their orientations on the screen. (D) Sounds, vibrations and player-specific information appear on the phone, directed by the game through the paired connection.

Finally, we developed an air-hockey game using CapCam. In this demo, two users pair their phones to the cap device to start a match. The phones are used as physical paddles to hit the virtual puck (Figure 16). Furthermore, the phones provide stereo audio feedback (e.g., puck hit sounds, goal sirens, and ambient audience sounds), and even individualized haptic feedback (e.g., short vibrations when the puck is hit, long vibrations when a goal is scored).

DISCUSSION

Having been the focus of more than a decade of research and development, NFC is a mature technology offering a useful gold standard. Perhaps the most important factor is pairing time, in which CapCam and NFC are comparable. However, compared with NFC-based approaches, CapCam inherently provides targeted and position-tracked interactions. With spatial differentiation, multi-device (and multi-person) interactions are readily supported, opening new and different interactive opportunities. Further, CapCam requires physical and direct contact to pair, as opposed to NFC, which can pair at a distance of up to 10 cm without line-of-sight (e.g., accidently through a pocket).

Although CapCam transmits data much slower than NFC (150 bits/sec vs. 424 kbits/sec), the main goal of CapCam's pairing phase is simply to establish a unique, secure, high-speed bidirectional link using wireless communication protocols already present on most devices, much like NFC does when attempting to transfer files. There are also avenues to boost CapCam's transmission rate, for example by transmitting different data across the pixels beneath the camera to achieve spatial modulation.

CapCam presently requires a special application to be downloaded to a phone before pairing can proceed. Thus, the first time a user wishes to pair using CapCam, an application would have to be downloaded and run, adding to the pairing time. This, of course, is a one-time cost. Moreover, there is no reason that CapCam could not be integrated into the OS as a system level feature, just like NFC on many phones. Thus, we see this limitation chiefly as an artifact of prototyping and not an inherent quality of the technique. Finally, due to the use of the rear camera, power usage is fairly high during the CapCam pairing process. This could be mitigated with custom hardware, such as a set of color photodiodes connected to a low-power dedicated decoder circuit, enabling always-on code detection.

CONCLUSION

We have presented CapCam, a technique that allows two devices to establish rapid and ad-hoc connections simply by pressing the camera of one device to the touchscreen of another. By exploiting capacitive sensing, CapCam tracks the precise position of the camera device, which combines with rapid pairing to enable a wide range of interactive functionality. From a technical perspective, we showed that CapCam can transfer data from the screen to the camera over 100 bits per second with negligible error, several times faster than prior display-to-camera transmission schemes. We use this to transmit data needed to establish a quicker and more stable connection. Finally, we demonstrated a wide range of fun and useful applications that showcase the capabilities of CapCam.

ACKNOWLEDGEMENTS

This research was generously supported by the David and Lucile Packard Foundation, a Google Faculty Research Award and Qualcomm.

REFERENCES

1. Bazo, A. and Echtler, F. Phone proxies: effortless content sharing between smartphones and interactive surfaces. In *Proc. EICS '14*. 229-234.

2. Bier, E., Stone, M., Pier, K., Buxton, W. and DeRose, T. Toolglass and magic lenses: the see-through interface. In *Proc. SIGGRAPH '93*. 73-80.

3. Boring, S., Altendorfer, M., Broll, G., Hilliges, O. and Butz, A. Shoot & copy: phonecam-based information transfer from public displays onto mobile phones. In *Proc. CHI '07*. 24-31.

4. Boring, S., Baur, D., Butz, A., Gustafson, S. and Baudisch, P. Touch projector: mobile interaction through video. In *Proc. CHI '10*. 2287-2296.

5. Bose, R.C. and Ray-Chaudhuri, D.K. On A Class of Error Correcting Binary Group Codes. Information and Control, 3(1), March 1960. 68–79.

6. Castelluccia C. and Mutaf, P. Shake them up!: A movement-based pairing protocol for CPU constrained devices. In *Proc. MobiSys '05*. 51–64.

7. Chan, L., Müller, S., Roudaut, A. and Baudisch, P. CapStones and ZebraWidgets: sensing stacks of building blocks, dials and sliders on capacitive touch screens. In *Proc. CHI '12*. 2189-2192.

8. Chong M. and Gellersen, H. Usability classification for spontaneous device association. *Pers. Ubi. Comput.* 16, 1 (Jan. 2012), 77–89.

9. Chong, M., Mayrhofer, R. and Gellersen, H. A Survey of User Interaction for Spontaneous Device Association. *ACM Comput. Surv.* 47, 1, Article 8 (May 2014), 40.

10. Echtler, F., Nestler, S., Dippon, A. and Klinker, G. Supporting casual interactions between board games on public tabletop displays and mobile devices. *Personal Ubiquitous Comput.* 13, 8 (November 2009), 609-617.

11. Guo, A., Xiao, R. and Harrison, C. CapAuth: Identifying and Differentiating User Handprints on Commodity Capacitive Touchscreens. In *Proc. ITS '15*. 59-62.

12. Hesselmann, T., Henze, N. and Boll, S. FlashLight: optical communication between mobile phones and interactive tabletops. In *Proc. ITS '10*. 135-138.

13. Hinckley, K. Synchronous gestures for multiple persons and computers. In *Proc. UIST '03*. 149–158.

14. Hinckley, K., Ramos, G., Guimbretiere, F., Baudisch, P. and Smith, M. Stitching: pen gestures that span multiple displays. In *Proc. AVI '04*. 23-31.

15. Holmquist, L.E., Mattern, F., Schiele, B., Alahuhta, P., Beigl, M. and Gellersen, H. Smart-Its Friends: A Technique for Users to Easily Establish Connections between Smart Artefacts. In *Proc. UbiComp '01*. 116-122.

16. Holz, C., Buthpitiya, S. and Knaust, M. Bodyprint: Biometric User Identification on Mobile Devices Using the Capacitive Touchscreen to Scan Body Parts. In *Proc. CHI '15*. 3011-3014.

17. Lakatos, D., Blackshaw, M., Olwal, A., Barryte, Z., Perlin, K. and Ishii, H. T(ether): spatially-aware handhelds, gestures and proprioception for multi-user 3D modeling and animation. In *Proc. SUI '14*. 90-93.

18. Leigh, S.-W., Schoessler, P., Heibeck, F., Maes, P. and Ishii, H. THAW: tangible interaction with see-through augmentation for smartphones on computer screens. In *Proc. TEI '15*. 55-56.

19. Li, F., Dearman, D., and Truong, K. Virtual shelves: interactions with orientation aware devices. In *Proc. UIST '09*. 125-128.

20. Lin, F. X., Ashbrook, D. and White, S. RhythmLink: securely pairing I/O-constrained devices by tapping. In *Proc. UIST '11*. 263-272.

21. McCune, J., Perrig, A. and Reiter, M. 2005. Seeing-is-believing: Using camera phones for human-verifiable authentication. In *Proc. IEEE S&P '05*. 110–124.

22. Miyaoku, K., Higashino, S. and Tonomura, Y. C-blink: a hue-difference-based light signal marker for large screen interaction via any mobile terminal. *Proc. UIST '04*. 147-156.

23. Olwal, A. LightSense: enabling spatially aware handheld interaction devices. In *Proc. ISMAR '06*. 119-122.

24. Park, D.G., Kim, J.K., Sung, J.B., Hwang, J.H., Hyung, C.H. and Kang, S.W. TAP: touch-and-play. In *Proc. CHI '06*. 677-680.

25. Patel, S., Pierce, S. and Abowd, G. A gesture-based authentication scheme for untrusted public terminals. In *Proc. UIST '04*, 157-160.

26. QR Code. Automatic identification and data capture techniques. Bar code symbology. BS ISO/IEC 18004:200.

27. Rekimoto, J. Pick-and-drop: a direct manipulation technique for multiple computer environments. In *Proc. UIST '97*. 31-39.

28. Rekimoto, J. SyncTap: Synchronous user operation for spontaneous network connection. *Pers. Ubi. Comput. 8, 2* (May 2004), 126–134.

29. Rohs, M. and Oulasvirta, A. Target acquisition with camera phones when used as magic lenses. In *Proc. CHI '08*. 1409-1418.

30. Roth, V., Schmidt, P. and Guldenring, B. The IR ring: authenticating users' touches on a multi-touch display. In *Proc. UIST '10*. 259-262.

31. Saxena, N., Ekberg, J., Kostiainen, K. and Asokan, N. 2006. Secure device pairing based on a visual channel. In *Proc. IEEE S&P '06*. 306–313.

32. Schmidt, D., Chehimi, F., Rukzio, E. and Gellersen, H. PhoneTouch: a technique for direct phone interaction on surfaces. In *Proc. UIST '10*. 13-16.

33. Schmidt, D., Seifert, J., Rukzio, E. and Gellersen, H. A cross-device interaction style for mobiles and surfaces. In *Proc. DIS '12*. 318-327.

34. Schwarz, J., Klionsky, D., Harrison, C., Dietz, P. and Wilson, A. Phone as a pixel: enabling ad-hoc, large-scale displays using mobile devices. In *Proc. CHI '12*. 2235-2238.

35. Seewoonauth, K., Rukzio, E., Hardy, R. and Holleis, P. Touch & connect and touch & select: interacting with a computer by touching it with a mobile phone. In *Proc. MobileHCI '09*. Article 36 , 9 pages.

36. Wang, J., Zhai, S. and Canny, J. Camera phone based motion sensing: interaction techniques, applications and performance study. In *Proc. UIST '06*. 101-110.

37. Wilson, A.D. and Sarin, R. BlueTable: connecting wireless mobile devices on interactive surfaces using vision-based handshaking. In *Proc. GI '07*. 119-125.

38. Woo, G., Lippman, A. and Raskar, R. VRCodes: Unobtrusive and active visual codes for interaction by exploiting rolling shutter. In *Proc. ISMAR '12*. 59-64.

39. Yee, K. Peephole displays: pen interaction on spatially aware handheld computers. In *Proc. CHI '03*. 1-8.

40. Yu, N., Chan, L., Lau, S. Y., Tsai, S., Hsiao, I., Tsai, D., Hsiao, F., Cheng, L., Chen, M., Huang, P. and Hung, Y. TUIC: enabling tangible interaction on capacitive multi-touch displays. In *Proc. CHI '11*. 2995-3004.

UI Testing Cross-Device Applications

Maria Husmann, Michael Spiegel, Alfonso Murolo, and Moira C. Norrie
Department of Computer Science, ETH Zurich
{husmann, murolo, norrie}@inf.ethz.ch, michael.spiegel@alumni.ethz.ch

ABSTRACT
The increasing number of devices available to a user has prompted the research community to explore how these can be used in combination. Frameworks and toolkits have been proposed to facilitate the design and implementation of these cross-device applications. Still, implementing cross-device applications remains complex because of the fragmentation of the user interface and logic across devices and the flexibility required to adapt to different combinations of devices. Testing in particular has been identified as a critical challenge. To address these issues, we introduce XD-Testing, a library that provides explicit and implicit device selectors, device templates and scenarios, as well as a visualiser for application screenshots. In a case study, we demonstrate how we used the library to author human-readable tests for a cross-device gallery that verify if a UI distributes correctly and if it works as expected *despite* being distributed.

Author Keywords
multi-device, distributed user interfaces; cross-device; ui testing; automated testing;

ACM Classification Keywords
H.5.2. Information Interfaces and Presentation : User Interfaces - Graphical user interfaces

INTRODUCTION
The number of computing devices available to a user has increased in recent years and now includes smartphones, smartwatches, smartTVs, tablets and even public screens. This move away from a single personal computer to an ecology of devices has prompted researchers to study how people currently use these in combination and how this combined use could be improved further [24]. To this end, a number of cross-device interaction techniques have been proposed (such as [19, 12]). Furthermore, applications that make use of and distribute their user interface (UI) across multiple devices have been implemented and studied. Proposed scenarios cover both single- and multi-user cases and range from travel planning [13, 7], (collaborative) sensemaking [10, 29], and interaction with geospatial data [27] to distributed video players and photo sharing [25].

ISS'16, November 06–09, 2016, Niagara Falls, ON, Canada

ACM 978-1-4503-4248-3/16/11...$15.00
DOI: **http://dx.doi.org/10.1145/2992154.2992177**

Some multi-device systems have been built for a specific, ideal set of devices (such as a combination of tabletops and tablets), whereas others aim to adapt to the set of devices at hand [20]. While the first approach is better suited to relatively controlled environments such as smart rooms, the second one is better for supporting adhoc interaction where the set of available devices might not be known in advance. For example, a system designed to include a tabletop might be hard to use when there is not one available, while a more flexible system could assign the role that the tabletop had to another device such as a tablet. Zagermann et al. have shown in [31] that this can be done without incurring a performance penalty in a sensemaking task.

Building these flexible cross-device applications is complex. While the design, prototyping, and implementation stages are supported by various cross-device frameworks and toolkits, in contrast, testing remains largely unaddressed. However, it has been identified recently as a critical challenge in the development of multi-device experiences [6]. Existing testing tools have not been built with cross-device applications in mind and offer limited support for their inherent challenges. These challenges include the large space of possible device combinations that could be used, in particular in multi-user scenarios. Testing all of them manually and repeatedly would be tedious. However, omitting tests for the sake of convenience could lead to regressions in later iterations. Another obstacle to testing is the fragmentation of the application across multiple devices. An interaction on one device can have an effect on another device and, given the flexibility of the application, it can be hard to predict in advance which device that will be as it could depend on the set of devices currently in use.

Given that testing is an integral part of established software engineering practice, we consider this lack of support of testing an obstacle to the wider dissemination of cross-device applications. To tackle this obstacle, we have created XD-Testing, a library for automated testing of web-based cross-device applications that makes the following contributions.

- A domain specific language for addressing devices in cross-device settings implicitly and explicitly, thus reducing the impact of the fragmentation on writing tests.
- Support for configuration and execution of tests with different sets of devices, which can be either crafted by the tester or generated by our system.
- Recording screenshots and visualising the application at critical checkpoints defined by the tester, allowing the comparison of behaviour on different sets of devices.

The rest of the paper is structured as follows. We first review related work on cross-device development and testing. We then introduce a motivating example to discuss the challenges particular to cross-device testing. Next we introduce our testing library and give a brief description of its architecture and implementation. Then, we report on the evaluation of the library in a case study with a cross-device application. We conclude with a discussion of the limitations and directions for future work.

BACKGROUND

Our research builds on two areas of related work: cross-device development and software testing. To understand the challenges associated with testing cross-device applications, we first introduce how these are built by discussing relevant cross-device frameworks and existing tools. Then we provide background on software testing with a focus on testing user interfaces.

Cross-Device Frameworks and Tools

Applications that distribute their interfaces across multiple devices have a long tradition in ubiquitous computing research (for example [28]). The more recent proliferation of internet-connected consumer devices such as tablets and smartphones has renewed interest in the topic (for example [9]). At the same time, increasingly powerful web technologies (such as WebSockets) have made the web a promising platform for building cross-device applications, eliminating the need to write separate code for each operating system and providing a lightweight delivery mechanism via URLs.

A new generation of frameworks and toolkits [16, 1, 25] has tapped into the potential of the web and provides abstractions for building cross-device applications. These frameworks typically provide concepts for connecting devices to form a group, specifying how the user interface should be distributed across them and keeping the application state synchronised among the devices. Some [23, 18, 4, 26] also abstract away sensors and provide higher-level proxemic and context information. For specifying the UI distribution, different approaches can be observed. Connichiwa [25] and Weave [4] provide an *event-based* mechanism to imperatively show and hide content on devices upon connection or disconnection of other devices. In contrast, Panelrama [30] allows developers to declare *affinity scores* for parts of the UI (panels) which the system uses to automatically assign that panel to a suitable device. For example, a video panel would be distributed to a device with a large screen, while a control panel would be distributed to one that is ready to hand. A third approach is to distribute the UI based on a more general model of *context rules* [8]. A context rule consists of a trigger and an action that will be executed upon the trigger. Proposed trigger dimensions are the device, the user, and the environment as well as social information, whereas actions include showing and hiding UI elements on specified devices.

Despite these mechanisms, it can be challenging for a developer to predict how the UI will be distributed given a set of devices. With *event-based* approaches, the distribution may depend on past interactions and the order that events (such as devices connecting) are received. To alleviate this issue, Weave was complemented with DemoScript [5] which generates previews of the step-by-step execution of the program. However, it assumes a given set of devices and cannot contrast how program execution may differ depending on the set of available devices. Using Panelrama, developers struggled with choosing suitable *affinity scores* and this prompted the authors to build a preview tool. Finally, a large set of *context rules* could make it challenging to understand which rules would be applied, possibly at the same time, and what the combined application of multiple rules would produce.

Given these insecurities, we consider it crucial that developers can easily test their applications with different sets of devices and verify that the distribution is acceptable in each case. This has been addressed in part by tools that emulate devices and thus allow developers to work with devices that are not physically present. XDStudio [21] supports the developer in specifying distribution profiles and checking them on emulated devices. However, the focus is on the design phase and there is no easy way to repeatedly test different sets of devices. Similarly, WatchConnect can emulate smartwatches for prototyping cross-device interactions, but also has no support for automated testing. In contrast, XDSession [22] explicitly addresses testing and debugging. It supports the emulation of one device at a time and allows recorded interactions to be replayed. Switching between different sets of devices is thus labour intensive and no automation is provided beyond the replay mechanism. The first issue has been addressed by XDTools [14] that allows sets of devices to be named, stored, and reloaded. However, XDTools focuses on manual testing and debugging rather than providing a mechanism for specifying formal tests and automating their execution.

Testing

Software testing can be executed at different levels of granularity and with different levels of coupling with the software being tested. On one end of the granularity spectrum are unit tests that verify isolated program behaviour at the smallest level of the system decomposition (such as single functions and classes) [2]. At the other end, there is system testing. A specific part of the latter, namely UI testing, also referred to as end-to-end testing, focuses on a whole, integrated system mimicking real-world interactions with the user interface.

UI testing also has less coupling with the underlying code, realising a black-box testing approach which focuses on the expected input/output behaviour of the system. Conversely, white-box testing approaches focus on the internal structure of the components, aiming at testing every possible state and interaction between the system components [2].

Unit tests do not suffer much from the fragmentation and distribution in cross-device applications, as they operate in isolation and at a high level of granularity and the behaviour under test would typically be executed on a single device. However, UI testing is highly impacted by the fact the application is distributed across multiple devices which need to be coordinated during testing. For example, input on one device can trigger output on another device. Thus in this paper, we focus our research on UI testing.

For UI testing, two main approaches can be observed [17]. Interactions with the UI can be recorded and replayed (for example as in Selenium[1] for browsers) or interactions can be scripted by the tester and executed by an automation tool. While the second approach requires more time from the developer to carefully craft the interactions, it is easier to adapt the scripts when the software changes [3], while recordings need to be re-captured if the changes are significant. A previous study [17] on web applications found that the scripted approach can cumulatively become less expensive than the record and replay already after one to three releases. These results show that the higher costs of scripting the test cases for UI testing can be quickly amortised with reduced costs of test maintenance in subsequent releases.

Cross-device applications typically aim to support a diverse set of devices, including tablets or phones, while they are often developed on desktop or notebook computers with larger screens. The challenges of testing mobile devices have been addressed by Testdroid [15], which allows testers to record scripts and replay them on multiple devices in parallel or alternatively on an emulated mobile device. Hesenius et al. [11] also provide support for testing on mobile devices with an extension to the test automation framework Calabash[2] for gesture-based interaction. However, coordination among the devices is considered in neither work and hence they are not adequate for cross-device testing.

MOTIVATING EXAMPLE

Two properties of cross-device applications introduce challenges into the testing process when compared to single-device applications: First, the fragmentation of the application across multiple devices, and second, the flexibility of the system to adapt to different device sets.

To illustrate these challenges we will use the example of a cross-device video player, similar to the one used in Panelrama [30]. The player consists of the actual video, a set of controls, and a search interface that lists videos matching a query. An example test for such a player could be to ensure that, when a video is selected from the list of search results, it will be displayed.

```
client
  .click('li=My Video')
  .getText('#title')
  .then(function(value) {
    assert(value === 'My Video');
    // true
  });
```

Listing 1: A simple test case that checks if a user clicks on a video in a list that the title of the video is displayed.

Listing 1 gives a simplified version of how such a test could be written. First, a click on the list element is triggered, then an assertion checks if the title element associated with the video shows the correct text. The example test will work fine, if both the search results and the video are on the same device. However, it cannot handle the case where these two elements are distributed across multiple devices. As a next step, the tester could script a test that contains two devices and explicitly test that particular case. They would need to pair the devices first, then the list item should be clicked on the device that shows the search. Identifying that device may not be trivial, as it can depend on properties of the device itself (such as its screen size), the other devices, or the context in general. Finally the tester needs to ensure that the title element is only checked after the changes have been propagated to the second device. In addition to the increased effort compared to writing the single-device test case, this would only test one particular combination of devices. However, selecting a video from the search results should *always* update the title, independent of how the UI is distributed and the number and type of devices involved. Existing testing libraries offer no constructs tailored towards expressing such tests that *implicitly* assume a distributed user interface and that could be written once and then be executed parametrised with different sets of devices.

While abstracting away the distribution of the UI could facilitate writing tests such as the one outlined above, addressing it *explicitly* would allow the developer to verify that the UI is distributed as expected. While cross-device applications often aim at supporting a diverse set of devices, they could still be tailored to support some combinations especially well. In the case of the video player, these could include {phone, TV}, {phone, tablet, TV}, {phone, phone, phone, TV}, and {phone, tablet}. An application could be tested with these combinations explicitly, similar to the way responsive web applications are typically tested on phones, tablets, and desktop PCs. As discussed in the previous section, it can be challenging for a developer to predict how the UI would be distributed across a given set of devices. Tweaking an affinity score or adding a context rule that attempts to cover one set of devices could influence the distribution of the UI on another set. Having this covered by an automated test spares the developer from having to test these distributions manually and can avoid regressions. A test for a cross-device application could also specify properties of a distribution that should always hold. For example, if a phone is among the devices, it should show the controls, and similarly, a TV should show the video. Also, each important part of the UI (the video, the search, and the controls in our example) should always be allocated to at least one device. Crafting tests of this kind with existing tools requires a lot of effort from the developer. They need to manually create a representation of each device in their test, connect all the devices to each other, ensure that state synchronisations are awaited and keep track of all devices in each individual test.

Finally, even if a tester carefully crafts tests for some combinations of devices, they would only test the device combinations they expected. While these are certainly important to test, it can be challenging for a developer to predict what devices might be used to access an application. The space of potential device combinations is huge, and continually evolving,

[1] **http://www.seleniumhq.org/**
[2] **http://calaba.sh/**

Template property	Supported values
name	Strings
type	*"watch"*, *"phone"*, *"tablet"*, *"desktop"*
size	*"xsmall"*, *"small"*, *"medium"*, *"large"*
width	Positive integer
height	Positive integer
desiredCapabilities	Accepted by Selenium

Table 1: Properties and supported values of device templates.

so trying to cover any possible combination is challenging if not impossible.

XD-TESTING

To address the challenges introduced by the fragmentation and flexibility of cross-device applications, we introduce XD-Testing, a testing library tailored towards web-based cross-device applications. XD-Testing consists of three main components: a JavaScript API for defining and randomly generating device scenarios for parametrised testing, a DSL for explicit and implicit testing of distributed UIs, and a mechanism for recording and visualising program flow in cross-device applications. XD-Testing extends WebDriverIO[3] which provides programmatic commands to remote control browsers with Selenium.

Device Templates and Scenarios

We offer a mechanism to parametrise a cross-device test with a set of devices so that the same test can be executed with different sets of devices. To this end we introduce *device templates* and *device scenarios*. A device template represents a reusable description of a device. We define a device scenario as a set of devices that interact with each other. Device scenarios can be built by instantiating devices from templates.

```
{
    name: "Nexus 5",
    type: "phone",
    size: "small",
    width: 360,
    height: 640,
    desiredCapabilities: {browserName:
        "chrome"}
}
```

Listing 2: An example device template for a Nexus 5 phone.

Table 1 lists all supported properties and values of a template and Lst. 2 shows an example. Each device template contains a human-readable name, the device type, the device screen dimensions with the assigned screen size and the desired capabilities as required by Selenium. *Width* and *height* need to be specified in density-independent pixels (dp), a measurement that reflects the physical size of a device rather than the pixel density. XD-Testing comes with a set of 8 predefined templates, more can be added by the tester.

[3]http://webdriver.io/

A tester can either craft a scenario directly in JavaScript (Lst. 3) or load it from a configuration file. The second approach supports easier reuse of scenarios across multiple tests and even across different projects. XD-Testing includes a command line tool for generating device scenarios. The aim of the tool is to provide the tester with a wide range of (possibly unexpected) combinations of devices but also to lessen the workload required for creating the scenarios. The tester can constrict the randomness to some extent by limiting the maximum number of devices per scenario and restricting their properties (as defined in the templates) to a given subset (for example to *small* and *medium* devices). Furthermore, the output is human-readable and can be edited by the tester.

```
1  var scenario = {
2    ctr: xdt.templates.devices.nexus4(),
3    dA: xdt.templates.large.nexus10(),
4    dB: xdt.templates.desktops.chrome()
5  };
6
7  xdTesting.multiremote(scenario).init()
8      // Load url on all devices
9      .url("http://myapp.com")
10     .click("button");
```

Listing 3: Creating a device scenario ad-hoc through JavaScript: Templates can be accessed from a general set (line 2) or by characterisation such as size (line 3) or type (line 4). A test is parametrised with the scenario (line 7) so that all following steps (line 9 and 10) are executed on the chosen devices.

Domain Specific Language

XD-Testing features a domain specific language providing a clear and concise syntax for testing cross-device applications. The DSL supports method chaining which means that each method returns an object that again can receive a method call. This allows several methods to be chained together and results in shorter code. Furthermore, the DSL abstracts away asynchronism, thus making it easier to read and write tests.

The main goal of our DSL is to facilitate the coordination of multiple devices when authoring tests. While our foundation, WebdriverIO, includes basic functionality to simultaneously control multiple browsers, it is restricted to either broadcast commands to all browsers or pick a single browser by its identifier. With XD-Testing, we introduce novel device selectors allowing a developer to choose a device subset explicitly or implicitly based on criteria such as device identifier, type, display size and accessible application elements, while maintaining readability and syntax consistency. Matching devices are passed to a callback function which executes clearly separated from the initial device set. Commands within the callback context are only executed on the selected device subset. The commands following the selection address the initial device set and are executed after the previous actions on the device selection are finished, allowing a test to leave a selected device subset and continue on the original set. Device selections can also be nested and support step-wise narrowing of the device specifications by combining several criteria, for example by first selecting devices by element and then restricting the resulting set to tablets only.

Explicit Device Selection

Explicit device selection is based on static device characteristics as defined in the device templates and on dynamic properties evaluated at run-time. This type of selection is used to explicitly choose a set of devices and address them with commands. The library provides several selector commands with different selection criteria. Supported criteria are the characteristics defined in the device scenario, such as device id, type and size, and the element selector (Table 2). The element selector matches all devices where a given HTML element is visible. These device selectors create a set of devices that consists of zero or more matching devices. Furthermore there is the `selectAny` command which selects a single arbitrary device or throws an error when called on an empty set. This is useful to ensure that only a single device is chosen. Nesting the *any* selection into another selection allows the tester to choose a single device from a set of devices which already matches certain criteria. Listing 4 illustrates this use case: first a button is clicked on all tablet devices, then it is clicked on just a single tablet device.

Command	Criteria Category	Criterion
selectById *selectBySize* *selectByType*	Device characteristic	One or multiple device Ids One or multiple screen sizes One or multiple device types
selectByElement *selectAny*	Dynamic	A element selector None, arbitrarily chosen

Table 2: Explicit device selection commands.

```
1 .selectByType("tablet", tablets =>
    tablets
2   .click("button")
3   .selectAny(device => device
4     .click("button")
5   )
6 );
```

Listing 4: First, all tablets are selected with a *type* selector (line 1), then the selection is constrained to a single device with the *any* selector (line 3).

Explicit device selection commands accept a second callback to address the *complementary device set*. This allows the original device set to be split into two subsets using the specified criterion. The first callback provides the devices matching the criterion (for example all tablets), while the second callback is applied to the complementary device set (the original device set minus all tablets). The complementary callback can be useful in combination with the `selectAny` command. In this case, the second callback returns all devices except the one returned in the first callback. This allows a developer to execute an action on one device and check results on all other devices. Listing 5 provides an example of use of the complementary callback with our video player example. If multiple devices show the controls, the state of the play/-pause button should be consistent across all of them. This can be tested by selecting all devices that have controls (line 1) and then picking a single one (line 2 and 3) and clicking the play button (line 4) on the selected device. The complimentary callback (lines 5 to 7) waits for all other devices that have controls to update their play button to display the text *Pause* and the test will fail if any device does not comply within the given timeout.

```
1 .selectByElement("#controls",
    controller => controller
2   .selectAny(
3     one => one
4       .click("#play"),
5     rest => rest
6       .waitForVisible("#play=Pause",
          2000)
7   )
8 );
```

Listing 5: Example usage of the complementary device set.

Implicit Device Selection

Implicit device selection handles cross-device behaviour of the application in an abstract way. It considers the distributed UI in its entirety by removing the need to address specific devices and instead it dynamically chooses the appropriate devices for each command. The test developer does not need to specify on which device the command should be executed. Instead, the system analyses the command and finds devices that can execute it. For example, if a command states that a specific UI element should be clicked, the system will find the devices that show the specified element and execute the command only on these devices. The semantics for implicit device selection are defined as follows:

- `implicitAll`: The system ensures that each command is executed on *at least one* device. Each command is guaranteed to be executed on all devices that match the selector given in a command.
- `implicitAny`: The system ensures that each command is executed on *exactly one* device. While `selectAny` chooses a device and then tries to execute all commands on the same device, `implicitAny` chooses a suitable device for each command.

In both case, the library throws an error, if no device is matched. Using our motivating example, we outline the differences in the semantics. Listing 6 uses the `implicitAny` and Lst. 7 the `implicitAll` selector. The `implicitAny` example first looks for a device that has the list item with the text *My Video*. It will click that item on exactly one device (or throw an error if there is no such device). Then it will select any single device that has the title element and check that the text matches *My Video*. The main difference of the `implicitAll` example compared to the `implicitAny` example is that each command will be executed on all devices that match the selector in the command, potentially resulting in multiple clicks. As each command could be executed on multiple devices, we cannot assume a single return value for commands that provide a result (such as `getText`). In our example, multiple devices could show the title element and all of them need to be checked. This is is done in lines 5 to 6 of Lst. 7 by accessing the `arguments` property of the function. The two selectors could also be combined to first click the list item on exactly one device and then verify that the title is correct on all devices that have the title element.

```
.implicitAny(device => device
  .click('li=My Video')
  .getText('#title')
  .then(function(value) {
    assert(value === 'My Video');
  }));
```

Listing 6: A simple test case using the `implicitAny` selector. Each command is executed on exactly one device.

```
1 .implicitAll(device => device
2   .click('li=My Video')
3   .getText('#title')
4   .then(function() {
5     var values = Array.prototype.slice
        .call(arguments);
6     values.forEach(value => assert(
        value === 'My Video'))
7   }));
```

Listing 7: A simple test case using the `implicitAll` selector. Each command is executed on one or more devices.

Device Set Commands

The XD-Testing library provides additional commands that provide control of the devices:

- `getCount` returns the number of devices contained in the device set.
- `forEach` provides access to each individual device in a set and accepts a callback with two parameters. The first parameter provides an individual device and allows the tester to execute commands on it. The second parameter gives a consecutive index for each device, i.e. the first device is identified by 0, the second by 1, etcetera.

Flow Recording and Visualisation

In addition to the formal testing that we address with the concepts introduced above, we also support more informal testing. We provide a visual representation of an application at interesting points in the execution. This allows a tester to visually verify the application behaviour. To this end, XD-Testing records the execution of each command on each device with a screenshot. We define a *flow* as the compound assembly containing information about the participating devices, the executed commands, and recorded screenshots.

Recording

Each library execution generates a flow and stores its JSON representation into a `.json` file. A flow file contains all necessary information about an execution and can be shared with other developers. The following commands are provided for flow recording.

- `name(name)`
- `checkpoint(name)`
- `addErrorCheckpoint()`

The `name` command is used to define a unique and human-readable name for each flow. It is used in the visualiser to identify flows. Developers can mark interesting points in the execution by defining a named checkpoint using the `checkpoint` command. While the checkpoint names for a single device need to be unique, different devices can use the same checkpoint name. Checkpoints with identical names will be grouped together across multiple devices in the visualisers. `addErrorCheckpoint` marks the flow as failed by adding an "ERROR" checkpoint with the remaining commands and screenshots. In addition to marking failures individually, this also allows a developer to add error checkpoints globally by creating a test hook that checks after each test if a failure has occurred (Lst. 8).

```
afterEach(function() {
  if (this.currentTest.state ==
      'failed') {
    return devices
      .addErrorCheckpoint()
  }
});
```

Listing 8: Adding error checkpoints globally.

Visualisation

XD-Testing provides a basic visualisation of recorded flows and allows the comparison of multiple flows side by side. The visualiser presents a list of all flows that are found in a specified directory. Flows that contain error checkpoints are marked visually. For a chosen flow, all checkpoints are listed and can be used to navigate through the flow. Optionally, all executed commands can be shown. Multiple flows can be displayed next to each other (Fig. 1), allowing the tester to visually compare flows. This could be useful for comparing the same interaction with different device scenarios or to identify visual regressions by comparing the same interaction with different versions of the code.

ARCHITECTURE AND IMPLEMENTATION

Since XD-Testing focuses on UI testing, its architecture has been conceived with the goal of controlling multiple browser instances at the same time, all of them running the client-side portion of the software under test (SUT). Figure 2 presents an overview of the architecture of the entire system.

XD-Testing is deployed as an NPM package running in Node.js[4] and it can execute the test case in a device scenario,

[4] **https://nodejs.org/en/**

Figure 1: Two flows being compared with the visualiser: The one on the left has been generated with a scenario consisting of a phone and a larger screen, the one on the right additionally contains a tablet.

Figure 2: Architecture of XD-Testing. On the left side, the Node.js server required to run XD-Testing; on the middle/right side, the integration with Selenium Server, its counterpart executing UI Testing through browser control.

coordinating the test-case steps across the different browsers. It is built on top of WebDriverIO, which can control any number of browser instances in a Selenium server by sending commands that follow the WebDriver protocol[5].

The Selenium server is able to process commands received through WebDriver to execute the corresponding operations on the browser instances. The connection between Selenium and each browser requires a separate driver for each browser type. For example, Chromedriver[6] is a driver that implements the WebDriver protocol, and is capable of controlling instances of Chrome. XD-Testing supports any browser in the device scenarios, as long as it can be managed through a Selenium server.

Browsers are the clients of a cross-device web application under test. They will be instantiated depending on the device scenario that has been specified for the test run; in addition, depending on the application and the device scenario, each browser may show similar or different user interfaces on which the test will be run.

XD-Testing extends the functionalities of WebDriverIO by adding the cross-device abstractions and introducing some additional tracking behaviour, which is required in implicit contexts and in screenshot generation. As an extension, XD-Testing can act as a replacement for WebDriverIO and is backwards compatible with it. This can be useful in a scenario in which a legacy application without cross-device features (which was tested with WebDriverIO) is extended with cross-device features. In this case, the developer only needs to replace the WebDriverIO object in their legacy test cases with the XD-Testing object, and then write new test cases that aim at supporting the new cross-device functionality.

The chosen architecture easily allows the integration of XD-Testing in more extensive and automated testing workflows, such as frameworks for test automation that can help systematically define test suites to be run repeatedly, for example for regression testing. In our case, we used Mocha[7] to define test suites written with XD-Testing, even those to validate XD-Testing itself. In addition to the definition of test suites, Mocha allows developers to attach hooks before and after individual test cases (or test suites) are executed. This can be used in combination with some useful interface abstractions that XD-Testing provides for the integration with test runners, such as a function to generate a checkpoint in the event that a test case in the runner has failed (see Lst. 8). Further interface abstractions allow the URL of the application under test to be globally set, or the length of timeouts to be waited when asserting effects of wait commands: for example, the test case in Lst. 9 would fail if no element with class `.controller` becomes visible within the specified timeout (line 19).

[5] **https://w3c.github.io/webdriver/webdriver-spec.html**

[6] **https://sites.google.com/a/chromium.org/chromedriver/**

[7] **http://mochajs.org/**

Since test runners like Mocha can be run from the command line, it is possible to create command-line scripts that perform automated regression testing on the SUT. These scripts are naturally suitable to be used in combination with a continuous integration system such as GitLab CI[8] or Travis CI[9]. XD-Testing itself has been tested throughout its versions in the GitLab continuous integration environment. A typical scenario of testing in continuous integration works as follows: once the developer commits a new version of the SUT, a command line script is automatically run to deploy the cross-device application (with all of its dependencies) on a testing system. Once the deployment is complete, the script can trigger the test runner, which in turn would start test cases written with XD-Testing.

Finally, while XD-Testing is framework-agnostic, it still supports the integration of specific application frameworks. The idea behind this is that sometimes it is critical to access abstractions and states of the development frameworks used in the SUT. For example, in cross-device applications it may be useful to query the number of connected devices, information usually contained in the internal state of the cross-device framework used for development.

For this reason, XD-Testing allows the definition of facades for individual frameworks that need to be accessed for testing purposes, in a way that their internal state can be accessed from within the test cases. It is even possible to define an adapter to group common functionalities of different frameworks (such as cross-device frameworks) behind a common interface, in such a way that different implementations can be dynamically switched if required. Currently, we have implemented a facade for a cross-device development framework that provides access to various functionalities, such as device pairing, querying connected devices, or handling events defined in the cross-device framework itself.

CASE STUDY

We used XD-Testing to test a cross-device gallery application. The gallery application consists of one controller and any number of viewer devices. The controller device presents a set of thumbnail images. Selecting an image on a controller device shows the image on a paired viewer devices. If more than one viewer is paired to a controller, it should show the subsequent image from the gallery. The controller role is dynamically assigned to the smallest device among the paired devices. In addition, if only a single device is present it will automatically assume both the viewer and controller roles, so that the application is always fully functional.

We have written a number of test cases using Mocha that verify this behaviour and present two of them in Lst. 9. The first one explicitly tests that the application is distributed correctly across devices, specifically it checks that the controller is on the smallest device for a given scenario. This is done by manually adding a phone and a desktop to a scenario (lines 2 to 4). The scenario is then loaded (line 5) and a function of the cross-device framework facade is called to pair the devices (line 6). Then the smaller device of the two is selected with an explicit selector (line 7) and finally the test waits 5 seconds for the controller to show up on the device (line 8). If it does not, the test fails.

The second test case handles the fragmentation implicitly. It checks that an image selected on the controller is always displayed on at least one device. This should hold across any given scenario, making this test suitable for testing with randomly generated scenarios. The scenarios are loaded from the configuration file and, for each scenario, the same test is executed (line 13). The devices are paired (line 16) and the state marked with a checkpoint for the flow recording (line 17). Then, an implicit block is started with the `implicitAny` selector (line 18) which ensures that the following commands are executed on exactly one device. As soon as the device shows the controller (line 19), the second image is clicked (line 20), and the test waits for a viewer to show the image (line 21) which is also recorded with a checkpoint (line 22). The flows generated by executing this test on two and three devices are displayed in the visualiser in Fig. 1.

The first test case benefits from the available device templates that make it easy to quickly instantiate a device with certain properties such as the screen size. It further demonstrates how a specific scenario can be tested with the provided explicit selectors. While the first test case is tailored to one specific scenario, it is relatively simple to add additional devices or exchange a device. The concept of a scenario combined with the device selectors eliminates the need to manually keep track of each device and reduces the required coordination.

The second test case would be even more challenging to write without XD-Testing. Writing this implicit test without the concepts from our DSL would mean that, for every command in the `implicitAny` block, the correct device needs to be identified first and the commands need to be properly synchronised to avoid checking the image before it has been selected. In addition to increasing the amount of code, this would impact readability. Using XD-Testing, the tester can focus on the behaviour while the device selection and synchronisation is handled by the library. Both test cases use the framework integration for pairing devices which facilitate the usage of this commonly used functionality and again makes the tests more concise.

In addition to the two test cases presented here, we have authored tests for checking if additional viewers show subsequent images, if this behaviour also works in corner cases (for example selecting the last image in the list with multiple viewers present), and tests that check the application behaviour when devices connect or disconnect from each other.

Students from our web engineering class had to implement a slightly simplified version of this cross-device gallery as a graded exercise. After they had received the grades, we asked for volunteers to submit their code to us for testing. Our test cases correctly identified issues, mostly related to redistributing the images correctly when devices disconnect.

[8] `https://about.gitlab.com/gitlab-ci/`

[9] `https://travis-ci.org/`

```
1  it('should show controller on the smallest device', () => {
2    let deviceSet = {
3      A: xdTesting.templates.devices.nexus4(),
4      B: xdTesting.templates.devices.chrome() };
5    return devices = xdTesting.multiremote(deviceSet).init()
6      .app().pairDevicesViaURL(baseUrl)
7      .selectBySize('xsmall', small => small
8        .waitForVisible('.controller', 5000)
9      )
10     .end()
11 });
12
13 xdTesting.loadScenarios().forEach(scenario => {
14   it('should show selected image', () => {
15     return devices = xdTesting.multiremote(scenario.devices).init()
16       .app().pairDevicesViaURL(baseUrl)
17       .checkpoint('paired')
18       .implicitAny(device => device
19         .waitForVisible('.controller', 5000)
20         .click('.controller img:nth-of-type(2)')
21         .waitForVisible('.viewer img[src="img/album/large/02.jpg"]', 3000)
22         .checkpoint('image clicked')
23       )
24   })
25 });
```

Listing 9: The first test (line 1 to 11) checks that the controller is displayed on the smallest device. The second one (line 13 to 25) checks if an image selected on a controller is displayed on a viewer device.

DISCUSSION

While our case study demonstrated the benefits of the concepts of XD-Testing, it also demonstrated some of its limitations and directions for future work. First, the explicit selectors are limited to a subset of device properties and only allow selection by one property at a time (such as size). While different types of selectors can be combined via nesting, another option could be to explore a query language for devices which would allow more expressive selectors, for example, *select the smallest device with a keyboard.*

In our case study, we only executed our tests on emulated devices and mainly focused on screen size as the main differentiator. However, there are other factors that could impact a test and thus testing on real devices with different hardware also has its merits. As XD-Testing builds on the standardised WebDriver protocol, it also allows tests to be executed on real devices and could even be used in combination with services like BrowserStack[10] or SauceLabs[11] that offer device farms as a service.

Finally, our visualiser has been optimised for comparing two flows at a time. While it is possible to display more than that, our experience showed that this risks visual overload. However, we would expect a tester to verify more than two scenarios. Visually comparing many different device scenarios at the same time remains a challenge and more options how this could best be presented to the tester need to be explored.

CONCLUSION

We have presented XD-Testing, a library for testing web-based cross-device applications. Our overall aim was to reduce the impact of the fragmentation and address the complexity stemming from the flexibility that is typically present in cross-device applications. To this end, we have introduced concepts for implicitly and explicitly selecting devices and allow tests to be parametrised by device scenarios, which can be randomly generated with our tool. Finally, we provided an option to record and visualise the application flow for informal checks. XD-Testing is lightweight and does not constrain a tester to a particular test runner or cross-device framework. To benefit other researchers and practitioners, we have made it available on NPM[12] and its source code has been released on GitHub[13].

Acknowledgements

This project was supported by grant No. 150189 of the Swiss National Science Foundation (SNF). We would like to thank all our web engineering students who have submitted their code for testing XD-Testing.

[10] **https://www.browserstack.com/**

[11] **https://saucelabs.com/**

[12] **https://www.npmjs.com/package/xd-testing**

[13] **https://github.com/mhusm/xd-testing**

REFERENCES

1. Badam, S. K., and Elmqvist, N. PolyChrome: A Cross-Device Framework for Collaborative Web Visualization. In *Proc. ITS* (2014).
2. Bruegge, B., and Dutoit, A. H. *Object-Oriented Software Engineering Using UML, Patterns and Java.* Prentice Hall, 2004.
3. Bruns, A., Kornstadt, A., and Wichmann, D. Web Application Tests with Selenium. *IEEE Software 26*, 5 (2009).
4. Chi, P. P., and Li, Y. Weave: Scripting Cross-Device Wearable Interaction. In *Proc. CHI* (2015).
5. Chi, P. P., Li, Y., and Hartmann, B. Enhancing Cross-Device Interaction Scripting with Interactive Illustrations. In *Proc. CHI* (2016).
6. Dong, T., Churchill, E. F., and Nichols, J. Understanding the Challenges of Designing and Developing Multi-Device Experiences. In *Proc. DIS* (2016).
7. Geronimo, L. D., Husmann, M., and Norrie, M. C. Surveying Personal Device Ecosystems with Cross-Device Applications in Mind. In *Proc. PerDis* (2016).
8. Ghiani, G., Manca, M., and Paternò, F. Authoring Context-dependent Cross-device User Interfaces Based on Trigger/Action Rules. In *Proc. MUM* (2015).
9. Gjerlufsen, T., Klokmose, C. N., Eagan, J., Pillias, C., and Beaudouin-Lafon, M. Shared Substance: Developing Flexible Multi-Surface Applications. In *Proc. CHI* (2011).
10. Hamilton, P., and Wigdor, D. J. Conductor: Enabling and Understanding Cross-Device Interaction. In *Proc. CHI* (2014).
11. Hesenius, M., Griebe, T., Gries, S., and Gruhn, V. Automating UI Tests for Mobile Applications with Formal Gesture Descriptions. In *Proc. MobileHCI* (2014).
12. Houben, S., Tell, P., and Bardram, J. E. ActivitySpace: Managing Device Ecologies in an Activity-Centric Configuration Space. In *Proc. ITS* (2014).
13. Husmann, M., Geronimo, L. D., and Norrie, M. C. XD-Bike: A Cross-Device Repository of Mountain Biking Routes. In *ICWE Workshops* (2016).
14. Husmann, M., Heyder, N., and Norrie, M. C. Is a Framework Enough? Cross-Device Testing and Debugging. In *Proc. EICS* (2016).
15. Kaasila, J., Ferreira, D., Kostakos, V., and Ojala, T. Testdroid: Automated Remote UI Testing on Android. In *Proc. MUM* (2012).
16. Klokmose, C. N., Eagan, J., Baader, S., Mackay, W., and Beaudouin-Lafon, M. Webstrates: Shareable Dynamic Media. In *Proc. UIST* (2015).
17. Leotta, M., Clerissi, D., Ricca, F., and Tonellla, P. Capture-Replay vs. Programmable Web Testing: an Empirical Assessment During Test Case Evolution. In *Proc. WCRE* (2013).
18. Marquardt, N., Diaz-Marino, R., Boring, S., and Greenberg, S. The Proximity Toolkit: Prototyping Proxemic Interactions in Ubiquitous Computing Ecologies. In *Proc. UIST* (2011).
19. Marquardt, N., Hinckley, K., and Greenberg, S. Cross-Device Interaction via Micro-Mobility and F-Formations. In *Proc. UIST* (2012).
20. Mikkonen, T., Systä, K., and Pautasso, C. Towards Liquid Web Applications. In *Proc. ICWE* (2015).
21. Nebeling, M., Husmann, M., and Norrie, M. C. Interactive Development of Cross-Device User Interfaces. In *Proc. CHI* (2014).
22. Nebeling, M., Husmann, M., Zimmerli, C., Valente, G., and Norrie, M. C. XDSession: Integrated Development and Testing of Cross-Device Applications. In *Proc. EICS* (2015).
23. Rädle, R., Jetter, H.-C., Marquardt, N., Reiterer, H., and Rogers, Y. HuddleLamp: Spatially-Aware Mobile Displays for Ad-hoc Around-the-Table Collaboration. In *Proc. ITS* (2014).
24. Santosa, S., and Wigdor, D. A Field Study of Multi-Device Workflows in Distributed Workspaces. In *Proc. UbiComp* (2013).
25. Schreiner, M., Rädle, R., Jetter, H., and Reiterer, H. Connichiwa: A Framework for Cross-Device Web Applications. In *Proc. CHI EA* (2015).
26. Seyed, T., Azazi, A., Chan, E., Wang, Y., and Maurer, F. SoD-Toolkit: A Toolkit for Interactively Prototyping and Developing Multi-Sensor, Multi-Device Environments. In *Proc. ITS* (2015).
27. Shakeri Hossein Abad, Z., Anslow, C., and Maurer, F. Multi Surface Interactions with Geospatial Data: A Systematic Review. In *Proc. ITS* (2014).
28. Streitz, N. A., Geissler, J., Holmer, T., Konomi, S., Müller-Tomfelde, C., Reischl, W., Rexroth, P., Seitz, P., and Steinmetz, R. i-land: An interactive landscape for creativity and innovation. In *Proc. CHI* (1999).
29. Wozniak, P., Goyal, N., Kucharski, P., Lischke, L., Mayer, S., and Fjeld, M. RAMPARTS: Supporting Sensemaking with Spatially-Aware Mobile Interactions. In *Proc. CHI* (2016).
30. Yang, J., and Wigdor, D. Panelrama: Enabling Easy Specification of Cross-Device Web Applications. In *Proc. CHI* (2014).
31. Zagermann, J., Pfeil, U., Rädle, R., Jetter, H.-C., Klokmose, C., and Reiterer, H. When Tablets Meet Tabletops: The Effect of Tabletop Size on Around-the-Table Collaboration with Personal Tablets. In *Proc. CHI* (2016).

LayerFish: Bimanual Layering with a Fisheye In-Place

Andrew M. Webb[1], Andruid Kerne[1], Zach Brown[1], Jun-Hyun Kim[2], Elizabeth Kellogg[1]
[1]Interface Ecology Lab, Deptartment of Computer Science and Engineering
[2]Department of Landscape Architecture and Urban Planning
Texas A&M University, College Station, Texas, United States
{andrew, andruid, zach, elizabeth}@ecologylab.net, jhkim@arch.tamu.edu

ABSTRACT

We introduce, LayerFish, a bimanual interaction technique for layering overlapping content in large 2D design spaces. Designers compose visual elements, often producing overlap and requiring layering in the z-dimension. A common approach in design tools is to provide a scene index, as an ordered list of layered elements. Scene indexes become difficult, in terms of physical effort and human cognition, to deal with when working with hundreds of elements. LayerFish renders an in-place scene index as a fisheye to reduce demands on effort and attention. Bimanual gestures support selection, scrolling, and manipulation. We evaluated layering task performance with LayerFish in comparison to a traditional scene index. Findings indicate that the fisheye reduces time to find an element and selection reduces layering time when elements do not heavily overlap.

Author Keywords

visual design; scene index; pen+touch; bimanual interaction

ACM Classification Keywords

H.5.2. Information Interfaces and Presentation: User Interfaces - Graphical User Interfaces

INTRODUCTION

Designers work with many visual elements, from 10s to 100s, in large 2D spaces. Elements overlap, requiring reordering of the visual stack, or *layering*, to place some elements in front of or behind others. As the number of overlapping elements increases in scale, the complexity of layering also increases. This requires more expressive forms of interaction than the common "bring to front" and "send to back" contextual menu options provided in tools such as Powerpoint.

Design tools, such as Adobe Illustrator, support complex layering through a *scene index*—an ordered list showing the visual stacking order of elements. Each element in the 2D design space is represented in the scene index by a *correspondent* thumbnail. Correspondents can be reordered to adjust the visual stacking of elements. They can also be selected

ISS'16, November 6–9, 2016, Niagara Falls, ON, Canada.

ACM ISBN 978-1-4503-4248-3/16/11 ...$15.00
DOI: http://dx.doi.org/10.1145/2992154.2992171

Figure 1. Example of bimanual interaction in LayerFish. The left hand touch has a correspondent selected and held in place, while the right hand drags to scroll the fisheye scene index.

to constrain direct manipulation to only corresponding elements, even those occluded by other elements. As the number of elements increases, the scene index must afford scrolling. Scrolling becomes tedious when working with hundreds of elements. Further, the index is often located out of the user's visual focus, requiring her to split attention between the design space and the index.

Prior work developed alternative techniques that provide *in-place* layering, addressing the split attention shortcomings of the scene index [11, 19]. However, these techniques are designed for working with a small number of elements, and will not scale well in design spaces with hundreds of elements.

LayerFish is a pen+touch interaction technique to support layering and manipulating overlapping content in a 2D design space on desktop and large collaborative surfaces (see Figure 1). LayerFish addresses issues of scene index scale and split attention through a fisheye visualization [6] and in-place positioning of the scene index at the user's point of focus. The fisheye distorts the visual space, decreasing the sizes of correspondents away from a focus element, and so enables more to be visible than a typical scene index. However, interaction issues arise, as the spatial distortion disrupts layering and scrolling operations. We develop bimanual techniques to address these issues, which keep the focus element fixed while the scene index reorders layers and scrolls. We hypothesize that the fisheye will reduce time to find desired correspondents, since the spatial distortion would help scrolling over large distances.

This paper begins with a discussion of prior work. Next, we present LayerFish. We follow with an evaluation comparing performance of LayerFish—when working with a large number of elements—to a traditional scene index. We discuss findings and derive implications for design.

RELATED WORK

Various layering techniques exist. Commercial design tools typically use either pop-up menus or scene indexes. HCI researchers have developed alternatives, investigating how spatial arrangement [19, 7, 10, 17] and sensing modalities [4, 11] can support interacting with dense and occluded content.

Commercial Design Tools

Many commercial design tools employ a contextual menu (e.g. Microsoft Powerpoint). The contextual menu includes several commands, not all of which are for accessing occluded content. In mouse-based interfaces, the contextual menu is activated by right clicking an element. The user must navigate a hierarchical menu and find the command to bring an element forward or backward. In touch-based interfaces, the contextual menu is activated by touching an element. Commands appear in a menu bar. The contextual menu approach requires the user to perform input on an element, which may be occluded, making it challenging to activate.

Alternatively, a scene index provides an ordered list of visual layers, which can be rearranged to adjust the z-ordering of elements. As the number of layers grows, the index becomes large. It can become difficult to find a layer. Thumbnails for each layer are used to support recognition. The thumbnails are all the same size, making it difficult to differentiate similar elements of different sizes [19]. LayerFish addresses issues of scale through a fisheye visualization and user selection.

HCI Researchers

Ramos et al. explored techniques that maintain the shape and size of elements, while creating spatial separation between layers, enabling novice users to interact with occluded content [19]. LayerFish addresses issues of scale while also maintaining element shape.

Herrlich et al. developed a touch technique for selecting occluded content [10]. The user resolves selection ambiguity by touching proxies arranged radially around the point of interaction. Handle Flags is an in-place technique for selecting overlapping ink strokes without complex lasso selections [7]. For LayerFish, ther user needs to not only select the element to be layered, but also nearby element(s) that it will be layered above or below. Therefore, we use lasso for selecting a region rather than one of these precise selection approaches.

Pen and multi-touch sensing technologies support additional input parameters that can be used to access and manipulate occluded content. Davidson and Han used touch pressure and points of contact to define layering gestures [4]. Hinckley et al. combined touch to select an element with pen tilt to reveal occluded elements [11]. These techniques are designed for working with a few overlapping elements.

Leithinger and Haller address occlusion issues of context menus on cluttered tabletops through user-drawn arrangements of menu items [17]. LayerFish's in-place scene index raises occlusion issues that could be mitigated through user-drawn arrangement. However, new interaction issues arise as scrolling the scene index and re-ordering correspondents involves two dimensions instead of one.

LAYERFISH

LayerFish is a bimanual interaction technique designed for desktop and large surfaces, including tabletops, where both hands are free to interact on the surface. We found, through discussions with visual designers, that these form-factors are commonly used when working with many layers. Smaller form factors are also used, but tended to involve fewer layers.

The LayerFish technique consists of a selection and activation gesture, a fisheye scene index, and interactions for layering elements and manipulating occluded content. For brevity and simplicity, we will describe our technique in terms of a right-handed user, where the *right* hand is their *preferred* hand and the *left* hand is their *non-preferred* hand. For left-handed users, interactions with LayerFish are mirrored, so that roles of preferred and non-preferred hand are consistent.

Selection and Activation

Using LayerFish begins with selecting elements on which to operate, followed by an activation gesture. Selection specifies the elements active in LayerFish. Unlike a traditional scene index that contains all elements, selection enables the user to work with a subset of elements, and so addresses scaling issues for human attention. To distinguish between normal selection for manipulating a group of elements versus selection for LayerFish, we use an activation gesture. LayerFish supports two bimanual input modalities for selection and activation, pen+touch and multi-touch.

Pen+Touch

When using the pen, LayerFish supports lasso selection of elements. LayerFish is activated with a Lasso'n'Cross gesture [1]. A lasso selection with the pen is followed by a vertical slash across the center of the circled selection (see Figure 2). We adhere to Hinckley et al.'s recommendation that the pen by itself creates ink, but when combined with touch performs alternative operations [12]. In order to use the pen as a selection tool, a modifier is needed. We provide an edge-constrained chorded gesture area for the left hand, called the *Hotpad*. Edge-constrained gestures with the non-preferred hand support efficient modal switching [9]. The Hotpad appears in the bottom corner on the left-hand side. Holding one finger down on the Hotpad modifies the pen to function as a lasso selection tool. After the user performs a Lasso'n'Cross gesture with a vertical slice, LayerFish's fisheye scene index appears adjacent to the bounding box of the selection area.

Multi-touch

Touch input is less precise than pen due to the fat finger problem [13]. We suspected this imprecision would make lasso

Figure 2. While holding a left-hand touch on the Hotpad, the user performs a Lasso'n'Cross gesture with a pen, selecting elements with a lasso, followed by a vertical slash to activate LayerFish.

Figure 3. Example of fisheye scene index in LayerFish. The focus of the fisheye is on the correspondent of the woman in a coat. Correspondents get smaller in size further from the focus.

selection involving dense overlapping content difficult with touch. We instead support rectangular selection with touch. Again, a left hand touch on the HotPad defines right-hand actions as selection. With a right-hand touch, the user drags a rectangular selection area that defines what elements LayerFish will select. Once the desired selection area is defined, with the left hand touch still down, the user lifts up the right hand and makes a vertical slash through the rectangular selection. The slash activates LayerFish's fisheye scene index with the elements within the selection bounds.

Fisheye Scene Index of Layered Elements

Upon activation, correspondents, representing the subset of selected elements, appear in an ordered list. Correspondents are ordered from top-most selected element to bottom-most.

Fisheye Visualization

A fisheye visualization is used to represent the list of correspondents (see Figure 3). Fisheyes are a focus+context technique that use spatial distortion to give larger visual emphasize to a focus while providing a smaller peripheral view of contextual details. In the case of LayerFish, the fisheye allows the user to see more correspondents at once than with a traditional scene index. The spatial distortion also makes the effect of scrolling non-linear, enabling direct-touch scrolling over larger distances than with a traditional scene index.

The fisheye visualization defines a focus, initially the top correspondent in LayerFish. The focus is given a fixed size (120 x 80 pixels at 94 dpi). Correspondents get progressively smaller as you move away from the focus. Pressing down with pen or touch on a correspondent makes it the focus of the fisheye. Through pen or touch drags, the scene index is scrolled, keeping the focus positioned under the drag input.

LayerFish supports inertial scrolling, a common technique used in touch interfaces for browsing large lists. With a quick flick, the fisheye scrolls based upon the velocity and direction of the flick, decelerating with time. We employ a form of speed-coupled flattening during inertial scrolling to address target acquisition issues [8]. That is, when the velocity of inertial scrolling exceeds a threshold, we flatten the fisheye scene index, making all correspondents equal in size. As the velocity falls back below the threshold, we redraw the fisheye with a focus on the top-most or bottom-most visible correspondent in the direction of the scroll.

Layering Interactions

The user adjusts an element's position in the visual stack by first selecting and then dragging and dropping, with pen or touch, its correspondent up or down the scene index. A correspondent is selected by briefly pressing down on it. The selected correspondent enlarges slightly, giving the effect of popping out of LayerFish. A rectangular placeholder highlights the current position of a selected correspondent in the scene index (Figure 4). As the selected correspondent is dragged up or down, the placeholder moves up and down the list accordingly, swapping positions with correspondents. The fisheye redraws, maintaining focus on the placeholder. When the user drops the selected correspondent, it is placed back in the scene index in the position of the placeholder.

Bimanual Scrolling

Drag and drop layering only supports layering above or below what is currently visible in the fisheye. As user the drags a selected correspondent, the focus changes, providing less space to visualize correspondents in the direction of the drag. To overcome this issue, the user can scroll the scene index without changing the focus, using a bimanual gesture. With a correspondent selected using the right hand, the user can drag the scene index using the left hand, causing the fisheye to scroll. The selected correspondent remains fixed below the right hand, while its position in the scene index changes as correspondents above or below it are scrolled up or down.

Figure 4. The correspondent for the woman in a coat is selected. A gray rectangle indicates the current position of the selected correspondent in the scene index. A rectangular outline in the design space shows the location of the element represented by the selected correspondent, even though the element is hidden behind the beige wall (the correspondent directly above in the scene index).

The user can scroll the fisheye scene index at a faster rate by dragging up or down with a left hand touch, beyond the bounds of LayerFish. This initiates automatic scrolling. The further away from LayerFish that the user drags the left hand touch, the faster the automatic scrolling happens.

EVALUATION DESIGN

To evaluate the effectiveness of LayerFish for adjusting the visual stacking order of overlapping content, we designed a repeated measures (within-subjects) evaluation comparing LayerFish with a traditional scene index, which we call *Sidebar*. We compare differences in task time between LayerFish and Sidebar. We vary several independent variables, including the number of elements and overlap density, to investigate in which situations LayerFish performs better than Sidebar.

Apparatus

The study apparatus consisted of a pre-questionnaire, two tutorial videos, 12 training tasks, and 48 study tasks. Participants began by answering the pre-questionnaire, which collected demographic information and details about their experiences using visual design tools and layering. Then, a tutorial video explained the task that participants would perform and demonstrated how to use either LayerFish or Sidebar. Next, participants performed 6 training tasks, followed by 24 study tasks using either LayerFish or Sidebar, depending on which tutorial video was shown. After completing the tasks, a second tutorial video demonstrated how to use the other technique, either LayerFish or Sidebar, that the participant had not yet used. Again, the participants performed 6 training tasks, followed by 24 study tasks. The study concluded with a post-questionnaire. Study sessions lasted approximately 30 minutes. Participants were given a $15 Amazon gift card.

Task

Each task consisted of a visual arrangement of overlapping elements (see Figures 6 and 7). Each element was a dancing figure from the artworks of Keith Haring [5], providing playfully engaging visuals with low complexity. The number of elements and how much they overlap was specified by independent variables (see *Independent Variables* section). The objective of each task was to layer a *task element* so that it resides between two goal elements in the z-dimension. The task and goal elements were uniquely colored with special fill patterns to make them easily distinguishable from the other elements (see Figure 5). The two goal elements always resided near the top of the visual stack, while the goal element resided near the middle or bottom. Performing a task consisted of three stages: (1) accessing the layering technique; (2) finding the task element; and (3) layering the task element between the two goal elements.

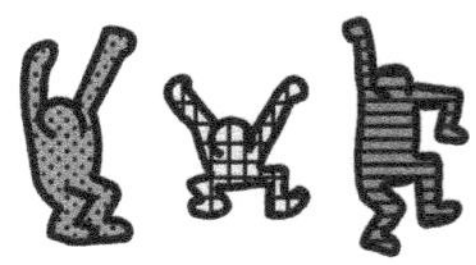

Figure 5. Yellow-gridded task element in the center, and two goal state elements (blue-dotted and red-striped) on left and right.

Sidebar

Sidebar represents a typical scene index used in visual design tools. In the study, Sidebar appears on the preferred hand side of the screen and contains correspondents for all elements (see Figure 6). Using a single touch drag, Sidebar is scrolled. The participant adjusts the layering of an element by dragging out the correspondent horizontally. The correspondent is removed from the scene index and appears under the participants dragging touch. Dragging the correspondent above or below the presented scene index will cause scroll the scene index in the dragged direction, beyond the initially visible subset of elements. Dropping the dragged correspondent back onto the scene index enables the participant to layer an element higher or lower in the visual stack. Dropping the correspondent outside the scene index cancels the operation, returning the correspondent to its original position.

Hardware Setup

The study workstation consisted of a Windows 8.1 PC with an Intel i7-5960X processor, 16GB RAM, and an NVIDIA GeForce GTX 680 Ti graphics card. Pen and touch input was supported through a Wacom Cintiq 24HD Touch display (1920 x 1200 pixels). Two cameras, one overhead and one on the right, captured participants' gestural interactions.

Independent Variables

Tasks involved 4 independent variables: Technique, Overlap Density, Number of Elements, and Layering Distance.

Technique

Technique was either LayerFish or Sidebar.

Overlap Density

Overlap Density is either *Low* or *High*. For Low Overlap Density, the task and goal elements only overlap with a few other elements (see Figure 7). This represents common layering tasks, such as when designing slides for a Powerpoint presentation. For High Overlap Density, all elements overlap. This represents the worst possible case for layering tasks.

Figure 6. Study task example with Sidebar and Low Overlap Density.

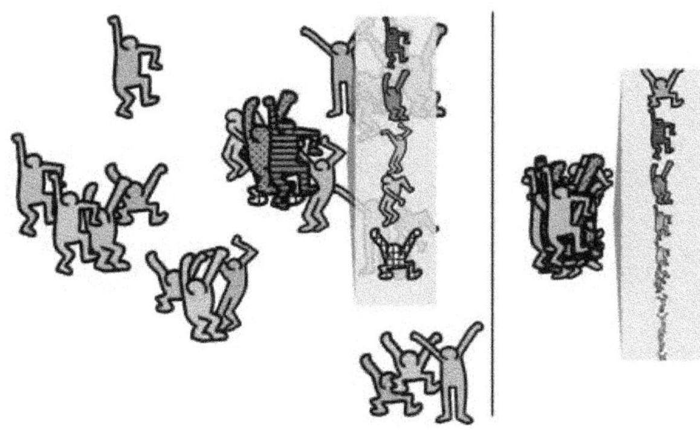

Figure 7. Low Overlap vs. High Overlap Density with LayerFish.

High Overlap Density focuses investigation on how LayerFish's fisheye visualization compares with a traditional scene index when the numbers of correspondents are the same. In Low Overlap Density tasks, LayerFish can be used to select a subset of elements. In High Overlap Density tasks, all elements overlap, so the user is unable to select a subset using LayerFish. As a result, both techniques present an equal number of correspondents, where the primary difference is how the correspondents are presented, either with fisheye or in a traditional scene index.

Number of Elements

The Number of Elements is either *25* or *100*. Through informal needs and requirements gathering sessions, Landscape Architecture students reported often creating design representations with around 100 layers. In the most extreme cases, all these layers overlapped. Thus, the condition with 100 elements and High overlap, represents a worst possible case scenario. While, 25 elements and High overlap represents the more common problematic scenario. One of our principle hypotheses is that LayerFish will scale better than Sidebar, as the number of elements increases.

Layering Distance (Relative)

Relative Layering Distance is the number of elements between the task element and the two goal elements at the start of the task. We use two possibilities for Layering Distance, *Medium* and *Far*. The absolute magnitude of these distances, in elements, varies directly with the Number of Elements. When Number of Elements is *25*, *Medium* is 7 and *Far* is 19. When Number of Elements is *100*, *Medium* is 44 and *Far* is 94. We vary Layering Distances so that participants do not know where the task element is located in each trial. Using two fixed distances for each Number of Elements reduces variability, and so facilitates comparison across techniques.

Tasks: Independent Variable Conditions

The 4 independent variables, each with 2 levels, produce 16 different conditions. Participants performed a total of 60 tasks, of which 12 were training and 48 were timed trials. For the timed trials, each condition was performed by each participant 3 times ($16 \times 3 = 48$).

Dependent Variables: Time Metrics

Layering tasks with scene indexes involve first finding a desired correspondent, and then adjusting that correspondent's position in the scene index. We wondered how a fisheye scene index would compare with a traditional scene index for this components of a layering task. Thus, we derive three time metrics for analyzing participants performance: Total Task Time, Find Time, and Layering Time. *Total Task Time* measures how long it took participants to perform the task in entirety. *Find Time* measures how long it took participants to find the task element that must be layered. Find Time is calculated as the time between the first touch down on the scene index (to scroll) to the first touch down on the task element. *Layering Time* measures how long it took participants upon finding the task element to reorder it to the goal state. Layering Time is calculated as the time after selection until the task element is positioned between the two goal elements.

We note that Find Time + Layering Time ≠ Total Task Time. Total Task Time includes additional time for selecting and activating LayerFish and for accessing Sidebar. We do not include a separate comparison of this additional time since LayerFish is expected to always be slower, because selection and activation requires a longer input sequence than the single touch required for accessing Sidebar.

PARTICIPANTS AND RESULTS

We recruited 47 participants (12 female) between 19 and 33 years old (22 mean). Participants were university students, primarily from Computer Science. We specifically invited participants from design-centric courses in Computer Science and Landscape Architecture to recruit participants with extensive experience working with layers. A majority (37) had worked with design tools at least once. Before investigating with expert visual designers, we sought to evaluate LayerFish with a more accessible population, as an intial usability study. Future work will examine expert visual designers.

We conducted a 2 (Technique) x 2 (Overlap Density) x 2 (Number of Elements) x 2 (Layering Distance) x 3 (trials) repeated measures analysis of variance (RM-ANOVA) on Total Task Time, Find Time, and Layering Time metrics for *All Participants*, the set of 47 participants. We performed pairwise comparison for each condition (see Table 1). Further, we examine a subset of All Participants identified as Experienced Layering Participants. We observe no order effects. Since a task was only completed when the task element was layered between the two goal elements, there is no measure

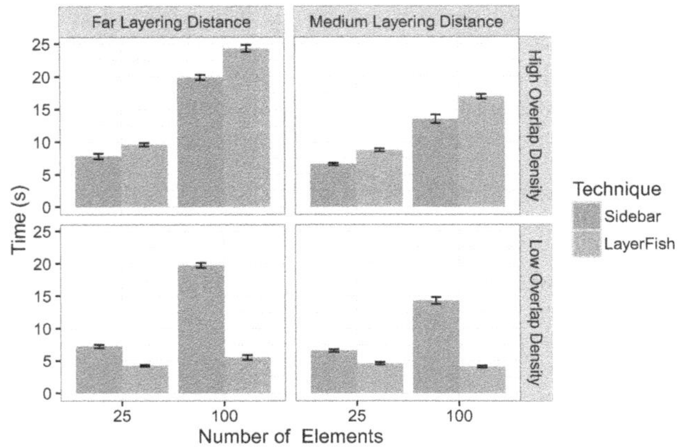

Figure 8. Mean Total Task Time for All Participants.

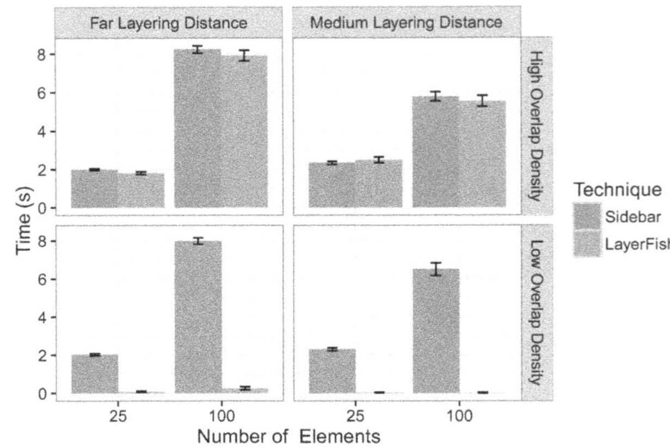

Figure 10. Mean Find Time for All Participants.

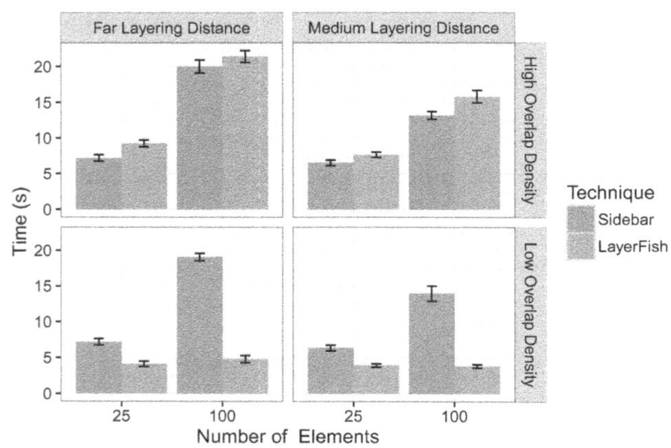

Figure 9. Mean Total Task Time for Experienced Layering Participants.

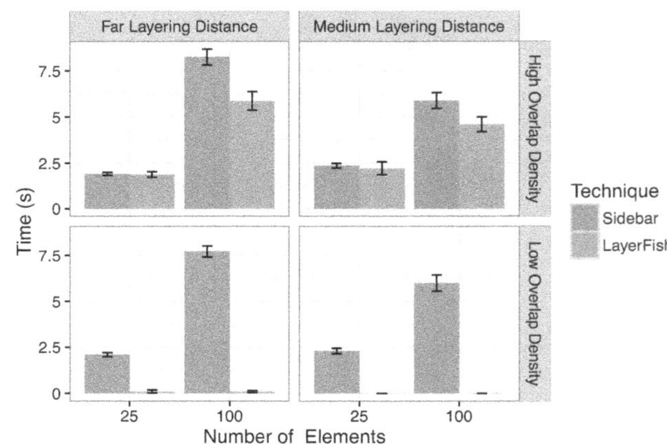

Figure 11. Mean Find Time for Experienced Layering Participants.

of errors. A post-questionnaire provides subjective experience report data.

Experienced Layering Participants

Through observations of participants during study sessions and variances in the data, we suspected that the participants more experienced with layering would performed tasks faster. From the All Participants set, we identify 12 Experienced Layering Participants based upon responses to two questions in the pre-questionnaires:

- How often do you use visual design tools?
- On average, how many layers do your projects contain?

These 12 participants responded that they often or frequently use visual design tools and typically work with at least 10 layers. The other 37 participants rarely used visual design tools, and on average, worked with 5 or less layers. For each time metric, we specifically compare times for these experienced users between the two techniques.

Total Task Time: All Participants

Total Task Time begins when a participant first touches and ends when the task is completed correctly. For LayerFish, this includes selection and activation time. Total Task Time using LayerFish was less than Sidebar with Low Overlap Density, but greater than with High Overlap Density (see Figure 8). Differences in means were statistically significant in all conditions (Table 1, A1-8). We observed a main effect for each independent variable: Technique ($F_{1,34} = 95.862$, $p < 0.001$), Overlap Density ($F_{1,34} = 918.01$, $p < 0.001$), Number of Elements ($F_{1,34} = 1938.316$, $p < 0.001$), and Layering Distance ($F_{1,34} = 154.541$, $p < 0.001$).

Total Task Time: Experienced Layer Participants

Experienced Layering Participants were on average faster for Total Task Time when compared with All Participants, particularly for LayerFish. In Low Overlap tasks, these participants were faster with LayerFish (see Figure 9). In High Overlap tasks, these participants were faster with Sidebar, but only some cases were statistically significant (Table 1, E6 and E7).

Find Time: All Participants

In Low Overlap Density tasks, participants were faster at finding the task element with LayerFish (Figure 10, Table 1 A1-4). In High Overlap Density tasks, participants averaged faster Find Time with LayerFish in most conditions. These results were statistically significant when Layering Distance is Far (Table 1, A6 and A8). We observed a main effect

Table 1. Pairwise comparison of Total Task Time, Find Time, and Layering Time between the two Techniques for each combination of Overlap Density, Number of Elements, Layering Distance. Rows A1-A8 (white background) show mean times with statistical significance for All Participants. Rows E1-E8 (gray background) show mean times with statistical significance for Experienced Layering Participants, a subset of All Participants.

				Total Task Time (s)			*Find Time (s)*			*Layering Time (s)*		
	Overlap Density	**Number of Elements**	**Layer-ing Distance**	**Layer Fish**	**Side-bar**	*p <* / *F =*	**Layer Fish**	**Side-bar**	*p <* / *F =*	**Layer Fish**	**Side-bar**	*p <* / *F =*
A1	Low	25	Medium	4.6	6.5	.001 / *98.5*	.036	2.3	.001 / *810.8*	1.61	4.22	.001 / *145.7*
E1	Low	25	Medium	4.01	6.35	.001 / *25.44*	0	2.1	.001 / *187.3*	1.08	4.00	.001 / *60.62*
A2	Low	25	Far	4.2	7.2	.001 / *53.7*	.081	2.03	.001 / *1036*	1.48	5.21	.001 / *189.8*
E2	Low	25	Far	4.12	7.18	.001 / *28.42*	0	2.09	.001 / *155.6*	1.14	5.10	.001 / *69.75*
A3	Low	100	Medium	4.1	14.3	.001 / *283*	.03	6.5	.001 / *397.1*	1.43	7.79	.001 / *163.7*
E3	Low	100	Medium	3.84	14.39	.001 / *71.66*	.03	5.43	.001 / *201.8*	1.03	8.03	.001 / *59.55*
A4	Low	100	Far	5.5	19.7	.001 / *797*	.10	7.98	.001 / *1858*	2.23	11.75	.001 / *556.1*
E4	Low	100	Far	4.80	19.16	.001 / *388.8*	.07	7.38	.001 / *437.6*	1.24	11.36	.001 / *414.7*
A5	High	25	Medium	8.7	6.6	.001 / *50.2*	2.33	2.34	.97 / *.002*	3.77	4.25	.20 / *5.07*
E5	High	25	Medium	7.6	6.54	.10 / *3.25*	2.2	2.35	.65 / *.212*	3.22	4.19	.05 / *3.63*
A6	High	25	Far	9.6	7.8	.01 / *7.51*	1.8	2.0	.02 / *5.67*	5.10	5.83	.11 / *2.59*
E6	High	25	Far	9.28	7.23	.001 / *25.44*	1.9	1.9	.83 / *.05*	3.97	5.34	.047 / *4.15*
A7	High	100	Medium	16.9	12.9	.001 / *20.2*	5.53	5.71	.54 / *.39*	8.41	7.16	.24 / *1.44*
E7	High	100	Medium	15.6	13.17	.05 / *4.22*	4.6	5.9	.10 / *2.49*	7.12	7.5	.70 / *.209*
A8	High	100	Far	23.2	19.9	.001 / *23.3*	7.46	8.22	.03 / *4.1*	13.39	11.64	.044 / *4.10*
E8	High	100	Far	21.39	20.0	.50 / *.477*	5.86	8.25	.017 / *6.18*	12. 69	11.78	.61 / *.268*

for all factors: Technique ($F_{1,34}$ = 1412.692, $p < 0.001$), Overlap Density ($F_{1,34}$ = 416.6, $p < 0.001$), Number of Elements ($F_{1,34}$ = 1175.654, $p < 0.001$), and Layering Distance ($F_{1,34}$ = 31.753, $p < 0.001$).

In Low Overlap Density tasks, Find Time for LayerFish can be zero seconds (Table 1, A1-4, E1-4). Find Time is intended to measure the scrolling time required to find the task element. Find Time is measured as the time between the first touch down within a technique and the first touch down on the task element. With LayerFish, these two touches may be the same touch, as selection allows the participant to see the task element without scrolling.

Find Time: Experienced Layering Participants

The Experienced Layering Participants were faster at finding the task element on average using LayerFish than Sidebar (see Figure 11). This result was statistically significant for all Low Overlap Density tasks and when Number of Elements was 100 and Layering Distance was Bottom for High Overlap Density tasks (Table 1, E1-4, E8). These participants also were on average faster at finding the task element than the average for All Participants.

Layering Time: All Participants

Layering Time measures long it takes to adjust the visual stack position of the task element so that it is between the two goal elements. The metric is derived by calculating the

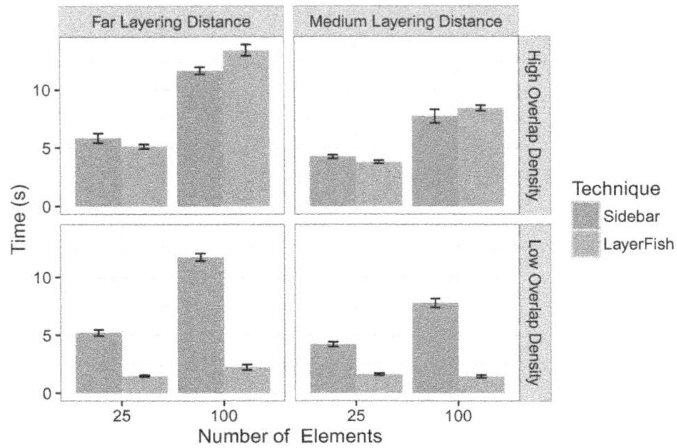

Figure 12. Mean Layering Time for All Participants.

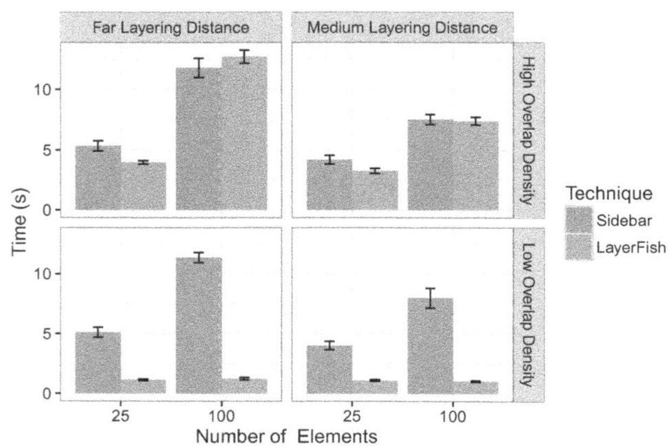

Figure 13. Mean Layering Time for Experienced Layering Participants.

difference in time between the selection of the task element and the finishing of the task. In Low Overlap Density tasks, participants had faster Layering Times when using LayerFish (see Figure 12). This result is statistically significant for all Low Overlap Density tasks (Table 1, A1-4). In High Overlap Density tasks, participants were faster with LayerFish when the Number of Elements was 25, but slower with LayerFish when the Number of Elements was 100. This result was statistically significant only in tasks with 100 elements and the Layering Distance is Far (Table 1, A8). We observed a main effect for all factors: Technique ($F_{1,34} = 247.403$, $p < 0.001$), Overlap Density ($F_{1,34} = 471.168$, $p < 0.001$), Number of Elements ($F_{1,34} = 1105.93$, $p < 0.001$), and Layering Distance ($F_{1,34} = 140.914$, $p < 0.001$).

Layering Time: Experienced Layering Participants

Experienced Layering Participants had faster Layering Times for Low Overlap Density tasks when using LayerFish (Figure 13). These results were statistically significant (Table 1, A1-4). In High Overlap Density tasks, these participants were faster with LayerFish in all cases, except when the Number of Elements was 100 and the Layering Distance was Far (E8). The results were statistically significant only when the Number of Elements was 25 (E5-6).

Experience Reports

Post-questionnaire responses provide reports of subjective experiences (see Figure 14). A majority of participants agreed that LayerFish was easy to use ($\chi^2 = 30.13$, $p < 0.001$), and they felt faster with LayerFish for both a few elements ($\chi^2 = 21.62$, $p < 0.003$) and many elements ($\chi^2 = 10.55$, $p < 0.05$). Participants agreed that LayerFish required less effort with only a few elements ($\chi^2 = 9.49$, $p < 0.05$). However, with many elements, only a slight majority agreed that LayerFish required less effort. This result was not statistically significant ($\chi^2 = 6.94$, $p < 0.14$). Participants agreed that they would use LayerFish in visual design tools like Adobe Photoshop ($\chi^2 = 20.55$, $p < 0.004$).

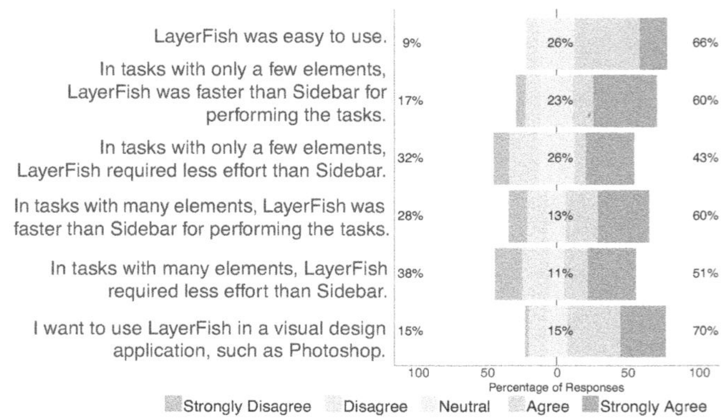

Figure 14. Results from post-questionnaire responses. Percentages show breakdowns participants' agreement (right), neutrality (middle), or disagreement (left) for each statement.

DISCUSSION

We hypothesized that our independent variables, which differentiate situations that users are likely to experience when working with overlapping content, would yield interesting findings. We observe significant differences between the two techniques for Overlap Density, Number of Elements, and Layering Distance. The most significant differences occur with Overlap Density. LayerFish was faster than Sidebar for Low Overlap tasks and slower in High Overlap tasks. We suspect that LayerFish requires additional learning time, as participants gain understanding of how interactions affect the fisheye representation. We also observed task performance differences for Experienced Layer Participants that indicate benefits of LayerFish for more expert users.

Low Overlap Density

In Low Overlap Density tasks, mean Total Task Time, Find Time, and Layering Time with LayerFish were all shorter than with Sidebar. Low Overlap Density means that the task element and goal elements only overlap with a few other elements. Selection in LayerFish allows the participant to engage only those few elements that overlap, unlike with Sidebar, where all elements are present in the scene index. Not surprisingly, this capability improves layering performance. After selection with LayerFish, the task element was immediately visible and could be quickly layered between the two goal elements, which were also visible. LayerFish does not require scrolling in this case, while Sidebar does.

LayerFish does not present a fisheye visualization in these low overlap tasks, instead using the common scene index representation. Ramos et al. suggested (but did not investigate) that an in-place scene index palette would improve layering times [19]. We have shown that this is true with at least 25 elements. We suspect that with fewer elements, the performance of a global scene index, like Sidebar, will be comparable to a contextual technique, like LayerFish. There exists a threshold in the number of elements, below which the selection and activation time for a contextual technique exceeds the time to move to the side to access a global technique.

High Overlap Density

We sought to understand the effects of the fisheye visualization on layering performance, by including a task condition, High Overlap, in which both LayerFish and Sidebar include a similar number of elements.

The Total Task Time results show that LayerFish is slower than Sidebar in high overlap tasks. LayerFish requires a selection gesture to activate. High Overlap tasks require that participants select (nearly) all elements using LayerFish. In this case, the selection takes time but doesn't help the user. When we further breakdown task time, for Find Time, we find that LayerFish is faster than Sidebar when there are 100 elements and Layering Distance is Far (Table 1, A8, E8). We suspect the fisheye's spatial distortion allows participants to scroll longer distances in a single touch gesture. As Layering Distance increases, so too does the difference in Find Time between LayerFish and Sidebar.

Meanwhile, for Layering Time with All Participants, LayerFish was slower when Number of Elements was 100 and Layering Distance was Far (Table 1, A8). When we look just at Experienced Layering Participants, LayerFish was faster when the Number of Elements was 25 (E5-6). We observe a larger variance in Layering Times when Layering Distance is Far, particularly for LayerFish. Bimanual scrolling was new to participants. We suspect that it may require more training for users to become comfortable at using it effectively.

Experienced Layer Participants

We observe a difference in the performance of the Experienced Layering Participants. Using LayerFish, these participants were faster than the average for All Participants. Yet, while using Sidebar, they performed, on average, similarly to All Participants. These performance differences for LayerFish are most evident in the Find Time metric with High Overlap tasks, particularly with 100 elements. In these cases, Experienced Layering Participants' mean Find Time is almost two seconds faster than the mean time for All Participants. The faster performance exhibited by Experienced Layering Particpants with LayerFish indicates that LayerFish has performance benefits for visual designers and others who work with many layers of overlapping elements. These participants seem more adept at learning to use LayerFish effectively. Novice layer users may also see improved performance with greater training and experience with layering.

The other significant difference was in Layering Time for High Overlap tasks with 25 elements. In these tasks, Experienced Layering Participants were faster using LayerFish than Sidebar. This matches the observed results for All Participants, except that, unlike for all, the differences for Experienced Layering Participants are statistically significant. All participants used bimanual scrolling in LayerFish to complete tasks with dense overlap. Again, bimanual scrolling is a new interaction, different from what participants are use to doing with touch devices. These results indicate that Experienced Layering Participants were among the quickest to learn how to effectively use the technique, emphasizing the benefits of LayerFish for visual designers who work with many layers.

Participant Experiences

Participants reported positive experiences using LayerFish. Interestingly, despite that participants were actually slower (in Total Task Time) using LayerFish with many elements, many participants felt that they were faster. When we exclude selection time for LayerFish, most participants were faster using LayerFish. This may have been part of participants' consideration when responding. Participants were not in agreement that LayerFish requires less effort than Sidebar when working with many elements. Since LayerFish requires additional touches for selection and bimanual scrolling, it is not surprising that participants felt it didn't require less effort.

IMPLICATIONS FOR DESIGN

We use the findings from the evaluation to derive implications for the design of pen+touch and multi-touch design tools that support layering operations.

Design tools with a scene index would benefit from transitioning to a fisheye visualization as the number of elements in the design space grows large. We saw benefits with LayerFish when the design space contained at least 25 elements, even when all elements overlapped. LayerFish was faster than Sidebar for Find Time in High Overlap tasks when Layering Distance was Far. We suspect that the spatial distortion of the fisheye allowed users to scroll longer distances more quickly. Prior work has used semantic zooming [18] as a form of spatial scaling to support speed-dependent scrolling rates in document browsing tasks [15]. We have shown that a fisheye view, as an alternate form of spatial scaling, can also improve scrolling performance in layering tasks with a scene index.

Design tools should support both in-place (i.e. LayerFish) and always-present (i.e. Sidebar) techniques for layering overlapping content. As the number of elements in a design grows large, the traditional scene index requires more effort and attention to effectively layer elements. An in-place technique, which enables selection to filter elements the user wishes to layer, can improve layering task performance time. However, when there are many elements that highly overlap, the user is unable to effectively select only the desired elements, reducing the benefits of selection. Additionally, when there are only a few elements, all are directly visible in the scene index, and scrolling is not required. In these cases, we recommend a traditional scene index that transitions to a fisheye when the number of elements grows large (at least 25).

Multi-touch scene indexes should support bimanual scrolling, particularly for tools in which users typically create 10 or more layers. Bimanual interactions have been shown to improve performance of compound tasks, in which each hand can adjust different parameters of interaction [16]. In LayerFish, the right hand layers a selected correspondent, while the left hand scrolls the fisheye scene index. Unimanual approaches require dragging the selected correspondent to the top or bottom of the scene index, requiring more total touch distance travel than with our bimanual technique.

ACKNOWLEDGEMENTS

This material is based upon work supported by the National Science Foundation, under grant IIS-1247126, and Wacom Technology Corporation. Any opinions, findings, and conclusions expressed in this material are those of the authors and do not reflect the views of the NSF or Wacom.

CONCLUSION

We present LayerFish, a new bimanual interaction technique for layering overlapping content. With a bimanual gesture, the user selects a subset of elements within a larger design space. When filtering out elements with selection, layering operations take less time than with a traditional scene index. A fisheye scene index increases the number of visible correspondents, while reducing time to find a desired element. Bimanual scrolling allows a selected correspondent, manipulated with the right hand, to remain as the focus of the fisheye while the left hand scrolls the view.

We apply a fisheye visualization to a traditional scene index. Prior work has investigated various advantages and disadvantages of fisheyes in numerous contexts [3]. Our findings show that fisheyes can be faster for finding the desired correspondent in a large scene index. One of the primary challenges with fisheyes is target acquisition, since targets are continuously moving due to changes in the fisheye focus. One solution is to use speed-coupled flattening to remove the fisheye effects as panning or scrolling velocities increase [8]. We employ speed-coupled flattening with inertial scrolling in LayerFish. For target acquisition with hierarchical structures of text, Fisheye Menus [2] are slower than traditional hierarchical menus [14]. Our present investigation focuses on flat scene index structures with thumbnail images. Future work can investigate hierarchical scene indexes.

In order to focus investigation on layering performance, participants were not able to zoom and pan the design space. The High Density Overlap tasks where all elements overlap completely, while representing extreme scenarios, would gain little benefit from zooming and panning. However, we presently use LayerFish in a design environment with an infinite, zoomable canvas. Future work will look at how a zoomable space affects selection and layering performance with LayerFish.

Designers are accustomed to working with their hands. While working with physical media, visual designers generate new ideas by exploring different arrangements of elements, moving them around and sketching over and amidst these elements. Future work will investigate LayerFish in architecture contexts, where designers create complex visual representations with overlapping content. We hypothesize that visual designers would benefit from interactive tools that allow them to directly gesture with their hands to explore a space of ideas.

RIGHTS FOR FIGURES

REFERENCES

1. Agarawala, A., and Balakrishnan, R. Keepin' it real: Pushing the desktop metaphor with physics, piles and the pen. In *Proc. ACM CHI* (2006), 1283–1292.
2. Bederson, B. B. Fisheye menus. In *Proc. ACM UIST* (2000), 217–225.
3. Cockburn, A., Karlson, A., and Bederson, B. B. A review of overview+detail, zooming, and focus+context interfaces. *ACM Comput. Surv. 41*, 1 (Jan. 2009).
4. Davidson, P. L., and Han, J. Y. Extending 2d object arrangement with pressure-sensitive layering cues. In *Proc. ACM UIST* (2008), 87–90.
5. Deitch, J., Geiss, S., and Gruen, J. *Keith Haring*. Rizzoli International Publications, 2014.
6. Furnas, G. W. Generalized fisheye views. *SIGCHI Bull. 17*, 4 (Apr. 1986), 16–23.
7. Grossman, T., Baudisch, P., and Hinckley, K. Handle flags: Efficient and flexible selections for inking applications. In *Proc. Graphics Interface* (2009).
8. Gutwin, C. Improving focus targeting in interactive fisheye views. In *Proc. ACM CHI* (2002), 267–274.
9. Hamilton, W., Kerne, A., and Robbins, T. High-performance pen + touch modality interactions: A real-time strategy game esports context. In *Proc. ACM UIST* (2012), 309–318.
10. Herrlich, M., Walther-Franks, B., Schröder-Kroll, R., Holthusen, J., and Malaka, R. Proxy-based selection for occluded and dynamic objects. In *Proc. of International Conference on Smart Graphics* (2011), 142–145.
11. Hinckley, K., Chen, X. A., and Benko, H. Motion and context sensing techniques for pen computing. In *Proceedings of Graphics Interface 2013* (2013), 71–78.
12. Hinckley, K., Yatani, K., Pahud, M., Coddington, N., Rodenhouse, J., Wilson, A., Benko, H., and Buxton, B. Pen + touch = new tools. In *Proc. ACM UIST* (2010).
13. Holz, C., and Baudisch, P. Understanding touch. In *Proc. ACM CHI* (2011), 2501–2510.
14. Hornbæk, K., and Hertzum, M. Untangling the usability of fisheye menus. *ACM Trans. Comput.-Hum. Interact. 14*, 2 (Aug. 2007).
15. Igarashi, T., and Hinckley, K. Speed-dependent automatic zooming for browsing large documents. In *Proc. ACM UIST* (2000), 139–148.
16. Kabbash, P., Buxton, W., and Sellen, A. Two-handed input in a compound task. In *Proc. ACM CHI* (1994).
17. Leithinger, D., and Haller, M. Improving menu interaction for cluttered tabletop setups with user-drawn path menus. In *Proc. ACM Tabletop* (Oct 2007).
18. Perlin, K., and Fox, D. Pad: an alternative approach to the computer interface. In *Proc. SIGGRAPH* (1993).
19. Ramos, G., Robertson, G., Czerwinski, M., Tan, D., Baudisch, P., Hinckley, K., and Agrawala, M. Tumble! splat! helping users access and manipulate occluded content in 2d drawings. In *Proc. of ACM AVI* (2006).

Talaria: Continuous Drag & Drop on a Wall Display

Hanae Rateau
University of Lille Sci. & Tech, CNRS, INRIA
hanae.rateau@inria.fr

Yosra Rekik
University of Lille Sci. & Tech, CNRS, INRIA
yosra.rekik@inria.fr

Laurent Grisoni
University of Lille Sci. & Tech, CNRS, INRIA
laurent.grisoni@univ-lille1.fr

Joaquim Jorge
INESC-ID / IST / U Lisboa
jorgej@acm.org

ABSTRACT
We present an interaction technique combining tactile actions and Midair pointing to access out-of-reach content on large displays without the need to walk across the display. Users can start through a Touch gesture on the display surface and finish Midair by pointing to push content away or inversely to retrieve a content. The technique takes advantage of well-known semantics of pointing in human-to-human interaction. These, coupled with the semantics of proximal relations and deictic proxemics make the proposed technique very powerful as it leverages on well-understood human-human interaction modalities. Experimental results show this technique to outperform direct tactile interaction on dragging tasks. From our experience we derive four guidelines for interaction with large-scale displays.

Author Keywords
Large display surfaces; Mid-air pointing; Direct interaction; Tactile Interaction; continuous interaction.

ACM Classification Keywords
H.5.2. Information Interfaces and Presentation (e.g. HCI): User Interfaces

INTRODUCTION
Large tactile displays are becoming ever more functional and affordable. This makes them increasingly adopted for public installations [18,21], as well as in small and medium-scale collaborative settings for a variety of tasks [20]. This is because the large display surface makes large quantities of information readily and visually accessible and easy to manipulate in natural ways by small groups.

However, the basic interactions currently afforded by large tactile displays are mostly limited to direct interaction [9]. This leads to major issues when manipulating information on such surfaces, that have been well revealed in research literature: (1) reaching content beyond arms' length is not easy. Accessing corners requires people either to squat/lean forward or to stand on tiptoe. And moving beyond arms reach requires users to walk along the display; (2) Interacting with other users on the same display. Indeed, when interacting with content on the display, people nearby can get on the way.

To alleviate these issues, Forlines et al [9] proposed a direct interaction technique allowing users to switch between absolute and relative actions. However, relative mapping poses other problems such as clutching that might prove cumbersome on very large displays, including movement discontinuities when switching modes, or adding external devices such as a tablet [16] to control indirect activation.

We propose to keep continuous interaction active throughout an operation without requiring users to move when their physical limits are reached, in order to preserve the naturalness of direct interaction on large displays. This is because in human-to-human interaction, gestural pointing arises naturally as it is one of the first gestures learned in life to point at objects out of reach [11]. We introduce TALARIA to leverage on natural deictic human ability and the directness of tactile interaction.

TALARIA is an interaction technique combining Touch actions and Midair pointing that enables accessing unreachable content on a large touch display without resorting to walk alongside its surface. The core idea is to start a Touch gesture on the display surface and to finish it by Midair pointing to push content away or inversely to retrieve out-of-reach content. This has two key advantages. First the transition between Touch and Midair is continuous. Therefore, users do not have to explicitly switch between the two modalities. Second, the semantics of pointing are well understood in human-to-human interaction [8]. These, coupled with the semantics of proximal relations and deixis make the proposed technique very powerful as it leverages on well-understood human-human interaction modalities [11]. Indeed, our technique leverages on contextual information given by proximity relations to the display as well as explicit spatial relations afforded by deixis to provide implicit arguments to most commands [1].

The contributions of this work are thus: (1) we propose TALARIA, a novel technique for direct interaction on large displays, (2) our experiment compares the performance of TALARIA with direct Touch interaction through a dragging task, (3) we report novel findings about direct interaction on large displays, and finally, (4) we derive four guidelines for designing interaction techniques on large displays. We hope that TALARIA and our results will prove useful to designers and practitioners interested in large display designs.

RELATED WORK

In this section, we review previous work on Touch interaction on large displays. We also present hybrid interaction techniques where Touch and Midair interaction appear intermixed.

Touch Interaction on Large Displays

Touch interaction on large displays suffers from the size factor. Reaching a target on a large surface can be easy if the area is in the user's physical reach. However, acquiring it can be tiring if the target position is distant from one's current position. In this case, users have to walk/jump/bend down, and in some cases it can be impossible for them to reach the target if someone or something obstructs the movement (*e.g.*, other users) or the target is simply out of reach (*e.g.*, too high). This has led to orthogonal techniques being developed. For example, some have proposed to switch between absolute and relative interaction by counting the number of fingers in contact with a surface [16] or by using a paper sheet [22] or by directly emulating a pad when needed through a multi-touch gesture [10] or by clicking on a widget with a pen [9]. However, those techniques require explicit switching between distinct interaction modes which can be quite frustrating. Others advocated for providing users with a miniature desktop to directly bring distant objects within reach or dragging closed objects to distant targets [6,12] or temporarily bring distant targets within arms reach to interact with them [3]. However, those techniques did not allow users to explore and navigate the whole display and require knowledge about the objects of interest. In parallel, others have proposed to use direct pen gesture to throw objects on a distant target [19] or by using foot gestures to bring distant bottom objects instead of bending down to reach them with ones' hands [13]. However, those techniques only allowed users to coarsely push away objects or bring bottom objects within reach.

Hybrid interaction: touch and mid-air interaction

Several works proposed to mix Midair with Touch actions to enrich interaction. Specific approaches adopt Midair interaction for users situated far away from the display and Touch interaction for those close to the display [2,14,23]. Other methods adopt a vocabulary mixing Midair gestures and Touch input devices [5]. However, those techniques, do not support continuity in gestures when switching from one mode to another. To deal with this limitation, in TractorBeam [17], pen-based interaction is the same whether operating on screen or above the tabletop. The cursor is determined by a raycast of the pen on the tabletop for Touch and Midair interaction. In [7,15] authors have proposed to continue the interaction when switching from surface to Midair manipulations. The surface of a tabletop and the space above it are thus considered as a continuum. In this configuration, several gestures are proposed. In particular, *extended continuous gestures*. The gesture begins in a certain space and continues or finishes in another. The transition between Touch and Midair does not alter the current action avoiding discontinuities while affording a more fluid operation. TALARIA builds upon this previous work to insure continuous control of the cursor.

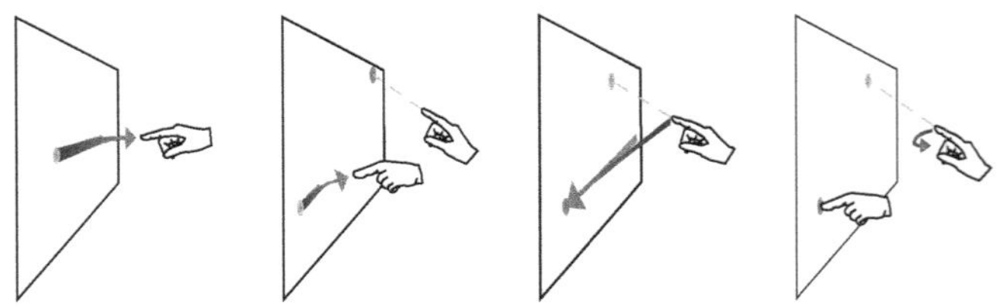

Figure 1: Push away ((a) one-handed and (b) two-handed) and retrieving ((c) one-handed and (d) two-handed) actions.

TALARIA DESIGN

TALARIA is designed to overcome the limitations of direct Touch interaction with large display surfaces. We were inspired by "Talaria", the winged sandals of Hermes that allowed to god to fly as a bird in Greek mythology. TALARIA allows one to reach past the boundaries of physical space and body abilities to enable two main actions: (1) pushing away an object and (2) retrieving a (possibly distant) object. In each interaction, we define two modalities: one-handed and two-handed.

In order to PUSH-AWAY an object when using the one-handed modality, users may start dragging the object by directly touching it and then continuously dragging the object when switching to Midair interaction (see Figure 1.a). We name the transition from Touch to Midair TAKE-OFF. To discriminate between TAKE-OFF and a finger release, we defined a velocity threshold. The velocity threshold was determined from preliminary tests conducted with three people. The threshold allows an effective discrimination between intended release and TAKE-OFF. When the finger is lifted off the display, if its velocity is above the threshold, then TAKE-OFF is activated and the object is then controlled in Midair. By doing so, TALARIA does not affect the standard Touch interaction. In both Touch and Midair modes, the mapping between the user's hand and the controlled object is absolute as we wanted to keep the directness of Touch interaction on large displays. In the two-handed modality, when users touch directly an object with their non-dominant hand (NDH) and then TAKE-OFF of the object while pointing at a display position with their dominant hand (DH) in Midair, the selected object is immediately dragged to the pointed-at position (see Figure 1.b).

As for retrieving objects, in the one-handed modality, the user has to select in Midair the object of interest, drag it in front of him/her and then touch it directly when the object is close to her/him (see Figure 1.c). Once in Touch interaction, the user can perform any standard Touch manipulation on the object. In the two-handed modality, when retrieving an object, users may select an object by pointing at it using their DH for example and then make a flick gesture with the DH while touching the display with their NDH, the selected object is immediately dragged to the touched position (see Figure 1.d).

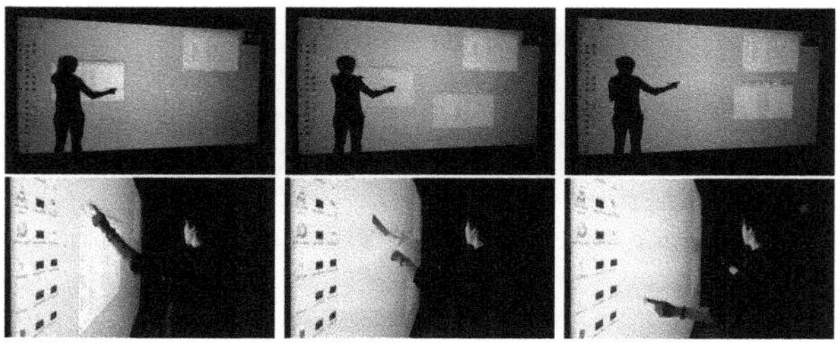

(a) (b) (c)

Figure 2: Two-Hand Push Away interaction example in use: (a) Touch the window with NDH while pointing at the screen, (b) Take-off happens; then the window moves to the pointed-at position, (c) Positioning the window and touching the screen to drop it.

Proof of concept. In order to test TALARIA in a real scenario, we simulate mouse input to integrate TALARIA in MS/Windows. We then added the two actions. As in Midair interaction, if we do not detect a click event then we generate a click event when pointing with one hand while the other hand is touching the display. By doing so, at the end of a PUSH-AWAY action, users have to click on the screen to drop the object being dragged (see Figure 2). Conversely, at the beginning of the RETRIEVING action, after pointing at an object, users should have to touch the screen to start dragging. Due to technical problems, we did not use the touch on the screen for the RETRIEVING but simply used the button of a mouse placed in the palm's hand. This way, users had a mean to click in Midair for the proof of concept. In the future, tapping the screen for selection should be done.

EXPERIMENT: DRAGGING AN OBJECT

We conducted an experiment to compare performance of TOUCH and TALARIA techniques. We hypothesize:

H1. The selection time will be lower for TALARIA than for TOUCH. Since, users can interact from the same place over all the task when using TALARIA.

H2. TALARIA will reduce dragging time compared to TOUCH. Since, contrary to TOUCH, users not have to move a lot when using TALARIA.

H3. TOUCH will be more accurate than TALARIA. The direct Touch interaction maximizes the opportunity to be the more accurate as Touch interaction is more familiar.

H4. TALARIA will reduce physical effort and increase the enjoyment compared to TOUCH. Since the body movement can be optimized when using TALARIA.

Participants

10 participants (4 females) volunteered to take part in our experiment. Participants' ages varied between 24 and 32 years (mean age 26.7, SD=2.71 years). All participants were right-handed. All participants were regular users of smart phones and tablet devices with multi-touch displays, and 3 participants were regular users of kinect games.

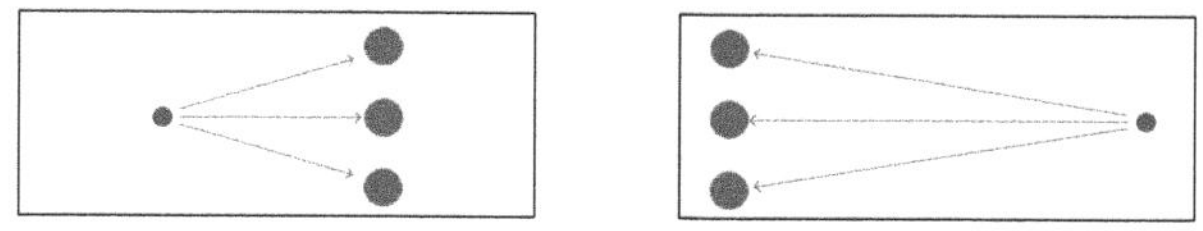

(a) (b)

Figure 3: Target acquisition task in (a) the LEFT-TO-RIGHT direction with the SHORTEST AMPLITUDE and (b) the RIGHT-TO-LEFT direction with the LARGEST AMPLITUDE with the different target positions.

Method

The experiment was conducted on a 4 m $\times$ 2 m multi-touch display starting from the ground. An infrared based touch frame sent touches to the operating system using TUIO protocol. In order to track the participant hand and forearm for TALARIA, we used an infrared motion capture system. We setup six cameras above and around the display allowing us to track the participants interacting on and far from the display (up to 1.5 m). One constellation of markers was strapped to the forearm and another one to a glove participants had to wear for TALARIA.

For TALARIA, detecting a TAKE-OFF was made when a touch release occurred. If at the release, the touch velocity was higher than a defined threshold, a raycast (forearm-hand) against the display yielded the cursor position and the touch release did not generate an event to the operating system. From that moment on, participants interacted with the control area in mid-air. There was no multi-touch support during the experiment. If multiple touches were detected, an error was triggered.

Task, Procedure & Design

Participants were instructed to perform a sequence of object dragging as quickly and accurately as possible. In the TALARIA technique, participant was only informed of the one-handed modality and the click action is activated after 0.2s of holding on the object. This way, we avoid false/lucky clicks to free the control area and the trial validation. Participant was then given the exact procedure to follow for each trial:

STATE 1. A blue circular control area with a diameter of 5 cm and a red circular target area appear on the display.

STATE 2. Touch the control area and hold it for 0.2 s to free it. Then after, the control area is free to move.

STATE 3. Drag control area over target area (see Figure 3). After holding for 0.2s, and if the center of mass of the control area was inside the target area, the target turns green to confirm the successful trial and the next trial started. If finger is raised off the control area or hand is pointing outside the display, during the dragging task, then an error was counted, the target flashes orange and the trial is repeated.

Dependent measures are analyzed using a $2 \times 2 \times 3 \times 2 \times 3$ repeated measures within-subjects analysis of variance for the factors: TECHNIQUE (TOUCH, and TALARIA), AMPLITUDE (SHORTEST :1.5m, and LONGEST: 3m, where AMPLITUDE corresponds to the distance between the center of the control area to the center of the target area), TOLERANCE (S:10 cm, M: 20 cm and L: 30 cm where TOLERANCE corresponds to target diameter), DIRECTION (LEFT-TO-RIGHT and RIGHT-TO-LEFT) and POSITION (TOP, MIDDLE, and BOTTOM, where POSITION corresponds to target position).

In the experiment phase, the order of TECHNIQUE, AMPLITUDE, TOLERANCES and DIRECTION was counterbalanced across participants. The experimental trials were then administered as 24 blocks of 15 trials, each block sharing a technique, an amplitude, a tolerance and a direction. Inside each block, 15 trials (3 POSITION $\times$ 5 repetitions) were randomly presented to each participant – a total of 360 trials per subject.

After each technique, participants responded to 5-point Likert-scale questions (strongly disagree to strongly agree): i) I performed well, ii) I accomplished the task rapidly, iii) I needed a lot effort to finish the task, iv) I needed to concentrate to accomplish the task; v) I felt frustrated/stressed/irritated/annoyed, vi) I felt confident in my ability to hit the target, vii) I enjoyed interacting with the device(s). At the end of the experiment, participants were asked to rank each technique according to their preferences. Experiments took on average 45 minutes.

RESULTS

The dependent measures are SELECTION TIME, DRAGGING TIME, ERROR RATE, and NUMBER OF FAILED ATTEMPTS. We also analyzed subjective responses using multi-way ANOVA and post-hoc Tukey tests for significant effects. Due to a technical issue, the data of two participants were not completely logged. Below, we report results for each of the dependent variables for eight participants.

Selection Time

SELECTION TIME is the total time taken by users to control selection, from the start of the trial, until the control area is successfully freed. TECHNIQUE ($F_{1,7} = 114.4$, $p < .0001$) affected selection time: TALARIA was significantly faster (mean 1258 ms, s.d. 65) than TOUCH (mean 2133, s.d. 102) by 40%.

As anticipated, there were significant main effects of AMPLITUDE ($F_{1,7}$= 88.3, p<.0001), TOLERANCE ($F_{2,14} = 8.50$, p < .0001), DIRECTION ($F_{1,7} = 9.58$, p = .017), and POSITION ($F_{2,14} = 6.16$, p = .001) on SELECTION TIME, but there was also a significant TECHNIQUE $\times$ AMPLITUDE ($F_{1,7} = 20.48$, p < .01), TECHNIQUE $\times$ DIRECTION ($F_{1,7}$ = 6.82, p = .034), and DIRECTION $\times$ POSITION ($F_{2,14}$ = 4.27, p = .035) interaction. Post-hoc tests revealed that selection time was significantly lower for TALARIA than for TOUCH ($p < .05$) with the LONGEST AMPLITUDE with no significant difference for the SHORTEST amplitude. We also found that selection time was significantly lower for the shortest AMPLITUDE than for the longest one when using TOUCH ($p < .05$). We correlate these findings with participants behavior: all our participants stayed between the control area and the target area when using TOUCH technique for the shortest AMPLITUDE to minimize their body movement and consequently reducing the selection time. Selection time was also found significantly lower with TALARIA than with TOUCH for both DIRECTION (p< .05). However, while there was no significant difference between the DIRECTION for TOUCH, we found that selection time was significantly lower when moving from LEFT-TO-RIGHT than the inverse direction when using TALARIA. We correlate this finding with technical issues: regardless of the movement direction, our participants must always use their dominant hand (right) to drag the control area which promotes movements from left to right. Interestingly, we found that there was no significant TECHNIQUE $\times$ TOLERANCE (p=.07) nor TECHNIQUE $\times$ POSITION (p=.07) interaction, suggesting that the benefits of TALARIA are consistent across the different TOLERANCES and POSITIONS. These results partially support **H1**.

Dragging Time

DRAGGING TIME is measured from the first control area movement, to target successfully selected. TECHNIQUE ($F_{1,7} = 5.87$, $p = .045$) significantly affected dragging time: TALARIA was significantly faster (mean 3256 ms, s.d. 128) than TOUCH (mean 4193, s.d. 322) by 22%.

We also found main effects of AMPLITUDE ($F_{1,7}$= 42.37, p<.0001), and TOLERANCE ($F_{2,14} = 7.44$, $p < .01$) on DRAGGING TIME and a significant TECHNIQUE $\times$ AMPLITUDE ($F_{1,7} = 6.57$, $p = .037$) and TOLERANCE $\times$ DIRECTION $\times$ POSITION ($F_{4,28} = 2.72$, $p = .045$) interaction. Post-hoc tests revealed that dragging time was significantly lower for TALARIA (mean 3725 ms , s.d. 185) than for TOUCH (mean 5665 ms , s.d. 530) ($p < .05$) with the longest AMPLITUDE. Without surprise, we found that participants were significantly faster when using shorter AMPLITUDE than with the longer one when using TOUCH technique. Again we correlate this finding with participants positions. Interestingly, we found that there was no significant TECHNIQUE $\times$ TOLERANCE ($p = .79$) nor TECHNIQUE $\times$ DIRECTION ($p = .56$) or TECHNIQUE $\times$ POSITION ($p = .84$), suggesting that the benefits of TALARIA are consistent across the different TOLERANCES, DIRECTIONS and POSITIONS. These results partially support **H2**.

Error rate and number of failed attempts

Targets that were not selected on first attempt were marked as errors. Surprisingly, TECHNIQUE had no significant effect ($F_{2,14} = 3.83$, $p = .09$) on ERROR RATE (TALARIA : mean 12%, s.d 1, TOUCH : mean 16%, s.d 2). There were significant AMPLITUDE $\times$ POSITION ($F_{2,14} = 4.18$, $p = .03$) and DIRECTION $\times$ POSITION ($F_{2,14} = 6.64$, $p < .01$) interactions.

Similarly to ERROR RATE, while we found that TALARIA (mean 15%, s.d 2) reduced the NUMBER OF FAILED ATTEMPTS as compared to TOUCH (mean 22%, s.d 3) by 31%, there was not a significant main effect of TECHNIQUE ($F_{2,14} = 26.8$, $p = .09$) on failed attempts. However, AMPLITUDE had a clear effect ($F_{1,7} = 6.75$, $p = .03$) on the number of failed attempts with significant DIRECTION $\times$ POSITION ($F_{2,14} = 4.50$, and TOLERANCE $\times$ DIRECTION $\times$ POSITION ($F_{4,28} = 2.77$, $p = .04$) $p = .03$) interaction. These results lead us to reject **H3**.

Subjective results and Observations

We recall that participants were asked to rank the two techniques after completing the experiment. Overall, the TALARIA technique was ranked 88% first and 12% second.

Participants were also asked to rate each technique condition. Overall, they found that TALARIA was faster, demanded less physical effort, implied less concentration and less frustration, while being more confident and more enjoyable than TOUCH technique. However, Wilcoxon-Signed-Rank tests showed that there were significant differences between the two TECHNIQUE conditions only for time, physical effort, frustration and enjoyment (see Table 1), supporting **H4**.

We correlate these findings with comments from participants that felt that the TOUCH technique was cumbersome and required more effort and time. Some quotes are: *"It is really tiring to move across the display"*, *"They should put those kind of big displays in gyms!"*. Additionally, in order to reduce effort, some participants were observed changing their hand as well as their fingers. Three participants were observed using their right hand when the DIRECTION was RIGHT-TO-LEFT and inversely using their left hand when the DIRECTION was LEFT-TO-RIGHT to reduce arm movement. Interestingly, all our participants tried to reduce their body movement (*e.g.*, walking). For instance, all participants stayed in the middle between the control area and the target area when the AMPLITUDE was 1.5 m and moved only their arm to accomplish the task. However, for the 3 m condition, all participants tried to minimize their walk by stretching their arms to select the control area or the target. One participant moved very slowly to avoid losing the control area and said *"this technique is the most frustrating, so I prefer to move slowly and be accurate to not repeat the trial!"*. Surprisingly, two participants decided to run alongside the display, to achieve faster execution. However, after a couple of tries they stopped running as they found that the task became too tiring. Another participant stepped back after selecting the target to save time.

In contrast, participants found TALARIA both easier and faster than direct interaction. All participants were enthusiastic to touch the surface and continue interacting when they switched to Midair interaction, and reported they felt *"freer"*, *"having super powers"*, *"like super heroes"*, while one participant said : *"when I take off, continuing to operate the control area feels like a dream"*. Surprisingly, while no time or distance constraints were given for Touch and Midair interaction (the only condition was to stay within 1.5m of the display when switching to Midair), all participants freed the control area and after a few seconds switched to Midair mode, which limited their touch distance. For instance, we found that the distance covered by Touch was on average 18.53 cm (s.d .76 cm) for the shortest AMPLITUDE and 36.07 cm (s.d 4.22 cm) for the longest AMPLITUDE. Wilcoxon-Signed-Rank tests showed the difference in AMPLITUDE ($Z=-16.52$, $p<.0001$) to be significant. Additionally, all participants limited their body movements to stay close to the start position of the control area (*i.e*, the viewing distance is similar to AMPLITUDE value and the viewing angle quite sharp) affecting the visual appearance of both control and target shapes. Consequently, participants felt that Midair required more concentration. Some quotes: *"it is simple to select the control area, but the dragging task was difficult in some cases as I didn't see clearly the other end of the display"*, *"as I am on the opposite edge of the display, I need to concentrate to correctly select the target, but this technique is funnier and easier."* They adopted two main strategies to achieve a better view. Four participants took a step backward or leaned back while the rest kept the screen at arm's length throughout the session.

	TOUCH		TALARIA		WILCOXON
	Mean	SD	Mean	SD	Z
Performance	3.37	.82	3.25	.61	.21
Time	2.5	.74	3.75	.88	-1.49
Physical	2.63	.90	1.63	.73	-1.34
Concentration	2.38	.97	2.13	.57	.35
Frustration	2.25	1.03	1.25	.80	-2.37
Confidence	3.5	1.28	3.75	1.03	-.15
Enjoyment	2.37	.90	4	.74	-1.9

NOTE: Wilcoxon-Signed-Rank tests are reported at p=.05 (*) significance levels. The significant tests are highlighted.

Table 1: Mean and SD questionnaire responses, with 1=strongly disagree, and 5 = strongly agree.

DISCUSSION AND DESIGN GUIDELINES

Our key finding is that the TALARIA technique improved both the selection and dragging times, increases the enjoyment and decreases the physical effort over conventional TOUCH techniques, without compromising accuracy. The performance benefits were consistent across different TOLERANCES and target POSITIONS. Our analysis suggest also that TALARIA is best combined with longer AMPLITUDE and LEFT-TO-RIGHT movement direction without decreasing performance on shorterAMPLITUDE and RIGHT-TO-LEFT movement direction. It is important to note that all participants were right-handed and that these results might differ with left-handed participants. Additionally, our findings indicate that Touch interaction on large displays is more appropriate when it occurs in front of the user. However, from the moment users must move along the display to complete tasks, Touch interactions became unsuitable and even boring in some cases.

Informed by our experimental findings and discussion, we outline relevant guidelines for designing interaction techniques on large displays:

- Touch interaction on large displays works best in a restricted space: in front of the user and targets must lie within users arms' reach. Indeed our participants often expressed dissatisfaction when making distant target selections requiring longer selection times and featuring lower accuracy on selection tasks.

- Midair interaction should be preferred for distant interactions (*i.e.*, beyond arms' length). Our findings indicate that beyond arms' length target selection, TALARIA outperforms Touch interaction.

- Design for flexible input by allowing users to combine Touch and Midair interaction. Our participants prefer TALARIA as it supports both modalities synergistically.

- Provide continuous transition between Touch and Midair interaction as our participants insisted on the fun brought about by this transition while reducing frustration.

CONCLUSION AND FUTURE WORK

We presented TALARIA, a novel interaction technique on large displays that combines Touch interaction with Midair pointing to access out-of-reach content. We conducted an experiment to evaluate and compare TALARIA with TOUCH interaction. Our findings show that TALARIA improved both the selection time and the enjoyment over TOUCH, without compromising accuracy. Finally, we hope that this work will advance our knowledge for direct dragging on large displays and that the TALARIA technique will prove useful by adding to the growing toolkit of large display interaction techniques as it is seemingly well-suited to perform casual tasks in both natural and appealing ways.

Future work will look at adopting multiple fingers simultaneously for Touch interaction with TALARIA as well as using the technique by multiple users at the same time. Finally, one potential usability issue of our technique is that, with TALARIA, when switching to the Midair modality, participants have a distorted view of both control and target shapes due to a sharp vision angle. To visually help users, an improved technique could add a magic distortion lens [4]. Future work will study the effect of adding this kind of lens on user perception around the manipulated object when using TALARIA. This should not detract from extending proxemics to other large-scale display interactions, a trend that we hope to have furthered with the present work.

ACKNOWLEDGMENTS

This work is partially supported by ERDF funds (CPER MAUVE project), ANR (equipex IRDIVE) and by the Portuguese Science Foundation under grant PTDC/EEI-SII/6038/2014 (IT-MEDEX).

REFERENCES

1. Ballendat, T., Marquardt, N., and Greenberg, S. Proxemic interaction: Designing for a proximity and orientation-aware environment. In *Proc. of ITS* (2010).
2. Banerjee, A., Burstyn, J., Girouard, A., and Vertegaal, R. Pointable: An in-air pointing technique to manipulate out-of-reach targets on tabletops. In *Proc. of ITS* (2011).
3. Baudisch, P., Cutrell, E., Robbins, D., Czerwinski, M., Tandler, P., Bederson, B., Zierlinger, A., et al. Drag-and-pop and drag-and-pick: Techniques for accessing remote screen content on touch-and pen-operated systems. In *Proc. of INTERACT* (2003).
4. Bier, E. A., Stone, M. C., Pier, K., Buxton, W., and DeRose, T. D. Toolglass and magic lenses: The see-through interface. In *Proc. of SIGGRAPH* (1993).
5. Chen, X. A., Schwarz, J., Harrison, C., Mankoff, J., and Hudson, S. E. Air+touch: Interweaving touch & in-air gestures. In *Proc. of UIST* (2014).
6. Collomb, M., Hascoët, M., Baudisch, P., and Lee, B. Improving drag-and-drop on wall-size displays. In *Proc. of GI* (2005).
7. De Araújo, B., Casiez, G., Jorge, J., and Hachet, M. Mockup Builder: 3D Modeling On and Above the Surface. *Computers & Graphics* (2013).
8. Ekman, P., and Friesen, W. V. The repertoire of nonverbal behavior: Categories, origins, usage, and coding. *Semiotica* (1969).
9. Forlines, C., Vogel, D., and Balakrishnan, R. Hybridpointing: Fluid switching between absolute and relative pointing with a direct input device. In *Proc. of UIST* (2006).
10. Gilliot, J., Casiez, G., and Roussel, N. Direct and Indirect Multi-Touch Interaction on a Wall Display. In *Proc. of IHM* (2014).
11. Hall, E. T. *The hidden dimension* . Doubleday & Co, 1966.
12. Hascoët, M. Throwing Models for Large Displays. In *Proc. of HCI* (2003).
13. Jota, R., Lopes, P., Wigdor, D., and Jorge, J. Let's kick it: How to stop wasting the bottom third of your large screen display. In *Proc. of CHI* (2014).
14. Liu, M., Nancel, M., and Vogel, D. Gunslinger: Subtle arms-down mid-air interaction. In *Proc. of UIST* (2015).
15. Marquardt, N., Jota, R., Greenberg, S., and Jorge, J. A. The continuous interaction space: Interaction techniques unifying touch and gesture on and above a digital surface. In *Proc. of INTERACT* (2011).
16. Nancel, M., Chapuis, O., Pietriga, E., Yang, X.-D., Irani, P. P., and Beaudouin-Lafon, M. High-precision pointing on large wall displays using small handheld devices. In *Proc. of CHI* (2013).
17. Parker, J. K., Mandryk, R. L., and Inkpen, K. M. Integrating point and touch for interaction with digital tabletop displays. *Proc. of CGA* (2006).
18. Peltonen, P., Kurvinen, E., Salovaara, A., Jacucci, G., Ilmonen, T., Evans, J., et al. It's mine, don't touch!: Interactions at a large multi-touch display in a city centre. In *Proc. of CHI* (2008).
19. Reetz, A., Gutwin, C., Stach, T., Nacenta, M., and Subramanian, S. Superflick: A natural and efficient technique for long-distance object placement on digital tables. In *Proc. of GI* (2006).
20. Rogers, Y., and Lindley, S. Collaborating around vertical and horizontal large interactive displays: which way is best? *Interacting with Computers* (2004).
21. Schmidt, C., Müller, J., and Bailly, G. Screenfinity: extending the perception area of content on very large public displays. In *Proc. of CHI* (2013).
22. Weibel, N., Piper, A. M., and Hollan, J. D. Hiperpaper: Introducing pen and paper interfaces for ultra-scale wall displays. In *Proc. of UIST* (2010).
23. Zhai, Y., Zhao, G., Alatalo, T., Heikkilä, J., Ojala, T., and Huang, X. Gesture interaction for wall-sized touchscreen display. In *Proc. of UbiComp* (2013).

Rapid Command Selection on Multi-Touch Tablets with Single-Handed HandMark Menus

Md. Sami Uddin
University of Saskatchewan
Saskatoon, Canada
sami.uddin@usask.ca

Carl Gutwin
University of Saskatchewan
Saskatoon, Canada
gutwin@cs.usask.ca

ABSTRACT
Fast command selection is important for touch devices, but there are few techniques that allow accelerated selection while still providing a large command set. HandMark menus [25] propose the use of the hands as landmarks for fast memory-based selection. However, the original HandMark menus rely on bimanual operation, and earlier studies provided only limited evidence for the value of hand-based landmarks as a reference frame for spatial memory. In this paper we address these limitations. We introduce adapted HandMark menus that can be operated with one hand (while the other hand holds the tablet); the new version changes bimanual selection operations into sequential actions with one hand. We carried out three studies of these HandMark menus. The first study showed that the adapted menus still allowed fast performance and the development of spatial memory, even with one-handed use. The second study focused on the value of hands as landmarks, by comparing HandMark menus against a hidden popup menu. This study showed that using the hand as a reference frame significantly improved performance, and was strongly preferred by participants. Our work extends HandMark menus and shows that they are an effective selection method for tablets, and provides new evidence about the value of the hands as a spatial landmark for interaction.

Author Keywords
Command selection; landmarks; tablets; spatial memory.

ACM Classification Keywords
H.5.2. Information interfaces (e.g., HCI): User Interfaces.

INTRODUCTION
Fast command selection is as important for touch devices as it is for traditional WIMP systems, but techniques that allow quick operation for experts are uncommon on touch interfaces. One promising approach to providing a higher performance ceiling for experts involves the use of spatial location memory (e.g., [10, 22, 25]) – once users learn command locations in a spatially-stable interface, they can make selections based on memory rather than visual search.

ISS '16, November 06 - 09, 2016, Niagara Falls, ON, Canada

ACM 978-1-4503-4248-3/16/11...$15.00
DOI: http://dx.doi.org/10.1145/2992154.2992172

In these techniques, an important element in the transition from search-based novice operation to memory-based expert operation is the support provided for the development of spatial memory. Landmarks play a critical role in this development, because they provide an external reference frame for remembering locations. Landmarks provide anchors for people's spatial memory as they move towards full "survey knowledge" [18] of command locations – for example, people can remember items at the corners of a grid better than they remember items in the middle.

A few touch-based selection techniques have considered landmarks and spatial memory as mechanisms for improving performance. For example, the FastTap technique [10] lets people make selections using a multi-touch tap on a grid of items; the structure of the grid provides an external reference frame for remembering command locations (e.g., "top left"). The limited structure and size of the grid, however, means that FastTap provides only a few landmarks, and cannot accommodate a large number of commands (20 items in a 4x5 grid [10]).

A more recent technique uses a rich source of landmarks on a touch interface – the user's hands – to assist the development of spatial learning and to increase the number of available commands. HandMark menus are a bi-manual technique that takes advantage of the user's knowledge of their own hand, and uses the hand as a reference frame for locating commands [25]. Two versions of HandMark menus have been introduced: one that lays out commands around the user's spread-out fingers, and one that arranges commands in a grid positioned between the thumb and forefinger. In both menus, one hand is used as the anchor for the menu, and the other hand is used to select an item.

Initial studies of these techniques showed that they were as fast or faster than equal-capacity standard toolbar techniques, and that they were strongly preferred by participants [25]. In addition, these studies provided early evidence that the benefits of the HandMark menus were associated with the value of the hand as a landmark.

However, there were several limitations to previous work on the HandMark approach. First, the techniques require bi-manual operation, which is feasible for tabletop systems but inappropriate for tablet use in mobile settings (where one hand is needed to hold the device). Second, the previous studies did not strongly focus on the spatial learning that takes place with HandMark menus – they compared HandMark menus only to toolbars at the edge of a table, rather than pop-up menus that are invoked at the user's work location. Therefore, it is still unclear whether HandMarks are fast because of the hand landmarks, or because of other factors such as the simple proximity of the commands.

In this paper we address these two limitations. We first present a new version of HandMark menus that works in a single-handed fashion, and is therefore appropriate for settings where a touch tablet is held in one hand and manipulated with the other. We then report on two studies: one that establishes a baseline for spatial learning with the one-handed versions of the technique, and one that compares the two HandMark techniques with a pop-up menu that does not provide hand-based landmarks.

Our results provide several new findings that argue for the use of hands as landmarks in touch interfaces. Our baseline study shows that both types of HandMark menus work well in single-hand operation, and both allow quick development of spatial memory. Second, our comparison study shows that both of the HandMark menus were significantly faster than the hidden popup menu (by more than 400ms per selection), and were strongly preferred by participants. In addition, the performance improvement arose from differences in the amount of time participants took to think about the spatial location of the item, not from the basic operation of the technique.

Our work makes two main contributions. First, our adaptation of bimanual HandMark menus provide two selection techniques for mobile tablets that are fast and that have high capacity. Second, our studies provide new evidence that using the hand as a landmark is feasible and effective for the development of spatial-memory based selection techniques, even with one-handed use.

RELATED WORK

Four areas of previous work influenced our design and analysis – multi-touch tablet interactions, rapid command selection techniques, use of hands as landmarks, and techniques support large command sets.

Interactions on Multi-Touch Tablets

Direct-touch interaction is the most common way to interact with multi-touch tablets [24]. Even though kinesthetic models suggest that humans are capable of using richer and more expressive forms of interaction with multiple fingers [12], most of the multi-touch gestures available in current tablets are typically limited to a small subset of one and two-finger gestures: tap, press, double tap, drag/flick, pinch/spread, bezel swipe, and rotate gestures [3]. Research projects have attempted to improve the multi-touch functionality of touch-based systems [2, 3].

Although modern tablets support numerous simultaneous touch points [3], users typically cannot use all the fingers from both hands, as the non-dominant hand is required to hold and orient the device [13]. A few projects have attempted to improve tablet interactions by introducing limited touch interaction for the holding hand – for example, in Wagner et al.'s BiTouch [26] users can interact with thumb or fingers of the supporting hand along with a finger from the dominant hand. Other research has shown how the back of the tablet can be used for meaningful tablet interactions [28]. Moreover, interaction with pen or stylus is also available [13], and several projects use the combination of pen and touch for advanced interaction [13].

Rapid Multi-Touch Command Selection

Rapid command selection is a primary goal in HCI. There are several ways of improving selection, such as the use of memory-based invocation, using proprioceptive memory, and reducing invocation steps.

Memory-based command invocation is generally faster than visually-guided navigation once commands are learned [7, 9]. Many researchers have used memory-based techniques such as gestures [15], hotkeys [19], spatial locations [10], or multi-touch chords [8]. For example, studies have shown that spatial memory is built up through interactions with a stable visual representation [10], and as people gain experience with a particular location, they can easily retrieve that location from memory [10, 25].

Proprioceptive memory can provide new opportunities for rich interactions with multi-touch surfaces. For example, multi-touch marking menus [17], finger-count menus [5], and HandMark menus [25] allow users to associate menu categories with specific combinations of fingers; and with practice, menu invocation becomes fast. However, since a more-complex control action (often requiring both hands) may take more time to recall and execute, these methods do not always improve performance [14] and may be inappropriate for mobile tablet use.

CommandMaps [21], HandMark menus [25] and FastTap [10] try to *reduce the number of steps* required for command invocation and execution. For fast command selection, these techniques use an overlay method to display all the commands at once, as opposed to hierarchical organizations of commands in toolbars, tabs, or standard menus. However, some of these advanced techniques are also unsuitable for hand-held multi-touch tablets – because of the physical characteristics of tablets, such as small screen size, or because of the need to hold the tablet with one hand, or the "fat finger" problem [23]. In our extension to the HandMark technique, we investigate the potential of a proprioceptive memory-based selection method that minimizes the steps required for invocation.

Using Hands as Landmarks

In GUI-based systems, landmarks help users build up spatial memory of different command locations by providing a strong external reference frame that can anchor retrieval. For example, Gutwin et al.'s FastTap [10], and Hidden Toolbars [22] use the edges and corners of hand-held devices (e.g., tablets) as landmarks to organize a grid menu and toolbar. However, these techniques provide only a few landmarks, and with larger command sets, many commands are not near any landmark (e.g., the middle regions of a grid). In some techniques, researchers have looked at adding artificial visual landmarks (e.g., Footprint Scrollbar [1]) to support spatial memory [25].

In all touch-based systems, however, a rich and natural visual landmark is always present – the user's own hands and fingers. Previous work on the HandMark technique [25] showed how hands and fingers can be used as landmarks to support the development of spatial memory for command locations. The two versions of HandMark menus use the space around each hand and its fingers to place command items. People can remember those spatially-stable locations by using the knowledge of their own hands and fingers. However, the bimanual operation of HandMark menus means that they are unsuitable for tablets when the non-dominant hand is used to hold the device.

A few techniques also use proprioceptive knowledge of the hands. For instance, Arpège [8], Multi-finger chords [27], and Finger Count menus [5] use the memory of different finger patterns for better command selection.

Supporting a Large Number of Commands

Many existing memory-based techniques for touch devices support a limited number of commands. For example, Finger Count menus [5] support only 25 commands, while FastTap can only accommodate 19 [10]. Researchers have tried to increase the number of commands through various approaches. HandMark menus use finger combinations of both hands to maximize the number of commands (the HM-Finger technique allows 42 commands, and the HM-Multi technique allows 160) [25]; other techniques such as Marking menus [15], Polygon menus [29], Flower menus [4], Arpège [8], Augmented letters [20] and Octopocus [6] try to increase the command vocabulary by extending gesture range, or allowing chained hierarchies of gestures.

In our work, we adapt HandMark menus [25] so that they can be operated with the dominant hand while the non-dominant hand holds the tablet. Our adaptation maintains the large number of commands possible in the technique, and attempts to maintain the spatial stability that allows users to capitalize on their intimate knowledge of their own hands as a reference frame for spatial command selection.

DESIGN OF HANDMARK MENUS FOR TABLETS

We describe the two adapted HandMark menu techniques, and then consider questions of enabling rapid execution, identifying fingers, and using hands as landmarks. Our work is strongly based on the original HandMark design [25], but several changes were required to enable one-handed use.

Design 1: HandMark-Finger for Tablets

Similar to the original version of HM-Finger for tables [25], our version of HM-Finger for tablets provides modal access to a set of commands (Figure 1). The need to hold a tablet with one hand means that we must we deviate from the bimanual technique and enable command selection using one hand only. In our adapted technique, commands can be displayed by touching down all the fingers of one hand in any order, spreading the hand to provide space between the fingers. The user can rotate and move the menu in any direction by moving the fingers. Unlike the earlier technique, however, command selection is carried out by lifting the fingers from the screen and touching the desired item with any finger. Command icons remain displayed until a selection is made (or until the menu is dismissed by touching on another part of the tablet).

As with the previous version, the spaces around the hand and between fingers are used to display commands (Figure 1). We place one command at the top of each finger (except the thumb), and pairs of commands between fingers. We utilize the large space between the thumb and index finger by placing eight commands in a 2x4 grid (20 items total).

Design 2: HandMark-Multi for Tablets

We also adapted the earlier HM-Multi technique for use on tablets. HM-Multi uses a similar command selection mechanism as HM-Finger, but differs in the placement and number of commands. There are four sets of commands, invoked by placing a specific number of fingers (in addition

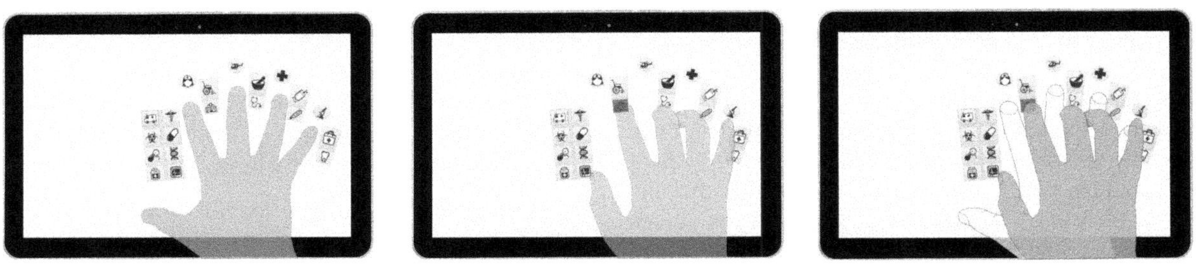

Figure 1. HandMark-Finger selection technique: (left) menu invocation, (middle) item selection after visual search, and (right) rapid selection with two sequential actions – one to invoke the menu, and another to select an item.

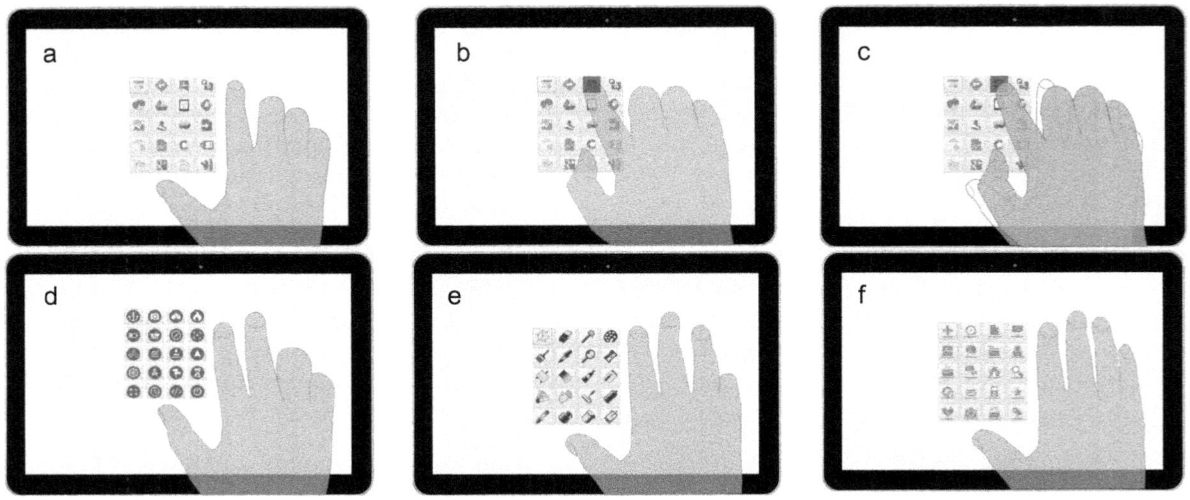

Figure 2. HandMark-Multi selection technique: (a) invoking the 1st item set by placing index and thumb in 'L' shape posture, (b) item selection after visual search, (c) rapid selection with two sequential actions – menu invocation, and item selection, and (d-f) invoking 2nd, 3rd, and 4th item sets with specific finger combinations respectively.

to the index finger and thumb) on the screen in an L-shaped posture (Figure 2). For example, to invoke the second set of commands, the index and middle fingers of one hand along with the thumb are placed on the tablet. The menu follows the user's hand as it rotates or moves. HM-Multi uses a spatially-stable 4x5 grid to show commands in the space between thumb and index finger (Figure 2). In total, HM-Multi supports 80 items (4 tabs, and 20 items in each tab).

Enabling Rapid Execution

Spatially-stable organization of commands helps users to build up spatial memory about those commands, and allows command execution by remembering their associated locations rather than searching for a command in the interface [16]. HandMark menus (both Finger and Multi) work on the simple principle of accelerating a basic interaction process. However, instead of the bimanual process used for the original HandMark menus (invoke the menu with one hand, and select with the other), our adapted menus require the user to invoke and select with the same hand (Figure 1, 2). Even though our adapted menus require two sequential actions rather than a bimanual parallel action, we hypothesize that as users become familiar with commands' locations, the two separate steps (menu invocation and command selection) will be integrated into a single learned motor chunk [16]. Chunking of sequential actions is well known in operations such as double clicking, which is considered as a single action for expert users.

Identifying Hand and Fingers

Current multi-touch tablets typically support only ten touch points, and the operating system typically only reports these as (X,Y) locations [3]. For accurate identification of hand and fingers, therefore, we have to rely on fingers' touch points. Previous research showed users' touch points based on distinctive geometric features of hands and comparative positions of different fingers can be used efficiently to identify specific hand and fingers [25]. For example, when the hand is pointing upwards, the lowermost position always belongs to the thumb, and the leftmost finger is the thumb of right hand (and reversed for left). We adapt this simple hand and finger detection approach used in the original HandMark technique [25] in our work.

Using Hands and Fingers as Landmarks

We designed our HandMark tablet techniques to maintain the use of hands and fingers as landmarks, as well as visual structures in the display of the menu items themselves. Both HM-Finger and HM-Multi provide visual guidance to assist command selection, including the user's hand, the display menu, the selected item, and the menu's gridlines. First, the techniques assign command sets to specific fingers. To invoke a command set, the HM-Finger technique requires all fingers to be touched down on the screen, while HM-Multi requires a specific finger combination.

Second, after invoking a command set, the commands for that menu are displayed on the screen as long as the menu fingers are touch down. Once the fingers are lifted, however, we set a timeout so that commands remain visible for 600ms. As the commands are shown in specific places around the hand, our hypothesis is that these techniques still allow users to remember locations of commands with reference to hand and fingers, even though the hand is lifted from the surface before the actual selection is made.

Third, when an item is selected after visual search, it is displayed in its position with different color for 500ms. This feedback provides confirmation of selection, which helps users to develop spatial memory.

Fourth, we place items in grids for the HM-Multi technique. Previous studies confirmed that grid marks are helpful for spatial memory development [10, 16]. We test people's ability to make selections based on landmarks (only the grid positions with reference to fingers are shown) in our studies, described below.

Figure 3. Mockup applications: Android system options in HM-Finger (left), and a drawing app in HM-Multi (right).

Usage Contexts

Our adapted HandMark techniques can be easily integrated with interaction paradigms and applications currently available on tablet platforms. For example, Figure 3 (left) shows a mock-up of an Android options menu with commonly used system settings and applications (using the HM-Finger method). Figure 3 (right) shows a color picker for a simple drawing application using HM-Multi. Other commands sets (accessed with different finger combinations) could be used for tools, shapes, or styles.

STUDY 1: SPATIAL LEARNING AND PERFORMANCE OF HANDMARK MENUS ON TABLETS

Changing HandMark menus from a bimanual to a single-handed technique means that selections are not made with the hand as a permanent reference frame. Since this may compromise people's proprioceptive spatial memory, we carried out a study to determine the baseline performance for the two adapted versions of HandMark. We designed the study to answer three questions:

- Does spatial learning occur when HandMark operation uses two serial touch actions with the same hand?
- What is the speed and accuracy of the adapted menus?
- What is the effect of overlapping item positions from different command sets (in HandMark-Multi)?

Tasks and stimulus. The study consisted of a series of trials, each involving the serial touch actions for both HM menus. In each trial, the participant pressed a start button, and then a stimulus icon appeared on the screen. The participant then invoked the HandMark menu and selected the item with any finger of the right hand (Figure 1, 2). Command icons were organized into sets by color and visual style.

HM-Finger shows 20 commands, of which six were used as study targets. HM-Multi shows four sets of 20 commands (in 4x5 grids); twelve of the 80 commands were used as targets (three from each set).

Procedure and study design. The study used a within-participants design, with order of menu counterbalanced. The menus were introduced to participants and they performed 36 sample selections using HM-Finger and 54 for HM-Multi. Participants then completed several blocks of trials with the same target items (random order, sampling without replacement).

The 15 blocks were grouped into three stages. At the end of each stage, participants performed a "blind" memory test with no feedback, where only the grid lines were visible, but not the icons. The aim of these blind blocks was to test the participant's spatial memory of the items. After each stage, participants were allowed to rest, and after finishing all the stages of each interface they completed a NASA-TLX [11] questionnaire.

Each selection was confirmed by visual feedback – changing the button background to green for correct, and red for incorrect. Incorrect selections could be corrected by simply selecting another item (except in the blind memory tests). Participants were instructed to complete trials as quickly and accurately as possible. For each trial, we recorded task completion time, errors, the number of incorrect sets opened (for HM-Multi only), and data describing individual touches.

Participants. We recruited 20 people (19 right-handed, and 1 ambidextrous) from a local university campus. We could not collect one person's data due to technical difficulties, leaving 19 participants (10 males, 9 females), ages 19-40 (mean 25.7). The same participants also took part in the second study discussed below. The two studies took ~60 minutes, and a $10 remuneration was paid to each participant. Eleven participants reported of owning and regularly using a tablet (> 10 hours per week).

Apparatus. The experiment was conducted on a Microsoft Surface Pro 4, with a 12.3-inch multi-touch 2736 x 1824 screen, and running Window 10. The interfaces were written in JavaFx. During the studies, we removed the physical keyboard, and participants held the tablet in landscape mode with their left hand and operated the system with right hand.

Study 1 – Results

Here we present completion time and error rates for both versions of the adapted HandMark menus without any comparison. We analyzed the 15 feedback-enabled blocks and the three 'blind' memory-test blocks separately.

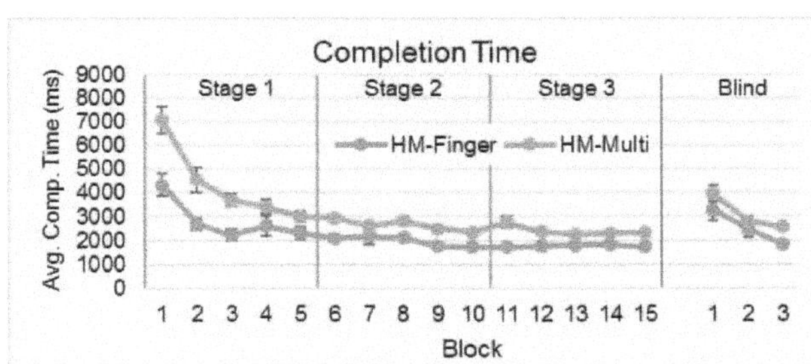

Figure 4. Average trial completion time by method and block.

Selection performance: HM-Finger

Average trial completion times for HM-Finger are shown in Figure 4. For the 15 feedback blocks, mean completion time was 2187ms (s.d. 1228ms); for the blind blocks, mean time was 2531ms (s.d. 1600ms). RM-ANOVA showed significant effect of *block* on completion time for both the feedback blocks ($F_{14,252}$=8.52, p<.0001) and for the blind blocks ($F_{2,36}$=5.08, p<.0001). Figure 4 clearly shows that trial completion time decreased significantly. In addition, completion time for the final memory-test block was similar to that of the feedback blocks (1848ms).

Selection performance: HM-Multi

Mean completion times for HM-Multi also decreased significantly for the feedback blocks ($F_{14,252}$=29.61, p<.0001) and the blind blocks ($F_{2,36}$=19.62, p<.0001) (see Figure 4). Average completion time with feedback was 3127.ms (s.d. 1648.ms).

Performance with both techniques closely followed the power law of learning: fitting power-law curves to the data in Figure 4 gives R-squared values of 0.88 for HM-Finger, and of 0.94 for HM-Multi. This correspondence suggests that participants were quickly developing spatial memory.

Error rates: HM-Finger and HM-Multi

We analyzed errors per trial by tracking incorrect selections for both techniques. Interestingly, participants made zero errors in the feedback blocks with HM-Finger. For blind blocks, mean errors per trial for HM-Finger were 0.28 in the first block, 0.05 in the second, and 0.03 in the third (overall 0.12 errors/trial, s.d. 0.21). RM-ANOVA showed a significant effect of *block* on errors ($F_{2,36}$=12.94, p<.0001).

HM-Multi had a slightly higher error rate in feedback blocks (mean 0.02 errors/trial, s.d. 0.04), but with no significant effect of block ($F_{14,252}$=0.63, p=.84). However, blind trials showed a significant effect of *block* ($F_{2,36}$=27.64, p<.0001). Means were 0.43 for the first block, 0.2 for the second, and 0.11 for the third (overall 0.25 errors/trial, s.d. 0.23).

Menu	Pos.	No Overlap	Overlap	Overall
Correct	Correct	896 (96.34%)	447 (97.17%)	1343 (96.62%)
Correct	Wrong	22 (2.3%)	8 (1.74%)	30 (2.26%)
Wrong	Correct	0	0	0
Wrong	Wrong	12 (1.29%)	5 (1.09%)	17 (1.22%)

Table 1. Error analysis for HM-Multi in few final blocks.

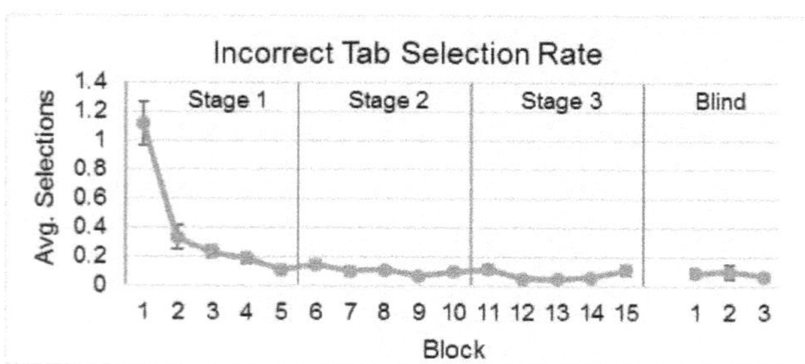

Figure 5. Average incorrect tab selection rate by block.

Impact of overlapping item positions in HM-Multi

We analyzed selection errors in HM-Multi to consider overlapping target positions (i.e., targets that were in the same grid location but different sets). Four of the 12 targets overlapped. We analyzed selections from the final stage (blocks 11-15) and last blind block (Table 1). Most errors occurred by tapping the wrong location in a correct menu (2.26% of selections). There were zero errors with the correct position but in the wrong menu, suggesting that overlapping targets are not a major source of errors.

Incorrect set selections: HM-Multi

There were four command sets in HM-Multi, each assigned to specific combinations of fingers. We recorded the number of times participants invoked an incorrect command set. For the 15 feedback, RM-ANOVA showed a significant effect of *block* on incorrect set selection ($F_{14,252}$=28.27, p<.0001) with 0.19 sets/trial (s.d. 0.34). Figure 5 shows that incorrect set selections reduced substantially by block three. The effect of *block* was not significant for blind trials ($F_{2,26}$=0.27, p=.77).

Subjective responses

Participants' gave positive responses for both HandMark interfaces in NASA-TLX scores (see Table 2). We did not perform a statistical comparison on these data (because of the large difference in the number of items), but it is clear that participants saw the HM-Multi technique as requiring additional effort – likely because of the increased capacity.

HM-Finger	Questions	HM-Multi
3.94(2.37)	**Mental**	5.52(2.44)
3.68(2.58)	**Physical**	4.58(2.69)
3.47(2.14)	**Temporal**	4.68(2.14)
8.21(1.13)	**Performance**	7.00(1.6)
4.89(2.31)	**Effort**	6.16(2.27)
2.11(2.02)	**Frustration**	3.00(2.4)

Table 2. Mean (s.d.) effort scores (0-10 scale, low to high).

In summary, our study showed that people were able to quickly and correctly learn both types of HandMark menus, even with single-handed use and serial (rather than bimanual) operation. Selection errors were very low, and overlapping targets did not cause additional errors.

STUDY 2: EFFECT OF LANDMARKS

Previous studies of HandMarks provide only limited evidence about the value of the hands as landmarks for anchoring spatial memory. In this study, we compared HM-Finger and HM-Multi against a version of the technique that does not strongly orient the grid menu to the position of the hand (the menu is posted underneath the user's hand). We were interested in which version of HandMark menus would perform best, and whether the two versions that are oriented towards the location of the hand performed better.

Study 2 – Method

This study tested three menu systems – HM-Finger, HM-Multi-1Tab (with only one tab of 20 items), and a pop-up menu called HM-Under. We restricted the HM-Multi technique to one tab to equal the number of commands available in HM-Finger. In this variant, all five fingers of the hand were required to display the menu (again, to equalize the invocation to that of HM-Finger). HM-Under was similar, with one set of commands in a 4x5 grid, but the menu was posted beneath the user's hand so that there was no clear association between the visual image of the hand and the location of items in the grid (Figure 6). We note, however, that this technique had a shorter average distance to commands than the other techniques.

Figure 6. HandMark-Under method used in Study 2: menu invocation (left), and item selection (right).

Tasks and stimulus. Similar to the study discussed above, each participant performed a series of selection trials with each of the three menu systems. In each trial, a stimulus item was displayed on the screen, and participants selected the corresponding item to complete the trial. Correct and incorrect selections were confirmed with color feedback. For incorrect selection, the trial continued until the correct item was selected. To avoid learning effects, we used new command icons for this study.

Procedure and study design. The study used a within-participants design. Each menu consisted of 18 blocks of trials (using 6 items as targets), divided into three stages (5 blocks of regular trials, followed by one blind block), as described above. Participants went through a practice session before starting each menu.

The order of the menu system was counterbalanced, and items of each block appeared in randomized fashion. At the end of each menu, participants took a break and filled out a NASA-TLX [11] questionnaire; after finishing all three menus, they gave their overall preferences.

Participants and apparatus. All 19 participants from our first study participated in this study as well, and the study was conducted with the same multi-touch tablet.

Study 2 – Results

Selection performance of the three techniques

We analyzed average trial completion time for the 15 feedback blocks and 3 blind blocks separately. For feedback blocks, HM-Multi-1Tab performed best (mean 1776ms, s.d. 1048ms) compared to HM-Finger (1960ms, s.d. 1182ms) and HM-Under (2365ms, s.d. 2257ms) (see Figure 7).

RM-ANOVA showed a main effect of *interface* ($F_{2,36}$=3.26, *p*=.05). As shown in Figure 7, completion times decreased across trial blocks for all the interfaces; RM-ANOVA showed a significant effect of *block* ($F_{14,252}$=19.16, *p*<.0001), and significant interaction effect between *interface* and *block* ($F_{28,504}$=2.03, *p*=.002). Performance with HM-Under was not as consistent as the other two methods, and was slower overall because of the occlusion. However, we suggest that although the menu was occluded by the fingers and hand, users could use the hand as a landmark to aid development of spatial memory.

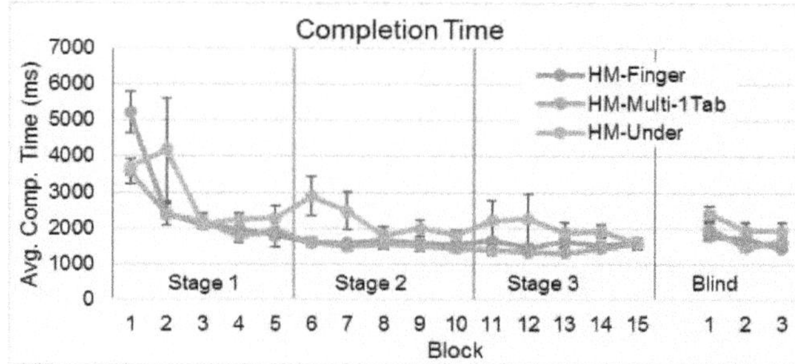

Figure 7. Average trial completion time by method and block.

We explored the issue of spatial-memory development for the three different techniques by again fitting the data to power-law curves corresponding to the classical power law of learning. The R-squared values were 0.90 for HM-Multi, 0.78 for HM-Finger, but only 0.64 for HM-Under – suggesting that participants were not able to learn item locations as well in the hidden pop-up menu.

For blind blocks, HM-Finger performed best (1653ms (s.d. 464ms), and the effect of *interface* was significant ($F_{2,36}$=5.4, *p*=.009). RM-ANOVA also showed significant effect of *block* ($F_{2,36}$=10.17, *p*<.0001), but no interaction between *block* and *interface*.

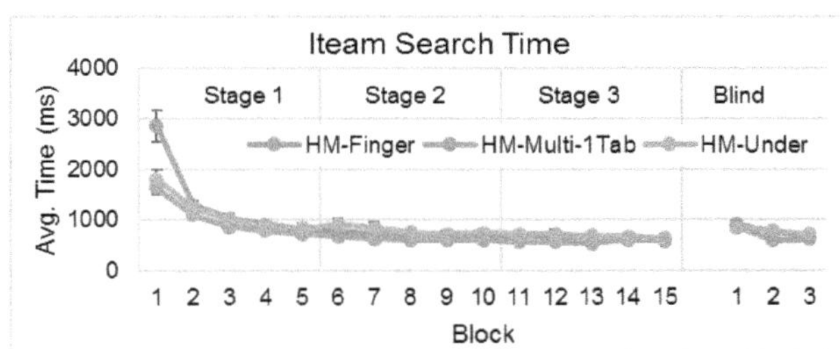

Figure 8. Average item search time by method and block.

We further analyzed performance by calculating the time from invocation of the menu to the selection (i.e., the time from stimulus appearance to menu invocation was removed). RM-ANOVA showed a significant effect of *interface* ($F_{2,36}$=8.19, *p*=.001); as shown in Figure 8, HM-Multi-1Tab was the fastest technique (mean 735ms, s.d. 390). HM-Finger was slow at the beginning (when users need to visually search for items) but by the second block performance with this technique was similar to the others.

This analysis shows that the additional time needed for the HM-Under technique (shown in Figure 7) arises primarily between stimulus appearance and menu invocation – and again we suggest that this indicates that users were having more difficulty remembering where the item was before starting the process of selection.

Error rates

Participants made zero errors in the feedback blocks. For the blind blocks, RM-ANOVA showed a similar pattern to study 1: HM-Finger had 0.053 errors/trial, s.d. 0.1, HM-Multi-1Tab had 0.099 errors/trial, s.d. 0.19, and HM-Under had 0.11 errors/trial, s.d. 0.16, with no main effect of *interface* ($F_{2,36}$=2.44, p=.101). There was a significant effect of *block* ($F_{2,36}$=17.73, p<.0001), and a significant interaction between *interface* and *block* ($F_{4,72}$=2.94, p=.026). These results also suggest that the presence of the hand as a landmark made the HM-Finger technique in particular less error-prone.

	HM-Finger	HM-Multi-1Tab	HM-Under	χ_r^2	p
Mental	3.47(2.04)	3.21(2.07)	4.0(2.65)	3.18	.2
Physical	3.79(2.88)	3.63(2.77)	5.21(2.74)	8.71	**.01**
Temporal	3.53(2.06)	3.37(1.92)	4.16(2.22)	5.08	.08
Performance	8.32(0.95)	8.53(1.17)	7.32(1.67)	9.03	**.01**
Effort	4.32(2.83)	4.68(3.13)	5.47(2.82)	8.84	**.01**
Frustration	1.58(1.8)	1.58(2.01)	3.21(2.66)	10.45	**.01**

Table 3. Mean (s.d.) effort scores (0-10 scale, low to high).

Subjective responses

Friedman tests on NASA-TLX responses showed several significant differences (see Table 3) in physical demand required, perceived performance, effort required, and level of frustration. In all cases, HM-Finger and HM-Multi-1Tab scored better than HM-Under.

Preference counts (see Table 4) showed that most participants (58%) preferred the HM-Finger and HM-Multi techniques. HM-Finger also preferred for facilitating easy memorization. Only one participant of the 19 preferred HM-Under on any measure.

	HM-Finger	HM-Multi-1Tab	HM-Under	None
Speed	8	10	0	1
Accuracy	8	8	0	3
Memorization	9	6	0	4
Comfort	8	10	1	0
Overall	11	8	0	0

Table 4. Count of participant preferences.

Participant comments

Participants preferred the HM-Finger and HM-Multi-1Tab almost equally, and these preferences were also reflected in the comments. HM-Finger method had more landmarks, allowing more opportunity to use proprioception: as one participant said, *"I can see every icon easily in the gaps between my fingers, and it requires an easy hand gesture."* Another person commented how their fingers facilitated memorization: *"I could use their location as reference."*

Others preferred HM-Multi as it required less visual search. One participant said *"everything was packed into one spot so I had to look only one spot."* Others commented about the occlusion problem with other methods: one stated that in HM-Finger *"I had to stretch my fingers apart to see all the icons."* Another participant commented that with HM-Under, *"I had less confidence in the location of icons."* Finally, all participants indicated that they used the hand and fingers as landmarks for all the three methods, even if the icons were partially occluded (HM-Finger and HM-Under).

STUDY 3: OVERLOADING SPATIAL MEMORY

When memory-based techniques are used in real life, there is a possibility that one application's command associations could interfere with another's commands. Because participants learned one set of icons for Study 1, and a different set for Study 2, we saw an opportunity to test this real-world issue.

As a final test at the end of the experiment, we asked our 19 participants to perform one final 'blind' memory test using all of the targets from both Study 1 and Study 2 (HM-Finger version). The 12 targets were used as stimuli in random order for the memory test. We were interested in whether participants' memory of the Study 1 command locations decayed after learning the locations in Study 2.

Study 3 – Results

As shown in Table 5, participants were able to recall a large majority of both command sets. However, items from Study 1 were recalled less accurately (72% overall) than items from Study 2 (91% overall). These results do not indicate whether the reduced accuracy is because of interference or simply the passage of time (participants had not used the Study 1 icons for about 20 minutes, whereas they had just used the Study 2 icons). However, this finding suggests that further research is needed on the issue of decay in memory-based techniques.

	No Overlapping		Overlapping		Overall	
Selection	**Study 1**	**Study 2**	**Study 1**	**Study 2**	**Study 1**	**Study 2**
Correct	60(79%)	69(91%)	22(58%)	35(92%)	82(72%)	104(91%)
Wrong	16(21%)	7(9%)	16(42%)	3(8%)	32(28%)	10(9%)

Table 5. Error analysis for Study 3.

DISCUSSION

Past research indicated that proprioceptive knowledge of hands and fingers can be used as landmarks for better bimanual multi-touch interaction on tabletops [25]. Our results suggest that the same approach can be used effectively for single-handed interactions on tablets:

- Study 1 showed that both HM-Finger and HM-Multi allowed rapid selections (completion time: ~2 seconds).
- Study 2 showed that using hands as landmarks improved performance: HM-Finger and HM-Multi outperformed HM-Under and were strongly preferred.
- Studies 2 and 3 showed that overlapping targets are not a main source of errors, but that location memory can degrade because of time or because of interference.

What Makes HM-Finger and HM-Multi Perform Well?

Study 1 and 2 showed that both HM-Finger and HM-Multi facilitate rapid command selection once participants are familiar with item locations (Figure 4, 7). The main reason for this performance is in the menu arrangement and item selection mechanism. For both techniques, menu items are placed in spatially-stable positions. When they are unfamiliar with the locations, users must visually search for a desired item (and explore multiple tabs with HM-Multi). After practice, users can use fingers as landmarks to remember item positions, and perform a "chunked" invoke-and-select sequence that is similar to double-clicking.

Overall, the adaptation of the HandMark menus to one-handed use was highly successful. The final performance of our serial version of the technique was very similar to results from previous studies (both versions of HM-Finger take approximately 2.0 sec/selection, and both versions of HM-Multi take approximately 2.5 sec/selection). It is worth noting that for each trial, we analyzed the completion time that started with the appearance of a stimulus, and stopped after a successful command selection.

In memory-based selection techniques, some errors are inevitable [10, 16]. However, our studies showed that the adapted HandMark menus had extremely low error rates. We believe that the low error rate arises from the switch from parallel bimanual to serial operation – the latter enforces a short period between invocation and selection where the visuals of the menu can be used to check the selection.

Relative Merits of HandMark Menus for Tablets

In general, both techniques have relative strengths and weaknesses depending on the usage situation. HM-Finger has the potential of higher performance in situations where fewer commands are used, as it can support only 20 items. However, sometimes items were partially occluded by parts of the hand (as reported by few participants); this was not a major problem, however, as the menu's display can be adjusted by moving the hand. A main advantage of HM-Finger technique is that each finger is very close to some of the locations – in future, we plan to test menus where frequently-used items are placed in easier-to-reach locations (such as around the index finger).

The HM-Multi technique is more suitable for interfaces where larger command sets are required. Our current design supports 80 items (20 in each set). The multiple tabs can be difficult to learn at first, because there is no clear indication of which finger combination is required (thus leading to the incorrect tab selection errors discussed in Study 1). However, our participants quickly overcame this limitation (and we note that moving between tabs is fast enough that even when users make tab errors it does not greatly slow the technique).

Another advantage of HM-Multi is that all the items are placed in one general location, making initial visual search easier. Additionally, HM-Multi does not suffer from the occlusion problem, and involves a simpler hand posture when invoking the menu. Even though HM-Multi does not have as rich a set of landmarks compared to HM-Finger, the modified single-tab version of it performed as well or better than HM-Finger in Study 2. Therefore, HM-Multi can also be used as a single menu for a small number of items.

Finally, more research is required with both single-handed HandMark techniques to explore integration with current multi-touch tablets or use in smaller touch devices.

Spatial Menus for Multi-Touch Tablets

Although some previous research has used spatial memory for tablet interactions [10, 22], our work is the first attempt to using the rich landmarks of hands and fingers on handheld touch devices. In addition, our work provides additional evidence for the value of spatial-memory-based interactions for touch screens. In future work, we plan to also compare learning rates and overall performance with other spatial and proprioceptive techniques such as Finger-count menus [5], Marking menus [15], and FastTap [10].

Limitations

We investigated only a subset of the likely issues present in real-life use. First, we designed and tested the prototype for right-handed people only; however, with simple changes the techniques can be used by left-handed users. Second, partial occlusion is an issue for HM-Finger, as some people with smaller fingers faced problem occasionally in the early stages of use. In future, we plan to explore this issue by exploring different arrangement of items or automatic scaling of items with finger size. Third, there is a limitation with the hand and finger detection process, in that our method assumes the origin of the user's hand; further work is required to allow HandMark menus with any hand orientation. Finally, advanced sensing could enable further exploration of HandMark-style interactions on and around the tablet, including the back or bezel of device.

CONCLUSIONS AND FUTURE WORK

The original HandMark menus were introduced as a way to provide both a large number of commands and a mechanism for spatial-memory-based acceleration. Two limitations of previous work were that the technique required bimanual use, making it unsuitable for handheld tablets, and that previous studies provided only initial evidence about the value of using hands as landmarks (in addition, the bimanual approach was considered to be an integral part of the landmarking in the original technique). We addressed both of these limitations in this paper – we adapted the technique to single-handed use by serializing the bimanual operation of the menu, and we carried out three studies to test the value of hands as landmarks (as well as several other practical aspects of the technique). Our results provide clear evidence that HandMark menus are a feasible and useful technique for tablets, and that they support development of spatial memory and fast performance even when used with a single hand. In addition, we clearly showed that having the hand as a reference frame for the menu contents provides significant performance and preference advantages.

In future work, we will continue the development of the HandMark approach, and will test the technique in real-world settings and compare it to other memory-based selection methods. We are developing an Android component to allow the use of HandMark menus in real tablet interfaces, and are building several example systems (including the applications mocked up above). We are also interested in improving the assignment of commands to the different spaces around the hand – for example, to put frequently-used commands around the index finger. We are also interested in comparing HandMark menus to systems that introduce artificial landmarks on the display surface, and potentially combining the two approaches. Finally, we will run studies that focus on issues of decay and interference in memory-based methods, to better understand how techniques like HandMarks can be deployed in the real world.

ACKNOWLEDGMENTS

This work was supported by NSERC. Our special thanks to Ashley Coveney who recruited and ran participants.

REFERENCES

1. Alexander, J., Cockburn, A., Fitchett, S., Gutwin, C. and Greenberg, S. Revisiting read wear. In *Proc. CHI '09*, 1665-1674.
2. Au, O. K. and Tai, C. Multitouch finger registration and its applications. In *Proc. OZCHI '10*, 41-48.
3. Avery, J. and Lank, E. Surveying Expert-Level Gesture Use and Adoption on Multi-Touch Tablets. In *Proc. DIS '16*, 577-581.
4. Bailly, G., Lecolinet, E. and Nigay, L. Flower menus. In *Proc. AVI '08*, 15-22.
5. Bailly, G., Müller, J. and Lecolinet, E. Design and evaluation of finger-count interaction: Combining multitouch gestures and menus. *Int. J. Hum.-Comput. Stud.* 70, 10 (2012), 673-689.
6. Bau, O. and Mackay, W.E. OctoPocus. In *Proc. UIST '08*, 37-46.
7. Cockburn, A., Quinn, P., Gutwin, C., Ramos, G. and Looser, J. Air pointing: Design and evaluation of spatial target acquisition with and without visual feedback. *Int. J. Hum-Comput. Stud.* 69, 6 (2011), 401-414.
8. Ghomi, E., Huot, S., Bau, O., Beaudouin-Lafon, M. and Mackay, W. E. Arpège: learning multitouch chord gestures vocabularies. In *Proc ITS '13*, 209-218.
9. Gustafson, S., Bierwirth, D. and Baudisch, P. Imaginary interfaces: spatial interaction with empty hands and without visual feedback. In *Proc. UIST '10*, 3-12.
10. Gutwin, C., Cockburn, A., Scarr, J., Malacria, S. and Olson, S.C. Faster command selection on tablets with FastTap. In *Proc. CHI '14*, 2617-2626.
11. Hart, S.G. and Staveland, L.E. Development of NASA-TLX (Task Load Index): Results of empirical and theoretical research. *Human Mental Workload.* 52, (1988), 139-183.
12. Hill, R., Rowley, P. and Buxton, W.1985. Issues and techniques in touch-sensitive tablet input. In *Proc. SIGGRAPH '85*, 215–224.
13. Hinckley, K. and Buxton, B. *Inking Outside the Box: How Context Sensing Affords More Natural Pen (and Touch) Computing*. Springer Int. Pub., Switzerland, '16.
14. Kin, K., Hartmann, B. and Agrawala, M. Two-handed marking menus for multitouch devices. *ACM Tran. on Computer-Human Interaction* 18, 3, Article 16 (2011).
15. Kurtenbach, G., Sellen, A. and Buxton, W. An Empirical Evaluation of Some Articulatory and Cognitive Aspects of Marking Menus. *Human-Comp. Interaction* 8, 1 (1993), 1-23.
16. Lafreniere, B., Gutwin, C., Cockburn, A. and Grossman, T. Faster command selection on touchscreen watches. In *Proc. CHI '16*, 4663-4674.
17. Lepinski, G.J., Grossman, T. and Fitzmaurice, G. The design and evaluation of multitouch marking menus. In *Proc. CHI '10*, 2233-2242.
18. Lynch, K., *The Image of the City*, MIT Press, 1960.
19. Malacria, S., Bailly, G., Harrison, J., Cockburn, A. and Gutwin, C. Promoting Hotkey use through rehearsal with ExposeHK. In *Proc. CHI '13*, 573-582.
20. Roy, Q., Malacria, S., Guiard, Y., Lecolinet, E. and Eagan, J. Augmented letters: mnemonic gesture-based shortcuts. In *Proc. CHI '13*, 2325-2328.
21. Scarr, J., Cockburn, A., Gutwin, C. and Bunt, A. Improving command selection with CommandMaps. In *Proc. CHI '12*, 257-266.
22. Schramm, K., Gutwin, C. and Cockburn, A. Supporting transactions to expertise in Hidden Toolbars. In *Proc. CHI '16*, 4687-4698.
23. Siek, K.A., Rogers, Y. and Connelly, K.H. Fat Finger Worries: How Older and Younger Users Physically Interact with PDAs. In *Proc. INTERACT '05*, 267-280.
24. Tuncer, Z., Selim, M., Liwicki, M., Kormann, G. and Allee, S. Evaluation of Multi-Touch Gestures. *gil-net.de.*
25. Uddin, M.S., Gutwin, C. and Lafreniere, B. HandMark Menus: Rapid command selection and large command sets on multi-touch displays. In *Proc. CHI '16*, 5836-5848.
26. Wagner, J., Huot, S. and Mackay, W.E. BiTouch and BiPad: Designing Bimanual Interaction for Handheld Tablets. In *Proc. CHI '12*, 2317-2326.
27. Wagner, J., Lecolinet, E. and Selker. T. Multi-finger chords for hand-held tablets: recognizable and memorable. In *Proc. CHI '14*, 2883-2892.
28. Wolf, K. *Interaction Areas on the Front and on the Back of Tablets*. Springer Int. Pub., Switzerland, 2015.
29. Zhao, S., Agrawala, M. and Hinckley, K. Zone and polygon menus. In *Proc. CHI '06*, 1077-1086.

GlassHands: Interaction Around Unmodified Mobile Devices Using Sunglasses

Jens Grubert[1,2], **Eyal Ofek**[3], **Michel Pahud**[3], **Matthias Kranz**[2], **Dieter Schmalstieg**[4]
[1]Coburg University [2]University of Passau [3]Microsoft Research [4]Graz University of Technology
jg@jensgrubert.de, eyalofek@microsoft.com, mpahud@microsoft.com, matthias.kranz@uni-passau.de, schmalstieg@tugraz.at

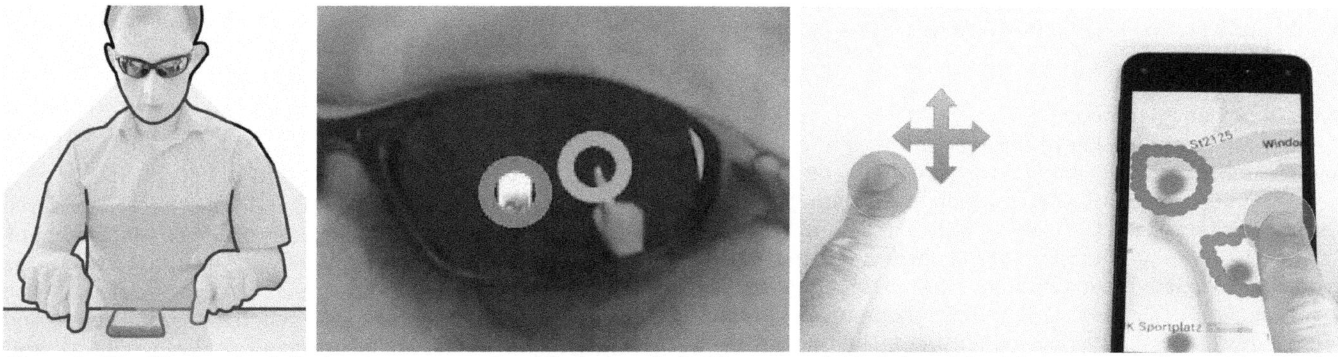

Figure 1. GlassHands extends the input space around mobile devices. Left: The narrow field-of-view of front facing cameras (orange) is extended through sunglasses reflections (green). Middle: Detected mobile phone (red) and finger tip (green) in glass area. Right: Users can continuously pan outside the display while simultaneously tracing over items on the device screen ©Jens Grubert.

ABSTRACT
We present a novel approach for extending the input space around unmodified mobile devices. Using built-in front-facing cameras of unmodified handheld devices, GlassHands estimates hand poses and gestures through reflections in sunglasses, ski goggles or visors. Thereby, GlassHands creates an enlarged input space, rivaling input reach on large touch displays. We introduce the idea along with its technical concept and implementation. We demonstrate the feasibility and potential of our proposed approach in several application scenarios, such as map browsing or drawing using a set of interaction techniques previously possible only with modified mobile devices or on large touch displays. Our research is backed up with a user study.

ACM Classification Keywords
H.5.2 [Information interfaces and presentation]: User Interfaces - Graphical user interfaces

INTRODUCTION
Handheld and wearable touch displays allow us to interact in a multitude of mobile contexts. However, shrinking device sizes, aiming at increased mobility [13], often sacrifice the interactive surface area. If devices shrink, while fingers stay the same, interaction may become inefficient. Hence, there is a need for compensating for the lack of physical interaction area.

One option is to decouple input and output area of interactive displays, using sensors to increase the input area around devices [16], extending it to near-by surfaces or to mid-air. Numerous research has sparked in the area of around-device interaction. So far, most research focused on equipping either mobiles [4], the environment [33] or the user [6, 14] with additional sensors. However, deployment of such hardware modifications is hard. Market size considerations discourage application developers, which limits technology acceptance in the real-world [5].

We present an approach that extends the input area of *unmodified* mobile devices to allow ample movements, including the environment around and to the sides of the device, without any additional sensing hardware. To do so, we propose to enrich the sensing capabilities of unmodified mobiles by everyday common apparels such as sunglasses or common reflective visors.

Our interactive system, called *GlassHands* (Figure 1), utilizes reflective glasses or visors to extend the field-of-view of front-facing cameras built into mobile devices, mimicking effects of catadioptric panorama cameras. Other reflective surfaces, such as ski goggles, diving masks or helmet visors, may enable gesture interaction with phones as well. This is of interest, when fine interaction with small screen is dangerous or impossible, for example, when the hands are covered with gloves. In fact, for some scenarios, such as skiing, reflective visors are so common, that a software-only deployment may also be economically feasible.

ISS 2016, November 6–9, 2016, Niagara Falls, ON, Canada.

ACM ISBN 978-1-4503-4248-3/16/11 ...$15.00.
http://dx.doi.org/10.1145/2992154.2992162

We hope that the suggested technology, enabling off-device sensing with a large interaction space without the need for any hardware changes, will open up the opportunity to deploy software-only applications to millions of existing mobile devices. All that is required from users is access to common apparel.

RELATED WORK

GlassHands is inspired by previous works on around-device interaction, around-the-body interaction and corneal imaging. In this section, we give an overview of these topics. In contrast to research extending the input and output of stationary displays [1, 26, 43], we focus on related work in *mobile scenarios*.

Around Device Interaction

Along with the reduction of the size and weight of mobile and wearable devices, the need for complementary interaction methods evolved. Research began investigating options for interaction next to [30], above [12, 23], behind [10, 42], across [9, 36], or around [45, 48] the device. The additional modalities are either substituting or complementing the devices' capabilities. These approaches rely on modifying existing devices using a variety of sensing techniques, which severely limits their deployment to mass audiences.

Surface Interaction

Appropriating *surfaces* around mobiles was investigated in several works. Butler et al. [4] showed compelling multi-touch input around a mobile phone lying on a flat surface, by equipping them with additional side-facing infrared sensors. In contrast, the proposed concept does not require to modify the mobile device and enables a larger input space. Avrahami et al. [3] extended the input space around tablets by using downward facing cameras on a stand. Their system was specifically designed to be portable, not mobile, as it requires a certain setup effort. Our approach can be used without prior setup time.

Harrison and Hudson [16] presented several approaches to appropriate surfaces for extending the input (and output) of mobiles. Recently, it was shown how acoustic sensing could be used to detect touch events on a hard surface around a device, using additionally mounted piezo sensors [45]. Several works also investigated how to extend touch input from touch screens to the human skin [25, 31, 41].

Free Space Interaction

Mobiles and wearables have been equipped with a variety of sensors to extend their input to *free space* gestures. Depth-sensors have been used to enhance interaction in front [23], at the side [37] or at the back [24] of mobile devices, enabling combined touch and free space interaction [7].

Magnetic sensing was used to extend the input space of mobile devices [2, 17]. Those approaches inspired us, as they allow the use of unmodified devices with built-in magnetometers, and instead rely on user worn magnets. However, these approaches mostly focus on in-air gestures or very coarse pointing in close proximity of the device [17].

Other approaches include equipping devices with additional cameras to extend the interaction space [3, 4].

Song et. al [38] enabled in-air gestures using the front and back facing cameras of unmodified mobile devices. However, their interaction space is limited to the field-of-view of the cameras, constraining the interaction space to two narrow cones in front and behind a device. Much of the interaction space around the mobile device, such as the areas to the sides of the device are not observed by these cameras (see figure 1, left). In contrast, our work focuses on a larger interaction space, covering positions around the device sides, as well as large hand gestures.

The closest work to ours is Surround See by Yang et al. [46]. They modified the front-facing camera of a mobile phone with an omnidirectional lens, extending its field of view to 360° horizontally. They showcased different application areas, including peripheral environment, object and activity detection, including hand gestures and pointing, but did not comment on the recognition accuracy.

Their approach, just like ours, supports a large interactive space around the device. The need to add non-standard hardware to the phone limits the deployment of this technology. Furthermore, the 360° lenses used by Yang et al. increase the size of the device thickness, making it hard to access and store a mobile device. In contrast, our approach only requires access to common and widely available apparels, which can result in a software only deployment to enable around-device interaction on millions of existing mobile devices.

Some approaches use stationary tracking systems to explore around-device interactions. Hasan et al. [19] presented AD-Binning, a technique for off-loading mobile content to the space around a device using finger movements. Jones et al. [22] explored free space interaction techniques for multi-scale navigation on mobile devices.

Around the Body Interaction

Similar to extending the interaction space around a device, researchers have investigated the interaction space around the human body. Wagner et al. [40] presented a body-centric design space for classifying multi-surface interaction techniques.

Chen et al. [8] studied how to appropriate body parts and free space around the users in a number of prototypes, including built-in sensors on a mobile phone. Grubert et al. [14] explored how to complement the input and output of multiple body-proximate wearable and mobile displays such as smartwatches and head-mounted displays. A number of works investigated re-purposing everyday objects and surfaces for input and output, turning them into opportunistic tangible user interfaces around the user [18, 20].

Corneal Reflective Imaging

Our approach to utilize reflections in the environment for camera-based sensing has been inspired by corneal imaging techniques [29]. The main idea thereof is to capture, unwarp and analyze the reflections in a human eye using catadioptric camera models [39].

We speculate that, in the future, using 4K or higher resolution front cameras, we may use corneal reflection instead of reflective glasses. Unfortunately, today's mobile phone sensors

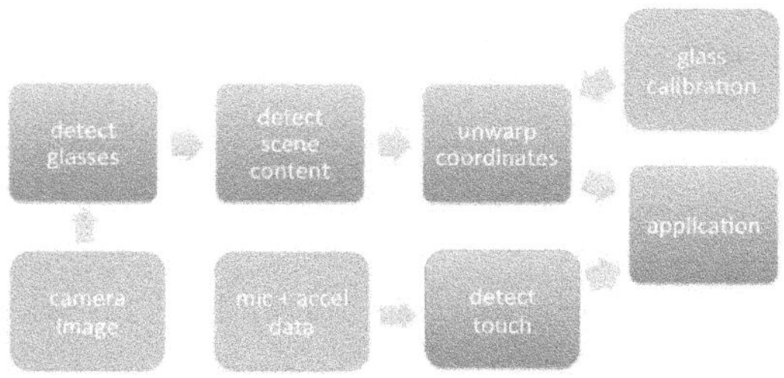

Figure 2. GlassHands processes image, microphone and accelerometer (green) to determine the glasses region, scene content and touch events. Calibration data (orange) is used to transform phone and hand coordinates from the camera's image space to the display space of the phone.

still do not deliver enough resolution for the practical use of those techniques, however, given the progress of camera technologies, it is not unlikely that such phones will be available in the future.

METHOD OVERVIEW

Off-phone interaction requires sensors that can observe the interaction, in our case, touch events on a surface and in-air events around the phone. However, the unmodified phone does not have any such sensing ability. GlassHands mimics a virtual external point-of-view (POV) that captures large areas of the workspace, by using the existing camera to observe a reflection from surface that lies in front of the camera. The reflection will contain the phone itself, the surface around the phone, and the user's hands.

Such a reflectors may be part of the environment, mounted on a ceiling or above a workstation. In this work, we look at *wearable* reflectors such as glasses or visors. Being worn in front of the user eyes, these reflectors are naturally positioned to face the phone. In many useful scenarios where normal touch interaction is difficult, for example, when the user has to wear gloves, or dangerous, such as skiing, bike riding, diving, manufacturing and more, such eye-wear is already common and can be leveraged.

To use the reflection image as an input modality, we need to be able to detect the reflected image in the camera image and extract the relative location of objects that need to be sensed. Specifically, we must detect the position of the user's hands next to the phone and, finally, map this information to world coordinates.

In the following sections, we will describe the components of the system, starting with detection of the user head and the area of the user's glasses where the reflection is visible, detection of the phone and the user hands in the reflection, and translation of all these locations to metric world coordinates around the phone. Finally, the implementation of a touch interface requires the ability to detect when the user's hands touch the surface, which will be described in the last section.

We have implemented the system on an Amazon fire phone using OpenCV for image processing and HTML5 and JavaScript for application development. We note, that while our system was implemented on an Amazon fire phone, it can be employed on other commodity smartphones as well. The system workflow is summarized in Figure 2.

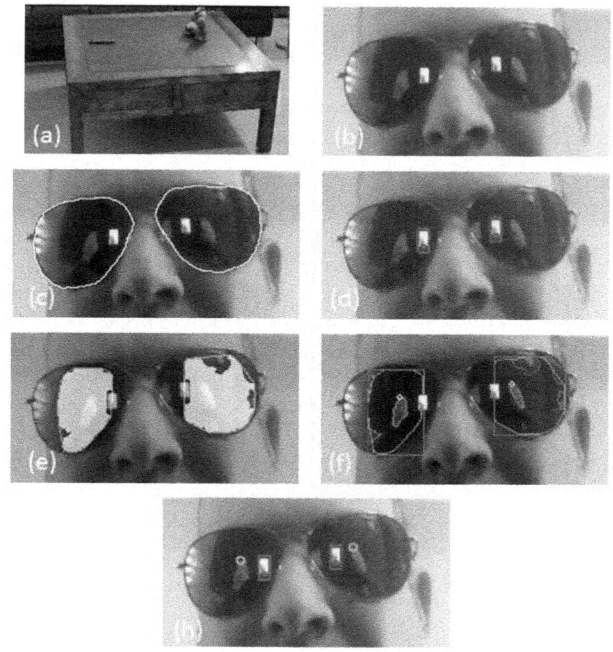

Figure 3. Detection of phones, interaction area (the table) and the hands. (a) A phone is lying on a table, facing the user. (b) A part of an original frame taken by the front facing camera. (c) Head is detected and glasses lenses, which are of different color than skin, are highlighted (d) Detected phones are highlighted. (e) Colors of the area around the phone are used to grow the table area (highlighted). This area is the interaction area. (f) Hands are detected as hand color areas (see explanation in the text), inside the table area. The curved tip of the hand define the hand position (marked by a green diamond). (h) Phones and hand locations as seen in the video.

Detecting the Glasses Area

The reflection of the workspace is seen in a relatively small part of the camera image. In a typical 2.1 megapixel image taken with an Amazon fire phone, the glasses cover less than five percent. It is important to limit the analysis of the video exclusively to this area, both for efficiency as well as to avoid false detections.

Amazon fire phone SDK supports recovery of the user's head position using its dedicated special cameras, offering a 5 degrees of freedom head pose. Estimation of the head position in the frame helps to constrain the search area for the glasses.

Specifically, we inspect a region of interest (ROI) around the expected eyes position, masking out human skin color helps to determine the glasses area (Figure 3 (c)).

Alternatively, when using different phones (some videos for this paper were captured by a Microsoft Lumia 550, and an iPhone 6s Plus), a software face detector (such as [28, 34]) can be used to recover head position and orientation. Recent developments ([34]) were able to display impressive performances of 300 fps face tracking on mobile phones, on par with the fire phone accuracy.

Scene content Detection

The scene content is detected with three steps: phone screen, background and hands detection, which are described next.

Phone Screen Detection

The position of the user's hands relative to the position of the phone determines the location of touch or in-air events. We are using simple and efficient computer vision techniques to detect both hands and the phone screen in the image of the reflections on the glasses.

The mobile device screen can be detected using a visual marker detection techniques [47]. In many environments, in particular, indoors (such as in Figure 3 (a)), the phone is easily detected as the brightest object on the surface, enabling arbitrary applications to run unmodified on the phone. A further verification of the phone size and rectangular shape can remove most false detections. In very bright environments (e.g., outdoors), we can detect the phone's shape, or may display markers such as a unique colored areas or codes, embedded in homogeneous areas of an application [44]. Figure 3 (b) shows a part of a single frame capture by a phone front camera, and Figure 3 (d) highlights detected phones in each of the glasses lenses.

Background Detection

Once the phone is detected, the system samples the environment around the phone and builds a model of the color histogram using a Gaussian mixture model [27]. Using these colors, we grow an area around the phone of similar colors which defines the work area for the interaction, for example, a surface that the phone is positioned on, the snow, when skiiing, or asphalt, when biking. Figure 3 (e) highlights the detected table area. Any holes inside this area are regarded as part of the work area as well. Note, that for simplicity, we detect the right hand in the right lens of the glasses, and right of the phone, and the left hand in the left lens of the glasses and left of the phone. As result, the detected work area is bounded by the phone location in each lens. We store the work area by an approximating polygon that bounds it's area (seen around the highlighted area in 3 (f)).

Hand Detection

Next, the user is asked to put the hands to the sides of the phones. The system samples the colors of the observed hands, and stores it again as a Gaussian mixture model. A hand is detected as a connected area of pixels of minimal size, with hand colors, that is located inside the work area polygon. Figure 3 (f) shows hands candidates as bright polygons, of which only the ones that lie inside the work area are regarded as valid hand candidates. The tip of the finger, which is a high point of large curvature along the hand boundary is regarded as the point of touch [11] (marked in Figure 3 (f) by green diamonds).

Further tracking of the hands over time can be used to eliminate sporadic false detection of hands, and focus on the true hands.

The above sampling of the environment and hand colors enhance robustness to the color of the environment lighting or to skin or gloves color (as long as they have a minimal difference from the environment color distribution), and gives the system flexibility to work both in dark environment (as seen in Figure 4, left) or a bright outdoor environment (Figure 4, right).

Figure 4. Detection of hands in different environments. Left: A dark room illuminated by a lamp. Right: Outdoor in full sunshine.

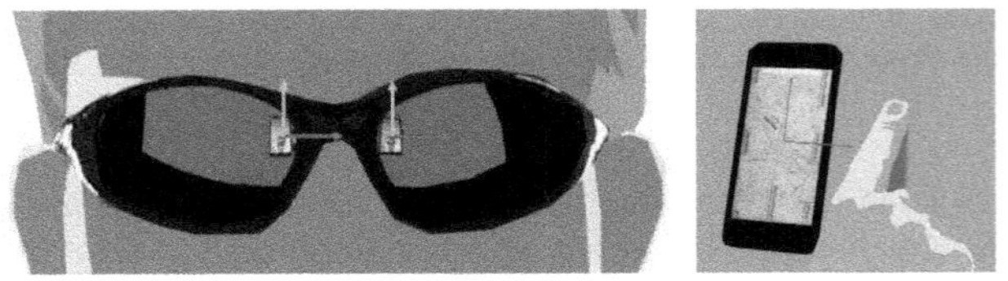

Figure 5. Origin of coordinate systems. Left: The coordinate system of each reflection originates at the center of the phone reflection, with axes parallel to the image axes. Right: The coordinate system of the surface originates at the center of the phone, and the axes are defined by the orientation of the calibration target ©Eyal Ofek.

Note that, during the user study, we used a blue work surface, which is the furthest from skin tone (see Figure 10), to ensure maximum robustness of detection during the study. Other methods could also be used, such as hand motion or machine learning of hands models [11], which enable hand detection in a large range of environments.

Unwarping of Image Points

Our goal is to use hand gestures over the planar surface around the phone, as an extension of the touch sensitive display of the phone. To do so, we need to map the position of any hand detected in the reflection in the glasses to the table surface. Let M be a mapping $s = M(p)$ from the position of a point in the camera frame, p, to a position of the surface, s. The coordinate system of the surface should have the same origin and same axes as the phone display (see Figure 5).

In some cases, the model of the reflector is known and the mapping is simple. For example, if the reflecting surface is planar, this mapping is a homography, defined by four points, such as the display corners of the phone. In the general case of curved glasses, the mapping is non-linear.

To estimate the reflection mapping, we place a checkerboard pattern on the working surface and position the phone at its center. Given an image of the reflection in the glasses, the transformation can be measured at the corners of the reflected pattern (see Figure 6) and mapping them to the actual dimensions of the target.

The mapping of other points is linearly interpolated between the known points. A point lying inside a checkerboard tile in the reflected image will be mapped to the corresponding surface point using a homography defined by the tile's corners. If fewer than four corners have a defined mapping, a simpler transformation is used (affine for three corners, and rotation plus scale for two).

The above mapping is depended on the head position and orientation relative to the phone. Let M_i be the mapping from

Figure 6. Left: A checkerboard is reflected in the glasses. Right: Area around the phone is unwrapped using recovered mapping for this glasses position.

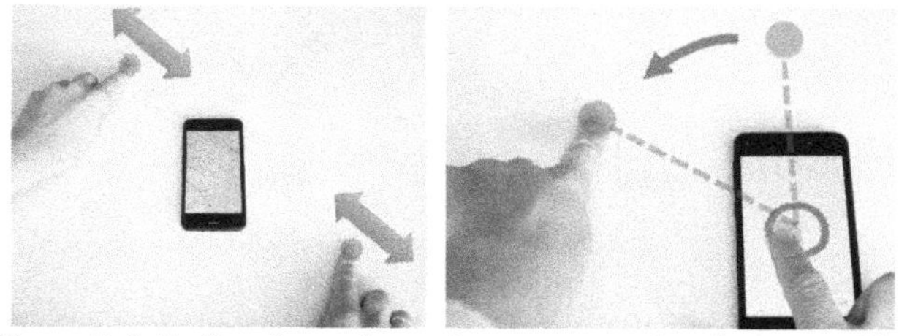

Figure 7. Left: Panning and zooming a map requires fewer repetitive gestures, compared to touch-screen only interaction and avoids screen occlusions. Right: The dominant hand draws on the touch display. The non-dominant hand rotates the virtual canvas around the screen center.

the image of the lens to the surface, when the phone center in the lens is visible at position q_i. Capturing the checkerboard and the phone images at k different position and orientation of the head enables the recovery of k mappings $\{M_i | i \in 1...k\}$. The mapping for a new position is interpolated from those known mappings using the current phone center location and radial basis functions.

However, in our trials, we found that the user face is constantly aimed at the phone display and the hands tend to be reflected by the central part of the lens (see Figure 3 (f)). The differences between the mapping of different frames, using our curved glasses, were quite small. As a result, we were able to use a fixed mapping, independent of the head position, for all our demos.

Detecting touch events

As a mobile device is lying on a surface, surface touch events may be detected by the peak they generate in the audio or accelerometer signals. Our touch detection algorithm is looking for a spike on the microphone data, similar to the way Hinckley et al. [21] detect spikes on the accelerometer or gyroscope of a grip sensing stylus. Touch-release events can not easily be detected this way. We used a gesture to signal it, such as opening the hand at the time of the release. The change in size of the hand relative to the mobile screen and a change in the number of detected convexity defects is used for the detection of touch-release events.

APPLICATIONS

We will demonstrate the potential of our concept by implementing four application prototypes: three uses bi-manual interaction around a supported phone, and one in-air application, where one hand is holding the phone. Furthermore, we have conceptualized new usage scenarios that are now feasible using the proposed technology.

The HTML5-based applications are integrated using an Android Web-View. Touch data is injected into the applications through JavaScript calls using the standard Android API.

Application 1: Map Navigation

Touch-based map navigation on mobiles is limited by the small screen space: Panning to distant objects or zooming large distances typically involves repeated drag and pinch gestures. Wearing gloves, for example while skying or biking, may prevent using touch to interact with the phone. Using GlassHands, one can pan and zoom utilizing the surface, or the air around the device (see Figure 7) or simultaneously pan and trace over an item of interest (see Figure 1, right). For the latter, the system detects if one touch is registered on the screen and one outside of the screen, classifying the touch on the display as trace action, whereas the touch (and subsequent movements) around the display trigger a pan action. This enables simultaneous panning and tracing compared to explicitly switching between panning and tracing on the device alone.

Moreover, navigating a map by outside device gestures avoids occlusion by the fingers, which is an advantage for small displays. Touching solely inside or outside the display causes the map to be paned and zoomed normally.

Application 2: Drawing

Drawing on paper is a task that involves both hands. Task execution is clearly separated between the dominant and non-dominant hand. Mimicking natural roles of hands, the non-dominant hand will be in charge of positioning the workspace, while the dominant hand is responsible for the precision task [15], such as writing or tracing.

One limitation of touch-based drawing applications on mobile devices are frequent switches of modes between workspace repositioning and drawing. The small size of the screen makes large workspace repositioning operations cumbersome, involving switching zooming, panning, and multiple flicks or ratcheting to cover large distances. Furthermore, there is no way to simultaneously draw and position the workspace.

We implemented a drawing application, in which transformations of the drawing canvas can happen simultaneously to drawing. For example, the canvas can be rotated outside the screen at the same time as a drawing action occurs on the screen, mimicking drawing on physical paper.

Application 3: Task Switching

Switching tasks on mobiles involves typically at least two touches and an additional pan action, searching for the requested application among a list of prior used applications. Furthermore, if task switching includes cutting and pasting items via a pop-up menu, at least six consecutive touch actions are needed.

We envision task switching utilizing the surface area around the device. Applications can be placed and retrieved through tapping on the locations, utilizing proprioceptive memory. The user can switch directly to a requested application by pointing on the location associated with that application (see Figure 8, left).

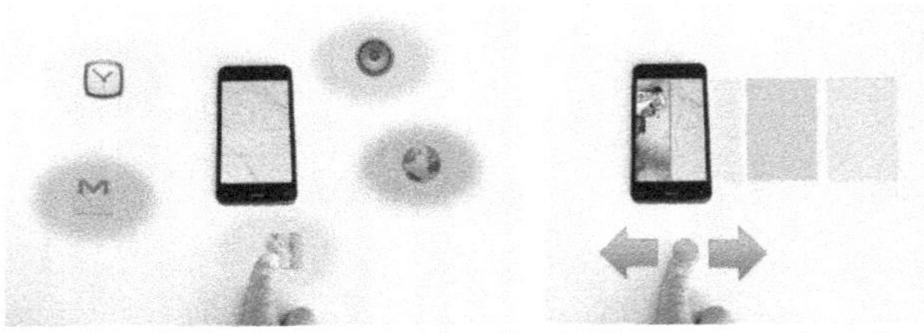

Figure 8. Left: Applications outside the visible screen can be activated through tapping. Right: A virtual ribbon allows browsing open applications, by panning outside the screen ©Eyal Ofek.

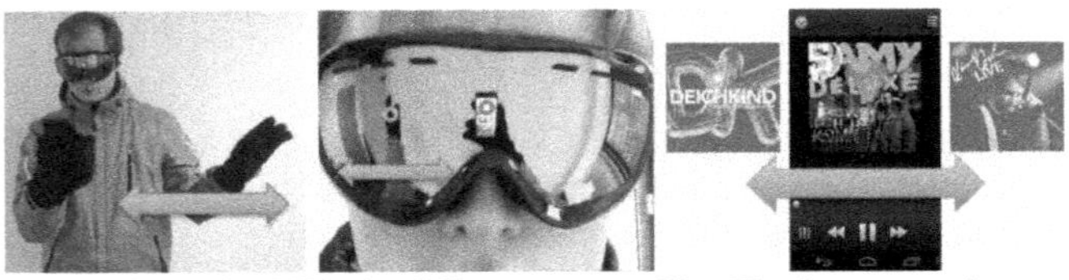

Figure 9. Left: Mid-air sliding gesture. GlassHands support large hand gestures, that enables continues scrolling or selection from a large list of options. Middle: Close-up with detected phone (red circle) and glove (green circle). Right: The album selection of a music player is operated with left and right sliding gestures.

We allow browsing application using a linear ribbon metaphor (see Figure 8, right), and enable fast cutting and pasting: The user selects an item to be moved, and holds it. Next, the user switches to the target application, either directly through tapping on locations as mentioned above or by panning the ribbon with a finger drag outside the phone. Upon reaching the target application, the user releases the item to paste it into the target. Prior to releasing, the user can place the item at the desired location within the target application by dragging it on the phone's display. This operation can also be done in mid-air, where the holding hand thumb is used for item selection.

Application 4: Music Player

Working with touch screens of mobile devices while wearing gloves, such as while skiing, viewing a map on a motorbike (at a traffic stop) or answering a phone while using work gloves, can be cumbersome. Users have to take off their gloves to operate common capacitive touch screens, e.g., when browsing through a music collection or when unlocking the screen. While touch screen capable gloves exist, they are definitely rarer than ski goggles. Furthermore, touching mobile screens with gloves can lead to an amplified fat finger problem. We have implemented a music player application that allows browsing music collections using mid-air gestures. The user can initiate a gesture by holding the hand next to the phone. Then, hand movements to either side of the phone are mapped to a scrolling list, as can be seen in Figure 9. The large available interaction space allows fine accuracy of selection. The same application can also be used with hand gestures on surfaces.

TECHNICAL EVALUATION

We carried out technical evaluations on the input accuracy of GlassHands.

Location Accuracy

As GlassHands relies on multiple image transformations, including cropping and warping of images, it is likely that the achievable input resolution is low compared to direct sensing

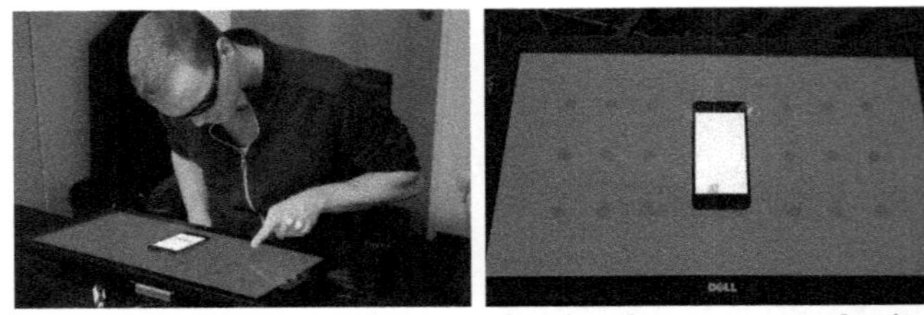

Figure 10. Left: A participant performing the accuracy evaluation. Right: Close up view on the fire phone, touch-enabled monitor and target points.

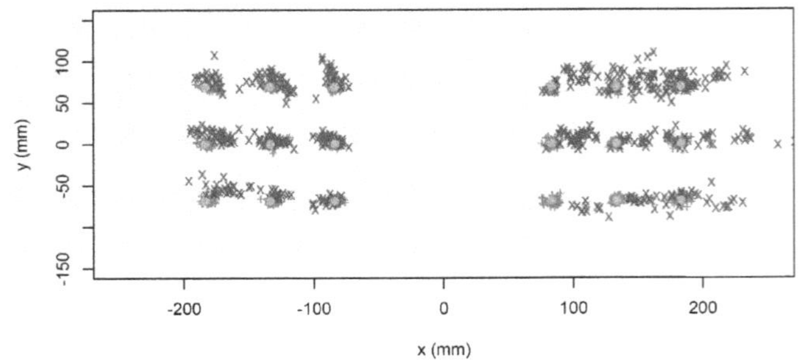

Figure 11. Plot showing a detected touch points on the Dell display. Blue crosses indicate the position of GlassHands touch input, red crosses indicate the detected baseline touches and green disks the target points.

of the scene using wearable cameras. To determine how accurate our approach could deliver touch input, we measured the input accuracy of GlassHands on a touch display. Six users participated in the study (4 male, 2 female).

We used a horizontally mounted Dell S2340T 23" multi-touch monitor as direct touch display, to associate detected touch points with target points. An Amazon fire phone was placed in the display center. The image resolution of the front camera was 1280x720 px. Users were placed in a chair in front of the touch display and wore reflective glasses, as seen in Figure 10. They were asked to position themselves so that the monitor would be completely visible in one of the lenses, to ensure a best-case estimate of the touch accuracy. To this end, they saw a video of the reflected area in the phone.

The users were asked to tap 18 fixed locations 10 times. The locations were indicated with blue circles distributed in a grid pattern, with three rows (on the top edge, middle and bottom edge of the phone) and six columns (three to the left at a distance of 5, 10 and 15 cm, same on the right side).

hor. target pos mm		-183.5		-133.5		-83.5		83.5		133.5		183.5	
condition		T	GH	T	GH	T	GH	T	GH	T	GH	T	GH
69	mean dev. mm	3.8	11.2	3.4	13	2.9	12	2.8	23.1	2.8	21.2	3.5	19.5
	sd	2.7	8.9	2.7	12.4	1.5	10.6	1.8	13.6	1.8	11.1	2.1	12
0		3.2	13.7	3.3	10.7	3.6	8.9	2.9	21.3	2.8	23	3.9	33.7
		1.7	8.2	3.1	5.9	2.8	4.1	2.1	7.8	1.5	10.5	2.1	22
-69		3.6	16.7	2.8	11.3	2.8	13.5	3.2	35.1	3.3	27.7	4.3	22.5
		2.4	7.1	1.7	8.7	1.7	6	2.4	8.7	1.5	17.5	2.2	15.9
vert. target pos mm													

Table 1. Mean errors and standard deviations for each target point (in mm) for the GlassHands (GH) detected fingers and the ground truth touch screen positions (T). Target positions are relative to the fire phone center.

The relative offsets between touch data on the large touch display and the ones detected by glasshands were determined in a common coordinate system, centered at the phone.

Figure 11 shows a plot with the individual touch down events detected using GlassHands (blue crosses), the ground truth touch data (red crosses) and the target points (green disks). Table 1 quantifies the deviations per target location compared to the ground truth touch data. The mean deviation over all target points was 18.3 mm (SD=13.2) using GlassHands; for ground truth touch data the mean error was 3.3 mm (SD=2.2).

To assess the accuracy in other environments, we measured accuracy for a regular room (shown in accompanying video) with manually labeling the fingertip (as ground truth data) for a single user. The hand was detected in 82% of frames with an average accuracy of 14mm (SD: 7.8). In all but one case tracking gaps were <4 frames, which can be addressed using dynamic tracking models (e.g., Kalman filter).

USER FEEDBACK

We conducted a user study, to learn from users' reactions to the GlassHands concept. Our goal was to examine the value proposition of GlassHands and discover potential social concerns. Twelve users (5 male, 7 female, mean age: 24 years, SD: 4 years, 10 with a social science background, 2 with an engineering background) participated in the study and were compensated with a small gratuity for their time. The same apparatus as in the technical evaluation was used.

Procedure

After a short introduction, users were asked to try out four prototypical applications in randomized order: map navigation using pan and zoom (MapPZ), combined map panning and tracing (MT), drawing (Draw), cut-paste (CP). Users tried both using GlassHands (GH) and a touch-screen only (OnDevice) interaction.

For the map applications, participants tried out navigation alone (pan, zoom) and a compound navigation task [32]. The latter task consisted of tracing six target regions and panning along a path. As simultaneous panning and tracing is not possible in the OnDevice condition, users could switch between both modes through a button. For the drawing application, participants were asked to trace a circle on screen. In the GH condition, users could rotate a virtual sheet of paper around the screen center as depicted in Figure 7. For the cut-paste scenario, users were asked to cut an image, embedded it in a word processor application, and paste it into a PowerPoint presentation and back again. For this scenario, we used the Android task manager, with Microsoft Word, Excel and PowerPoint applications opened in the touch-screen only condition. For each application, participants tried out the OnDevice and the GH version (counterbalanced).

They rated the ease of use and usefulness of the applications through 2-item questionnaires with 5-items Likert scales and selected the preferred way of interacting. After trying both applications, they were asked about the challenges and merits of GlassHands in semi-structured interviews. In a second part of the study, users were presented with the two mid-air concepts using verbal descriptions and pictures. They were then also asked to comment on the potential usefulness of

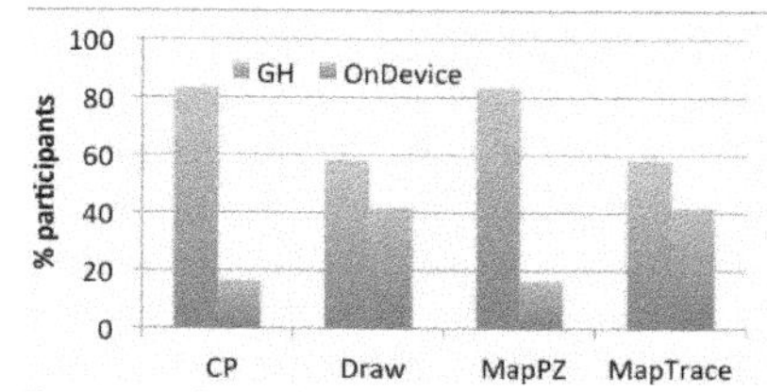

Figure 12. Percent of participants preferring GlassHands (GH) or touch-screen only (OnDevice) interaction for the same tasks as in Figure 14.

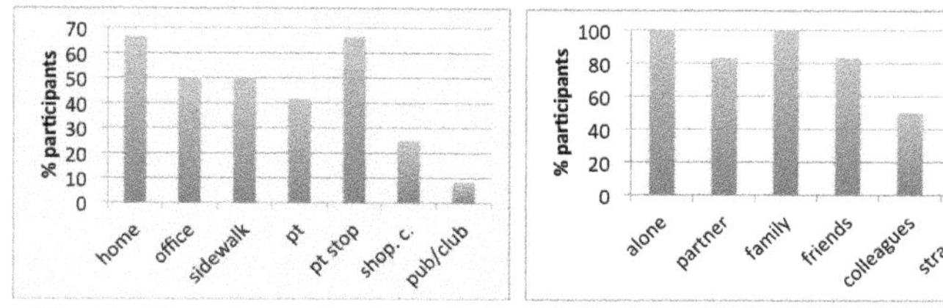

Figure 13. Percent of participants who could imagine using GlassHands at various locations (left) and in front of various audiences (right).

GlassHands interaction and about applications they would like to use with GlassHands in those scenarios.

Findings

Ease of use and usefulness ratings are shown in Figure 14. For ease of use, two-sided Wilcoxon signed-rank tests indicated significant differences for CP ($W=45$, $Z=2.87$, $p<0.01$, Cohen's $d=1.45$) and MT ($W=15$, $Z=2.23$, $p=0.026$, Cohen's $d=1.02$). For usefulness, two-sided Wilcoxon signed-rank tests indicated significant differences with large effect sizes for cut-paste ($W=28$, $Z=2.60$, $p=0.017$, Cohen's $d=1.26$) and MT ($W=15$, $Z=2.23$, $p=0.026$, Cohen's $d=1.02$, same results as for ease of use). Preferences are depicted in Figure 12.

Most participants preferred GlassHands for CP and and MT. For CP, users mentioned time savings and fewer number of required interactions compared to on-device usage. One user said "it is convenient to just use the hand and swipe to switch applications." Another mentioned that GlassHands interaction is "pretty easy, like on your desktop computer" and that this technique seems specifically useful, if one needs to switch applications often. Similarly, for MT, users mentioned that they preferred the modeless interaction enabled by GlassHands, with one stating "there is no need to switch" the interaction mode, another one mentioning "it is very annoying, if I have to switch between tracking and panning" in the on-device condition.

For the drawing application, users agreed that GlassHands enables more precise tracing of template figures. One highlighted the fact that he was able to draw "more accurate, clean and beautiful." However, while some users liked this features, other users were feeling that this approach hinders artistic expression. One participant mentioned that "for beginners [GlassHands] might be better due to its constraints, while professionals would probably prefer the freedom of on-screen drawing." Users also saw potential for GlassHands for more complex drawing scenarios than tracing a circle. One mentioned "I could concentrate on drawing complex shapes at the top of the screen without worrying about other parts of the canvas."

For map navigation using pan and zoom, participants preferred GlassHands, but did not rate the ease of use or usefulness higher compared to on-device usage. Several users mentioned that the on-device interaction is "already quite easy" and "familiar." Four users mentioned that they felt more confident using GlassHands, as there is a smaller chance for unexpected effects of finger movements (specifically, pinch gestures) due to the larger space. Occlusion free navigation of the map was mentioned as an advantage of GlassHands by five participants. One user also mentioned that it is more fun to use the GlassHands approach, as it "feels like StarTrek."

With a questionnaire on social acceptability [35], we asked participants about suitable locations and audiences (Figure 13) for using GlassHands.

Social issues were primarily mentioned by participants who would not wear sunglasses for fashion purposes (three do not wear sunglasses, seven only for sun protection, two also inside buildings for fashion purposes). Five users mentioned that (in the words of one participant) it would "feel awkward to wear sunglasses, when the sun is not shining," but also mentioned that it would be "inappropriate not to look others in the eyes while interacting with them." Interestingly, the target audience for this inappropriate behavior differed between participants, with some mentioning strangers, while others, partners and friends, as individuals in front of whom they would not wear sunglasses. Three users explicitly mentioned spatial constraints for using GlassHands in public space as "I would be worried to bump into another person." One user also mentioned privacy concerns as "it would be more visible what I am doing with my phone." One participant mentioned to be a trend follower and said that "if everyone would wear sunglasses to interact with their phones, I would do it, too."

We asked participants about their opinion on using mid-air GlassHands while wearing gloves or while biking. Users mentioned that this kind of interaction would be ideal for situations in which they would have to concentrate on a demanding primary task, to trigger secondary tasks. Examples included operating a music player, answering incoming calls or coarse map navigation. However, several participants also mentioned that they would not use GlassHands (or an ordinary phone) while biking at all, due to safety reasons. Finally, two users mentioned that they really like the concepts, but, ultimately, would like to use use the space around an unmodified phone without sunglasses.

DISCUSSION AND CONCLUSION

We have presented GlassHands, an interactive system for around-device interaction on unmodified mobile devices. We demonstrated that interaction at the periphery of a mobile device is feasible given a front-facing RGB camera and a user wearing sunglasses, or any other reflector. In contrast to previous work [38], we significantly broaden the interaction space around an unmodified mobile device. In contrast to Surround-See [46], we enable large interaction space, without the need for special hardware, just everyday common apparel, and with keeping the phone thin and small. Removing the need for special hardware enable us to easily deploy this solution, such as through a store application.

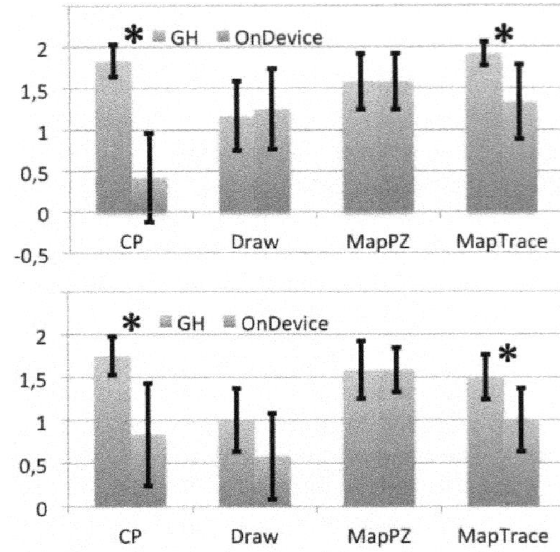

Figure 14. Ease of use (top) and usefulness (bottom) for GlassHands (GH) and Touch-screen only (OnDevice) interaction for cut and paste (CP), drawing (Draw), map pan and zoom (MapPZ) and map tracing (MT) on a 5-point Likert scale (-2 very difficult ... 2 very easy). Statistically significant differences at $\alpha = .05$ indicated with a *.

We demonstrated interaction techniques and applications for GlassHands, among them, mode-less panning and tracing on maps, cut and paste by dragging between applications, and drawing with the non-dominant hand controlling the canvas. A group of users have tried these applications, and found their interaction preferable over their common interaction. The consensus was that the higher potential savings in effort, the more participants were willing to use it.

The proposed system has several limitations, some which may be addressed in future work:

An inherent limitation of our approach is that users have to wear reflective glasses, which have to be visible in the field of view of the front camera (typically 70-80 degrees field of view). Dark glasses allows the camera to view a clear reflection without the view of the user eyes behind them. If the user face is relatively dark, such as in the case of a desk lamp illuminating the table, while the user's head stays in the dark, then regular glasses can be used just as well.

In general, the usage of dark glasses in low-light environments, like indoor offices, might not be appropriate, both due to perceptual and social reasons. However, there are many situations, both indoors and outdoors, where wearing reflective eye-wear is common: workers wearing safety goggles, skiers, divers, motorcyclists and so on.

On-surface interactions as described above enable comfortable work, where the users hands are supported by the surface, and the tap of a finger on the surface can be used to detect touch. However, the technology is not limited to surface-based interaction. The same 2D interaction may be used in mid-air around the phone with ample gestures. Such in-air interaction with Glasshands could help skiers operate their mobiles without the need to take off their gloves.

Also, GlassHands could be used by bikers, who have mounted their phone on the handle bar. Sliding the hands along the handle bar, relatively far from the phone, could be utilized to steer on-screen applications (see Figure 9, right). A possible application may sense the direction of a pointed hand, reflected in the helmet visor, and use the phone GPS and orientation to announce the street number of the house the biker is pointing at. Divers could use GlassHands to interact with their phone, stored inside a watertight casing. In a similar fashion, workers who wear protective glasses and gloves may interact using large gestures around the phones.

Measuring the hand positioning accuracy shows that a minimal distance of at least 5 cm is needed to reliably separate two individual touch down events on the surface, when a single frame is used for measurement. It is possible to increase the measurement accuracy, for example, using temporal filtering.

Furthermore, we deliberately employed simple and efficient computer vision techniques throughout our pipeline to demonstrate the feasibility of the GlassHands concept. These simple algorithms can not cope well with complex environments, typically found in real-world situations. For practical implementations in commercial applications, more robust algorithms should be used (see also below).

FUTURE WORK

At the camera resolution we used (0.9 megapixel), the image of each lens is about 130 by 170 pixels, which limits the maximum accuracy of the hands location to about 0.5 cm. Better front cameras are already available and should improve the quality of detection and location estimation.

In the future, we want to support a wider variety of glasses models with different reflection and curvature properties. Moreover, the use of reflections directly of the user's eye using corneal imaging [29] could overcome the need for eyewear.

Any method that uses a camera depends on sufficient lighting. We could use the flashlight LED on the phone itself to illuminate the glasses. An interesting alternative would be the reflection of a time-of-flight sensor to determine the 3D position of objects above the surface.

Furthermore, by using both lenses of the glasses, one could model two catadioptric camera systems and apply stereo techniques to recover depth values. We plan to investigate how to estimate such camera models on the fly. Depending on the quality of the stereo reconstruction, usage may range from determining the height of the user's hands above the surface to possible replacement of body-worn depth sensors.

GlassHands allows to sense an ample area in a phone's vicinity. There are options to recognize objects in space and react accordingly. The interaction may involve everyday objects, such as toys on a table, a board-game, or ingredients on a kitchen counter.

We believe that new sensing capabilities for phones will help spreading spatially aware applications. In many cases, the development of such applications is hampered by the limited distribution of required hardware. Hardware manufacturers, on the other hand, may hesitate to include new technology without proven value for applications [5]. We hope that an approach such as GlassHands may break this circle by enabling applications aimed at a specific scenario, such as Skiing, to be commercially successful using existing hardware. Ultimately, this may encourage the development of new dedicated sensors integrated in consumer phones.

REFERENCES

1. Annett, M., Grossman, T., Wigdor, D., and Fitzmaurice, G. Medusa: a proximity-aware multi-touch tabletop. *Proc. UIST '11*, 337–346.
2. Ashbrook, D., Baudisch, P., and White, S. Nenya: subtle and eyes-free mobile input with a magnetically-tracked finger ring. *Proc. CHI '11*, 2043–2046.
3. Avrahami, D., Wobbrock, J. O., and Izadi, S. Portico: tangible interaction on and around a tablet. *Proc. UIST '11*, 347–356.
4. Butler, A., Izadi, S., and Hodges, S. Sidesight: multi-"touch" interaction around small devices. *Proc. UIST '08*, 201–204.
5. Buxton, B. The long nose of innovation. *Insight*, 11, 2008: 27.
6. Chan, L., Hsieh, C.-H., Chen, Y.-L., Yang, S., Huang, D.-Y., Liang, R.-H., and Chen, B.-Y. Cyclops: wearable and single-piece full-body gesture input devices. *Proc. CHI '15*, 3001–3009.
7. Chen, X. A., Schwarz, J., Harrison, C., Mankoff, J., and Hudson, S. E. Air+touch: interweaving touch and in-air gestures. *Proc. UIST '14*, 519–525.
8. Chen, X. A., Schwarz, J., Harrison, C., Mankoff, J., and Hudson, S. Around-body interaction: sensing and interaction techniques for proprioception-enhanced input with mobile devices. *Proc. MobileHCI '14*, 287–290.
9. Chen, X. A., Grossman, T., Wigdor, D. J., and Fitzmaurice, G. Duet: exploring joint interactions on a smart phone and a smart watch. *Proc. CHI '14*, 159–168.
10. De Luca, A., Zezschwitz, E. von, Nguyen, N. D. H., Maurer, M.-E., Rubegni, E., Scipioni, M. P., and Langheinrich, M. Back-of-device authentication on smartphones. *Proc. CHI '13*, 2389–2398.
11. Erol, A., Bebis, G., Nicolescu, M., Boyle, R. D., and Twombly, X. Vision-based hand pose estimation: a review. *Comput. Vis. Image Underst.* 108(1-2), Oct. 2007: 52–73.
12. Freeman, E., Brewster, S., and Lantz, V. Towards usable and acceptable above-device interactions. *Proc. MobileHCI '14*, 459–464.
13. Gemperle, F., Kasabach, C., Stivoric, J., Bauer, M., and Martin, R. Design for wearability. *Proc. ISCW'98*. 1998, 116–122.
14. Grubert, J., Heinisch, M., Quigley, A., and Schmalstieg, D. Multifi: multi fidelity interaction with displays on and around the body. *Proc. CHI '15*, 3933–3942.
15. Guiard, Y. Asymmetric division of labor in human skilled bimanual action. *Journal of Motor Behavior*, 19(4), 1987: 486–517.

16. Harrison, C. Appropriated interaction surfaces. *Computer*, 43(6), June 2010: 86–89.
17. Harrison, C., and Hudson, S. E. Abracadabra: wireless, high-precision, and unpowered finger input for very small mobile devices. *Proc. UIST '09*, 121–124.
18. Harrison, C., Benko, H., and Wilson, A. D. Omnitouch: wearable multitouch interaction everywhere. *Proc. UIST '11*, 441–450.
19. Hasan, K., Ahlström, D., and Irani, P. Ad-binning: leveraging around device space for storing, browsing and retrieving mobile device content. *Proc. CHI '13*, 899–908.
20. Henderson, S. J., and Feiner, S. Opportunistic controls: leveraging natural affordances as tangible user interfaces for augmented reality. *Proc. VRST '08*, 211–218.
21. Hinckley, K., Pahud, M., Benko, H., Irani, P., Guimbretière, F., Gavriliu, M., Chen, X. A., Matulic, F., Buxton, W., and Wilson, A. Sensing techniques for tablet+stylus interaction. *Proc. UIST '14*, 605–614.
22. Jones, B., Sodhi, R., Forsyth, D., Bailey, B., and Maciocci, G. Around device interaction for multiscale navigation. *Proc. MobileHCI '12*, 83–92.
23. Kratz, S., and Rohs, M. Hoverflow: exploring around-device interaction with ir distance sensors. *Proc. MobileHCI '09*, 42:1–42:4.
24. Kratz, S., Rohs, M., Guse, D., Müller, J., Bailly, G., and Nischt, M. Palmspace: continuous around-device gestures vs. multitouch for 3d rotation tasks on mobile devices. *Proc. AVI '12*, 181–188.
25. Laput, G., Xiao, R., Chen, X. A., Hudson, S. E., and Harrison, C. Skin buttons: cheap, small, low-powered and clickable fixed-icon laser projectors. *Proc. UIST '14*, 389–394.
26. Marquardt, N., Jota, R., Greenberg, S., and Jorge, J. The continuous interaction space: interaction techniques unifying touch and gesture on and above a digital surface. In: *Proc. INTERACT '11*. Vol. 6948. 2011. ISBN: 978-3-642-23764-5.
27. McLachlan, G. J., and Basford, K. E. Mixture models : inference and applications to clustering. M. Dekker, 1998.
28. Murphy-Chutorian, E., and Trivedi, M. Head pose estimation in computer vision: a survey. *PAMI*, 31(4), 2009: 607–626.
29. Nitschke, C., Nakazawa, A., and Takemura, H. Corneal imaging revisited: an overview of corneal reflection analysis and applications. *Information and Media Technologies*, 8(2), 2013: 389–406.
30. Oakley, I., and Lee, D. Interaction on the edge: offset sensing for small devices. *Proc. CHI '14*, 169–178.
31. Ogata, M., and Imai, M. Skinwatch: skin gesture interaction for smart watch. *Proc. AH '15*, 21–24.
32. Pahud, M., Hinckley, K., Iqbal, S., Sellen, A., and Buxton, B. Toward compound navigation tasks on mobiles via spatial manipulation. *Proc. MobileHCI '13*, 113–122.
33. Rädle, R., Jetter, H.-C., Marquardt, N., Reiterer, H., and Rogers, Y. Huddlelamp: spatially-aware mobile displays for ad-hoc around-the-table collaboration. *Proc. ITS '14*, 45–54.
34. Ren, S., Cao, X., Wei, Y., and Sun, J. Face alignment at 3000 fps via regressing local binary features. *Proc. CVPR 2014*. 2014.
35. Rico, J., and Brewster, S. Gestures all around us: user differences in social acceptability perceptions of gesture based interfaces. *MobileHCI 09*. 2009, 64:1–64:2.
36. Schmidt, D., Seifert, J., Rukzio, E., and Gellersen, H. A cross-device interaction style for mobiles and surfaces. *Proc. DIS '12*, 318–327.
37. Sodhi, R. S., Jones, B. R., Forsyth, D., Bailey, B. P., and Maciocci, G. Bethere: 3d mobile collaboration with spatial input. *Proc. CHI '13*, 179–188.
38. Song, J., Sörös, G., Pece, F., Fanello, S. R., Izadi, S., Keskin, C., and Hilliges, O. In-air gestures around unmodified mobile devices. *Proc. UIST '14*, 319–329.
39. Sturm, P., Ramalingam, S., Tardif, J.-P., Gasparini, S., and Barreto, J. a. Camera models and fundamental concepts used in geometric computer vision. *FTCGV*, 6(1-211;2), Jan. 2011: 1–183.
40. Wagner, J., Nancel, M., Gustafson, S. G., Huot, S., and Mackay, W. E. Body-centric design space for multi-surface interaction. *Proc. CHI '13*, 1299–1308.
41. Weigel, M., Lu, T., Bailly, G., Oulasvirta, A., Majidi, C., and Steimle, J. Iskin: flexible, stretchable and visually customizable on-body touch sensors for mobile computing. *Proc. CHI '15*, 2991–3000.
42. Wigdor, D., Forlines, C., Baudisch, P., Barnwell, J., and Shen, C. Lucid touch: a see-through mobile device. *Proc. UIST '07*, 269–278.
43. Wilson, A. D., and Benko, H. Combining multiple depth cameras and projectors for interactions on, above and between surfaces. *Proc. UIST '10*, 273–282.
44. Woo, G., Lippman, A., and Raskar, R. Vrcodes: unobtrusive and active visual codes for interaction by exploiting rolling shutter. *Proc. ISMAR '12*, 59–64.
45. Xiao, R., Lew, G., Marsanico, J., Hariharan, D., Hudson, S., and Harrison, C. Toffee: enabling ad hoc, around-device interaction with acoustic time-of-arrival correlation. *Proc. MobileHCI '14*, 67–76.
46. Yang, X.-D., Hasan, K., Bruce, N., and Irani, P. Surround-see: enabling peripheral vision on smartphones during active use. *Proc. UIST '13*, 291–300.
47. Zhang, X., Fronz, S., and Navab, N. Visual marker detection and decoding in ar systems: a comparative study. *Proc. ISMAR '02*. 2002, 97–106.
48. Zhao, C., Chen, K.-Y., Aumi, M. T. I., Patel, S., and Reynolds, M. S. Sideswipe: detecting in-air gestures around mobile devices using actual gsm signal. *Proc. UIST '14*, 527–534.

Differentiating in-Game Frustration from at-Game Frustration using Touch Pressure

Matthew K. Miller and Regan L. Mandryk
Department of Computer Science, University of Saskatchewan
Saskatoon, SK, S7N 0Y7, Canada
{firstname.lastname}@usask.ca

ABSTRACT
Games are engaging in part because players experience competence from overcoming challenges. Although this process can feel frustrating, it is often experienced as a positive frustration that results in further engagement. Motivating frustration can be difficult to differentiate from the disheartening frustration that occurs when games are poorly designed or are much too difficult, yet understanding this difference is important for designers to make informed decisions on how to address player experience problems. We conducted an experiment to determine whether touch pressure from game interaction can differentiate between motivating in-game frustration and disheartening at-game frustration. Our results showed that although in-game and at-game frustration were of similar magnitude, enjoyment was higher and attribution was more internal for in-game frustration. Both peak pressure and mean pressure were also higher for in-game frustration, showing the potential of touch pressure as a game experience evaluation metric.

Author Keywords
Touch pressure; games; frustration; player experience.

ACM Classification Keywords
H.5.m. Information interfaces and presentation (e.g., HCI): Miscellaneous.

INTRODUCTION
People now spend more time and money playing digital games than on other leisure media, such as listening to music or watching movies [12,13]. There are several theories that explain why games are so engaging – the most prevalent (self-determination theory [32]) suggests that one reason games are motivating to play is because players experience a feeling of competence from overcoming in-game challenges [33]. Repeatedly trying (and failing) to beat game elements can feel frustrating, but then triumphing over the challenge is rewarding [2]. This type of *motivating frustration* (in which players want to persevere and overcome in-game challenges) can be called *in-game frustration* [16] and is desirable in a game. However, frustration during game play is not always positive. For example, players can be so frustrated by poor game controllers or a ridiculously difficult boss that they 'rage quit' and potentially do not return to play again. This type of *disheartening frustration* (in which players disengage from game play) can be called at-game frustration [16] and is something that game designers want to avoid in their game design. Designers try to avoid negative frustration by using good design principles and by employing iterative evaluation throughout the design lifecycle to identify frustrating moments that can be balanced or fixed during development.

There are several methods to infer frustration during gameplay. Researchers can visualize player death locations [11,4], or quitting behavior; can observe players [22] and look for signs that are based in physiology (e.g., red face, sweating) or behavior (e.g., agitation, swearing); can ask questions that explicitly ask players to recall frustrating moments [6]; or can record physiological signals that indicate negative arousal [23]. However, these methods either do not scale for use after commercial release or have a resolution too low to trigger adaptation. In addition, although these methods may indicate that a player is frustrated, they do not differentiate whether players will be motivated or disheartened as a result. Knowing whether the experienced frustration is motivating or disheartening is vital for game researchers and designers to be able to choose a course of action – for example, whether the in-game challenge should be reduced or whether the controls need to be fixed.

The problem that we address is that by using standard approaches for detecting frustration, researchers cannot reliably differentiate between motivating frustration that may encourage players to overcome in-game challenges and disheartening frustration that may result in players quitting. Previous research has shown that the pressure that players exert on controller buttons increases with increasing game difficulty [34]. As such, we propose that although the magnitude of frustration may be similar, the pressure exerted by players during touch-based game interaction will differentiate between these two types of frustration. Specifically, we hypothesized that motivating in-game frustration will result in greater touch pressure (reflecting engagement) and disheartening at-game frustration will result in lower touch pressure (reflecting disengagement).

ISS '16, November 06-09, 2016, Niagara Falls, ON, Canada
© 2016 ACM. ISBN 978-1-4503-4248-3/16/11…$15.00
DOI: http://dx.doi.org/10.1145/2992154.2992185

To differentiate frustration type using touch pressure, we designed a game that allowed us to vary the in-game challenge and responsiveness of the input controls. We created four experimental conditions: a training condition, in-game frustration (created through challenging obstacles), at-game frustration (created through unresponsive and laggy controls), and an easy condition (created through boring and repetitive obstacles) that was used as a comparison condition. In a study with 42 participants, we gathered data on player experience from several validated scales. We also collected touch pressure; however, because pressure-sensitive displays are not ubiquitous, we operationalized touch pressure as the size of the finger contact area, which can be sensed using a standard touch-sensitive display.

Our results showed that:

- There was no difference in the frustration ratings between the motivating and disheartening conditions, showing that the two types were similar in terms of the magnitude of experienced frustration;
- Players perceived in-game frustration as more difficult and attributed it more internally, which shows that our experimental manipulation of game challenge was successful at eliciting different experiences and that players blamed the system more for their performance during at-game frustration.
- In-game frustration was rated as more enjoyable than at-game frustration, which lends support to the distinction between positive motivating frustration and negative disheartening frustration.
- Competence, attribution, and difficulty were significant predictors of enjoyment; whereas frustration was not, suggesting that the root cause of the frustration (i.e., in-game or at-game) yields different experiences that could result in feeling motivated or disheartened.
- Most importantly, players pressed harder on average and also had higher peak pressures when the frustration was derived from in-game challenges (i.e., challenging level design) as opposed to at-game challenges (i.e., laggy controls), showing that motivating frustration can be objectively differentiated from disheartening frustration through an analysis of touch pressure.

Our results differentiate in-game and at-game frustration using subjective measures (e.g., enjoyment, attribution). More notably, our research is the first that we know of to use touch pressure to objectively distinguish between these interaction patterns. Understanding the degree of frustration is important for designers to create adaptive games; however, understanding the orientation of the frustration is equally important for making decisions on how to address the player experience problems through game design changes or difficulty adaptations. By using touch pressure to differentiate between in-game and at-game frustration, game designers will have a continuous and high-resolution indicator of player experience that complements the useful and robust tools already in the game user research toolbox.

RELATED WORK

In this section, we present an overview of positive and negative frustration in games and how it is measured along with an overview of touch input and touch pressure input in games, and how touch pressure is measured.

Frustration in Games

Frustration in game play can either be positive for player experience or negative for player experience, and researchers have suggested several ways of describing this distinction.

Positive frustration arises under various circumstances. For example, players may be positively frustrated when in-game challenges are slightly beyond a player's abilities – such as when playing against an opponent who is slightly superior in skill [1,2]. Players may also be positively frustrated when they do not know exactly what needs to be done to complete an in-game challenge [16]. Gilleade and Dix call this *in-game frustration*, defined as "a failure to know how a challenge is to be completed" [16]. Nyland and Landfors call this positive frustration, defined as frustration whose cause can be entirely ascribed to the player [28]. This desirable frustration has been argued as either originating from a particular source [16] or being attributed to the player [28]. We argue a distinction based on the resulting outcome of the frustrating experience. As such, we define *positive frustration as frustration that motivates the player to engage further with the game, i.e., motivating frustration.* Designers create positive frustration by producing well-balanced games with difficulty levels, by providing in-game assists either explicitly (e.g., health packs) or covertly (e.g., bullet magnetism) [36], by implementing dynamic difficulty adjustments that tailor to an individual's performance [18], or by scaffolding players to learn the mechanics and controls at an appropriate pace [20].

Negative frustration, on the other hand, arises when challenges are well beyond a player's capabilities (e.g., the enemy is too strong and the player has no chance of beating it) [6,36], the competition in multi-player games is unbalanced (e.g., the opponents have much greater skill and the player gets badly beaten) [36], or the game or controls do not behave in a way that the player expects (e.g., the mappings of the controller buttons to in-game actions are non-standard or unintuitive) [16,33]. Gilleade and Dix call this *at-game frustration* [16], defined as a "failure to operate the input device," which could be caused by poor command mapping, unresponsive input, complex input patterns, or the player's skill level. Nyland and Landfors call this negative frustration, whose cause can be attributed to the game itself [28]. We define *negative frustration as frustration that motivates the player to disengage with the game, i.e., disheartening frustration.* Designers try to avoid at-game frustration by using good design principles and by employing iterative evaluation throughout design to identify frustrating moments that can be balanced or fixed during development.

Although good design and iterative evaluation should help to avoid at-game frustration, it may also occur in a well-designed but poorly balanced game. Ijsselsteijn et al. [19] note that while in-game frustration can add to the satisfaction of completing a challenge, if it becomes too much, it may negatively impact player experience. As a result, they suggest that there is a need for real-time indicators of frustration [19]. In addition, we suggest that knowing whether the experienced frustration is motivating or disheartening is vital for game researchers and designers to be able to choose a course of action – for example, whether the in-game challenge should be reduced or whether the controls need to be adapted.

Measuring Frustration

There are several methods to infer frustration during gameplay. Researchers can visualize player death locations (indicating in-game chokepoints) [11,4], or quitting behavior; however, this only works after-the-fact and cannot be used to trigger an intervention. Researchers can infer frustration by observing players and looking for signs that are based in physiology (e.g., red face, sweating) or behavior (e.g., agitation, swearing); however, this requires a researcher to observe all gameplay and doesn't scale to dynamically adapt games in real time. Researchers can ask survey questions that explicitly ask players to recall frustration within a game [6,33], but the resolution of this method is low. Researchers can record physiological signals that detect arousal through, for example, heart rate or galvanic skin response [23]; however, this requires participants to be connected to expensive sensors and does not work for players in their natural environments. In addition, although these methods may indicate the degree of frustration experienced by a player, they do not differentiate whether players will be motivated or disheartened.

Touch in Games

In this section, we discuss touch as input, touch as an evaluation approach, and how to measure touch pressure.

Touch as Input

With the advent of smartphones, touch interaction has become a predominant mode of interaction with mobile systems. Although game controller or mouse/keyboard interactions still comprise the majority of game input, touch input continues to gain prominence through mobile gaming – recent estimates suggest that 35% of U.S. gamers play on a smartphone [13]. And although touch-based game interaction may be viewed as non-standard, research by Watson et al. [37] demonstrated that experience in a targeting game improved when using a multi-touch display over a mouse. In particular, participants experienced greater positive affect, felt more competent, in control, related to other people, and immersed when using touch input. They also showed that the results could not be explained by the intuitiveness of the controls, by discussing their findings within the framework of needs satisfaction [32,33].

Although touch is a common in-game interaction, touch pressure has not been leveraged as an input approach in the context of games. Several mobile gaming devices have pressure-sensitive screens (e.g., Wii U, 3DS); however, neither device exposes an application programming interface (API) to developers that would allow them to incorporate touch pressure as input mechanism. As the new iPhones have pressure-sensitive screens and allow developers to access this parameter, we may see an increase in the number of games that incorporate touch pressure as an input approach. Outside of the context of games, Cechanowicz and Gutwin [8] give several design examples of how click pressure exerted on a mouse could augment interactions with a computer interface. For example, they suggest that increased pressure could bypass dialog box confirmations or unlock locked folders. Similarly, Ramos and Balakrishnan [31] present several designs and a framework of how pressure exerted by a stylus on an interactive display could be used to augment interactions. Ramos and Balakrishnan also explored integrated panning and zooming using input pressure of a stylus while sliding in x-y space [30].

Touch as Evaluation

As opposed to being used as input to a game, the quality of touch interaction can also be used to evaluate interaction with a system. Pressure on game controller devices has been proposed to be linked to frustration. Sykes and Brown found that pressure on a gamepad increases with emotional arousal [34], while Octavia et al. showed that pressure exerted on a joystick indicates frustration [29]. Outside of the context of games, researchers have shown that frustration can be predicted by pressure exerted on chairs [35], keyboards [17,35], mice [9,21,17,35], and trackpads [25,26]. As such, touch pressure seems to be a good candidate for measuring frustration. In a study with touch gestures in Fruit Ninja played on an iPod, Gao et al., [15] found that pressure features discriminated frustration from excitement, relaxation, and boredom, whereas features related to stroke speed discriminated between levels of arousal. Using these features, the authors created a model that differentiated between low and high arousal and between low and high valence with 89% accuracy. Although indicative that great touch pressure should indicate frustration, this work does not differ between motivating and disheartening frustration.

Integrating Touch Pressure into Interaction

Most touchscreens afford a constrained 2-dimensional input space in which x- and y- locations are translated into on-screen actions. Touch pressure could act as a third dimension to this space. Using specially designed hardware that senses touch pressure, prior research has shown touch pressure to be useful for augmenting touch input, for example to speed up typing [5] or create more flexible gestures [31]. Because displays that have pressure-sensing capabilities are not yet ubiquitous, Ramos and Balakrishnan also suggest using the size of a fingertip's contact area with a touchscreen as a proxy for pressure [30]; this approach was also used by Gao et al. [15] in their examination of emotion during play of a touch-base game on an iPod and by Hernandez et al. [17] to operationalize pressure on a mouse through contact area.

EXPERIMENT

We conducted an experiment to determine whether pressure can differentiate between at-game and in-game frustration.

Game Design

The goal of our work was to differentiate between in-game and at-game frustration using both objective and subjective measures, and thus the game chosen for our experiments had to be able to be manipulated in terms of generating both kinds of frustration. Also, as with all games used in controlled experiments, we had to balance the need to get into the game quickly (unlike, for example, a complicated role-playing game) with the need to feel engaged. Finally, our game also required repeated touch input so that we could determine whether the pressure of touch input changed with frustration. As such, we wanted to choose a casual game – defined as games that are "fun, quick to access, easy to learn and require no previous special video game skills, expertise or regular time commitment to play" [7, pg. 3] – that used touch input regularly during the game. To meet these requirements, we chose an infinite runner game for our experiment. Infinite runners, also called endless runners, represent a very popular game type available on mobile devices (e.g., Temple Run [39]). We developed a game based on a version downloaded from the Unity 3D asset store [40]. Our game, called *City Run*, is very similar to commercial games, but developing our own version gave us the flexibility needed to introduce touch gestures to control the avatar, to introduce different types of frustration into the game, and to implement all of the touch event and game event logging needed to answer our research questions.

Figure 1. Our infinite runner game, called City Run.

In City Run, players control an avatar that runs along an infinite track, which is divided into three lanes (see Figure 1). As the avatar runs down the track, players must collect coins and avoid obstacles through a combination of jumping, ducking, and switching lanes. These avatar movements are accomplished using touch gestures: swiping left and right to switch lanes, swiping up to jump, and swiping down to duck. If the avatar hits an obstacle, it loses ten coins to a minimum of zero, but continues running. The avatar moves at a fixed speed, which increases over the course of the game. Rather than procedurally generating the obstacles (which would then be different each time the game was played), we scripted the locations and types of obstacles by hand-designing short patterns of obstacles. We created 11 patterns: 1 easy pattern with few obstacles, 8 medium patterns with a manageable numbers of obstacles, and 2 hard patterns with high numbers of obstacles. We then created the levels by piecing together a series of patterns. To create an easy level, we used the single easy pattern repeatedly. In the medium level, we used only the medium patterns. To create the hard level, we used half medium patterns and half hard patterns.

Frustration Conditions

To facilitate our manipulation of frustration, we modified the game to add three configurable parameters. *Input Lag* allowed us to introduce a configurable amount of lag to the touch input, meaning that the game's reaction to a player touching the screen could be delayed by an adjustable amount. *Input Fail* allowed us to introduce a configurable amount of failure into the gesture recognizer; failure was implemented as a specified percentage of the user's gestures on the touch screen simply being ignored by the game. *Difficulty* allowed us to adjust the difficulty of the game itself. We created three discrete levels of difficulty by varying the number of obstacles that the user had to avoid. This is similar to the way in which comparable commercial games create higher levels of difficulty.

Using these parameters, we created the following five experimental conditions.

1. **Training:** no modifications to the game, medium difficulty level
2. **Lag (at-game):** for each gesture the response was delayed by a random amount between 0 and 300ms, medium difficulty level
3. **Fail (at-game):** 1 of every 10 gestures were ignored, medium difficulty level
4. **Easy:** the appearance of obstacles was infrequent and repetitive compared to the other conditions
5. **Hard (in-game):** the appearance of obstacles was very frequent compared to the other conditions

A small pilot study helped to determine that the lag and fail conditions yielded very similar patterns of behaviour, and thus we only considered the Training, Easy, Lag, and Hard conditions moving forward with our full experiment. Our hypothesis was that lag would yield disheartening at-game frustration and game difficulty (i.e., hard) would yield motivating in-game frustration. The easy condition was included as a comparator and the training condition introduced players to the game mechanics and input. As such, our full experiment used four conditions: Training, In-game frustration (i.e., Hard), at-game frustration (i.e., Lag), and the Easy condition as the baseline.

In each condition, the game lasted until the player reached a fixed in-game distance of 800, which translated into approximately two minutes of play time. We chose this distance because it kept the duration of the entire experiment manageable, and also because it reflects the typical length of casual game play levels for mobile phone games.

We used a within-subjects design so participants played each condition. All participants began with the Training condition, and the order of presentation of the remaining three conditions was controlled using a Latin Square.

Participants and Procedure

We had 42 participants in the study (20 females, aged 18-49). Of our participants, 33 reported playing videos games at least once per week, and 37 reported playing mobile games on a phone or tablet previously. Participants were recruited though mailing lists at the University of Saskatchewan.

After providing informed consent, participants were introduced to the game and played the Training condition. Following completion of the game play, participants filled out a series of game experience questionnaires (see Measures section) about the condition they just played. This approach was repeated for the three remaining experimental conditions (presented in a Latin Square). Following all four conditions, participants completed a background survey that collected information on their basic demographics and game playing experience. We then debriefed participants on the nature of the experiment, and compensated them with $10.

The experiment was conducted on a Microsoft Surface Pro 3 computer using a connected multitouch-enabled monitor (positioned horizontally on the desktop) with a resolution of 1920x1080. Halfway through the experiment, we switched to the integrated screen of the Surface (resolution of 2160x1440), as we found that the pressure sensitivity of the touch monitor was inferior to the Surface. Because of the within-subjects design, in which we compare participants' performances to themselves across conditions, the fact that the technology was different for about half of the participants is not a major issue in our analyses; however, we return to this aspect in the discussion of the limitations of the study.

The game required that the computer use Windows 8 or higher. We instrumented the game so that each game event (e.g., obstacle hit) was logged to a file, each touch event was logged to a file, and we generated a summary log of overall game performance and touch pressure for ease of analysis. The experiment was conducted in a private room in a laboratory at the University of Saskatchewan.

Measures

We collected subjective measures of experience and objective measures of touch pressure.

Player Performance & Experience

We gathered the following validated measures of experience.

Perceived competence was gathered using the Player Experience of Needs Satisfaction (PENS) instrument [33]. Participants rated their agreement (on a 5-point scale from strongly disagree to strongly agree) with three items related to how well they felt they demonstrated mastery over the game's challenges (e.g., "I feel very capable and effective when playing"). The scale had good internal consistency (Cronbach's α=0.81).

Intuitive control was gathered also using PENS and reflects how well the game controls support interaction with the system. Three items (e.g., "When I wanted to do something in the game, it was easy to remember the corresponding control") rated on a 5-point scale from strongly disagree to strongly agree exhibited good internal consistency (Cronbach's α=0.69).

Enjoyment was measured using the interest-enjoyment subscale of the Intrinsic Motivation Inventory [24]. Five items (e.g., "Playing the game was fun") rated on a 5-point scale from strongly disagree to strongly agree exhibited good internal consistency (Cronbach's α=0.88).

Internal attribution was measured using three items (e.g., "The score of the round was mostly caused by things other than myself": recoded) adapted from [10]. Measured using a 5-point scale from strongly disagree to strongly agree, the Attribution scale exhibited good internal consistency (Cronbach's α=0.81). Attribution was collected to determine whether participants felt that their performance was attributable more to internal causes (e.g., skills and abilities) or more to external causes (e.g., game mechanics, system) [10]; a higher number indicates more internal attribution.

Difficulty was measured using the single item "How difficult was the game you just played?", rated on a 5-point scale from easy to hard.

Subjective performance was rated using the single item "How well do you think you did at the game?", rated on a 5-point scale from poor to excellent.

Frustration was measured using the single item "How frustrated did you feel with the game?", rated on a 5-point scale from not at all frustrated to very frustrated.

Touch Pressure

A pressure gesture generally follows a normal distribution over time – pressure increases to a peak and then decreases. We operationalized touch pressure metrics in three ways.

Peak pressure considers the peak of each individual touch gesture in a condition and averages those for an indicator of the central tendency of peak pressure.

Average pressure takes the average pressure of each gesture and returns the mean of those for an indicator of central tendency of average pressure.

We also considered the overall pressure – operationalized as the average of all pressure values in a condition, but found that it was almost identical to average pressure, and thus we only report average pressure.

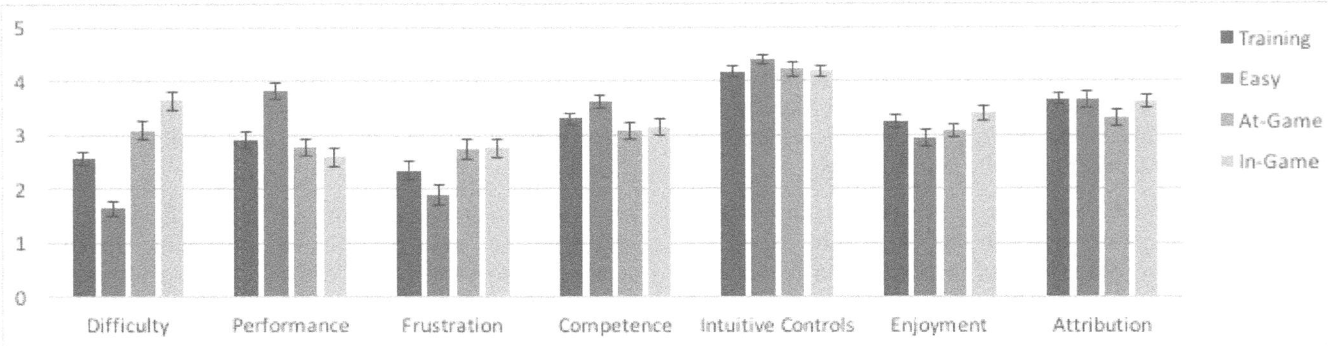

Figure 2. Means (±SE) of the subjective measures on a 5-pt scale (higher number indicates greater value).

Demographics

Demographic information was collected at the end of the study, including participant age, sex, gaming frequency, gaming devices used, and touchscreen experience.

Data Analyses

All data analysis was performed with IBM SPSS Statistics 24. It was important that participants included in the analyses were able to control the game with a base level of competence, thus we removed outlier participants who were three standard deviations below the mean on both subjective performance and objective performance (i.e., score). This resulted in the removal of a single participant who rated themselves as very low competence in all conditions and whose game score ranged between 0 and 18 (for comparison, the average score in the Training condition was 146). We performed a Multivariate Analysis of Variance with condition (easy, at-game, in-game) as a within-subjects factor on the subjective scales, (difficulty, frustration, performance, competence, intuitive controls, enjoyment, and attribution) and the touch pressure data (average pressure, average peak pressure). When the sphericity assumption was violated, we used the Greenhouse-Geisser correction.

RESULTS

We first present the results of player experience followed by the results from the touch data.

Player Experience

Our results showed main effects of condition on Competence ($F_{2,80}$=7.0, p=.002, η^2=.15), Enjoyment ($F_{2.85,64.5}$=5.8, p=.008, η^2=.13), Attribution ($F_{2,80}$=3.02, p=.05, η^2=.07), Frustration ($F_{2,80}$=13.1, p≈.000, η^2=.25), Difficulty ($F_{1.74,69.7}$=42.9, p≈.000, η^2=.52), and Performance ($F_{2,80}$=17.1, p≈.000, η^2=.30). See Figure 2. There were no main effects of condition on intuitive control ($F_{2,80}$=2.3, p=.105) or overall score ($F_{2,80}$=0.5, p=.624).

Participants felt less frustrated in the easy condition than in the in-game (p≈.000) or at-game (p≈.000) conditions. There was no difference in subjective frustration between in-game and at-game (p=.897). Similarly, participants felt more competent and that they performed better in the easy condition than the in-game (competence: p=.008; performance: p≈.000) or at-game (competence: p=.002; performance: p≈.000) conditions, with no differences between in-game and at-game (competence: p=.686; performance: p=.460). These results suggest that both in-game and at-game frustration yielded similar levels of frustration and that those two conditions did not produce differing levels of perceived performance or competence.

In terms of perceived difficulty, players felt that the in-game condition was more difficult than the at-game condition (p=.004), which was in turn more difficult than the easy condition (p≈.000), suggesting that the condition designed to yield in-game frustration was perceived as more challenging than the condition designed to yield at-game frustration. These results are expected as the frustration that arose from increasing the game's challenges (the in-game condition) should translate into an experience of a difficult game; whereas the frustration that arose from the game feeling laggy should not translate into an experience of difficulty.

In terms of the player experience, participants enjoyed the in-game condition more than the easy condition (p=.009) or the at-game condition (p=.003), with no differences observed between easy and at-game (p=.366). This suggests that in-game frustration yielded an enjoyable play experience, whereas at-game frustration yielded a less enjoyable play experience – even though there were no differences in the perceived levels of frustration for these two conditions.

Finally, participants attributed the cause of their performance more externally in the at-game condition than the easy condition (p=.029) or in-game condition (p=.035), but there was no difference between easy and in-game (p=.969). This suggests that regardless of actual performance, participants do not differentiate in their attribution of the cause of that performance when the game is easy or more challenging (attributing success and failure internally), but do distinguish when the game is affected by laggy controls (attributing more externally – likely to the system). Players attribute more externally for at-game frustration and more internally for in-game frustration.

Touch Pressure

In terms of the touch pressure data, we found a main effect of condition on both the average touch pressure ($F_{2,80}$=5.2, p=.008, η^2=.11) and the average peak pressure ($F_{2,80}$=4.5, p=.014, η^2=.10). In both cases, the results show that the in-game condition yielded more pressure than the at-game condition (average: p=.039; peak: p=.049) or the easy condition (average: p=.008; peak: p=.011), with no differences between the at-game and easy conditions (average: p=.190; peak: p=.247). These results suggest that participants press harder when they experience in-game frustration derived from the game's challenges than when they experience at-game frustration as a result of laggy controls. See Figure 3 (note that although the error bars seem large, it is due to using two different displays in the study; because participants were compared to themselves in a repeated-measures test (from a within-subjects design), the differences in display sensitivity affect the standard error and means, but not the statistical tests).

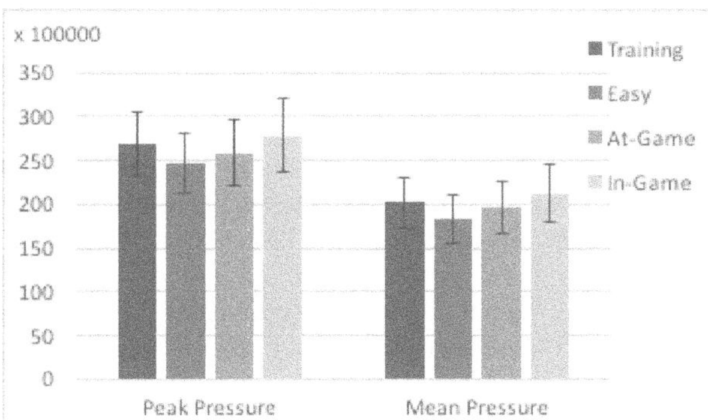

Figure 3. Means (±SE) of the peak and average pressure.

Predicting Enjoyment

Our results suggest that although frustration levels are similar for the in-game and at-game frustration conditions, the experience of participants varies depending on the source of the frustration. To determine the relative predictive value of the experiential variables on perceived enjoyment of the game, we conducted a hierarchical regression analysis in which we first entered the player satisfaction of needs variables (i.e., competence, intuitive control) and in a second step entered the variables frustration, difficulty and attribution. We began with the needs satisfaction variables because of the large body of work that suggests how satisfaction of needs during play translates into increased game enjoyment (e.g., [3]).

As shown in Table 1, perceived competence predicts enjoyment in the first step, whereas intuitive control did not. This is not surprising in our data set because we saw little variance in intuitive control overall. In the second step, both game difficulty and attribution predict enjoyment; however, frustration does not play a significant role. This reaffirms the idea that the amount of frustration is not as important in determining enjoyment as the source of that frustration. When the frustration stems from challenging in-game activities toward which players can internally attribute their performance (i.e., feel that the cause of their success is within themselves), the game is still enjoyable. On the other hand, when similar levels of frustration stem from problems or issues with the game environment that are not part of the game's mechanics or challenges, the game is less enjoyable.

Table 1. Unstandardized β values, t-statistic, and p-values for individual predictors of game enjoyment. R(m) and P(m) refer to the R and significance of the overall model fit for each step.

	Predicting Enjoyment				
	β	*t*	*p*	*R(m)*	*P(m)*
Step One	**Player Experience of Need Satisfaction (PENS)**				
Competence	0.543	6.80	**<.001**	0.526	**<.001**
Intuitive Control	-0.170	1.56	0.121		
Step Two	**Difficulty, Attribution, and Frustration**				
Difficulty	0.213	3.59	**<.001**		
Attribution	0.252	3.49	**0.001**	0.663	**<.001**
Frustration	0.003	0.05	0.963		

DISCUSSION

In this section, we summarize the results and provide possible explanations for the patterns of behavior that we observed. We then describe implications for the design and evaluation of games and other media, followed by a discussion of the limitations and future opportunities enabled by the research.

Summary and Explanation for Results

As expected, the easy condition was rated as least difficult, with the best performance, lowest frustration, and highest competence. In terms of differentiating between in-game and at-game frustration, people found the level of frustration to be similar in the in-game and at-game conditions; however, they found that in-game frustration was perceived as more difficult and more enjoyable than at-game frustration. They also attributed more internally for in-game frustration than at-game frustration and pressed harder on average and also at the peak when the frustration was derived from in-game challenges (i.e., challenging level design) as opposed to at-game annoyances (i.e., laggy controls). Finally, competence, attribution, and difficulty were significant predictors of enjoyment, whereas frustration was not.

We did not see any differences in the ratings of intuitive control between the conditions and it was also not a predictor of enjoyment. This is not surprising as the interface to the game was the same in each condition – players made directional gestures to jump, duck, and switch lanes. As such, we would expect their ratings of intuitive controls to not vary with the amount of game challenge. We may have expected the lack of responsiveness in the at-game condition to affect ratings for intuitive control; however, the participants were rating the input mappings and not the laggy response. This was also made clear in that players attributed their performance more externally in the laggy condition – suggesting that they perceived that it was the system's fault that they did not perform well and not their own fault.

Contextualizing within Current Literature

The idea that games offer different types of challenges, which result in different types of experiences has been established. Gilleade and Dix differentiated between in-game and at-game frustration [16] as frustration that is derived from the game's challenges versus frustration that stems from an inability to operate the game controls. Nyland and Landfors [28] distinguish between positive and negative frustration depending on the attribution of the source of that frustration (user or game respectively). Lazzaro [22] differentiates between four types of fun in games, referring to hard fun (i.e., in-the-moment personal triumph over adversity), easy fun (i.e., curiosity), serious fun (i.e., relaxation and excitement), and people fun (i.e., amusement). In describing hard fun, she notes how the in-game challenges focus a player's attention and reward their progress, which creates emotions such as frustration and fiero – a feeling of personal triumph. In self-determination theory, Ryan et al. [33] describe that games have motivational pull because they allow people to experience a sense of mastery over challenges (i.e., competence) by offering choice and volitional engagement (i.e., autonomy), in an environment that supports connections to other players and characters in the game (i.e., relatedness). The act of volitionally overcoming challenges creates a sense of competence, even if frustration at the failure of repeated attempts is experienced along the way.

Touch Pressure as an Indication of Frustration

Our results show that when frustration stems from challenging in-game activities, and players are able to internally attribute their performance (i.e., feel that the cause of their success in the game is within themselves), the game experience is enjoyable. On the other hand, when similar levels of frustration stem from problems or issues with the game environment that are not part of the game's mechanics or challenges, the game experience is less enjoyable. As such, it isn't the degree of frustration experienced by the players, but the source of that frustration that is more important for determining future engagement.

More importantly, we showed that touch pressure (both average pressure and peak pressure) can differentiate between an enjoyable type of frustration and a less enjoyable type of frustration. Players pressed harder when the frustration was experienced as a result of in-game challenges. When the frustration was experienced at the game itself, the players pressed less hard – similar in degree to the pressure exerted in the easy condition. Although we cannot say for certain, the lower pressure in the laggy response condition may have been prompted by a feeling of disengagement from the participants. This disengagement may have been the driving factor behind not pressing as hard when frustrated with the game.

Implications for Design and Games User Research

Games offer players a relatively risk-free environment in which they can try new things and fail multiple times before experiencing the joy of triumphing over adversity. Differentiating between the negative frustration that arises when players are challenged well beyond their capacity or when controls do not operate as expected, and the positive frustration that results from getting so close to overcoming a challenge before failing and trying again is essential for game designers and researchers. The negative frustration should be prevented through better game design, better game balance [36], or scaffolding player skill development [20]. The positive frustration should be maintained so long as it does not start to turn into negative frustration. Our results move toward a method of distinguishing in real-time whether a player is positively frustrated through in-game challenges or whether they are negatively frustrated by poor design. If designers can detect these states during game play, they can provide games that better adapt to a player's emotional state and ability – which would ultimately create more engaging and successful games.

Although our work is grounded in the need for frustration detection in game user research, there are also applications beyond games. There are many productivity applications that could offer assistance if they detected that a user is struggling or could adapt the interface if it is detected that a user is overwhelmed [14]. Although we cannot generalize our results beyond games, there is an opportunity to determine how touch pressure can be used a metric for evaluation in serious applications.

Limitations and Future Work

Our research provides initial support for the idea that touch pressure is valuable for differentiating between types of frustration in gameplay. There are limitations in the generalization of our results and many opportunities afforded by the work.

First, as discussed in the methods section, we did not use a pressure-sensitive display, but operationalized pressure as the contact area of the finger. We chose this approach because touch-sensitive displays are prevalent, but true pressure-sensitive displays are only now becoming more accessible, which makes our method more practical for application. However, the accuracy of this method may vary on different devices because the resolution of touch digitizers varies. Further, contact area is more commonly used in differentiating between fingertips and palms, which requires a very low degree of accuracy, reducing the incentive for device manufacturers to increase the accuracy of touch digitizers. Device manufacturers also rarely document the specifications of their touch digitizers, making it difficult to know how well our method of pressure sensing will perform across all devices. The initial display that we used in our study is not as sensitive as Microsoft's Surface, which we switched to part way through collecting our data. As we used a within-subjects design, we compared participants' performance to themselves, and the display was kept consistent for an individual participant. However, future work should use the most sensitive displays.

Second, we adjusted difficulty to create in-game frustration using two factors – the number of obstacles and the repetitiveness of obstacles. It is possible that are results are driven by one of these factors – that people press harder when they are more engaged through novelty or more engaged through challenge. Future research should deconstruct the increased pressure further – we showed that pressure was higher in the more challenging and more enjoyable condition; however, investigating the source of the enjoyment and how variations in that source affect touch pressure would be valuable.

Third, along these lines, we investigated touch pressure in the context of a popular genre of mobile games – an infinite runner game. The infinite runner uses gestures (i.e., swiping) and investigating whether our results extend to other interaction techniques (e.g., tapping, pinching, marking) is an important future extension of our work.

Finally, we looked at touch pressure as an objective measure of player experience. Although we characterized the data in the subjective experience of players, comparing the information provided by touch pressure with other objective data sources (e.g., logging and visualization of game events [11], player physiological responses [23], eyetracking [38], or posture sensing [27]) would further help game user researchers characterize player experience using objective and continuous real-time metrics.

CONCLUSION

Frustration in game play can be both a motivating and positive source of engagement for players and a disheartening and negative reason to quit. There are various methods of determining the frustration level of people playing games; however, the existing methods are either too low in resolution (e.g., survey data), do not scale for games after release (e.g., observation), or require expensive sensors that are not appropriate for use in people's homes (e.g., physiology). In this paper, we describe an objective and non-disruptive method for differentiating between types of frustration in a touch-based game – by using the average or average peak pressure of the touch gestures.

We demonstrated how touch pressure can be used to detect the positive challenging frustration that is desired in game design. Used in combination with other existing methods, player frustration and its type can be characterized, yielding opportunities for game designers to adapt their systems and create more engaging and successful games.

ACKNOWLEDGMENTS

We acknowledge NSERC for funding, the Interaction Lab for support, cats for being awesome, and our participants.

REFERENCES

1. Abuhamdeh, S., & Csikszentmihalyi, M. The importance of challenge for the enjoyment of intrinsically motivated, goal-directed activities. *Pers. & Soc. Psych. Bull.*, 38 (3), (2012), 317-330.
2. Abuhamdeh, S., Csikszentmihalyi, M., & Jalal, B. Enjoying the possibility of defeat: Outcome uncertainty, suspense, and intrinsic motivation. *Motiv. & Emot.*, 1-10, (2014). Published online.
3. Birk, M. V., Mandryk, R. L., Miller, M. K., & Gerling, K. M. How self-esteem shapes our interactions with play technologies. In *Proc. CHI Play'15, (2015)*, 35-45.
4. Birk, M. V., Lürig, C., & Mandryk, R. L. A metric for automatically flagging problem levels in games from prototype walkthrough data. In *Proc. of the 19th International Academic Mindtrek Conference*, ACM Press, (2015), 33-40.
5. Brewster, S. A. and Hughes, M. Pressure-based text entry for mobile devices. In *Proceedings of the 11th International Conference on Human-Computer Interaction with Mobile Devices and Services*, ACM Press, (2009), 9.
6. Canossa, A., Drachen, A., & Sørensen, J. R. M. Arrrgghh!!!: blending quantitative and qualitative methods to detect player frustration. In Proc. of Fun and Games (2011), 61-68.
7. Casual Games Market Report 2007. Casual Games Association.
8. Cechanowicz, J., Irani, P., and Subramanian, S. Augmenting the Mouse with Pressure Sensitive Input. In *Proc. CHI 2007*, ACM Press, (2007), 1385-1394.
9. Dennerlein, J., Becker, T., Johnson, P., Reynolds, C., and Picard, R. W. Frustrating computer users increases exposure to physical factors. In *Proc. International Ergonomics Association*, Seoul, Korea (2003).
10. Depping, A., Mandryk, R.L., Li, C., Gutwin, C., Vicencio-Moreira, R. How Disclosing Skill Assistance Affects Play Experience in a Multiplayer First-Person Shooter Game. In Proc. *CHI 2016*, (2016), 3462-3472.
11. Drachen, A., & Canossa, A. Analyzing spatial user behavior in computer games using geographic information systems. In Proc. of MindTrek'13, (2009), 182-189.
12. Dring, C. More money is spent on games then on movies or music combined, says IHS (Blog post, 2015). Retrieved from: http://www.mcvuk.com/news/read/more-money-is-spent-on-games-than-movies-and-music-combined-says-ihs/0151059.
13. Entertainment Software Association. Essential Facts 2015. Retrieved from: http://www.theesa.com/wp-content/uploads/2015/04/ESA-Essential-Facts-2015.pdf
14. Findlater, L., Moffatt, K., McGrenere, J., & Dawson, J. Ephemeral adaptation: The use of gradual onset to improve menu selection performance. In *Proc. CHI'09,* (2009), 1655-1664. ACM.
15. Gao, Y., Bianchi-Berthouze, N., & Meng, H. What does touch tell us about emotions in touchscreen-based

gameplay? *ACM Transactions on Computer-Human Interaction (TOCHI)*, 2012, *19*(4), 31.

16. Gilleade, K. M., and Dix, A. Using frustration in the design of adaptive videogames. In *Proc. ACE'04*, ACM Press (2004), 228-232.

17. Hernandez, J., Paredes, P., Roseway, A., & Czerwinski, M. Under pressure: sensing stress of computer users. In *Proc. CHI'14*, 2014, 51-60.

18. Hunicke, R. The case for dynamic difficulty adjustment in games. *In Proc. ACE'05*, (2005), 429-433.

19. IJsselsteijn, W., De Kort, Y., Poels, K., Jurgelionis, A., and Bellotti, F. Characterising and measuring user experiences in digital games. In *Proc. ACE'07,* (2007), 27.

20. Johanson, C., Mandryk, R.L. 2016. Scaffolding Player Location Awareness through Audio Cues in First-Person Shooters. *In Proc. CHI'2016*, (2016), 3450-3461.

21. Kapoor, A., Burleson, W., & Picard, R. W. Automatic prediction of frustration. *International journal of human-computer studies,* 65(8), (2007), 724-736.

22. Lazzaro, N. (2004, March). Why we play games: 4 keys to more emotion. In Proc. Game Dev. Conf.

23. Mandryk, R. L., Atkins, M. S., & Inkpen, K. M. A continuous and objective evaluation of emotional experience with interactive play environments. In *Proc. of CHI'06*, (2006), 1027-1036.

24. McAuley, E., Duncan, T., & Tammen, V. V. Psychometric properties of the Intrinsic Motivation Inventory in a competitive sport setting: A confirmatory factor analysis. *Research Quarterly for Exercise and Sport*, 60, 1989, 48-58.

25. McLaughlin, M., Chen, Y. S., Park, N., Zhu, W., and Yoon, H. Recognizing user state from haptic data. In *International Conference on Information Systems Analysis and Synthesis* (2005).

26. Mentis, H. M. Using touchpad pressure to detect negative affect. In *Proceedings of the 4th IEEE International Conference on Multimodal Interfaces*, IEEE Computer Society (2002), 406.

27. Mutlu, B., Krause, A., Forlizzi, J., Guestrin, C., and Hodgins, J. Robust, low-cost, non-intrusive sensing and recognition of seated postures. In *Proc. UIST'07,* (2007), 149-158.

28. Nylund, A., and Landfors, O. Frustration and its effect on immersion in games: A developer viewpoint on the good and bad aspects of frustration. Master's Thesis. Umeå University, Sweden. (2015).

29. Octavia, J. R., Coninx, K., & Luyten, K. Squeeze me and i'll change: An exploration of frustration-triggered adaptation for multimodal interaction. In *3D User Interfaces (3DUI)*, (2011), 79-86.

30. Ramos, G., and Balakrishnan, R. Zliding: fluid zooming and sliding for high precision parameter manipulation. In *Proc. UIST'05*, ACM Press, (2005), 143-152.

31. Ramos, G. A., and Balakrishnan, R. Pressure marks. In *Proc. CHI'07*, ACM Press (2007), 1375-1384.

32. Ryan, R. M., & Deci, E. L. Self-determination theory and the facilitation of intrinsic motivation, social development, and well-being. *American Psychologist*, 55(1), 2000, 68.

33. Ryan, R.M., Rigby, C.S., & Przybylski, A. The motivational pull of video games: A self-determination theory approach. *Motivation and Emotion*, 30(4), 2006, 344-360.

34. Sykes, J., and Brown, S. Affective gaming: measuring emotion through the gamepad. In *CHI'03 extended abstracts on Human factors in computing systems*, ACM Press (2003), 732-733.

35. Van den Hoogen, W. M., IJsselsteijn, W. A., De Kort, Y. A. W., and Poels, K. Toward real-time behavioral indicators of player experiences: Pressure patterns and postural responses. In *Proceedings of Measuring Behaviour* (2008), 100-101.

36. Rodrigo Vicencio-Moreira, Regan L. Mandryk, and Carl Gutwin. 2015. Now You Can Compete With Anyone: Balancing Players of Different Skill Levels in a First-Person Shooter Game. In Proc. *CHI 2015*, (2015), 2255-2264.

37. Watson, D., Hancock, M., Mandryk, R. L., & Birk, M. Deconstructing the touch experience. In *Proc. of ITS'13*, (2013), 199-208.

38. Zammitto, V., Seif El-Nasr, M., & Newton, P. (2010). Exploring quantitative methods for evaluating sports games. In *Proc. CHI 2010 Workshop on Brain, Body and Bytes.*

39. http://imangistudios.com/

40. 3D Infinite Runner Toolkit – Unity Asset Store. http://u3d.as/5Nh.

Miners: Communication and Awareness in Collaborative Gaming at an Interactive Display Wall

Ulrich von Zadow, Daniel Bösel, Duc Dung Dam,
Anke Lehmann, Patrick Reipschläger, Raimund Dachselt
Interactive Media Lab Dresden
Technische Universität Dresden
Dresden, Germany
{firstname}.{lastname}@tu-dresden.de

ABSTRACT
Research on interactive wall displays has thus far focused mostly on professional use. However, as large displays with support for touch and other input modalities become more common, it becomes reasonable to assume use in more casual settings as well. We present *Miners*, one of the first collaborative games for a touch-sensitive display wall, and investigate multimodal, multi-user interaction in this context. In this fast-paced game, four players cooperate to rescue workers trapped in an underground cave, with each player being able to influence the game world in a different way. In an exploratory study using Miners, we found that players enjoyed the game and showed very high engagement. On the other hand, awareness suffered: Players often missed events in other areas. In addition, we found limited awareness of other players' actions and social cues. We report on these results in detail and discuss implications for touch-based wall interaction in general as well as in other application contexts.

ACM Classification Keywords
H.5.m. Information Interfaces and Presentation (e.g. HCI): Miscellaneous

Author Keywords
Collaborative games, display wall, tangible interaction, wall interaction, multitouch, awareness

INTRODUCTION
As display technology advances, wall-sized interactive displays will become usable in more and more settings. Current high-resolution displays often support input modalities such as touch, pen and marker-based tangible input. Research in this area has focused mostly on professional use, e.g., for visualization [1]. Work on wall interaction has found them well-suited for collaboration [13], with physical navigation – locomotion to access data – being a central aspect [3, 15]. It is reasonable to assume that broader usage scenarios and more informal use will become feasible as equipment prices decline. At the same time, there is only little research that covers such casual use (e.g., [17]), and even less gaming [22] on touch-sensitive walls. While there is some research on casual use of large displays in the tabletop domain (e.g., [11, 25]), it is unclear whether the results apply to interactive vertical displays as well. This also applies to research on awareness: While others have, e.g., compared mouse and touch input on tabletops with regard to awareness of collaborators' actions [12], awareness is to our knowledge only mentioned in passing in wall-related work (e.g., [9, 14]).

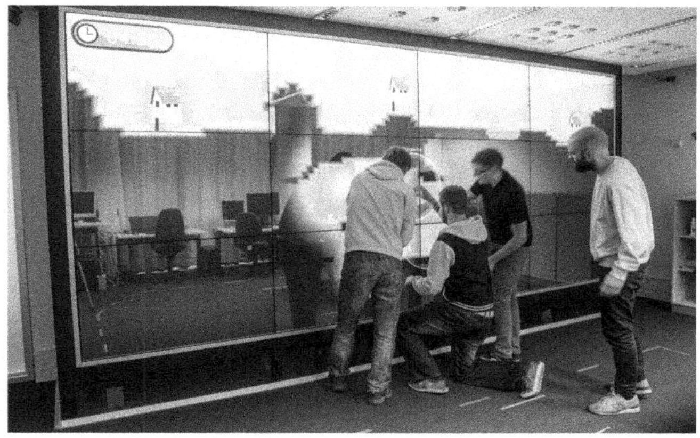

Figure 1. Typical Miners gameplay scene

We therefore designed and implemented a fast-paced, collaborative multi-player game for a large wall display, *Miners* (Figure 1). Miners uses a bimanual, combined tangible-touch interface with physical navigation, where players interact in a game world similar to the game Lemmings. With Miners, we contribute novel game mechanics and an interaction concept which – to the best of our knowledge – has not been described before. To investigate aspects of collaboration and awareness in this exemplary setting, we conducted an exploratory observational study using this game. While players enjoyed the game and showed very high engagement, we also found a number of awareness and communication issues which we believe are relevant beyond our specific application case.

ISS '16, November 06 - 09, 2016, Niagara Falls, ON, Canada

ACM 978-1-4503-4248-3/16/11... $15.00
DOI: http://dx.doi.org/10.1145/2992154.2992174

MINERS

Miners is a game for four players that revolves around rescuing miners from a cavern displayed in cross-section on a wall display. Injured and initially immobile miners are dispersed through the dark cavern, and the goal of the players is to rescue them by sending additional miners down from the surface given limited time. Each of the players has a different tool to interact with: One player can build bridges, another ladders, the third has a pickaxe to remove obstacles, and the last can place lights. Consequently, players need to cooperate to succeed. Our game development was iterative, user-centered, and involved regular tests by new users to ensure easy learnability. To identify users (and thus determine the tool in use), we use tangible markers. These are held in one hand and open up a circular interaction lens when they touch the wall (Figure 2). The player can then touch inside the lens to activate the tool (and, e.g., build a bridge).

Each game level starts with a 30-second *Planning Phase* in which the mine is lit in its entirety, allowing the players to orient themselves. In this phase, no interaction with the game world or the miners is possible. In the following five-minute *Interaction Phase*, the mine is completely dark and lit only through player actions. To win, players need to bring all miners to the surface. Miners follow simple rules while moving: They walk in one direction, turning around when they reach an obstacle. They can fall without hurting themselves, but there are lava pits that injure them. When they meet a regular miner, injured miners in the caverns start walking as well. Significantly, the size of the wall display allows us to show the complete game board, making a minimap superfluous.

Although there is ongoing research on this (e.g., [27]), most current touch-sensitive surfaces do not detect who is interacting. Therefore, we support player-specific interaction using tangibles to open an *Interaction Lens* specific to that player (Figure 2). The lens temporarily lights up the immediate surroundings, and touches inside the lens trigger actions. When two interaction lenses overlap, the area turns red and interaction becomes impossible. This constitutes a convenient means of bimanual interaction: In general, the user's non-dominant hand creates an interaction zone, allowing the dominant hand to interact. To our knowledge, using tangibles for this purpose, while similar to, e.g., Schmidt et al.'s IdLenses [20] and Kister et al.'s BodyLenses [15], is novel in a game context.

Bridge and Ladder components have a limited lifetime, so they need to be placed shortly before miners arrive. Further, the number of concurrently placed Bridge, Ladder and Light components is limited, with the current use count displayed at the top of the Interaction Lens. Besides removing obstacles, the Pickaxe can also be used to destroy placed components. While any tool produces a small, temporary light, the Light tool can place permanent lamps that illuminate a larger area.

Our game is designed to put a focus on teamwork and communication and clearly requires a group effort to succeed. It therefore implements typical cooperative game mechanics such as heterogenous resources, common goals and collaborative tasks [18, 21, 24]. At the same time, it is interesting because enforces physical navigation close to the display wall, uses bimanual tangible+touch interaction, and thus has the potential to significantly change mechanisms for collaboration.

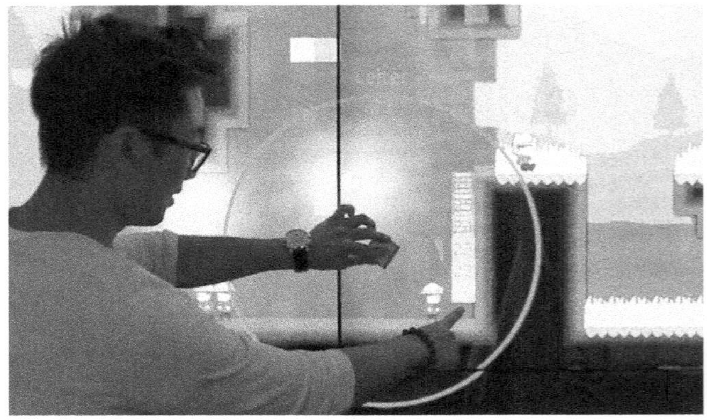

Figure 2. Miners interface: The player opens an Interaction Lens using the tangible in his left hand. Touches in this lens then activate his tool.

Miners is implemented in Python using the media application framework libavg[1]. Our prototype runs on a display wall consisting of twelve 55" multi-touch displays with a total dimension of 5x2 meters and 24 megapixels resolution. The wall supports touch and pen input as well as marker-based tangibles.

RELATED WORK ON GAMES

A number of papers have covered gaming at large display walls. Most involve interaction at a distance using various input modalities; touch is seldom used. Multi-player games include Polar Defence, Tabula Rasa and PyBomber. While Polar Defence [7] uses text messaging in a public walk-up-and-use setting and focuses on engaging bystanders, Tabula Rasa [8] is a two-player game with a single player interacting at a large display using a game controller and the second player interacting using touch at a separate tabletop. Machaj et al. investigate 4- and 12-player interaction at a large display wall using Wiimotes as input devices in PyBomber [16]. This game involves physical navigation, and the authors find some of the same issues with occlusion that we do. Additionally, Hoare et al. [10] investigated a single-user wall game for children using a smartphone camera for interaction, and Vepsäläinen et al. [23] report on an in-the-wild deployment of a game for a large public display controlled using smartphones. None of these publications involve interaction close to the wall, nor do they report results on awareness.

The only wall game involving touch known to us is Toprak et al.'s [22] Bubble Popper, which focuses on physical contact between players as gameplay mechanic. To our knowledge, Miners is the first cooperative multi-user game based on a touch-sensitive display wall.

USER STUDY

To learn about the behavior of groups closely collaborating at a large display wall, we conducted an exploratory, largely qualitative study using Miners. We focused on two major

[1] http://www.libavg.de

research questions: First, how do the physical environment (a large display wall) and interaction modality (tangible+touch, interaction close to the wall) impact collaboration? Second, do the insights from prior work on wall displays – especially those pertaining to awareness and collaboration – hold in a casual, fast-paced game environment? This is interesting because collaborative games in other environments don't have this amount of body involvement and physical navigation.

Method

Our study involved four groups of four players each (recruited from the local university, ages 19-30, 25% female, avg. 45 min per group, various levels of acquaintance within the groups.), with an additional two groups in a pre-study to adjust study parameters. Subjects are designated using 1A-4D in the following, with the initial digit signifying the group and the letter indicating a specific group member. After an explanation of the game and signing informed consent, subjects played a total of five levels: a tutorial level, three levels with increasing difficulty, and a final level where speaking was prohibited to provoke use of non-verbal communication. We conducted a semi-structured interview with each group, each participant answered a short questionnaire (see the most important questions in Figure 3), and we video-taped the sessions. Finally, we recorded head position and direction of the participants using an Optitrack system (head positions and directions are not evaluated in this work). There were at least three observers per group, which discussed and compared notes immediately after each session to iteratively build understanding.

Based on these observations and related work [6, 21], one person conducted a video analysis, with the results again discussed among all researchers. During analysis, we looked for interaction and awareness issues, observed players' focus of attention and mechanisms for communication (verbal, gestural, eye contact). We further analysed communication content and studied the movement of players in front of the wall.

Findings

In general, subjects enjoyed the game very much, with two of the groups asking to play again post-study without being prompted. This was visible in high engagement and motivation, as well as bodily involvement such as running or kneeling down to interact or to get out of the way. It was also reflected in the questionnaire results (Figure 3): The game was rated very highly for fun, with an average of 6.125 (SD: 0.806) on a 7-point scale. In interviews, several players commented that

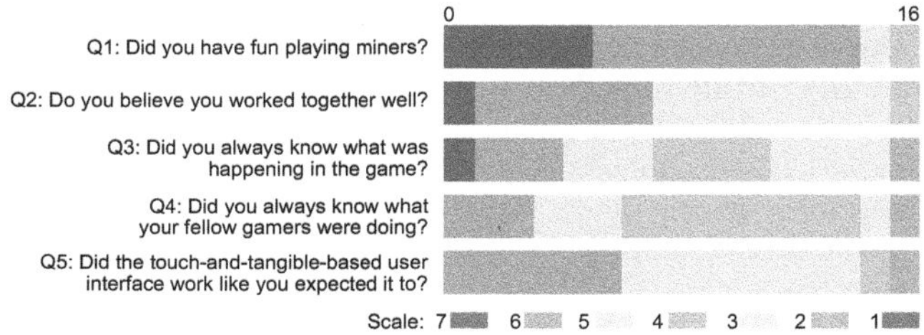

Figure 3. Excerpt of the questionnaire results with 7 signifying strong agreement, 1 strong disagreement.

they particularly liked the physical aspects of the game, including the whole-body movement needed, and that the sheer size of the wall helped immersion. The Interaction Lens-based interface as well as the basic game mechanics were generally understood during the tutorial level, but some specifics (e.g., the minimum tunnel height above ladders) took longer for players to grasp.

Note that given the number of study participants, the quantitative results should not be overinterpreted and are therefore only reported in excerpts. On the other hand, the qualitative results were largely uniform across the four groups, so we assume that additional participants would not have yielded additional insights.

Positioning and Locomotion

During the planning phase, players generally stood at an overview distance from the wall and discussed possible interactions, while respecting others' personal zones. This changed in the interaction phase: When players cooperated well, they stood in a group close to the wall, sharing a focus of attention and following miners moving through the caves. Interaction proceeded in turns, with the Light tool often scouting the way. However, there were frequent departures from this ideal: Players would often break off of the group to pursue individual goals or scout ahead.

Through video analysis, we found three possible states for players (with many fluid changes between states and between shared and individual foci of attention):

- *Active*: Directly interacting. Close to the wall and generally focused on their Interaction Lenses. Generally, no more than two people could interact at once.
- *Ready*: Still close to the wall, but focused on the active players' interaction lenses. Ready state players were able to interact at moment's notice.
- *Observing*: One or two steps behind the Active and Ready state players. Observing players hovered on the periphery, getting an overview of the other players and the game state but unable to interact immediately. In general, occlusion by other players caused Observing state players to keep changing their viewpoint by moving. These players were also most likely to take on leader or coordinator roles.

Figure 1 shows a typical configuration: The two center players are in Active state, the left player is Ready, and the right player is Observing. Note that states are closely related to the role the players take on as well as their physical distance from the wall and the observed center of interaction.

Significantly, no more than three players could share a focus of attention in Active or Ready states at once for space reasons. This is visible in Figure 1, where the Observing player would have had a hard time interacting without physically displacing one of the other players. In the Active and Ready states, there was also no evidence of territoriality [2] and much interaction in very close proximity (Player 4B: "Twister-like") – even among strangers. Players physically got in each other's way, but several players stated that this actually added to the fun in the interview.

Figure 4. Awareness issues: The player at the right cannot see what the other players are doing.

Awareness

We observed many instances of tunnel vision, where players were unaware of the game state or other players' actions. In addition, the corresponding questions in the survey (Figure 3, Q3 and Q4) got much less positive results than the other questions. This was less an issue when players shared a single focus of attention. Conversely, it was most severe when players interacted apart from the group close to the wall (e.g., Figure 4), where only the game state in the player's immediate center of attention was seen. In some instances, players missed changes directly outside their respective Interaction Lenses. Global game state such as the time left was in most cases ignored completely, with players acting surprised when the time was up. Interestingly, even the 'Game Over' state, where the complete wall darkens and a corresponding text is displayed that spans several displays, was ignored once in the study (Player 3B continued interaction attempts for more than 5 seconds) and several times during playtesting.

In Observing state, players were in most cases aware of the events in their general area. This was visible in the videos and commented on several times in the interviews (2B: "I could get an overview by stepping back", 2C: "Stepping back worked, but there were occlusion issues", 4C: "I had the choice to either interact or get an overview"). Also, Observing players were sometimes able to help with awareness issues that the immediately involved players had. One example of this would be the display of a tool usage count which was missed by the interacting player, with the observer pointing out the issue.

Communication

Communication in Miners was generally used to to tell a player to use her tool, to explain game mechanics, or to discuss strategy. As mechanisms, we observed:

- Verbalisation: Often short and in command form ("Ladder here!"), with very context-dependent content.
- Pointing: Generally using the complete arm. Pointing was mostly seen in the planning phase, less often during hectic gameplay.
- Interaction Lens: Players would place their tangible on the wall to show locations, sometimes moving it around to mark an area.
- Bodily contact such as a tap on the shoulder, usually to gain someone's attention.

In the planning phase, verbalisation and pointing were commonly used. There were no issues with getting other players' attention. Again, this changed during the interaction phase, where getting other's attention was an issue, and, in consequence, players ignored other's needs regularly. Notably, there was very little eye contact between players, since players mostly focused on the wall and the game state. Eye contact was also not used as often as expected when asking for attention (e.g., when action by another player was needed), and co-verbal gestures were seldom used for communication.

There were issues with getting attention in all groups, with repeated and in some cases drastic measures taken to resolve this. In approximate order of urgency, we observed the following methods of getting attention:

- Calling the player's or the tool's name.
- Repeated tool names (e.g., 1C: "Pick, pick", 3B: "Light light light"), louder words and commands (e.g., 1A: "Get going!", 3B: "Quickly!").
- Light bodily contact.
- Exertion of force: We observed one case where a player didn't react to other cues and was forcefully pushed in the direction required.

In addition, when getting attention failed, other players would often intervene.

Not surprisingly, in the level without speaking, communication became even harder and getting others' attention was very difficult. In many cases, gestures were used to communicate intent (e.g., 'ladder' indicated by an up-down hand movement.), but this was often ignored since the intended recipient's attention was elsewhere.

DISCUSSION

Our case study describes interactions and behavior specific to one game, and by themselves it is not clear to what degree the findings can be applied to more general cases. However, some of our results are interesting because they confirm and emphasize findings by other researchers in a new usage context. In addition, several aspects have been seen in other areas but not put into a broader perspective – the most important of these being that social awareness is likely limited when interacting close to a wall display.

Awareness

One fundamental fact about wall interaction is that when users are close to the wall, they see only a small part of the interface. It is clear that this is a potential cause for *blindness to changes in the display contents*, and findings by other researchers support this: Among others, Sabri et al. [19] observed issues with awareness of peripheral information with larger displays in a single-user game played on different-sized displays, Andrews et al. [1] hypothesize that change blindness will become an issue when interacting at close proximity to wall displays, and Bezerianos et al. [4] find that content further away is hard to perceive because of reflections, low contrast, and distortions when users are close to the wall. In the case of our game, where people can only interact when close to the wall, these findings become even more evident.

Additionally, our observations show a related but separate issue: Users interacting within touching distance of the wall suffered from limited *awareness of other users*. This pertains to awareness of other's interactions with the software as well as awareness of social cues such as gestures, body posture, facial expressions and eye contact. There are some hints at similar issues in related work. E.g., Jakobsen and Hornbæk [14] found "more negative signs of awareness" when interacting close to a large vertical display, and Hawkey et al. [9] found similar awareness issues at a vertical display when one participant was further away than the other.

However, the issues we observed were much more pronounced. High engagement with the game world and stress caused by the time-critical interaction, as well as the Interaction Lens concept probably contributed to this. Also, Miners only supports interaction when in direct proximity to the wall. Still, we assume that awareness issues will appear elsewhere: If users remain close to the wall, the wall takes up the complete field of view, preventing users from perceiving social cues (gestures, body posture, facial expressions, eye contact) of others in addition to causing blindness to interface changes. In contrast, consider the other main collaborative single-device setting, the tabletop: Tabletop users can see each other's arms, so pointing and touch interactions remain visible. In addition, body posture and gestures can be observed through peripheral vision and eye contact can be established more easily (see, e.g., [25, 26]). These mechanisms facilitate collaboration and are missing in our as well as likely most other wall-based scenarios with direct interaction. A further contributing factor may have been that our wall is significantly larger than in many other studies (e.g., [5, 8, 9, 14]) and thus allowed for multiple foci of interaction and true physical navigation.

In a game such as Miners, the issues observed add to the challenge and don't necessarily detract from the players' enjoyment. Still, in general, a challenge in wall interaction will probably be to design interaction mechanisms that counteract change blindness and social awareness issues. Others (e.g., [3, 19]) have suggested moving information closer to the respective user, and this does help in the case of blindness to interface changes. However, it does not alleviate social awareness issues, and we believe that one important tool here is to allow interaction when at a distance from the wall, e.g., using freehand gestures, remote controllers (e.g., [10, 16]) or body movements [15].

Positioning and Locomotion

Some of our findings regarding positioning and locomotion were likely the result of our specific scenario – including, e.g., the lack of territoriality and work in close proximity.

On the other hand, the observation that no more than three players were able use touch interaction with a single center of attention at once in Miners probably applies to other scenarios as well, since it involves natural physical limits. Additional users would have had a hard time reaching the display, even when interacting in very close proximity (cf. Figure 1). In fact, the issue can be seen in other work as well, (e.g., Clayphan et al. [5], Fig. 9) , though it is only hinted at in the text.

Finally, we believe that our observations of occlusion issues for players at a distance are important. Others have found similar issues as well [14, 16], so this is probably a general phenomenon when users interact at differing distances. Consequently, when designing a system involving interaction at differing distances to a display wall, occlusion needs to be taken into account. In fact, since there was nearly always someone in the way, occlusion issues should be treated as a rule, not an exception. As one solution, we propose displaying additional overview content above user's heads when appropriate, where they can be seen even if others stand in front of the wall.

CONCLUSION

We have presented the first cooperative, multi-user game for a touch-sensitive display wall. *Miners* is a fast-paced game that employs a novel bimanual tangible+touch interface for multimodal interaction. We performed an exploratory study to investigate communication and awareness in this context, and results indicate a very high level of engagement and fun while playing. Also, our study revealed awareness issues for users interacting close to the wall: Not only changes in display contents, but also others' interactions and social cues were often ignored. Further, players that stepped back to get an overview expericenced occlusion issues. In our opinion, it is probable that both awareness and occlusion issues are applicable to more general use cases. Therefore, for further work, we propose additional comparative studies to isolate dependent variables, e.g., by comparing touch-only with touch and distant interaction for collaborative work.

ACKNOWLEDGMENTS

We would like to thank our study participants for taking part. This project was in part funded by the DFG (DA 1319/3-1) and the Excellence Initiative of the German Federal and State Governments (Institutional Strategy, measure "support the best").

REFERENCES

1. Andrews, C., Endert, A., Yost, B., and North, C. Information visualization on large, high-resolution displays: Issues, challenges, and opportunities. *Information Visualization 10*, 4 (Oct. 2011), 341–355.
2. Azad, A., Ruiz, J., Vogel, D., Hancock, M., and Lank, E. Territoriality and behaviour on and around large vertical publicly-shared displays. In *Proc. DIS*, ACM (2012), 468–477.
3. Ball, R., North, C., and Bowman, D. A. Move to improve: Promoting physical navigation to increase user performance with large displays. In *Proc. CHI*, ACM (2007), 191–200.
4. Bezerianos, A., and Isenberg, P. Perception of visual variables on tiled wall-sized displays for information

visualization applications. *IEEE Trans. Vis. Comput. Graphics 18*, 12 (Dec. 2012), 2516–2525.

5. Clayphan, A., Martinez-Maldonado, R., Tomitsch, M., Atkinson, S., and Kay, J. An In-the-Wild Study of Learning to Brainstorm: Comparing Cards, Tabletops and Wall Displays in the Classroom. *Interacting with Computers* (2016), 1–23.
6. de Kort, Y. A. W., IJsselsteijn, W. A., and Poels, K. Digital games as social presence technology: Development of the Social Presence in Gaming Questionnaire (SPGQ). In *Proc. PRESENCE 2007* (2007), 195–203.
7. Finke, M., Tang, A., Leung, R., and Blackstock, M. Lessons learned: Game design for large public displays. In *Proc DIMEA*, ACM (2008), 26–33.
8. Graham, T. N., Schumann, I., Patel, M., Bellay, Q., and Dachselt, R. Villains, architects and micro-managers: What tabula rasa teaches us about game orchestration. In *Proc. CHI*, ACM (2013), 705–714.
9. Hawkey, K., Kellar, M., Reilly, D., Whalen, T., and Inkpen, K. M. The proximity factor: Impact of distance on co-located collaboration. In *Proc. GROUP*, ACM (2005), 31–40.
10. Hoare, C., Campbell, R., Felton, R., and Betsworth, L. Hide and seek: Exploring interaction with smart wallpaper. In *Proc. CHI PLAY*, ACM (2015), 129–133.
11. Horn, M., Atrash Leong, Z., Block, F., Diamond, J., Evans, E. M., Phillips, B., and Shen, C. Of bats and apes: an interactive tabletop game for natural history museums. In *Proc. CHI 2012*, ACM (2012), 2059–2068.
12. Hornecker, E., Marshall, P., Dalton, N. S., and Rogers, Y. Collaboration and interference: Awareness with mice or touch input. In *Proc. CSCV*, ACM (2008), 167–176.
13. Jakobsen, M. R., and Hornbæk, K. Up close and personal: Collaborative work on a high-resolution multitouch wall display. *ACM Trans. Comput.-Hum. Interact. 21*, 2 (Feb. 2014), 11:1–11:34.
14. Jakobsen, M. R., and Hornbæk, K. Negotiating for space?: Collaborative work using a wall display with mouse and touch input. In *Proc. CHI*, ACM (2016), 2050–2061.
15. Kister, U., Reipschläger, P., Matulic, F., and Dachselt, R. Bodylenses: Embodied magic lenses and personal territories for wall displays. In *Proc. ITS*, ACM (2015), 117–126.
16. Machaj, D., Andrews, C., and North, C. Co-located many-player gaming on large high-resolution displays. In *Proc. CSE*, IEEE Computer Society (2009), 697–704.
17. Peltonen, P., Kurvinen, E., Salovaara, A., Jacucci, G., Ilmonen, T., Evans, J., Oulasvirta, A., and Saarikko, P. It's mine, don't touch!: interactions at a large multi-touch display in a city centre. In *Proc. CHI*, ACM (2008), 1285–1294.
18. Rocha, J. B., Mascarenhas, S., and Prada, R. Game mechanics for cooperative games. *ZON Digital Games* (2008), 72–80.
19. Sabri, A. J., Ball, R. G., Fabian, A., Bhatia, S., and North, C. High-resolution gaming: Interfaces, notifications, and the user experience. *Interact. Comput. 19*, 2 (Mar. 2007), 151–166.
20. Schmidt, D., Chong, M. K., and Gellersen, H. Idlenses: Dynamic personal areas on shared surfaces. In *Proc. ITS*, ACM (2010), 131–134.
21. Seif El-Nasr, M., Aghabeigi, B., Milam, D., Erfani, M., Lameman, B., Maygoli, H., and Mah, S. Understanding and evaluating cooperative games. In *Proc. CHI*, ACM (2010), 253–262.
22. Toprak, C., Platt, J., and Mueller, F. Bubble popper: Considering body contact in games. In *Proc. Fun and Games*, ACM (2012), 97–100.
23. Vepsäläinen, J., Savolainen, P., Ojala, J., Rienzo, A. D., Nelimarkka, M., Kuikkaniemi, K., Tarkoma, S., and Jacucci, G. Web-based public-screen gaming: Insights from deployments. *IEEE Pervasive Computing 15*, 3 (July 2016), 40–46.
24. Wendel, V., Gutjahr, M., Göbel, S., and Steinmetz, R. Designing collaborative multiplayer serious games. *Education and Information Technologies 18*, 2 (2013), 287–308.
25. Xambó, A., Hornecker, E., Marshall, P., Jordà, S., Dobbyn, C., and Laney, R. Let's jam the reactable: Peer learning during musical improvisation with a tabletop tangible interface. *ACM TOCHI 20*, 6 (Dec. 2013), 36:1–36:34.
26. Zadow, U. v., Buron, S., Harms, T., Behringer, F., Sostmann, K., and Dachselt, R. Simmed: Combining simulation and interactive tabletops for medical education. In *Proc. CHI*, ACM (2013), 1469–1478.
27. Zadow, U. v., Reipschläger, P., Bösel, D., Sellent, A., and Dachselt, R. YouTouch! Low-cost user identification at an interactive display wall. In *Proc. AVI*, ACM (2016), 144–151.

The Effect of Visual Distractors in Peripheral Vision on User Performance in Large Display Wall Systems

Anton Sigitov
Bonn-Rhein-Sieg University
of Applied Sciences
Sankt Augustin, Germany
anton.sigitov@h-brs.de

Ernst Kruijff
Bonn-Rhein-Sieg University
of Applied Sciences
Sankt Augustin, Germany
ernst.kruijff@h-brs.de

Christina Trepkowski
Bonn-Rhein-Sieg University
of Applied Sciences
Sankt Augustin, Germany
christina.trepkowski@gmail.com

Oliver Staadt
University of Rostock
Rostock, Germany
oliver.staadt@uni-rostock.de

André Hinkenjann
Bonn-Rhein-Sieg University
of Applied Sciences
Sankt Augustin, Germany
andre.hinkenjann@h-brs.de

ABSTRACT

Supported by their large size and high resolution, display walls suit well for different collaboration types. However, in order to foster instead of impede collaboration processes, interaction techniques need to be carefully designed, taking into regard the possibilities and limitations of the display size, and their effects on human perception and performance. In this paper we investigate the impact of visual distractors (which, for instance, might be caused by other collaborators' input) in peripheral vision on short-term memory and attention. The distractors occur frequently when multiple users collaborate in large wall display systems and may draw attention away from the main task, as such potentially affecting performance and cognitive load. Yet, the effect of these distractors is hardly understood. Gaining a better understanding thus may provide valuable input for designing more effective user interfaces. In this article, we report on two interrelated studies that investigated the effect of distractors. Depending on when the distractor is inserted in the task performance sequence, as well as the location of the distractor, user performance can be disturbed: we will show that distractors may not affect short term memory, but do have an effect on attention. We will closely look into the effects, and identify future directions to design more effective interfaces.

ACM Classification Keywords

H.1.2 User/Machine Systems: Human Factors; H.5.3 Group and Organization Interfaces: Computer-supported cooperative work; H.5.3 Group and Organization Interfaces: Evaluation/Methodology; H.5.2 User Interfaces: User-centered design

Author Keywords

Large, high-resolution displays; short-term memory; peripheral vision; collaboration

ISS'16, November 06-09, 2016, Niagara Falls, ON, Canada.

DOI: http://dx.doi.org/10.1145/2992154.2992165

INTRODUCTION

Large display environments such as high-resolution tiled-display walls are highly suitable for different types of collaborative work, including remote and partially distributed, but in particular also co-located collaboration. Systems often implement a whiteboard metaphor with novel interaction techniques and devices to resemble collaboration principles that have been known to be effective over decades.

Enabling multi-user collaboration in such systems, however, will raise the necessity for rendering visual feedback for each user independently. Due to the inherent characteristics of large wall displays, it will often occur that co-user's visual feedback will appear in the peripheral visual area of the other user: users are frequently aware of most parts of the visual display other than their active working area as it often falls within the human visual field. In this paper, we regard the peripheral vision as the visual field area outside central vision defined by the macula, from 17 degrees field of view extending outwards to the border of the visual field. Feedback for other users will be perceived and processed by the user's brain, as peripheral vision is sensitive to motion and visual changes [14, 18, 25, 30]. There is no drawback if collaborators are working tightly coupled. In fact, it has been shown that such workspace awareness is apt to facilitate groups' task performance [5].

Collaborative processes, however, consist not only of tightly-coupled shared activity. Various studies have investigated user behavior during collaborative work in single display environments, partly looking into the specific underlying processes and stages [4, 8, 13, 23, 27]. These studies have shown that collaboration processes consist of multiple work phases: loosely-coupled (individual) work, and tightly-coupled (shared) work.

While loosely-coupled work exhibits processing of multiple tasks in parallel (for instance, datasets are often split to support users to process only a part of the data, a typical approach to process input data more effectively), tightly-coupled work targets effective combination of gained knowledge into a solution. Such collaboration processes where users alternate between tightly-coupled and loosely-coupled work are called mixed-focus. Mixed-focus collaboration is typical for different collaborative tasks, e.g. sensemaking, construction, design, planning. During the parallel work stage, however, interaction of co-located users might result in recurrent system generated visual feedback that does not carry any relevant information for the user's current task, or work coordination. Thus, this visual feedback becomes task-irrelevant distractor. This is the category of distractors our studies look into.

Collaborative frameworks often only consider tightly-coupled interaction, while ignoring of phases of individual work is seen as a trade-off in favor of workspace awareness. Moreover, computer-supported cooperative work (CSCW) researchers often consider only the focus / working area of the user as critical. For instance, users can cause interference when invading a co-user's working area [31]. The peripheral area, on the other hand, was considered as safe. There is, however, no empirical evidence that confirms this assumption. For instance, previous work in the psychology domain has provided indications that distractors can negatively affect human performance and efficiency [21, 28]. Also, Gutwin et al. [5] argued that increased workspace awareness will likely decrease effectiveness of individual users. Such tendency might be ascribed to distractors' impact as well. We believe that better understanding of how system generated visual events affects users will allow for better performing collaborative interfaces.

In context of tasks that heavily depend on memory capabilities, there are two ways distractors may impact efficiency, either through attention capturing [10] (start of memorization process is delayed, because attention was driven away) or through memorization impairment (memorization process is interrupted) [19, 32]. In the latter case a distractor interferes with the process of storing information in short term memory, affecting immediate recall of the information.

The design of user interfaces for collaborative environments used at large display walls has to consider human perceptual abilities as a critical factor in order to ensure effective collaboration. As such, distractors should be taken into regard, in case a truly negative effect can be shown. In this paper, we base our research on insights gained in [11] that implies short-term memory is prone to interruptions, and in [3, 16] that showed that task-irrelevant feedback could not be ignored and decreased task efficiency. Yet, these studies only provide initial indications on how to design interfaces, and were mostly focused on smaller display types. We extend the understanding provided by this and other related studies by providing following **contributions**

- Through two user studies, we explore the effect of distractors in peripheral vision for the user working on a large display wall. Doing so, we specifically focus on visual distractors caused by visual system feedback, not on other distractors caused by collaborators themselves, such as motions. Such visual distractors are typical for loosely-coupled work stages in mixed-focus collaboration scenarios.
- We assess the effects of the distractors on short-term memory and attention, and show that distractors can have an effect depending on when the event occurs. However, and surprisingly, in comparison to non-stimuli conditions, we could not find a significant effect of distractors on performance (Levenshtein distance, see section *Results*). However, overall cue-insertion time (the moment the distractor becomes visible to the user) does have some effect when solely looking at the conditions including distractors. As a result, we extend the understanding of the effects of visual events in peripheral vision on user performance, looking specifically into factors associated with display area, learning curve, distractor awareness and workload.
- Based on the outcomes, we identify fruitful directions of future research through a set of research questions.

RELATED WORK

In this section, we explore related work that has considered the effect of visual distractors on user performance.

Interferences in display environments. Zanella and Greenberg [31] defined interference as *"the act of one person hindering, obstructing, or impeding another's view or actions on a single shared display"*. Pinelle et al. [20] listed interference issues that can occur in single-display environments, and proposed mechanisms for counteraction. Also, Izadi et. al [9] identified some "overlap"-situations where one user's interactions interfered with another's. Hornecke et al. [7] determined that touch input leads to more interferences than mouse input. Tse et al. [26] conducted a comprehensive study to investigate if interferences are common in practice. He identified that participants often avoid interferences by spatially separating their actions. Still, he argued that interaction techniques have to be designed with interferences in mind in order to mitigate the latter.

Multiple attempts targeted the mitigation of interferences: new strategies and techniques were proposed and evaluated [17, 20, 31]. Yet, researchers have considered only interferences that have a direct impact on user's performance (e.g. a user cannot execute an action because a co-user's interface component occludes his working area). Moreover, a general assumption has been prevailed - without any empirical evidence - that interferences can only occur in the user's focus / working area. In this paper, we will look at interferences that occur in peripheral visual area. Based on indications in related work, we assume they might have an indirect impact on user's performance, such as causing attention, memory, or mental workload issues.

Effects of task-irrelevant and task-relevant stimuli. In this paper, we differ between task-relevant and task-irrelevant distractors. Bundesen defined task-relevant distractors as stimuli that are similar to the target along the defining characteristics of the target [1]. By contrast, task-irrelevant distractors carry no information with regard to the task. Both task-relevant and task-irrelevant distractors may be of two conditions: congruent and incongruent. Congruent distractors activate the same response as the target for the trial, while incongruent distractors activate incorrect response. For instance, imagine a scenario where two symbols - one on the left side of the display, and one on the right side - are presented to the user. One symbol is a predefined trigger symbol the user was instructed to look for. Depending on the position of the trigger symbol (left or right) the user has to push the left or the right button. In addition, each time the symbols are shown one side of the display becomes highlighted, thus drawing attention of the user. If the highlight distractor draws attention of the user to the display side where the trigger symbol is, then the distractor is congruent. Otherwise it is incongruent.

Forster et al. [3] conducted a number of experiments on a 15" screen and showed that task-irrelevant stimuli can distract the user. As a result, decrease of effectiveness could be observed. Task-relevant peripheral stimuli can also decrease task performance. Chewar et al. [2] investigated secondary task display attributes (e.g. position, color) aiming to lessen interference of peripheral task-relevant stimuli with the primary task. The conducted experiments showed that users' primary task performance decreased due to peripheral stimuli. In contrast, Mori et al. [16] showed the effect of windows in the peripheral visual field on user task performance. They found that peripheral windows impair user's efficiency the stronger the closer peripheral windows are to foveal vision. It was also shown that dynamic stimuli have more negative impact in comparison to static stimuli.

The above described experiments were conducted on common desktop displays. Thus they investigated effects in very near peripheral vision area only. Moreover, the experiments did not consider high load tasks that make heavy use of humans' memory (in particular short-term memory) and attention resources.

Interferences with indirect impact. We differ between interferences with direct impact and interferences with indirect impact. Interferences with direct impact make task execution impossible. For instances, a pop-up window that occludes a text, or a loud noise that prevents the user to make a verbal report are interferences with direct impact. The user is not able to work on the task until the interference is resolved. By contrast, interferences with indirect impact rather slow down the user during task completion. For instance, a semi-transparent pop-up window will allow the user to read the text, or a high frequency, faint noise will allow the user to make a verbal report, mental load of the task will be much higher due to interferences though. Interferences with indirect impact might have immediate or delayed effect. For instance, interruption of memorization process, or drawing of user's attention represents an immediate effect. In contrast, overloading of user's awareness through irrelevant visual events represents a delayed effect that accumulates over time, and which might, for instance, lead to fatigue, and subsequent to performance decrease. Both, short-term memory and attention are important factors for analytical work (e.g. compare objects, find relationships, find an object based on information just gained from another object), and multiple studies have shown that both can be affected by distractors [3, 10, 11].

In conclusion, while some studies indicate a negative effect of visual distractors on human performance in interactive systems, the effects of distractors in the peripheral visual field during task performance are not fully understood. It is here our studies tie in, extending previous work, to better understand potential effects of distractors on task performance in large display walls.

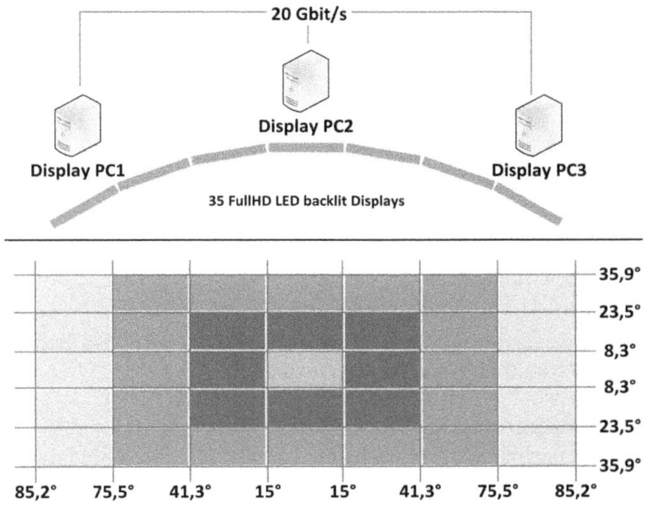

Figure 1. Large wall display: (top) View from the top - the display shapes a slight curve; (bottom) View from the front with angle range for each screen. Angles are given with regards to the user's head position defined in meters as (0, 0, 2) with the origin in the middle of the middle screen (grey), and Z-Axis orthogonal to it and showing away from the display. The color zones depict the three areas used for analysis with their associated degrees: blue (near peripheral visual field, area 1), orange (middle peripheral visual field, area 2) and yellow (far peripheral visual field, area 3).

EXPERIMENTS

In order to address the gap in understanding on the effect of visual distractors, we performed two interrelated user experiments. In these experiments, we explored the effect of visual task-irrelevant events such as caused by visual feedback to co-workers in peripheral vision during accomplishment of high-load tasks. Doing so, we specifically targeted display area location effects, learning issues, distractor awareness and workload issues to address the various dimensions distractors can affect user performance. We chose high-load tasks to explore the effect of distractors in cognitively demanding applications, an area in which large wall displays are often deployed. We performed the experiments by contrasting **short-term memory** and **attention**-driven distractors, two directions that have been focused on in previous work. The underlying assumption is, that information stored in short-term memory might get lost while being distracted, resulting in decreased effectiveness by complex tasks, which require memorization of intermediate results. On the other hand, since the humans' peripheral vision system is movement oriented [14], dynamic visual events have an increased potential to

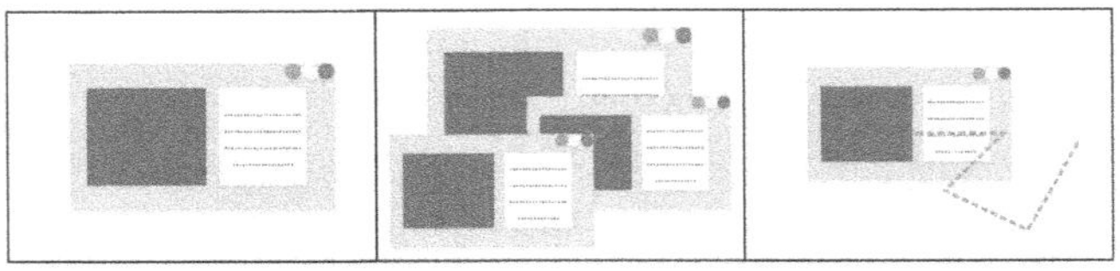

Figure 2. Stimuli: (left) pop-up window, (middle) multiple pop-up window, (right) pop-up and move window

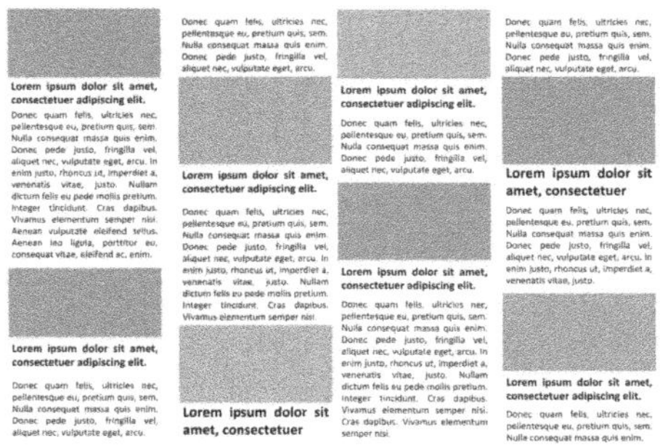

Figure 3. Schematic depiction of a background image as shown at a single display

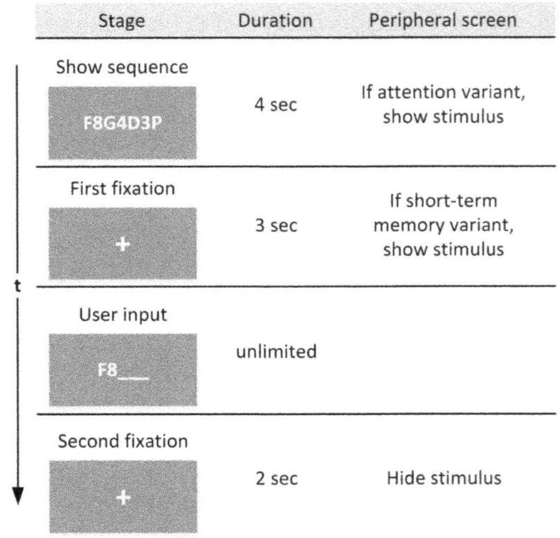

Figure 4. Trial loop, with insertion of distractors in the first fixation (short-term memory experiment 1) or during the show of the sequence (attention experiment 2)

attract user attention at an unconscious level, thus become distractors that can affect performance.

Apparatus

The experiments were performed at a large curved tiled display wall comprising 35 LCD displays (Figure 1), ordered through a seven (column) by five (row) grid. Each of the columns has a relative angle difference of 10 degrees along the Y-axis to adjacent columns, as such creating a slight curvature. Each LCD display has a bezel of less than three millimeters, minimizing the visual rim effect. The LCD displays are 46" panels with a 1080p resolution, resulting in a total of 72 megapixels.

Participants sat in front of the display at a distance of 2 meters. The height of the stool was adjusted in such a way that participant's eyes were at the same level as the center display. The distance was chosen to cover most of the user's peripheral vision with the display, approximately 170 degrees horizontal and 72 degrees vertical (Figure 1). In front of the participant a console with a keyboard was placed, used for typing in the results of the memory task.

Procedure and design

Both experiments were conducted as a within-subject study, employing a 3 x 4 factorial design, consisting of the factorial combination of four different event types (pop-up, multiple pop-up, move and no stimulus, Figure 2) that would appear in one of the 34 displays ordered in one of the three different areas (Figure 1). Of course, it should be clearly noted that "no stimulus" was not associated with any display area, and as such was analysed accordingly. Each window contained an image field and a text field. During the experiment each stimulus was shown exactly one time on each peripheral screen.

The 34 locations were associated with each single screen that makes up the tiled display wall, with the exception of the center screen, which was used for the memory task itself. Screens were clustered in three areas, to analyze the effect of cues in the near, middle and far peripheral visual field (Figure 1). The areas were defined through angular distances with some tolerance due to apparatus geometry. As a result, 136 samples per participant were recorded. The order of trials was fully randomized. All screens showed 1 of 15 static background images (see Figure 3), representing a newsfeed. The background images were different, though very similar in structure and usage of color and text, containing a number of news notes as text with a corresponding image. Design of background images and used stimuli was akin on purpose in order to lower contrast between them.

The difference between the two experiments was the point of time at which a specific distractor was inserted. As described in Figure 4, each trial spans 4 stages. First, a character sequence was shown to the user in the middle of the focal screen for 4 seconds. The main task was comprised of remembering this particular sequence, and recalling it from memory afterwards. Next, the sequence was hidden and a fixation point in form of small cross appeared for 3 seconds. Directly afterwards the screen contents blanked and the participant had to recall and enter the sequence using the provided keyboard. During the input, the participant was able to observe the sequence she is entering on the center screen, and correct if needed. No time limits were set for that stage, however, users were requested to start input directly after the screen blanked, to avoid differences in memory decay. The input stage was finalized by the participant by pressing the Enter key and followed by a second fixation point stage, which lasted for 2 seconds, after which a new trial began. Users were requested to focus on the center screen or the keyboard during the full experiment, specifically avoiding the direct focus of attention at the distractors.

In case of the first experiment (labeled **short-term memory** or STM), a distractor was shown during the first fixation point stage. This means that the participant had 4 seconds to remember a sequence. After it becomes hidden, the system tries to clear the content of short-term memory using a distractor. In case of the second experiment, called the **attention** experiment, a stimulus was shown during the stage of sequence showing. This means that the system tried to distract the participant while she was trying to remember a sequence, thus drawing their attention away and reducing the time for the task. Regardless of the experiment variant, shown stimuli remained static on the screen after animation until the second fixation point stage and were erased at the beginning of it.

Each sequence had a length of 7 tokens with the pattern *LDLDLDL*, where L stands for letter token, and D stands for digit token. All letters were upper case. For the sake of clarity, we omitted the digits 0, 1, 5 and characters O, L and S during the process of sequence generation. We also rejected the digit 7 and the letters W and Y since their words have more than one syllable.

The participants were instructed not to look at other screens apart from the focus screen in the center of the display wall. Each participant could practice the memorization task up to 20 trials and ask questions beforehand. No stimuli were shown during the practice stage.

At the beginning of the experiment, each participant filled in a survey that contained questions regarding age, gender, eyesight, color blindness, LHRDs experience, and computer games experience. The question about LHRDs experience was a single choice question with the following options: have never seen before; have seen a couple of times; have worked with them. The question about computer game experience was a Likert scale question with a 7-point scale from 1 (novice) to 7 (professional). During the experiment users were asked 2 questions after each block of 34 trials:

1. How mentally demanding was the last series of the trials?

2. How well could you concentrate during the last series of the trials?

The participants had to answer the questions using a 7-point Likert scale from 1 to 7, with seven being very high or very good, using the provided track pad. At the end of the experiment, each participant had to fill in a standard NASA TLX [6] survey, and a questionnaire regarding stimuli awareness and the application static background. The question about stimuli awareness was a Likert scale question with three Likert items (one for each stimulus type). Each Likert item had a 7-point scale from 1 (low level of awareness) and 7 (high level of awareness). In addition, an oral interview was made. Through these questions, we addressed issues related to mental demand, stimuli, background (level of distraction), and their strategy of remembering the sequences. Furthermore, users were observed, looking specifically at indications of concentration and distraction.

The rational behind the experiment is as follows. First, we choose a single user controlled experiment as we wanted to investigate the effect of particular stimuli in particular areas of a large display. Such an investigation with multiple users would be barely possible, as the presence of additional users would result into uncontrollable variables: co-users might make sounds or motions in peripheral area that affect the user, thus distorting the results. As such, we only focus on visual distractors caused by system feedback, instead of also focusing on other visual distractors that can be caused by for example users. Second, we chose high-load tasks to explore the effect of distractors in cognitively demanding applications, an area in which large wall displays are often deployed. The task seems to be very specific, however, remembering and recalling of small information chunks underlies multiple general tasks such as comparing, searching or determining relationships. Third, we decided to use a highly visual with information saturated background for two reasons: to reduce contrast between stimuli and background, and to emulate an information rich environment, which is typical for large display applications. Fourth, we are aware of the fact that curved displays have a higher potential to increase visual distraction in comparison to flat displays. In our study, however, we made use of a large display to cover as much of the human FOV as possible, for which the used curved display was an excellent option. Though likely covering a smaller FOV, similar negative effects are to be expected at flat wall displays, as the results particularly showed that distractors in the near peripheral field had the highest negative impact.

Participants and demographics

Experiment 1 was performed with 8 participants (2 females) aged between 22 and 33 years ($M = 27.00, SD = 4.10$), with normal or corrected-to-normal vision. The participants had rather a high level of computer games experience ($M = 5.00, SD = 1.41$) and most participants had seen large, high-resolution displays a couple of times before or worked with them (7 participants 87.5%). Similarly, experiment 2 comprised 8 participants (1 female) aged between 22 and 40 years ($M = 27.75, SD = 5.52$), with normal or corrected-to-normal vision. The participants also had rather a high level of computer games experience ($M = 4.50, SD = 2.00$) and most participants had seen large, high-resolution displays a couple of times before or have worked with them (6 participants 75%). All participants had an academic background (students or research associates). The participants were paid for taking part in the experiment. Each participant took part only in one experiment (either short-term memory or attention).

RESULTS

Data of 816 trials per experiment (102 trials per participant, totalling 1632 trials) was analyzed using two-way repeated measures ANOVA for each experiment separately with within-factors display area (near peripheral, mid peripheral, far peripheral) and stimulus type (pop-up window, multiple pop-up window, pop-up and move window). As noted before, "no stimulus" was not associated with a display area, and as such corresponding trials were not included in this ANOVA. Levenshtein distance [12] was used to calculate the difference between two sequences: the correct sequence, and the sequence provided by the user. As explanation, for sequences A and B Levenshtein distance is defined as $LD(A,B) = min(a(i)+b(i)+c(i))$. Here B is obtained from A by the minimal number of $a(i)$ replacements, $b(i)$ insertions and $c(i)$ deletions of characters. For example, the Levenshtein distance between "ocean" and "means"

	STM		ATT	
Condition	Mean	SD	Mean	SD
Stimuli				
Display Area 1	0,88	1,19	1,33	1,59
Display Area 2	0,83	1,26	1,15	1,47
Display Area 3	0,87	1,34	1,09	1,40
No Stimuli	0,82	1,21	1,16	1,35

Table 1. Stimuli vs. No-Stimuli condition for Levenshtein distance)

is 3, since the following three edits change one into the other, and there is no way to do it with fewer than three edits: Deleting "o", replacing "c" by "m" and inserting "s". Finally, as we noted, displays were clustered in areas (Figure 1) to analyze the effect of distractors in specific areas of the peripheral vision, ranging from near (1) to the far (3) peripheral field. While the display areas contain different amount of displays, the number of trials per area was high enough to warrant no negative effects. Mean values for each participant for each display area were finally included in the analysis. The population mean values for each display area can be estimated through the sample mean values. The mean value is more precise if it is based on many trials. As a great number of trials was used for each display area to calculate the mean values, differences in the number of trials should not affect the results as we can assume representative values for each display area. The Šidák correction was used to counteract the problem of multiple comparisons. Within the following we compare the results of both short-term memory and attention experiments, identifying the differences of the cue effects.

General performance. Analysing the general performance as based on Levenschtein distance, we found a surprising result: there was only a marginal difference between the no-stimili conditions, and the stimuli conditions in the attention and STM groups (see Table 1). As we will note in the discussion, this result is not in line with previous findings, and needs further research. However, we did find a significant difference between the attention and STM group, when performing a between-subjects analysis over ANOVA: the attention group produced significantly more errors than the STM group ($F(1,1630) = 21.58, p < .001$).

Display area. There was no main effect of display area or stimulus type (pop-up, multiple pop-up, pop-up and move) on recall time, number of correct tokens from position 0 till the first error and Levenshtein distance in both experiments. Display area, but not stimulus type showed marginal influence on the number of correct tokens at proper position ($F(2,14) = 3.606, p = .055, \eta_p^2 = .34$) only in the attention experiment. With respect to the different areas in peripheral vision, for this experiment, post-hoc pairwise comparisons show a greater number of correct tokens at proper position for display area 3 ($M = 5.21, SD = .2.22$) than 1 ($M = 4.84, SD = 2.40$) than, $p < .001$ (Šidák corrected). These results indicate that distractors in far peripheral vision did affect performance less than distractors in near peripheral vision. Interestingly enough, the stimulus "pop-up and move window" had almost the same effect in areas 1 and 3 in both experiments. However, in the display area 2 the effect was lesser in attention experiment, and stronger in the short-term memory experiment. Overall, and also in reflection to the errors produced by non-stimuli conditions, the effect of display area can be disregarded.

Learning. To gain better insights in learning effects, trial data from 136 trials was categorized in 4 equal time periods of 34 trials. To compare both experiments, we performed repeated measures ANOVA for each experiment with the within factor time period, which showed a significant effect on Levenshtein Distance in the STM group, $F(3,21) = 12.11, p < .001, \eta_p^2 = .634$. Mean Levenshtein Distance decreased from $M = 1.24(SD = 0.88)$ for the first 34 trails to $M = 0.59(SD = 0.56)$ for the last time period (see Figure 5). Post-hoc pairwise comparisons of time periods (Šidák adjusted) showed a significant difference of Levenshtein Distance between period 1 and 3 ($M = 0.64, SD = 0.67$), $p = .024$ and period 1 and 4, $p = .033$. As can be seen clearly in Figure 5, performance increased over time, showing a strong learning effect. Additionally, a comparison of learning curves has yielded that the overall distraction level was higher in the attention experiment. This is in line with the results of ANOVA between-subjects analysis.

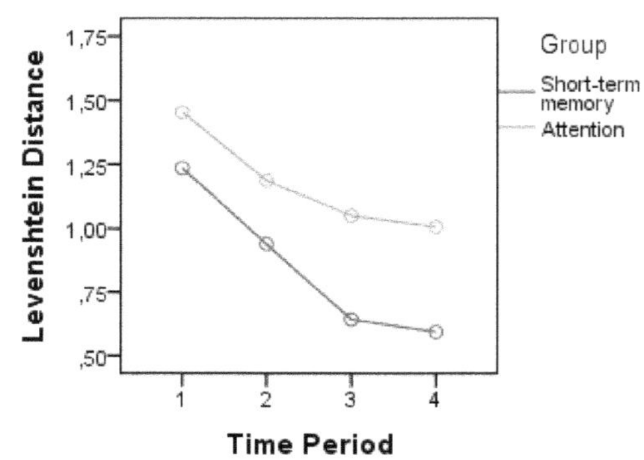

Figure 5. Mean Levensthein Distance over time

Awareness. A repeated measures ANOVA was conducted for both experiments to assess the effect of stimulus type on the level of awareness rating. Stimulus type affected awareness ratings only in the attention group ($F(2,14) = 4.688, p = .028, \eta_p^2 = .401$) as awareness seemed to differ between windows: Moving windows showed rather high awareness ($M = 5.63, SD = 1.30$) followed by multiple windows ($M = 3.63, SD = 2.2$) and single windows ($M = 3.38, SD = 2.33$). However adjusted post-hoc comparisons were not significant here. In the STM group the awareness of stimuli seemed to be similar for different distractor types.

Workload. Overall workload as depicted by NASA TLX (all subscales) was located in the center on a 21-point scale ($M = 11.56, SD = 3.26$). Mental demand, temporal demand and effort showed above-average mean values and thus seemed to be more relevant to the task than the other subscales (see Table 2). Standard deviations of all subscales are remarkable and vary from 4.07 (Mental Demand) to 5.29 (Frustration).

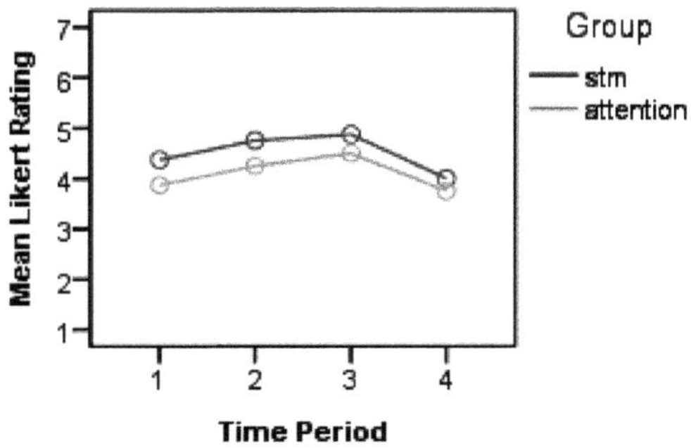

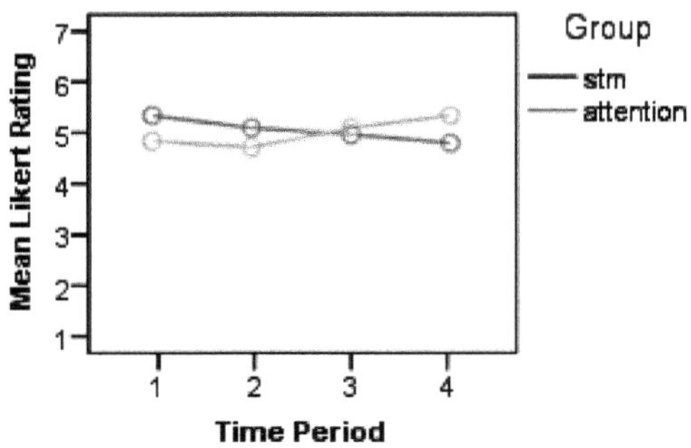

Figure 6. Mean Likert rating for frustration (top) and mental demand (bottom) for different time periods

The NASA TLX ratings show that the memory task was quite demanding, and as such can be rated as moderately high-load.

Repeated measures ANOVA showed no significant influence of time period on mental demand or mental frustration in both groups (see Figure 6). Mean mental demand was constantly high over time ranging from 4.83 to 5.83 in the STM group and from 4.75 to 5.38 in the attention group with standard deviations between 0.75 and 1.55. Mean mental frustration showed similar values ranging from 4 to 4.83 in the STM group and from 3.75 to 4.5 in the attention group with standard deviations from 1.17 to 1.94.

In oral interviews participants were asked about different aspects of the experiment. Most participants found the experiment mentally demanding: 75% of participants in attention group and 87.5% in the STM group said that the experiment was either "demanding from the start" or "became demanding throughout the experiment". Only few participants were distracted by the static background, as 37.5% and 25% of participants in attention and STM group respectively gave positive answer. On the other hand, all participants agreed the dynamic distractors did indeed distract them. The answers to the question which area of distraction was most distracting were fully in line with their performance: 100% of participants of the attention group indicated the near peripheral area, while in the short-term memory group 75% of the participants indicated the near peripheral area, 12.5% indicated all three areas, and 12.5% said that "stimuli were not distracting". Finally, participants were asked if they recognized disappearance of the stimuli during the second fixation phase and if it was distracting. In the attention group 75% of participants as well as 62.5% of participants in the STM group did not recognize

	Min	Max	Mean	SD
Mental Demand	5	20	15.0	4.07
Physical Demand	1	17	7.19	5.95
Temporal Demand	1	19	12.63	4.88
Performance	4	16	9.63	4,05
Effort	3	20	15.00	4.43
Frustration	2	19	9.94	5.29
Overall Workload	4.33	16.83	11.56	3.26

Table 2. Descriptive statistics for NASA-TLX subscales

the disappearance. The remaining participants stated that they recognized, it was not distracting though.

DISCUSSION

As a result of the study, we showed that distractors similar to those in mixed-focus collaborative scenarios could affect performance negatively. Even though no further person was in view, the distractor design was chosen as such that similar effects can be expected in true multi-user scenarios. Still, the optical flow produced by a nearby user while interacting can also potentially cause further distraction, which is an interesting issue to follow up in further research. These distractions could be counteracted by tunneling effects, an issue we discuss in the paper, but also this warrants further research.

While we assumed that task-irrelevant distractors would affect short-term memory and attention, we could determine some effects of stimuli on user performance during experiments, mostly related to the area in peripheral vision the distractor would appear.

Short-term memory. The mental load of our task was high: by design, character sequences were constructed in a way that makes it harder to apply chunking as memory aid, while also the number of elements the participant had to keep in mind was rather high [15]. The level of task load was supported by the feedback acquired through questioning during (see Figure 5) and directly after (see Table 2) the experiment, as users noted (moderately) high cognitive demands. Another indication of high mental demand was gained through observation, as participants exhibited clear lip movement throughout the experiment. The results of short-term memory group revealed that the stimuli effect remained more or less constant regardless in what area in peripheral vision it was. As such, we conclude that the provided stimuli did not impair short-term memory.

Attention. In contrast to the short-term memory experiment, the results we obtained in the attention experiment only endorsed our anticipation of a negative effect when comparing to the STM group, but not to the conditions excluding a distractors.

The gained results are surprising: with respect to previously performed studies, we could not show that task-irrelevant stimuli did always affect performance in our moderately high-load tasks, as shown by Forster et al [3], even though a higher task load was confirmed. However, it should be noted that Forster et al noted that especially low-load tasks were affected. Interestingly, the oral interviews showed that stimuli in near periphery distracted most, while in far periphery were barely perceived consciously, which would be in line with results achieved by [16] - yet, performance results did not confirm the latter. Let us look more closely at how these results can be explained, by looking at both the cue (distractor) and task design.

Distractor design. It is possible that perception and effect of far-off stimuli could be amplified through increased contrast between stimuli and background. With respect to stimulus type, the stimulus pop-up and move window distracted most as expected, as it exhibits the highest level of visual change. Interestingly enough, it is followed not by the stimulus multiple pop-up windows, but by single pop-up window. However, the effect of the distractors was not significant enough, as we showed while comparing our results to the no stimuli conditions. The question remains if other types of distractors (e.g. more salient distractors) will produce different results. While literature only provides limited indications, the peripheral visual field is more receptive to, for example, to blue colours [18]. Furthermore, issues such as transparency, and the size of cues can also have a larger effect, as at least large size cues would produce more optical flow in the peripheral visual field to which it is receptive.

Task design. One possible explanation for our results is that high cognitive load has been shown to produce attention tunneling, in which a human is less receptive to events outside the central visual area: mental workload is known to reduce the area of one's visual field (perceptual tunneling [24, 29]), but little is known about its effects on the shape of the visual field. Initial studies seem to indicate the expected limitation of the visual field and a potential shape distortion [22]. Hence, due to the high-cognitive load, attention may have been tunneled, as such that distractors could have a lower impact than if a low cognitive load task would have been deployed. If tunneling would have occurred, distractors in area 2 and 3 would have less effect than distractors in area 1, which is in line with Mori's experiment [16] and which users noted orally. However, as we showed, performance was not affected significantly by display area. Hence, it would be appropriate to perform the same experiment, however, with a lower cognitive load task to be able to confirm this assumption.

CONCLUSION

To foster effective collaboration in large wall display systems, apt graphical user interfaces need to be designed in a way that afford concentration on the primary task, especially in cognitively demanding applications. Visual feedback caused by the actions of a collaborative user can draw attention from the main task, as visual distractors can trigger attention towards other areas of the screen. In this article, we reported on two interrelated experiments to improve the understanding of the effects of dynamic visual task-irrelevant stimuli in far, mid, and near peripheral vision areas on users' efficiency at very high-load memorization tasks. The experiments showed that in some conditions such stimuli might impair users' performance and as such can place requirements on the design of the graphical user interface. For example, the partitioning of private and public spaces on large wall displays could be affected, as in particular attention effects could be shown for the near peripheral visual field. We have also shown that insertion time of visual stimuli may have a significant impact on users' performance. Since there is no way to control time of visual feedback emergence, we can try to mitigate interference through visual attributes' manipulation of stimuli.

Results also show that this experiment is a first step towards fully understanding the effects: it is clear further research has to be performed with an aim to minimize negative impact. In our future work, we intend to investigate the analysis of effects of stimulus attributes, e.g. color, transparency or size, on users' performance, and the study of various dynamic screen partitioning methods. Knowing the impact intensity of different attributes, we can experiment with their values to detect if impairment factor can be reduced, e.g. to make a pointer of co-user semi-transparent if it nears the near area of user's peripheral vision.

REFERENCES

1. Bundesen, C. A theory of visual attention. *Psychological Review 97*, 4 (Oct. 1990), 523–547.
2. Chewar, C. M., McCrickard, D. Scott, Ndiwalana, Ali, North, Chris, Pryor, Jon, and Tessendorf, David. Secondary Task Display Attributes - Optimizing Visualizations for Cognitive Task Suitability and Interference Avoidance. In *Proc. Eurographics / IEEE VGTC Symposium on Visualization 2002* (2002).
3. Forster, S., and Lavie, N. Failures to ignore entirely irrelevant distractors: The role of load. *Journal of Experimental Psychology: Applied 14*, 1 (2008), 73–83.
4. Gutwin, C., and Greenberg, S. Design for individuals, design for groups: tradeoffs between power and workspace awareness. In *Proc. CSCW 1998*, ACM Press (1998), 207–216.
5. Gutwin, C., and Greenberg, S. A Descriptive Framework of Workspace Awareness for Real-Time Groupware. *Computer Supported Cooperative Work (CSCW) 11*, 3 (2002), 411–446.
6. Hart, S. G., and Staveland, L. E. Development of NASA-TLX (Task Load Index): Results of Empirical and Theoretical Research. In *Advances in Psychology*, vol. 52. Elsevier, 1988, 139–183.
7. Hornecker, E., Marshall, P., Dalton, N. S., and Rogers, Y. Collaboration and interference: awareness with mice or touch input. In *Proc. CSCW 2008*, ACM Press (2008), 167.
8. Isenberg, P., Fisher, D., Morris, M. R., Inkpen, K., and Czerwinski, M. An Exploratory Study of Co-located Collaborative Visual Analytics around a Tabletop Display. In *Proc. Visual Analytics Science and Technology (VAST) 2010*, IEEE Computer Society (Los Alamitos, CA, USA, Nov. 2010).
9. Izadi, S., Brignull, H., Rodden, T., Rogers, Y., and Underwood, M. Dynamo: a public interactive surface supporting the cooperative sharing and exchange of media. In *Proc. UIST 2003*, ACM Press (2003), 159–168.

10. Jonides, J., and Yantis, S. Uniqueness of abrupt visual onset in capturing attention. *Perception & Psychophysics 43*, 4 (1986), 346–354.

11. Keppel, G., and Underwood, B. J. Proactive inhibition in short-term retention of single items. *Journal of Verbal Learning and Verbal Behavior 1*, 3 (1962), 153 – 161.

12. Levenshtein, V. Binary codes capable of correcting deletions, insertions, and reversals. Tech. rep., 1966.

13. Lissermann, R., Huber, J., Steimle, J., and Mhlhuser, M. Permulin: collaboration on interactive surfaces with personal in- and output. In *Proc. CHI EA 2013*, ACM Press (2013), 1533.

14. Mckee, S. P., and Nakayama, K. The detection of motion in the peripheral visual field. *Vision Research 24*, 1 (Jan. 1984), 25–32.

15. Miller, G. A. The magical number seven plus or minus two: some limits on our capacity for processing information. *Psychological Review 63*, 2 (Mar. 1956), 81–97.

16. Mori, H., and Hayashi, Y. Visual interference with users tasks on multiwindow systems. *International Journal of Human-Computer Interaction 7*, 4 (Oct. 1995), 329–340.

17. Morris, M. R., Ryall, K., Shen, C., Forlines, C., and Vernier, F. Beyond "social protocols": multi-user coordination policies for co-located groupware. In *Proc. CSCW 2004*, ACM Press (2004), 262.

18. Osterberg, G. *Topography of the Layer of Rods and Cones in the Human Retina*. Supplementum. A. Busck, 1935.

19. Perfect, T. J., Andrade, J., and Syrett, L. Environmental Visual Distraction during Retrieval Affects the Quality, Not the Quantity, of Eyewitness Recall: Visual distraction. *Applied Cognitive Psychology 26*, 2 (Mar. 2012), 296–300.

20. Pinelle, D., Barjawi, M., Nacenta, M., and Mandryk, R. An evaluation of coordination techniques for protecting objects and territories in tabletop groupware. In *Proc. CHI 2009*, ACM Press (2009), 2129.

21. Rabiner, D. L., Murray, D. W., Schmid, L., and Malone, P. S. An exploration of the relationship between ethnicity, attention problems, and academic achievement. *School Psychology Review 33*, 4 (2004), 498–509.

22. Rantanen, E. M., and Goldberg, J. H. The effect of mental workload on the visual field size and shape. *Ergonomics 42*, 6 (June 1999), 816–834.

23. Scott, S. D., Sheelagh, M., Carpendale, T., and Inkpen, K. M. Territoriality in collaborative tabletop workspaces. In *Proc. CSCW 2004*, ACM Press (2004), 294.

24. Tonnis, M., Lange, C., and Klinker, G. Visual Longitudinal and Lateral Driving Assistance in the Head-Up Display of Cars. In *Proc. ISMAR 2007*, IEEE (Nov. 2007), 1–4.

25. Torralba, A., Oliva, A., Castelhano, M. S., and Henderson, J. M. Contextual guidance of eye movements and attention in real-world scenes: The role of global features in object search. *Psychological Review 113*, 4 (2006), 766–786.

26. Tse, E., Histon, J., Scott, S. D., and Greenberg, S. Avoiding interference: how people use spatial separation and partitioning in SDG workspaces. In *Proc. CSCW 2004*, ACM Press (2004), 252.

27. Vogt, K., Bradel, L., Andrews, C., North, C., Endert, A., and Hutchings, D. Co-located Collaborative Sensemaking on a Large High-Resolution Display with Multiple Input Devices. In *Proc. INTERACT 2011*, vol. 6947 of *Lecture Notes in Computer Science*, Springer (2011), 589–604.

28. Wallace, J. C., and Vodanovich, S. J. Can Accidents and Industrial Mishaps Be Predicted? Further Investigation into the Relationship Between Cognitive Failure and Reports of Accidents. *Journal of Business and Psychology 17*, 4 (2003), 503–514.

29. Wickens, C. D., and Alexander, A. L. Attentional Tunneling and Task Management in Synthetic Vision Displays. *The International Journal of Aviation Psychology 19*, 2 (Mar. 2009), 182–199.

30. Wolfe, J. M. Guided Search 2.0 A revised model of visual search. *Psychonomic Bulletin & Review 1*, 2 (June 1994), 202–238.

31. Zanella, A., and Greenberg, S. Reducing Interference in Single Display Groupware through Transparency. In *ECSCW 2001: Proceedings of the Seventh European Conference on Computer Supported Cooperative Work 1620 September 2001, Bonn, Germany*, W. Prinz, M. Jarke, Y. Rogers, K. Schmidt, and V. Wulf, Eds. Springer Netherlands, Dordrecht, 2001, 339–358.

32. Zeamer, C., and Fox Tree, J. E. The process of auditory distraction: disrupted attention and impaired recall in a simulated lecture environment. *Journal of Experimental Psychology. Learning, Memory, and Cognition 39*, 5 (Sept. 2013), 1463–1472.

Multimodal Segmentation on a Large Interactive Tabletop: Extending Interaction on Horizontal Surfaces with Gaze

Joshua Newn, Eduardo Velloso, Marcus Carter, Frank Vetere
Microsoft Research Centre for Social NUI
The University of Melbourne
[joshua.newn][evelloso][marcusc][f.vetere]@unimelb.edu.au

ABSTRACT
Eye tracking is a promising input modality for interactive tabletops. However, issues such as eyelid occlusion and the viewing angle at distant positions present significant challenges for remote gaze tracking in this setting. We present the results of two studies that explore the way gaze interaction can be enabled. Our first study contributes the results from an empirical investigation of gaze accuracy on a large horizontal surface, finding gaze to be unusable close to the user (due to eyelid occlusion), accurate at arm's length, and only precise horizontally at large distances. In consideration of these results, we propose two solutions for the design of interactive systems that utilise remote gaze-tracking on the tabletop; multimodal segmentation and the use of *X-Gaze*—our novel technique—to interact with out-of-reach objects. Our second study evaluates and validates both these solutions in a *Video-on-Demand* application, presenting immediate opportunities for remote-gaze interaction on horizontal surfaces.

Author Keywords
Interactive tabletop; large horizontal surfaces; eye tracking; smooth pursuit; gaze interaction; multimodal interaction.

ACM Classification Keywords
H.5.2. Information Interfaces and Presentation: User Interfaces: Input devices and strategies

INTRODUCTION
Touch is the most widely supported input modality for interactive tabletops, providing a precise, spatial, and natural means of interacting with digital content [2, 6]. As the sizes of interactive surfaces increase, reachability starts becoming a problem as touch input can be only used within physical reach [31]. To minimise this, various novel interaction techniques have been proposed in the literature, which extend touch on tabletops: through emulation of a mouse [5], the use of tools/widgets [1, 7], or by introducing an additional input device/modality [4, 16, 18, 32].

ISS '16, November 06-09, 2016, Niagara Falls, ON, Canada
© 2016 ACM. ISBN 978-1-4503-4248-3/16/11...$15.00
DOI: http://dx.doi.org/10.1145/2992154.2992179

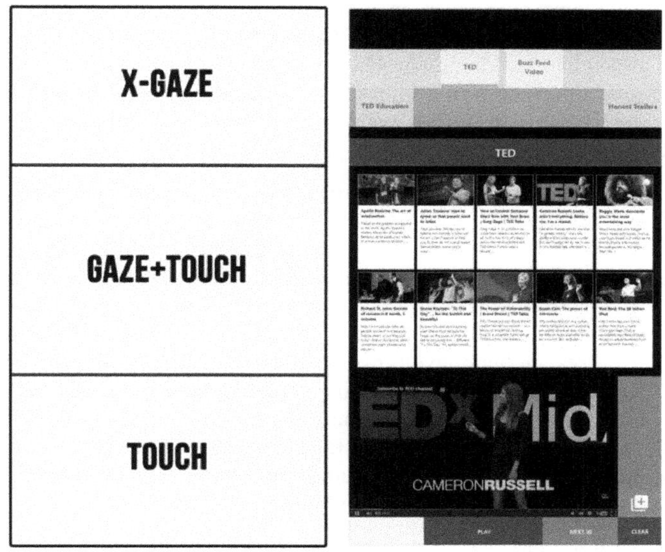

Figure 1: Multimodal Segmentation. Left: Input modalities for each region segmented. Right: The application built in relation to where each modality/interaction technique works best. This is an animated figure and it is best viewed in Adobe Reader.

Recently, eye tracking has been shown to be a promising technology for remote interaction with very large vertical displays, as gaze is fast, naturally drawn to objects of interest, and able to interact with objects beyond our reach [29, 30, 34]. However, remote gaze-tracking is inaccurate on large horizontal surfaces. As the results from our first study demonstrate, this is constrained for two reasons. At the far end, the wide visual angle leads to inaccuracies, while in the closer end to the user, the eyelid tends to cover the pupil as the user looks down. To get around these constraints, HCI researchers have typically used wearable eye-trackers to simulate perfect gaze tracking on tabletops [3, 14]. This approach limits actual implementation where remote gaze tracking is often the only suitable option, e.g., in unsupervised walk-up-and-use interactive surfaces found in museums [10] or in collaborative spaces where impromptu interactions take place [39].

This paper contributes the initial steps for enabling interaction on a large interactive tabletop with gaze input. Our first study identifies the gaze estimation accuracy and precision on a large tabletop display with a low-cost remote eye tracker. The results show that, whereas gaze pointing works well at the centre of the screen, the accuracy decreases exponentially with distance. However, even at the far end of the table, horizontal eye movements are still tracked with high precision. Based on these results we contribute a multi-level interaction architecture in which we divide the table into three regions that employ different input modalities i.e. multimodal segmentation (see Figure 1-Left). In the first—the *Touch Region*—users interact using touch gestures. In the second—the *Gaze+Touch Region*—users point with gaze combined with indirect touch gestures. In the third—the *X-Gaze Region*—users select targets with *X-Gaze*, a novel technique we developed in this work using a horizontal smooth pursuit tracking algorithm adapted from Vidal et al. [36]. Our second study evaluates both solutions—multimodal segmentation and *X-Gaze*—through a *Video-on-Demand* application (see Figure 1-Right) that demonstrates how they can be used in a cohesive interface on an interactive tabletop. Lastly, we present the immediate future opportunities from these solutions.

RELATED WORK

A considerable amount of research in HCI has explored the use and design of large ($> 1m^2$) interactive tabletops. Touch input on tabletops has been the common modality, reflective of its ease of use, intuitiveness, and social advantages [2, 6]. However, touch is limited by the user's reach, limiting these advantages. Gaze input presents a possible solution [12], and HCI researchers have typically used wearable eye trackers to simulate perfect gaze-tracking on tabletops [3, 14, 37]. This approach is likely due to the inherent challenge of remotely detecting gaze on a horizontal plane. Therefore, few studies have explored the use of remote gaze tracking on tabletops and predominantly in the context of intent prediction [17, 41].

Holman [12] first proposed the idea of using remote gaze as a possible solution to address inherent problems when interacting with large tabletop surfaces (e.g. reachability). Based on this idea, an eye-tracking tabletop interface (ETTI) and an accompanying game were developed and evaluated by Yamamoto et al. [40, 41]. Beyond demonstrating the ability to predict a user's intention based on gaze detection, their experiment highlighted two developments for interaction with horizontal surfaces using gaze. First, it showed the potential for unsupervised walk-up-and-use interaction using remote gaze, such as in museums: the natural habitat of multi-user large horizontal surfaces [10]. Second, it showed that remote gaze could be used in a horizontal configuration with high accuracy when they conducted their initial empirical gaze detection accuracy study. However, their system was designed so that all parts of the projected surface could be reached (within arm's length) by any single user.

Mauderer et al. [17] demonstrated the use of remote gaze on a larger surface (53-inch) where reachability starts to become a problem in which their proposed technique attempted to address. By combining the use of touch and gaze using two existing interaction techniques—MAGIC [42] and Superflick [20]—the operable area was extended allowing gaze-assisted object placement through a flick gesture. Their results showed a high error in the y-axis compared to the x-axis in different conditions, warranting further investigation. Accordingly, our first study sets out to empirically characterise

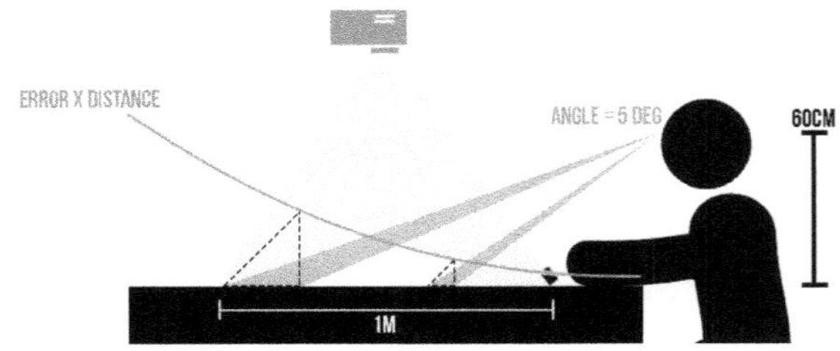

Figure 2: The diagram illustrates the theoretical regions on the tabletop corresponding to 5 degrees of visual angle close and far to the user on a 1m projected surface.

remote gaze tracking on a large horizontal surface. Nevertheless, these works highlight two challenges faced when using remote gaze tracking on horizontal surfaces. First, commercial eye trackers are built for vertical displays, thus their underlying algorithms start from this assumption. Second, the differences in visual angle when a user is positioned on one side of the surface causes difficulties in gaze tracking.

The combination of remote gaze and touch have been explored in various ways. Stellmach and Dachselt [29] combined touch (using a hand-held device) and remote gaze input with distant displays, demonstrating the potential for multimodal gaze-supported interaction. Pfeuffer et al. [19]'s work emphasises the complementary combination of gaze for selection and multi-touch for manipulation on the same horizontal surface. Their *Gaze-touch* technique allowed objects within reach to be interacted with using touch while objects out of reach were selectable using gaze and manipulated by touch gestures in the reachable space. Results showed that when touch is combined with gaze, interaction speed increased, and as physical mid-air hand movements were decreased, fatigue decreased as well. Serim and Jacucci [25] illustrated that gaze input could be used to extend interaction beyond 'gaze pointing' as seen in related works (e.g. [19, 29, 30, 34]). Their results show that gaze can support interface use with decreased reliance on visual guidance. For large interfaces, this means that touch input combined with gaze could be used differently i.e. the user touches where she is looking versus not looking. As demonstrated in the literature, combining touch with gaze shows great promise, motivating us to explore this area further. Thus, the contributions in this paper aim to extend this existing area of literature.

STUDY 1: CHARACTERISING EYE GAZE ON TABLETOPS

We noted two significant challenges for remote gaze tracking in this setting. First, commercial eye trackers are built for vertical displays, so their underlying algorithms start from this assumption. Second, the gaze inaccuracy increases with distance from the user on a horizontal surface due to the differences in visual angle. Here, we identify a third challenge: when users look down at the edge of the table closest to them, the eyelids cover the pupil thereby, deteriorating the accuracy. Focusing on the second challenge, the further from the user, the wider the estimation error is for a given visual angle (see Figure 2). Using the derived equation below, it is possible to predict how inaccurate ($Error$) the gaze estimation will be depending on the $Distance$ to the user, the given visual angle θ and the $Height$ of the eyes.

$$Error = Height \times \tan\left(\theta + \arctan\left(\frac{Distance}{Height}\right)\right) - 100$$

Figure 2 shows the theoretical error curve at scale for a 5-degree visual angle at a 60cm height on a 1m surface. To characterise the gaze estimation on the tabletop in practice, we designed a study that builds on the gaze estimation accuracy evaluation by Yamamoto et al. [41] but on a much larger surface, simultaneously investigating the high error rates in the y-axis found in Mauderer et al. [17]'s evaluation. Therefore, the aim of this study is to empirically characterise the limitations of remote gaze on a large horizontal surface. This was done by comparing the tracking error between the estimated gaze point for each ground truth point displayed.

Hardware Configuration

As shown in Figure 2, a face-down short-throw projector was used to create a 45-inch (1000x563mm) horizontal display with a resolution of 1920x1080px on the tabletop. A low-cost eye tracker (Tobii EyeX ($30Hz$)) was mounted on the table surface on the edge of the projection facing the user at 40-50 degree angle and $25cm$ away from the short edge of the table. As the eye tracker specified working distance is 45–80cm (tracker to eyes), this positioning was suitable and able to accommodate to participants of different seated heights but for each participant, the angle of the tracker was adjusted to point towards her eyes from below for better tracking performance.

Study Procedure

Upon arrival, participants signed an informed consent form and completed a simple demographics questionnaire. Participants were asked to sit comfortably in front of the eye tracker, which we first calibrated using its default 9-point procedure. Participants were then asked to look at 63 circular target points (size: 20px, approx. 1cm in diameter) displayed sequentially for 4 seconds each. All participants looked at the same sequence row by row. To make it more comfortable, each point was presented with a grow/shrink animation.

Results

We recruited 10 participants (7M/3F), aged 25 to 52 years (mean=32), 6 participants wore glasses, and only 2 had previous experience with eye tracking. For each of the 63 points, we computed the difference between the estimated coordinates of the gaze point and the corresponding coordinates of the ground truth. Figure 3 shows that the error in each direction depends on the position of the ground truth on the tabletop. To elaborate, vertical error refers to the deviation of the estimated coordinates of the gaze point for each point (in pixels) from the coordinates of the ground truth point in terms of the *Y* coordinate. Likewise, the horizontal error refers to the deviation in the *X* coordinate. Arranged in 9 rows of 7, Figure 3(a) shows the error for the 9 rows in terms of the y-axis, while Figure 3(b) shows in terms of the x-axis accordingly.

We found that in the y-axis, the error increases exponentially with the angle between the gaze direction and the tabletop, as predicted by the error estimation equation. However, it is noted that there is a slight increase in the error at the positions immediately closer to the user, likely due to the eyelids covering the eyes. The x-axis presented a much smaller

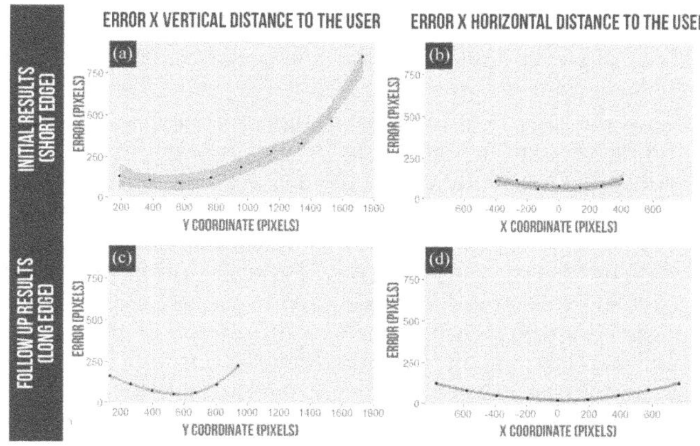

Figure 3: Horizontal and vertical error. The vertical error increases exponentially with the distance to the user. The horizontal error is much smaller in magnitude and follows a slender 'U' shape curve.

estimation error, with a curve following a slender U-shape. This is also expected, as the distance is at its minimum when users are looking straight ahead, increasing as they look towards either side. In any case, this represents consistently low error throughout the x-axis in comparison to the y-axis. We then evaluated how the distance to the user affects the tracking precision. The effects of the *Y* coordinate of the ground truth points on the mean horizontal and vertical standard deviations of the measurements was tested using Pearson's product-moment correlation. A significant correlation between the *Y* coordinate and the vertical standard deviation was found (Pearson's $r(7) = 0.84$, $p = 0.0045$), but no significant correlation with the horizontal standard deviation ($p = 0.22$). This means that for each target point further away from the user, the recorded gaze estimation points deviated more from the target point. As it is highly significant ($p < 0.01$), the results confirm our original prediction where the gaze inaccuracy is likely to increase with distance in this setting. As mentioned, there is no statistical significance in the x-axis, meaning that the deviations remained consistent throughout and was not affected by changes in horizontal distance, showing that the *X* coordinate remained fairly accurate and usable for all 63 points.

To confirm this, we conducted a follow-up study in which the eye tracker was moved to the centre of the long edge of the table to obtain a wider surface. We collected the gaze data from 10 participants (6M/4F), aged 22 to 52 years (mean=33.2). Four participants wore glasses and three had no experience with eye trackers. In addition, three participants took part in our initial study. Figure 3(c) shows a similar plot as Figure 3(a), showing the consistency of error at the positions closest to the user in both studies. More importantly, Figure 3(d) shows that the tracking error remains consistently low in this configuration, and we tested the correlation between the *Y* coordinate and the horizontal standard deviation and found no significant correlation ($p = 0.8955$). These results furthered our confidence in using the *X* coordinate for interaction on a large tabletop, especially at the end furthest from the user.

In summary, these results show that the gaze estimation in the far end of the tabletop is highly inaccurate and that the accuracy decreases exponentially. However, the results also show that even though the vertical precision deteriorates as the distance to the user increases, the horizontal precision remains the same. For interface design, this suggests that techniques that require high accuracy (e.g. gaze pointing) are not well suited for the far end of the tabletop, but techniques that only require a consistently precise estimate—such as *Pursuits* [36]—can still work if only the horizontal direction is considered. Instead of comparing the absolute position of the gaze point and the target, *Pursuits* compares the relative movement of the eyes with moving targets on the screen. In the next section, we elaborate and describe how *Pursuits* can be adapted to extend interaction at the far end of the tabletop with gaze. Finally, it appears that there is some tracking deterioration at the edge closer to the user due to eyelid occlusion.

STUDY 2: INTERACTIVE SYSTEM EVALUATION

The results from our first study showed that vertical gaze estimation is considerably affected by the distance to the user, but the relative movement in the horizontal axis can still be used for interaction, even at the furthest area of the tabletop. Moreover, the findings also showed that the estimation error is at its minimum at the centre of the table, increasing again as it gets closer to the user due to eyelid occlusion. With knowledge of these constraints, we designed a system that segments the tabletop in three distinct regions, each with an interaction technique that overcomes its inherent shortfalls and builds on its opportunities—what we call *multimodal segmentation*. Further, we draw on guidelines by Shen et al. [27] that consider occlusion and reach—the two overarching problems in our work aims to address. The purpose of the system is to evaluate the viability of (1) gaze-only interaction on the far end of the tabletop and (2) interacting with a large surface using multimodal segmentation.

Segmented Regions

In the region closest to the user (*Touch Region*), the gaze estimation error is high due to eyelid occlusion, but this is not necessarily a problem since the user can still interact with the region using touch. Touch is a well suited interaction modality in reachable areas on horizontal surfaces, it is, highly applicable and suited for use in this region. For this reason, only *touch* was adopted in this region. In the central region of the tabletop (*Gaze+Touch Region*), touch-based interaction techniques become awkward due to the need to 'reach out', whereby the user needs to move in order to be able to reach sufficiently far. However, it is the region with the smallest gaze estimation error, meaning that both the *X* and *Y* gaze coordinates are the most accurate and thus usable for gaze pointing in this region. Therefore, the interaction technique used in this region draws from Pfeuffer et al.'s *Gaze-touch* where we combine gaze pointing with indirect touch confirmation i.e. the touch is used for manipulation in the region close to the user while gaze is used for selection beyond the reach of the user [19].

In the area furthest from the user (*X-Gaze Region*), the user cannot physically reach targets and gaze estimation error is high in the vertical axis. However, the still precise horizontal axis can be taken advantage of by displaying targets that move only in the horizontal direction and correlating their *X* coordinate with the *X* coordinate of the eyes. This approach has been used in previous works using 2D movements to enable interaction with public displays [36] and with smart watches [9], using both *X* and *Y* coordinates. We adapted the approach by solely using the *X* coordinate to overcome the limitations of remote gaze estimation at far distances on horizontal surfaces that we identified in our first study.

Smooth Pursuit Eye Movements

Smooth pursuit eye movements have recently been proposed as a solution for contexts where calibration and precise pointing are challenging, such as in public displays, smart watches, and smart homes [9, 35, 36]. The technique works by correlating the smooth movement of the eyes with moving targets on the interface to detect where the user is looking, leveraging the smooth movement our eyes naturally perform when we follow a moving object. It is known that our eyes naturally are drawn towards objects of interest such as moving objects [13]. The *Pursuits* technique is suitable for scenarios where gaze tracking is inherently inaccurate such as on horizontal surfaces as it is not a concern where exactly the user is looking, but in the movement that the eye makes when fixated on a moving object. The details of how the *Pursuits* algorithm works can be found in Vidal et al. [36].

Here, we note that in the *X-Gaze Region*, the optimised parameters are not known, as the *Pursuits* algorithm has not been implemented on a horizontal surface, let alone one that is large in size. In theory, a horizontal adaptation of the algorithm is ideal for visual interaction. Collewijn and Tamminga [8] suggested that due to the extensive use in following everyday objects that tend to be horizontal, our ability to perform horizontal smooth pursuit is likely to be better than vertical smooth pursuit. Similar results are also seen in Rottach et. al's study [22] where horizontal, vertical and diagonal smooth pursuit eye movements were compared. Furthermore, existing implementations of *Pursuits* solely use gaze as an input. This paper presents an example of how *Pursuits* can be combined as part of a multimodal system.

Application

To illustrate how these regions can be combined into one cohesive application, we built a *Video-on-Demand* application that allows users to explore an on-line video library in a multimodal fashion (see Figure 1). In the *X-Gaze Region*, multiple tags are displayed that correspond to different video channels. These tags move left and right in distinct patterns and the smooth pursuit correlation algorithm [36] is used to select them. However, by not considering the *Y* coordinate of the eye gaze and tag movements, this substantially reduces the number of possible trajectories for different targets. For example, in 2D, even if two objects present the same horizontal movement, the selection can be disambiguated by the vertical axis. To compensate for this, the *X-Gaze* region is divided in two side-by-side sub-regions (see Figure 4). The absolute *X* coordinate is then used to estimate at which sub-region the user is looking, only presenting moving targets in that sub-region. The relative movement of the targets is compared with the relative movement of the eyes to select a specific tag. This way, only one of the sub-regions presents any movements at

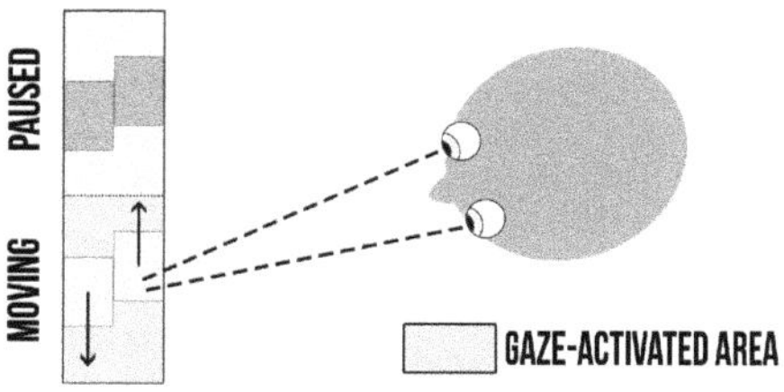

Figure 4: X-Gaze technique illustration.

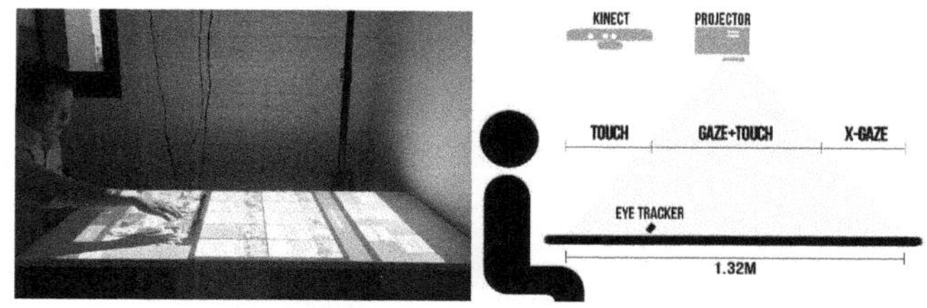

Figure 5: Study 2 application and hardware configuration. Left: Highlight selection used in Gaze+Touch Region with reachability demonstration shown. Right: Enhanced setup used with added touch capabilities.

a time, which start depending on the absolute horizontal coordinate of the gaze point. Moreover, by sub-regioning, the visible number of possible tags doubles, presenting more selectable channel options.

When a tag is selected, the *Gaze+Touch Region* is populated with videos that satisfy that query. The thumbnails of the videos are displayed along with their titles and summary descriptions. To select a video, the user looks at its thumbnail and touches the *Play* button displayed in the *Touch Region* at the very bottom of the table together with other playback controls. The video is shown in the *Touch Region*. The user can also use the *Next 10* button in the *Touch Region* to repopulate the *Gaze+Touch Region* with another 10 videos.

Hardware Configuration

We used the same hardware configuration as in the previous study, but with added touch capabilities using an overhead Kinect mounted on top of the projector (see Figure 5-Right). The touch events were detected using the *Ubi Displays Toolkit* [11], which matched touch points on the table to the pixels being projected. The eye tracker is moved to the bottom of the *Gaze+Touch Region*, as there is no longer a need to track the users' eyes in the *Touch Region* and the touch gestures could occlude the eye tracking if the location remains. By moving the eye tracker further away, the ability to use gaze increases and therefore increasing the possible area for interaction. In the enhanced setup used in this study, a 25% increase in display size (45-inch to 60-inch) was created by moving the eye tracker forward further from the user. A larger display size means that more content can be displayed at any one time. The placement of the segmented regions in relation to the hardware and user is shown in Figure 5-Right.

Data Collection

The screen was recorded using Open Broadcaster Software (OBS), along side the recording from the video camera that recorded the side view of the user and the interface, as shown in Figure 5-Right. This generated video recordings for analysis, showing the actions of the users synchronised with what they saw on the display. Throughout the tasks, participants were asked to employ the 'think-aloud' technique. The data primarily provides insights into the participants' thinking and whether they understood the system. Both interview and 'think-aloud' data were included as part of the combined video recording which was transcribed and coded using thematic analysis. Observations were made from a desk placed behind the participant, viewing the actions on the interface through a display clone. Notes were taken during both the tasks and the semi-structured interviews to be used for data analysis. Participants were then asked to complete a post-study questionnaire with a five-point semantic differential scale consisting of 15 dimensions (e.g. *I felt uncomfortable* versus *I felt comfortable*) (see Figure 6) that focuses on the *X-Gaze Technique*, the *Multimodal Segmentation* and the *Overall User Experience* in line with the goals of the evaluation.

Study Procedure

Upon arrival, participants were asked to complete the consent form and a simple demographics questionnaire. Participants were then asked to sit comfortably in front of the eye tracker and undergo a standard calibration procedure using the default 9-point procedure. Upon a successful calibration, participants were then asked to perform three tasks sequentially. Each task was designed with increasing difficulty, encouraged the participant to use the system as a whole, and are adapted from the functionality (i.e. find similar, remove odd) of a prior study on video searching [28]. In the first task, we explained how the system worked through a live tutorial, guiding participant through steps before inviting participants to explore the video library. Here, participants were encouraged to use all regions on the tabletop to familiarise themselves and to get over the initial learning curve while not giving away how the interface should be used. We were able to observe how participants initially approached the techniques without the complexities of a difficult task. This was followed by a short semi-structured interview to gain insights into participants' impressions, their overall perception of the system, the interaction techniques used in each region, and any difficulties that they experienced so far.

The following tasks were presented one after another and participants were asked to stop if they could not find all videos after 5 minutes. In the second task, the participant was asked to find similar videos, requiring the user to jump between the channels as they look for e.g. 'cat videos', which are not all in a single channel. The 'cat' video will be one that belongs to the channel but may not be immediately obvious at first. For example, in one channel, the thumbnail is a cartoon illustration of a cat instead of a picture while in another, the word 'cat' appears in the video title but the thumbnail does not display a cat. In the third task, the videos were shuffled among the channels and the participants were asked to find the videos that did not belong to that respective channel. Among the 10 videos displayed, there can be any number of videos that do not belong to that channel, encouraging participants to go back and forth between the channels to contrast the videos with the dominant type of videos in that channel. Therefore, the placement of the content in relation to the tasks required participants to not only navigate within the channel but also to switch between different channels, encouraging the use of the *X-Gaze* technique implicitly rather than explicitly. Once

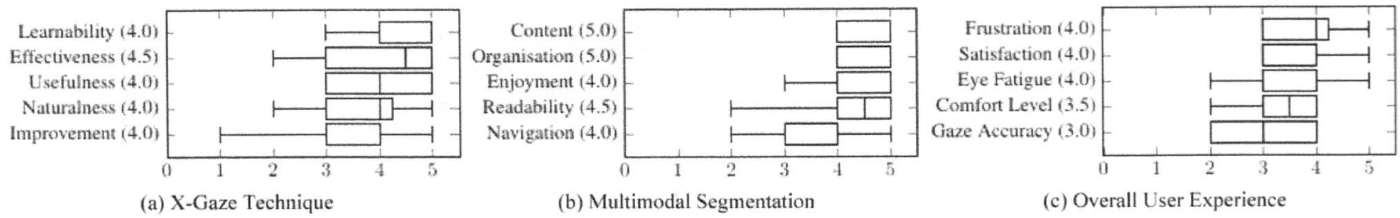

Figure 6: Study 2 Post-Study Questionnaire Results. The median score is shown for each dimension.

completed, the participants were asked to complete the post-study questionnaire followed by a second semi-structured interview.

Results

A total of 13 participants took part in the study (4F/9M), aged between 24 and 38 years (mean=28.2). However, 1 participant (P7) was omitted due the inability to calibrate with the eye tracker's default calibration. All participants had little to no experience with eye tracking. Two participants wore corrective contact lenses and one wore glasses. All participants either completed all tasks within 5 minutes or gave up by asking where the remaining videos were located. Figure 6 shows the results of the post-study questionnaire where participants rated between 1 (strongly unfavourable) to 5 (strongly favourable) for each dimension. The semi-structured interviews provided further insight into these scores.

The *X-Gaze* technique in the distant region was quickly highlighted with 10 out of 12 participants reporting that the technique being "minimal" was "easy to learn", and that it felt natural enough that there was little room for improvement (e.g. *I looked at things and it worked right away* [P8]). This corresponds with the low improvement scores but high learnability scores in the questionnaire. However, three participants (P4, P9, P13) reported that they felt the technique was somewhat slow. Overall, participants praised the novelty of the technique, along with the ability to accurately select distant targets solely with gaze, despite the unusual technique. For example, P3 mentioned *"you follow something with your eyes and it then selects. There is no real-world equivalent. It's easy and its effective but it doesn't feel like something normally I would do in my life. Thought, it was intuitive so I wasn't thinking about it too much."*

In the *Gaze+Touch Region*, we have chosen not to use a gaze pointer (or cursor), instead, the tiles were highlighted (blue) when selected by dwell time shown in Figure 5-Left. When the gaze estimate was accurate, this provided effective, subtle feedback, but when the tracking was particularly inaccurate, it created a flickering nuisance as noted in observation and confirmed in our video analysis. This is despite the centre of the screen being the area of the tabletop where gaze is most accurate. This shows that gaze tracking in this configuration is still substantially less accurate than on vertical screens. This was expected to some extent and was compensated by the use of large targets for the video thumbnails. However, half the participants still reported that the targets at the edges of the screen were more difficult to select that the ones in the centre. A subset of these participants (P3, P8, P12) also reported that it was sometimes harder to select videos on the bottom row (closer to the user) than compared to the top row (further from the user). This difficulty in selection led to the low gaze accuracy score. On the other hand, Participant P4 and P5 mentioned when reading the video titles, the button will highlight suddenly (due delayed dwell-time activation) causing a 'shock' to the eyes contributing to eye fatigue. Further, P4 mentioned *"When I wanted to look at something, I just wanted to look but when I wanted to select something, I wanted it to be fast."* This is reflective of the *Midas Touch* problem, an expected inherent problem when using eye gaze modality for interaction [13].

In contrast, a few participants (P3, P4, P12) explicitly noted the ability to select further than their physical reach when interacting with out of reach areas, which is reflective of our motivation to use eye gaze to extend reachability on large tabletops. Their positive responses are as follows:

> P3: *"It made sense that you can touch things in front of you and everything else [demonstrated the use of eye gaze by selecting objects that were out of reach]". "It's pretty unique to be able to select stuff that is so far away."*
>
> P4: *"I think it works when its a big screen like that. Like you don't want to go all the way and touch it."*
>
> P12: *"When it's here [shows touch area], it's easy to use your hands, but when it's over there [points at out-of-reach area], its hard, so yeah.", "It's actually very good. I really like it, it's easy and I don't want to be [participant stretches hand out]"*

Overall, participants enjoyed using the system through the seamless transition between the regions, receiving high ratings in all dimensions as shown in Figure 6. In the next section, we will discuss the issues that have risen from our evaluation followed by the implications of our solutions.

DISCUSSION

This paper demonstrates the immediate opportunities for enabling gaze interaction on large horizontal surfaces. The findings from the first study characterised the use of remote gaze on large interactive surfaces, in this case a large tabletop. This empirical investigation showed the different accuracies in the different parts of the tabletop. The highest accuracy was found in the centre while at the far end of the tabletop, accuracy only remains along the horizontal axis. This led to *multimodal segmentation*, the formation of regions with each region employing an interaction technique in accordance with the strengths and limitations. Subsequently, the characterisation informed the development of *X-Gaze*—our novel interaction technique—that enables the interaction on a large tabletop where the vertical axis is unusable especially at the far end. In the second study, both multimodal segmentation and

X-Gaze were evaluated through a *Video-on-Demand* application that illustrates how these regions can be used together in a cohesive interface on a large interactive tabletop. The evaluation showed positive results, yielding many interesting insights presenting how the system can be implemented in the future. In this section, we draw attention to both solutions and discuss their implications in light of our findings.

X-Gaze: Findings and Opportunities

We presented the design, development and evaluation of *X-Gaze*, a novel interaction technique we developed directly to respond to the need to interact with distant targets using only *X* coordinates. In our evaluation, the technique was found to be favourable by participants as the low overhead made it "minimal" and therefore "easy to learn" with little room for improvement as well as the ability to select out-of-reach targets. This highlights the fact that even techniques as such may look unusual at first, can still provide an effective means of providing input to interactive systems.

Some participants found that using the technique became slower after adapting to the technique, especially after completing the first task. This is a common effect in eyes-only techniques that require the user to follow a target or to dwell on it for a certain amount of time, due to a trade-off between the system's responsiveness and its robustness to errors [15]. Another possibility is that participants transitioned to being expert users after successfully using the technique during the first task. This caused these 'expert' users feel "slow" due to the thresholds in place to prevent false activations. Our implementation privileged robustness, using a 2-second activation window and a .95 correlation threshold, substantially higher than previous works [9, 36], which came at the cost of responsiveness. Future implementations could consider giving participant's control over the activation window time, reducing it as users become more adept at using the technique.

The *Pursuits* technique [36], in which *X-Gaze* has been adapted from, relies on interfaces that are highly dynamic i.e. interfaces with objects of interest moving with different trajectories and speeds. The authors referred to as a potential limitation as the constant movement might be a source of confusion or fatigue for users if used for longer periods of time. *X-Gaze* provides a possible solution to this by leveraging the use of 'gaze-aware' regions which is possible with large surfaces as the general gaze direction and point-of-regard can be estimated. When a gaze-aware region is activated, only then objects will start to move which further provides the user feedback that gaze has been detected in that region. Our application used in the evaluation used two gaze-aware subregions which could have been easily increased.

Furthermore, Vidal et al. [36] states that their technique 'is potentially unsuitable for objects that contain more than a short segment of text as it may be difficult to read and follow the moving text at the same time' and that objects that move too slowly may also cause bad performance. In our implementation, we demonstrated that text could be read as it only moves in one direction with the combination of a slow speed. As the coordinates of only one axis is used, the slow speed of the objects does not have an impact on performance, rather provided users with more control. As mentioned, a high correlation threshold was achieved. This is likely attributed to the fact that humans perform horizontal smooth pursuit better than vertical smooth pursuit [8, 22]. Thus, addressing some limitations of *Pursuits*, particularly in situations where gaze accuracy starts to becomes a problem with distance and consequently, where reachability becomes a problem too. We note that reachability is present when interacting with vertical surfaces as well [10]. This presents opportunities for exploring the use of *X-Gaze* on large vertical displays especially for use in public settings.

Multimodal Segmentation: A Viable Strategy

The informed decision to divide the tabletop into segmented regions can be viewed as a 'divide and conquer' strategy taken where an interaction technique was employed to 'conquer' each segment in accordance to their strengths. Our *Video-on-Demand* application illustrated how each of these different regions could cohesively work together. This cohesion was largely achieved by the use of a flat hierarchical structure that formed a natural division between each level. This was also possible as there were at least three levels where each level is progressively further from the user. These levels are visible at all times afforded by the large display that encouraged the serendipitous discovery of content. Moreover, this afforded visibility and the techniques employed in each region allowed the user to quickly jump between the different channels. This means that the user does not need to traverse up and down the hierarchy. For instance, while watching a video in the region closest to the user, the user can select another channel and scan for the next video while the current video remains played. The seamless transition between the regions builds on the use of a familiar drill down navigational structure commonly seen in interface design. This allowed users to bring the desired content within their reach as their interaction moves from the furthers region to the closest region to them. The two highest median scores in the questionnaire were given to content and organisation as it was well received by participants.

However, the evaluation encountered some difficulties with gaze tracking especially in the *Gaze+Touch Region* (centre of the tabletop). The deterioration in accuracy reflects the curve in Figure 3(b), which shows how the accuracy deteriorates towards the edges. Likewise, some participants encountered difficulty in selecting the videos closer to them, and this is most likely due to the error between 200 to 400 pixels in the vertical axis shown in Figure 3(a) where there is some degree of tracking deterioration due to eyelid occlusion.

Focusing on interaction techniques employed in the regions, this work presents the first instance where two types of gaze interaction were combined on the same interface i.e. gaze pointing and a natural gaze behaviour (e.g. smooth pursuit eye movement). Previous works that employ the former typically relied on accurate tracking while those that employ the latter were used in scenarios where accurate pointing was challenging. In this study, both types were identified through the characterisation and the intended use of a large surface, leading to the employment of the both. In the evaluation, participants did not have any issues switching between both

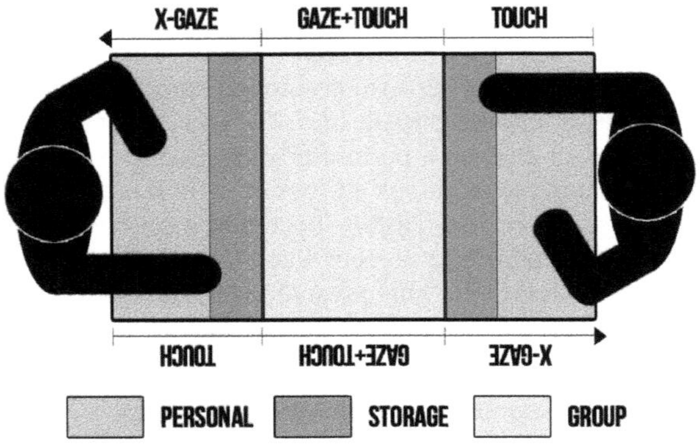

Figure 7: Regions in relation to the *Theory of Tabletop Territoriality* by Scott et al. [28] in a multi-user setting.

types of interaction and was observed to have been performed somewhat unconsciously. This proves that there are opportunities in combining both types of interaction. Lastly, humans naturally divide spaces on computers, such as grouping windows and icons on desktop computers. On tabletops, whether digital or non-digital, it has been shown that there is a natural segmentation which we aimed to investigate as part of our future work and is discussed further in the next section.

EXTENSIONS TO MULTIUSER TABLETOP SCENARIOS

Previous studies have articulated numerous advantages of using tabletops for collaborative work. Tables in general provide a large and natural interface for supporting human-to-human interactions whereby its characteristics provide affordances that allow the gathering of people for face-to-face communication as they surround a shared surface [26]. However, sharing the surface has certain negative connotations despite having advantages for subtle communication and this has to do with both 'space' and 'access'. Ryall et al. [23] observed that the actions of people in this setting often conflict with one another, both intentionally and accidentally. On occasion, users want to use the whole table, but sometimes privacy becomes an issue when users want to interact with displayed elements without sharing them with other users, which raises the problem of undesired access in specific situations [21]. Therefore, multiuser tabletops should allow users to protect their data against undesired access.

A potential solution for this is to increase the size of the interactive surface and divide the tabletop interface into territories in accordance to the *Theory of Tabletop Territoriality* [24]. The authors observed three distinct territories on the table, namely *personal*, *storage* and *group (shared)*. This division limits other users from reaching into the personal space of another user. The personal territory is typically determined by the users' reach while storage territory is within their extended reach [31]. However, placing and reaching for objects outside their personal and storage territories (e.g. group territory) now becomes a problem. Likewise, placing or obtaining an object in another user's personal territory with agreement from the owner also becomes a problem. Current proposed techniques such as *I-Grabber* [1] allows the user to seamlessly interact with both out-of-reach territories from the user's current location without blocking the territory of another user. This once again raises the problem of undesired access and that it might be useful to implement authorisation and privacy protocols to avoid distant users to see or manipulate one's workspace without permission [38].

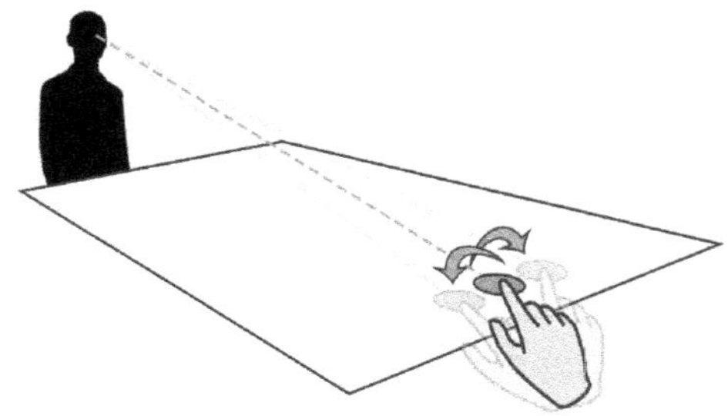

Figure 8: Potential application of *X-Gaze* in a multi-user setting. A user can initiate the movement while the other user selects using *X-Gaze*.

Our contributions present immediate opportunities to balance the issues of private personal territory, reachability, and having a form of authorisation protocol for seeking permission to access content from another user. Coincidentally, the regions defined in this work echo the territories of the tabletop presented by Scott et al. [24] (see Figure 7). In relation to these regions, the *X-Gaze* technique can be used to support multi-user sessions in both terms of 'passing objects' and as a method of authentication. In their *personal* and immediate *storage* territory, users can interact using touch gestures, which is well suited for private tasks such as reading, writing, annotating. In the *group* territory users interact using the combination of gaze and touch. This not only makes users aware of each other's attention but allows them to directly interact with public content at a distance. Users can also use combinations of gaze and indirect touch gestures as exemplified in Gaze+RST [34] to move items back and forth between this space and their personal space. Finally, *X-Gaze* elegantly supports protecting a user's *personal* territory from interference by other users [33]. For the user on the other side of the table to select an item, it is necessary for that item to move. If the owner of the personal space authorises the other user to interact with that content, she can move the object side-to-side a few times. If the other user follows it with her eyes, she is able to select that object and can be transferred over to her *personal* territory. To avoid unwanted selections, the user moving the object can casually gaze into the other user's *personal* territory which also naturally facilitates feedback, an important function in human-computer interaction. For instance, the user 'passing' the object will anticipate the object reappearing in the other user's *personal* territory and when this occurs it provides the user with a closure that the interaction has been successful.

Consequently, this form of authentication presents a form of 'social contract' and can be expanded to facilitate simultaneous exchange between two users, and this is best demonstrated by way of example. Take Monopoly, and picture a digitised version on a large interactive tabletop with two users sitting opposite one another. The *group* space displays the board while each user holds virtual deed cards to their properties and their virtual money notes in their *personal* territories. In the scenario where one user purchases a property from another, one user can move the virtual deed card while the other moves the money notes. Both users will consequently gaze into *personal* territory of one another, forming a 'social contract' where both users authenticate one another simultaneous upon agreed terms, therefore, facilitating a 'natural' exchange. Without neglecting the opportunities in *group* territory, it is possible that gaze awareness can be employed here which could change the social experience in this setting collaboratively. Tse et al. [32] mentions that monitoring the gaze of others lets us know where they are looking and where attention is directed. More importantly, gaze awareness happens easily and naturally in co-located tabletop settings as users can easily gauge what another user is gazing towards to in addition to being a great indicator for attention. Therefore, making gaze explicitly visible on a shared surface has some interesting connotations. For example, one user can say to another when solving a large jigsaw puzzle collaboratively, *"Can you get me that piece?"*. The other user will know which piece was refereed to by simply looking where the user is looking on the surface, serving as an implicit pointing method. Alternatively, it can be used competitively in a game of chess such that if one user is aware of the other user's intentions through their visible gaze and whether they will change their strategy or trick their opponent. Nevertheless, we hope to further explore how a multi-user gaze-enabled tabletop can support collaborative tasks using our interaction architecture.

CONCLUSION

This paper contributes a first step in enabling gaze interaction on large tabletops and for the first time, gaze-based interaction has been used effectively over a large distance on a horizontal surface ($1m^2$). This was achieved by initially identifying that the relative accuracy of the gaze along x-axis (parallel to user) was usable rather than y-axis (perpendicular to user) in our first study. We highlight that this first time characterisation to be a key contribution of this paper.

This informed the development of two solutions in which we evaluated in a second study. First, *X-Gaze*, a novel gaze-based interaction technique that leverage natural gaze behaviour was developed to enable gaze-only interaction at the far end of the tabletop. It is important to note that there are natural limitations of gaze, and despite the maturing enabling technology, it will not change the way our eyes work and it crucial that gaze-based techniques adhere to this fact. Consequently, novel techniques such as *X-Gaze* show great potential, such as enabling users to select of out-of-reach objects with low overhead and high precision. Secondly, we demonstrated how multimodal segmentation and *X-Gaze* can be incorporated in an interface design through a *Video-on-Demand* application, which we evaluated in a user study. Our findings showed that participants overall enjoyed using the system through the seamless transition between the regions but more importantly, showed that our solutions can be used in practice. Therefore, addressing two specific problems with respect to remote eye tracking, (1) the accuracy of eye-tracking on horizontal surfaces *at long distances* (i.e. beyond physical reach) and (2) the problem of eyelid occlusion *at short distances*. For our future work, we will expand our solutions formed in this paper to support collaborative multi-user environments.

REFERENCES

1. Abednego, M., Lee, J.-H., Moon, W., and Park, J.-H. I-grabber: Expanding physical reach in a large-display tabletop environment through the use of a virtual grabber. In *Proc. of ITS '09*, ACM (2009), 61–64.
2. Ardito, C., Buono, P., Costabile, M. F., and Desolda, G. Interaction with large displays: A survey. *ACM Comput. Surv. 47*, 3 (Feb. 2015), 46:1–46:38.
3. Bader, T., Vogelgesang, M., and Klaus, E. Multimodal integration of natural gaze behavior for intention recognition during object manipulation. In *Proc. of the 2009 Int. Conf. on Multimodal Interfaces*, ICMI-MLMI '09, ACM (2009), 199–206.
4. Banerjee, A., Burstyn, J., Girouard, A., and Vertegaal, R. Pointable: An in-air pointing technique to manipulate out-of-reach targets on tabletops. In *Proc. of ITS '11*, ACM (2011), 11–20.
5. Bartindale, T., Harrison, C., Olivier, P., and Hudson, S. E. Surfacemouse: Supplementing multi-touch interaction with a virtual mouse. In *Proc. of TEI '11*, ACM (2011), 293–296.
6. Benko, H., Morris, M. R., Brush, A. B., and Wilson, A. D. Insights on interactive tabletops: A survey of researchers and developers. Tech. Rep. MSR-TR-2009-22, March 2009.
7. Bezerianos, A., and Balakrishnan, R. The vacuum: Facilitating the manipulation of distant objects. In *Proc. of CHI '05*, ACM (2005), 361–370.
8. Collewijn, H., and Tamminga, E. P. Human smooth and saccadic eye movements during voluntary pursuit of different target motions on different backgrounds. *The Journal of Physiology 351*, 1 (1984), 217–250.
9. Esteves, A., Velloso, E., Bulling, A., and Gellersen, H. Orbits: Gaze interaction for smart watches using smooth pursuit eye movements. In *Proc. of UIST '15*, ACM (2015), 457–466.
10. Geller, T. Interactive tabletop exhibits in museums and galleries. *Computer Graphics and Applications, IEEE 26*, 5 (Sept 2006), 6–11.
11. Hardy, J., and Alexander, J. Toolkit support for interactive projected displays. In *Proc. of MUM '12*, ACM (2012), 42:1–42:10.
12. Holman, D. Gazetop: Interaction techniques for gaze-aware tabletops. In *CHI '07 Extended Abstracts on Human Factors in Computing Systems*, CHI EA '07, ACM (2007), 1657–1660.
13. Jacob, R. J. K. What you look at is what you get: Eye movement-based interaction techniques. In *Proc. of CHI '90*, ACM (1990), 11–18.
14. Lander, C., Gehring, S., Krüger, A., Boring, S., and Bulling, A. Gazeprojector: Accurate gaze estimation and seamless gaze interaction across multiple displays. In *Proc. of UIST 2015* (2015), 395–404.

15. Majaranta, P. *Communication and Text Entry by Gaze.* IGI Global, 2012.

16. Marquardt, N., Jota, R., Greenberg, S., and Jorge, J. A. The continuous interaction space: Interaction techniques unifying touch and gesture on and above a digital surface. In *Proc. of INTERACT'11*, Springer-Verlag (2011), 461–476.

17. Mauderer, M., Daiber, F., and Krüger, A. Combining touch and gaze for distant selection in a tabletop setting. In *CHI 2013: Workshop on Gaze Interaction in the Post-WIMP World* (2013).

18. Parker, J. K., Mandryk, R. L., and Inkpen, K. M. Integrating point and touch for interaction with digital tabletop displays. *Computer Graphics and Applications, IEEE 26*, 5 (Sept 2006), 28–35.

19. Pfeuffer, K., Alexander, J., Chong, M. K., and Gellersen, H. Gaze-touch: Combining gaze with multi-touch for interaction on the same surface. In *Proc. of UIST '14*, ACM (2014), 509–518.

20. Reetz, A., Gutwin, C., Stach, T., Nacenta, M., and Subramanian, S. Superflick: A natural and efficient technique for long-distance object placement on digital tables. In *Proc. of GI '06*, Canadian Information Processing Society (2006), 163–170.

21. Remy, C., Weiss, M., Ziefle, M., and Borchers, J. A pattern language for interactive tabletops in collaborative workspaces. In *Proc. of EuroPLoP '10*, ACM (2010), 9:1–9:48.

22. Rottach, K. G., Zivotofsky, A. Z., Das, V. E., Averbuch-Heller, L., Discenna, A. O., Poonyathalang, A., and Leigh, R. Comparison of horizontal, vertical and diagonal smooth pursuit eye movements in normal human subjects. *Vision Research 36*, 14 (1996), 2189–2195.

23. Ryall, K., Forlines, C., Shen, C., Morris, M. R., and Everitt, K. Experiences with and observations of direct-touch tabletops. In *Proc. of TABLETOP '06*, IEEE Computer Society (2006), 89–96.

24. Scott, S. D., Carpendale, S., and Inkpen, K. M. Territoriality in collaborative tabletop workspaces. In *Proc. of CSCW '04*, ACM (2004), 294–303.

25. Serim, B., and Jacucci, G. Pointing while looking elsewhere: Designing for varying degrees of visual guidance during manual input. In *Proceedings of CHI '16*, ACM (2016), 5789–5800.

26. Shen, C. From clicks to touches: Enabling face-to-face shared social interface on multi-touch tabletops. In *Proc. of OCSC'07*, Springer-Verlag (2007), 169–175.

27. Shen, C., Ryall, K., Forlines, C., Esenther, A., Vernier, F. D., Everitt, K., Wu, M., Wigdor, D., Morris, M. R., Hancock, M., and Tse, E. Informing the design of direct-touch tabletops. *IEEE Comput. Graph. Appl. 26*, 5 (Sept. 2006), 36–46.

28. Smeaton, A. F., Lee, H., Foley, C., and Mcgivney, S. Collaborative video searching on a tabletop. *Multimedia Syst. 12*, 4-5 (Mar. 2007), 375–391.

29. Stellmach, S., and Dachselt, R. Look & touch: Gaze-supported target acquisition. In *Proc. of CHI '12*, ACM (2012), 2981–2990.

30. Stellmach, S., and Dachselt, R. Still looking: Investigating seamless gaze-supported selection, positioning, and manipulation of distant targets. In *Proc. of CHI '13*, ACM (2013), 285–294.

31. Toney, A., and Thomas, B. H. Considering reach in tangible and table top design. In *Proc. of TABLETOP '06*, IEEE (2006), 2–pp.

32. Tse, E., Greenberg, S., Shen, C., and Forlines, C. Multimodal multiplayer tabletop gaming. *Computers in Entertainment (CIE) 5*, 2 (Apr. 2007).

33. Tse, E., Histon, J., Scott, S. D., and Greenberg, S. Avoiding interference: How people use spatial separation and partitioning in sdg workspaces. In *Proc. of CSCW '04*, ACM (2004), 252–261.

34. Turner, J., Alexander, J., Bulling, A., and Gellersen, H. Gaze+rst: Integrating gaze and multitouch for remote rotate-scale-translate tasks. In *Proc. of CHI '15*, ACM (2015), 4179–4188.

35. Velloso, E., Wirth, M., Weichel, C., Esteves, A., and Gellersen, H. AmbiGaze: Direct Control of Ambient Devices by Gaze. In *Proc. of DIS'16*, ACM (2016), 812–817.

36. Vidal, M., Bulling, A., and Gellersen, H. Pursuits: Spontaneous interaction with displays based on smooth pursuit eye movement and moving targets. In *Proc. of UbiComp '13*, ACM (2013), 439–448.

37. Voelker, S., Matviienko, A., Schöning, J., and Borchers, J. Combining direct and indirect touch input for interactive workspaces using gaze input. In *Proc. of SUI '15*, ACM (2015), 79–88.

38. Voelker, S., Weiss, M., Wacharamanotham, C., and Borchers, J. Dynamic portals: A lightweight metaphor for fast object transfer on interactive surfaces. In *Proc. of ITS '11*, ACM (2011), 158–161.

39. Wigdor, D., Jiang, H., Forlines, C., Borkin, M., and Shen, C. Wespace: The design development and deployment of a walk-up and share multi-surface visual collaboration system. In *Proc. of CHI '09*, ACM (2009), 1237–1246.

40. Yamamoto, M., Komeda, M., Nagamatsu, T., and Watanabe, T. Development of eye-tracking tabletop interface for media art works. In *Proc. of ITS '10*, ACM (2010), 295–296.

41. Yamamoto, M., Komeda, M., Nagamatsu, T., and Watanabe, T. Hyakunin-eyesshu: A tabletop hyakunin-isshu game with computer opponent by the action prediction based on gaze detection. In *Proc. of NGCA '11*, ACM (2011), 5:1–5:4.

42. Zhai, S., Morimoto, C., and Ihde, S. Manual and gaze input cascaded (magic) pointing. In *Proc. of CHI '99*, ACM (1999), 246–253.

Physical-Digital Privacy for Mixed Reality Collaboration: An Exploratory Study

Mohamad Salimian, Derek Reilly, Stephen Brooks, Bonnie MacKay
Dalhousie University
Halifax, Nova Scotia, Canada
{rizi, reilly, sbrooks, bmackay}@cs.dal.ca

ABSTRACT
We present a study exploring privacy behaviours in mixed reality collaborative environments. We consider two scenarios involving hiding and sharing blended physical-virtual documents around a tabletop, under two vertical display conditions: a solo display showing the remote collaborator as an avatar, and circumambient displays showing the rest of the connected virtual environment. We explore four types of cues (interactive, communication-based, ambient, and infrastructure) and their impact on how collaborators hide and share blended physical-virtual documents. Many participants did not obviously develop a sense that the physical and virtual surroundings were fused; as a result, certain physical privacy behaviours (e.g., orienting one's body to shield documents from the remote collaborator) were less apparent in the study. However, the circumambient displays generated curiosity about how the spaces were connected, and episodes where breaches were enacted or the spatial correlation was otherwise suggested led some participants to trust the environment less. On the table, the presence of fiducial markers and digital document "shadows" served to cue participants about the impact of hiding and sharing physical documents, however accidental breaches usually went unnoticed.

Author Keywords
Collaborative environments; Mixed reality; Tabletop; Privacy and Security; User Study; Human Factors

ACM Classification Keywords
H.1.2; H.2.1

INTRODUCTION
Blended interaction [1] promises forms of cooperative work that effectively integrate the physical and digital, maintaining the primacy of physical actions in co-located collaboration when using digital tools and services. By integrating physical workspaces with virtual workspaces, mixed reality may promote blended interaction in mixed presence work configurations (involving both co-located and remote collaborators). In our work we explore how privacy-related actions with physical documents—sharing a document with all or some in a group, and sharing a portion of a document with a group—can be understood as intentional privacy-related actions and manifested in a mixed reality collaborative environment (MRCE).

ISS '16, November 06-09, 2016, Niagara Falls, ON, Canada
 ISBN 978-1-4503-4248-3/16/11...$15.00
DOI: http://dx.doi.org/10.1145/2992154.2992167

A range of approaches have been considered to support mixed presence collaboration, including the early media space work [23], display-sharing [2][3], telepresence [4] systems, blended interaction spaces [5], mixed reality [6][7] and collaborative virtual environments [8][9]. Each tries to achieve a sense of co-presence to facilitate collaboration between co-located and remote collaborators and to reduce *presence disparity* [10]. In many cases, this is done by creating a work environment that is accessible to all collaborators in an *experientially similar* way. VideoArms [11], Almost Touching [12], WaaZam! [13], Clearboard [14] and Carpeno [8] are examples of research projects using shared space environments to permit remote or mixed presence collaboration. These systems require that all participants have symmetric hardware and software setups to collaborate. While having identical interfaces can make it more straightforward to see and interpret the actions of a collaborator, this limits how and where collaborators can connect and can be costly for users.

In the mixed reality approach that we consider, remote collaborators connect to a virtual world mapped to a physical co-located ("local") collaboration space. This mapping is achieved through a high level spatial correspondence between the two spaces, and through one or more tightly interwoven ("fused") collaboration surfaces. For example, documents placed on a physical tabletop display become visible and available to remote collaborators on a mapped virtual table, and digital documents that the remote collaborator shares on the virtual table appear on the tabletop display. While the experiences of remote and local collaborators are not identical (and perhaps even dissimilar), remote collaborators require limited technical infrastructure (laptop and headphones) and can connect anywhere, while co-located collaborators can still use the facilities of the entire physical workspace. Using a mixed reality collaborative environment can benefit collaborators in a number of ways: indicating the location of collaborators, allowing a shared perspective on documents (if desired) to remote and co-located collaborators, mapping between digital and physical work artifacts, and encouraging a sense of co-presence[15] [16][17].

In an MRCE, privacy needs to be managed across multiple spaces and multiple interaction channels. Difficulties with either can reduce reliability and fragment collaboration[9], making it difficult to both use and trust the system. We address the former by having the physical and virtual spaces spatially correspond, as with blended interaction spaces and collaborative virtual environments. Using blended interaction techniques, we address the latter by designing interfaces that allow physical actions to be translated into digital actions, and for corresponding virtual actions to be manifested similarly in the physical space.

For example, consider a meeting where a participant shares documents with selected colleagues by breaking away from the main workspace with those colleagues and orienting her documents so only they can view them. Knowing the "locations" of remote collaborators in a mixed reality collaborative space may allow her to achieve the same effect with only minimal changes in behavior, avoiding unintentional exposure of information.

While designing around existing physical privacy management behaviours seems promising, it also introduces a number of challenges. How do we communicate spatial correspondence to local and remote collaborators? Will collaborators exploit spatial correspondence? How do local collaborators know the effect of their physical actions in the virtual space, and remote collaborators in the physical space?

Inspired by these challenges, we conducted an exploratory study, where we considered two generic document-centric privacy needs:

- Sharing one or more documents with all collaborators while withholding other documents from the group.
- Sharing one or more documents with a subset of collaborators.

We built a blended interaction prototype supporting each need. The prototype binds physical documents to virtual counterparts, and allows remote and local collaborators to share their documents on a physical tabletop display that is itself mapped to a virtual tabletop. Placing a physical document on the tabletop causes its virtual counterpart to be presented beneath it and slightly displaced, as a *digital shadow* indicating that the document is now visible in the virtual space. Remote collaborators can "walk" around the virtual tabletop to view content and collaborate just as local collaborators can walk around the physical table.

Study participants used the prototype to engage in two collaborative activities, each focused on one of the two privacy needs identified above. We were interested to know how collaborators would interpret information suggesting how physical and virtual are connected: we call these *correspondence cues*. Activities were conducted under two conditions: one in which the spatial correspondence between physical and virtual was visually emphasized using circumambient displays, and another without these displays.

Our study produced two main findings. First, participants exhibited expected physical privacy behaviours in relation to co-located collaborators (e.g. holding playing cards close), but in general considered physical-virtual document privacy only in relation to the tabletop workspace. Environmental cues revealing the connected virtual space were mostly viewed as providing information about what the virtual space looked like and what was going on within it, and/or as a means of communicating with their remote collaborator, versus indicating that the physical and virtual spaces were spatially integrated.

Second, the extent to which participants sought information about how physical and virtual are connected varied, as did which correspondence cues participants considered and the weight they ascribed to each. Cues intended to indicate mappings between physical actions and virtual effects were even ignored during tasks by some participants, including the circumambient displays and digital shadows on the tabletop. Participants more concerned about privacy found it stressful to use the mixed reality environment without verifying the completeness of their mental models. This is challenging when correspondence cues are weak, ambiguous, or if they conflict with each other.

BACKGROUND AND MOTIVATION

Privacy and Security in Collaborative Environments

Privacy is a term that harbors a variety of meanings and connotations [18]. In this paper we employ Culnan's succinct definition of privacy [19]: "the ability of an individual to control the terms under which their personal information is acquired and used".

People often utilize their prior experiences, strategies, and practices to make sense of new encounters with digital artifacts [20]. Privacy management in physical collaborative environments involves continuous and dynamic interaction with the environment and managing the boundaries between different actions and degrees of disclosure in different circumstances [21]. This offers opportunities for the design of privacy solutions for collaborative environments, however such environments do not always allow one to apply prior experience when managing privacy, or to dynamically negotiate their privacy. Instead, many establish secure procedures that users should follow, specifying proper security policies, and providing end-user assistance with these procedures or specifications when requested [22]. Mixed presence also does not automatically support applying prior experience and it is important to find ways to support privacy and security through conscious design choices [12].

Our prototype centers collaboration around a fused physical-virtual tabletop and a range of privacy approaches have been considered for shared surfaces in general. UbiTable [23] attempts to support most common privacy needs by defining three levels of access for sharing information: private, personal and public. Semi–Public Displays [24] are targeted toward small co-located groups that require a high level of mutual awareness. A semi–public display divides a display into regions with different purposes such reminders and notifications, and active collaboration. Rather than enforce privacy rules, the display itself is intended to be used in shared workspaces in a manner very similar to whiteboards and bulletin boards, relying on existing social protocols and practices for privacy management. By contrast, in Virtual Walls [25] collaborators define rules on the visibility of data in different regions of the physical space. In our work, we attempt to map the actions of hiding or sharing a physical document on a tabletop to the visibility of digital copies.

Mapping physical privacy actions to virtual privacy actions in MRCE spaces may yield collaborative environments that allow users to manage their privacy and security in a manner that is both familiar and dynamic. Conceptually similar privacy actions in physical and virtual spaces must be carefully blended to avoid coordination problems arising from a fragmented workspace, however [9]. Several requirements of MRCEs make this challenging: managing interface differences between collocated and remote collaborators, maintaining group awareness across both physical and virtual spaces, and supporting accurate mental model formation.

Mental Models in Mixed Reality Spaces

An individual's mental representation of a physical environment is known as a spatial mental model. Spatial mental models are map-like mental constructs that are gradually built and updated by moving and acting in the world and through inspection [26].

In MRCEs the spatial mental model and the user's model of the system are closely intertwined. Therefore, individuals build a mental model that contains both spatial and system elements. Reilly et al. [27] demonstrated that the physical and virtual elements of a MRCE, including the layout of furniture, logical groupings of content and interface cues (such as dial controls) all influence a collaborator's mental model of a connected virtual space, and ultimately impacts how they collaborate. A correct mental model can increase contextual awareness and help collaborators manage security and privacy more effectively by using the knowledge they acquire while building their mental model. In this paper, we use the term mental model to refer to this hybrid form of mental model.

Dix et al. [28] identify three type of spaces in a mixed reality system: the physical space, positioning relative to physical and virtual space (the "sensed space"), and the virtual space. Building a mental model in this case includes the additional task of understanding the relationships among all three spaces. In an MRCE, local collaborators acquire a mental model of the physical space most readily, but through collaboration must build a model of both the connected virtual space and of the fidelity, accuracy, range, etc. of the sensed space. Remote collaborators start from the virtual space, and work toward a model that includes the mapped physical space as well. An MRCE can increase group awareness and decrease presence disparity. This helps collaborators build a more accurate mental model such that they can allocate their attention more effectively.

EXPERIMENT

Research Questions

We explore how methods that people regularly use for handling privacy in physical environments can ground the designs of privacy mechanisms for mixed reality collaboration. These include simple yet effective physical actions such as tilting a document to hide content from others or positioning oneself at a distance from others. In this study we considered two research questions:

- How do cues indicating physical-virtual correspondence impact privacy-related behaviour?
- How readily do collaborators transfer their physical document-centric privacy behaviors to an MRCE?

We consider these questions in terms of both environment-centric physical privacy behaviours (positioning one's self relative to others) as facilitated through physical-virtual spatial correspondence, and document-centric physical privacy behaviours, facilitated by blended physical-virtual documents.

Environment

Virtual Environment: We designed a virtual café scenario where the co-located and remote collaborators met. Participants were told that the remote collaborator (actually a research confederate) was participating from another city and connected via the virtual café, which was being used as a collaborative distributed workspace by labs in several universities. During the experiment, prerecorded avatars could be seen walking around the virtual café, occasionally opening documents, and speaking with each other. By doing this, we aimed to infuse the feeling of being connected to a public place and so encourage participants to be more aware of the virtual environment and consider potential privacy implications.

Physical Environment: The study was conducted in a lab space approximately $6m^2$ in size. We used a bottom-projected 70" tabletop display as the document sharing interface. Participants stood around the tabletop during the study. On one side of the tabletop, a 62" wall display presented the location of the remote collaborator in the virtual world; the intended effect was to communicate the spatial correspondence between the physical table and the virtual tabletop in the cafe. Projectors were used to show the virtual café on walls approximately 2.5m from each of the remaining three sides of the table; each projection was >100" diagonal. Figure 1 shows a sketch of the setup wherein each

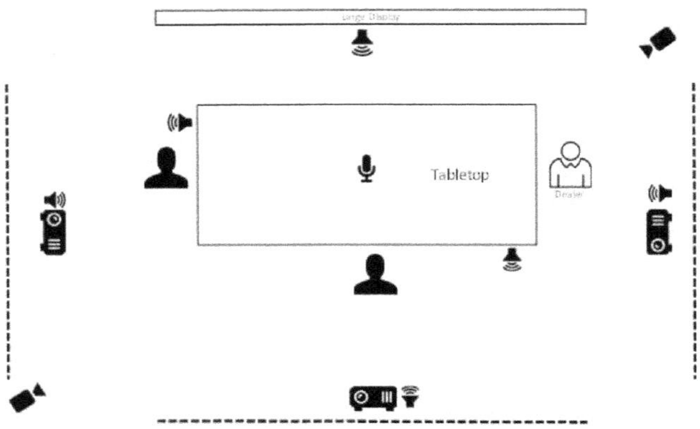

Figure 1. Room setup for the collocated collaborators. Each projector presents one side of the virtual café, the large display (top) shows the remote collaborator's avatar in their "place" at the table.

projector displays one side of the café on the wall of the physical room. Figure 3 shows each side of the café.

We used four cameras during the study. Camera 1 was used to record the study, camera 2 provided a live stream to the remote collaborator, camera 3 tracked fiducials above the table, and camera 4 was a fake camera placed opposite to camera 2 to suggest that participants could be observed from multiple angles.

We installed six pairs of speakers around the room, as shown in Figure 1. These speakers were connected to the virtual café to provide spatialized audio. In all conditions, participants could hear ambient café noise and the spatialized voice of the remote collaborator.

In a separate room, a research associate sat with three screens to play the remote collaborator. One screen showed a top-down view of the virtual table, another allowed him to navigate his avatar in the virtual café, showing his perspective of the virtual world, and a third provided a video feed of the physical lab. By having these three views, the remote collaborator could act as though the local collaborators were represented as avatars at the virtual table (they were not), and was able to walk (virtually) to where they stood (physically).

Fiducial markers (visual markers that can be recognized by cameras) were attached to all documents used during the study. A Logitech 1080p webcam was set 1.5m above the tabletop to identify the fiducials. When a fiducial was recognized, a digital copy of the document appeared on the tabletop display, indicating that it was recognized and shared: that is, visible on the virtual tabletop in the same position and orientation. Figure 3 shows the tabletop setup.

Population

We recruited university students majoring in a variety of disciplines. 16 participant pairs (14 females, 18 males, and 19-35 years old) played the part of the local collaborators. Participants completed a short background questionnaire asking how often they work in groups and how often they share paper and digital documents. The majority reported that they did both: 28/32 participants work as a group at least ten times per year, 25/32 participants share paper documents at least five times per month, and all 32 participants share digital documents at least five times per month. Only 3 participants had prior experiences with MRCEs.

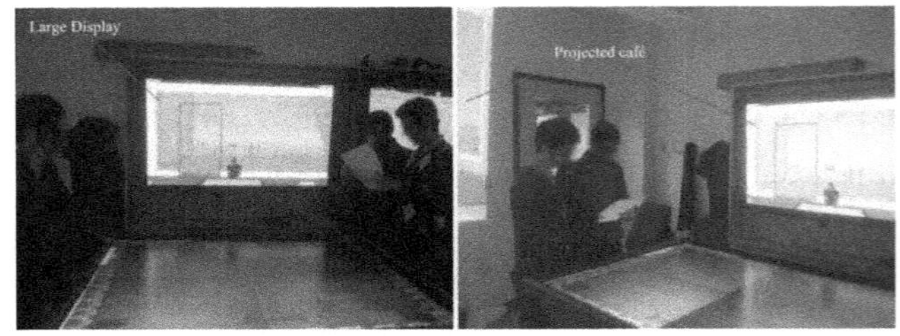

Figure 2. Left: solo display con. Right: circumambient con.

Figure 3. Four sides of the café in the circuit ambient condition; these were projected around the room.

Disclosure and Environment Conditions

Participants were told how physical documents were shared using the tabletop; at the outset of each activity the facilitator demonstrated how the document set specific to the activity is used. Aside from saying that the virtual café was connected to the lab, and that the remote collaborator could "see them", we gave no explanation to participants about how the physical and virtual spaces were linked. For example, we did not disclose whether participants were represented as avatars in the virtual world and/or visible by a video camera, but if they explicitly asked, we told them that we would explain it after the study. We employed this protocol because we wanted to observe which cues participants used to interpret how the physical and virtual settings were connected, to explore what those interpretations would be, and to see if the interpretations had any impact on privacy-related behavior during the activities.

We defined two environment configurations for the study. In the *solo display* condition, participants saw one side of the virtual café on the wall display, showing a small extension of the physical table indicating the remote collaborator's "place at the table" (see Figure 2). In the *circumambient* condition, we projected the rest of the café around the physical tabletop on the remaining three sides. In addition to the background sounds of the café, participants could see the activities of other avatars, and keep track of their collaborator's avatar if

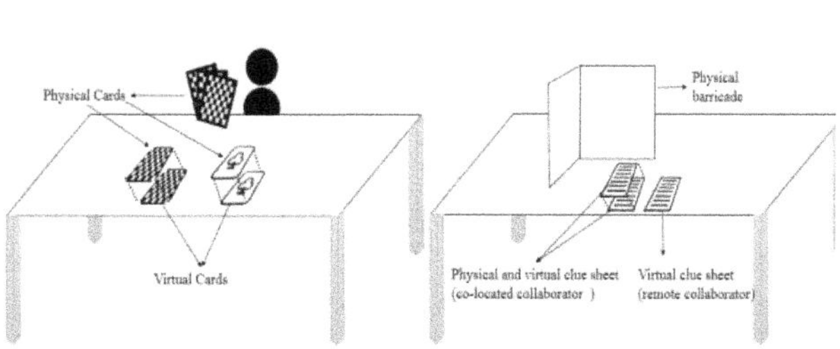

Figure 4. Left: Card game. Right: Guessing game.

he moved away from or around the table (see Figure 3). The conditions provided different information about the virtual world and how it is connected to the physical environment in order to explore how users build an understanding of the operation of the system with respect to privacy.

Activities

In piloting we tested roleplaying [29] using a credit card scenario to motivate participants to protect their data, even though data was fictitious [30]. However, we found the mechanisms we needed to support privacy in that scenario were unwieldy, affecting participant engagement. We designed game scenarios that while not real-world examples, require privacy management and encourage engagement.

Card Game (sharing with all/none): This activity is an example of a situation in which documents (cards) are shared with all or hidden from all in a group. The dealer (experiment facilitator) and two co-located collaborators stood on three sides of the tabletop, and the remote collaborator's space was displayed on the remaining side, in front of the large display showing the remote player's avatar. The game played was *31* (*Banking* variant), a turn-based game whereby collaborators try to obtain a total card value as close as possible to 31 without going over. After an open hand was played for training, three rounds of the game were played.

When physical cards were placed over or on the table a digital version of the card appeared on the screen below it but displaced slightly (face up or down, depending on how the physical card was held). The card was then visible in the same relative position and orientation to the remote collaborator. The remote collaborator's cards remained face down on their side of the table, but their digital counterpart's were displayed face-up on the remote collaborator's table view. When he clicked on 2 digital cards (1 from his hand and 1 from the center), the region around the physical cards flashed on the table, indicating they should be exchanged. The dealer then exchanged the physical cards on behalf of the remote collaborator. Figure 4 (left) shows the setup.

Guessing Game (sharing with some but not all): The guessing game was used as an example of needing to share a document with some but not all in a group. In this activity, two collaborators worked together as clue givers and the other collaborator played as a guesser. The clue givers each were given clue sheets with five clues about a topic. They began by sharing their clues with each other and deciding the order of the 10 clues to give to the guesser. The clue givers' aim is to give as many clues as possible before a correct guess is made, while the guesser aims to guess correctly with the fewest clues provided. After the facilitator described the objective and mechanics of the game, three rounds were played: one where the remote collaborator guessed, and two where the remote collaborator paired with one of the co-located collaborators as a clue-giver.

When playing as a clue-giver, the remote collaborator verbally indicated where on the table he would place his digital clue sheet. The co-located clue giver would then place their physical clue sheet beside it, and use a physical blind to hide both clue sheets from the co-located guesser. As with the playing cards, physical clue sheets were tracked using fiducials and when placed on the table a digital version was displayed below it on the table at a slight offset. When the remote collaborator was guessing, co-located participants could hold their clue sheets as they wished. Figure 4 (right) shows the setup for the guessing game when a co-located participant played as guesser.

We fully counterbalanced the environment configurations and the activities.

Scripted Events

During the experiment, a number of scripted events were performed to help participants infer physical-virtual correspondence. We suggest correspondence through cues only, rather than explicitly describe them to participants, to observe what cues are picked up and how they are interpreted.

Throughout the experiment, avatars were shown moving around the virtual café, sitting down, entering and leaving, and opening virtual documents to share with other avatars.

Before the 1st activity, the remote collaborator would enter the café from the entrance door after a delay and would walk to the virtual tabletop while talking to collaborators. For example, he would say, *"Hey, how are you? Sorry that I am late, I was busy with..."* The remote collaborator's voice would be heard from different speakers as he entered in the virtual café to help emphasize the spatialized audio. The remote collaborator would also walk away from the table at the end of the first activity and return in a similar fashion when the next activity began.

During the first activity, the remote collaborator would make indirect references suggesting they could see his collaborators (*"nice hat", "no, not that one, the one to your left")*. During the second activity, he would walk around the virtual table, suggesting the possibility of a privacy breach.

Data Collection

After performing each activity participants answered five 5-point Likert-scale questions (anchored with Strongly Agree and Strongly Disagree, see Table 1). We also interviewed participant groups after each activity to get more detail about their experiences and their opinions about using the environment for collaboration with sensitive documents.

We transcribed and coded the recorded video of the study and interviews. Four researchers met prior to coding and derived a preliminary coding scheme. After this, one video was chosen at random and was coded by all researchers. Then researchers came together and discussed their codes to reach consensus on the coding scheme. We captured privacy-relevant actions and behaviours such as holding, exchanging and sharing documents, moving about the table, asking questions about the setup, and paying visual attention to other collaborators and the virtual environment.

Table 1. Post-activity questionnaire

It was easy to hide documents from the other person at the table.
It was easy to hide documents from the remote person.
It was easy to share documents with the other person at the table.
It was easy to share documents with the remote person.
It was easy to tell if there was someone near me or near the table in the virtual Cafe.

RESULTS

Questionnaires

We found no main effect of display condition on responses to any questions. A significant effect of activity was found only for hiding documents from the player at the table ($F(1,32)=15.328$, $p<0.001$), with the guessing game viewed as more difficult. An interaction effect (display X activity) was found for hiding documents from the remote player ($F(1,32=5.282$, $p=.025$), with more difficulty perceived in the circumambient condition for the guessing game. We anticipated but did not see an effect of display condition on the last question ("...tell if there was someone near me...").

We next considered differences in ratings for ease of sharing and hiding documents with collocated and remote collaborators, regardless of display condition. We did not find significant differences for the card game. For the guessing game, there was a significant difference ($F(1,32)=11.029$, $p=0.001$) in ratings for hiding documents: participants found it easier to hide the clue sheet from the remote collaborator. There was also a significant difference ($F(1,32)=13.086$, $p=0.0005$) for sharing: participants found it easier to share their clue sheet with the local collaborator.

Card Game Behaviours

Our results suggest that the fiducials on the cards did not impact privacy related behaviors in a significant way, and that the digital shadows enforced physical-digital correspondence. Out of a total 193 card-exchanging events, no participants covered the marker of the card they wanted to exchange while they were extending their arm over the tabletop. During exchanges the player's card was being tracked, but the digital shadow appearing on the table corresponded to whether the card was held face up or down. Similarly, in the nine cases where participants exchanged a card but changed their mind, it was apparent by whether their card was held face up or down whether they had revealed one of their cards to both players.

As with exchanging cards, the broader physical behaviours of our participants largely corresponded with how people play cards around a table. We also didn't observe participants acting any more protective of their cards in the circumambient or solo display conditions. 23/32 participants (10 participants in solo-display and 13 participants in circumambient display) leaned over the tabletop to exchange their cards. These participants held two cards in one hand and held the card they wanted to change in the other. They were careful to keep the two cards close to their chest before they leaned over the table. They then drew away from the table and lowered their cards from their chest at the same time. The remaining nine participants (six participants in solo-display condition and three participants in circumambient display) moved their hand over the table first, then leaned over the tabletop and brought the hand close to their chest. Therefore, the system could detect the cards for a moment and show the virtual cards that corresponded with real cards on the table. Only in one case, the participant noticed that his cards were being tracked and said "*oh*". The other participants concentrated on changing cards and did not notice that corresponding virtual cards appeared on the table. We also noted that 14/32 participants at least once rested their cards on the edge of the table during the game. This position limited the co-located opponent's ability to see their cards but increased the possibility of revealing the fiducial to the table tracker unintentionally.

Guessing Game Behaviours

The absence of fiducials seemed to influence behavior in the guessing game. When the remote player was the guesser, most (14/16) groups put their clue sheets directly on the tabletop. Fiducial markers were not placed on the clue sheets when co-located collaborators worked together, and it seems that participants interpreted this to mean that the remote collaborator would not be able to see them. Fiducials *were* used when one of the co-located participants was guessing. In these cases, an opaque plastic barrier was used to block the virtual and physical clue sheets from the guesser's view; all co-located teammates put their clue sheet on the tabletop beside the remote collaborator's virtual clue sheet, behind the divider. On occasion, the fiducial would not be tracked due to occlusion by the barrier, and so the clue sheet's digital shadow would not appear. Participants did not remark when this occurred, relying instead on feedback from the remote collaborator indicating that they could see the sheet.

As for broader physical behaviours, these were evident and reasonable in relation to local collaborators, but generally absent in relation to the remote collaborator. Most (26/32) guessers stood away from the tabletop while others were working on the clues with the remote collaborator, to ensure they couldn't see the clues, sometimes making themselves busy by looking at their cell phones, talking with the facilitator, or looking at the virtual world. When the remote collaborator was guessing, the participants moved together at the corner of the tabletop to decide on the order to give the clues. Most groups did not pay much attention to the location of the remote collaborator's avatar when he was guessing, however one group was noticeably vigilant about the location of the remote collaborator when he virtually walked around the café. Participants in this group stood shoulder-to-shoulder, to protect their documents from being seen.

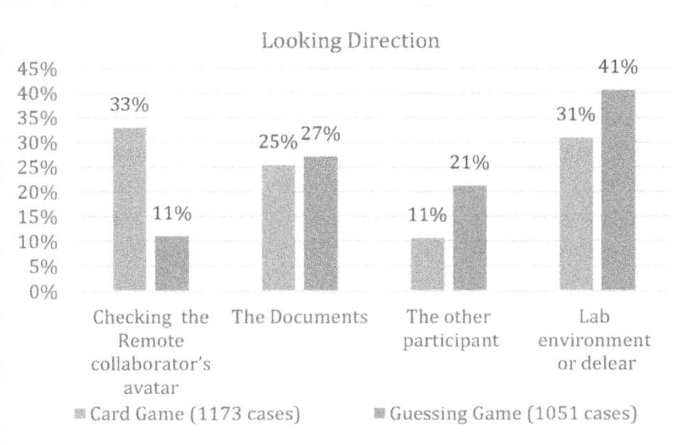

Figure 5: Visual attention

Participant Mental Models

During video coding we logged the amount of time spent attending visually to the surroundings, the facilitator, the remote collaborator's avatar, and the local collaborator (see Figure 5). In particular, visually exploring the environment may help in forming a mental model.

Most often, participants paid attention to the circumambient displays at the very outset of the condition/activity in which they were used, before the activity began.

In contrast, we observed no obvious instances of this once the card game was underway. Instead, shifts in visual attention away from the documents were very game-focused: toward the remote collaborator's avatar during their turn, to the other local player, or to the facilitator/dealer, even in the circumambient condition.

During the guessing game, a majority (10/16) of participants did not pay attention to the circumambient displays. These participants occupied themselves with activities such as checking their cell phones or talking to the facilitator until it was their turn to guess, and did not ask questions or make comments about the setup. The remaining 6 participants used this "off time" to explore the setup and ask questions about the setup and the projected café, while sharing their ideas and assumptions with others, *"how [does] the system work? [Can you] set up a private server?"*–p18, *"it is neat to be [an] avatar"*–p19, *"I think he can see us as [an] avatar like we are seeing him"*–p15, *"it is cool to do a high five on the table with Brian [remote collaborator]"*–p23. In the solo display condition, no participants showed any sign of interest in exploring the setup.

At the end of the study, we asked participants about their preference for the display conditions and whether they helped them to increase their awareness of events happening around them. 22/32 participants preferred to have the circumambient condition during the card game and guessing game. Surprisingly, many expressed that the circumambient condition helped them feel immersed in the café. For example, *"I think the whole view is cool. It feels like you are in the location with the person"–p30, "I can talk to him[and] see him. It ... kinda feel[s] like real world."–P17, "I think, when we could see entire cafe, it makes you feel closer to the person regardless of the physical distance between you, so if I want to share something with somebody ... not necessary in the same area, this would make it more real."–p29.* Even though many participants seemed to like the circumambient condition for the enhanced immersion, they did not in general attempt to use spatial correspondence as a medium for hiding and sharing documents.

14/32 participants thought it inappropriate to have circumambient displays when sharing confidential documents. For some, this was due to privacy concerns, but for others it was simply a matter of propriety. For activities like the card game and guessing game, the circumambient condition had value: *"... good when you want to socialize but for sharing information, or when you want to get down to business, I think you don't need this."–p29, "it is ok, I didn't feel anything, because it was a game, it wasn't something that I would be asking him about his personal life"–p13; "I'm sharing my personal information and I have the feeling that this information might, or some other people might hear this information but [not] for card game guessing game."–p31.*

11/32 participants mentioned that if turning the projectors off in the circumambient condition meant that people in the virtual environment could not view their documents, then they would prefer to share confidential documents with the projectors off (i.e., in the solo display). *"If they can see my cards then just front view"–p28, "if it is a big game, or money or gambling is going then yea just front view"–p22.*

4/32 participants preferred the solo display condition so that they could concentrate on the activities, *"I think the front view is fine, I really didn't use the other views." P11, "I think only usable stuff here is this monitor"–p24, "I like front view, I don't care about the projected cafe."–p12.*

From the comments, interviews and observations it is apparent that some participants believed that the remote collaborator could only see their documents if they chose to show them over the tabletop. For example, *"He couldn't see my hand"*– p2, *"he is not here and he cannot see my cards"* – p3. They also thought that it was easier to hide documents from the remote participant, because he would not have a chance to look at their documents even if they held them improperly. For example, *"there is some chance for real person to see my cards but there is no chance for him [the remote collaborator]. Very secure"* – p7, *"in actual world p1 can see my cards, for example if card drop from my hand, but for virtual there is no chance"* – p23.

DISCUSSION

In a dialectic process, privacy regulation is formed from our expectations, as well as our experience with and observations of other collaborators' behavior [21]. In a dynamic process, privacy forms through continuous negotiation and management, and boundary definitions for collaboration under different circumstances [21]. Our strategy was to retain the tangible nature of cards and clue sheets, and take advantage of privacy–related protocols that have emerged with the physical documents, while designing a relatively unconstrained space for mixed reality collaboration; therefore, users are able to manage their privacy as a continuation of their experiences in similar situations.

Mapping Physical Privacy Behaviors

MRCEs are still quite rare, and there is no commercial example in use by the general public. Therefore, individuals usually do not have enough collaboration experience and knowledge of a MRCE. For example, there is a deficit of knowledge about how the mapping between physical and virtual documents works, how they can be aware of events and changes in the environment, if there is any mechanism to increase their awareness and how they can use them, etc. This lack of experience makes it challenging to manage privacy simultaneously in both physical and virtual environments [9]. The background questionnaire indicated that only three participants had heard about mixed reality and none had experienced it.

Deploying well-practiced physical interactive methods and actions in virtual environments minimizes or potentially even removes the learning stage and provides a more integrated collaborative environment between the virtual and physical world. Our observations suggest that collaborators can effectively use an MRCE that translates physical privacy behaviors to virtual actions even without prior collaboration experiences, though issues persist.

Accidental exposure of private documents needs to be properly flagged or else it can easily go unnoticed. In our study we observed many accidental incidents such as leaving physical documents unprotected under view of the tracking system which resulted in exposing the collaborator's information. In many cases it was not obvious that local collaborators even noticed the breach.

Managing Privacy and Security across Multiple Spaces

After examining the interview responses and coded videos, we classified the collaborator's questions into three main categories. These three categories can be used as basic guidelines to design a mixed reality collaborative system to help collaborators build a mental model and trust the system. Our findings are in line with guidelines for privacy in mixed reality suggested by [27] and Dix et al.'s definition of the three spaces in mixed reality [28].

The relation between physical and virtual spaces: A number of collaborators showed an interest to learn how their actions were manifested in the virtual world, and if they needed to do anything specific to protect their document. This is the sensed space of Dix et al. [28]. We tried to provide different cues to help collaborators to understand the transference of their action between the mediums. For example, if they extend their hand to the center of the table with the card face down. As an equal action, we showed the back of the digital version of the cards on the tabletop to provide a cue that suggests the remote collaborator only sees the back of the card. *"What angles to put my paper?"– p1.*

The participants' comments and activities imply that they assumed the remote collaborator's view was limited to the tabletop such that hiding from the remote collaborator is easier and safer. Even when they did not protect the document well (e.g. drop it on the floor), they assumed the remote person could not see it. For example, *"because the only information which I was trying to share [on the tabletop] ...I am sharing only that information [on the tabletop] it was perfectly safe for sharing.", "only when I put them on the table he could see that"– p3.* Also, 12/16 groups mentioned at different times that they would like to know what the remote collaborator could see so that they could trust the system to manage their privacy.

Virtual space: Co-located collaborators showed a lot of interest in learning how they were presented to the remote collaborator. For example, they asked if the remote collaborator saw them as an avatar inside the virtual world or if the remote collaborator saw their real faces. Again, we used different cues to help collaborators to learn about the MRCE. For instance, the remote collaborator commented on what the collaborators around the table wore and there were cameras set up around the physical room. *"I don't [feel safe] because I don't know like what other participants [remote collaborator] can see." – p11, "I wish I could see what he was seeing to confirm what I am sharing"–p31.*

Physical space: After establishing the boundaries of the shared work region in the co-located space, 25/32 participants asked for details about their remote collaborator's physical environment. While our MRCE was designed as a combination of a virtual and a physical space, our participants based their trust partly on an understanding of the remote collaborator's physical context. Co-located collaborators wanted to know where the remote collaborator was physically located, i.e., were they in their office, a private room, a meeting room, or in a public place like a café. Participants also asked if the remote collaborator was alone. To facilitate participant understanding, we provided cues to make the café feel like a public environment. For example, we explained our MRCE is shared between different universities for collaboration. Still, co-located participants wanted to know more about what was happening physically on the other side. *"He can google the answers."*–p4, *"I don't know if he is alone. That is my only concern."* – p12.

A Classification of Correspondence Cues

From our video coded analyses and interviews we learned that collaborators start the activities with a mental model close to their previous collaboration activities such as display sharing and video conference collaborative environments. They continually updated this mental model with different cues that we provided during the study. We identified cues that help collaborators form a mental model of the environment into four categories, and assess the effectiveness of each in our study.

Communication-based cues: communication between collaborators can impact mental model formation. For example, when the remote collaborator waved to co-located collaborators, most waved back while looking at the avatar. The remote collaborator's comments on their dress or actions reinforced the idea that they were visible, but didn't necessarily suggest spatial correspondence. In the guessing game, collaborators relied on verbal communication to verify that documents were visible.

Interactive cues: In a physical environment people expect specific results for their actions. Responsive cues follow from a collaborator's actions in the physical space. For example, in our prototype, if a co-located collaborator put her document on the table, the system displayed the digital version on the table to indicate it is also visible to those "nearby" in the virtual world. In our study, these cues were sometimes ignored in favour of expected or understood physical-virtual correspondences, as when cards were sometimes tracked when not directly over the table.

Ambient cues: For example, we used spatialized audio to give co-located collaborators a sense of "where" the remote collaborator was relative to the table. Our circumambient displays offered a window into the connected virtual world, but this did not obviously translate into a sense of "fused space" and did not encourage corresponding privacy behaviours such as using body orientation or distance.

Infrastructure cues: visible system infrastructure (e.g., fiducials, cameras) can be a source of inference during mental model formation. For example, the absence of fiducials encouraged some groups to freely place their clue sheets on the tabletop. In our study, unexpected cues, which break people's focus on a collaborative activity, and cues that infuse the feeling of being insecure had a greater influence on collaborators than ambient cues such as spatialized audio and background activities. However, such "ambient" cues were enough for some participants to become aware of their environment or more cautious about their actions. *"We could hear his sound.... so this is good to see he is walking around;"*-p2, *"If I don't exactly understand how the virtual room works if someone else joined this room and they are standing over there can they see what is on the table?"*-p7.

Limitations
We note that our study prototype is not a polished collaboration tool. For example, we did not use a fully immersive closed cave with professional surround sound to provide high quality visuals and sound effects of the café. We believe the lack of a fully immersive space could be a reason some participants did not show interest in all the cues. In particular, we saw very few instances where participants watched the activity of avatars moving about the café; there were also a number of cases where the remote collaborator would move around the virtual table yet the local collaborators did not seem to notice. Several participants also expressed that the games did not encourage them to concentrate on maintaining privacy while playing; other activities should be considered in future work.

Facial expressions and other non-verbal cues are a source of social and emotional information [31], conveying information such as an individual's internal emotional state and a person's identity [32][33]. Viewing others faces encourages trust, which has implications for managing privacy. *"I can't see his face; if I had met the person, and now he is virtual to me I could share the document with him."*-p27 *"I can trust the person because I can see him. In this virtual I can see only these pictures; that doesn't feel the same...you cannot read their emotions, ... or what they are thinking."*-P19. Using an engine that integrates facial feature tracking and body gestures into the avatars might introduce important emotional components into the MRCE.

Finally, we concentrated on co-located participants and did not study the remote collaborator's experience. Further research should explore how mixed co-located and remote groups manage privacy together in such environments.

CONCLUSION
Our study supports the idea that physical privacy behaviors can be effectively applied in MRCEs, however designers must ensure that cues clearly convey the consequences of these actions to the instigator. We provided a range of cues to help collaborators build an understanding of the environment, and observed how cues impacted how collaborators physically managed privacy. Collaborators applied mental models based on experiences with other collaboration tools, but using the cues many participants actively built a mental model of the MRCE. These participants tried to acquire information about the virtual space and its relation to the physical space. Other participants seemed less observant of the cues, focusing on completing the activities and missing indications that their information privacy may be compromised. Providing explicit visibility about how privacy-related actions are translated across physical and virtual will help mental model formation about the collaborative environment, which is necessary to build trust when sharing sensitive information. Collaborators do not fully trust a MRCE when they are unsure of how their privacy-related actions are interpreted, and how they are manifested in the virtual space.

ACKNOWLEDGEMENTS
We thank our study participants, and the reviewers for their valuable feedback. This research was funded by a collaboration grant from Boeing and NSERC.

REFERENCES

1. H.Jetter, H. Reiterer, and F. Geyer, "Blended Interaction: understanding natural human–computer interaction in post-WIMP interactive spaces," *Pers. Ubiquitous Comput.*, vol. 18, no. 5, pp. 1139–58, Oct. 2013.
2. K. Lyons, T. Pering, B. Rosario, S. Sud, and R. Want, "Multi-display Composition: Supporting Display Sharing for Collocated Mobile Devices," vol. 5726, Berlin, Heidelberg: Springer, 2009, pp. 758–771.
3. Y. Liu, O. J. Anshus, P. H. Ha, T. Larsen, and J. M. Bjorndalen, "MultiStream: A Cross-Platform Display Sharing System Using Multiple Video Streams," in *Distributed Computing Systems*, 2008, pp. 90–95.
4. P. Garner, M. Collins, S. M. Webster, and D. A. D. Rose, "The application of telepresence in medicine," *BT Technol. J.*, vol. 15, no. 4, pp. 181–187, Oct. 1997.
5. K. O'hara, J. Kjeldskov, and J. Paay, "Blended interaction spaces for distributed team collaboration," *ACM Trans. Comput. Interact.*, vol. 18, no. 1, pp. 1–28, Apr. 2011.
6. D. F. Reilly, H. Rouzati, A. Wu, J. Y. Hwang, J. Brudvik, and W. K. Edwards, "TwinSpace: an infrastructure for cross-reality team spaces," *UIST '10*, 2010, pp. 119–28.
7. C. Weichel, M. Lau, D. Kim, N. Villar, and H. W. Gellersen, "MixFab: A Mixed-Reality Environment for Personal Fabrication," in *SIGCHI*, 2014, pp. 3855–64.
8. H. Regenbrecht, M. Haller, J. Hauber, and M. Billinghurst, "Carpeno: Interfacing remote collaborative virtual environments with table-top interaction," *Virtual Real.*, vol. 10, no. 2, pp. 95–107, Sep. 2006.
9. J. Hindmarsh, M. Fraser, C. Heath, S. Benford, and C. Greenhalgh, "Fragmented interaction:establishing mutual orientation in virtual environments," in *CSCW*, 1998, pp. 217–226.
10. A. Tang, M. Boyle, and S. Greenberg, "Display and presence disparity in Mixed Presence Groupware," vol. 28, pp. 73–82, Jan. 2004.
11. A. Tang, C. Neustaedter, and S. Greenberg, "VideoArms:Embodiments for Mixed Presence Groupware," *People Comput.*, pp. 85–102, 2006.
12. S. Yarosh, A. Tang, S. Mokashi, and G. D. Abowd, "'Almost Touching': parent-child remote communication using the sharetable system," in *CSCW*, 2013, pp. 181–192.
13. S. E. Hunter, P. Maes, A. Tang, K. M. Inkpen, and S. S. M. Hessey, "WaaZam! Supporting Creative Play at a Distance in Customized Video Environments.," in *SIGCHI*, 2014, no. Figure 1, pp. 1197–06.
14. H. Ishii, M. Kobayashi, and J. Grudin, "Integration of inter-personal space and shared workspace," in *CSCW*, 1992, pp. 33–42.
15. J. Hauber, H. Regenbrecht, M. Billinghurst, and A. Cockburn, "Spatiality in videoconferencing:trade-offs between efficiency and social presence," in *CSCW*, 2006, pp. 413–422.
16. P. Van Schaik, T. Turnbull, A. Van Wersch, and S. Drummond, "Presence Within a Mixed Reality Environment," *CyberPsychology Behav.*, vol. 7, no. 5, pp. 540–552, Oct. 2004.
17. J. Hauber, H. Regenbrecht, A. Cockburn, and M. Billinghurst, "The Impact of Collaborative Style on the Perception of 2D and 3D Videoconferencing Interfaces," *Open Softw. Eng. J.*, vol. 6, no. 1, pp. 1–20, Jun. 2012.
18. M. Ackerman and S. Mainwaring, *Privacy Issues & Human-Computer Interaction*. Cambridge: O'Reilly, 2005.
19. M. J. Culnan, "Protecting Privacy Online: Is Self-Regulation Working?," *J. Public Policy Mark.*, vol. 19, no. 1, pp. 20–26, Mar. 2000.
20. J. McCarthy and P. Wright, "Technology as experience," *interactions*, vol. 11, no. 5, pp. 42–43, Sep. 2004.
21. L. Palen and P. Dourish, "Unpacking 'privacy' for a networked world," in *SIGCHI*, 2003, pp. 129–136.
22. E. Chin, A. P. Felt, V. Sekar, and D. Wagner, "Measuring user confidence in smartphone security and privacy," in *SOUPS*, 2012, pp. 1–16.
23. C.Shen, K. Everitt, and K. Ryall, "UbiTable: Impromptu Face-to-Face Collaboration on Horizontal Interactive Surfaces," in *UbiComp*, 2003, vol. 2864, pp. 281–88.
24. E. M. Huang and E. D. Mynatt, "Semi-public displays for small, co-located groups," *SIGCHI*, 2003, pp. 49–56.
25. A. Kapadia, T. Henderson, J. J. Fielding, and D. Kotz, "Virtual walls: protecting digital privacy in pervasive environments," *Pervasive computing*, 2007, pp. 162–79.
26. B. Tversky, "Cognitive maps, cognitive collages, and spatial mental models," in *Spatial Information Theory A Theoretical Basis for GIS*, vol. 716, A. U. Frank and I. Campari, Eds. Heidelberg: Springer, 1993, pp. 14–24.
27. D. Reilly, M. Salimian, B. MacKay, N. Mathiasen, W. K. Edwards, and J. Franz, "SecSpace: Prototyping Usable Privacy and Security for Mixed Reality Collaborative Environments," *EICS*, 2014, pp. 273–82.
28. A. Dix, A. Friday, B. Koleva, T. Rodden, H. Muller, C. Randell, and A. Steed, "Managing Multiple Spaces," in *Spaces, Spatiality and Technology*, vol. 5, Dordrecht: Springer Netherlands, 2005, pp. 151–172.
29. J. S. Downs, M. Holbrook, and L. F. Cranor, "Behavioral response to phishing risk," in *eCrime*, 2007, pp. 37–44.
30. D. S. Tan, P. Keyani, and M. Czerwinski, "Spy-resistant keyboard: more secure password entry on public touch screen displays," in *OZCHI*, 2005, pp. 1–10.
31. R. Adolphs, "Cognitive neuroscience of human social behaviour.," *Nat. Rev. Neurosci.*, vol. 4, no. 3, pp. 165–78, Mar. 2003.
32. M. Ellamil, J. M. Susskind, and A. K. Anderson, "Examinations of identity invariance in facial expression adaptation.," *Cogn. Affect. Behav. Neurosci.*, vol. 8, no. 3, pp. 273–81, Sep. 2008.
33. V. Chan, "The Perception and Recognition of Emotions and Facial Expression," *Univ. Toronto J. Undergrad. Life Sci.*, vol. 3, no. 1, Mar. 2009.

ControllAR: Appropriation of Visual Feedback on Control Surfaces

Florent Berthaut
Univ. Lille, Inria, UMR 9189 - CRIStAL
florent.berthaut@univ-lille1.fr

Alex Jones
University of West England
alexander9.jones@live.uwe.ac.uk

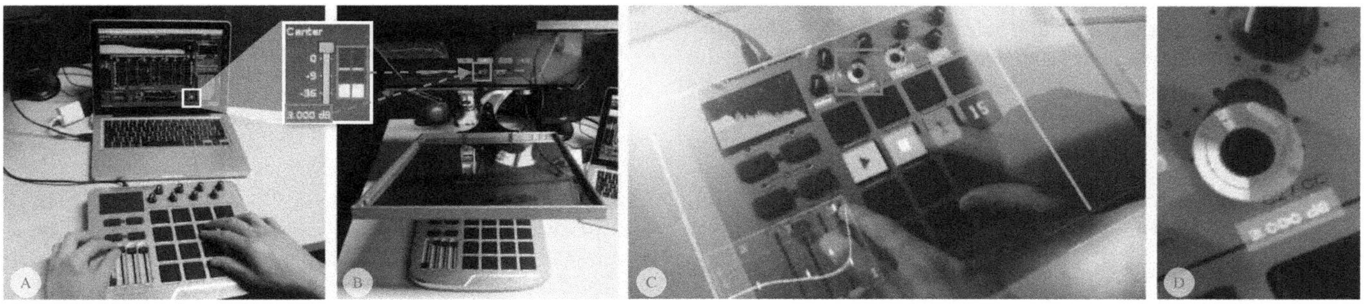

Figure 1. ControllAR enables the appropriation of visual feedback on control surfaces. Elements from the GUIs of controlled applications (A) can be cut, transformed and rearranged (B) by users. They can then be placed on/around sensors on the controller using an optical combiner (C). Close-ups show the value of the volume parameter of a track and the resulting VU meter being placed around the knob that controls it (D), illustrating both process and parameter feedback.

ABSTRACT
Despite the development of touchscreens, many expert systems for working with digital multimedia content, such as in music composition and performance, video editing or visual performance, still rely on control surfaces. This can be due to the accuracy and appropriateness of their sensors, the haptic feedback that they offer, and most importantly the way they can be adapted to the specific subset of gestures and tasks that users need to perform. On the other hand, visual feedback on controllers remains limited and/or fixed, preventing similar personalizing. In this paper, we propose ControllAR, a novel system that facilitates the appropriation of rich visual feedback on control surfaces through remixing of graphical user interfaces and augmented reality display. We then use our system to study current and potential appropriation of visual feedback in the case of digital musical instruments and derive guidelines for designers and developers.

Author Keywords
ControllAR; Augmented Reality; Visual Feedback; Appropriation; Hardware controllers; Control surfaces;

ACM Classification Keywords
H.5.2. Information Interfaces and Presentation (e.g. HCI): User Interfaces

ISS '16, November 06 - 09, 2016, Niagara Falls, ON, Canada

ACM 978-1-4503-4248-3/16/11$15.00
DOI: http://dx.doi.org/10.1145/2992154.2992170

INTRODUCTION
Following on from analog devices for the control of video and audio signals, many software applications for the creation and processing of digital media rely on control surfaces / hardware controllers composed of sensors such as groups of buttons, rotary and linear encoders. They are often preferred to touchscreens because of the variety of gestures that the sensors allow and because of the haptic feedback that they provide and to tabletops with tangibles because of their compactness. Combined with software applications with graphical user interfaces (GUI), these controllers are now used in many contexts : live electronic music performances, music recording/mixing/composition, visual performances, video editing, lights control, and so on.

Control surfaces and appropriation
Over time, users of these systems develop expert skills specific to the hardware and software components. Most importantly, they also customize the systems to match the specific subset of gestures and tasks that they need to perform. As pointed out by Findlater and McGrenere [4], "*the focus of personalized interfaces is generally to improve core task performance, that is, performance of completing known or routine tasks*". This appropriation happens at multiple levels. First the sensors themselves can be modified, either by spatially assembling/arranging existing control surfaces, as depicted in Figure 2.C, or by designing and building them from scratch using dedicated kits or generic components, as described by Greenberg et al. [6]. Gestures applied to these sensors may then vary from user to user. In the case of digital musical instruments (DMI), appropriation may lead to very different playing techniques on the same instrument as

demonstrated by Gurevitch et al. [7]. In many cases, the controller and software are interconnected using standard communication protocols such as MIDI and OpenSoundControl. While presets are sometimes available for widespread controllers, users may also freely decide on the mappings between sensors and parameters. The choice of these mappings is essential for the efficiency and expressiveness of the system, as explained in the context of DMIs by Hunt et al. [10]. Mappings may change during the interaction with the system. For instance, multiple sets (or pages) of mappings can be created in a preparatory phase and selected in real time, therefore allowing the user to access a different set of functions with the same sensors. Furthermore, changing mappings may be part of the actual interaction either when the set of functions available in the application changes, e.g. when tracks are added in a video mixing software, or in the case of "hackable" instruments [13]. These levels of appropriation relate to the control, i.e. the flow of data from the user to the system.

In any interactive system, the feedback, that is the flow of data from the system, is essential to an expert user. In particular, visual feedback plays an important role in the interaction with the system as for example demonstrated by Liu et al. [11]. However, compared to other components described above, the appropriation of visual feedback remains limited. GUIs usually include detailed representations of application content and parameters such as waveform and spectrum displays, tracks and video clips preview, dynamic labels and widgets. They however constrain visual feedback : a) their arrangement can not be modified to fit the controller or users' actions; b) they may present more details than actually needed during actions, leading to cognitive overload; c) they are distant from the physical sensors and from the performed gestures. Therefore visual feedback on control surfaces is a growing request from users, as suggested by the apparition of embedded LEDs on most commercial controllers and of screens on the most expensive ones. However appropriation of this feedback is constrained either in the choice of the displayed feedback, the resolution of this feedback or its placement on the controller. For example, in the case of MIDI controllers, some include a limited number of programmable color LEDs (Keith McMillen Quneo, Berhinger BCR 2000) around/behind sensors, others a higher-resolution screen with fixed (Ableton Push, M-audio Trigger Finger) or even programmable content (Akai MPC Touch), but distant from the sensors.

In this paper, we propose a solution that enables the appropriation of rich and co-located visual feedback on control surfaces through GUI remixing and augmented reality displays.

GUI remixing

Research on GUIs has demonstrated the usefulness of appropriation of graphical interfaces in many contexts. By transforming visual elements, data can be visualized in new ways as demonstrated by Brosz et al. [2], Mendez et al. [14] and Tan et al. [16]. Novel GUIs can be designed by composing elements from existing interfaces as demonstrated by Sturzlinger et al. [15] and Fujima et al. [5]. Extraction of GUI widgets can be informed or decided by the user or even

Figure 2. Example hardware controllers and associated applications: A) Digital Audio Workstation, B) Visual performance. C) Appropriation of controllers arrangement and D) of the mappings between sensors and parameters. Visual feedback available on controllers is limited in content or position to fixed screens (E) and LEDs (F).

done automatically through pixel based analysis [3]. In contrast, our project focuses not on the graphical interaction with remixed interfaces but on using these interfaces as dynamic visual feedback.

Visual augmentations for expert interfaces

Adding visual feedback on expert interfaces has been shown to have various benefits. Liu et al. demonstrated an improvement in performance on a value selection task with hardware controllers when adding feedback through an augmented reality display [11]. Augmentation of hardware controllers also opens novel interaction techniques as demonstrated for computer keyboards by Block et al. [1].

In the specific context of DMIs, visual augmentations have been designed for various instruments such as turntables [9], removing the need for musicians to look at their laptop screen. With ControllAR we investigate how custom visual augmentations can be designed by expert users themselves.

Contribution

Our contribution is two-fold. First, we propose ControllAR, a novel approach that facilitates the appropriation of rich visual feedback on control surfaces by remixing graphical user interfaces. We describe its implementation and provide insights on key elements of the software pipeline. Second, we use ControllAR to investigate users practices during a study on digital musical instruments. Based on the results, we provide insights and guidelines to inform the design of applications and hardware that would help appropriation of visual feedback.

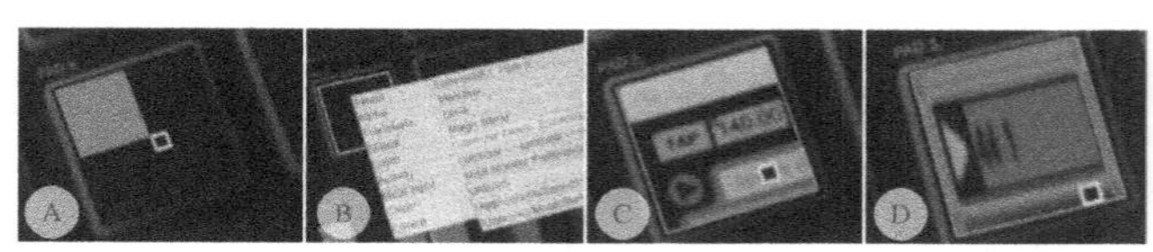

Figure 3. Appropriation process with ControllAR : A) Users draw a *zone* (overlapping a sensor or not) on the controller, and B) select one of the opened desktop windows. C) A *cut* of the selected window is then mapped inside the zone and D) can be dragged and zoomed to match any part or widget of the GUI

CONTROLLAR

Contrary to existing controllers for which the choice of content and spatial organization of visual feedback is limited, ControllAR allows users to select and place freely graphical elements on any controller. It relies on the fact that the GUIs of multimedia software applications, designed for mouse and keyboard interaction, provide rich and high resolution feedback on the manipulated content. With ControllAR, *cuts* can be made in these GUIs and placed in *zones* directly on the controller with either a projector or an optical combiner. This design process is detailed in Figure 3. However, our approach requires a series of steps to ensure that the GUI content can be transformed and displayed as visual feedback on the controllers.

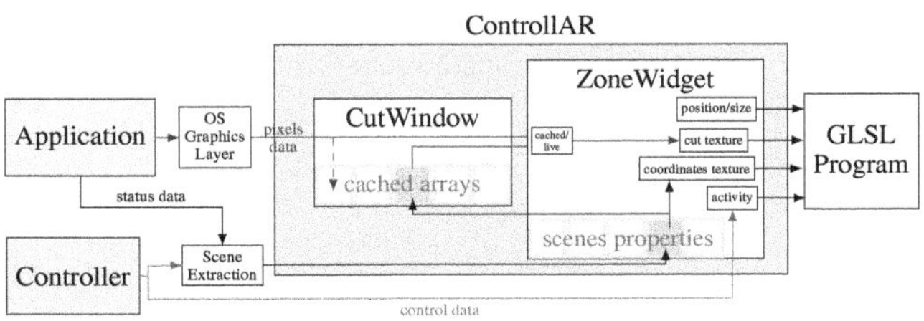

Figure 4. Visual feedback appropriation pipeline: Applications GUIs are captured in CutWindows, transformed in ZoneWidgets and rendered through a GLSL program. Control messages from the controller and data from the application are also captured to handle changing scenes and adapt to user activity.

Appropriation pipeline

In the next sections, we describe the visual appropriation pipeline, depicted in Figure 4, and the key steps that we contribute.

Capturing application GUIs

ControllAR runs on the Mac OS X, GNU/Linux and Microsoft Windows operating systems (OS). Lists of opened application windows and arrays of pixels for each of them can be accessed through the respective system graphics layers and software libraries: CoreGraphics, Xlib, GDI. These three OS feature compositing window managers. In order to allow for visual effects on the windows (such as transparency, blur, live preview ...), the window managers render all windows to offscreen buffers. It is therefore possible to access the pixels of windows even when they are not visible and combine *cuts* from multiple GUIs. This proves to be useful for software applications that rely on multiple windows (e.g. plugins, video preview) which are not always all visible at once. As shown in Figure 4, in ControllAR a dedicated CutWindow manages the pixels array of each currently accessed OS window.

Adaptation to changes in GUIs

Within each application window the arrangement and selection of visual content may change during the interaction. For example, in music production / performance software such as Renoise, a section of the GUI is often dedicated to effects and parameters of the selected audio track. Whenever the selected track changes, all the graphical elements are replaced by the ones associated with the new track. Therefore, the *cut* displayed by a *zone* might be hidden after the change. A key element of our appropriation pipeline is the detection and management of these changes in GUIs. To that extent, ControllAR allows for the creation of multiple *scenes* for each *zone*. Each *scene* can be associated to a state of the GUI and to a set of properties of the *zone*, such as the cut position and size. *Zones* can then be updated only when a specific *scene* is selected, i.e. when the correct content is visible on the GUI. When the *scene* is about to change, the current pixels array for the CutWindow is then cached as shown in Figure 4. Changes in the GUI can be detected either from the controller or from the application. When a sensor on the controller signals a change, the control data sent can be assigned in ControllAR to the selection of *scenes*. When the changes originate from the application, it is not always possible to detect them. However, some applications provide an API which can be used by plugins (for example Max For Live patches in the case of Ableton Live) to retrieve status data, as shown in Figure 4. OpenSoundControl messages can then be sent to ControllAR in order to select the corresponding *scene*. Detection could also be done through pixel-based analysis [3], although with a more variable accuracy and more setup required from users.

Adaptation to changes in mappings

Scenes can also be used to follow changes in mappings rather than changes in the GUIs. Many controllers and applications allow for multiple banks of mappings, i.e. with the same sensors associated to different parameters of the application depending on the bank. By defining *scenes* for each bank of mappings, users may display on the *zones* the correct parts of the GUI for the current bank, for example the labels of parameters for a group of knobs. Changes of banks that are internal to the controller, i.e. sensors simply send different messages/values depending on the bank, require an additional extraction step. For example, we use a Pure-Data patch to detect the apparition of specific messages from the control surface that indicate a change in bank. This patch then sends an OpenSoundControl message to ControllAR in order to set the corresponding *scene* for one or all of the *zones*.

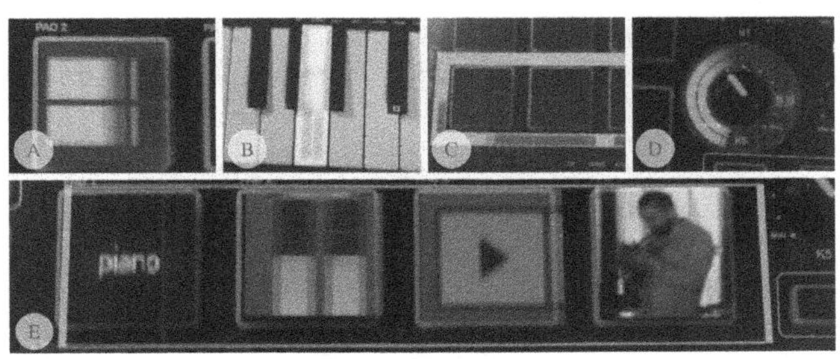

Figure 5. (A-B-C-D) Adaptation of a VU meter *cut* to four different sensors: Single pad, piano key with inverted color, groups of pads, knob. E) Different types of *cut* content on four pads: static output, dynamic output, input/output and external

Adaptation to sensors shape and color

GUIs provide a great variety of graphical elements, which can all be used as visual feedback on the control surfaces. As depicted in Figure 5.E, *cuts* can be : static (e.g. text labels) or dynamic (e.g. VU meter); input only (e.g. buttons), output only, or input and output (e.g. video clips in visual performance software); internal to the application or external (e.g. from a live camera filming a stage). On the contrary to most research on GUI remixing, in ControllAR this content needs to be transformed to match the sensors on which users want to add visual feedback. We draw inspiration from the Transmogrification project [2] and propose a set of transformations that correspond to the shapes of sensors commonly found on hardware controllers. As depicted in Figure 5, a filled square cut of a VU meter that fits a rubber pad (5.A), can be stretched and rotated to fit a piano key (5.B) . It may also be transformed to a frame that surrounds a group of sensors (5.C) or to a circle that wraps around a knob (5.D). Users choose from the sets of shapes and orientations either with a contextual menu or shortcut. They may also resize and move *zones* by dragging them so that they match the sensors once transformed, for example to make a circle shaped zone large enough to surround a knob. In order to render transformed *cuts*, a coordinates texture is first generated for the properties defined for the zone, e.g. transformation and shape, possibly specific to each scene, as depicted in Figure 4. It contains the coordinate inside the window pixels array computed for each pixel of the resulting *zone*. This coordinates image is passed as a texture to the GLSL program together with the texture containing the pixels array of the CutWindow, thus ensuring minimal computation at each frame. Colors of the *cuts* also often need to be modified in order to improve their perception when displayed over sensors with different materials and colors. To that extent, their opacity can be modified and their color inverted, for example to go from light content displayed over a black key, to dark content over a white key. These parameters are passed as uniforms to the GLSL program.

Adaptation to activity

Finally, our pipeline allows for *zones* to be updated dynamically to adapt to the activity of users. ControllAR can be connected to the controller and *zones* associated to messages from corresponding sensors. *Zones* that identify the mappings on sensors can then be hidden when these sensors are used so as to guide gestures but limit visual overload during interaction. Symmetrically, *zones* can be displayed only when the corresponding sensors are used, for example to obtain feedback regarding the exact values of controlled parameters. To that extent, *zones* can be associated with a specific message from the controller, through a learn function, to trigger the corresponding activity.

Augmenting controllers

Appropriation of visual feedback is also limited by the displays of existing control surfaces. We experimented with two hardware solutions that aim at minimizing the constraints on placement of the feedback while ensuring correct perceptual alignment of sensors and augmentations. In addition, we discuss these hardware issues in more details in the guidelines section. The first solution to place a projector above the controller and project zones directly onto its surface. The second solution is the use of an optical combiner. Drawing inspiration from [8], a half-silvered mirror is placed between a screen displaying the cuts and the controller, as shown in Figure 6. Moreover we designed it with adjustable orientations and positions for the mirror and screen so that the angles between them and between the mirror and control surface are equal. When looking through the mirror, the screen and controller surface align perfectly. As explained by Martinez et al. [12], because the optical combiner has a flat surface, this alignment remains consistent at all positions of the observer. This solution preserves the visual quality (i.e. resolution and shape) of the *cuts* and prevents occlusions. When interacting with the controller, users see both their hands and augmentations, therefore ensuring that the visual feedback remains visible at all time. To ensure compactness, in the case of performance applications, the user's laptop can itself be used as the screen above the mirror, removing the need for an additional screen.

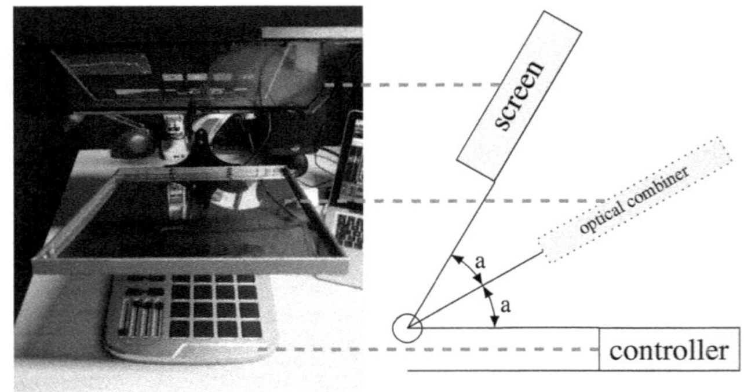

Figure 6. Front view (left) and side schematic view (right) of our hardware solution. We augment the control surfaces with the remixed GUI elements using an optical combiner and a screen. The angles (a) between screen surface and combiner and between combiner and controller surface need to be equal for the augmentation to remain consistent at all viewing positions.

ANALYSIS AND GUIDELINES

In this section, we use ControllAR to investigate the current and potential practices of appropriation of visual feedback. We first conduct a study on users of digital musical instruments, provide an analysis of visual feedback created by the participants, and derive guidelines to facilitate appropriation.

Study on digital musical instruments

This study focuses on current practices of musicians and how these could be expanded using ControllAR. While participants demonstrated and experimented with their instruments and usual performance settings, this study does not provide insights on longer term impact of facilitated appropriation of visual feedback on the way participants design or play their instruments. We conducted the study on ten musicians, aged from 21 to 45 (mean=31.8, sd=9.3). They had been playing music for between 4 and 31 years (mean=16.1, sd=8.6), a digital musical instrument for between 2 and 20 years (mean=9.7, sd=6.5) and the instrument used in the study for between 1 and 14 years (mean=5.2, sd=4.1, only two of them for one year). Seven participants used their instrument for performance only, one for composition only, and two for both composition and performance. Six participants used only one controller, three participants used an arrangement of two controllers and one of three controllers. The participants' control

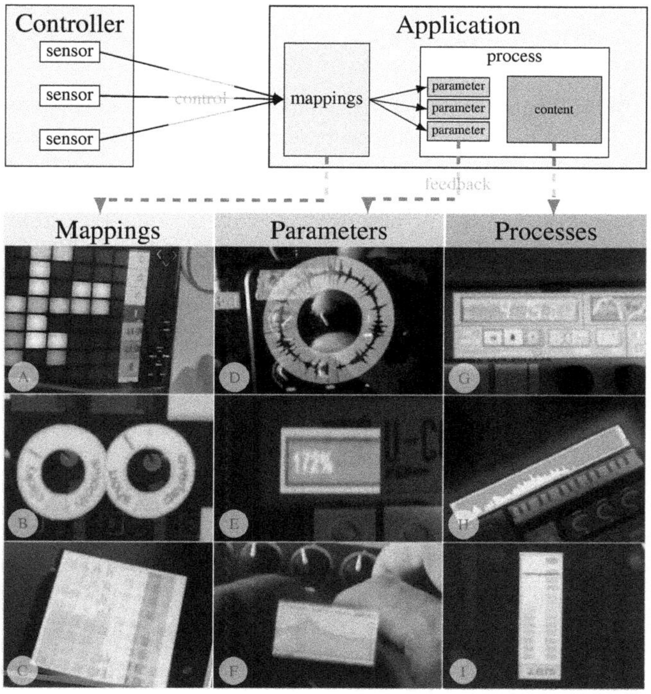

Figure 7. Examples of visual feedback created by the participants during the study grouped by category.

surfaces were composed of between 0 and 24 rotary encoders / knobs (mean=12.4, sd=7), between 0 and 17 linear potentiometers / faders (mean=4.7, sd=6.5), between 8 and 110 buttons (mean=50.6, sd=37.2) and between 0 and 64 pressure and velocity sensitive rubber pads (mean=16.8, sd=26). Other sensors included keys, one ribbon (position) sensor, one leap motion controller and one joystick. Regarding applications, six participants were using Ableton Live (including one with Max For Live plugins), two were using Max/MSP and two were using FL Studio.

The study was composed of four phases and lasted between one and two hours. In the first phase, we used a questionnaire to gather information on the participants' level of musical expertise and their use of DMIs. Then we asked the participants to demonstrate their instrument and explain their use of visual feedback with a guided interview. This phase was filmed for further analysis. We demonstrated the use of ControllAR with a simple instrument created in Pure Data and composed of eight drum loops, a four bands EQ, a delay effect and a soundfile player. Finally, we installed ControllAR on the participants' laptop, placed their controller below the mirror and filmed/interviewed them while they explored its use with their DMI. The study was run only with the optical combiner solution for augmenting the controllers. This choice was made to ensure that visual feedback would be displayed correctly regardless of the material and shape of the sensors on the participants' controllers.

Results and analysis

Participants had positive reactions to the system and saw many possibilities of appropriation of the visual feedback that could help them while playing. P4 stated that "*visual feedback is really important*" for performance/composition , and comparing with touchscreens: "*I find this more interesting than many other options*". Relating to the fact that normal practice is to get used to not having any visual feedback on parameter changes with a controller, so that introducing them aided manipulation, P3 says "*It's quite nice to be able to see what you're doing*". Participants also expressed their interest in using ControllAR to prepare their future performances. P2 says "*you would need to start projects with it, for me at least, because I don't have a fixed instrument*". P1 also commented that an interesting aim for him was to play without needing the screen and that ControllAR was a possible way to do it. P2 pointed out the possibilities of exchanging information with other musicians through ControllAR : "*the guitarist i am playing with, on his midi foot controller, he could have feedback on the various effects*". Participants also highlighted a few limitations of the current hardware solution such as: the size of the area that can be augmented, which may be too small for some large or composite controllers; the size and shape of the mirror which constrains hands and head position of the user; the fact that augmentations would not visible for an audience.

Current practices were extracted from the guided interviews and questionnaires from the first two phases, completed with the analysis of the filmed interviews and demonstrations. The potential practices were extracted from the filmed experimentation with the system in the fourth phase, by extracting and classifying both the *zones* they designed and their comments on the system. During the exploration, each participant created between one and twelve *zones* (mean=5.4, sd=3.7). The results suggest that the visual feedback both currently used by participants and explored during the study with ControllAR originates from three specific sections of the software application: the mappings layer, application parameters and application processes/content. Figure 7 illustrates these three sections with examples taken from the study and indicates their origin in the application. Our results suggest that for each of these categories, feedback can be improved by the use of ControllAR. Although this study was conducted for DMIs, we believe these categories may also apply to other applications.

Mappings feedback reveals the *mappings* section of the application, that is the set of connections between sensors and application parameters. Here feedback is mostly composed of static content such as text, icons or colors. It is used for identifying *static mappings*, either permanently or only temporarily to learn the use of a controller or to remember the mappings when switching between controllers/applications. In their usual practices, two participants used tape with written labels under the sensors to remember the mappings, with several layers when they had to change mappings. One participants had color coded stickers to identify parameters and tracks. Another participant had manuals in PDF format to remember the functions for each button of their control surface.

Feedback of the *mappings* category can also help identify *dynamic or changing mappings*. On the controller used by P9, buttons' LEDs change color to identify which track they control when scrolling through a large number of them.

With ControllAR static labels could easily be stored / removed / retrieved by participants, and placed directly over the sensors. Figure 7.B shows labels used by a participant to permanently identify the mappings around two knobs (P1) and Figure 7.C a user manual in PDF format displayed directly above a group of buttons indicating the function assigned to each (P10). For the *dynamic mappings* on P9's control surface, the LEDs did not exactly match the colors of tracks on screen and provided less information than text labels. As depicted in Figure 7.A, P9 used ControllAR to add labels with correct colors on the right side of the rows of buttons, that will be updated when scrolling through the tracks.

Parameters feedback helps during the interaction by providing visual feedback on the applications *parameters*. They can be subdivided into three types of feedback. *Contextual feedback* provides information on the context of the parameter. This information is usually only available on the application GUI, so participants had to look at their laptop screen. *Value feedback* provides the exact value to which application parameters are set, with the corresponding unit, which allows for reaching specific values. On participants' control surfaces, this feedback is given either for one sensor at a time and at one position, or individually but only for the sensors below the screen (P9). *Interaction feedback* reveals the interaction between application parameters. In their current practice, participants only had access to this feedback on the application GUI on the computer screen.

With ControllAR, *parameters feedback* can be directly integrated with the sensors, allowing users to focus on the control surface instead of having to look at their laptop screen. Examples of *contextual feedback* designed during the study include displaying the changes in linearity or continuity between sensor and parameter values by overlapping the graphical sliders of the application GUI with the physical faders, or as depicted in Figure 7.D showing the control of a range within a waveform (P1). With ControllAR participants placed *value feedback* for each parameter directly over the corresponding sensor, as depicted in Figure 7.E (P4). Finally participants used ControllAR to display *interaction feedback* over the group of corresponding sensors, for example controlling two points on an interpolated curve with two knobs as shown in Figure 7.F.

Processes feedback helps users perceive the global or local state of the application and its processes, in order to guide interaction. It complements other feedback, such as auditory perception in the case of our study. This feedback is usually only displayed on the application GUI, forcing participants to look at their screen, although one control surface allowed for displaying vu-meters when other feedback was hidden. *Local feedback* provides information on the status of more or less autonomous processes within the application, e.g. the progression in a video sequence or waveform or the status of an audio or visual clip. *Global feedback* helps perceive the general state of the application, in order to guide or inform interaction with its components. In their current practices some participants would for example look at their screen for upcoming cues on a timeline or the global pulse.

With ControllAR, *local feedback* was overlapped or placed close to the sensors that were used to control various parameters of a process. For instance, P1 chose to display the VU meter for a track as shown in Figure 7.I. For *global feedback*, participants tried or proposed displaying temporal information such as the bar and beat count used in Figure 7.G (P4), but also information specific to the application such as the global spectrum shown in Figure 7.H, or levels of audio inputs from musicians around the faders controlling their volume during live mixing.

Guidelines for facilitating appropriation

Results from our study highlight the need of appropriation of visual feedback. Although we focused on digital musical instruments, we believe that this conclusion also applies to other fields. However, while our approach enables this appropriation, it remains constrained by design choices of multimedia production applications and could be improved by following three main guidelines.

Facilitate GUI remixing: Appropriation of feedback from GUIs can be simplified if applications enable detaching parts of the interface as separate windows (as done in FL Studio) so that they are continuously rendered for compositing. Otherwise scene mechanisms such as those implemented in ControllAR must be used but cannot guarantee that all GUI elements can be captured at all times. **Expose sections of the application:** To further improve appropriation, by enabling more customized visualizations than remixed GUIs, software applications should provide easy access, via a protocol or API to all information about the three sections used for appropriation : list of mappings, parameters values and contexts, activity of processes and application. **Ensure correct augmentations:** The hardware setup used for augmenting control surfaces must ensure that gestures can be done correctly, for example with enough room for the hands and no visual occlusions, and that augmentations can cover sufficiently large areas, both for large or composite control surfaces, and when the controllers need to be moved during use, for example in music recording/mastering studio contexts.

CONCLUSION

We presented ControllAR, a novel system for the appropriation of visual feedback on control surfaces for multimedia software applications. We also provided an analysis of the current and potential appropriation possibilities leading to guidelines for design. A first perspective for this work is the study of the long-term impact of ControllAR on how musicians design and play their instrument. Another perspective is the extension to handheld / gestural controllers. In fact, many users now combine traditional sensors with gestural sensing (i.e. distance, 3D position, poses, gestures) which provide even less visual feedback on their impact on application parameters. Tracking these controllers or body parts and projecting correctly transformed *cuts* on them could lead to better integration in multimedia production systems.

REFERENCES

1. Block, F., Gellersen, H., and Villar, N. Touch-display keyboards: transforming keyboards into interactive surfaces. In *Proceedings of the SIGCHI Conference on Human Factors in Computing Systems*, ACM (2010), 1145–1154.

2. Brosz, J., Nacenta, M. A., Pusch, R., Carpendale, S., and Hurter, C. Transmogrification: Causal manipulation of visualizations. In *Proceedings of the 26th Annual ACM Symposium on User Interface Software and Technology*, UIST '13, ACM (New York, NY, USA, 2013), 97–106.

3. Dixon, M., and Fogarty, J. Prefab: implementing advanced behaviors using pixel-based reverse engineering of interface structure. In *Proceedings of the SIGCHI Conference on Human Factors in Computing Systems*, ACM (2010), 1525–1534.

4. Findlater, L., and McGrenere, J. Beyond performance: Feature awareness in personalized interfaces. *Int. J. Hum.-Comput. Stud. 68*, 3 (Mar. 2010), 121–137.

5. Fujima, J., Lunzer, A., Hornbæk, K., and Tanaka, Y. Clip, connect, clone: combining application elements to build custom interfaces for information access. In *Proceedings of the 17th annual ACM symposium on User interface software and technology*, ACM (2004), 175–184.

6. Greenberg, S., and Boyle, M. Customizable physical interfaces for interacting with conventional applications. In *Proceedings of the 15th annual ACM symposium on User interface software and technology*, ACM (2002), 31–40.

7. Gurevich, M., Stapleton, P., and Marquez-Borbon, A. Style and constraint in electronic musical instruments. In *International Conference on New Interfaces for Musical Expression* (2010), 106–111.

8. Hachet, M., Bossavit, B., Cohé, A., and de la Rivière, J.-B. Toucheo: Multitouch and stereo combined in a seamless workspace. In *Proceedings of the 24th Annual ACM Symposium on User Interface Software and Technology*, UIST '11, ACM (New York, NY, USA, 2011), 587–592.

9. Heller, F., and Borchers, J. Diskplay: In-track navigation on turntables. In *Proceedings of the SIGCHI Conference on Human Factors in Computing Systems*, CHI '12, ACM (New York, NY, USA, 2012), 1829–1832.

10. Hunt, A., and Kirk, R. Mapping strategies for musical performance. *Trends in Gestural Control of Music* (2000), 231–258.

11. Liu, C., Huot, S., Diehl, J., Mackay, W., and Beaudouin-Lafon, M. Evaluating the benefits of real-time feedback in mobile augmented reality with hand-held devices. In *Proceedings of the SIGCHI Conference on Human Factors in Computing Systems*, CHI '12, ACM (New York, NY, USA, 2012), 2973–2976.

12. Martinez Plasencia, D., Berthaut, F., Karnik, A., and Subramanian, S. Through the combining glass. In *Proceedings of the 27th Annual ACM Symposium on User Interface Software and Technology*, UIST '14, ACM (New York, NY, USA, 2014), 341–350.

13. McPherson, A. P., and Zappi, V. Exposing the scaffolding of digital instruments with hardware-software feedback loops. In *International Conference on New Interfaces for Musical Expression* (Baton Rouge, United States, 2015).

14. Méndez, G. G., Nacenta, M. A., and Vandenheste, S. ivolver: Interactive visual language for visualization extraction and reconstruction. In *Proceedings of the 2016 CHI Conference on Human Factors in Computing Systems*, CHI '16, ACM (New York, NY, USA, 2016), 4073–4085.

15. Stuerzlinger, W., Chapuis, O., Phillips, D., and Roussel, N. User interface façades: towards fully adaptable user interfaces. In *Proceedings of the 19th annual ACM symposium on User interface software and technology*, ACM (2006), 309–318.

16. Tan, D. S., Meyers, B., and Czerwinski, M. Wincuts: Manipulating arbitrary window regions for more effective use of screen space. In *CHI '04 Extended Abstracts on Human Factors in Computing Systems*, CHI EA '04, ACM (New York, NY, USA, 2004), 1525–1528.

A Dynamic 3D Performance Space for Control of Virtual Musical Instruments

Andrew Hollenbach
Dept. of Computer Science
Rochester Institute of Technology
Rochester, NY, 14623 USA
hollenbach.andrew@gmail.com

Matthew Cox
Eastman School of Music
Rochester, NY 14604, USA
mcoxvla@gmail.com

Joe Geigel
Dept. of Computer Science
Rochester Institute of Technology
Rochester, NY, 14623 USA
jmg@cs.rit.edu

ABSTRACT
This work explores developing an intuitive, real-time music generation system and interface. We present a system that uses the real-time skeletal tracking provided by the Kinect to generate complex musical compositions containing up to four tracks, with instruments represented in distinct physical spaces. The performer's position and movements are translated into cues that are relayed to Ableton Live for music generation. Finally, we experiment with an interface projected in physical space to provide real-time feedback to the user.

Author Keywords
Music generation; interactive projection; virtual music instrument; Kinect; Ableton Live

ACM Classification Keywords
H.5.1 [Artificial, augmented, and virtual realities]; H.5.2 [User Interfaces]; H.5.5 [Sound and Music Computing]

INTRODUCTION
Motion capture systems have tremendous application potential in the form of virtual musical instruments (VMIs). Three dimensional sensing allows for the creation of instruments with unconventional design and ability. At the core of a VMI is the mapping of movement to sound in order to generate music [12]. This mapping can range from tracking small finger movements to tracking dancing across a stage. The inherent flexibility that comes with motion capture systems allows for a variety of VMIs, and musical interaction can mean fine-grained note control, as well as more interpretive approaches where direct mapping of movement to music is less apparent. VMIs can also provide an outlet for individuals who may have difficulty with fine motor skills. Many common instruments (violins, guitars, pianos, etc.) rely on precise finger control to generate notes, but such instruments can be adapted to instead harness gross motor skills in the form of a VMI. Furthermore, VMIs can be used as a non-traditional music education tool, engaging students through full body movement.

ISS 2016, November 6–9, 2016, Niagara Falls, ON, Canada.

ACM ISBN 978-1-4503-4248-3/16/11 ...$15.00.
http://dx.doi.org/10.1145/2992154.2992178

One deficiency commonly found in VMIs is a lack of a proper feedback system. With many different controls and no tactile response, it is important to present the user with an effective way to understand the state of the system. Arm fatigue is also a common issue with VMIs, as there is often no surface to rest on [5].

The movements and gestures that control a VMI are then used as inputs, usually to some form of a software music sequencer that can be used to generate and record notes. More advanced sequencers provide a variety of ways to further modulate notes, adjust instrument playback parameters, control loops, and more. These sequencers can be custom or commercially available. The benefit of the latter is the accessibility and robustness that comes with widely-used products. However, commercially available sequencers may not be readily integrated, and thus a drawback is that this approach is not as transparent as a VMI using an integrated sequencer.

The contribution of this paper is three-fold. First, it presents a fine-grained VMI control system using the Kinect complete with pitch, volume, and filtering control. Second, it presents stage partitioning and looping control, allowing a single performer to control up to four instruments in physically discrete spaces. Third, it presents a visual interface in physical space to provide feedback to the performer on the 3D stage.

RELATED WORK

Kinect Based VMIs
There are many approaches to creating VMIs leveraging many different technologies, including webcam approaches [13], complex motion capture systems such as the Vicon system [4], as well as small-scale RGB-D sensors such as the Leap Motion [10]. One interesting technology to emerge has been the Microsoft Kinect, an RGB-D system which has been established as a low-cost markerless sensing system for many purposes, including music generation.

Sentrk, Sertan, et al. use hand pose and hand actions (open, close, etc.) to interact with a primarily 2D grid or crossword interface playing notes and chords on a fixed loop. However, this provides coarse control overall, and the interface does not inherently reflect the full 3D interaction that can be provided by the Kinect. They do present a dynamic timbral manipulation mode, which fully leverages 3D pose to distort the underlying note/chord loop [15].

Gillian and Paradiso [5] present a Kinect-based VMI that focuses on finger and hand reading. A tradeoff is that in order to gain the precision for finger and hand sensing, they are unable to fully realize the large sensing area of the Kinect for full-body tracking.

Hsu, Mu-Hsen, et al. present three VMIs using the Kinect—drums, guitar, and a novel instrument coined Spider King. The drums use hit points to activate MIDI signals, while the guitar provides a 3D chord selection interface. The Spider King instrument provides individual note control, although only within a single octave [7].

Lu, Ming-Fong, et al. extend this concept by proposing an interface using the Kinect to generate MIDI notes by creating a 3D sphere around the user. Notes are triggered by body parts/joints from the Kinect skeleton enter regions of the sphere. This provides a very dynamic form of note generation. Additionally, they are able to improve the sensing accuracy by placing two Kinect sensors at 90 degrees to each other [9].

The Synapse for Kinect project provides a general approach to mapping joints retrieved from the Kinect skeleton to control applications that can receive OSC messages such as Ableton Live, Quartz Composer, and more. This has extreme flexibility in that any joint's movement can be easily mapped to instruments, and thus offloads instrument setup to the third party software [1].

Berg, Tamara, et al. describe a system similar to the Synapse system, in which the skeletal joint information was sent over OSC and the information unpacked as x, y, and z coordinates without orientation; this information is then placed into the range of 0 to 127, the standard MIDI range. The x, y, and z values were assigned to carrier frequency, modulator frequency, and amplitude, respectively in a manner that is scalable [2].

Many other demonstrations of the Kinect in use as a musical instrument can be found across the web, although we generally found that these systems were focused more on abstract or coarse music generation, rather than fine-grained note control.

Spatial Interfaces for VMIs

The use of spatial positioning in VMIs has also been well explored. Systems such as Sync'n'Move [16], the Music Room [11], and the Orchestra Explorer [3] define interactive and collaborative social listening spaces that can allow for music manipulation based on the position of users in a physical 3D space.

Systems that provide control for the position of audio sources in a spatialized sound environment have been introduced that make use of 2D table top interface [8, 14] or a 3D physical space [6].

In our system, we combine a gestural interface as afforded by the motion capture capabilities of the Kinect sensor with the use of spatial positioning to enable looping, instrument selection, and incremental musical composition. Although there is a rich collection of work in the literature in each of these areas, we feel our system is novel in the way it combines advances in these two arenas into an integrated music creation and composition system.

SYSTEM OVERVIEW

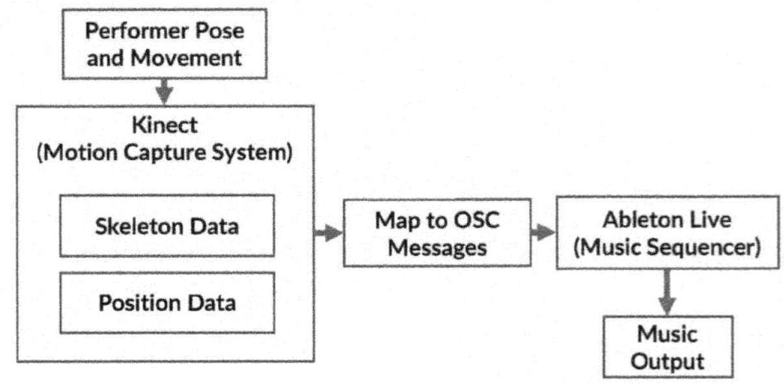

Figure 1. A high level architecture diagram of the full system.

A high level overview of our system can be seen in Figure 1. The release of the Microsoft Kinect provided an extremely affordable and accessible platform for markerless human pose tracking. The Kinect v2 uses an RGB-D camera system to generate data streams containing a host of information about the scene. Our primary use is the skeletal tracking, which provides a skeleton containing 25 joints tracked across a stage area of considerable size. The ample sensing area of the Kinect can be partitioned based on the user's location on the stage, and these partitions can be used to intuitively control up to four different instruments. This 3D interaction between the Kinect and a performer's movements is converted into Open Sound Control (OSC) packets and passed to Ableton Live, a robust music generation software. OSC packets are then registered as a musical note, looping effect, or modulation signal and a resulting sound is produced. We have worked with a musician to create an intuitive, yet fine-grained music generation system based on movement in 3D space. To reinforce the performer's interaction with the system, we augment a monitor-based interface with a projection-based interface to allow for a more physical feedback. The entire system is designed with live performance in mind, such that the performer is able to engage an audience visually while producing acoustically pleasing music.

There are three core subsystems: the tracking and mapping of gestures from the Kinect, the conversion from OSC packet to music in Ableton Live and Max, and the interface used to provide feedback to the performer.

Mapping the Kinect to OSC

Skeletal tracking data is gathered from the Kinect and accessed via the Kinect SDK. We use the skeletal data for many aspects of the music generation process, including arm location and movement for pitch, intensity, and modulation, as well as for instrument selection, the core of the body for determining staging—which instrument the performer is playing, and leg data for controlling looping.

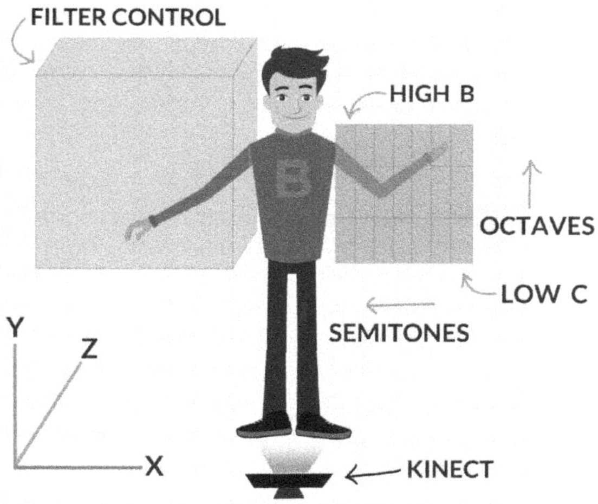

Figure 2. The coordinate system and gestures. As seen from the perspective of the Kinect, the x-axis extends to the left and right, the y-axis is the vertical axis, and the z-axis is the depth measure. The note grid shown represents the notes from the C Major scale. If the performer's left hand were closed, the grid would change to 5 by 3, with the five horizontal bins now representing the five remaining semitones not found in the C Major scale.

Note Generation

Note generation uses a combination of the left and right hands for pitch and actuation. The location of the left hand determines the pitch, and it is assumed that the performer is facing the Kinect directly. The coordinate system used and gestures are demonstrated in Figure 2. The system provides three octaves by altering the the left hand along the y-axis, and horizontally sub-divided bins for selecting specific semitones along the x-axis. An open left hand allows for the selection of notes from the C Major scale—the white keys of a piano, while a closed hand allows for selection of the five remaining notes—the black keys of a piano. By altering the notes depending on the state of the left hand, we are able to provide sufficient space for each note bin, reducing the chance of inaccurate notes being played. This interface was generated to closely mirror that of a piano, and provides fine-grained control of all 36 semitones of three octaves.

All of the information is captured, processed, and transformed into the appropriate note in the form of an OSC packet. For note generation, we use an OSC bundle, which allows us to pass multiple arguments to an address. An OSC bundle addressed to the appropriate instrument endpoint is sent, containing pitch, velocity, duration, and midiChannel for the note. All values aside from pitch draw from defaults, but could be easily mapped to sensed movements. We experimented with adjusting velocity and duration based on right hand actuation, but found that the costs outweighed the benefits (accidental variations in velocity, inconsistent durations, and never-ending notes).

Note Modulation

In addition to using the right hand to actuate notes, the position of the right hand can be taken into account for note modulation. OSC messages are passed containing the relative x, y, and z coordinates of the hand to the shoulder, which can be used for dynamic filters, adjusting volume or duration, and more.

Looping

The system supports sending looping messages with the intention of interfacing with the Ableton Live Looper, but as with all aspects of the system, the messages can theoretically be placed in any sequencer that supports looping.

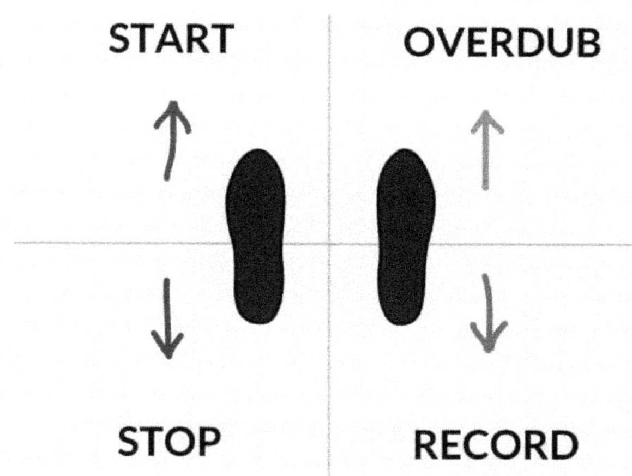

Figure 3. The loop controls from the point of view of the performer looking down at their feet. Note that in Ableton, playing a loop automatically stops recording, so no stop recording gesture is needed (the start and stop actions represent starting and stopping playback).

As seen in Figure 3, four different looping actions can be activated, and the one selected is based on where the feet are moved. We considered using a threshold distance from the resting foot position, but this failed when the performer was walking around. Instead, the performer makes a quick lasso shape with the right hand and keeps their left hand open and then makes the desired foot movement. We found that this was relatively unobtrusive and prevented false positives.

The Virtual Stage

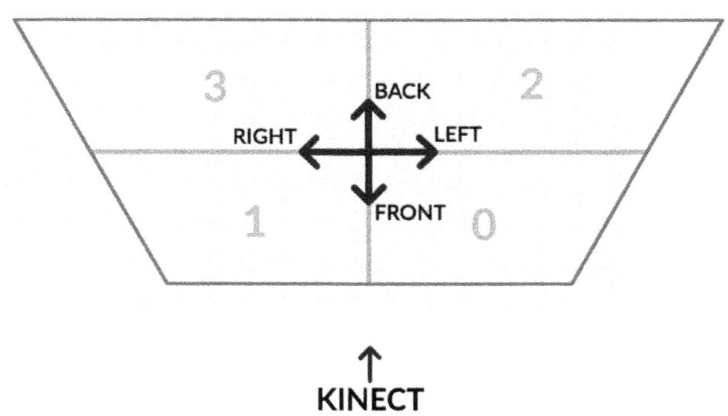

Figure 4. The layout of the virtual stage. The stage can have no divisions (the entire stage is one instrument), two divisions (front and back, or left and right), or four divisions (pictured).

At the core of the system is a staging mechanism which allows for the division of the Kinect's sensing region into up to four parts as demonstrated in Figure 4. The performer's physical position on the stage is determined by the position of the SPINE_MID, a joint defined by the Kinect SDK roughly approximating the center of the body, assuming a standing position. As notes are actuated, the quadrant is determined by the performer's position and an OSC packet is sent to the instrument associated with that quadrant.

Experimentally, we found the effective stage area of the Kinect to be trapezoidal, roughly 2 meters deep, 2.5 meters in width at the closest point, and 4 meters at the furthest, assuming the performer is an adult of average height. Outside of this range, sensing was not consistent enough for quality results.

Music Generation Using Ableton Live and Max

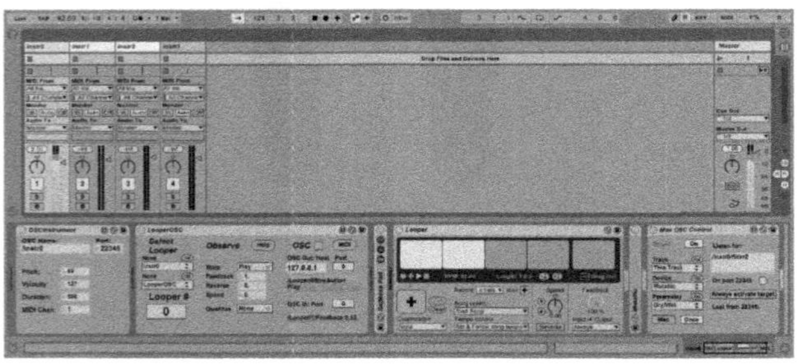

Figure 5. The Ableton Live interface. Several Max for Live patches used for receiving OSC messages can be seen on the bottom of the screen.

Ableton Live is an extremely powerful music sequencer. This power can be further supplemented by Max for Live, a toolkit that allows customization and interaction with Ableton using the visual Max language. We use a combination of Max patches to interact with Ableton Live using OSC. Each track in Ableton is set up to receive a different namespace of OSC packets. For example, track one may be a piano track, and therefore will be set up to receive any OSC packets that come in with the /piano namespace. OSC packets are sent via the network, and thus Ableton Live can be either on a remote machine or the same machine connected to the Kinect.

Note Generation

OSC packets are received in a custom patch pictured in the bottom left of Figure 5. This patch generates MIDI signals for the current track.

Note Modulation

Note modulation is received via standard OSC messages in the *Max OSC Control* [1] patch pictured in the bottom right of Figure 5. Ableton allows this input to then be mapped to nearly any button or value seen in the interface.

Looping

As of Ableton Live 9 (used in development), normal mapping methods do not work for the Ableton Live Looper. Thus, we route messages through a Max for Live patch called LooperOSC, which then forwards the commands to the Live Looper. LooperOSC can be seen in the bottom center of Figure 5, and Ableton Live Looper is pictured just to the right.

Interface

The system provides two forms of visual feedback to the performer, an interface that is best viewed on a computer monitor, as well as a projection that is intended to augment the monitor interface.

Monitor

The monitor interface shown in Figure 6 is the primary interaction between the performer and the system. It provides a visualization of the Kinect-provided skeleton and useful information about the state of the system. We also experimented with displaying the note grid over the skeleton in real time to help the user better understand which note they were playing. Additionally, we found it useful if the Ableton Live window was also viewable for the performer to provide additional state of the system information.

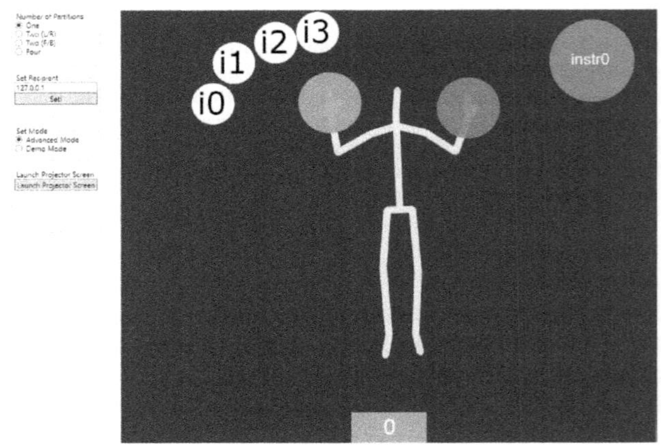

Figure 6. The monitor interface. The green circle indicates an open hand is sensed, while the red circle indicates a closed hand is sensed. The current quadrant is displayed in the gray box (bottom center), and the current instrument is displayed in the darker blue circle (top right). The stage can be partitioned on the fly (top left), and a target recipient can be set if another device is receiving the OSC messages, or can be set to the local machine. Users can toggle between the advanced mode (described in this paper), or a demo mode, which reduces the amount of controls and is intended for musical exploration.

Projection

The projection is intended to augment the primary interface. A standard projector can be used and is pointed towards the ground as seen in Figure 7. The projector will likely be distorted. We provide a simple interface to move the four bounding corners and centroid of the staging area. Unfortunately, this is a manual process and needs to be approximated. The interface is meant to provide feedback in the physical space to counteract the lack of tactile response from a VMI. Our initial work focuses on the basics—providing information on the quadrant the performer is currently in, as well as the active instrument in that quadrant. We use a single projector angled towards the ground, attached to the main computer as a secondary monitor.

RESULTS

Our main subject from which we derive the majority of the feedback is a musician trained in many instruments, but specializing in viola and ukulele. Non-musicians also experimented with the system to provide an alternative perspective.

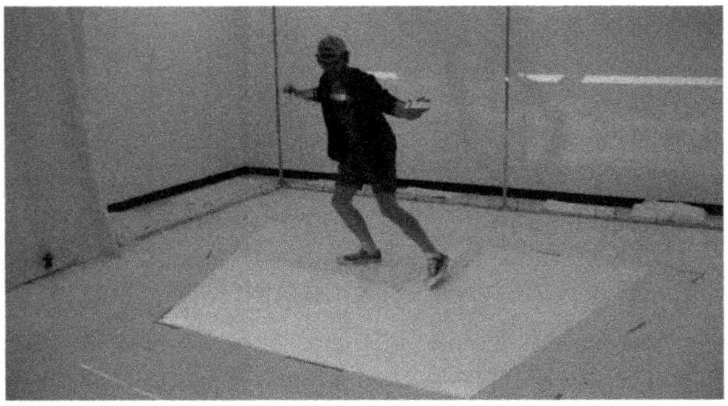

Figure 7. Interactive stage projection. The green represents the active stage area, while the red represents the active partition. The current instrument is displayed. The green tape on the floor is no longer needed with the projection interface.

Musician Biography

Co-author and musician Matthew Cox has a uniquely specialized skill set that made him the optimal candidate for developing and testing this work. He has a Viola Performance degree from the Eastman School of Music, and a minor in American Sign Language (ASL) from the University of Rochester. Disparate as the two fields may be, both are incredibly expressive, and it would be difficult to say which skill requires more dexterity in the hands. Eventually, Matthew developed an overuse injury that made it incredibly difficult to play the viola for extended periods of time, so he shifted his focus towards computers and started exploring their potential as expressive tools. He needed to find another way to make music.

Matthew is an advanced musician who has been studying the principles of music theory and instrumental performance since he was very young, which was a significant advantage when determining how to construct the instrument. Not only was he able to anticipate whether or not specific gestures could be learned by other musically inclined users, he learned how to control the instrument very efficiently. Additionally, his background in American Sign Language proved to be a significant asset when cataloguing gesture combinations.

Instrument Control

Within 30 minutes of his first interaction with our VMI, the musician was able to play *Twinkle Twinkle Little Star* with relatively little error and even felt comfortable enough to add small flourishes to the melody. Comparatively, we found that the non-musicians generally were not as accurate as the musician and took longer to become acquainted with the controls. We were not particularly surprised, as it follows naturally that a skilled musician would be more efficient and effective when learning new instruments.

One of the musician's primary concerns regarding the instrument control is that it can be mentally and physically exhausting to play for long durations of time (greater than roughly 30 minutes). We believe there are a few contributing factors to this effect, and as previously mentioned, this is not unique to our system.

First off, the system has a diverse set of controls, which can be hard to track. For a power user who has experience with the system, it becomes easier over time, but for a person just starting out, the system can be very confusing and frustrating. Interestingly, the general consensus from non-musicians trying the system has been that even though the system was not inherently doing what they wanted, they were still really enjoying it.

The lack of physical feedback and support can also cause strain. Users have to maintain their left arm in a lifted position for playing accurate notes. Some approaches discussed previously attempt to address this, but at the sacrifice of what we see as some of the key differentiators of a VMI and our system in particular.

Earlier we mentioned experimentation with displaying a note grid to assist the performer in playing the correct note. However, this was found to be more difficult to use than simply building up muscle memory through playing the instrument. We believe that this is due to the unavoidable small amount of lag from the Kinect sensor processing step.

Stage Partitioning and Loop Control

In observing the musician and through feedback he provided us, we found that stage partitioning was extremely effective. Physically partitioning out the space allows for the performer to quickly switch between instruments. We found that physical partitioning also enhanced the viewer experience, as it made it easier to understand the effects the performer's movements were having on the music generated.

One drawback is that without the projection interface, the active partition in which the performer was standing was not always apparent, both to the performer and viewers, especially around the edges of partitions. The projection was effective at communicating the active partition, and the issue was generally not observed following the introduction of the projection interface.

The musician was also able to effectively utilize the looping aspect of the system, generating both multi-part covers of existing songs, as well as producing his own orchestral compositions by stacking loops of audio. The musician initially struggled with the procedure necessary to manipulate loops, which requires both hands and a foot movement. Furthermore, we found that the system did not provide sufficient feedback when loop actions were sensed and activated, especially given the hand and foot configuration necessary to activate loop actions. We believe that integrating loop feedback in the projection interface might provide a better experience.

Interface

Our aim to reduce mental strain, as well as potentially improve overall system tactility by adding a projection element was successful. By providing additional information to the performer directly below them, the performer can focus more on what their hands are doing and are not straining to see what the small monitor is trying to convey.

Initially, the instrument was developed without a projection interface. With its addition, the musician reported that the interface did provide some useful context, but the positive effect of the projection interface was more noticeable with non-musicians. We believe this is likely correlated to the musician's mastery of the instrument relative to the non-musicians, and as such, he did not require as much of a visual cue in regards to active partition and current instrument.

When looking at Figure 7, you can see tape laid down to mark the sensed area by the Kinect. This was initially done to help the performer understand their workable area, but by introducing the projection component, this is no longer necessary.

A supplementary video has been provided to demonstrate the capabilities of the system.

FUTURE WORK

Ease of setup of the system could be improved through auto-calibration of the projection. There is also the possibility of experimenting with more complex visual feedback on the projection surface, such as visualization of potential actions such as loop status, notes to be played, and more, which were not as effective when placed on the monitor interface.

Future Applications

This instrument has a broad array of applications, particularly in the fields of live performance and music education. It is designed to allow the user to compose and perform live music, either as a soloist or as a supplement to a larger ensemble. As motion-capture technology develops, newer devices can be combined with (or replace) the Kinect to increase the instrument's sensitivity and functionality. The system can also function as a tool for teaching children about music. It presents an opportunity for kids to play, all while correlating movement with sound and developing fine motor skills. While the Kinect has some technical limitations (latency, precision, etc.), the instrument interface itself gives the performer a massive toolkit for spatial expression, and can create a virtually limitless range of sounds.

CONCLUSION

We present a dynamic system for music generation and performance using a low-cost and relatively easy to setup system. The performer is capable of in-depth control of up to four instruments and can generate full compositions in support of a larger musical performance or as an individual performer. The interface provides both an informative screen interface, as well as an interactive projection element, providing the performer with sufficient feedback in order to easily understand and control the state of the system.

ACKNOWLEDGMENTS

This work was developed as a component part of the 01X Project (`http://www.project01x.com/`). The authors would like to thank Susan Lakin, Katie Verrant, and the Sound Exchange Project for their support of the work. Emily Abele, Ameya Lonkar, and Vishwanath Raman contributed to an earlier version of the interface and we are thankful for their contributions. Finally, the authors would also like to thank Marla Schweppe and the 3D Digital Design Department at RIT for allowing us the use of their motion capture suite for this project.

REFERENCES

1. Synapse for kinect. `http://synapsekinect.tumblr.com/`. Accessed: 2016-06-27.
2. Berg, T., Chattopadhyay, D., Schedel, M., and Vallier, T. Interactive music: Human motion initiated music generation using skeletal tracking by kinect. In *Proc. Conf. Soc. Electro-Acoustic Music United States* (2012).
3. Camurri, A., Canepa, C., and Volpe, G. Active listening to a virtual orchestra through an expressive gestural interface: The orchestra explorer. In *Proceedings of the 7th International Conference on New Interfaces for Musical Expression*, NIME '07, ACM (New York, NY, USA, 2007), 56–61.
4. Dobrian, C., and Bevilacqua, F. Gestural control of music: using the vicon 8 motion capture system. In *Proceedings of the 2003 conference on New interfaces for musical expression*, National University of Singapore (2003), 161–163.
5. Gillian, N., and Paradiso, J. A. Digito: A fine-grain gesturally controlled virtual musical instrument. In *Nime* (2012).
6. Honigman, C., Walton, A., and Kapur, A. The third room: A 3d virtual music paradigm. In *Proceedings of the International Conference on New Interfaces for Musical Expression* (2013), 29–34.
7. Hsu, M.-H., Kumara, W., Shih, T. K., and Cheng, Z. Spider king: Virtual musical instruments based on microsoft kinect. In *Awareness Science and Technology and Ubi-Media Computing (iCAST-UMEDIA), 2013 International Joint Conference on*, IEEE (2013), 707–713.
8. Lam, J., Kapralos, B., Kanev, K., Collins, K., Hogue, A., and Jenkin, M. Sound localization on a horizontal surface: virtual and real sound source localization. *Virtual Reality 19*, 3 (2015), 213–222.
9. Lu, M.-F., Chiang, J.-S., Shih, T. K., and Wu, S. 3d sphere virtual instrument with kinect and midi. In *Ubi-Media Computing (UMEDIA), 2015 8th International Conference on*, IEEE (2015), 140–145.
10. Moore, A. G., Howell, M. J., Stiles, A. W., Herrera, N. S., and McMahan, R. P. Wedge: A musical interface for building and playing composition-appropriate immersive environments. In *3D User Interfaces (3DUI), 2015 IEEE Symposium on*, IEEE (2015), 205–206.
11. Morreale, F., De Angeli, A., Masu, R., Rota, P., and Conci, N. Collaborative creativity: The music room. *Personal and Ubiquitous Computing 18*, 5 (2014), 1187–1199.
12. Mulder, A. Virtual musical instruments: Accessing the sound synthesis universe as a performer. In *Proceedings of the First Brazilian Symposium on Computer Music* (1994), 243–250.

13. Olivieri, D., Conde, I. G., and Vila-Sobrino, X. A. Ar-based virtual musical instruments using smc tracking. In *6th Iberian Conference on Information Systems and Technologies (CISTI 2011)* (2011).

14. Sasamoto, Y., Cohen, M., and Villegas, J. Controlling spatial sound with table-top interface. In *Awareness Science and Technology and Ubi-Media Computing (iCAST-UMEDIA), 2013 International Joint Conference on*, IEEE (2013), 713–718.

15. Sentürk, S., Lee, S. W., Sastry, A., Daruwalla, A., and Weinberg, G. Crossole: A gestural interface for composition, improvisation and performance using kinect. In *NIME* (2012).

16. Varni, G., Mancini, M., Volpe, G., and Camurri, A. *Sync'n'Move: Social Interaction Based on Music and Gesture*. Springer Berlin Heidelberg, Berlin, Heidelberg, 2010, 31–38.

Shared Interactive Music Experiences in Public Spaces: User Engagement and Motivations

Maximilian Müller[*] **Nuno Otero**[*+] **Marcelo Milrad**[*]

[*]Department of Media Technology, Linnaeus University, Sweden

[+]Instituto Universitário de Lisboa, CIS-IUL, Portugal

maximilian.muller@lnu.se; nuno.otero@lnu.se; marcelo.milrad@lnu.se

ABSTRACT

The recent development and distribution of interactive pervasive computing systems, especially those incorporating digital public displays, facilitate a variety of new interactive scenarios in shared public spaces where people gather and spend time to enjoy a social experience. Integrating novel interaction mechanisms related to the sharing and listening of music with digital displays is a good example of the potential of using current technologies to enhance physical and social spaces. This paper explores the design and impact of shared situated interactive systems, combining public display installations with a collaborative music player. To explore the design space of these systems, we conducted two studies involving the deployment of a particular system at different venues. The analysis of our results allowed us to identify specific (group) interactions and events, which were fostered by the system under consideration. Based on these outcomes, we propose a set of features that should foster further engagement with such systems and promote new ways of social interaction.

Author Keywords

Public displays; collaborative music player; multi-user interaction; exploratory study; field study; user engagement; social interaction.

ACM Classification Keywords

H.5.1 [**Multimedia Information Systems**]: Audio input/output, evaluation/methodology; H.5.2 [**User Interfaces**]: User-centered design;

INTRODUCTION AND MOTIVATION

Music has and will always play an important role in most people's everyday life influencing moods, actions and events [7], as well as social practices [13]. Recent developments in the music industry have made music more easily accessible and thus changing the ways how people consume it [14]. Nevertheless, one crucial aspect of music consumption practices has remained the same: music consumed in shared spaces is frequently curated by a single person. And as Likkanen et al. [15] point out, research around music consumption is almost extinct and needs a revival.

New pervasive technologies and ways of acquiring music (streaming, unlimited access) suggest the potential for different new scenarios to be explored. Interactive digital displays can provide a simple and effective way for supporting shared experiences in public spaces by fostering information exchanges between multiple users that will enrich music consumption practices and usage patterns. However, these emerging scenarios and applications around novel interactive music consumption also demand more research regarding the role and impact such systems play in altering people's music consumption patterns in (semi-) public settings.

In this work we explore the impact that public interactive digital displays have on physical and social settings they are situated in by utilizing a collaborative music player. Prior studies in this particular topic have demonstrated the importance of the social context and social interactions around public displays [11, 22, 23, 25], engaging people not only to interact with the system per se but also with each other. The music player incorporating a collaborative playlist is a democratic music curating system, which lets people choose, add and vote on songs they would like to hear and share with co-habitants of the (semi-) public spaces. Such systems have a fair potential for being deployed at public venues by providing a democratic way of selecting music (compared to regular DJs). This way, the interactive system can turn passive listeners into active music selecting actors in public spaces. However, to promote democratic voting and representation of the users preferences, it is especially crucial for the majority of the audience to be engaged to interact with the systems.

Engaging users to interact and keeping them motivated to do so is still one of the biggest challenges in the design of public display systems [1, 2, 9, 18]. And it has been pointed out that users' incentives and motivations for interacting with public displays are often far from being understood [19].

ISS '16, November 06 - 09, 2016, Niagara Falls, ON, Canada

ACM 978-1-4503-4248-3/16/11...$15.00
DOI: http://dx.doi.org/10.1145/2992154.2992183

Our approach for tackling this challenge is by investigating users' incentives and motivations for using the shared and public interactive music systems. In order to deepen our understanding of the dynamics of these interaction processes and further explore this distinct design space, we conducted two in-the-wild studies that involved deployments at two events (~270 attendees). These studies allowed us to explore people's usage of the system and investigate the distinct engaging factors of the application under consideration. A system's design should exploit and facilitate these situated behaviors with the goal of providing richer and more fulfilling experiences [1, 19]. The results enable us to propose system features that should foster (multi-) user interactions, towards engaging public interactive systems incorporating display installations.

Our exploratory studies were guided by the following set of research questions:

- How and why do people interact with the public music system?
- How does the system affect the public space and social context it is situated in?

In the remaining of the paper, we give an overview of related work and present the display system used in our study. We then describe settings and methodology of the conducted studies, before we introduce and discuss the results.

RELATED WORK

Applications of digital situated displays around music experiences in public spaces are still not widespread. Still, some projects were designed for and deployed in scenarios similar to the work at hand.

The *Jukola* music system [24] by O'Hara et al. is a mp3 jukebox including a public display and fixed PDA handheld devices allowing users to select music and vote on it. The authors deployed the system at a pub and the results showed that the processes of voting and choosing music enhanced the social value in form of discussions about the music and identity aspects in the community. Kukka et al. [10] presented the *UbiRockMachine*, a prototype application designed for local bands and artists to share and exchange about their music on public displays in urban spaces. The music system *MEET* by Sørensen and Kjeldskov [29], a multi device music player and curating system, focuses on the use of multiple mobile devices and multiple simultaneous users of the system. MEET also incorporates a situated display showing the music playlist of the system.

The jukebox of Chen et al. [5] is a collaborative music sharing system that allows users to share music they actually have on their mobile devices to a public sound system. This work focuses on the opportunistic sharing of music and is limited to what content the users have stored on their mobile phones. Music selection using the *PartyVote* system by Sprague et al. [30] explores a democratic jukebox that selects music from a shared music library according to the users' votes. This system focuses on the usage among small, established social groups. Lenz at al. [12] investigated shared music experiences in smaller social groups using *Mo*, a handheld music player with speaker that can be connected to other players for joint music listening. They report the joint listening is driven by the themes of sharing and influencing music as well as relating memories to the music.

While there are works describing the distinct social value of music in different settings and situations [6, 7, 13] and research demonstrating the capabilities of public display installations to enrich physical spaces fostering the social communities [17, 28], research and systems investigating novel interactive scenarios combining both fields are still rare.

In other scenarios than music consumption, research carried out by Memarovic et al. [17] has categorized how users behave around interactive displays (passive engagement, active engagement and discovery) and also how they influence and benefit the social communities. Akpan et al. [2] showed the importance of situation and environment around displays, comparing interactions with an application in different situations. Regarding the user engagement with a public display, the results demonstrated that a beneficial place (social context) could encourage interactions in poor physical space. The importance of understanding the context and interaction processes around display systems is further described by Terrenghi et al. [32]. The authors present a taxonomy for multi-display-person ecosystems that allows to design different user-display constellations.

Even though different approaches of designs and deployments in the field of public interactive systems and pervasive displays exist and have been studied, generating engagement is still a key challenge [1, 9, 18, 20]. Agamanolis [1] describes in his work that a major part of the design of an interactive public display system needs to focus on the way the system invites users to interact. On the one hand, in order to overcome the first hurdle of interaction, users need to be invited explicitly and implicitly. And on the other, the interactive features must provide an obvious value to the user. Simply offering interactive features is not sufficient to the users. Huang et al. [9], Müller et al. [20] as well as Müller et al. [23] described the positive effect of exposing other people's interactions and social awareness on the user engagement, thus utilizing the social context around the display.

The examples for shared music systems mentioned in this section did not specifically investigate or report the distinct engaging factors of the applications and the crucial role of a shared screen in the applications' public settings. Further did they not sufficiently investigate the user engagement and incentives of interacting with the music systems in real settings. The present paper explores and investigates such factors to gather requirements for the system design and exploit these insights for a more engaging experience with interactive display applications in public spaces.

APPLICATION SYSTEM DESCRIPTION

For the deployments of the studies presented in this paper, we utilized an existing music curating system called *festify*[1], since the main goal of our study was of exploratory nature. This application allowed us to initiate our work in the field of shared interactive music systems. Making use of this application allowed us to focus on the investigation of the interactions with such system and around it in public settings. Festify is an application which allows several users to democratically decide and dynamically influence the music that is being played at a location. Compared to the systems mentioned in [5, 24], festify accesses music from Spotify's[2] library containing over 30 million songs, and is thus not limited to priorly added or the users' local libraries. Still, one needs to bear in mind that the system is not developed specifically for public spaces, or based on research from the field of pervasive displays or interactive installations. This circumstance will be further discussed later in this paper.

The application has three main components: a music player with a view showing the music playlist and short instructions, a mobile web app that facilitates interactions with the playlist, and an admin view. The views of the player screen and the mobile endpoint can be seen in Figure 1. The music player streams the music directly from Spotify. It also provides the option to add a fallback playlist, which is played if no user adds songs. Users can (anonymously) add songs to a shared playlist and vote on songs already in the playlist using their mobile phones. Using the audience's mobile phones for interactions has also proven to be a suitable interaction technique for many-to-many social contexts in public settings [32], in which several users interact with information on a large screen that is visible for several others. The songs in the playlists are played in the order they were added. But if a song receives votes, it will jump up in the playlist order, passing all songs with fewer votes. Each user device can vote once on each song. Users can follow the progression of the playlist and the amounts of votes on the shared view and mobile devices. We showed the shared view of the playlist on a public display to communicate the visual output of the music system and make the audience aware of the system's functionality. All interactions immediately result in changes in the playlist on the display, making it a key component in the system (i.e. songs, durations, amounts of votes, and movements of voted songs up and down in the list). Furthermore, the admin view allows to delete (inappropriate) songs and maintain the fallback playlist.

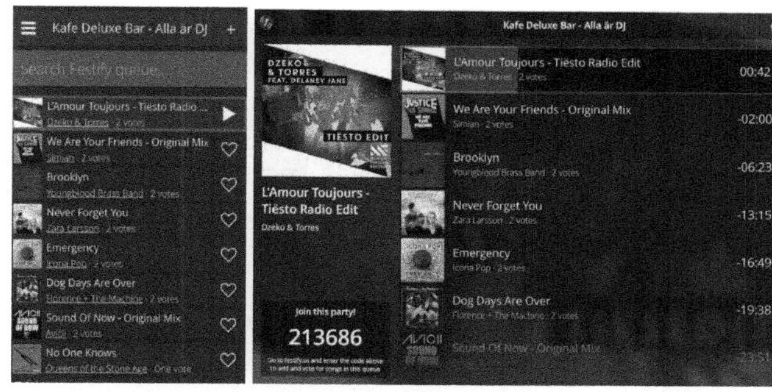

Figure 1. Mobile (left) and shared screen view of festify

EXPLORATORY DEPLOYMENT STUDIES

In order to evaluate and explore the usage and impact of a public music system with a collaborative playlist and explore the engagement and incentives of people to interact with such system, we conducted two in-the-wild user studies. In-the-wild studies are an established method for the evaluation of the interaction processes of public display systems, deploying a system in the settings for which they are envisioned [3, 27]. During the in-the-wild user studies we conducted observations and in-situ interviews. The following sections will describe the settings and the methodology of the studies.

Study Settings and Display Environments

The public displays used during the studies were situated in two very different settings, not only regarding the physical space but also the type of the events. These different characteristics define the role of the music at the venue, as well as the interactions to be expected.

The first venue for one of our studies is Kafé Deluxe in Växjö, Sweden, a venue with several bars and dance floors, spread across two floors. The venue is categorized as indie/alternative with a strong music profile. During the evening of the study, the club was hosting the theme night "Gay Deluxe". The music system deployed by us was responsible for the music at the top floor pub/restaurant. The study was conducted during one night between 23:30 to 3:00 in October 2015. There were ~200 people at Kafé Deluxe during this time. Around the public display, we estimated 80 people in the vicinity that were affected by it. We had orders from the venue owner that the display should not interfere with the retro environment. We used a window of a door as the (rear) projection surface for the public display (size around 80x80cm; see Figure 2). The public display was placed opposite the bar, where the club has several tables around for people to sit. It is common for this area in front of the display to be transformed into a dance floor at later hours, when the staff removes some tables. This also happened during our study.

[1] www.getfestify.com

[2] www.spotify.com

Figure 2. Public display at Kafé Deluxe

Figure 3. Public display at Garage48 during the WUD event

The second venue was the afterparty event of the World Usability Day (WUD) in Tallinn, Estonia. This event took place at Garage48 HUB in Tallinn, which is mainly a co-working space for tech start-ups. But used for social events, it provides two open spaces. Due to the nature of the event, the international audience present (e.g. Russia, Iran, India, Nigeria, Finland, Columbia, Estonia, Germany) was mostly people working in and/or studying the design and development of software applications. During the informal networking event, there were ~70 people present at the venue. The event and the study took place from 18:00 to 21:30 during an evening in November 2015. The public display during this study was a projection on a prominent wall at the venue with a size of approximately 160x120cm. The venue and the public display can be seen in Figure 3.

Compared to the event at Kafé Deluxe, the music had a different role at Garage48. At Kafé Deluxe, it was a leisure party where the music is used and needed to provoke a specific atmosphere to entertain the partying audience [7]. But the music at Garage48 had a more ambient character, providing some musical background (soundscape) for people networking at the afterparty event, but also enjoying some leisure time after the conference. These two different characteristics allowed us to gather insights about different settings to get more valuable information regarding the potential role of a collaborative music installation as well as its design.

To spread information about the system and bring it into focal awareness of the people at the venues [4], 8 DIN A4-sized posters were placed at different locations at the venues with short instructions regarding the functionalities and purpose of the system (see red box Figure 3); including a QR-code leading to the mobile web app for more quickly accessing and interacting with the system. Besides that we did not advertise the system. We chose this method since it did not require any changes to the software and the actual pre-engagement was not subject of further investigation. Furthermore, we can easily imagine that such practice could be close to a realistic situation, where people would encounter such system for the first time.

Study Methodology

We combined several different qualitative and quantitative methods to collect the data. Our methodology of field deployments combined with in-situ observations, interviews and technical logging provides us access to crucial temporal information important to evaluate the impact of the system under consideration. The ludic contexts where the studies took place pose some challenges concerning how one could observe and approach people and engage in interviewing. Naturally, we did not want to become too intrusive and the overall flow of the interview was very much conditional to the perceived availability of the interviewees to be interrupted on their on-going highly social dealings.

In-situ Observations

In both studies, two researchers were present at the venues to do in-situ observations. The observations were conducted in the vicinity of the public display to be able to get a clear picture of what the users and bystanders were doing with and around the system. Our locations were adapted to the happenings and attendee constellations at the venues. Furthermore, the observations were driven by our research questions. Building up on Robson's framework [26] for observations, we derived categories from our research questions that were applied to elicit our interest and foci. These categories were: people near the public display, looking at or avoiding the public display; people using mobile phones, reading/scanning the info posters; a new song is played; the display content changes. The observations were done during the whole scope of the deployments, which resulted in 3.5h of observations at Kafé Deluxe and 3.5h at Garage48. In total, we collected 49 observation instances at Kafé Deluxe and 28 observation instances at Garage48. A observational grid was created and used for the in-situ observations [31]. This grid included guiding questions that allowed the observers to focus their detailed description of the situation, the events, as well as the context around the public display. The questions were: T*ime-stamp of event; Who was present (individuals? groups?); Which activity is being observed (how do they interact? with the system, with each other, as a group, as individuals?).* The observations were recorded with hand-written notes on the observational grid. In addition, observations were accompanied by photographs when possible.

Semi-structured In-situ Interviews

In addition to the observations at the venues, two researchers conducted semi-structured in-situ interviews. Venue visitors who participated in activities related to the system under consideration were interviewed when the researchers observed something that was of interest for the study (cf. categories for the observations). In such situations, participants were carefully approached after the event/interaction of interest was finished to not interfere with it. To get structure in the interviews, a template with guideline questions was used (*Why did you (did not) interact with the system? Did you observe how the system affected the space? Do you have any other comments about the system?*). During the in-situ interviews, the researchers took handwritten notes on paper into the template that provided sections for the guiding questions as well as space for further elaborations, additions and comments. All of the interviews were conducted in-the-wild, in ludic environments (dark ambient light, loud music; see Figure 2 and 3). The duration of the interviews differed from each other driven by the dynamics of the environments and the concern to not interfere with the actual flow of events.

Participants of the Semi-structured In-situ Interviews

We conducted 24 interviews during the two deployments – 14 at Kafé Deluxe (11 male), 10 at Garage48 (7 male). The participants were picked based on the explicitness of their behavior, but also depended on their availability (as mentioned above). At Kafé Deluxe, the average age of the interviewees was 25.1 years (ranging from 20 to 30), while at Garage48 it was 27.3 years (ranging from 21 to 37). Regarding the system interactions of the interviewees, at Kafé Deluxe 4 did not use the system and at Garage48 3 did not use it. In the following sections, interviewees from Kafé Deluxe are marked with "KD", from Garage48 with "GA".

System Logs

In order to support the qualitative data collected from the observations and interviews, we collected technical logs of interactions with the system. These comprised information from festify's developers regarding the usage during the events (i.e. amount of unique devices, and amounts of songs added and votes given), as well as our own logging in form of screenshots of the system's music playlist taken every 15 seconds. To further comprehend the interactions and happenings from the system point of view, we then created time-lapse videos with the snapshots we took.

RESULTS OF THE DEPLOYMENT STUDIES

During our investigation and the analysis of the data collected, we were mostly interested in ways how and why people used the system, how they perceived the system and specifically the public display, as well as how the system affected the space and what this encouraged in the audience (such as social interactions). The results are based on a qualitative data analysis, in which we conducted open-ended coding on the data collected during the observations and interviews. During this process, two researchers analyzed the observation and interview data and generated as many themes as possible. The emerging themes were then further analyzed and combined into a smaller set of categories.

In terms of users and interactions logged during the studies, we could identify 18 unique devices used that did 129 interactions in total (songs added and votes on songs) at Kafé Deluxe, while at Garage48 10 unique devices did 94 interactions in total. It needs to be mentioned that we observed groups interacting with only one (shared) mobile device. This probably led to some noisy data in our log files, since it counted only unique devices. Out of the 53 songs played during the study at Kafé Deluxe, 51 had user interactions, i.e. were added by users or were an initial track voted on by users (plus 14 user songs still in the queue at the end of the event). At Garage48, out of the 58 songs played, 55 had user interactions (plus 7 user songs left in the queue). Due to these high numbers of user-interacted tracks played, one can conclude that the system was generally used throughout the events in both studies. Furthermore, in both events, the fallback tracks were only played during the first 10 minutes. In peak times, at Kafé Deluxe, a song needed 5 votes to be played next directly (overall: 5 songs had 4 votes, 12 had 3, 17 had 2, 17 had 1, and 2 had 0 votes, i.e. fallback tracks), while at Garage48, a song would have needed 4 votes to jump to the top of the playlist (5 songs had 3 votes, 22 had 2, 28 had 1, and 3 had 0 votes).

At both deployments, we did not encounter any problems with the system or with the music being played. During a potentially sensitive song played at Kafé Deluxe, where the word "gay" was used in a derogatory way, people laughed instead of being upset about it. So we interpreted this to be an ironic approach teasing the audience. In general, the music being played at both events reportedly fit the occasion and was diverse, which points to several people influencing it, instead of individuals taking over the system, e.g. only playing their favorite band repeatedly.

System and Group Interactions Observed

The observations helped to identify how people engaged with the system and with each other, as well as indications of the impact the system and the interactions had on the (social) context around it.

Competitive Behavior Fostered Interactions Among Users

In both events people showed a competitive behavior. This competitive behavior was observed in several occasions and its nature was confirmed in interviews (KD11: "I was happy when my song was on top of the list and was played"; GA10: "It is really cool that everybody can decide and compete"; GA3: "It was interesting to vote and decide on the music"). Firstly, we noticed people trying to convince others (familiar and unfamiliar people) to vote on the songs added to get them higher up in the playlist (observed 6 occasions; GA3: "I tried to get more votes for my song, because I wanted to listen to it"). Furthermore, they asked to borrow and use others' devices to vote. This tactical approach was also observed several times during the studies. Secondly, people teamed up to coordinate the songs they add and support each other's songs/votes (observed and reported in 12 occasions). Such situation can be seen in Figure 4, showing several users closely gathered discussing and sharing their votes. From the logs, we could see the participation increased considerably in the second half of both events, which then again increased the competitiveness at that point, since songs needed more votes to be played directly (average votes on songs first/second half: 1.4/2.7 at Kafé Deluxe, 1.1/1.9 at Garage48). This increase is also supported by the interviews with most of the participants stating they started to use the system because someone else informed them about it (GA9: "I told my friend about the system and then he also used it"; KD1: "I saw my friend using it"). These observations in the logs and the comments from the interviews suggest that the more users interacted, the higher the conversion rate of new users was.

Group Interactions and Discussions

We observed that it was mostly groups being engaged with the system (observed group sizes 2-6 people), whether it was looking at the screen and discussing about the playlist or what music to add to it. This also often happened using/sharing a single mobile device for interacting (observed 7 occasions). Besides this, we observed that the content on the display and the music being played triggered discussions about it among bystanders (see Figure 6). It was also clear that the system had a positive impact on the users, with cheering about specific songs at both events and dancing taking place throughout the evening at Kafé Deluxe on the dance floor directly in front of the public display especially.

Interactions Around and Fostered by the Public Display

In several situations, the importance and central role of the public display for the users became obvious at both events. We could observe users constantly pointing at and coming to the display and checking the changing playlist to see when their song would be played (observed 10 occasions; GA5: "It was exciting to wait for my song and see others vote for it"). They then also reacted positively/negatively to up-/down-movements of songs in the list. Another reoccurring engagement with the public display was that people took photos of the display or of themselves in front of it at both events (observed in 11 occasions). These events happened reportedly when a user's added song or another for them interesting song was played. As the interviews showed, users did this to remember the songs, but also especially to memorize the whole experience at the venue, which they also intended to share with other people later on.

Figure 4. Group teaming up and supporting each other's songs at Kafé Deluxe

Figure 5. Individual user interacting with the system after seeing the public display at Garage48

Figure 6. Group discussing around the public display about its content at Garage48

Differences and Commonalities at the Two Venues

The type of the events and therefore also the role of the music at the two study locations was different. Deploying the system in these diverse contexts enabled us to gather valuable insights about the usage and also the influence of the settings on the observed interactions.

As the results presented above showed, we could identify in general the same interactions and behaviors, as well as a similar impact the system had on the physical and social space during both studies.

To complement the results presented, the differences we could point out were expected due to the types of the events. On one hand, Kafé Deluxe is a pub and nightclub. People usually visit it in groups of friends and are in general more open to dancing and other celebratory recreative activities (as the observed cheering). This open attitude (i.e. being in "party mode") could explain the higher participation numbers - the music had a more present role in this context and people were keen to experiment with the interactive music player. On the other hand, the nature of the event at Garage48 was more professional. The main aim of the event attendees was to network and socialize with colleagues and acquaintances. This made the atmosphere in the venue more laid back and slightly less formal. Nevertheless, the background of the attendees being ICT related, made them also curious about the new system and willing to try it out.

The main difference between the observed behaviors at the two venues was that in Kafé Deluxe the people interacted with the system in groups from the start of the event, while at Garage48 group interactions emerged with the progression of the event (because most of the attendees arrived in the event initially alone or in pairs). In the beginning, at Garage48, we could observe more individuals interacting with the system at first (see Figure 5).

Engaging and Motivating Features and User Incentives

Based on the interviews, we were able to identify several features and incentives for users to interact with the system. The topics mentioned in the next sections are valid for both venues of the studies.

Sharing the Taste in Music and thus Personalizing and Affecting the Physical and Social Space

One of the main reasons for interacting was the possibility to share one's own (taste in) music and thus expose this preference to the people sharing the physical and social space with them (mentioned by 11 participants) (KD13: "I wanted to listen to songs I liked"; G10: "I wanted to share my taste in music"; KD4: "I want others to hear my great music taste"). Providing this feature, the users had a chance to express themselves and also personalize the place they were in. They reported experiencing an engaging feeling of making an impact and influencing the space (GA5: "It is great to have an impact"). The system allowed them to be part of the event at another level by being present through the interaction (GA3: "I can participate in the party on another level"; GA8: "It allows to take part in the party").

Entertainment Through Participation and Competition

Furthermore, people who interacted with the system considered themselves to be very interested in music and they were eager to share this interest with people around them (7 participants). At Kafé Deluxe especially, the music was not only for listening but also for dancing. The main incentive here was to enrich the experience at the place with playing music they liked (GA2: "It made me happy"; GA2: "I would leave a party with bad music"; KD8: "I wanted to dance to song [x] tonight and hoped it would be played – now I had the chance to add it myself"). Furthermore, the application provided them additional entertainment while the event was at some point failing to engage them (GA9: "[it] gave me and my friends an activity at the event"; GA9: "I was bored"; KD2: "I wanted to try what the song sounded like here with the sound system"). This behavior from single users could especially be observed at Garage48 (see Figure 5). Given by the type of event that took place there, many people attended alone and they appreciated the interaction with the system in between conversations. The voting system encouraged competition between the users and this reportedly drove other people to interact too. A similar behavior was also experienced in prior studies [23].

Importance of the Situatedness of the Interactions

Participants emphasized that they liked the fact that they were able to observe and experience people around them being directly and immediately affected by and exposed to the system they were able to influence (KD11: "Others were dancing and cheering when my song was played"; G10: "People liked my music"). They contrasted this to other types of online sharing, where everybody consumes music/content individually and expresses reactions only through text or "likes".

Issues and Concerns Encountered at the Studies

Besides the positive engagements with and positive elements of the system described above, the studies uncovered factors at both events, which had a negative influence on the users' engagement and showed possible concerns regarding the application scenario and thus its adoption.

Awareness of the System and its Interactive Features

People who did not interact with the system reported that the interactive features were not conveyed well enough (GA6: "I did not know about the features"; KD3: "The screen did not catch my attention"; GA7: "The system should show its functionalities better"). Thus most of the people did not know about the functionality and interactions possible, but saw the public display, expecting to just see Spotify running. This issue is an example of "display blindness" [21] and is mostly due to the fact that the application used is not developed specifically for public spaces or based on research from the field of pervasive displays, e.g. [9, 21]. The instructions on the screen were too small and unnoticeable and it did not catch bystanders' attention. This claim is well supported by the fact that all 3 participants at Garage48 who did not interact with the system before the interview did interact after they learned more about its features. Participants also mentioned having several public displays at the venue could have raised their awareness of the interactive system. Concerning the awareness of the system and its usage, one needs to consider it was the first time deploying such system at either of the venues and the system was not promoted before the deployment. Thus people did probably not expect to have an influence on the music, since these kinds of systems are not common.

Consciously Avoiding the System

The interviews uncovered also other important issues that kept people from using the system. Firstly people reported they were not interested enough in music in general and the music at pubs did not matter much to them (3 participants). Their main goal at the event was to socialize with people (KD14: "I just want to have a drink and talk to people"). On top of that, as another crucial point for the design of such system, event participants mentioned that using a phone could disturb the original person-to-person interactions at the events and it would be impolite towards other people they socialized with (3 participants) (GA7: "I would not use my phone at a party"; KD14: "It is too much effort to interact while I am at a pub").

Unwanted Exposure

In contrast to the users who reported being actively engaged with the system, participants who did not interact with it stated they were too shy and did not want to be exposed to the audience through the public display and music (3 participants; KD12: "It could be embarrassing if people don't like the song"). They mentioned concerns regarding their choice of music and preference being shared, since it could be embarrassing if people did not like their choice in music. This concern was mentioned even with the interactions being anonymous at the studies. Further, people were also reportedly discouraged if they felt their choice would not fit the rest of the playlist (GA7: "It discourages me if my choice does not fit the other songs").

Potential Risks for the Democratic Process

The concerns mentioned above could mean potential risk for the nature of the system aiming at a democratic way to take part in the event and thus decide the music together. At our study at Kafé Deluxe, 18 users (22% of audience) chose the music for ~80 people directly affected at the display location, while at Garage48 10 (14%) users decided the music for ~70 people. Even though this is a high overall participation based on our experience from prior studies deploying public display systems, these concerns could lead to a minority deciding in the "democratic" music system.

CONSIDERING NEW FEATURES

Based on the results presented in the last sections, we introduce a set of design proposals and new features for fostering further engagement with the system, as well as inducing and enabling new ways of situated social interactions around the public display installation.

Features and Mechanisms to Draw Attention to and Foster Engagement with the System

In order to draw more attention to the system, the public display needs a more prominent role, since it is the main discovery point for the system. The participants asked for more obvious instructions, as well as more dynamic content and feedback to interactions (GA1: "It should show more dynamic content on the display"; GA3: "Users should be represented"). More screens at the venues could further care for a more immersive experience. In terms of more dynamic and engaging content, the main entities in the interaction process, i.e. users and votes, need to be emphasized.

Self-expression and Having an Impact

It became obvious that the incentive of self-expression needs to be further supported by the system. Users liked the exposure and possible attention, which enriched their experience while being at the event. In order to foster self-expression, user names (nicknames) could be introduced in the system. This would emphasize the individuality of the users and bring their interactions to the forefront. Further, this would clearly raise awareness of the interaction possibilities for other people, thus engaging more people in potential interaction [23].

Recording and Sharing the Experience

It was a common action of users to take photos of the screen and themselves in front of it. Their aim was to remember and to further share the experience at the location and beyond. This scenario could be further expanded by allowing users to share their photos via the public display. It was also very important to the users to make other people aware of their preferences and their presence at the physical and social space. Photo-sharing could give more context and personal appeal to the interactions. Saving the playlist would be another option for allowing users to add new discoveries to personal playlists and thus to take mementos from the event.

Competition

The observations and interviews indicated clearly that the competitive nature of the voting system was an important factor in engaging users to interact with the system, but also to reach out to other people at the venue. To further foster this behavior and make use of it, features such as rankings for successful additions to the playlist, i.e. receiving many votes by others, could be rewarded. Furthermore, the system could provide functionalities to reach out to others asking for support/votes for ones own entries to the playlist.

Features and Mechanisms to Foster Social Engagement

Group Interactions and Social Encounters

Similarly to prior studies [23] we were able to create some sense of group belonging and provoke specific social interactions around the display installation at both events. Even though the events had different purposes and different character, the system and the music could foster these interactions at both events already with its basic functionality of opening up the music playlist to the audience. Given the nature of such social events, the interactions in these contexts are often influenced and conducted by groups. This was also observed during the studies. The system should further support these groupings (of familiar and unfamiliar people) providing features to directly interact as groups and promote the possibilities to connect to others. As mentioned in the prior sections, reaching out to other participants via the system could bring (unfamiliar) people together through display interactions. Also when individual users and their interactions are represented on the public display with more context, other people could possibly relate to that, thus connecting to the respective user. In this case the system would foster social interactions of people sharing the same (situated) experiences. This could especially be beneficial for situations like the afterparty event at Garage48 with one of the main purposes being to network and socialize with people.

Focus on the Social Interactions in the Place

While introducing new features to the system, it is important to design them with a clear focus on the interactions between people in the real physical and social space, without over-emphasizing the digital and virtual experience. An out of balance system emphasis could potentially isolate the venue visitors from each other, which could be a harm for the interactions in the physical and social space. This potential isolation through interactions with/via mobile devices is a common threat to social interactions in shared physical spaces, also known as the "heads-down phenomenon" [8, 16]. Thus the system features should support the social interactions in the real space to exploit the scenario to its full potential, facilitated by physical interfaces such as the public display.

CONCLUSION AND FUTURE WORK

In the presented in-the-wild studies, we deployed a public display system with a shared music player and a collaborative playlist in two venues hosting social events of different character. Our results based on in-situ observations and interviews indicated that shared interactive music systems could potentially enhance public spaces by engaging users in self-expression and influencing the physical space they are at. Deploying the system introduced a range of new dynamics into the users' practices, which reportedly enriched the experience for them at the venue. The system engaged participants to form groups and teams, induced discussions on music related topics, enabled individuals to express themselves, share their preferences and compete with friends as well as strangers in curating the playlist in new and playful ways. Furthermore, the in-the-wild studies allowed us to acquire valuable insights and acquire requirements that can now be used for designing new features for our own public display applications and projects. The gathered insights are already being used as input in a participatory design process of a new collaborative music system facilitating situated shared experiences around public displays.

In our research, we are particularly interested not only in the ways people engage with shared public interactive displays, but also in how the systems affect the physically and socially shared spaces they are located in. In conclusion, we can say that our study supported the claim that music has a big impact on people's practices and the social dynamics in the shared spaces such systems are deployed. We will make use of this scenario in future work to further investigate these dynamics.

ACKNOWLEDGEMENTS

We thank Marcus Knutsson, LNU, for his help organizing and conducting the study at Kafé Deluxe, and Hanna-Liisa Pender, Tallinn University, helping use to conduct the study at Garage48. We also thank all participants of the studies.

REFERENCES

1. Agamanolis, S. 2003. Designing Displays For Human Connectedness. *Public and Situated Displays*. K. O'Hara, M. Perry, E. Churchill, and D. Russell, eds. Springer Netherlands. 309–334.
2. Akpan, I., Marshall, P., Bird, J. and Harrison, D. 2013. Exploring the Effects of Space and Place on Engagement with an Interactive Installation. *Proc. of the CHI '13*, 2213–2222.
3. Alt, F., Schneegaß, S., Schmidt, A., Müller, J. and Memarovic, N. 2012. How to evaluate public displays. *Proc. of PerDis '12*.
4. Brignull, H. and Rogers, Y. 2003. Enticing people to interact with large public displays in public spaces. *Proc. of INTERACT. 3*, 17–24.
5. Chen, Z., Yavuz, E.A. and Karlsson, G. 2012. What a juke! A collaborative music sharing system. *IEEE International Symposium on a World of Wireless, Mobile and Multimedia Networks*.
6. Cunningham, S.J. and Nichols, D.M. 2009. Exploring Social Music Behavior: An Investigation of Music Selection at Parties. *Proc. of the 10th International Society for Music Information Retrieval Conference (ISMIR '09)*, 747–752.
7. DeNora, T. 2006. Music and Emotion in Real Time. *Consuming Music Together: Social and Collaborative Aspects of Music Consumption Technologies*. K. O'Hara and B. Brown, eds. Springer Netherlands.
8. Hsi, S. 2003. A study of user experiences mediated by nomadic web content in a museum. *Journal of Computer Assisted Learning*. 19, 1, 308–319.
9. Huang, E.M., Koster, A. and Borchers, J. 2008. Overcoming assumptions and uncovering practices: When does the public really look at public displays? *Pervasive Computing*. 228–243.
10. Kukka, H. and Patino, R. 2009. UbiRockMachine: A Multimodal Music Voting Service for Shared Urban Spaces. *Proc. of MUM '09*.
11. Leikas, J., Stromberg, H., Ikonen, V., Suomela, R. and Heinila, J. 2006. Multi-User Mobile Applications and a Public Display: Novel Ways for Social Interaction. *IEEE International Conference on Pervasive Computing and Communications*, 66–70.

12. Lenz, E., Diefenbach, S., Hassenzahl, M. and Lienhard, S. 2012. Mo. shared music, shared moment. *Proc. of NordiCHI '12*, 736.
13. Leong, T.W. and Wright, P.C. 2013. Revisiting social practices surrounding music. *Proc. of CHI '13*, 951.
14. Liikkanen, L.A. and Åman, P. 2015. Shuffling Services: Current Trends in Interacting with Digital Music. *Interacting with Computers*.
15. Liikkanen, L.A., Amos, C., Cunningham, S.J., Downie, J.S. and McDonald, D. 2012. Music interaction research in HCI: Let's Get the Band Back Together. *CHI '12 EA - Extended Abstracts*.
16. Lyons, L. 2009. Designing Opportunistic User Interfaces to Support a Collaborative Museum Exhibit. *CSCL '09 Proc. of the 9th international conference on Computer supported collaborative learning*, 375–384.
17. Memarovic, N., Langheinrich, M., Alt, F., Elhart, I., Hosio, S. and Rubegni, E. 2012. Using public displays to stimulate passive engagement, active engagement, and discovery in public spaces. *Proceedings of the 4th Media Architecture Biennale Conference on Participation (MAB '12)*, 55–64.
18. Michelis, D. and Müller, J. 2011. The Audience Funnel: Observations of Gesture Based Interaction With Multiple Large Displays in a City Center. *International Journal of Human-Computer Interaction*. 27, 6 (Jun. 2011), 562–579.
19. Müller, J., Alt, F., Michelis, D. and Schmidt, A. 2010. Requirements and design space for interactive public displays. *Proceedings of the international conference on Multimedia '10*.
20. Müller, J., Eberle, D. and Tollmar, K. 2014. Communiplay: A Field Study of a Public Display Media Space. *Proc. of CHI 2014*.
21. Müller, J., Wilmsmann, D., Exeler, J., Buzeck, M., Schmidt, A. and Krüger, A. 2009. Display blindness: The effect of expectations on attention towards digital signage. *Pervasive Computing*.
22. Müller, M., Otero, N., Alissandrakis, A. and Milrad, M. 2014. Evaluating usage patterns and adoption of an interactive video installation on public displays in school contexts. *Proc. of MUM '14*, 160–169.
23. Müller, M., Otero, N., Alissandrakis, A. and Milrad, M. 2015. Increasing user engagement with distributed public displays through the awareness of peer interactions. *Proc. of PerDis 2015*, 23–29.
24. O'Hara, K., Lipson, M., Jansen, M., Unger, A., Jeffries, H. and Macer, P. 2004. Jukola: Democratic Music Choice in a Public Space. *Proc. of DIS '04*.
25. Robles, E., Nass, C. and Kahn, A. 2009. The Social Life of Information Displays: How Screens Shape Psychological Responses in Social Contexts. *Human-Computer Interaction*. 24, 1 (2009), 48–78.
26. Robson, C. 2011. *Real World Research*. John Wiley & Sons.
27. Rogers, Y., Connelly, K., Tedesco, L., Hazlewood, W., Kurtz, A., Hall, R.E., Hursey, J. and Toscos, T. 2007. Why It's Worth the Hassle - The Value of In-Situ Studies When Designing Ubicomp. *Proc. of UbiComp '07*, 336–353.
28. Rubegni, E., Memarovic, N. and Langheinrich, M. 2011. Talking to Strangers: Using Large Public Displays to Facilitate Social Interaction. *Design, User Experience, and Usability. Theory, Methods, Tools and Practice*. (2011), 195–204.
29. Sørensen, H. and Kjeldskov, J. 2012. The interaction space of a multi-device, multi-user music experience. *Proc. of NordiCHI '12*, 504–513.
30. Sprague, D., Wu, F. and Tory, M. 2008. Music selection using the PartyVote democratic jukebox. *Proceedings of the working conference on Advanced visual interfaces - AVI '08*, 433.
31. Strauss, A. and Corbin, J. 2008. *Basics of qualitative research: Techniques and procedures for developing grounded theory*. Sage Publications, Inc.
32. Terrenghi, L., Quigley, A. and Dix, A. 2009. A taxonomy for and analysis of multi-person-display ecosystems. *Personal and Ubiquitous Computing*. 13, 8 (2009), 583–598.

Felines, Foragers, and Physicists: Supporting Scientific Outreach with Multi-Surface and Multi-Space Games

Victor Cheung
Games Institute
University of Waterloo
victor.cheung@uwaterloo.ca

James R. Wallace
School of Public Health and Health Systems
University of Waterloo
james.wallace@uwaterloo.ca

ABSTRACT
We describe the design, development, and deployment of two scientific outreach games to support an open house event at an Institute for Quantum Computing (IQC) by an 11-member team of academics and practitioners over a one-year period. We overview our collaborative design process, the development of design goals aligned with facilitating scientific outreach during a one-day open house, and report on how successfully our final prototypes achieved those goals. We then reflect on implications for the use of interactive surfaces and spaces as a platform for scientific outreach, and in particular, the effectiveness of large displays as 'honey pots', the immaturity of technologies for creating interactive spaces, and extending the reach of outreach activities through technology.

ACM Classification Keywords
H.5.2. Information Interfaces and Presentation (e.g. HCI): User-centered design

Author Keywords
Games; Outreach; Large Displays; Mobile Devices

INTRODUCTION
The rapid adoption and evolution of interactive surfaces have provided an accessible, malleable, and engaging medium for scientific outreach. In particular, applications in scientific and educational outreach have been actively explored [9, 11], since interactive surfaces provide a familiar means by which lay audiences can be enticed to engage, interact, and ultimately learn about science. Furthermore, diversity in display size, display configuration (e.g., handheld, large format), and interaction modalities (e.g., touch, proxemics) enables scientific institutions to develop custom-built applications that better engage visitors with their research, personnel, and facilities.

Multi-surface and multi-space scientific outreach applications have the potential to help educate the public about local scientific activities, to act as a 'honey pot' and draw in otherwise uninterested audiences [5, 18, 20, 22], and to take advantage of

ISS '16, November 06 - 09, 2016, Niagara Falls, ON, Canada

ACM 978-1-4503-4248-3/16/11 ... $15.00
DOI: http://dx.doi.org/10.1145/2992154.2992156

Figure 1: We implemented two games to support scientific outreach. (top) Quantum Cats, an Angry Birds-like game that introduces guests to basic quantum mechanics. (bottom) Alice and Schrödinger's Excellent Adventure, a locative game that teaches guests about the IQC's research, staff, and facilities.

the growing number of smartphones and tablets to engage individuals and extend an institution's reach beyond their physical space [12]. However, to effectively engage an audience with an institution's research, staff, and facilities, custom-built hardware and/or software is often necessary. And while software tools for gaming and multi-touch development (e.g., Unity) are available, there is a lack of guidance towards how they should be developed and deployed in practice to maximize their benefits for outreach applications.

We describe the design and deployment of two applications developed over a one-year period by a cross-disciplinary team of 11 researchers and practitioners, aiming to educate and engage the general public with research at an Institute for Quantum Computing (IQC) during a one-day outreach event. As the surface applications were designed to support engagement with complex scientific material, we incorporated gameplay elements (e.g., puzzle-solving, item-collecting) for a more accessible and enjoyable experience. The first game, *Quantum Cats* (Figure 1, top), is similar to Angry Birds but was implemented on large multi-touch displays and later made available for download to personal smartphones and tablets. The second game, *Alice and Schrödinger's Excellent Adventure* (Figure 1, bottom), is a locative game designed with the intention to encourage exploration of the IQC's facilities.

We first describe our development process, which included a review of related work in the area of scientific outreach applications, an overview of our collaborative design process conducted with members of the IQC, and the development of design goals that guided the application development. We then describe each of the designs in depth, link each application's design to our stated goals, and describe use during the open house. We conclude with a reflection on our design process and goals, and discuss implications for the use of multi-surfaces and multi-space games as a platform for scientific outreach: the effectiveness of large displays as 'honey pots', the immaturity of technologies for creating interactive spaces, and extending the reach of outreach activities through technology.

SUPPORTING SCIENTIFIC OUTREACH

For decades, institutions such as museums, art galleries, and libraries have explored how new technologies can facilitate and promote engagement with their archives. For example, modern museums and art galleries often provide visitors with location-aware personal audio devices, or more recently smartphone applications [1, 16, 23], to augment their visiting experiences and provide details on an exhibit-by-exhibit basis as visitors move through a collection. Such use of technology to augment and enhance the visiting experience not only improves a visitor's experience by making the materials more accessible and enjoyable, but can also benefit institutions like museums through the development of brand and loyalty [25]. Thus, technology-enhanced exhibits have been developed for a wide range of topics such as science [3], natural history [15, 19], cultural learning [7, 8], and sustainability [2, 9].

A challenge in deploying these technologies, however, is that they often have limited interactivity, such as playing an audio track for each exhibit, and alone cannot make scientific, and often dry, materials more engaging. In response to this need, gamification, or the application of gaming elements to non-game domains [11], has recently been explored as a means of encouraging engagement with scientific outreach. For example, D'Angelo et al. [9] created a game to educate aquarium visitors about the dangers of overfishing. They noted that while such games could help to motivate interactions with educational or outreach exhibits, shallow learning experiences might be more appropriate. That is, outreach games may be most effective when they are designed for short playtimes of about 5 minutes, but encourage the player to continue exploring the subject matter at a later time. In this work, we explore the use of novel technologies, such as large interactive surfaces and spaces, as well as gamification to support scientific outreach. In particular, we explore the implementation of games on these platforms to support outreach activities at an Institute for Quantum Computing.

Scientific outreach activities, such as our open house event, also have requirements beyond those for typical exhibits. For example, besides providing educational value and engaging experience to visitors, the open house aims at promoting the hosting institute as a whole, thereby developing a stronger relationship with the outside community. These additional requirements have led to design criteria unique to scientific outreach activities, as discussed later.

Interactive Surfaces and Spaces

Many novel technologies, including interactive surfaces and spaces, have been explored as support tools for scientific outreach as they become technologically and economically feasible. For example, large interactive displays have been leveraged to provide interactive exhibit content for museum visitors [18, 20]. Similarly, emerging trends in mobile devices and augmented reality have been explored as a means of making physical spaces more supportive of outreach activities [1, 16, 23]. In this work, we explore using two technologies in these domains: large interactive displays, and location-aware mobile devices.

Interactive Surfaces: Multi-Touch Displays

Large interactive displays have been recognized by the HCI community as providing a number of opportunities and challenges for interaction in a public environments. For example, a large display often entices users to approach and engage with content [18, 20] and supports interaction through the now-familiar touch-interaction metaphor. Conversely, requiring users to interact publicly may deter some individuals from participating due to the risk of public embarrassment [5].

In the context of scientific outreach, a common theme is designing for short-lived, ephemeral interactions with large interactive displays. For example, Hornecker [20] noted that while their museum display attracted significant attention from guests, visitors were likely to spend only a few minutes exploring an exhibit, and thus only have a short time "to experience success ... and to understand the purpose, scope and properties" of the activity (p. 116). Similarly, D'Angelo et al. [9] reported that interactions with their fishing game rarely extended beyond a 5-minute timeframe, after which players moved on to explore other exhibits at the aquarium.

When designing our outreach applications, we paid careful attention to the benefits and limitations of large interactive displays. In particular, we designed a game to introduce quantum mechanics concepts and encourage further explorations with other open house exhibits. By deploying the game on a large interactive surface we encouraged brief interactions with the content, and expected visitors to then move on and explore other exhibits at the open house event. To further facilitate learning at the event, we designed complementary experiences using location-aware mobile devices.

Interactive Spaces: Location-Aware Mobile Devices

Another technology frequently explored to support outreach is a location-aware mobile device, such as a smartphone or tablet [1, 12, 16, 23]. These devices provide an opportunity to deliver additional materials to individuals on an on-demand basis, based on their location within an institution. For example, many art galleries use personal devices to provide information about nearby artwork to a visitor. Similarly, evoGuide [17], a system for guided factory tours, provided visitors access to a variety of multimedia content, such as videos and textual descriptions of nearby objects that were otherwise available only to trained professionals wearing safety equipment. Recent work has explored benefits of providing such immersive experiences, particularly in the context of location-aware gaming with mobile devices (e.g., [4, 10, 14]), and help providing a 'socially safe' and engaging experience in public places [6].

When designing our own applications, we faced a situation similar to Hable et al. [17] where many research laboratories at the IQC were only accessible to trained personnel using proper safety equipment. To overcome this barrier, and to make the facilities and research more accessible to guests, we decided to develop a location-aware game that provided content via mobile devices as the guests explored the facilities. This location-aware game provided an opportunity to explore the IQC in more depth than our interactive surface game, and thus provided a complementary learning experience.

THE INSTITUTE FOR QUANTUM COMPUTING

The Institute for Quantum Computing (IQC) is a scientific research institute at a local university. As a research institute, the IQC's primary function is to facilitate research, and is home to about 25 faculty, 45 postdoctoral fellows, and 100 students exploring topics such as optics, nanoelectronics, nuclear magnetic resonance, and quantum sensors. As a university institution, the IQC also engages in outreach activities with the local community and hosts an annual open house event, where the general public is invited to meet IQC researchers and learn about their research.

The open house event features many outreach activities, including a tour of the facility which highlights many of the design features of the building that houses the IQC. For example, the "state-of-the-art facility is built to the most stringent scientific controls against vibration, temperature fluctuations, and electromagnetic radiation" [24]; a feature that would later impact our design since WiFi technologies rely on transmitted electromagnetic radiation. In addition to the building tour, featured activities include scientific demonstrations by graduate students and public lectures by eminent quantum physicists.

About a year before the open house event, our team was assembled to develop custom applications to support scientific outreach during the one-day event. While Human-Computer Interaction researchers were included on the team, no assumptions were made as to the specific technologies to be adopted for use in the project.

THE OPEN HOUSE PROJECT

Over an approximately one-year design cycle, we collaboratively developed a series of interactive experiences designed to inform, entertain, and educate open house guests about the IQC's personnel and research. The event was part of the university campus's larger Fall outreach activities, and featured scientific demonstrations by graduate students, a tour of the IQC facilities including laboratories, and guest lectures by world-renowned quantum physicists. As an outreach activity, the focus of the event was to develop engagement with the outside community, to make the research more accessible to non-scientists, and to foster an interest in science in visiting children and young adults who might one day become researchers themselves.

Our design team comprised 11 faculty, staff, and students from a games research group. Our student and faculty members brought perspectives from research backgrounds in English, Engineering, and Applied Health Science. They were responsible for the majority of the requirements gathering and initial scoping and design work on the project. Throughout this process, approximately 10 student outreach members from the IQC were consulted regularly for feedback on how to best engage guests with the interactive experiences. For example, multiple brainstorming and focus group sessions were held over the first 3-month period to determine what genres would be most effective in engaging guests with Quantum Mechanics principles. Approximately 6 months before the open house, two full-time developers and one artist were brought onto the project as dedicated development staff.

Design Criteria

Through our requirements gathering activities with IQC staff, we first identified past outreach activities at the IQC. For example, past open house events had featured a 'Plinko' game that was used to demonstrate the principle of quantum uncertainty. The game was played on a large display with input via a smartphone, but had many limitations: it demonstrated only a single quantum principle, was not strongly related to the IQC or its researchers, and was not perceived by IQC staff as being particularly engaging.

Using this feedback from the IQC administration and student outreach staff as design requirements, we developed a set of goals to inform and guide our design process:

(D1) Educational Value The primary function of the open house is to educate, to make IQC research accessible to the public, and to encourage exploration of quantum mechanics principles.

(D2) Personal/Local Information In addition to educating about quantum mechanics, the open house strives to teach about the IQC itself, including the research projects, personnel, and physical building. Where possible, installations should aim to highlight these more personal aspects of on-campus research.

(D3) Approachable and Accessible In addition to the above goals, installations at the open house should do so in a way that is approachable by a diverse group of open house guests, including children, individuals whose first language is not English, and those with physical disabilities.

(D4) Engaging One of the most significant challenges faced in previous open houses was making the (difficult) scientific content not only accessible to guests, but also engaging, and for guests to leave the event with a positive experience. An oft-cited goal was to have guests "Google 'quantum mechanics' " when they arrived home after the event.

(D5) Integrated The open house is a large event, spanning three research labs, and four floors of the IQC building.

Thus, IQC staff wanted to ensure that our installations were not a stand-alone experience, and worked to complement the other experiences taking place throughout the building.

(D6) Logistical Constraints A final design consideration arose from the IQC building's unique construction. Due to interference with nearby labs, the building does not have strong WiFi signals. Temporary wireless access points were provided in the lobby, but our design and development processes has to assume no WiFi access within the building.

We initially identified challenges in developing game applications that met all of these goals. For example, there are design tensions in making an installation that is both informative (D2) and approachable (D3). Similarly, integration (D5) across the entire open house may detract from engagement (D4) with a single installation. Thus, each of these goals was realized to a different degree in each of the subsequent projects.

THE GAMES

After gathering requirements and developing our design goals, we sought to determine which types of installations would best meet those goals. We followed a collaborative design process where our team consulted, brainstormed, designed, and tested iterations of each game in collaboration with IQC administration and outreach staff over a period of 8 months. Our first round of collaborative design, following our requirements gathering, explored the design space and identified the types of games that might best suit the open house with outreach staff. We eventually determined two installations to be developed:

Quantum Cats

Given the focus of the open house to educate and to make quantum computing research more accessible to the general public **(D1,3)**, the first installation was determined to be a classical game that would incorporate quantum computing aspects into its core mechanics. The motivation behind developing a game was that it would have broad appeal to a large group of guests, and would provide an approachable, accessible **(D3)**, and engaging **(D4)** experience while providing an opportunity to informally introduce quantum computing concepts to visitors **(D1)**. We hoped that this experience would spark interest in quantum computing, and foster engagement with other parts of the tour **(D5)** rather than be a stand-alone educational tool, and thus were not concerned with developing deeply educational experience.

Through a series of focus groups and seminars, we first proposed adaptations of classical arcade games, such as PacMan or Asteroids. Yet these suggestions did not receive much positive feedback. However, during a brainstorming session, IQC outreach staff proposed an "Angry Birds-like" game. This idea was well-received by IQC staff, administration, and our design team because of its familiar interface, and the opportunity to incorporate quantum mechanics into birds' flight properties. Over a series of design exercises we developed concepts for the quantum principles that should be incorporated into the game, and game mechanics that would be representative of the research at the IQC. In particular, three concepts that drove much of the IQC's research were identified: Super-positioning, Quantum Tunnelling, and Uncertainty.

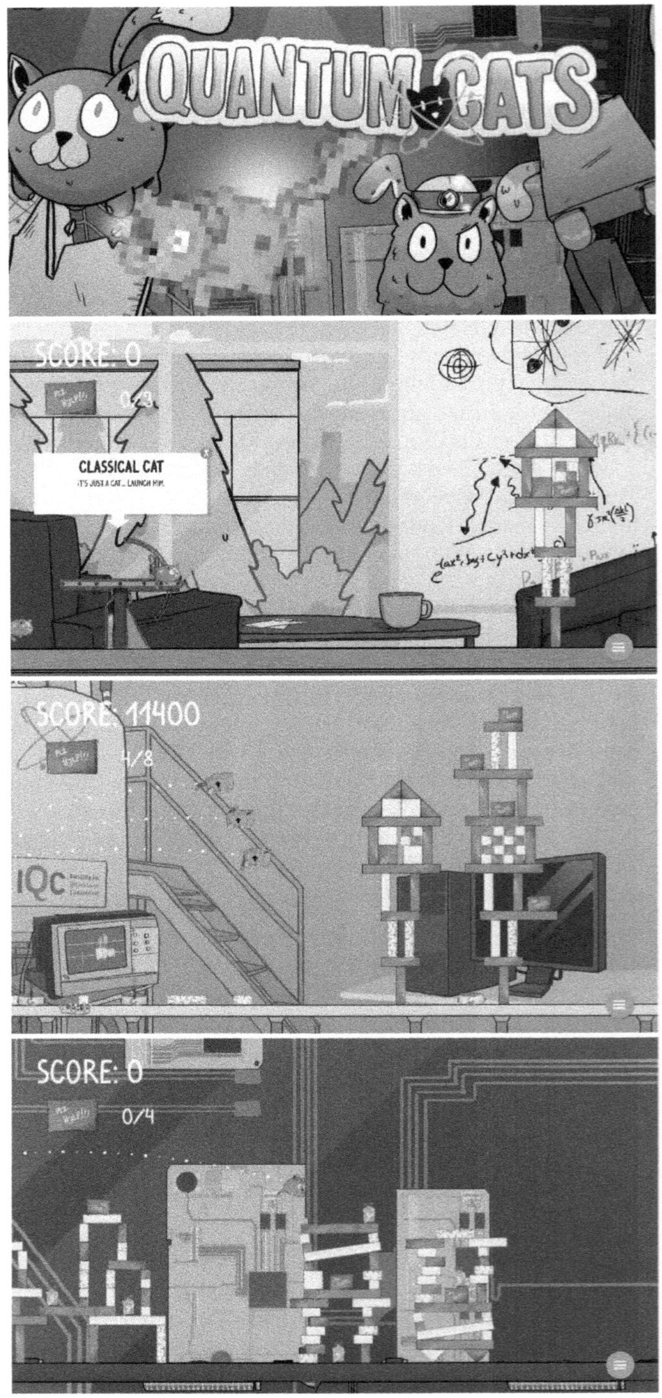

Figure 2: Quantum Cats, a puzzle game that employs many of the same mechanics and interaction metaphors as Angry Birds. **(Panel 1)** The Quantum Cats welcome screen, featuring each of the 4 in-game characters. **(Panels 2-4)** Players launch cats associated with quantum properties such as Uncertainty, Quantum Tunnelling, and Superposition to rescue kittens trapped in nearby boxes. As cats are launched on each level, obstacles have to be either avoided or knocked over.

Our game, called *Quantum Cats*[1] (Figure 2) is an Angry Birds clone that features four cats, who are launched using an electromagnetic catapult across levels to rescue the world's kittens (who are coincidentally trapped in nearby boxes). Each cat's game mechanics correspond to different quantum computing concepts: Classy represents classical physics and is a traditional ballistic projectile; Schrö represents superposition, and splits into three projectiles when fired, only one of which (picked by a tap) will ultimately strike a target; Digger embodies quantum tunnelling, and can pass through obstacles as he flies through the level; and Fuzzy represents quantum uncertainty, and flies through the level as a cloud of uncertainty, when tapped she will strike a randomly-determined nearby object at random speed. Each cat is illustrated in order in Figure 2, Panel 1. We created a series of 7 levels of varying difficulty to showcase each of the quantum mechanics and engage guests for an expected playtime of about 5 minutes.

Since existing research points towards brief interactions with game content [9, 20], the educational focus **(D1)** of Quantum Cats was on introducing quantum mechanics fundamentals to players through each of the cat's game mechanics (i.e., superposition, quantum tunnelling, uncertainty). Care was taken throughout the design process to represent these mechanics as accurately as possible. However, players were not expected to gain an understanding of their meaning through gameplay. Instead, the goal was to spark a player's curiosity, and, later on, engagement and conversation with exhibits and researchers. For example, by featuring different labs throughout the IQC, we hoped that players would later visit and inquire about their research and the quantum mechanics featured in-game.

Quantum Cats was developed in Unity 5[2] by our full-time development team over the 5-month period leading up to the open house. A benefit of developing in Unity was the ability to cross-compile for different platforms. We ultimately released the Quantum Cats app on the Google Play and iOS App stores, and could re-release on myriad additional platforms based on need. In addition to development in Unity, the game featured custom artwork by our in-house cartoonist with minimal text usage **(D3)**. The artwork was created to reflect the IQC and its research labs **(D2,5)**, particularly the Optics, Nuclear Magnetic Resonance, and Integrated Circuit laboratories.

To address our goals surrounding feasibility **(D6)**, the game was developed as a stand-alone installation on three 60" multitouch displays. Each display was mounted on a mobile, height-adjustable stand **(D3)** and equipped with a PQ Labs G4 infrared touch frame connected to an Android A300 series iStick computer[3] (Figure 1, top) to run the game.

Alice and Schrodinger's Excellent Adventure

Throughout our collaborative design cycles, we also identified a need to enhance the previous year's guided tour, to better describe the research conducted in-house and convey the uniqueness of the IQC facility's construction **(D2)**. We decided to develop a self-guided, locative, and augmented reality tour that

[1]Available at http://quantumcats.ca
[2]http://unity3d.com
[3]http://multitouch.com/

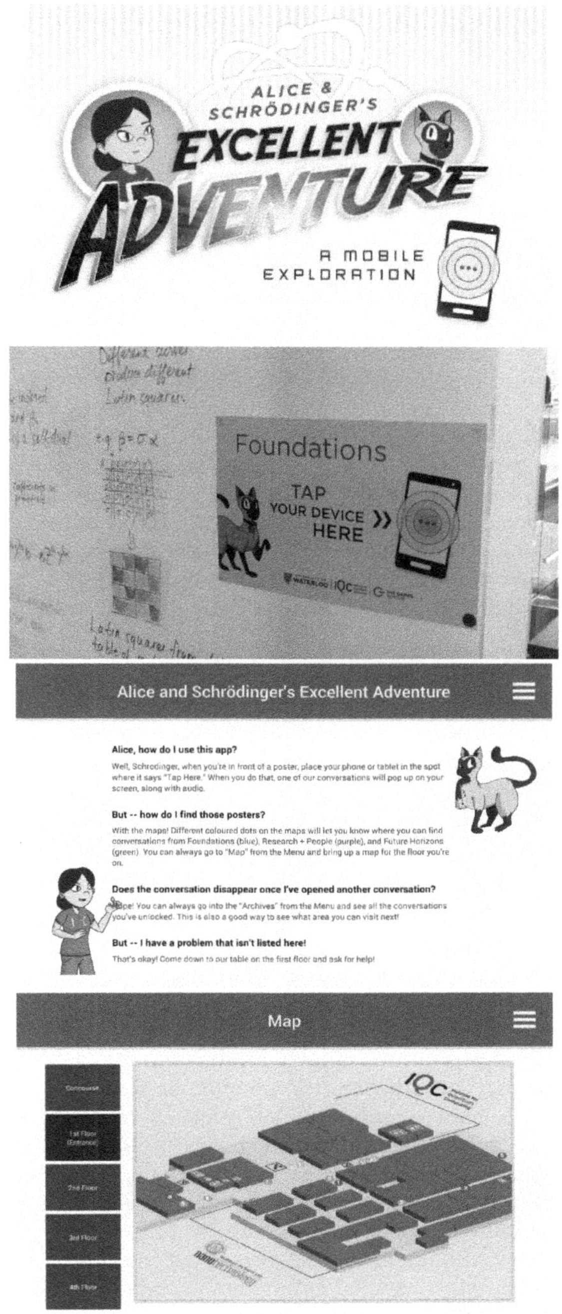

Figure 3: Alice and Schrödinger's Excellent Adventure is a locative game that encourages players to move around the IQC facilities. **(Panel 1)** Game's title screen. **(Panel 2)** Players scan NFC-enabled posters with their personal smartphone or tablet, or play the game using provided tablets attached to plinths located at key game locations. **(Panel 3)** As players move throughout the building, they reveal new conversations between a fictional IQC researcher, Alice, and her cat Schrödinger at each station. **(Panel 4)** An in-game map showing poster locations on one floor of the IQC's building.

would provide visitors an opportunity to explore the building at their own pace, and investigate their own points of interest in more depth than would be typically afforded by a guided tour. We sought to encourage visitors to explore the building in more depth, and support integration across the venue by connecting the locations with other open house events **(D5)**.

Alice and Schrödinger's key game mechanic relied on players scanning up to 34 interactive posters placed around the building with a smartphone or tablet's built-in NFC reader (Figure 3, Panel 1). As players scanned each poster, they experienced conversations between Alice, a fictional IQC researcher and her cat Schrödinger (Figure 3, Panels 2 and 3). Thus, the game leveraged a 'foraging' metaphor whereby players were free to move around the building and complete as few or as many of the locations as they wished. These locations were indicated as in-game maps (Figure 3, Panel 4), and were revealed to players as 'achievements' that were unlocked as they visited each location and experienced the associated dialog. In addition to experiencing each conversation in text, voice actors were hired to record a full version of the game, improving accessibility and engagement **(D3,4)**.

The 34 game posters were organized around 3 themes: Foundations, Research and People, and Future Horizons. The Foundations theme focused on providing information about the IQC facility; the Research and People theme focused on providing information about the people working at the IQC; and the Future Horizons theme provided in-depth details about research conducted in specific labs, and the anticipated practical implications of quantum computing. Each of the three themes had a total of 11 posters, with one 'Start' poster in the concourse.

Unlike Quantum Cats, the mobile nature of the adventure meant that logistical constraints of the IQC also needed to be considered in our game design **(D6)**. In particular, the physical design of the IQC facility prevented the use of WiFi throughout the building, and required all content to be loaded onto the devices prior to engaging on the tour. To enable players to use their own devices for the tour, we set up a local WiFi access point in the building's lobby and encouraged visitors to download a local copy of the app before exploring the building. For those individuals who wished to play the game but did not own a compatible device, we provided two additional options: 1) 20 Android Nexus 7 tablets were available to sign out from the lobby with pre-installed copies of the game, and 2) a series of plinths were installed throughout the building at key game locations with a tablet set to permanently display the associated portion of dialog. However, regardless of which device was used to play the game, the building's WiFi limitations impacted our ability to monitor progress through the tour, or to collect usage data over the course of the open house.

As with Quantum Cats, the game was developed by our team in Unity 5. However, due to restrictions on use of NFC technologies in iOS, the game was only available to Android devices.

EXPERIENCES AT THE OPEN HOUSE

In the lead-up to the open house event, we found that IQC administration staff were excited about the development of our custom applications, and the potential to provide a new, engaging, and accessible experience during the open house event. In preparation for the event, the IQC invested additional marketing resources in creating Quantum Cats-themed merchandise that would accompany and better promote the game, including t-shirts, science kits, and a series of collectible stickers that featured the four Quantum Cats. The t-shirts and science kits were available for purchase at-cost at a nearby merchandise table, while the stickers were handed out for free next to the Quantum Cats displays.

Furthermore, many resources were dedicated to promoting the event. For example, the `quantumcats.ca` domain was purchased, and a companion website was developed to enable interested visitors to further explore the game and its content.

Finally, during a soft launch event at a nearby museum approximately two weeks prior to the open house, discussions with reporters generated additional interest and a request to feature the Quantum Cats game in an upcoming article. Based on this interest a decision was made to make the Quantum Cats game available for download as an app. While this decision came late in our development process, we felt confident that we could deliver the cross-compiled applications in-time for the event, due to the flexibility afforded by Unity's development environment. Ultimately, Quantum Cats was available on Google's Play Store on the day of the open house event. It was however not available on Apple's iOS App Store until a week later due to delays in the approval process.

We now reflect on our experiences at the open house event, and in particular how the two games helped support scientific outreach activities. Due to nature of the open house, more traditional evaluation methods, such as video recordings and on-site interviews, were not available to us. Instead, our presentation of results focuses on observations and field notes, event and post-event usage and download numbers, and post-event discussions with IQC staff.

Quantum Cats

Quantum Cats was largely considered a success by IQC staff and administrators. Since the game was played on our own large displays, we were able to collect some usage data from the event. Our logs showed that over the course of the day more than 2,400 cats were 'launched' in-game, representing an average rate of more than 8 cats per minute. This level of use exceeded our expectations for the event, but matched observations by the researchers throughout the day; the three displays running identical copies of the game were a popular destination during the open house, particularly for younger children and families (Figure 4).

While we had intended for the Quantum Cats play experience to be short in duration, we noticed that many players stayed long enough to attempt most, if not all of the available levels. Many players stayed until they were able to complete each level before moving on to a new exhibit. In one case, a parent ready to leave the open house event and head home literally dragged their child away from the display.

We did not observe many usability issues with the game over the course of the event, however two issues were identified. First, the Uncertainty Cat was notoriously difficult to use, and

Figure 4: Quantum Cats was played throughout the day by visitors. In front of the displays, Quantum Cats-themed stickers were handed out to visitors at no cost.

Figure 5: An open house volunteer demonstrates how to scan an NFC-enabled poster for Alice and Schrödinger's Excellent Adventure using a guest's smartphone.

we observed that players frequently did not understand that to 'activate' the cat's ability one needed to tap the screen. This usability issue was identified as a priority in our next development iteration. Second, the IR touch frames that we used for the installation occasionally started generating spurious 'ghost' touch points. While we were unable to diagnose the issue on-site, we found that rebooting the iStick hardware resolved the issue temporarily; a procedure we followed throughout the day as needed to keep the games up and running.

In the week following the open house, Quantum Cats was downloaded more than 5,000 times on the Google Play Store, vastly exceeding the approximately 300 in attendance at the event. These downloads can be attributed in part to open house guests downloading the app while on-site or when returning home. However, more significantly the app was featured on various media such as `phys.org`, a leading scientific research and technology website with a large audience. We discuss this exposure later, in our Implications for Design section. Unfortunately, since the game did not launch immediately on Apple's iOS App Store, only 300 downloads were registered for iOS devices two weeks after the event.

Alice and Schrodinger's Excellent Adventure

As previously mentioned, poor WiFi reception within the building limited the amount of data we could collect (e.g., real-time usage) for the locative game Alice and Schrödinger's Excellent Adventure. These limitations meant that all content was downloaded to a player's tablet or smartphone prior to gameplay, and we had to rely on experience sampling over the course of the open house to determine how well the game served its purpose of providing a deeper learning experience during the event.

While we had made the application available for download prior to the event, based on our observations, however, very few visitors installed and used the application. Inspection of our Google Play account confirmed this hypothesis, and only 12 individuals installed the application to their personal device during the event. Nevertheless, 38 visitors signed out one of the tablets from the front desk, and played the pre-installed game using the borrowed tablet.

We attribute the relative shortage of players to four possible issues. First, many visitors did not understand that the posters were connected to a game, and never sought to download the application or sign out a tablet. Second, due to restrictions on NFC usage, our application was not available on the iOS platform, and was restricted to be used by individuals with an NFC-equipped Android device. This restriction likely limited users to about 60% of visitors, based on recent adoption numbers [13]. Third, we encountered a number of users who had downloaded the app to an Android device but did not have the NFC functionality enabled; in these cases we assisted those players that we could, but some may have simply given up. Finally, some individuals may not have found the self-guided tour to be engaging or worth the effort to download, or may not have had an interest in learning about the IQC.

We were, however, able to inspect the game state of the 38 players who borrowed an Android tablet on the day of the event. While some took the time to explore all 34 posters, most explored only a handful of nearby points. One usability issue that arose from a conversation with one 'Completionist' player was that the in-game numbering the posters was extremely inefficient to visit in-order (though not required), which took the determined player an extraordinary long time to complete.

REFLECTIONS ON DESIGN GOALS

We strove to balance scientific learning with creating engaging, technology-enhanced, and fun exhibits for the IQC's open house event. In developing Quantum Cats and Alice and Schrödinger's Excellent Adventure, we worked directly with IQC staff to develop a set of six design goals to inform our design process. We also carefully considered how interactive surfaces and spaces could serve the event, and placed an emphasis on developing applications that addressed the design goals identified through our initial consultations with the IQC. We now reflect on some of the tensions that arose between these design goals as we progressed through the development process, how we resolved those tensions, and the overall outcome of our design process.

Educational Value (D1) vs. Engagement (D4)

Perhaps the most immediate tension that we tried to address was the issue of creating a Quantum Cats game that was both educational **(D1)** and engaging **(D4)**. We acknowledged early on, in line with other outreach research [9, 20], that players were unlikely to spend more than a few minutes playing the game, and thus were able to focus on delivering a "superficially educational" game that aimed to introduce the player to various fundamental quantum mechanics concepts, rather than develop in-depth knowledge about one particular concept.

The choice to leverage Angry Birds' gameplay helped significantly in supporting ephemeral play sessions for a number of reasons. For example, the game remained extremely popular amongst the general public and allowed for many people to 'walk-up-and-play', overcoming existing research challenges such as interaction blindness [21]. The physics-based gameplay also helped scaffold players' advancement through each of the included quantum mechanics concepts, starting with classical Newtonian physics and then moving on to more advanced concepts such as Superposition, Quantum Tunnelling, and Uncertainty. Usage numbers collected during the event suggested that our design was engaging.

However, assessing the educational value of the game was more difficult, particularly for the 'shallow' learning experience that we targeted. In post-event discussions with IQC outreach staff there was a general agreement that the game had achieved its goals, and administration staff decided to invest additional resources into development for Quantum Cats. In particular, they extended the development team's contract and approved the creation of new artwork for the game. While specific design goals are still in development for this iteration of the software, initial discussions have focused on how additional educational content could be introduced to gameplay, particularly for those who downloaded the game to a personal device. We interpret these outcomes as a tacit acknowledgment of both the achievement of our initial goals surrounding engagement, but also that outreach is an ongoing process.

Personalization (D2) vs. Logistics (D6)

On the other hand, our work on Alice and Schrödinger's Excellent Adventure largely focused on addressing tensions between creating a personalized tour of the IQC's facilities and research **(D2)** and logistical constraints at the event **(D6)**. In particular, we identified issues around WiFi connectivity early on in our design process and worked to create a locative game that would work without internet connection. We took inspiration from personal curator devices used in museums, and incorporated an 'item-collecting' gameplay element where visitors 'unlocked' dialogs by physically visiting locations in the IQC.

However, Alice and Schrödinger's Excellent Adventure was not played by many visitors at the event; a shortfall we attribute, at least in part, to the logistics surrounding deploying games to personal devices in a setting without reliable wireless connectivity. Our observations of players at the open house event pointed to at least three contributing failure points: 1) that the application (70MB) must be downloaded in its entirety to a personal device, 2) that the NFC functionality must be enabled on the personal device, and 3) that the IQC had limited resources to distribute tablets to visitors.

In retrospect, we underestimated the degree to which these relatively small logistical issues would interfere with providing a personalized tour of the facility. We had expected a mature ecosystem on which to deploy a locative game, and that users would be familiar enough with their personal smartphones to manage NFC functionality. Instead, we found that these technically minor issues were significant barriers to visitors playing our game. While we had anticipated these barriers to some degree, and that some visitors would benefit from signing out a tablet for the tour, the IQC's resources were limited to purchasing 20 tablets to loan out during the event. We discuss the implications of this tension in the next section.

IMPLICATIONS FOR DESIGN

Our results provided an opportunity to reflect on our design process and outcomes, and discuss implications for the design of surfaces and spaces that support scientific outreach.

Can a Honey Pot Encourage Pollination?

Our design experience and review of the literature point to interactive surfaces as supporting relatively short-lived, engaging interactions. If this is the case, a number of implications for the design and value of large, interactive surfaces arise – particularly in outreach settings such as those explored in this work. For example, how can the monetary and development costs for installations such as Quantum Cats be justified as educational tools? In justifying the often high development costs, institutions such as museums and art galleries, which often are working with constrained budgets, must answer the question of whether such large display installations provide sufficient value to justify their expenses.

One potential answer to this question is engagement. The 'Honey-Pot' effect of large displays is well documented in the literature [5, 18, 20, 22], and large displays are often able to attract an audience to important content. This effect is particularly appealing for scientific outreach applications, and for example, was a critical factor in the decision to continue development for Quantum Cats. However, what remains to be shown is whether a corresponding '*pollination*' effect may also take place. That is, can nearby or associated attractions also benefit from the 'honey pot' effect surrounding a large display.

While we set out to design for this effect in our work, we were unable to perform a formal study to verify our success, and leave answering this question to future work.

Creating Interactive Spaces

We developed Alice and Schrödinger's Excellent Adventure with the hope of providing a deeper, more personal tour and learning experience at the open house event. While Unity provided comprehensive support for most aspects of game development, we found that a number of technical/logistical issues were obstacles to the development of our interactive spaces. In particular, our work points to some very practical difficulties in creating locative content that is available to all attendees, and can be integrated with surrounding exhibits. For example, even though NFC readers have been integrated with many smartphones for a number of years now, they are not consistently available on all devices, and in many cases are disabled and difficult to enable via nested or hidden settings.

We settled on NFC to determine a player's location because it provided a simple interface/interaction mechanism, could be embedded in other artefacts, and was natively supported on many Android devices. Other technologies such as QR Codes, iBeacon, or camera-based toolkits offered different combinations of trade-offs which we felt were less appropriate for this application. Our experience suggests that the technologies available to create these experiences have yet to mature, and there is an opportunity for research to provide support to developers, and perhaps more importantly, to end users.

Extending an Event's Reach

Our experience with Quantum Cats illustrates the potential of custom-built games not only to encourage learning on-site, but also after visitors had left the open house event, and to individuals who were not able to attend at all. Data from our Google Play account suggested that Quantum Cats was installed on more than 5,000 devices in the week following the event, compared to the approximately 300 guests that attended the event in-person. Even downloads from Apple's iOS App Store reached more than 300 unique devices, despite the launch being delayed by more than a week.

Enabling visitors to download their own souvenir copy of the app provided a means of making these experiences available to them after the event had taken place, an advantage not mentioned in previous research around companion apps [12], and was positively perceived by IQC administrators. However, the capability to download and install the app was only included later in our design phase due to concerns around compatibility and testing on the wide variety of expected devices, particularly within the Android ecosystem. The decision to upload versions to app stores and allow installation on personal devices was only feasible due to the flexibly afforded by Unity's development environment, and the capability to port code quickly and easily. In addition, our lead developer had the foresight to anticipate that the user interface may need to scale to different display sizes, thus only minimal revisions and testing were required for mobile devices.

Following the open house event, IQC administration expressed interest in continuing development on Quantum Cats, which we interpret as largely arising from the media interest and downloads of the game following the event. This new direction has, not surprisingly, led to different design criteria as compared to a large interactive display for a one-day event. For example, the expected duration of play, the much smaller form factor, and the further educational value the game provides; some of which are reflected in the reviews in the app stores.

CONCLUSION

We described the design, development, and deployment of two scientific outreach games for a local Institute for Quantum Computing (IQC). By combining surface technologies and gameplay mechanics, we created a touch-centric game for both large displays and personal devices. We also created a locative game designed with the intention to encourage visitors to physically explore the IQC's facilities, research, and staff. Our collaborative design process allowed us to work with stakeholders in establishing six design criteria that guided the design and development, leading to a successful deployment on the event date, and opportunities for further developments. By reflecting on our design experience, we also discussed tensions between educational value and engagement, and personalization and logistics. Finally, we discussed implications for the design of interactive surface and space applications to support scientific outreach.

Our work highlights both the potential and the challenges to the use of interactive surfaces and spaces as platforms for scientific outreach. Large interactive surfaces provide an engaging, easily understood platform on which complex materials can be presented to a lay audience, but may only be used for a few minutes at a time. On the other hand, locative games provide an opportunity for learning over longer periods, and engagement with more complex materials, but may be inhibited by logistical and hardware constraints related to personal devices. We see multi-surface and multi-space games as a promising vehicle to engage the public with scientific outreach activities, and foster lasting interests beyond a day-long event.

ACKNOWLEDGMENTS

We thank the rest of the development team for their work on the project: Mike Brown, Jagger Nast, Keith McLean, Elise Vist, Lauren Burr, Erica Robinson, Neil Randall, Agata Antkiewicz, Tobi Day-Hamilton, and Angela Olano. We also thank our financial sponsors: The Mike and Ophelia Lazaridis Institiute for Quantum Computing, and the Social Sciences and Humanities Research Council of Canada.

REFERENCES

1. Abowd, G. D., Atkeson, C. G., Hong, J., Long, S., Kooper, R., and Pinkerton, M. Cyberguide: A mobile context-aware tour guide. *Wirel. Netw. 3*, 5 (Oct. 1997), 421–433.

2. Antle, A. N., Wise, A. F., Hall, A., Nowroozi, S., Tan, P., Warren, J., Eckersley, R., and Fan, M. Youtopia: A collaborative, tangible, multi-touch, sustainability learning activity. In *Proceedings of the 12th International Conference on Interaction Design and Children*, IDC '13, ACM (New York, NY, USA, 2013), 565–568.

3. Block, F., Hammerman, J., Horn, M., Spiegel, A., Christiansen, J., Phillips, B., Diamond, J., Evans, E. M., and Shen, C. Fluid grouping: Quantifying group engagement around interactive tabletop exhibits in the wild. In *Proceedings of the 33rd Annual ACM Conference on Human Factors in Computing Systems*, CHI '15, ACM (New York, NY, USA, 2015), 867–876.

4. Blum, L., Wetzel, R., McCall, R., Oppermann, L., and Broll, W. The final timewarp: Using form and content to support player experience and presence when designing location-aware mobile augmented reality games. In *Proceedings of the Designing Interactive Systems Conference*, DIS '12, ACM (New York, NY, USA, 2012), 711–720.

5. Brignull, H., and Rogers, Y. Enticing people to interact with large public displays in public spaces. In *Proceedings of the IFIP International Conference on Human-Computer Interaction (INTERACT)* (2003), 17–24.

6. Cheung, V., Watson, D., Vermeulen, J., Hancock, M., and Scott, S. Overcoming interaction barriers in large public displays using personal devices. In *Proceedings of the Ninth ACM International Conference on Interactive Tabletops and Surfaces*, ITS '14, ACM (New York, NY, USA, 2014), 375–380.

7. Chu, J. H., Clifton, P., Harley, D., Pavao, J., and Mazalek, A. Mapping place: Supporting cultural learning through a lukasa-inspired tangible tabletop museum exhibit. In *Proceedings of the Ninth International Conference on Tangible, Embedded, and Embodied Interaction*, TEI '15, ACM (New York, NY, USA, 2015), 261–268.

8. Ciolfi, L., Avram, G., Maye, L., Dulake, N., Marshall, M. T., van Dijk, D., and McDermott, F. Articulating co-design in museums: Reflections on two participatory processes. In *Proceedings of the 19th ACM Conference on Computer-Supported Cooperative Work & Social Computing*, CSCW '16, ACM (New York, NY, USA, 2016), 13–25.

9. D'Angelo, S., Pollock, D. H., and Horn, M. Fishing with friends: Using tabletop games to raise environmental awareness in aquariums. In *Proceedings of the 14th International Conference on Interaction Design and Children*, IDC '15, ACM (New York, NY, USA, 2015), 29–38.

10. De Lange, M. From always on to always there: Locative media as playful technologies. *A. de Souza e Silva & DM Sutko (eds.), Digital cityscapes: merging digital and urban playspaces* (2009), 55–70.

11. Deterding, S., Dixon, D., Khaled, R., and Nacke, L. From game design elements to gamefulness: Defining "gamification". In *Proceedings of the 15th International Academic MindTrek Conference: Envisioning Future Media Environments*, MindTrek '11, ACM (New York, NY, USA, 2011), 9–15.

12. Economou, M., and Meintani, E. Promising beginning? evaluating museum mobile phone apps. In *Rethinking Technology in Museums 2011: Emerging experiences*, University of Limerick, Ireland (2011).

13. Epstein, Z. September data shows sharpest iOS market share drop in months as android gains. *Boy Genius Report* (2016).

14. Farman, J. Locative life: Geocaching, mobile gaming, and embodiment. *Digital Arts and Culture 2009* (2009).

15. Fosh, L., Benford, S., and Koleva, B. Supporting group coherence in a museum visit. In *Proceedings of the 19th ACM Conference on Computer-Supported Cooperative Work & Social Computing*, CSCW '16, ACM (New York, NY, USA, 2016), 1–12.

16. Ghiani, G., Paternò, F., Santoro, C., and Spano, L. D. Ubicicero: A location-aware, multi-device museum guide. *Interacting with Computers 21*, 4 (2009), 288–303.

17. Hable, R., Rössler, T., and Schuller, C. evoguide: Implementation of a tour guide support solution with multimedia and augmented-reality content. In *Proceedings of the 11th International Conference on Mobile and Ubiquitous Multimedia*, MUM '12, ACM (New York, NY, USA, 2012), 29:1–29:7.

18. Hinrichs, U., Schmidt, H., and Carpendale, S. Emdialog: Bringing information visualization into the museum. *IEEE Transactions on Visualization and Computer Graphics 14*, 6 (Nov. 2008), 1181–1188.

19. Horn, M., Atrash Leong, Z., Block, F., Diamond, J., Evans, E. M., Phillips, B., and Shen, C. Of bats and apes: An interactive tabletop game for natural history museums. In *Proceedings of the SIGCHI Conference on Human Factors in Computing Systems*, CHI '12, ACM (New York, NY, USA, 2012), 2059–2068.

20. Hornecker, E. "i don't understand it either, but it is cool"-visitor interactions with a multi-touch table in a museum. In *Horizontal Interactive Human Computer Systems, 2008. TABLETOP 2008. 3rd IEEE International Workshop on*, IEEE (2008), 113–120.

21. Ojala, T., Kostakos, V., Kukka, H., Heikkinen, T., Linden, T., Jurmu, M., Hosio, S., Kruger, F., and Zanni, D. Multipurpose interactive public displays in the wild: Three years later. *Computer 45*, 5 (May 2012), 42–49.

22. Peltonen, P., Kurvinen, E., Salovaara, A., Jacucci, G., Ilmonen, T., Evans, J., Oulasvirta, A., and Saarikko, P. It's mine, don't touch!: interactions at a large multi-touch display in a city centre. In *Proceedings of the SIGCHI Conference on Human Factors in Computing Systems*, ACM (2008), 1285–1294.

23. Tesoriero, R., Gallud, J. A., Lozano, M., and Penichet, V. M. R. A location-aware system using rfid and mobile devices for art museums. In *Autonomic and Autonomous Systems, 2008. ICAS 2008. Fourth International Conference on*, IEEE (2008), 76–81.

24. University of Waterloo. Mike & Ophelia Lazaridis Quantum-Nano Centre.

25. Wallace, M. A. *Museum branding: how to create and maintain image, loyalty, and support*. AltaMira Press, 2006.

Lightweight Capacitance-based Block System for 3D Space Interaction

Koshi Ikegawa
University of Tsukuba
1-1-1 Tennodai, Tsukuba,
Ibaraki, 305-8573 Japan
ikegawa@iplab.cs.tsukuba.ac.jp

Arika Yoshida
University of Tsukuba
1-1-1 Tennodai, Tsukuba,
Ibaraki, 305-8573 Japan
yoshida@iplab.cs.tsukuba.ac.jp

Masaya Tsuruta
University of Tsukuba
1-1-1 Tennodai, Tsukuba,
Ibaraki, 305-8573 Japan
tsuruta@iplab.cs.tsukuba.ac.jp

Buntarou Shizuki
University of Tsukuba
1-1-1 Tennodai, Tsukuba,
Ibaraki, 305-8573 Japan
shizuki@cs.tsukuba.ac.jp

Tetsuya Abe
University of Tsukuba
1-1-1 Tennodai, Tsukuba,
Ibaraki, 305-8573 Japan
abe@iplab.cs.tsukuba.ac.jp

Shin Takahashi
University of Tsukuba
1-1-1 Tennodai, Tsukuba,
Ibaraki, 305-8573 Japan
shin@cs.tsukuba.ac.jp

ISS '16, November 06-09, 2016, Niagara Falls, ON, Canada
ACM 978-1-4503-4248-3/16/11.
http://dx.doi.org/10.1145/2992154.2996772

Abstract
Capacitive Blocks is a block-shaped tangible user interface that connects the physical space to the virtual space, allowing users to build 3D models in the virtual space by handling tangible blocks. The system counts the number of stacked blocks by measuring the capacitance with a capacitance meter; the system recognizes the structure of stacked blocks arranged in a grid using the capacitance meter and generates 3D models. In this study, we improved the stability of Capacitive Blocks, presented by Yoshida et al. at UIST '15, by revising the block design: each block of the new system has a built-in capacitor. To evaluate the improvement, we conducted an experiment. The result showed a counting accuracy of 96.5%.

Author Keywords
Tangible; building block; stacking; 3D modeling; computational devices; interactive devices.

ACM Classification Keywords
H.5.2 [Information Interfaces and Presentation (e.g. HCI)]: User Interfaces - Input devices and strategies, Prototyping

Introduction
A tangible user interface (TUI) (e.g., [5, 8, 11]) allows users to operate intangible materials in the virtual space

by operating tangible objects in the physical space. Especially, a block-shaped TUI (e.g., [1, 13, 15]) allows users to build 3D models in the virtual space by handling tangible blocks such as LEGO[1] in the physical space. This can be done even without expert knowledge, which makes the block-shaped TUI a suitable 3D modeling method for beginners and children.

Block-shaped TUIs have mechanisms to recognize the position of the placed blocks and the connections among the blocks. The mechanisms can be classified into two approaches. The first approach embeds a microcontroller and a complex circuit into the blocks (e.g., [1, 13]). The second approach uses cameras around the blocks (e.g., [3, 9]); however, its setup occupies space and the camera image suffers from occlusion by the user's hand.

To explore an alternative approach, Yoshida et al. [14, 15] developed a capacitance-based block-shaped TUI called Capacitive Blocks. Their block is 3D-printed only with filaments (i.e., conductive and nonconductive ones), which forms a capacitor. Their system counts the number of stacked blocks by measuring the capacitance of the stacked blocks. However, Yoshida et al. stated that the system sometimes fails to count the number accurately when blocks are stacked over three layers because the blocks' capacitances differ from each other owing to the inaccuracy of 3D-printing and abrasion of blocks.

In this study, we improved the stability of Capacitive Blocks by revising the block design: each block of the new system has a built-in capacitor (i.e., laminated ceramic chip capacitor). This results in all the blocks having the same capacitance with high accuracy. To evaluate the improvement, we conducted an experiment. The result revealed that our system allows the blocks to be stacked up to 17 layers. In addition, we implemented a 3D modeling application that allows users to change the viewpoint and zooming level in the virtual 3D space so that they can examine the structure of stacked blocks.

[1]https://www.lego.com

Related Work
Block-shaped TUIs have been intensively researched. Among them, there was much research that embedded microcontrollers in blocks. The systems by Anderson et al. [1] and Watanabe et al. [13] recognize the structures of blocks by using embedded microcontrollers that communicate with each other. StackBlock [2] uses blocks with an embedded array of infrared (IR) LEDs and photo transistors to recognize the connection. Glauser et al. [6] embedded microcontrollers in the joints of a structure, which synchronizes to 3D models in a computer. By contrast, our block has no microcontroller but only a capacitor, which is a passive component making our blocks and block system lightweight.

Some research studies used cameras to recognize the connections of blocks in a block-shaped TUI. Baudisch et al. [3] used a table's built-in camera to recognize the height of stacked blocks, each of which has a glass fiber bundle and markers. Miller et al. [9] and Gupta et al. [7] recognized the structure of stacked blocks using a depth camera and reproduced them in a computer as a 3D model. By contrast, our system counts the number of stacked blocks by measuring the capacitance instead of using cameras, thus solving the occlusion problem.

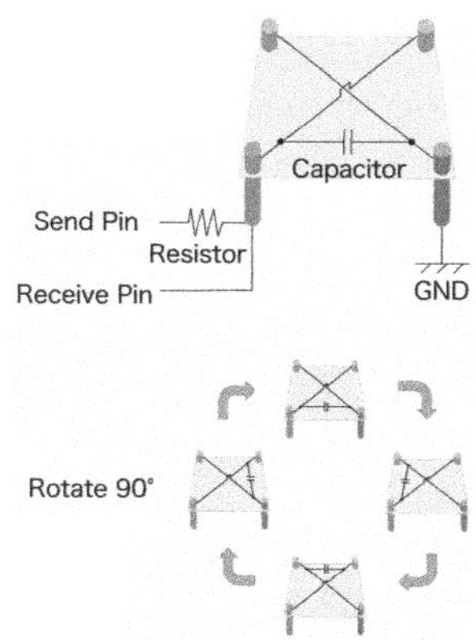

Figure 2: The wiring of our block. It can be detected even when rotated by 90°.

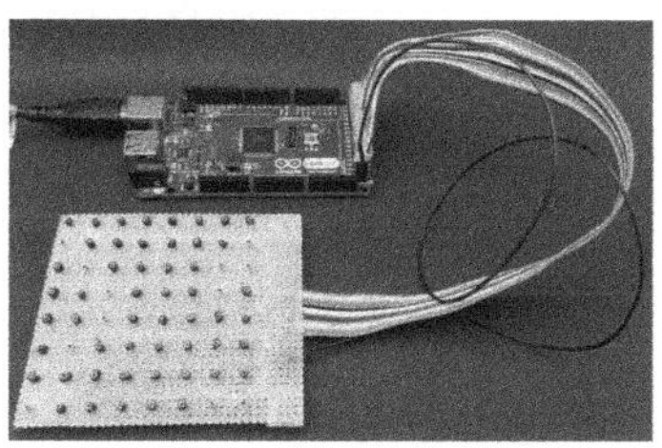

Figure 3: Construction of our sensing circuit consisting of a baseplate and a capacitance meter.

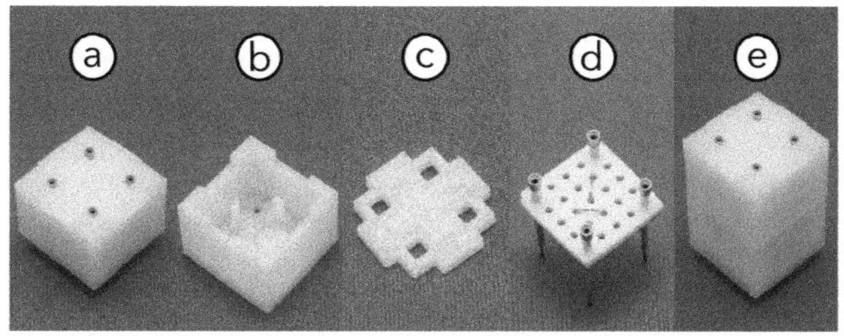

Figure 1: Construction of our blocks: a) block consisting of b-d, b) box, c) lid, d) core circuit, e) stacked blocks.

There are some research studies that detected placed objects on the basis of capacitive sensing. For example, Voelker et al. [12] realized a marker that generates touch events without power (i.e., passive) on capacitive touchscreens, which can be detected by unmodified capacitive touchscreens. On the other hand, we focused on applying capacitive sensing to count the number of stacked blocks. Chen et al. [4] developed a method that can detect coordinates and the number of stacked blocks on a touchscreen by touching blocks. However, the detection occurs only when the user touches the block because the system uses capacitance that is charged by touching. Moreover, because of the limited number of contacts and the threshold of capacitance that a touchscreen detects, the number of stacked blocks is limited. By contrast, our system can detect blocks without touching and extends the number of blocks that the user can stack.

Yoshida et al. [14, 15] developed a method for block detection without touching, using unique blocks that have capacitance themselves and capacitance meters arranged in a grid. In this paper, we reviced their blocks and found that the capacitance was accurate enough to extend the number of blocks that can be stacked.

Revised Capacitive Blocks

Block

Our blocks (Figure 1a) consist of a box (Figure 1b), lid (Figure 1c), and core circuit (Figure 1d). The circuit consists of a $10\,\mathrm{nF}$ chip capacitor (manufacturing error of 1% or less) and four pin-sockets that connect the blocks to each other (Figure 1e). We chose $10\,\mathrm{nF}$, which is much larger than the capacitance of the user's body (approximately $200\,\mathrm{pF}$ [10]), to eliminate the effect of the user's body. The wiring of the core circuit shown in Figure 2 enables two blocks to form a circuit even when they are rotated by 90°, although two pin-sockets are enough for measuring a block's capacitance (one connected to the sensing circuit and one connected to the ground). We 3D-printed the box and lid. Combining the three parts forms a $20 \times 20 \times 15\,\mathrm{mm}$ rectangular cuboid.

Sensing Circuit

We created a sensing circuit to detect the stacked blocks (Figure 3). The sensing circuit consists of a baseplate and a capacitance meter. A set of four pin-sockets forms a capacitance meter. Among the four pin-sockets, one is connected to an Arduino MEGA microcontroller board and one is grounded. The remaining two are open: they are necessary for the connection of stacked blocks. We used the Capacitive Sensing Library[2] running on Arduino MEGA to measure the capacitance. This library realizes capacitance by measuring the charging time of the capacitor.

We describe a mechanism to count stacked blocks by measuring the capacitance. As shown in Figure 4, the capacitors in stacked blocks are connected in parallel. Generally, the total capacitance of capacitors connected in parallel is the sum of all the capacitors' capacitances.

[2] `http://playground.arduino.cc/Main/CapacitiveSensor`

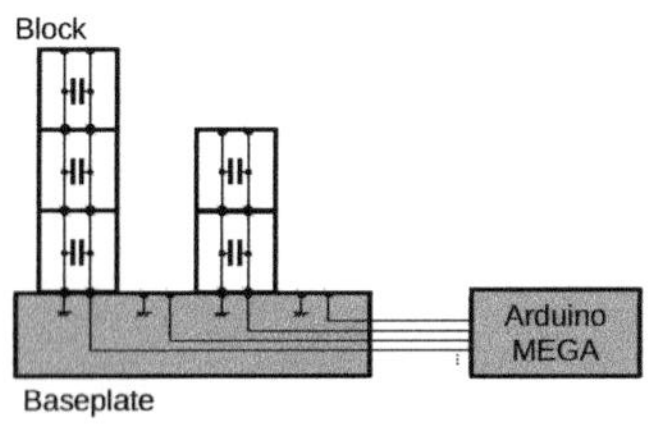

Figure 4: Schematic diagram of our circuit. The capacitors in the stacked blocks are connected in parallel.

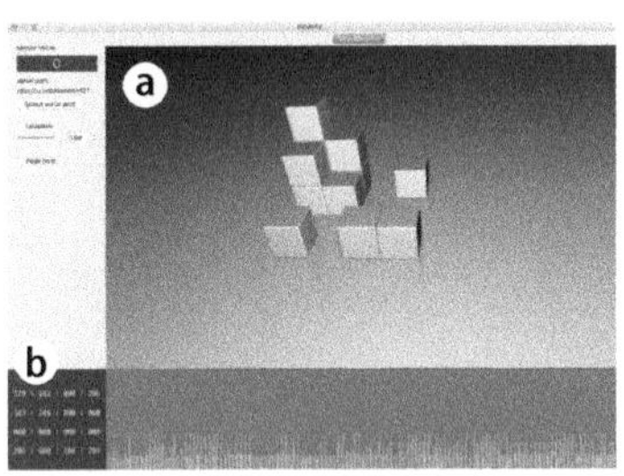

Figure 6: Screenshot of the 3D modeling application. a) A reconstructed 3D model of the blocks. b) The interface also displays the number of stacked blocks and the sensor values of each capacitance meter.

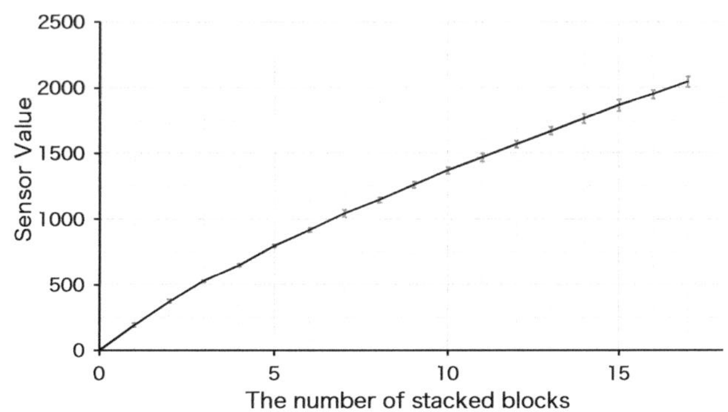

Figure 5: Sensor values of our sensing circuit for each number of stacked blocks.

Therefore, the total number of stacked blocks (n) can be calculated by $n = C/C_b$. Here, C is the measured capacitance of the stacked blocks and C_b is the capacitance of a block. However, our test result showed that the sensor value measured by the sensing circuit did not increase linearly, as shown in Figure 5 (this would be due to a characteristic of the Capacitive Sensing Library). Therefore, for the method of mapping between the sensor value and the number of stacked blocks, we adopted a quadratic function fitted to the sensor values.

3D Modeling Application

We implemented a 3D modeling application running on a PC (Figure 6) that shows the structure of stacked blocks in the virtual space and allows users to change the viewpoint and zooming level so that they can examine the model.

To reconstruct the 3D model in real time, the software reads the sensor values from the sensing circuit via a USB port, uses the quadratic function to count the stacked blocks on each grid position of the baseplate, and reconstructs a 3D model of the blocks. With this software, the user can now build a 3D model in the virtual space interactively by using blocks in the physical space. We show example 3D models that we created using the software shown in Figure 7.

Evaluation

We conducted an experiment using our 3D modeling application to examine whether the coordinates and number of stacked blocks were detected accurately.

Three participants including the authors took part in this experiment. For the task, a participant stacked blocks one by one from 0 to 17 on a specified grid position of the baseplate. After that, the participant performed this task on another grid and repeated this for all 16 grid positions. We define these 16 tasks as a session. The participants repeated the session three times. Through the experiment, we recorded the results of the detection.

The accuracy in detecting the stacked coordinates (grid positions) was 100% on average. On the other hand, the accuracy in detecting the number of stacked blocks, shown in Figure 8, was 96.5% on average up to 17 layers.

Discussion and Future Work

The experiment result showed that the accuracy in detecting the number of stacked blocks was generally high but not 100%, which was 96.5% on average up to 17 layers. This would be because the standard deviation of sensor values increases when the number of stacked blocks increases, as shown in Figure 5. Therefore, we plan to implement a capacitance meter that senses the capacitance more accurately. Specifically, we will change

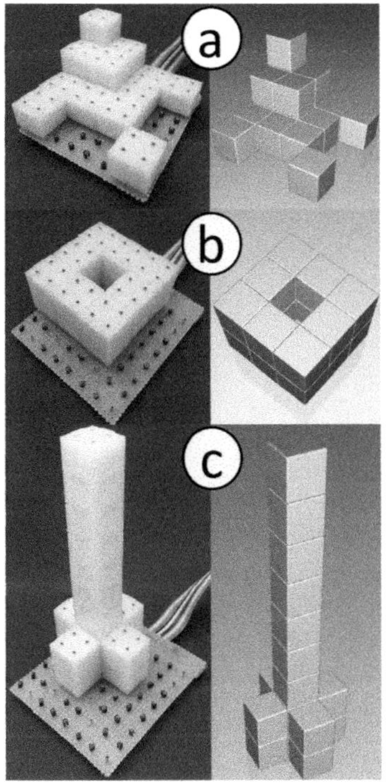

Figure 7: 3D modeling examples: a) steps, b) doughnut, c) rocket.

the capacitive meter from a software implementation using Capacitive Sensing Library to a hardware implementation.

Moreover, in our current implementation, because the pin-sockets we used were too thin and made of metal, their tips were bent frequently. As a future work, we plan to implement our blocks using thicker and robust connectors to stabilize the connection.

For the above improvement, we plan to re-evaluate the accuracy of the revised Capacitive Blocks and conduct a user study to explore how users would actually go about using these blocks.

In addition, as a step to support more realistic 3D modeling, we plan to adopt a sculpt modeling function to our system. In sculpt modeling, users first make a rough model and then smarten up the detailed parts. Because our system could be useful for making such rough models, we plan to explore such possibility by combining our system to a commercial software with a sculpt modeling function.

Conclusions

In this paper, we presented Capacitive Blocks, a block-shaped TUI that allows users to build 3D models in the virtual space by handling tangible blocks. We made Capacitive Blocks count stacked blocks by measuring the capacitance with a capacitance meter; the system recognizes the structure of stacked blocks arranged in a grid using the capacitance meter and generates 3D models. In this paper, we improved the stability of Capacitive Blocks by revising the block design over our previous work: each block of the new system has a built-in capacitor, which is a passive component. The result of an experiment to evaluate the improvement showed that the accuracy in detecting the number of stacked blocks was 96.5% up to 17 layers.

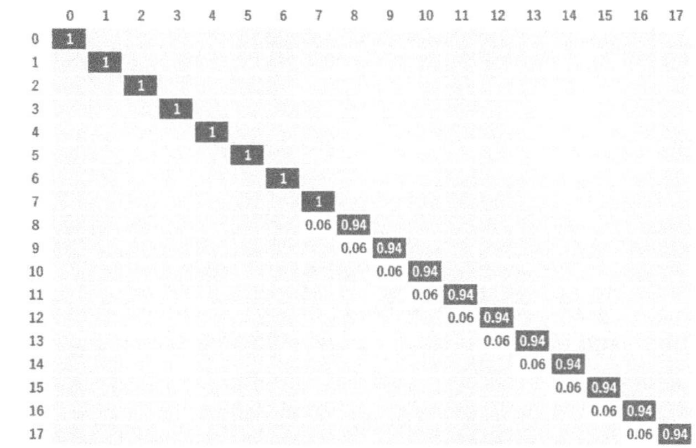

Figure 8: Accuracy of the number of stacked blocks. Vertical axis: actual count. Horizontal axis: detected count.

References

[1] Anderson, D., Frankel, J. L., Marks, J., Agarwala, A., Beardsley, P., Hodgins, J., Leigh, D., Ryall, K., Sullivan, E., and Yedidia, J. S. Tangible Interaction + Graphical Interpretation: A new approach to 3D modeling. In *Proc. of SIGGRAPH '00* (2000), 393–402.

[2] Ando, M., Itoh, Y., Hosoi, T., Takashima, K., Nakajima, K., and Kitamura, Y. StackBlock: Block-shaped interface for flexible stacking. In *Proc. of UIST '14 Adjunct* (2014), 41–42.

[3] Baudisch, P., Becker, T., and Rudeck, F. Lumino: Tangible blocks for tabletop computers based on glass fiber bundles. In *Proc. of CHI '10* (2010), 1165–1174.

[4] Chan, L., Müller, S., Roudaut, A., and Baudisch, P. CapStones and ZebraWidgets: Sensing stacks of building blocks, dials and sliders on capacitive touch screens. In *Proc. of CHI '12* (2012), 2189–2192.

[5] Fitzmaurice, G. W., Ishii, H., and Buxton, W. A. S. Bricks: Laying the foundations for graspable user interfaces. In *Proc. of CHI '95* (1995), 442–449.

[6] Glauser, O., Ma, W.-C., Panozzo, D., Jacobson, A., Hilliges, O., and Sorkine-Hornung, O. Rig Animation with a Tangible and Modular Input Device. *ACM Trans. Graph. 35*, 4 (2016), 144:1–144:11.

[7] Gupta, A., Fox, D., Curless, B., and Cohen, M. DuploTrack: A real-time system for authoring and guiding duplo block assembly. In *Proc. of UIST '12* (2012), 389–402.

[8] Ishii, H., and Ullmer, B. Tangible Bits: Towards seamless interfaces between people, bits and atoms. In *Proc. of CHI '97* (1997), 234–241.

[9] Miller, A., White, B., Charbonneau, E., Kanzler, Z., and Jr., J. J. L. Interactive 3D model acquisition and tracking of building block structures. *IEEE TVCG 18*, 4 (2012), 651–659.

[10] Ott, H. W. *Electromagnetic Compatibility Engineering*. Wiley, 2009.

[11] Ullmer, B., and Ishii, H. Emerging Frameworks for Tangible User Interfaces. *IBM Systems Journal 39*, 3-4 (2000), 915–931.

[12] Voelker, S., Nakajima, K., Thoresen, C., Itoh, Y., Øvergård, K. I., and Borchers, J. PUCs: Detecting transparent, passive untouched capacitive widgets on unmodified multi-touch displays. In *Proc. of UIST '13 Adjunct* (2013), 1–2.

[13] Watanabe, R., Itoh, Y., Asai, M., Kitamura, Y., Kishino, F., and Kikuchi, H. The Soul of ActiveCube: Implementing a flexible, multimodal, three-dimensional spatial tangible interface. *Computers in Entertainment 2*, 4 (2004), 15–15.

[14] Yoshida, A., Shizuki, B., and Tanaka, J. Capacitive Blocks: a block system based on capacitance. In *WISS '15* (2015), 1–6. in Japanese.

[15] Yoshida, A., Shizuki, B., and Tanaka, J. Capacitive Blocks: A block system that connects the physical with the virtual using changes of capacitance. In *Proc. of UIST '15 Adjunct* (2015), 85–86.

A Distributed Framework for Location-oriented Motion-based Interactive Public Installations and Games

Ali Arya
Carleton University
1125 Colonel By Drive,
Ottawa, ON, K1S5B6 Canada
arya@carleton.ca

Ryan Bottriell
Carleton University
1125 Colonel By Drive,
Ottawa, ON, K1S5B6 Canada
ryanbottriell@live.ca

ISS '16, November 06-09, 2016, Niagara Falls, ON, Canada
ACM 978-1-4503-4248-3/16/11.
http://dx.doi.org/10.1145/2992154.2996773

Abstract
This paper proposes a framework for developing and accessing distributed multiplayer motion-based interactive applications. The framework provides an API for programmers to easily access users' motion data through a Kinect sensor, connect to a network of stations with similar features, and share the motion data. Using this framework, developers can create multiplayer motion-based games or other apps, and share them. The framework allows users to select both apps to play and the stations with which to play. The location-oriented nature of the framework (choosing station vs. user) makes it particularly useful for public installations. We demonstrate the functionalities of our proposed framework with a sample game.

Author Keywords
Motion; Network; API; Game

ACM Classification Keywords
H.5.2 [User Interfaces]: Input Devices and Strategies; I.3.2 [Graphics Systems]: Distributed/network graphics; I.3.6 [Methodology and Techniques]: Interaction Techniques; I.6.8 [Types of Simulation]: Gaming

Figure 1: Two Stations Running RSF-based Game

Introduction

Hardware and software advances since late 90's and particularly in the last decade, have made significant changes in digital art and entertainment [13]. Among these changes are multiplayer online games, natural user interfaces, and interactive public installations [3, 16].

The increased availability and reliability of high-speed Internet connections have made it possible for game players to have more engaging experiences through interaction with others. On the other hand, starting with Nintendo Wii, and continued with Microsoft Kinect, Leap Motion, and other devices, natural user interfaces not only allow a more intuitive way of interacting with computer systems but also can provide health benefits by encouraging active play [2]. This is demonstrated particularly in interactive public installations such as those in libraries, airports, museums, or significant outdoor urban locations. Such installations frequently utilize large displays, and motion tracking and other natural interaction methods instead of traditional mouse and keyboard, in order to provide flexible mobility and visibility [5,13,14]. These installations are also increasingly relying on network connectivity by mechanisms such as using data collected from the Internet or communicating with users through a mobile device [18].

Many software technologies, middleware, and tools have been developed to help create and share apps with network connection, multiplayer features, and access to various sensor devices [1, 6, 19]. While these products provide frameworks that simplify application development, they lack certain features that can be very beneficial particularly for public installations.

The primary motivation of our research is the notion of "location-oriented" game, i.e. one where players are identified as the location they log in from rather than who they are. This is particularly useful for public installations that want to promote certain locations such as libraries, airports, etc, so the user identifies as Ottawa-Airport-Arrivals or Beijing-Central-Library. On the other hand, most games are either multiplayer or use natural interfaces such as motion and gesture. Very few communicate the users' natural input over the network. Those that do are usually specific games and do not provide a general Application Programming Interface (API) to be used easily by others. Such API can provide a standard way to communicate users' motion data (or other natural input) between a network of computers with motion-tracking ability, and identify such computers with which user can play. This in turn helps establish a developer community and provide more options (games), and so attract more users.

Based on the above motivations, and with the goal of simplifying the development of games for interactive public installations, we propose the Reactive Spaces Framework (RSF). RSF relies on "stations" (i.e. computers with motion sensor and usually a large screen to allow users' free movement), a group of apps, and a client-server structure that allows connecting stations, sharing motion data, and selecting stations and apps. A typical example of using RSF is a series of public installations, e.g. in libraries, where players can stop by, choose a game and another station with active player, and then play a game by moving in front of a large screen (Figure 1). Using RSF, developers can create applications that connect to other stations, read the local and remote motion data, and implement any game logic in popular programming languages and environments. The users can access any RSF station, choose from available apps, and select the station(s) to play with from the list of currently active stations. While particularly suitable for public installations, RSF can be used for any other distributed application scenario, or even local applications that require motion input. In the following sections, we briefly review the related work, the general structure of RSF, some implementation notes, and concluding remarks.

Related Work

Many interactive and public installations use the advances in connectivity, mobility, and natural interfaces. Weißker et al. [18] have recently proposed a general framework that allows large number of users to interact with a public display through their mobile devices. Onna: Past, Present, and Future [5] is an interactive art installation that also uses mobile plus natural interaction to personalize visitor's experience. Wall Relief [14] is another example that uses upper body motion tracking to interact with a TaiChi-themed game on wall display.

Many frameworks and middleware systems have been proposed for multiplayer games [1, 6]. While successful in providing different architectures for multiplayer games, these approaches are not aimed at sharing motion data. On the other hand, individual games and applications have been developed that use motion tracking, force detection, and other natural inputs while connecting to remote users to implement games like tug of war over network [8, 10, 11, 19]. Motion tracking using 3D cameras, particularly Kinect, have been used in multiple distributed applications. Parajuli, et al. [12] have used Kinect in a distributed monitoring application. Tang and Wang [17] used Kinect in a multiplayer ball-passing game. To the best of our knowledge though, none of these projects have resulted in a general purpose API for sharing motion data over network or allowing each app/station to find and connect to other similar stations and apps.

While majority of interactive applications and games are developed as stand-alone platform-dependent programs, the advances in browser and web technologies have resulted in the idea of platform-independent browser-based web apps and games, mostly based on HTML5 [4, 7]. Since JavaScript, the most common programming tool for HTML5, does not directly support access to devices such as Kinect, stand-alone local programs are usually used in addition to the web app [15]. Hou, et al. [9] have used this approach to develop a browser-based distributed game using Kinect input. While they suggest a new approach that allows development of cross-platform distributed games with motion data, they have only developed a sample game and no actual framework.

Proposed Framework

The Reactive Spaces Framework (RSF) is designed to help develop games (or other apps) for interactive public installations that can work in a distributed fashion, i.e. with remote players, and use motion input. It is based on the following fundamental concepts:

- An interactive public installation can be considered a location-oriented system, where the main identifier in a network is the location, not the user.
- An interactive public installation can benefit from natural motion as input (and potentially a large display/work area) to allow flexibility in movement and number of users.

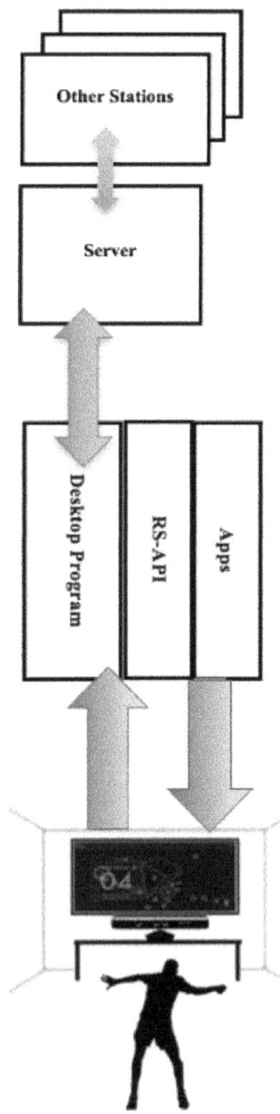

Figure 2: General Structure of RFS-based Systems

- An API can help establish a developer community and provide more apps/games to attract more users.

Location-Oriented vs. User-Oriented
Public installations are available to random groups of users and have a strong association with location. While the user of such installation may want to connect to another particular user, it is more likely that designers and users will be interested in connection to other similar locations, for example a network of airports or libraries. RSF provides an interface for programmers and users to select other RSF stations to connect to and play with. These locations are listed on a server, as described later. Groups of stations may set up their own server and start their own RSF-based network.

Natural Interaction
While many public kiosks use traditional interfaces, public installations generally occupy a bigger space and a more free-style and natural interface seems more appropriate for them. This is particularly relevant when using large screens (projected or TV) where users stand farther and so will not be able to use mouse and keyboard. Also the public nature will make audio-based interaction less effective. RSF uses body motion and gestures as the primary input mechanism. In theory, various methods can be used for motion tracking but currently this is limited to Kinect sensor. This choice allows the system to work with more than one local user.

Simple App Creation and Distribution
RSF relies on a easy-to-use API that exposes the following basic functionality:

- Connecting to a network
- Identifying available stations and apps
- Accessing local and remote user motion (number of users and type of data depends on the sensor)
- Uploading new apps
- Basic RSF user interface

The apps are developed in platform-independent formats such as JavaScript while each station will need a platform dependent RSF base code that provides the above functionality to the apps.

Framework Implementation
Figure 2 shows the general structure of RSF-based systems. The system consists of a desktop program, a server, and a series of apps created using RS-API.

The desktop program is platform dependent, will manage a socket connection to the server, and will expose a local websocket connection over which to exchange data with the apps. It will also be responsible for passing messages to and from the server and apps as well as reading from and passing Kinect input data. Our current implementation is on Windows stations and the desktop program is a .NET application written in C# and using Kinect SDK. Future extensions could use other operating systems and devices, as long as the program follows the RSF communication protocol. Figure 3 shows an example screen from the desktop program.

RS-API is a software library that allows apps to communicate with desktop program. It will deal with connecting to, sending data to, and receiving data from the desktop program. It will also define data types specific to the API (such as Kinect motion data, skeleton, station, etc) as well as providing utility

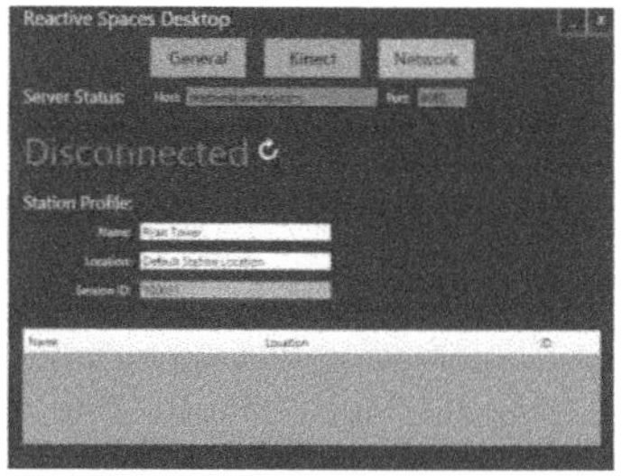

Figure 3: Station Setting in Desktop Program

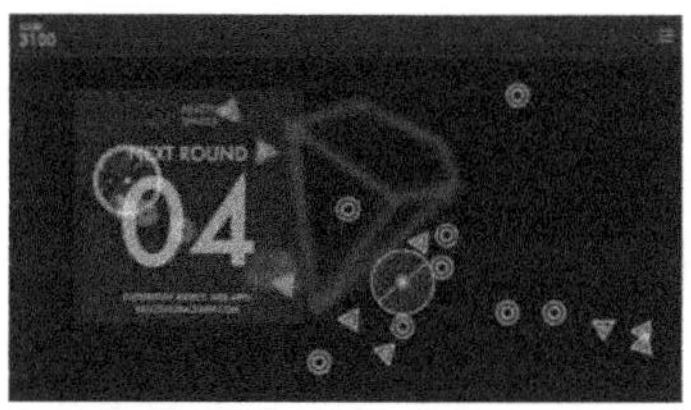

Figure 4. Sample Game Screen. The player uses body movement to grab moving shapes. Remote player's movement, on the other hand, can affect the movement of the shapes. So every player's moves has two effects: grabbing a shape and interfering with other player. Different shapes have different values and properties (speed and difficulty of capturing).

functions related to those data types. RS-API is currently available only in JavaScript.

The main part of RS-API is the RS class which includes the following items:

- Settings: URL, Port, Number of Players, etc
- Data Members: Station, Players, Messenger, etc
- Methods: Connect, Activate, DrawSkeleton, etc
- Types: Skeleton, Station, Message, etc

The server manages connections between all running instances of the desktop program, and matches them into sessions based on app types. The server will also be responsible for passing messages between appropriate clients in each session. It is currently implemented using Node.js on a Linux server. The main functionality includes:

- Accept and manage connections from client apps
- Match clients into sessions based on games/apps
- Pass messages between clients
- Notify clients of changes in their session

All messages in the system will take the form of JSON objects. They include a message type and actual data. A web browser with web socket support is required.

Each set of related stations who want to form a network (such as groups of universities, libraries, airports, community centres, etc) will require to set up a server and install the desktop program on each station. The apps can be installed locally, or uploaded to a server and downloaded from it by each station. Either way, the desktop program will list all the available apps. Our test implementation included only one server and a few stations on university campus.

To demonstrate the features of Reactive Spaces Framework, we have developed a sample game (Figure 4). The game involves multiple stations participating and playing against each other. It is an arcade-style game where players aim to reach a high score by collecting shapes. The game uses the API to provide input via the Microsoft Kinect. It also uses the API to share data between peers. The moving shapes are influenced by the other running stations.

Discussion and Conclusion

While RSF can be used for any distributed (or even local) app that uses motion input, it is motivated by the idea of establishing a community to develop "location-oriented" games for public installations, through connecting to different "stations" and sharing motion data. RSF is a work in progress, and as a result has not been publicly evaluated yet. It is available for download (http://rsapi.ryanbottriell.com) and we intend to create a developer community, and through that evaluate and improve the framework. Future extensions to this project include but are not limited to adding personal communication (text, voice, video), supporting other platform-independent options such as Unity3D, support for other motion-tracking devices, adding location-dependent features, and including more game development tools to simplify app creation. Uploading and sharing RSF apps currently have no security measures. Streamlining and securing this process will be another major direction of future work.

References

1. Balan, R.K., Ebling, M., Castro, P. and Misra, A., 2005, November. Matrix: Adaptive middleware for distributed multiplayer games. In International Conference on Distributed Systems Platforms and Open Distributed Processing.

2. Biddiss, E. and Irwin, J., 2010. Active video games to promote physical activity in children and youth: a systematic review. Archives of pediatrics & adolescent medicine, 164(7), pp.664-672.
3. Bozgeyikli, G., Bozgeyikli, E. and İşler, V., 2013. Introducing tangible objects into motion controlled gameplay using Microsoft® Kinect TM. Computer Animation and Virtual Worlds.
4. Chen, B., Xu, Z., 2011, A framework for browser-based Multiplayer Online Games using WebGL and WebSocket. In International Conference on Multimedia Technology (ICMT)
5. D'Amico, G., Del Bimbo, A., Ferracani, A., Landucci, L. and Pezzatini, D., 2015. Onna project: a natural interaction installation and mobile solution for cultural heritage. In Built Heritage: Monitoring Conservation Management
6. Diot, C. and Gautier, L., 1999. A distributed architecture for multiplayer interactive applications on the Internet. IEEE network, 13(4), pp.6-15.
7. Feng, K., Wang, H., Lian, J., Liu, W., Jia, H., 2013, Design of 3D browser-based multiplayer online game based on HTML5. Software Technology
8. Harfield, A., Jormanainen, I. and Shujau, H., 2009, June. First steps in distributed tangible technologies: a virtual tug of war. In Proceedings of the 8th International Conference on Interaction Design and Children (pp. 178-181). ACM.
9. Hou, W., Sun, Z., Li, T. and Zhao, L., 2014, November. A Framework for Browser-Based Multiplayer Online Interaction by Kinect and HTML5--with "Flying Kite" as a Case Example. In International Conference on Human Centered Computing (pp. 415-426). Springer International Publishing.
10. Laine, T.H. and Sedano, C.I., 2015. Distributed Pervasive Worlds: The Case of Exergames. Educational Technology & Society, 18(1), pp.50-66.
11. Mueller, F., Agamanolis, S. and Picard, R., 2003, April. Exertion interfaces: sports over a distance for social bonding and fun. In Proceedings of the SIGCHI conference on Human factors in computing systems (pp. 561-568). ACM.
12. Parajuli, M., Tran, D., Ma, W., et al., 2012, Senior health monitoring using Kinect. In: The Fourth International Conference on Communications and Electronics (ICCE), pp. 309–312. IEEE Press, Hanoi
13. Paul, C., 2015. Digital art. London: Thames & Hudson.
14. Profita, H., Brinkman, D., Lim, A. and Smith, R., 2015, January. Wall Relief: A Health-Oriented Interactive Installation for the Workplace Environment. In Proceedings of the Ninth International Conference on Tangible, Embedded, and Embodied Interaction (pp. 607-611). ACM.
15. Pterneas, V. 2013. Kinect and HTML5 using WebSockets and Canvas. http://www.codeproject.com/Articles/309306/Kinect-HTML5-using-WebSockets-and-Canvas
16. Simanowski, R., 2011. Digital art and meaning. Reading Kinetic Poetry, Text Machines, Mapping Art and Interactive Installations.
17. Tang, T.Y. and Wang, Y., 2015, February. Alone Together: Multiplayer Online Ball Passing using Kinect-An Experimental Study. In 18th ACM Conference Companion on Computer Supported Cooperative Work & Social Computing
18. Weißker, T., Berst, A., Hartmann, J. and Echtler, F., 2016, May. MMM Ball: Showcasing the Massive Mobile Multiuser Framework. In CHI-16 Extended Abstracts on Human Factors in Computing Systems
19. Yao, L., Dasgupta, S., Cheng, N., Spingarn-Koff, J., Rudakevych, O. and Ishii, H., 2011, May. Multi-jump: jump roping over distances. In CHI'11 Extended Abstracts on Human Factors in Computing Systems

Presenting Business Data: Challenges during Board Meetings in Multi-Display Environments

Tom Horak
Interactive Media Lab
Technische Universität Dresden
Dresden, Germany
horakt@acm.org

Ulrike Kister
Interactive Media Lab
Technische Universität Dresden
Dresden, Germany
ukister@acm.org

Raimund Dachselt
Interactive Media Lab
Technische Universität Dresden
Dresden, Germany
dachselt@acm.org

ISS '16, November 06-09, 2016, Niagara Falls, ON, Canada
ACM 978-1-4503-4248-3/16/11.
http://dx.doi.org/10.1145/2992154.2996774

Abstract
In this work, we discuss important challenges arising when presenting business data in board meetings. After firstly considering the specific characteristic of board meetings, we have identified challenges concerning the following four topics emerging from the multi-display setup of (digital) boardrooms as well as the social situation in those board meetings: Control Presentations (Interaction), Content Presentation (Visualization), Discussion with Audience (Communication), and Remote Presence. Focusing on selected challenges, we propose first ideas how existing HCI research can help to tackle those challenges and thus help to improve efficiency of board meetings.

Author Keywords
Presentation; Business Data; Multi-Display Environments

ACM Classification Keywords
H.5.m [Information interfaces and presentation (e.g., HCI)]: Miscellaneous.

Introduction
Board meetings are a very important component in managing large companies, regularly evaluating, e.g., the current progress, target compliance, or competitiveness of specific projects, departments, or the company as a whole. Additionally to supervising tasks, the board of directors

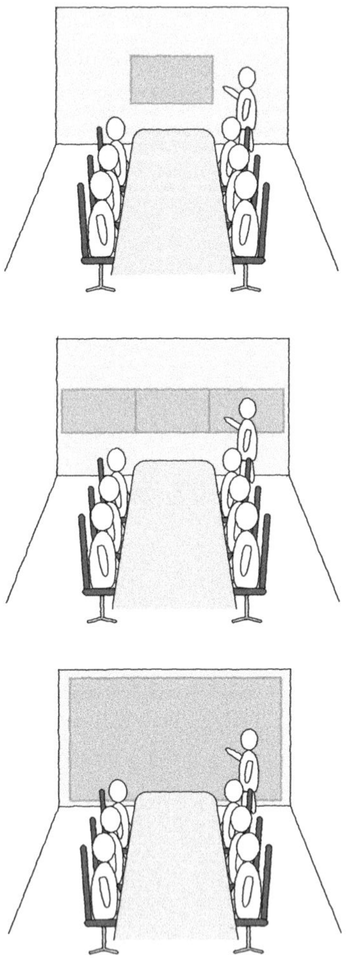

Figure 1: Different display setups in a boardroom ranging from a TV-sized display to a display wall.

also has to decide on managerial issues [11]. During the meetings, the *C-suite* (e.g., CEO, CFO) or representatives of individual departments report on current business data. Usually, this involves a presentation of numbers, measures taken, and existing challenges or possibilities.

Owing to the importance of the board meetings for companies, there is a special need to properly present data and being able to efficiently identify the best decisions. Although there is already research in HCI on, e.g., multi-display environments in general [1], handling visualization in ordinary meetings [10], or supporting the presenter [2], board meetings have unique characteristics and incorporate further HCI challenges that need to be considered. By identifying and analyzing these challenges, we plan to support the development of efficient systems that incorporate principles of natural interaction and user-centered interfaces. In the following, we will describe the challenges and categorize them into four major topics.

HCI Challenges in Board Meetings

Before focusing on the specific challenges, we want to stress the unique circumstances and resulting social situation that characterize the board meeting scenario. Firstly, board meetings are regular, but non-frequent meetings that need to condense major activities and future plans of a company into a very strict agenda. Additionally, the presenter has to face the pressure to report in the best possible way as the consequences can be far-reaching: jobs, budget, powers and also his own position can rely on the presentation. This also means that the audience is very invested as well as critical and has itself experiences in managerial tasks [11].

Depending on the company, the board can differ in size mostly ranging between eight and 30 directors. Since large companies have branches around the world, the board members may speak different languages and may take part by video-conference or telepresence. The boardrooms used often incorporate a long table that directors sit around (Figure 1 and Figure 2) and a display to present information or to show remote participants. These displays can be a projection, one or multiple TV-sized displays, or even a complete display wall. Furthermore, the table may be equipped with additional smaller displays for each member (Figure 3), thus forming a complex multi-display environment.

Figure 2: Image of a boardroom with a large display on one side (right), ©*reynermedia*[1].

Control Presentations (Interaction)
As a key feature for a successful report, the presenter has to be able to control the distribution of the content as well as to control the presentation in general—especially when using large, wall-sized displays or multiple displays. The presenter has to balance between making use of the

[1](CC BY 2.0) *Empty Boardroom*. https://flic.kr/p/hT9nnA

Figure 3: Additional displays for audience: large displays on the sides, built-in monitors or personal tablets.

available display space and reducing unnecessary walking to different display areas.

As a result, already the preparation of the presentation brings additional challenges as the space on the different displays has to be taken into account for content arrangement. This can be even more difficult when the presenter has no previous access or incomplete knowledge of the display setup. Hence, the presenter needs a well-equipped tool to define where each content item should be shown, possibly making content distribution flexible for the presentation. Furthermore, content is often provided by other colleagues and subordinates, extracting the data and preparing a story for the presentation (c.f. [8]) in groups to guarantee the best possible outcome where the presenter might not always be involved.

Depending on the software used (e.g., Powerpoint, Prezi), presentations can be linear or non-linear resulting in different ways of navigating through the presentation. There also exists proprietary software of companies for easily accessing business data (e.g., SAP Digital Boardroom) that can support both linear and non-linear presentation paths. Especially in non-linear presentations it can be challenging for the presenters to remember the current position as well as the next topics of their presentation. Thus, similar to presentations in other scenarios, the presenters may require a preview of the next content, their own presentation notes, the current time, or schedule of their talk.

Further, the presenter may use additional portable hardware (e.g., wireless presenter), fixed hardware (e.g., PC/laptop), or the capabilities of the display (e.g., touch) to control the presentation steps like loading subsequent content, highlighting specific aspects, or transferring parts to other displays. It's a challenge to support managing these tasks during presentation with minimal effort. For instance, whereas touch enables a more explicit interaction (i.e., enhanced comprehensibility for presenter and audience), it may require more movements, can cause occlusions, or can even not supported by the display. Also, additional laptops cannot be used in some cases due to a complex technical setup. This can also involve technicians sitting in a side room and starting the presentation software, thus limiting controllability for the presenter.

Content Presentation (Visualization)
A further challenge in boardroom presentations lies in the readability of data and content. Due to the number of people involved, the distance between presented data and audience member may be very large, so that individual data points cannot be properly identified on the larger display. Additional displays, either larger ones to the sides or individual displays for each participant (Figure 3), can help presenting the actual content. However, this further increases the number of attention switches required: focus switches between the presenter (i.e., facial expressions and words, gestures and pointing), content on the large display referenced by the presenter or otherwise visible (e.g., overview), the personal display (i.e., details), or the telepresence of remote collaborators (Figure 4).

While text is an essential part of presentations, it has been shown that visualizations improve attention, agreement, and recall of business strategies [5]. However, a challenging aspect to consider is the type and complexity of visualization used for presentation to allow accurate insights. Visualizations in board meetings have to be designed for domain experts, not data analysis experts. Explanations of visual mappings should not be required to understand the message of the visualization. An essential factor for this is using business communication

Figure 4: Participants need to switch focus, e.g., between the presenter, the content on the large display, remote participants, or their personal device/display.

standards (e.g., IBCS[2]), however, challenges regarding large display space and distances are not in their focus.

Furthermore, data of different aspects of a company are often interconnected and decisions have to be evaluated based on these connections, so that large display spaces are required to show individual aspects of these complex processes. The challenge here is to find appropriate smart visualization techniques and use coordinated views to present the data while also supporting interactions with these visualizations in the context of presentation, e.g., showing details or different time layers. Furthermore, dynamic and flexible visualizing that describe past events or even present predictions to indicate the consequences of certain decisions are an additional challenge.

Discussion with Audience (Communication)
While listening to the presentation, the board members might interrupt to ask questions and discuss aspects of the presented data. It is a challenge to design flexible ways to allow each audience member to annotate content in this large presentation space in preparation of a question and to manage and organize their personal annotations. Furthermore, members require the ability to point to a specific data item visible to each board member when referring to specific data during discussion. Similarly, the presenter might want to highlight certain data points on the individual displays of each audience member when making a point.

As participants also ask for more detailed data [11], the presenter might need to adapt his presentation triggering either previously prepared back-up slides or manipulate visualizations to load additional information, e.g., a previous year or another sales area with which to compare data. Providing this additional information live is essential as the board members are almost always required to make decisions in this very meeting and thus to avoid a deferral.

Remote Presence
In many cases not all board members are able to attend in person but via video-conference or telepresence. In addition to general challenges of such systems [6], there are several boardroom-specific aspects: The placement of the remote participants' avatar or video may differ between the presentation and discussion part: For the latter one, it is beneficial to use a telepresence system providing an immersive experience, i.e., enhancing the impression the participant is sitting at the table [12]. However, this restricts the visibility of the previously presented content. During the presentation the content is central, thus the avatar can be placed less prominently or even hidden. In both cases, attention switches for the other board members are required. Of course, complexity increases as more remote participants collaborate.

Vice versa, it can also be challenging to determine what content is displayed to remote participants and how it can be controlled. Similar to co-located participants, remote participants can switch attention between presented content, the presenter, or other participants. Depending on their used setup (e.g., desktop, other boardroom), it may not be possible to display all things at the same time resulting in manual switches between views. These switches could be triggered by remote participants or the presenter (similar to personal devices of all participants).

Tackling the Challenges

The presented challenges incorporate many aspects that can be addressed with knowledge from existing research in business communication, human-computer interaction as

[2] http://www.ibcs-a.org

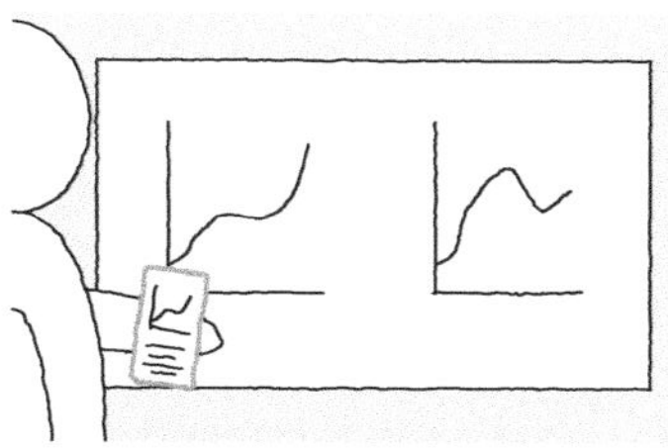

Figure 5: Showing hints and notes for the presenter on a smartphone.

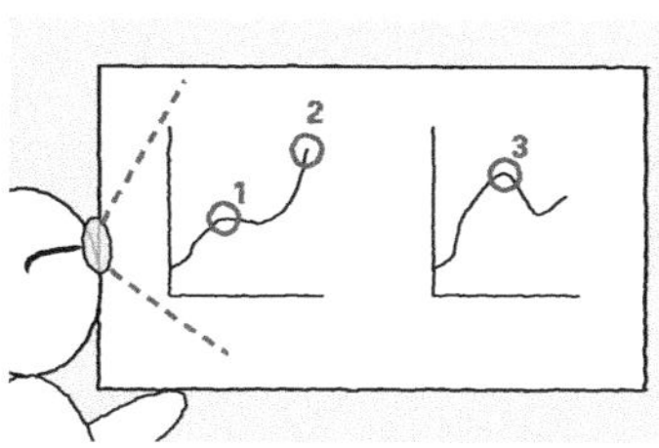

Figure 6: Providing enhanced in-place hints and notes through AR glasses.

well as information visualization. Especially focusing on HCI, we want to indicate a few selected possibilities to tackle the challenges based on work about multi-display environments and cross-device interaction.

Additional notes, hints, and previews for the presenter
Using research of interaction on large displays and multi-device environment as a basis (e.g., [1, 7]), we propose using an additional smartphone (or smartwatch) to guide the presenter in his presentation. As smartphones and even watches are wide-spread and the presenter will very likely own such a device, these can be used to allow showing hints and notes as well as triggering special functions like highlighting, moving content or loading next slides (Figure 5; c.f. [2]). To allow better use of both hands and freedom of gesturing during the presentation the device can also be attached to the presenter's wrist or arm [13]. Taking this further, augmented reality (AR) glasses can provide hints, the order of points to discuss, and next slide information in-place on the actual content (only visible to the presenter; Figure 6).

Recognition of content in focus and transfer to audience
Especially in larger boards with enhanced distance between participants and the presenter, the challenge of controlling which part of the presentation is transferred to audience members' displays (both co-located or remote) is another interesting point to address. We suggest using additional sensors, e.g., a mobile's location in the presenter's pocket, Kinect data, or simply the current touch on the touch-enabled large display, to detect the presenter's current focus of the presentation. Based on this focus, the system could automatically decide what content needs to be transferred, e.g., the current data graph, multiple graphs, or the whole page (Figure 7). In this way, the need to prepare in advance which part of the content is transferred is reduced. This allows flexible presentation paths adapted to previous discussions.

Reducing awareness switches
As previously discussed, attention switches are an issue for audience members (Figure 4). By transferring the content in focus to the mobile device in front of the audience, we enhance the readability of the currently focused data but increase the need of attention switches at the same time (i.e., between presenter and content). To reduce attention switches again, we support the notion of integrating multiple views into one by merging the presenter and his motions into the presentation (Figure 7; similar to [9]). This may be of even greater importance for remote participants where integrating the presenter or even a present member in discussion into the content can help focus the conversation and reduce necessary management of views. However, focusing on the personal device instead of the presenter for a longer time could be felt as impolite for co-located participants.

Integrating the audience's mobile devices
To provide audience better insights, we suggest connecting the audience devices to the system and thereby allowing access to presentation content and data (Figure 8). As a result the audience can freely annotate (draw and write) and explore content on their devices (interaction similar to, e.g., [3]). Further, we propose allowing the audience to push annotations to the large display for question clarification and discussion (using known cross-device concepts, e.g., [4]). This might require management of user roles (e.g., presenter and audience) as well as system states (e.g., presentation or discussion) to restrict the audience's access, making sure the presenter stays in control and has the ability to focus the audience on the current presentation.

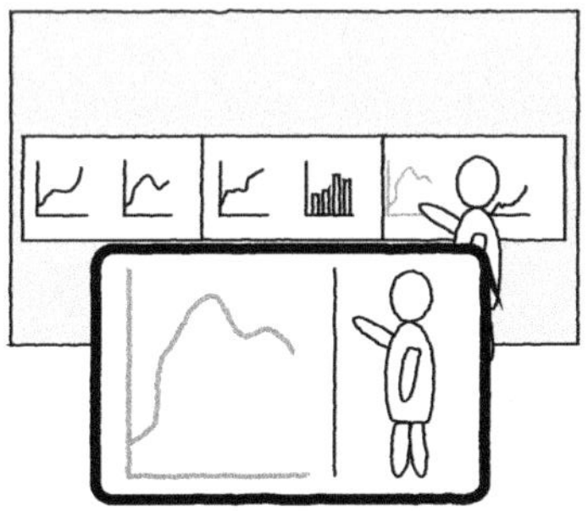

Figure 7: Transferring parts of the presentation onto the participants mobile device and embedding the presenter and his motions.

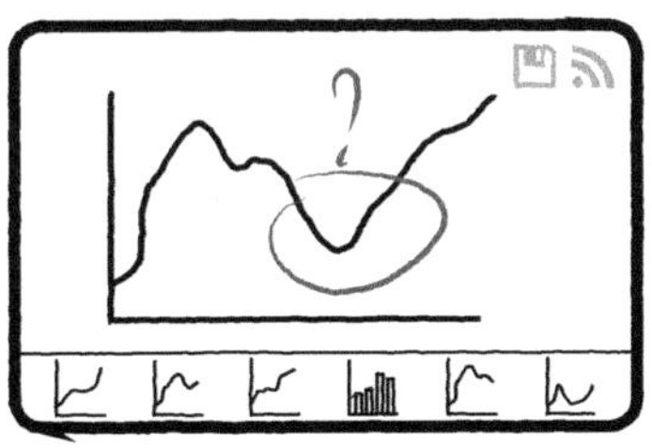

Figure 8: Providing access to presentation content on the participants mobile device with annotation support.

Conclusion

We identified four topics of challenges arising in the specific scenario of presenting business data in board meetings. By considering these challenges, the development of presentation systems as well as the design of boardroom setups could be guided and thus enhance the experience for both presenter and audience as well as efficiency of board meetings in general. Incorporating existing research, we outlined different concepts how the scenario can be further supported in future with both additional hardware and unchanged setup. Of course, these are only a few selected possibilities how HCI research can help address the challenges, however, we are confident that these serve as a foundation for future discussion and research.

References

[1] Boring, S., Baur, D., Butz, A., Gustafson, S., and Baudisch, P. Touch projector: mobile interaction through video. In *Proc. CHI '10*, ACM (2010), 2287–2296.

[2] Bragdon, A., DeLine, R., Hinckley, K., and Morris, M. R. Code space: Touch + air gesture hybrid interactions for supporting developer meetings. In *Proc. ITS '11*, ACM (2011), 212–221.

[3] Drucker, S. M., Fisher, D., Sadana, R., Herron, J., and others. TouchViz: a case study comparing two interfaces for data analytics on tablets. In *Proc. CHI 2013*, ACM (2013), 2301–2310.

[4] Hamilton, P., and Wigdor, D. J. Conductor: enabling and understanding cross-device interaction. In *Proc. CHI 2014*, ACM (2014), 2773–2782.

[5] Kernbach, S., Eppler, M. J., and Bresciani, S. The use of visualization in the communication of business strategies an experimental evaluation. *International Journal of Business Communication 52*, 2 (2015), 164–187.

[6] Larsen, S. Videoconferencing in business meetings: An affordance perspective. *International Journal of e-Collaboration 11*, 4 (10 2015), 64–79.

[7] Ledo, D., Greenberg, S., Marquardt, N., and Boring, S. Proxemic-aware controls: Designing remote controls for ubiquitous computing ecologies. In *Proc. CHI '15*, ACM (2015), 187–198.

[8] Lee, B., Riche, N. H., Isenberg, P., and Carpendale, S. More than telling a story: Transforming data into visually shared stories. *IEEE Computer Graphics and Applications 35*, 5 (Sept 2015), 84–90.

[9] Matulic, F., Engeln, L., Träger, C., and Dachselt, R. Embodied interactions for novel immersive presentational experiences. In *Proc. CHI EA '16*, ACM (2016), 1713–1720.

[10] Radloff, A., Tominski, C., Nocke, T., and Schumann, H. Supporting presentation and discussion of visualization results in smart meeting rooms. *The Visual Computer 31*, 9 (2015), 1271–1286.

[11] Schwartz-Ziv, M., and Weisbach, M. S. What do boards really do? evidence from minutes of board meetings. *Journal of Financial Economics 108*, 2 (5 2013), 349–366.

[12] Standaert, W., Muylle, S., and Basu, A. An empirical study of the effectiveness of telepresence as a business meeting mode. *Information Technology and Management* (4 2015), 1–17.

[13] von Zadow, U., Büschel, W., Langner, R., and Dachselt, R. Sleed: Using a sleeve display to interact with touch-sensitive display walls. In *Proc. ITS '14*, ACM (2014), 129–138.

Combining Mobile, Tangible and Virtual World Platforms to Support Participatory Campus Planning

Haley Coppins
School of Professional
Communication
Ryerson University
hcoppins@ryerson.ca

Tudor Tibu
Synaesthetic Media Lab
Ryerson University
tudor.tibu@ryerson.ca

Jack Shen-Kuen Chang
Synaesthetic Media Lab
Ryerson University
College of Technology
Purdue University
JackSKChang@gmail.com

Ali Mazalek
Synaesthetic Media Lab
Ryerson University
mazalek@ryerson.ca

Frauke Zeller
School of Professional
Communication
Ryerson University
fzeller@ryerson.ca

ISS '16, November 06-09, 2016, Niagara Falls, ON, Canada
ACM 978-1-4503-4248-3/16/11.
http://dx.doi.org/10.1145/2992154.2996775

Abstract
Urban planning, and campus planning in particular, can benefit greatly from technology that fosters and leverages collaborative, participatory planning which includes all affected stakeholders. Interactive surfaces such as tabletops and walls, and spaces such as 3D environments are examples of such technologies. Our research aims to explore and assess the appropriateness and effectiveness of such technologies in participatory campus planning. We present here a prototype system that combines the tangible and multi-touch surfaces with a virtual world platform to provide a participatory planning approach for campus development projects.

Author Keywords
Participatory urban planning; interactive tabletops; virtual environments; tangible interaction; multitouch interaction; mobile technologies.

ACM Classification Keywords
H.5.2 [Information Interfaces and Presentation]: User Interfaces—*Input devices and strategies*, *interaction styles*; H.5.3 [Information Interfaces and Presentation]: Group and Organization Interfaces—*Collaborative computing*.

Introduction

Our research explores participatory urban planning with 3D and tangible media. We present a prototype system that uses an interactive tabletop with tangible and multitouch interaction in combination with a virtual world platform to create a more complete participatory planning approach for campus development projects, using Ryerson University in Toronto, Canada, as a first practical example.

Universities in densely populated urban areas often face severe spatial problems in their expansion and evolving processes. Ryerson University, an urban metropolitan university is also facing challenges and thus is exploring means of expanding its physical capacity, while at once constrained by geography. Its physical location in the busy downtown Toronto core creates considerable challenges in meeting the needs of its users, both in optimizing navigation throughout the whole of the campus and in adding sufficient physical space to account for classroom, lab space, and residential requirements for a university of its size. Thus, space is a particular challenge for Ryerson: specifically, the inability to grow "out" as it is courted on four sides by dense urban development. As a result, Ryerson is looking into ways that space can be added— by growing vertically, creating spaces that serve a number of purposes, and placing people first.

In expanding and growing Ryerson's campus, participatory planning will be imperative. Participatory planning follows the idea to let relevant stakeholders—from business owners, city planners, to residents—participate in the planning and shaping of urban environments. Successful collaborative planning promotes trust-building and educative endeavours, employs unbiased and inclusive processes, and uses methods that empower local citizens and facilitate growth [7].

This research project develops a participatory approach for the future planning of Ryerson's campus and its social ecology. The project merges mobile computing and social media, 3D virtual environments, and tangible, tabletop interaction technologies. The central question driving our research is: how can we leverage mobile, virtual and tangible media technologies to motivate community participation in campus planning?

We aim to make a difference in two ways: firstly, by using a holistic social ecology approach that includes communication, safety, health and ecological aspects; secondly, applying a synergetic model that combines novel tools and interaction techniques for community urban planning consisting of mobile and media, tangible and tabletop interactions, and virtual worlds.

Related Work

This literature review provides an overview of the methods that have contributed to our prototype: traditional participatory planning, virtual worlds, interactive tabletops and mobile participation.

Traditional Participatory Planning Methods

Traditional methods of participatory planning have been challenging for planners as they require the physical presence of participants [4] and dominant voices often control the conversation [6]. As a result of these difficulties, neighbourhood groups have traditionally been inactive in planning processes [1]. The emergence and establishment of mobile phones, improved GIS data, and integration of virtual environments and interactive tabletops have challenged the shortcomings of traditional methods [4].

Virtual Worlds

Virtual world platforms developed by massively multiplayer online games (MMOGs) such as Second Life, allow users to both participate in, and visualize an environment. These virtual three-dimensional (3D) public spaces promote a new form of civic engagement. Unlike traditional workshops that require the physical presence of participants, virtual world platforms allow participants to take part in workshops remotely [3]. They permit anyone with access to the internet to log-in and join other participants in virtual environments that may be models of their communities.

For example, researchers at Tufts University in Acton, Massachusetts used Second Life to increase public understanding of their plan [3]. This "Master Planning" involved the use of Second Life to develop computer visualizations of various locations. Similarly, researchers at McMaster University in Hamilton, Ontario, are using macGRID— a 3D simulation research platform that uses avatar virtual worlds and mixed reality systems— to encourage community participation in the planning and re-design of Hamilton [8]. This platform is used for a number of purposes, such as demonstrating proposed developments.

Virtual world platforms are beneficial for a number of reasons. Because they are constructed in three dimensions, they allow average residents to comprehend and engage with virtual worlds and their constructed environments— something that in the past could only be done with physical models of cities and 3D perspective drawings [3]. Virtual world platforms are particularly attractive to a young demographic of technologically savvy individuals who enjoy gaming platforms. As a result, these platforms become useful for engaging students, many of whom make up the Ryerson community.

Interactive Tabletops

Interactive tabletops offer a new mode that allows planners to explore design ideas and implement complicated projects, while also including the community in the planning process. Recently, there has been a shift in urban planning to the implementation of interactive and tangible interfaces [9]. These interfaces are beneficial in a number of ways. They facilitate active and interactive participation by allowing participants to express their suggestions and better understand the implications of different housing types and other infrastructure. They also act as a mediator by allowing participants to discuss planning by placing objects, modifying and commenting, rather than in a confrontational face-to-face manner.

For example, a participatory workshop involving an urban planning project of the Caserne Bossut in the city of Pontoise used an interactive tabletop to facilitate discussion surrounding new construction that was replacing 90% of the existing buildings [9]. By placing objects such as roads to decide on future locations and by using a sketching tool, participants used the interactive tabletop to illustrate their ideas and develop their own vision of their community. Another example was the Augmented Urban Planning Workbench, which integrated 2D drawings, 3D physical models, and digital simulation into a single tabletop information space in order to support the urban design process [5]. The system was used in an urban design class at MIT's

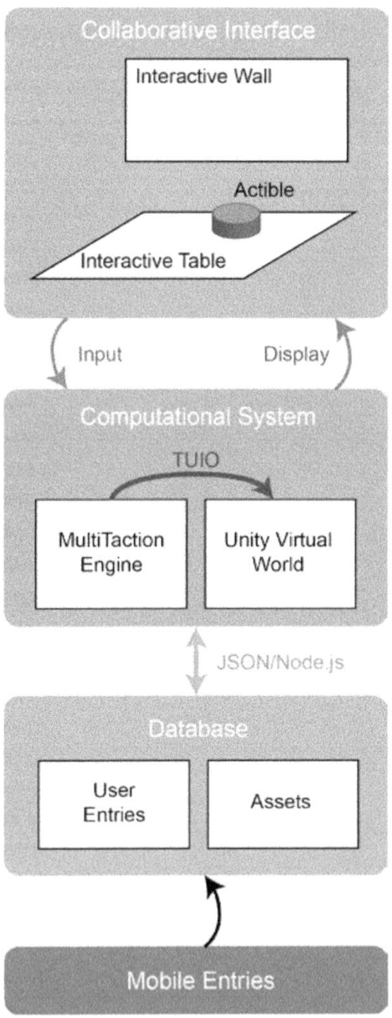

Figure 1: Diagram showing the setup of the prototype system.

School of Architecture and Planning. Although the planning process in this case did not involve community members, student designers found that the layering of physical and digital representations supported the creation of more informed designs.

Mobile Participation
Mobile participation has included the integration of web-based participation into mobile phones, which further aims to use mobile devices to broaden citizen participation through the connection to other users and offers the ability to generate and share information [4]. This method demonstrates sufficient promise, largely due to the wide proliferation of smartphones and ownership across social groups, thus increasing the chance that participants from a wide range of demographics have the opportunity to participate equally in the planning process. Mobile apps are also far cheaper to develop than computer programs. Their various functions allow participants to simply walk around a neighbourhood, take pictures, and record comments without having to worry about the technological details of the app [6]. Crowdsourcing, then, of proposed urban or campus changes and improvements, may be highly conducive in the university environment, as it is expected that the user groups have a correspondingly higher rate of cellphone ownership and therefore ability to participate.

Mobile apps are easily appropriated by certain groups because they require little training [6]. This allows citizens with little spatial and planning background to get involved. Rather than relying on the physical presence of participants at traditional meetings, mobile apps also allow more freedom on the part of the user by allowing them to participate remotely. Therefore, mobile participation represents a major advancement, largely because it gives individuals the chance to discuss locations while physically there and saves time and money by not needing a professional facilitator [6].

While each of these methods offers sufficient promise, they also have certain limitations. For example, using technologies for participatory planning can result in quantitative data that over simplifies findings and loses the detailed and insightful opinions of community members [2]. Our work aims to overcome these limitations and support the campus planning process through a combination of methods, integrating mobile data collection with collaborative interaction through interactive tabletops and virtual worlds — allowing for both quantitative and qualitative data to be collected.

Participatory Campus Planning System

Our prototype system combines mobile participation to collect feedback on a university campus, with a 3D virtual environment displayed on an interactive tabletop and wall displays to allow community members to collaboratively re-design the campus space (see Fig. 1).

Community members first use a web-based form on their mobile devices to submit their comments about the campus, relating to categories such as safety, accessibility, green space, etc. For each comment, they must provide a brief description of the problem they wish to address. These comments can be entered as users navigate the campus space, with the location determined using GPS and geolocation, and are then stored in a database and visualized within the 3D virtual environment. For example, a student walking home late at night might enter the comment "This corner is too dark. I don't feel safe." and flag it as a

Figure 2: Users interacting with the interactive tabletop and wall display. The tabletop shows a map view, while the wall display shows a perspective view of the urban space.

Figure 3: A user interacting with the wall display. The flags in the virtual space show comments and suggestions

Figure 4: An actible being used by a user on the tabletop surface.

safety concern. Their comment then appears as a small red flag within the virtual environment at the location where it was set. The flags in the virtual environment are colour-coded based on the category (e.g., red for safety, green for green space, etc.). In future, the mobile application will present a top-down map view of the campus with the user's location indicated by a marker. A menu will be available for users to flag areas that require attention and submit suggestions for changes. Users will also be able to submit pictures along with their comments.

Community members can then interact with the system through the tabletop and wall display setup (see Fig. 2). The tabletop surface shows a top-down map view of the urban space being re-designed, while the wall display shows a 3D perspective view of the same space (see Fig. 3). The flags showing community members' comments can be seen in both views. Users interact with the system through multi-touch interactions on the tabletop and wall displays, as well as through the manipulation of tangible objects on the tabletop. Two kinds of tangible objects are used for the tabletop interaction: a passive tangible object shaped like a camera controls the view shown on the vertical display, while a set of active tangible objects (called Actibles) are used to select and place assets in the virtual environment (see Fig. 4). The Actibles provide a small integrated display and can be used both on and off the tabletop surface. Users first browse a menu of virtual assets (e.g., lamp posts, benches, trees, etc.) on the Actible, make a selection, and then place the Actible on the table to position the asset within the virtual environment. The Actibles allow flexible binding of tangible objects to many different assets. This helps to avoid the need for large numbers of dedicated asset tangibles, while also minimizing the tabletop screen real estate used for asset selection. Multitouch interactions on the tabletop and wall displays are also used to select and edit the virtual assets, e.g. to scale items or fine-tune their positioning.

The prototype system makes use of MultiTaction Ultra-Thin Bezel Cells (MT553UTB) for the tabletop and wall displays, which are able to interpret touch and fiducial marker input (MultiTaction Codice markers). The Actibles are hand-held devices that employ LG G smartwatches as their core, contained within a 3D printed custom case that includes additional hardware to support interactions such as stacking, rotating, shaking, and bumping. The virtual environment is implemented using the Unity 3D game engine and all Unity related events are coded using C#. Both the table and wall show the same instance of the Unity environment by using two separate in-game cameras that capture the scene from different angles. Touch and fiducial input data is interpreted using a Unity Asset called TouchScript. Communication of data between the Actibles and the Unity instance is done through a JavaScript node server using Socket.IO data. A Unity asset called Socket.IO for Unity was used to convert the JSON package data from the socket server into data that is compliable with the Unity engine.

Future Work

The prototype system will be first presented at an open-house event at Ryerson University in October 2016. This venue will be used to recruit participants from various parts of the Ryerson community (e.g., students, faculty, staff) for a focus group study on the prototype. Our aim is to gain insights about the system design and to gauge its usefulness and applicability to the continuous re-design of Ryerson's campus environment. We have scheduled three focus group sessions of about 12 to 15 participants each. During each session, the prototype will be introduced and participants will be invited to use it. During and after the interaction, participants will be asked to discuss their thoughts and opinions about the prototype and provide feedback to researchers.

Conclusion
With our approach we aim to assist Ryerson university planners in integrating a participatory campus planning approach that involves all stakeholders in the process. By making use of a holistic participatory planning design process, we hope to allow users to not only discuss their visions, but also execute them. We also hope this system will reach more people, attracting students and other stakeholders who otherwise may not have been involved in planning. More generally, we believe this approach has the potential to help urban and campus planning by developing a process that combines the advantages of each method, while accounting for their challenges. In doing so, we aim to provide an approach for planners to follow when attempting to integrate a diverse range of participants into planning.

Acknowledgements
This project has been supported in part by the Ryerson Faculty of Communication Design's Creative Innovation Fund, the Social Sciences and Humanities Research Council, the Canada Foundation for Innovation, and the Ontario Ministry for Research and Innovation.

References
[1] Afzalan, N., & Evans-Cowley, J. (2015). Planning and social media: Facebook for planning at the neighbourhood scale. *Planning Practice & Research, 30*(3), 270-285.

[2] Dennis, S. F. (2006). Prospects for qualitative GIS at the intersection of youth development and participatory urban planning. *Environment and Planning A*, 38(11), 2039-2054. doi:10.1068/a3861

[3] Evans-Cowley, J., & Hollander, J. (2010). The new generation of public participation: Internet-based participation tools. *Planning Practice & Research, 25*(3), 397-408.

[4] Ertiö, T.P. (2015). Participatory Apps for Urban Planning—Space for Improvement. *Planning Practice & Research, 30*(3), 303-321.

[5] Ishii, H., Ben-Joseph, E., Underkoffler, J., Yeung, L., Chak, D., Kanji, Z., & Piper, B. (2002). Augmented urban planning workbench: Overlaying drawings, physical models and digital simulation. In *Proc. 1st international symposium on mixed and augmented reality* (p. 203). IEEE Computer Society.

[6] Jones, P., Layard, A., Speed, C., & Lorne, C. (2015). MapLocal: use of smartphones for crowdsourced planning. *Planning, Practice & Research, 30*(3), 322-336.

[7] Sirianni, C. (2007) Neighbourhood planning as collaborative democratic design. *Journal of the American Planning Association, 73*(4), 373-387. doi:10.1080/01944360708978519.

[8] Smith, D. H., Zeller, F., Eyles, J., Eyles, E., Dwyer, L. J., and Smith, H. (2016). Using 3D social worlds to enhance participatory urban planning. *Social Media & Society Conference*, 11-13 July, London, UK.

[9] Wagner, I., Basile, M., Ehrenstrasser, L., Maquil, V., Terrin, J.J., & Wagner, M. (2009). Supporting community engagement in the city: urban planning in the MR-tent. In *Proc. fourth international conference on communities and technologies* (pp.185-194). ACM.

Pose Estimation for a Cuboid with Regular Patterns in an Interactive Assembly-support Projection System

Yuya Obinata
FUJITSU LABORATORIES LTD.
Kanagawa, JAPAN
obinata.yuya@jp.fujitsu.com

Yusaku Fujii
FUJITSU LABORATORIES LTD.
Kanagawa, JAPAN
fujii.yusaku@jp.fujitsu.com

Genta Suzuki
FUJITSU LABORATORIES LTD.
Kanagawa, JAPAN
suzuki.genta@jp.fujitsu.com

Taichi Murase
FUJITSU LABORATORIES LTD.
Kanagawa, JAPAN
murase.taichi@jp.fujitsu.com

ISS '16, November 06-09, 2016, Niagara Falls, ON, Canada
ACM 978-1-4503-4248-3/16/11.
http://dx.doi.org/10.1145/2992154.2996776

Abstract
Workers in factories often have to stop an operation to confirm various assembly instructions, for example, component numbers and/or the location to place a component; this is particularly the case with exceptional or inexperienced operations in a mixed-flow production line. These types of operation interruptions are one of the most significant factors linked to a decreasing productivity rate. In this study, we propose a novel method that estimates, in real time, the pose of a manufactured product on a production line without any augmented reality (AR) markers. This system projects instructions and/or component positions to help a worker process production information quickly. In this paper, we produced assembly-support system experimentally using projection-based AR. We develop a highly accurate object pose estimation method for manufactured products. The result of this experimental evaluation indicates that the combination of ORB and our algorithm can detect an object's pose more precisely than ORB only. We also develop an algorithm that is robust even if a part of an object is occluded by a worker's hand. We consider that this system helps workers understand instructions and component positions without the need to stop and confirm

assembly instructions, thus enabling more efficient operation of tasks.

Author Keywords
Augmented reality; Assembly-support system;

ACM Classification Keywords
H.5.1 Multimedia Information Systems: Artificial, augmented, and virtual realities; H.5.2 User Interface: Prototyping; I.4.8 Scene Analysis: Object recognition;

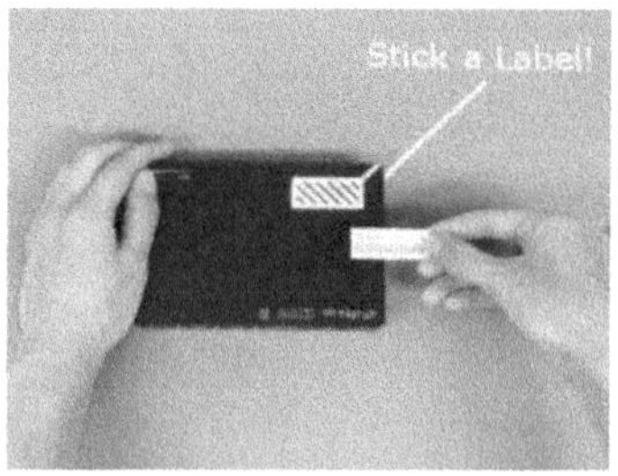

Figure 1. Projecting operating position and assembly instructions.

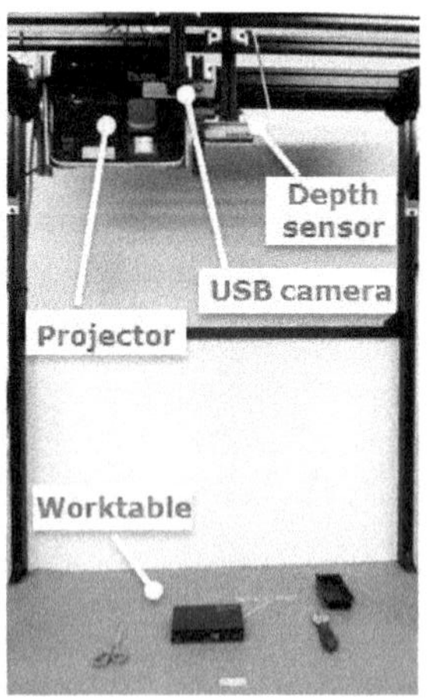

Figure 2. Assembly-support system.

Introduction
Many factories have mixed-flow production lines for operating custom tasks according to specific customer requests. Custom tasks are tasks that modify mass-produced products based on specific customer requests, for example, sticking labels printed with serial numbers or product control numbers and inserting cables into manufactured products at specific points. During the work flows of these custom tasks, workers often have to stop and read assembly instructions to confirm specific details, for example, the position of labels or cables. Moreover, these instructions can be different for each customer request even if the workers are operating the tasks onto different populations of the same manufactured products. This means that the workers have to interrupt their tasks and confirm every position each time; this can take a considerable amount of time. This creates a serious problem since the workers are not operating efficiently, thus factory production efficiency levels will decrease.

Our goal is that workers can operate their tasks efficiently. We focused on a workplace and installed a projector to project various instructions, for example, where to place objects, what to do, and how to do it etc., onto real objects. This was designed to help the workers understand how to operate their tasks intuitively and quickly without interrupting the task in progress. In our previous paper, we proposed a projector–camera system that helps workers understand how to move their hands intuitively by projecting hand movements of experts with the real size and at normal speed onto real objects [7]. The system users tended to copy the hand movements of the experts and this improved user awareness. In this paper, we propose a method that estimates object pose (in the case of manufactured products) to create an interactive assembly-support system that projects instructions and positions onto real objects in accordance with its pose to help the workers understand these quickly without having to refer to assembly instruction (see Figure 1). We consider that the system can help workers operate their tasks more efficiently because the workers do not have to interrupt their tasks to confirm specific instructions and positioning. Object pose estimations method using augmented reality (AR) markers already exist. We focused on using markerless object pose estimation method as it was not realistic to stick a unique AR marker onto each object precisely. Therefore, we decided using feature-based object pose estimation method. Through in situ observation in a factory we found that many manufactured products (e.g., a desktop personal computer and a network router) are almost cuboid in shape with a regular pattern (e.g., a hole for dissipating heat). The problem is that the accuracy of estimating an object's pose decreases when the object has a simple and geometrically symmetrical shape, such as a cuboid, and similar local features are extracted from a regular pattern in the object image. We also found that objects could be occluded by a worker's hand while they were operating tasks. This caused a problem in detecting the object. We thus focused on overcoming these problems to create an interactive assembly-support system.

This paper introduces (1) an interactive assembly-support system using projection-based AR for improving workers' efficiency levels, (2) an algorithm for estimating object pose, where similar local features are extracted and the object is almost cuboid in shape, and (3) an algorithm for detecting an object even if this object is occluded by a worker's hand.

Related Work

Many people have researched work-support system using projection-based AR. Funk et al. [1] developed a picking support system, which used a depth sensor to highlight the area where component parts are located. Sato et al. [6] developed a cooking support system, which detected the location of utensils using a depth sensor and projected cooking instructions onto a kitchen counter. These systems can detect the space that an object is in or locate an object. However, these systems do not detect an object's pose.

Many people have also researched markerless object pose estimation method; this includes feature-based object pose estimation method, using color camera, depth sensor, or both of them. SIFT [3] and ORB (oriented FAST and rotated BRIEF) [5] detect keypoints, extract local features from pixels in a smoothed image patch, and create correspondences between extracted local features and local features in template image to estimate object pose using color camera. Kobori et al. [2] used a SIFT keypoint detector and local descriptor to estimate a mobile robot's pose. SHOT [8] extracts local features from 3D coordinates of k-nearest neighbors of the keypoint and creates correspondences between local features extracted and local features in template 3D shape using depth sensor. CSHOT [9] extracts local features that combine a feature of histograms of shape-related measurements together with a feature of texture-related measurements from spherical support around keypoint and creates correspondences between local features extracted and local features in template colored 3D shape using color camera and depth sensor. However, these algorithms cannot distinguish between keypoints that similar local features are extracted from in one image and/or shape. Therefore, it could be difficult to estimate manufactured product's pose because manufactured products have a simple and geometrically symmetrical shape, such as a cuboid, with regular pattern, many keypoints that similar local features are extracted from are detected, and thus incorrect correspondences are created.

An interactive assembly-support system using projection-based AR

Figure 2 shows the proposed interactive assembly-support system using projection-based AR to improve workers' efficiency rates. The system includes a USB camera, a depth sensor, and a projector to estimate an object's pose on a worktable and to project any instructions and operating positions onto it in accordance with its pose. These devices are calibrated to transform their images into coordinates.

We explain how to project an operating position onto object according to its pose in this system as follows.

1. Obtain a color image and depth image from a USB camera and a depth sensor.

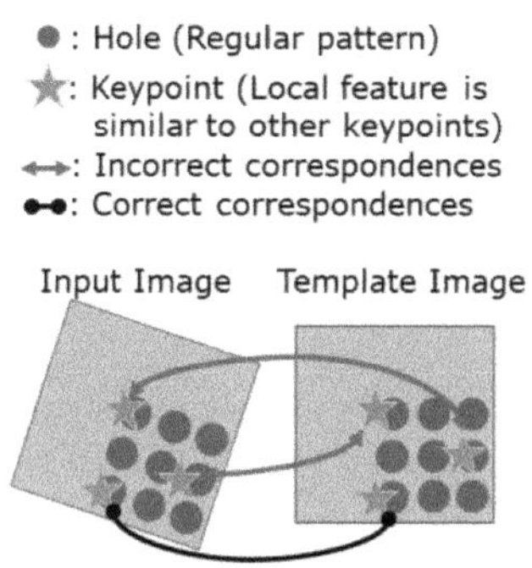

Figure 3. Creating the incorrect correspondences because of a regular pattern.

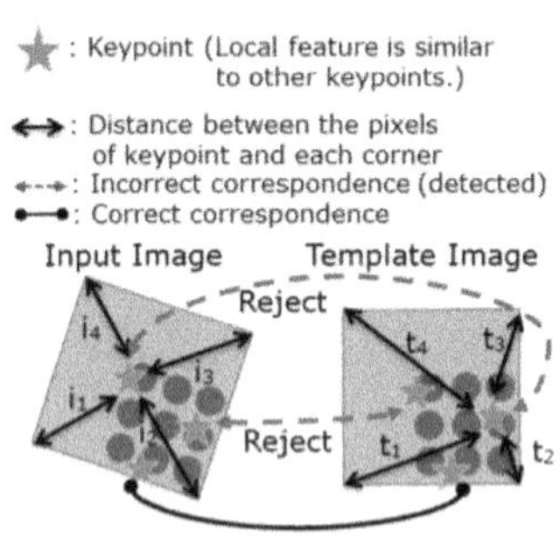

Figure 4. Overview of our method.

2. Detect an object in the depth image using the object's size, then transform the object's region into a color camera two-dimensional (2D) coordinate, and extract the object in the color image.

3. Detect the keypoint and extract the local features in the extracted image. We chose an ORB keypoint detector and a local descriptor [5] for real-time systems.

4. Perform brute-force matching to create the best correspondences between the extracted local features and the object's local features extracted from a template image and find the homography matrix for pose estimation using the correspondences and the position of object detected. This object pose estimation implements a conventional object pose estimation pipeline similar to Martinez et al. [4].

5. Project the operating position onto the object as per its estimated pose.

We focus on estimating the pose of manufactured products because projecting operating instructions onto these according to their pose can help workers find operating positions intuitively.

Estimating the pose of a manufactured product

We need to know the current pose of a manufactured product to be able to project an operating instruction or position onto it. It is not difficult to estimate the pose of an object when the correct correspondences for estimating an object's pose are created. However, incorrect correspondences can be created when an object has a regular pattern (for design conformity). For example, let's consider estimating the pose of a desktop personal computer with the aim of sticking a label in a certain location (e.g., serial number labels and/or product control number labels). Figure 3 illustrates the creation of correspondences between extracted local features in the input image and the extracted local features in the template image. The side of the computer has similar holes (i.e., holes that are the color and shape) and, thus, extracted local features are similar to other local features. Incorrect correspondences could be created because the local features cannot be distinguished. Incorrect correspondences create an incorrect homography matrix for estimating pose. As a result, we could not precisely estimate the pose of the desktop personal computer and project operating position precisely.

Incorrect correspondence detection using global information of correspondence

We developed a new algorithm to detect any incorrect correspondences and reject these using global information of correspondence and estimate object's pose using the rest of the correspondences. We found that the distance between the pixels of the keypoint and each corner in input image and the distance between the pixels of the keypoint and each corner in template image is different in an incorrect correspondence (see Figure 4). Therefore, we developed the algorithm that judged incorrect correspondences using distance between the pixels of the keypoint and each corner in these images (see Figure 5). In our algorithm, the outline of objects in a depth image is approximately rectangle and four corners are detected. We assume that the outlines of many manufactured products (e.g., a desktop personal computer and a router) are cuboid in shape. Next, the pixels of the four corners are transformed into a color camera 2D coordinate. After that, the vectors $\mathbf{V} = \mathbf{d}_i - \mathbf{d}_t$, where $\mathbf{d}_i = (i_1, i_2, i_3, i_4)$ indicates the vector that

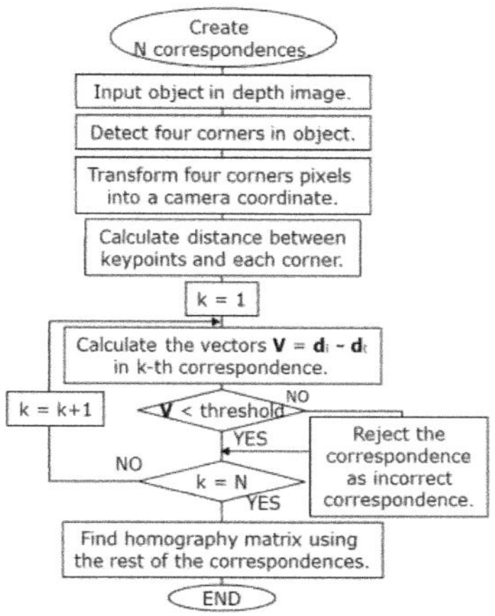

Figure 5. Flow chart for detecting incorrect correspondences and rejecting these.

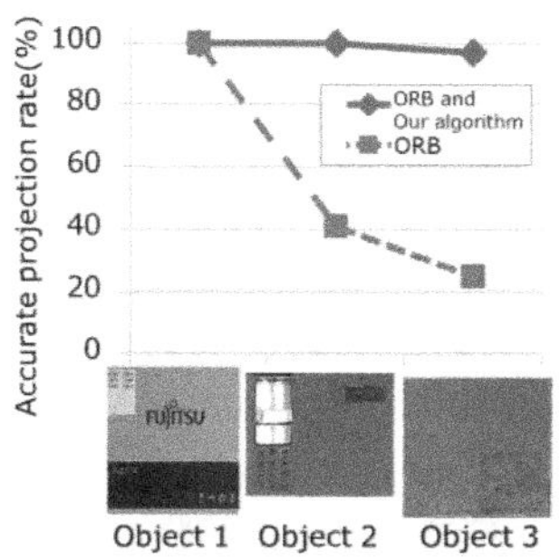

Figure 6. Accurate projection rate for object pose estimation method.

include value of distance between the pixels of a keypoint and each corner in input image and $\mathbf{d}_t = (t_1, t_2, t_3, t_4)$ indicates the vector that include the distance between the pixels of a keypoint and each corner in template image are calculated for every correspondence (see Figure 4). Correspondences of elements of $\mathbf{d}_i$ and $\mathbf{d}_t$ is decided using maximum value of cosine similarity in total number of trials. Then, the correspondences of two keypoints with absolute value of any element of $\mathbf{V}$ above a threshold (that we chose) is judged as incorrect correspondences and rejected these (see Figure 5). Finally, homography matrix for pose estimation is found using the rest of the correspondences.

Experimental evaluation

We evaluated the accurate projection rate in accordance with object's pose in our assembly-support system using the combination of ORB [5] and our algorithm and ORB only. We put an actual object on the worktable in various positions and rotations; rotation about the vertical axis and horizontal and vertical translations were estimated. Then, operating position that is fixed area of a rectangle for sticking label is projected as per its estimated pose and we measured errors from correct position.

Figure 6 shows the result, with the *x*-axis representing the evaluated objects and the *y*-axis representing the accurate projection rate using the object pose estimation method. We chose manufactured products and packing box with which workers operate tasks as the evaluated objects. A number of similar local features differ with these objects. The number of similar local features in object 1 is less than the other objects and the number of similar local features in object 3 is more than the other objects. We determined success as being when the maximum difference between the operating position's corners calculated from estimated object's pose and the correct position of the corners was less than 5 mm. The accurate projection rate was determined as the number of successful outcomes compared to the total number of trials. We decided that thresholds for object 1, object 2 and object 3 are 100, 25 and 10 pixels in our algorithm experimentally. The accurate projection rate for the combination and ORB were the same for object 1 because the number of similar local features in object 1 is low. However, the accurate projection rate using ORB decreases for object 2 and object 3 because the number of similar local features is high and thus incorrect correspondences are created. Conversely, the accurate projection rate with the combination is higher (compared with ORB) for object 2 and object 3 because our algorithm detects any incorrect correspondences and rejects them.

Detecting an object even if an object is occluded by a worker's hand

We also need to include any interaction between workers and the system. However, this interaction could not continue when part of an object is occluded by a worker's hand and thus the object is not detected in the depth and color images. This often happens because workers' hands are above the manufactured products when they are operating tasks.

Hand removal using previous images

We also developed an algorithm to ignore any hand shapes in current depth and color images using previous images to continue the interaction with the workers. In our algorithm, a hand is detected in the current depth image using the hand shape and incident

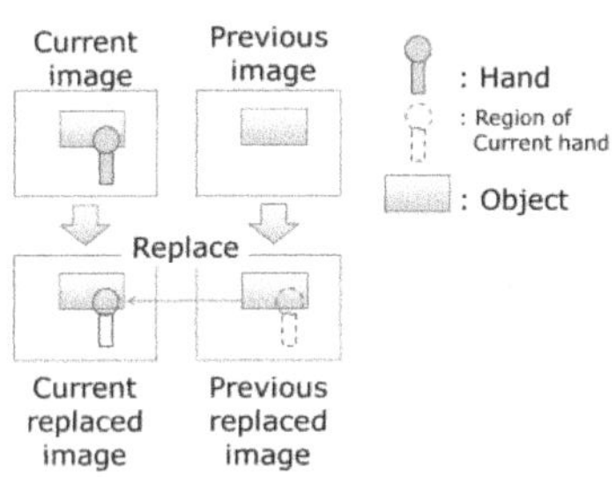

Figure 7. The algorithm rejecting hand movement.

direction. Next, the pixels of the hand image are replaced with pixels of the same region from the previous depth image that did not show the hand (see Figure 7). We assume that workers do not move the manufactured products when they are operating tasks. Pixels of the hand in the current color image are also replaced in the same way. Finally, the object is detected in these replaced images.

Conclusion and Future Work

In this study, we proposed an object pose estimation method for manufactured products. The result of this experimental evaluation indicates that the combination of ORB and our algorithm can detect an object's pose more precisely than ORB only. We also proposed hand removal method by taking into account the interaction with the worker.

Future work will include an increased variety of object. We also need to consider other global information (e.g., the distance between a keypoint and the center of gravity of an object). Moreover, we need to evaluate continuous interaction with workers using our hand removal method. Additionally, we need to evaluate interference with the RGB/IR tracking by projection. In experimental evaluation, we consider that it is no problem because there is a long distance between a keypoint and a position of projection. However, we also consider that projecting instructions and positions near keypoints could cause extraction of incorrect local features. Furthermore, we plan to set our system in an actual factory and evaluate how efficiently the workers operate their tasks.

References

[1] Funk, M., Shirazi, A. S., Mayer, S., Lischke, L., and Schmidt, A. Pick from here!: an interactive mobile cart using in-situ projection for order picking. In *Proc. UbiComp 2015*, ACM Press (2015), 601-609.

[2] Kobori, N., Deguchi, D., Takahashi, T., Ide, I., and Murase, H. High Accuracy Pose Estimation for a Mobile Robot fusing a Camera and Gyro Sensors. In *Proc. MIRU 2009*.

[3] Lowe, D. G. Distinctive image features from scale-invariant keypoints. *International Journal of Computer Vision*, 60(2004), 91–110.

[4] Martinez, M., Collet, A., and Srinivasa, S.S. MOPED: A Scalable and Low Latency Object Recognition and Pose Estimation System. In *Proc. ICRA 2010*, IEEE Press (2010), 2043-2049.

[5] Rublee, E., Rabaud, V., Konolige, K., and Bradski, G. ORB: An efficient alternative to SIFT or SURF. In *Proc. ICCV 2011*, IEEE Computer Society Press (2011).

[6] Sato, A., Watanabe, K., and Rekimoto, J. MimiCook: a cooking assistant system with situated guidance. In *Proc. TEI 2014*, ACM Press (2013).

[7] Suzuki, G., Fujii, Y., and Murase, T. Projecting Recorded Expert Hands at Real Size, at Real Speed, and onto Real Objects for Manual Work. In *Proc. IUI 2016*, ACM Press (2016), 13-17.

[8] Tombari, F., Salti, S. and Stefano, L. D. Unique Signatures of Histograms for Local Surface Description. In *Proc. ECCV 2010*, Springer Press (2010), 356-369.

[9] Tombari, F., Salti, S. and Stefano, L. D. A COMBINED TEXTURE-SHAPE DESCRIPTOR FOR ENHANCED 3D FEATURE MATCHING. In *Proc. ICIP 2011*, IEEE Press (2011).

Touch Detection Technique for Various Surfaces Using Shadow of Finger

Takehiro Niikura
Hitachi, Ltd. Research & Development Group
1-280, Higashi-koigakubo
Kokubunji-shi, Tokyo, Japan
takehiro.niikura.xh@hitachi.com

Takashi Matsubara
Hitachi, Ltd. Research & Development Group
1-280, Higashi-koigakubo
Kokubunji-shi, Tokyo, Japan
takashi.matsubara.pw@hitachi.com

Naoki Mori
Hitachi, Ltd. Research & Development Group
1-280, Higashi-koigakubo
Kokubunji-shi, Tokyo, Japan
naoki.mori.xn@hitachi.com

ISS'16, November 06-09, 2016, Niagara Falls, ON, Canada
ACM 978-1-4503-4248-3/16/11.
http://dx.doi.org/10.1145/2992154.2996777

Abstract
In this paper we try to realize a system that enables users to interact with surrounding surfaces using touch interactions. For this purpose, we propose new touch detection technique which utilizes the shadows of a finger, and developed a prototype system with an infrared (IR) camera and two IR lights. Since the shapes of a finger's shadows vary drastically depending on the distance between the surface and finger, our prototype system can detect touch. To improve the accuracy of the estimated touch position, we also introduce multiple regression analysis into the estimation algorithm of the touch position. We conducted two experiments on the accuracy of estimated touch position, and the results shows that the target accuracy was within an error of less than 5 mm.

Author Keywords
vision-based UIs; touch interaction; shadow detection

ACM Classification Keywords
H.5.2. [User Interfaces]: Input devices and strategies (e.g., mouse, touchscreen).

Introduction
Tablet PCs and smartphones are used throughout the world, and touch interactions are commonly used for such devices. Some display devices such as see-through

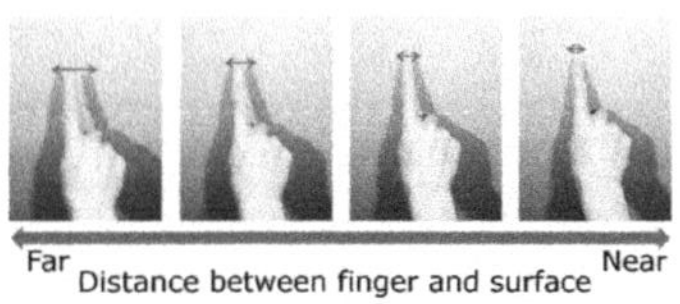

Figure 1: Shapes of finger's shadows vary depending on distance between surface and finger

head-mount displays (HMDs) or projectors have also been developed that enables us to visualize information on various surrounding surfaces. Since touch interactions have become a natural operation method, a system in which users can manipulate information on surrounding surfaces with touch interactions will be required.

To develop such a system, touch detection on various surfaces is an important underlying technology. Various surfaces means surrounding surfaces such as walls, desks, and screens. Additionally, these surfaces are not always flat but curved or have protruding objects. Therefore, to enable useful touch interactions regardless of the environment, it is desirable for a system to detect touch even on non-flat surfaces.

There have been many studies on enabling touch interaction on surrounding surfaces. Roeber et al. [4] proposed a system that uses a line laser. The line laser emits light parallel to the surface, and the system detects touch by recognizing the reflected light, which is diffused from the touching finger. Today, many optical touch panels that use a similar algorithm are widely used. However, this system has some constraints, such as a surface must be flat and the sensors must be settled stably on a surface.

To overcome these constraints, some researchers proposed touch detection techniques using 3D cameras (e.g. Kinect) [2, 3, 7]. Most of these systems capture the 3D geometry of a surface beforehand and detect touch by recognizing the distance between the surface and the approaching finger. Some researchers also used the information from a color camera to prevent a system from detecting the touch of other approaching objects.

Even though we can easily detect touch interaction between a finger and various surfaces with 3D cameras, there are some disadvantages. For example, low accuracy of depth estimation with 3D cameras may cause mis-detection of a touch. Additionally, such a system requires relatively large space due to the narrow field of view (FOV) of a 3D camera. In principle the gap between a finger and a surface cannot be detected by a camera; therefore, a touch is more likely to be mis-detected.

From the above background, we propose a new touch detection technique that uses shadows of a finger, and developed a prototype touch detection system. Since the shapes of a finger's shadows vary depending on the distance between the finger and a surface, we can detect a touch, as shown in Figure 1. Additionally, a touch on a curved surface or surface with protruding objects can be detected because we can observe shadows even on these surfaces.

Wilson[6] proposed a system that consists of an IR camera and an IR light and detects touch by using the shapes of a finger's shadows. However, the shapes of a finger's shadows can drastically change for many reasons. For instance, the shapes will change depending on the positional relationship between a camera and the finger or on the posture of the finger to the surface. Therefore, it is difficult to precisely detect touch with only one side shadow.

Our prototype system overcomes this issue by using two IR lights and detects touch by recognizing both side shadows of a finger. The system can operate in a wide operation area by using wide-angle lens. To precisely detect a touch position, we also introduced multiple regression analysis (MRA) into the touch position

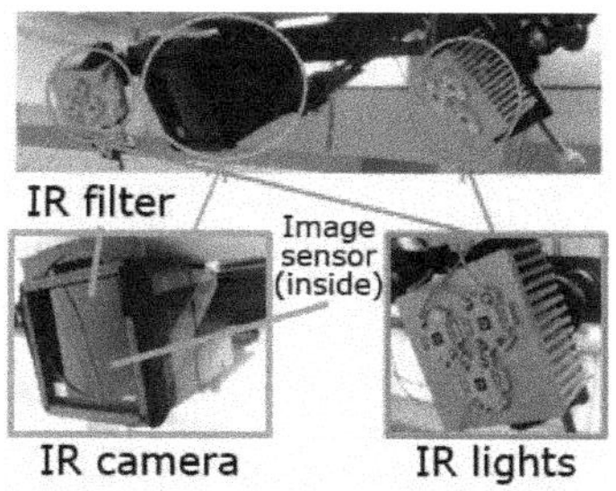

Figure 2: System configuration: our prototype system consists of two IR lights and one IR camera.

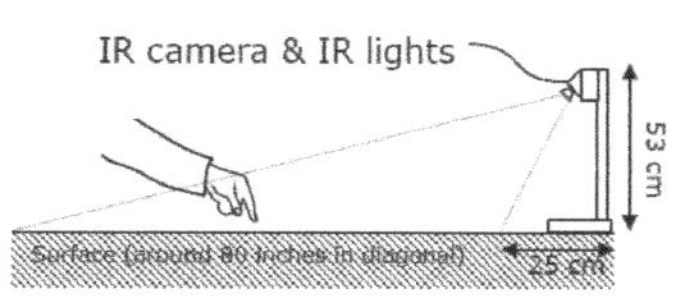

Figure 3: Configuration of our prototype system. Size of operation area is around 80 inches in diagonal.

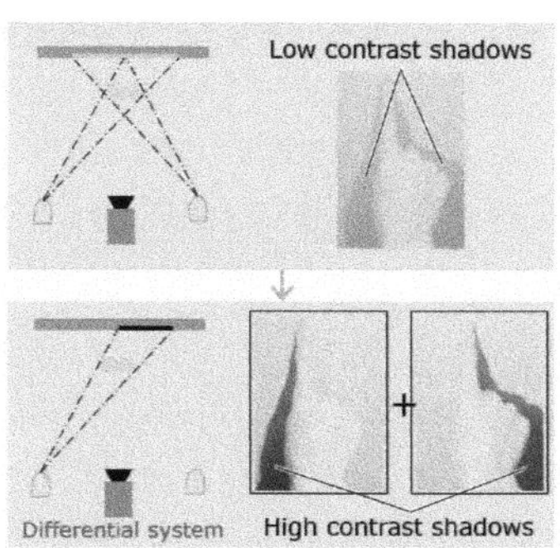

Figure 4: Shadow extraction with differential system

estimation. The system estimates precise touch position from the shapes of a finger's shadows.

There are two main contributions of this paper. First, we propose a new touch detection technique and developed a prototype system with an IR camera and two IR lights, which requires no sensors on a surface and can detect touch even on non-flat surfaces. Second, we experimentally confirmed that estimating touch position based on MRA significantly improves the accuracy of the estimated touch position.

Proposed Technique and Prototype System

Hardware

Figure 2 shows the configuration of our prototype system. The system consists of an IR camera and two IR lights, and the camera captures the shadows of a finger generated by the IR lights. The resolution of the camera is 1920×1080 pixels, and the camera runs at 30 fps. Since we use a wide-angle lens with 120-degree FOV, the system can detect touch in a wide area. We configured the lights to be at a distance of about 20 cm from the camera.

The positional relationship between the prototype system and a surface is shown in Figure 3. We configured the size of the operation area to be around 80 inches in diagonal, which is commonly used for large displays and is large enough for daily activities. The system was installed 25 cm horizontally from the edge of the operation surface and 53 cm vertically from the surface. We fixed the orientation of the camera and lights to the surface so that the camera can observe the entire operating area.

Shadow Extraction and Touch Detection

To precisely detect touch, the shadows of a finger must be extracted stably from images. In other words, it is important for our prototype system to capture shadows with high contrast. If a shadow generated by an IR light is canceled out with the other IR light, the contrast of the shadows becomes low.

Therefore, we introduced a differential system that controls two IR lights to flash alternately, synchronized with the camera's frame. Since a shadow will not be canceled out, we can obtain high contrast shadows, as shown in Figure 4.

To obtain shadow regions from captured image, we adopted background subtraction. First, we capture some background images then, while a user interacts with the surface, the system subtracts the captured image from the background image. If a pixel in the subtracted image has a higher brightness value than that of noise, the system extracts that pixel as a shadow region.

Next, we explain touch detection. First, the system traces contours of the shadow regions. Then, it extracts various features from the contours. For example, as shown in Figure 5, the coordinates of a shadow's tip, distance between the shadow's tips, angle of a shadow's tip, and orientation of the shadows are extracted as features. Since there are some shadow regions per image, here we have some sets of extracted features.

Finally, the system detects whether the finger is touching based on extracted features. Our system utilizes both sides' shadow of the finger to detect a touch. However, since we introduced a differential system, we can obtain one side shadow of the finger per image. Therefore, the system combines sets of features of the latest frame and that of the previous frame to detect a touch. Thus, the system can detect a touch at the same rate as the camera's frame rate.

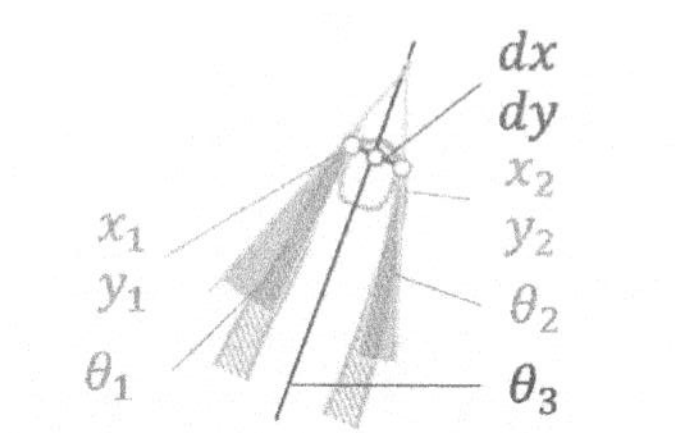

Figure 5: Feature example. The system extracts various features from shadow such as the coordinates of a shadow's tip, distance between the shadow's tips, angle of a shadow's tip, and orientation of the shadows.

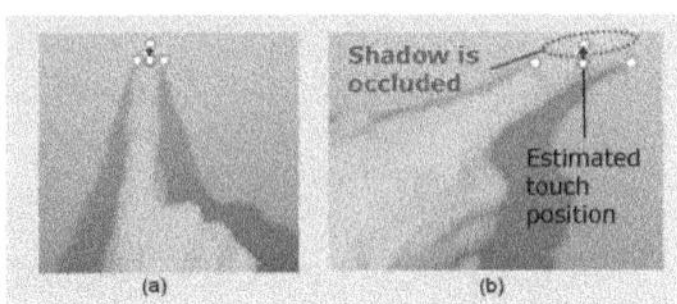

Figure 7: Occlusion of shadow. If shadow of finger is occluded, system fails to correctly estimate touch position.

We configured threshold conditions for the extracted features, and if a combination of set of features meets the conditions, the system recognize it as a touch.

Figure 6 illustrates an example of touch interactions on non-flat surfaces with our prototype system and a projector. Our system can detect a touch even on curved surface or surface with protruding object unless the shadow is occluded or strongly deformed.

Figure 6: Detecting touch on a non-flat surface. Three characters (A, B and C) are written on flat surface, curved surface, and protruding object (slope), respectively.

Touch Position Estimation

In this section, we explain touch position estimation. Touch panels are widely used in smartphones and tablet PCs, and companies that provide the operating systems for mobile devices, such as Apple, Google, and Microsoft, publish the design guidelines [1] for the minimum size for the touch interaction area. In these guidelines, the recommended minimum size for the touch interaction area is around $7 \sim 10$ mm. Also, Wang et al. [5] reported that the upper level of the 95% confidence interval for tapping deviation of the index finger is about 4.4 mm.

We assume that users can interact naturally if the misalignment between the true touch position and estimated touch position is nearly equal to the above values. Therefore, we aimed to detect touch position with an error of less than 5 mm.

To precisely estimate touch position, we first assumed that the touch position is slightly higher than the midpoint of the shadows' tips. In fact, as shown in Figure 7 (a), if a user touches the surface with a straight finger, the touch position can be precisely estimated. However, as shown in Figure 7 (b), if the user touches the surface with the finger inclined, the shadow is occluded by the finger and the system will fail to estimate the touch position. In particular, through a preliminary experiment we conducted, we found that misalignment on the x-axis is significantly large.

This problem occurs when the system uses only a shadows' tip for touch position estimation. To resolve this problem, the system needs to correct touch position considering the position and posture of the finger.

Therefore, we introduced MRA for touch position estimation. The system extracts various features from the shape of a shadow, some of which are the same used in touch detection. The system then calculates the correction value according to the following equation.

$$dx = \boldsymbol{w}^{\boldsymbol{t}}\boldsymbol{\theta} + b = w_1\theta_1 + w_2\theta_2 \cdots w_n\theta_n + b \qquad (1)$$

Here, dx is a correction value, $\boldsymbol{w}$ is weight vector, $\boldsymbol{\theta}$ is a vector of a shadows' feature, and b is an intercept, and we call this equation a multiple regression model.

We first collected a set of correction values and shadow features. We collected data at nine locations in the operating area, as shown in Figure 8(a). As we mentioned

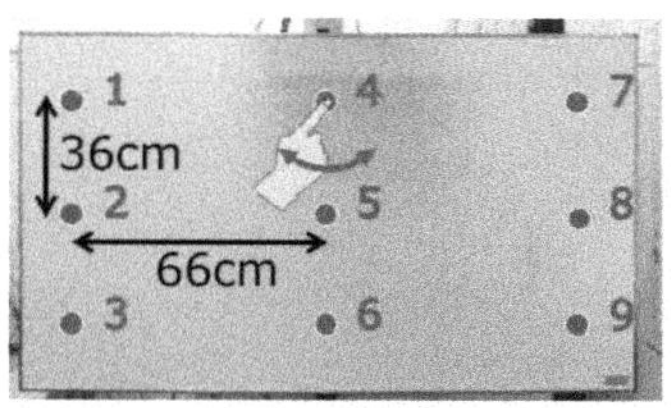

(a)

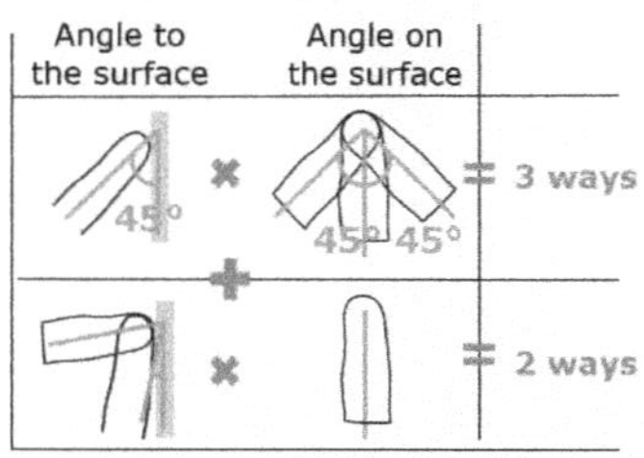

(b)

Figure 8: Conditions of collecting data for multiple regression analysis

in Figure 3, the size of operation area was around 80 inches. We also varied the posture of the finger five ways: (1) varying the angle on the surface in three ways $(-45°, -0°, 45°)$ while maintaining the angle to the surface and (2) varying the angle to the surface in two ways $(0°, 90°)$ while maintaining the angle on the surface. Throughout data collection, we used only index finger to touch the surface. Under each condition, we visually confirmed the true touch position and recorded the position and the shadow features twice.

We collected data for MRA as stated above, and built a model with 13 features extracted from shadows. We then evaluated the model with backward elimination based on the Akaike information criterion and finally obtained a multiple regression model with eight features.

Evaluation

We carried out an experiment to evaluate the accuracy of touch position estimation. Before evaluating the effectiveness of MRA, we measured the deviations in estimating touch position when a user touches a surface with straight finger.

The posture of the finger was similar to that shown in Figure 7(a): The angle to the surface was about $45°$ and the angle on the surface was about $0°$. We divided the operating area into 36 equal parts (6 parts vertically and 6 parts horizontally) and measured the deviation of estimated touch position at the center of each part. Half of the center of each part corresponds to the locations shown in Figure 8. One subject participated in this experiment, and he touched each part once. We recorded the estimated touch position in 100 successive frames for each position.

Table 1 lists the results of the measured standard deviation (SD) of the estimated touch position. The units of the results are the pixels in the captured image. The average SD of the entire operation area was 0.52 pixels on the x-axis and 0.76 pixels on the y-axis. If the resolution of the displayed image on the surface is 1920 × 1080, a misalignment of 1 pixel in the captured image would correspond to a misalignment of 0.9 mm in the real world at worst. (Since the camera image plane is not parallel to the surface, the scale between the pixels and real world would change depending on the position in the camera.) Therefore, our prototype system detects touch with high position accuracy compared to the misalignment target of less than 5 mm.

Next, we carried out an experiment to evaluate the effect of introducing MRA. We evaluated the deviations in estimated touch position with various positions and finger postures.

The locations and postures of the finger were the same as those shown in Figure 8. In this experiment, we considered the estimated touch position of a straight finger as a reference position and measured the deviations in the estimated touch position from the reference position while changing the finger posture.

Another subject participated in this experiment, and he had 10 trials for each location. In one trial, the subject changed the finger posture while keeping touching the surface, and we recorded the touch position data for each posture. Therefore, we collected 900 touch position data (9 locations × 5 posture × 2 conditions(applying MRA or not) × 10 reputation) for this experiment. As mentioned above, since the misalignment caused by the change in posture occurs mainly on the x-axis, we evaluated only the x coordinate of the estimated touch position.

	x	y
Average	0.52	0.76
Max	0.56	1.47
Min	0.14	0.39

Table 1: Standard deviation [pixels] of estimated touch position with straight finger

Figure 9 shows the experimental results. All results are shown in millimeters for easy observability, following the correspondence of misalignment between the captured image and the real world. Specifically, before applying MRA, the average root mean squared error(RMSE) was 7.5 mm, whereas that after applying MRA was 2.9 mm. In other words, the average RMSE significantly decreased by about 57%. From these results, we confirmed that the target accuracy of estimated touch position with a misalignment of less than 5 mm was achieved.

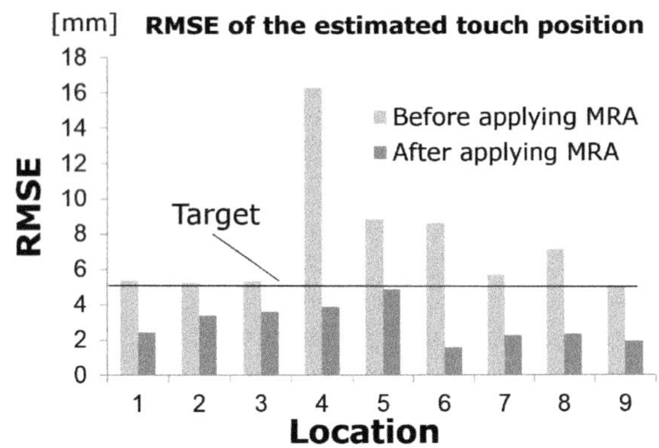

Figure 9: Root mean squared error of detected touch position with and without MRA

Conclusion

We proposed new touch detection technique which utilizes the shadows of a finger, and developed a prototype touch detection system with an IR camera and two IR lights. We also introduced MRA for touch position estimation. The results of the experiment on the accuracy of estimated touch position show that estimating touch position based on MRA significantly improves the accuracy and target accuracy of touch position with an error of less than 5 mm.

Future work will include improvement in touch detection accuracy, evaluation on various surfaces, and considerations necessary for practical use of the system.

References

[1] Design - Apple Developer. https://developer.apple.com/design/.

[2] Dippon, A., and Klinker, G. Kinecttouch: Accuracy test for a very low-cost 2.5d multitouch tracking system. In *Proc. ITS '11*, ACM (2011), 49–52.

[3] Kim, D., Izadi, S., Dostal, J., Rhemann, C., Keskin, C., Zach, C., Shotton, J., Large, T., Bathiche, S., Nießner, M., Butler, D. A., Fanello, S., and Pradeep, V. Retrodepth: 3d silhouette sensing for high-precision input on and above physical surfaces. In *Proc. CHI '14*, ACM (2014), 1377–1386.

[4] Roeber, H., Bacus, J., and Tomasi, C. Typing in thin air: The canesta projection keyboard - a new method of interaction with electronic devices. In *CHI '03 Extended Abstracts on Human Factors in Computing Systems*, ACM (2003), 712–713.

[5] Wang, F., and Ren, X. Empirical evaluation for finger input properties in multi-touch interaction. In *Proc. CHI 2003*, ACM (2009), 1063–1072.

[6] Wilson, A. D. Playanywhere: A compact interactive tabletop projection-vision system. In *Proc. UIST '05*, ACM (2005), 83–92.

[7] Wilson, A. D. Using a depth camera as a touch sensor. In *Proc. ITS '10*, ACM (2010), 69–72.

SUR40 Linux: Reanimating an Obsolete Tangible Interaction Platform

Florian Echtler
Mobile Media Group
Bauhaus University
Weimar, Germany
florian.echtler@uni-weimar.de

Martin Kaltenbrunner
Interface Culture Lab
University of Art and Design
Linz, Austria
martin.kaltenbrunnner@ufg.at

ISS '16, November 06-09, 2016, Niagara Falls, ON, Canada
ACM 978-1-4503-4248-3/16/11.
http://dx.doi.org/10.1145/2992154.2996778

Abstract

Optical sensing technologies are among the most versatile hardware solutions for interactive surfaces, as they are capable of recognizing touch as well as (limited) hover state in addition to printed tokens. One widely used system is the Pixelsense/SUR40, currently one of very few devices which provides these capabilities in the form factor of a regular table, thereby allowing working at the device in a sitting position. Unfortunately, the device has been discontinued by the manufacturer, provides only an unsupported SDK on an outdated operating system, and has a gathered a reputation for high latency as well as sensitivity to environment light.

In this paper, we present our research into modernizing and extending the SUR40 system. By switching to a Linux operating system running a custom video driver, we are able to provide lower latency, support other types of optical tags and improve the system's robustness, particularly regarding external lighting conditions. We present an analysis of the device's internals, a comparison of quantitative performance measurements, and an outlook into extending the tangible interaction capabilities with an improved cross-platform development framework.

ACM Classification Keywords

H.5.m. [Information Interfaces and Presentation (e.g. HCI)]: Miscellaneous

Author Keywords
SUR40; Linux; computer vision; touch sensing; tangible interaction

Introduction & Related Work
After a decade of fundamental tangible interaction research initiated by Ishii et.al. [3], large-scale interactive surfaces became popular in 2005 following the seminal publication by Han [2]. Initially, most research setups were custom-built constructions based on infrared cameras and consequently employed optical sensing using techniques such as FTIR, diffuse illumination or combinations thereof [6].

Although capacitive sensing has been widely used for small-scale touch sensors, large-scale capacitive surfaces have only recently started to become available. Even if capacitive surfaces are generally perceived to have more robust touch detection than optical systems, tangible interaction with, e.g., fiducial tokens is still a domain where optical sensing has distinct advantages.

One major drawback of many existing optical systems, however, is their bulkiness. Camera-based systems require a certain amount of distance and space for the light path, and therefore often take the form of large boxes with closed sides. Very few systems with optical sensing exist which don't have this limitation, either by arranging a large number of cameras close to the surface (e.g. MultiTaction[1] systems) or by integrating the sensor directly into the display.

In this paper, we present our results from reverse engineering one of the latter systems, the SUR40 tabletop system. This was the only commercially available system with optical sensing that has directly been integrated into the display, and therefore provides an unique combination

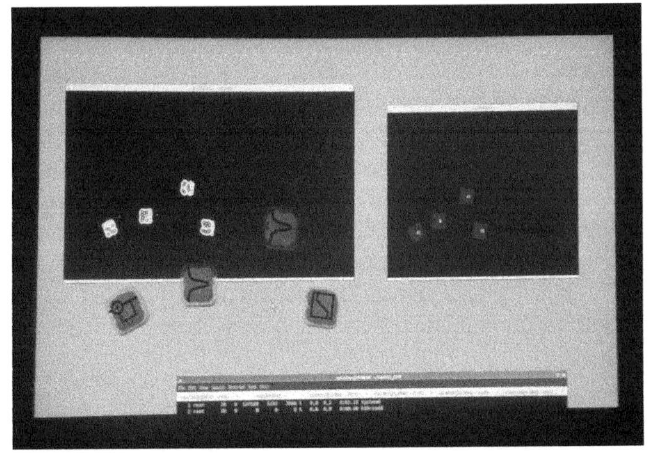

Figure 1: reacTIVision running natively under SUR40 Linux.

of features, such as the ability for the user to work on the system like at a regular table, and the ability to detect optical tags and hovering hands. As this system is still very popular in a research context, even though it has been discontinued by the manufacturer, we believe that the background information we are able to provide on the system's hardware and software will help other researchers to optimize their applications and to continue using the device for their research.

Hardware Description
The SUR40 is one of the few commercial examples of an optical in-cell sensor, i.e. an infrared sensor which is directly integrated with a flat-panel display. The LCD screen of the SUR40 has a standard resolution of 1920x1080 pixels at a diagonal size of 40 inch, while the sensor covers the same screen area at half resolution, i.e. 960x540 pixels. The screen dimensions are approximately 89x50 cm, resulting in

[1] https://www.multitaction.com/

a sensor resolution of 0.93 mm. The sensor is connected to the integrated host computer via an USB 2.0 connection and delivers 8-bit greyscale images at a constant rate of 60 Hz.

One interesting aspect of the SUR40 hardware is that blob/touch detection is performed directly in the panel controller through a custom FPGA chip. This is in contrast to most custom-built systems, where only a raw camera stream is provided and then interpreted by computer-vision software. On the SUR40, however, detected blobs are sent to the host system over a separate USB channel and can directly be interpreted as touch events without having to expend significant CPU power for image-processing tasks.

Reverse Engineering
Most of the presented information was gathered by booting the SUR40 with a Linux operating system, running the native Windows environment inside a virtual machine and observing the USB traffic between the hardware and the driver running inside the VM. As a result of this process[2], we were also able to write a native Linux driver providing standard system interface access to both the processed touch data (evdev) and the raw video stream (V4L2). This driver has been included into the official mainline Linux kernel since version 4.1 and enables users to run an unmodified Linux OS directly on the SUR40 hardware with full access to all features of the device (including native touch support). A standalone and continuously improved version of this driver is available on Github[3].

Performance Evaluation
As noted earlier, in contrast to its innovative hardware design the SUR40 is not without performance issues. In particular, it has developed a bad reputation for its high

[2]Details at http://floe.butterbrot.org/matrix/hacking/surface/
[3]https://github.com/floe/surface-2.0/

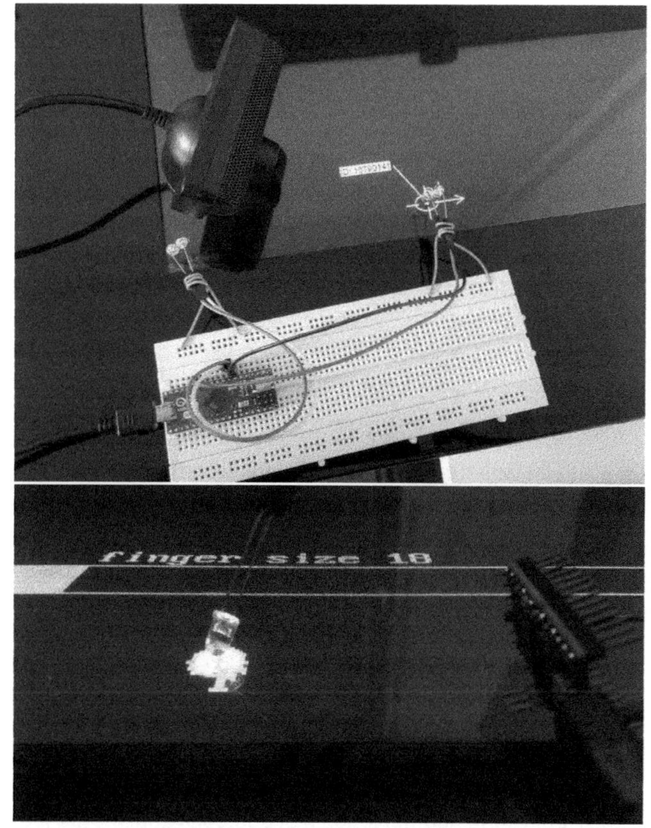

Figure 2: top: End-to-end optical latency measurement tool. bottom: USB-based optical latency measurement tool.

sensitivity to environmental light and its significant latency. While those issues are common to most optical tabletop setups, current camera based systems provide lower latency and can be better shielded from environmental light through optical filtering.

Touchscreen latency is difficult to measure directly, as it is hard to determine the exact moment of contact between the touching object and the screen. Deber et al. presented he "Latency Hammer", a mechanical measurement device for capacitive touch screens[1]. However, this approach is not directly applicable to optical screens such as the SUR40.

To obtain objective measurements of the perceived overall system latency, we created an optical measurement device based on an Arduino and infrared LEDs. This device alternatingly illuminates two spots on the SUR40 surface, thereby triggering a simulated touch event. We run the standard software designed to visualize incoming touch events. The entire setup is recorded with a PS3Eye infrared camera at 187 frames per second, which then allows a custom OpenCV application to compute the delay between lighting up the IR LED and its on-screen visual response. This enables us to measure the entire end-to-end latency with a temporal resolution of 5.3 ms (see also figure 2).

Under the original Windows environment, we used the provided "Touch Input Visualizer" and adjusted our software to detect the appearance of a touch label after the LEDs had been turned on. We repeated this process for 10 measurements and calculated a total end-to-end latency of 153 ms (+- 10 ms). This is noticeably higher than the generally agreed-upon upper latency bound of 100 ms and provides one explanation for the high perceived latency.

Repeating the same experiment under Linux, we measured the total latency of our video-based driver implementation, based on the raw video data provided by the SUR40 device and its processing by a local reacTIVision installation. In this case, we achieve a comparable result of 163 ms (+- 10 ms), although the video data is now already being processed on the host computer.

In a second experimental setup we have created a similar device comprised of a Teensy Board and a single LED simulating an alternating touch event triggered every second (see also figure 2). Before the LED is illuminated, the device sends a simultaneous event through a USB/serial connection. We chose the Teensy board for its real-time capabilities and low serial latency of around 1ms, allowing the precise measurement of the delay until the first raw image showing a bright spot. For comparison we conducted a similar experiment with a PS3Eye camera connected through a standard USB port. While the USB camera showed a constant delay of roughly one frame, our SUR40 measurements revealed a minimum delay of roughly three frames (50ms) before the touch point became visible. Due to the asynchronous signalling, the maximum measured latency was gradually shifting towards four frames (66ms) as expected. The total acquisition latency can be considered as the sum of sensor latency, image processing and USB transport of the raw image data.

We subsequently also measured the "headless" latency with a modified TUIO client, which provided the total delay for the above V4L2 image acquisition, plus the reacTIVision image analysis and TUIO transport without display. This measurement exposed an expected latency of roughly one additional frame, resulting in an average minimum latency of 66 ms and a maximum of 82 ms by average.

LCD panel refresh (sensor readout) at 60 Hz	1 frame
internal image buffer + processing	1 frame
USB transfer (506 kB/frame at 480 MBps)	1 frame
reacTIVision and TUIO	1 frame
66ms Total Latency (before display)	4 frames

Table 1: Latency analysis (average case)

Based on our experiments the perceived overall latency can be interpreted as a combination of individual delays accumulated by data acquisition, image processing, API communication and finally the display. We can also conclude that the majority of the total latency is caused by the sensor processing itself as well as a considerable delay of the display, which both eventually could be improved with an extended knowledge of the hardware internals. Table1, analyzes the average latency of these individual sources and how much they contribute to the observed total latency.

User Space Interaction

By having direct access to the raw video stream over the standard V4L2 interface, it is now possible to run vision-based interaction frameworks such as reacTIVision [4] directly on the SUR40. In turn, this enables the detection of alternative fiducial markers in addition to the original byte tags. It is now also possible to adjust parameters of the software-based touch detection algorithm on the fly and thereby react to changing external lighting conditions. Finally, this more modular and open software stack allows researchers to experiment with different touch, hover and token detection algorithms on a high-performance platform.

Integrating reacTIVision and TUIO

Due to our standard V4L2 driver, the current reacTIVision 1.5.1 release can be run the SUR40 Linux platform. The image processing in user space allows a much more flexible and expandable analysis of the tangible interaction on the tabletop surface, without adding significant overhead to the overall system performance as our above measurements have shown. reacTIVision currently consumes roughly 30-40 percent of the dual core 2.9GHz AMD Athlon CPU, easily processing the provided 960x540 raw image frames at 60fps. The current development version 1.6 now also implements the full TUIO 1.1 specification, providing raw blob analysis in addition to the standard fiducial and finger tracking. In controlled lighting condition the overall tracking performance is considerably more robust and easier to calibrate than compared to camera based systems. Compared to the limited possibilities of the original Windows .NET SDK, this native implementation of the TUIO framework[5] also provides a widely extended choice of programming languages and environments that can now be used on the SUR40 platform.

Environment Light

The original Windows environment provides a calibration tool for the SUR40 which requires alternate placement of a black and a white board on the surface. This establishes minimum and maximum values for the brightness and then uses these values to configure a simple normalization step in the device hardware. However, large changes in the dynamic brightness of the environment (e.g. sudden appearance of sunlight in the room) will usually cause this static threshold to result in very noisy touch data, thereby sometimes rendering the device unusable.

The realtime frame-equalization and adaptive threshold of the reacTIVision engine generally provides a more flexible and robust approach to changing light conditions, which is still able to track fiducial markers in brighter environments. Therefore we observed a more robust tracking performance even with an uncalibrated raw camera image.

Pending Improvements

Due to our reverse-engineering approach, we still have limited access to some of the internal configuration, features and processing details of the SUR40 sensor component, which has not been sufficiently exposed by the manufacturer. Based on the provided functionality and observed latencies, we assume that the overall system performance could be significantly improved by a deactivation of the hardware image processing, resulting in an earlier delivery of the raw sensor data for user-space processing. This step could potentially reduce the acquisition latency by roughly one frame (16ms), in equivalent to our USB camera measurements. In addition to a desirable reduction of the system latency, we are also looking in the possible adjustment of the "sensor camera" parameters, such as exposure, brightness and contrast if possible, as well as the implementation of a user-space tool for the overall device configuration and calibration.

Conclusion & Outlook

In this paper, we have presented an in-depth look at the hardware and software of the widely installed SUR40 device in order to provide previously undocumented background information on its inner workings. We also present a production-ready Linux kernel driver for the device, thereby enabling a contemporary operating system to run on the hardware. This, in turn, enables a wider range of alternative interaction frameworks to run on the device as well as the development of custom experiments, thereby greatly expanding the functionality, flexibility and future sustainability of the device.

As we will continue the ongoing development of the kernel-level drivers as well as the user-space TUI tools, we are also looking for collaborators, testers and users on this platform. At this occasion we'd also like to encourage the original Samsung and Microsoft developers to support the completion of this open source effort.

Acknowledgments

We'd like to thank the Linux-Media kernel developers and especially Hans Verkuil for their help in testing, debugging and improving the V4L2 driver for publication.

REFERENCES

1. Jonathan Deber, Bruno Araujo, Ricardo Jota, Clifton Forlines, Darren Leigh, Steven Sanders, and Daniel Wigdor. 2016. Hammer Time!: A Low-Cost, High Precision, High Accuracy Tool to Measure the Latency of Touchscreen Devices. In *Proceedings of the 2016 CHI Conference on Human Factors in Computing Systems (CHI '16)*. ACM, New York, NY, USA, 2857–2868. DOI: http://dx.doi.org/10.1145/2858036.2858394
2. Jefferson Y. Han. 2005. Low-Cost Multi-Touch Sensing through Frustrated Total Internal Reflection. In *UIST '05: Proceedings of the 18th Annual ACM Symposium on User Interface Software and Technology*. 115–118.
3. H. Ishii and B. Ullmer. 1997. Tangible Bits: Towards Seamless Interfaces between People, Bits and Atoms. In *CHI '97: Proceedings of the Conference on Human Factors in Computing Systems*. 234–241. citeseer.ist.psu.edu/ishii97tangible.html
4. M. Kaltenbrunner and R. Bencina. 2007. reacTIVision: A Computer-Vision Framework for Table-Based Tangible Interaction. In *TEI '07: Proceedings of the 1st International Conference on Tangible and Embedded Interaction*. 69–74.
5. M. Kaltenbrunner, T. Bovermann, R. Bencina, and E. Costanza. 2005. TUIO: A Protocol for Table-Top Tangible User Interfaces. In *Proceedings of Gesture Workshop 2005 (GW '05)*.
6. Johannes Schöning, Peter Brandl, Florian Daiber, Florian Echtler, Otmar Hilliges, Jonathan Hook, Markus Löchtefeld, Nima Motamedi, Laurence Muller, Patrick Olivier, Tim Roth, and Ulrich von Zadow. 2008. *Multi-Touch Surfaces: A Technical Guide*. Techreport. Technische Universität München.

Exploring Time-dependent Scientific Data Using Spatially Aware Mobiles and Large Displays

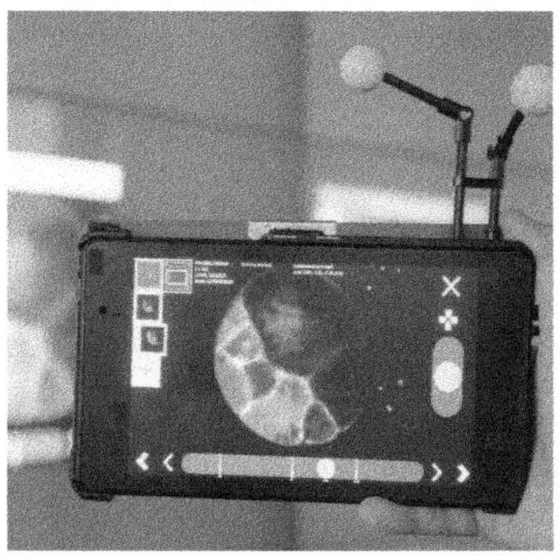

Figure 1: Current prototype showing biological data using a spatially aware mobile and a large interactive display.

Hendrik Sollich
Interactive Media Lab
Technische Universität Dresden
Dresden, Germany
hendrik.sollich@tu-dresden.de

Pavel Tomancak
MPI-CBG Dresden
Dresden, Germany
tomancak@mpi-cbg.de

Ulrich von Zadow
Interactive Media Lab
Technische Universität Dresden
Dresden, Germany
uzadow@acm.org

Raimund Dachselt
Interactive Media Lab
Technische Universität Dresden
Dresden, Germany
dachselt@acm.org

Tobias Pietzsch
MPI-CBG Dresden
Dresden, Germany
pietzsch@mpi-cbg.de

ISS '16, November 06-09, 2016, Niagara Falls, ON, Canada
ACM 978-1-4503-4248-3/16/11
http://dx.doi.org/10.1145/2992154.2996779

Abstract
Scientific Visualization is generally based on very large and often high-dimensional data sets. In many cases (e.g., in the biomedical domain), high-resolution 3D data that changes over time and multiple data sets are involved. One important task in making sense of this data is finding interesting 2D views in the 3D space and additionally finding ways to handle changes over time. We explore how the combination of spatially aware mobiles and large displays can be used in this context. Specifically, we contribute both a precise selection technique for 2D cross sections and a concept for time-dependent 4D bookmarks that follow a point of interest over time. We implemented these techniques in a prototype application that visualizes biological Light Sheet Fluorescence Microscopy data and report on initial user feedback.

Author Keywords
Tangible views; large display; display wall; multi-display environment; spatial interaction; information visualization

ACM Classification Keywords
H.5.2 [Information interfaces and presentation (e.g., HCI)]: User Interfaces - Input devices and strategies; Interaction styles.

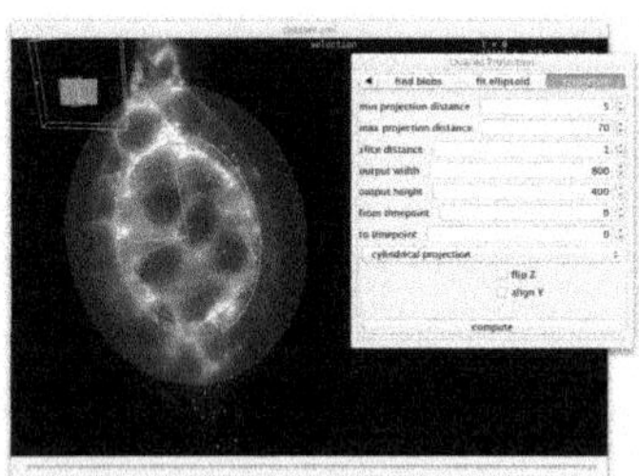

Figure 2: Conventional user interface based on BigDataViewer [7] showing LSFM data.

Introduction

Exploration of time-dependent 3D data is an important topic in scientific visualization, e.g., in the biomedical field [7] and in fluid dynamics [2]. Challenges include finding 2D cross sections in 3D and in time that display salient features of the data [6]. The combination of a spatially aware mobile display and a large contextual display has been shown to support interaction with cross sections of 3D data well [2, 9]. In these cases, the mobile display's position and orientation in space are used to specify a cross section to show and the large display serves to provide context and a frame of reference. We extend this to cover effective selection using three-way clutching and contribute a novel concept for selection and bookmarking in time-dependent data. Our interaction concepts are based on observations of and discussions with developmental biologists, and our prototype (Figure 1), which displays microscopy time-series, reflects this.

Related Work

Our work builds on previous work on tangible displays for infovis. A salient example is Spindler et al.'s work on Tangible Views [9], which used projection onto passive tangible surfaces tracked in 3D space for information visualization (later expanded to spatially-aware mobile devices [8]). More recently, Besancon et al. [2] investigated hybrid tactile/tangible interaction in the context of fluid dynamics visualization, again using a spatially-aware mobile device to specify cutting planes. Both these works included an additional stationary display for context visualization. Closer to our application domain, Bertelsen et al. [1] investigated medical volume visualization using a larger display mounted on a movable mechanical arm. None of these works specifically consider time-dependent 3D data or bookmarking.

Additionally, there are several overviews that consider the use of novel user interface techniques in the context of scientific visualization. Keefe and Isenberg's 'Reimagining the Scientific Visualization Interaction Paradigm' [6] gives a good concise introduction, including an overview of low-level interactions that these systems should support. Two overviews covering specific modalities are van Dam et al.'s report on VR in scientific visualization [4] and Isenberg et al.'s paper on the use of data visualization on interactive surfaces [5].

Application Scenario: Visualization of LSFM Microscopy Data

Although we designed them to be generalizable, our interaction concepts are based on the analysis of the workflows of a specific group of users: Developmental Biologists working with Light Sheet Fluorescence Microscopy (LSFM) data. LSFM produces high-resolution, 3D time-series recordings of the development of living biological specimens, enabling scientists to examine anatomical structures close enough to observe miniscule details as small as cell membranes or nuclei in motion during cell division. Our concepts and prototype were developed in an iterative fashion, involving several meetings with prospective users and observations of their work using current tools (e.g., Figure 2). The following user scenario is derived from these observations:

A developmental biologist, Alice, wants to analyze the effects of different treatments on the development of Platynereis, a marine ragworm. Accordingly, her goal is to compare certain biological aspects of these ***specimens****. These aspects emerge in certain spatial regions of the embryo and at certain times in the development, so Alice selects appropriate views (called* ***samples****: 2D cross sections at a point in time, i.e., a 2D plane in 4D space)* *for comparison (Figure 3a). Additionally, to demonstrate the expected development of a specimen, she compares the same aspects in different stages of development of the same specimen (Figure 3b). In both cases, the samples she selects must be located both in time and in space.*

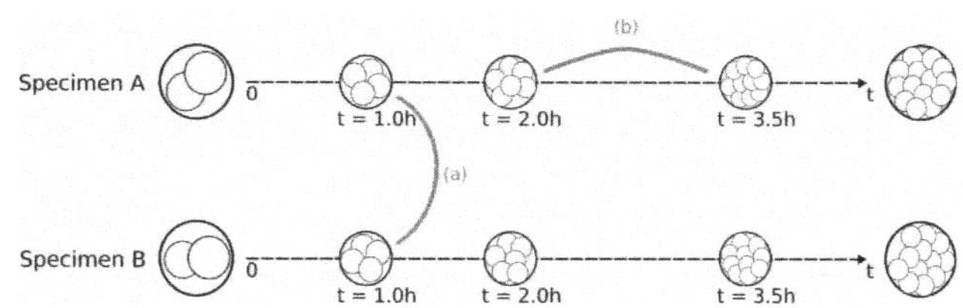

Figure 3: Comparing two samples: (a - red line) two specimens at the same stage of development or (b - blue line) two stages of development in the same specimen

Selection in time is aided by the fact that Platynereis development is stereotypic and roughly synchronous across specimens, but the location in space involves precise selection of a **cross section** *that involves three translational and three rotational degrees of freedom (DOF). This is more difficult, especially if using a 2D input device such as the mouse. An additional issue appears when she needs to be able to follow the aspects over time: With the development of the organism, the interesting points move in space. She therefore needs to be able to adjust cross sections accordingly. Further, when she compares different specimens, it helps if she can transfer sample locations from one specimen to another to have an initial starting point.*

After selecting samples for comparison alone, Alice wants to present and discuss her analysis with colleagues. For this stage, Alice would like to have a larger screen for better overview of the data, as well as easy access to bookmarks.

Thus, challenges are the precise yet intuitive and quick selection of a cross section to display and seamless support of time-dependent data, including bookmarking of areas of interest that move over time.

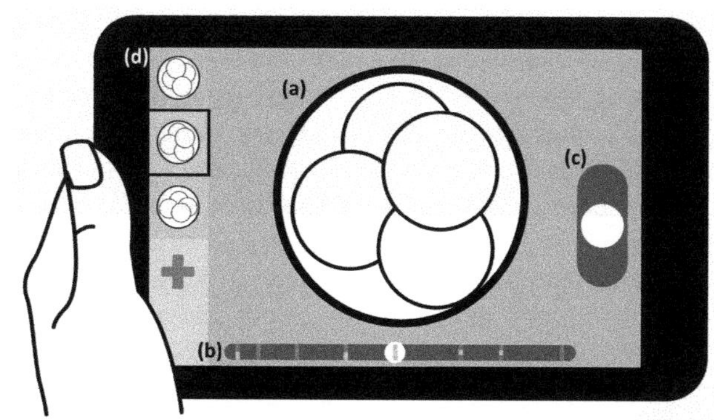

Figure 4: Mobile user interface concept. (a) Sample (2D view), (b) Timeline showing current point in time and bookmark keyframes, (c) Clutch for positioning in 3D, (d) Bookmarks.

Interaction Concept

Our interaction concept supports the user scenario above and involves a spatially-aware mobile device as well as a large touch-sensitive display. Users can intuitively select cross sections and in general work with a single sample on the mobile device, while the larger screen enables work with multiple samples and specimens, comparison of samples, and group work.

The mobile UI is structured around a rendering of the currently selected sample (Figure 4a). In addition, it displays a timeline at the bottom (b) that allows selecting the point in time to view. At the right and left sides of the screen – easily accessible by thumb if the device is held in two hands – are further interface elements: A clutch that controls cross section selection (c), and a list of bookmarks (d).

The contextual display (Figure 7) is large and therefore capable of displaying numerous samples (from the same or different specimen) in multiple views. The individual wall views are similar to the mobile UI: They have the same timeline and bookmark selection functionality (but no facility for specifying cross sections). In addition, they can display a volumetric view of the data that visualizes the positions of the currently configured cross sections. The contextual display also supports a comparison view that superimposes two samples.

Cross Section Selection
Cross section selection – configuration of the 2D cutting plane in the 3D volumetric data – is performed via spatial input (Figure 5). In essence, the position and rotation of the mobile device in 3D space represents the cross section the user wishes to view, and movement of the device changes the cross section (as in [2, 8]). However, it must be possible to enable and disable these view changes. Further, it is not effective to control 6 DOF at once.

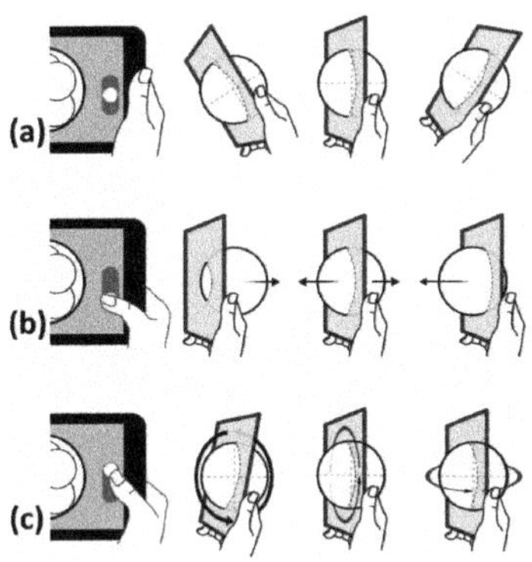

Figure 5: Clutch usage: (a) In neutral state, the dataset does not move in relation to the tablet's screen, (b) Clutch down: Translation of the cross section within the dataset by moving the tablet along its z-axis, (c) Clutch up: Rotating the selected cross section by tilting or rotating the handheld.

We approach both issues by using a three-way clutch (Figure 5) that disables cross section changes when in neutral position (a). Two other modes can be enabled by sliding and holding the clutch down or up, respectively enabling translation (b) or rotation (c). This separation of DOF allows more effective interaction [6]. Additionally, if more precision is needed, it should be straightforward to combine three-way clutching with a mechanism that modifies control-display (CD) gain or with nudging.

An additional issue appears when the current cross section is visualized both on the mobile and the large stationary screen: While looking at the mobile, users expect the plane to move through a stationary virtual object (the *egocentric* view [3]). However, when looking at a stationary screen, users expect the inverse, with the mobile representing the virtual object while the cross section remains stationary in space (the *exocentric* view [3]). Thus, displaying the moving cross section on both displays is confusing, and one view should be disabled during the interaction.

Figure 6: Single bookmark with four keyframes at different points in time

Bookmarking
The interface described in the previous section allows specifying cross sections for single points in time. However, one of our goals was to support working with points of interest that move over time. Our bookmark concept (Figure 6) enables this. Besides supporting traditional bookmarks that reference single samples, it allows the user to specify multiple cross sections for different points in time. These are then used as *keyframes* for interpolation. An interface at the left side of the screen (Figure 4d) allows the user to manage bookmarks. It supports adding and removing bookmarks and highlights the currently selected bookmark. Keyframes are displayed and configured on the timeline (Figure 4b), with color coding used to identify different bookmarks.

Prototype
Our prototype implements the bulk of the concepts described above. We tested the prototype using an interactive display wall comprised of twelve 55" displays with a total size of 5x2 meters and a resolution of 24

Figure 7: View of complete multi-device prototype.

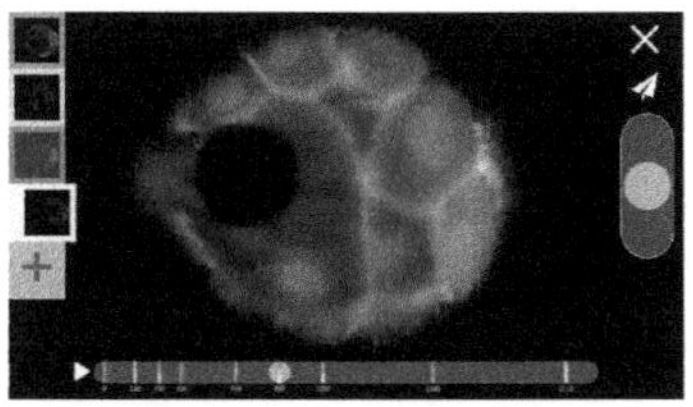

Figure 8: Prototype mobile interface.

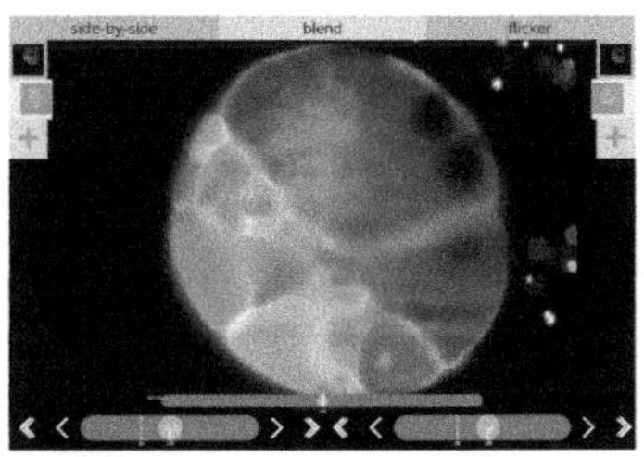

Figure 9: Comparison view on large display using color coding to show differences between samples.

megapixels running Ubuntu. As mobile device, we used a Google Nexus 7 tablet.

On the large display, the prototype supports multiple cross section views (of the same or different specimen) as well as volumetric views and a comparison view (Figure 9). The mobile device displays the currently selected sample and supports cross section selection using clutching. Currently, we assume that the user looks at the mobile device when specifying a cross section and therefore implement an egocentric perspective. To avoid confusing users, we disable view updates on the large screen as long as the clutch is active. Further, nudging and configurable CD gain are currently not implemented. Both mobile and large display views fully support bookmark management.

The UI of the prototype is implemented in Python using the media application framework libavg[1]. It is a single multi-device application: Both display wall and mobile interfaces are rendered on the display wall workstation. The mobile interface is compressed to h264 in realtime and streamed to the device. Conversely, touch data is streamed from mobile to workstation. Mobile location data is obtained using a marker-based optical tracking system, OptiTrack.

For rendering of the actual LSFM images, we use BigDataViewer (BDV), an extensible open source solution for interactive visualization of very large volumes and time series of volumes [7]. Individual image stacks are arbitrarily arranged in global 3D coordinate space, and can be displayed independently or as color composite. The software renders arbitrarily oriented virtual slices through the global space. An intelligent tile-based loading and caching scheme allows smooth navigation in multi-terabyte image datasets. The data can be provided by both local and remote sources, and is easily extended to handle new data sources such as 3rd party file formats or online data stores.

BDV is implemented as a java library. To make it usable in our context, we implemented a libavg plugin in C++ using the Java Native Interface. Using this plugin, an application can request rendered frames from BDV, specifying parameters such as timepoint, transformation, visible channels, etc. On the Java side, BDV fetches and caches the data from an arbitrary backend (in our experiments we remotely access data provided by a server at the MPI-CBG). Rendered frames are asynchronously passed back to libavg where they are loaded to textures for display.

Initial User Feedback

As initial validation of our prototype, we solicited feedback from several domain experts (developmental biologists) who are potential users of our system. For this feedback session we used an LSFM dataset of Platynereis that had a size of 1.4 terabytes. The session included a presentation of the interface, informal tests by the domain experts, and a discussion about future directions.

The general reaction was very positive for both tangible-based cross section selection and time-series bookmarking. There were few precision issues in cross section selection with the current three-way clutch. However, users pointed out that this might change for higher resolution data sets. Further, users would like the ability to set a pivot point for rotations, as the current rotation around the center of the specimen causes them to frequently lose their point of interest.

[1]http://www.libavg.de

Discussion

Based on the initial user feedback, we are confident that our concept is sound and that development is proceeding in the right direction in general. However, there are a number of directions for future work. One very interesting topic is the distribution of the interaction between the mobile and the large display. While the mobile device is clearly more suitable for sample selection, the wall display is good for work with multiple views and presentation of results. However, other interactions can be done on both devices, and sample selection could potentially be done with the mobile device while viewing the results on the wall display in exocentric mode. Aspects such as necessary attention switches, egocentric versus exocentric visualization, and single- versus multi-user interaction all play a role here, so we believe that a good solution requires the exploration of several alternatives.

Conclusion

We presented an interaction concept for exploration of large scientific time-dependent 3D data sets, validated through a prototype and initial user feedback from domain experts. The presented interactions include both a precise selection technique for 2D cross sections and a concept for time-dependent bookmarks that allows following a point of interest through time.

Acknowledgements

We would like to thank the scientists of the Max Planck Institute of Molecular Cell Biology and Genetics who provided valuable domain knowledge and user feedback, namely Ulrik Günther, Mette Handberg-Thorsager, Yu-Wen Hsieh, Akanksha Jain, Helena Jambor, and Christopher Schmied. Additional thanks to Mette Handberg-Thorsager and Yu-Wen Hsieh for providing LSFM data of Platynereis development.

References

[1] Bertelsen, A., Irarrazaval, P., and Cadiz, R. F. Volume visualization using a spatially aware mobile display device. *Computerized Medical Imaging and Graphics 36*, 1 (2012), 66 – 71.

[2] Besancon, L., Issartel, P., Ammi, M., and Isenberg, T. Hybrid tactile/tangible interaction for 3d data exploration. *IEEE Trans. Vis. Comp. Graph. PP*, 99 (2016), 1–10.

[3] Bowman, D. A., Kruijff, E., LaViola, J. J., and Poupyrev, I. *3D User Interfaces: Theory and Practice.* Addison Wesley Longman Publishing Co., Inc., Redwood City, CA, USA, 2004.

[4] Dam, A. v., Forsberg, A. S., Laidlaw, D. H., LaViola, J. J., and Simpson, R. M. Immersive VR for scientific visualization: A progress report. *IEEE Comput. Graph. Appl. 20*, 6 (Nov. 2000), 26–52.

[5] Isenberg, P., Isenberg, T., Hesselmann, T., Lee, B., von Zadow, U., and Tang, A. Data visualization on interactive surfaces: A research agenda. *IEEE Comput. Graph. Appl. 33*, 2 (2013).

[6] Keefe, D. F., and Isenberg, T. Reimagining the scientific visualization interaction paradigm. *Computer 46*, 5 (May 2013), 51–57.

[7] Pietzsch, T., Saalfeld, S., Preibisch, S., and Tomancak, P. BigDataViewer: visualization and processing for large image data sets. *Nature Methods 12*, 6 (06 2015), 481–483.

[8] Spindler, M., Büschel, W., Winkler, C., and Dachselt, R. Tangible displays for the masses: Spatial interaction with handheld displays by using consumer depth cameras. *Personal Ubiquitous Comput. 18*, 5 (June 2014), 1213–1225.

[9] Spindler, M., Tominski, C., Schumann, H., and Dachselt, R. Tangible views for information visualization. In *Proc. ITS*, ACM (2010), 157–166.

Synchronized Mixed Presence Data-Conferencing Using Large-Scale Shared Displays

Thomas Marrinan
Argonne National Laboratory
9700 Cass Ave.
Lemont, IL 60439 USA
tmarrinan@anl.gov

Luc Renambot
University of Illinois at Chicago
851 S. Morgan St.
Chicago, IL 60607 USA
renambot@uic.edu

Jason Leigh
University of Hawai'i at Mānoa
2500 Campus Rd.
Honolulu, HI 96822 USA
leighj@hawaii.edu

Angus Forbes
University of Illinois at Chicago
851 S. Morgan St.
Chicago, IL 60607 USA
aforbes@uic.edu

Steve Jones
University of Illinois at Chicago
851 S. Morgan St.
Chicago, IL 60607 USA
sjones@uic.edu

Andrew Johnson
University of Illinois at Chicago
851 S. Morgan St.
Chicago, IL 60607 USA
ajohnson@uic.edu

ISS '16, November 06-09, 2016, Niagara Falls, ON, Canada
ACM 978-1-4503-4248-3/16/11.
http://dx.doi.org/10.1145/2992154.2996780

Abstract
Real world group-to-group collaboration often occurs between partially distributed interdisciplinary teams, with each discipline working in a unique environment suited for its needs. Groupware must be flexible so that it can be incorporated into a variety of workspaces in order to successfully facilitate this type of mixed presence collaboration. We have developed two new techniques for sharing and synchronizing multi-user applications between heterogeneous large-scale shared displays. The first new technique partitions displays into a perfectly mirrored public space and a local private space. The second new technique enables user-controlled partial synchronization, where different attributes of an application can be synchronized or controlled independently. This paper presents two main contributions of our work: 1) identifying deficiencies in current groupware for interacting with data during mixed presence collaboration, and 2) developing two multi-user data synchronization techniques to address these deficiencies and extend current collaborative infrastructure for large-scale shared displays.

Author Keywords
Mixed presence collaboration; computer-supported cooperative work; large-scale displays; multi-user interaction; data synchronization.

ACM Classification Keywords
H.5.3. Information Interfaces and Presentation: Group and Organization Interfaces: Computer-supported cooperative work, synchronous interaction.

Introduction
Commercial software, such as Google Hangouts, Skype, and WebEx [3,9,10] has made significant strides to enhance remote collaboration between single users. Other systems, such as Oblong's Mezzanine [7], have enabled mixed presence collaboration (remote collaboration between multiple collocated groups), but only when the display environment is cloned in all locations. These configurations are not always practical in the real world since collaboration is often interdisciplinary, with each discipline having a unique work environment suited for its needs.

Research endeavors have also attempted to enhance collaboration over distance. CollaBoard [5] augments video and audio with shared applications to create a data-conferencing system that imitates a life-sized face-to-face meeting. However, CollaBoard only supports one-on-one remote collaboration and requires a special setup of cameras and displays. Hugin [4] is a framework for mixed presence collaborative information visualization. Networked tabletop displays are utilized to allow multiple users located at various sites to collaboratively view and analyze visualizations. While Hugin doesn't fully restrict hardware and allows each group to choose what content is shared publicly, it represents a domain specific solution for collaborative information visualization. PolyChrome [1] synchronizes web applications between heterogeneous devices such as a large-scale display and a tablet. This allows multiple users to interact in a shared application simultaneously. However, PolyChrome only handles one web application at a time and enforces full synchronization between devices.

Since many other existing systems enforced hardware or content limitations and large-scale displays have been shown to foster collaboration [2], we identified SAGE2™, the Scalable Amplified Group Environment [6,8], as the most suitable collaborative infrastructure for researching mixed presence data-conferencing using shared displays. SAGE2 provides a windowing environment that allows simultaneous multi-user interaction with documents and applications on large high-resolution shared displays of any size. Prior to the work presented in this paper, SAGE2 enabled limited forms of mixed presence collaboration: *data-pushing*, and *perfect-mirror*. *Data-pushing* allows collaborators at one SAGE2 site to share any application or document that is currently on the display with another SAGE2 site. A copy of the application is sent to the remote site, and each group can interact independently without affecting the remote instance. In *perfect-mirror* mode, collaborators at a remote location can view an exact copy of an entire SAGE2 display. In this scenario, users at both locations interact with and manipulate the same instances of applications and data. Additionally, SAGE2 has already been adopted at more than 200 sites worldwide, and builds upon more than 10 years of research surrounding large-scale shared display collaboration.

Since SAGE2 already had a basic mixed presence collaboration infrastructure in place and had an active user community, we decided to leverage its framework and extend its capabilities. However, the techniques described in the rest of this paper can broadly apply to mixed presence groupware in general.

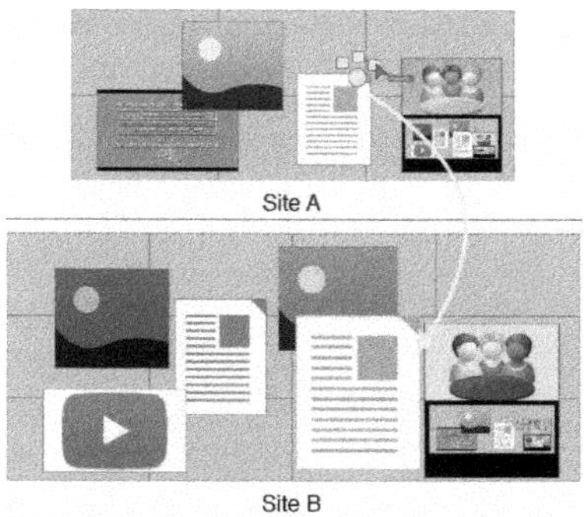

Figure 1. Illustration of *data-pushing*. Two sites are using heterogeneous shared displays and viewing separate content, private to the local group. Site A has shared the blue document causing a copy to appear at Site B. Further interaction with this document will not be synchronized.

Unlike video and audio, data-conferencing with fully synchronized content may not always be ideal. Groups or individuals may be analyzing different portions of the same data, and therefore desire unsynchronized interactions in certain situations. We have supplemented one of the existing remote collaboration techniques of SAGE2 and designed two new data-conferencing techniques to allow various forms of semi-synchronized content sharing. First, we enhanced the existing *data-pushing* technique by augmenting a shared application with its current state. This enables a shared application to be initialized on the remote site as a snapshot of its original application. Further interaction within the shared application from either site would still be unsynchronized.

The first new technique developed was *data-duplication*, where one section of the shared display contains local unsynchronized versions of private data-conferencing content and a second portion of the shared display contains fully synchronized copies of public data-conferencing content. This technique partitions the shared display into two spaces – public content that would be perfectly mirrored with the remote collaborators and private content that would be viewed and controlled independently. The second new technique developed was to use *advanced data-synchronization options*, where collaborators chose which aspects of each shared application are synchronized and which are controlled independently. This technique allows for independent window management by each site and enables continuous synchronization of some or all aspects for each shared application.

Methods

The work previously done on SAGE2 made it a powerful and flexible system to better enable collocated and remote collaboration. However, there was still a need to develop and evaluate more advanced means of supporting groups working together across distance in a mixed presence environment. In order to mirror content and have all interactions synchronized between multiple sites, SAGE2 required matching hardware configurations at all locations. For collaboration between heterogeneous shared displays where groups are working on separate but related pieces of a problem, collaborators were limited to *data-pushing*: sending unsynchronized applications between locations. Multiple sites could not simultaneously interact with a shared application in this situation; each site could only interact with their own local copy. For example, if one site pushed a PDF to another site, the same document would be shown on each shared display. However, the position and size of the document and which page of the PDF was being viewed would be completely independent between the two sites. We have supplemented this technique by initializing a shared application with its current state so that it serves as a snapshot of what the original collaborators were viewing (Figure 1). Extending the above example, when a PDF currently showing its third page is shared with a remote site, a copy of that PDF will open on the remote site showing page three. However, further changes to which page is visible will only affect the local site since interaction is still unsynchronized.

SAGE2 natively supports screen sharing from remote machines. This feature can be utilized in a mixed presence collaboration setting to share a videoconference application, such as Skype or Google

Figure 2. Mixed presence collaboration using the *data-duplication technique*. The yellow highlight in each photo shows the shared portal on each shared display with synchronized applications and pointer icons.

Hangouts, on the shared display. In order to provide remote collaborator awareness, we determined that sharing two videoconference windows, one with the camera showing the collaborators and one with the camera showing the remote shared display, would work well for mixed presence collaboration.

To improve coordination and user awareness by allowing users at different sites to collaborate on a shared application, we developed two new techniques to handle synchronizing applications across remote sites. These two techniques have been termed *data-duplication* and *advanced data-synchronization options*.

Data-Duplication

The first new technique we developed was *data-duplication*, where one section of the shared display contains local unsynchronized versions of private data-conferencing content and a second portion of the shared display acts as a shared portal that contains the fully synchronized copies of public data-conferencing content. These sections partition the overall screen space of the shared display. At any time, any user can move an application from the local space to a remote partition in order to share the application. The application will appear in the corresponding partition on the remote site's shared display. Users at both locations are able to simultaneously interact with the shared application. Both window management actions, such as window movement and resize, and interactions inside the application are fully synchronized across sites. Additionally, interaction icons for pointers and touch events in the shared partition are displayed at both locations (Figure 2). This gives the appearance of both groups working on the same application simultaneously, and is designed to improve remote collaborator awareness.

Unlike perfect-mirror sites, this technique allows for both a shared and a private space for data. Additionally, remotely located shared displays do not need to be homogenous. Any two shared displays using our *data-duplication* technique could create a shared data portal regardless of size, resolution, or aspect ratio. Additionally, the shared portal can be freely moved and resized on each shared display independently – only relative positions and sizes of applications inside the portal remain constant. This allows each group to scale the shared portal to a size that is best for their technology.

Since applications are executing separately at each site, the application's state, which defines all properties necessary to fully reproduce the application, is observed at all sites. Any time an aspect of the state is modified, its value is streamed to the linked remote application. This ensures that the state of shared applications at both sites remain the same. Since each site has its own instance of the application, other aspects of the application can vary between sites, such as frame rate. This gives users the appearance that the groups are interacting with the same application, while optimizing performance for each site's local hardware.

Since SAGE2 is a multi-user collaborative platform, multiple pointers can be used for simultaneous interaction. All pointers from the remote shared display are also added to the local shared display (and vice-versa) so that collaborators at both sites can view local and remote pointers within the portal. Whenever a remote pointer enters the portal, a message is sent from the remote site instructing the local display to make that pointer visible, and whenever a remote pointer exits the portal, another message is sent from the remote site instructing the local display to make that pointer invisible. Therefore remote pointers only appear within the shared area and do not

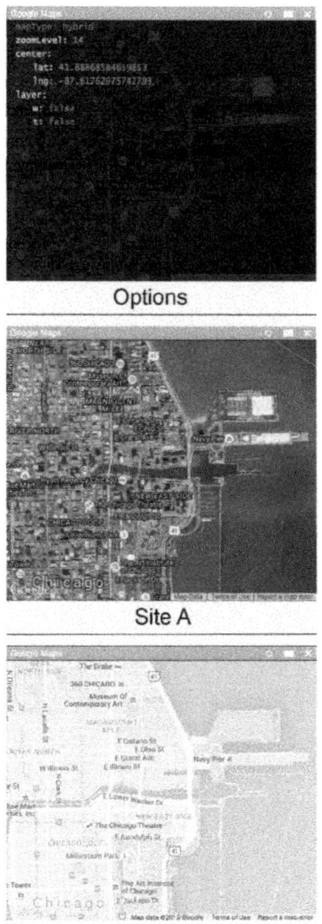

Figure 3. Mixed presence collaboration using the *advanced data-synchronization options* technique. Top – application state and selected options (all properties except for 'mapType' are synchronized). Middle – the shared application at Site A with 'mapType' showing satellite imagery. Bottom– the shared application at Site B with 'mapType' showing roadmap imagery. Other properties, such as the map's center (latitude, longitude) and zoom are synchronized between the sites.

interfere with the private content on the rest of the shared display.

Advanced Data-Synchronization Options

The second new technique we developed uses *advanced data-synchronization options*, where collaborators can choose which aspects of each shared application will be synchronized and which will be controlled independently. Users are given access to independent variables within an application's state and are able to choose whether or not to synchronize each individual property when sharing with a remote site (Figure 3). This technique was designed to allow teams at each location to coordinate their efforts based on individual needs versus whole group needs. For example, when watching a video across multiple sites it may be beneficial to synchronize the location of the play head and whether the video is playing or paused. However, different sites may wish to have independent control on the volume level.

In order to keep users from manually selecting whether to synchronize each individual property, the state is ordered hierarchically. For example, the camera position in a 3D model viewing application can be the parent of x, y, and z positions. Therefore, to synchronize or desynchronize the camera position, a user would simply need to make one selection rather than three.

Similar to the *data-duplication* technique, applications will be executing separately at each site. Any time a synchronized aspect of the state is modified, its value will be streamed to each remote application. Since each site has its own instance of the application, unsynchronized aspects of the state never get streamed to the remote instances. This gives users the appearance that they are interacting with a shared application that allows the freedom to control certain properties locally.

We designed a graphical user interface that overlays a shared application depicting its state. Aspects of the application state are organized hierarchically. Properties that are not synchronized are visually grayed out, whereas synchronized properties are visualized in full color. Users can display or hide this interface and select or unselect any property at any time. Whenever a user at either site synchronizes or desynchronizes a property, this option is streamed to the other site so that changes to this property are handled accordingly.

Conclusion

Physical distance between collaborators has created a barrier that has fueled the research and development of technology that can enable groups of people to connect and share data. While existing commercial software has begun to address the issues surrounding mixed presence collaboration, many of the solutions are limited to a particular task or a particular set of hardware.

Our research has sought to create a more flexible solution that provides a platform for researchers to share arbitrary data and collaborate in real-time with other remotely located teams. The two new techniques we developed, *data-duplication* and *advanced data-synchronization options*, enable users to engage in mixed presence collaboration in manner previously not supported in any groupware system. Using *data-duplication*, distributed teams can see exact replicas of shared data at both sites while still maintaining private workspace. Using *advanced data-synchronization options*, distributed teams can partially desynchronize and resynchronize various aspects of a shared application at any point during the collaborative session to enhance coordination and work on tasks in parallel.

Future Work

Our research and development does have certain limitations. All data sharing techniques are one-to-one, enabling two shared displays to share data with each other. In order to communicate between three or more sites, multiple one-to-one sharing connections would be required. Moving forward, the *data-duplication* and *advanced data-synchronization options* techniques could be expanded to allow for any application to be shared with any number of other shared displays. This way three or more groups involved in a mixed presence collaboration could all see and work on synchronized copies of the same applications.

Acknowledgements

This publication is based on the work supported in part by the National Science Foundation (NSF), awards ACI-1339772, OCI-0943559 and CNS-0959053. SAGE2 is a trademark of the University of Illinois Board of Trustees.

References

[1] Badam, S. K. and Elmqvist, N. 2014. PolyChrome: A Cross-Device Framework for Collaborative Web Visualization. In *Proceedings of the ACM International Conference on Interactive Tabletops and Surfaces* (ITS '14), (2014), 109-118. http://dx.doi.org/10.1145/2669485.2669518

[2] Czerwinski, M., Smith, G., Regan, T., Meyers, B., Robertson, G., and Starkweather, G. Toward Characterizing the Productivity Benefits of Very Large Displays. In *Proceedings of the 2003 IFIP TC13 international conference on Human-Computer Interaction* (INTERACT '03), vol. 3 (2003), 9-16.

[3] Google Hangouts. Retrieved August 25, 2016 from https://hangouts.google.com/.

[4] Kim, K., Javed, W., Williams, C., Elmqvist, N., and Irani, P. Hugin: a Framework for Awareness and Coordination in Mixed-presence Collaborative Information Visualization. In *Proceedings of the ACM International Conference on Interactive Tabletops and Surfaces* (ITS '10), (2010), 231-240. http://doi.acm.org/10.1145/1936652.1936694

[5] Kuechler, M. and Kunz, A. M. Collaboard: a Remote Collaboration Groupware Device Featuring an Embodiment-enriched Shared Workspace. In *Proceedings of the 16th ACM International Conference on Supporting Group Work* (GROUP '10), (2010), 211-214. http://dx.doi.org/10.1145/1880071.1880107

[6] Marrinan, T., Aurisano, J., Nishimoto, A., Bharadwaj, K., Mateevitsi, V., Renambot, L., Long, L., Johnson, A., and Leigh, J. SAGE2: A New Approach for Data Intensive Collaboration Using Scalable Resolution Shared Displays. In *Proceedings of the IEEE International Conference on Collaborative Computing: Networking, Applications and Worksharing* (CollaborateCom '14), (2014), 177-186. http://dx.doi.org/10.4108/icst.collaboratecom.2014.257337

[7] Oblong Industries, Inc. Introducing Mezzanine: the Future of Conference Room Collaboration. *White Paper* (2013).

[8] Renambot, L., Marrinan, T., Aurisano, J., Nishimoto, A., Mateevitsi, V., Bharadwaj, K., Long, L., Johnson, A., Brown, M., and Leigh, J. SAGE2: A Collaboration Portal for Scalable Resolution Displays. In *Future Generation Computer Systems*, vol. 54 (2016), 296-305. http://dx.doi.org/10.1016/j.future.2015.05.014

[9] Skype. Retrieved August 25, 2016 from http://www.skype.com/en/.

[10] WebEx. Retrieved August 25, 2016 from https://www.webex.com/.

Sports Support System: Augmented Ball Game for Filling Gap between Player Skill Levels

Yuji Sano
Koya Sato
Ryoichiro Shiraishi
Mai Otsuki
University of Tsukuba
1-1-1 Tennodai, Tsukuba, Ibaraki
305-8577 Japan
sano@aclab.esys.tsukuba.ac.jp
koya@osss.cs.tsukuba.ac.jp
shiraishi_r@golem.kz.tsukuba.ac.jp
otsuki@emp.tsukuba.ac.jp

ISS '16, November 06-09, 2016, Niagara Falls, ON, Canada
ACM 978-1-4503-4248-3/16/11.
http://dx.doi.org/10.1145/2992154.2996781

Abstract
In order to fill the gap between various levels of ball game players, we propose the Sports Support System that can reduce the difference among the skills of various players by augmenting the traditional ball game. We implemented a system that visualizes the trajectory and velocity of the ball for soccer games, as one example of ball games. This visualization and the enhancement of the player positions in the field can help beginner players recognize what they should do next and improve their playing skills.

Figure 1: Overview of Sport Support System, that is a projection-based augmented reality system for supporting ball game training, provides the trajectory and velocity of the ball and players on a marker projection on the floor.

This paper introduces the proposed system and discusses, through a user study, its effectiveness for improving reaction speed and enhancing the pleasure of playing sports. Based on the experiment results, the proposed system contributes to reaction time improvements in passing and receiving the ball, i.e., one of the most important skills in playing soccer.

Author Keywords
Visualization; Augmented Reality; Sports; Augmented Sports; Sports Support System;

ACM Classification Keywords
H.5.1 Multimedia Information Systems: Artificial, augmented, and virtual realities

Introduction
Sports have positive effects on health, including mental, emotional, and physical benefits such as disease prevention. In addition, we can enjoy playing sports with others. Additional benefits include the fact that participating in team sports can provide players with a method for meeting new people and expanding social networks.

A sports game includes aspects of victory and defeat, tactics, and reaction speed; furthermore, some skills are very important for obtaining advantages of a game. There are large differences among the skills of various levels of players.

The purpose of this study is to develop a Sports Support System that can reduce the differences among the skills of various players by augmenting traditional sports (Figure 1). The proposed system visualizes the trajectory and velocity of the ball for soccer games, as one example of ball games. This visualization and the enhancement of the player positions in the field can help beginner players recognize what they should do next and improve their playing skills.

This paper introduces the proposed system and discusses, through a user study, its effectiveness for improving reaction speed and enhancing the pleasure of playing sports.

Related Work
Augmented reality technologies provide additional information for assisting with recognition and perception [10]. There is a study that applied an interactive projection system to help learn to play the piano fast [1]. The system provided enhanced piano roll notations and a natural leaning process with live feedback, and those interactions improved the user's performance. Augmented reality technologies are also effective in improving skills to play drums [11], climb walls [7], or other physical activities, such as dancing [2, 3].

On the other hand, an interactive augmented reality technology has been applied to basketball, table hockey, and dodgeball to create new game content [4, 9]. Those approaches indicate that the collaboration between sports and augmented reality technologies can enhance the pleasure of playing sports. Augmented reality is suitable for team games because encouragement of the social interaction among players is one of the important benefits of games [4]. However, how effective augmented reality technologies are for improving skills has not been made clear. Therefore, we focus on the skill improvement of playing sports,

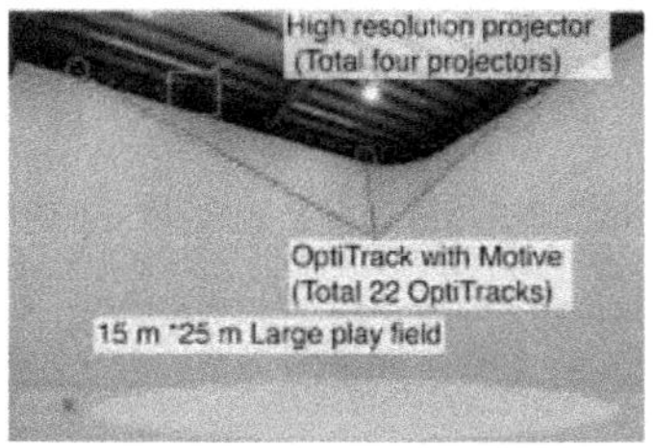

Figure 2: Large Space equipment for the proposed system, that is the world's largest immersive virtual environment with full surround and floor projections.

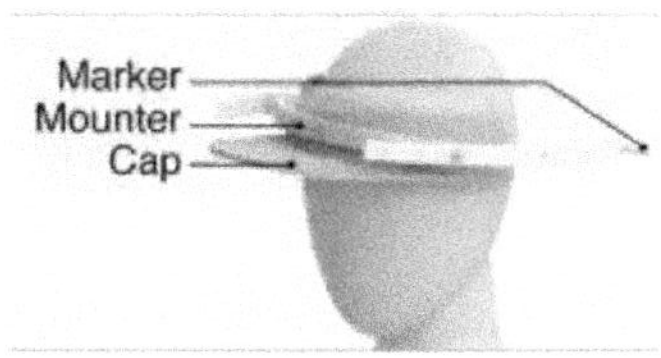

Figure 3, Mounter for infrared reflective markers that has six mounting holes to be set markers in various position combinations.

and this paper discusses the feasibility and effectiveness of the proposed system.

Sports Support System

Design

From the perspective of soccer training, the ability to pass a ball is one of the most important skills, and it consists of accuracy and timing. In particular, the goalkeeper should pay attention to the motion of four or five players simultaneously, and thus training for goalkeeping focuses on the cognition of player position and motion. Passing and receiving the ball are also required skills, as are imagining the game progress and place management [6] .

Because the standard operation of soccer training is almost always based on group practices that share the same field [5], we developed a projection-based augmented reality system for supporting soccer training, which is the Sports Support System, that allows multiple users to play in the same field at the same time. In addition, in order to support passing and receiving the ball and cognition of the ball and player movements, the Sports Support System provides the trajectory and velocity of the ball and players on a marker projection on the floor.

System Configuration

Figure 2 shows a system overview of the Sports Support System. The system uses 22 motion capture cameras and four projectors within the Large Space. The Large Space is the world's largest immersive virtual environment with full surround and floor projections. It covers a space of 7.7 m in height, 25 m in width, and 15 m in length.

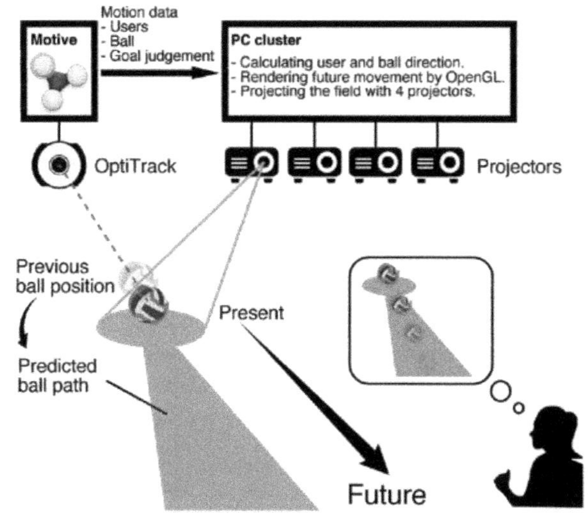

Figure 4: System Configuration of Sport Support System that have 22 motion capture cameras for tracking the ball and users at very high accuracy less than 1mm and four FHD projectors for projecting ball path and players position.

Tracking System

We use the motion tracking system (Optitrack with Motive) to detect the position and direction of the ball and players with infrared reflective materials. In order to distinguish each player, we made a 3D-printed mounter (Figure 3) that has six mounting holes for infrared reflective materials to be set in various position combinations.

Projection System

We developed a projection system for visualizing the position and direction of the ball and players in order to enhance predictions of ball path (Figure 4). This system renders on the floor a predicted path calculated by the

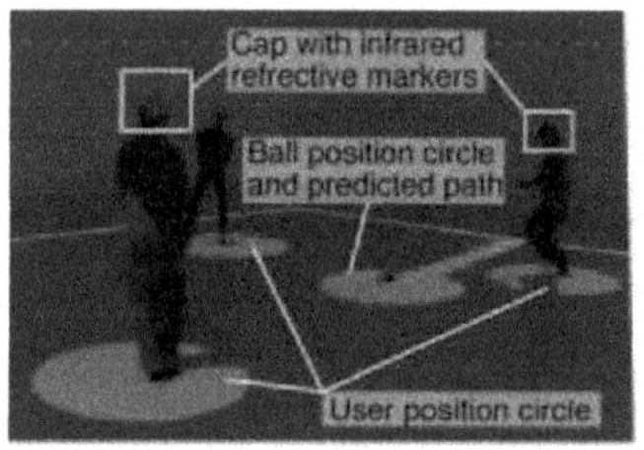

Figure 5: Implementation results for Sports Support System for soccer, the proposed system can track six of players and the ball and visualize those positions and predicted direction.

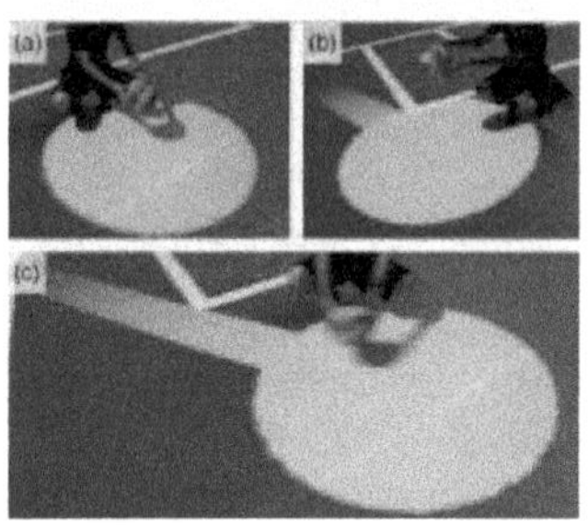

Figure 6, Predicted path of a ball (a) stopping, (b) moving slowly, (c) moving quickly, the length of predicted path scales linearly with the velocity.

previous ball position; it also renders player directions in the same way as the ball. The rendering task is managed by OpenGL, and four PCs (CPU: Intel Core-i7 4790K, GPU: NVIDIA Quadro K5000) in a PC cluster run the OpenGL program. Each computer calculates the ball path on the floor allocated to each projector. A player would predict not only the ball path, but also the velocity. The length of the ball path represents the velocity of the ball.

Implementation Results

Six players can simultaneously play a mini-soccer game in this space (Figure 5). Figure 6 shows the difference in the length of the predicting path based on ball velocity. The tracking error is less than 1 mm according to the system datasheet.

Experiment

Purpose and Procedure

The purpose of this experiment is to clarify the effectiveness of the proposed system for improving skills. We assume that the gap among the various player levels can fall into two categories: the skill of ball-path-prediction and width of the field of view. The skill of ball-path-prediction can be confirmed by comparing the cases with or without the proposed system, and width of the field of view can be confirmed by comparing the cases of passing the ball from the front or from out of view.

In order to evaluate the effectiveness of the proposed system for these factors, we recorded reaction times from the moment of passing the ball to the participant's initial reaction in the case of passing from the front or from out of view, and with or without the system.

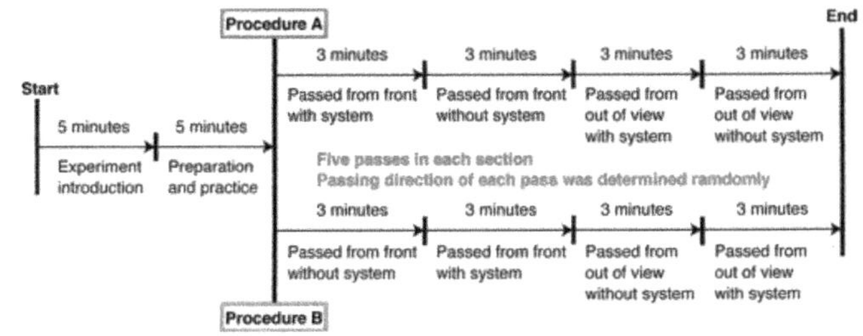

Figure 7: Experiment procedure for evaluating effectiveness of proposed method for improving reaction time

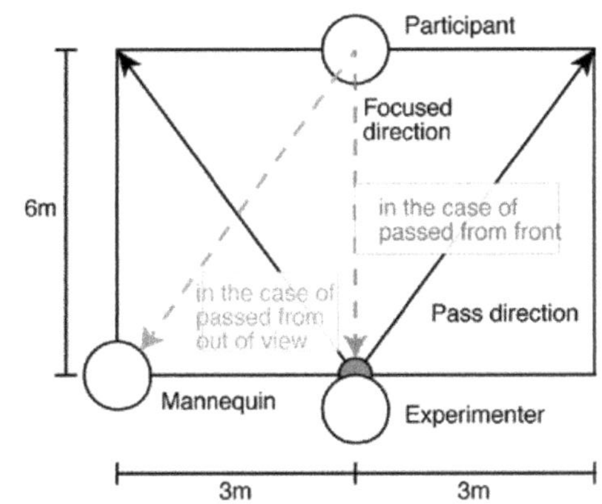

Figure 8: Experiment environment and position of each mannequin, participant, and experimenter

The experiment procedure is shown in Figure 7, and eight university students (22-25 years of age) participated in this experiment. The students were divided into two groups, and they were subjected to the experiment in different order, starting from the case with the proposed system or from the case without the system, in order to avoid an order effect.

The experiment was divided into four sections in each procedures, and the experimenter randomly passed a ball to the participant's left or right side from 6 m away in each sections (Figure 8). In the case of passing from out of view, in order to create a situation where the participant received the ball passed from out of view, we set a mannequin 3 m to the left of the experimenter, and required the participant to focus on the mannequin.

Results

We focused on the differences in reaction time between the cases of passing from the front or from out of view, with or without the system (Figure 9). A two-way factorial repeated-measures ANOVA indicated a significant main effect for both with or without the system ($F(1,1) = 113.7$, $p < 0.01$) and the focused direction ($F(1,1) = 42.53$, $p < 0.01$). Their interaction showed no significant difference.

The average reaction time in the case of passing from out of view is longer by 114 ms compared with the case of passing from the front for all participants, both with and without the system. On the other hand, the proposed system improved the reaction time by 88 ms on average. Note that the difference of ball speed between each trial was so small that there was weak correlation between the ball speed and the reaction time in this experiment.

Discussion

The results of ANOVA indicate that the proposed system contributes to improvements in reaction time when passing the ball; therefore, the proposed system can improve the skill of passing and receiving the ball, i.e., one of the most important skills in playing soccer.

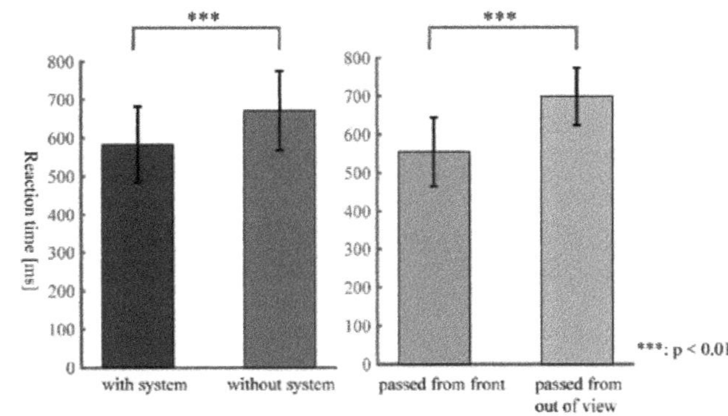

Figure 9: The reaction time between in the case of whether passed from front or from out of view, with or without the system.

In addition, the proposed system might be effective for low-skilled players because none of participants exercise actively in their daily life. On the other hand, the proposed system does not support the player's field of view because there is no significant difference between the cases of passing from the front or from out of view. From this result, in order to improve the proposed system, we plan to implement a function that can visually suggest the moving path for the player to receive the ball.

Conclusion

We focused on the gap among various levels of ball game players, and proposed the Sports Support System. We realized the idea of reducing this gap by helping with the cognition of what a player should do next. For implementation, the proposed system provides the trajectories and velocities of the ball and players as projections on the floor of a soccer game.

As demonstrated by the experiment results, the proposed system contributes to reaction time improvements when passing the ball. Our approach found that the interactive visualization in sports could help various levels of players to improve their skills.

For future work, because the results of the experiment also showed only the effect of short-term skill improvement, we plan to clarify the effectiveness of the proposed system for long-term skill training.

References

1. Alt F., Schneegass S., Girgis M., and Schmidt A. Cognitive effects of interactive public display applications. In *Proceedings of the 2nd ACM International Symposium on Pervasive Displays* (PerDis '13), 13-18.
2. Anderson F. and Bischof W. F. Learning and performance with gesture guides. In *Proceedings of the SIGCHI Conference on Human Factors in Computing Systems* (CHI '13), 1109-1118.
3. Anderson F., Grossman T., Matejka J., and Fitzmaurice G. YouMove: enhancing movement training with an augmented reality mirror. In *Proceedings of the 26th annual ACM symposium on User interface software and technology* (UIST '13), 311-320.
4. Baudisch P., Pohl H., Reinicke S., Wittmers E., Lühne P., et al. Imaginary reality gaming: ball games without a ball. In *Proceedings of the 26th annual ACM symposium on User interface software and technology* (UIST '13), 405-410.
5. Cook, Malcolm. Soccer Training: Games, Drills and Fitness Practices. Bloomsbury Publishing, 2015.
6. Docherty, T. The ABC of soccer sense: strategy & tactics today. Arco Pub. Co., 1978.
7. Kajastila R., Holsti L., and Hämäläinen P. The Augmented Climbing Wall: High-exertion proximity interaction on a wall-sized interactive surface. In *Proceedings of the 2016 CHI Conference on Human Factors in Computing Systems*, CHI '16, 758-769.
8. Mueller S., Dippon A., and Klinker G. Capture The Flag: Engaging in a multi-device augmented reality game. In *Proceedings of the 2015 International Conference on Interactive Tabletops & Surfaces*, ITS '15, 277-282.
9. Nojima T., Phuong N., Kai T., Sato T., and Koike H. Augmented dodgeball: an approach to designing augmented sports. In *Proceedings of the 6th Augmented Human International Conference*, AH '15, 137-140.
10. Van Krevelen D. W. F. and Poelman R. A survey of augmented reality technologies, applications and limitations. *International Journal of Virtual Reality*, *9,2*, (2010), 1.
11. Yamabe T. and Nakajima T. Playful training with augmented reality games: case studies towards reality-oriented system design. *Multimedia Tools and Applications*, *62,1*, (2013), 259-286.

Foldable3D: Interacting with 3D Content Using Dual-Display Devices

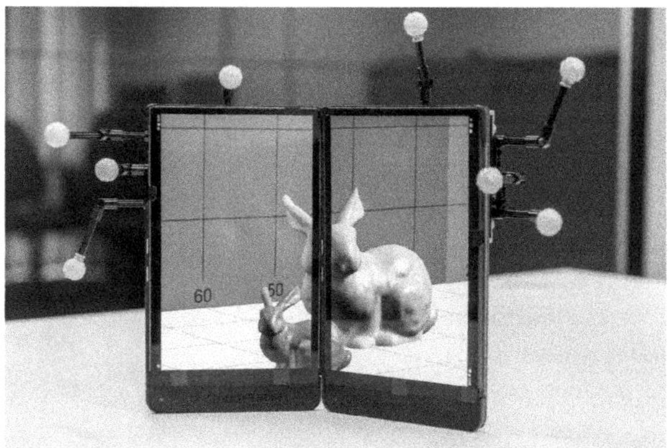

Figure 1: The current prototype running on two Android tablets and using an optical tracking system. The scene in this photo is shown as it would be perceived by a user.

Wolfgang Büschel
Interactive Media Lab
Technische Universität Dresden
Dresden, Germany
bueschel@acm.org

Patrick Reipschläger
Interactive Media Lab
Technische Universität Dresden
Dresden, Germany
preipschlager@acm.org

Raimund Dachselt
Interactive Media Lab
Technische Universität Dresden
Dresden, Germany
dachselt@acm.org

ISS 2016, November 6–9, 2016, Niagara Falls, ON, Canada.
ACM ISBN 978-1-4503-4248-3/16/11.
http://dx.doi.org/10.1145/2992154.2996782

Abstract
By now, mobile 3D interaction is often limited to simple multi-touch input on standard devices and less expressive or hard to use. We present the concept of mobile dual-display devices which can be folded for the exploration of 3D content. We examine different display modes and introduce new presentation and 3D interaction techniques that make use of the special form factor and the added input modality of folding two displays. In particular, we also consider the advantages of our proposed device for head-coupled perspective rendering – virtually extending the view and providing independent perspectives for two users.

Author Keywords
3D Interaction; Head-Coupled Perspective; Dual-Display Device; Virtual Reality; Augmented Reality

ACM Classification Keywords
H.5.2 [User Interfaces]: Input devices and strategies (e. g., mouse, touchscreen)

Introduction
Using mobile devices for 3D interaction and visualization is increasingly popular and has a lot of potential in fields such as presentation of 3D content, games or Augmented

Figure 2: Pictures of our prototype showing the effect of HCP for different folding angles and viewer positions.

Reality applications. However, so far, interaction is mostly limited to multi-touch input and ordinary form factors and is not taking into account, e. g., spatial input or head-coupled perspective. On the other hand, while dual-screen mobile devices have been proposed and studied in the past (i. e., [5, 6]), their potential for 3D interaction and visualization has not been realized yet. Existing commercial devices, e. g., the *Nintendo DS* portable game console and its successors, also generally limit the use of the second screen to straight-forward input and output techniques.

For head-coupled perspective (HCP), also called fishtank VR or user-centered perspective, instead of a fixed perspective that is bound to the display device, the user's position in relation to the screen is used to determine a dynamic off-axis perspective that creates the immersion of the screen being a window through which the 3D scene is observed. However, most solutions that are available today are limited by the field of view of the camera that tracks the user and the viewing angle of the display.

We envision to combine two displays into a foldable dual-display mobile device for 3D interaction and visualization. Our research goals are to examine if such devices can benefit the exploration and manipulation of 3D content by providing new ways for spatial interaction and to investigate if HCP for mobile devices is improved by having two linked but spatially flexible displays. To this end, we analyzed the design space of the proposed form factor for 3D interaction. Specifically, we conducted iterative brainstorming sessions and discussed possible concepts in-depth, also making use of a functional device mockup and first software prototypes.

In this work we present our first steps towards these research goals. We introduce the novel concept of using HCP on a dual-display mobile device for interacting with 3D content. We also present display modes and several techniques for 3D interaction and presentation with such a device, taking into consideration both HCP and the additional input modality of folding.

Related Work

Multi-Display and Foldable Mobile Devices

Mobile devices with two or more displays have already been proposed and studied in the past: Hinckley et al. presented *Codex* [5] as a dual-screen mobile device with embedded sensors and pen input capabilities. Besides presenting the prototype, the authors also proposed a taxonomy of dual-screen postures, organizing the different classes of postures for dual-screen devices. Spindler et al. [14] used passive, projected displays for the prototype of foldable tangible GUI palettes (TUIP). Unfolding allowed users to adaptively show more GUI elements on the palette. *FoldMe* [6] by Khalilbeigi et al. is a similar foldable device. The authors investigated different types of folds and the combination of folding with touch. They also proposed continuous value adjustment by folding.

Several other works have examined folding and bending for interaction, such as [4, 8, 12, 18]. While most of these display prototypes are independent of the specific content that they show, few have specifically looked at 3D content and its particular requirements. For the *FlexPad* by Steimle et al. [15], volumetric 3D datasets where one application example, classic 3D interaction however was not investigated. Kratz & Rohs [7] examined 3D object rotation with a dual-screen device supporting simultaneous front and back multi-touch input.

Besides such research prototypes, several design concepts (e. g., Microsoft's *Courier*) and also off-the-shelf consumer

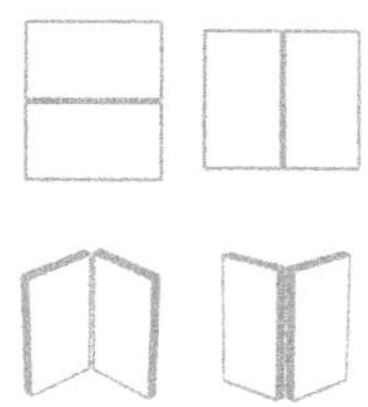

Figure 3: Top: Device orientation in landscape (left) and portrait mode (right). Bottom: Folding inward (left) and outward (right)

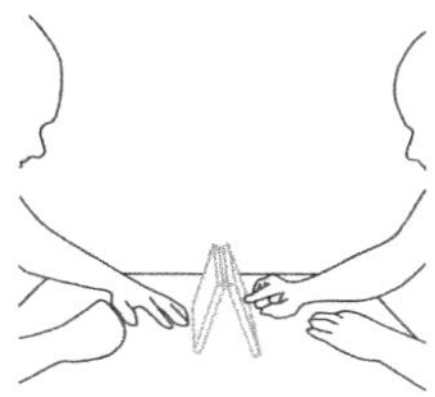

Figure 4: Two users working with the system. Each one has a dedicated screen.

Figure 5: Collaborative usage, users either have a dedicated display or share a unified workspace.

products such as the *Nintendo DS* portable game console or Acer's *ICONIA* dual-display notebook from 2010 have been developed. One of the earliest examples is the *Knowledge Navigator*[1] by Apple, a 1987 conceptional video showcasing concepts for future computers. One of the concepts already shows a a portable device with a large, foldable display.

Head-coupled Perspective
Head-coupled perspective (HCP) has already been proposed in the early 1980s [2] and has in recent years been studied for mobile devices as well (e. g. [3, 13]). Spindler et al. [13] used HCP to support spatial interaction with 3D tracked tangible lenses in a tabletop environment. A positive effect compared to a standard device-centric perspective has been observed by Pucihar & Coulton [11]. Baričević et al. [1] and Tomioka et al. [17] combine tablets with RGB-D cameras to capture a 3D representation of the environment for correct HCP in (video see-through) AR applications. All these systems however only use planar, single-display devices, limiting the user's view into the 3D scene. The *pCubee* device [16] addresses this issue. It is a cube of displays that allows to view virtual content placed inside correctly rendered from all sides. The display configuration is however static, limiting the use of the device to this specific application case. A dynamic, shape-changing interface supporting HCP has recently been presented by Lindlbauer et al. [9].

Principal Concept
We assume a device consisting of two screens flexibly connected with a hinge on the long side, similar to a book. We envision each of the displays to be touch capable, enabling standard multi-touch input.

[1]http://www.digibarn.com/collections/movies/knowledge-navigator.html

Additionally, the folding angle can be measured with a rotary encoder in the hinge and cameras in each device can track the user's face to support HCP. For our mockups and early prototype (see Figures 1 and 2), we combined two commercially available Android tablets with a screen size of 8 inches each in a self-built case. We use an external optical tracking system to determine the positions of the device and the user's head, as well as the angle of the hinge between the two displays. However most presented concepts could instead be implemented using the cameras of the envisioned hardware. The device can either be held in hands in portrait or landscape orientation (see Figure 3), or placed on a table in different ways (see Figures 4 and 5) and supports both a single user or two users simultaneously.

Among the use cases for our proposed device are 3D games, the inspection of 3D content in a mobile setting, or Augmented Reality applications, e. g., for interior design and decoration. We identify three main advantages of our concept for those use cases: (1) The combination of two angled screens provides a larger viewing angle, allowing for a more flexible use of HCP. (2) Folding serves as an additional degree of freedom for interaction, providing another input modality. (3) Two individual but connected screens support both the meaningful arrangement of content and new interaction techniques. In the following we will discuss possible screen modes and how switching between those modes can be benefitial for different use cases. We will also present specific 3D interaction techniques.

Screen Usage & Mode Changes
Having two connected but otherwise independent displays lends itself to a variety of different display modes. As briefly mentioned by Hinckley et al. [5], interaction with a

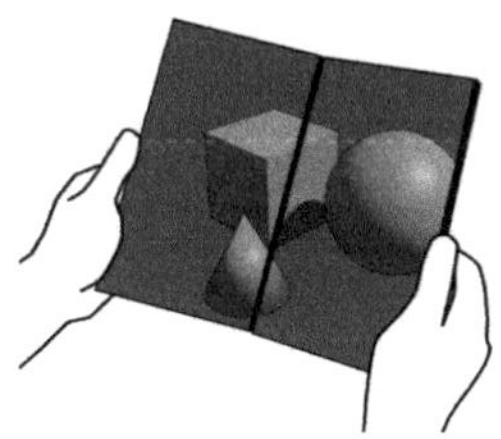

Figure 6: Unified workspace for a continuous canvas, showing one large HCP view into the 3D scene.

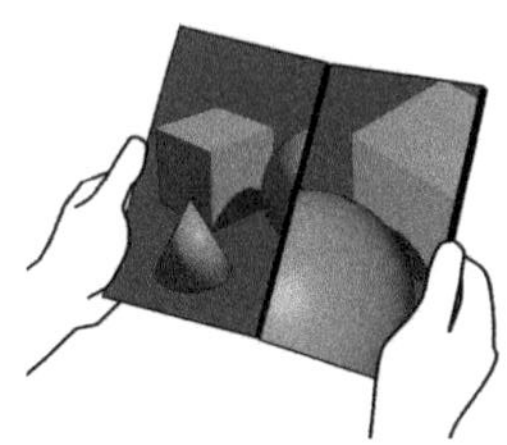

Figure 7: Connected workspace showing a dual perspective view, allowing the user to inspect a scene from two directions.

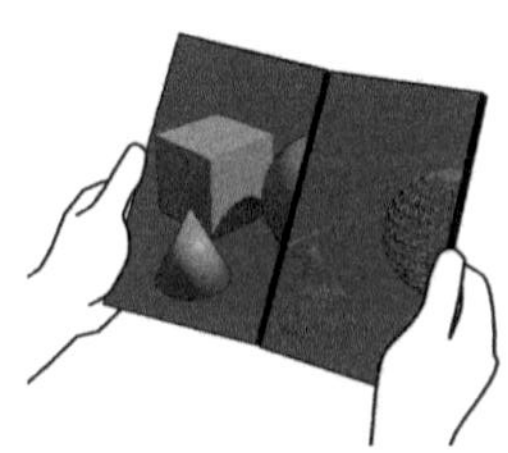

Figure 8: Connected workspace showing an alternative wireframe view for easier object inspection.

dual-display device can be classified according to the relationship between the content of the two screens. Based on this, for 3D interaction we propose to differentiate between three classes of content relations:

In *Unified Workspaces*, both screens are used for one large, unified viewport. In such a continuous canvas both displays are showing a HCP view of the same scene (see Figure 6 and our prototype in Figures 1 and 2). This mode not only provides a larger viewing angle for HCP compared to single-display devices, it also gives the user two spatially configurable input surfaces that can be used for interaction with the 3D content (see below), as well as the additional input modality of the folding itself.

One the other hand, *Connected Workspaces* are two separate viewports into the same scene (see Figures 7 and 8). Among other possibilities, this addresses one of the limitations of typical HCP systems: Normally, with the perspective adapted to one point of view, they only support one user. However, the two separate displays allow the system to be used for *co-located multiuser tasks* (see Figure 4 and Figure 5) in a way not possible with a singular display.

Finally, in *Extended Workspaces*, one screen is a viewport into the scene, while the other one is a secondary screen with completely independent, different functionality. For example, this can be used to offload user interface palettes (see Figure 9).

The analysis of the use of multi-screen devices in the related work shows that different display configurations (folding angle, screen orientation) may be used for different use cases. Thus, we propose to choose the active mode according to the context. The main mode described above, using a continuous, unified workspace for 3D content, is the default and used in *portrait orientation*. We propose to change to one of the other modes in the following situations: When the device is used in *landscape orientation* with an *inward fold* (i. e., like using a laptop computer), the mode switches to an extended workspace with the 3D content being shown on the upper screen and controls displayed on the lower screen. This type of configuration has been used for adaptable multitouch tool spaces in 3D interaction [10]. It would also be possible to use the angle to differentiate between modes in *portrait orientation*. This however comes at the cost of losing the folding angle as an input parameter. We therefore suggest to not use automatic mode changes for handheld portrait orientation.

When *placed on a surface* however, we propose to switch to a multi-user mode: A configuration in *landscape orientation* using an *outward fold* supports a scenario where the device is placed between two users (or two small groups of users). The 3D content is shown on both devices using dual-perspective rendering in a connected workspaces pattern. With two independent views into the same scene, users can interact with the content independently of each other (see Figure 4). If HCP is to be used, both users can have their own perspective, limited to one screen. We propose to use this mode for two-player games and similar applications where collaboration on the same representation of the content is not crucial. In contrast, when placed in *portrait orientation* in a book-like fashion, collaborative work on the same content is easily supported. Again, both users can have their own perspectives but in this configuration, the other display is in sight and reachable (see Figure 5).

Figure 9: Extended workspace combining a 3D viewport and a user interface palette.

Figure 10: Object translation on all three axes with the help of angled displays.

Figure 11: Manipulation of a clipping plane parallel to one of the displays.

Techniques for 3D Interaction

Besides the different display modes made possible by the device, we also propose to use folding as an additional input parameter in combination with multi-touch and thus use the potential of the dual display configuration for interaction purposes. The following techniques all make use of the non-standard input modalities of a foldable dual-screen device

Camera Control by Folding

Folding displays towards or away from the user has been used for changing the zoom level, e. g., in [12]. Bringing this technique to 3D interaction means changing the camera's field of view/focal length depending on the fold. When using HCP however, the camera's FOV is determined by the user's relative position to the displays. Thus, we propose to instead move the scene closer or farther away from the camera (dolly), a movement that is often employed for "zooming" in 3D applications anyhow.

Rotation and Translation Frame of Reference

Rotation and translation of selected objects is done via touch with one or two fingers, respectively. The two dimensions of each display are mapped to the best fitting axes of the 3D camera coordinate system. For example, for a display facing the user, translation and rotation would be on/around the X and Y axes (see Figure 10). Thus, by configuring the device for a folding angle of around $90°$, all six degrees of freedom for translation and rotation of a selected object can be supported by touch on both the front and the side facing displays. If no object is selected, the camera is rotated or translated instead, in the same manner as described above. As a drawback, by having one display not facing the user, content can only be displayed on the remaining one.

Clipping and Snapping Planes

For the exploration of complex scenes, it can be useful to filter the objects to be displayed using clipping planes. Also, snapping objects to previously defined snapping planes (e. g., a ground plane) can support the user in placing and arranging objects. We therefore support the easy manipulation of such planes. By swiping inwards from the screen bezel, an axis-aligned plane is created quasi-orthogonal to the display (e. g. on the x-z-plane for an upwards swipe on the front-facing display) and can then be moved like any other object. Consequently, with our proposed device, such planes can be manipulated on one display without obstructing the view on the other one (see Figure 11).

Conclusion and Future Work

We have presented the concept of using a dual-display, foldable mobile device for 3D interaction. By making use of two independent but connected displays, we virtually extend the field of view for head-coupled perspective and, at the same time, allow for exciting ways to display 3D content for one or multiple users. We examined concepts of different possible screen configurations and their usage, as well as new interaction techniques that make use of the special capabilities of the envisioned system. Initial, in-house feedback on our concepts has been promising. We have begun to implement our concepts in a hard- and software prototype (see Figures 1 and 2). One of the main challenges is to combine existing techniques and different new concepts into one consistent system. We are already partially addressing this issue in this work by our proposal of mode switches depending on the usage context. We plan to expand on this in the future and to evaluate our prototype in appropriate user studies.

Acknowledgements

This work was in part funded by grant no. 03ZZ0514C of the German Federal Ministry of Education and Research (measure Twenty20 – Partnership for Innovation, project Fast), grant no. DA 1319/2-1 of the German Research Foundation (DFG), and the Excellence Initiative by the German Government (measure "Support the best").

References

[1] Baričević, D., Lee, C., Turk, M., Höllerer, T., and Bowman, D. A. A hand-held AR magic lens with user-perspective rendering. In *Proc. ISMAR '12*, IEEE (2012), 197–206.

[2] Fisher, S. Viewpoint Dependent Imaging: An Interactive Stereoscopic Display. In *Proc. SPIE*, vol. 0367 (1983), 41–45.

[3] Francone, J., and Nigay, L. Using the User's Point of View for Interaction on Mobile Devices. In *Proc. IHM '11*, ACM (2011), 4:1–4:8.

[4] Gomes, A., and Vertegaal, R. PaperFold: Evaluating Shape Changes for Viewport Transformations in Foldable Thin-Film Display Devices. In *Proc. TEI '15*, ACM (2015), 153–160.

[5] Hinckley, K., Dixon, M., Sarin, R., Guimbretiere, F., and Balakrishnan, R. Codex: A Dual Screen Tablet Computer. In *Proc. CHI '09*, ACM (2009), 1933–1942.

[6] Khalilbeigi, M., Lissermann, R., Kleine, W., and Steimle, J. FoldMe: Interacting with Double-sided Foldable Displays. In *Proc. TEI '12*, ACM (2012), 33–40.

[7] Kratz, S., and Rohs, M. Extending the virtual trackball metaphor to rear touch input. In *Proc. 3DUI '10*, IEEE (2010), 111–114.

[8] Lee, J. C., Hudson, S. E., and Tse, E. Foldable Interactive Displays. In *Proc. UIST '08*, ACM (2008), 287–290.

[9] Lindlbauer, D., Grønbæk, J. E., Birk, M., Halskov, K., Alexa, M., and Müller, J. Combining Shape-Changing Interfaces and Spatial Augmented Reality Enables Extended Object Appearance. In *Proc. CHI '16*, 791–802.

[10] Palleis, H., Wagner, J., and Hussmann, H. Novel indirect touch input techniques applied to finger-forming 3d models. In *Proc. AVI '16*, ACM (2016), 228–235.

[11] Pucihar, K. Č., and Coulton, P. Contact-view: A magic-lens paradigm designed to solve the dual-view problem. In *Proc. ISMAR '14*, IEEE (2014), 297–298.

[12] Schwesig, C., Poupyrev, I., and Mori, E. Gummi: A Bendable Computer. In *Proc. CHI '04*, ACM (2004), 263–270.

[13] Spindler, M., Büschel, W., and Dachselt, R. Use Your Head: Tangible Windows for 3D Information Spaces in a Tabletop Environment. In *Proc. ITS '12*, ACM (2012), 245–254.

[14] Spindler, M., Hauschild, M., and Dachselt, R. Towards making graphical user interfaces tangible. In *Proc. ITS '10*, ACM (2010), 291–292.

[15] Steimle, J., Jordt, A., and Maes, P. Flexpad: Highly Flexible Bending Interactions for Projected Handheld Displays. In *Proc. CHI '13*, ACM (2013), 237–246.

[16] Tang, Y., Stavness, I., and Fels, S. The New pCubee: Multi-touch Perspective-corrected Cubic Display. In *Proc. CHI EA '14*, ACM (2014), 419–422.

[17] Tomioka, M., Ikeda, S., and Sato, K. Approximated user-perspective rendering in tablet-based augmented reality. In *Proc. ISMAR '13*, IEEE (2013), 21–28.

[18] Watanabe, J.-i., Mochizuki, A., and Horry, Y. Bookisheet: Bendable Device for Browsing Content Using the Metaphor of Leafing Through the Pages. In *Proc. UbiComp '08*, ACM (2008), 360–369.

Twosome Coloring: Designing a Playful Coloring System on Dual-sided Transparent Surfaces

Heesun Kim
Korea Institute of Science and Technology
5, 14-gil, Hwarang-ro, Sungbuk-gu, Seoul, Korea
pure4eva@gmail.com

Hyoyoung Kim
Korea Institute of Science and Technology
5, 14-gil, Hwarang-ro, Sungbuk-gu, Seoul, Korea
090752@kist.re.kr

Seung A Lee
Korea Institute of Science and Technology
5, 14-gil, Hwarang-ro, Sungbuk-gu, Seoul, Korea
090778@kist.re.kr

Ji-hyung Park
Korea Institute of Science and Technology
5, 14-gil, Hwarang-ro, Sungbuk-gu, Seoul, Korea
jhpark@kist.re.kr

ISS '16, November 06-09, 2016, Niagara Falls, ON, Canada
ACM 978-1-4503-4248-3/16/11.
http://dx.doi.org/10.1145/2992154.2996783

Abstract
This paper introduces a coloring application for dual-sided transparent surfaces. It extends the traditional coloring experience with see-through display technology and dual-sided interaction techniques that enable a playful user experience. Twosome Coloring allows two users to interact with a see-through color picker and twosome interaction techniques on dual-sided transparent surfaces. We describe design concerns related to see-through technology, dual-sided interaction and application design, and present the results from a preliminary user study that indicates the benefit of see-through interface and twosome interactions.

Author Keywords
Dual-sided transparent displays; See-through interface; Twosome interaction; Coloring application

ACM Classification Keywords
H.5.2 Information interfaces and presentation (e.g., HCI): User Interfaces – Interaction styles

Introduction
Transparent surfaces could be employed as a communication medium to enable people to have access to the each side of a transparent screen. The

technological systems of dual-sided transparent displays used for collaboration have been unveiled [1, 3]. Since dual-sided transparent surfaces induce people's interest and new user experiences, this merit of dual-sided transparent surfaces shows that they can be applied for entertainment systems, especially interactive games [1, 8]. However, the fundamental challenge for these interactive systems is the lack of considerations for transparent interfaces and interaction techniques: how the form properties of dual-sided transparent display can change user experience with them.

Since there are only a few devices and other enablers for see-through technologies, the applications of those devices are still scarce. Particularly, the end users' viewpoints have yet been thoroughly investigated [2]. In order to solve this challenge, it is crucial to design, implement and evaluate a practical application for dual-sided transparent displays. One potential solution to practical applications is to offer users on each side a collaborated task that includes dual-sided transparent interfaces and interaction techniques.

In this paper, we study user interfaces and interaction techniques that enhance user experience by implementing interactive coloring system on dual-sided transparent surfaces. We briefly investigate design requirements for a dual-sided prototype development and describe in detail our system's features. We examine the results of our preliminary user study and discuss the system's reception for future usages.

Related Work

While several systems indicate that dual-sided transparent displays are technically developed [10], and well suited as communication devices for interpersonal interaction [4], a question remains which applications for communication and interaction techniques would be practical. To go beyond the current offerings, based on the review of other research issues, we suggest (1) the design principles for dual-sided transparent interfaces based on the form characteristics and (2) the appropriate interactive application as a willing-to-use system in reality.

Design principles

Our early designs are guided by a number of principles related to primary aspects of dual-sided transparent surfaces:

- Create rich user experience with see-through characteristic. Most transparent interfaces researches focus on the visibility of the screen with different transparency [6]. However, these studies do not address the issues in terms of user experience. Transparent surfaces can provide a new user experience of playful design and aesthetics that technological advances of the transparent surfaces would bring out. Therefore, when designing the system and the user interface on transparent surfaces, new functions and applications reflecting the see-through characteristic should be considered by default.
- Provide collaborative interaction techniques. The dual-sided characteristic provides an interaction environment where people could use both front and back sides of the display. Furthermore, when two people use a dual-sided transparent surface, they can experience face-to-face interaction through the transparent screen. Despite this aesthetical advantage, most studies employed the touch input on both sides respectively, and contemplated the reversible

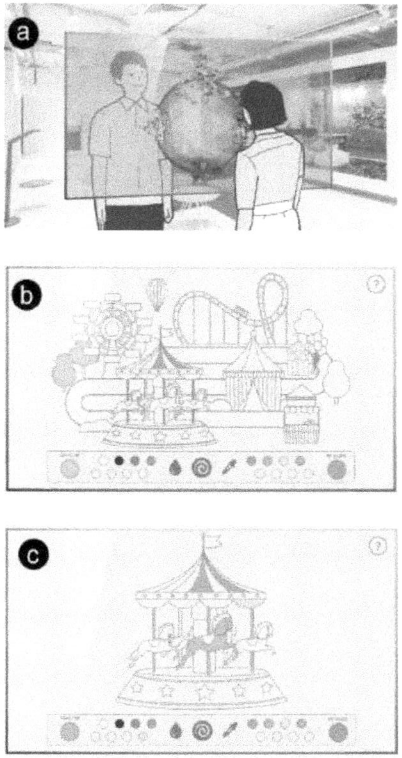

Figure 1. User interfaces for Twosome Coloring. (a) A 3D spherical land interface for choosing one template to color shows three attractions including amusement park, zoo and botanic garden, (b) a 2D non-directional template and its palette is provided to color and (c) is offered an expanded view to color the objects in detail.

information to provide individual user interface [4, 6, 7, 10]. However, it is questionable whether there is a need for each user to see the different contents and control respectively on dual-sided transparent surfaces. To support the mutual collaboration between co-located users, research on the appropriate content and interaction techniques seems to be necessary for facilitation of collaborative interaction.

Application design

We consider a drawing application for dual-sided transparent displays due to many dedicated drawing applications in previous works [1, 4, 8, 9]. VideoDraw [9] and ClearBoard [4] are shared drawing mediums that used projectors. In addition, Microsoft Office Labs [8] and Corning [1] introduced a future scenario which shows that children could draw a figure on a glass-like transparent display and share the figure with another user.

Digitalization of coloring activity could provide users an experience of expressing their creativity by generating an unlimited number of colors. Moreover, by allowing face-to-face interaction, self-expression as well as emotional communication between two facing users will be reinforced.

Therefore, we propose that a coloring application could be used as a useful application of dual-sided transparent display at a break room or a conference venue during a coffee break in the future. It could also be used at public places such as at a birthday party or at a playground for children.

Twosome Coloring

Twosome Coloring was inspired by traditional coloring books. We designed the key features of the interactive coloring system based on the three steps of conventional coloring books and we also added novel ways to color and communicate that are only enabled on this system.

Key features based on traditional coloring books

- Selecting coloring theme. In order to choose the template to color, users pick one template among three represented as attractions on the 3D spherical land (Figure 1-a).
- Choosing colors on palette. Users can choose one color over several primary colors provided in palette interface (Figure 1-b). When users need more colors to use, they can generate new colors by blending two colors at the blending area where it is center of the palette. They can use those blended colors after adding them on the empty area of the palette. Users also can extract colors from the real environment.
- Coloring. Users can color the attraction scene. Using clicking water icon, they can add watercolor painting effect by touching the parts where they already painted. Also, users can easily move from an attraction to another attraction. In one attraction, users also magnify one object in order to paint it in detail. Once one object is painted completely, it will animate the object.

Novel interactions for dual-sided transparent surfaces

- See-through color picker. This technology augments the color information from the real environment beyond the screen which is viewable through the transparent screen. Users can extract the color from the physical objects or from people's clothes by pointing the specific position on the transparent screen (Figure 2). This function is enabled by two cameras in tune with the field of vision of each user, and allows the users to extract the colors from the real environment intuitively.

- Twosome zooming interaction. This interaction enables two users to switch the scene on screen when there is a consensus among users. When a user wants to switch or scale the scene, both users must collaboratively complete one command, such as zoom in or out.
- Twosome blending interaction. This interaction allows two users to create new color from the default colors. It reflects the analog metaphor and affordance from conventional coloring experience. We designed a color blending area in center of the palette on screen as a common workspace separated from an individual workspace. Blending color can only be carried out when two users agree to create a new color by communicating during the coloring activity.

Implementation
The hardware of our prototype consisted of a transparent surface with two high-lumen projectors

Figure 2. Color picking technology to extract the color information from the real environment

mounted on an aluminum frame, connected to a PC (Figure 3).

For the transparent surface, we made a 42-inch projection screen by attaching a holographic projection film between two plexi-glasses (3mm). It enables us to display a vivid image while maintaining high transparency. For dual-sided interaction on the transparent surface, we used two PQ Labs touch sensor frames (G5S 42"Multi-Touch Sensors) and embedded at the top and bottom on each side of the projection screen. This allows users to stand face-to-face in front of the transparent surface and intuitively participate in coloring with their fingers. In addition, two webcams are positioned to capture the real environment scene around the prototype for the see-through color picker function what we mentioned above.

Preliminary User Evaluation
We conducted a preliminary user evaluation of Twosome Coloring with 26 participants (age 22-34, 15 female) were recruited from Korea Institute of Science and Technology. The participants volunteered in a

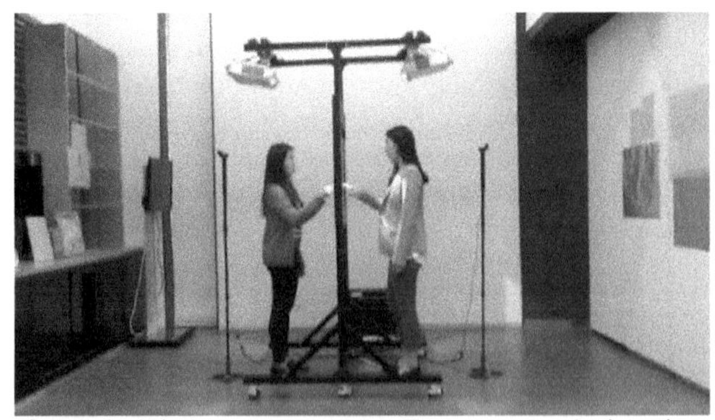

Figure 3. Coloring system set up. Two users manipulate the system on opposite sides of the display surface.

group of two. Among the 13 pairs, five pairs were female-female, three pairs were male-male and five pairs were female-male pair. All participants reported to have normal color vision. All participants were right-handed except one participant.

The purpose of evaluating the satisfaction of the interfaces was to examine in which aspects users are satisfied with Twosome Coloring. A questionnaire which evaluates aesthetic, usability, playfulness, pleasant and service quality was used at the end of the study to assess the overall satisfaction of the interfaces [5].

After a brief overview of how the system worked, both participants of each group played with the coloring system for 15 minutes. Although they were instructed to use the system freely, they were asked to use each functions at least once. The experimenter observed and recorded participants' interaction.

Questionnaire responses (7-point Likert scale) indicate that the Twosome Coloring were pleasing (5.9).

Figure 4. Examples of see-through interfaces and twosome interaction techniques. (a) Before and after twosome zoom-in interaction and (b) one of colored scene with watering effect.

Participants also find it playful (5.6) and good in service quality (5.4). However, they reported a relatively lower aesthetics (5.1) and usability (4.8), compared to other aspects.

See-through function and effect give pleasure
As revealed from the interface questionnaire results, participants reported that they enjoyed using the system. Among the five aspects of the interface satisfaction, pleasure showed the highest score among all aspects. According to the interview and observation, some participants reported that see-through interfaces such as the watering effect and the picker gave a new user experience.

Some used watering effect more frequently than other effects. They stated that "watering effect made the drawing more beautiful...the effect is similar to the real water-color painting". Moreover, although the color picker was not frequently used as expected, one of the participants stated "The picker function was really fascinating and interesting" and another comment included that "This (picker) is what I liked the most during coloring".

Twosome interactions induce cooperation and communication
Through the observation, twosome interaction seems to enhance collaboration between two users. Particularly, it was often observed that once participants used the zoom in feature to color an object in more detail, they used the twosome zooming more frequently and conversation was increased.

It was also observed that some participants were likely to be more conversational because they can gain a new perspective about counterpart. For instance, some participants were surprised by their counterpart's art talent and praised them. Some also revealed their personal stories to others. For instance, one participant disclosed that "I actually used to take an art course when I was in university" or "I used to do this sort of thing with my daughter". This shows that the coloring system provides emotional communication and could give an opportunity for two users to bring them closer to each other.

Limitation and Future work

The limitation of this study is that there was a relatively short time to explore several different effects. A long-term study would be necessary to observe more users behaviors and effects of the coloring system. We plan to continue design iteration, evaluation and field deployment for dual-sided transparent surfaces.

Conclusion

Twosome Coloring presents early investigations of designing an application to provide pleasing emotions and playful experience on dual-sided transparent surfaces. By augmenting traditional coloring book features with novel interaction techniques, our implementation represents design concerns for see-through interfaces and collaborated interaction based on the characteristics of the dual-sided transparent display. We hope that this exploration offers initial insights for designing dual-sided transparent interfaces and interaction techniques, and could further support real user needs in the near future.

Acknowledgements

This work was supported by the IT R&D program of MOTIE/KEIT.[10042418, UI and User Interaction Technology for more than 60"HD-level Transparent Flexible Display Applied Product Using Eyetracking and Space Recognition].

References

[1] Corning, Inc. A Day Made of Glass I and II. https://www.youtube.com/watch?v=6Cf7IL_eZ38 and https://www.youtube.com/watch?v=jZkHpNnXLB0.

[2] Häkkilä, J., Olsson, T., Colley, A., Pederson, T., and Grubert, J. Interactions and applications for see-through technologies. In Proc. NordiCHI'14. ACM, New York, NY (2014), 793-796.

[3] Heo, H, Kim, S., Park, H., Chung, J., Lee, G., and Lee, W. TransWall. In Proceedings of ACM SIGGRAPH '13 Emerging Technologies. Article No. 14. (2013).

[4] Ishii, H. and Kobayashi, M. ClearBoard: A seamless medium for shared drawing and conversation with eye contact. In Proc. CHI '92 (1992), 525–532.

[5] Lavie, T. and Tractinsky, N. Assessing dimensions of perceived visual aesthetics of web sites. International journal of human-computer studies 60, 3 (2004), 269-298.

[6] Li, J., Greenberg, S. and Sharlin, E. Enhancing Workspace Awareness on Collaborative Transparent Displays. Research Report 2015-1065-16, Department of Computer Science, University of Calgary, Calgary, Alberta, Canada. (2014).

[7] Li, J., Greenberg, S., Sharlin, E., and Jorge, J. Interactive Two-Sided Transparent Displays: Designing for Collaboration. In Proc. DIS '14 (2014), 395–404.

[8] Microsoft OfficeLabs. (2009) Productivity Future Vision. https://www.youtube.com/watch?v=t5X2PxtvMsU

[9] Tang, J. C., and Minneman, S. L. VideoDraw : A Video Interface For Collaborative Drawing. In Proc. CHI '90 (1990), 313–320.

[10] Lindlbauer, D., Aoki, T., Walter, R., Uema, Y., Höchtl, A., Haller, M. & Müller, J. Tracs: transparency-control for see-through displays. In Proceedings of the 27th annual ACM symposium on User interface software and technology (2014), 657-661.

Finding the Minimum Perceivable Size of a Tactile Element on an Ultrasonic Based Haptic Tablet

Farzan Kalantari
University of Lille 1 - Science and Technology
CRIStAL, INRIA Lille
Villeneuve d'Ascq, France
farzan.kalantari@inria.fr

Yosra Rekik
University of Lille 1 - Science and Technology
INRIA Lille
Villeneuve d'Ascq, France
yosra.rekik@inria.fr

Laurent Grisoni
University of Lille 1 - Science and Technology
CRIStAL, CNRS, INRIA Lille
Villeneuve d'Ascq, France
laurent.grisoni@univ-lille1.fr

Frédéric Giraud
University of Lille 1 - Science and Technology
L2EP, CNRS
Villeneuve d'Ascq, France
frederic.giraud@univ-lille1.fr

ISS '16, November 06-09, 2016, Niagara Falls, ON, Canada
ACM 978-1-4503-4248-3/16/11.
http://dx.doi.org/10.1145/2992154.2996785

Abstract
Tactile devices with ultrasonic vibrations (based on squeeze film effect) using piezoelectric actuators are one of the existing haptic feedback technologies. In this study we have performed two psychophysical experiments on an ultrasonic haptic tablet, in order to find the minimum size of a tactile element on which all the users are able to perfectly identify different types of textures. Our results show that the spatial resolution of the tactile element on haptic touchscreen actually varies, depending on the number and types of tactile feedback information. A first experiment exhibits three different tactile textures, chosen as being easily recognized by users. We use these textures in a second experiment, and evaluate minimal spatial area on which the chosen set of textures can be recognized. Among other, we find the minimal size depends on the texture nature.

Author Keywords
Haptic; Tactile device; Friction modulation; Ultrasonic vibrations; Minimum size; Texture rendering.

ACM Classification Keywords
H.5.2 [User Interfaces]: Input devices and strategies.

Introduction

Eye and ear are used by humans for retrieving most of information in the real, physical, world; both sense channels are quite well handled by technology. But the sense of touch in human is still complex and varies on different people and is not an absolute phenomenon. The tactile information perception might be influenced by environmental conditions such as temperature and strongly based on the skin mechanoreceptors of the human finger. Therefore the existing interactive technologies allowing to provide user to retrieve information through tactile sense are still emerging and many parameters appear to make it difficult for applications to handle tactile feedback in a shared, generic way. In particular, each tactile technology still demands a specific development and adaptation [13].

In the field of technologies for visual feedback, the concept of *pixel* had a huge consequence on display technology and provides a conceptual common basis between higher level software architectures, and lower-level, electronic systems that is used for display. Such common concept is still missing for tactile feedback; we still lack a common, shared reference of an elementary tactile information, both in terms of spatial resolution, and information nature; can we go up to a normalization level comparable to the one that pixels provide for visual information?

In this study we introduce a step toward the concept of *taxel* (Tactile Element), by suggesting an up-down response protocol (adaptive procedure) in psychophysics [5] that allows, for a specific tactile feedback technology, to measure the minimum size on which tactile information can be retrieved. We define the notion of *texture waveform* as the elementary signal shape that we provide to the tactile feedback technology, that is used as periodical signal for tactile stimulation. Such notion is a standard, usable term for all existing tactile feedback technologies (see related work section). We provide a first experiment that identifies few elementary textures that can be easily identified by user. Among the 24 textures proposed to user, we identify three that all users can identify accurately. From this experiment, we derive a second experiment that evaluates the minimum size of the tactile element at which user can differentiate textures accurately. We conclude that the texture type influences the minimum size of the tactile element.

Related Work

In the recent years, touchscreen interfaces with haptic feedback to the user's finger have become more and more popular.This haptic feedback permits the users to enrich the feeling of what they touch and can improve the performances of their interactions.[3, 6, 14]

Generally, we can divide the haptic feedback technology on touchscreen interfaces in to 4 categories. These technologies mostly use various friction modulation between the fingertip and the interaction surface for texture rendering. The first class of devices are based on electro-vibration effect which use electrostatic force, generated by applying a voltage to the surface for haptic feedback [2, 8]. The second category create haptic feedback through electroadhesion technique, which also use electrostatic force generated by DC excitation to the haptic surface. [9]. Both of these two classes of devices increase the friction between the fingertip and the interaction surface. The third class of devices are based on friction reduction using ultrasonic vibration via the squeeze film effect [1, 12, 7]. This effect reduces the friction, which is opposite to electrostatic force in the two previous technologies. The fourth class of devices utilize vibrotactile actuators for tactile rendering which is widely used in smartphones and tablets since several years now [4]. Furthermore, in [10] the differences in haptic perception of object size when exploring the inside or outside the objects is investigated by means of psychophysical experiments. But there is still no studies to show the minimum object size for tactile perception while using a touchscreen device with haptic feedback.

Experiment 1: Finding the Three Perceivable and Distinguishable Textures

At first we have done an experiment in order to find at least 3 different textures that could be perceived and distinguished properly by all users. We have selected 3 types of textures due to the time constraints for performing the two experiments by participants.

Apparatus

We used a haptic tablet based on ultrasonic vibrations for texture rendering [11] which is developed on a Banana Pi, a single-board computer with 1 GHz ARM Cortex-A7, dual-core CPU and 1 GB of RAM working in parallel with STM32f4 microcontroller. The communication between the singleboard computer and the microcontroller is provided via the Serial Peripheral Interface (SPI) bus at 10 kHz. This singleboard computer is connected to a 5 inches capacitive touchscreen in order to detect the finger position on the display with the sampling frequency of 50 Hz. The two piezoceramic actuators are placed at each side of the display.

Design and Procedure

In order to design our first experiment, we have defined 4 types of texture waveforms as *square*, *sine*, *dirac* and *sawtooth* with the constant amplitude of 1 μm and the spatial frequencies of 50 μm , 100 μm, 500 μm, 1000 μm, 5000 μm and 10000 μm. The setup of the first experiment is illustrated in figure 1 which was coded with Java and Processing language and the display is divided to 4 equal sections. On each part there is a specific texture waveform and so the value of spatial frequency can be selected. Ten participants (4 female and 6 male) were free to explore the surface as long as they wanted and then choose 3 or 4 textures that could be accurately sensed and distinguished among all the 24 provided textures.

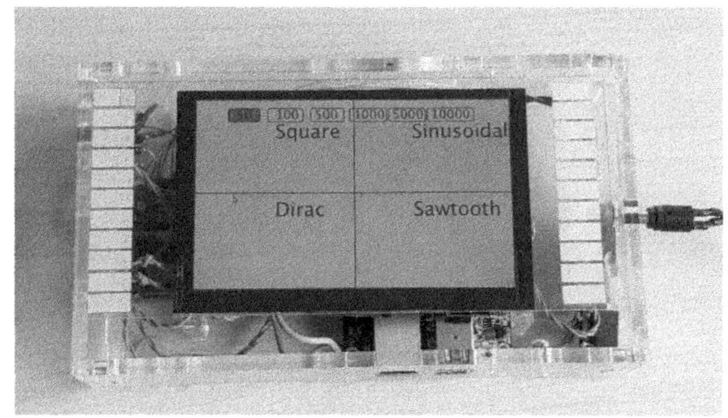

Figure 1: The setup of the Experiment 1

Results

The analysis of results as we can see in table 1, show that several participants could distinguish between 5 to 7 different textures. In overall the results demonstrate that all 100% of participants could perceive and distinguish the following textures perfectly: square texture, sinusoidal texture and dirac texture with the spatial frequency of 50 μm, 1000 μm and 1000 μm respectively and the constant amplitude of 1 μm for all of the textures. The feeling perception of the dirac and sawtooth texture waveforms were more or less similar for the participants and therefore rather hard to be distinguished appropriately. These results are used for our second experiment.

Participants	Square (μm)	Sinusoidal (μm)	Dirac (μm)	Sawtooth (μm)
1	50	1000	1000	5000
2	50	1000	1000	10000
3	50	1000	1000	5000
4	50	500,1000	1000	500,1000,5000
5	50,1000,5000	1000	1000	5000
6	50,1000	500,1000	1000	5000,10000
7	50,1000	500,1000	500,1000	10000
8	50,1000	1000	500,1000	10000
9	50	1000	500,1000	1000
10	50	1000	1000	10000

Table 1: The results of the chosen textures from experiment 1

Experiment 2: Finding the Minimum Size of a Tactile Element

The goal of our second experiment is to determine the minimum size of a tactile element (taxel) on the touchscreen on which the participants are able to distinguish the 3 textures found from the results of the experiment 1. As before we have used the same haptic tablet based on ultrasonic vibrations and defined 3 textures due to the time constraints to accomplish the task by the participants

Figure 2: The setup of the minimum size experiment

The participants were demanded to find the accurate corresponding texture of the first taxel among the 3 other taxels and clicked on (1), (2) or (3) on the keyboard for the correct answer.

Design and Procedure

We have used an up-down response protocol (adaptive procedure) in psychophysics [5] with the total number of 25 tries for each of 3 trials. Thus the minimum size of the tactile elements is considered to be the last size as the ten participants obtained after 25 tests for each trial (10 participants $\times$ 3 textures $\times$ 25 times $=$ 750). We have displayed 4 tactile elements of square shapes with the identical initial size of 10 mm (1cm) that are situated in parallel as shown in figure 2. At each try if the participants has a correct answer for the texture detection, the size of all squares decrease by 0.5 mm simultaneously and for the wrong answers it will increased by 0.5 mm. At each step there is a specific texture on the first tactile element and the textures on the other taxels are assigned

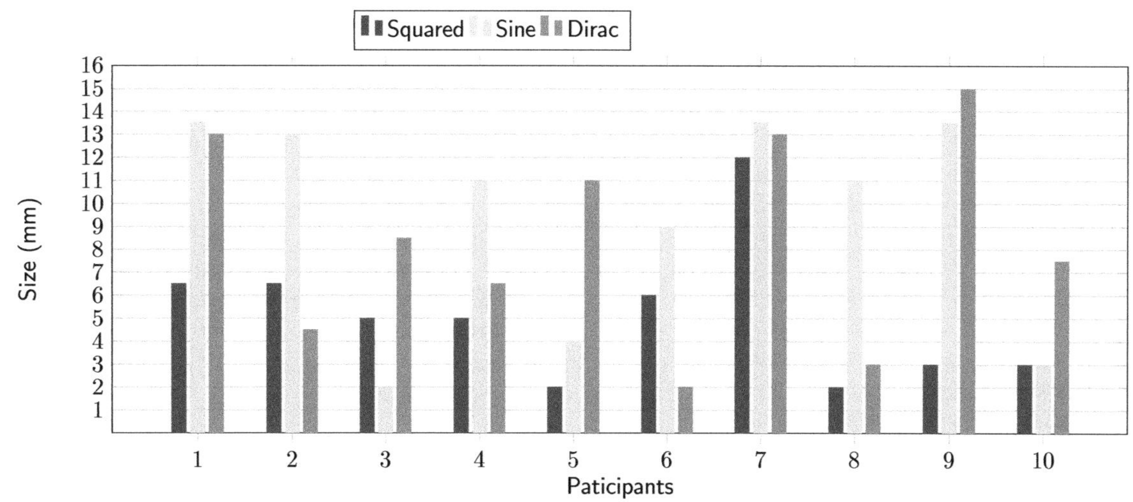

Figure 3: The results of each participant for the minimum size of the tactile element for the 3 given textures

with the randomized manner, in order to obtain the ideal validity of the experiment.

Results and Discussions

For the first trial we applied a square signal waveform (texture) with the spatial frequency of 50 μm and the constant amplitude of 1 μm to the first square object (taxel) and asked the participants to find it among the 3 following squares with a randomized texture on each one. As it is illustrated in figure 3, all of 10 participants were able to distinguish the given square texture with the other textures for the minimum size of 12mm. (6.5 mm for 9 participant)

In the second trial we have exerted a sine wave with the spatial frequency of 1000 μm and the amplitude of 1 μm to the first square. The procedure is the same as the first trial. The result is illustrated in the figure 3. As we find out from figure 3, the minimum size of the square is 13.5 mm for all 100% of the participants to distinguish the provided texture.

In the third trial with the same procedure as before, we applied a dirac texture with the spatial frequency of 1000 μm and the constant amplitude of 1 μm to the first square. The minimum size of the taxel is 15mm. (see figure 3)

Conclusion and Future work

Our results show that the minimum perceivable size of the tactile element depends on the nature of texture signal waveform. The standard range in our case is from few millimeters to about one centimeter, depending on the texture waveform. Our results also demonstrate that the textures with square signal might be more perceivable with small sizes (6.5 mm for the majority of the participants). Hence, textures with square signal waveform is the most suitable texture for tactile rendering of small size of virtual objects on the ultrasonic based haptic feedback touchscreens.

As the future work we target to do the same study with the other haptic feedback technologies on touchscreens and try to compare the results. It is also possible to change the tactile element (square in our case) with other geometrical shapes.

Acknowledgements

This work is partially funded by European ERDF funds (IRCICA, CPER MAUVE, SCV) and ANR funding agency (equipex IRDIVE). The authors would like to appreciate Nicolas Bremard for his useful help and discussion for developing the experiments in our study.

References

[1] Amberg, M., Giraud, F., Semail, B., Olivo, P., Casiez, G., and Roussel, N. Stimtac: A tactile input device with programmable friction. In *UIST 2011* (2011).

[2] Bau, O., Poupyrev, I., Israr, A., and Harrison, C. Teslatouch: Electrovibration for touch surfaces. In *Proc. UIST 2010* (2010).

[3] Casiez, G., Roussel, N., Vanbelleghem, R., and Giraud, F. Surfpad: Riding Towards Targets on a Squeeze Film Effect. In *Proc. CHI '11* (2011).

[4] Choi, S., and Kuchenbecker, K. J. Vibrotactile display: Perception, technology, and applications. *Proc. IEEE 2013 Volume 101*, No. 9 (2013).

[5] Leek, M. R. Adaptive procedures in psychophysical research. *Perception & Psychophysics* (2001).

[6] Levesque, V., Oram, L., MacLean, K., Cockburn, A., Marchuk, N. D., Johnson, D., Colgate, J. E., and Peshkin, M. A. Enhancing physicality in touch interaction with programmable friction. In *Proc. CHI 2011* (2011).

[7] Long, B., Seah, S. A., Carter, T., and Subramanian, S. Rendering volumetric haptic shapes in mid-air using ultrasound. *ACM Trans. Graph.* (2014).

[8] Senseg. Inc. http://senseg.com/.

[9] Shultz, C. D., Peshkin, M. A., and Colgate, J. E. Surface haptics via electroadhesion: Expanding electrovibration with johnsen and rahbek. IEEE (2015).

[10] Tiest, W. M. B., and Hayward, V. Inside vs. outside: Haptic perception of object size. In *Proc. WHC 2015*, IEEE (2015).

[11] Vezzoli, E., Sednaoui, T., Amberg, M., Giraud, F., and Lemaire-Semail, B. Texture rendering strategies with a high fidelity - capacitive visual-haptic friction control device. In *Haptics: Perception, Devices, Control, and Applications* (2016).

[12] Winfield, L., Glassmire, J., Colgate, J. E., and Peshkin, M. T-pad: Tactile pattern display through variable friction reduction. IEEE (2007).

[13] Yi, B., Cao, X., Fjeld, M., and Zhao, S. Exploring user motivations for eyes-free interaction on mobile devices. CHI '12 (2012).

[14] Zhang, Y., and Harrison, C. Quantifying the targeting performance benefit of electrostatic haptic feedback on touchscreens. In *Proc. ITS 2015* (2015).

Accessing Mobile Apps with User Defined Gesture Shortcuts: An Exploratory Study

Chi Zhang
Bournemouth University
BH12 5BB
United Kingdom
czhang@bournemouth.ac.uk

Nan Jiang
Bournemouth University
BH12 5BB
United Kingdom
njiang@bournemouth.ac.uk

Feng Tian
Bournemouth University
BH12 5BB
United Kingdom
ftian@bournemouth.ac.uk

ISS '16, November 06-09, 2016, Niagara Falls, ON, Canada
ACM 978-1-4503-4248-3/16/11.
http://dx.doi.org/10.1145/2992154.2996786

Abstract
Smart phones have become the hub of people lives due to the overwhelming number and extensive range of apps available in app stores that are available to support their daily tasks. On average, smart phone users have around 100 apps installed on their devices and the number is ever growing. Thus, it becomes crucial to make sure they can quickly access these apps. In this paper, we present an exploratory study to understand users' memorability of their self-defined gestures for 15 frequently used mobile apps. The results show that although participants recalled their self-defined gestures most of the time, there are still certain factors that can influence their recall. The paper further analyses the underlining reasons and discusses how such issues could be addressed from a technical perspective.

Author Keywords
Smart phones; gesture interface; gesture shortcuts; user-defined gestures; recall; memorability

ACM Classification Keywords
H.5.m. Information interfaces and presentation (e.g., HCI): Miscellaneous.

Strategy	Icon	Gesture Shortcut
Visual		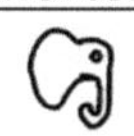
Textual		
Functional		
Other		

Table 1. Examples of Definition Strategy.

Introduction

With the support of an enormous number and extensive range of apps available in app stores, smart phones have become the hub of people's live [12]. In the UK, two-thirds of adults now own smart phones and use them for nearly 2 hours a day to support their daily activities [10]. On average, smart phone users have around 100 apps installed on their devices and this number is ever growing [14]. With only system-defined mechanisms such as searching [1] and browsing, accessing an app can become very time-consuming and inconvenient [4]. For example, the performance of searching an app via built-in/third-party search tools for a smart phone relies on how accurate a user can remember the name of the app. Similarly, the performance of locating an app through browsing the app list on a smart phone interface is determined by user's familiarity with the app as well as the way how the app list is organized [3].

Recent research on touch screen gestures has acknowledged the convenience of using gesture shortcuts to access system functions (e.g., wireless on/off), execute system commands (e.g., rotate) [8] [13] and even perform specific tasks (e.g., web browsing) on touch screen devices [2]. Further to this, several studies have noted that user-defined gesture shortcuts are easier to be memorized by users when compared with system-defined gesture shortcuts [9].

Despite the merits of user-defined gesture shortcuts, current studies only focus on system functions. So it is still unclear whether similar approaches can also be applied to mobile apps. One may argue that the representation of system functions is very similar to the representation of mobile apps on the smart phone user interface (e.g., icons with/without textual information). The fact is, apps present a much higher degree of complexity and diversity than system functions as users can choose what apps to install, how many they want to install and even how many similar ones they want to install (e.g., Skype and LINE are both commonly installed as instant messengers). The "freedom of choice" can trigger an immediate question, which is: although the user can define a gesture shortcut for a mobile app freely, can they always recall the gesture easily?

In this paper, we present an exploratory study that aims to understand user memorability of self-defined gesture shortcuts for accessing mobile apps. Starting with 15 commonly used mobile apps to identify several factors that may influence the recall performance and discussed how the performance could be improved from a technical perspective.

Methodology

Gesture shortcut definition strategy

A previous study on understanding how users define gesture shortcuts for common tasks on mobiles has noticed that users are selective but they tend to use only certain strategies instead of drawing gestures randomly [11]. These strategies can be differentiated into three types: name based strategy, system icon based strategy, and function/purpose based strategy. Accordingly, we add "other" strategy to cover these gestures with unknown user behaviors and define four definition strategy categories based on the ways mobile apps are displayed as well as their purposes, as given in Table 1.

Gesture shortcut capture

Several attempts related to using gesture shortcuts to access apps have been made [5, 7] but there is no

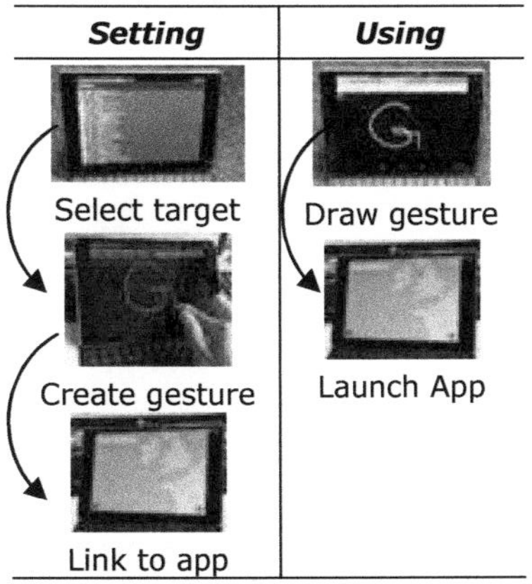

Figure 1. Workflow of Agile Search app. *Setting* and *Using* are two working modes and can be toggled by a button on the right top of the app.

Category	Name	Abbreviation
Communication	Wechat	wcht.
	Messenger	msgr.
	Whatsapp	wapp.
	Facebook	fb.
	Skype	skyp.
	Chrome	chrm.
	Outlook	otlk.
	Gmail	gml.
Travel	Tripadvisor	trip.
	Booking	bk.
	Maps	map.
Entertainment	YouTube	ytub.
Finance	PayPal	pp.
Photography	Instagram	ins.
Shopping	Amazon shopping	ashp.

Table 2. Apps selected for the experiment.

native support for user-defined gesture shortcuts offered by current smart device systems. In order to enable the support and capture user-defined gesture shortcuts, we developed the Agile Search, a standalone Android app that allows the user to define gesture shortcuts to launch associated apps. Agile Search uses Google's gesture recognition algorithm [6] so it supports defining and recognizing uni-stroke and multi-stroke gestures [15].

Two steps are needed to pre-define a gesture shortcut under the *Setting* mode. First, a user needs to select an app that they intend to access via gesture shortcuts among the installed apps' list populated in Agile Search. Second, the user draws a gesture shortcut for the app and confirms whether they are satisfied with the gesture. If the user is not satisfied with the gesture shortcut, they can redraw it. Once the gesture is confirmed, Agile Search opens the target app and saves the gesture as PNG files locally. After defining the gesture, the user can launch the app by redrawing the gesture in Agile Search under the *Using* mode. If the gesture matches what the user defined earlier, Agile Search will then launch the app associated with the gesture (see Figure 1).

App sampling

Due to the diversity and a large number of installed apps, it is impractical to ask users to draw gestures for each installed apps for this exploratory study. A user survey aims to sample the apps was developed, in which participants were asked to select the apps they use for at least once a day from a list of 40 apps extracted from Google Play's top downloads chart. 67 students responded to the survey. Eventually, 15 apps commonly used by 33 students were selected, as shown in Table 2. The categories in this table are based on Google Play's categorization. These 33 students were also invited to participate in the experiment later.

Measurement

To understand users' recall of their self-defined gesture shortcuts and explore factors that may influence their recall, two measures are defined: (1) gesture shortcut recall rate and (2) definition strategy recall rate. For (1), it is defined as the proportion of gesture shortcuts for a specific number of apps that are recalled successfully by a specific number of users. For (2), it is defined as the proportion of definition strategy for gesture shortcuts that are recalled successfully by users. Note that this calculation does not consider whether a user has successfully recalled gesture shortcut or not.

Experiment design

Participants

During the app sampling process mentioned in the Methodology section, 33 university students who studied different subjects nominated 15 common apps. These students were then invited to take part in this experiment. They are all active smart phones and tablets users for over 3 years and own at least one smart phone or tablet.

Testing device

A Google Nexus 9 tablet with Agile Search pre-installed was given to the participants during the experiment to avoid compatibility issues when installing the app on their own devices.

Procedure

Participants were asked to familiarize themselves with the device first if they had not used a Nexus 9 tablet before. After that, they were demonstrated the use of

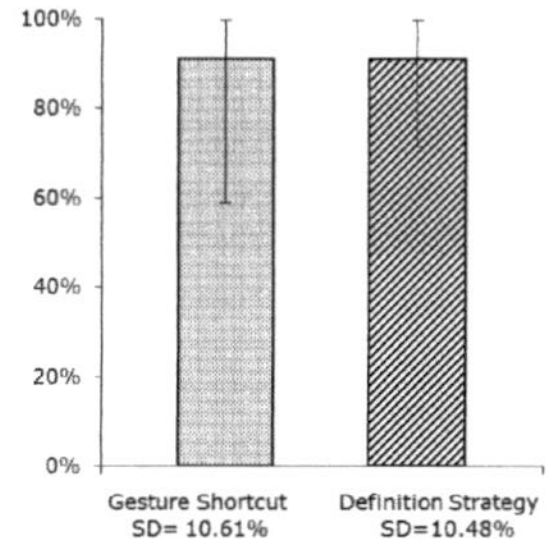

Figure 2. Overview of Participants' Recall Rate on Gesture Shortcut and Definition Strategy.

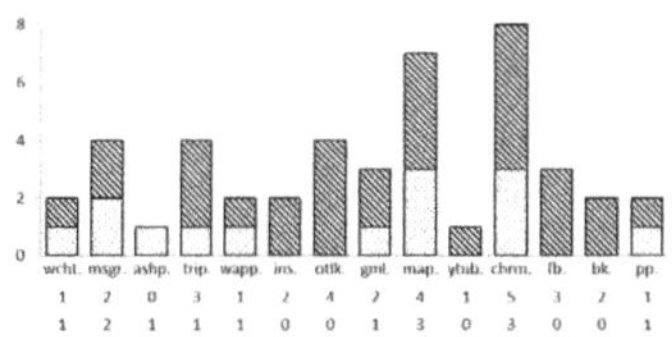

Figure 3. Detailed Breakdown of Gesture Shortcut Recall Failures. over Apps.

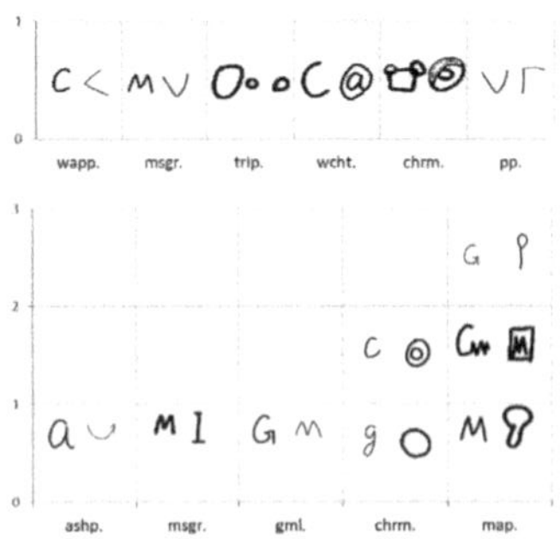

Figure 4. Detailed Breakdowns of Incorrect Gesture Shortcut Pairs based on Different Definition Strategies.

Agile Search and offered a 15-minute self-practice session to try Agile Search with five apps (not included in sample apps' list) installed on the device. The experiment began when participants confirmed that they were ready for the test after the practice. Then the participants were asked to draw or recall the gesture by Agile Search. Each participant was asked to come to the lab for 2 consecutive days to complete a trial consisting of three sequenced phases: gesture shortcut definition (Day 1), reinforcement (Day 1) and next-day recall test (Day 2). The time interval between the two days was set to 24 hours.

Results

Gesture shortcut recall

The overview of participants' gesture shortcut recall rate is shown in Figure 2 (left bar). The averages recall rate is 90.9% (SD= 10.61%, range of 60% to 100%). Out of 33 participants, 16 correctly recalled all gesture shortcuts, they defined and for the rest of them, only two had a recall rate under 80% (P11: 60%, P23: 67%).

Definition strategy recall

The overview recall rate of participants' gesture shortcut definition strategy is shown in Figure 2 (right bar). The averages recall rate is 91% (SD=10.48%, range of 73.3% to 100%) indicating most participants remember the strategy used for defining gesture shortcuts. In detail, 12 participants remembered all strategies they used correctly while 4 participants remembered less than 80% of the strategies they used.

Recall failures over apps

Figure 3 shows the detailed breakdown of gesture shortcut recall failures over apps. The bar chart is divided into two parts: the top part represents the number of failures resulted from the same gesture shortcut definition strategy and the bottom part represents the number of failures resulted from misremembered strategies. Note that the height of each bar represents the total number of failures registered for each app among 33 participants in the recall test.

Figure 4 shows the detailed breakdown of failures in the recall of the gesture shortcut pairs (definition vs. recall) recorded for apps when definition strategies were misremembered. The results reveal that 8 recall failures were the cases that participants misremembering the textual strategy used in the definition phase as the visual strategy in recall test phase, and 6 failures were related to misremembering visual strategy as functional strategy.

Figure 5 shows the detailed breakdown of failures in the recall of the gesture shortcut pairs (definition vs. recall) recorded for apps when the definition strategies were remembered. There were 17 failures related to the textual strategy, 6 failures related to the visual strategy and 5 pairs related to the functional strategy. Note there were also 3 failures related to "other" strategy that is not presented in the figure but they are discussed in next section.

Discussion

The experiment results show that participants recalled the gesture shortcuts effectively in most of the time. This indicates the effectiveness of using self-defined gesture shortcuts to access frequently used mobile apps. However, the failures should not be ignored as they were found with almost all apps (14 out of 15) in the sample list. After examining the link between

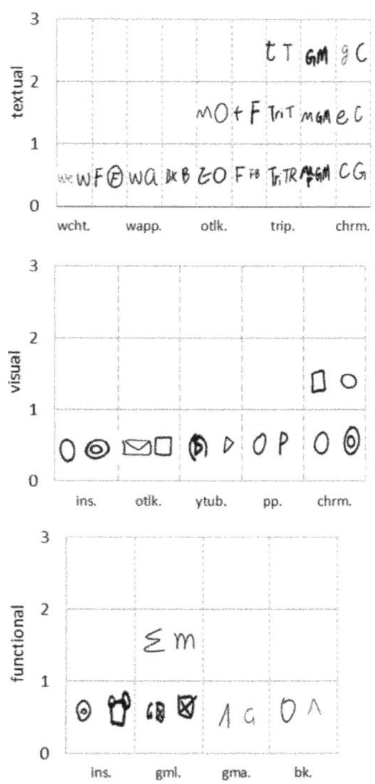

Figure 5. Detailed Breakdowns of Incorrect Gesture Shortcut Pairs based on Same Definition Strategy.

definition strategy recall and gesture shortcut recall, we found that when participants remembered the definition strategies they used, they were very likely to remember the gesture shortcuts they defined (gesture shortcut recall rate: 96.4%); otherwise, the recall rate dropped significantly to 31.1%. This suggests that a mechanism to help users better remember the definition strategy they have used is needed to improve their gesture shortcut recall. For example, if users' choices of strategies can be limited to just one option, the option can be provided as a hint when a user is trying to recall the gesture shortcuts.

It was also found that many failures were related to the textual strategy (i.e., app's name) as participants could not remember the exact letter they used when defining the gesture shortcuts. For example, "G" was defined for Google Map but it was recalled as "M" or "GM". The cases suggest that the gesture matching algorithm for any interface like Agile Search should be more flexible to allow the use of either capital or lowercase of a letter, and any letter or combinations of letters from an app's name as correct gesture shortcuts, regardless of what was defined as the initial gesture shortcut.

Participants' confusions with uni-stroke and multi-stroke were another cause of recall failure. For example, the circle gesture shortcut was first drawn for Instagram but then changed to a nest circle gesture shortcut later. This suggests that only allowing uni-stroke gesture could be used to reduce the probability of gesture shortcut recall failure.

It is also worth to mention that a very few number of failures were related to the "functional" and "other" strategy (e.g., PayPal in Figure 4). Unlike the textual and visual strategy where cues can be easily drawn from app's name and icon, the "functional" and "other" are very vague. For example, users may think Google Map is a map app but they can change their mind to think it as a navigation app over time depending on their main usage (Figure 4). Therefore a possible solution is to limit the definition strategy to the textual and visual only to avoid the confusion.

Limitation and future work

This exploratory study has some limitations due to the controlled environment the experiment has.

First, the time interval for running the recall task was set to 24 hours for all participants. This does not seem to represent the real life scenario very well as in reality, users may be able to launch an app using their self-defined gesture shortcuts more often, which may help them remember the shortcuts better. Therefore, different intervals based on user's actual app use behaviors need to be considered in future experiments to obtain a more accurate understanding of their memorability of self-defined gesture shortcuts.

Second, the sample apps in this exploratory study were the most frequently used apps by participants. It remains unclear whether such findings can be applied to infrequently used apps as users may have more memorability issues with these apps.

Third, in this exploratory study, our analysis was mainly focused on strategies that were clearly identified such as visual strategy, textual strategy and functional strategy. Although "other" strategy was also used, we did not look into these strategies due to the very small number of incorrect gesture shortcut pairs presented. In the future, we may also look into this category when more sample apps are used in the experiment.

Last, the recall of definition strategies was only checked within 24 hours. It remains unclear whether users would change their definition strategies after a period of using or which definition strategy is more effective. Therefore, future experiments focusing on single strategy need to be considered.

Conclusion

An exploratory study has been conducted to study users' abilities on recalling their self-defined gesture shortcuts to access mobile apps as well as understanding the strategies based on which they used to define these gesture shortcuts. The results were quite promising with an average recall rate of 90%, which demonstrated the effectiveness of using self-defined gesture shortcuts to access an app. Certain factors that may influence users' recall rate have also been noticed in the experiment and possible solutions to improve recall are also discussed. Despite the findings, the study clearly has some limitations. So our further study will focus on addressing these limitations and aiming to provide recommendations on the design of gesture shortcut definition interfaces and icon designs.

References

[1] Apple. https://support.apple.com/en-gb/HT201285.

[2] Billinghurst, S. S., and Vu, K.-P. L. Touch screen gestures for web browsing tasks. Computers in Human Behavior 53 (2015), 71–81.

[3] Chen C.-C. User recognition and preference of app icon stylization design on the smartphone. In Proc. HCI 2015, Springer (2015), 9–15.

[4] Lavid Ben Lulu, D. and Kuflik, T. Functionality-based clustering using short textual description: Helping users to find apps installed on their mobile device. In Proc. IUI 2013, ACM Press (2013), 297–306.

[5] Li, Y. Gesture search: a tool for fast mobile data access. In Proc. UIST 2010, ACM Press (2010), 87–96.

[6] Lu, H., and Li, Y. Gesture coder: a tool for programming multi-touch gestures by demonstration. In Proc. CHI 2012, ACM Press (2012), 2875–2884.

[7] Lu, H., and Li, Y. Gesture on: Enabling always-on touch gestures for fast mobile access from the device standby mode. In Proc. CHI 2015, ACM (2015), 3355–3364.

[8] Morris, M. R., Wobbrock, J. O., and Wilson, A. D. Understanding users' preferences for surface gestures. In Proc. GI 2010, CIPS (2010), 261–268.

[9] Nacenta, M. A., Kamber, Y., Qiang, Y., and Kristensson, P. O. Memorability of pre-designed and user-defined gesture sets. In Proc. CHI 2013 , ACM Press (2013), 1099–1108.

[10] Ofcom. http://stakeholders.ofcom.org.uk/binaries/research/cmr/cmr15/CMR_UK_2015.pdf

[11] Poppinga, B., Sahami Shirazi, A., Henze, N., Heuten, W., and Boll, S. Understanding shortcut gestures on mobile touch devices. In Proc. MobileHCI, ACM Press (2014), 173–182.

[12] Statista.http://www.statista.com/statistics/330695/number-of-smartphone-users-worldwide/.

[13] Wobbrock, J. O., Morris, M. R., and Wilson, A. D. User-defined gestures for surface computing. In Proc. CHI 2009, ACM (2009), 1083–1092.

[14] Yahoo.http://www.androidcentral.com/yahooaviate-data-shows-95-apps-are installed/

[15] Zhai, S., Kristensson, P. O., Appert, C., Andersen, T. H., and Cao, X. Foundational issues in touch-screen stroke gesture design-an integrative review. FTHC 5 (2012), 97–205.

Fun-f! Game-furniture Experimenting Interactive Surfaces for Children's Sensory Learning

Nicola Corona
CRS4
Science and Technology Park
Sardinia, Pula CA, Italy
ncorona@crs4.it

Roberto Foddai
CRS4
Science and Technology Park
Sardinia, Pula CA, Italy
foddai@crs4.it

Samuel Aldo Iacolina
CRS4
Science and Technology Park
Sardinia, Pula CA, Italy
samuel@crs4.it

Agnese Mannai
CRS4
Science and Technology Park
Sardinia, Pula CA, Italy
mannai@crs4.it

ISS '16, November 06-09, 2016, Niagara Falls, ON, Canada.
ACM 978-1-4503-4248-3/16/11.
http://dx.doi.org/10.1145/2992154.2996787

Abstract
This work describes Fun-f, a game-furniture for kids designed as a tool of sensory and relational discovery. We introduce the Montessori 2.0 concept, mixing technology and pedagogical theories on the relationships between objects, senses and child growth. Offering a complete sensory experience, our project consists in a sensory labyrinth composed by different modules related to all of the five primary senses. The Fun-f prototype follows a modular design allowing to create different labyrinths with the aim to propose personalized sensory paths and interactive experiences. Its design defines spaces supporting both personal and collaborative experiences, helping kids of different ages to increase their own cognitive, sensory and relational abilities by means of a learning-through-play environment.

Author Keywords
Game; furniture; sensory; interactive; responsive; design; learning-through-play; education; learning;

ACM Classification Keywords
J.4 [Social and behavioral sciences]: Psychology; J.5 [Art and humanities]: Architecture; K.3.1 [Computer Uses in Education]: Collaborative learning

Figure 1: An assembled version of Fun-f prototype as a sensory labyrinth.

Figure 2: The inner spaces are related to sensory discovery.

Figure 3: The external spaces are designed to social practices and collaborative activities.

Introduction

Nowadays new challenges are emerging about the creation of multisensory learning spaces for children, designed to stimulate self-discovery and sensory discovery, promoting at the same time collaborative activities and social practices. The discovery model [10, 9] compared with other approaches [8], proposes learning-by-doing and learning-through-play methods [1, 4] and environments where children can develop their senses working directly with materials. The play itself is considered as a central thread in learning, and large spaces [6] (eg. room-sized [2]) are exploited as immersive and collaborative spaces allowing children to learn concepts [14] from manipulative and practical activities supporting multi-age groupings for peer learning. Well-finished spaces encourage independence, exploration, collaboration (eg. non planar interactive surfaces [5]). Some projects integrate technology [7] to provide interaction and sensory discovery [12, 11] through large interactive spaces eliciting sensations and encouraging movements. This project wants to face these challenges by creating a fully responsive environment, capable of stimulating all of five primary senses, supporting also relational practices and playful activities, integrating innovative kids friendly design and technology to realise a dynamic and modular environment.

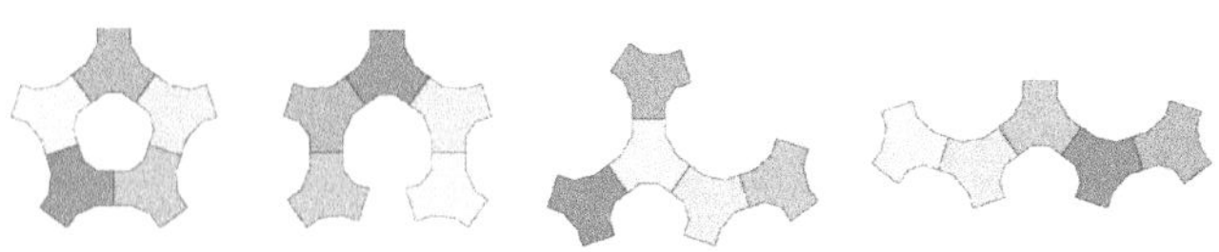

Figure 4: Example of different module configurations.

Project

Fun-f is basically a sensory labyrinth (figure 1) made up by different modules that can be arranged to create an always different configuration of the environment (figure 4). Each module is related to a different sense, but they are structurally identical: a module is composed by three walls, arranged to guarantee three possible connections to other modules. Our prototype covers an area of 12 square meters (more than 2 square meters for each module). The walls, one meter tall, are conceived to divide the space into an inside and an outside. The outer spaces (figure 3) are characterized by three seats (one for each wall) in order to make clear the relational purpose of the project; the concave shape of each wall is made to guarantee intimate spaces for relationship. The inner spaces are those of the sensory discovery (see figure 2), made up to be playful, interactive and responsive; the convex shape enhance the interest of children in movement and interactivity through the whole surface and module [5]. Colours define the main sensory characteristics of each module:

- the **white** one is the sight module (figure 5), where the kid can experience the connections between movement and lights; interactive surfaces act as touch displays, allowing the kid to play with light creating combinations of colors;
- the **yellow** one is the hearing module (figure 6), where children can understand the connections between touch and sound and try to compose music. In fact every wall of the module has three instruments families sounds (percussions, chordophones, aerophones) which allow to create music in a collaborative way;
- the **green** one is the smelling module (figure 7), with different types of fragrances. Also in this case the children try to guess the nature of the element

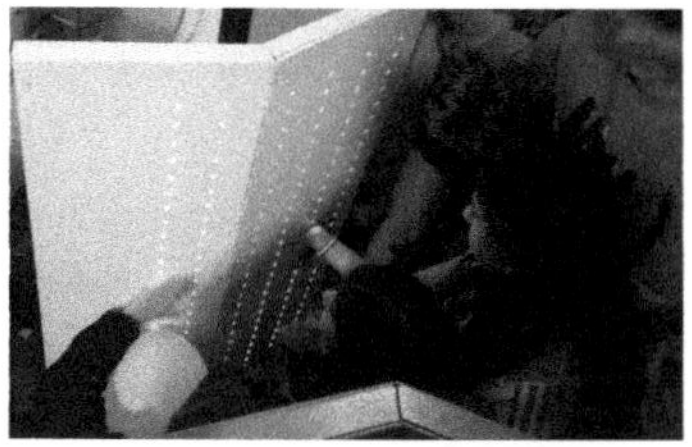
Figure 5: First evaluations at *Maker Faire Rome 2015* and *Science Festival 2015*. Children playing with the sight surface.

Figure 6: Children playing with the hearing surface.

Figure 7: Children playing with the smell module.

that creates the smell and describes the different sensations that come in their minds;

- the **blue** module is the touching one (figure 8), where children play with materials, describing to the teacher these differences and characteristics (e.g. smooth, rough, hot, cold etc.) and trying to guess from which material the texture come from, and comparing the texture to those who are familiar to them.

- the **orange** is the tasting one (figure 9), for hygienic reasons we developed it differently. There is a set of gears on each wall, each gear has different food representation on the external part in predefined positions. When all gears are selected on the same food type (sweet, salty, etc) a candy with related taste is released to the child letting him to associate the taste to known food.

Children are free to interact with a surface, observe the results and then choose another one: this action loop defines the children's interaction experience. Fun-f prototype has been designed to be easily assembled and reassembled, built using low-cost materials that however guaranteed an high resistance during the whole testing phase. Inner surfaces had been cutted and decorated in various ways (depending on the module purpose) by laser cutting (figure 11). We preserved a large interactive surface for each module, in order to create an immersive sensory experience for children, but giving also intimate spaces allowing a small set of children to explore and interact directly with the surfaces.

Technology
The modular approach followed in the Fun-f design has been adopted also for the technological side. Each wall (three per module) holds a set of components enabling the interactive capabilities: sensors, actuators, a battery, a microcontroller, a wifi module and some breakout boards. The specific electronic components have been selected to satisfy the following set of criterias: low cost, readily available, flexibility, simplicity, low power consumption, standard compliant.

Different sensors and actuators had been adopted for each sense: for the **sight** a motion detection sensor (passive infrared and photoresistors) allows to detect the presence of some children nearby and activate the associated RGB LED strip, using random or predefined lighting patterns.
For the **hearing** a motion detection sensor is associated to a specific musical instrument (drawn on the wall) allowing to play a track. A child (or a group) can use his hands on different walls to create musical compositions.
For the **smell** each motion detection sensor allows to turn on a small fan allowing the flow of the air (with a fragrance) to the child. Fragrances flow out from walls interspace through some holes on the wall surface.
For the **touch** there is a pressure sensor on each material sampling (e.g. metal, organic, fabric, etc.) that allows to heat or cool the sampling through a peltier cell adding the hot/cold perception.
For the **taste** each gear is connected to a rotary encoder that allows to know which food picture has been selected by the child; a specific combination of foods enable a servo motor that will release one candy from a bin. Different candy types can be used to evaluate and compare different tastes (related to food pictures).

Instead of using existing integrated kits (like CC2541 SensorTag [1]), we chose the Arduino Nano version as

[1]SensorTag Development Kit http://www.ti.com/tool/cc2541dk-sensor

Figure 8: Children playing with the touch surface.

Figure 9: The taste module.

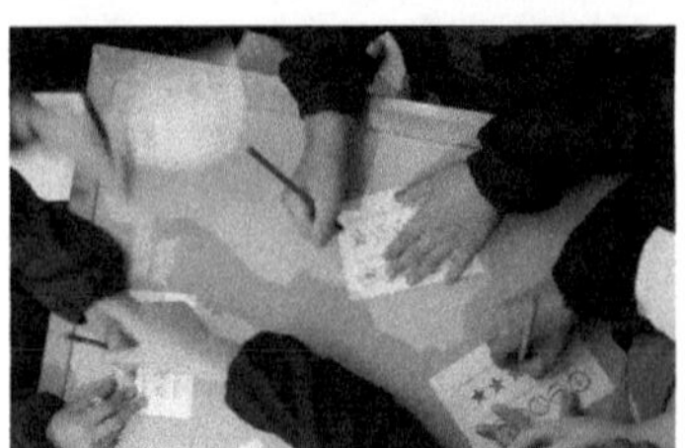

Figure 10: Kids are filling in the evaluation form.

microcontroller for its tiny size, low-cost, extensibility. Currently we developed a firmware with a predefined interaction feedback for each sense; through the adoption of standard technologies (like the 802.11b/g/n and the HTTP protocol) it will be possible to develop other services or devices that will easily interact with Fun-f modules, letting two modules cooperate each other (even remotely) or dynamically changing the modules behavior for customizing the sensorial experience.

In figure 12 it has been reported a logic architecture of interactive components, introducing also incoming and outgoing network requests. In this scenario it will be possible to evolve the sensory path to an immersive synesthetic experience for the children.

Case Study

Our project has been designed as a modular interactive sensory experience that can be used for different purposes and can be reconfigured when needed. Taking into account the stages of cognitive development Piaget [13][10], we propose an environment that can be experienced in different ways:

- Up to 2 years (sensorimotor stage) - sensory learning environment. Babies approach the sensory labyrinth as a discovery process, where their senses are stimulated. Modules can be used by tutors as a pedagogic tool, explaining how to interact with each module during the sensory experience.
- 2 to 7 years (preoperational stage) - sensory play and relational environment. The sensory path is considered as an entertainment environment where children can play with modules and socialize, comparing and exchanging their own knowledge with peers.
- 7 to 11 years (concrete operational stage) - learn-by-doing environment. The entire project can be used as learn-by-doing platform, letting children to understand how each module works and to apply changes on existing modules. Moreover if it is used in schools, it can be integrated in the existing courses in order to teach children programming and electronics basics. Older grades create new modules for the younger grades, validating their work and ideas.

The entire project is suitable for being used as a didactic tool, an entertainment installation or a multi sectoral project. The main application context can be:

- schools and museums, where the didactic aspect is predominant. In these cases Fun-f can be a tool to help teachers and museum guides in their work. The exterior spaces are those for the frontal lessons, while interior spaces are suited to self discovery;
- hospitals and waiting rooms, where the most important thing is the relational and fun aspect. Fun-f become a self sufficient element, with no need for facilitators or guides. The exterior spaces guarantee relational environments, both intimate or more public, and interior spaces define sensory games;
- special needs environments for kids, since sensory surfaces help sense comprehension and ease exploration by means of interaction with materials, even in a collaborative way [3].

It is also possible to create vertical solutions (e.g. specific contexts, from food production to storytelling) changing

Figure 11: The interactive surfaces are realized through laser cutter.

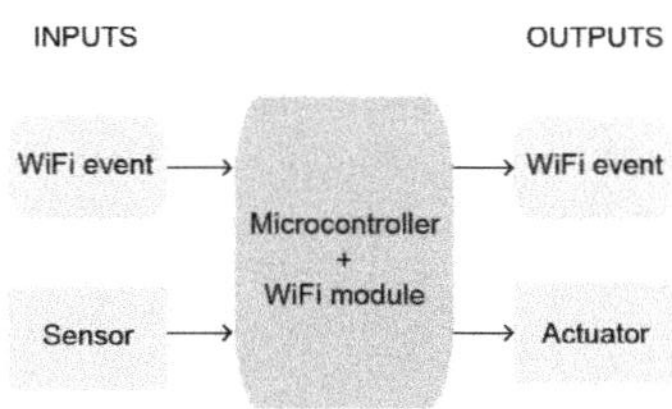

Figure 12: Illustration of the logic functional architecture.

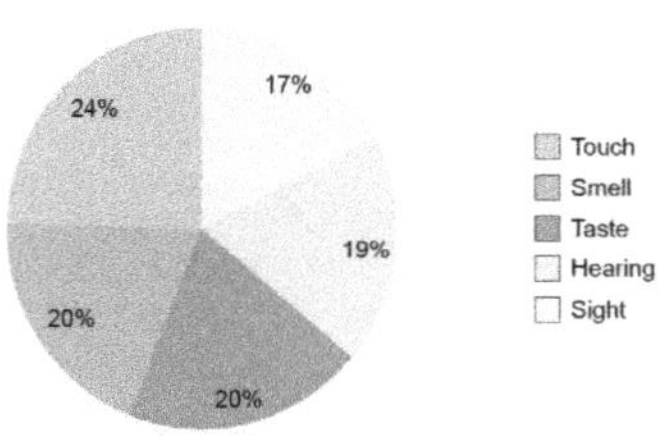

Figure 13: Index of appreciation of the different modules.

hardware and software component, using different material samplings (related to the context) and electronics.

Evaluation

Fun-f project has been validated in various fairs (*Maker Faire Rome 2015*, *Science Festival 2015* at Cagliari, etc.), where we observed the reactions of a high number of children (8000 kids, as estimated by the MFR2015 organization). Absence of malfunctioning and/or broken modules confirms the correct design of the structure (the wall interspaces contain electronic devices, protected and not accessible to children). The modular approach allows us to assemble and try different configurations during the faire (free sensory labyrinth or defined path). Due to the large number of participants it has been very difficult to collect opinions from all children and their parents and we limited ourselves to observe the approval rating of the children (most between 5 and 10 years old): children were very focused at the tactile module,trying to guess which materials has been used; the smell module has been appreciated especially from female users which recognized most of the fragrances. Furthermore most of the children were able to understand how to interact with each module, teaching their mates and explaining them the main features of each module (spontaneous activity, independency and communication expected by learn-through-play educational approach).
A short survey (figure 10) was submitted to the children (574 kids) in order to detect how much they enjoyed Fun-f and which module was the funniest one (the favourite sense experience); the evaluation (figure 13) reconfirms that touch module collected most of the preferences, highlighting children's interest in tactile sensory experience.
During both events, some limits related to the adopted technologies has been detected: (i) light based motion detection sensors can be too sensitive in case of low light environments and (ii) power consumption of some modules is very high so it is necessary to recharge frequently all batteries.

Conclusion

With Fun-f we introduce the concept of Montessori 2.0 proposing and environment specifically designed for kids, integrating technology with design, and supporting sensory discovery by means of interaction with materials, mixing social and collaborative activities in a learning-through-play environment.
Although it has not been possible to compare any result with similar existing solutions (due to the lack of objective measures), we observed that children were very involved and enthusiastic about the provided sensory experience.
The homogeneity of the hardware architecture (similar sensors) setted to zero the learning curve, so children were immediately able to play on the entire installation, confirming the correct design of the interaction pattern.
The overall impressions have been very good both for children and for their parents and teachers; the former were evidently excited and the latter were very enthusiast about the project objective and they asked for custom versions of the modules (reducing the size in order to fit children rooms or editing the sensory effects).
For future works we will develop a new firmware for each module improving connectivity for IoT purposes (data transmitting, remote configuration), solving sensors and batteries problems. We would like also to participate to other events (and/or creating a permanent installation of Fun-f) in order to measure the effectiveness of Fun-f project compared to similar existing projects and measure the children's response to different adopted materials, design and interaction patterns (which are the subjects of our studies).

Acknowledgments

The team wants to thank Simone Spiga (a talented local woodworker) and Sardinia Research Fab-Lab[2].

References

[1] Adams, M., and Moussouri, T. The interactive experience: Linking research and practice. In *Proceedings of International Conference on Interactive Learning in Museums of Art and Design* (2002).

[2] Alborzi, H., Druin, A., Montemayor, J., Platner, M., Porteous, J., Sherman, L., Boltman, A., Taxén, G., Best, J., Hammer, J., et al. Designing storyrooms: interactive storytelling spaces for children. In *Proceedings of the 3rd conference on Designing interactive systems: processes, practices, methods, and techniques*, ACM (2000), 95–104.

[3] Alper, M., Hourcade, J. P., and Gilutz, S. Interactive technologies for children with special needs. In *Proceedings of the 11th International Conference on Interaction Design and Children*, ACM (2012), 363–366.

[4] Barker, P. Designing interactive learning. In *Design and production of multimedia and simulation-based learning material*. Springer, 1994, 1–30.

[5] Beyer, G., Alt, F., Müller, J., Schmidt, A., Isakovic, K., Klose, S., Schiewe, M., and Haulsen, I. Audience behavior around large interactive cylindrical screens. In *Proceedings of the SIGCHI Conference on Human Factors in Computing Systems*, ACM (2011), 1021–1030.

[6] Bobick, A. F., Intille, S. S., Davis, J. W., Baird, F., Pinhanez, C. S., Campbell, L. W., Ivanov, Y. A., Schütte, A., and Wilson, A. The kidsroom: A perceptually-based interactive and immersive story environment. *Presence: Teleoperators and Virtual Environments 8*, 4 (1999), 369–393.

[7] Druin, A. The role of children in the design of new technology. *Behaviour and information technology 21*, 1 (2002), 1–25.

[8] Lopata, C., Wallace, N. V., and Finn, K. V. Comparison of academic achievement between montessori and traditional education programs. *Journal of research in childhood education 20*, 1 (2005), 5–13.

[9] Montessori, M. *The discovery of the child*. Aakar books, 2004.

[10] Montessori, M. *The Montessori Method*. Transaction Publishers, 2013.

[11] Morrison, A., Manresa-Yee, C., Jensen, W., and Eshraghi, N. The humming wall: Vibrotactile and vibroacoustic interactions in an urban environment. In *Proceedings of the 2016 ACM Conference on Designing Interactive Systems*, ACM (2016), 818–822.

[12] Morrison, A. J., Manresa-Yee, C., Jensen, B. W. S., and Eshraghi, N. The humming wall. *Dis2016* (2016).

[13] Piaget, J., and Cook, M. *The origins of intelligence in children*, vol. 8. International Universities Press New York, 1952.

[14] Roussou, M. Learning by doing and learning through play: an exploration of interactivity in virtual environments for children. *Computers in Entertainment (CIE) 2*, 1 (2004), 10–10.

[2] http://www.sardegnaricerche.it/fablab/

HABITAT EXPLORER: Designing Educational Games for Collaborative Learning on Interactive Surfaces

Anne Schwartz*
Wellesley College
aschwar3@wellesley.edu

Clara Sorensen*
Wellesley College
csorense@wellesley.edu

Eni Mustafaraj
Wellesley College
eni.mustafaraj@wellesley.edu

ISS '16, November 06-09, 2016, Niagara Falls, ON, Canada
ACM 978-1-4503-4248-3/16/11.
http://dx.doi.org/10.1145/2992154.2996788

Abstract
Data science is an interdisciplinary field at the intersection of computer science, mathematics, and subject matter expertise with the purpose to gain insights from relatively large sets of data. With elementary school age children as the target audience, we developed an educational collaborative game, Habitat Explorer for the MultiTaction display to introduce users to the core data science cycle components of data collection, exploration, and visualization. Users capture "sea creatures" in a collection jar, sort their collection into a data table, and then are able to create a bar chart visualization using their data. These components are interspersed with questions assessing user comprehension of the simple biological and data science concepts introduced during the game. The main goal of this research is to understand the potential of multi-touch displays to facilitate data science education with future aims to develop more complicated data exploration applications.

Author Keywords
Interactive surfaces; Multi-touch interaction; Collaborative Learning; Data visualization

ACM Classification Keywords
H.5.m. Information interfaces and presentation (e.g., HCI): Miscellaneous.

Introduction
Data science is an interdisciplinary field that makes use of computer science, mathematics, and specific subject matter expertise in an effort to gain insights from relatively large sets of data. Data exploration and analysis is currently most commonly performed using many different non-collaborative, non-interactive applications such as Excel, hosted on hardware that also does not facilitate collaboration or exploration. Tangible interfaces have been found to allow people to actively explore and learn as touch and object manipulation helps introduce users to difficult content [5]. MultiTaction displays are large scale touch screen displays that can process input from multiple users. The aim of the multi-touch nature of MultiTaction displays is collaboration between users with an emphasis on user exploration.

We have developed an educational collaborative game, Habitat Explorer, for the MultiTaction display that introduces users to some of the core data science process steps, concretely, data collection, exploration, and visualization. We built this application as a tool to determine the potential of MultiTaction displays to host interactive and collaborative data science applications. In this paper we will describe the design and implementation of Habitat Explorer, as well as our goals for future development and testing. We will begin by discussing related work.

Related Work
Tangible interfaces have been found beneficial for teaching difficult content as their ability for spatial manipulation allows for different viewpoints to analyze particular problems [5]. These systems have been found to be more intuitive, easy to learn, and more free of performance errors than existing keyboard-and-mouse interfaces. Additionally, students have been found to have difficulties with understanding patterns of unfamiliar data, but being able to show students an entire view of the data, making use of large, high-resolution displays has proven useful [6]. Multi-touch technologies, furthermore, have been demonstrated previously to be intuitive and to allow for clear visualization of data [1].

Playing educational games collaboratively, too, has been found to be an effective and valuable learning method, particularly when coupled with traditional education methods [2]. Successful design of these educational games, however, requires a difficult balance between educational elements and a "fun-factor" [3]. Generic gameplay design is often later enhanced with real-time adaptation that caters to a specific user with ongoing assessment.

The current state of educational technologies is such that there is often limited user input capabilities and a need to improve support for active, expressive, and flexible user input with a compelling educational game design [3, 5]. We seek to accomplish this with Habitat Explorer by making use of MultiTaction displays that promote collaborative learning.

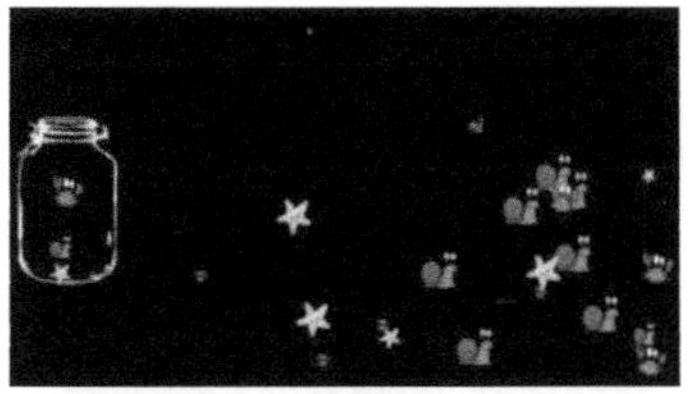

Figure 1: Users begin the game by collecting "sea creatures".

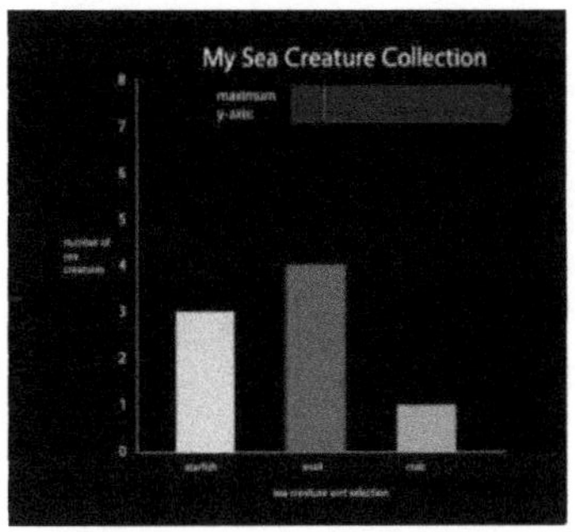

Figure 2: The user builds a simple data visualization.

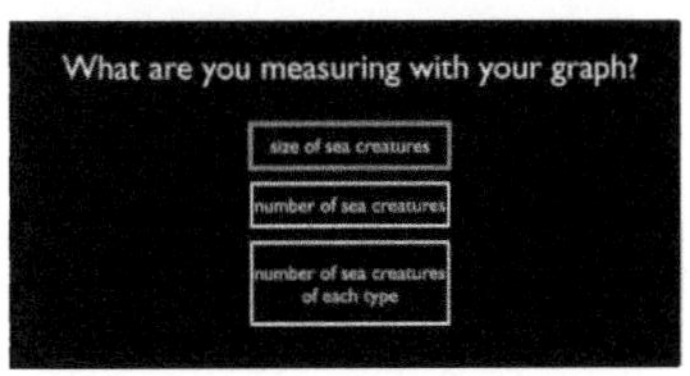

Figure 3: Users are asked comprehension questions between stages of the game.

Habitat Explorer Prototype

Habitat explorer is currently implemented using a vertical MultiTaction cell with the application written in JavaScript using the Cornerstone Software Development Kit. It is designed as a 2-3 player game with the intention of having an instructor present to facilitate and monitor use. The application simplifies the data science cycle into three straightforward steps: data collection, in which users capture sea creatures, data exploration, in which users sort their collection of sea creatures into a simplified data table, and data communication (by way of a simple visualization) of exploration results.

Game Components

1. Data Collection: The first component of Habitat Explorer presents users with many moving "sea creatures" that vary in size and type (species) that they must capture within the span of 10 seconds by tapping the creatures to trap them in a collection jar. See Figure 1.

2. Data Organization and Exploration: Users are asked whether they want to sort their collected sea creatures by their size or by their type. An empty simplified data table is created based upon the user's sorting type choice and users are instructed to drag their collected sea creatures to the correct spot in the table. The table increments the count of number of sea creatures in each category (size or type) when the user drags a sea creature to the correct location in the chart. When the user drags a sea creature to the correct location in the chart the creature is given a green border to indicate the correctness of its location.

3. Data Visualization: Using their completed data table, Habitat Explorer users create a simple bar chart. First they build the outline of the chart by dragging the chart's labels to a provided set of axes. After they finish the outline, they populate the chart with the data they have in their data table by tapping on each one of the sea creatures to add its data to the bar chart. Users are able to adjust the scale of the bar chart to see how that impacts the height of the bars. See Figure 2.

4. Comprehension Questions: Between stages of the Habitat Explorer game users are prompted to answer questions that assess their understanding of the topics introduced in the game such as what the user is measuring with their graph, or what type or size of sea creature might be hardest to catch based on how many of each the user collected. With these comprehension questions Habitat Explorer introduces both data science topics such as visualization and data organization as well as simple biological concepts like representative sampling and habitat diversity. See Figure 3.

5. User Data Collection: When it runs, Habitat Explorer collects data about the interactions that users have with the MultiTaction and the different components of the game. The console keeps track of users answering assessments questions right or wrong, the time it takes for users to complete each section of the game, as well as the type of sorting the user chooses for their collected "sea creatures". This internal data collection is a way of assessing user understanding as they progresses through Habitat Explorer, and the general type of interaction that users have with MultiTaction displays.

Figure 4: Collaborative user testing of Habitat Explorer.

Implementation

Habitat Explorer is implemented on a 55" MultiTaction display cell using JavaScript following the framework of MultiTaction's Cornerstone Software Development Kit. The application runs through a command line-based shell from a laptop connected to the cell.

Preliminary User Testing

During a public poster session, visitors were invited to play Habitat Explorer (see Figure 4). We observed that participants were excited and eager to progress through the application, successfully navigating their way through all stages of the game while collaboratively working with one another by talking about their thoughts and simultaneously interacting with the MultiTaction display to complete application tasks. However participants were almost too eager to move from one stage of the game to another so rather than actively thinking about comprehension components, they tended to click whatever they thought might allow them to proceed. As a result, initial testing demonstrated a need to simplify the game and make the questions more engaging, though the game itself proved successfully collaborative and engaging.

Apart from the Habitat Explorer game itself, the MultiTaction display posed some difficulties. Although the MultiTaction website states that their displays are considered "the most responsive in the world" [4], the display we used was often not sensitive enough to user interaction that users could smoothly complete the tasks posed by Habitat Explorer. Users would often have to drag items in multiple short bursts to get them to move where they wanted and sometimes they were not even able to drag objects that were supposed to be draggable, because they were too small. Application design for the MultiTaction must take into account its lack of responsiveness through adjusting the size of draggable items. With further development we will most likely discover more design challenges associated with MultiTaction displays.

Programming for MultiTaction and the MultiTaction Community

The MultiTaction displays at Wellesley College run on MultiTaction's Cornerstone software. Cornerstone is a software development kit based on C++. MultiTaction's website states that while you can program for the Cornerstone SDK using JavaScript, a basic understanding of C++ is very helpful. When exploring the documentation for Cornerstone, we discovered code for many example applications, nearly all in C++, with just a few in JavaScript. The lack of JavaScript documentation made it very difficult to simply begin programming in JavaScript without first exploring the Cornerstone SDK and programming simple applications in C++.

There is very little community surrounding the development of applications for MultiTaction displays. The only forum specifically concerning programming using the Cornerstone SDK is on the Cornerstone SDK site itself, and is not very active. We have found very minimal public communication between MultiTaction developers and most Cornerstone programs are designed to meet an individualized, private project by MultiTaction itself and not by individual developers.

Conclusion and Next Steps

Habitat Explorer is an educational game for MultiTaction displays that we hope to use as a tool to test the potential of multi-touch displays to host more complicated data science applications. We plan to continue to develop Habitat Explorer before and after further user testing in the Human Computer Interaction (HCI) Lab at Wellesley College.

More specifically, we would like to introduce more biological concepts by providing the user the ability to select a specific habitat at the beginning of the game, allowing them to "explore" organism variation in different ecosystems. We also want to allow the user more flexibility in exploration and movement through the different stages of the game. Rather than solely progressing forward, the user should be able to move back and forth between stages of the game, as well as store their progress at any point.

We additionally want to be able to analyze user-produced data in a more efficient way that provides immediate feedback to the application administrators telling them where a group of users struggled the most during use of the application. These administrators should also be able to select the type of data visualization they want to teach with the game or have the option to teach a variety with a single gameplay. The expanded variety in options should help improve user interest and collaborative engagement.

Acknowledgements
We would like to thank our sponsors Mrs. Jenkins, Mr. Bartels and Ms. Condon, and our technical support guides Lauren Wesendorf from the Wellesley HCI Lab and Borys Plyenkov from MultiTaction support.

References
[1] Liu, Sirui, Kara Lu, Nahum Seifeselassie, Casey Grote, Nicole Francisco, Veronica Lin, Linda Ding, Consuelo Valdes, Robert Kincaid, and Orit Shaer. "MoClo planner: supporting innovation in bio-design through multi-touch interaction." In Proceedings of the 2012 ACM international conference on Interactive tabletops and surfaces, pp. 307-310. ACM, 2012.

[2] Martín-SanJosé, J., Juan, M., Seguí, I. and García-García, I. The effects of computer-based games and collaboration in large groups vs. collaboration in pairs or traditional methods. Computers & Education 87, (2015), 42-54.

[3] Moreno-Ger, P., Burgos, D., Martínez-Ortiz, I., Sierra, J. and Fernández-Manjón, B. Educational game design for online education. Computers in Human Behavior 24, 6 (2008), 2530-2540.

[4] Multitaction | Our Technology. Multitaction.com, 2016. https://www.multitaction.com/technology.

[5] Oviatt, S. The design of future educational interfaces. Routledge, New York, 2013.

[6] Rajabiyazdi, Fateme, Jagoda Walny, Carrie Mah, John Brosz, and Sheelagh Carpendale. "Understanding Researchers' Use of a Large, High-Resolution Display Across Disciplines." In Proceedings of the 2015 International Conference on Interactive Tabletops & Surfaces, pp. 107-116. ACM, 2015.

Exploring Interactive Surface Designs for Eliciting Social Activity from Elderly Adults

Richard J. Wirth
Pennsylvania State University
University Park, PA 16801 USA
rvw5292@psu.edu

John M. Carroll
Pennsylvania State University
University Park, PA 16801 USA
jmcarroll@psu.edu

Chien Wen Yuan
Pennsylvania State University
University Park, PA 16801 USA
tuy11@psu.edu

Mary Beth Rosson
Pennsylvania State University
University Park, PA 16801 USA
mrosson@psu.edu

Benjamin V. Hanrahan
Pennsylvania State University
University Park, PA 16801 USA
banrahan@ist.psu.edu

Jomara Bindá
Pennsylvania State University
University Park, PA 16801 USA
jmb89@ist.psu.edu

ISS '16, November 06-09, 2016, Niagara Falls, ON, Canada
ACM 978-1-4503-4248-3/16/11.
http://dx.doi.org/10.1145/2992154.2996789

Abstract
Isolation and loneliness has been shown to be a significant cause of disease and mortality among elderly adults. The coproduction of activity is one potential method of prevention, through the promotion of social interaction and community engagement. The present study aims to facilitate coproduction in a continuing care retirement community, promoting health and wellness in elderly adults. To achieve this, we engage in the participatory design of a public interactive display for organizing community activity. We explore design needs and usability concerns from elderly residents, and discuss the trajectory of co-design work to realize this technological intervention.

Author Keywords
Coproduction; elderly adults; health; participatory design

ACM Classification Keywords
H.5.m. Information interfaces and presentation (e.g., HCI): Miscellaneous.

Introduction
The design of technological interventions for healthy aging in elderly communities is a growing need, as this

Figure 1. Our researchers lead a participatory design session at a Continuing Care Retirement Community, prompting users for desired features and interface layouts.

demographic represents an increasing portion of the population [16, 18]. Today's elderly population is in general healthier, with higher levels of independence and education than prior generations [3]. However, little research has taken into account the potential for technology to leverage this independence for self-care and the coproduction of services [19]. Coproduction is a social practice in which individuals enact services together, using their everyday resources [19]. Research has shown that social isolation and loneliness play a significant role in disease and mortality rates among the elderly [14, 15]. Designing technology to elicit social interaction and coproduction may lead to improvements in health and wellness for elderly adults.

Social software interventions have been shown to affect general positive changes on individuals' engagement, sense of community, and sociability [1, 6, 10]. Research has additionally explored the ability for interactive surfaces to leverage social software in public spaces [8, 10]. However, this research is generally targeted at tech-savvy users and conventional locations, with the design needs of elderly adults frequently left unaddressed [13]. Information communication technologies (ICTs) are regularly employed to promote healthy behaviors, however, they are often centered on the treatment and detection of poor health, rather than on enhancing good health [4, 17].

The present study aims to fill this gap by designing an interactive surface for coproduction activities in a Continuing Care Retirement Community (CCRC). Our work promotes coproduction in elderly adults through activity planning, particularly activities done together. In developing a public technology for older adults, designers must account for cognitive and physical decline, a lack of technological fluency, and the needs of an underexplored demographic [1, 3, 11, 13]. We employ participatory design methods to overcome these challenges by eliciting desired features, improving accessibility, and uncovering emergent factors through mutual learning (shown in Figure 1). What we present here are the trajectory and design implications of an ongoing long-term participatory design study. These early findings will be guided by observations and interviews from a six-month engagement with elderly communities. Implications for design and future work will be discussed.

Related Work

Designing interactive systems for older adults requires an understanding of their usability and information-processing needs. Mutual learning and understanding between users and designers is a key feature of participatory design. Here we present relevant literature on the role of user participation in usability and design for older adults.

Designer specifications and user behavior are often misaligned in the design of new systems of interaction. This notion is seen in Wobbrock et al.'s [20] study of gesture interaction for surface computing, wherein users evidenced a variety of expectations and intuitions about how to use a system. This becomes problematic in elderly adults, who have been shown to have significantly different needs for information usability than typical technology users [12].

Eisma et al. [5] identified the importance of hands-on and group-oriented approaches for eliciting feedback and participation from older adults. Applying this

Figure 2. Prototype board installed in a high-traffic public mailroom so that the majority of residents encounter it on a daily basis. Goal is to encourage reflection and active participation.

method to the design of a large-screen display for a care home, Müller et al. [11] identified sociality, trust, and memory as important factors for usability. These factors contribute to building confidence in older users, which prior research has concluded is important in keeping them open to the design process [5, 13]. Researchers have concluded that the design of interactive systems for elderly users benefits from mutual understanding and learning, for which co-design methods are an apt choice [2, 13]. Prior research has explored the issue of usability in elderly adults, as the aging process introduces unique considerations such as cognitive and ambulatory decline [7, 9, 12]. Studies have shown that while technology usage generally declines with age, the perception of technology as useful and functional significantly slows this decline [5]. Because of this, positioning a display or interactive system as useful may serve to encourage learning and adoption. Given the importance of social activity to both enjoyment and wellness, the present study seeks to design a public installation of interactive event organizing software for the purpose of promoting activity in the residents of a CCRC.

User Study

The goal of our study was to identify desired functionality and address both new and previously identified usability issues in a community of elderly adults, ranging in age from 65-95 years old. As part of our ongoing Smart and Connected Health (SACH) project, we have conducted a number of activities towards understanding the design of technological interventions for elderly communities. In the present study, researchers conducted a series of participatory design sessions in an effort to identify early prototype requirements, assess opinions towards traditional features, and gain perspective from our elderly stakeholders.

Procedure

Four researchers engaged a group of elderly adults in conversations of design for an interactive display. The purpose of this display to assist them in organizing events with other residents of their retirement community. Facility staff installed a whiteboard for prototyping purposes in a high-traffic public space (see Figures 2 and 3), and researchers used mock-ups to relate interfaces and functionality for this future software. In addition to the whiteboard, we supplied a collection of widgets (e.g. magnetized objects, stickers, and labels) to help participants conceptualize what their designs might appear as. In doing so, our goal was to minimize technology-related jargon and maintain confidence in understanding from our audience, as compromising this has been shown to reduce cooperation and willingness to learn [1, 5, 13].

An additional benefit of paper prototyping with elderly users is that the benefits of software can be highlighted. Users and facility staff alike communicated a number of design concerns that we aim to highlight through prototyping, and encourage solving through systems design. Doing so may help to alleviate the persistent issue of technology resistance among older adults [18]. Our initial participatory design session aimed to keep aspects of the interface, interactions, and system design open to discussion. Researchers primarily highlighted the purpose of the whiteboard, the reason for participatory design, and its role in future development.

Figure 3. Whiteboard installed in the public mail room of the retirement community, located centrally in a high-traffic hallway. Participants are invited to design and organize the board over a long-term participatory design effort.

Results

We received a variety of feedback from participants, with interesting findings related to usage, system notifications, the creation of social events and invitations, and the physical space in which the display is situated. The general interface design for the whiteboard, such as the basic organization of content based on date, time, or activity, received a great deal of commentary. Most of the participants expressed the desire for no organization at all. Users wanted to be able to put notices wherever they want on the board with no regard for formatting or organization.

Potential Usage

Participants in the design session focused usage conversation on the topics of function and potential activities. These results have a significant implication for the transition from a fixed to an interactive digital display. In designing the whiteboard prototype, one participant expressed the concern that when an individual sees an event or activity they would like to attend, they might simply take the notice back to their room. This is a common practice in traditional public displays, such as posters and fliers, to have contact information torn off in small pieces. Users generally agreed that interaction should be as simplified as possible, and that a minimalist design would prevent distraction by color-coding, categories, and positioning. Finally, participants provided a number of unforeseen use cases that may inform future design. Users were concerned about privacy and public display of interest, the role of official groups and regularly scheduled events, and confrontational events-planning such as discussion of religious culture.

Notifications and Communication

Many participants expressed concerns with being notified about event postings and invitations, claiming that they already receive too many notifications. Others commented that residents ignore their phones, or receive too much email. Generally, residents agreed that they wanted to browse and express interest, rather than receive invitations directly from other people. Others still were concerned that their interests were too broad and varied, and that to satisfy them all there would be an overload of information. Participants offered design solutions such as quickly fading event postings, open perusal of events with no organization, and communication going back to the organizer, but not to interested parties.

Spatial Considerations

One of the most prominent concerns from participants was the concern for space and presentation, both from a practical and aesthetics perspective. Many people expressed concern that in posting an event, users would write too much, not follow an understandable format, or not include crucial location and contact information. As a solution, participants suggested that event postings be structured similarly to an RSVP card, using a template that was universally understood by the community (see Figure 4). They asserted that this would help to reduce clutter and prevent individuals from taking up too much space. Similarly, space concerns prompted questions about limitations on event postings, particularly for recurring and regular activity. Users worried that if somebody wanted to go on daily walks, that portions of the whiteboard would remain dedicated to that activity and become unusable. Some participants were concerned about the space limitations of the display location, rather than just the

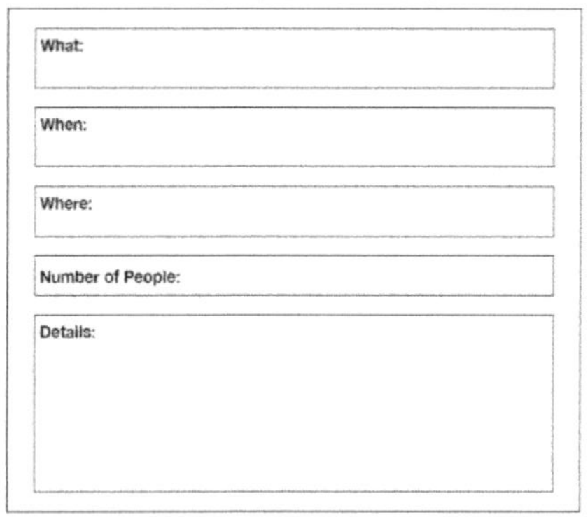

Figure 4. Template proposed by the participants of an initial design session. Users felt that simplicity and resemblance to RSVPs, a convention they are all familiar with, would improve usability and communication.

interface. One person worried that the popularity and frequent usage of the display could lead to crowding in the mail room or even the hallway itself. This raised interesting related questions about personal routines. One participant shared that many of the residents would pass by the mail room and be able to see if they had anything in their personal mailbox. However, with the presence of the display and an increase in traffic, they were concerned that this routine may no longer be possible.

Conclusions and Future Work

Our participatory design sessions raised a number of interesting concerns about the features and implementation of an interactive display for the coproduction of social activity. In conducting the study, we were confronted by an unexpected variety of social and technical concerns, as well as a wide gap in the technological fluency of our participants. Based on these preliminary results, the trajectory of future participatory design sessions must balance concerns of usability, spatial limitations, technological fluency, a desire for privacy, and varying attitudes towards channels of communication and notification.

Moving forward, the initial feedback and usability concerns generated by participatory design will influence the development of our interactive display software. Issues of organization and clutter, as well as uniformity of postings, may prove to be a venue for more structured co-design opportunities. Additionally, concerns of privacy and communication can be framed as a benefit of digital displays over traditional bulletin boards, with users having control over visibility and channels of communication.

Due to the variance in technology fluency, the design session conversation was dominated by the more proficient residents. Additionally, only a portion of the facility's 154 elderly adults were able to attend. Based on our findings and these limitations, we have devised a long term design installation, where residents may repeatedly encounter the prototype during their daily routines. It is our hope that residents that have lesser technical aptitude may be able to provide feedback through repeated encounters and observations, and that design-oriented participants may have more clear ideas about structure and interaction with the display. We will engage in regular design sessions to elicit feedback from residents and find the ideal end product for promoting the coproduction of activity and wellness.

References

[1] Blythe, M., Wright, P., Bowers, J., Boucher, A., Jarvis, N., Reynolds, P., & Gaver, B. (2010). Age and experience. *Proceedings of the 8th ACM Conference on Designing Interactive Systems - DIS '10*, 161-170.

[2] Coleman, G. W., Gibson, L., Hanson, V. L., Bobrowicz, A., & McKay, A. (2010). Engaging the Disengaged: How do we Design Technology for Digitally Excluded Older Adults? *Proceedings of the 8th ACM Conference on Designing Interactive Systems*, 175–178.

[3] Czaja, S. J. (2005). The impact of aging on access to technology. *ACM SIGACCESS Accessibility and Computing*, (83), 7–11. http://doi.org/10.1145/1102187.1102189

[4] Dayer, L., Heldenbrand, S., Anderson, P., Gubbins, P. O., & Martin, B. C. (2013). Smartphone medication adherence apps: Potential benefits to patients and providers. *Journal of the American Pharmacists Association*, *53*(2), 172-181.

[5] Eisma, R., Dickinson, a., Goodman, J., Syme, a., Tiwari, L., & Newell, a. F. (2004). Early user involvement in the development of information technology-related products for older people. *Universal Access in the Information Society*, *3*(2), 131–140.

[6] Farnham, S., Zaner, M., & Cheng, L. (2001). Supporting Sociability in a Shared Browser. *Proceedings of Interact Conference, Tokyo, Japan*.

[7] Holzinger, A., Searle, G., Kleinberger, T., Seffah, A., & Jevahery, H. (2008). Investigating Usability Metrics for the Design and. In *International Conference on Computers for Handicapped Persons* (pp. 98–105).

[8] Hosio, S., Kukka, H., Jurmu, M., Ojala, T., & Riekki, J. (2010). Enhancing interactive public displays with social networking services. *Proceedings of the 9th International Conference on Mobile and Ubiquitous Multimedia - MUM '10*, 1–9.

[9] Ijsselsteijn, W., Nap, H. H., De Kort, Y., & Poels, K. (2007). Digital game design for elderly users. In *Proceedings of the 2007 Conference on Future Play, Future Play '07* (pp. 17–22).

[10] McCarthy, J. F., Farnham, S. D., Patel, Y., Ahuja, S., Norman, D., Hazlewood, W. R., & Lind, J. (2009). Supporting Community in Third Places with Situated Social Software. *Communities and Technologies*, 225–234.

[11] Müller, C., Neufeldt, C., Randall, D., & Wulf, V. (2012). ICT-development in residential care settings: sensitizing design to the life circumstances of the residents of a care home. *Proceedings of the SIGCHI ...*, 2639–2648.

[12] Murata, A., & Iwase, H. (2015). Usability of Touch-Panel Interfaces for Older Adults, *47*(4), 767–776.

[13] Newell, A., Arnott, J., Carmichael, A., & Morgan, M. (2007). Methodologies for involving older adults in the design process. *Proceedings of HCII 2007, 4554*, 22–27.

[14] Steptoe, A., Shankar, A., Demakakos, P., & Wardle, J. (2013). Social isolation, loneliness, and all-cause mortality in older men and women. In *Proceedings of the National Academy of Sciences of the United States of America* (Vol. 110, pp. 5797–5801).

[15] Tomaka, J., Thompson, S., & Palacios, R. (2006). The Relation of Social Isolation, Loneliness, and Social Support to Disease Outcomes Among the Elderly. *Journal of Aging and Health*, *18*(3), 359–384.

[16] U.S. Department of Health and Human Services. Administration on Aging. 2012. Retrieved September 1, 2016 http://www.aoa.acl.gov/aging_statistics/index.aspx

[17] Vervloet, M., Linn, A. J., van Weert, J. C. M., de Bakker, D. H., Bouvy, M. L., & van Dijk, L. (2012). The effectiveness of interventions using electronic reminders to improve adherence to chronic medication: a systematic review of the literature. *Journal of the American Medical Informatics Association : JAMIA*, *19*(5), 696–704.

[18] Vines, J., Pritchard, G., Wright, P., & Olivier, P. (2015). An Age-Old Problem : Examining the Discourses of Ageing in HCI and Strategies for Future Research. *ACM Transactions on Computer-Human Interaction (TOCHI)*, *22*(1), 1–27.

[19] Wilson, G. (1994). Co-Production and Self-Care: New Approaches to Managing Community Care Services for Older People. *Social Policy & Administration*, *28*(3), 236–250.

[20] Wobbrock, J. O., Morris, M. R., & Wilson, A. D. (2009). User-defined gestures for surface computing. *Proceedings of the 27th International Conference on Human Factors in Computing Systems - CHI 09*, 1083.

Learning New Words and Spelling with Autocorrections

Ahmed Sabbir Arif
Ryerson University
Toronto, Ontario, Canada
a.s.arif@gmail.com

Cristina Sylla
University of Minho
Braga, Portugal
sylla@engagelab.org

Ali Mazalek
Ryerson University
Toronto, Ontario, Canada
mazalek@ryerson.ca

ISS '16, November 06-09, 2016, Niagara Falls, ON, Canada
ACM 978-1-4503-4248-3/16/11.
http://dx.doi.org/10.1145/2992154.2996790

Abstract
We present a novel color-coded feedback method that highlights the types of corrections made by autocorrections. We then present results of a longitudinal user study with 7-8-year-old children that compared the new method with the conventional autocorrection feedback method, in terms of leaning new words and spelling. Results suggested that the new method better accommodates learning new words. Interestingly, learning was observed with the conventional feedback method as well, demanding further investigation into whether predictive methods are truly a barrier to learning new words and spelling.

Author Keywords
Child; children; prediction; predictive keyboard; spelling; autocorrection; color-coded autocorrect.

ACM Classification Keywords
H.5.2. Information interfaces and presentation (e.g., HCI): User Interfaces – Graphical user interfaces (GUI).

Introduction
Mobile devices are becoming increasingly popular among children. A survey revealed that about 72% of children aged eight and under in the U.S. have access to mobile devices, including tablets, which they are using for various purposes, such as to play games, watch videos,

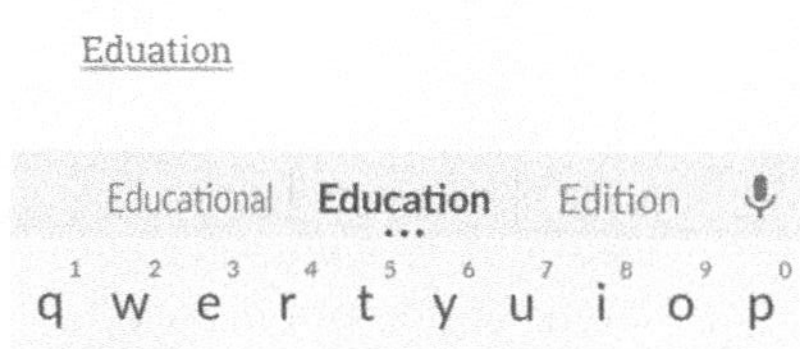

Figure 1. Current autocorrection feedback.

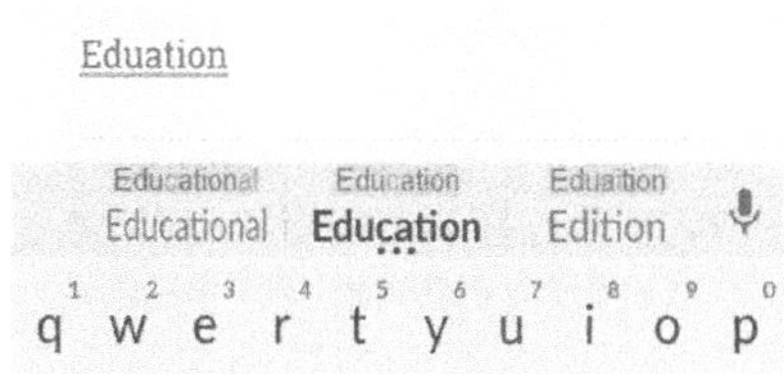

Figure 2. Color-coded autocorrection feedback.

Figure 3. A child participating in the user study.

take pictures, and gain access to social networks and mobile applications [19]. Many of these activities require text entry. Yet most current mobile devices do not include children-friendly keyboards. There are some third-party virtual keyboards available for children. However, the effort and technical expertise required to find and install these keyboards are often discouraging to mobile owners. As a result, most children are forced to use keyboards that are primarily designed for adults. Research suggests that composing text with a conventional keyboard can play a role in the language learning process of young children. Conventional keyboards require children to revise, rework, and discuss their work, encouraging critical thinking. This assists children to improve their writing [11], narrative [21] and spelling [15] skills. Most current mobile keyboards, however, are augmented with predictive systems that suggest the most probable next word/s based on prefix and context, and automatically correct all probable misspelled words. Studies showed that these techniques have made mobile text entry much easier for both children [14] and adults [4]. Yet, predictive systems, particularly autocorrect, have long been considered a barrier to learning spelling by popular media, teachers, and parents [16, 22]. The argument is that because of autocorrections, children no longer have to review their input to identify and correct misspelled words [22], thus cannot learn from their mistakes. As a first step towards investigating this popular belief, here we explore whether or not learning of new words and spelling occurs with autocorrections.

Related Work

Most current text entry techniques for children are full-length physical keyboards that use the standard QWERTY layout with larger key-prints and brightly colored vowel and numeric keys to enable learning [20]. Some use alphabetic layouts to facilitate a faster transition from novice to expert [9]. Several virtual keyboards are also available that are practically virtual versions of the existing physical keyboards [6]. Unfortunately, most of these keyboards do not account for the variable spelling abilities of children [17].

Several studies have found relationships between text entry and language skills. Papert [15] suggested that text entry accommodates critical thinking and learning by allowing children to revise and rework their ideas. Kurth [11] argued that the high visibility of text on the screen can passively improve children's spelling skills by igniting more conversation about the writing. Sturm [21] showed that text entry can improve users' narrative skills. Newell et al. [14] showed that predictive text can improve the quantity and quality of their written work. Wood et al. [23] confirmed this in a separate study, where they showed that the use of word prediction can improve spelling skills. Yet none of these works explored the impact of autocorrection on language skills.

Many have highlighted the need for providing children with meaningful visual feedback to facilitate learning. Anthony et al. [1] argued that visual feedback can help children learn a new system, especially when they are still developing the skills required to interact with it. Druin [7] showed that feedback facilitates learning by providing children with the means to evaluate themselves.

Current Visual Feedback on Autocorrections

Most current virtual keyboards provide visual feedback on autocorrections. They display the most probable word/s in a prediction bar or above the text as the user types, and highlight an autocorrected word by changing its font or background to a different color for about one second.

Color-Coded Visual Feedback

We designed a new feedback method for autocorrection to inform users of how an incorrect input was fixed. When an autocorrection occurs, it highlights the corrections made in the prediction bar and in a bubble above the autocorrected word. It characterizes all edits as insertions or deletions, because substitutions are practically combinations of these two operations. It highlights all deletions with a red font and all insertions with a green, however different colors can be used to address colorblindness. The method does not highlight the types of errors, but the types of edits made by the autocorrection method. Figure 1 and 2 illustrates the current and the proposed methods, respectively.

An Experiment

The study explored whether current autocorrection feedback facilitates learning new words and spelling, and if the proposed method improves these learning rates.

Apparatus

We used two LG Optimus L7 II P710 smartphones, 121.5× 66.6×9.7 mm and 118 g. They ran on Android 4.1.2 at 480×800 (Figure 4). A custom application, developed with the default Android SDK was used. It displayed drawings of people, animals, and various objects on the screen and asked children to enter the name of the entity in the picture using the default Google Android keyboard. For this, we collected 25 nouns, and the drawings associated with them, from a workbook for young children [10]. We included a narrator feature to address unknown words, implemented using the Google Translate API [8]. When children could not recognize the subject of a picture, they could tap on the picture to hear its name. We used words instead of short phrases for better control of the variables and to reduce the possibility of fatigue. We used nouns, as children's first learned words are usually names of people, animals, and objects [13]. We used a custom autocorrection method [3], since the default SDK does not allow access to its predictive system. We implemented the color-coded feedback using the Levenshtein distance algorithm [12]. The prediction bar was disabled to eliminate a confound.

Participants and Design

We recruited 26 grade two students from a school where English is taught as a second language, reducing the possibility of learning new words outside the classroom. We only recruited students with comparable academic standings. We used a between-subjects design with two groups: *basic* (current feedback) and *color-coded*. Each group had 13 children, 7 males and 6 females, aged 7-8, on average 7.5. There were 3 sessions, with about a day in between. Children entered the same 25 words in all sessions in random order. In summary, the design was: 2 groups × 13 children × 3 sessions × 25 words = 1,950 words, in total. Figure 3 shows the study setup.

Procedure

During the study, children entered words using the custom application. It displayed one drawing at a time and asked them to enter the name of the entity in the picture. When done, they had to press the "ENTER" button to see the next drawing. They were instructed to tap on the drawing if they could not identify/remember the entity in the picture to hear its name. They were asked to input as fast and accurately as possible, but informed that it is alright to forget/misspell words, so that they would not feel under pressure. Error correction

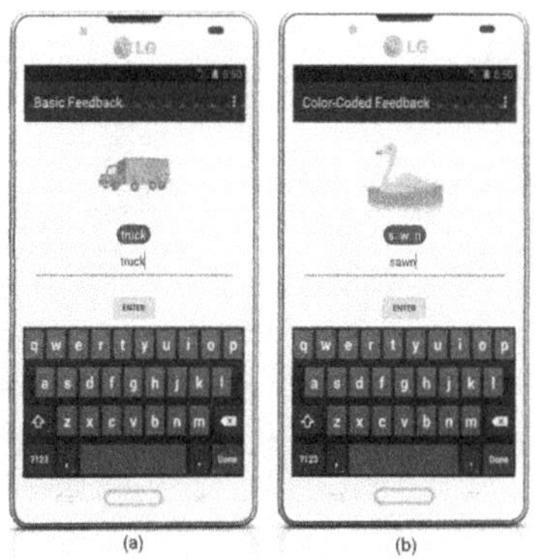

Figure 4. The device and the (a) current and (b) color-coded

Words per Minute (WPM) measures how many words can be produced in one minute [2].

Success rate (%) represents the rate at which correctly spelled words were inputted. This was calculated as the ratio of the total number of correctly spelled words to the total number of words entered.

Recall rate (%) measures the proportion of new words that were correctly recalled by the users. This was calculated as the ratio of the total number of correctly recalled words to the total number of words entered.

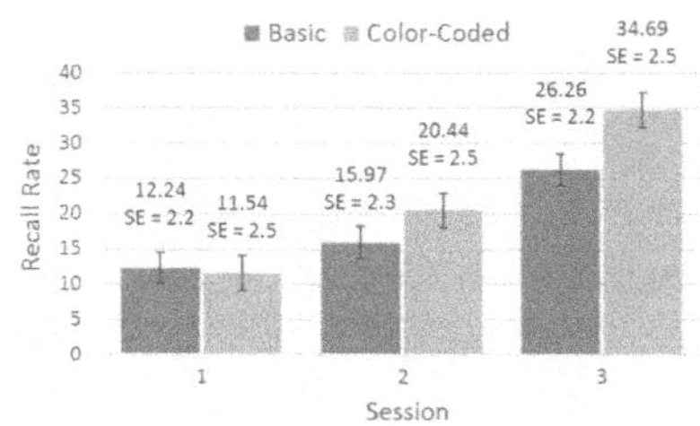

Figure 5. Average recall rate by session. Error bars represent ±1 standard error (σ_x).

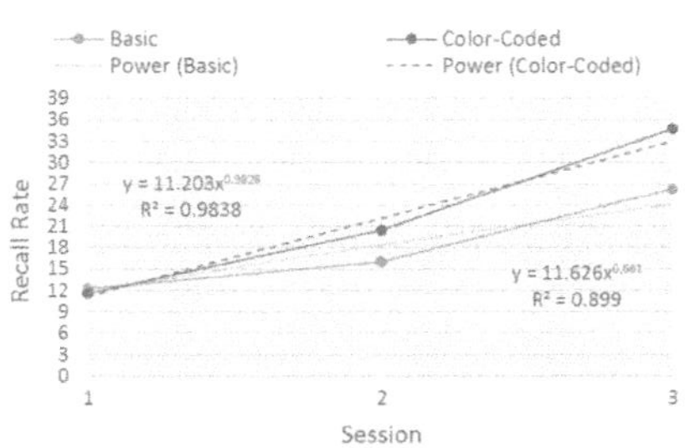

Figure 6. Average recall rate by session fitted to the power law of practice [5].

was recommended, but not enforced, thus they could submit incorrect/misspelled words. We took permission from the school to run the study during class-hours in an empty room at the school. Children also had to have consent from their parents to participate. When they arrived for the first session, we demonstrated the application and the feedback method assigned to them. We also allowed them to practice with the application using a different set of words. We started the study when they felt confident. The following sessions used the same structure, excluding the demonstration and practice. The sessions were scheduled with about a day in between. After the last session, children were asked to fill out a questionnaire, where they could rate the feedback methods on a 5-point Smileyometer scale [18].

Results

We used a Mixed-Design ANOVA on the study data and a Mann-Whitney U Test on the questionnaire data.

Recall Rate

An ANOVA identified a significant effect of condition on recall rate ($F_{1,24} = 4.51$, $p < .05$). On average recall rate was 18.2% ($\sigma_{\bar{x}} = 1.4$) and 22.4% ($\sigma_{\bar{x}} = 1.4$) in basic and color-coded, respectively. There was also a significant effect of session in both basic ($F_{2,12} = 10.7$, $p < .0001$) and color-coded ($F_{2,12} = 21.9$, $p < .0001$). See Figure 5. To study learning, we fitted power functions to sessional success rates to model the power law of practice [5]. In Figure 6, one can see that the data correlates well to the power functions for both basic ($R^2 = 0.89$) and color-coded ($R^2 = 0.98$).

Success Rate

An ANOVA failed to identify a significant effect of condition on success rate ($F_{1,24} = 0.84$, ns). The basic and color-coded yielded on average 63.8% ($\sigma_{\bar{x}} = 1.6$) and 65.9% ($\sigma_{\bar{x}} = 1.7$) success rate, respectively. There was also no significant effect of session in basic ($F_{2,12} = 1.6$, ns) or color-coded ($F_{2,12} = 1.2$, ns). See Figure 7. Results also revealed that both groups yielded comparable success rates in the first session: 61% ($\sigma_{\bar{x}} = 2.8$) and 63% ($\sigma_{\bar{x}} = 2.9$) in basic and color-coded, respectively ($F_{1,24} = 0.11$, ns). This suggests that one group was not substantially better at spelling than the other group when they started the study.

Investigation also revealed that 28% of all errors were caused by missing or incorrectly entered characters, 16% of all errors were caused by entering extra characters, while the remaining 56% were caused by the combination of the both. A Kruskal-Wallis test failed to find a significant effect of condition on this ($H_1 = 0.6$, ns). To explore learning, we fitted power functions to sessional success rates to model the power law of practice [5]. In Figure 8, one can see that the data correlates well to the power functions for both basic ($R^2 = 0.92$) and color-coded ($R^2 = 0.99$) conditions.

Entry Speed

An ANOVA failed to identify a significant effect of condition on entry speed ($F_{1,24} = 0.03$, ns). The basic and color-coded groups yielded on average 52.9 ($\sigma_{\bar{x}} = 0.8$) and 52.7 ($\sigma_{\bar{x}} = 0.8$) WPM, respectively. There was also no significant effect of session in basic ($F_{2,12} = 1.3$, ns) and color-coded ($F_{2,12} = 0.6$, ns) groups. See Figure 9.

User Feedback

A Mann-Whitney U test failed to identify a significance with respect to children's overall rating of the feedback systems ($U = 75.5$, $Z = -0.523$, $p > .05$). About 92% and 85% children from basic and color-coded liked the

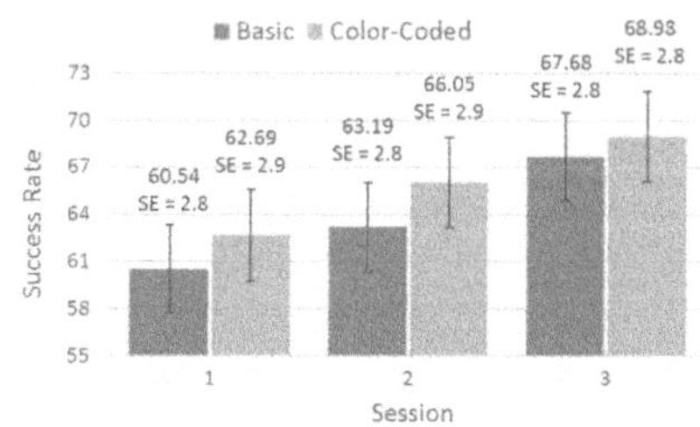

Figure 7. Average success rate by session. Error bars represent ±1 standard error (σ_x).

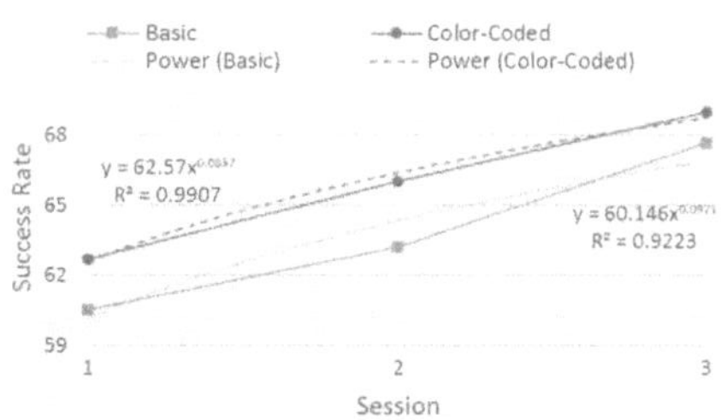

Figure 8. Average success rate by session fitted to the power law of practice [5].

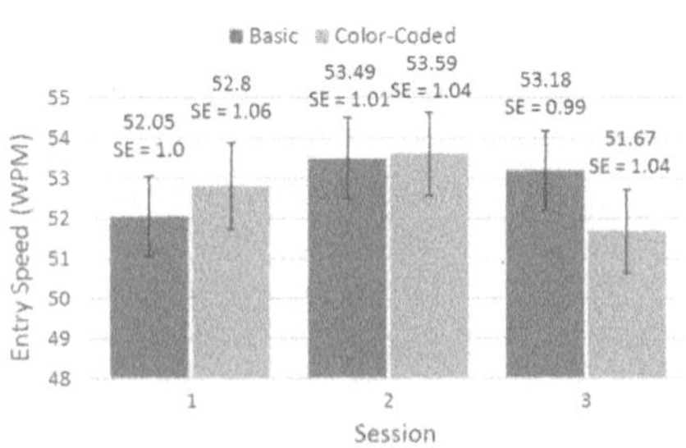

Figure 9. Average entry speed by session. Error bars represent ±1 standard error (σ_x).

corresponding feedback methods. The remaining 8% and 15% children were mostly neutral (Figure 10).

A Mann-Whitney U test failed to identify a significance with respect to children's perception of if the feedback methods helped them learn new words and spelling ($U = 82.0$, $Z = -0.150$, $p > .05$). 100% and 92% children from basic and color-coded felt that the corresponding feedback methods facilitated learning of new words and spelling. The remaining 8% were impartial (Figure 11). A Mann-Whitney U test failed to identify a significance with respect to willingness to use the feedback methods ($U = 75.0$, $Z = -0.552$ $p > .05$). 100% and 92% children from basic and color-coded wanted to keep using the corresponding feedback methods. The remaining 8% were neutral (Figure 12).

Discussion

There was no significant effect of condition on success rate, although on average about 3% more words were correctly spelled with color-coded than basic. Further, there was no significant effect of session in either of the groups. Figure 8 fits average success rate of both groups in all sessions to the power law of practice that shows that the data correlates well to the power functions for both groups. Hence, it is possible that learning of spelling occurs with autocorrections augmented with both feedback methods, but at too slow a pace to explore in the study. Interestingly, a significant effect of feedback was identified on recall rate. On average recall rate was about 23% higher with color-coded. There was also an effect of session. Recall rate improved substantially with time. Figure 6 fits average recall rate for both groups in all sessions to the power law of practice that shows that the data correlates well to the power functions for both groups. Both groups started with a comparable recall rate (~12%), but in the last two sessions color-coded outperformed basic. In the final session, recall rate for color-coded was about 32% higher than basic. Yet, the fact that learning occurred in both groups with new words and spelling, although likely not at as fast a pace as conventional keyboards, demands further investigation into whether autocorrection can improve children's language skills. There was no significant effect of condition on entry speed. Both groups yielded on average 53 WPM. There was also no significant effect of session in either of the groups, suggesting that children did not take extra time to process the information on the color-coded feedback. User feedback was also positive for both feedback methods. Most children liked the examined methods, felt that the methods helped them to learn new words and spelling, and thus wanted to keep using them.

Conclusion and Future Work

We presented a novel color-coded feedback method that highlights the corrections made by autocorrections. We then presented results of a user study with 7-8-year-old children that compared the proposed method with the conventional autocorrection feedback method, in terms of leaning new words and spelling. Results suggested that the new method significantly improves learning new words. Interestingly, learning was also observed with the conventional method, demanding further investigation into if predictive methods are truly a barrier to learning new words and spelling. In the future, we will investigate this in another study that will compare learning rates with predictive and non-predictive input techniques.

Acknowledgments

We thank all students, teachers, and staffs of Colégio Teresiano Braga for their support. This work has been

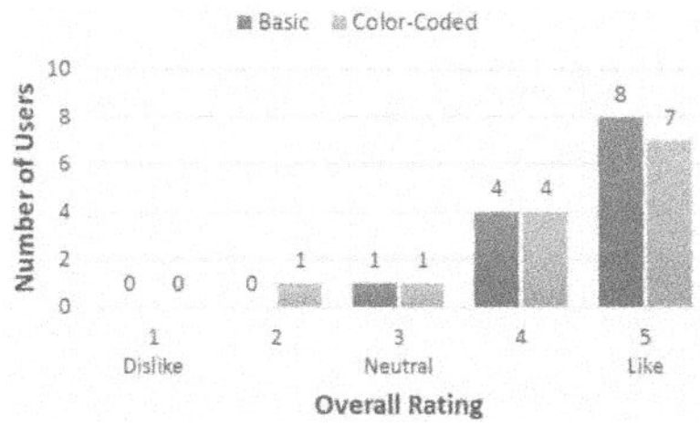

Figure 10. User feedback on if they liked the feedback systems.

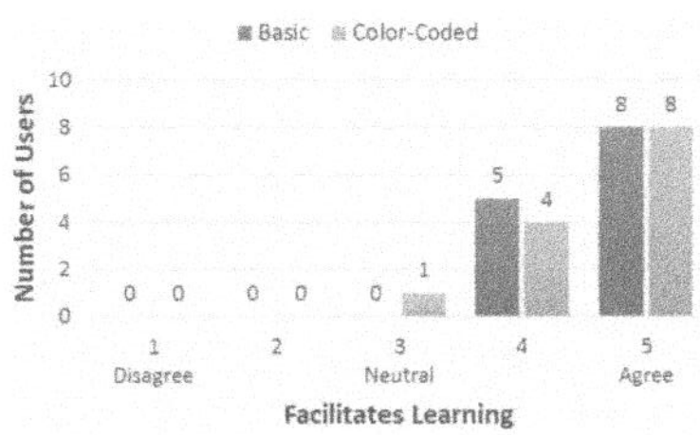

Figure 11. User feedback on whether the feedback facilitated learning new words and spelling.

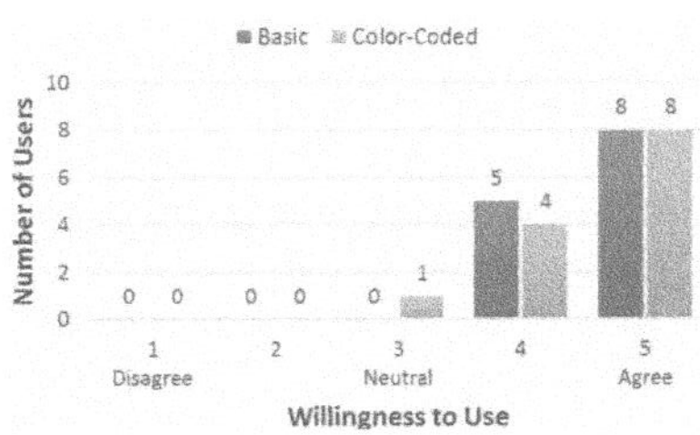

Figure 12. User feedback on if they are willing to use the examined feedback systems on their mobile devices

supported in part by the Canada Research Chairs (CRC) Program, the Human Potential Operating Programme (HPOP) of the European Social Fund, and the Portuguese Ministry for Science, Technology and Higher Education (MCTES) Postdoctoral Grant SFRH/BPD/111891/2015.

References

[1] Anthony, L., Brown, Q., Nias, J., and Tate, B. Examining the need for visual feedback during gesture interaction on mobile touchscreen devices for kids. *Proc. IDC 2013*, ACM (2013), 157-164.

[2] Arif, A. S. and Stuerzlinger, W. Analysis of text entry performance metrics. Proc. TIC-STH '09, IEEE (2009), 100-105.

[3] Arif, A. S. and Stuerzlinger, W. Pseudo-pressure detection and its use in predictive text entry on touchscreens. *Proc. OzCHI 2013*, ACM (2013), 383-392.

[4] Arif, A. S. *Predicting and Reducing the Impact of Errors in Character-Based Text Entry*. York University, 2013.

[5] Card, S. K., Newell, A., and Moran, T. P. *The Psychology of Human-Computer Interaction*. Lawrence Erlbaum, 1983.

[6] Cintero Systems. Kids Keyboard. https://play.google.com/store/apps/details?id=com.cintero.kidskeyboard

[7] Druin, A. Mobile Technology for Children: Designing for Interaction and Learning. Morgan Kaufmann, 2009.

[8] Google Translate API. https://cloud.google.com/translate

[9] KidTech, Inc. The PC Computer Keyboard Designed Just for Kids (2015). http://www.kidtech.com

[10] Kumon Publishing. *My Book of Sample Sentences: Learning about Nouns and Verbs*. Kumon Publishing North America, Inc., 2005.

[11] Kurth, R. J. Using word processing to enhance revision strategies during student writing activities. *Educational Technology 27*, 1 (1987), 13-19.

[12] Levenshtein, V. I. Binary codes capable of correcting deletions, insertions, and reversals. *Soviet Physics Doklady 10*, 8 (1966), 707-710.

[13] Nelson, K. Structure and strategy in learning to talk. *Monographs of the Society for Research in Child Development 38*, 1/2 (1973), 1-135.

[14] Newell, A. F., Booth, L., Arnott, J., and Beattie, W. Increasing literacy levels by the use of linguistic prediction. *Child Language Teaching and Therapy 8*, 2 (1992), 138-187.

[15] Papert, S. Mindstorms: Children, Computers, and Powerful Ideas. Basic Books, Inc, 1980.

[16] Paton, G. Over-reliance on technology is undermining spelling skills. The Telegraph (May 22, 2012). http://goo.gl/2MJz8c

[17] Read, J. C. Text input for the elderly and the young. In *Text Entry Systems: Mobility, Accessibility, Universality*. Morgan Kaufmann, 2007, 271-288.

[18] Read, J. C. Validating the Fun Toolkit: an instrument for measuring children's opinions of technology. *Cognition, Technology a Work 10*, 2 (2008), 119-128.

[19] Rideout, V. Zero to eight: children's media use in America. Common Sense Research Study (2013). https://www.commonsensemedia.org/research/zero-to-eight-childrens-media-use-in-america-2013

[20] Solutions for Individuals with Disabilities (1998). https://www.ablenetinc.com

[21] Sturm, J. Using computer software tools to facilitate narrative skills. *The Clinical Connection 11*, 4 (1988), 6-9.

[22] University of Alabama at Birmingham. Could texting and autocorrect affect kids' writing skills? ScienceDaily (May 19, 2014). https://goo.gl/WOdFSz

[23] Wood, L. A., Rankin, J. L., and Beukelman, D. R. Word prompt programs: current uses and future possibilities. *American Journal of Speech-Language Pathology 6*, 3 (1997), 57-65.

WebTEM: A Web Application to Record Text Entry Metrics

Ahmed Sabbir Arif
Ryerson University
Toronto, Ontario, Canada
a.s.arif@gmail.com

Ali Mazalek
Ryerson University
Toronto, Ontario, Canada
mazalek@ryerson.ca

ISS '16, November 06-09, 2016, Niagara Falls, ON, Canada
ACM 978-1-4503-4248-3/16/11.
http://dx.doi.org/10.1145/2992154.2996791

Abstract

WebTEM is a Web application to record text entry metrics. It is developed with common Web technologies, thus works on any device with a modern Web browser, and with any keyboard. We evaluated its effectiveness in an empirical study that compared the default Apple iOS, Google Android, and Microsoft Windows Phone keyboards. Results of the study highlighted mobile users' increased dependency on autocorrections.

Author Keywords

Text entry; performance; metrics; Web app; prediction; autocorrection; predictive text; keyboard; evaluation.

ACM Classification Keywords

H.5.m. Information interfaces and presentation (e.g., HCI): Evaluation/methodology.

Introduction

Text entry techniques are usually evaluated by measuring entry speed and accuracy in transcription tasks. Participants are presented with phrases of text from a corpus that they have to transcribe as quickly and accurately as possible [2]. Yet due to the unavailability of tools to record performance metrics with different devices, operating systems, and text entry techniques, researchers are often forced to develop custom evaluation tools. Since these tools are

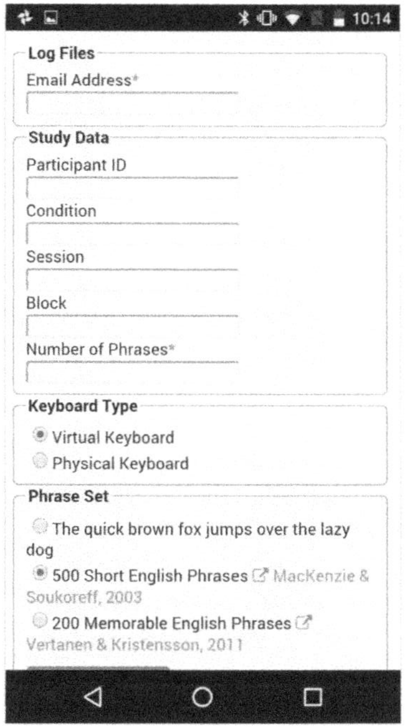

Figure 1. Partial view of WebTEM settings.

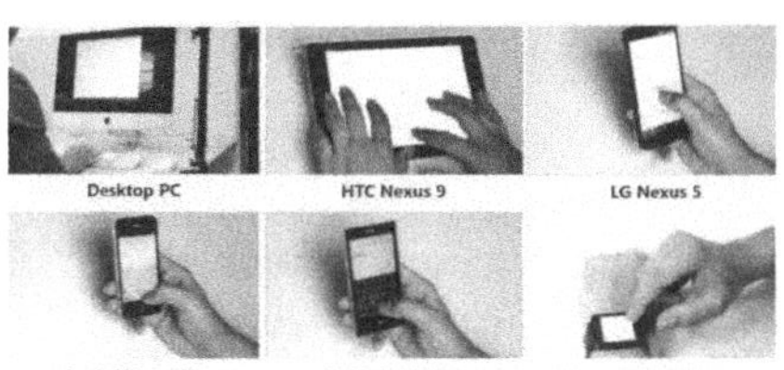

Figure 2. WebTEM on different devices.

tailored to fit the needs of a particular evaluation, usually they cannot be used in other studies. Further, developing these tools can be a challenge, since it requires, as a minimum, programming skills and an understanding of the existing corpora, metrics, and mechanism of the techniques under investigation. This can restrict researchers from quickly evaluating novel text entry techniques. Besides, when developing these tools, they have to decide which metrics to record. If calculating additional metrics becomes necessary after conducting the study, but the existing data sets do not provide the means, they have to first modify the tool and then conduct a new study. As a result, evaluation of text entry techniques is laborious, and depends largely on a researcher's programming skills and knowledge of the existing text entry research. To address this, we present WebTEM, a Web application to record text entry metrics. It is developed with common Web technologies, thus works with any device with a modern Web browser, regardless of the operating system or text entry technique. It allows researchers to select from a large set of metrics and settings. Its goal is to make text entry research easier by reducing the efforts necessary to setup a user study.

Related Work

Some applications are available to collect text entry metrics. However, they all are either specific to an operating system or text entry technique. Wobbrock and Myers [15] developed TextTest, an application that supports most keyboards, but works only on Windows PC. Castellucci and MacKenzie [4] developed TEMA that works with most text entry techniques, but runs only on Google Android. Besides, in an informal test, the current version (v2.1) failed to record metrics on devices running on Android OS 6. Arif et al. [3] developed an application that works only with QWERTY on Apple iOS.

WebTEM

WebTEM is developed with HTML5, CSS3, JavaScript, and PHP. It uses jQuery [8], Diff-match-patch [5], and Grapheme-Splitter [7] JavaScript libraries to perform Ajax requests, analyze plain text, and break strings into their individual user-perceived characters, respectively. WebTEM processes all user interactions on the client side, but periodically pushes all data to the server using PHP for faster performance and to reduce data loss. It also uses PHPMailer PHP library [11] for its integrated SMTP implementation. WebTEM allows researchers to select from a large set of metrics and settings, discussed below. It is freely accessible from http://www.asarif.com/resources/WebTEM.

Study-specific data. Researchers can enter optional session-specific data for recordkeeping, such as participant ID, condition, session, and block (Figure 1). But they must enter the total number of phrases in the session for the application to display the phrases in a randomized order. It also requires a valid email address to send all log files to researchers upon completion of the session. The device must also have access to the Internet throughout the study to avoid any data loss.

Keyboard type. Researchers must select whether they are evaluating a physical or a virtual keyboard. The application detects and records all predictive actions, such as word prediction, autocorrection, and auto-capitalization, for virtual keyboards. However, if detection of these features is desirable for a physical keyboard, researchers could select "Virtual Keyboard", regardless of the actual keyboard type (Figure 1).

Confidentiality. To maintain participant confidentiality, the application does not store any data on the server.

It generates anonymous temporary files at runtime that are automatically emailed to the researcher, and then deleted. The application also deletes all temporary files when the researcher leaves the application, such as exits, refreshes, and/or reloads the application.

Limitations. WebTEM detects all input based on the events in the input area. As a result, it cannot detect modifier and special keys, such as Shift, Ctrl, Alt, etc., for virtual keyboards that do not emulate actual key events.

Further, it detects predictions based on patterns and entry time. While in our tests it was able to detect all predictions, it may misrecognize some in some scenarios. Hence, the predictive metrics reported by the application should be treated as estimations.

WebTEM detects predictive features based on input patterns and event time. For this, we recorded different prediction patterns and event times from informal user studies with multiple devices and keyboards. Results revealed that regular taps on virtual keyboards always take more than 90 milliseconds, while automated events always take less. We used this as a threshold, together with input patterns, to detect predictive behaviors.

Phrase sets. WebTEM includes the three most popular phrase sets, two for adults [13, 14] and one for children [9]. It also includes the "The quick brown fox jumps over the lazy dog" pangram that is frequently used in quick evaluations, since it contains all letters of the English alphabet.

Performance metrics. WebTEM records all commonly used metrics, including Words per Minute (WPM) and Characters per Second (CPS) for entry speed, and Error Rate (ER), Minimum String Distance Error Rate (MSD ER), Keystrokes per Character (KSPC), Corrected Error Rate (CER), and Total Error Rate (TER) for accuracy [2, 13]. Apart from these popular metrics, it can also record the following.

Visual Scan Time (VST) signifies the time (in milliseconds) users took to visually scan a recently completed phrase, mainly to proofread, before submitting it.

Cursor Control Count (CCC) is the total number of times users repositioned the cursor using the arrow keys, the mouse, direct touch, or a digital pen to correct errors or to edit text in a text entry episode.

Backspace Count (BC) is the total number of backspaces in a text entry episode.

Prediction Rate (PR) is calculated as the ratio (%) of the total number of characters automatically entered by the predictive system and the total number of characters entered in a text entry episode. It does not account for incorrect predictions, since they are difficult to identify.

International text entry. WebTEM supports non-Latin text entry evaluations. Currently, it includes a Bengali corpus [1] and several performance metrics for non-Latin scripts, calculated using the output stream convention [12]. In the future, we will include more corpora and metrics to further accommodate the international text entry community.

Additional options. WebTEM includes the following options for researchers to customize a study condition.

Disable predictive features. This disables the browser's spell checker and the keyboard's predictive features, i.e., word prediction, autocorrection, and auto-capitalization.

Present all phrases in lowercase. This converts all uppercase letters in the presented text to lowercase.

Ignore letter case and extra spaces in metrics calculation. This ignores letter case mismatch and extra spaces in metrics calculation. This option is useful for predictive techniques that auto-capitalize words and automatically enter a space after each prediction.

Present all phrases without special characters. Some phrase sets include punctuation and other characters to increase the external validity of the work. However, if the techniques under investigation use the same mechanism to enter special characters, it is better to exclude these from the study to eliminate a potential

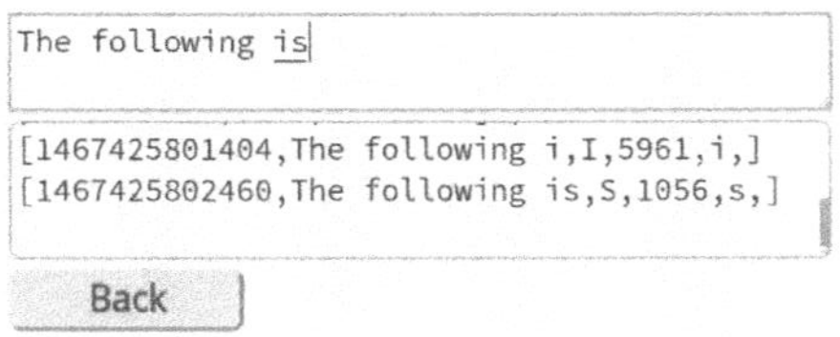

Figure 3. WebTEM works with almost all operating systems, browsers, and keyboards. Yet to verify compatibility, researchers can press the "Check" button and type a chunk of text in the input area to see all events in the aforementioned format.

Figure 4. WebTEM is freely accessible from http://www.asarif.com/resources/WebTEM

confound. This option allows researchers to present all phrases without special characters.

Display the number of phrases entered. Participants often query the number of phrases they still have to enter, especially in longer sessions. This interrupts the study and disrupts the natural flow of text entry. To avoid this, this option displays the number of phrases entered below the input area.

Display performance summary. This displays speed and accuracy rates for the last entered phrase, and the session averages, below the input area. We, however, recommend against using this, since it makes participants aware of their performance, compromising their input behavior and reducing the external validity. Yet we included this for better comparisons between data collected using different tools, since some existing tools [4] include this feature.

Hide presented text when users start typing. In text entry studies, participants are usually asked to take the time to read, understand, and memorize the phrases before entering them. Researchers can enforce this by using this option that hides the presented phrase when the user starts typing.

Force error-free submissions. Some user studies may require participants to enter error-free text, especially when an error correction method is being evaluated. This option disables the entry of text containing errors. Selecting this also enables auditory feedback. That is, the system makes a noise when the user attempts to enter phrases with errors.

WebTEM preselects the most popular phrase set, metrics, and settings for convenience. It also stores cookies on the devices to assure that researchers do not have to reselect the options at each visit.

Log files. The application generates one information (.INFO) and two tab-delimited files (.TSV) to record all settings, timestamped events, and performance metrics, respectively. Each row of the metrics log represents a phrase and each column a metric. The last row holds average values. Events are recorded as [time,text,event,duration,insertion,deletion], where time is the number of milliseconds since Jan 1, 1970, text is the current state of the transcribed text, event is a user or system action, e.g., a tap, an autocorrection, etc., duration is the time for the action in milliseconds, and insertion and deletion are character/s entered and deleted by the action, respectively. See Figure 3.

A User Study

We tested WebTEM with multiple devices, e.g., desktop computers, tablets, smartphones, and smartwatches, operating systems, e.g., Android, iOS, Mac, Windows, and Windows Phone, browsers, e.g., Chrome, Firefox, Safari, Internet Explorer, and Microsoft Edge, and keyboards. Figure 2 shows some examples. We also tested its effectiveness in an empirical study.

Apparatus

The study used an Apple iPhone 4S, 115.2×58.6×9.3 mm, 140 g, running on iOS 9.3.2, an LG Nexus 5, 137.9×69.2×8.6 mm, 130 g, running on Android 6.0.1, and a Nokia Lumia 520, 119.9×64×9.9 mm, 124 g, running on Windows Phone 8.1 (Figure 5). The devices accessed WebTEM using their default browsers, namely Safari, Chrome, Internet Explorer, respectively. To our knowledge, no studies have compared these keyboards.

Participants

Twelve participants, aged from 18 to 33 years, average 24.6, took part in the study. Four of them were female

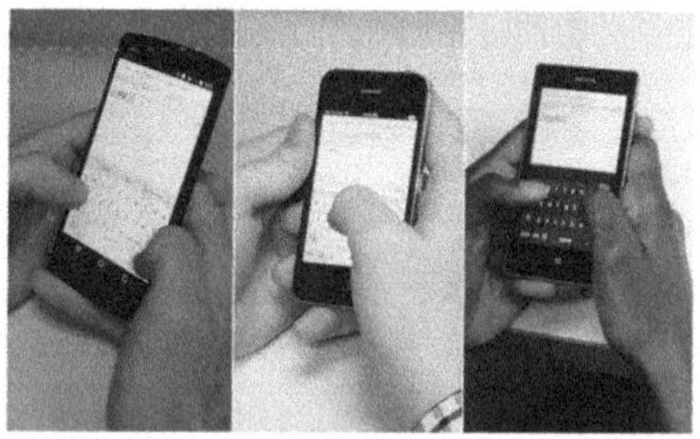

Figure 5. Participants transcribing phrases with WebTEM using the three devices and keyboards.

	Android	Apple	Windows
WPM*	30.31* σ = 10.9	29.87 σ = 11.7	24.98 σ = 8.8
ER*	6.8 σ = 13.9	1.86* σ = 4.6	4.75 σ = 2.9
TER*	10.29 σ = 9.5	9.72* σ = 11.5	13.9 σ = 9.9
PR*	37.98* σ = 30.2	6.62 σ = 8.6	29.32* σ = 37.1

Table 1. Average Words per Minute (WPM), Error Rate (ER), Total Error Rate (TER), and Prediction Rate (PR) for the three keyboards. The symbol "σ" signifies standard deviation, while "*" marks statistically significance.

and all were right-handed. They were all experienced touchscreen users. Most of them (84%) owned at least one Google Android device. The others owned either/both an Apple iOS (17%) or a Windows Phone (8%) device.

Procedure and Deign

In the study, participants were asked to transcribe ten short English phrases from the MacKenzie and Soukoreff [10] set on each device using the respective keyboard. The application displayed all phrases in lowercase and in random order. Participants were asked to hold the device and enter the phrases as they usually would on their own devices. The keyboards enabled word prediction and autocorrection. However, personalized prediction was disabled to eliminate a potential confounding factor. Participants could also gesture type on the default Android and Windows Phone keyboard, but the default iOS keyboard does not support this feature. There was no auditory feedback. Error correction was encouraged but not forced. Participants were asked to enter the phrases as fast and accurately as possible. There was no practice block, but the keyboards were demonstrated before the study. The study used a within-subjects design for the three factors: the three devices and their respective virtual keyboards. The factors were counterbalanced. In summary, the design was, 12 participants × 3 conditions × 10 phrases = 360 phrases, in total.

Results

We used a repeated measures ANOVA for all analysis. Table 1 displays the results.

ENTRY SPEED (WPM)

An ANOVA identified a significant effect of keyboard on WPM ($F_{2,11} = 4.56$, $p < .05$). A Tukey-Kramer Test revealed that Android was significantly faster than Windows.

ERROR RATE (ER)

An ANOVA identified a significant effect of keyboard on ER ($F_{2,11} = 9.71$, $p < .001$). A Tukey-Kramer Test revealed that Apple was significantly more accurate than Android and Windows.

TOTAL ERROR RATE (TER)

An ANOVA identified a significant effect of keyboard on TER ($F_{2,11} = 3.84$, $p < .05$). A Tukey-Kramer Test revealed that Apple was significantly faster than Windows.

PREDICTION RATE (PR)

An ANOVA identified a significant effect of keyboard on PR ($F_{2,11} = 7.88$, $p < .005$). A Tukey-Kramer Test revealed that PR was significantly lower for Apple than Android and Windows.

Subjective Analysis

Most participants (84%) selected Android as one of their most preferred keyboards, followed by Apple (17%) and Windows (8%). Further enquiry revealed that they preferred Android mostly due to familiarity (84% of them were Android users) and its predictive system – 60% of them felt that Android's predictive system was more reliable. Interestingly, only about 25% picked a keyboard they are unfamiliar with as one of their most preferred, again primarily for its superior predictive system (67%), secondarily for its design (33%).

Windows was the least preferred keyboard (67%), followed by Apple (25%) and Android (8%). When enquired about the reasons, most participants (75%) blamed the keyboard's unreliable predictive system. Some also complained about the device itself, such as it is smaller (25%) and its screen is not as responsive as the other devices (13%).

Additional Observations

We asked participants if they gesture type on their devices. About 67% responded that they never gesture type, while 25% responded that they sometimes do. The remaining 8% use gesture typing almost exclusively. We also observed the posture used to input text. About 84% of participants used the two-thumb, while 16% used one thumb (8% of them were gesture typists). They all held their devices in portrait position.

Support

Researchers could report bugs or request new features, performance metrics, and/or corpora for their user studies via email to textentry@asarif.com.

Acknowledgments

We thank the members of RE/Lab at Ryerson University, particularly Jason Nolan, for helping us with the user study. This work has been supported in part by the Canada Research Chairs (CRC) program.

Discussion

Results revealed that there was a significant effect of keyboard on WPM, ER, TER, and PR. Android was significantly faster, while Apple was significantly more accurate. Interestingly, PR was substantially lower for Apple, suggesting that users rarely used the keyboard's predictive features. The fact that it did not include a prediction bar like the other keyboards may have caused this. It is possible that some users did not realize that it also provides predictive features like autocorrect, thus were more careful while typing, increasing its accuracy rate. This shows how dependent users are nowadays on predictive features. Post-study survey also highlights this, where participants picked the keyboards they felt has the most reliable predictive systems as their most preferred. Yet, we suggest caution when interpreting the results considering our Android-heavy user base.

Conclusion and Future Work

We presented WebTEM, a cross-platform customizable Web application to record text entry metrics that works with almost all devices and keyboards. We demonstrated its effectiveness in a study that compared the default Apple iOS, Google Android, and Microsoft Windows Phone keyboards. Results reveled that the default Android keyboard is significantly faster and Apple is significantly more accurate. Results also highlighted mobile users' increased dependency on autocorrections. In the future, we will include more corpora and metrics for ultra-small devices, e.g., smartwatches, and non-Latin text entry. We will also include additional settings.

References

[1] Arif, A. S. and Fardeen, S. A phrase set for Bengali text entry evaluations based on actual text messages. *Ext. Abstracts CHI '16*, ACM (2016), 2992-2998.

[2] Arif, A. S. and Stuerzlinger, W. Analysis of text entry performance metrics. TIC-STH '09. IEEE (2009), 100-105.

[3] Arif, A. S., Lopez, M. H., and Stuerzlinger, W. Two new mobile touchscreen text entry techniques. *Poster GI '10*, CEUR-WS.org/Vol-588, 22-23.

[4] Castellucci, S. J. and MacKenzie, I. S. Gathering text entry metrics on Android devices. *Ext. Abstracts CHI '11*, ACM (2011), 1507-1512.

[5] Diff-match-patch. https://code.google.com/p/google-diff-match-patch

[6] Font Awesome. http://fontawesome.io

[7] Grapheme-Splitter. https://github.com/orling/grapheme-splitter

[8] jQuery. https://jquery.com

[9] Kano, A., Read, J. C., and Dix, A. Children's phrase set for text input method evaluations. *NordiCHI '06*, ACM (2006), 449-452.

[10] MacKenzie, I. S. and Soukoreff, R. W. Phrase sets for evaluating text entry techniques. *Ext. Abstracts CHI '03*, ACM (2003), 754-755.

[11] PHPMailer. https://github.com/PHPMailer/PHPMailer

[12] Sarcar, S., Arif, A. S., and Mazalek, A. Metrics for Bengali text entry research. *CHI 2015 Workshop on Text Entry on the Edge* (2015). Seoul, South Korea.

[13] Soukoreff, R. W. and MacKenzie, I. S. Metrics for text entry research: An evaluation of MSD and KSPC, and a new unified error metric. CHI '03, ACM (2003), 113-120.

[14] Vertanen, K. and Kristensson, P. O. A versatile dataset for text entry evaluations based on genuine mobile emails. *MobileHCI '11*, ACM (2011), 295-298.

[15] Wobbrock, J. O. and Myers, B. A. Analyzing the input stream for character-level errors in unconstrained text entry evaluations. *ACM Trans. Comput.-Hum. Interact. 13*, 4 (2006), 458-489.

Interactive Multi-Modal Display Spaces for Visual Analysis

Thomas Marrinan
Argonne National Laboratory
Illinois USA
tmarrinan@anl.gov

Silvio Rizzi
Argonne National Laboratory
Illinois USA
srizzi@alcf.anl.gov

Arthur Nishimoto
University of Illinois at Chicago
Illinois USA
anishi2@uic.edu

Andrew Johnson
University of Illinois at Chicago
Illinois USA
ajohnson@uic.edu

Joseph A. Insley
Argonne National Laboratory
Illinois USA
insley@anl.gov

Michael E. Papka
Argonne National Laboratory &
Northern Illinois University
Illinois USA
papka@{anl.gov, nui.edu}

ISS '16, November 06-09, 2016, Niagara Falls, ON, Canada
ACM 978-1-4503-4248-3/16/11.
http://dx.doi.org/10.1145/2992154.2996792

Abstract
Classic visual analysis relies on a single medium for displaying and interacting with data. Large-scale tiled display walls, virtual reality using head-mounted displays or CAVE systems, and collaborative touch screens have all been utilized for data exploration and analysis. We present our initial findings of combining numerous display environments and input modalities to create an interactive multi-modal display space that enables researchers to leverage various pieces of technology that will best suit specific sub-tasks. Our main contributions are 1) the deployment of an input server that interfaces with a wide array of interaction devices to create a single uniform stream of data usable by custom visual applications, and 2) three real-world use cases of leveraging multiple display environments in conjunction with one another to enhance scientific discovery and data dissemination.

Author Keywords
Multiple Display Environments; multi-user interaction; collaboration; input devices; large-scale displays; virtual reality; multi-touch screens; motion capture.

ACM Classification Keywords
H.5.2. User Interfaces: Input devices and strategies, user centered design.

Introduction

Scientific data exploration, analysis, and dissemination have been aided by the use of specialized display technologies and interaction techniques. Large high-resolution displays have been shown to amplify sensemaking abilities and foster collaborative task execution [1]; Virtual Reality (VR) environments, such as head-mounted displays (HMDs), provide additional depth cues and a sense of immersion for three-dimensional data [8]; and GPU enabled clusters allow big data problems to be visualized with ultra-fine detail [7]. Interaction devices also play a role in benefiting exploration, analysis, and dissemination tasks. Devices such as a multi-touch screen, gaming controller, gyromouse, and motion capture system enable users to collaborate and move around a display environment's space freely, without being tied to a desk with a mouse and keyboard. While each of these technologies have provided some level of benefit to scientists, researchers have begun examining the combination of multiple pieces of technology.

Much of the research on Multiple Display Environments (MDEs) surrounds interaction paradigms to support cross-display navigation [10], the development of tools that leverage disparate screens [2,9], and studies to determine MDEs impact on collaborative tasks [5]. In each of these cases, users interface with a single application using multiple display technologies. However, when performing real-world analysis, researchers often require comparing multiple pieces of data from multiple applications to gain meaningful insight. Therefore, we investigated the use of multiple applications networked together with the ability to share certain data, rather than using just one application that runs in a MDE.

Specialized hardware, such as ultra high-resolution displays, HMDs, and collaborative touch screens, are specifically designed to enable analysis for specialized tasks. Ultra high-resolution displays enable scientific visualizations to show extraordinary detail while still being able to provide context to viewers. HMDs block out objects in the physical world and provide additional depth cues to users viewing three-dimensional data, thereby creating an immersive virtual experience. Large touch screen displays, on a tabletop device or vertical flat-screen monitor, enable collaborative interaction since they support multiple simultaneous touch events. Each of these specialized devices, along with personal devices such as laptops and tablets, can be leveraged to support various sub-tasks of an overall data exploration and analysis task. We present our initial findings on three our use cases where data is distributed amongst computing resources, and each display technology in a MDE is running a separate application to fully leverage the affordances of its hardware for exploration, analysis, and dissemination tasks.

Prior to discussing real-world uses of MDEs running networked applications, we present the development and deployment of an input server that interfaces with a wide array of interaction devices to create a single uniform stream of data usable by these custom visual applications. Enabling multiple modes of interaction is important for data exploration and analysis, especially when done collaboratively. Typical computer systems only allow a single user to interact at a time using a mouse and keyboard. Large touch screens are an exception to this general case, where multiple users can simultaneously interact with content on the display. However, enabling collaborative tasks on non-multi-

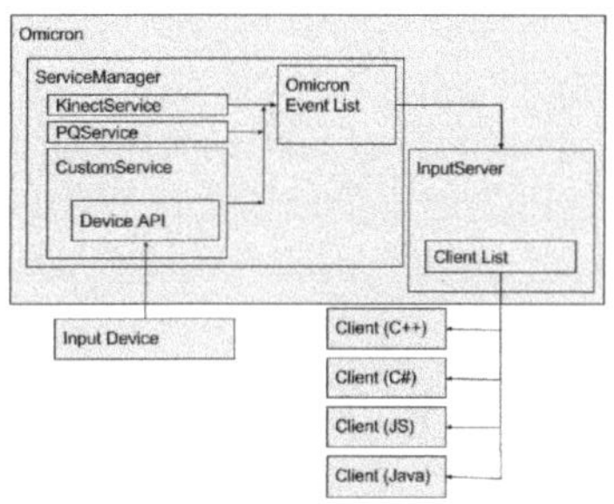

Figure 1. Architecture for the Omicron input abstraction library. The Service Manager receives native events from a variety of input devices and converts them to an Omicron event list. An Input Server application can be launched to stream these events to multiple simultaneous clients (currently implemented in C++, C#, Java, and JavaScript).

touch display environments and not tethering users to a mouse, keyboard, or touchscreen required integrating multiple non-standard input devices, such as gaming controllers and motion tracking systems, into visualization applications. Additionally, by deploying an input service, we allow separate applications to receive input from the same devices simultaneously, thereby enabling multiple applications to receive synchronized updates from a series of input devices.

Multi-Input Service

An input abstraction library, Omicron, was designed to integrate multiple different input modalities. These inputs are abstracted using modular event services, providing clients access to a specific set of input devices. The Omicron library can be used to directly integrate the event stream into a C++ application as a static library or run as a standalone Input Server to stream events using the Omicron connector API to multiple applications or across display clusters. The connector API client interface has been implemented for C++, C#, Java, and JavaScript. The entire library is open-source at https://github.com/uic-evl/omicron.

Omicron is comprised of two major elements: the Service Manager and the Input Server. The Service Manager prioritizes the various input service modules that can be attached to the Omicron API. Each service implements the native API of the input device to receive events and is then categorized into a more general Service Type, which identifies similar event types. For example a mouse and touch event share similar base structure such as a 2D position, ID, and an event action (down, move, drag, click). Both these devices would fall under the 'Pointer' Service Type. Similarly a motion tracked object from an optical tracking system and a Kinect skeleton share 3D positional information and would be categorized as a 'Mocap' Service Type. Other supported Service Types are 'Controllers' (Xbox 360, PS3, Wiimote, gyromouse), 'Keyboard', 'Brainwave' (NeuroSky), and 'Speech' (Microsoft Speech API).

Once native events are received from a device, the Service Manager converts incoming information to Omicron input events, which are time stamped and inserted into an event queue. Omicron's architecture is illustrated in Figure 1.

Applications using Omicron as a static library can access the queue and process events directly. To stream events to other applications or across a computing cluster, an Input Server application is launched and listens for incoming clients using the Omicron connector API. The Input Server manages client connections and Service Type requests, then streams requested events to the clients in either UDP or TCP depending on the priority of an event. Single command events like a button click will be sent on the TCP stream, while continually updating events like a motion tracked 3D position will be sent via UDP.

Multi-Application MDE Use Cases

Networking applications in MDEs and providing an array of collaborative input modalities to users has proven itself as a useful paradigm for a variety of scientific exploration, analysis, and dissemination tasks. This section will cover three unique use cases where multiple separate applications are run and displayed on various computing resources with networked communication. In each case, applications can connect to Omicron's Input Server to support multi-user interaction with input devices best suited for their task (in addition to using native controls such as a mouse and keyboard). Additionally, we are beginning to use the motion capture data to track users during these tasks so that we can start to understand how researchers utilize the physical space in a MDE.

Visual Exploration for Large Volumetric Data
Interactive exploration of large volumetric data presents a number of challenges that can be addressed using multiple applications in a MDE. Our architecture consists of three main elements: (i) visualization cluster and parallel rendering framework, (ii) tiled display, and (iii) interaction client. We use Cooley, the visualization cluster at Argonne National Laboratory, consisting of 126 nodes (12 CPU cores and 384 GB RAM per node). We run vl3, a framework for large-scale visualization and analysis [3], on Cooley to execute a ray casting volume renderer. We stream images from Cooley to the tiled display using high-bandwidth links. Our tiled display is an 8x4 arrangement of 1080p LCD panels, with a total resolution of 15360x4320 pixels, driven by a Linux workstation containing four GPUs. The workstation runs a streaming client to receive rendered images from Cooley. The final component is the interaction client, which runs on a laptop that communicates with vl3, controlling the position of the camera, the transfer function for volume rendering, and other parameters such as light positions and material properties. Devices such as a keyboard, mouse, or gyromouse are used for interaction.

Figure 2. A multidisciplinary team of scientists is shown interactively exploring a 2048^3 voxel micro CT scan of a primate tooth. The left half of the large-scale tiled display is showing a high-resolution image of 3x3 tiles (total image size of 5760x3240 pixels) streamed from ANL's Cooley visualization cluster. A laptop running the interaction client is mirrored on the right half of the large display so the entire group can view the visualization parameters such as the transfer function, material properties, and light positions.

This setup has been used for interactive exploration of a micro CT scan of a primate tooth. The process delivers a regular grid of 2048^3 voxels. In this experiment, vl3 was run on 16 Cooley GPUs, using a distributed ray casting algorithm with global illumination for soft shadows. vl3 composited images in a 3x3 arrangement, streaming the partial images to individual monitors on the tiled display. As a result, the total image size was 5760x3240 pixels.

Figure 2 shows Argonne scientists interactively exploring the primate tooth. Among the lessons learned from this experience, it is worth mentioning: (i) soft shadows substantially helped scientists perceive depth in the visualizations; (ii) the large pixel count was crucial to identify regions of interest; (iii) mirroring the laptop user interface on the tiled display was helpful for scientists to understand and tweak visualization parameters, getting immediate feedback on the visual results; (iv) returning to a console to use a keyboard and mouse for interaction was cumbersome, whereas mobile input devices, such as a gyromouse, enable the scientists to interact fom anywhere in the room; and (v) scientists quickly learned how to interact with the system, which enabled them to identify regions of interest for further modeling and numerical simulation.

Analysis of 3D Reconstructed Geometric Objects
As described in the previous sub-section, a large-scale tiled display can be coupled with an advanced visualization cluster to stream an interactive visualization session. In addition to using such a configuration for data exploration, it can also be extended to include an HMD, such as the Oculus Rift, to perform further data analysis in VR. For example, we work with a team of neuroscience researchers investigating the mapping of neurons in the brain. An electron microscope is used to capture ultrahigh resolution images of slices from a section of a mouse brain. A supercomputer is then used to segment the data into axons, dendrites, and other structures, creating individual geometric models of each, resulting in an extremely large data set.

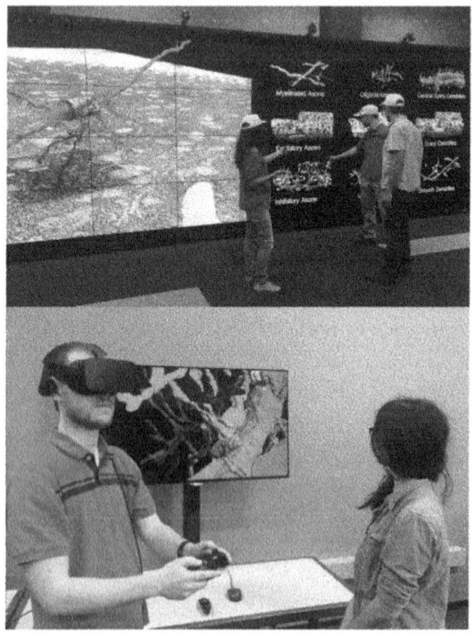

Figure 3. On the top we see researchers using a large-scale tiled display to explore models of neurons extracted from electron microscopy images. A subset of these models could be selected for further investigation using a virtual reality head mounted display available across the room. On the bottom, while one investigator explores the data in stereo 3D, others can see a non-stereo version displayed on a large monitor. In addition, each of the researchers in the view on top wears a hat, outfitted with tracking tokens that enables us to uniquely identify and track them. This information will be used as part of a separate effort to investigate how users interact in collaborative spaces such as these.

Leveraging the visualization cluster, which has large amounts of memory and multiple GPUs, several thousand of these complex models could be rendered at interactive rates and displayed on the tiled display. While this in itself could help provide insight, investigating these structures in further detail in stereoscopic 3D could prove to be even more beneficial. For this we use an Oculus Rift. A single workstation is used to drive the VR application, which limits the number of models that can be rendered at a time. Therefore only a subset of structures can be analyzed in further detail at a time. Researchers are able to utilize the tiled display to identify and select a subset of structures to transfer to the Oculus Rift for further investigation. Currently, this process has been done offline, but networking the two applications together and using Omicron would allow researchers to use a controller to select and transfer data from the tiled display to the Oculus in real-time (Figure 3).

Collaborative Meeting for Data Dissemination
After exploration and analysis, researchers must disseminate their findings to collaborators and brainstorm next steps. In this case, we highlight the use of a large ultra high-resolution display, multi-touch screen, and multiple input devices. We have used SAGE2 [4,6], a democratic multi-user windowing environment, for displaying and interacting with content on the large ultra high-resolution display. These meetings are supplemented with a large multi-touch screen used as a digital whiteboard, as well as laptops and tablets for personal use. SAGE2 enables any collaborator to upload new material from their personal device, such as images or PDF documents, as well as reorganize content on the large ultra high-resolution display. Collaborators can also interact with content on the SAGE2 display by using a variety of input devices enabled through the Omicron Input Server, such as a Wii remote or direct on-screen touch.

The secondary large display, used as a multi-touch digital whiteboard, fosters ad-hoc discussion by enabling any user to generate digital artifacts on-the-fly. In contrast to presenting prepared material, this form of interaction is critical to dissemination and brainstorming sessions, which are less formal and often require adaptation as the group discussion evolves. Since a digital whiteboard application is utilized over a traditional whiteboard, information can easily be recorded and archived. This facilitates data dissemination in two ways: 1) collaborators can easily revisit the manually created artifacts generated during the meeting, and 2) individuals not present at the meeting can view the ad-hoc artifacts from the digital whiteboard in addition to the prepared material shared via SAGE2. Figure 4 illustrates a sample collaborative meeting that uses a MDE for data dissemination.

Conclusion
MDEs present unique opportunities for collaboration and enhancing data exploration, analysis, and dissemination. We have presented our work on enabling scientists to leverage disparate computing and display technologies to facilitate research tasks. Omicron, our multi-input service, enables custom applications to integrate a variety of unique devices for collaborative user interaction. These input devices are leveraged by various applications to allow users to interact with data on display environments ranging from multi-touch screens to ultra high-resolution large-scale displays and immersive HMDs.

Figure 4. Collaborators gather in front of a large-scale display to share research findings and utilize a multi-touch digital whiteboard to brainstorm next steps to advance their work.

We have presented three authentic use cases that highlight how MDEs running separate, but often interconnected, applications enhance scientists' ability to explore, analyze, and disseminate their data. Future work includes analyzing motion capture data to investigate how users utilize the space within an MDE and how to further leverage additional display technologies, including augmented reality systems and mobile devices.

Acknowledgements

This work was supported in part by the DOE (contract DE-AC02-06CH11357), and the NSF (awards OCI-0943559, CNS-0959053, and CNS-0821121).

References

[1] Andrews, C., Endert, A., and North, C. Space to Think: Large High-resolution Displays for Sensemaking. In Proceedings of the SIGCHI Conference on Human Factors in Computing Systems (CHI '10), (2010), ACM, New York, NY, USA, 55-64.

[2] Geyer, F., Jetter, H., Pfeil, U., and Reiterer, H. Collaborative Sketching with Distributed Displays and Multimodal Interfaces. In ACM International Conference on Interactive Tabletops and Surfaces (ITS '10), (2010), ACM, New York, NY, USA, 259-260.

[3] Jiang, J., Hereld, M., Insley, J., Papka, M. E., Rizzi, S., Uram, T., and Vishwanath, V. Streaming Ultra High Resolution Images to Large Tiled Display at Nearly Interactive Frame Rate with vl3. In IEEE 5th Symposium on Large Data Analysis and Visualization (LDAV), (2015), 133-134.

[4] Marrinan, T., Aurisano, J., Nishimoto, A., Bharadwaj, K., Mateevitsi, V., Renambot, L., Long, L., Johnson, A., and Leigh, J. SAGE2: A New Approach for Data Intensive Collaboration Using Scalable Resolution Shared Displays. In Proceedings of the IEEE International Conference on Collaborative Computing: Networking, Applications and Worksharing (CollaborateCom '14), (2014), 177-186.

[5] Plaue, C. and Stasko, J. Presence & Placement: Exploring the Benefits of Multiple Shared Displays on an Intellective Sensemaking Task. In Proceedings of the ACM 2009 International Conference on Supporting Group Work (GROUP '09), (2009), ACM, New York, NY, USA, 179-188.

[6] Renambot, L., Marrinan, T., Aurisano, J., Nishimoto, A., Mateevitsi, V., Bharadwaj, K., Long, L., Johnson, A., Brown, M., and Leigh, J. SAGE2: A Collaboration Portal for Scalable Resolution Displays. In Future Generation Computer Systems, (2016), Vol. 54, 296-305.

[7] Strengert, M., Magallón, M., Weiskopf, D., Guthe, S., and Ertl, T. Hierarchical Visualization and Compression of Large Volume Datasets using GPU Clusters. In Proceedings of the 5th Eurographics conference on Parallel Graphics and Visualization (EGPGV '04), (2004), Dirk Bartz, Bruno Raffin, and Han-Wei Shen (Eds.). Eurographics Association, Aire-la-Ville, Switzerland, Switzerland, 41-48.

[8] Sutherland, I. E. A Head-mounted Three Dimensional Display. In Proceedings of the December 9-11, 1968, Fall Joint Computer Conference, Part I (AFIPS '68 (Fall, part I)), (1968), ACM, New York, NY, USA, 757-764.

[9] Van der Laan, M., Kellet, R., Girling, C., Senbel, M., and Su, T. A Collaborative Multi-touch, Multi-display, Urban Futures Tool. In Proceedings of the Symposium on Simulation for Architecture & Urban Design (SimAUD '13), (2013), Society for Computer Simulation International, San Diego, CA, USA, Article 10 , 4 pages.

[10] Waldner, M., Pirchheim, C., Kruijff, E., and Schmalstieg, D. Automatic Configuration of Spatially Consistent Mouse Pointer Navigation in Multi-display Environments. In Proceedings of the 15th International Conference on Intelligent User Interfaces (IUI '10), (2010), ACM, New York, NY, USA, 397-400.

The Use of a Multi-Display System in University Classroom Lectures

Bingyi Cao
Freie Universität Berlin
caobingyi@inf.fu-berlin.de

Margarita Esponda-Argüero
Freie Universität Berlin
esponda@inf.fu-berlin.de

Raúl Rojas
Freie Universität Berlin
rojas@inf.fu-berlin.de

ISS '16, November 06-09, 2016, Niagara Falls, ON, Canada
ACM 978-1-4503-4248-3/16/11.
http://dx.doi.org/10.1145/2992154.2996793

Abstract
We have built a display wall system with four liquid crystal displays to provide a very large visual area for university lectures. A program was developed to transform the display wall into an electronic blackboard. It has been used in a long-term classroom practice. Based on the research results, we demonstrate the benefits of the digital multi-display system for classroom learning.

Author Keywords
Multi-Display; Classroom Lecture; Electronic Blackboard

ACM Classification Keywords
H.5.2 [Information Interfaces and Presentation (e.g., HCI)]: User Interfaces—Graphical User Interfaces (GUI)

Introduction
The slide presentation is the most common form of teaching in current university classrooms. It has advantages, including the ability to structure material in advance, prepare high-quality examples and illustrations, and easily reuse material [2]. However, since the most frequently used presentation tools such as Microsoft PowerPoint and Apple Keynote currently support only one public screen, the area of visual aids dramatically decreased when moving from traditional blackboard to a single projector. Therefore, the amount

of information that can be displayed each time is limited by the screen resolution, forcing the instructors to split the related information into several parts. The information is stacked over time instead of space, which makes it difficult to understand the context and internal relationships [10]. A study [11] mentioned that the lack of history information may lead to students' "lost" of the lecture as the context was no longer available when the lecturer moved to a new slide.

Researchers try to adopt more and larger displays to regain the lost visual area and the related benefits. Different tools have been developed to make use of the increased screen space to enhance classroom learning [5, 9, 11]. These systems usually used two or more projectors to increase the public display area. The extra screens were used to display history information or other environments such as a browser window. These projects all used projectors to display lecture content since large digital displays were not even available when they were conducting their studies. Different from our approach, these systems were based on slides since the "slideware" just started getting popular at that time.

We have built a display wall system with four liquid crystal displays, providing 5.5 meters of space for classroom teaching since 2013. A canvas-based presentation system was developed to transform the screen wall into an electronic blackboard. It completely abandoned the slide metaphor. Instead, independent elements such as digital ink, texts and images can be freely placed on an infinite canvas. Lecturers from the Department of Mathematics and Computer Science in our university can use this system for their courses. Our aim is to study how teachers use the large display surfaces in real educational practices and to find out the benefits of such surfaces for classroom learning. We deployed the system in a classroom and collected students' feedback from the courses. Then we analyzed the results and discussed the benefits of such systems.

Related Work

The most convenient way to study the impact of the increased display area on learning is to use a dual-projector system. The advantages of this method are the low cost, the basic requirement of computer skills for the teachers, and easy to implement in classrooms. Therefore, numerous studies in this area are related to dual-projector systems [3, 7, 8]. The most frequently reported benefits of increased visual area include improved students' learning effectiveness [7, 8] and reduced cognitive loads [3].

However, the information can be presented in dual projection screens is still far less than a typical traditional blackboard. Other researchers adopted three or more displays as visual aids for teaching, aiming to understand the benefits of using larger displays. ModSlideShow [5] is a presentation system on which users can use a gestural interface to manipulate the flow of slides on multi-displays. It was an early study about multi-display usage for presentations and meetings. A study [4] introduced a three-projector presentation system and compared the use of it with one single projector for four weeks period lecture and concluded that the multi-display system significantly reduced the students' cognitive load and enhanced their learning effectiveness. Virtual MultiBoard [11] simulates traditional sliding blackboards with multiple digital projectors. It provides a "history" of the lecture notes for students. E-Chalk [6] was based on the chalkboard-metaphor and provided teachers with a familiar environment. Lectures on that system were highly praised by teachers and students.

In summary, most studies we can find about multi-display (more than two) systems for classroom use were completed more than ten years ago. They are unlikely to involve large digital display walls. These studies commonly used digital projection of slides to present information. However, we believe that the traditional blackboard support many teaching techniques than slides. The combination of traditional blackboards and digital display systems may produce more suitable tools for classroom learning. We present our study and the preliminary findings of such a system.

Intellichalk

We believe that traditional blackboard has many advantages for teaching compared to slide presentations, especially in the disciplines of STEM (Science, Technology, Engineering and Mathematics) where complex reasoning and interpretations are needed. We have developed Intellichalk, an electronic blackboard teaching system.

The basic functionality of the system is to support writing. With the digital ink technology and high-quality input devices, we provide users with a smooth writing experience like writing on the paper. A variety of colors are readily available. Users can also paste images from the local disk, removable storage or the Internet. Figure 1 shows the user interface of Intellichalk.

In addition to these basic and commonly used functions, the system also provides advanced features, such as a gallery of graphic elements, handwriting recognition, and other plug-ins.

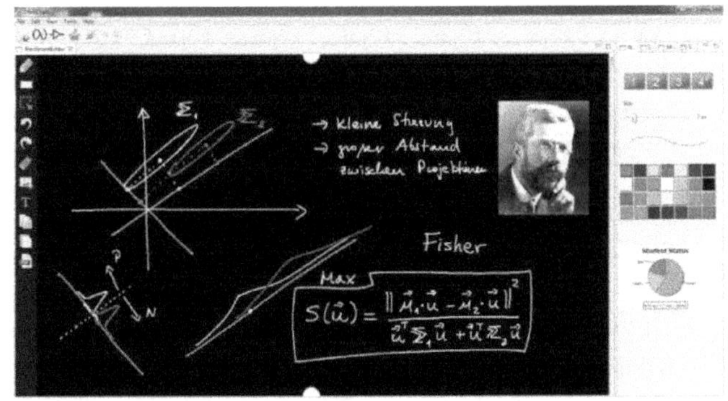

Figure 1. The user interface of the Intellichalk system.

As shown in Figure 2, an extra graphical tablet and a stylus are used as the input devices and the four screens are turned into an electronic blackboard. Figure 3 shows how we arrange the screens. The writing area extends vertically to fit the writing habits of the human. The content is mapped to the horizontally positioned four screens. The instructor can get unlimited writing space by pushing up the old contents.

According to our default settings, the fourth screen is the focus area, where new teaching contents are created. When the focus screen is full of information, the older content can be gradually pushed to the former screens. All users accepted this default setting in our study.

Figure 2. A professor was delivering a lecture with Intellichalk.

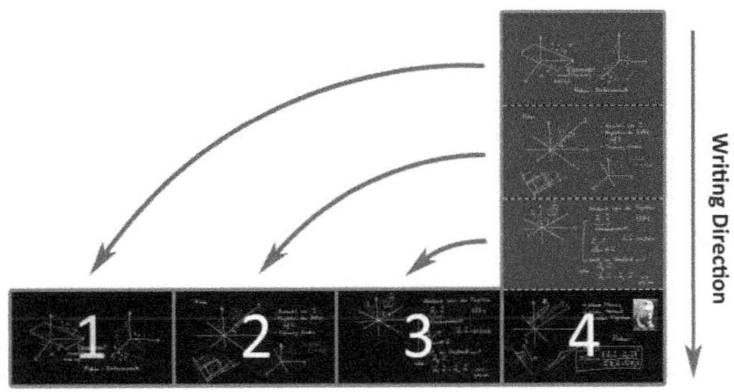

Figure 3. The arrangement of the displays.

Study

We deployed the Intellichalk system in a multimedia classroom. Three lecturers used the system for their courses for a period of one semester. At the end of each course, we sent questionnaires to investigate students' opinion towards the system.

Results

Figure 4 shows parts the screenshots of each course. The first lecturer drew lots of colorful diagrams to explain algorithms (see Figure 4 (a) for example). The second lecturer heavily used attention marks on the textual lecture content. It looks like writing on a traditional blackboard (Figure 4 (b)). The third lecturer frequently added images of code during his programming language course (Figure 4 (c)).

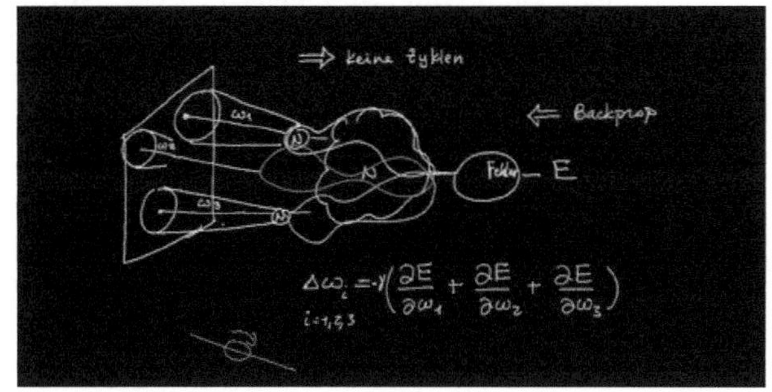

(a)

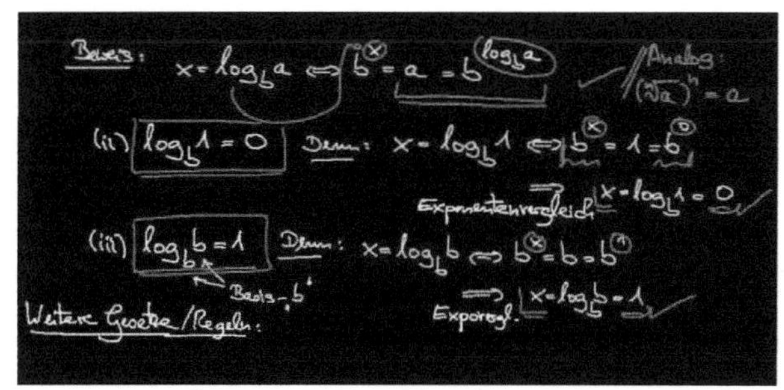

(b)

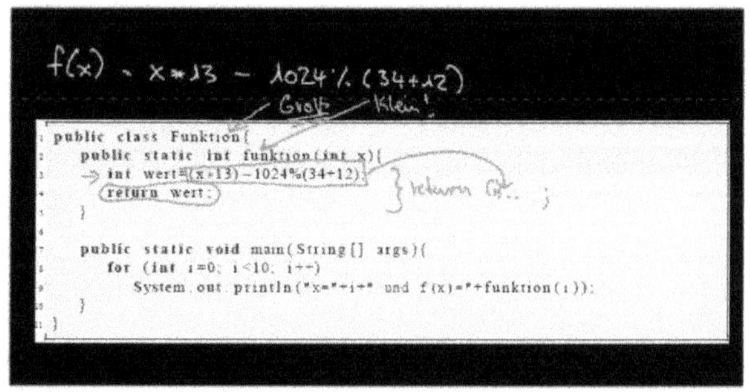

(c)

Figure 4. Screenshots from the three courses.

56 valid questionnaires were collected from the three courses. We list the students' evaluations about the Intellichalk system as follows (5 = strongly agree, 1 = strongly disagree):

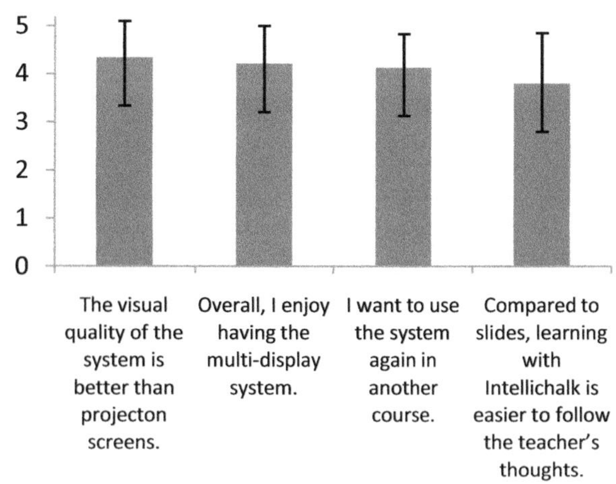

Figure 5. Students' evaluations about the Intellichalk system.

The questionnaire results (Figure 5) indicate that students thought the visual quality of the multi-display system was better than projection displays (Mean = 4.34, SD = 0.76), they enjoyed having the system in classroom (Mean = 4.21, SD = 0.79), and they showed their willingness to use the system in the future (Mean = 4.13, SD = 0.70). 38 of the 56 students (67.9%) agreed that learning with the Intellichalk system was easier to follow the teacher's thoughts compared to slide presentations (Mean = 3.80, SD = 1.05).

Discussion

We have implemented a digital multi-display system and deployed it for real classroom learning. Students' evaluations have been collected to analyze their experience with the system. Based on our study, we summarize the benefits of digital multi-display system for teaching as follows:

Better visual quality

The evaluation results show that the students were satisfied with the visual quality of the system. Actually, digital displays have many advantages over projection displays. For example, they offer higher luminance and contrast, easier to calibrate, and do not require dimming down the classroom lights. Compared with slide projection, teachers can naturally use physical gestures like when using a traditional blackboard, without the problem of casting shadows on the screen. As the display technology develops rapidly, large high-resolution displays are becoming increasingly affordable. It is highly likely that in the near future large digital displays will be used in more classrooms. We presented a vision of the digital future of the classroom.

Students' preference

Students showed very positive attitudes towards the multi-display system for both current and future use. It is possible that the results were affected by the novelty of new technology. But it is a great encourage for us to continue our study.

Support flexible ways of teaching

From the screenshots taken from three lectures, we can find that the lecturers used different visual elements for teaching. The canvas based lecturing area gives the users the flexibility to organize lecture materials according to the nature interconnection of knowledge, rather than mapping it to linear slide pages. This flexibility encourages instructors to deliver lectures in the ways which are suitable for the subjects, and the ways they like. The preliminary observation shows that the Intellichalk system may support flexible ways of teaching.

Easier to follow the lecture

Around two third of the students reported that they felt learning with Intellichalk was easier to follow the teacher's thoughts. We believe the inking process on the electronic blackboard exhibits the built up of information. It gives students chance to observe the instructor's mind, rather than showing the final results. Also, the increased display area keeps the old information available for a longer time, giving students opportunity to catch up the lecture from the short absence of mind or note-taking.

References

[1] Abowd, Gregory D., et al. Classroom 2000: Enhancing classroom interaction and review. 1996.

[2] Bligh, Donald A. *What's the Use of Lectures?*. Intellect books, 1998.

[3] Chang, T. W., Hsu, J. M., and Yu, P. T. A Comparison of Single-and Dual-Screen Environment in Programming Language: Cognitive Loads and Learning Effects. *Educational Technology & Society*, *14*, 2, (2011), 188-200.

[4] Cheng, T. S., Lu, Y. C., and Yang, C. S. Using the multi-display teaching system to lower cognitive load. *Journal of Educational Technology & Society 18,* 4 (2015), 128-140.

[5] Chiu, P., Liu, Q., Boreczky, J. S., Foote, J., Kimber, D., Lertsithichai, S., and Liao, C. Manipulating and Annotating Slides in a Multi-Display Environment. In *INTERACT*. 2003.

[6] Friedland, G., Knipping, L., Rojas, R., and Tapia, E. Teaching with an intelligent electronic chalkboard. In *Proceedings of the 2004 ACM SIGMM workshop on Effective telepresence,* ACM Press, (2004), 16-23.

[7] Lai, Y. S., Tsai, H. H., and Yu, P. T. Integrating Annotations into a Dual-slide PowerPoint Presentation for Classroom Learning. *Educational Technology & Society*, *14*, 2 (2011), 43-57.

[8] Lanir, J., Booth, K. S., and Hawkey, K. The benefits of more electronic screen space on students' retention of material in classroom lectures. *Computers & Education*, *55,* 2 (2010), 892-903.

[9] Lanir, J., Booth, K. S., and Tang, A. MultiPresenter: a presentation system for (very) large display surfaces. In *Proceedings of the 16th ACM international conference on MultiMedia,* ACM Press *(2008),* 519-528.

[10] Tufte, E. R. *The cognitive style of PowerPoint*. Graphics Press, Cheshire, CT 2003.

[11] Rößling, G., Trompler, C., Mühlhäuser, M., Köbler, S., and Wolf, S. Enhancing classroom lectures with digital sliding blackboards. In *ACM SIGCSE Bulletin* 36, 3 (2004), 218-222.

Grab This, Swipe That: Combining Tangible and Gestural Interaction in Multiple Display Collaborative Gameplay

Aniruddha Waje
Dalhousie University
6299 South Street.
Halifax, NS B3H 4R2
waje@cs.dal.ca

Raghav V. Sampangi
Dalhousie University
6299 South Street.
Halifax, NS B3H 4R2
raghav@cs.dal.ca

Khalid Tearo
Dalhousie University
6299 South Street.
Halifax, NS B3H 4R2
tearo@cs.dal.ca

Derek Reilly
Dalhousie University
6299 South Street.
Halifax, NS B3H 4R2
reilly@cs.dal.ca

Abstract
In this paper, we explore the use of multimodal interfaces (tangible and gestural) in collaborative gameplay. In our setup, gestural interaction is performed to control tasks using reference content to support tangible interaction on a tabletop display. We designed two games allowing us to explore the impact of multimodal interfaces on collaborative gameplay in multiple display environments. We conducted a pilot within-subjects user study, piloting the games with 35 children between the ages of 8 and 15, and considered the impact of a number of factors (group size, age range, game type and interaction style) on collaboration. We present the lessons learned from designing such multimodal (tangible and gestural) system from design standpoint, and the refinements made iteratively in the system. Also we conducted a pilot study and based on our observations, refined the study design to explore our system.

Author Keywords
Tangible and gestural interaction; Multimodal interaction; Collaboration in collocated workspaces; Collaborative gameplay.

ISS '16, November 06-09, 2016, Niagara Falls, ON, Canada
ACM 978-1-4503-4248-3/16/11.
http://dx.doi.org/10.1145/2992154.2996794

Figure 1: Game Setup

Figure 2: Tangibles with fiducial markers

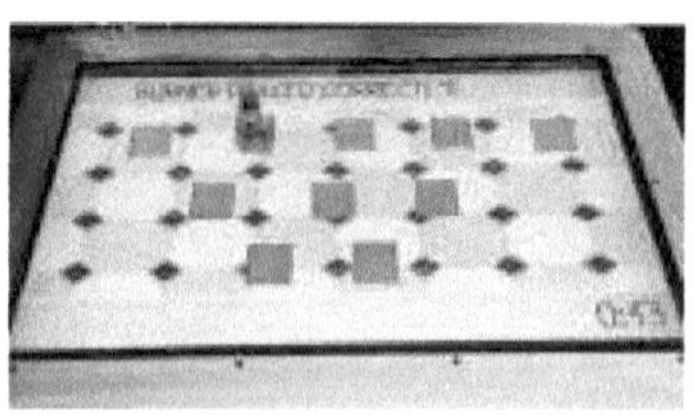

Figure 3: Game Scene with message board on top and timer on bottom right corner

(a) (b)

Figure 4: (a) Open hand (b) Closed hand – grab gesture.

Gesture	Action	Descriptio
Rotate Left	Swipe right hand to left	Rotates 3D model clockwise 90 degrees
Rotate Right	Swipe left hand to right	Rotates 3D model counter-clockwise 90 degrees

Table 1: Swipe Gestures

ACM Classification Keywords

H.5.2. Information interfaces and presentation: User interfaces

Introduction

Affordable devices supporting gestural interaction such as Microsoft Kinect, PlayStation Move, and Wiimote [1] are becoming commonplace. Furthermore, commercialization of multi-touch tabletops has led to their deployment in community settings such as museums and schools [5]. Tangible User Interaction (TUI) makes it possible to use physical objects as interaction tools to manipulate digital content. The gaming industry has begun exploring the use of tabletops and embodied interaction [1] to provide unique, compelling gaming experiences. The games typically employ unimodal interaction, using either only gesture or tangible/touch-based interactions [4].

Our work explores the potential of using a combination of gestural and tangible interfaces in a multimodal design, as a way to facilitate collaborative gameplay. Gestural interactions are performed by users to interact with supportive digital model that is projected on a wall-mounted display and are recorded using a Kinect [8]. The contributions of our work are the following: we explore one such multimodal interaction setup on collaborative gameplay. We also identify a number of factors that affect collaboration, namely – group size (2 v. 3 members), age range (8-15 years), game type and interactions (swipe and grab), and consider implications for design.

We developed two games, *Furniture Finder* and *Block Rock*, where users use hand gestures to manipulate content on the wall-mounted display and receive information, and use this information to place tangibles on the tabletop display to complete the requirements of the game. In both *Furniture Finder* and *Block Rock*, users place tangible objects to complete the layout displayed on the tabletop. In *Furniture Finder*, we used the strategy of "hiding" the tangibles in the3D model being projected on the wall-mounted display and revealing them when the user *grabs* them individually using their hands. However, in *Block Rock*, the entire layout of the 3D model was visible, and users used *swipe* gesture to rotate the model and complete the layout on the tabletop, or *grabbed* the model and rotated it to a suitable view.

Background

Tangible and Gestural Interactions

Rossol et al.[2]explored the use of mid-air gestural interaction to control visual displays while using handheld objects. Their study showed that workflow is more fluid and uninterrupted while using mid-air hand gestures as compared to a touchscreen interface. When designing interactive collaborative systems, users and their attributes such as age, familiarity with technology, technology needs and so on, are important aspects to consider. Anthony et al. [5] emphasize the importance of considering several categories of users, including children, while designing gesture controlled systems.

With the reference being a 3D model, we considered allowing participants to interact with it as it would allow them to better identify tangibles to be placed at a certain location. Using a touch interaction on the vertical display would necessitate delegating one member of the group to manage the reference model manipulation, which could possibly block another

Furniture Finder

In Furniture Finder, wooden models of dollhouse furniture were used as the tangibles. Furniture is displayed in 3D on the wall-mounted display, but they are hidden or covered by 3D boxes; each to be revealed when users grab the corresponding box. Using this model as reference, users were required to place corresponding elements on the tabletop. Furniture Finder is designed to encourage sequential collaborative gameplay: when a 3D model is uncovered by one player, another player can then place the tangible in the correct place on the tabletop.

Figure 5: Group of two playing Furniture Finder Game, with each participant controlling one interaction

participants' view of the model. On the other hand, placing control buttons on the tabletop would restrict our ability to use the full area of the tabletop display for tangible interaction. We evaluated the possibility of using gestural controls for 3D model manipulation as explored by Rossol et al.[2].

Collaboration among users

Ryall et al. [7]conducted a study of groups on re-creating a poem tasks. They conclude that, group size needs to be considered relative to the task that is being attempted by the group. Interactive collaborative systems represent designs that embody three essential characteristics as identified by Hornecker et al. [6] namely – embodied constraints, shared transaction spaces and multiple access points. Embodied constraints is defined as "the physical system set-up or configuration of space and objects" [6]. Applying such theory helps in defining the game's rules by constraining the role of each participants, thereby promoting collaboration and limiting the solitary decisions. We considered these constraints as guidelines for our design, such as constraints to distribute tasks, constraints to promote collaboration and constraints to coordinate action.

Shared transaction space is the area that can be fully utilized by a person to perform actions and interact with surroundings within reach [6]. Having more than one participant in the same space will create a shared transaction space that might promote collaboration, especially if the transaction rules require a coordinated input by all participants. According to Hornecker, the shared transaction space increases the focus on the central objects as well as the peripheral awareness. The shape, access to objects and rules of the shared transaction space define the relationship among users.

Furthermore, multiple access points are identified in terms of the ability of all members in a group to access and manipulate objects in the interactive system via various "access points". Each object (e.g. tangible, touch points, etc.) can be considered as an access point to the game. Accessibility to the game's objects increases the power of players and influences the way they play the game by creating a sense of competition or collaboration among players.

Children as Technology Users

User interactions with any system depend on one's ability to understand what is expected and to make decisions to lead towards a goal. As children move through different stages of cognitive development, designing interactions and interactive activities for a broad age range can be challenging. The stages of cognitive development in children as identified by Piaget [9] include the *sensorimotor* stage (birth to age 2), the *preoperational* stage (ages 2 through 7), the *concrete operational* stage (ages 7 through 11) and the *formal operational* stage (ages 11 and above).

In our work, we set out to study interaction behaviours in collaborative environments; specifically, collaborative gameplay for children. We were motivated by Ryall et al.'s suggestion about augmenting collaborative actions on a tabletop display with task related information on a vertical display [7], to enhance engagement of group members and improve the overall experience

Block Rock Swipe

In Block Rock (Swipe), wooden blocks were used as tangibles and users were required to interact with the 3D model using the swipe gesture. A corresponding empty scene "top-view" layout is displayed on the tabletop display. Users were required to place tangibles as seen on the 3D model to reconstruct the layout on the tabletop display. The swipe gesture provides ease of control to user(s), but limits the view to four 90 degree rotations along the x-axis. This is aimed at facilitating discrete gestural interaction events by any collaborator.

Figure 6: Group of two playing Block Rock Swipe, with one participant performing the swipe and the other placing the tangible.

Design and implementation

System Implementation

We designed our system to support tangible interaction on a 55-inch *MultiTaction* multi-touch tabletop display MultiTaction Tabletop and gestural interactions with a 70-inch wall-mounted LCD display, providing gameplay support. Users interacted with the information displayed on the wall-mounted display using a Microsoft Kinect V2 sensor[8]. The system set up is illustrated in Figure 1. The tabletop display is housed in a custom-built aluminum frame with a 6-inch surface surrounding the display, which was used to place tangibles when not in use. The tabletop display is connected to a PC (Intel Core i5 2.66 GHz processor, running Microsoft Windows 7) with cross Ethernet cable, while the wall display is connected to a different PC (AMD Athlon A10 2.66 processor, running Windows 8). The PCs were running applications programmed using Unity3D, which represented two different views of the same layout.

While the application on the wall-mounted display presented the goal state for the current game, the tabletop display displayed only a floor layout (or a top-down view) that enabled users to place tangibles at the appropriate locations using the design on the wall-mounted display as reference. The tabletop display was able to register the identity, position and orientation of the tangibles by tracking fiducial markers attached to the underside of the tangibles. The *Unidicial* library for Unity3D [3] facilitated reception and processing of the tracking data by the tabletop application. The interactive application on the wall-mounted display included support for two types of gestural interactions, *grab* and *swipe*.

Grab requires users to perform a hand grab or closing their hands to make a fist (illustrated in Figure 4) over a target object to make a selection. In our case, the 3D model is projected on a 3D board which has a handle on each side. In order to rotate the model, user has to grab a handle. Once a handle is grabbed, user can rotate the model. The swipe gesture allowed users to perform fixed (90 degree) rotations to rotate the 3D model either clockwise or counterclockwise. The translation of hand movement actions into 3D model rotations are summarized in Table 1.

We developed two games for the purposes of our study, namely, a dollhouse game called *Furniture Finder* and a block-based game called *Block Rock*. In both games, a 3D model is projected on the wall-mounted display. Users are required to reconstruct the 3D model on the tabletop display using tangible objects. As a way to provide feedback for user actions of placing or moving the tangible, a digital "shadow" of the tangible is displayed on the tabletop. The table top application as shown in Figure 3, displayed on the tabletop display contains triggers (green squares). The games are described in the sidebar.

Design Iterations

We made design iterations to the system, revisiting the various design elements of the games during each iteration. In the initial design, we did not have distinct triggers (as shown in Figure 3) on the tabletop layout, and the tangibles could be placed anywhere on the tabletop. Instead of triggers, we relied on relative digital placement of the tangibles to detect if a tangible was correctly placed. However, when playing in a group, the lack of distinct placeholders for tangible

Block Rock Grab

In Block Rock (Grab), wooden blocks were used as tangibles and users were required to interact with the 3D model using a grab gesture. A corresponding empty scene "top-view" layout is displayed on the tabletop display. Users were required to place tangibles as seen on the 3D model to reconstruct the layout on the tabletop display. The grab gesture affords 360 degree view but needs precision to control from users. This is aimed at facilitating continuous gestural interaction events by any collaborator.

Figure 6: Group of two playing Block Rock Grab, with one participant performing the swipe and the other placing the tangible.

would not allow equal access to all participants in the group. Thus, we decided to have a representative layout with triggers on the tabletop. Furthermore, we decided to add virtual handles to the 3D model in block rock with grab, whereas in our earlier version, the entire 3D model could be grabbed and then rotated. Our motivation in designing virtual handles was to afford a 360 view of the 3D model, but is also meant that users were required to use precision and control when interacting with the model. Furthermore, with successive iterations we refined the design of the elements on the tabletop to allow participants to keep track of their actions. For example, having a message board as shown in Figure 3, adding countdown timer in the bottom right corner where participants could see it easily, and so on.

Sample and Recruitment

All the participants were part of SuperNova, an annual summer camp in Dalhousie University. Participants were in the age range of 8 to 15 years.

Pilot Study

The pilot study required participants to interact with our system and provide their comments during a post-game interview. We conducted a pilot with 35 participants, divided into 11 diads, 3 triads and 1 group of 4. Note that the first 18 participants (9 diads) only played Furniture Finder and Block Rock with Swipe, while the rest played Furniture Finder and two variants of the Block Rock games (swipe and grab).

Lessons Learnt

Participants in groups of 2, 3 and 4 successfully completed all the games. However, we observed that in the group of 4, one participant did not have an access point to the shared space, and found it difficult to interact during gameplay. This participant stood on the side of the tabletop and watched the other three participants play the games. This forced us to reconsider our strategy regarding group sizes and we decided to restrict our study to include only groups of two and three. While interacting with the wall display we observed that participants could not figure out who was in control of the gestures. Participants overcame this by each participant in a group performing the gesture to see if they are in control of the gesture. To help participants determine who was in control we decided to add control indicator. We did this by having the digital silhouette of the participant, on the wall display in control of gesture, highlighted in a distinct color.

Study Design

Our primary interest in designing the user study was to study how small groups of youth (groups of two - *diads* and three – *triads*) collaborate in an environment with multimodal displays, where gestural interaction aided tangible interaction. A between-subjects study was employed. For each group, the overall system setup and game rules were explained. Each team played three games (*Furniture Finder* and two variants of *Block Rock*). At the beginning of each game, rules of the game were explained and a participants were allowed to try a demonstration of the game, to help them get familiar. After each group finished playing the three games, a post-game interview was conducted. We video-recorded the gameplay and audio recorded the interviews. In order to mitigate ordering effect, the order of games was randomized for each group.

The nature of the sample was such that all groups in a batch were present in the study area at the same time, and could observe other groups as they played the games. This prompted us to require groups who were not playing games to be asked to interact with other exhibits (augmented reality games on Oculus Rift, whole body interaction games with Kinect 0 and Leap Motion games to minimize the risk of learning effect

Conclusion

In this paper, we conducted an initial exploration of multimodal (tangible and gestural) interfaces for collaborative gameplay. We performed our pilot with a sample of children between the ages 8 – 15 years. Based on our motivation, we iterated on our design process building up a refined system that we evaluated by conducting a pilot study. Based on our observations of our pilot study, we refine our study design to further explore the interactions in such multimodal (tangible and gestural) interfaces.

References

[1] Poor, G. M., Tomlinson, B. J., Guinness, D., Jaffee, S. D., Leventhal, L. M., Zimmerman, G., & Klopfer, D. S. (2013). Tangible or gestural: comparing tangible vs. Kinect™ interactions with an object manipulation task. In 7th International Conference on Tangible, Embedded and Embodied Interaction.

[2] Rossol, N., Cheng, I., Shen, R., & Basu, A. (2014, August). Touchfree medical interfaces. In Engineering in Medicine and Biology Society (EMBC), 2014 3 Rossol, N., Cheng, I., Shen, R., & Basu, A. (2014, August). Touchfree medical interfaces. In Engineering in Medicine and Biology Society (EMBC), 2014 36th Annual International Conference of the IEEE (pp. 6597-6600).

[3] Downloads - unidućial - Fiducial Marker support for the Unity3d engine - Google Project Hosting. (n.d.). Retrieved from https://code.google.com/p/unidućial/downloads/list

[4] Antle, A. N., Bevans, A., Tanenbaum, J., Seaborn, K., & Wang, S. (2011, January). Futura: design for collaborative learning and game play on a multi-touch digital tabletop. In Proceedings of the fifth international conference on Tangible, embedded, and embodied interaction (pp. 93-100).

[5] Anthony, L., Brown, Q., Nias, J., Tate, B., & Mohan, S. (2012, November). Interaction and recognition challenges in interpreting children's touch and gesture input on mobile devices. In Proceedings of the 2012 ACM international conference on Interactive tabletops and surfaces (pp. 225-234). ACM.

[6] Hornecker, E. "A Design Theme for Tangible Interaction: Embodied Facilitation." *ECSCW*. Vol. 5. 2005.

[7] Ryall, K., Forlines, C., Shen, C., & Morris, M. R. (2004, November). Exploring the effects of group size and table size on interactions with tabletop shared-display groupware.

[8] http://www.microsoft.com/en us/kinectforwindows/

[9] Piaget, J. (1977). The role of action in the development of thinking. In Knowledge and development (pp. 17-42). Springer

Carbon Copy Metaphor: Mode Switching Technique for Trackpad-based Manipulations

kaori Ikematsu
Ochanomizu University
2-1-1 Otsuka, Bunkyo-ku, Tokyo
112-8610, Japan
g0920502@gmail.com

Itiro Siio
Ochanomizu University
2-1-1 Otsuka, Bunkyo-ku, Tokyo
112-8610, Japan
siio@acm.org

Abstract

Drawing characters or images using smartphones and tablets is much easier than drawing using trackpads commonly equipped in laptops and desktop computers. The reason is that tablets are absolute coordinate input devices, whereas trackpads are relative coordinates input devices similar to conventional mouse. However, most of the modern laptops have trackpads approximately the same size as a smartphone screen, and they have enough space for hand-writing. We believe that modern trackpads would allow users to write easily as smartphones or tablets, if they properly provide an absolute coordinates input mode. This paper proposes a novel input technique that aims to switch between relative and absolute coordinates input methods seamlessly based on the "carbon copy" metaphor. We display a small workspace ("carbon copy area") on a computer screen that corresponds one-to-one with the handy trackpad. The user can input hand-written characters or images using absolute coordinates input on this virtual carbon copy paper and move it anywhere using relative coordinates.
Our technique allows a user to call both absolute and relative coordinates input methods and use them appropriately with arbitrary timing. We developed a prototype application software to utilize this technique based on a preliminary experiment.

ISS '16, November 06-09, 2016, Niagara Falls, ON, Canada
ACM 978-1-4503-4248-3/16/11.
http://dx.doi.org/10.1145/2992154.2996795

Author Keywords
Touch/Pointing/Gesture; User Interface Design.

ACM Classification Keywords
H.5.2 [User Interface]: Input devices and strategies.

General Terms
Human Factors; Design.

Introduction
Owing to the widespread use of touch surfaces, such as in smartphones, tablets, and trackpads, touch inputs can be seen in everyday life. At present, two input methods are used for touch surfaces. One is the relative coordinates input method, which calculates the distance between the current cursor location and destination point. Like the conventional mouse, a trackpad engages the relative coordinates. When a user moves a finger on the input surface, a cursor in the display moves according to the finger movement. By performing a clutching operation on the surface and adding pseudo acceleration to the moving speed of the cursor, a user can relatively easily operate a large screen even if the input surface is small. Relative coordinate input method is suitable for common GUI operation. Even small finger movement can be used for large cursor movement, and precise operations can be performed, as mentioned before. Another one is the absolute coordinates input method, in which the coordinates of an input surface correspond directly to the coordinates of the display. Writing characters or drawing a painting is much easier compared to using the relative coordinates input method because it provides similar pen tip movement as writing characters or drawing a picture on paper. We presume many people would have wished they could write or draw characters or pictures on the trackpad easily, for example, in cases wherein: jotting down numerical formulas, writing short comments in the margin or figure when correcting a document, making an electronic signature and sharing a laugh idea sketch with colleagues, etc. It would be surely useful if modern trackpads allow users to write as easily as smartphones or tablets do.

We implemented a new input interface focusing on the two methods of entering coordinates. Particular input equipment such as a pen tablet is required when a user performs absolute coordinates pointing. It allows a user to hand-draw or paint easily by providing absolute coordinates input to devices based on the relative coordinate input method. Typical trackpads and computer screens are different in size. If a computer screen corresponds one-to-one with the handy trackpad, precise operation becomes difficult because of size difference between the screen and trackpad in a large screen environment. On the other hand, if only a part of a computer screen corresponds one-to-one with trackpad, the workspace will be limited. By providing a small area that corresponds directly to a trackpad on the screen and allowing a user to input absolute coordinates only in this area, the problem can be resolved. However, a user interface for moving the small area and setting it on the screen is required.

In this study, we propose a new interface method based on the “carbon copy” metaphor for three easily-switchable mode:

1. Conventional pointer mode with relative coordinates
2. Absolute coordinate mode to input rectangle sub-area on the screen
3. Moving mode for this input sub-area

Related Work

Various methods combine relative and absolute coordinate inputs for a desktop/laptop PC or a large screen environment have been proposed. ARC-Pad[3] provides implicit mode switching, it provides absolute input mode by finger tapping on a smartphone screen and relative input mod by finger dragging. In [2], it enables fluid switching between the two modes by using a pen device. In [5], a pointing gesture with a user's hand for absolute-ray casting mode and opens a his/her hand to enable relative input mode by using a motion-tracked glove. Our proposed method targets to a widespread touchpad without any special hardwares or sensors. Inklet [1] is a utility that also allows a common trackpad to emulate virtual absolute coordinates input area by using predefined shortcut keys. Similar to above approaches, our proposed technique is designed as explicit mode switching interfaces. However these approaches tend to address specific use cases where a user is locked into a dedicated mode, thus these are not intend to switch between the two modes frequently. Further more the " carbon copy " metaphor will make the operation more understandable than using pre-defined shortcut keys.

Researchers have studied interfaces for gestures of both hands. ToolStone[4] utilizes a physical tool widget to switch zooming, 3D rotating, and camera controlling modes. [1] provides virtual filters to modify input and output manipulated by non-dominant hand. In our approach, non dominant hand is used temporal function switching similar to a modifier key on a keyboard.

Carbon Copy Metaphor

Our proposed method provides following operations, (1) mode-switching operation between relative and absolute

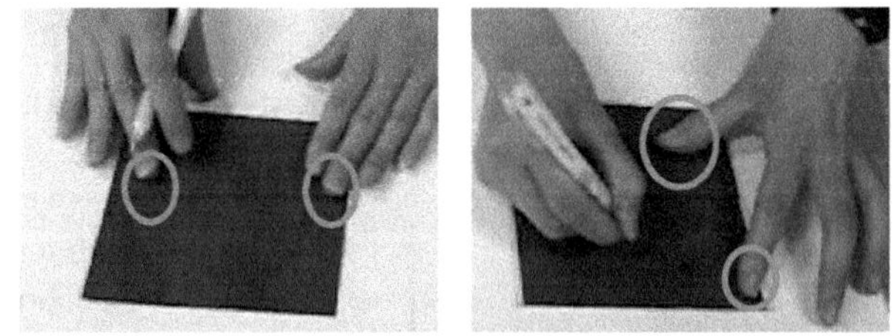

Figure 1: Fingertip positions when handling a carbon paper.

Figure 2: Setup for the preliminary experiment.

coordinates input and (2) an operation of moving the absolute coordinates input area. This method allows users to absolute input for the limited area on a screen, and the area can be moved to any optional place. Aiming to achieve it, we adopted the "carbon copy" metaphor similarly to using a carbon paper. Namely, we have implemented user-operations similar to real world activities of adjusting the position of a small carbon paper and writing on it. A virtual "carbon paper" appears on the display when the users touch the trackpad with their non dominant hand. The virtual carbon paper on the computer display is a metaphor of the actual carbon paper. In the real world, we can move the carbon paper by slightly pressing it with our fingers, and we can transfer it below a paper by holding and fixing it. Our proposed method is based on this hand motion: a user can

[1] https://tenonedesign.com/inklet.php

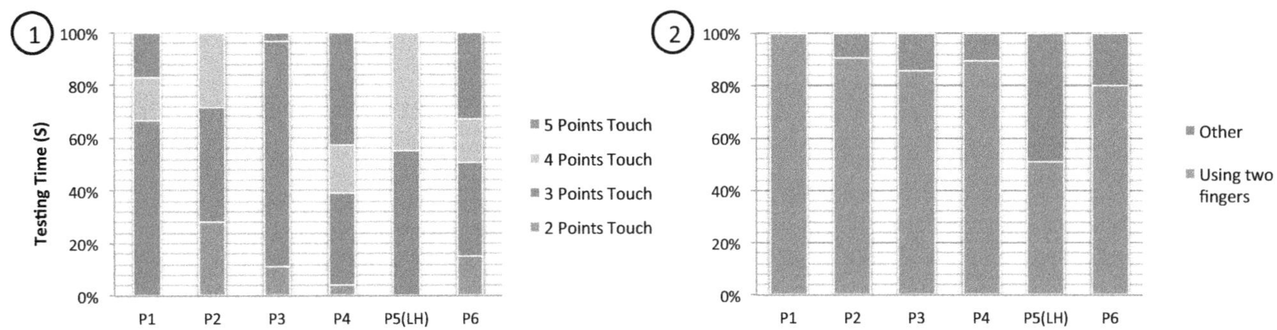

Figure 3: Frequency of (1) the number of fingers used to hold the carbon paper. (2) drawing between or outside the fingers used for holding the paper.

manipulate the virtual "carbon paper" using similar actions, which they would apply to a physical carbon paper (Fig.1).

Preliminary Experiments

To design user actions on a touch surface of an interface based on the carbon copy metaphor, we conducted an observational study regarding the manipulation of a carbon paper in the real world. We assigned a drawing task to six participants (five right-handed, one left-handed, ages 21 to 24). We used a drawing paper ($500mm \times 400mm$), small carbon paper ($130mm \times 130mm$), and ballpoint pen that ran out of ink (Fig. 2). Participants sign their own name on the left half of the drawing paper and paint freely on the right half. We recorded this experiment and looked for patterns in which the fingers were used for handling a carbon paper.

When participants carried out the task, to write or draw on the paper, they pressed the edge of the carbon paper with their non dominant hand. This indicates that the participants utilized a wide drawing area and prevented the carbon paper from floating or peeling off. Fig. 3 (1) shows the ratio of the time fingers touched the carbon paper to that taken for the execution of the entire task. There are significant differences in frequencies of pairs of three fingers and other touches. The t-test calculation showed that there are significant differences in frequencies of pairs of three fingers and other touches, such as between a three-finger touch and two-finger touch ($t(5) = 4.028, p < 0.001$), three-finger touch and four-finger touch ($t(5) = 3.007, p < 0.005$) and three-finger touch and five-finger touch ($t(5) = 3.466, p < 0.005$). All the other pairs are not considered significant. As shown in Fig. 3 (2), we found that the participants tended to open certain two fingers widely, which means they decisively used two fingers for holding a carbon paper. Conversely, various finger movements were observed when they moved the carbon paper.

Interface Design

We designed the interface based on the preliminary experiment as follows. Focusing on the writing behavior of the participants on a carbon paper, we adopted "Pressing the edge of a carbon paper with two spreading fingers of the

Figure 4: Black-framed carbon copy area corresponds to the input area on the trackpad.

Figure 5: Trackpad divided into two areas. A case for a right-handed person.

non dominant hand" as a condition for the writing operation. When a user uses two spreading fingers of the non dominant hand to press the edge of a trackpad while moving the cursor with one finger, a small working area with the same aspect ratio as a trackpad appears at the cursor location on the screen. This small working area (carbon copy area) is enabling absolute coordinates inputs. The absolute coordinates input mode is called the "carbon copy mode." When the user removes the two non dominant fingers, the carbon copy area disappears, and the input mode switches to the conventional relative coordinates input mode.

Implementation

To test the efficiency of our proposed method, we implemented a prototype, a painting application, in Objective-C for use on a OS X 10.9 operating system. Touching the trigger area with one finger activates the carbon copy area (the black-edged area on the screen, as shown in Fig.4). When compared with the preliminary experiment, in the prototype, the entire desktop area corresponds to the drawing paper and the black-framed carbon copy area corresponds to the carbon paper. As Fig.5 shows, we divided a trackpad into two parts (non dominant hand side: trigger area, dominant hand side: input area) to define a gesture set for fixing/moving the carbon copy area and switching relative/absolute coordinates inputs.

The mapping between the gesture set and functions of the application is shown in Figure 6. The circles in Figure 6 indicate the fingertip position of a user (blue: fixed fingertip, red: moving fingertip).

- No.1 shows one moving finger on a trackpad. It corresponds to the cursor movement with conventional relative coordinate inputs.
- No.2 shows two fixed fingers on the trigger area. By this operation, the fixed carbon copy area appears on the screen.
- No.3 shows two fixed fingers on the trigger area and one moving finger on the input area. By this operation, a user manipulate the pointer inside the carbon copy area with absolute coordinates input mode. Our prototype provides cursor movement by touching on the input area and drawing by dragging (moving while pressing) on the input area. That is, when a user activates the carbon copy mode, tracing the input area

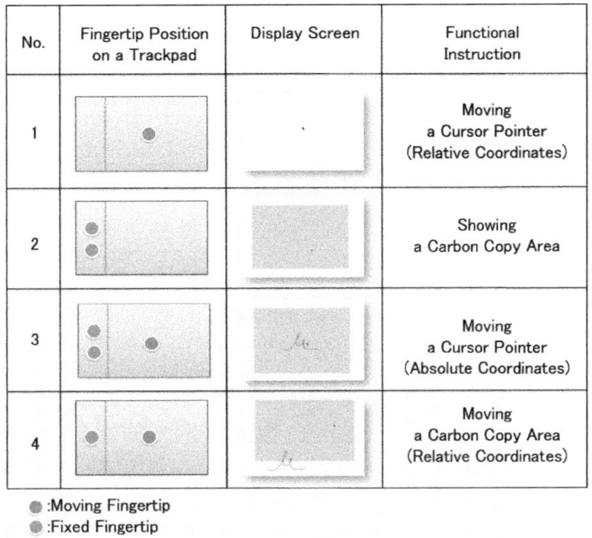

Figure 6: Mapping between the fingertip position on the trackpad and carbon copy metaphor function

provides preview of cursor movement, and then dragging provides drawing lines on the paint application. A cursor follows the movement of the finger on the input area.

- No.4 shows one finger on the trigger area and one fixed finger on the input area. It corresponds to moving the carbon copy area in relative coordinates.

In this way, our proposed method switches two coordinates input modes simply by following the manner of writing on a carbon copy paper is carried out.

Conclusion and Future Work

In this paper, we proposed novel mode switching technique based on the carbon copy metaphor. It provides relative and absolute coordinates inputs by using a trackpad embedded in a laptop or a consumer trackpad. We developed the prototype application based on the observational study for the user's manipulation of a carbon paper in the real world. We are planning to carry out comparison experiments to assess the effectiveness of our idea.

acknowledgement

This work was supported by JSPS KAKENHI Grant Number 26330219.

References

[1] Eric A. Bier, Maureen C. Stone, Ken Pier, William Buxton, and Tony D. DeRose. 1993. Toolglass and Magic Lenses: The See-through Interface. In *Proc. SIGGRAPH'93*. ACM, New York, NY, USA, 73–80.

[2] Clifton Forlines, Daniel Vogel, and Ravin Balakrishnan. 2006. HybridPointing: Fluid Switching Between Absolute and Relative Pointing with a Direct Input Device. In *Proc. UIST'06*. ACM, New York, NY, USA, 211–220.

[3] David C. McCallum and Pourang Irani. 2009. ARC-Pad: Absolute+Relative Cursor Positioning for Large Displays with a Mobile Touchscreen. In *Proc. UIST '09*. ACM, New York, NY, USA, 153–156.

[4] Jun Rekimoto and Eduardo Sciammarella. 2000. ToolStone: Effective Use of the Physical Manipulation Vocabularies of Input Devices. In *Proc. UIST'00 (UIST '00)*. ACM, New York, NY, USA, 109–117. DOI: http://dx.doi.org/10.1145/354401.354421

[5] Daniel Vogel and Ravin Balakrishnan. 2005. Distant Freehand Pointing and Clicking on Very Large, High Resolution Displays. In *Proc. UIST'05*. ACM, New York, NY, USA, 33–42.

Quantum Cats: The Demo

Victor Cheung
Systems Design Engineering
University of Waterloo
Waterloo, Ontario, Canada
victor.cheung@uwaterloo.ca

James R. Wallace
School of Public Health and Health Systems
University of Waterloo
Waterloo, Ontario, Canada
james.wallace@uwaterloo.ca

ISS'16, November 06-09, 2016, Niagara Falls, ON, Canada
ACM 978-1-4503-4248-3/16/11.
http://dx.doi.org/10.1145/2992154.2996869

Abstract
We describe the design, development, and deployment of a scientific outreach game to support an open house event at an Institute for Quantum Computing (IQC) by an 11-member team of academics and practitioners over a one-year period. We overview our design process, the development of design goals that aligned with facilitating scientific outreach during a one-day open house, and report on how successfully our final prototype achieved those goals. We then reflect on the effectiveness of large displays as 'honey pots' and extending the reach of outreach activities through technology. This demonstration accompanies our ISS 2016 paper.

Author Keywords
Science; Outreach; Games; Large Displays

ACM Classification Keywords
H.5.m [Information interfaces and presentation (e.g., HCI)]: Miscellaneous.

Introduction
The rapid adoption and evolution of interactive surfaces have provided an accessible, malleable, and engaging medium for scientific outreach. In particular, applications in scientific and educational outreach have been actively explored, since interactive surfaces provide a familiar

Figure 1: Quantum Cats is an Angry Birds-like game played on large, multi-touch displays that introduces guests to basic quantum mechanics principles. The game was subsequently made available for play on smartphones and tablets.

means by which lay audiences can be enticed to engage, interact, and ultimately learn about science. Furthermore, diversity in display size, display configuration (e.g., handheld, large format), and interaction modalities (e.g., touch, proxemics) enables scientific institutions to develop custom-built applications that better engage visitors with their research, personnel, and facilities.

Multi-surface scientific outreach applications have the potential to help educate the public about local scientific activities, to act as a 'honey pot' and draw in otherwise uninterested audiences, and to take advantage of the growing number of smartphones and tablets to engage individuals and extend an institution's reach beyond their physical space. However, to effectively engage an audience with an institution's research, staff, and facilities, custom-built hardware and/or software is often necessary. And while software tools for gaming and multi-touch development are available, there is a lack of guidance towards how they should be developed and deployed in practice.

We describe the design, development, and deployment of *Quantum Cats* (Figure 1) over a one-year period by a cross-disciplinary team of 11 researchers and practitioners. The game aims to educate and engage the general public with research at an Institute for Quantum Computing (IQC) during a one-day outreach (open house) event. As the surface application was designed to support engagement with complex scientific material, we incorporated gameplay elements (e.g., puzzle-solving) for a more engaging and enjoyable experience.

Design Process and Criteria

Through requirements gathering activities with IQC staff, we first identified past outreach activities at the IQC. Then, using feedback from the IQC administration and student outreach staff, we developed a set of goals to guide our design process [2], a subset of which is:

(D1) Educational Value The event aims to educate, make IQC research accessible to the public, and to encourage exploration of quantum mechanics.

(D3) Approachable and Accessible Installations at the event should be accessible to a diverse group of guests, e.g., children, individuals with non-English backgrounds, and those with physical disabilities.

(D4) Engaging One of the most significant challenges faced previously was making scientific content accessible and engaging to guests, and for them to leave the event with a positive experience. An oft-cited goal was to have guests "Google 'quantum mechanics'" when they arrived home afterwards.

Quantum Cats: Gameplay

Given the focus of the open house to educate and to make quantum computing research more accessible to the general public **(D1,3)**, the first identified installation was determined to be a classical game that would incorporate quantum computing aspects into its core mechanics. The motivation behind developing a game was that it would have broad appeal to a large group of guests, and would provide an approachable, accessible **(D3)**, and engaging **(D4)** experience while providing an opportunity to informally introduce quantum computing concepts to visitors **(D1)**. We hoped that this experience would spark interest in quantum computing, and foster engagement with other parts of the tour rather than being a stand-alone educational tool.

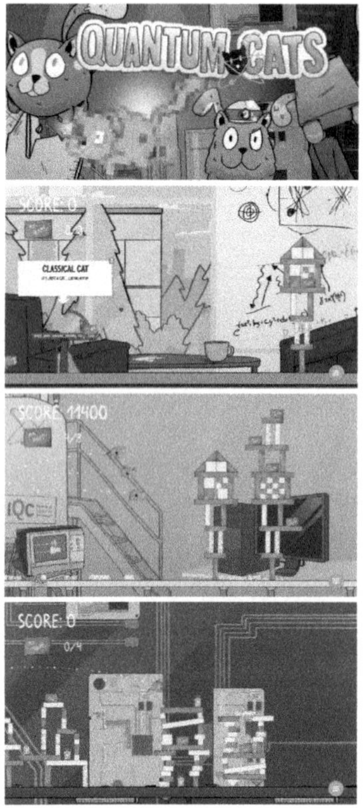

Figure 2: Quantum Cats employs many of the same mechanics and interaction metaphors as Angry Birds. **(Panel 1)** The welcome screen, featuring each of the 4 in-game characters. **(Panels 2-4)** Players launch cats associated with quantum properties such as Uncertainty, Quantum Tunnelling, and Superposition to rescue kittens trapped in nearby boxes.

Through a series of focus groups and seminars, we first proposed adaptations of classical arcade games, such as PacMan or Asteroids. These suggestions did not receive much positive feedback. However, during a brainstorming session, IQC outreach staff proposed an "Angry Birds-like" game. This idea was well-received by IQC staff, administration, and our design team because of its familiar interface, and the opportunity to incorporate quantum mechanics into birds' flight properties. Over a series of design exercises we developed concepts for the quantum principles that should be incorporated into the game, and game mechanics that would be representative of the research at the IQC. In particular, three concepts that drove much of the IQC's research were identified: Super-positioning, Quantum Tunnelling, and Uncertainty.

Our game, called *Quantum Cats*[1] (Figure 2) is an Angry Birds clone that features four cats, who are launched using an electromagnetic catapult across levels to rescue the world's kittens (who are coincidentally trapped in nearby boxes). Each cat's game mechanics correspond to different quantum computing concepts: Classy represents classical physics and is a traditional ballistic projectile; Schrö represents superposition and splits into three projectiles when fired, only one of which will ultimately strike a target; Digger embodies quantum tunnelling, and can pass through obstacles as he flies through the level; and Fuzzy represents quantum uncertainty and flies through the level as a cloud of uncertainty, when tapped she will strike a randomly-determined nearby object at random speed. Each cat is illustrated in order in Figure 2, Panel 1. We created 7 levels of varying difficulty to showcase each of the quantum mechanics and engage guests for an expected playtime of about 5 minutes.

[1] Available at http://quantumcats.ca

Quantum Cats was developed in Unity 5 over the 5-month period leading up to the open house. A benefit of developing in Unity was the ability to cross-compile for different platforms. We ultimately released the Quantum Cats app on the Google Play and iOS App stores. The game features custom artwork by our in-house cartoonist, which reflects the IQC and its Optics, Nuclear Magnetic Resonance (NMR), and Integrated Circuit laboratories.

At the Open House

Our logs showed that throughout the day more than 2,400 cats were 'launched' in-game, representing an average rate of more than 8 cats per minute. This level of use exceeded our expectations for the event, but matched observations made by the researchers; the three displays running identical copies of the game were a popular destination during the event, particularly for younger children and families (Figure 3).

In the following week, Quantum Cats was downloaded more than 5,000 times on the Google Play Store, vastly exceeding the approximately 300 in attendance at the event. These downloads can be attributed in part to guests downloading the app on-site or back at home. However, more significantly the app was featured on various media such as `phys.org`, a leading scientific research and technology website with a large audience. We discuss this exposure later in the next section. Unfortunately, since the game did not launch immediately on Apple's iOS App Store, downloads on this platform only registered about 300 two weeks after the event.

Implications for Design

Our experience at the open house event suggests two implications for the design of interactive surfaces that support scientific outreach:

Figure 3: Quantum Cats was played throughout the day by visitors. In front of the displays, Quantum Cats-themed stickers were handed out to visitors at no cost, adding to our effort to extend the event's reach afterwards.

Can a Honey Pot Encourage Pollination?
Our design experience and review of the literature point to interactive surfaces as supporting relatively short-lived, engaging interactions. If this is the case, how can the monetary and development costs for installations such as Quantum Cats be justified as educational tools? One potential answer to this question is engagement. The 'honey pot' effect of large displays is well documented in the literature [1], and large displays are often able to attract an audience to important content. This effect is particularly appealing for scientific outreach applications. Yet, what remains to be shown is whether a corresponding '*pollination*' effect may also take place. That is, can nearby or associated attractions also benefit from the 'honey pot' effect surrounding a large display?

Extending an Event's Reach
Our experience with Quantum Cats illustrates the potential of custom-built games not only to encourage learning on-site, but also after visitors had left the event, and to individuals who were not able to attend at all. Our Google Play account reported that Quantum Cats was installed on more than 5,000 devices in the week following the event, compared to the approximately 300 guests that attended the event in-person. Even downloads from Apple's iOS App Store reached more than 300 devices, despite the launch being delayed by more than a week. Enabling visitors to download their own souvenir copy of the app provided a means of making these experiences available to them after the event, an advantage not mentioned in previous research using companion apps [3].

Conclusion
We described the design, development, and deployment of a scientific outreach game for a local Institute for Quantum Computing (IQC). By combining surface technologies and gameplay mechanics, we created a touch-centric game for both large displays and personal devices. Our work highlights both the potential and challenges to the use of interactive surfaces and spaces as platforms for scientific outreach. Large interactive surfaces provide an engaging, easily understood platform on which complex materials can be presented to a lay audience, but may only be used for a few minutes at a time. We see multi-surface games as a promising vehicle to engage the public with scientific outreach activities, and foster lasting interests beyond a day-long event.

Acknowledgements
The authors would like to thank the rest of the development team for their immense work throughout the project: Mike Brown, Jagger Nast, Keith McLean, Elise Vist, Lauren Burr, Erica Robinson, Neil Randall, Agata Antkiewicz, Tobi Day-Hamilton, and Angela Olano. We would also like to thank our financial sponsors: The Mike and Ophelia Lazaridis Institute for Quantum Computing and the Social Sciences and Humanities Research Council of Canada.

References
[1] Brignull, H., and Rogers, Y. Enticing people to interact with large public displays in public spaces. In *INTERACT* (2003), 17–24.
[2] Cheung, V., and Wallace, J. R. Felines, foragers, and physicists: Supporting scientific outreach with multi-surface and multi-space games. In *Proceedings of the ACM Conference on Interactive Surfaces and Spaces*, ISS 2016, ACM (2016).
[3] Economou, M., and Meintani, E. Promising beginning? evaluating museum mobile phone apps. In *Rethinking Technology in Museums 2011: Emerging experiences* (2011).

CHI PLAYGUE: A Mobile Conference Networking Game

Gustavo F. Tondello
HCI Games Group,
Games Institute,
Cheriton School of Computer Science
University of Waterloo
Waterloo, ON, Canada
gustavo@tondello.com

Lennart E. Nacke
HCI Games Group,
Games Institute,
Department of Drama and Speech Communication,
Stratford Campus,
University of Waterloo
Waterloo, ON, Canada
lennart.nacke@acm.org

Rina R. Wehbe
HCI Games Group,
Games Institute,
Cheriton School of Computer Science
University of Waterloo
Waterloo, ON, Canada
rina.wehbe@uwaterloo.ca

ISS '16, November 06-09, 2016, Niagara Falls, ON, Canada
ACM 978-1-4503-4248-3/16/11.
http://dx.doi.org/10.1145/2992154.2996870

Abstract
Modern professional networking relies on social media. To take advantage of this fact, we present CHI PLAYGUE, a conference game designed to facilitate interaction among strangers and encourage social networking to create a community. The game integrates digital technology (mobile devices and large displays) within the space of the conference venue, combined with a mixed-reality narrative and people's social interactions to facilitate the emergence of social dynamics. By providing a platform for large-scale, playful interaction, the game creates an experience that fosters the development of mutually beneficial, personal, and professional relationships among players.

Author Keywords
Social networking game; mobile game; mixed-reality game; social game; gamification.

ACM Classification Keywords
H.5.1 Information interfaces and presentation (e.g., HCI): Multimedia information systems; K.8.0 Personal Computing: Games.

Introduction
The increasing ubiquity of mobile and online technologies allows game designers to seamlessly integrate real-life social interactions in digital games. Traditional

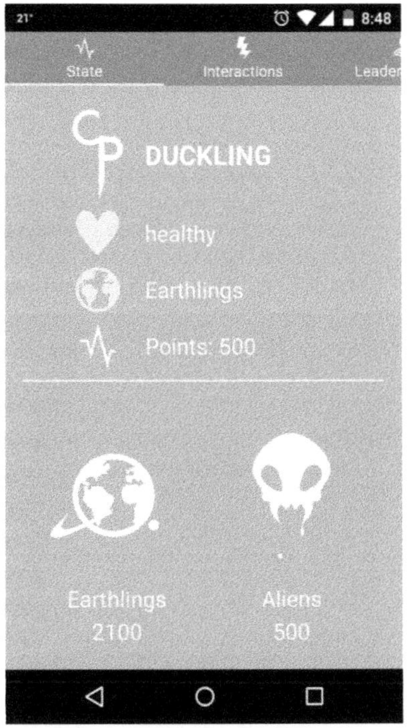

Figure 1. The status screen, where players can see their points, team, infection status, and the total score for both teams. The blue background colour is displayed to players with a healthy status.

The game application and video are available at: http://play.hcigames.com/playgue

methods of networking, such as the exchange of business cards or social media accounts, are still necessary but have become somewhat tedious. CHI PLAYGUE [4] is a mobile digital game designed to facilitate networking among conference attendees, encouraging them to build personal and professional connections with members of the community. It is designed to augment the conference space with an alternate reality, creating a narrative scenario of a virtual alien invasion that can be influenced by the players' actions. Players can decide to aid the alien invaders or defend against them by interacting and networking with other conference attendees. This way, CHI PLAYGUE gamifies conference networking by exploring social interactions on a shared physical space.

Similar applications or games have been previously presented aiming to increase social interaction and networking. *Flashbulb* [1] casts players into the role of *paparazzi*, requiring them to photograph specific attendees as a conversational icebreaker. However, this concept only encourages players to interact with particular targets. In CHI PLAYGUE, interaction with any other attendee yields in-game progress, providing an incentive to form as many connections as possible. *Snag'em* [3] provided similar motivation, offering points to players for growing their social network. CHI PLAYGUE enhances this motivation by embedding in-game rewards in an exciting narrative context. Cooperative team mechanics further enhance sociality, maximizing the design's social impact. *Whova* [5] is a mobile application for event networking that includes features such as business card exchange, chat, and agenda. However, it does not feature a gamified layer to motivate attendee engagement as CHI PLAYGUE does. Ku and Spruyt [2] have designed a game to help break the ice for starting conversations between conference attendees. However, their game did not support people to truly get to know each other.

Gameplay

CHI PLAYGUE facilitates social interaction for participants. The game's narrative emphasizes that players must form social connections to create a structured data cloud protecting the planet from alien invaders. Aliens were chosen as an universally accessible narrative context, giving players of diverse cultural backgrounds a recognizable antagonist to unite their efforts. The invaders are also carriers of a highly contagious biological agent, which has invisibly contaminated a small, random subsample of the player population. This creates a dynamic similar to the virus transmission themes of the wildly popular *zombie* genre. As gameplay develops, sick players are able to infect healthy players, flipping their allegiance to the invading alien forces. Defected players can also be cured, rejoining the Earth defences. As the game progresses, the two teams (*Earthlings* and *Aliens*) struggle to keep hold of their ranks, forming social connections to increase their score. The ultimate goal is to secure the victory of a player's chosen faction. At the end of the conference event, the team with the strongest network (highest cumulative score) wins, determining the fate of the planet within the narrative context of the game.

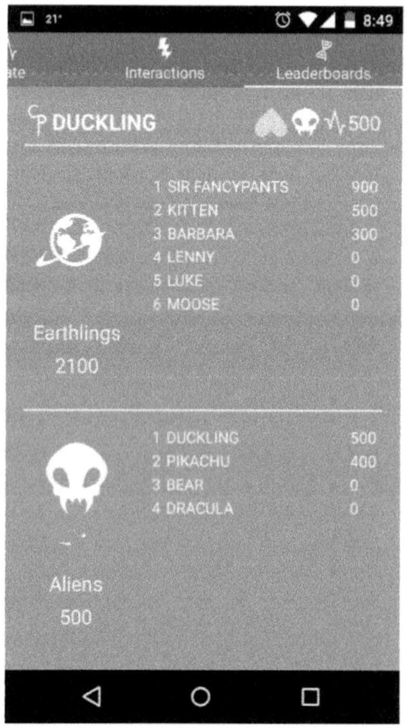

Figure 2. The leaderboards screen, where players can view the best scores of players from each team. The red background colour is displayed for turned players.

CHI PLAYGUE gameplay has the potential to evolve rapidly. The population begins as healthy members of the Earth faction; however, a small portion of players are randomly selected to be infected. The outbreak is handled by the server backend. The initial infection is invisible, so these players have a chance to unknowingly spread the infection. After six hours, silently infected players progress to a visibly sick state. Those that have interacted with these players, then find themselves in an uncertain situation. As interactions continue to occur, the infection and the cure both possess the potential to spread rapidly through the population. Players can adopt different social strategies lead their team to victory, as described by Tondello et al. [4].

New to this version: While players strive for their team's supremacy, CHI PLAYGUE encourages them to talk with other players (with whom they interact) to learn about them and their research. At random intervals, the game asks the player a random question about one of the other players they have scanned before. If they answer the question correctly in the allowed time, both players earn points. If they did not gather the required information when the players first talked, they have the chance to seek the other person out to ask for the missing. However, since time has passed, players earn less points when this happens. Players are able to see the business card information of other players they have scanned. They are also able to automatically follow other players' Twitter account or connect with them on LinkedIn. Additionally, players can leave short testimonials or comments about other people they have scanned. The testimonials can be read by people who received it in the game's interface.

Surfaces and Spaces

Players are invited to download CHI PLAYGUE on their *iOS* or *Android* devices. They receive a business card with a unique QR code serving as in-game identification. Player motivation comes from the promise of a shared social experience occurring inside the conference venue and the competitive drive to see themselves, or their team, rise to the top of the leaderboards and emerge victorious in the game's narrative. During registration for the game, CHI PLAYGUE asks players to enter their business card, LinkedIn, and Twitter information, and some questions about their research or facts about them. This enables a deeper networking experience between players. The game's user interface consists of the *status screen* (see Figure 1), the *history screen*, and *leaderboards* (see Figure 2). The gameplay mechanics consist of interactions between players. During interactions, a player scans the identification of another (see Figure 3), earning points for both players and potentially changing their health status based on each player's current condition. The rate at which the alien infection is spread or cured depends on each players' current infection status. A more thorough description was presented by Tondello et al. [4]. At any one time, the cumulative score of a team is determined by the scores of its current members.

A large monitor display needs to be set up at a prominent location of the conference venue to show the teams' scores. The display highlights the new social connections that were made or strengthened by players by randomly showing some of the testimonials people left in the game (see Figure 4).

Figure 3. A player scans the QR code of other player to earn points for their teams.

Figure 4. A large monitor display is used to show players the overall progress of the *Earthlings* and *Aliens* factions, the conference attendees business cards (to encourage other players to seek them out and talk to them) and the testimonials players have entered after interacting with other players.

Innovations

Since portability and accessibility were essential qualities in a game targeting a large active population, the mobile platform was a natural choice. CHI PLAYGUE is run through server-side operations and a mobile app. The mobile application, which runs on most *iOS* or *Android* devices, is a lightweight layer that retrieves information from the web server and presents it within the app's user interface. It handles the scanning of other players' QR codes and the server processes them.

The simplicity of the interaction mechanic is designed to provide opportunities for conference attendees to meet, converse, create new contacts, and have positive, playful, and social experiences. Thus, technological devices help to foster real-world interactions between the conference attendees. Players are provided with an open invitation to initiate conversations with others. Leaderboards encourage engagement and progression, conferring special gameplay advantages to socially prolific players. The exchange of business cards and the questions about people's research encourage the development of meaningful social connections, which may result in real-world collaboration.

CHI PLAYGUE uses the space of a conference venue, augmented with the attendees' own mobile devices and a mixed-reality virtual narrative, to motivate attendees into social networking. The use of a public large display can further redirect the attendees' attention to the game and provide an extra fun and motivation layer. In the future, we plan to collect data to evaluate how effective CHI PLAYGUE is at engaging conference attendees in new social interactions.

Conclusion

The main goal of CHI PLAYGUE is to liven up the casual social interaction essential to conferences. The innovative gameplay provides playful ways to meet and interact with people. As a result, conference attendees have additional opportunities to become familiar with one another's works and to form new social and professional connections. CHI PLAY integrates digital technology through mobile devices and large displays, the shared space of the conference venue, and social interactions to foster social networking.

Acknowledgements

Gustavo Tondello thanks the CNPq, Brazil, and the University of Waterloo for his funding. Rina Wehbe thanks the Cheriton School of Computer Science, University of Waterloo, and NSERC for her funding. Dr. Nacke's research is supported by his NSERC Discovery Grant (RGPIN-418622-2012), NSERC CREATE: SWaGUR, Mitacs Accelerate, and SSHRC IMMERSe (895-2011-1014, IMMERSe).

References

[1] Entrepreneurial Game Studio. *Flashbulb*. http://egs.excite.drexel.edu/flashbulb/.

[2] Ku, D. & Spruyt, J. *Designing of ICE: Interactive Co-located Events*. Independent thesis Advanced level. Umeå University (2016).

[3] Powell, E., Stukes, F., Barnes, T., and Lipford, H.R. Snag'em: Creating Community Connections through Games. In *IEEE PASSAT and SocialCom 2011*, IEEE (2011) 591-594. doi:10.1109/PASSAT/SocialCom.2011.229.

[4] Tondello, G.F., Wehbe, R.R., Stahlke, S.N., Leo, A., Koroluk, R., Nacke L.E. CHI PLAYGUE: A Networking Game of Emergent Sociality. In *Proc. of CHI PLAY 2015*, ACM (2015) 791-794. doi:10.1145/2793107.2810265.

[5] Whova. *Whova*. https://whova.com/

Single-Handed HandMark Menus: Rapid Command Selection on Tablets

Md. Sami Uddin
Department of Computer Science
University of Saskatchewan
Saskatoon, SK S7N 5C9, Canada
sami.uddin@usask.ca

Carl Gutwin
Department of Computer Science
University of Saskatchewan
Saskatoon, SK S7N 5C9, Canada
gutwin@cs.usask.ca

ISS '16, November 06-09, 2016, Niagara Falls, ON, Canada
ACM 978-1-4503-4248-3/16/11.
http://dx.doi.org/10.1145/2992154.2996871

***Please Note**: This is an Extended Abstract entry for Demo at ISS 2016. It accompanies a fully refereed article that can be found in the ISS 2016 Main Proceedings.*

Abstract
Although rapid command selection is important for touch devices, only a few techniques allow accelerated selection while still providing a large command set. HandMark menus [3] propose the use of the hands as landmarks for fast memory-based selection. However, the original HandMark menus for tables rely on bimanual operation - not suitable for tablets, and earlier studies provided only limited evidence for the value of hand-based landmarks as a reference frame for spatial memory. We introduce adapted HandMark menus that can be operated with one hand (while the other hand holds the tablet); the new version changes bimanual selection operations into sequential actions with one hand. Three studies of these HandMark menus showed that using the hand as a landmark significantly improved performance and allowed fast spatial memory development, even with one-handed use. Our work extends HandMark menus and shows that they are an effective selection method for tablets, and provides new evidence about the value of the hands as a spatial landmark for interaction.

Author Keywords
Command selection; landmarks; tablets; spatial memory.

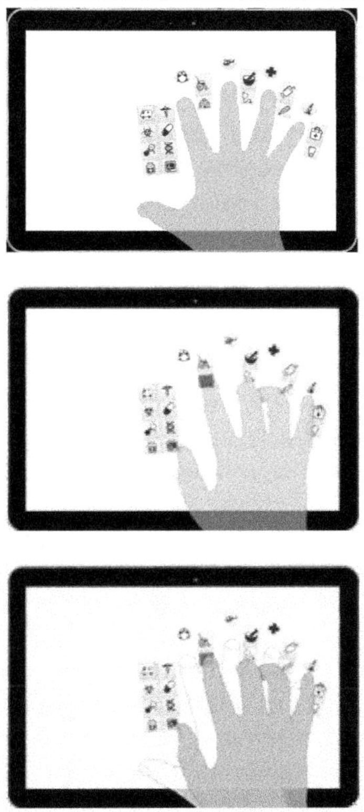

Figure 1. HandMark-Finger selection technique: (top) menu invocation, (middle) item selection after visual search, and (bottom) rapid selection with two sequential actions – one to invoke the menu, and another to select an item.

ACM Classification Keywords

H.5.2. Information interfaces (e.g., HCI): User Interfaces.

Introduction

Similar to traditional WIMP systems, fast command selection is also important for touch devices, but techniques that allow quick operation for experts (e.g., shortcuts, hotkeys) are uncommon on touch interfaces. One promising approach to providing a higher performance ceiling for experts involves the use of spatial location memory (e.g., [1, 2, 3]) – once users learn command locations in a spatially-stable interface, they can make quick selections based on memory rather than visual search.

Landmarks provide anchors for people's spatial memory when they move from novice to expert command selections – for example, people can remember items at the corners of a grid better than they remember items in the middle. A few touch-based selection techniques have considered landmarks and spatial memory as mechanisms for improving performance. For example, the FastTap technique [1] lets people make selections using a multi-touch tap on a grid of items; the structure of the grid provides an external reference frame for remembering command locations (e.g., "top left"). The limited structure and size of the grid, however, means that FastTap provides only a few landmarks, and cannot accommodate a large number of commands (only 20 items in a 4x5 grid [1]).

A more recent technique uses a rich source of landmarks on a touch interface – the user's hands – to assist the development of spatial learning and to increase the number of available commands. *HandMark menus* are a bi-manual technique that takes advantage of the user's knowledge of their own hand, and uses the hand as a reference frame (i.e., a landmark) for locating commands [3]. In these techniques, one hand is used as the anchor for the menu, and the other hand is used to perform rapid selection of an item.

However, there are several limitations to previous work on the HandMark approach. First, the techniques require bi-manual operation, which is feasible for tabletop systems but inappropriate for tablet use in mobile settings (where one hand is needed to hold the device). Second, previous studies did not strongly focus on the spatial learning that takes place with HandMark menus – they compared HandMark menus only to toolbars at the edge of a table, rather than pop-up menus that are invoked at the user's work location. Therefore, it is still unclear whether HandMarks are fast because of the hand landmarks, or because of other factors such as the simple proximity of the commands.

We address these limitations by presenting two new versions of HandMark menus (Figures 1 and 2) that work in a single-handed fashion, and are therefore appropriate for settings where a touch tablet is held in one hand and manipulated with the other. We then report on studies that we conducted to understand spatial learning performance and the value of the hand as a landmark with the one-handed versions of the technique. Our results show that both types of HandMark menus work well in single-hand operation, both allow quick development of spatial memory, and both are strongly preferred by participants.

Our work makes two main contributions. First, our adaptation of bimanual HandMark menus provide two

Design Goals: The goal was to build a spatial memory-based interaction technique that will accelerate the command selection process. It should be feasible for one-handed mobile tablet use: menu can be operated with the dominant hand while the non-dominant hand holds the tablet. In addition, it should support large number of commands.

Menu Capacity and Layout: *HM-Finger* uses the spaces around the hand (top of fingers) and between fingers to display **20** items. *HM-Multi* uses a spatially-stable 4x5 grid to show **80** items (**4 tabs**, and **20** items in each tab) in the space between thumb and index finger.

Chunking Actions: HM uses chunking of two sequential steps (*menu invocation* and *item selection*), rather than a bimanual parallel action. It works as double clicking for expert users.

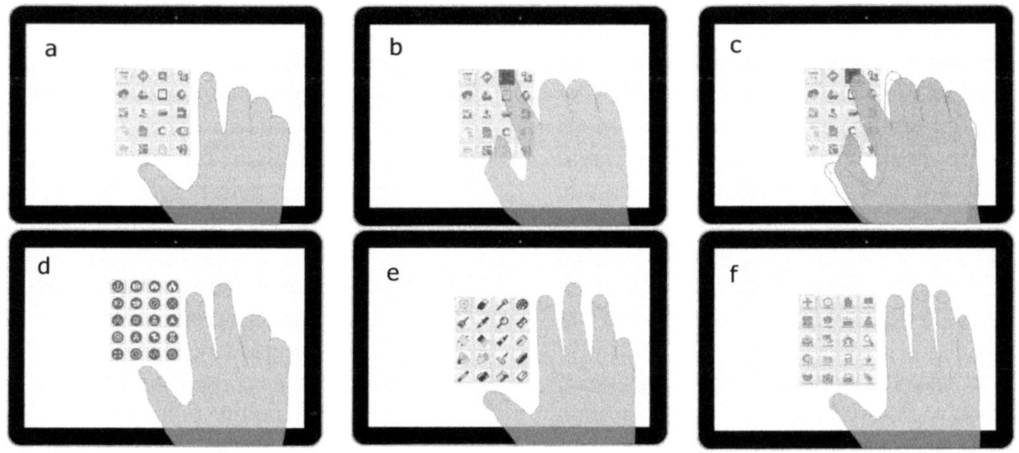

Figure 2. HandMark-Multi selection technique: (a) invoking the 1st item set by placing index and thumb in 'L' shape posture, (b) item selection after visual search, (c) rapid selection with two sequential actions – menu invocation, and item selection, and (d-f) invoking 2nd, 3rd, and 4th item sets with specific finger combinations respectively.

selection techniques for mobile tablets that are fast and that have high capacity. Second, our studies provide new evidence that using the hand as a landmark is feasible and effective for the development of spatial-memory based selection techniques, even with one-handed use.

Design 1: HandMark-Finger for Tablets

Similar to the original version of HM-Finger for tables [3], our version of HM-Finger for tablets provides modal access to a set of commands (Figure 1). The need to hold a tablet with one hand requires to deviate from the bimanual technique and enable command selection using one hand only. In our adapted technique, commands can be displayed by touching down all the fingers of one hand in any order, spreading the hand to provide space between the fingers. The user can rotate and move the menu in any direction by moving their fingers. Unlike the earlier technique, however, command selection is carried out by lifting the fingers from the screen and touching the desired item with any finger. Command icons remain displayed until a selection is made (or until the menu is dismissed by touching on another part of the tablet).

Design 2: HandMark-Multi for Tablets

We also adapted the earlier HM-Multi technique for use on tablets. HM-Multi uses a similar command selection mechanism as HM-Finger, but differs in the placement and number of commands. There are four sets of commands, invoked by placing a specific number of fingers (in addition to the index finger and thumb) on the screen in an L-shaped posture (Figure 2). The menu follows the user's hand as it rotates or moves. HM-Multi uses a spatially-stable 4x5 grid to show commands in the space between thumb and index.

Demo Task: An icon appears on the middle of the screen after pressing *start* button. The user then needs to invoke the HM menus and select the item with any finger of the right hand.

Three Studies: *Study 1* was conducted to understand the performance of the two single-handed HM menus. *Study 2* explored the value of hands as landmarks for both HMs. *Study 3* analyzed the interference of item associations between two applications.

Demonstration Setup

The demonstration setup consists of two versions of the single-handed HM menus, which were implemented for a Microsoft Surface Pro 4, with a 12.3-inch multi-touch 2736 x 1824 screen, and running Windows 10. The interfaces were written in JavaFx. The demo consists of a series of tasks, each involving serial touch actions for both HM menus.

Discussion & Future Work

After the implementation, we conducted three studies with 19 participants on both HM techniques. Our studies clearly revealed that our adapted HandMark menus can be used effectively for single-handed interactions on tablets, and they support rapid spatial memory development. The main results from the studies are:

- Study 1 showed that both HM-Finger and HM-Multi allowed rapid selections.
- Study 2 showed that using hands as landmarks improved performance: HM-Finger and HM-Multi outperformed a non-landmarked technique, and were strongly preferred by participants.
- Studies 2 and 3 showed that overlapping targets are not a main source of errors, but that location memory can degrade because of time or because of interference.

Despite the limitations of single-handed use, our adapted HM menus for tablets performed similarly to the original HM menus for tables. Therefore, we believe that interaction designers, as well as people interested in spatial-memory-based rapid selections in HCI can benefit from this demonstration.

In future work, we will continue the development of the HandMark approach, and will test the technique in real-world settings and compare it to other memory-based selection methods. We are also interested in comparing HandMark menus to systems that introduce artificial landmarks on the display surface, and in potentially combining the two approaches. Finally, we will run studies that focus on issues of decay and interference in memory-based methods, to better understand how techniques like HMs can be deployed in the real world.

Acknowledgements

This work was supported by NSERC. Our special thanks to Ashley Coveney who recruited participants and ran the studies for this work.

References

[1] Gutwin, C., Cockburn, A., Scarr, J., Malacria, S. and Olson, S.C. Faster command selection on tablets with FastTap. In *Proc. CHI '14*, 2617-2626.

[2] Scarr, J., Cockburn, A., Gutwin, C. and Bunt, A. Improving command selection with CommandMaps. In Proc. *CHI '12*, 257-266.

[3] Uddin, M.S., Gutwin, C. and Lafreniere, B. HandMark Menus: Rapid command selection and large command sets on multi-touch displays. In *Proc. CHI '16*, 5836-5848.

Instruction for Paper-cutting : A System for Learning Experts' Skills

Takafumi Higashi
Japan Advanced Institute of Science and Technology
1-1, Asahidai, Nomi
ishikawa, Japan
s1620021@jaist.ac.jp

Hideaki Kanai
Japan Advanced Institute of Science and Technology
1-1, Asahidai, Nomi
ishikawa, Japan
hideaki@acm.org

Abstract
In this study, we contribute to the support of skills for novices making handmade crafts. We focus on the craft steps that involve paper-cutting. Novice has to take long time to get skillful. The study of this area has problems in that it is difficult to learn the experts' skill. We examined about the differences between novices and experts. As a result, we have identified that *Maintaining Suitable Pressure with Knife* is the most important basic factor for novices. Moreover, *frequency of knife usage* considerably determines whether sufficient or insufficient pressure is applied. The novices exhibit a greater frequency than the experts. Therefore, we developed a system based on a tablet computer and a stylus. The system has a function : *Displaying Applied Pressure*. This function helps a novice to apply the correct pressure with the stylus as an expert would do. Moreover, we have experimented with the system with several groups. As a result, the subjects who practiced with the system could be better close to experts' that.

Author Keywords
Paper-cutting; Craft art; Handmade crafts; Study supporting; Supporting for producing handmade items; Creative activity support

ISS '16, November 06-09, 2016, Niagara Falls, ON, Canada
ACM 978-1-4503-4248-3/16/11.
http://dx.doi.org/10.1145/2992154.2996872

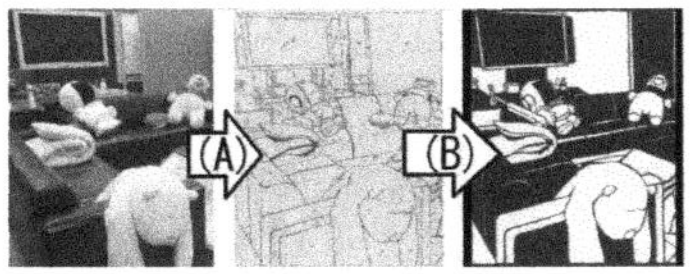

Figure 1: Steps of performing paper-cutting (A) output design, (B) output creation.

Figure 2: Examples of the utility knife.

Figure 3: Experimental pattern configures.

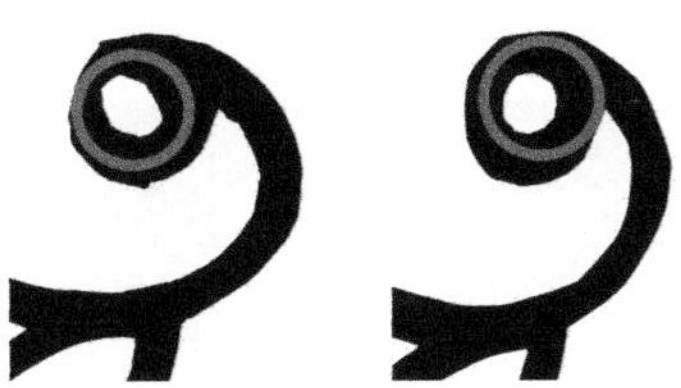

Figure 4: Circles which cut by novice (Left) and expert (Right).

ACM Classification Keywords
H.5.m [Information interfaces and presentation (e.g., HCI)]: Miscellaneous.

Introduction
Paper-cutting involves two steps (Figure 1), (A) *output design* : the creator outputs a design for paper-cutting, and (B) *output creation* : the creator cuts the paper with a utility knife. Many researchers have studied (A), that is, the automatic output of a design like paper- cutting by computer graphics (CG). This study proposed a method to produce artistic paper-cutting renderings of human portraits from photographs [4]. One study proposed a system that could render a paper-cutting design from anything from a line drawing to a painting [1]. Especially, we focused on the steps of (B) output creation in paper-cutting. Paper-cutting is a painting technique for production only in the action to cut. Paper-cutting, that is, the cutting of paper with a utility knife, is involved in the creation of handmade crafts. Utility knife is better suited for cutting of fine details (Figure 2). Action to cut using the tool is one of the dexterity to be natured from craftwork. The production of the paper-cutting is very important to maintain the sufficient pressure on the knife. The pressure is adjusted by the movement of a fingertip. Such dexterity is not only in manufacturing, including the paper-cutting, the ability to use the fingertip skillfully is important. Using a hand dexterity is important in thinking the development of childhood. The hand is concentrated peripheral nerves, to encourage the development of the brain by the stimulus to the fingertip, the child's intelligence is enhanced. Many researchers have studied tearing and drawing on dexterity. This researcher has shown to be effective in the control of the muscles of the fingertip dexterity by utilizing tablet computer [3]. One studies, as haptic studies using objects, have developed something called Tako-pen [2]. This is to be the suction pressure stimulation to the user's finger by adding the pressure to the pen, let the learned of the technique for controlling the delicate force to the user. In addition, study conducted by a brush-like input device to the tablet terminal [5]. We focused on the adjustment of the pressure of the knife when creating the paper-cutting, the development of a system for foster the dexterity of the fingertip as a basic stage to develop the system. We have been planning to develop a system whereby the user cut a paper with a knife on a tablet computer screen that displays the pressure applied. In this paper, we propose the support system that displays the pressure the user applies.

Differences between novices and experts
We examined the importance of the pressure. Our subjects were 5 experts and 5 novices. The experts (males, with an average age of 26.5 years, three of whom had four years' experience, while the others had six and nine years' experience, respectively) were working as artists and teachers in paper-cutting courses. The novices (males, with an average age of 23 years) had never attempted paper-cutting. The subjects cut a pattern has A4 in size, with a line thickness of 5mm and 70 negative spaces. (Figure 3).

As a result, the novices have a greater *frequency of knife usage* than the expert. In this examination, the results showed the average of the frequency and the standard deviation(SD) (Table 1). The novices exhibit a greater frequency because they can not maintain the ideal pressure with the knife (Figure 4). Some novices cut coarse curves with enough pressure to cut smooth curves. Moreover, if the novices apply insufficient pressure, they have to repeatedly make the same cut. The experts, being

Figure 5: Materials used for practicing paper-cutting ; A : Cat, B : Frog, C : Koala, D : Gorilla, E : Camel, F : Lion.

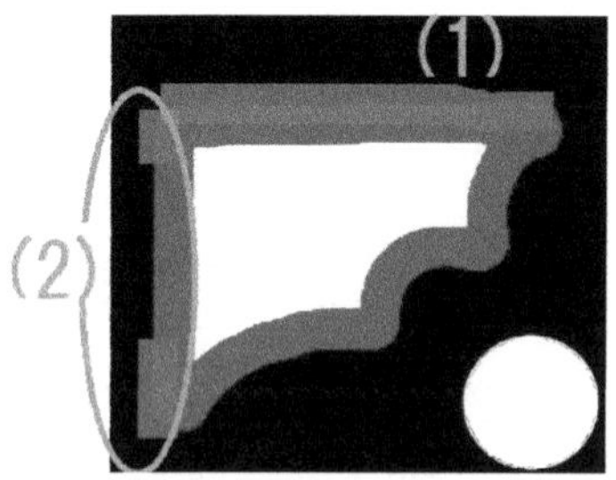

Figure 6: The function displaying tracer; (1) appropriate pressure, (2) inappropriate pressure.

conscious of the pressure needed for the paper-cutting, can produce work of high quality. We found that the experts were able to make a cut with a single pass through *maintaining suitable pressure* in an experiment.

Table 1: Average time and standard deviation for task shown in Figure 3 for novices and experts.

subjects	the frequency		the cutting time (minitues)	
	average	SD	average	SD
novices	436.3	41.5	96.5	30.1
experts	112.8	15.6	35.7	5.5

Rouded to the first decimal place

Support system

We developed a system based on a tablet computer (iPad by Apple) and a stylus (Jot Touch4 by Adonit) for learning the experts' skill. This stylus can measure pressure. The system has a function : *Displaying Applied Pressure* and six patterns (Figure 5). The users use the tablet computer and the stylus instead of the paper and the knife. They trace the pattern displayed on the tablet computer. The system displays the pressure traced by the users.

The system has six patterns which measures 10 cm x 10 cm. These patterns were devised by experts for novices. Each pattern introduces the factors affected by pressure. If one pattern incorporates many factors, the pattern is categorized as being difficult. One of pattern has large polygons to learn user to use.

Function : Displaying Applied Pressure
This stylus can measure pressure in the 2048 levels. In particular, range of pressures between 1300 and 2000 should normally be applied. This range is an area close to the pen pressure of a skilled person. This function displayed user's pressure of stylus by applying an appropriate pressure (Figure 6). However, it does not display any line if user applies with inappropriate pressure The users repeat the tracing of the spaces indicated by the red lines with applying a suitable pressure. Therefore, the user can learn one of experts' skills : maintaining suitable pressure with the knife.

Experiment

We applied the system to 3 groups, each with 5 subjects Our experiment is straightforward: 1) the subjects perform paper-cutting in the traditional manner, with Figure 8 and a knife; 2) each subject practices with six patterns, and 3) they repeat the first step. In Step 2, three groups of six subjects each were given varying practice methods: G1 (practice the system with the functions (Figure 9)); G2 (practice only performed with knife and paper); G3 (practice only perform paper-cutting as given explanations experts' skill) in Step2.

We compared changes observed exhibited between Step1 and Step3. The results showed the average of the frequency and the SD (Table 2). The results vary in terms of the average and SD of the frequency (Figure 10). Only members of G1 were able to apply sufficient pressure in Step 3; the others cut coarse curves with insufficient pressure. Moreover, G1 subjects were able to apply sufficient pressure in Step 3 (Figure 7 (A)) and maintain the stylus pressure in Step2. Measurements from G1 revealed that the system helps users to improve their skill levels, such that the pressure they apply in paper-cutting approaches that of experts (Figure 7 (B)).

Figure 8: Experiment pattern.

Figure 9: The system in use.

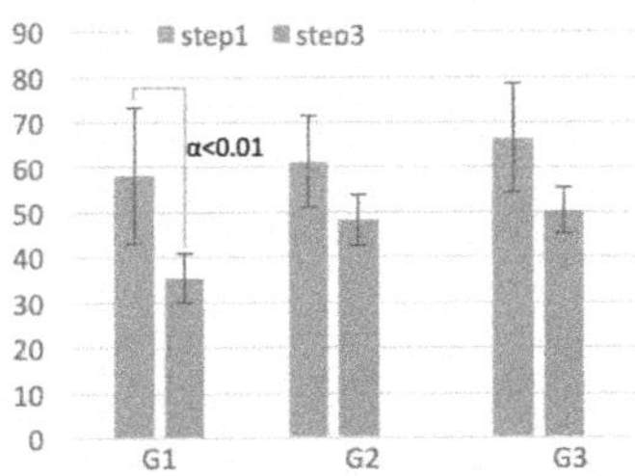

Figure 10: Change in the average frequency of knife usage.

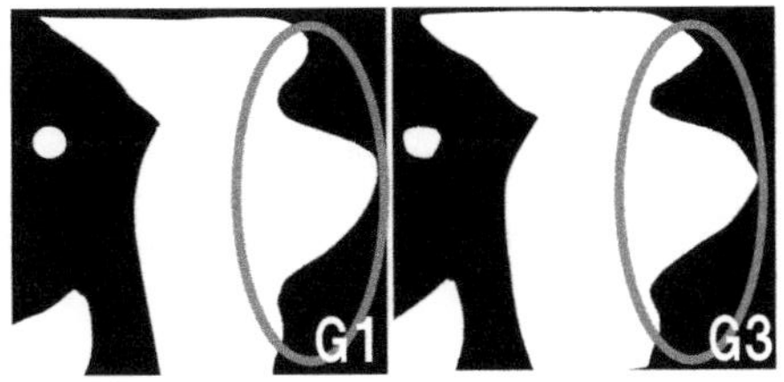

Figure 7: Experiment pattern and example of results, created by G1 (instruction from the system) and by G3 (instructed by an expert).

Table 2: Average frequency of knife usage.

subjects	Step1		Step3	
	average	SD	average	SD
G1	58.2	15.0	35.4	4.3
G2	61.3	10.2	48.2	5.7
G3	66.4	12.1	50.3	5.1

Rouded to the first decimal place

Conclusion and future works

We proposed a support system for assisting with the learning of experts' skills for paper-cutting. We experimented with the differences between novices and experts. As a result, *maintaining suitable pressure with the knife* is the most important basic skill that a novice should master. The frequency of knife usage is closely related to whether sufficient pressure is applied. Therefore, we developed a system based on a tablet computer and a stylus. The system has a function : Displaying Applied Pressure. This function helps a novice to apply the correct pressure with the stylus as an expert would do. Moreover, we performed experiments with the system with several groups. As a result, the subjects who practiced with the system could decrease the frequency of knife usage. In our future studies, we will research the degree of difficulty for attaining those skills that are somewhat more difficult to attain than the basic skills, with the goal of allowing users to attain a skill level that more closely approximates that of an expert. We have been planning to develop a system whereby the user cut a paper with a knife on a tablet computer screen that displays the pressure applied.

Acknowledgment

This work was supported by JSPS KAKENHI Grant Number JP16K00269.

References

[1] Hongyuan, L., and Weilin, Q. The conversion from line drawings to paintings with paper-cutting designs. In *Computer Science and Network Technology (ICCSNT), 2011 International Conference on*, vol. 4 (Dec 2011), 2783–2786.

[2] Konyo, M. Tako-pen: A pen-type pseudo-haptic interface using multipoint suction pressures. In *SIGGRAPH Asia 2015 Haptic Media And Contents Design*, SA '15, ACM (New York, NY, USA, 2015), 16:1–16:2.

[3] Larsen, L., Jensen, T., Christensen, M., Langberg, H., and Nielsen, J. Changes in corticospinal drive to spinal motoneurones following tablet-based practice of manual dexterity. *Physiological Reports 4*, 2 (2016). CURIS 2016 NEXS 044.

[4] Meng, M., Zhao, M., and Zhu, S.-C. Artistic paper-cut of human portraits. In *Proceedings of the 18th ACM International Conference on Multimedia*, MM '10, ACM (New York, NY, USA, 2010), 931–934.

[5] Ryokai, K., Marti, S., and Ishii, H. I/o brush: Drawing with everyday objects as ink. In *Proceedings of the SIGCHI Conference on Human Factors in Computing Systems*, CHI '04, ACM (New York, NY, USA, 2004), 303–310.

Exploring Genetic Mutations on Mitochondrial DNA Cancer Data with Interactive Tabletops and Active Tangibles

Roozbeh Manshaei
Nauman Baig
Sean Delong
Shahin Khayyer
Brien East
Synaesthetic Media Lab
Ryerson University
Toronto, ON, Canada
roozbeh.manshaei@ryerson.ca
nauman.m.baig@ryerson.ca
sean.delong@ryerson.ca
skhayyer@ryerspn.ca
beast@ryerson.ca

Ali Mazalek
Synaesthetic Media Lab
Ryerson University
Toronto, ON, Canada
Georgia Tech
Atlanta, GA, US
mazalek@ryerson.ca

ISS '16, November 06-09, 2016, Niagara Falls, ON, Canada
ACM 978-1-4503-4248-3/16/11.
http://dx.doi.org/10.1145/2992154.2996873

Abstract
Biological data is becoming so complex, it is difficult for scientists and other professionals to interpret and understand it. New tools are needed to better support the manipulation and understanding of data in order to improve analyses and the formation of new hypotheses. Tangible mtDNA is an active tangible and tabletop system that allows multiple users with diverse expertise to collaborate in exploring and understanding mitochondrial DNA sequencing data in breast cancer patients. In an evaluation of the system, 5 expert biologists found it to be effective for data exploration and useful in supporting understanding, collaboration and discussion of DNA datasets.

Author Keywords
Tangible interaction; tabletop interaction; active tangibles; bioinformatics; visualization; genetic mutations; cancer; clinicopathological features; collaboration; exploration.

ACM Classification Keywords
H.5.2 Information Interfaces and Presentation (e.g., HCI): User Interfaces—*input devices and strategies*, *interaction styles*, *user-centered design*; I.6.7 Simulation and Modeling: Simulation Support Systems—*environments*.

Challenge: Scientists have driven the creation of increasingly complex and sophisticated biological datasets, but the ability to understand and interpret this data remains limited.

Need: New methodologies that link insights from the fields of data-visualization, human-computer interaction (HCI), machine learning, and genomics.

Our solution: Design, develop and evaluate tangible interaction techniques for visualizing, analyzing, and interpreting cancer genomic data. Our system is called **Tangible mtDNA**.

Introduction

The significant growth of biological data in recent years has resulted in a need for new tools that can assist scientists and clinicians in interpreting this data in order to support decision-making and the formation of hypotheses. We present Tangible mtDNA, a tangible tabletop system for exploring large sets of genomic mutation data of cancer patients. When dealing with large datasets, such as genomic data, it is difficult to understand its significance and make appropriate hypotheses unless the data is effectively visualized. Through the use of active tangibles and an interactive tabletop, users are able to visualize the data while manipulating its parameters. Our research provides three main research contributions. First, the system introduces novel visualizations and interactions to encourage collaborative exploration of clinicopathological feature effects on mutation trends; users of varying expertise are provided with a common language for understanding and discovery. Second, the system contributes to the use of active tangibles for data exploration; active tangibles provide fast and efficient methods for manipulating and filtering data through a combination of tangible and gestural interactions, both on and off the table. Third, the visualization of gene-based and patient-based networks through clustering methods that are accessed via tangible and tabletop interactions provides insight into the relationships between mitochondrial genes or between patients based on mutation patterns.

Background

One of the most important organelles present within eukaryotic cells is the Mitochondria. It is responsible for energy production through the process of cellular respiration and has several other crucial functions that have a direct effect on different parts of the body. A dysfunctional mitochondria can result in diseases such as Cardiomyopathy, Alzheimer's and Breast cancer. It is caused by mutations within the mitochondria DNA (mtDNA) sequence. Mutations are processes by which a person's DNA sequence is permanently altered. When they occur in certain regions of the DNA sequence called genes, they are referred to as genetic mutations. Each gene codes for unique functional proteins within a tissue, thus a genetic mutation can cause an abnormality in the tissue's functions and result in the mentioned diseases. The aim of our research is to develop a tangible platform that facilitates collaborative analysis of mtDNA sequence mutation data to understand its effects on such diseases.

Related Work

With the rise of complex biological data, there has been an emphasis on the importance of GUI visualization techniques for the understanding and accessibility of such data. A comprehensive review by Schroeder et al. [1] provides a selection of effective and common genomics visualization tools and discusses their limitations, such as the lack of data comparison and collaborative exploration.

Many of the tangible and/or tabletop systems that have been developed for biological data visualization partially implement the suggestions discussed by Schroeder et al. [1]. G-nome Surfer [2] is a multi-touch tabletop interface for browsing gene expression data, but is limited to on-screen interactions and was designed for non-experts. SynFlo [3] is a tangible museum exhibit that allows visitors to engage in a bio-design activity through passive and active tangibles. However, its focus is on teaching concepts of synthetic biology

Figure 1: When two active tangibles are placed on the multi-touch surface, available CP features are displayed.

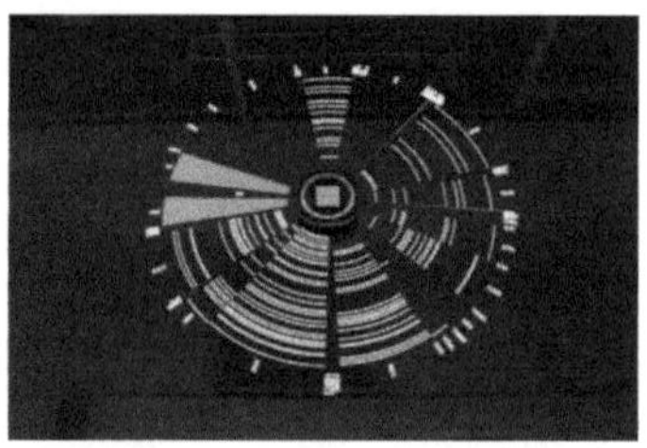

Figure 2: mtDNA genes and number of mutations for each patient arc in those genes.

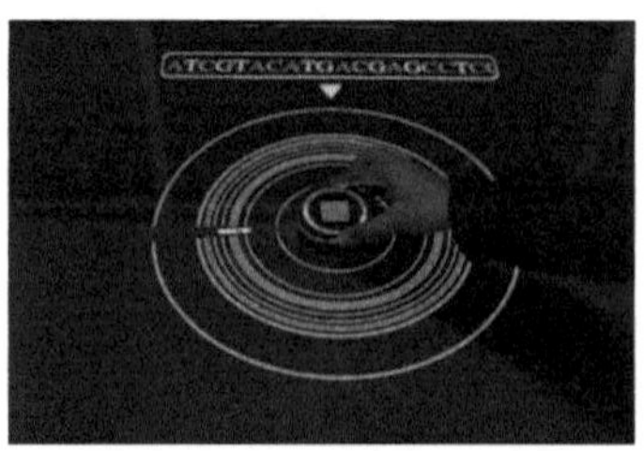

Figure 3: Mutation location, along with the nucleotide fraction at the pointer.

rather than on exploration and investigation of big data by experts. Eugenie [4] is multi-touch and tangible interface for browsing big datasets. Its limitations include restricted table space, along with users' lack of understanding of the system's designed interactions. Sparse Tangibles [5] is a collaborative system that employs an interactive tabletop and custom active tangibles to assist expert users in better understanding experimentally extracted gene interactions. The system provides a limited number of filters and computational methods for exploration and does not support the comparison of organisms in terms of interactions.

In contrast to previous work, our system allows users to access large-scale cancer sequencing datasets along with associated CP features, compare the DNA sequences of large numbers of cancer patients, and explore the relationships between CP features and mutation patterns, all while supporting collaborative exploration of the data. It also supports clustering as a computational method for further exploration.

Tangible Mitochondrial DNA

Tangible mtDNA uses an interactive tabletop that supports multi-touch interactions, as well as the manipulation of active tangibles on the screen. The system also supports off-screen interactions through the active tangibles, which include a small multi-touch screen and additional sensors. These interactions include stacking, shaking, and on-screen gestures such as tapping, swiping, dragging, rotating and pinching.

The system consists of three main layers of dynamic visualizations, which are displayed as doughnut charts around the active tangibles. Upon placement of an active tangible on the tabletop, the user is presented with the first layer of visualization, namely the clinical feature selection menu. This layer prompts the user to select one of the different CP feature options, which are displayed as segments around the doughnut chart (Fig.1). Upon selection of a feature in the first layer, the visualization transitions to the second layer, namely the gene selection menu. This layer displays the mutation data while acting as the selection menu for genes (Fig.2). The doughnut chart is partitioned based on the number and size of regions (genes, gene overlaps, and introns) within the mtDNA, which have labels positioned on the outside of the arc. The chart consists of multiple arcs, each of which represents a patient affected by breast cancer. If a patient has a mutation in a region, it is given a color based on a color scale ranging from yellow to red, where yellow represents a single mutation whereas red represents the maximum number of mutations. Users can also select a specific region for individual viewing by simply tapping on it. This takes them to the third layer, which visualizes the mutation data for only the selected region. Aside from colored arcs, this layer also indicates the location of each mutation using red dots (Fig.3). It also displays a dynamic sequence bar at the top of the chart, which changes as the active tangible is rotated.

The system also allows for query construction through stacking of the active tangibles. Upon selecting the CP features on two tangibles, users can stack the tangibles to display the visualizations in parallel, allowing them to compare the mutation data filtered by the two CP features (Fig.4). They can also perform K-means clustering of data, which displays a force directed network of genes or patients, allowing users to observe any gene-gene or patient-patient relationships based on the mutation data sample. This is done by selecting

Figure 4: mtDNA region mutation counts in parallel after stacking two active tangibles.

Figure 5: The result of gene-based (left) and patient-based (right) clustering.

either gene-based or patient-based clustering on the mobile menu along with the *K* number of clusters. Selecting gene-based clustering clusters the data into K clusters according to their similarities between genes based on the mutation trends. Patient-based clustering does the same procedure but performs clustering between patients rather than genes (Fig.5).

Technical Implementation

Tangible mtDNA is a mainly web-based platform implemented using front-end web development tools such as HTML, CSS, and JavaScript. System components include the active tangibles, the interactive tabletop, and communication processes. The active tangibles, called Actibles, consist of a smartwatch and built-in sensors within a custom case. They allow for interactions such as stacking, tilting, and on-screen gestures. The interactive table uses a LCD MultiTaction display, with built-in IR sensors for touch and marker detection. A fiducial marker is placed on the bottom of each Actible for detection purposes. A Node.js server on the table allows real-time bidirectional communication between the table and the Actibles.

Expert Feedback

Five biological experts from distinguished clinical research facilities were invited to evaluate the system. Overall the experts found the concept to be novel and important to the exploration of genetic mutations. They mentioned that the system was unique, intuitive, and effective for navigating through data. They especially appreciated certain aspects of the system, such as stacking to compare mutation trends and the ability to explore the dataset collaboratively. However, they felt the system needed to include more statistical analysis tools in order to be truly useful in their practice.

Conclusion and Future Work

We presented a novel tangible and tabletop visualization system for exploring mtDNA mutation data within a breast cancer dataset. The system aims to support biologists and physicians by allowing them to collaboratively investigate large-scale cancer data. Five experts found the system to be intuitive, to be effective for information navigation, and to facilitate learning and collaboration between users. In future, we will expand the system to support the study of the whole human genome, include mutation datasets from different cancers to allow comparison of mutation patterns across diseases, and incorporate more statistical tools.

Acknowledgements

This work is supported by NSF grant IIS 1320350, NSERC, and the Canada Research Chairs program. We thank Dr. Hopkins and Dr. Boutros (Ontario Institute for Cancer Research) and Dr. Kyan (York University).

References

1. Schroeder, M.P., et al (2013). Visualizing multidimensional cancer genomics data. *Genome medicine*, 5(1), 1.
2. Shaer, O., et al (2010, April). G-nome surfer: a tabletop interface for collaborative exploration of genomic data. *CHI'10* (pp. 1427-1436). ACM.
3. Okerlund, J., et al (2016, February). SynFlo: A Tangible Museum Exhibit for Exploring Bio-Design. *TEI'16,* (pp. 141-149). ACM.
4. Grote, C., et al (2015, January). Eugenie: Multi-Touch and Tangible Interaction for Bio-Design. *TEI'15,* (pp. 217-224). ACM.
5. Arif, A.S., et al (2016, February). Sparse Tangibles: Collaborative Exploration of Gene Networks using Active Tangibles and Interactive Tabletops. *TEI'16,* (pp. 287-295). ACM.

ControllAR: Appropriation of Visual Feedback on Control Surfaces

Alex Jones
University of West England
alexander9.jones@live.uwe.ac.uk

Florent Berthaut
Univ. Lille, Inria, UMR 9189 - CRIStAL
florent.berthaut@univ-lille1.fr

ISS '16, November 06-09, 2016, Niagara Falls, ON, Canada
ACM 978-1-4503-4248-3/16/11.
http://dx.doi.org/10.1145/2992154.2998580

Abstract
Despite the development of touchscreens, many expert systems for working with digital multimedia content, such as in music composition and performance, video editing or visual performance, still rely on control surfaces. This can be due to the accuracy and appropriateness of their sensors, the haptic feedback that they offer, and most importantly the way they can be adapted to the specific subset of gestures and tasks that users need to perform. On the other hand, visual feedback on controllers remains limited and/or fixed, preventing similar personalizing. Here we present ControllAR, a novel system that facilitates the appropriation of rich visual feedback on control surfaces through remixing of graphical user interfaces and augmented reality display.

Author Keywords
ControllAR; Augmented Reality; Visual Feedback; Appropriation; Hardware controllers; Control surfaces;

ACM Classification Keywords
H.5.m [Information interfaces and presentation (e.g., HCI)]: Miscellaneous.

Introduction
Following on from analog devices for the control of video and audio signals, many software applications for the

creation and processing of digital media rely on control surfaces / hardware controllers composed of sensors such as groups of buttons, rotary and linear encoders. They are often preferred to touchscreens because of the variety of gestures that the sensors allow and because of the haptic feedback that they provide and to tabletops with tangibles because of their compactness. Combined with software applications with graphical user interfaces (GUI), these controllers are now used in many contexts : live electronic music performances, music recording/mixing/composition, visual performances, video editing, lights control, and so on. Over time, users of these systems develop expert skills specific to the hardware and software components.

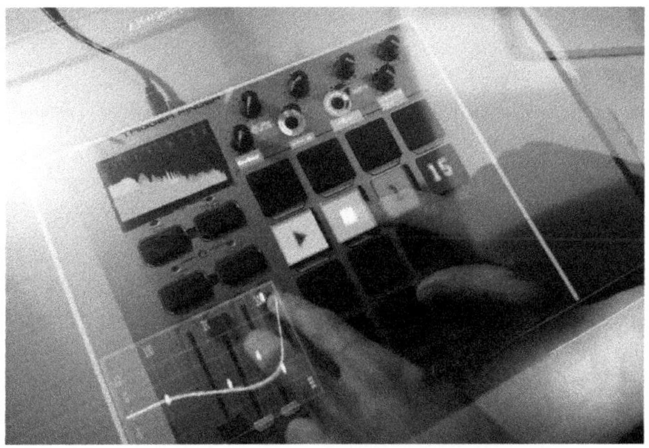

Figure 1: ControllAR allows for the appropriation of visual feedback on control surfaces. When looking through the optical combiner, remixed elements from the GUI appear overlapped with sensors on the control surface.

Most importantly, they also customize the systems to match the specific subset of gestures and tasks that they need to perform. As pointed out by [2], *"the focus of personalized interfaces is generally to improve core task performance, that is, performance of completing known or routine tasks"*. This appropriation happens at multiple levels: choice/design of the control surfaces, choice of the mappings between the sensors and the application parameters, choice of content in the application. These levels of appropriation relate to the control, i.e. the flow of data from the user to the system. In any interactive system, the feedback, that is the flow of data from the system, is essential to an expert user. In particular, visual feedback plays an important role in the interaction with the system as for example demonstrated by Liu et al. [4].

However, compared to other components described above, the appropriation of visual feedback remains limited. GUIs usually include detailed representations of application content and parameters but: a) their arrangement can not be modified to fit the controller or users' actions; b) they may present more details than actually needed during actions, leading to cognitive overload; c) they are distant from the physical sensors and from the performed gestures. Therefore visual feedback on control surfaces is a growing request from users, as suggested by the apparition of embedded LEDs on most commercial controllers and of screen on the most expensive ones. However appropriation of this feedback is constrained either in the choice of the displayed feedback, the resolution of this feedback or its placement on the controller. For example, in the case of MIDI controllers, some include a limited number of programmable color LEDs (Keith McMillen Quneo, Berhinger BCR 2000) around/behind sensors, others a higher-resolution screen with fixed (Ableton Push, M-audio Trigger Finger) or even programmable content (Akai MPC Touch), but distant from the sensors.

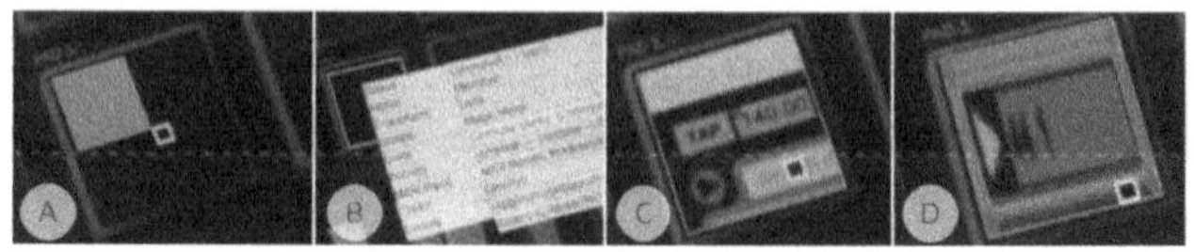

Figure 2: Appropriation process with ControllAR : A) Users draw a *zone* (overlapping a sensor or not) on the controller, and B) select one of the opened desktop windows. C) A *cut* of the selected window is then mapped inside the zone and D) can be dragged and zoomed to match any part or widget of the GUI

ControllAR

Contrary to existing controllers for which the choice of content and spatial organization of visual feedback is limited, ControllAR allows users to select and place freely graphical elements on any controller. It relies on the fact that the GUIs of multimedia software applications, designed for mouse and keyboard interaction, provide rich and high resolution feedback on the manipulated content. With ControllAR, *cuts* can be made in these GUIs and placed in *zones* directly on the controller with either a projector or an optical combiner. This design process is detailed on Figure 2. Figure 1 depicts a control surface augmented with a number of visual elements designed by the user.

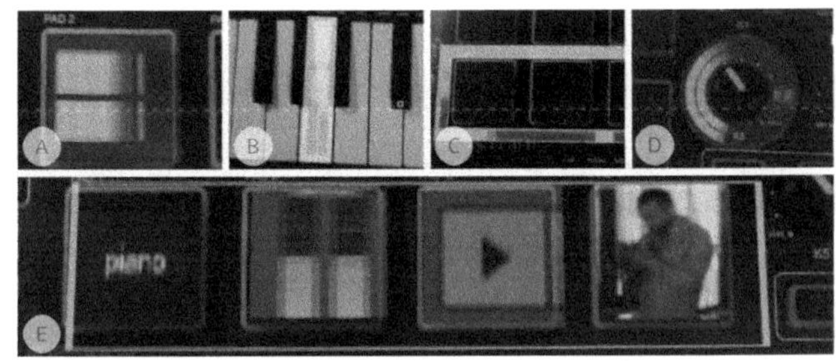

Figure 3: (A-B-C-D) Adaptation of a VU meter *cut* to four different sensors. E) Different types of *cut* content on similar sensors: static output, dynamic output, input/output and external

Our approach requires a series of steps to ensure that the GUI content can be transformed and displayed as visual feedback on the controllers. On the contrary to most research on GUI remixing (see [5] or [6]), in ControllAR this content needs to be transformed to match the sensors on which users want to add visual feedback. We draw inspiration from the Transmogrification project [1] and propose a set of transformations that correspond to the shapes of sensors commonly found on hardware controllers. As depicted on Figure 3, a filled square cut of a VU meter that fits a rubber pad (3.A), can be stretched and rotated to fit a piano key (3.B) . It may also be transformed to a frame that surrounds a group of sensors (3.C) or to a circle that wraps around a knob (3.D) .

Hardware setup

Appropriation of visual feedback is also limited by the displays used on existing control surfaces. The solution we present here is the use of an optical combiner. Drawing inspiration from [3], a half-silvered mirror is placed between a screen displaying the cuts and the controller, as

Figure 4: A two-monitors arm holds a monitor and an optical combiner. Their orientation are set so that the reflection of the screen in the combiner overlaps with the control surface placed below it.

shown on Figure 4. Moreover we designed it with adjustable orientations and positions for the mirror and screen so that the angles between them and between the mirror and control surface are equal. When looking through the mirror, the screen and controller surface align perfectly. This solution preserves the visual quality (i.e. resolution and shape) of the *cuts* and prevents occlusions. When interacting with the controller, users see both their hands and augmentations, therefore ensuring that the visual feedback remains visible at all time. To ensure compactness, in the case of performance applications, the user's laptop can itself be used as the screen above the mirror, removing the need for an additional screen.

Perspectives

ControllAR makes it possible to investigate current and potential practices of appropriation of visual feedback by allowing users to quickly design the feedback from existing visual components. Studying the long-term effect of this appropriation on users' practices is one of the main goals of the project. Another interesting perspective for this work is the extension to handheld / gestural controllers. In fact, many users now combine traditional sensors with gestural sensing (i.e. distance, 3D position, poses, gestures) which provide even less visual feedback on their impact on application parameters. Tracking these controllers or body parts and projecting correctly transformed *cuts* on them could lead to better integration in multimedia production systems.

References

[1] Brosz, J., Nacenta, M. A., Pusch, R., Carpendale, S., and Hurter, C. Transmogrification: Causal manipulation of visualizations. In *Proceedings of the 26th Annual ACM Symposium on User Interface Software and Technology*, UIST '13, ACM (New York, NY, USA, 2013), 97–106.

[2] Findlater, L., and McGrenere, J. Beyond performance: Feature awareness in personalized interfaces. *International Journal of Human-Computer Studies 68*, 3 (2010), 121–137.

[3] Hachet, M., Bossavit, B., Cohé, A., and de la Rivière, J.-B. Toucheo: Multitouch and stereo combined in a seamless workspace. In *Proceedings of the 24th Annual ACM Symposium on User Interface Software and Technology*, UIST '11, ACM (New York, NY, USA, 2011), 587–592.

[4] Liu, C., Huot, S., Diehl, J., Mackay, W., and Beaudouin-Lafon, M. Evaluating the benefits of real-time feedback in mobile augmented reality with hand-held devices. In *Proceedings of the SIGCHI Conference on Human Factors in Computing Systems*, CHI '12, ACM (New York, NY, USA, 2012), 2973–2976.

[5] Stuerzlinger, W., Chapuis, O., Phillips, D., and Roussel, N. User interface façades: towards fully adaptable user interfaces. In *Proceedings of the 19th annual ACM symposium on User interface software and technology*, ACM (2006), 309–318.

[6] Tan, D. S., Meyers, B., and Czerwinski, M. Wincuts: Manipulating arbitrary window regions for more effective use of screen space. In *CHI '04 Extended Abstracts on Human Factors in Computing Systems*, CHI EA '04, ACM (New York, NY, USA, 2004), 1525–1528.

Actibles: Open Source Active Tangibles

Brien East
Synaesthetic Media Lab
Ryerson University
beast@ryerson.ca

Ahmed Arif
Synaesthetic Media Lab
Ryerson Universtiy
asarif@ryerson.ca

Sean DeLong
Synaesthetic Media Lab
Ryerson Universtiy
sean.delong@ryerson.ca

Ali Mazalek
Synaesthetic Media Lab
Ryerson University
mazalek@ryerson.ca

Roozbeh Manshaei
Synaesthetic Media Lab
Ryerson University
roozbeh.manshaei@ryerson.ca

ISS '16, November 06-09, 2016, Niagara Falls, ON, Canada
ACM 978-1-4503-4248-3/16/11.
http://dx.doi.org/10.1145/2992154.2996874

Abstract
Actibles are an open source hardware/software platform for creating active tangibles. Actibles contain a smartwatch core, which eases both hardware and software development, and enables application developers to leverage various web technologies. The smartwatch core is augmented by custom hardware that enables an expanded set of tangible interactions, including shaking, tilting, stacking and neighboring, as well as on-screen gestures and integrated LED feedback. Actibles can be used both independently or in conjunction with other devices, such as interactive tabletops. We describe the Actible's technical specifications and demonstrate several example applications.

Author Keywords
Active tangibles; tangible interaction; tabletop interaction; open source platform; smartwatch; LED feedback.

ACM Classification Keywords
H.5.2 [Information Interfaces and Presentation (e.g., HCI)]: User interfaces – *input devices and strategies*, *interaction styles*, *prototyping*.

Introduction
Tangible, embedded and embodied interaction (TEI) is emerging as an important field within human-computer interaction research. TEI often enlists the use of physical

Figure 1: Actibles are a smartwatch-based active tangibles platform that incorporates additional sensors to detect stacking and neighboring, as well as LED feedback. The image shows an assembled Actible.

Figure 2: Three Actibles in the Sparse Tangibles application. The Two Actibles in the forefront are stacked to filter datasets on the tabletop surface.

objects, or "tangibles", to control and represent digital information [7]. Many TEI applications utilize passive (i.e. unpowered) tangibles. When augmented with a fiducial marker on their base, these tangibles can be tracked on interactive display surfaces (e.g., [2]). Today, there is an increased interest in active (i.e., powered) tangibles due to the increased number of interactive capabilities they can provide both independently and in combination with other interactive devices and surfaces.

Related Work

Building on existing work on active tokens [9] and active tangibles [1], we define active tangibles as physical input-feedback devices that can be used independently or in conjunction with other hardware or software to tangibly augment interaction with integrated displays, sensing, or actuation capabilities. Data querying and browsing (e.g., [1, 3, 8]), media content editing (e.g., [12]), and scientific discovery (e.g., [5]), are some of the tasks that have been explored using active tangibles.

While most applications that employ active tangibles have created custom built devices with interactive capabilities designed for specific application scenarios, there are also some examples of active tangibles that aim to serve as a general platform for diverse applications. The most notable example are the Siftables [4], which were later offered commercially as 'Sifteo Cubes'. Sifteo cubes were small cube-shaped units that included wireless communication, IrDA communication, a graphical display and sensing. They could detect a variety of interactions including shaking, neighboring, tilting, and tapping. However, Sifteo cubes did not offer support for multi-touch or stacking.

Interactions

Actibles (Fig. 1) are capable of five major types of interactions. These include tangible interactions, on-screen interactions, physical controls, tabletop interactions, and visual feedback. Developers can combine these interactions to yield new innovative interactions for specific applications.

Tangible Interactions
The following gestural interactions [10] with a single Actible are supported: tilting shaking and flipping. Additionally, gestural interactions with multiple Actibles include: bumping, neighboring and stacking.

On-Screen Interactions
Actibles incorporate a smartwatch display, and as a result, all common on-screen manipulations are offered to the end user. These on-screen interactions include double-tap, swipe and pinch/spread.

Physical Controls
Only one physical control is available on an Actible. This is a tactile button. Its main purpose is to switch power on or off, but it can also be used as a selector. This selector could be used in an application to confirm menu selection while scrolling via tilting or dialing.

Visual Feedback
Two types of visual feedback are offered on the Actible platform, namely a smartwatch display and an RGB LED array arranged in a ring. The smartwatch display may be used to view menus, messages or images, while the LED ring may be used to display colorful animations, dial feedback, or to affirm interaction detection.

Tabletop Interactions
By attaching fiducial markers to the bottom of the Actibles, they can be tracked on the surface of interactive displays such as ReacTIVision [2] or MultiTaction. All common tabletop interactions are supported on the surface such as moving, placing, removing and rotating, as well as all the Actible interactions described above.

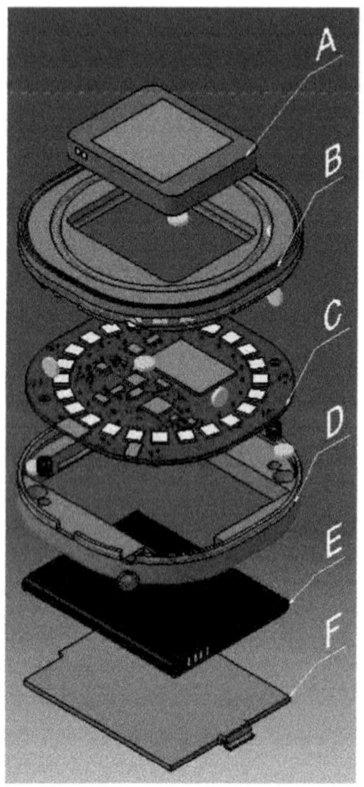

Figure 3: An exploded assembly view of the Actible showing: A) smartwatch, B) upper case, C) circuit board, D) lower case, E) smartphone battery, and F) battery cover.

Technical Implementation

The four main components that make up an Actible are the case, LG G smartwatch, circuit board, and battery (see Fig. 3). The case (Fig. 3, parts B, D and F) is designed to house the circuit board and battery. A battery access panel at the bottom of the Actible allows for quick battery removal (Fig. 3, part F). The inside walls of the case are designed with small inserts to house the magnets required for hall effect magnetic detection. This magnetic detection is what allows for stacking, bumping and neighboring.

A squircular shape was selected for the Actible's geometry. This design encourages intuitive neighboring, stacking and bumping alignment, while maintaining a circular geometry for dials and other circular or concentric applications.

In order for an Actible to function, basic software and firmware must be installed. The firmware is written in Arduino, however AVR support is inherent. Firmware is provided to interface the microcontroller with the power supervisory circuit in order to power on and shut down. Also, wifi module communication routines serve to establish wireless communication. Libraries are provided to enable developers to build applications based on the interactions described above.

Application Examples

Two existing projects, Active Pathways [6, 11] and Sparse Tangibles [1], were updated to use Actibles, demonstrating how previous active tangible implementations (in this case Sifteo cubes and custom tangibles, respectively) can be replaced with the Actibles platform. Tangible mtDNA is a new project that demonstrates the versatility of the Actibles.

Active Pathways

Active Pathways (Fig. 4) is a tangible tabletop biochemical modeling application. This application enables the construction and simulation of biochemical reaction networks using the Actibles both on and off the tabletop. A reaction network is constructed by "binding" the Actibles to components of the model (e.g., molecules, enzymes, reactions) and then touching them together to create connections between them. The tabletop interface allows the users to "fit" (i.e. match) of their model to selected experimental datasets by tweaking parameters such as reaction speeds and molecule concentrations with the Actibles.

Sparse Tangibles

Sparse Tangibles (Fig. 2) is a collaborative gene interaction network exploration application that employs Actibles for both on- and off-table interactions. Swipe and touch interactions on the Actibles are used to browse the BioGrid database and select genes/organisms. Actibles can also be associated with different filters (e.g., filter by number of connections), whose parameters are adjusted on the Actible display. A filter is then applied by stacking the given Actible on top of another Actible that is bound to a specific gene or organism. Placing gene/organism Actibles on the table displays the selected part of the network on the surface around them.

Tangible mtDNA

Tangible mtDNA (Fig. 5) allows users to gain insight into mitochondrial DNA sequencing mutation data for breast cancer patients using Actibles in combination with an interactive tabletop. Interactions such as shaking, stacking, and on-screen gestures with the Actibles both on- and off-table are used to query and visualize the dataset, which includes both DNA sequence/mutation data and clinicopathological features of patients. Users can also bind multiple Actibles to different queries within the dataset, and compare them by stacking the Actibles and placing them on the table. This results in a visualization that aligns the queries, so that users can, for example, compare mutations across genes based on different clinical features of patients.

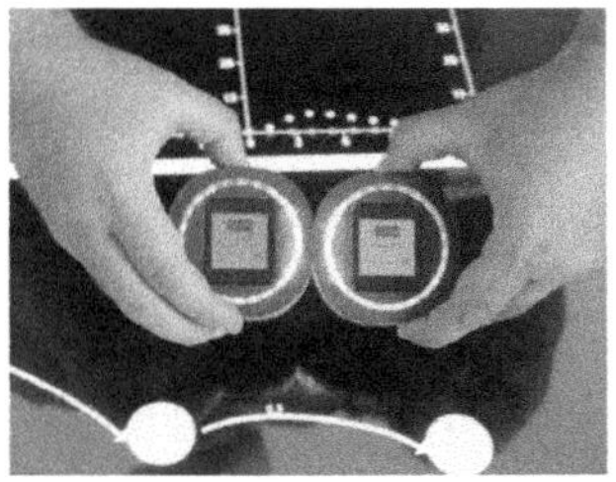

Figure 4: Two Actibles in an off-table interaction in the Active Pathways application. Each Actible is bound to a molecule and touching them together creates a reaction between the two molecules.

Figure 5: An Actible being used on table to view DNA sequence mutation data in the mtDNA application

Conclusion

We presented Actibles, an open-source platform that enables researchers and developers to better explore the use of active tangibles in their applications. We described the interactions and technical implementation of the platform, and demonstrated its use in three application scenarios. Future work will involve hardware improvements, including the exploration of newer smartwatch models as well as open source/open hardware single board solutions.

Acknowledgements

This work has been supported by in part by NSF-IIS grant 1320350, the Canada Research Chairs program, NSERC, the Canada Foundation for Innovation, and the Ontario Ministry of Research and Innovation.

REFERENCES

[1] Arif, A. S., Manshaei, R., Delong, S., East, B., Kyan, M., and Mazalek, A. Sparse tangibles: Collaborative exploration of gene networks using active tangibles and interactive tabletops. In *Proc. TEI '16*, ACM (2016), 287–295.

[2] Kaltenbrunner, M., and Bencina, R. reactivision: a computer-vision framework for table-based tangible interaction. In *Proc. TEI '07*, ACM (2007), 69–74.

[3] Klum, S., Isenberg, P., Langner, R., Fekete, J.-D., and Dachselt, R. Stackables: Combining tangibles for faceted browsing. In *Proc. AVI '12*, ACM (2012), 241–248.

[4] Merrill, D., Kalanithi, J., and Maes, P. Siftables: Towards sensor network user interfaces. In *Proc. TEI '07*, ACM (2007), 75–78.

[5] Okerlund, J., Segreto, E., Grote, C., Westendorf, L., Scholze, A., Littrell, R., and Shaer, O. Synflo: A tangible museum exhibit for exploring bio-design. In *Proc. TEI '16*, ACM (2016), 141–149.

[6] Shaer, O., Mazalek, A., Okerlund, J., Grote, C., and Ullmer, B. Tangible interaction with large data sets using active tokens. In *CHI '15 Workshop, Exploring the Challenges of Making Data Physical* (2015).

[7] Ullmer, B., and Ishii, H. Emerging frameworks for tangible user interfaces. *IBM Syst. J. 39*, 3-4 (July 2000), 915–931.

[8] Ullmer, B., Ishii, H., and Jacob, R. J. Tangible query interfaces: Physically constrained tokens for manipulating database queries. In *Proc. INTERACT*, vol. 3 (2003), 279–286.

[9] Ullmer, B., Ishii, H., and Jacob, R. J. K. Token+constraint systems for tangible interaction with digital information. *ACM Trans. Comput.-Hum. Interact. 12*, 1 (Mar. 2005), 81–118.

[10] Valdes, C., Eastman, D., Grote, C., Thatte, S., Shaer, O., Mazalek, A., Ullmer, B., and Konkel, M. K. Exploring the design space of gestural interaction with active tokens through user-defined gestures. In *Proc. CHI '14*, ACM (2014), 4107–4116.

[11] Wu, A., Yim, J.-B., Caspary, E., Mazalek, A., Chandrasekharan, S., and Nersessian, N. J. Kinesthetic pathways: A tabletop visualization to support discovery in systems biology. In *Proc. C&C '11*, ACM (2011), 21–30.

[12] Zigelbaum, J., Horn, M. S., Shaer, O., and Jacob, R. J. K. The tangible video editor: Collaborative video editing with active tokens. In *Proc. TEI '07*, ACM (2007), 43–46.

Proxemics-Based Visual Concepts to Attract and Engage Public Display Users: Adaptive Content Motion and Adaptive User Shadow

Victor Cheung
Systems Design Engineering
University of Waterloo
Waterloo, Ontario, Canada
victor.cheung@uwaterloo.ca

Stacey Scott
Systems Design Engineering
University of Waterloo
Waterloo, Ontario, Canada
stacey.scott@uwaterloo.ca

ISS '16, November 06-09, 2016, Niagara Falls, ON, Canada
ACM 978-1-4503-4248-3/16/11.
http://dx.doi.org/10.1145/2992154.2996875

Abstract

Large interactive displays presenting useful content responding to users' actions are becoming ubiquitous in public places such as museums and campuses. Being an integral part of the surrounding environment, a major design challenge is to first attract passersby's attention and entice them to interact. One promising approach is to incorporate proxemics parameters to guide how the content are visually presented. In this paper we describe the design of a field experiment using user-display distances in determining how visual content was displayed, and its deployment at a university campus with frequent foot traffic. We also offer some selection criteria for reference when conducting a field experiment with public large interactive displays.

Author Keywords

Public Large Interactive Displays; Proxemics; Interface Design; Field Experiment

ACM Classification Keywords

H.5.m. Information interfaces and presentation (e.g., HCI): Miscellaneous.

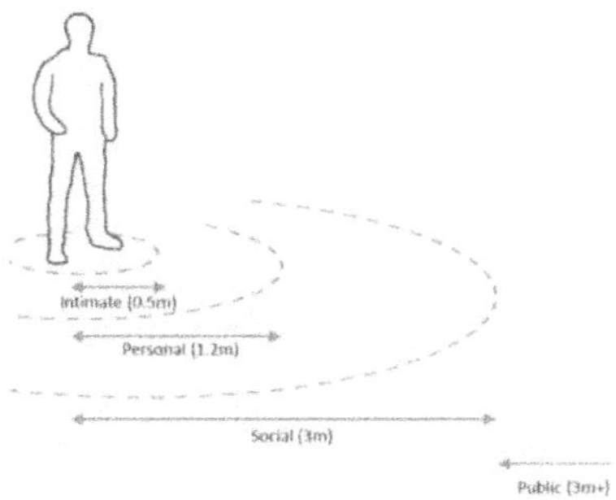

Figure 1. Depict of Hall's Proxemics Theory separating a person's behaviour into discrete proxemics zones of proximity.

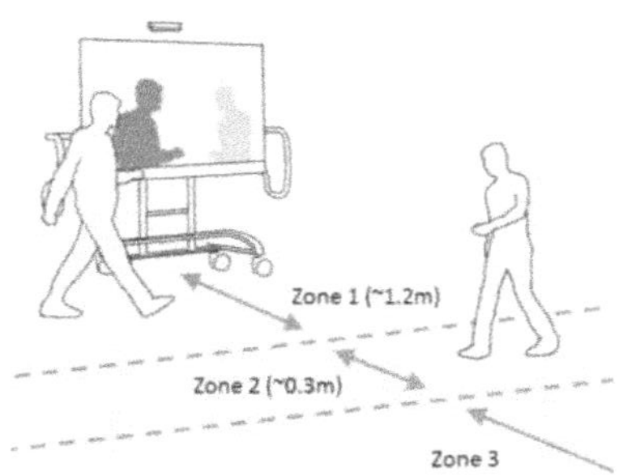

Figure 2. Zonal setup in the field experiment.

Introduction

Public Large Interactive Displays (PLIDs) have recently been adopted in many public places such as museums and campus, providing useful information (e.g. as part of an exhibit, campus map), and/or entertainment (e.g., mini-games). A commonly observed issue with such deployments, however, is that these displays often go unnoticed, and thus are underutilized [4, 6]. PLID designs must therefore first attract the attention of potential users and entice them to interact, or the display's usefulness will never be realized.

As more interactive techniques are available beyond multi-touch, PLIDs can now support various types of interactivity, for example, gestures [4], and proxemic interactions [1]. While allowing a greater interaction variety, these techniques might also help notifying passersby. In particular, the proxemic interactions system proposed by Ballendat et al. [1] provides proxemics parameters (e.g., distance, and orientation) that can be used to estimate the level of attention of a passerby, and adjust the visual content accordingly [7].

In previous work exploring the notion of combining proxemics parameters with visual content presentation to attract and entice users to a large display, we found that showing a user shadow, together with application content responding and adapting to user's proximity, showed promise in a laboratory setting [2]. Building on this result, we wished to further investigate the potential of these proxemics-based visual effects, both together and independently, in a more realistic public setting. This interactive demonstration showcases the proxemics-based visual concepts, namely Adaptive Content Motion and Adaptive User Shadow, that we developed and deployed as part of a field experiment to better understand their effectiveness in a public setting.

Proxemics Zones

Proxemic interactions are based on the *proxemics zones* by Hall [3] (see Figure 1), with which one can use the distance values to guide what level of details to be shown [7], or how visual stimuli are presented [2].

While other proxemics parameters (e.g., orientation, movement, identity) have been proposed [1] and could also be useful for such purpose [8], they often require more setup effort to be available (e.g., an elaborate tracking system with users wearing beacons [7, 8]). In balancing practicality and the information available, we opted to only use proximity (relatively simple to obtain with a depth sensor) as the proxemics parameter.

Combining proxemics zones and space available at the deployment location (discussed in the Deployment section), three zones were setup with boundaries of approximately 1.2m away, 1.5m away, and above 1.5m away from the display, as shown in Figure 2. As our research was primarily focused on the earliest stages of interaction (i.e., attracting attention and intriguing potential users to consider interacting with the display), we did not distinguish Intimate zone from Personal zone (see Figure 1), and combined them into a single zone (Zone 1 in Figure 2).

Visual Concepts

Extending our prior laboratory study [2], our field experiment focused on two main visual concepts, Adaptive Content Motion and Adaptive User Shadow.

In the Adaptive Content Motion concept, the speed of application content (images of our university campus) decreased in a stepwise manner as a passerby approached the PLID, so as to provide sufficient opportunities for interaction to occur, and the change

Figure 3. Illustration of the Adaptive User Shadow concept: Contrast of shadow increases when the passerby approaches the display, together with a natural scaling-up effect (proximity decreases from top to bottom).

more likely to be noticed. Speed for each content item was randomly chosen from between 11.3 to 22.5 cm/s as the starting speed, and was used when the passerby was at Zone 3 (furthest away from the PLID). When the passerby was at Zone 2, content would move at 60% of its starting speed; and at Zone 1 (closest to the display), it would move at 20% of its starting speed.

In the Adaptive User Shadow concept, a silhouette of the passerby was projected as if they were casting a shadow on the PLID. In contrast to a similar technique being used by Müller et al. [5] to increase the attraction power of a display and communicate its interactivity, we increased the contrast of the shadow continuously as a passerby approached the PLID. This visual contrast change was implemented by mapping the shadow's alpha value to 0 at 0.4m and 255 at 3.15m from the display. Furthermore, as a result of the perspective view of the camera used to render the silhouette, a passerby further away would project a smaller shadow, hence providing a natural scaling effect (Figure 3).

The field experiment also included a control condition, in which displayed content moved in a constant speed, and no user shadow was displayed.

Hardware and Software

A 164cm, multi-touch display (SMART[1] Kapp iQ 6065i) was used as the PLID, reporting up to four multi-touches as touch events to a connected Windows 8 PC (3.5GHz CPU, 16GB RAM, NVDIA Quadro K2200 display card) at a 1920x1080-pixels resolution. The surface was made using reinforced glass with metal enclosure, making it robust to frequent use and was mounted on a mobile stand of adjustable height (see Figure 4).

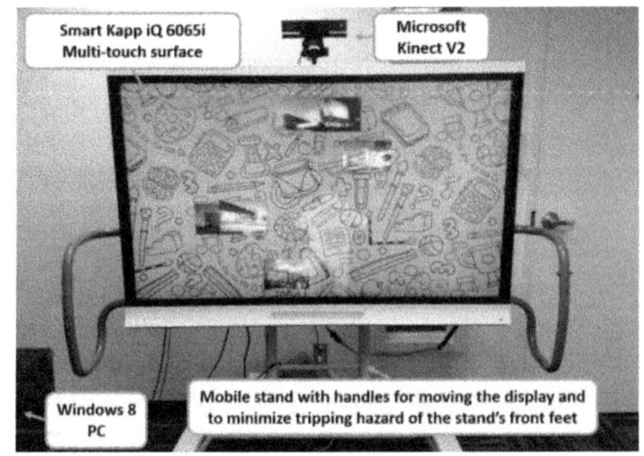

Figure 4. Hardware setup for the field experiment. The Kinect device was made visible by being installed on the top of the display. Content was photos of a university campus.

Visibly installed on top of the surface was a Microsoft Kinect V2, which measured the proximity of up to six passersby to a distance of 4.5m of millimetre precision. The proximity values were used by a custom software application developed using Unity 5[2] to determine the changes in speed for Adaptive Content Motion, and the changes in contrast for Adaptive User Shadow.

Summary of Deployment and Observations

Several criteria had to be met when determining a location for the field experiment, including 1) frequent foot traffic while possible for passersby to stay for a short period of time to interact, 2) a place for the researchers to observe the site unobtrusively, 3) power supply for the display to operate for several hours, and be accessible for transportation and storage of equipment over the duration of the experiment, and 4) legally and institutionally accessible to the researchers.

[1] http://smartkapp.com/en/products/kapp-iq

[2] http://unity3d.com/

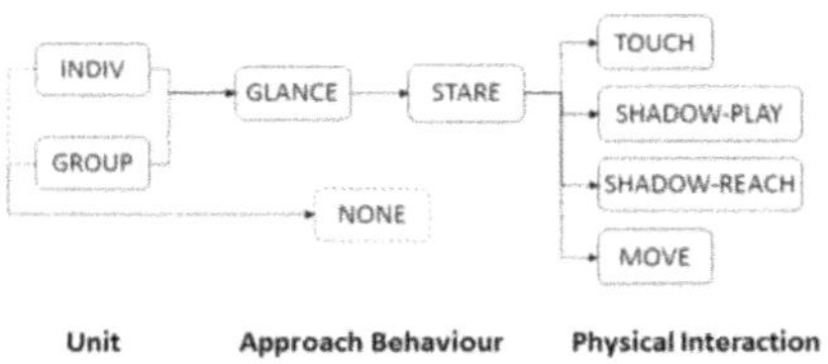

Figure 6. Annotation scheme of observable passersby behaviour used in the video analysis, indicating increasing levels of engagement from unknowing to attracted, and from attracted to engaged.

Figure 5. Deployment of the field experiment. The researchers (not shown in the figure) were stationed opposite to the display without any indication of a study in progress.

We decided to deploy the PLID in a lobby area of an Engineering building on our university campus that had an above-ground pedestrian pathway link between campus buildings (see Figure 5). Besides frequently traveled, this location satisfied all the above criteria.

The field experiment was conducted in an "in-the-wild" manner typical to studies of PLIDs [4–6], where interactions were captured using field notes, computer logs, and video recordings. Two researchers also observed from an unobtrusive location nearby, where students commonly sat at tables to study or complete assignments between classes. The collected video data was analyzed using an annotation scheme developed to identify recurring passerby behaviour. Log data were used to analyze system interaction, including user movement and dwelling in the space, and hand and body gestures made in front of the display. Overall, both visual concepts (independently and combined) were found to attract and entice interaction with the PLID, compared to the control condition. Both proxemics-based visual concepts increased users' length of stay (often called "holding power" in museum contexts) at the display over the control condition. The findings also showed that the visible Kinect device may have also attracted and enticed interaction from users, as many hand and body gestures in front of the display were observed, even in the absence of user shadows.

Conclusion

We present proxemics-based visual concept designs that adapt content's properties, namely, content speed and user shadow contrast and scale, based on users' proximity. Our deployment of these visual concepts found that they both effectively attracted passersby's attention in a public setting, and that they also showed some promise in enticing interaction. We hope to demonstrate their design and interactivity to conference participants and discuss potential strategies for refining their designs. We also hope to discuss extending the proxemic interactions approach to better facilitate user engagement, thereby leading to better utilization of public large interactive displays.

References

[1] Ballendat, T., Marquardt, N., et al. Proxemic interaction: designing for a proximity and orientation-aware environment. *Proc. ITS '10*, 121–130.

[2] Cheung, V. and Scott, S.D. Studying Attraction Power in Proxemics-Based Visual Concepts for Large Public Interactive Displays. *Proc. ITS '15*, 93–102.

[3] Hall, E.T. *The Hidden Dimension*. Anchor.

[4] Michelis, D. and Müller, J. The Audience Funnel: Observations of Gesture Based Interaction With Multiple Large Displays in a City Center. *Int. J. Hum. Comput. Interact.* 27, 6 (2011), 562–579.

[5] Müller, J., Walter, R., et al. Looking glass: a field study on noticing interactivity of a shop window. *Proc. CHI '12*, 297–306.

[6] Peltonen, P., Kurvinen, E., et al. "It's mine, don't touch!": interactions at a large multi-touch display in a city centre. *Proc. CHI '08*, 1285–1294.

[7] Vogel, D. and Balakrishnan, R. Interactive public ambient displays: transitioning from implicit to explicit, public to personal, interaction with multiple users. *Proc. UIST '04*, 137–146.

A Dynamic 3D Performance Space for Control of Virtual Musical Instruments

Matthew Cox
Eastman School of Music
Rochester, NY 14604, USA
mcoxvla@gmail.com

Andrew Hollenbach
Dept. of Computer Science
Rochester Institute of Technology
Rochester, NY 14623, USA
hollenbach.andrew@gmail.com

Joe Geigel
Dept. of Computer Science
Rochester Institute of Technology
Rochester, NY 14623, USA
jmg@cs.rit.edu

ISS '16, November 06-09, 2016, Niagara Falls, ON, Canada
ACM 978-1-4503-4248-3/16/11.
http://dx.doi.org/10.1145/2992154.2996877

Abstract
This work explores an intuitive, real-time music generation system and interface. We present a system that uses the real-time skeletal tracking provided by a Microsoft Kinect to generate complex musical compositions containing up to four tracks, with instruments represented in distinct physical spaces. The performer's position and movements are translated into cues that are relayed to Ableton Live for music generation. Finally, we experiment with an interface overlayed in physical space to provide real-time feedback to the user.

Author Keywords
Music; music generation; Kinect; projection interface; Ableton; virtual music instrument; VMI

ACM Classification Keywords
H.5.5 [Information interfaces and presentation (e.g., HCI)]: Sound and Music Computing - Systems

Introduction
In this demo, we present a virtual musical instrument (VMIs) [1] system that utilizes motion capture as the primary means of interface and control. The novelty of this system is three-fold. First, it presents a fine-grained VMI control system using the Kinect complete with pitch, volume, and filtering control. Second, it presents stage partitioning and looping

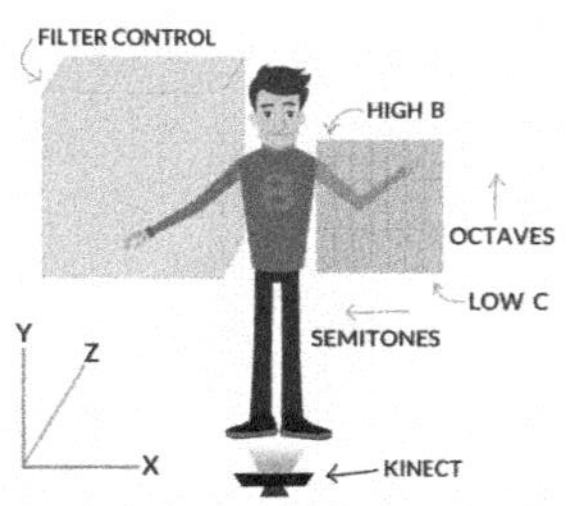

Figure 1: The coordinate system and gestures. As seen from the perspective of the Kinect, the x-axis extends to the left and right, the y-axis is the vertical axis, and the z-axis is the depth measure. The note grid shown represents the notes from the C Major scale. If the performer's left hand were closed, the grid would change to 5 by 3, with the five horizontal bins now representing the five remaining semitones not found in the C Major scale.

control, allowing a single performer to control up to four instruments in physically discrete spaces. Third, it presents a visual interface in physical space to provide feedback to the performer on the 3D stage.

System Overview

A high level overview of our system can be seen in Figure 2. The Microsoft Kinect sensor provides an extremely affordable and accessible platform for markerless human pose tracking. The ample sensing area of the Kinect is partitioned based on the user's location on the stage, and these partitions can be used to intuitively control up to four different instruments. This 3D interaction between the Kinect and a performer's movements is converted into Open Sound Control (OSC) packets and passed to Ableton Live, a robust music generation software. OSC packets are then registered as a musical note, looping effect, or modulation signal and a resulting sound is produced. To reinforce the performer's interaction with the system, we augment a monitor-based interface with a projection-based interface to allow for a more physical feedback. The entire system is designed with live performance in mind, such that the performer is able to engage an audience visually while producing acoustically pleasing music.

Mapping the Kinect to OSC

Skeletal tracking data is gathered from the Kinect and accessed via the Kinect SDK. We use the skeletal data for many aspects of the music generation process, including arm location and movement for pitch, intensity, and modulation, as well as for instrument selection, the core of the body for determining staging—which instrument the performer is playing, and leg data for controlling looping.

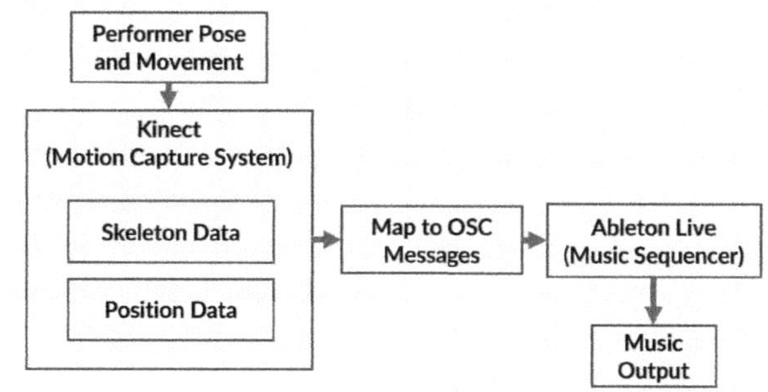

Figure 2: A high level architecture diagram of the full system.

Note Generation

Note generation uses a combination of the left and right hands for pitch and actuation. The location of the left hand determines the pitch, and it is assumed that the performer is facing the Kinect directly. The coordinate system used and gestures are demonstrated in Figure 1. The system provides three octaves by altering the the left hand along the y-axis, and horizontally sub-divided bins for selecting specific semitones along the x-axis. An open left hand allows for the selection of notes from the C Major scale—the white keys of a piano, while a closed hand allows for selection of the five remaining notes—the black keys of a piano. By altering the notes depending on the state of the left hand, we are able to provide sufficient space for each note bin, reducing the chance of inaccurate notes being played. This interface was generated to closely mirror that of a piano, and provides fine-grained control of all 36 semitones of three octaves.

Note Modulation

In addition to using the right hand to actuate notes, the position of the right hand can be taken into account for note modulation. OSC messages are passed containing the rel-

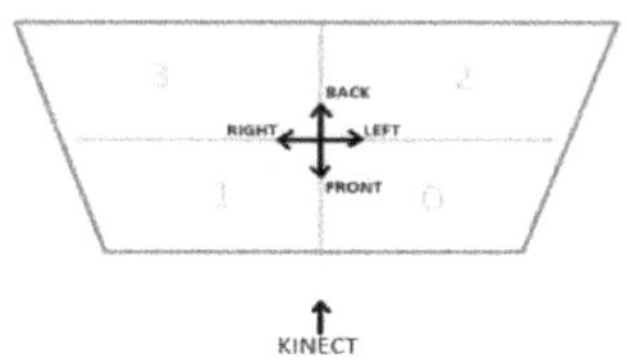

Figure 3: The layout of the virtual stage. The stage can have no divisions (the entire stage is one instrument), two divisions (front and back, or left and right), or four divisions (pictured).

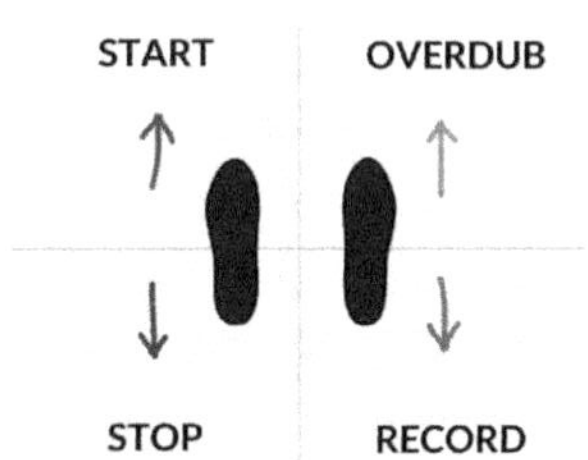

Figure 4: The loop controls from the point of view of the performer looking down at their feet. Note that in Ableton, playing a loop automatically stops recording, so no stop recording gesture is needed (the start and stop actions represent starting and stopping playback).

ative x, y, and z coordinates of the hand to the shoulder, which can be used for dynamic filters, adjusting volume or duration, and more.

The Virtual Stage

At the core of the system is a staging mechanism which allows for the division of the Kinect's sensing region into up to four parts as demonstrated in Figure 3. The performer's physical position on the stage is determined by the position of the spine joint, defined by the Kinect as roughly approximating the center of the body, assuming a standing position. As notes are actuated, the quadrant is determined by the performer's position and an OSC packet is sent to the instrument associated with that quadrant.

Looping

As seen in Figure 4, four different looping actions can be activated, and the one selected is based on where the feet are moved. The performer makes a quick lasso shape with the right hand and keeps their left hand open and then makes the desired foot movement.

Projection

The monitor interface shown in Figure 6 is the primary interaction between the performer and the system. It provides a visualization of the Kinect-provided skeleton, overlayed with useful information about the state of the system. We also experimented with displaying the note grid over the skeleton in real time to help the user better understand which note they were playing.

A projection in the physical space is intended to augment the primary interface. A standard projector can be used and is pointed towards the ground as seen in Figure 5. We provide a simple interface to move the four bounding corners and centroid of the staging area. The interface is meant to provide feedback in the physical space to counteract the lack of tactile response from a VMI. Our initial work focuses on the basics—providing information on the quadrant the performer is currently in, as well as the active instrument in that quadrant.

Results

Our main subject from which we derive the majority of the feedback is a musician trained in many instruments, but specializing in viola and ukelele. Non-musicians also experimented with the system to provide an alternative perspective.

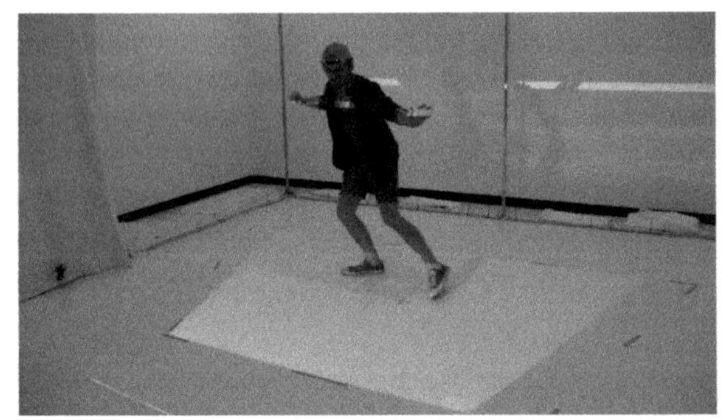

Figure 5: Interactive stage projection. The green represents the active stage area, while the red represents the active partition. The current instrument is displayed.

Instrument Control

Within 30 minutes of his first interaction with our VMI, the musician was able to play *Twinkle Twinkle Little Star* with relatively little error and even felt comfortable enought to add small flourishes to the melody. Comparatively, we found that the non-musicians generally were not as accurate as the musician and took longer to become acquainted with the controls. We were not particularly surprised, as it fol-

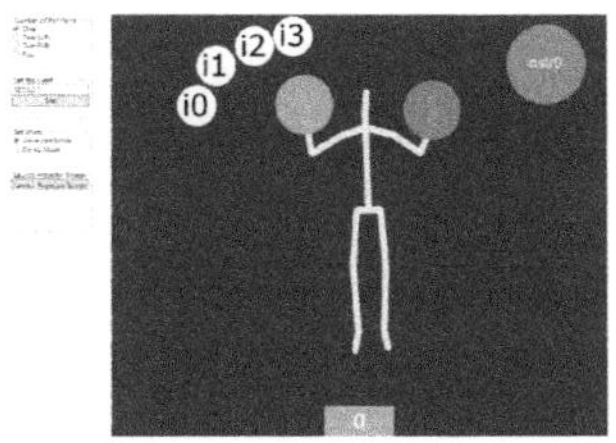

Figure 6: The monitor interface. The green circle indicates an open hand is sensed, while the red circle indicates a closed hand is sensed. The current quadrant is displayed in the gray box (bottom center), and the current instrument is displayed in the darker blue circle (top right). The stage can be partitioned on the fly (top left), and a target recipient can be set if another device is receiving the OSC messages, or can be set to the local machine. Users can toggle between the advanced mode, or a demo mode, which reduces the amount of controls and is intended for musical exploration..

lows naturally that a skilled musician would be more efficient and effective when learning new instruments.

Stage Partitioning and Loop Control
In observing the musician and through feedback he provided us, we found that stage partitioning was extremely effective. Physically partitioning out the space allows for the performer to quickly switch between instruments. We found that physical partitioning also enhanced the viewer experience, as it made it easier to understand the effects the performer's movements were having on the music generated.

The musician was also able to effectively utilize the looping aspect of the system, generating both multi-part covers of existing songs, as well as producing his own orchestral compositions by stacking loops of audio. The musician initially struggled with the procedure necessary to manipulate loops, which requires both hands and a foot movement. Furthermore, we found that the system did not provide sufficient feedback when loop actions were sensed and activated, especially given the hand and foot configuration necessary to activate loop actions. We believe that integrating loop feedback in the projection interface might provide a better experience.

Interface
Our aim to reduce mental strain, as well as potentially improve overall system tactility by adding a projection element was successful. By providing additional information to the performer directly below them, the performer can focus more on what their hands are doing and are not straining to see what the small monitor is trying to convey.

When looking at Figure 5, you can see tape laid down to mark the sensed area by the Kinect. This was initially done to help the performer understand their workable area, but by introducing the projection component, this is no longer necessary.

A supplementary video has been provided to demonstrate the capabilities of the system.

Conclusion
We present a dynamic system for music generation and performance using a low-cost and relatively easy to setup system. The performer is capable of in-depth control of up to four instruments and can generate full compositions in support of a larger musical performance or as an individual performer. The interface provides both an informative screen interface, as well as an interactive projection element, providing the performer with sufficient feedback in order to easily understand and control the state of the system.

Acknowledgments
This work was developed as a component part of the 01X Project (http://www.project01x.com/). The authors would like to thank Susan Lakin, Katie Verrant, and the Sound Exchange Project for their support of the work. Emily Abele, Ameya Lonkar, and Vishwanath Raman contributed to an earlier version of the interface and we are thankful for their contributions. Finally, the authors would also like to thank Marla Schweppe and the 3D Digital Design Department at RIT for allowing us the use of their motion capture suite for this project.

REFERENCES
1. Axel Mulder. 1994. Virtual musical instruments: Accessing the sound synthesis universe as a performer. In *Proceedings of the First Brazilian Symposium on Computer Music*. 243–250.

BacPack for New Frontiers: A Tangible Tabletop Museum Exhibit Exploring Synthetic Biology

Anna Loparev
Wellesley College
Wellesley, MA 02481
aloparev@wellesley.edu

Lauren Westendorf
Margaret Flemings
Jennifer Cho
Wellesley College
Wellesley, MA 02481
{lwestend, mfleming, jcho7}
@wellesley.edu

Romie Littrell
Anja Scholze
The Tech Museum of Innovation
San Jose, CA 95113
{rlittrell, ascholze}@thetech.org

Orit Shaer
Wellesley College
Wellesley, MA 02481
oshaer@wellesley.edu

ISS '16, November 06-09, 2016, Niagara Falls, ON, Canada
ACM 978-1-4503-4248-3/16/11.
http://dx.doi.org/10.1145/2992154.2996878

Abstract
We present BacPack for New Frontiers, an interactive museum exhibit that introduces core synthetic biology concepts to visitors through tangible, multi-touch, and physical interaction. The exhibit engages users in the design and engineering of bacteria, which are helpful in extreme environments like Mars. This project aims to allow museum visitors to play and tinker with biology through tangible and multi-touch interactions that bridge size and time scales. Here we present the design, implementation, and preliminary evaluation of this exhibit.

Author Keywords
Interactive Surfaces; Tangible Interaction; Tabletop

ACM Classification Keywords
H.5.2. [Information Interfaces and Presentation]: User Interfaces

Introduction
Synthetic Biology is an emerging field that combines science and engineering in innovative ways to address critical real-world problems such as food shortage, waste disposal, and access to clean water. Synthetic

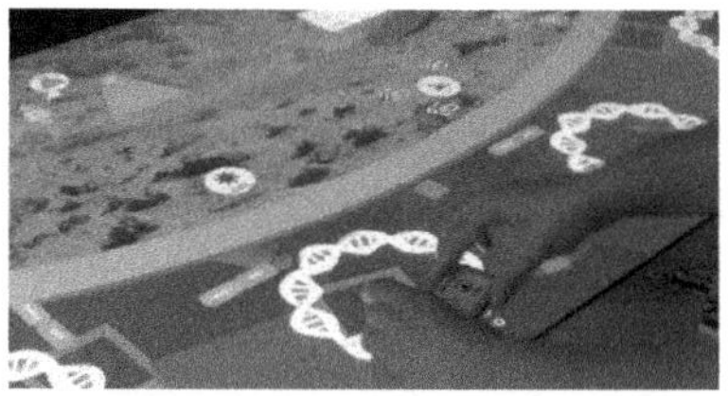

Figure 1. Visitors select genes by placing corresponding tangibles into a loop of DNA.

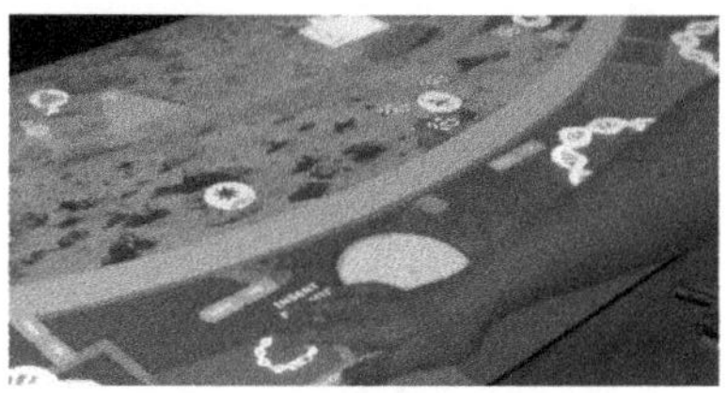

Figure 2. Visitors insert their custom designed DNA loop into a bacterium by dragging it over.

Figure 3. After custom-designed bacteria multiply, visitors can send their bacteria to Mars.

biologists apply engineering principles such as standardization, abstraction, and modularity to design and build new living organisms with particular properties or functions. To create new biological designs, complex genetic sequences are broken down into standardized biological parts called BioBricks, which are used like "Lego Bricks" based on their function and can be inserted into living cells.

The process of creating interactive and exploratory educational activities that expose wide audiences to the promise and limitations of synthetic biology is confounded by several factors, including the long time scales of biology, the complexity of the topic, and the unique behaviors of living organisms (often occurring at the nanometer level). Our goal is to create novel interfaces for exploring synthetic biology that bridge the goals of design and tinkering (tangible, responsive, and open ended) and the confounding factors of biology (invisible, unintuitive, slow, and prescriptive). In designing such activities, virtual augmentation is necessary to bring time and size scales into the range of a play session and to allow users to design with biology.

In this abstract, we present BacPack for New Frontiers, an interactive museum exhibit created in collaboration with the Tech Museum of Innovation. The system consists of a tabletop multi-touch display and a set of tangible BioBricks that allow users to collaboratively design and tinker with digital bacteria. Below we discuss how we used the tabletop and tangible interaction in this exhibit to bridge the confounds of biology through a collaborative platform for exploring biological-design. We also describe findings from a preliminary evaluation in the museum.

Related Work

A number of museum exhibits allow younger audiences to interact with biological concepts through experimentation like the observation of how bacteria react to light [2] and the analysis of multi-colored bacteria [1]. Most closely related to our work is SynFlo [7], a tangible museum exhibit for synthetic biology that utilizes active tangible tokens to simulate a biology experiment. BacPack seeks to examine how combining tabletop and tangible interaction can support collaborative open inquiry, design, and tinkering with biology.

Exhibit Design

We designed BacPack in close collaboration with synthetic biologists and educators. Informed by these professionals, as well as by the Tech Museum's constructionist educational philosophy, we defined the following design goals: G1) Supporting the development of inquiry skills through a collaborative and playful experience; G2) Conveying the excitement and application of synthetic biology by allowing visitors to design and tinker with biology. Through the exhibit, museum visitors take on the role of a scientist tasked with engineering bacteria to help an astronaut survive on Mars. This concept is inspired by a research paper that demonstrates synthetic biology can be used to harness available resources in such a scenario [3].

Museum visitors use tangible representations of BioBricks from the Registry of Standard Biological Parts [5] to design bacteria that can produce necessary materials from existing resources, and through touch gestures release their bio-designs to a virtual Mars (see Figures 1 – 4). Our design choices were informed by an iterative design process, as well as by design

Figure 4. Children interact with the BacPack exhibit in a museum setting. (Bottom picture curtesy of Ashley McCabe, Ashley Daubenmire Photography.)

frameworks for learning with tabletop and tangible user interfaces [6]. We encountered several design challenges as we built our system:

Supporting parallel and collaborative work – To facilitate the flow of museum visitors, BacPack provides four virtual workbenches where users can work in parallel on different biological designs. The application invites all users to release their designs to a common environment (i.e. Mars) and observe the impact. Users are encouraged to collaborate on solving pressing problems, such as severe lack of oxygen and dwindling fuel supplies.

Fostering strategy development – The goal of the exhibit, survival on Mars through efficient utilization of resources, aims to encourage strategy development. We provide users with contextual hints, as well as dynamic representations of resources and state, to help them develop a strategy within the activity's short time span.

Facilitating group dynamics – Virtual workbenches are required to support each visitor group as a whole. Visitor groups vary in size, composition, and age. Through the use of tangibles, visibility of actions, and a visualization of previous interactions, we aim to facilitate group dynamics that allow visitors to learn together.

Bridging time and size scales – We use animation to bridge the size and scale of biology. Animations allow us to expose visitors to essential biological processes (e.g. transformation) and provide a dynamic simulation of resource consumption and production.

Museum setting – Interactions with museum exhibits are typically short and casual. To draw users in and to ensure their success, we present intuitive controls and provide clear, immediate feedback.

Implementation

BacPack for New Frontiers was developed for the 55" Multitaction Cell. It was programmed in JavaScript using the Multitouch Cornerstone 2 SDK. Tangibles were assembled from laser-cut layers and incorporated into the design using the MultiTaction fiducial markers.

Evaluation

We conducted a preliminary evaluation of BacPack at the Tech Museum of Innovation over the span of 4 days. The 67 visitor groups that interacted with the exhibit varied in composition and size: the largest group had 7 active participants, while over half of groups (55%) consisted of a single user. Adults not directly engaged with the exhibit often provided direct and indirect support to groups with children. User ages ranged from 4 to adulthood, and they collaborated not just within, but also across visitor groups.

Visitors were briefed about the general premise of the exhibit, but were not given explicit step-by-step instructions unless it was clear they needed support. Most visitors engaged with the system for over 4.5 minutes, with 20% interacting for longer than 7 minutes and a couple for over half an hour. All but three groups completed at least one round of interaction successfully.

Through observations and video data, we established that the exhibit was successful in facilitating collaborative engagement. For example, we found evidence of verbal strategizing, as well as passing and sharing tokens. In addition, in about 24% of groups, visitors observed someone else at least briefly interact with the exhibit before starting to interact with the exhibit themselves. In 14 out of the 26 groups with more than one member, we observed physical interventions like pointing or directly interacting with someone else's station, and in 2 groups, visitors actively shared stations.

After completing the interaction, users reported their age and rated how difficult and enjoyable they found the application on a scale of 1 to 10. They found the exhibit not particularly difficult to figure out and interact with ($M = 3.40$) and in general enjoyed their experience with it ($M = 7.41$). One 8-year-old chose to break the difficulty assessment into two parts, explaining that the tangible tabletop functionality was really easy (1) but the concept it taught was really hard (10).

We also asked open-ended questions about the exhibit's content to gauge learning. Visitors used terminology introduced by the exhibit and showed a grasp of learning goals through their overall response to post-task questions. For example, "I'm making bacteria to go on Mars, so I choose something and make something else. Yeah. Telling you what we need" (age 9). Visitors were also able to describe aspects of the process: "We made poop bricks.; We put genes together" (age 13); "I found that the poop is the best thing to make ... the water and the energy" (age 11) and "There's a DNA, and then you put the DNA into those thingies, and then you send it to Mars" (school age girl).

Conclusion and Future Work

BacPack for New Frontiers is an interactive installation that incorporates tangible and tabletop interaction to illustrate core concepts of synthetic biology to non-expert users. We will continue refining BacPack to provide more complex inquiry and interaction. We also plan to conduct a further evaluation at the Tech Museum before its launch fall 2016.

Acknowledgements

This work is partially funded by NSF grant no. IIS-1149530 and by NSF grant no. CNS-1513077.

References

[1] E. pixels. http://2014.igem.org/Team:The_Tech_Museum

[2] Lee, S., Bumbacher, E., Chung, A., et al. Trap it!: A Playful Human-Biology Interaction for a Museum Installation. In *Proc. CHI '15*. 2593-2602.

[3] Menezes A., et al. (2014). Towards Synthetic Biological Approaches to Resource Utilization on Space Missions. *J R Soc Interface*, 12, 102 (2015).

[4] Multitaction, Inc. http://www.multitaction.com

[5] Registry of Standardized Biological Parts. http://parts.igem.org/Catalog

[6] Antle, A. N. and Wise, A.F. Getting down to details: Using learning theory to inform tangibles research and design for children, *Interacting with Computers*, 25, 1 (2013).

[7] Okerlund J. et al. SynFlo: A Tangible Museum Exhibit for Exploring Bio-Design. In *Proc. TEI '16*. 141-149.

A Toolkit for Building Collaborative Immersive Multi-Surface Application

Cooper Davies [1]
Cooper.Davies@agilesoftwareengineering.org

Jade White [1]
whitejk@ucalgary.ca

Alec McAllister [1]
Alec.McAllister@agilesoftwareengineering.org

Adam Saroka [1]
asaroka@ucalgary.ca

Omar Addam [1]
omaddam@ucalgary.ca

Fatemeh Hendijani Fard [1]
fhendija@ucalgary.ca

Frank Maurer [1]
fmaurer@ucalgary.ca

[1] University of Calgary
2500 University Drive NW
Calgary AB, Canada

Abstract
The paper describes a toolkit that integrates spatially-aware multi-surface systems with mixed-reality approaches to create immersive collaborative environments. The toolkit integrates multiple digital displays and multiple Microsoft HoloLens devices with multiple Kinects. The HoloLens' allow several users to look at the same virtual hologram while the Kinects enable them to use body movements to interact with these holograms as well as with other digital surfaces in a space. Effectively, the toolkit enables its users to build collaborative applications that utilize digital displays as well as the space between them to interact with information. Our approach also facilitates the management of virtual objects and overcomes gesture restrictions of HoloLens. We use the toolkit in a prototype application for improving the efficiency and response time in emergency management.

ISS '16, November 06-09, 2016, Niagara Falls, ON, Canada
ACM 978-1-4503-4248-3/16/11.
http://dx.doi.org/10.1145/2992154.2996879

Author Keywords
Augmented Reality; gestures; multiple devices; interaction; hand tracking.

ACM Classification Keywords
I.3.6

Introduction
Interacting with 3D mixed-reality models requires substantial amounts of technology and/or usability trade-offs. While head mounted devices such as HoloLens offer a limited gesture set for interactions [1], depth cameras such as Microsoft Kinect provide a full body interaction along with a variety of gestures that

can be useful for interacting with 3D models. The usability of complex multi-surface systems can be enhanced if this society of devices is treated as a single environment [2,3]. To go beyond showing information on digital surfaces, the 3-dimensional space between different surfaces can be utilized for mixed-reality models. To help developers, we developed a tool that manages 3D mixed reality models and enables users to interact with these virtual objects. This paper focuses on how we use the Microsoft HoloLens and Kinects to create the immersive collaborative experience.[1] Combining the interface of the HoloLens with the functionality of the Kinect has introduced many opportunities for information handling or manipulation. We have created an infrastructure by which the two devices are able to communicate. The toolkit utilizes multiple HoloLens and/or Kinect devices to enable multiple users to view the same data within the same space. Our framework can be expanded even further to include multiple other devices, restricted only by their ability to connect to our server. By defining a standard message format, there are potentially a limitless number of devices that can be connected and integrated. We have previously published part of this toolkit (SoD) [3]. We use the toolkit in a collaborative industry project to prototype technology for an Emergency Operations Centre (EOC) of the Future to supports analyze and plan emergency situations.

Related Work

Various applications and frameworks have been developed that use head mounted devices, wearables, Kinect, etc., to interact with the 3D mixed reality models and create seamless interaction of devices.

[1] See ***SoD ITS 2015 paper*** for details on the multi-surface aspect of the approach.

Mayer and Soros use smart glasses and watches to select objects and interact with them in the real world [4]. XDKinect is a framework that uses Microsoft Kinect as a mediate for cross device interaction (allow users to interact with multiple devices) [5]. In [6] authors study how to manipulate or interact with virtual objects using various gesture control systems or gesture interactions via Kinect or other devices. Different projects are explained in [7] that separately use Kinect and GearVR headset as well as other devices to interact with virtual objects. The most similar work to ours is HoloR [1], an augmented reality system that uses projectors, goggles, and Kinect. It tracks the data and forwards the Kinect primary gestures to the app. However, the use of HoloLens and the details of Kinect and lens interactions are not mentioned in [1]. The main difference of our work with HoloR is the ability to use SoD built in gestures on the HoloLens to manage a virtual object and overcome the restriction of HoloLens to create new gestures.

Engine

The HoloLens is tied in with the Unity Engine for model creation. Unity uses a type of file (AssetBundle) which automates the process of 3D model serialization and deserialization. Integrating these capabilities allows us to shift focus from data optimization, to how the data is transferred.

Framework

To allow for cross-device communication, we use our "Society of Devices" (SoD) toolkit [3]. SoD is a message relay server to which multiple devices connect, and register themselves with. SoD relays

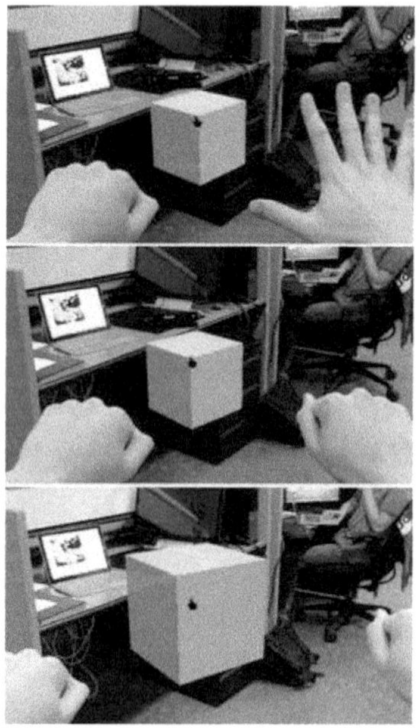

Figure 1. Real-time use of the Kinect in coordination with the HoloLens. In frame one, the user anchors the object by closing one hand. In frame two, the user positions his second hand in order to calculate relative distance between hands. In frame three, the user enlarges the object by widening his hand position.

messages between connected devices. Currently, similar to standardized network socket libraries, SoD contains commands such as Connect, On, and Emit, has the ability to exchange information, and implement additional commands (e.g. declaring the single target of a message, asking for the number of people the Kinect are able to see, etc.). SoD can be used as a file server. We serialize data from files and upload them through Emit messages to be stored on the server. Multiple HoloLens are then able to download these files, deserialize them, and use the information accordingly. This allows for the sharing of 3D models and their location in physical space amongst multiple HoloLens devices in real time.

Gestures

One of the limitations of the HoloLens (restrictions placed on its API by Microsoft) is that it does not allow for the creation or addition of new gestures and provides exactly two gestures. Because users feel comfortable using more than two gestures [8] we decided to integrate Kinect gestures that are already distributed by SoD to overcome this limitation. Using the Kinect, we can place the users' hands within the 3D realm of the HoloLens. By giving their real-world hands a virtual position in the same space as the mixed reality objects, interaction within that 3D world becomes possible. To interact with virtual objects, a "grab" gesture seems to be an obvious choice. The HoloLens already supports a grab gesture, but we found it to be very unnatural feeling during its use. It requires a very awkward, and deliberate motion, which goes against our intuitive approach. We felt this to be very contradictory, and attempted to create alternatives.

Along the way, we implemented a mechanism which determines the specified object we are attempting to interact with. This raised a number of issues. If we were to use hand positions, we could not assume that the world the HoloLens views is comparable in scale or position as the world the Kinect views. Neither device knows how the other interprets the physical world. We cannot be sure that the HoloLens has the room mapped similarly to that of the Kinect to any degree of accuracy. SoD merely relays along what the Kinect tells it to. We use the standard gaze mechanism used in the HoloLens to decide which object the user is interacting with. A ray is cast from the current camera perspective, down the line of sight, until it collides with an object that we have tagged as interactable. The collided object becomes considered the current focused object. When a user performs a grab, the focused object is what they interact with. This cross-device integration enabled us to provide intuitive interactions with 3D models.

Interaction

Implementing the Kinect allows for a more fluid and natural interaction between the 3D world and the user. The user has to simply close their hand to instantiate a grab event and the system handles the rest. The Kinect invokes an emit function which sends a "Grab started" message to SoD passing the users/hand position, current gestures, etc. The HoloLens receives the message from SoD, looks at the hand positions, and then invokes its own grab event. If the User then opens their hand, invoking a "Grab released" event, this process is repeated. While the grab released event is not sent, the HoloLens will poll SoD every 100ms to ask the Kinect the current position of hands. Every time the HoloLens receives the hand positions from SoD, it uses these positions to determine how to alter the virtual world. For example, in Figure 1, we have the HoloLens set to recognize that a grab indicates we are attempting to interact with the focused object. We then begin polling to find the relative distance between the users' hands with respect to their original distance. We can also do the same for rotating as shown in figure 2. By implementing more gestures via the Kinect, there is essentially a large number of body movements to signify commands. By extending the model from that of a simple 3D cube, we can allow for users to manipulate individual buildings on a map. By introducing different gestures, the user can clone, move, orient, scale, and rotate buildings with our current design.

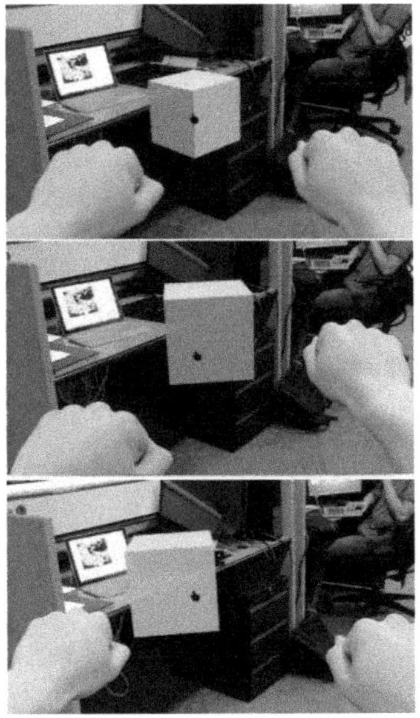

Figure 2. Real-time use of the Kinect in coordination with the HoloLens. Similar to Figure 1 except that the gesture is used to rotate the cube rather than enlarge it

Conclusion & Future Work

Based on current state of the project, we believe that there is a significant number of applications for this technology. The toolkit will substantially decrease the amount of time taken build immersive multi-surface applications. In the future, we will explore immersive analytics applications with a focus on enhancing EOCs.

In addition, we will integrate Google Tango tablets to view the same virtual holograms. This would be a low cost alternative to look at virtual holograms but will also require to rethink gesture interactions. On the technical side, we will store 3D objects and their positions in a database, enabling us to show or hide parts of an object. By storing the information as opposed to an AssetBundle file, we would be able to download the models to a non-unity engine if need be.

Acknowledgements

We would like to thank our industry partner, C4i Consultants Inc. for their support.

References

[1] Schwede, C. and Hermann, T. HoloR: Interactive mixed-reality rooms. CogInfoCom,IEEE 2015,517-522.

[2] Rädle, R., Jetter, H.C., Schreiner, M., Lu, Z., Reiterer, H. and Rogers, Y. Spatially-aware or spatially-agnostic?: Elicitation and evaluation of user-defined cross-device interactions. In Proc. Human Factors in Computing Systems, ACM (2015), 3913-3922.

[3] Seyed T, Azazi A, Chan E, Wang Y, Maurer F. SoD-Toolkit: A Toolkit for Interactively Prototyping and Developing Multi-Sensor, Multi-Device Environments. In Proc. ITS 2015, ACM (2015), 171-180.

[4] Mayer, S. and Sörös, G. User Interface Beaming--Seamless Interaction with Smart Things Using Personal Wearable Computers. In Wearable and Implantable Body Sensor Networks Workshops, 2014 11th International Conference, IEEE (2014), 46-49.

[5] Nebeling, M., Teunissen, E., Husmann, M. and Norrie, M.C. XDKinect: development framework for cross-device interaction using kinect. In Proc. 2014 ACM SIGCHIsymposium on Engineering interactive computing systems, ACM (2014), 65-74.

[6] Fernandes, L., Nunes, R.R., Matos, G., Azevedo, D., Pedrosa, D., Morgado, L., Paredes, H., Barbosa, L., Fonseca, B., Martins, P. and Cardoso, B. Bringing user experience empirical data to gesture-control and somatic interaction in virtual reality videogames: an exploratory study with a multimodal interaction prototype. In SciTecIn15, 2015.

[7] Perlin, K. Future Reality: How emerging technologies will change language itself. IEEE Computer Graphics and Applications, 36.3 (2016), 84-89.

[8] Chan, E., Seyed, T., Stuerzlinger, W., Yang, X. D., & Maurer, F. User Elicitation on Single-hand Microgestures. In Proc. CHI 2016, ACM Press (2016), 3403-3414.

ERWear: Wearables System Design through the Lens of First Responders

Edwin Chan [1]
chane@ucalgary.ca

Yuxi Wang [1]
yuxwang@ucalgary.ca

Teddy Seyed [1]
teddy.seyed@ucalgary.ca

Frank Maurer [1]
frank.maurer@ucalgary.ca

[1] University of Calgary
2500 University Drive NW
Calgary, Alberta, Canada

ISS '16, November 06-09, 2016, Niagara Falls, ON, Canada
ACM 978-1-4503-4248-3/16/11.
http://dx.doi.org/10.1145/2992154.2996880

Abstract
We explore the design of a wearable computing solution for first responders. Wearable devices have many uses, but commercial devices are not suitable for emergency response. First responders face high risk and volatile situations, and wearables possess significant potential to keep responders safe. A lack of understanding exists when designing wearables for first responders. Existing research focuses on the physical implementation of various sensors, rather than usability. Combining literature and extensive interviews, we devise design guidelines for responder-oriented wearable systems. We propose a prototype system, and discuss early feedback from responders.

Author Keywords
Wearable devices; first responder; emergency management; head-mounted display.

ACM Classification Keywords
H.5.2 [Information Storage and Retrieval]: User Interfaces---User-centered design; H.5.3 [Group and Organization Interfaces]: Computer-supported cooperative work

Introduction
Emergencies happen frequently and unpredictably, with potentially devastating results. First responders are

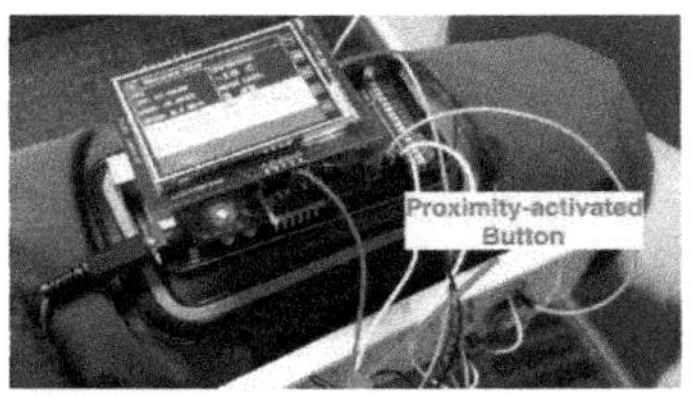

Figure 1: An early wearable prototype for emergency management, by Cernea et al. [1], was found to be too heavy and bulky for practical use.

tasked with gathering information during volatile situations, and protecting the safety of impacted victims. Despite constantly being exposed to risk, responders are often ill-equipped for the task, relying on aging technology with limited capabilities. In recent years, wearable devices have proliferated, becoming easily accessible in many form factors. Despite the potential of wearables to keep users safe, most existing wearables are designed for everyday use, not suitable for emergency situations.

Wearable computing enables the constant and automated collection of information, keeping dispatch informed of a responder's health status, location, and surrounding environment. Head-mounted displays can help visualize mission-related information, increasing situational awareness of responders. Cameras embedded in various wearable devices help responders convey information quickly and accurately. To bring these benefits to responders, we carry out extensive interviews over the course of a year to understand their needs. From the resulting design guidelines, we propose a prototype wearable system made for responders. We then discuss early critique and feedback from responders.

Related Work

Lachner et al. found that mission-related data, information about incidents, clinical data, medical treatments, and spatial awareness data are necessary for emergency response [6]. Of these, health and spatial data play especially significant roles [3, 5].

Magenes et al. introduced ProeTEX, a wearable system for field operators that detects physiological and environmental status [7]. The study demonstrated the use of many sensors, without investigating how they can benefit responders. Cemea et al. developed a wearable device with a color display, which tracked GPS location, ground speed, and ambient noise levels [1]. The system lacked user involvement in the design phase, and was too heavy and bulky for practical use (Figure 1). Curone et al. used sensor data to classify responders' activities, showing that sensor data can help dispatch monitor responders to improve safety and awareness [4].

User Requirements

Interviews with 21 emergency responders were conducted in three stages, over the course of one year [2]. The first two stages helped us identify four themes to designing wearables for responders, while the last stage elicited early feedback to our prototype. The first theme, *System Usability*, provides context about the operating conditions of responders and presents several requirements for such a system to be feasible. The remaining three themes relate to the collection, exchange, and presentation of data. *Responder Safety* describes the types of information the EOC needs to receive from responders, in order to monitor and maintain their safety and well-being. Next, *Responder Awareness* is about how responders can be supported in their tasks through a greater understanding of their surroundings. Finally, *Media and Communications* discusses several tools which can help better convey information, as an alternative to traditional communications via radio.

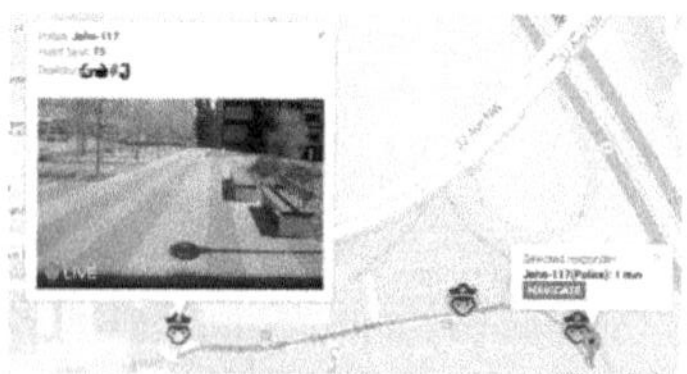

Figure 2: EOC operators can see geotagged photos and live video captured by first responders, displayed directly on the map.

Figure 3: Color indicators alert EOC operators to abnormal heartrates, helping operators monitor the status of responders and ensuring backup can be dispatched in a timely manner.

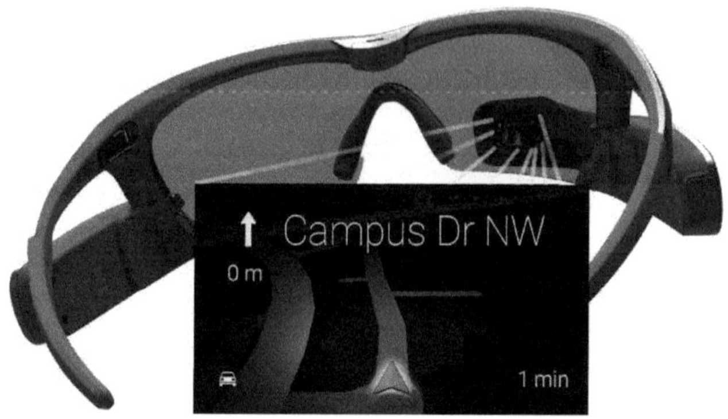

Figure 4: The Recon Jet eyewear used in *ERWear* provides always-on and hands-free access to visual and geographical information, such as navigation support.

ERWear

The *ERWear* wearables prototype tries to address the requirements of emergency responders, and consists of the Recon Jet eyewear and the Motorola 360 smartwatch.

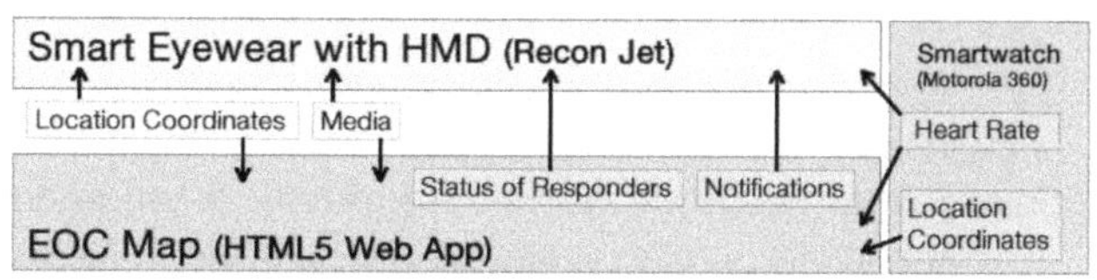

Figure 5: Information exchange between *ERWear* components.

The Recon Jet is a pair of wirelessly connected sunglasses, equipped with a head-mounted display positioned over the right eye (Figure 4). It is always on and hands-free, allowing responders to focus on their tasks. Responders' locations are always tracked by GPS, as part of the safety requirements. Using the built-in camera, responders can record and stream videos to dispatch (Figure 2). Compared to traditional bodycams, a head-mounted camera reflects exactly what the user sees, which is important when presenting video evidence in litigation. On the display, responders can visualize spatial and graphical information, which is difficult to convey verbally over the radio. Maps and navigation guide responders to objectives or fellow responders, increasing situational awareness and efficiency. The Recon Jet is extendable with numerous sensors by connecting to ANT+ peripherals.

The Motorola 360 smartwatch is used primarily for its heart rate sensor, and compliments the Recon Jet (Figure 3). The built-in GPS sensor acts as a backup to Recon Jet's positioning system, providing redundancy for tracking responder locations to ensure their safety.

We also implemented a simple EOC Map, to demonstrate how dispatch operators could interact with and monitor first responders through the equipped wearables.

Early Discussion and Critique

Responders were able to operate the devices with minimal help. Walking with the HUD equipped, participants found the device usable for prolonged use. "*The weight, it's very comfortable, I think you could wear it for several hours.*" However, they expressed some discomfort due to the small size and position of the display. Having located the controls, users were able to respond to notifications and start navigation with ease. Although interactions were simple, users still emphasized the need for minimal interactions during emergency scenarios.

Users appreciated navigation support, and particularly liked knowing locations of other responders. Recording and sharing geotagged photos and videos was seen as

Figure 6: A participant tries on the Recon Jet during an interview.

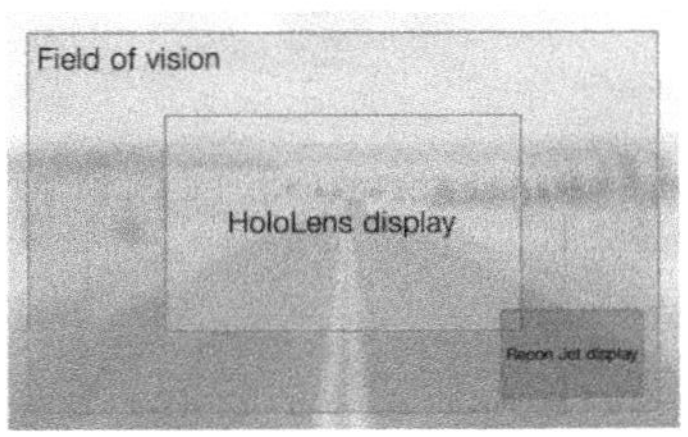

Figure 7: Content overlaid in the center of a user's field of vision allows them to stay focused on a task, without shifting their focus.

a necessity to provide elevated situational awareness to decision makers.

Heavy emphasis was placed on designing a minimalistic interface, with only critical information being shown during operations. Functionality and comprehensibility were prioritized over aesthetics, as the system must remain operable by responders under stress, when cognitive ability may be reduced.

Future Work

From our interviews, it became apparent that wearable devices can help first responders be safe and efficient. We discovered significant enthusiasm for bringing wearables into emergency response.

A continuation of our *ERWear* prototype may use augmented reality displays like the Microsoft HoloLens [7], as suggested by many participants. Showing content directly in a user's view will prevent responders from having to repeatedly shift their focus (Figure 7). It will also be crucial to investigate how information should be visualized to responders, in a clear and concise manner.

Conclusion

We addressed the lack of understanding in designing wearable devices for first responders. We extensively interviewed responders and supporting roles in three stages over a yearlong period. Resulting design guidelines led to our *ERWear* wearables prototype for first responders. We conducted usability testing with responders, and presented early feedback. We hope to extend our prototype to include augmented reality HUDs in the future, while refining the visual elements to be clearer for responders. We hope this initial work will encourage greater use of wearables in emergency response, as a powerful and versatile tool to support responders and keep them safe.

References

[1] Cernea, D., Mora, S. and Perez, A. et al. Tangible and Wearable User Interfaces for Supporting Collaboration among Emergency Workers. *Lecture Notes in Computer Science*, (2012), 192-199.

[2] Chan, E. and Pratte, S. Integrating Wearables in Emergency Management. 2015.

[3] Chang, J., Henry, M., Burtner, R., Love, O. and Corley, C. The Heroes' Problems. In Proc of. *33rd Annual ACM Conference Extended Abstracts on Human Factors in Computing Systems - CHI EA '15*, (2015), 1531-1536.

[4] Curone, D., Tognetti, A. and Secco, E. et al. Heart Rate and Accelerometer Data Fusion for Activity Assessment of Rescuers During Emergency Interventions. *IEEE Transactions on Information Technology in Biomedicine 14*, 3 (2010), 702-710.

[5] Fischer, C. and Gellersen, H. Location and Navigation Support for Emergency Responders: A Survey. *IEEE Pervasive Comput. 9*, 1 (2010), 38-47.

[6] Lachner, J. and Hellwagner, H. Information and Communication Systems for Mobile Emergency Response. *Lecture Notes in Business Information Processing*, (2008), 213-224.

[7] Magenes, G., Curone, D., Lanati, M. and Secco, E. Long-distance monitoring of physiological and environmental parameters for emergency operators. In Proc. of *2009 Annual International Conference of the IEEE Engineering in Medicine and Biology Society*, (2009), 5159-5162.

Tunnel Divisions: Interactive Sound Mapping of Transitory Public Spaces

Cayley MacArthur
Systems Design Engineering
University of Waterloo
Waterloo, ON, Canada
cayley.macarthur@uwaterloo.ca

Stephen Trothen
Critical Media Lab
University of Waterloo
Waterloo, ON, Canada
strothen@uwaterloo.ca

Mark Hancock
Department of Management Sciences
University of Waterloo
Waterloo, ON, Canada
mark.hancock@uwaterloo.ca

ISS '16, November 06-09, 2016, Niagara Falls, ON, Canada
ACM 978-1-4503-4248-3/16/11.
http://dx.doi.org/10.1145/2992154.2996881

Abstract
We present *Tunnel Divisions*, an interactive musical installation designed for ephemeral interaction in public spaces. Informed by concepts from cultural and media studies along with existing literature on interactive public displays, we designed the installation as an intervention meant for the monotonous parts of everyday life. Our demonstration uses low-cost sensors and musical theory to create a generative sound composition unique to the particular space and the people moving through it. By experiencing the installation, we hope to promote critical thinking about the nature and form of interaction with public spaces.

ACM Classification Keywords
H.5.2 User Interfaces: Auditory (non-speech) feedback.

Introduction
A persistent focus of the human-computer interaction (HCI) community has been how to better engage passersby with interactive devices in public spaces, spurring thorough design requirements [8] and interaction models [4]. We designed *Tunnel Divisions* as a *critical making exercise* to explore musical rather than visual systems for public spaces. *Critical making* is a methodology used in design to connect critical thinking, which is traditionally thought of as conceptually and linguistically based, and physical

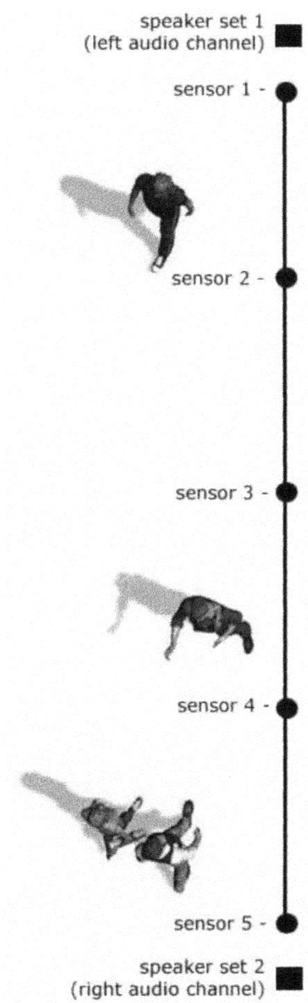

Figure 1. Arrangement of the five PIR sensors and 2 sets of speakers in a corridor. Sensors are 20 feet apart, but can be adjusted to fit other spaces.

making, using making practices as processes of material and conceptual exploration [10]. In designing the piece, we aimed to question trends in HCI literature such as the persistence of visual displays, the prizing of audience attention, and the characterization of "public spaces" as significant places punctuating daily movements as opposed to forgotten spaces in between.

The resulting installation is a low-cost augmentation that adds to the experience of a space without stopping the people moving through it, generating a fleeting sonic map of these transitory spaces through a process we term *data phonolization*. Taking cues from the practice of data visualization in which information is collected and mapped to present a clear visual representation of data, data phonolization similarly draws from large and complex data and distils this information into an organized, perceivable structure. The intent of data phonolization is to encourage listening to sounds within an environment which otherwise promotes the perceptual filtering of noise.

Motivation

Studies of interaction in the context of public and semi-public environments have a continuing presence in HCI. Review of the literature revealed trends in the following three areas: how urban spaces were characterized [4, 6]; which types of technologies proliferate in public settings [3, 9]; and predominant interaction paradigms [7, 11]. Tunnel Divisions is a response to all three.

Tunnel Divisions: Design Goals

Tunnel Divisions is an interactive music installation that uses the rhythms of a public space to organize a generative sound composition. The goal of the installation is to prompt contemplation about the role of interactive surfaces and spaces (ISS) in public life, while creating a sense of joy or wonder for those who participate in the installation. The use of ISS in public spaces carries a set of challenges, such as smooth integration into people's day-to-day movements [5], accumulation of visual clutter [8], and how to solicit attention to convert passersby into "users" of an interactive system in a public space [4]. *Tunnel Divisions* explores these challenges as follows:

1. We use the concept of a "non-place" [1] as a new context for public interaction. These are the places often ignored as we move between lobbies, train stations, offices and other spaces where interactive public systems are usually found. By using this concept, we ask how interactive spaces can enhance or augment people's experiences of the "in-between" without fundamentally changing the identity of that space.

2. We avoid visual primacy in the design, relying on the physical movement of passersby as input, with a musical output response. This is similar to the concept of proxemic interaction [2] in that the space is divided into "zones" which affect system activity as people move through them and trigger sensors. The zones however do not hold different meanings, nor are they imbued with social or cultural significance. The auditory output is specifically designed to preserve the integrity of non-places by not changing their meaning.

3. It does not rely on attracting or holding the attention of passersby, as is a main concern in implementations of public displays [6]. This design decision was made to ask whether attention, or lack thereof, is required for "successful" interactions in public spaces, and how the

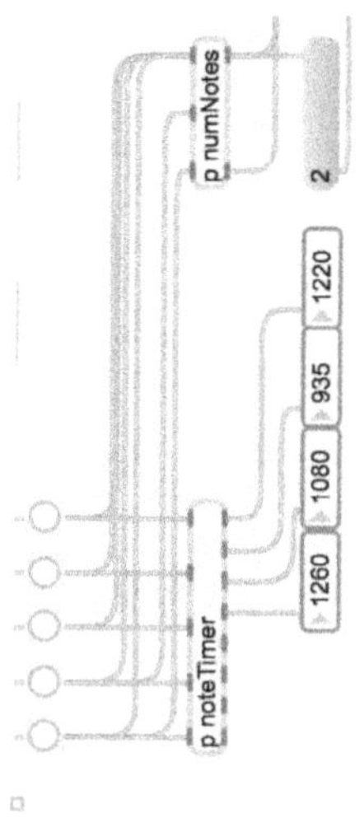

Figure 2. Detail of the Max/MSP patch where sensor input feeds into the noteTimer and numNotes subpatchers, which determine the timing of note patterns and the number of notes to be output.

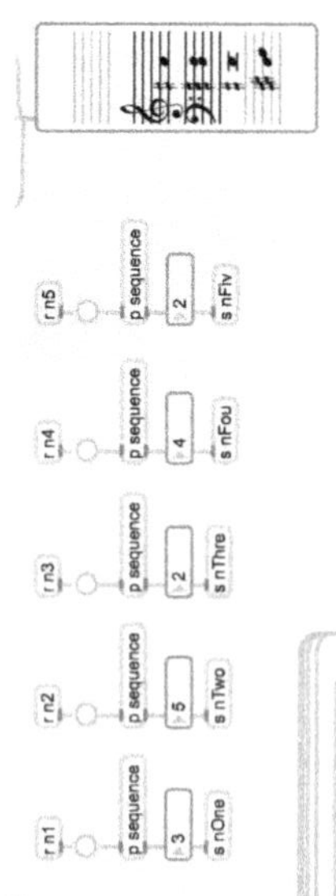

Figure 3. A detail of the sequence subpatchers which are used to select notes from the current key. The output in notation format can be seen on the far right.

current interaction models used to describe public interaction [7, 11] are affected when design goals shift.

Tunnel Divisions is a physical expression of studies within the digital humanities of the tension between technology and culture in constructing the social meaning of spaces, created with the intent of raising issues for contemplation within the HCI community. We encourage those with an interest in designing interactive systems for public spaces or those with an interest in designing public spaces that may incorporate interactive technologies to experience this demo.

Tunnel Divisions: System Design

Tunnel Divisions is set up in a long hallway-like space such as a corridor or tunnel, where people are moving through as opposed to congregating within the space. The system uses five passive infrared (PIR) motion sensors, an Arduino microcontroller, Max/MSP[1] and Ableton Live[2]. The five sensors are used to divide a space into four measures of music, hence its name: *Tunnel Divisions*. The name also refers to the expression "tunnel vision" where an individual has narrow or limited attention to their surroundings. Individuals moving through the tunnel trigger piano notes, which are output through two sets of speakers.

The speed with which individuals move between sensors determines both the tempo of the subdivision of notes, as well as the complexity of note phrases, and scheduling of key changes. The major pentatonic scale is used to select from five musical notes, the set of which subtly evolves between closely related keys over time based on the density of traffic. The left and right audio channels are positioned at opposite ends of the tunnel, and rhythmically echo each other across different octaves and playing dynamics. The resulting musical composition is an indeterminate, evolving and ephemeral map of a space. Those passing through hear ambient-sounding piano notes echoing in response to the sensors being triggered, and as more people follow or cross paths, these notes develop in frequency and complexity. The system parameters (length/spacing, patches and timers triggered by the sensors, number of sensors, and so on) can be adjusted to fit spaces of different lengths and amounts of traffic.

Observations

To initially evaluate our design, *Tunnel Divisions* was installed for four hours in an underground 100-foot tunnel (with sensors spaced at 20 feet each) connecting two buildings on the University of Waterloo campus chosen for its "non-place" qualities. We observed some of the expected effects of deliberate design decisions, such as the slowing of pace, but not stopping or reversing direction. This supports our goal of becoming part of the space as opposed to overriding or changing the experience of the space. By using music in this drab setting, some passersby commented to their friends that we "really liven[ed] it up", suggesting the idea that the space otherwise ceases to exist when not in use. The sound generated and recordings captured during this instance of Tunnel Divisions act as a data phonolization particular to a time and place.

In this design, we did not aim to interrupt the flow of traffic or disengage people from their environment, but rather connect them to the space. We attempted to challenge existing concepts of motivation for interaction

[1] Max/MSP: https://cycling74.com/products/max/

[2] Ableton Live: https://www.ableton.com/en/live/

Figure 4. A student passes through *Tunnel Divisions* in an underground tunnel on the University of Waterloo campus.

Figure 5. As more people traversed the tunnel, the music reflected this increased traffic through complexity of musical components such as key changes and note phrases.

in public spaces by inverting the sense of choice or control, while leaving the door open to curiosity and exploration [8]. In some cases people appeared uncomfortable and mediated their experiences with technology by staying focussed on their phones, or left headphones on and did not engage. It was unclear whether this was a reaction to being observed, or to the experience itself. The means of moving from indirect to intentional interaction with the system was not a matter of stopping and paying attention, but of removing barriers separating person and environment.

Conclusion

This interactive demo is a response to the way that large public displays can arrest movement and demand the attention of passersby. With *Tunnel Divisions*, we aim to augment the unfolding human experience between point A and point B, as opposed to disrupting the natural flow of bodies through a space. We use sound to emphasize "non-places" by mapping it to transitory environments. We hope the demo participants will question the ways that technology can be used to relate people to the spaces around them, the ways that interactive technologies change the meaning of the spaces they inhabit, and alternative ways to think about the forms and functions that interaction in public spaces can take.

Acknowledgements

We thank NSERC; SSHRC IMMERSe; Ontario Ministry of Research, Innovation and Science; Betty Chang and Victor Cheung; and ENGL 799 at University of Waterloo.

References

[1] Augé, M. 1995. *Non-places: introduction to an anthropology of supermodernity*. Verso.

[2] Ballendat, T. et al. 2010. Proxemic interaction: designing for a proximity and orientation-aware environment. *Proc. ITS 2010* (2010), 121–130.

[3] Brignull, H. and Rogers, Y. 2003. Enticing People to Interact with Large Public Displays in Public Spaces. *Proc. INTERACT 2003* (2003), IOS Press.

[4] Cheung, V. 2014. Improving Interaction Discoverability in Large Public Interactive Displays. *Proc. ITS 2014* (2014), 467–472.

[5] Dourish, P. and Bell, G. 2014. *Divining a digital future: mess and mythology in ubiquitous computing.* MIT Press.

[6] Huang, E. et al. 2008. Overcoming Assumptions and Uncovering Practices: When Does the Public Really Look at Public Displays? *Proc. Pervasive 2008* (2008), 228–243.

[7] Michelis, D. and Müller, J. 2011. The audience funnel: Observations of gesture based interaction with multiple large displays in a city center. *Intl. Journal of Human–Computer Interaction*. 27, 6 (2011), 562–579.

[8] Müller, J. et al. 2010. Requirements and design space for interactive public displays. *Proc. Multimedia 2010* (2010), 1285–1294.

[9] Peltonen, P. et al. 2008. It's Mine, Don't Touch!: interactions at a large multi-touch display in a city centre. *Proc. CHI 2008* (2008), 1285–1294.

[10] Ratto, M. 2011. Critical Making. *Open Design Now: Why Design Cannot Remain Exclusive*. BIS Publishers.

[11] Streitz, N.A. et al. 2003. Situated interaction with ambient information: Facilitating awareness and communication in ubiquitous work environments. *Proc. HCI International 2003* (2003).

ABOVE WATER: Extending the Play Space for Health

Rina R. Wehbe
HCI Games Group, Games Institute, Cheriton School of Computer Science, University of Waterloo
Waterloo, ON, Canada
rina.wehbe@uwaterloo.ca

Diane K. Watson
TouchLab, Games Institute, Cheriton School of Computer Science, University of Waterloo,
Waterloo, ON, Canada
diane.watson@uwaterloo.ca

Gustavo F. Tondello
HCI Games Group, Games Institute, Cheriton School of Computer Science, University of Waterloo
Waterloo, ON, Canada
gustavo@tondello.com

Lennart E. Nacke
HCI Games Group, Games Institute, Department of Drama and Speech Communication, Stratford Campus, University of Waterloo
Waterloo, ON, Canada
lennart.nacke@acm.org

ISS '16, November 06-09, 2016, Niagara Falls, ON, Canada
ACM 978-1-4503-4248-3/16/11.
http://dx.doi.org/10.1145/2992154.2996882

Abstract
ABOVE WATER is a game that disseminates information about Clinical Anxiety Disorders, particularly Generalized Anxiety Disorder and Panic Disorder. This game focuses on teaching players about treatments as well as providing a safe space for discussion of personal experiences. This game focuses on using the physical world (physical space, physical and tangible cards) and the digital world (accessible by any phone or tablet with a modern web browser) as part of its gameplay.

Author Keywords
Games for Health, Mobile Games, Psychology

ACM Classification Keywords
J.3 [Computer Applications]: Health; K.8 [Personal Computing]: Games.

Introduction
Clinical anxiety is characterized as an anxiety experienced by an individual that becomes pervasive and affects their day-to-day behavioural functioning. The physical, mental, and social symptoms of anxiety disorders may include sweating, increased heart rate, and feelings of fear [1, 2]. Symptoms of anxiety are different for each subcategory of the disorder, and may be experienced differently by each individual. For someone that may be suffering from problems

Figure 1: Here an anxiety card is directing players to the digital component to play the mini-game myth busting.

with anxiety, gathering information about anxiety disorders, possible treatments, and places to seek help is the first step on the road to recovery. However, lack of support internalized by stigma surrounding mental health can often be a barrier. The game ABOVE WATER [3] was designed to help disseminate information about clinical anxiety disorders, particularly generalized anxiety disorder, and panic disorder.

The Game

The game[1] is designed to be simple. Four players gather around the deck and take turns drawing cards. There are four types of cards: treatment cards, which provide information on specific treatments for further inquiry; anxiety cards, which symbolize the challenge presented by anxiety disorder; goal cards, which present different life goals players may be inspired to collect; and share cards, which encourage community and conversation. To win the game, players must collect the four life goal cards they choose to target at the beginning of the game and have no anxiety cards in their hand.

The digital component extends gameplay and encourages conversation, sharing, and collaboration by asking questions, thus allowing the discussion of experiences, presenting useful information, and 'myth busting'. The application also helps regulate the game by tracking players' in game collection goals. Additionally, the online digital component points to trusted sources of information and places where one can seek help from professionals.

ABOVE WATER presents information, but it is not a treatment itself. Instead, the possibilities for treatment are presented as puzzle pieces to health. Seeking professional help is emphasized.

[1]See the video of the project by accessing the ACM reference [3]

Gameplay

The game is a mixture of both a physical card game, as well as digital component which can be accessed from any personal device with a modern web browser.[2] The application extends the space of the gameplay beyond the scope of the tabletop by adding mini-games that use the physical space. For example, the exercise mini-game Yoga is designed to demonstrate how changes to life style, including increase in physical activities, may be part of a full treatment plan.

Yoga Mini-game: Players do yoga poses for a short period of time. This is meant to stress the benefits of exercise.

Deep Breathing Mini-game: Players are lead through a collective meditative experience focusing on breathing patterns. This is to stress the benefits of mindfulness and relaxation.

Information is provided about treatments requiring the help of professionals, but are not represented in an active minigame. To provide further information and allow for discussion of these treatments, as well as, other information such as reducing stigma, there is also games that focus on discussion. This includes myth busting and sharing.

Sharing Mini-game: Players either collectively answer a question from a list, each provide a question and have one be chosen randomly, or each one answer the same question and have the answer be selected for discussion. Collection of the content is done on the device, while discussion is done face to face. For example, players might be asked to provide a 'tip for a friend' about how to manage a panic attack in a public location, and a random 'tip' will be picked and discussed. This personalizes each play experience and allows players to share their own experiences.

[2]The online game is available at: http://play.hcigames.com/abovewater/

Figure 2: A gameplay session with four players.

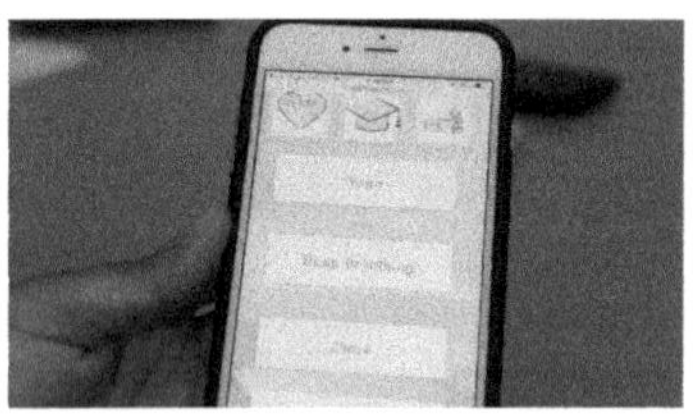

Figure 3: The digital component can be accessed on any device with a modern browser.

Myth Busting Mini-game: Players must discuss a 'mental health myth' and decide whether it is true or false. Feedback is provided to their answer such that the player can learn why a myth is true or false. Often these myths are true in some situations, or based on a false premise and it is important to provide this information.

Combining Physical and Digital Spaces

The main innovation of ABOVE WATER is the combination of both physical cards, physical space, and digital content to expand the play space beyond the regular scope of a card game.

Yoga Device Interaction: Players hold their device in their hand as they do yoga and it vibrates if they move to much while in the pose. This uses the physical space in the room. While the mini-game is in effect, the players are doing more than a simple card game and this may make them consider the reality of the content provided in game.

Deep Breathing Gameplay: The deep breathing mini-game has players breath in and out in response to instructions on the screen. A meditative ocean sound is played. As players are doing the activity at the same time, this stresses collaboration.

Sharing Card Digital Enablement: Personal content is collected on their personal device. Using a personal device makes players more likely to enter personalized information (rather than saying it out-loud) and also allows the game to choose a random entered response to discuss, allowing for some privacy (the players will not know who's content is being discussed unless the player self-identifies).

Myth Busting: Players read a myth on their own device, then vote 'True' or 'False'. Players can discuss as a group, or simple enter their own responses. Having a digital device means we can have a very large library of myths to be discussed (as opposed to only being able to print one myth per physical card).

Conclusion

ABOVE WATER is a game that seeks to help by providing information about clinical anxiety. The innovations of this game go beyond health by expanding the play space of this tangible card game using digital devices.

Acknowledgments

Thank you to Lennart Nacke's NSERC Discovery Grant, SSHRC IMMERSe, Cheriton School of Computer Science, University of Waterloo, The Games Institute, and CNPq, Brazil for funding and support of this research.

REFERENCES

1. Gavin Andrews, Megan J. Hobbs, Thomas D. Borkovec, Katja Beesdo, Michelle G. Craske, Richard G. Heimberg, Ronald M. Rapee, Ayelet Meron Ruscio, and Melinda A. Stanley. 2010. Generalized worry disorder: a review of DSM-IV generalized anxiety disorder and options for DSM-V. *Depression and Anxiety* 27, 2 (2010), 134–147. DOI: http://dx.doi.org/10.1002/da.20658
2. R. Parekh. 2015. What are Anxiety Disorders? American Psychiatric Association. (2015). http://www.psychiatry.org/patients-families/anxiety-disorders/what-are-anxiety-disorders
3. Rina R. Wehbe, Diane K. Watson, Gustavo F. Tondello, Marim Ganaba, Melissa Stocco, Alvin Lee, and Lennart E. Nacke. 2016. ABOVE WATER: An Educational Game for Anxiety.. In *CHI PLAY'16 Extended Abstracts*. Austin, TX, USA. DOI: http://dx.doi.org/10.1145/2968120.2971804

A Demonstration of Haptic Retargeting: Dynamic Repurposing of Passive Haptics for Enhanced Virtual Reality Experiences

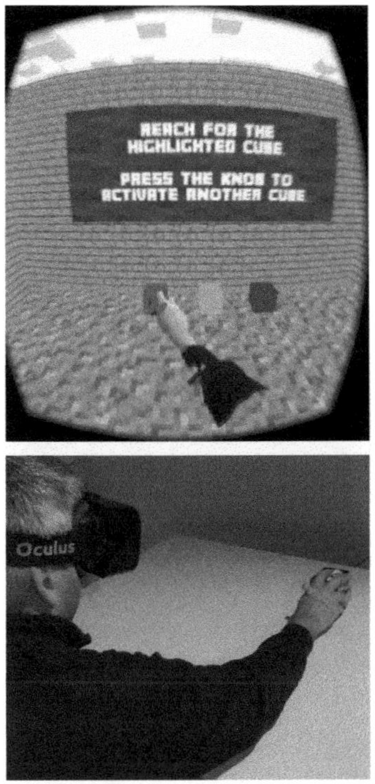

Figure 1. Our haptic retargeting framework in action: User touches three different virtual cubes while in reality the same cube is touched each time.

Mahdi Azmandian
University of Southern California
Los Angeles, CA, USA
mazmandian@ict.usc.edu

Mark Hancock
University of Waterloo
Waterloo, ON, Canada
mark.hancock@uwaterloo.ca

Hrvoje Benko
Eyal Ofek
Andrew D. Wilson
Microsoft Research
Redmond, WA, USA
{benko, eyalofek, awilson}@microsoft.com

ISS '16, November 06-09, 2016, Niagara Falls, ON, Canada
ACM 978-1-4503-4248-3/16/11.
http://dx.doi.org/10.1145/2992154.2996883

Abstract

Manipulating a virtual object with appropriate passive haptic cues provides a satisfying sense of presence in virtual reality. However, scaling such experiences to support multiple virtual objects is a challenge as each one needs to be accompanied with a precisely-located haptic proxy object. We showcase a solution that overcomes this limitation by hacking human perception. Our framework for repurposing passive haptics, called *haptic retargeting*, leverages the dominance of vision when our senses conflict. With haptic retargeting, a single physical prop can provide passive haptics for multiple virtual objects. We introduce three approaches for dynamically aligning physical and virtual objects: body manipulation, world manipulation and a hybrid technique which combines both world and body manipulation. This demo has been presented previously at CHI 2016 [1,2].

ACM Classification Keywords

H.5.1 [Information Interfaces and Presentation]: Multimedia Information Systems-Artificial, Augmented, and Virtual Realities; H.5.2 [User Interfaces]: Haptic I/O.

Figure 2. Arrangement of three cubes before the demonstration task begins (top) and with two cubes removed once the HMD is put on (bottom). The user handles only a single physical cube.

Introduction

Over the past few years, virtual reality (VR) has experienced a resurgence. Though optics, rendering, and audio technologies have improved substantially, a component that has remained underdeveloped is haptics—the sense of touch expected when reaching out and grabbing virtual objects. Users may describe a VR experience as immersive and life-like, but when reaching out to touch a virtual object, the illusion can be shattered when their hand unexpectedly passes through the rendered visuals.

One way to add a sense of touch to virtual objects is through the use of *passive haptics* [3], where physical props are placed in the environment to match their virtual counterparts. The result can be a compelling tactile sensation when reaching and touching an object. However, this technique requires each virtual object to have a physical prop of the same size and shape, in the correct position, to create this illusion. Furthermore, each time the virtual scene is changed, the infrastructure must be modified and possibly rebuilt. This limits the ability to develop complex virtual environments with passive haptics.

We explore a solution that overcomes these limitations by hacking human perception. We have created a framework for repurposing passive haptics, called *haptic retargeting,* that leverages the dominance of vision when our senses conflict. In essence, our approach repurposes a single physical prop to provide a passive haptic sensation for a variety of virtual world objects thus increasing the user's sense of presence and improving the overall quality of the experience. We do this by dynamically aligning physical and virtual objects as the user interacts with the environment. We investigate three approaches:

- **Body Warping** – Manipulating the virtual representation of the person's body (e.g., arms) such that, at the point of contact with the real object, the body part also appears to be at the virtual object;
- **World Warping** – Manipulating the virtual world's coordinate system to align virtual and physical objects;
- **Hybrid Warping** – A dynamic combination of Body and World Warping.

Body warping

Consider a simple arrangement with a real cube A positioned on the desk in front of the user, and the virtual cube A' shifted slightly to the right. In this case, as the user reaches for the cube, to ensure that the virtual hand meets the real cube, a translation to the right must be applied. A straightforward way of achieving this is to shift the entire rendering of the body to the right, effectively translating the user's hands and arms to the right.

Applying an overall shift, the user's virtual representation of their hands and arms may be noticeable and possibly disruptive. To avoid this, we apply the warp *incrementally* to respect the hands' position at the beginning of the warp, yet still align the cubes once the hand reaches the physical cube.

1 for 3 Illusion

We developed a demonstration task that involves reaching to touch one of three static virtual cubes aligned in front of the user (Figure 1). At each phase, the user is instructed to tap a button placed in front of them on the desk. Once pressed, an instruction appears

Figure 3. User building a virtual castle by arranging and stacking multiple virtual cubes mapped to a single physical cube.

directing them to reach for and touch one of the cubes. Before the demo, they see three cubes placed on the desk, leading them to believe that the three virtual cubes correspond to the same three physical cubes (Figure 3). Once the user puts on the HMD, unbeknownst to them, the left and right cubes are removed from the desk, leaving only the center cube on the table. In each phase, pressing the button initiates a new trial, mapping the single physical cube to one of the three virtual cubes using Body Warping.

Observing users' behavior, we noticed that as they reach to grab a cube, the virtual hand starts warping and they—perhaps subconsciously—correct the hand trajectory, effectively countering the warp to meet the real cube. Users typically report that as they perform the task, they are uncertain what the purpose of the demonstration was and found it repetitive; but once they are instructed to take off the HMD, they realize what has happened.

Cube Stacking with Body Warping

Body Warping can also be used to simulate stacking cubes on a table. The task is to grab a virtual cube resting on the table, and place it on top of another cube, also sitting on the table. Under normal circumstances, if the user were to perform this task with the tracked cube, when the user brings the cube above the bottom virtual cube, not only would there be no haptic feedback indicating the cube's placement on the lower cube, the cube would fall to the table once released. To properly simulate the haptics of stacking the cube, the idea is to add an upward translation to the body warp, so that when the user attempts to place the upper cube, the user sees the virtual cube resting on the lower cube. Meanwhile, haptic feedback indicating that the upper cube is stacked on the lower cube is provided by the table's surface. This creates the illusion that the cubes are being stacked (Figure 3).

World Warping

World warping involves manipulating the virtual world to align virtual objects with the real. In the cube alignment example, where physical cube A is placed on the table, and the virtual cube A' is positioned to the right of A, alignment using World Warping involves translating the entire virtual world to the left, so that A' meets A. Users would likely find this change jarring if applied instantaneously. However, from the redirected walking literature [4] we know that a user's head motions can be scaled by certain factors without being noticed. For instance, if the user rotates 90º to the right, the virtual world can also rotate with/against the user's head rotation, resulting in a rightward/leftward 10º rotation about the user's head position.

The Ring of Cubes Illusion

To demonstrate the functionality of world warping, we created a demonstration similar to the 1 for 3 Illusion. In this task, the user is instructed to look to their right to view a billboard to trigger the next instruction. The user sees an arrangement of cubes forming a quarter circle and in each phase, one cube is deactivated and the adjacent cube is activated. As before, the user is instructed to touch the active cube in each trial.

The cubes are arranged so that mapping one cube to the other can be accomplished by rotating the world around the button placed in front of the user. Each time the user looks to the board and looks back, the required scale factor is calculated and applied. The rotations are applied about the position of the button in

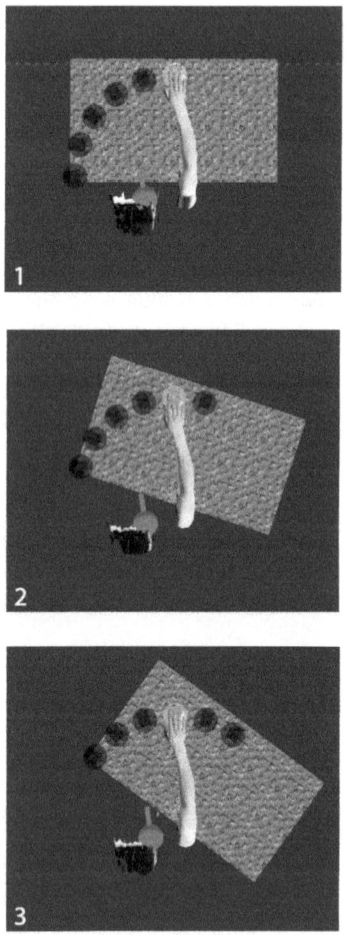

Figure 4. Ring of Cubes Illusion - World warping progressively maps a single physical cube to different virtual cubes arranged in an arc around the button, and within the user's reach.

the scene since the button is always the starting location of the manipulating hand (Figure 4). Since the button itself is cylindrical, its own rotation during the warp is not easily detectable.

The Ring of Cubes Illusion demonstrates how World Warping manipulations can be compounded and extended as long as there are sufficient head motions. This contrasts with Body Warping, where manipulations are constrained by physical limitations of the body.

Hybrid Warping

Both Body Warping and World Warping can produce a noticeable distortion in the user's sense of space for large warps. To minimize artifacts of each approach and thereby improve the user's overall sense of presence, we propose a Hybrid Warping technique which distributes the alignment task between both Body Warping and World Warping techniques simultaneously.

With Hybrid Warping, the user's head translation and rotation enables our World Warping technique to inject some small amounts of translations and rotations that assist in the alignment. The algorithm also simultaneously employs Body Warping to aid in task completion: the required warp is calculated based on the current hand position and the difference between positions of the target object and its virtual representation. Scaling factors are set so that users are typically unable to detect either of the warping.

Hybrid Warping works by World Warping to improve the alignment as possible, while any remaining warp is accommodated by Body Warping. In theory, if enough head motions are observed, the alignment may be completed entirely by World Warping.

User Reaction

Naïve users generally react to the experience of using haptic retargeting with enthusiasm and surprise, making comments such as "knowing that the cube was just placed there and it appeared somewhere else freaked me out", "this is surreal; it's definitely messing with me", and "my mind is blown".

Conclusion

We present a system for providing haptic feedback in a virtual reality environment by warping the virtual space to match the location of a physical prop in a person's immediate surroundings. Haptic Retargeting techniques allow a person to experience passive haptics in a virtual environment that differs from the physical one in potentially dramatic ways, allowing the designer to consider more complex virtual scenes and experiences, while still providing a sense of touch.

References

1. Mahdi Azmandian, Mark Hancock, Hrvoje Benko, Eyal Ofek, Andrew D. Wilson. Haptic Retargeting: Dynamic Repurposing of Passive Haptics for Enhanced Virtual Reality Experiences. In *Proc. of CHI 2016.* http://dx.doi.org/10.1145/2858036.2858226
2. Mahdi Azmandian, Mark Hancock, Hrvoje Benko, Eyal Ofek, and Andrew D. Wilson. 2016. A Demonstration of Haptic Retargeting: Dynamic Repurposing of Passive Haptics for Enhanced Virtual Reality Experience. In *Proc. CHI EA '16*. http://dx.doi.org/10.1145/2851581.2890265
3. Brent E. Insko. 2001. Passive haptics significantly enhances virtual environments. Computer: 100.
4. Sharif Razzaque, Zachariah Kohn, and Mary C Whitton. 2001. Redirected Walking. *Proceedings of EUROGRAPHICS*: 289–294.

Collaboration Meets Interactive Surfaces and Spaces (CMIS): Walls, Tables, Mobiles, and Wearables

Craig Anslow
Department of Computer Science
Middlesex University
London, UK
c.anslow@mdx.ac.uk

Pedro Campos
Madeira Interactive Technologies Institute
University of Madeira
Madeira, Portugal
pcampos@uma.pt

Andrés Lucero
SDU Design
University of Southern Denmark
Kolding, Denmark
lucero@acm.org

Laurent Grisoni
Computer Science Laboratory
University of Lille
Lille, France
laurent.grisoni@univ-lille1.fr

Mirjam Augstein
Department of Communication and Knowledge Media
University of Applied Sciences Upper Austria
Hagenberg, Austria
Mirjam.Augstein@fh-hagenberg.at

Jim Wallace
School of Public Health and Health Systems
University of Waterloo
Ontario, Canada
james.wallace@uwaterloo.ca

ISS '16, November 06-09, 2016, Niagara Falls, ON, Canada
ACM 978-1-4503-4248-3/16/11.
http://dx.doi.org/10.1145/2992154.2996359

Abstract
The CMIS workshop proposes to bring together researchers who are interested in improving collaborative experiences through the combination of multiple interaction surfaces with diverse sizes and formats, ranging from large-scale walls, to tables, mobiles, and wearables. The opportunities for innovation exist, but the ISS, CHI, CSCW, and other HCI communities have not yet thoroughly addressed the problem of bringing effective collaboration activities together using multiple interactive surfaces, especially in complex work domains. Of particular interest is the potential synergy that one can obtain by effectively combining different-sized surfaces and sharing information between devices.

Author Keywords
Collaboration, interactive surfaces, large display walls, tabletops, mobile, multi-touch interaction, wearables.

ACM Classification Keywords
H.5.m [Information interfaces and presentation (HCI)]: Miscellaneous.

General Terms
Design; Human Factors

Figure 1: Eery Space: a remote user controls the wall, two users in different physical spaces engage in a collaborative activity (indicated by the same color of their auras) and a fourth user looks at them through a virtual window.

Figure 2: Bancada: multiple users collaboratively exploring geospatial information space with an overview map displayed on a tabletop.

Introduction

Large scale displays and interactive surfaces offer a unique visualization environment favorable to both individual and collaborative design tasks [4, 6]. During the last decade these devices have become both affordable and easier to setup, providing highly interactive environments with high resolution and support for stereoscopic images. Combined with emerging input devices, these provide new ways to interact with content as well as enabling new applications to support collaborative engineering tasks as well as many other activities [5].

Additionally, new devices have become available to enhance these interactions, including tablets combining several sensors [3], non-intrusive tracking solutions based on depth cameras, wearable devices, and other equipment. Despite this rapid technological advance, however, it still remains an unsolved problem how to bring effective collaboration capabilities to this myriad of heterogeneous interactive surfaces. This workshop aims at bringing together the most advanced techniques, user interfaces, and technological issues that are crucial in fostering co-located collaboration and remote communication between users across different facilities simultaneously [7].

Following the success of previous Collaboration Meets Interactive Surfaces (CMIS) workshops co-located at ITS 2013–2015 [1, 2], we propose to host another workshop at ISS 2016. In the 2015 edition of the workshop a total of 25 participants attended, in 2014 21 participants attended, and in 2013 27 participants attended. Participants exchanged experiences regarding collaborative user interface design and evaluation techniques involving interactive surfaces, in both remote and co-located settings. Some previous CMIS workshop papers discussed issues focusing on collaborative design space with proxemics [8] (see Figure 1), geospatial interaction on tabletops [10] (see Figure 2), collaborative medical visualization on tabletops [11] (see Figure 3), and multi-user presentation software on large high resolution touch walls [9] (see Figure 4).

Topics of Workshop

Topics of the workshop include (but not limited to):

- Design and evaluation of collaborative environments with interactive surfaces, either remotely or co-located;
- Collaborative applications on interactive surfaces for different domains (e.g. meeting rooms, 3D visualization, mechanical engineering, medical visualizations)
- Communication, cooperation and coordination as well as social protocols;
- Interactive surfaces to enhance spatial perception of content and support navigation during collaboration;
- Issues when moving from desktop-based collaboration to large-scale walls, tabletops, touch-based mobile devices, and wearables;
- Integration of different devices and surfaces (Walls, Tables, Mobiles, Wearables) for collaboration;
- Physical navigation between different devices;
- Collaboration paradigms and user interface designs that address enhancement of collaborative activities using interactive surfaces and tabletops;
- Collaborative sense making and visual analytics with different interactive surfaces and devices;
- Theories and applications of social science for interactive surfaces and devices.

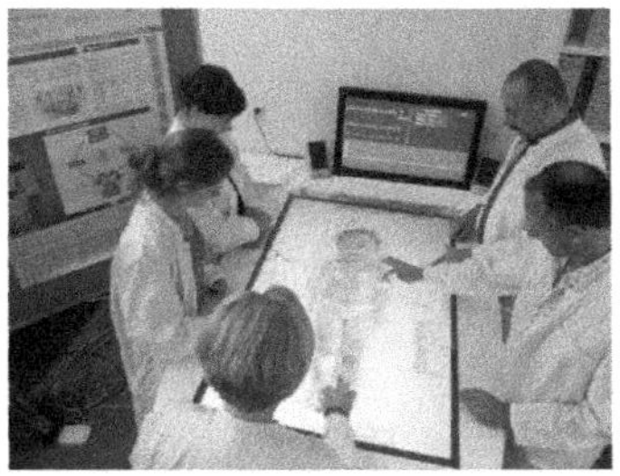

Figure 3: SimMed: multiple students collaborating around a tabletop for medical training.

Figure 4: The Cube: running CubIT a large scale multi-user presentation and collaboration platform.

Organizing Committee

The following people form the organizing committee:

Craig Anslow is a Senior Postdoctoral Research Fellow at Middlesex University, UK. His research interests include multi-surface environments for emergency management and criminal intelligence as well as engineering novel visual analytics applications.

Pedro Campos is an Assistant Professor at the University of Madeira, Portugal. His research interests include interaction design, augmented reality, natural interaction, and museums and cultural heritage.

Laurent Grisoni Laurent Grisoni is a Professor in computer science at University of Lille, France. He is also associated to CNRS and INRIA (MINT research group). His research interests include tactile and gesture-based interaction, in the fields of virtual reality and HCI.

Andrés Lucero is an Associate Professor at the University of Southern Denmark in Kolding. His research interests lie in the areas of mobile human-computer interaction, co-design, and design research.

Mirjam Augstein is a Professor for personalized and collaborative systems at the University of Applied Sciences Upper Austria in Hagenberg. Her research interests lie in the areas of adaptive systems, assistive technologies, interaction methods and techniques and collaboration support in interactive systems.

Jim Wallace is an Assistant Professor at the University of Waterloo, Canada. His research interests include health informatics, decision-making in healthcare, and interactive data exploration and analysis.

Program Committee

The following people form the program committee:

- Alfredo Ferreira, University of Lisbon, Portugal
- Nick Graham, Queens University, Canada
- Uta Hinrichs, University of St Andrews, United Kingdom
- Kris Luyten, Hasselt University, Belgium
- Roberto Martinez, University of Technology Sydney, Australia
- Narges Mayhar, University of British Columbia, Canada
- Alexander Nolte, University of Bochum, Germany
- Ian Oakley, Ulsan National Institute of Science and Technology, Korea
- Alberto Raposo, Pontifical Catholic University of Rio de Janeiro, Brazil
- Luciano Soares, Insper Instituto de Ensino e Pesquisa, Brazil
- Theophanis Tsandilas, INRIA, France

Planned Activities and Format

Table 1 outlines the proposed planned activities of the one-day workshop. In the first session we will have welcome and introductions by all attendees, followed by an invited talk. After the morning break the second session will have lightning talks of workshop papers from attendees. Lunch will follow to allow attendees to meet and mingle. In the third session attendees will split into groups based on themes related to the goals of the workshop. Once the groups have been formed discussions will happen amongst attendees and the groups will report back about this discussions. The fourth session will involve a group design activity based on the discussions from the previous session. Finally there will be some closing remarks from the organizing committee as well as feedback from attendees.

Time	Activity
0900–0930	Welcome and introductions
0930–1030	Invited Talk - Stacey Scott, University of Waterloo
1030–1100	*Morning Break*
1100–1230	Presentation of workshop papers (lightning talks)
1230–1400	*Lunch Break*
1400–1530	Split into groups based on themes: from the workshop and discuss
1530–1600	*Afternoon Break*
1600–1730	Group design activity Closing remarks from OC

Table 1: Workshop Activities

REFERENCES

1. C. Anslow, P. Campos, and A. Ferreira. 2014. Collaboration Meets Interactive Surfaces (CMIS): Walls, Tables, Tablets, and Phones. In *Proc. of International Conference on Interactive Tabletops and Surfaces (ITS)*. ACM, 495–498.
2. P. Campos, A. Ferreira, and A. Lucero. 2013. Collaboration Meets Interactive Surfaces (CMIS): Walls, Tables, Tablets, and Phones. In *Proc. of International Conference on Interactive Tabletops and Surfaces (ITS)*. ACM, 481–482.
3. K. Cheng, J. Li, and C. Müller-Tomfelde. 2012. Supporting Interaction and Collaboration on Large Displays Using Tablet Devices. In *Proc. of International Working Conference on Advanced Visual Interfaces (AVI)*. ACM, 774–775.
4. R. Jota, J. Pereira, and J. Jorge. 2009. A Comparative Study of Interaction Metaphors for Large-scale Displays. In *Proc. of Extended Abstracts on Human Factors in Computing Systems (CHI EA)*. ACM, 4135–4140.
5. J. Klimke and J. Döllner. 2010. Combining Synchronous and Asynchronous Collaboration Within 3D City Models. In *Proc. of International Conference on Geographic Information Science (GIScience)*. Springer-Verlag, 115–129.
6. E. Lantz. 2007. A Survey of Large-scale Immersive Displays. In *Proc. of Workshop on Emerging Displays Technologies: Images and Beyond: The Future of Displays and Interacton (EDT)*. ACM, Article 1.
7. A. Lucero, J. Holopainen, and T. Jokela. 2012. MobiComics: Collaborative Use of Mobile Phones and Large Displays for Public Expression. In *Proc. of International Conference on Human-computer Interaction with Mobile Devices and Services (MobileHCI)*. ACM, 383–392.
8. D. Mendes, M. Sousa, J. Pereira, A. Ferreira, and J. Jorge. 2014. Enabling Remote Proxemics through Multiple Surfaces. In *Proc. of Workshop on CMIS at ITS*. ACM.
9. M. Rittenbruch, A. Sorensen, J. Donovan, D. Polson, M. Docherty, and J. Jones. 2013. The Cube: A Very Large-scale Interactive Engagement Space. In *Proc. of International Conference on Interactive Tabletops and Surfaces (ITS)*. ACM, 1–10.
10. F. Rodrigues, T. Seyed, F. Maurer, and S. Carpendale. 2014. Bancada: Using Mobile Zoomable Lenses for Geospatial Exploration. In *Proc. of International Conference on Interactive Tabletops and Surfaces (ITS)*. ACM, 409–414.
11. U. von Zadow, R. Martinez-Maldonado, and R. Dachselt. 2014. Tabletop Territoriality and Social Context: Examining Medical Simulation. In *Proc. of Workshop on CMIS at ITS*. ACM.

Cross-Surface: Challenges and Opportunities of Spatial and Proxemic Interaction

Steven Houben
University College London
UCL Interaction Centre / ICRI Cities
s.houben@ucl.ac.uk

Jo Vermeulen
Department of Computer Science
University of Calgary
jo.vermeulen@ucalgary.ca

Clemens Klokmose
Department of Computer Science
Aarhus University
clemens@cs.au.dk

Johannes Schöning
Expertise Centre for Digital Media,
Hasselt University - tUL - iMinds
johannes.schoening@uhasselt.be

Nicolai Marquardt
University College London
UCL Interaction Centre / ICRI Cities
n.marquardt@ucl.ac.uk

Harald Reiterer
HCI Group,
University of Konstanz
harald.reiterer@uni-konstanz.de

ISS '16, November 06-09, 2016, Niagara Falls, ON, Canada
ACM 978-1-4503-4248-3/16/11.
http://dx.doi.org/10.1145/2992154.2996360

Abstract
In this workshop, we will review and discuss open issues, technical challenges and conceptual models for multi-device spatial or proxemic interaction. We aim to bring together researchers, students and practitioners working on technical infrastructures, studies and designs of spatial interfaces, or domain specific multi-device applications that use space as a unit of analysis. We focus specifically on analysing how such interfaces, tools and tracking technology can be deployed "in the wild". The workshop will facilitate knowledge exchange about the current state of spatial and proxemic interactive systems, identify application domains and enabling technologies for cross-surface interactions in the wild, and establish a research community to develop effective strategies for successful design of cross-device interactions.

Keywords
Cross-surface interaction, ubicomp ecologies, multi-surface interactions, multi-device interactions, spatial reconfigurations of displays, spatially distributed interfaces, multi-screen workplaces, wearable devices, proxemic interaction, configuration

ACM Classification Keywords
H.5.m. Information interfaces and presentation (e.g., HCI): Miscellaneous.

Introduction

People increasingly carry more interactive and interconnected devices that operate as a portal into their personal or shared information space. These devices are primarily general-purpose devices such as tablets, phones and laptops but recently we have also seen many new wearable devices, such as smartwatches or head-mounted displays, being introduced into people's device ecology. This expanding device ecology provides new opportunities for better collaboration, ad hoc information exchange, or data representations. However, this *device multiplicity* and the changing *context of use* lead to increasing more complex configuration problems associated with (i) discovering and pairing devices, (ii) tracking existing device ecologies, (iii) security and privacy in device ecologies, and (iv) creating stable distributed information and data representations that transcend the individual device.

Prior work has introduced a range of systems, techniques and tools aimed at facilitating cross-surface interaction. Examples include sensing of nearby devices [11, 15] device pairing [2,5, 7, 14, 15], information exchange [13, 15] and configuration of cross-device ecologies [6]. On common denominator in most of these approaches is the either implicit or explicit use of *space* and *spatial relations between devices and people* (Proxemics) as a way to create multi-device multi-user configurations [1]. Most of this technology has been successfully designed, deployed and evaluated in lab conditions, but a large number of open issues around its wider applicability to handle known multi-device problems [3,4] is unclear. We need a more in depth understanding of the role of space and proxemics as mediator in cross-surface interaction on a technologic, social and domain-specific level.

Objectives

This workshop is the third instalment in a series of workshops around interacting with multi-device ecologies in the wild with previous editions at ITS 2015 [8] and CHI 2016 [9] (cross-surface.com). This workshop series is aimed to tackling fundamental issues and challenges in cross-surface interaction in the wild. This third Cross-Surface workshop aims to provide interaction designers, researchers, students and practitioners with an open, creative and structure forum to discuss the current state of the art in spatial and proxemic interaction and tackle open issues and challenges. The central goal of this workshop is to *map out a design space, interaction vocabulary and conceptual models for spatially-aware cross-surface systems.* The workshop will be structured around three main topics:

Conceptual Models For Spatial Interactions

How can we conceptualize, describe and model multi-device interaction within a space? Which social, spatial or psychological theories and frameworks can be employ to help characterize spatial interactions? How do we translate such theories to interaction design, system research and multi-device representations?

Spatial Tracking "in the wild"

Which tracking technologies and tools can be used to support "in the wild" spatial interfaces and designs? How can these technologies be deployed, democratized and shared with a broader audience?

Control and Intelligibility

How do people make sense of spatially aware cross-surface ecologies? How can we support discoverability and learnability of interactions, inform users of action possibilities and provide feedback about cross-surface connections?

Participants

We aim to bring together 10-20 participants from academia and industry that are working on cross-surface systems. Participants will be selected based on the position papers and their relevance to the scope and goal of the workshop. We will solicit position papers of up to 7 pages in the ACM SIGCHI EA format that describe original research and outline a person's interest and experience in the topic of the workshop. Selected papers will serve as introductions for discussions and will be made available to the participants on the workshop website. Submissions will be reviewed by the organizing committee based on originality and relevance.

Workshop Format

As indicated in Table 1, we propose a one-day, 8-hour workshop focused on a combination of brainstorming, discussions and design activities in groups of 4 or 5 people.

Time	*Activity*
09:00	Madness session
09:30	Keynote by TBC
10:00	Brainstorm in 3 subgroups + design brief
10:30	Coffee break
11:00	Continue brainstorm Sketch/storyboard/prototype designs
13:00	Lunch
14:00	Present ideas + map out design space
16:00	Coffee break
16:30	Group reflections
17:30	Close

Table 1. Timeline of the workshop day

Publication Venue

The results of the workshop will be communicated to the larger HCI community by submitting an article to a magazine (e.g., *ACM interactions*). In this article, we hope to define future design spaces for cross-surface interactions in Ubicomp ecologies based on the collage of topics discussed and challenges identified in the different breakout groups. We will also invite all workshop participants to submit an extended article of their submission for a special issue on *"Interacting across Surfaces: Multi-Device Ecologies in the Wild"* in the Personal and Ubiquitous Computing journal that will appear mid-2017. This information and call for papers will also be shared on the website and will be open to the community.

Organizers and Program Committee

Steven Houben *is a Research Associate at University College London. He works at the ICRI-Cities and UCL Interaction Centre on projects related to multi-device environments, physical computing and sensor-based systems.*

Jo Vermeulen *is a Postdoctoral Fellow in the InnoVis research group at the Interactions Lab of the University of Calgary. He is interested in addressing interaction challenges within ubicomp spaces, including providing intelligibility, discoverability, feedback and feedforward for proxemic interaction and cross-device interactions.*

Clemens Klokmose *is an Associate Professor at the Computer Science department at Aarhus University and is associated with the center for Participatory Information Technology. His main interest is human-computer interaction that goes beyond personal computing.*

Johannes Schöning *is Professor of computer science at Hasselt University working at the Expertise centre for Digital Media (EDM). His main research interests lie at the intersection between human-computer interaction (HCI), geographic information science and ubiquitous interface technologies.*

Nicolai Marquardt *is a Lecturer at the University College London. At the UCL Interaction Centre he works on projects in the research areas of ubiquitous computing, interactive surfaces, toolkits, and physical user interfaces.*

Harald Reiterer *is Professor at the Computer and Information Science Department of the University of Konstanz. His main research interests include different fields of Human-Computer Interaction, like Interaction Design, Usability Engineering, and Information Visualization.*

References

1. Ballendat, Till, Nicolai Marquardt, and Saul Greenberg. "Proxemic interaction: designing for a proximity and orientation-aware environment."*ACM International Conference on Interactive Tabletops and Surfaces*. ACM, 2010.
2. Bernaerts, Yannick, et al. "The office smartwatch: development and design of a smartwatch app to digitally augment interactions in an office environment." Proceedings of the 2014 companion publication on Designing interactive systems. ACM, 2014.
3. Dearman, David, and Jeffery S. Pierce. "It's on my other computer!: computing with multiple devices." *Proc. Of CHI'08.* ACM.
4. Greenberg, Saul, Boring, Sebastian, Vermeulen, Jo and Dostal, Jakub. "Dark Patterns in Proxemic Interactions: A Critical Perspective." *Proc. of DIS '14*. ACM.
5. Hinckley, Ken. "Synchronous gestures for multiple persons and computers." *Proc. UIST '03*. ACM.
6. Houben, Steven, Paolo Tell, and Jakob E. Bardram. "ActivitySpace: Managing Device Ecologies in an Activity-Centric Configuration Space." *Proc. ITS '14*. ACM.
7. Houben, Steven, and Nicolai Marquardt. "WatchConnect: A Toolkit for Prototyping Smartwatch-Centric Cross-Device Applications." *Proc. CHI'15.* ACM, 2015.
8. Houben, Steven, Jo Vermeulen, Clemens Klokmose, Nicolai Marquardt, Johannes Schöning, and Harald Reiterer. "Cross-Surface: Workshop on Interacting with Multi-Device Ecologies in the Wild." In Proceedings of the 2015 International Conference on Interactive Tabletops & Surfaces, pp. 485-489. ACM, 2015.
9. Houben, Steven, Nicolai Marquardt, Jo Vermeulen, Johannes Schöning, Clemens Klokmose, Harald Reiterer, Henrik Korsgaard, and Mario Schreiner. "Cross-Surface: Challenges and Opportunities for 'bring your own device' in the wild." (2016).
10. Jokela, Tero, Jarno Ojala, and Thomas Olsson. "A Diary Study on Combining Multiple Information Devices in Everyday Activities and Tasks." *Proc. CHI '15*. ACM, 2015.
11. Kortuem, Gerd, Christian Kray, and Hans Gellersen. "Sensing and visualizing spatial relations of mobile devices." *Proc UIST '05*. ACM.
12. Kolko, Jon. Methods of design synthesis: moving from data to innovation. *Proc. CHI '14*. ACM.
13. Marquardt, Nicolai, Till Ballendat, Sebastian Boring, Saul Greenberg, and Ken Hinckley "Gradual engagement: facilitating information exchange between digital devices as a function of proximity." *Proc. ITS '12*. ACM.
14. Mayrhofer, Rene, and Hans Gellersen. "Shake well before use: Authentication based on accelerometer data." Pervasive computing. Springer Berlin Heidelberg, 2007. pp. 144-161.
15. Rädle, Roman, Hans-Christian Jetter, Nicolai Marquardt, Harald Reiterer, and Yvonne Roger. "HuddleLamp: Spatially-Aware Mobile Displays for Ad-hoc Around-the-Table Collaboration." *Proc. ITS '14*. ACM.
16. Schmidt, Dominik, Julian Seifert, Enrico Rukzio, and Hans Gellersen. "A cross-device interaction style for mobiles and surfaces." *Proc. DIS '12*. ACM.

Cross-Device Interfaces: Existing Research, Current Tools, Outlook

Michael Nebeling
Information Interaction Lab
School of Information
University of Michigan
Ann Arbor, MI 48109 USA
nebeling@umich.edu

ISS '16, November 06-09, 2016, Niagara Falls, ON, Canada
ACM 978-1-4503-4248-3/16/11.
http://dx.doi.org/10.1145/2992154.2996361

Abstract
In this tutorial, I will describe key technical and design challenges of developing cross-device interfaces, which are not only able to adapt to a wide variety of device characteristics and user preferences, but can actually migrate a user's tasks from one device to another and even distribute the interface between multiple devices jointly used by one or more users. Starting with a review of the cross-device design concepts, authoring tools and interaction techniques presented in the ISS and larger HCI literature, I will give a comprehensive overview of the state of the art. I will then analyze the current tools for design and development of cross-device interfaces, and present one of these tools, XDBrowser, in detail.
Participants will get hands-on experience with designing cross-device versions of existing interfaces using such authoring tools created for non-technical users. Finally, I will discuss open issues and provide an outlook based on the results from recent cross-device workshops I co-organized or participated in at CHI, EICS, and DIS.

Author Keywords
cross-device interface research overview; hands-on design session; open discussion and outlook

Introduction
The current proliferation of new devices ranging from smartwatches and phones, to tablets, to interactive tabletops and walls challenges designers to create flexible and adaptive interfaces. It has also prompted researchers to investigate how to best support designing for the combined use of multiple such devices. In particular, three main research streams can be identified.

First, a number of studies have been conducted on multi-device workflows [6, 14] and specifically cross-device web use [7, 8]. These studies clearly identified a need to support sequential and parallel use of multiple devices to more easily share tasks and interfaces between them.

Second, many different cross-device interaction techniques [1, 3, 4, 13] have been explored. Together, they render a very rich design space for cross-device interfaces. However, at this stage, most techniques are still limited to particular sets of applications or combinations of devices, and are typically not available in the interfaces we commonly use.

A third stream of research has investigated new cross-device programming toolkits and authoring tools [2, 3, 9, 16]. Many of these tools are targeted at web developers, allowing them to specify distributed web-based interfaces between two or more devices.

As part of the XDBrowser project, I am investigating how existing web browsers can be extended to support parallel usage of multiple devices as motivated by previous studies. A recent paper [8] presents a first prototype that enables non-technical users to adapt existing single-device interfaces for cross-device use. The paper explores XDBrowser as an end-user customization tool allowing users to try out alternative cross-device designs during active use. The main contribution of the project so far is a study of seven common multi-device interface patterns.

It is important to have an overview of these three research streams to understand the capabilities and limitations of existing tools, and be aware of the open issues before designing yet another method or tool. This tutorial aims to provide this overview as well as a forum for discussion with designers and researchers working in the broad area of multi-device interaction. Interested participants will benefit from a thorough review of the existing solutions, including but not limited to the family of XD tools I have designed and studied over the past few years. I will also share insights from a number of workshops I co-organized or attended over the past two years at CHI, EICS and DIS. The tutorial will also include demos of the tools currently available to the community, as well as a hands-on session allowing participants to explore the cross-device design space for an interesting set of interfaces using a tool such as XDBrowser.

Tutorial Synopsis
In the following, I will outline the topics covered and hands-on activities planned for the tutorial.

This tutorial will be organized in three blocks: *(1)* the three streams of cross-device research, *(2)* the tool landscape and the design space so far, *(3)* a discussion of the open issues, and outlook.

The first block gives participants an overview of the state of the art in cross-device user interface research. Going back to the early research, I will introduce participants to the early notions of multi-device, distributed user interfaces (e.g., using a single mobile device to control various appliances [11], redirecting input across devices [5]). Given the recent proliferation of many new forms of devices, I will then cover the more recent research efforts from the three streams mentioned earlier. In particular, I will present the most promising models, languages, frameworks and tools explored in research. The review will consider the technical aspects using Paternò and Santoro's multi-device development framework [12] as well as the design and user experience aspects based on Wljas et al.'s multi-device user experience framework [15].

This first block of the tutorial will build a comprehensive list of references useful to anyone interested in working in this field. An initial bibliography will be provided by the organizer, but participants will be asked to provide their input and help it become more complete.

The second block will be devoted to the impressive number of tools created by the community and the design space explored so far in research and practice. I will review existing tools and show interesting cross-device scenarios and applications they support according to the literature. This block will involve a practical component, where participants can try out a recent cross-device tool, XDBrowser [8], for themselves. Participants will be given examples of popular single-device web interfaces, such as GMail, YouTube and Maps, that they can then customize for cross-device use. We will then discuss the results produced by workshop participants and compare the interfaces they designed with those produced by 15 participants in a recent study presented at CHI 2016.

This second block will allow participants to get hands-on experience with recent tools such as XDBrowser to experiment with alternative cross-device designs of existing web-based interfaces while browsing them.

The third block opens the floor for discussion with participants. Participants can reflect on their experience with existing solutions, including the tools they tried in the second block. To drive the discussion, it will be moderated by the organizer and structured around three important questions: *(1)* What are promising concepts and techniques for authoring cross-device user interfaces? *(2)* What is the role of designers and developers in the process, and how does it need to change to give more power to the end-users themselves? *(3)* What may the future research agenda in cross-device user interfaces, in general and specific to ISS, look like? Here, it will be interesting to hear from participants about the research questions that they are interested in and how they would try to answer them. The organizer will then wrap up the discussion and provide an outlook based on his own research experience from the past few years and the results from four workshops recently held at CHI, EICS, and DIS.

This third block of the tutorial will foster discussion among participants. It will also be informed by the results from recent cross-device workshops held outside of, but very relevant to, ISS and the former ITS series.

Biography

Michael Nebeling is an Assistant Professor at the University of Michigan School of Information, where he leads the Information Interaction Lab, investigating more natural interfaces to information. As part of his research, he has created a family of cross-device user interface tools, including XDStudio [9], a distributed interface builder; XDKinect [10] a multi-device interaction mediation toolkit; and XDBrowser [8], which enables end-users to construct cross-device interfaces as they are browsing the web. He has recently given a number of guest lectures and research talks on his cross-device user interface research at Carnegie Mellon University, ETH Zurich, TU Munich, University of Washington, Adobe and Google.

Acknowledgements

I would like to acknowledge the support from the Swiss National Science Foundation under mobility grants, P300P2_154571 and P300P2_164646. I also want to thank Anind Dey for his support while at CMU.

References

[1] Chen, X. A., Grossman, T., Wigdor, D. J., and Fitzmaurice, G. W. Duet: Exploring Joint Interactions on a Smart Phone and a Smart Watch. In *Proc. CHI* (2014), 159–168.

[2] Chi, P. P., and Li, Y. Weave: Scripting Cross-Device Wearable Interaction. In *Proc. CHI* (2015), 3923–3932.

[3] Hamilton, P., and Wigdor, D. J. Conductor: Enabling and Understanding Cross-Device Interaction. In *Proc. CHI* (2014), 2773–2782.

[4] Houben, S., and Marquardt, N. WatchConnect: A Toolkit for Prototyping Smartwatch-Centric Cross-Device Applications. In *Proc. CHI* (2015), 1247–1256.

[5] Johanson, B., Hutchins, G., Winograd, T., and Stone, M. C. Pointright: experience with flexible input redirection in interactive workspaces. In *Proc. UIST* (2002), 227–234.

[6] Jokela, T., Ojala, J., and Olsson, T. A Diary Study on Combining Multiple Information Devices in Everyday Activities and Tasks. In *Proc. CHI* (2015), 3903–3912.

[7] Karlson, A. K., Iqbal, S. T., Meyers, B., Ramos, G., Lee, K., and Tang, J. C. Mobile Taskflow in Context: A Screenshot Study of Smartphone Usage. In *Proc. CHI* (2010), 2009–2018.

[8] Nebeling, M., and Dey, A. K. XDBrowser: User-Defined Cross-Device Web Page Designs. In *Proc. CHI* (2016), 5494–5505.

[9] Nebeling, M., Mintsi, T., Husmann, M., and Norrie, M. C. Interactive Development of Cross-Device User Interfaces. In *Proc. CHI* (2014), 2793–2802.

[10] Nebeling, M., Teunissen, E., Husmann, M., and Norrie, M. C. XDKinect: Development Framework for Cross-Device Interaction using Kinect. In *Proc. EICS* (2014).

[11] Nichols, J., Myers, B. A., Higgins, M., Hughes, J., Harris, T. K., Rosenfeld, R., and Pignol, M. Generating remote control interfaces for complex appliances. In *Proc. UIST* (2002), 161–170.

[12] Paternò, F., and Santoro, C. A logical framework for multi-device user interfaces. In *Proc. EICS* (2012), 45–50.

[13] Rädle, R., Jetter, H., Schreiner, M., Lu, Z., Reiterer, H., and Rogers, Y. Spatially-aware or Spatially-agnostic?: Elicitation and Evaluation of User-Defined Cross-Device Interactions. In *Proc. CHI* (2015), 3913–3922.

[14] Santosa, S., and Wigdor, D. A Field Study of Multi-Device Workflows in Distributed Workspaces. In *Proc. UbiComp* (2013), 63–72.

[15] Wäljas, M., Segerståhl, K., Väänänen-Vainio-Mattila, K., and Oinas-Kukkonen, H. Cross-Platform Service User Experience: A Field Study and an Initial Framework. In *Proc. Mobile HCI* (2010), 219–228.

[16] Yang, J., and Wigdor, D. Panelrama: Enabling Easy Specification of Cross-Device Web Applications. In *Proc. CHI* (2014), 2783–2792.

Projected Augmented Reality with the RoomAlive Toolkit

Andrew D. Wilson
Microsoft Research
One Microsoft Way
Redmond, WA 98052
awilson@microsoft.com

Hrvoje Benko
Microsoft Research
One Microsoft Way
Redmond, WA 98052
benko@microsoft.com

ISS '16, November 06-09, 2016, Niagara Falls, ON, Canada
ACM 978-1-4503-4248-3/16/11.
http://dx.doi.org/10.1145/2992154.2996362

Abstract
The RoomAlive Toolkit is an open source SDK that enables developers to create interactive projection mapping applications. The toolkit focuses on calibrating a network of multiple Kinect sensors and video projectors. It also provides a simple projection mapping sample that can be used as a basis to develop new immersive augmented reality experiences similar to those of the IllumiRoom [2] and RoomAlive [3] research projects. In this tutorial we will describe the RoomAlive Toolkit in detail, demonstrate its basic use and discuss integration with Unity3D.

Author Keywords
Projection mapping; spatial augmented reality; projector-camera system.

ACM Classification Keywords
H.5.2 User Interfaces: Graphical user interfaces, Input devices and strategies, Interaction styles.

Introduction
In this tutorial we present the RoomAlive Toolkit, an open source SDK that enables developers to create interactive, immersive augmented reality experiences using multiple projectors and commodity depth cameras. We will discuss the unique aspects of the RoomAlive Toolkit, such as its ability to handle dynamic

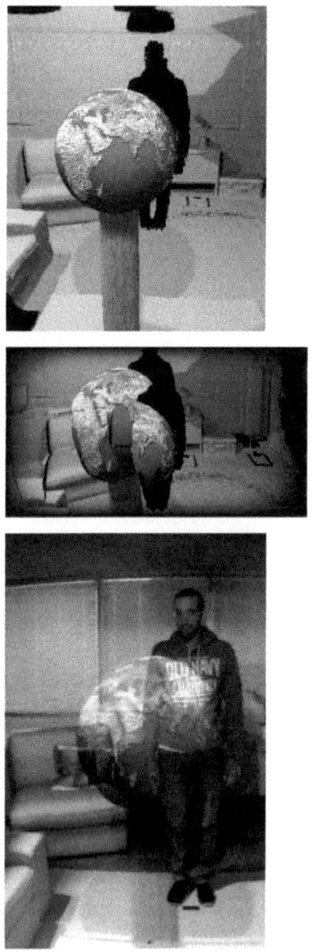

Figure 1. Dynamic projection mapping can be used to project onto moving bodies, for example. Top: desired view; middle: projected graphics; bottom: resulting view.

projection surfaces. We will present the SDK in detail, focusing on the calibration of multiple projectors and cameras, as well as basic projection mapping techniques and integration with Unity3D. The RoomAlive Toolkit is provided as open source under the MIT License. The code is available for download at GithHub: https://github.com/Kinect/RoomAliveToolkit.

The RoomAlive Toolkit allows for the use of multiple, calibrated projectors and depth cameras, and unlike most projection mapping formulations, allows for the movement of projection surfaces.

Dynamic Projection Mapping

The use of projection mapping techniques to create artistic and entertaining installations and performance works is now popular and familiar, and there are several professional software tools available to author projection mapping content [4]. A basic assumption of many of these tools is that the projection surface is static (as when projecting onto the façade of a building), or if it moves, that its motion is deterministic (as when projecting onto robots). Critically, this assumption simplifies the projection mapping problem to a 2D mapping from content images to projected pixels.

Meanwhile, a number of our projects demonstrate the application of projection mapping onto dynamic surfaces to create interactive, immersive augmented reality experiences using multiple video projectors and commodity depth cameras. In these systems, the projection must be continually adjusted to respond to dynamic, moving surfaces sensed by depth cameras. The projection mapping problem is no longer a fixed 2D mapping.

The RoomAlive Toolkit supports dynamic projection mapping where surfaces are sensed frame-to-frame by depth cameras. Camera and projector poses are determined in 3D, allowing the real time transformation of depth image geometry for accurate projection mapping of virtual objects onto moving surfaces. For example, it is possible to project a viewpoint-corrected 3D graphic onto a person's moving body (see Figure 1).

Multi Projector and Camera Calibration

A truly immersive interactive dynamic projection will require multiple projectors and depth cameras. Our most recent installation, for example, uses five projectors and eight Kinect cameras to cover most surfaces of a corporate conference room (see Figure 2).

The RoomAlive Toolkit provides routines to automatically calibrate a network of multiple projectors and cameras. The initial release of the RoomAlive Toolkit focuses on calibration, as this task be a particularly daunting for content creators. This calibration procedure determines the precise 3D pose of each camera and projector in the room, as well as standard parameters such as focal length and principal point for both cameras and projectors. The Toolkit also provides a Kinect server, as a means to distribute Kinect data over the network. This server also calculates a standard camera model for the Kinect camera.

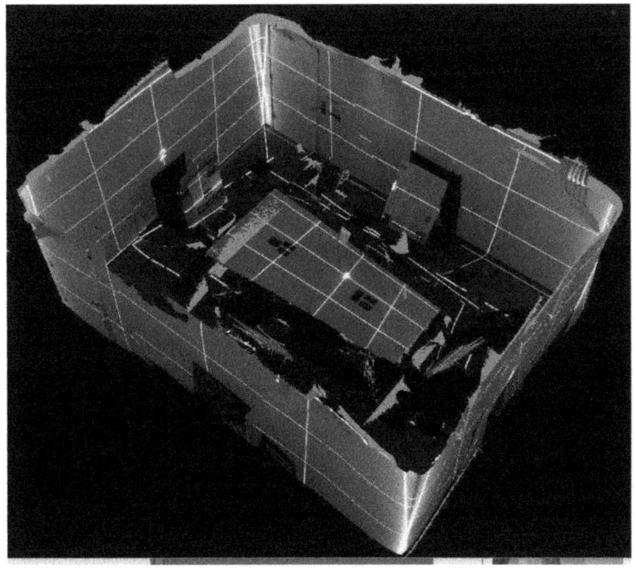

Figure 2. Calibration tool shows calibrated room using eight cameras and five projectors.

Planned Activities

We will demonstrate the use of the RoomAlive Toolkit to calibrate a multi-projector and multi-camera configuration. Attendees are encouraged to download and build the toolkit to follow along. We will use calibration data collected beforehand, but if possible we will also bring a single projector and camera to demonstrate the full calibration process. After calibrating, we will discuss and demonstrate projection mapping techniques, covering the theory of projection mapping as well as shader (HLSL) implementation.

Presenter Biographies

Andrew D. Wilson

Andy Wilson is a Principal Researcher and Research Manager at Microsoft Research. There he has been applying sensing technologies to enable new modes of human-computer interaction. His interests include gesture-based interfaces, display technologies, computer vision, and AR/VR. He helped found the Surface Computing group at Microsoft, and pioneered early efforts to commercialize depth cameras at Microsoft. He served as general chair of IEEE ITS (2007), ACM UIST (2009), and ACM SUI (2014). Before joining Microsoft, Andy obtained his BA at Cornell University, and MS and PhD at the MIT Media Laboratory. He currently directs the Natural Interaction Research group at Microsoft Research. More detail can be found at: http://research.microsoft.com/~awilson/.

Hrvoje Benko

Hrvoje Benko is a senior researcher at Microsoft Research. He explores novel interactive computing technologies and their impact on human-computer interaction. In particular, his research interests include augmented reality, computational illumination, surface computing, new input form factors and devices, as well as touch and freehand gestural input. Dr. Benko is the author of more than 30 scientific papers and journal articles. He served as General Chair (2014) and Program Chair (2012) of the ACM User Interface Systems and Technology conference. For his publications he received the best paper awards at both ACM UIST and ACM SIGCHI. His work has been featured in the mainstream media and on popular technology blogs. In 2010, he worked with Microsoft Hardware to turn one of his research projects into a product called Microsoft Touch Mouse. He received his

Ph.D. in Computer Science from Columbia University in 2007 with prof. Steven Feiner. More detail can be found at: http://research.microsoft.com/~benko/.

References

[1] Benko, H., Jota, R. and Wilson, A. D. (2012). MirageTable: Freehand Interaction on a Projected Augmented Reality Tabletop. In Proc. of ACM CHI 2012. p. 199-208.

[2] Jones, B., Benko, H., Ofek, E., and Wilson, A. D. (2013). IllumiRoom: Peripheral Projected Illusions for Interactive Experiences. In Proc. of ACM CHI 2013.

[3] Jones, B., Sodhi, R., Murdock, M., Mehra, R., Benko, H., Wilson, A., Ofek, E., MacIntryre, B., Raghuvanshi, N., Shapira, L. (2014). RoomAlive: Magical Experiences Enabled by Scalable, Adaptive Projector-Camera Units. In Proc. of ACM UIST 2014.

[4] Projection Mapping Central http://projectionmapping.org/tools/

[5] Tomislav Pejsa, Julian Kantor, Hrvoje Benko, Eyal Ofek, and Andy Wilson. (2016). Room2Room: Enabling Life-Size Telepresence in a Projected Augmented Reality Environment. In Proc. of ACM Conference on Computer Supported Cooperative Work (CSCW 2016).

[6] RoomAlive Toolkit https://github.com/Kinect/RoomAliveToolkit

[7] Wilson, A. and Benko, H. (2010). Combining Multiple Depth Cameras and Projectors for Interactions On, Above, and Between Surfaces. In Proceedings of ACM UIST '10. pp. 273-282.

[8] Wilson, A. D., Benko, H., Izadi, S., and Hilliges, O. (2012). Steerable Augmented Reality with the Beamatron. In Proc. of ACM UIST 2012. p. 413-422.

Let's Talk Architecture: An Introduction to Glass Buildings

Edward Tse
SMART Technologies
3636 Research Road NW
Calgary, Alberta, Canada
edwardtse@smarttech.com

ISS '16, November 06-09, 2016, Niagara Falls, ON, Canada
ACM 978-1-4503-4248-3/16/11.
http://dx.doi.org/10.1145/2992154.2996363

Abstract

A rise in room-sized interaction research and responsive architecture is increasing the need for collaboration between HCI researchers and architects. These two communities use language in very different ways making it difficult to maintain a common understanding of terms such as interactive architecture. As a result, there is a need for the interaction research community to become familiar with the industry-standard language used in the Architecture, Engineering, and Construction industries. To this end, we propose a tutorial to aid in the understanding of this language in the specific area of glass facades and new architecture styles. Increasingly, transparent displays and glass are used in interactions research and it is natural to expect that some of this technology will be integrated into the architecture of future buildings. This not only provides HCI researchers with a foundation for collaboration but it also reveals some of the key customer needs that concern architects and may inspire future research.

Author Keywords

Architecture, Curtain Walls, Mullions, Glazings, Spandrels, ANSI Z79.1, SHGC, NFRC

ACM Classification Keywords
H.5.m. Information interfaces and presentation (e.g., HCI): Miscellaneous.

Introduction
Significant growth in interaction research over large murals, museums, and buildings (e.g. [6]) has driven the need for collaboration with the architecture community. Similarly, architectural research in the area of reactive bio-mimicry such as roofs that open up when it is warm [7], and architecture that responds to the movement of crowds [5] have increased the need for collaboration with the HCI community. The challenge is that these two communities use language and terms in different ways making it challenging to obtain common ground for collaboration. Terms such as glass mullions, and post-modernism may have different meanings to architects and HCI researchers.

As a result, we wanted to focus specifically on the meaning of terms that are common in the world of large building facades. These terms are used not only by architects but also those in the engineering and construction industries. This enables the HCI interaction research community to interact with a wide array of people in the construction industries. We will also discuss key aspects of safety and efficiency standards as these are key areas of customer need that can inspire future HCI research.

We begin with a brief history describing the transition from windows to modern curtain walls.

From windows to curtain walls
While early windows (i.e. wind eye) were simply holes in a wall people in the Far East used paper to cover these holes. Glass (i.e. to shine) was demonstrated around 100AD through blown glass jars that were flattened to sheets. However, it took till around 1100AD for the first see through glass to be introduced. Glazed windows fortified with Iron were introduced around 1500AD at which point glass became affordable for the middle class [3]. Chemical strengthening such as Lead Oxide was introduced in the 1600s (Ravenscroft, 1674). Float Glass was explored in the 1800s with Rolled Cast Plate Glass (Hartley, 1848) followed by Tin Bath Float Glass (Pilkington, 1953). Today almost 90% of flat glass production uses the Tin Bath Float Glass method.

The term *curtain wall* comes from the Latin 'courtina' which means Court. Curtain walls were part of the defense of medieval castles. Originally they were made of timber and were susceptible to rot and fire. Later they were made of stone with crenels (old French term that means a notch) that were used for defense of a castle [2]. Glass curtain wall manufacture was introduced in the 1800s with steel mullions and plate Glass. An inspirational example was the Crystal Palace in London (Paxton, J., 1851) and Oriel Chambers in London (1864). Glass mullions were introduced into JFK Airport Terminal 6 in New York City in 1970 (Pei, I.M., 1970).

Curtain Wall Systems

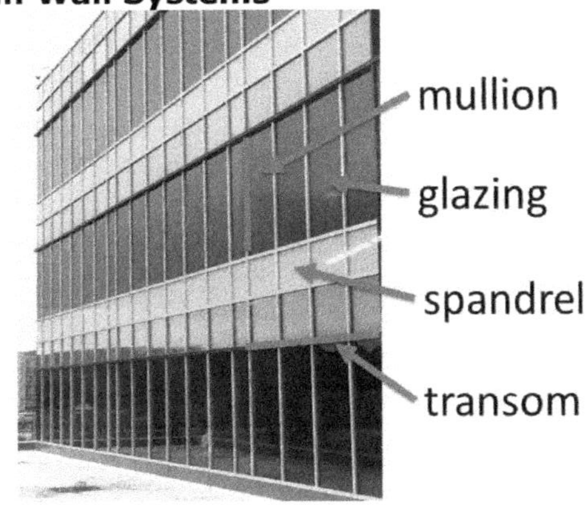

Figure 1. Components of a Stick curtain wall

Modern curtain wall systems fall into two categories: stick and unitized. *Stick* systems are generally used for smaller scale projects as construction is done on site, while *unitized* systems allow for quicker production speed due to scale manufacturing. A curtain walls is typically composed of vertical structural members called *mullions* (i.e. middle) that divide windows and transfer horizontal wind loads and glazing weight to the floor. Transoms (i.e. to cross) are horizontal structural members that hold windows above a floor. Glazings (i.e. to fit with glass) are structural glass that can be composed of different types (e.g. tempered, laminated) and layers (e.g. double, triple). Spandrels (i.e. expand) hide the floor structure and the mounting hardware.

Glass Production and Safety

Generally float glass is mixed in a melting furnace and then mixture is sent to a bath of molten tin for leveling. Float glass is cooled slowly in an annealing lehr to ensure that the final glass is smooth and clear. The final continuous sheet of mother glass can then be cut according to customer need. Tempered glass uses a similar process to float glass except the glass is rapidly cooled or strengthening chemicals are added to induce compressive stresses on the glass surface balanced with tensile stresses on the inside of the glass.

Tempered glass is commonly used in applications where strength and safety are required. When shattered tempered glass tends to break into small cubes instead of large shards for float glass. Further safety can be provided by adding a layer of polyvinyl butyral (PVB) or ethylene-vinyl acetate (EVA) as this tends to hold the glass cubes upon impact.

Figure 2. Example safety label for Architectural glass

In the 1960s there were 320K injuries a year from structural glass, this prompted the creation of the ANSI Z97.1 standard. The number of injuries was reduced to 73K in the 1970s when the Consumer Product Safety Commission (CPSC) 16 CFR 1201 standard was introduced [4]. In Figure 2 we can see the writing 16

CFR 1201 – I. II this means that the glazing can withstand 400 ft/lbs of impact.

Managing Heat and Moisture

The thermal transmittance of windows is a key factor in the amount of energy used for heating and cooling spaces. As a result, significant effort has been put into making windows more insulating and heat reflecting while still maintaining visual clarity.

Energy star labels on new windows list details such as Solar Heat Gain Coefficients (SGHC) the ratio of solar heat divided by incident solar heat. SHGC values of <0.40 are desired for hot climates and >0.55 for colder climates [ref]. Visual Transmittance (VT) measure the ratio of visible light compared to incident visible light. VT values of >0.60 are required for glass to look clear (the best Transparent OLED displays today have VT of 0.40) while clear glass has VT of 0.90 [1].

Improved energy ratings are provided in several ways in insulated glazing units (IGU) for example: Increasing the number of layers of glass can improve insulation and reduce condensation in cold temperatures. Wood frames are relatively good insulators but are susceptible to rot, and frame rot is the most common failure of windows. Low emissivity materials increase the amount of reflected radiant heat sources.

Modern smart windows have enabled computer control of when the windows and blinds are opened. A PDLC window has SHGC 0.71 and VT 0.81 while clear and SHGC 0.10 and VT 0.10 when Frosted. Similarly electrochromic windows typically seen on airplanes have SHGC 0.48 VT 0.62 when clear and SHGC 0.09 VT 0.04 when tinted.

Conclusion

The need for collaboration between HCI researchers and architects is growing and their use of language is quite different. The aim of this tutorial is to provide common ground with the hope of furthering collaborations between HCI research and Architecture.

References

[1] Cascadia Windows & Doors (2013) NAFS-08 & CSA A440S1-09 Fenestration Standards http://www.cascadiawindows.com/database/files/library/2013_11_29___Cascadia_Windows_Ltd___NAFS_Presentation___BOABC.pdf

[2] Curtain wall (architecture). https://en.wikipedia.org/wiki/Curtain_wall_(architecture).

[3] "Glass Online: The History of Glass". Archived from the original on April 15, 2011. Retrieved 2007-10-29.

[4] Hansen, D. (2011) Safety Glazing http://www.codecheck.com/cc/ccimages/PDFs/SafetyGlazingHansenOctober2011.pdf

[5] Petersen, K. Y., Kongshaug, J., & Søndergaard, K. (2015). Adaptive Lighting.

[6] Russell, D. M., Streitz, N. A., & Winograd, T. (2005). Building disappearing computers. Communications of the ACM, 48(3), 42-48.

[7] Sung, D. K. (2007) Skin Deep: Breathing Life into the Layer between Man and Nature. AIA Report of University Research Volume 3, USC.

SIVARG: Spatial Interaction in Virtual/Augmented Reality and Games

Robert J. Teather
Carleton University
1125 Colonel By Drive
Ottawa, ON, K1S 5B6
Canada
rob.teather@carleton.ca
www.csit.carleton.ca/~rteather

Wolfgang Stuerzlinger
Simon Fraser University
250-13450 102nd Avenue
Surrey, BC V3T 0A3
Canada
w.s@sfu.ca
http://ws.iat.sfu.ca/

ISS '16, November 06-09, 2016, Niagara Falls, ON, Canada
ACM 978-1-4503-4248-3/16/11.
http://dx.doi.org/10.1145/2992154.2996364

Workshop Topics

We propose a workshop soliciting submissions on the topics of spatial and 3D interaction in highly fidelity graphical interactive systems, especially video games and virtual reality systems. This workshop is the first of its kind on the topic of Spatial Interaction in Virtual/Augmented Reality (VR/AR) and Games. Topics will cover all aspects of interaction in these systems, including input-related issues such as efficient control mappings, spatial input device features (e.g., low latency, input noise, etc.), as well as output-related issues such as display hardware features (e.g., stereoscopic rendering, head-tracking), and information visualization (e.g., game HUDs for status information). We propose to include both position papers, as well as papers including at least preliminary studies on issues in these areas.

State of the Art

Recent work in spatial interaction has revealed the comparative ineffectiveness of spatial input devices (e.g., 3D trackers) compared to equivalent tasks performed with a mouse [1, 2, 3]. Yet 3D input devices and interaction techniques are still useful in situations where the user may be standing or walking, particularly in virtual reality systems. Gamers are also interested in these technologies, and VR and AR games are a growing market. Our workshop looks at the interplay between virtual reality and game-based interaction, to encourage discussion between researchers on these topics. This will help plot the way forward in the design of intuitive and effective spatial user interfaces that can be adopted in VR/AR systems and games alike.

Relevance to ISS Community

Interactive Surfaces are becoming more and more important. There are many examples where surface- or constraint-based interaction in 3D games or 3D User Interfaces for VR are advantageous. Moreover, various AR systems, including the Microsoft Hololens head-mounted display, now use the surfaces of the surroundings to display content and to enable interaction with it.

Topics Covered

We plan to cover a range of topics relating to spatial interaction in games, virtual reality (VR) and augmented reality (AR). This will include both hardware and software related issues, across both input and output related issues. We thus propose to consider topics that fall within four combinations of these two axes. Topics areas may include, for example:

Output/Hardware:

- Effects of stereo 3D display or head-tracking in common gaming tasks (e.g., shooting targets) or genres (e.g., strategy vs. first-person shooter)
- Addressing display issues, such as the convergence/accommodation or field of view problems in VR and AR

Input/Hardware:

- Effectiveness of spatial input devices relative to game controllers, touch screens, or the mouse in common 3D tasks, e.g., selection, manipulation, navigation, etc.
- "Cost" of factors like tracker latency or noise

Output/Software:

- Design considerations of game status information visualization (e.g., HUDs, diegetic displays)
- Wayfinding and other spatial task aids in games and VR

Input/Software:

- Software mappings for desktop input devices (e.g., mouse, touchscreen) for effective spatial navigation in games or VR
- Novel interaction techniques for controlling spatial data with surface-constrained input devices

Planned activities primarily focus on a technical content track presented by authors of accepted submissions. We expect to include 15 minute presentations organized into sessions of similar content, with ample time for discussion between presentations (10 minutes).

Depending on submission numbers, we will also include a brainstorming session. This session would focus on novel forms of spatial input and output techniques in the key contexts (games, VR, AR) outlined above.

Equipment Requested

Since the workshop will be primarily presentation-based, we will only require a room with a projector and screen.

Organizers

Robert J. Teather is an assistant professor in the School of Information Technology at Carleton University. His research primarily focuses on spatial interaction in virtual reality systems, especially as compared to equivalent tasks with mouse-based interfaces (e.g., selection tasks). While a postdoc at McMaster University, he expanded his research program to include various aspects of game user interfaces, notably including scale (i.e., how do game UIs change across drastically different sized displays/devices?). He has published over 20 peer-reviewed papers in venues such as the ACM CHI Conference, IEEE 3D User Interfaces Symposium, and Graphics Interface.

Wolfgang Stuerzlinger is a professor at the School of Interactive Arts + Technology at Simon Fraser University. The work in his research group spans spatial and three-dimensional user interfaces, virtual reality, human-computer interaction, and visual analytics. His work aims to find innovative solutions for real-world problems and is often interdisciplinary. He has published more than 100 refereed scientific papers and has supervised more than 40 graduate students to completion, many of which now work in leading positions around the world.

Draft Call for Participation

We invite your submission to our workshop on Spatial Interaction in Games and VR, to be held at ISS 2016 in Niagara Falls, Canada (Nov. 6–9). We seek original position papers or technical papers documenting research contributions, practice and experience, or novel applications, from all areas of spatial interaction relating to games or VR. User interface evaluations are strongly encouraged for all technical publications.

Submissions are of variable length, and paper length must be based on the weight of the contribution. Full papers up to 7 formatted pages and should describe research or design within the scope of spatial interaction in games and/or VR/AR. Submitted papers should be anonymous. Submissions must not be previously published or accepted for publication elsewhere and must not be under review by any other publication venue during the review period.

All submissions should be prepared in SIGCHI Extended Abstracts publication format (see http://www.sigchi.org/publications/chipubform/sigchi-extended-abstracts-word-template/view/). Supplementary videos are strongly encouraged. Submissions should address one or more of the following topics within spatial user interaction. Topics should be somehow linked to games and or virtual/reality. Unlisted but strongly related topics are also welcome.

- Spatial interaction techniques
- Spatial user interface metaphors
- Spatial input devices and technology
- Interaction on spatial, stereoscopic, and 3D displays
- Evaluation methods for spatial user interaction
- Collaborative interaction in 3D space
- Design and user experience (UX) for spatial user interaction
- Applications of human spatial perception to interaction

- Adaptive and perceptual-inspired spatial user interaction
- Applications of spatial UIs, such as games, entertainment, CAD, education
- Gesture-based spatial interaction
- Tangible spatial user interaction
- Multi-touch technologies for spatial user interaction
- Desktop interfaces for spatial interaction
- Multisensory and other novel forms of spatial user interaction

Accepted work will be published in non-archival companion proceedings indexed in the ACM Digital Library. Please note that at least one author of each accepted submission will be required to register for the workshop and ISS conference.

More information is available at www.csit.carleton.ca/SIVARG.

Submission date: Sept. 24
Notification: Oct. 7

References

1. Bérard, F., Ip, J., Benovoy, M., El-Shimy, D., Blum, J., and Cooperstock, J. (2009). Did "Minority Report" get it wrong? Superiority of the mouse over 3D input devices in a 3D placement task, INTERACT 2009, 400-414.
2. Teather, R. J. and Stuerzlinger, W. (2011). Pointing at 3D targets in a stereo head-tracked virtual environment, IEEE 3D User Interfaces - 3DUI 2011, 87-94.
3. Teather, R. J. and Stuerzlinger, W. (2013). Pointing at 3D target projections using one-eyed and stereo cursors, ACM Conference on Human Factors in Computing Systems - CHI 2013, 159 - 168.

Immersive Analytics: Exploring Future Interaction and Visualization Technologies for Data Analytics

Benjamin Bach
Monash University
900 Dandenong Rd
Caulfield East, Victoria, Australia
benj.bach@googlemail.com

Raimund Dachselt
Interactive Media Lab
Technische Universität Dresden
01062 Dresden, Germany
dachselt@acm.org

Sheelagh Carpendale
University of Calgary
2500 University Dr. NW
Calgary, AB, Canada
sheelagh@ucalgary.ca

Tim Dwyer
Monash University
900 Dandenong Rd
Caulfield East, Victoria, Australia
tim.dwyer@monash.edu

Christopher Collins
University of Ontario
Institute of Technology
2000 Simcoe St. N
Oshawa, ON Canada
christopher.collins@uoit.ca

Bongshin Lee
Microsoft Research
One Microsoft Way
Redmond, WA 98052, USA
bongshin@microsoft.com

ISS 2016, November 6–9, 2016, Niagara Falls, ON, Canada.
ACM ISBN 978-1-4503-4248-3/16/11.
http://dx.doi.org/10.1145/2992154.2996365

Abstract
We propose to conduct a workshop on the topic of *Immersive Analytics*: a new multidisciplinary initiative to explore future interaction technologies for data analytics. Immersive Analytics aims to bring together researchers in Information Visualisation, Visual Analytics, Virtual and Augmented Reality and Natural User Interfaces.
http://immersiveanalytics.net

Author Keywords
Visualization, Interaction, Virtual and Augmented Reality, Visual Analytics

Relevance to ISS
Due to the recent advances in immersive technologies (VR, AR, large displays, tangible surfaces), we see new opportunities to using these technologies to analyse and explore data. Several research areas are concerned with the development of methods to support the analysis of such data, including information visualisation, data sciences, and visual analytics. Visual analytics, introduced a decade ago as “the science of analytical reasoning facilitated by interactive visual interfaces” [1], has now become a key technology for dealing with big data [2], and there is massive potential for its use in further emerging application areas like health informatics, business intelligence; transport and logistics; scientific applications including

Figure 1: A possible use-case to be explored by immersive analytics: data analysis in Augmented Reality.

astronomy and physics; environmental monitoring; and personal information management.

The definition for visual analytics given above is agnostic of the actual interface devices employed by visual analysis systems. Nevertheless, the affordances of the display and input devices used for analyzing data strongly affect the experience of the users of such systems, and so, their degree of engagement and productivity. Ultimately, therefore, it affects the adoption and ubiquity of sophisticated data analysis tools. For practical visual analysis tools used in the industries and areas of data science described above, the platform for interaction is almost always a standard desktop computer: a single average-sized display, keyboard and mouse.

While visual analytics and information visualisation researchers sometimes publish studies exploring some data visualisation application in 3D or using natural user interfaces, this has never been a core topic. By contrast, 3D user interface researchers have tended to focus more on lower-level technologies rather than practical applications. Therefore, a systematic approach to developing visual analytic tools that move beyond the desktop is lacking. We propose a new facet of data analytics research that seeks to unify these efforts to identify the most enabling aspects of these emerging natural-user-interface and augmented-reality technologies for real-world analysis of data. We call this new research thrust *"Immersive Analytics"*, a topic that will explore the applicability and development of emerging user-interface technologies for creating more engaging experiences and seamless work-flows for data analysis applications.

We feel that this workshop is a perfect fit for collocation with the 2016 ISS conference with its focus on different emerging display, interaction and natural user-interface technologies. The workshop differs from the more general ISS themes by being focused in collaboration between Information Visualisation, Visual Analytics, novel display/interaction and Virtual and Augmented Reality researchers. This basic definition of Immersive Analytics has already been explored in some depth at meetings at NII Shonan, Japan and a seminar at Dagstuhl, Germany. The goal of these meetings was to establish the field with by authoring an introductory book and "manifesto". This book is now in production. This workshop would differ by being a forum for researchers to prevent their work-in-progress on this topic, position papers, and original research.

Topics Covered in the Workshop

The overarching goal of immersive analytics research is to understand how (and whether) new interface and display technologies can be used to create a more immersive kind of data analysis and exploration. The kinds of devices and environments include augmented and virtual reality displays, large high-resolution 2- and 3-D displays, haptic and audio feedback, and gesture and touch controlled interaction. These potentially require very different interaction and visualisation models and techniques to those used in standard visual analytics. Some of the main research questions are:

Real-World VA: What questions do technologies like augmented reality raise for visual analytics? Traditional information visualization supports open-ended exploration based on Shneiderman's information mantra: overview first, zoom and filter, then details on demand. In our view a different model is required for analytical applications grounded in the physical world. In this case objects in the physical environment provide the immediate and primary focus and so the natural model is to provide detailed

Figure 2: "Immersing people in their data" does not necessarily involve 3D or stereo display. In this concept, analysts work in a purpose-built, collaborative data analytics room.

information about these objects and only provide contextual information on demand.

Collaboration: Much research has been devoted to computer-assisted collaboration both synchronous and asynchronous, local and remote. These new devices and environments potentially support new models for collaboration as shown in Figures 1 and 2. What paradigms are potentially enabled by these new interaction modalities? How de we evaluate them?

Hybrid 2D/3D: Traditionally 3D visualisation has been used in the physical sciences, engineering and design; while 2D visualisations have been used to display statistical and abstract data in information visualisations. Increasingly there is a need to combine both sorts of visualisation in holistic visualisations. For instance in the life sciences different aspects of a cell are displayed using 2- and 3-D images, 2-D network data and the various -omics. Can these new technologies support more holistic visualisations of such data incorporating 3-D spatial information as well as abstract data?

Affordances for Immersion: What are the interface "tricks" and affordances such as high-resolution displays, sound, touch, responsive interaction that change the user perception from an allocentric view of the data to a more egocentric and immersive view of the data?

Changing Technologies: What are the lessons that can be learnt from previous research into the use of 3D visualisation for information visualisation? Do the new technologies invalidate the current wisdom that it is better to use 2D visualisation for abstract data since the designer of the visualisation has complete freedom to map data to an occlusion free 2D display?

Application Areas What are the most fertile application areas for immersive analytics? For example, these could be in life-sciences, disaster and emergency management, archaeology, and many more.

Platforms and Toolkits: How do we develop generic platforms that support immersive analytics? Currently there is a wide range of different development platforms and existing cross-platform tools however they do not quite have a broad enough focus for immersive analytics. For example, Unity[1] is designed for gaming applications rather than analytics while the Visualization Toolkit (VTK)[2] is targeted at scientific visualisation applications.

Nature of the Workshop

The aims of the workshop are as follows:

1. To bring together experts from the Human Computer Interaction, Information Visualisation, Augmented Reality and Visual Analytics communities; as well as industry representatives, and domain experts from application areas that require analysis of complex data.
2. To investigate the potential and the challenges of immersive analytics in research and industry.
3. To investigate how existing interaction models and techniques can be adapted to new environments, and where new approaches are necessary. Based on this to formulate guidelines for the use of such interaction models and techniques in immersive analytics.
4. Initial design of open-source tools and platforms for supporting immersive analytics research and practice.
5. To investigate how the evaluation of new concepts can be done, including interaction efficiency.
6. To explore the design space for immersive analytics for effective collaborative data analysis in various forms, e.g. distributed or local, synchronous or asynchronous.

[1]unity3d.org
[2]www.vtk.org

Schedule	
9:00	Intro. & overview of the workshop structure
9:15	One minute introductions from participants
9:45	Invited talks
10:30	Submitted paper talks
12:00	Lunch
13:00	Topic Brainstorming
13:45	Group Formation
14:00	Group Discussions
16:00	Group Reports
16:30	Community Building
17:00	Closing

Outcomes
We plan to prepare a special journal issue (IEEE Computer Graphics and Applications would be appropriate) compiling expanded versions of the submitted workshop papers and also inviting new papers evolved from the discussions at the workshop.

Another goal of the workshop is to "test the waters" to see if there is sufficient interest to develop a continuing symposium on Immersive Analytics. This will be a focus of the "Community Building" activities scheduled for the afternoon session.

Format of the Workshop
We propose to run a one-day workshop collocated with the 2016 ISS conference. The workshop would be a forum for:

- Invited talks from one or two important figures in the relevant communities.
- Work-in-Progress and novel research presentations (with submitted and reviewed short papers).
- Brain storming activities and new project formation around the themes of the workshop.
- Community building and panel discussions about how to progress the topic of Immersive Analytics.

A possible schedule is provided in the left margin.

Program Committee
We invited a mixture of Information Visualization, Virtual and Augmented Reality and HCI researchers to join our program committee. Each is asked to review 2-3 submissions on work-in-progress and novel research in Immersive Analytics. We initially invite attendees from the Shonan and Dagstuhl workshops, beginning with the following:

Steve Drucker, Microsoft Research, USA
Bruce Thomas, University of South Australia, Australia
Mark Billinghurst, University of South Australia, Australia
Petra Isenberg, Inria, France
Emmanuel Pietriga, Inria, France
Christophe Hurter, ENAC, France
Carla Freitas, Fed. University of Rio Grande do Sul, Brazil
Falk Schreiber, Konstanz University, Germany
Chris North, Virginia Tech, USA
Gerik Scheuermann, University of Leipzig, Germany
Wolfgang Stuerzlinger, Simon Fraser University, Canada
Aurélien Tabard, University Claude Bernard – Lyon, France
Maxime Cordeil, Monash University, Australia
Wolfgang Buesche, Dresden University, Germany
Karsten Klein, Konstanz University, Germany
Kim Marriott, Monash University, Australia
Jon McCormack, Monash University, Australia
Aaron Quigley, University of St. Andrews, UK
Wolfgang Stuerzlinger, Simon Fraser University, Canada

REFERENCES

1. Thomas, James J., and Kristin A. Cook, eds. Illuminating the path: The research and development agenda for visual analytics. IEEE Computer Society Press, 2005.
2. Keim, Daniel A., Florian Mansmann, Jörn Schneidewind, Jim Thomas, and Hartmut Ziegler. Visual analytics: Scope and challenges. Springer Berlin Heidelberg, 2008.

Call-for-papers

The CfP summarizes the oultline and topics of the workshop as stated in this proposal. It will be distributed on the ISS website, mailing-lists for IEEE VIS, ACM CHI, and UIST, as well as on the internal mailing lists of the organizer's respective institutions, on the organizers' webpages and social media. The call-for-papers is as follows:

Due to the recent advances in immersive technologies (VR, AR, large displays, tangible surfaces, etc.), we see new opportunities to leverage these technologies to analyse and explore data. Visual analytics is concerned with analytical reasoning facilitated by interactive visual interfaces. This definition is agnostic of the actual interface devices employed by visual analysis systems. Nevertheless, the affordances of the display and input devices used for analyzing data strongly affect the experience of the users of such systems, and so, their degree of engagement and productivity. However, a systematic approach to developing visual analytic tools that move beyond the desktop is yet lacking.

In this call, we are looking for innovative research, design, and view-points, mature or work-in-progress, that fall into or are related to the following topics: Real-world VA, Collaboration, Hybrid 2D/3D, Affordances for Immersion, Changing Technologies, Application Areas, Platforms and Toolkits. We call this new research thrust "Immersive Analytics", a topic that will explore the applicability and development of emerging user-interface technologies for creating more engaging experiences and seamless work-flows for data analysis applications.

Submissions will be peer-reviewed and accepted submissions will be published as a special issue of IEEE Computer Graphics and Application in early 2017.

Room Requirements

We expect around 30 participants for the workshop and the room should provide tables for participants to gather into groups (5-6 persons per group and table). We also need a standard projector for talks to be held. Whiteboards for group discussions.

Author Index

www.ingramcontent.com/pod-product-compliance
Ingram Content Group UK Ltd.
Pitfield, Milton Keynes, MK11 3LW, UK
UKHW051416290926
15471UKWH00009B/1630